YACHT BOY 207

Imagine. A radio that sits comfortably in the palm of your hand that can tune 9 short-wave bands plus AM, FM, and Longwave. The shortwave bands encompass all significant world-wide shortwave broadcasting from 3.90 to 21.40 MHz; 75m, 49m, 41m, 31m, 25m, 22m, 19m, 16m, and 13m. Comes with carrying pouch, headphone jack and *Grundig Shortwave Listening Guide.*

YACHT BOY 305

Finally, a well-built, high-quality, inexpensive digital shortwave radio. The YB-305 features a large cavity speaker enclosure for true rich sound. The 30-memories are easy to program; with tuning features including direct entry tuning, autoscan and up and down slewing. Coupled with continuous short-wave coverage from 2.30-21.85 MHz, you truly have a portable shortwave radio that even the critics will love. Comes with carrying pouch, batteries and *Grundig Shortwave Listening Guide*.

GRUNDIG

Call for information: U.S. 1-800-872-2228 or 415-361-1611
Canada 800-637-1648 • Fax: 415-361-1724

1996 PASSPORT
TO WORLD BAND RADIO

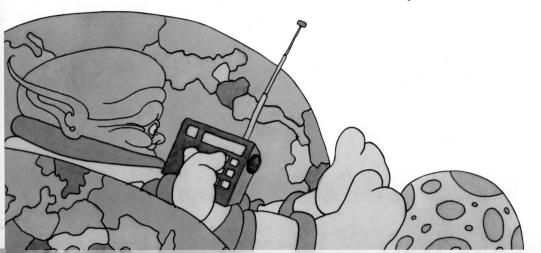

WHEN AND WHERE WORLDSCAN®

CHANNEL-BY-CHANNEL

MAKING CONTACT

ISSN 0897-0157

International Broadcasting Services, Ltd.

Passport® To World Band Radio

1996

Our reader is the most important person in the world!

EDITORIAL

Editor-in-Chief	Lawrence Magne
Editor	Tony Jones
Contributing Editors	Jock Elliott (U.S.) • Craig Tyson (Australia)
Consulting Editors	John Campbell (England) • Don Jensen (U.S.)
WorldScan Contributors	James Conrad (U.S.) • Frederick Gordts (Belgium) • Manosij Guha (India) • Anatoly Klepov (Russia) • Marie Lamb (U.S.) • *Número Uno*/John Herkimer (U.S.) • Toshimichi Ohtake (Japan) • *Radio Nuevo Mundo*/Tetsuya Hirahara (Japan) • Takayuki Inoue (Japan) • Henrik Klemetz (Colombia) • Nikolai Rudnev (Russia) • Don Swampo (Uruguay) • Vladimir Titarev (Ukraine) • David Walcutt (U.S.)
WorldScan® Software	Richard Mayell
Laboratory	Sherwood Engineering Inc.
Cover Artwork	Gahan Wilson
Graphic Arts	Bad Cat Design; Ruttle, Shaw & Wetherill, Inc.
Printing	Quebecor Printing

ADMINISTRATION

Publisher	Lawrence Magne
Associate Publisher	Jane Brinker
Advertising & Distribution	Mary Kroszner, MWK
Offices	IBS North America, Box 300, Penn's Park PA 18943, USA • Advertising & Distribution: Phone +1 (215) 794-3410; Fax +1 (215) 794 3396 • Editorial: Fax +1 (215) 598 3794 •Orders (24 hours): Phone +1 (215) 794-8252; Fax +1 (215) 794-3396
Media Communications	Jock Elliott, Pickering Lane, Troy NY 12180, USA • +1 (518) 271-1761 • Fax +1 (518) 271 6131

BUREAUS

IBS Latin America	Tony Jones, Casilla 1844, Asunción, Paraguay • Fax +595 (21) 446 373
IBS Australia	Craig Tyson, Box 2145, Malaga WA 6062 • Fax +61 (9) 342 9158
IBS Japan	Toshimichi Ohtake, 5-31-6 Tamanawa, Kamakura 247 • Fax +81 (467) 43 2167

Library of Congress Cataloging-in-Publication Data

Passport to World Band Radio.
   1. Radio Stations, Shortwave—Directories. I. Magne, Lawrence
TK9956.P27   1995   384.54'5   95-22739
ISBN 0-914941-37-2

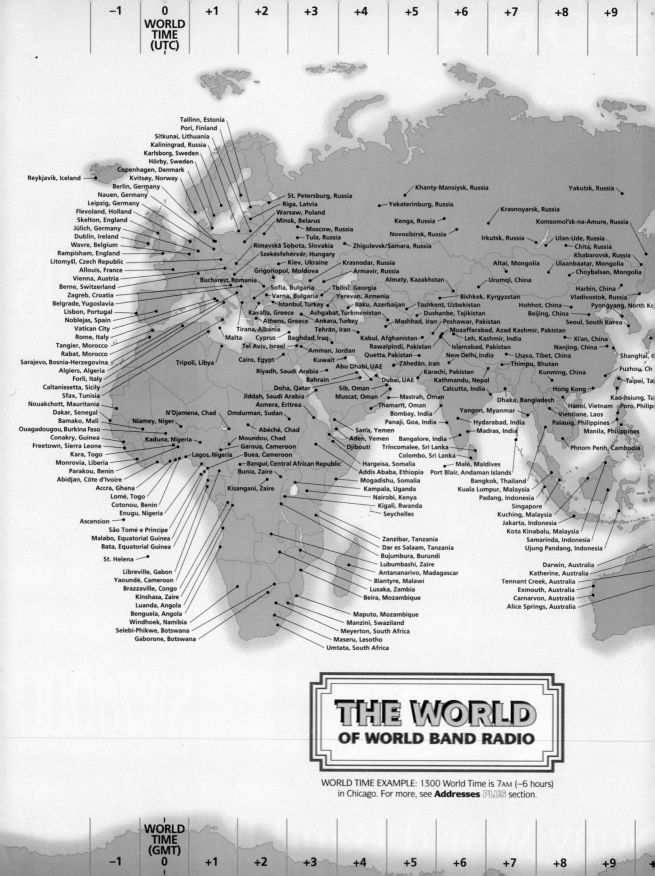

| −1 | 0 WORLD TIME (UTC) | +1 | +2 | +3 | +4 | +5 | +6 | +7 | +8 | +9 |

Reykjavik, Iceland

Tallinn, Estonia
Pori, Finland
Sitkunai, Lithuania
Kaliningrad, Russia
Karlsborg, Sweden
Hörby, Sweden
Copenhagen, Denmark
Kvitsøy, Norway
Berlin, Germany
Nauen, Germany
Leipzig, Germany
Flevoland, Holland
Skelton, England
Jülich, Germany
Dublin, Ireland
Wavre, Belgium
Rampisham, England
Litomyšl, Czech Republic
Allouis, France
Vienna, Austria
Berne, Switzerland
Zagreb, Croatia
Belgrade, Yugoslavia
Lisbon, Portugal
Noblejas, Spain
Vatican City
Rome, Italy
Tangier, Morocco
Rabat, Morocco
Sarajevo, Bosnia-Herzegovina
Algiers, Algeria
Forlì, Italy
Caltanissetta, Sicily
Sfax, Tunisia
Nouakchott, Mauritania
Dakar, Senegal
Bamako, Mali
Ouagadougou, Burkina Faso
Conakry, Guinea
Freetown, Sierra Leone
Kara, Togo
Monrovia, Liberia
Parakou, Benin
Abidjan, Côte d'Ivoire
Accra, Ghana
Lomé, Togo
Cotonou, Benin
Enugu, Nigeria
Ascension
São Tomé e Principe
Malabo, Equatorial Guinea
Bata, Equatorial Guinea
St. Helena
Libreville, Gabon
Yaoundé, Cameroon
Brazzaville, Congo
Kinshasa, Zaire
Luanda, Angola
Benguela, Angola
Windhoek, Namibia
Selebi-Phikwe, Botswana
Gaborone, Botswana

St. Petersburg, Russia
Riga, Latvia
Warsaw, Poland
Minsk, Belarus
Moscow, Russia
Tula, Russia
Rimavská Sobota, Slovakia
Szekésfehérvár, Hungary
Kiev, Ukraine
Grigoriopol, Moldova
Bucharest, Romania
Sofia, Bulgaria
Varna, Bulgaria
Istanbul, Turkey
Kaválla, Greece
Athens, Greece
Ankara, Turkey
Tirana, Albania
Malta
Cyprus
Tehrān, Iran
Baghdad, Iraq
Tel Aviv, Israel
Amman, Jordan
Tripoli, Libya
Cairo, Egypt
Kuwait
Riyadh, Saudi Arabia
Bahrain
Doha, Qatar
Jiddah, Saudi Arabia
N'Djamena, Chad
Omdurman, Sudan
Abéché, Chad
Moundou, Chad
Garoua, Cameroon
Buea, Cameroon
Bangui, Central African Republic
Bunia, Zaire
Kisangani, Zaire
Niamey, Niger
Kaduna, Nigeria
Lagos, Nigeria

Khanty-Mansiysk, Russia
Yekaterinburg, Russia
Kenga, Russia
Novosibirsk, Russia
Zhigulevsk/Samara, Russia
Krasnodar, Russia
Armavir, Russia
Almaty, Kazakhstan
Tbilisi, Georgia
Yerevan, Armenia
Baku, Azerbaijan
Tashkent, Uzbekistan
Ashgabat, Turkmenistan
Mashhad, Iran
Dushanbe, Tajikistan
Peshawar, Pakistan
Muzaffarabad, Azad Kashmir, Pakistan
Kabul, Afghanistan
Rawalpindi, Pakistan
Islamabad, Pakistan
Quetta, Pakistan
Zāhedān, Iran
New Delhi, India
Abu Dhabi, UAE
Dubai, UAE
Karachi, Pakistan
Kathmandu, Nepal
Sib, Oman
Muscat, Oman
Maslrah, Oman
Thamarīt, Oman
San'a, Yemen
Aden, Yemen
Djibouti
Hargeisa, Somalia
Addis Ababa, Ethiopia
Mogadishu, Somalia
Kampala, Uganda
Nairobi, Kenya
Kigali, Rwanda
Seychelles
Asmera, Eritrea
Bishkek, Kyrgyzstan
Bombay, India
Panaji, Goa, India
Hydarabad, India
Madras, India
Bangalore, India
Trincomalee, Sri Lanka
Colombo, Sri Lanka
Malé, Maldives
Port Blair, Andaman Islands
Calcutta, India
Lhasa, Tibet, China
Thimpu, Bhutan
Dhaka, Bangladesh
Yangon, Myanmar
Bangkok, Thailand
Kuala Lumpur, Malaysia
Padang, Indonesia
Singapore
Kuching, Malaysia
Jakarta, Indonesia
Kota Kinabalu, Malaysia
Samarinda, Indonesia
Ujung Pandang, Indonesia

Yakutsk, Russia
Krasnoyarsk, Russia
Komsomol'sk-na-Amure, Russia
Irkutsk, Russia
Ulan-Ude, Russia
Chita, Russia
Khabarovsk, Russia
Altai, Mongolia
Ulaanbaatar, Mongolia
Choybalsan, Mongolia
Urumqi, China
Hohhot, China
Harbin, China
Vladivostok, Russia
Pyongyang, North Korea
Beijing, China
Seoul, South Korea
Xi'an, China
Nanjing, China
Shanghai, China
Lhasa, Tibet, China
Kunming, China
Fuzhou, China
Hong Kong
Taipei, Taiwan
Kao-hsiung, Taiwan
Poro, Philippines
Hanoi, Vietnam
Vientiane, Laos
Palauig, Philippines
Manila, Philippines
Phnom Penh, Cambodia
Darwin, Australia
Katherine, Australia
Tennant Creek, Australia
Exmouth, Australia
Carnarvon, Australia
Alice Springs, Australia

Zanzibar, Tanzania
Dar es Salaam, Tanzania
Bujumbura, Burundi
Lubumbashi, Zaire
Antananarivo, Madagascar
Blantyre, Malawi
Lusaka, Zambia
Beira, Mozambique
Maputo, Mozambique
Manzini, Swaziland
Meyerton, South Africa
Maseru, Lesotho
Umtata, South Africa

THE WORLD
OF WORLD BAND RADIO

WORLD TIME EXAMPLE: 1300 World Time is 7AM (−6 hours)
in Chicago. For more, see **Addresses** PLUS section.

| −1 | 0 WORLD TIME (GMT) | +1 | +2 | +3 | +4 | +5 | +6 | +7 | +8 | +9 |

| +11 | +12 | −11 | −10 | −9 | −8 | −7 | −6 | −5 | −4 | −3 | −2 |

Anchor Point, Alaska, USA

Calgary AB, Canada
Salmon Arm BC, Canada

Petropavlovsk-Kamchatskiy, Russia
Magadan, Russia

Vancouver BC, Canada

Toronto ON, Canada
Montréal PQ, Canada
Scotts Corners ME, USA
St. John's NF, Canada
Sackville NB, Canada
Halifax NS, Canada
Noblesville IN, USA
Bethel PA, USA
Red Lion PA, USA
Cincinnati OH, USA
Upton KY, USA
Nashville TN, USA
Greenville NC, USA
Cypress Creek SC, USA
Birmingham AL, USA
New Orleans LA, USA
Okeechobee FL, USA
Miami FL, USA
Havana, Cuba

Sapporo, Japan

Salt Lake City UT, USA
Boulder CO, USA
San Francisco CA, USA
Redwood City CA, USA
Delano CA, USA
Los Angeles CA, USA
Mesquite NM, USA
Dallas TX, USA
Hermosillo, Mexico
Linares, Mexico
Mérida, Mexico
México City, Mexico
Veracruz, Mexico
Belize City, Belize
Guatemala City, Guatemala
San Salvador, El Salvador
Puerto Cabezas, Nicaragua
Managua, Nicaragua
Maracaibo, Venezuela
Mérida, Venezuela
Santa Fé de Bogotá, Colombia
Villavicencio, Colombia
Florencia, Colombia

Tokyo, Japan

Osaka, Japan

Hiroshima, Japan

Kekaha, Kauai Island, Hawai'i, USA

Naalehu, "Big Island," Hawai'i, USA

Saipan, Northern Mariana Islands
Guam

Palau

Biak, Indonesia
Wewak, Papua New Guinea
Madang, Papua New Guinea
Rabaul, Papua New Guinea
Mendi, Papua New Guinea

Honiara, Solomon Islands

Morobe, Papua New Guinea
Port Moresby, Papua New Guinea

Tarawa, Kiribati

Santo Domingo, Dominican Republic
Antigua

Tegucigalpa, Honduras
San José, Costa Rica

Bonaire, Netherlands Antilles
Caracas, Venezuela
Maturín, Venezuela
Georgetown, Guyana
Paramaribo, Surinam
Cayenne, French Guiana

Montsinéry, French Guiana
Belem, Brazil
Manaus, Brazil
Pôrto Velho, Brazil
Recife, Brazil
Salvador, Brazil
Cuiabá, Brazil
Brasília, Brazil
Goiânia, Brazil

Quito, Ecuador
Iquitos, Perú
Cajamarca, Perú
Pucallpa, Perú
Cobija, Bolivia
Guayaramerín, Bolivia
Cusco, Perú
Arequipa, Perú
La Paz, Bolivia
Santa Cruz, Bolivia
Sucre, Bolivia

Belo Horizonte, Brazil
Rio de Janeiro, Brazil
São Paulo, Brazil
Curitiba, Brazil
Foz do Iguaçú, Brazil
Florianópolis, Brazil
Pôrto Alegre, Brazil
Artigas, Uruguay

Tahiti, French Polynesia

Port-Vila, Vanuatu

Brandon, Australia

Nuku'alofa, Tonga

Asunción, Paraguay
Encarnación, Paraguay
Mendoza, Argentina

Santiago, Chile

Malargüe, Argentina
Temuco, Chile

Montevideo, Uruguay
Buenos Aires, Argentina

Canberra, Australia

Shepparton, Australia

Melbourne, Australia

Rangitaiki, New Zealand

Levin, New Zealand

Coyhaique, Chile

McMurdo, Antarctica (+13)

Base Esperanza, Antarctica (−3)

| +11 | +12 | −11 | −10 | −9 | −8 | −7 | −6 | −5 | −4 | −3 | −2 |

Ten of the Best: 1996's Top Shows

World band radio offers so much information that the problem isn't availability—it's getting what you want. There are many programs of uncommon excellence, but it takes some doing to ferret these out from the hundreds of others.

Soup-to-nuts coverage is in PASSPORT'S "What's On Tonight." That "TV Guide" type section leads you through the full gamut of choices of what's aired in English around the clock. But if you want to home in quickly on real gems, here are our panelists' choices. As always, schedules are in World Time.

"Brain of Britain"
BBC World Service

Here's the quiz to end all quizzes, and probably the longest-running of them all. It has a worldwide audience of millions of listeners, one of the most enthusiastic being U.S. television personality David Letterman, who's had the winners on his show.

So what's so special about it? First, the half-hour "Brain of Britain" is no radio equivalent of a TV game show. Instead, it is one of the stiffest tests of general knowledge ever to hit the airwaves. That's part of its appeal, but what makes it a top-notch entertainment package is the inimitable style and "black" humor of its long-time host, Robert Robinson.

"Brain of Britain" is a serious test of knowledge and intuition, but it's also irreverent and often downright amusing. The series runs for approximately four months of the year, most of May through September, and culminates in a grand finale, "Brain of Brains." The questions seem

United Nations official Abdel-Kader Abbadi, right, and Moroccan colleagues use world band to follow international events. *(Kader Abbadi.)*

9

CBC

Bob McDonald, host of CBC's irreverent Quirks and Quarks.

1030 Thursday on 6195 and 9740 kHz. For *Australasia*, it's 2115 Sunday on 9740 and 11955 kHz.

Officially, listeners in *North America* have just the one opportunity, at 0330 Monday (Sunday evening, local date) on 5975 and 6175 kHz. However, in eastern North America also try the European release at 2130 Sunday; farther west, check the Asian release on 9740 kHz at 1030 Thursday.

"Quirks and Quarks"
Canadian Broadcasting Corporation

There are a number of excellent science programs on the international airwaves, not least of which are the BBC's "Discovery" and "Science in Action," Radio Nederland's "Research File," and the Voice of America's "New Horizons." But there's nothing quite like the Canadian Broadcasting Corporation's "Quirks and Quarks." It's not that the CBC program is any better—we've selected the others as "Ten of the Best" in years past—it's just that it is both different and entertaining.

Although some topics are naturally serious, a light touch keeps away visions of Science 101. For example, deadly bacteria in Britain are "flesh-eating bugs." And chosen topics include clouds, thousands of light-years away, that are full of alcohol ("the bar at the end of the universe"), and the sexual selection of snakes (nothing to do with shedding your mate).

There's a spirit of irreverence, too. About God, for example, "We know that She has a sense of humor. Otherwise, why do men have nipples?" But if you like your science treated with wit, "Quirks and Quarks" is for you.

Listeners in the northeastern *United States* can tune to the CBC Northern Québec Service at 1210 Saturday (one hour earlier in summer) on 9625 kHz. Otherwise, it's a case of listening to the

to cover virtually all fields of human knowledge, including music, sport, literature, geography and current affairs. Even the Anatomical Snuff-Box (we'll leave *that* one to your imagination).

Around the program's halftime, the contestants join forces and try to answer a pair of questions sent in by a listener. If the listener manages to beat the panel on one or both of the questions, he or she receives a prize. During the eight or so months of the year when the program heads for the hills, it is replaced by other quiz shows, often lighthearted.

For *Europe* it's at 1230 Saturday on 9410, 12095 and 15070 kHz; with a repeat at 2130 Sunday on 6180, 6195, 7325, 9410 and 12095 kHz. In the *Middle East*, choose from 1230 Saturday on 11760 and 15575 kHz, and 2130 Sunday on 9410 kHz.

East Asia is the best served of all, with three slots: 2115 Sunday on 3915, 6195, 9580, 11945 and 11955 kHz; 0430 Wednesday on 11955 and 15280 kHz; and

IF YOU LISTEN TO BBC WORLD SERVICE, YOU SHOULD READ THIS.

Wherever you are in the world, and whether you are travelling or resident abroad, BBC World Service will keep you informed and entertained.

Broadcasting 24 hours a day, seven days a week, it provides not only the highest standards of news and current affairs, but also many hours a week of top quality sport, drama, science and business features, comedy, and music ranging from Handel to hip-hop.

A subscription to new BBC Worldwide, BBC World Service's own magazine, will make sure you don't miss a thing.

Published monthly in full colour, it contains within its 100 pages comprehensive details of all BBC World Service TV and radio programmes broadcast in English – together with a lively and well written blend of in-depth previews and special features, reflecting all the many facets of the BBC's world.

And if you take out a subscription now, at just £24 or $40 per annum, you'll also pick up a free BBC World Service World Time alarm clock, showing the time in 22 different countries around the world.

To take advantage of this very special offer, which will only last for a limited period, please complete the coupon now.

For further information please insert 222 on the Reader Reply Card

BBC WORLD SERVICE

relay via Radio Canada International. Because of the show's 50-minute length, it is only available to RCI listeners in the *Americas*.

Winters, the program goes out at 0205 Monday (Sunday evening, local date) on 6120, 9535, 9755, 11725 and 11845 kHz; summers, at 2305 Saturday on 5960, 9755, 11940, 13670 and 15305 kHz.

"The Greenfield Collection" BBC World Service

For many years, the voice of music critic Edward Greenfield has been familiar to followers of the BBC World Service's classical music programs. But it's only recently that he has been given his own 45-minute show, and along with it the opportunity to share his masterful collection of classical recordings with an appreciative audience.

Although "The Greenfield Collection"

Angel Records

The incomparable Kathleen Ferrier, heard on the BBC's "The Greenfield Collection."

is nominally a request program, many of the musical pieces are selected to suit the tastes of the listeners who write in, but are not necessarily those requested.

The choice of music, composers and musicians is all-encompassing, ranging from old favorites to rare sessions from as far back as the 1920s. One of the strongest arguments for listening is that nowhere else are you likely to hear as many recordings of one of the greatest female voices of all time, that of the incomparable Kathleen Ferrier. Or the now-rare 1950 recording of her duet with another vocal great, Elizabeth Schwarzkopf.

The first slot for *Europe* is at 0815 Sunday on 9410, 12095 and 15070 kHz, with a repeat at 1615 the same day and on the same frequencies. These two airings are also available for the *Middle East* at 0815 on 9410 (or 15070), 11760 and 15575 kHz; and at 1615 on 9410, 12095 and 15070 kHz.

Listeners in *East Asia* have just the one opportunity, at 0810 Sunday on 11955 and 15280 kHz, with 11955 kHz also available for *Australasia*.

Unfortunately, the timing for *North America* is dreadful. First shot is for the West Coast at 0715 Tuesday (around midnight Monday night, local time) on 9640 kHz, with a repeat to all areas during the day at 1515 on 9515, 11775 and 11865 kHz.

"VOA Business Report" Voice of America

The BBC World Service has always been walls and streets ahead of other broadcasters for up-to-the-minute business and financial news, and it is unlikely that any serious competitor will emerge anytime soon.

Full marks, then, to the Voice of America for not going head-to-head with the BBC when it decided to add a

ATS-606

ATS-800A

SG-631

DT 200V
DT 300VW
w/Weather Band

ATS-808

ATS-818CS

Be there now.

Sangean World Band Receivers, Multiple Band, Multiple Choice...

Whether traveling around the world or simply across town, **Sangean** portables keep you informed. And **Sangean** has it all from the world's only full featured ATS-818CS Digital Receiver with built-in Programmable Cassette Recorder to the world's most advanced ultra-compact digital receiver, our ATS-606 with Automatic Preset Tuning which automatically sets up your memory presets at the push of a button. **Sangean's** complete line of full featured analog and digital receivers offer the utmost in reliability and performance at a price just right for your budget.

Sangean portables, it gets you where you want to be!

Call or write for more information.

WRTH Radio Industry Award
Most Innovative Receiver Manufacturer 1993!
WRTH is a trademark of Watson-Guptill
Publications and is used with express permission

WORLD 21 YEARS LEADERSHIP
1974 to 1995

SANGEAN
A M E R I C A ,   I N C .
A WORLD OF LISTENING
2651 Troy Ave, S. El Monte, CA 91733
(818) 579-1600 FAX (818) 579-6806

The VOA Business Report presents first-rate analysis of business and economic affairs. Shown, Paul Westpheling, co-anchor.

regular business section to its lineup. Although it took a while to find its niche, the 20-minute "VOA Business Report" has developed into a useful and interesting program about business and finance. Because it takes the time to explain things in plain English, it appeals to ordinary folks, as well as those versed in the minutiae of business and finance.

Unlike the BBC's financial and business output, that of the VOA gives relatively little prominence to the world's stock and futures markets. Instead, it delves thoughtfully into the larger picture of business and financial matters without reciting price quotations. Too, while the BBC's approach is unmistakably international, the VOA leans more towards events and trends affecting the United States and its interests.

Europeans have to be early risers, indeed, to catch the program, as it goes out at a time better suited to farmers than financiers: 0410 Monday through Friday, on 5995, 6040 and 7170 kHz. There are no designated winter frequencies for the *Middle East*, but 11965 and 15205 kHz should be easily audible in summer.

In *East Asia*, it's at 0010 Sunday through Thursday (Monday through Friday, local dates) on 7215, 11760, 15185, 15290, 17735 and 17820 kHz. The same slot is also available to *Australasia* on 15185 and 17735 kHz.

Although there are no transmissions specifically directed their way, listeners in *North America* have a choice of options, depending on their location. Try 0010 Tuesday through Friday (Monday through Thursday, local dates) on 5995,

JRC NRD-535D

"Best Communications Receiver"

World Radio TV Handbook 1992

"Unsurpassed DX Performance"

Passport to World Band Radio 1992

Setting the industry standard once again for shortwave receivers, the NRD-535D is the most advanced HF communications receiver ever designed for the serious DXer and shortwave listener. Its unparalleled performance in all modes makes it the ultimate receiver for diversified monitoring applications.

Designed for DXers by DXers! The NRD-535D (shown above with optional NVA-319 speaker) strikes the perfect balance between form and function with its professional-grade design and critically acclaimed ergonomics. The NRD-535D is the recipient of the prestigious World Radio TV Handbook Industry Award for "Best Communications Receiver."

- Phase-lock ECSS system for selectable-sideband AM reception.
- Maximum IF bandwidth flexibility! The Variable Bandwidth Control (BWC) adjusts the wide and intermediate IF filter bandwidths from 5.5 to 2.0 kHz and 2.0 to 0.5 kHz—continuously.
- Stock fixed-width IF filters include a 5.5 kHz (wide), a 2.0 kHz (intermediate), and a 1.0 kHz (narrow). Optional JRC filters include 2.4 kHz, 300 Hz, and 500 Hz crystal type.
- All mode 100 kHz – 30 MHz coverage. Tuning accuracy to 1 Hz, using JRC's advanced Direct Digital Synthesis (DDS) PLL system and a high-precision magnetic rotary encoder. The tuning is so smooth you will swear it's analog! An optional high-stability crystal oscillator kit is also available for ±0.5 ppm stability.
- A superior front-end variable double tuning circuit is continuously controlled by the CPU to vary with the receive frequency automatically. The result: Outstanding 106 dB Dynamic Range and +20 dBm Third-Order Intercept Point.
- Memory capacity of 200 channels, each storing frequency, mode, filter, AGC and ATT settings. Scan and sweep functions built in. All memory channels are tunable, making "MEM to VFO" switching unnecessary.
- A state-of-the-art RS-232C computer interface is built into every NRD-535D receiver.
- Fully modular design, featuring plug-in circuit boards and high-quality surface-mount components. No other manufacturer can offer such professional-quality design and construction at so affordable a price.

JRC *Japan Radio Co., Ltd.*

Japan Radio Company, Ltd., New York Branch Office – 430 Park Avenue (2nd Floor), New York, NY 10022, USA Fax: (212) 319-5227

Japan Radio Company, Ltd. – Akasaka Twin Tower (Main), 17-22, Akasaka 2-chome, Minato-ku, Tokyo 107, JAPAN Fax: (03) 3584-8878

7405, 9775 and 13740 kHz, when the program is beamed to Latin America; 0010 Monday (Sunday evening in the Americas) on 6130, 9455 and 11695 kHz (targeted at the Caribbean); or 0410 Monday through Friday on the African Service, on 7405 kHz, plus 7280, 7340 and 9575 kHz.

"On The March"
Radio New Zealand International

With satellite-delivered entertainment and glitzy television spectaculars, it is easy to forget that people succeeded in enjoying themselves for centuries without the technological trappings of today. "Enjoyment," once synonymous with "entertainment," has now been almost totally overtaken by the latter.

Every once in a while, though, something comes up that is both entertaining

Strike up the band, with Radio New Zealand International's Rudi Hill!

and pleasurable, with all the technological bustle of a hand-rolled cigar. Such is the case with "On the March," a weekly offering from Radio New Zealand International, and presented by veteran host Rudi Hill. It features no less than recordings of military and other parade bands—the sort of entertainment that captured the fancy of generations past, and not all that long ago. It's wholesome, as wholesome was before people said it with a snicker. And it's from a country which still retains core values that so many other societies are trying to recapture.

Although beaming to listeners in the South Pacific, friendly Radio New Zealand International also provides a decent signal in many other parts of the world, including *North America*. "On the March" can be heard at 0910 Thursday, winters (summers in the Southern Hemisphere) on 9700 kHz, and summers on 6100 kHz.

"Insight"
Deutsche Welle

One of the major strengths of world band programming is the amount of in-depth analysis that's aired. Not surprisingly, much of it comes from broadcasting giants, as their human and financial resources are far in excess of those available to smaller stations.

Deutsche Welle, one of the front-runners when it comes to news and news analysis, offers several features dedicated to analyzing political and economic issues. Most are concerned with local or regional affairs, but one, "Insight," is truly international.

Unlike some other programs of this kind, which project opposing viewpoints, "Insight" tends to rely on interviews with one or more persons of a like mind who are closely connected to the international topic under review. Extracts of interviews are then interwo-

Gabriele Fromm, DW

Deutsche Welle's "Insight" brings together the ethos of the new Germany with the confidence of the old.

ven into a prepared script, so as to produce a flowing, in-depth feature that gives a solid background to the chosen subject.

There is no limit to the variety of topics, which range from a look at Arab banking practices, to economic development in the Mekong Delta. And the dreaded "W" word is no longer in the closet. Witness the show's thoughtful and incisive reassessment of the allied bombing of Dresden in 1945. Whatever the subject, the end result is always the same—a full justification of the program's title.

The first airing is for *North America* at 0332 Wednesday (Tuesday evening, local date). Winter frequencies are 6045, 6085, 6120, 9535 and 9650 kHz; in summer, go for 6085, 6185, 9615, 9640 and 11750 kHz.

Listeners in Europe are brushed off,

and the *Middle East* fares little better. Either place, try 1932 Wednesday, winters on 13790 kHz and summers on 13690 kHz.

East and Southeast Asia and Australasia get their opportunity at 0932 Wednesday. Winter channels are 6160, 9875 (East Asia only), 11715, 17780, 17820, 21650 and 21680 kHz; in summer, choose from 6160, 11730, 12055 (East Asia only), 15245, 17715 and 21680 kHz.

"Off The Shelf"
BBC World Service

Tired of surfing the Internet? TV putting you to sleep? Football team in the cellar? Can't fly to the Islands?

It's time to put up your feet, switch on your radio, and discover "Off the Shelf," the weekday 15-minute literary offering from the BBC World Service. If there is anything like reading a good book, it's having it read to you. By a BBC professional, which is what you get.

If you're a fan of Dorothy Sayers, there's *Strong Poison*. Prefer a classic? Try Jane Austen's *Northanger Abbey* or Gaston Leroux's *The Phantom of the Opera*. A bio? Hard to beat Nelson Mandela's *Long Walk to Freedom*. And who would want to miss Edna O'Brien reading her own intensely powerful *House of Splendid Isolation*?

Some of the *oeuvres* last for as long as three weeks, but others occupy only two or three programs. The problem with any serialization is whether or not you can hear all the episodes—and the BBC, regrettably, has not done much towards providing repeat broadcasts. In Europe, the Middle East and North America, there is no second chance. Listeners in South Asia, on the other hand, have three opportunities to hear the program. Lucky them.

In *Europe*, tune in at 1045 on 9410, 12095 and 15070 kHz, and in the *Middle*

Now The Company That Takes You Around The World Lets You Take The World Around With You.

The Drake SW8 – Finally, Professional Desktop Performance In An Affordable, Portable World Band Shortwave.

The company that has been setting the standards in premium-quality world band shortwave performance now puts top-of-the-line features and technology at your fingertips with the SW8…wherever you want to take it. Designed for both desktop use and easy portability, the Drake SW8 includes many of the same features that have made Drake a perennial favorite of experts – superb audio, versatility, and the unique combination of professional quality and functional simplicity. So tune in the world and get the best of all worlds – quality and affordability, desktop technology and portability. The Drake SW8.

To order your SW8 direct, for more information, or for the dealer nearest you call:

1-800-568-3426

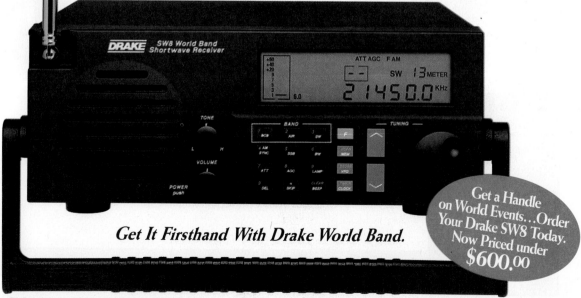

Get It Firsthand With Drake World Band.

Get a Handle on World Events…Order Your Drake SW8 Today. Now Priced under $600.00

R.L. Drake Company • P.O. Box 3006 • Miamisburg, OH 45343 • U.S.A.

ANYPLACE.
ANYWHERE.
ANYTIME.

Once again, Grundig revolutionizes the art of radio technology! Introducing the newest and most advanced shortwave radio available today. If you are serious about shortwave radio, the **Satellit 900** is for you!

Years of experience and technology were brought together to create the Satellit 900. Although it is technically advanced, featuring a PC interface, synchronous detection and RDS radio text, the Satellit 900 is one of the easiest-to-use products on the market today!

The Satellit 900 boasts advanced features:

- A personal computer interface which allows direct programming of radio memory functions.
- A large, high-contrast dot matrix LCD allows for clear reading of all radio functions. The display screen is adjustable for better viewing.
- Incorporating a technical enhancement, the Satellit 900 utilizes an RDS radio text feature which allows broadcasted text to be received and displayed.

After all is said and done, the Satellit 900 is one of the best radios available today!

SATELLIT 900

Advanced Features:
- PC Interface
- Adjustable Display Viewing Angle
- Sound Boost
- RDS Radio Text
- Dot Matrix LCD

Standard Features:
- AM/FM
- Continuous Shortwave 1.6–30 MHz
- PLL Tuning
- Synchronous Detector
- Upper/Lower Sideband
- Expandable Memory
- Dual Alarm
- Programmable Sleep Timer

Size: 13-1/8"L x 7"H x 2-1/8"

Weight: 4 lbs

GRUNDIG

Call for information: U.S. 1-800-872-2228 or 415-361-1611
Canada 800-637-1648 • Fax: 415-361-1724

East try 11760 and 15575 kHz. *East Asia* has two opportunities: at 0330 on 11955 and 15280 kHz, and at 0715 on 11955, 15280 and 15360 kHz. This second slot is also available for *Australasia* on 11955 and 15360 kHz.

In eastern and southern *North America*, you can listen at 2130 on 5975 kHz, but there is no specific broadcast for folks out west. (Hello, Bush House— human life forms have been spotted west of the Mississippi!)

If "On the Shelf" is not available to your area, try times and frequencies intended for other regions. Apart from the broadcasts already mentioned, other editions of the program go out at 0430 on 9605 and 15310 kHz (South Asia); 0715 on 15310 and 17790 kHz (South Asia); 1045 on 11940, 15400, 17830 and 17885 kHz (Africa); 1315 on 15420 and 17885 kHz (East Africa); 1445 on 11940, 15400, 17830 and 21660 kHz (West Africa);

and 1730 on 5975, 9510, 9740 and 11750 kHz (South Asia). Several of these channels provide fair-to-good reception well beyond their intended target areas.

"Newsline" Radio Nederland

Radio Nederland must be a major candidate for "The Jekyll and Hyde of world band radio." While some former favorites have either disappeared or degenerated into uninteresting shows of dubious taste, others have established themselves as offerings of the highest quality.

One of the best is the anchor program, "Newsline," usually available six days a week. However, if you are looking for a rival to the BBC's incomparable "Newshour," or the VOA's outstanding "Report to the Americas," you might be disappointed, because it's a lot short-

"Newsline's" award-winning team from Holland. Shown: (front, glasses) Mike Shea, Network Manager; Jimmy Ocotti; (rear) Michèle Ernsting, Jaldeep Katwala, James McDonald and Theo Tamis.

er. But what it does, it does very well—like a first-rate appetizer, rather than a main course. For some, in a hurry, that's a plus.

"Newsline" is a 14-minute no-frills package of interviews, commentaries and on-the-spot correspondents' reports. Although particularly strong on events in Europe, there are also special editions for Africa and Asia. Thanks to Radio Nederland's outstanding shortwave facilities, these can also be heard well beyond the intended target areas.

All transmissions are Monday through Saturday, unless stated otherwise.

In *Europe*, "Newsline" is heard at 1137 and 1237 winters on 6045 and 7130 kHz; summers one hour earlier on 6045 and 9650 kHz. For the *Middle East*, try at 1337 on 13700 kHz.

Listeners in *East Asia* should aim for the 0937 and 1037 editions, winters on 7260 and 9810 kHz, and summers on 12065 kHz. In *Australasia*, shoot for 0737 on 9700 (or 11895) and 9720 kHz; 0837 on 9720 and (winters only) 13700 kHz; 0937 on 9720 and (summers only) 13700 kHz; and 1037 (summers only) on 9820 and 12065 kHz.

First slots for *North America* are at 2337 and 0037 on 6020, 6165 and 9845 kHz. There is a third broadcast, for western areas, at 0437 Tuesday through Sunday (Monday through Saturday evenings, local dates) on 5995 (or 9590) and 6165 kHz.

The special Asian edition of the program goes out at 1337, 1437 and 1537, and is targeted at the southern part of the continent. Try 9890 (or 9895), 13700 (at 1337) and 15150 kHz.

The alternative version for Africa can be heard at 1737, 1837, 1937 and 2037. The second and third releases are heard over a wide area outside Africa, including parts of *North America*, on 9860, 9895, 15315 and 17605 kHz.

"Folk Routes"
BBC World Service

Like *The Little Train That Could*, this is a "keep trying" success story of world band radio. When the program was introduced some years ago, under a different and awful name, all they played was British folk music, along with English bands playing American and other ethnic music.

You can imagine the result. A band from the North of England playing Cajun music creates about the same effect as Professor Longhair performing an Irish jig. So the format was changed to include recordings of overseas artists currently performing in Britain.

That didn't fly, either, so caution was thrown to the wind. On its third try, the program wound up with its present format, and it's a winner.

So, what can you expect? Basically, five tracks from currently available compact discs. Sounds mundane? Well, yes, until you actually hear the CDs: folk-rock from Ontario, country-folk from Nashville, exotic tunes from Mali, Nothumberland pipes from England, Delta blues from Mississippi—all chosen with a certain *je ne sais quoi*. Truly eclectic, perhaps *too* eclectic for some, but it comes off with aplomb.

Unlike some of the BBC's other offerings, "Folk Routes" is easily heard in virtually all areas. For *Europe*, there's 2030 Sunday on 6180, 6195, 7325, 9410 and 12095 kHz; and 1645 Wednesday on 9410, 12095 and 15070 kHz. These times are also available for the *Middle East*— 9410, 12095 and 15070 kHz are available for both slots.

Listeners in *East Asia* have two opportunities: 0030 Tuesday on 15360 kHz, and 0445 Friday on 11955, 15280 and 15360 kHz. For *Australasia*, it's 2030 Sunday on 9740 and 11955 kHz.

North America, for a change, is the best served of all: 0030 Tuesday

(Monday evening, local date) on 5975, 6175 and 7325 kHz; 1615 Tuesday on 9515 and 11755 kHz; and 1130 Wednesday on 6195 and 9515 kHz.

"Israel News Magazine"
Kol Israel

News from the Middle East is so commonplace that the last thing that would seem to make sense is yet another source from that part of the world. Especially from one of the most active and partisan players.

Yet, this show, which made its debut in the summer of 1995, succeeds better than anything else we've come across. The high level of professionalism shown by Kol Israel journalists, combined with on-the-spot reporting, produces a half hour of comprehensive, superior-quality reporting rarely found even in larger broadcasting organizations. It's news the way news should be presented—but otherwise rarely is, especially where Israel is concerned.

Veteran correspondent Sara Manobla is one of "Israel News Magazine's" several outstanding journalists.

> "Israel News Magazine" is news the way news should be presented.

Not only does "Israel News Magazine" inform about the country and its people, it also provides insight into many of the region's problems, which otherwise can seem baffling to outsiders. Interviews are widely used to create a sense of "being there," but their length is kept to just the necessary minimum, ensuring that this fast-moving program rarely falters.

Alas, governing authorities have so badly mishandled this station for the past few years that its voice is but a whisper of what it could and should be, and to some extent once was. The decline began in 1991, when a former manager claimed, falsely, and the *Jerusalem Post* echoed, that virtually nobody outside Russia was listening. This allowed external service funds to be diverted into a new domestic service he was to head. Then, with the demise of the Soviet Union, the Jewish Agency withdrew most of its financial support. Finally, the parent Israel Broadcasting Authority decided that they wanted no part of paying for a service for foreigners, so in early 1995 nearly terminated the external service altogether.

Fortunately, Kol Israel continues to soldier on in the best journalistic tradition, thanks in large part to letters, faxes and calls of support it and the Israeli government has received from its vast worldwide listening audience— believed to be roughly half Jewish, half non-Jewish, and numbering in the millions.

"Israel News Magazine" runs a half hour except Saturdays, when it's abbreviated to an eight-minute news bulletin, followed by a 20-minute news interview. Listeners in *Europe* can tune in evenings, and in *Eastern North America* afternoons, at 2000 (1900 in summer) on 7405 (winter), 7465, 9465, 11603 and (summer) 11685 kHz. A year-round frequency of 15640 kHz is also available for Central and South America.

Prepared by the staff of PASSPORT TO WORLD BAND RADIO.

Did we say "Ten of the Best"?

Well, every rule has to have an exception, so here is our "baker's tenth"...sort of. Normally, we only select individual programs, but here we have an entire broadcast. It's the hour-long information package produced by Radio France Internationale, and released, in separate editions, three times each day.

What makes the broadcast exceptional, apart from its excellence of content, is that it is streamlined and fast-moving—there's rarely time to breathe! Each edition is geared to a particular audience: North America and Eastern Europe at 1200, the Middle East and Asia at 1400, and Africa at 1600, plus the scattering properties of shortwave allow for transcontinental eavesdropping.

The first half hour is devoted to the latest news, extensive reports and interviews, and a review of items from the French press. These are followed by a regional feature, with the final part being a cultural, scientific or ecological feature.

The 1200 transmission to *North America* is available year-round on 13625 kHz. For another channel, try either 11615, 15530 or 17575 kHz—or 15325 kHz via RFI's relay in Gabon. Though targeted at West Africa, its signal can be heard in parts of eastern North America and the Caribbean. The 1600 broadcast to Africa, once easily heard in eastern North America, is now much more iffy. Try 11615, 11700, 12015 and 15530 kHz at 1600-1655, and 15210 (or 17795) and 15460 kHz at 1600-1730; the extra half hour has additional programming for East Africa.

In *Europe*, you can listen at 1200-1255 on 9805, 15155 and 15195 kHz; and at 1600-1655 a relay of the African Service is on 6175 kHz. Listeners in the *Middle East* can try 1400-1455 on 17560 kHz; 1600-1655 on 9485 or 11615 kHz, and 1600-1730 (nominally for East Africa) on 15460 kHz.

Best bet for *Asia* is 1400-1455 on 7110 and 12030 (or 15405) kHz. Listeners in the southeastern part of the continent can also try at 1200-1255 winters on 11615 kHz. There is no specific broadcast for *Australasia*, but listeners in that part of the world should try the 12030 (or 15405) kHz channel targeted at Asia.

Radio France International's Jean Maurice de Montremy hosts French culture with a touch of class.

RADIO VATICANA
ESPERANTO-SEKCIO
Piazza Pia 3
00193 ROMA

Herrn Pater E.v.Genninger
Deutschsprachige
Radio V~·

CAMILUS,
CE,

ABIA·

The Vatican Ra
Indian Section
001~~CAN CIT
00

VIA AIR MAIL

1490 ☩ 1990
100

Pater
EBERHARD VON GENNINGEN SJ
Radio Vaticana

I- 00120 Vatikanstadt
(Città del Vaticano)
-Italia

Service
dio
tican City.

NIGERIA
NIGERIA
NIGERIA
20k

Radio
Inter

Compleat Idiot's Guide to Getting Started

Welcome to World Band Radio!

World band radio—it's your direct connection to what's going on just about everywhere. Facts and perspectives appear before they can be filtered and molded by editorial arbiters. It's news you want to know—not what you're supposed to know.

That, plus remarkable entertainment, is what you can expect. Here's how to go about getting them...

"Must" #1: Set Clock for World Time

Research has shown that world band listeners who try to wing it without PASSPORT have about a 50-50 chance of dropping out within their first year of listening. Yet, less than one person in 20 who uses PASSPORT gives up. That's mainly because PASSPORT's schedule details take away the "hit-and-miss" of shortwave radio purchases and schedules.

But to make this work, these schedules use the *World Time* standard. That's because world band radio is global, with nations broadcasting around-the-clock from virtually every time zone.

Imagine the chaos if each broadcaster used its own local time for scheduling. In England, 9 PM is different from nine in the evening in Japan or Canada. How would anybody know when to tune in?

To eliminate confusion, international broadcasters use World Time, or UTC, as a standard reference. Formerly and in some circles still known as Greenwich Mean Time (GMT), it is keyed to the Greenwich meridian in England and is announced in 24-hour format, like military time. So 2 PM, say, is 1400 ("fourteen hundred") hours.

There are three easy ways to know World Time. First, you can tune in one of the standard time stations, such as WWV in Colorado and WWVH in Hawaii in the United States. These are on 5000, 10000 and 15000 kHz around-the-clock, with

Letters are welcomed at Vatican Radio. "Addresses PLUS" explains how you can contact stations.   *(Vatican Radio)*

29

WWV also on 2500 and 20000 kHz. There, you will hear time "pips" every second, followed just before the beginning of each minute by an announcement of the exact World Time. Boring, yes, but very handy when you need it.

Second, you can tune in one of the major international broadcasters, such as London's BBC World Service or Washington's Voice of America. Most announce World Time at the top of the hour.

Third, here's some quick calculations.

If you live on the East Coast of the United States, *add* five hours winter (four hours summer) to your local time to get World Time. So, if it is 8 PM EST (the 20th hour of the day) in New York, it is 0100 hours World Time.

On the U.S. West Coast, add eight hours winter (seven hours summer).

In Britain, it's easy—World Time (oops, Greenwich Mean Time) is the same as local winter time. However, you'll have to subtract one hour from local summer time to get World Time.

Elsewhere in Western Europe, subtract one hour winter (two hours summer) from local time.

Live elsewhere? Flip through the next pages until you come to "How to Set Your World Time Clock."

A World Time clock is a "must."

Heath Company.

Once you know the correct World Time, set your radio's clock so you'll have it handy whenever you want to listen. No 24-hour clock? Pick up the phone and order one (world band specialty firms sell them for as little as $10, see box). Unless you enjoy doing weird computations in your head (it's 6:00 PM here, so add five hours to make it 11:00 PM, which on a 24-hour clock converts to 23:00 World Time—but, whoops, I forgot that it's summer and I should have added four hours instead of five...), it'll be the best ten bucks you ever spent.

"Must" #2: Understand World Day

There's a trick to World Time that can occasionally catch even the most experienced listener. What happens at midnight? A new day, *World Day*, arrives as well.

First Taste: Passport's Five-Minute Start

In a hurry? Here's how to get to first base pronto:

1. Wait until evening. If you live in a concrete-and-steel building, put the radio by a window.

2. Make sure your radio is plugged in or has fresh batteries. Extend the telescopic antenna fully and vertically. Set the DX/local switch (if there is one) to "DX," but otherwise leave the controls the way they came from the factory.

3. Turn on your radio. Set it to 5900 kHz and begin tuning slowly toward 6200 kHz. You will now begin to encounter a number of stations from around the world. Adjust the volume to a level that is comfortable for you. *Voilà!* You are now an initiate of world band radio.

Other times? Read this article. It tells you where to tune day and night. Too, refer to the handy "Best Times and Frequencies for 1996" box at the end of this chapter.

ANYPLACE.
ANYWHERE.
ANYTIME.

GRUNDIG

40—STATION MEMORIES

Travel the airwaves with Grundig's portable digital Yacht Boy 400. Listening has never been easier... the BBC commentary from London, the news from Berlin, Beijing, the Balkans and more. Imagine!

Only Grundig with its reputation for world class electronics could offer a radio so advanced and compact: AM/FM Stereo/Shortwave, digital tuning, auto scan and 40-memories, clock alarm and timer. Also includes *Grundig Shortwave Listening Guide*, batteries, external antenna, earphones and carrying case.

Rated best in its class!

YACHT BOY 400

Features:

- Shortwave/AM/FM and Longwave
- Continuous shortwave from 1.6–30 MHz
- Clock, alarm and timer
- 40 randomly programmable memories
- Multifunction liquid crystal display
- Phase-lock-loop tuning
- Size: 7-3/4"L x 4-5/8"H x 1-1/4"W
- Weight: 1 lb. 5 oz.

GRUNDIG

Call for information: U.S. 1-800-872-2228 or 415-361-1611
Canada 800-637-1648 • Fax: 415-361-1724

Remember: Midnight World Time means a new day, too. So if it is 9 PM EST Wednesday in New York, it is 0200 hours World Time *Thursday*. Don't forget to "wind your calendar."

"Must" #3: Know How to Find Stations

You can find world band stations by looking them up in PASSPORT'S by-country or "What's On Tonight" sections. Or you can flip through PASSPORT'S vast Blue Pages to surf within the several *segments*, or "bands"—neighborhoods within the shortwave spectrum where stations are found. Information on what segments to tune at which times appears later in this chapter.

Incidentally, frequencies may be given in kilohertz, kHz, or Megahertz, MHz. The only difference is three decimal places, so 6175 kHz is the same as 6.175 MHz. But forget all the technobabble. All you need to know is that 6175, with or without decimals, refers to a certain spot on your radio's dial.

If you have never before experienced world band radio, you will be accustomed to hearing local stations at the same place on the dial day and night. Things are very different when you roam the international airwaves.

World band radio is like a global

Iveta Pustajovská, editor/announcer for Radio Slovakia International—a new station from a new country.

bazaar where merchants come and go at different times. Stations enter and leave the same spot on the dial throughout the day and night. Where you once tuned in, say, a British station, hours later you might find a Russian or Chinese broadcaster roosting on that same spot.

Or on a nearby perch. If you suddenly hear interference from a station on an adjacent channel, it doesn't mean something is wrong with your radio; it means another station has begun broadcasting on a nearby frequency. There are more stations on the air than there is space for them, so sometimes they try to outshout each other, like merchants in a bazaar: "Come over here! Listen to me!"

The best way to cope with this is to purchase a radio with superior adjacent-channel rejection, also known as selectivity. Read PASSPORT REPORTS to find out what's what in this regard.

One of the most enjoyable things about world band radio is cruising up and down the airwaves. Daytime, you'll find most stations above 11500 kHz; night, below 10000 kHz.

Tune slowly, savor the sound of foreign tongues cuddled alongside the regular English shows. Enjoy the music, weigh the opinions of other peoples.

If a station disappears, there is probably nothing wrong with your radio. The atmosphere's *ionosphere* reflects world band signals, and it changes constantly. The result is that broadcasters operate in different parts of the world band spectrum, depending upon the time of day and season of the year. PASSPORT'S schedules show you where to tune and retune. On advanced radios, you can store these favorite channels on presets for immediate call-up, day-after-day.

That same changeability can also work in your favor, especially if you like to eavesdrop on signals not intended to be heard by you. Sometimes stations from exotic locales—places you would not ordinarily hear—arrive at your radio,

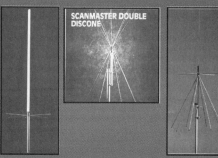

Evaristo Mercado Pérez, director of Nicaragua's Radio Miskut, with Allan Zavala. Hundreds of intriguing stations lie off the beaten path for talented listeners to enjoy.

thanks to the shifting characteristics of the ionosphere. Unlike other media, world band radio sometimes allows stations to be heard thousands of miles beyond where they are beamed.

"Must" #4: Obtain A Radio That Works Properly

If you haven't yet purchased a world band radio, here's some good news: Although cheap radios should be avoided—they suffer from one or more major defects—you don't need an expensive set to enjoy exploring the world's airwaves. With one of the better-rated portables, about the price of an ordinary VCR, you'll be able to hear much of what world band has to offer.

You won't need an outside antenna, either, unless you're using a tabletop model. All portables, and to some extent portatops, are designed to work off the built-in telescopic antenna. Try, though, to purchase a radio with digital frequency display. Its accuracy will make tuning around the bands far easier than with outmoded slide-rule tuning.

Does that mean you should avoid a tabletop or portatop model? Hardly, especially if you listen during the day, when signals are weaker, or to hard-to-hear stations. The best-rated tabletop, and even portatop, models can bring faint and difficult signals to life—especially when they're connected to a good external antenna. But if you just want to hear the big stations, you'll do fine with a moderately priced portable. PASSPORT REPORTS rates nearly all available models.

Radio in hand, read your owner's manual. You'll find that, despite a few unfamiliar controls, your new world band receiver isn't all that much different from radios you have used all your life. Experiment with the controls so you'll become comfortable with them. After all, you can't harm your radio by twiddling switches and knobs.

Prepared by Jock Elliott, Tony Jones and Lawrence Magne.

Bargains in World Time Clocks

Each of the following simple clocks contains identical "mechanisms"...

★ ★ ★ **MFJ-24-107B**, $9.95. Despite its paucity of features, this "Volksclock" does the trick.

★ ★ ★ **NI8F LCD**, $14.95. Same as the MFJ, above, but with a handsome walnut frame instead of aluminum. It is less likely than MFJ models to scratch surfaces. From Universal Radio.

★ ★ ★ **MFJ-108**, $19.95. For those who also want local time. Two LCD clocks—24-hour format for World Time, separate 12-hour display for local time—side-by-side.

OUT OF THIN AIR AND INTO THE THICK OF THINGS.

THE DRAKE R8A

The Drake R8A World Band Communications Receiver. Turn it on, tune it in, and as easy as that, you're hearing world events as they happen… uncensored and complete. And with the R8A's astounding clarity, it's almost as if you're there. In fact, no other communications receiver puts you closer to the action in even the most distant parts of the world.

If you're a hobbyist, you'll marvel at the R8A's simplicity of operation. If you're an expert, you'll admire the high-powered features. The Drake R8A offers superior performance in a complete package that includes built-in filters and other unique features that have made Drake the foremost name in world band communications. The R8A from Drake…you've got to hear it to believe it.

DRAKE, FOR A WORLD OF DIFFERENCE.

R.L. Drake Company, P.O. Box 3006, Miamisburg, Ohio 45343, U.S.A. ▪ Sales Office: 513.866.2421 ▪ Fax: 513.866.0806 ▪ Service and Parts: 513.746.6990 ▪ In Canada: 705.742.3122
© 1995 The R.L. Drake Company   **DRAKE** is a registered trademark of The R.L. Drake Company.

MONITOR MORE WITH ADVANCED EQUIPMENT FROM UNIVERSAL!

MULTI-MODE CONVERTERS AND READERS

■ Universal M-8000v5

The professional grade M-8000 was designed primarily for the military, commercial and diplomatic user. It can also be used by the hobbyist who requires maximum intercept capability. The M-8000 provides modes and features not available on other units. The color VGA output includes a spectral display and simulated tuning scope plus five tuning bars. Modes currently supported include: **CW, Baudot, SITOR A & B, ARQ-M2/4, ARQ-E/3, ARQ6-90, ARQ-S, SWED-ARQ, FEC-A, FEC-S, ASCII, Packet, Pactor, Piccolo, VFT, ACARS, POCSAG** and **GOLAY.** Plus display modes for: Russian Cyrillic, Literal and Databit analysis mode. Breathtaking **FAX** images to screen or printer. 115/230 AC 50/60 Hz. This unit is a favorite with military, diplomatic and hobby users worldwide. Too many features to list here. Contact Universal for full specifications. *#0085* **$1349.00** (+$10)

■ Universal M-400

Forget the limitations you have come to expect from most "readers". The self-contained Universal M-400 is a sophisticated decoder *and* tone reader offering exceptional capabilities. The shortwave listener can decode: **Baudot, SITOR A&B, FEC-A, ASCII** and **SWED-ARQ.** Weather **FAX** can also be decoded to the printer port. The VHF-UHF listener will be able to copy the **ACARS** VHF aviation teletype mode plus **GOLAY** and **POCSAG** digital pager modes. Off-the-air decoding of **DTMF, CTCSS** and **DCS** is also supported. Big two-line, 20 character LCD. The M-400 can even be programmed to pass only the audio you want to hear based on CTCSS, DCS or DTMF codes of your choosing. The M-400 runs from 12 VDC or with the supplied AC adapter. No computer or monitor is required. The American-made M-400 is *the* affordable accessory for every shortwave or scanner enthusiast. *#0400* **$399.95** (+$6)

■ Universal M-1200

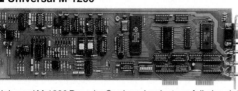

Turn your IBM computer (or compatible) into a powerful intercept device! The Universal M-1200 Decoder Card requires just one full-size slot in your PC. Your computer can open up a new world of listening (... or *seeing*) opportunities! Reception modes include: **Morse, Baudot RTTY** and **SITOR A/B, FEC-A, ARQ-M2, ARQ-E,** and **ARQ-E3** plus **ASCII** and **Packet.** VHF enthusiasts can copy **ACARS** aviation mode, **POCSAG** and **GOLAY.** Advanced RTTY DXer's will appreciate the *Databit* and *Literal* modes, helpful in protocol identification and analysis. The video quality of your **FAX** intercepts will amaze you. Advanced FAX imaging includes pseudo-color and zoom features. FAX images as well as text traffic can be saved to disk. Operation is easy through on-screen menus, status indicators and help windows. A new *datascope* feature operates in both RTTY and FAX modes. The Universal M-1200 comes complete with an informative manual and software on a 3°" 720K disk. Requires *PC* computer with EGA or VGA monitor. Made in the U.S.A. *#1200* **$399.95** (+$6)

COMMUNICATIONS BOOKS

● **Passport To Worldband Radio** *By L. Magne*
Graphic presentation of all shortwave broadcast stations and hard hitting receiver reviews. A *must have* book. *#1000* **$19.95** (+$2)

● **World Radio TV Handbook**
All shortwave broadcast stations organized by country with schedules, addresses, power, etc. Some FM/TV. *#2000* **$24.95** (+$2)

● **The WRTH Satellite Broadcasting Guide**
Covers satellite dishes, equipment reviews, 160 satellite coverage maps, transponder survey, glossary & more. *#2311* **$24.95** (+$2)

● **Shortwave Receivers Past & Present** *By F. Osterman*
Your guide to over 200 receivers with new and used values, specifications and features. Photos for most. *#2948* **$8.95** (+$2)

● **Joe Carr's Receiving Antenna Handbook** *By J. Carr*
A complete guide to high performance receiving antennas for long wave through shortwave. Includes: loops, rhombics, beverages and directional designs. Excellent. *#3113* **$19.95** (+$2)

● **Guide to Utility Stations** *By J. Klingenfuss*
The definitive guide to shortwave utility stations including CW, SSB, FAX and radioteletype. 20,000+ frequencies. *#1481* **$39.95** (+$2)

● **Shortwave Listening Guidebook** *By H. Helms*
This noted author provides a readable book on all aspects of shortwave listening. Expanded Second Ed. *#2984* **$19.95** (+$2)

● **Worldwide Aeronautical Frequency Directory** *By R.E. Evans*
Over 260 pages on commercial and military aero monitoring with 2350 frequencies. Covers shortwave and VHF/UHF voice and digital communications including ACARS. This book features detailed maps and an extensive glossary. *#0042* **$19.95** (+$2)

● **Discover DXing!** *By J. Zondlo*
A readable introduction to DXing AM, FM & TV. *#0009* **$4.95** (+$2)

● **Now You're Talking!** *By the A.R.R.L.*
Everything you need to know to get your first amateur license and get on the air. Expanded Second Edition. *#1780* **$18.95** (+$2)

● **The World Below 500 KiloHertz** *By P. Carron*
An introduction to longwave DXing. *#0289* **$4.95** (+$2)

● **Easy-Up Antennas for Listeners & Hams** *By E. Noll*
Learn about low-cost, easy to erect antennas for LW, MW, SW, FM and ham radio. A highly acclaimed title. *#0005* **$16.95** (+$2)

● **Shortwave Radio Listening for Beginners** *By A. McCormick*
Here is the understandable information you need to get off to a quick start in the hobby of world band radio. *#0394* **$10.95** (+$2)

● **Shortwave Listener's Q & A Book** *By A. McCormick*
The author uses a question and answer format to explain many aspects of listening. Informative appendices include station addresses, radio club list, sources and book list. *#2548* **$12.95** (+$2)

● **Comprehensive Guide to Military Monitoring** *By S. Douglass*
This huge title covers monitoring equipment, shortwave and VHF/UHF frequencies, identifiers, playbook, military bases with layouts, black projects and much more. *#3301* **$19.95** (+$2)

● **National Radio Club AM Radio Log** *By National Radio Club*
The most accurate and comprehensive guide to American and Canadian AM stations. With addresses too! *#0078* **$19.95** (+$2)

● **FM Atlas and Station Directory** *By B. Elving*
The best guide to N. American FM stations. *#0983* **$15.95** (+$2)

☞ *Be sure to include $2 per title for shipping.*

Showroom Hours
Mon.-Fri. 10:00 - 5:30
Thursday 10:00 - 8:00
Saturday 10:00 - 3:00

Universal Radio, Inc.
6830 Americana Pkwy.
Reynoldsburg, OH 43068
➤ 800 431-3939 **Orders**
➤ 614 866-4267 **Information**
➤ 614 866-2339 **Fax**

universal radio inc.

MONITOR MORE WITH ADVANCED EQUIPMENT FROM UNIVERSAL!

COMMUNICATIONS RECEIVERS

The **Drake SW-8** doubles as a portable and a desktop radio. Complete coverage of AM and SW *plus* FM and VHF Aircraft! (Shown above.) The new **Drake R-8A** is our most popular communications receiver.

KENWOOD

The **Kenwood R-5000** is a powerful receiver for the serious DX'er. Keypad, notch, IF shift, 100 memories, 10 Hz display, dual VFOs.

The **Japan Radio NRD-535D** is for the communications connoisseur. Rated 5 stars & *Editor's Choice* in *Passport '93*. The "D" deluxe version includes BWC, ECSS and three filters. Universal also carries the affordable *standard* **NRD-535** plus their new line of transceivers.

YAESU

Don't let the compact size and affordable price tag fool you. The **Yaesu FRG-100B** is a full featured, high performance receiver. The French made, self-powered, wired **keypad** is now available for only $59.95.

The **Watkins-Johnson HF-1000** is *the* ultimate receiver! Advanced D.S.P. technology, 58 bandwidths, 1 Hz display. The pro's choice.

The British-made **Lowe HF-150** performs like a full-sized communications receiver but is only 8"x 3"x6.5". Universal also carries the Lowe HF-225, the HF-225 *Europa* and the brand new HF-250.

DIGITAL PORTABLE RECEIVERS

■ Sony ICF-SW100S
Truly the ultimate in miniaturization. Full coverage, synchronous detection, 1 kHz readout, stereo FM, 50 alpha memories, SSB, tone, more. *#0111*

■ Grundig Satellit 700
Outstanding fidelity, features & style. 512 alpha memories expandable to 2048. Selected *Editor's Choice* in *Passport '93, '94* and *'95. #0798*

■ Grundig YB-400
Praised in *Passport '94* as providing "the best performance for price-size category ... right up there with the very best". Great value.*#0040*

■ Sangean ATS-818
The proud successor to the ATS-803, the ATS-818 features 45 memories, BFO, clock, etc. Great SSB. Includes AC adapter. *#2754*

■ Sangean ATS-818CS
Finally ... a quality digital receiver with a built-in cassette for easy off-the-air recording. Full coverage of LW, MW, SW and FM. *#0367*

■ Sony ICF-SW77
Sophisticated performance and features that rival a table top receiver. Sony's top-of-the-line. Brochure available on request. *#2493*

■ Sony ICF-SW7600G
A true price breakthrough! Synchronous detection, 1 kHz digital tuning, SSB, 22 memories, keypad, scanning and clock timer! *#0760*

■ Grundig YB-305
This affordable new digital portable provides continuous coverage from 2.3 - 21.85 MHz., has 30 memories and keypad entry. *#3305*

Note: Many other models available. Please see catalog.

ANTENNAS
Universal is pleased to offer an excellent selection of antennas by manufacturers such as: Alpha-Delta, Barker & Williamson, Antenna Supermarket, RF Systems, Diamond, MFJ, McKay Dymek, Sony, Sangean and Palomar. Please request our free catalog.

USED SHORTWAVE EQUIPMENT
Universal offers a wide selection of used shortwave receivers, amateur gear and radioteletype receiving equipment. All items have been tested by our service center and are protected by a thirty day limited warranty. Our computerized used list is published twice a month. Please send one or more self-addressed stamped envelopes to receive this free list. Universal also buys used equipment.

★ HUGE FREE CATALOG ★
Universal offers a huge **100 page** catalog covering all types of shortwave, amateur and scanner equipment. An unbeatable selection of antennas, books, parts and accessories is also featured. Radioteletype and facsimile decoders are fully explained. This informative publication covers absolutely everything for the radio enthusiast. With prices, photos and full descriptions. This giant catalog is available **FREE** in North America. (Also available for five IRCs - International Reply Coupons, outside of North America).

Universal Radio, Inc.
6830 Americana Pkwy.
Reynoldsburg, OH 43068
➤ 800 431-3939 Orders
➤ 614 866-4267 Information
➤ 614 866-2339 Fax

◆ **Serving radio enthusiasts since 1942.**
◆ **Universal is happy to ship worldwide.**
◆ **Visa, MasterCard and Discover accepted.**
◆ **Visit our fully operational showroom.**
◆ **Used equipment list available.**
◆ **Prices and specifications are subject to change.**
◆ **Returns are subject to a 15% restocking fee.**

First Tries: Ten Easy Catches

Tuning around world band is like touring the United Nations. Among all the exotic tongues, one comes through loud and clear: English. So here are ten stations in English you can enjoy on nearly any world band radio. All times are World Time.

EUROPE

France

Radio France Internationale is one of the most frequently heard stations on world band, usually in French. But RFI has a growing output in English, and it's got one of the best program packages to grace the airwaves.

North America: 1200-1255, year-round, on 13625 kHz. For a second and seasonal channel, try 11615, 15530 or 17575 kHz. No joy? Try 15325 kHz via the relay in Gabon. Though targeted at West Africa, the signal can be heard in parts of eastern North America and the Caribbean. The 1600 broadcast to Africa is also sometimes audible in eastern North America.

RFI

The Sports Service of Radio France Internationale never drops the ball!

Europe: 1200-1255 on 9805, 15155 and 15195 kHz. The 1600 African Service is also on 6175 kHz for European listeners.

Middle East: 1400-1455 on 17560 kHz; 1600-1655 on 9485 or 11615 kHz, and 1600-1730 (targeted at East Africa) on 15460 kHz.

Asia: 1400-1455 on 7110 and 12030 (or 15405) kHz. Listeners in the south-eastern part of the continent can also try at 1200-1255 winters on 11615 kHz.

Africa: Surveys show that most Westerners don't want to hear news about Africa, so the media tends to ignore it. But RFI is an exception. Its programs for Africa are among the best for news about that continent, and can often be heard well outside the intended target area. Audible at 1600-1655 on 6175, 11615, 11700, 12015 and 15530 kHz; and at 1600-1730 on 15210 (or 17795) and 15460 kHz.

Germany

Deutsche Welle, the mighty "Voice of Germany," is a prime source for news and analysis of European events. It also reports on developments in Africa, Asia and the Pacific in its broadcasts targeted at those areas. A mix of technical excellence and journalistic professionalism makes the station a listening "must" for people interested in world events.

North and Central America: 0100-0150 winters on 6040, 6085, 6120, 6145, 9565, 9670 and 9700 kHz; summers on 6040, 6085, 6145, 9555, 9640, 11740 and 11865 kHz. The next edition is at 0300-0350: winters on 6045, 6085, 6120, 9535 and 9560 kHz; summers on 6085, 6185, 9615 9640 and 11750 kHz. The third and final broadcast goes out at 0500-

0550, winters on 5960, 6045, 6120 and 6185 kHz; and summers on 5960, 6185, 9515 and 11705 kHz. This last slot is best for western North America.

Europe: 2000-2050, winters on 5960 and 7285 kHz, and summers on 7170 and 9615 kHz. Enjoy this while it lasts, as DW intends to deep-six its European services. (*See* Germany in "Addresses PLUS.")

Middle East: 1900-1950 on 13690 or 13790 kHz.

East Asia and the Pacific: 0900-0950, winters on 6160, 9875, 11715, 17780, 17820, 21650 and 21680 kHz; summers on 6160, 11730, 12055, 15245, 17715, 17780, 21600 and 21680 kHz. A second broadcast goes out at 2100-2150 on 6185 (winter), 7115 (summer), 9670, 9765 and 11785 kHz. A third broadcast, at 2300-2350 (for East Asia), was introduced in 1995 on 7235, 9690 and 11705 kHz. However, some of these frequencies may change in 1996.

Holland

Radio Nederland, known in English as Radio Netherlands, is the big voice from the little land. It is also one of several stations to have increased its English output at the expense of other, less-widely used, languages. The result: a better choice of times and programs for many of its faithful listeners.

North America: The station is easily heard throughout much of North America at 2330-0125 on 6020, 6165 and 9840 (or 9845) kHz. Out West, try 0430-0525 on 6015 (or 9590) and 6165 kHz. Too, for Africa at 1830-2025 on 15315 and 17605 kHz it's often well heard in parts of North America.

Europe: 1030-1225 summers on 6045

Holland embraces the world through the voices of Radio Nederland. Shown: David Swatling, Maggie Ayre and Dherra Sujan, winners of the international broadcasting New York Festival Awards for 1995.

and 9650 kHz; 1130-1325 winters on 6045 and 7130 kHz.

Middle East: 1330-1425 on 13700 kHz.

East Asia: 0930-1125, winters on 7260 and 9810 kHz, and summers on 12065 and 13705 kHz.

Australia and the Pacific: 0730-0825 on 9720 (or 9700) and 11895 kHz, and 0830-1025 on 9720 kHz. In addition, the channels for East Asia at 0930-1125 are often well heard in parts of Australasia.

Russia

Voice of Russia (formerly Radio Moscow) has suffered drastic budget cuts in recent years, just as the program quality has risen to its highest level ever. In a relatively short space of time, the world's most omnipresent broadcaster has been reduced to a small number of channels for each of its target areas. In a move to try and keep its audience, the VOR has concentrated its resources into fewer, but more powerful, transmitters. While harder to hear, the station still provides a rea-

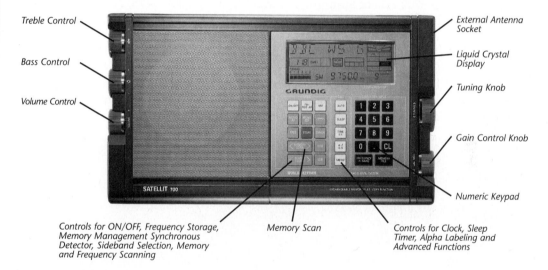

sonable signal to most areas of the world, except eastern North America.

VOR's frequencies change often, and are difficult to predict. Fortunately, it tends to broadcast within certain segments at given times, so a little dialing around should produce at least one usable channel.

Eastern North America: Reception quality varies, but best is late afternoon and early evening. Winter, go for 7105-7260 and 9600-9750 kHz, with the 9530-9750 and 11650-11900 kHz ranges the best bets in summer. For late evening (0300 onwards) try the 5905-6050 and 7105-7200 kHz segments in winter, and 9500-9700 kHz in summer.

Too vague? Then try the following times and frequencies for winter: 1700-2100 on 7180 kHz; 2100-2400 on 7150, 7180, 9620 and 9750 kHz; 0030-0600 on 5940, 7105, 7165 and 7180 kHz. In summer, check 1500-2000 on 15105 kHz; 2000-2400 on 9530 (or 11805), 9720, 11730 and 11750 kHz; 0000-0300 on 9530 (or 11805), 9620 and 11750 kHz; and 0300-0500 on 9620 and 9665 kHz.

Not all frequencies are available during any given time slot; for more specific information, see "Worldwide Broadcasts in English" or the "Blue Pages" elsewhere in this book.

Western North America is much better served, with 12050 and 15425 kHz available throughout the year, albeit for just one hour (0200-0300) in winter. Thereafter, try the 9800-9850 kHz range, with the 5900-5940 and 7150-7350 kHz segments a good bet at 0400-0800. Available channels should include 5905, 6065, 7175, 7270, 7345, 9825 and 9850 kHz, though actual times will vary. For good summer reception, try 12050, 13645, 13665, 15180, 15425 and 15580 kHz from 0100 onwards, plus 12010 kHz from 0430. Most of these frequencies are available until 0700.

Voice of Russia

Eugene Nikitenko (left), presenter of Newmarket; Clara Belousova, editor, and Tatyana Shvetsova, author, Audio Book Club and Moscow Yesterday and Today; and Vladimir Zhamkin, Editor-in-Chief.

Europe has seen its options reduced to just a few hours in the late afternoon and evening. It's now limited to 1600-2300 (one hour earlier in summer), a far cry from the former 19-hour schedule. In winter, dial around the 6 and 7 MHz segments (especially 5900-6110 and 7105-7350 kHz), while 9890 kHz should also be available at 1600-2200. For summer, try the 9480-9820 and 11630-11980 kHz ranges, with 7350 kHz an additional option for northern areas.

Middle East: 1500-2100 (one hour earlier in summer). Best bets for winter are 6035, 9830 and 12015 kHz early in the evening, and 11945 kHz later. In summer, try 11715, 11835, 11910, 11945, 15320, 15340, 15425 and 15480 kHz between 1400 and 1700; 11715 and 15480 kHz at 1700-1900; and 7210, 7275, 11910 and 11945 kHz for the final couple of hours.

East Asia: Reception varies, but is usually best between 1000 and 1400. Winters, try 5960, 6000, 7135, 7205, 9480 and 9540 kHz; summers on 5960, 9800, 9895, 11940 and 17590 kHz. Some of these channels carry other languages

You can tour Switzerland daily by radio over SRI. Shown, the Castle of Aigle, in the Lac Léman region.

Schweiz Tourismus

part of the time, so you might have to tune around a bit.

Southeast Asia and Australasia: A much reduced service, following the latest cuts. Try between 0700 and 1400, winter on 9550, 9800, 11710, 12015, 17840 and 17860 kHz; and summer on 9835, 11800, 17560 and 17570 kHz. Additional winter options for Southeast Asia include 7205, 11675, 11760 and 17560 kHz; in summer, check out 11940, 17590, 17675 and 17695 kHz.

Switzerland

Sometimes even world band stations can sound like the stuff you hear at home, but not always. Here's a good example. Because it is cheek-to-jowl with important international agencies and the Red Cross, **Swiss Radio International** pumps out news with a difference. In particular, there's lots on "Third World" issues rarely reported on elsewhere, including coverage of armed conflicts in out-of-the-way places. And, of course, there's always the latest on what's happening in the colorful cantons of Switzerland.

North America: 0100-0130 on 5885, 6135, 9885 and 9905 kHz; 0400-0430 on 6135 and 9885 kHz; and 0400-0500 on 9905 kHz.

Europe: (one hour earlier in summer) 0600-0615, 0700-0730, 1100-1130, 1200-1230 and 1330-1400 on 6165 and 9535 kHz; and 2000-2030 on 6165 kHz.

Middle East: 1700-1730 on 6205 (12075 summer), 9885 and 13635 kHz.

East Asia: 1100-1130 on 9885 (winter), 11640 (winter), 13635 and (summer) 15545 and 17515 kHz; and 1300-1330 on 7230 (or 7250), 7480, 11640 (15460 or 15545 in summer) and 13635 kHz.

RCSS™ REMOTE

RCSS™ Remote pictured with optional wideband receiver internally installed.

Simultaneous High Speed Data and Full Duplex Audio Over a Single Phone Line.

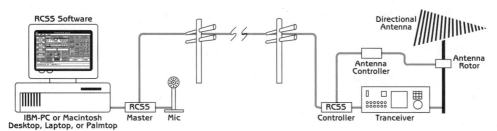

RCSS™ Remote provides a unique solution to remote systems control. It enables high speed data and full duplex wideband audio over any standard or cellular phone line. Audio and data are transferred simultaneously, not time sliced, providing true real time control.

Remote operation can be fully automated with RCSS™ software. A simple point and click graphical user interface via Microsoft Win-dows™ provides quick learning and easy operation. RCSS™ software is also available separately to provide automated control of AOR and ICOM receivers, among others.

The RCSS™ master unit can be used with any serial terminal including desktops, laptops, and the new palmtops. RCSS™ Remote is housed in a rugged aluminum case for military style dependability. It is constructed using several processors and the latest DSP technology available. All RCSS™ components are fully shielded from RF leakage. Power is supplied from either AC or DC sources for portability.

The RCSS™ modular design allows the configuration to be modified as user needs expand. Special user developed programs can be uploaded for custom applications.

For more information call, write, fax, or e-mail today. Or, via computer, visit our web page at http://www.sasiltd.com/sasi

SYSTEMS & SOFTWARE
INTERNATIONAL · LTD

Systems & Software International is in its 10th year, and manufactures all equipment in the USA. Please contact us at:
4639 Timber Ridge Drive, Dumfries, Virginia, 22026-1059, USA; **(703) 680-3559**; Fax (703) 878-1460; E-mail 74065.1140@compuserve.com

Australasia: 0900-0930 on 9885, 13685 and 17515 kHz.

United Kingdom

The **BBC World Service** ensures that Britannia rules the airwaves, despite its introduction in 1995 of "streaming"—beaming programs at different times to different parts of the world. This has caused heartburn in North America, where the timing of some key programs is now less convenient, although improvement is promised in short order. Fortunately, world band signals often scatter beyond their intended area, so North Americans can fish for BBC signals in different streams, even if the resulting signals are beamed elsewhere and tend to be weaker. While the BBC World Service may not always get it right, it remains the best and most popular of all international broadcasters.

North America: In the mornings, easterners can listen at 1100-1200 on 5965, 6195 and 9515 kHz; 1200-1400 on 6195, 9515 and 11865 kHz; 1400-1500 on 9515 and 11865 kHz; 1500-1615 on 9515, 11775 and 11865 kHz; and 1615-1715 on 9515 and 11775 kHz. Listeners in or near the Caribbean area can tune in at 1100-1200 on 6195 kHz; 1200-1400 on 6195 and 11865 kHz; and 1400-1615 on 11865 kHz.

Early risers in western North America can try 1200-1500 on 11865 kHz; 1500-1615 on 11775 and 11865 kHz; and 1615-1715 on 11775 kHz. If you prefer the Asia-Pacific stream, tune to 9740 kHz between 1130 and 1615.

Early evenings in eastern North America, go for 5975 kHz at 2100-2200. Also worth hearing is "Caribbean Report," aired at 2115-2130 Monday through Friday on 15390 and 17715 kHz. It's a good way to keep up with events in the Islands.

Throughout the evening, North Americans can listen at 2200-0600 on a number of frequencies. Best bets are 5975 kHz (to 0600), 6175 kHz (2300-0330, summers to 0430), 7325 kHz (2300-0330) and 9590 kHz (2200-0030). For the West Coast, 9640 kHz is also available at 0500-0815.

Europe: A powerhouse 0300-2330 on 3955 (winter), 6180, 6195, 7325, 9410, 12095 and 15070 kHz (times vary on each channel).

BBC

The BBC World Service's newsroom, where emanate what is widely considered to be the best news analysis anywhere.

YACHT BOY 400

THE ULTIMATE IN DIGITAL TECHNOLOGY

Noted for: its exacting controls, including fine tuning, volume and high/low tone controls.

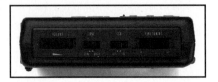

Multi-Function Liquid Crystal Display: The LCD shows simultaneous displays of time, frequency, band, alarm function and sleep timer.

The Digital Key Pad: The key pad itself is a marvel of performance with 40 memories. It's intelligently designed and easy to use.

GRUNDIG
made for you

Grundig's Yacht Boy 400 has received rave reviews from the shortwave press for combining a wealth of sophisticated features in one compact, portable package that doesn't cost a fortune. It incorporates features found on stationary shortwave systems that cost thousands, such as outstanding audio quality, precise 1 kHz increment tuning, up/down slewing, frequency scanning, signal strength indication, and single-sideband signal demodulation.

But the Yacht Boy advantage mentioned most often in reviews is its ease of use for the novice listener. Following the included Grundig *Shortwave Listening Guide*, in moments you can be listening to foreign broadcasts beamed to North America.

Soon, you will be scanning the airwaves to tune in exotic music programs and sports events from faraway locales. The Yacht Boy 400 even picks up shortwave amateur (ham radio) broadcasts and shortwave aeronautical/maritime frequencies. The possibilities for family fun, education, and enjoyment are boundless.

For travel or home use, Grundig adds a dual-time travel clock with snooze and sleep timer. FM band is stereophonic with your headphones. The lighted LCD panel is easy to read in the dark. Comes with a form-fitting pouch, integral telescoping antenna and advanced external antenna on a compact reel, carry-strap, batteries, and complete instructions.

GRUNDIG
made for you

SATELLIT 700
WORLD'S MOST ADVANCED SHORTWAVE PORTABLE

German shortwave technology in its most advanced form. For serious listening to international broadcasts and long distance two-way communications. More flexibility than any other shortwave portable.

Digital/Alphanumeric display with PLL tuning, general coverage shortwave receiver, with SSB and advanced synchronous detector. Dual clocks and turn on/off timers. Sleep timer. Eight character memory page labeling. 512 memories standard; 2048 possible with optional memofiles. Multi-voltage adapter.

Continuous shortwave tuning from 1.6 to 30 megahertz covers all shortwave bands, plus FM-stereo, AM and LW. Single sideband (SSB) circuitry allows for reception of shortwave amateur, aeronautical and maritime two-way communications. 120 factory pre-programmed frequencies for world-wide reception. Dual conversion superheterodyne receiver design.

Multifunction Liquid Crystal Display: The LCD shows time, frequency band, alphanumeric memory labels, automatic turn on/off, sleep timer, bandwidth select position, synchronous detector status and USB/LSB status.

Tuning Made Simple: With both a tuning dial, and direct entry keypad, tuning into your favorite broadcast is both quick and easy.

Synchronous Detector: is but one of the many functions available with the Satellit 700. The synchronous detector helps to eliminate interference so that what you hear is as ear pleasing as possible.

Universal Radio, Inc.
6830 Americana Pkwy.   800 431-3939 Orders
Reynoldsburg, Ohio   614 866-4267 Info.
430068 U.S.A.   614 866-2339 Fax

First Tries: Ten Easy Catches, *Continued*

Middle East: 0300 (0200 in summer)-0700 (or later) and 1500-2230 on 9410 kHz; 0300-0930 and 1000-1400 on 11760 kHz; 0400-0730 and 0900-1500 (continuous at weekends) on 15575 kHz; 0600-0800 (or later) and 1500-2030 on 15070 kHz; 1400 (or 1500)-2030 on 12095 kHz; and 1715-1830 and 1900-2000 on 7160 kHz.

East Asia: 0000-0030 on 7180, 9580, 11945 and 15360 kHz; 0030-0330 on 15360 kHz; 0330-0500 on 11955 and 15280 kHz; 0500-0800 on 11955, 15280 and 15360 kHz; 0800-0900 on 11955 and 15280 kHz; 0900-1030 on 9740, 15280 and 17830 kHz; 1030-1100 on 9740 kHz; 1100-1300 on 9575, 9740, 11765, 11955 and 15360 kHz; 1300-1615 on 7180 and 9740 kHz; 1615-1745 on 7180 kHz; 2100-2200 on 3915, 6195, 9580 and 11945 kHz; 2200-2300 on 6195, 7110 and 9890 kHz; and 2300-2400 on 7250, 9580, 11945 and 11955 kHz.

Australia and New Zealand: 0500-0800 on 11955 and 15360 kHz; 0800-0900 on 11955 kHz; 0900-1030 on 15280 kHz; 1100-1130 (via Radio New Zealand International) on 6100 or 9700 kHz; 1130-1615 on 9740 kHz; 1800-1830 on 11955 kHz; 1830-2200 on 9740 and 11955

Yuko Chibata, friendly host of "Radio Japan Guide."

kHz; 2200-2300 on 11695 and 11955 kHz; and 2300-2400 on 11955 kHz.

ASIA

Japan

Radio Japan has improved its transmitting facilities both in Japan and overseas, so it's now an easy catch. For followers of the East Asian scene, the station is custom-made for keeping up with what is happening there. Most broadcasts last one hour, although there is the occasional 30-minute exception. Don't expect lots of snap and pizzazz, though—this is a good, gray operation of the Japanese establishment, not a Yoko Ono thing.

Eastern North America: 1100 on 6120 kHz, and again at 0300 (0100 summers) on 5960 kHz.

Western North America: 0100 and 0300 winters on 9565 kHz, and summers on 9680 (or 11790) kHz; 0500 winters on 6025 and 9565 kHz, summers on 6110 and 9680 (or 11790) kHz, and year-round on 11885 kHz; 1400 on 9535 and 11705 kHz; and 1500, 1700 and 1900 on 9535 kHz. There is a separate broadcast to Hawaii, western North America and Central America at 0300-0330 on 11885, 11895 and 15230 kHz.

Europe: 0500 on 5975 and 7230 kHz; 0700 on 5975, 7230 and 15335 kHz; 2100

Oui Mei takes a break from her work at China Radio International.

on 11865 (or 11925) kHz, and 2300 on any two channels from 5965, 6055 and 6155 kHz.

Middle East: 0700 on 15335 kHz, and 1700 on 11930 kHz.

Asia: 0100 on 11840 (or 15195), 11860, 11900, 11910, 17810 and 17845 kHz; 0300 on 11840 (or 15210) and 17810 kHz; 0500 on 11725 (or 11955), 11740 and 17810 kHz; 0600 on 11725 (or 11955) and 17810 kHz; 0700 on 11725 (or 11955), 11740, 17810 and 21610 kHz; 0900 on 9610 and 15190 kHz; 1100 on 9610 and 15350 (or 15295) kHz; 1400 on 9610, 11895 (or 11840) and 11915 kHz; 1500 on 11955 kHz; 1700 on 6150, 9570 (or 11840) and 9580 kHz; 1900 on 6150 and 9580 kHz; 2100 on 6035, 7140 and 9580 kHz; and 2300 on 7140 and 9580 kHz. Transmissions to Asia can also be heard in other parts of the world.

Australasia: 0700 and 0900 on 11850 (or 15270) kHz; 1900 on 7140 and 11850 kHz; and 2100 and 2300 on 11850 kHz.

NORTH AMERICA

Canada

Despite annual Perils of Pauline reruns about who will provide funding—and how much—**Radio Canada International** soldiers on with informative and entertaining programs. Many shows are lifted from the domestic service of its large parent organization (Canadian Broadcasting Corporation), but it's still pleasant listening for Canadians and non-Canadians, alike.

North America: Morning reception is better in eastern North America than farther west, but virtually the whole United States gets a fair shot at the evening broadcasts. Try Monday through Friday at 1300-1400 on 9635 (summer only), 11855 and 13650 (or 17820) kHz; and 1400-1700 Sunday on 11955 and 17820 kHz.

Radio Canada International's popular announcer/producer Ian McFarland (center), now retired, ruminates with PASSPORT's Editor-in-Chief Lawrence Magne (left) and the Voice of America's Audience Research Officer Kim Andrew Elliott.

With the ALPHA DELTA Model DX-ULTRA Full Spectrum Dipole you don't have to imagine anymore! We designed it for "knock-your-socks-off" performance with an absolutely no-compromise attitude — with full frequency access from AM Broadcast through 30MHz!

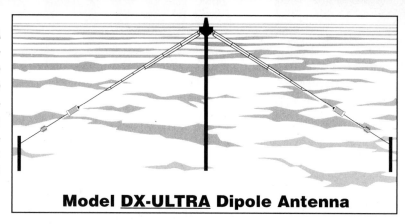

Model <u>DX-ULTRA</u> Dipole Antenna

- Absolutely remarkable performance for Medium Wave, Tropical, International Shortwave, Government, Military, Embassy, Maritime, Aircraft, Commercial and all other Utility communication frequency ranges.

- The DX-ULTRA design provides extremely low-noise performance for maximum sensitivity to weak DX signals.

- The wire elements' "Tapered Wing" design allows broadband operation on 1/2 wavelength and 3/4 wavelength multiples of various frequency ranges.

- The DX-ULTRA is designed with a pair of ISO-RES inductors and parallel wire elements for maximum broadband, efficient performance - no lossy narrowband traps. The difference on your S-meter can be phenomenal!

- Our exclusive Model DELTA-C Center Insulator with the built-in Model SEP ARC-PLUG® Static Electricity Protector provides effective protection for your sensitive receiver components. Connectors accept either coax or balanced line.

- Overall length of the DX-ULTRA is only 80 feet with dipole, inverted-vee, or full sloper configurations possible!

- Fully assembled - no cutting or soldering required. All components are rated for 2kW of power with all stainless-steel hardware. Can be used with a wide-range antenna tuner for commercial, military, or embassy operation.

- The DX-ULTRA is designed specifically for full spectrum shortwave performance, not just for the narrower amateur or international shortwave bands.

Alpha Delta Model DX-ULTRA, 80 ft. in length $119.95

If your space does not permit the full 80 ft. length of the DX-ULTRA, we suggest our Model DX-SWL 1/4 wave sloper (60 ft.) or our DX-SWL-S 1/4 wave sloper (40 ft.). These antennas have similar design philosophies.

At your Alpha Delta dealer or add $5.00 for shipping and handling in the continental United States. Export orders - please call for quote.

ANYPLACE.
ANYWHERE.
ANYTIME.

No matter where you go, the Grundig Satellit 700 is there for you. The Satellit 700 is the world's most advanced shortwave portable radio. This is the portable for serious listening to international broadcasts and long distance shortwave two-way communications.

Covers all shortwave bands, plus FM-stereo, AM and LW. Single sideband (SSB) circuitry allows for reception of two-way shortwave amateur, shortwave maritime and shortwave aeronautical communications.

"The best portable introduced this year is Grundig's Satellit 700."
PWBR, 1993

SATELLIT 700

Features:

Unprecedented memory capacity. 512 user-programmable positions, plus 120 preprogrammed frequencies.

Advanced synchronous detector minimizes broadcast interference.

Excellent sensitivity. Even weak signals come in more clearly.

Superior sideband performance. Helps eliminate unwanted noises providing clear, natural voice quality.

Multi-function liquid crystal display. Including frequency, band, mode, TIME I and II, battery strength, antenna and more.

Size: 12-1/4"L x 7-1/4"H x 3"

Weight: 4 lbs

GRUNDIG

Call for information: U.S. 1-800-872-2228 or 415-361-1611
Canada 800-637-1648 • Fax: 415-361-1724

During winter, evening broadcasts air at 2300-0100 on 5960 and 9755 kHz, and 0200-0300 on 6120 and 9755 kHz. Summer frequency usage is the same as winter, except for the addition of 11895 kHz at 2200-2230. All broadcasts are one hour earlier in summer.

Something different? A special 30-minute week night program, complete with messages from the folks back home, goes out to Canadian peacekeepers in the Caribbean (replaced weekends by an hour of CBC programming). It can also be heard throughout much of North America. Winters, it starts at 0300 on 6000, 9725 and 9755 kHz; and summers at 0200 on 6120, 9535 and 11940 kHz.

The evening transmission for Africa is also audible in parts of North America; winters at 2100-2230 on 13690, 15140 and 17820 kHz; and summers one hour earlier on 13670, 15150 and 17820 kHz.

Europe: Winters at 1430-1500 on 9555, 11915, 11935, 15325 and (Monday through Saturday) 17820 kHz; 1745-1800 (Monday through Friday only) on 9555, 11935, 15325 and 17820 kHz; and 2100-2230 on 5995, 7260, 9725 (or 15325), 11945 and 13650 kHz. Summer broadcasts are one hour earlier: 1330-1400 Monday through Saturday on 15315, 17820 and 17895 kHz, and daily on 15325 and 21455 kHz; 1645-1700 (weekdays only) on the same channels as the 1745 winter broadcast; 2000-2100 on 5995, 7235, 11985, 13650 and 15325 kHz; and 2100-2130 on the same frequencies, except that 11690 replaces 11985 kHz.

Europe, Middle East and Africa: There is a special program for Canadian peacekeeping forces (*see* four paragraphs up), which is broadcast winter weekdays at 0600-0630 on 6050, 6150, 9740, 9760 and 11905 kHz. Summers, it goes out one hour earlier on 6050, 7295, 15430 and 17840 kHz.

Middle East: Winters, at 0400-0430 on 6150, 9505 and 9670 kHz; 1430-1500 on 9555, 11935 and 15325 kHz; and 1745-1800 (Monday through Friday only) on 9555, 11935, 15325 and 17820 kHz. In summer, try 0400-0430 on 9650, 11835, 11905 and 15275 kHz; 1330-1400 on 15325 and 21455 kHz; 1645-1700 (weekdays only) on 9555, 11935, 15325 and 17820 kHz; and 2000-2130 on 5995 and 7235 kHz.

Asia: To East Asia at 1330-1400 on 6150 (summers on 11795) and 9535 kHz; and to Southeast Asia at 2200-2230 on 11705 kHz.

United States

The Voice of Russia was not the only international broadcaster to suffer draconian cuts in funding during 1995. Its American counterpart, the venerable **Voice of America**, also fell victim to well-meaning, but short-sighted, political thinking resulting from a national budget crisis. Although virtually all languages were affected, the VOA's English output suffered less than most.

Voice of America offers well-produced and popular programs.

The station offers several well-produced and popular regional variations of its mainstream programming. These are targeted at Africa, Latin America, the Caribbean and the Pacific, but are also widely heard elsewhere (including within North America).

North America: The two best times to listen are at 0000-0200 to South America and the Caribbean on 5995,

6130, 7405, 9455, 9775 and 13740 kHz (with 11695 kHz also available at 0000-0100); and 1000-1200 on 6165, 7405 and 9590 kHz. The African Service can also be heard in much of North America—try the morning broadcast at 0300-0630 (0700 weekends) on 6035 (from 0500), 7405, 9575 (0300-0600) and (from 0500) 9630 kHz; at 1630 (1600 weekends)-1800 on 13710, 15445 and 17895 kHz; and 1800-2200 (Saturday to 2130) on 15410 and 15580 kHz.

Europe: 0400-0700 on 5995, 6040, 6140 (winter), 7170 and (summer only) 7200 and 11965 kHz; evenings on 1700-2200 on 6040, 9760 and 15205 kHz.

Middle East: Winters at 0500-0700 on 11825 and 15205 kHz; summers at 0400-0600 on 11965 and 15205 kHz, and 0600-0700 on 11965 kHz. Later in the day, try 1500-1700 on 9700 and 15205 kHz; 1700-1800 on 9700 kHz; and 1800-2100 on 9700 (or 9770) kHz.

Australasia: 1000-1200 on 5985, 11720 and 15425 kHz; 1200-1330 on 11715 and 15425 kHz, 1330-1500 on 15425 kHz; 1900-2000 on 9525, 11870 and 15180 kHz; 2100-2200 on 11870, 15185 and 17735 kHz; and 2200-0100 on 15185 and 17735 kHz.

East Asia: 1100-1500 on 9760 and 15160 kHz; 2200-2400 on 15290, 15305, 17735 and 17820 kHz; and 0000-0100 on 15290, 17735 and 17820 kHz.

Monitor Radio International, formerly the World Service of the Christian Science Monitor, is one of the world's best sources of in-depth news coverage. Weekday broadcasts are full of news-related fare, plus short listener-response and religious features closing out the hour-long broadcasts. Weekends, it's religious programming, not all of it in English.

North America: In eastern North America, try 0000 on 7375 kHz; 1000, 1100 and 1200 on 6095 kHz; and 2200 and 2300 on (winters) 9355 or (summers) 13770 kHz. Farther west, listen at 0100 on 7535 kHz, 0200 and 0300 on 5850 kHz, and at 1300 on 6095 kHz. Although beamed elsewhere, 9430 kHz also provides good reception within much of North America at 0000-0300.

Europe: 0400, 0500, 0600, 0700, 0800 and 0900 on 7535 kHz; 1800 and 1900 on 9355, 13770 or 15665 kHz; 2000 and 2100 on any two channels from 7510, 9355 and 13770 kHz; and 2200 and 2300 on 7510 or 13770 kHz.

Middle East: 1800 and 1900 on (winters) 9355 or (summers) 13770 kHz.

East Asia: 0900 and 1000 on 9430 kHz; 1100, 1400 and 1500 on 9355 kHz; and 2200 and 2300 on (winters) 9430 or (summers) 15405 kHz. The 2200 broadcast is also available year-round on 13625 kHz.

Australasia: 0800 on 9425 or 13615 kHz; 0900 on 13615 kHz; 1000 on 13625 kHz; 1100 and 1200 on 9425 kHz, 1800 on 9355 kHz; 1900 (winters only) also on 9355 kHz; 2100 (summers only) on 13840 kHz; and 2300 on 13625 kHz.

Howard Gammon

Pakistani men sewing women's clothes at Karachi Bazaar. The influential Voice of America has a substantial audience in Pakistan.

GRUNDIG

DIGITAL WORLD RECEIVER

THE ULTIMATE IN DIGITAL TECHNOLOGY

YACHT BOY 400

- Shortwave, AM and FM-stereo
- PLL synthesized tuning for rock-solid frequency stability.
- Continuous shortwave from 1.6-30 megahertz, covering all existing shortwave bands. Plus FM-stereo, AM and Longwave.
- No tuning gaps in its shortwave receiver means that all frequencies can be monitored.
- Single sideband (SSB) circuitry allows for reception of shortwave long distance two-way communication such as amateur radio and shortwave aeronautical/maritime.

PROGRAMMABLE MEMORIES

- 40 randomly programmable memories allow for quick access to favorite stations. The memory "FREE" feature automatically shows which memories are unoccupied and ready to program.

MULTI-FUNCTION LIQUID CRYSTAL DISPLAY

- The LCD shows simultaneous display of time, frequency, band, automatic turn-on and sleep timer.

CLOCK, ALARM AND TIMER

- Liquid crystal display (LCD) shows time and clock/timer modes.
- Dual alarm modes: beeper & radio.
- Dual clocks show time in 24 hour format.
- Sleep timer programmable in 10 minute increments to 60 minutes.

GRUNDIG ANNOUNCES ANOTHER BREAKTHROUGH IN DIGITAL TECHNOLOGY — THE YACHT BOY 305
Packed with features: Direct key in AM, FM and Shortwave with continuous coverage, 30 memory presets.

GRUNDIG

DIGITAL WORLD RECEIVER

THE ULTIMATE IN DIGITAL TECHNOLOGY

SATELLIT 700 — the latest and most sophisticated portable world receiver available! Featuring phased lock loop digital circuitry for seamless AM, FM-stereo, LW, and SW reception from 1.6 – 30 Mhz. From London to Lithuania to San Francisco, tune in the world easily with its unique digital or manual tuning. With Grundig, the world is at your fingertips.

GERMAN ENGINEERING ANNOUNCES BREAKTHROUGH IN MEMORY

The unprecedented 120 factory pre-programmed frequencies for worldwide reception makes tuning into the world's shortwave radio broadcast almost as simple as touching a button. You also have 512 alpha numeric user-programmable memory positions which can be expanded to 2048 memory positions so you can build your own favorite-station radio archive!

WORLD CLASS RECEPTION

With PLL Tuning, selectable wide/narrow band width filter, and synchronous detector, the Satellit 700 offers unparalleled reception, sensitivity and selectivity. The 700 comes equipped with a built-in NiCad battery charger, the Grundig *Shortwave Listening Guide*, and a one-year warranty covering parts and labor. If you have any questions regarding the Satellit 700, please call our shortwave Hotline and talk to the experts, U.S. (800) 872-2228, and Canada (800) 637-1648 (9am to 4pm PST).

HIGH PERFORMANCE FEATURES INCLUDE:

- Unprecedented Memory Capacity
- Advanced Synchronous Detector
- Superior Sideband Performance
- Multi-function Liquid Display
- RDS Capability for FM Stations

With world band, if you dial around randomly, you're almost as likely to get dead air as you are a favorite program. For one thing, a number of world band segments are alive and kicking by day, while others are nocturnal. Too, some fare better at specific times of the year.

Official and "Outside" Segments

Segments of the shortwave spectrum are set aside for world band radio by the International Telecommunication Union (see), headquartered in Geneva. However, the ITU also countenances some world band broadcasts outside these parameters. Stations operating within these "outside" portions tend to encounter less interference from competing broadcasters. However, as these portions are also shared with utility stations (see), they sometimes suffer from other forms of interference.

"Real-world" segments—those actually being used, regardless of official status—are shown in bold (e.g., **5730-6250 kHz**). These are where you should tune to hear world band programs. For the record, official ITU segments are shown in ordinary small type (e.g., 5950-6200 kHz).

What you'll actually hear will vary. It depends on your location, where the station is, the time of year, your radio, and so on. (For more on this, see Propagation). Although stations can be heard 24 hours a day, signals are usually best from around sunset until sometime after midnight. Too, try a couple of hours on either side of dawn.

Here, then, are the most attractive times and frequencies for world band listening, based on reception conditions forecast for the coming year.

Rare Reception

2 MHz (120 meters) **2300-2500 kHz**[1,2]
  ITU: 2300–2498 kHz[3] (Tropical domestic transmissions only.)

Limited Reception Winter Nights

3 MHz (90 meters) **3200-3400 kHz**[1]
  ITU: 3200–3400 kHz (Tropical domestic transmissions only.)

Good-to-Fair during Winter Nights in Europe and Asia

4 MHz (75 meters) **3900-4080 kHz**[4]
  ITU: 3900-3950 kHz (Asian & Pacific transmissions only.)
    3950-4000 kHz (European, African, Asian & Pacific transmissions only.)

Some Reception during Nights

5 MHz (60 meters) **4700-5100 kHz**[1,2]
  ITU: 4750–4995/5005-5060 kHz[2] (Mainly Tropical domestic transmissions.)

Excellent during Nights
Regional Reception Daytime

6 MHz (49 meters) **5730-6250 kHz**
  ITU: 5950–6200 kHz now, 5900-6200 kHz[5] from April 2007

Good during Nights except Mid-Winter
Variable during Mid-Winter Nights
Regional Reception Daytime

7 MHz (41 meters) **7100-7600 kHz**[6]
    ITU: 7100–7300 kHz now, 7100-7350 kHz[5] from April 2007 (No American-based transmissions below 7300 kHz.)

Good during Summer Nights
Some Reception Daytime and Winter Nights
Good Asian and Pacific Reception Mornings in America

9 MHz (31 meters) **9020-9080 kHz/9250-10000 kHz**[2]
    ITU: 9500–9775 kHz now, 9400-9900 kHz[5] from April 2007[7]
11 MHz (25 meters) **11500-12160 kHz**
    ITU: 11700–11975 kHz now, 11600-12100 kHz[5] from April 2007[7]

Good during Daytime
Generally Good during Summer Nights

13 MHz (22 meters) **13570-13870 kHz**[1]
    ITU: 13570-13870 kHz in full official use from April 2007[7]
15 MHz (19 meters) **15000-15800 kHz**[2]
    ITU: 15100–15450 kHz now, 15100-15800 kHz[5] from April 2007[7]
17 MHz (16 meters) **17480-17900 kHz**
    ITU: 17700–17900 kHz now, 17480-17900 kHz[5] from April 2007[7]
19 MHz (15 meters) **18900-19020 kHz**[1] (virtually no stations for now)
    ITU: 18900-19020 kHz in official use from April 2007
21 MHz (13 meters) **21450-21850 kHz**
    ITU: 21450–21750 kHz now, 21450-21850 kHz[5] eventually

Variable, Limited Reception Daytime

25 MHz (11 meters) **25670-26100 kHz**
ITU: 25600–26100 kHz now, 25670-26100 kHz eventually

---

[1]Entire segment shared with utility stations for the time being.
[2]2498-2505, 4995-5005, 9995-10005 and 14990-15005 kHz are reserved for standard time and frequency signals, such as WWV/WWVH.
[3]2300-2495 kHz within Central and South America and the Caribbean.
[4]Shared with American ham stations.
[5]Expansion portions—5900-5950, 7300-7350, 9400-9500, 9775-9900, 11600-11700, 11975-12100, 15450-15800, 17480-17700 and 21750-21850 kHz—will continue to be shared with utility stations until these portions are made official for broadcasting.
[6]7100-7300 kHz shared with American ham stations; 7300-7600 kHz shared with utility stations.
[7]Certain portions of the expanded segments may be implemented before April 2007, provided an appropriate frequency-planning procedure can be agreed upon and implemented by the ITU.

The Old Record Shop:

A World Band Wax Museum

R usty dusties? Moldy oldies? Maybe so, but Ken Berryhill makes no apologies for his music, even though some of it has been around for more than 90 years.

There's a worldwide audience out there, he says, and a surprisingly young audience at that, for "The Old Record Shop," his weekly half-hour radio show on mighty WWCR in Nashville, Tennessee.

"I play some of the really great old music," says Berryhill. "That's really great, and really old!"

In 1922, Rudy Vallee broke down laughing in mid-record.

1901-1930s: "Jass" to Joplin

You never know what you'll hear on "The Old Record Shop." Since the program first aired on WWCR in early 1994, listeners have heard everything from the very first Victor Talking Machine Record ever released—a banjo solo recorded in 1901—to the Original Dixieland Jass Band, for that's how jazz was spelled 'way back when.

He's also played a 1907 piano roll by Scott Joplin, and the first Columbia "double disc"—before that, each 78-rpm record had a song on one side only. "The Old Record Shop" has also aired the first authenticated recording of a radio broadcast, vintage 1922, and a classic early "blooper": Rudy Vallee's "Tavern in the Town," in which the nasal crooner breaks down laughing in mid-record.

"There's a real interest overseas in American music, and in old American recorded music—say, from the earliest days to the 1930's. I've heard from listeners with more than a few gray hairs, but what has really amazed me is that many

Ken Berryhill, "the world's oldest living DJ," is heard regularly with turn-of-the-century recordings. *(Ken Berryhill)*

65

of those I hear from are in their Twenties."

"Maybe I shouldn't be so surprised, though. That's the age when I first became interested in this old music."

"World's Oldest Living Disc Jockey"

Berryhill bills himself as "the world's oldest living disc jockey." Not anxious to blow his gimmick, he declines, politely, to reveal his actual age, preferring to say only that he has lived in eight different decades. A tricky answer, since other comments suggest that his life span includes only a scant few hours in the decade of the 1920's.

Being called "the world's oldest living disc jockey" started, he says, as a gag, years ago.

"I was doing an early version of this show on AM radio, and one of the other DJs started calling me that because I was playing all these old records. Later, when I realized I'd grown into the part, I started calling myself the world's oldest."

"Funny part is, nobody has ever argued the point with me, which bothers me somewhat," he adds with a laugh.

Berryhill knows his way around a laugh. His long and varied career in entertainment has included stints as a stand-up comic. He's even written a how-to book for would-be come-dians.

Humor makes a regular appearance on "The Old Record Shop," as well. Ken's shows sometimes feature bits of old-time comedy radio—Lum 'n' Abner, for instance, or Fibber McGee and Molly. He's aired vintage novelty numbers by Bob Burns and his Bazooka, a home-made musical instrument whose tube-like shape gave name to the U.S. Army's World War II anti-tank weapon. Listeners guffaw again at classic record-ed routines like Abbott and Costello's "Who's on First," and vintage vaudeville shticks by the Two Black Crows.

Over the years, Berryhill has also worked as a public relations man, TV puppeteer, radio station manager and broadcast consultant. He's even man-aged the careers of country music stars and circus performers, including the famous Flying Wallendas.

HISTORY RECORDED

THE OLD RECORD SHOP is vintage American music, all right, but with much more. Host Ken Berryhill also draws upon his collection of rare bits of recorded history and nostalgia, including:

- Commander Robert E. Perry describing his 1912 discovery of the North Pole.
- Perennial presidential candidate William Jennings Bryan reciting the 23rd Psalm.
- The voices of U.S. presidents Teddy Roosevelt, Woodrow Wilson and Warren G. Harding.
- News bulletins announcing the attack on Pearl Harbor.
- Recordings of old-time steam calliope and antique music boxes.
- Opening announcements from famous old radio shows.
- Interviews with Hoagy Carmichael, entertainer Donald O'Connor, Charlie Chaplin Jr., "Girl O' My Dreams" songwriter Sunny Clapp, and many more.

Berryhill can be reached through WWCR (see Addresses PLUS), or direct at 1322 Pine Needle Road, Venice FL 34292 in the United States.

Oldies Aficionado Since 1942

But he keeps coming back to old-time music.

It started, he says, in 1942, when he found a stack of old records and a wind-up phonograph in a house his dad bought. He kept adding to that collection.

"I just can't tell you how many recordings I have. Back in 1960 it was at least 5,000, but I haven't counted them in years."

Berryhill's radio program began in the early 1950's on a mediumwave AM station in Jackson, Tennessee. Later it was aired by other stations where he worked in Nashville. At one point, "The Old Record Shop" was syndicated on more than 100 stations in a twelve-state area.

As Ken moved about the broadcasting world, his old-time music show would also pop up from time to time, revived at different radio stations across the southeastern United States.

Old Friend Offers WWCR Show

The current reincarnation of "The Old Record Shop" on WWCR came as a surprise even to Berryhill.

In 1993, living on Florida's west coast, he got to wondering whatever had happened to a broadcaster named George McClintock whom he had known years before in Memphis, Tennessee. He tracked down his old friend to Nashville, then sent him a Christmas card.

Not long after, he got a call from McClintock, now WWCR general manager. "I've been looking for you for five years," he told Berryhill. "Why don't we put your old music show on shortwave?"

"I put together an audition tape," Ken recounts. "He liked it so much he said, 'It's going on the air this week.' 'Whoa,' I said. 'It's the only show I've got on tape

WWCR, Home Sweet Home for "The Old Record Shop."

now.' 'Then you'd better get busy,' he said."

Berryhill has been cranking out his weekly taped programs ever since.

That first WWCR program led off with the musical oldie "Ain't Misbehavin'," sung by Gene Austin—not surprising, since that top recording star of the Roarin' Twenties was, in later years, one of Berryhill's best friends in the entertainment business. It was through Austin that Berryhill met other entertainment luminaries, past and present, including Elvis Presley and his manager, Col. Tom Parker.

"Gene sold 87 million records, an amazing total in its day," Ken says. "I have what I believe is the last recording of his voice, talking to me on the phone when he was dying from lung cancer in 1972. 'God Bless you,' were his last words to me. It was very touching."

Over the years Ken has recorded interviews with many other musical stars, from old-time crooner Nick Lucas and "Heartaches" whistler Elmo Tanner, to "Sugar Blues" wha-wha trombonist Clyde McCoy and big band singer Helen Forrest. Some of those interviews also find their way onto "The Old Record Shop."

"It's a sustaining program on WWCR," Berryhill says, "so it does get moved around in the schedule. But it's usually on, with a repeat, twice a week." At this writing, "The Old Record Shop" airs

2030 to 2100 Tuesdays on 15685 kHz, and 1000 to 1030 Saturdays on 5065 kHz.

"I've loved the feedback to the program over the months we've been on shortwave," he says. "Nigeria! I got a card from a fellow in Nigeria, and another from a fellow in northern Norway, above the Arctic Circle. Just great!"

Mail has also come from England and all over the United States, from Florida to New Hampshire, Texas to Minnesota. "For a guy who just loves radio," Berryhill says, "it is the ultimate to be heard worldwide."

Second Passion is International Radio

But shortwave radio is nothing new to Ken.

"I started in shortwave back in 1947, when a buddy in the neighborhood, a friend who lived on the next street, called me over to see the Hallicrafters S-38 receiver he'd just got. He had the antenna up already, and it was incredible what he was picking up."

"I went home and told my dad that I had to have an S-38 too. I saved the fifty bucks it cost, and got my Hallicrafters. It lasted for years. I remember HCJB in Quito, Ecuador. That was one of the first long distance stations I heard back then."

Today, Berryhill still considers himself a "serious listener," though now he tunes the world using a Panasonic world band receiver.

"It's a few years old, but it does a good job for me. Besides my own taped program on WWCR—naturally I listen to that—I tune in to Radio Nederland, Switzerland, Australia, Japan. I like the Voice of America, too, because of the variety of programming."

_____

Prepared by Don Jensen.

BRITAIN'S BEST SELLING RADIO MAGAZINES

ARE NOW AVAILABLE WORLDWIDE

TO SUBSCRIBE TO *PW* OR *SWM* JUST COMPLETE THE FORM BELOW AND MAIL OR FAX IT THROUGH - OR CALL US WITH YOUR CREDIT CARD NUMBER AND WE'LL START YOUR SUBSCRIPTION IMMEDIATELY

Practical Wireless

The #1 selling radio magazine in the UK is *the* magazine for anyone interested in the world of amateur radio.

* News & reviews of the latest equipment
* Antenna Workshop
* Bits & Bytes - the computer in your shack
* Novice Natter
* Focal Point - the world of ATV
* Valve & Vintage
* Equipment construction

And much, much more. *PW* covers all aspects of this fascinating international hobby.

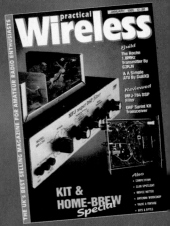

Short Wave Magazine

For everyone, from the newcomer to the experienced radio monitor, *SWM* is *the* listener's magazine with articles and features written specifically to help the listener find out what to buy and where and how to listen. Regular features include:

* News & reviews of the latest equipment
* Utility receiving & decoding
* Reflections
* Bandscan Europe
* Airband
* Info in Orbit
* Scanning

Sony ICF-SW100S, the ultimate in pocket portables.

1996 PASSPORT REPORTS

How To Choose a World Band Radio

*U*nlike, say, VCRs, world band receivers vary greatly from model to model. As usual, money talks—but even that's a fickle barometer. Some models still use old technology, or misuse new technology, and are unhandy or function poorly. Others, more advanced, perform nicely.

World band radio is a jungle: 1,100 channels, with stations scrunched cheek-by-jowl. This crowding is much greater than on FM or mediumwave AM. To make matters worse, the international voyage often causes signals to be weak and quivery. To cope, a radio has to perform some tough electronic gymnastics. Some succeed, others don't.

This is why PASSPORT REPORTS was created. Since 1977 we've tested hundreds of world band products. These evaluations include rigorous hands-on use by veteran listeners and newcomers alike, plus specialized lab tests we've developed over the years. These form the basis of this PASSPORT REPORTS, and are detailed even more fully in the various Radio Database International White Papers®.

HRH Prince of Wales, a long-time world band listener, is presented with a Grundig Yacht Boy 400.   *(BBC)*

Checklist: What to Consider

Before you get into the specifics of which radio does what, here's a basic checklist to help you get oriented.

What to spend? Don't be fooled by the word "radio"—able world band radios are surprisingly sophisticated devices. Yet, for all they do, they cost only about as much as a VCR, usually less.

If you're just starting out, figure the equivalent of what sells in the United States for $100-200, and which sells for £60-130 in the United Kingdom, in a model with two-and-a-half stars or more. If you're looking for top performance, shoot for a portable with three-and-a-half stars—at least $350 or £360—or look into one of the sophisticated portatop or tabletop models that cost at least twice as much.

If price isn't a reliable guide, why not go for the cheapest? Research shows that once the novelty wears off, most people quit using cheap radios, especially those under $80 or £60. On most stations they sound terrible, and they're clumsy to tune.

What kind of stations do you want to hear? Just the main ones? Or do you also hanker for softer voices from exotic lands? Determine what you feel is the minimum performance you want, then choose a model that surpasses that by a good notch or so. This helps ensure against disappointment without wasting money.

Determine your minimum, then choose one notch better.

On the other hand, portables usually don't do well with tougher signals—those that are weaker, or hemmed in by interference from other stations. To ferret out as much as possible, think four stars—perhaps five—in a $600 (£400) or more portatop or tabletop.

Where are you located? Signals are strongest in and around Europe, second-best in eastern North America. If

---

Ethics: The PASSPORT Road to Rome

Our reviewers, and no one else, have written everything in PASSPORT's reviews. These include our laboratory findings, all of which are done independently for us by a specialized contract laboratory that is recognized as the world's leader in this field. (For more on this, please see the RDI White Paper, *How to Interpret Receiver Lab Tests and Measurements*.)

Our review process is completely separate from any advertising, and our reviewers may not accept review fees from manufacturers, or "permanently borrow" radios. And neither International Broadcasting Services nor any of its editors owns any stake in firms which manufacture, sell or distribute world band radios, antennas or related hardware.

PASSPORT recognizes superior products regardless of when they first happen to appear on the market. For this reason, we do not bestow annual awards, which recognize only models released during a given year. Some years, many worthy models are introduced, whereas in other years virtually none appear. Thus, a "best" receiver for one year may be markedly inferior to a "non-best" receiver from another year.

you live in either place, you might get by with any of a number of reasonably rated models.

However, elsewhere in the Americas, or in Hawaii or Australasia, choose with more care. You'll need a receiver that's unusually sensitive to weak signals—some sort of extra antenna will help, too.

In many places, you'll need a radio sensitive to weak signals.

Urban listeners in high-rise buildings may find ordinary portable radios to be insufficient, so should buy these on a money-back basis. Sometimes the best bet is a tabletop or portatop model fed by a simple outboard antenna mounted at or just outside a window or balcony. For more on this, see the introduction to the tabletop section of this PASSPORT REPORTS.

What features make sense to you? Separate these into those that affect performance and those that don't (see box). Don't rely on performance features alone, though. As PASSPORT REPORTS show, much more besides features goes into performance.

World band radios don't test well in stores.

Where to buy? Unlike TVs and ordinary radios, world band sets don't test well in stores other than specialty showrooms with outdoor antennas. Even there, given the fluctuations in world band reception, long-term satisfaction is hard to gauge from a spot test.

Exceptions are audio quality and ergonomics. Even if a radio can't pick up world band stations in the store, you

can get a thumbnail idea of fidelity by catching some mediumwave AM stations. By playing with the radio, you can also get a feel for handiness of operation.

If you're not familiar with a particular store, a good way to judge it is to bring along or mention your PASSPORT. Reputable dealers—reader feedback suggests most are—welcome it as a sign you are serious and knowledgeable. The rest react accordingly.

Otherwise, whether you buy in a mall or through the mail makes little difference. Use the same horse sense you would for any other appliance.

If possible, buy on some sort of money-back or exchange basis—even if it includes a reasonable re-stocking fee—from a vendor with a wide choice of portables, portatops and tabletops, alike. This way, if you're not satisfied and you're willing to cough up more money, you can step up to a higher-rated model.

"Street prices" are virtually a norm with world band.

"Street prices" are now pretty much the norm with world band, just as with computers. Price differences, if any, between everyday outlets and world band specialty stores are usually mini-

Performance Features

Some performance features can be genuinely useful. For example, *multiple conversion* (also called *double conversion*, *up conversion*, *dual conversion* or *two IFs*) is important to rejecting spurious "image" signals—unwanted growls, whistles, dih-dah sounds and the like. Few models under $100 or £70 have it; most over $150 or £100 do.

Also look for two or more *bandwidths* for superior rejection of stations on adjacent channels; properly functioning *synchronous selection (with selectable sideband)* for yet greater adjacent-channel rejection and also to reduce fading; and *continuously tunable tone* controls, preferably with separate bass and treble. For world band reception, *single-sideband* (SSB) reception capability is unimportant; but it is essential if you want to tune in utility or "ham" signals.

On heavy-hitting tabletop models or their portatop cousins, designed to flush out virtually the most stubborn signal, you pay more so you expect more. Look for a tunable *notch filter* to zap howls; *passband offset*, also known as *IF shift*, for superior adjacent-channel rejection and audio contouring; and multiple *AGC* rates, perhaps with selectable *AGC off*.

A *noise blanker* sounds like a better idea than it really is, given the technology world band manufacturers use. Noises that are equal to or lower in strength than the received signal aren't chopped out by a noise blanker until they become stronger than the signal. Innovative circuits exist that can do much better, but this sort of noise-reduction technology is, as yet, nowhere to be found on world band radios.

Digital signal processing (DSP) is the latest attempt to enhance mediocre signal quality. This feature is only now just starting to become available on

mal, with the latter sometimes having the better deal because of volume purchasing.

Are repairs important? Judging from our experience and reports from readers, the quality or availability of repairs tends to correlate with price. At one extreme, some off-brand portables from China are essentially unserviceable, although most outlets will replace a defective unit within warranty.

Better portables are almost always serviced or replaced within warranty. If you can possibly swing it, insist upon replacement, as repairs even from major manufacturers usually are a nightmare.

After warranty expiration, nearly all factory-authorized service departments tend to fall woefully short, sometimes making radios worse, rather than better. Grundig worldwide—and, in the United States, Sangean and Radio Shack—spring to mind as exceptions, mainly because they have been shown to be unusually willing to replace faulty products from dissatisfied customers.

> Quality of repairs tends to correlate with price.

On the other hand, for tabletop models factory-authorized service is usually available to keep them purring for many years to come. Drake and

Continued

the costliest tabletop models, but it should become more commonplace as the decade unfolds. Outboard DSP devices already exist, but thus far only the most costly do much good. DSP has been improving of late, and probably will improve more as new designs emerge. Prices should drop, too.

Looking ahead, the exciting possibility exists that *digital shortwave transmissions* could supplement the current analog system by around the end of the decade. If successful—right now, it looks like a long shot—it might result in much-improved reception quality for the listener, with reduced transmission costs for the broadcaster. But don't look anytime soon for radios that can receive these transmissions. They don't exist yet, even as concepts.

Operating Features

Desirable operating features for any world band radio include *digital frequency readout*, a virtual "must"; 24-hour *World Time* clock, especially one that is always displayed; direct-access tuning via *keypad* and *presets* ("memories"); and any combination of *"signal-seek" scanning*, a *tuning knob* or up/down *slewing controls* to "fish around" for stations.

Useful, but less important, are an *on/off timer*, especially if it can control a tape recorder; *illuminated display*; *single-keystroke callup* (a separate button for each preset), rather than having to use the 1-0 keypad; *numerically displayed seconds* on the 24-hour clock; and a good *signal-strength indicator*. Travelers should stick to portables with locks that keep the power from coming on accidentally in suitcases.

Watkins-Johnson are legendary in this regard within North America, as is Lowe in Europe. Service can also be first-rate at a number of other firms, such as Japan Radio, Kenwood and Yaesu. Yet, Drake, Watkins-Johnson and Lowe stand apart because they also tend to maintain a healthy parts inventory, even for older models.

Of course, nothing quite equals service at the factory itself. So if repair is especially important to you, bend a little toward the home team: Drake and Watkins-Johnson in the United States, Grundig in Germany, Lowe in the United Kingdom, Japan Radio in Japan, and so on.

Outdoor Antennas: Do You Need One?

If you're wondering what accessory antenna you'll need for your new radio, the answer for portables and portatops is usually simple: none or almost none, as all come with built-in telescopic antennas. Indeed, for evening use in Eastern North America or Europe nearly all portables perform *less* well with sophisticated outboard antennas than with their built-in ones.

But if you listen during the day, or live in such places as the North American Midwest or West, your portable may need more oomph. The best solution in the United States is also the cheapest: less than ten bucks for Radio Shack's 75-foot (23-meter) "SW Antenna Kit," which comes with insulators and other goodies, plus $2 for a claw clip. The antenna itself may be a bit too long for your circumstances, but you can always trim it.

Alternatively, many electronics and world band specialty firms sell the necessary parts and wire for you to make your own. An appendix in the Radio Database International White Paper® *Evaluation of Popular Outdoor Antennas* gives minutely detailed step-by-step instructions on making and erecting such an antenna.

Basically, you attach the claw clip onto your radio's rod antenna (this is usually better than the set's external antenna input socket, which may have a desensitizing circuit), then run it out your window, as high as is safe and practical, to something like a tree. Unless you want to become Crispy the Cadaver, *keep your antenna clear of any hazardous wiring—the electrical service to your house, in particular—and respect heights.* If you live in an apartment, run it to your balcony or window—as close to the fresh outdoors as possible.

This "volksantenna"—best disconnected when you're not listening, or when thunder, snow or sand storms are nearby—will probably help with most signals. But if it occasionally makes a station sound worse, disconnect the claw clip and use your radio's telescopic antenna.

It's a different story with tabletop receivers. They require an external antenna, either passive or electrically amplified (so-called "active"). Although portatop models don't require an outboard antenna, they invariably work better with one.

Amplified antennas use small wire or rod elements that aren't very efficient, but make up for it with electronic circuitry. For apartment dwellers and some others, they can be a godsend—provided they work right. Choosing a suitable amplified antenna for your tabletop or portatop receiver takes some care,

Coconuts operate radio station! Rebel station "Radio Free Bougainville" is powered entirely by electricity generated from coconuts.

Continued

as some are pretty awful. Yet, certain models—notably, Britain's Datong AD 370, and to a lesser extent California's McKay Dymek DA100D—work relatively well. These sell at world band specialty outlets, usually for under $200 or £125.

If you have space outdoors, a passive outdoor wire antenna is much better, especially when it's designed for world band frequencies. Besides not needing problematic electronic circuits, a good passive antenna also tends to reduce interference from the likes of fluorescent lights and electric shavers—noises which amplified antennas boost, right along with the signal. As the cognoscenti put it, the "signal-to-noise ratio" tends to be better with passive antennas.

With any outdoor antenna, especially if it is high out in the open, disconnect it and affix it to something like an outdoor ground rod if there is lightning nearby. Handier, and nearly as effective except for a direct strike, is a modestly priced "gas-pill" lightning protector, such as is made by Alpha Delta. Or, if you have deep pockets, the $295 Ten-Tec Model 100 protector, which automatically shuts out your antenna and power cord when lightning appears nearby. Otherwise, sooner or later, you may be facing a costly repair bill.

A surge protector on the radio's power cord is good insurance, too. These are available at any computer store, and cheap MOV-based ones are usually good enough. But you can also go for the whole hog, as we do, with the innovative $150 Zero Surge ZS 900 (U.S. phone 800/996-6696; elsewhere +1 908/996-7700).

Many firms—some large, some tiny—manufacture world band antennas. Among the best passive models—all under $100 or £60—are those made by Antenna Supermarket and Alpha Delta Communications, available from world band stores. A detailed report on these is available as the same Radio Database International White Paper® mentioned above, *Evaluation of Popular Outdoor Antennas*. We also have a special update report in "Tabletop Receivers for 1996," farther on in this edition.

GRUNDIG

TUNE

SW BROADCAST BAND

LOCK

SW

5.000 kHz

MEMORY

10

PLL SW BROADCAST BAND

30 STATION MEMORIES

POWER

ON/OFF

AUTO OFF

SLEEP

PRESET/DIRECT ACCESS

120m 90m 75m

1 2 3

60m 49m 41m

4 5 6

31m 25m 22m

7 8 9

19m 16m 13m

0

BAND

METER

SW

ENTER

MEMORY

SCAN STORE

RESET

TUNING

LOCK

YB 305
MW/SW/FM-STEREO
PLL SYNTHESIZED RECEIVER

GRUNDIG

SATELLIT 900

TREBLE

BASS

BOOST

VOLUME

LOCAL

UTC

07:15 22.30 08.45

RDS

STEREO

MEMORY

2.02

TUNING

BOOST

ACCU

CHARGE

FM 100.60 MHz

DLF-INFO

88.9   DW D   BBC   CARIVARI

AM ROM

RDS

LEARN

MONO

AF

A-Z

MENU

PUSH
OFF/ON

LOCK UNLOCK

TUNING

FAST

Chr

SLEEP

TIME

AUTO

WORLD RECEIVER

Portables for 1996

*I*nterested in programs from major world band stations? If so, a good portable is the value way to go. Unless you live in a high-rise, the best digitally tuned portables will almost certainly meet your needs—especially evenings, when signals are strongest.

That's especially true in Europe and the Near East, or even eastern North America. Signals tend to come in well there, so virtually any well-rated portable will probably satisfy.

Where Signals Are Weak

Elsewhere, signals might be weaker, especially in such places as central and western North America, Australasia, Caribbean or Pacific islands. There, you need to concentrate on models PASSPORT has found to be unusually sensitive to weak signals. (Look under "Advantages.")

Yet, even in Europe and eastern North America, daytime signals tend to be weaker than at night. If you listen then—some stations and programs are heard in North America only during the day—weak-signal performance should be a priority.

Signals Now Harder to Hear

Almost everywhere, anything governmental is being scaled back—and international broadcasting is no exception, especially since the end of the Cold War. Too, as government broadcasters are relatively free from accountability to their audiences, some have been substituting other technologies in lieu of shortwave—even when this causes audiences virtually to disappear. The result is that world band voices are sometimes harder to hear, or can be heard only when beamed away from where you live. To enjoy these tougher signals, you need a better receiver than in the past. Another reception

New for Grundig in 1996 is the Yacht Boy 305. The Satellit 900, not yet on the market, is expected to be introduced shortly.

challenge results from our being in the trough of the 11-year sunspot cycle. This limits the number of world band channels available for use, especially in the evening, but this will begin to improve in a couple of years. Until then, daytime listening will be a relatively attractive supplement to evening listening.

Tabletop and portatop models with first-rate antennas flush out most weak signals better than even the best of portables. However, you can use an alligator or claw clip to connect a hank of wire to your portable's telescopic antenna to obtain at least some benefit on the cheap. If your antenna has to be indoors, that wire can work to best advantage if you affix it along the middle of a window, such as with Velcro, tape or suction cups. Another signal-boosting trick that sometimes helps is to operate your portable off AC, rather than batteries. (See blue box in "How to Choose a World Band Radio.") Beware, though, of cheap electronic "signal-booster" devices.

Avoiding Batteries

AC adaptors pay for themselves quickly, while also giving the environment a friendly boost. It's best to use adaptors approved by the appropriate safety authorities, such as Underwriters Laboratories. If you travel abroad, look for a multi-voltage version—standard on a few models.

Longwave Useful for Some

The longwave band is still used for some domestic broadcasts in Europe, North Africa and Russia. If you live in or travel to these parts of the world, longwave coverage is a slight plus. Otherwise, forget it.

Keep in mind, though, that when a low-cost model is available with longwave, that band may be included at the expense of some world band coverage.

Shelling Out

For the United States, suggested retail ("list") prices, or a street-list range of prices, are given. Discounts from list are common, although those sold under the "Radio Shack" brand name are usually discounted only during special Radio Shack sales.

For Canada, the European Union, Australia and some other parts of the world, observed selling prices (including VAT, where applicable) are usually given.

Duty-free shopping? For the time being, in some parts of the EU it may save you ten percent or more, *provided* you don't have to declare the radio at your destination. Check on warranty coverage, though. In the United States, where prices are already among the world's lowest, you're better off buying from shortwave specialty outlets and regular stores. Canada, as well—and, to an increasing extent, the United Kingdom and Germany.

In Japan, however, the go-go days of bargain hunting in Tokyo's famous Akihabara are over—at least for the time being. World band radios are no longer widely available, with only a few outlets, such as X-One and T-Zone, having much selection. Even Japanese-made radios are now usually cheaper in the United States than in the Akihabara!

Naturally, all prices are as we go to press and may fluctuate. Some may change before the ink dries.

We try to stick to plain English, but some specialized terms have to be used. If you come across something that's not clear, check it out in the Glossary farther back in this edition.

Nearly All Available Models Included

Here are the results of this year's hands-on and laboratory testing. We've scoured the earth, and evaluated nearly

With the world band market growing, a number of new models are looming on the horizon. As with anything else, the promise found in the manufacturers' advance publicity may not resemble the reality of performance.

Grundig Satellit 900

Due out in early 1996, this high-end model reportedly will feature sophisticated computer-assisted tuning. One to watch, and we'll be testing it for PASSPORT '97 later in 1996, once the "shakedown cruise" is over and any possible initial bugs cleaned up. Around DM1000 in Germany.

Sony ICF-SW1000T

Due out just before January, 1996, this programmable radio-with-stereo-cassette should be the first serious alternative to Sangean's top-selling ATS-818CS. Unusual features include two-event recording and synchronous selectable sideband. To list at $699.95 in the United States. Another one to watch.

Sangean ATS 909

The Great Mystery Radio. Initially to have appeared in mid-1994, then mid-1995. Sangean continues to promise that this pride-of-the-fleet model will be introduced before long. As always with Sangean products, the 909 is likely to appear under a variety of other brand names. Price? No idea, but something in the $300-400 range would seem probable.

Sangean ATS-303

Here's a new digitally tuned portable from Sangean that *is* to appear soon, probably on or before January, 1996. According to the manufacturer, it will tune 2.3-7.3 and 9.5-26.1 MHz, incredibly missing gobs of important stations between 7305-7600 kHz and 9350-9495 kHz. Apparently single-conversion, with a clock and alarm/timer. List in the United States is scheduled to be $119.00.

Radio Shack DX-395

A Spartan, low-cost digital portable with ten world band presets, clock and timing facilities. Presumably single-conversion, and world band tuning range not yet specified by the manufacturer. Will be out by the time you read this, with a list price in the United States of $79.99.

every digital portable currently produced and reasonably available that meets our minimum specifications for performance.

What Passport's Ratings Mean

Star ratings: ★ ★ ★ ★ ★ is best. We award stars solely for overall performance and meaningful features; price, appearance and the like are not taken into account. To facilitate comparison, the same rating system is used for portable and portatop models, reviewed elsewhere in this PASSPORT. Whether a radio is portable, a portatop or a tabletop model, a given rating—three stars, say—means largely the same thing.

A rating of three stars or more should please most who listen regularly during the evening to the major stations. However, for occasional use on trips, a small portable with as little as one-and-a-half stars may suffice.

If you are listening from a weak-signal part of the world, such as central and western North America or Australasia, lean strongly towards models that have sensitivity among the listed advantages. Too, check out the portatop and tabletop sections of this PASSPORT REPORTS.

Passport's Choice models are our test team's personal picks of the litter—digital portables that we would buy for ourselves.

Ç: denotes a price-for-performance value.

Models in **(parentheses)** have not been tested by us, but appear to be essentially identical to model(s) tested.

How Models Are Listed

Models are listed by size; and, within size, in order of world band listening suitability. Unless otherwise indicated, each digital model includes:

- Tuning by keypad, up/down slewing, presets and scanning.
- Digital frequency readout.
- Coverage the world band shortwave spectrum from at least 3200-26100 kHz.
- Coverage of the usual 87.5-108 MHz FM band.
- Coverage of the AM (mediumwave) band in selectable 9 and 10 kHz channel increments from 513-1705 kHz.

POCKET PORTABLES

Handy for Travel, Poor for Home

Pocket portables weigh under a pound, or half-kilogram, and are somewhere between the size of an audio cassette box and one of the larger hand-held calculators. They operate off two to four ordinary small "AA" (UM-3 penlite) batteries. These diminutive models do one job well: provide news and entertainment when you're traveling, especially abroad.

Don't expect much more, once the novelty has worn off. Listening to tiny speakers can be tiring, so most pocket portables aren't suitable for hour-after-hour listening, except through good headphones. This isn't an attractive option, given that none has the full array of Walkman-type features, such as a hidden antenna.

Too, none of the available digitally tuned pocket portables is as sensitive to weak signals as they could be. Outboard antennas, sometimes supplied, help, but defeat the point of having a pocket model: hassle-free portability.

Best bet? If price and sound quality through the speaker are paramount, try Sangean's relatively affordable ATS 606p and ATS 606, also available as the

Siemens RK 659. Otherwise, check out Sony's innovative, but pricey, ICF-SW100S and ICF-SW100E.

Don't forget to look over the large selection of compact models, just after the pocket portables reviewed in this PASSPORT REPORTS. They're not much larger than pocket versions, so they also travel well. But, unlike their smaller cousins, compacts usually have more sizable speakers, and so tend to sound better.

Price: $479.95 in the United States. CAN$599.00 in Canada. £179.95 in the United Kingdom.

Advantages: Extremely small. Superior overall world band performance for size. Excellent synchronous detection with selectable sideband. High-quality audio when earpieces (supplied) are used. FM stereo through earpieces. Exceptional number of helpful tuning features, including "page" storage. Tunes in precise 100 Hz increments. Worthy ergonomics for size and features. Illuminated display. Clock for many world cities,

For the gadget-loving traveler, nothing beats the itsy Sony ICF-SW100.

which can be made to work as a *de facto* World Time clock. Timer/sleep features. Travel power lock. Receives longwave and Japanese FM bands. Amplified outboard antenna (supplied), in addition to usual built-in antenna, enhances weak-signal reception. High-quality travel case for radio. *Except for North America:* Self-regulating AC adaptor, with American and European plugs, adjusts automatically to all local voltages worldwide.

Disadvantages: Tiny speaker, although an innovative design, has mediocre sound and limited loudness. Weak-signal sensitivity could be better, although outboard active antenna (supplied) helps. Expensive. No tuning knob. Clock not readable when station frequency is being displayed. Rejection of certain spurious signals ("images") could be better. No meaningful signal-strength indicator. Earbuds less comfortable than foam-padded headphones. Mediumwave AM channel spacing adjusts peculiarly. Batteries run down faster than usual when radio off. Flimsy battery cover. *North America:* AC adaptor 120 Volts only.

Bottom Line: What an engineering *tour de force!* Speaker and, to a lesser extent, weak-signal sensitivity keep it from being all it could have been. Yet, it's still is the handiest pocket portable around, and one of the niftiest gift ideas in years.

Price: £179.95 in the United Kingdom. Currently not distributed by Sony within North America.

Bottom Line: This version, available in Europe (where the "S" version is currently not available), but not North

America, nominally includes a case, tape-reel-type passive antenna and earbuds. Otherwise, it is identical to the Sony ICF-SW100S, above.

★ ★ ★ *Passport's Choice*

Sangean ATS 606p
Sangean ATS 606
(Siemens RK 659)

Price: *ATS 606p:* $269.00 in the United States and Continental European Community. CAN$259.95 in Canada. *ATS 606:* $249.00 in the United States and Continental European Community. CAN$259.95 in Canada. AUS$249.00 in Australia.

Advantages: Exceptional simplicity of operation for technology class. Speaker audio quality superior for size class, improves with (usually supplied) earpieces. Various helpful tuning features. Keypad has exceptional feel and tactile response. Longwave. World Time clock, displayed separately from frequency, and local clock. Alarm/sleep features. Travel power lock. Clear warning when batteries weak. Stereo FM via earpieces. Superior FM reception. *ATS 606p:* Reel-in passive wire antenna.

Sangean's ATS 606 is the best deal in a pocket portable.

Self-regulating AC adaptor, with American and European plugs, adjusts automatically to most local voltages worldwide.

Disadvantages: No tuning knob. Tunes only in coarse 5 kHz increments. World Time clock readable only when radio is switched off. Display not illuminated. Keypad not in telephone format. No meaningful signal-strength indicator. No carrying strap or handle. Supplied earpieces inferior to comparable foam-padded headphones. *ATS 606:* AC adaptor extra.

Bottom Line: A sensible choice, thanks to its superior sound through the speaker. If the regular "606" Sangean version seems Spartan, there's the "606p" version, complete with handy goodies. It's well worth the small extra price.

★ ★

Sangean ATS-202

Price: $149.00 in the United States. CAN$119.95 in Canada.

Advantages: Weak-signal sensitivity a bit better than most. World Time clock. Travel power lock. Alarm and sleep-delay. Illuminated display. Tunes using ten presets, signal-seek scanning and up/down slewing.

Disadvantages: Doesn't tune important 7300-7600 kHz and 9020-9495 kHz ranges. Adjacent-channel rejection (selectivity) mediocre. Spurious-signal ("image") rejection poor. Lacks keypad and tuning knob. Sometimes requires adjusting band switch when changing world band frequencies. Tunes only in coarse 5 kHz increments. World Time clock readable only when radio is switched off. Audio, although otherwise reasonable, somewhat tinny. Batteries can run down more quickly than usual with radio off.

The Sangean ATS-202 is inexpensive and small, but not much else.

Bottom Line: Least-costly digital pocket portable currently available, but otherwise lackluster.

COMPACT PORTABLES

Good for Travel, Fair for Home

Compacts tip in at 1.0-1.5 pounds, or 0.5-0.7 kg, and are typically sized 8 x 5 x 1.5", or 20 x 13 x 4 cm. Like pocket models, they feed off "AA" (UM-3 penlite) batteries—but more of them. They travel almost as well as smaller models, but sound better and usually receive better, too. For some travelers, they also suffice as home sets—something pocket units can't really do. However, if you don't travel abroad often, you will probably find better value and performance in a lap portable.

Which stand out? For general listening, Grundig's Yacht Boy 400 has superior audio quality and two bandwidths. For hearing signals hemmed in by interference, the Sony ICF-7600G brings real affordability to synchronous detection. Both are outstanding buys, especially if you don't live where signals are relatively weak. (If you do, consider the new Grundig Yacht Boy 305, the larger Sony ICF-2010, or a portatop or tabletop model; but between the YB 400 and ICF-7600G, the latter has a slight edge in such weak-signal parts of the world as central and western North America.) The various three-star models are no slouches, either...but why bother?

On the cheap? The new Grundig

Tips for Globetrotting

Customs and airport security people are used to world band portables, which are now a staple among world travelers. Yet, a few simple practices will help in avoiding hassles:

- Stow your radio in a carry-on bag, not checked luggage.
- Take along batteries so you can demonstrate that the radio actually works, as gutted radios can be used to carry illegal material.
- Travel outside Europe, North America, the Caribbean, Pacific islands and Australasia with nothing larger than a compact model.
- Avoid models with built-in tape recorders.
- If asked what the radio is for, state that it is for your personal use.
- If traveling in war zones or off the beaten path in East Africa, take along a radio you can afford to lose.

Finally, remember that radios, cameras, binoculars and the like are almost always stolen to be resold. The more used it looks—affixing worn stickers helps—the less likely it is to be "confiscated" by corrupt inspectors or stolen by thieves.

Yacht Boy 305 is nigh ideal for tightfisted Americans, whereas elsewhere the Sony ICF-SW30 provides pretty good performance with mediocre tuning. Another to consider is the Radio Shack/Realistic DX-375, which provides okay performance with more-versatile tuning.

Passport's Choice ¢

Grundig Yacht Boy 400

Price: $199.95-249.95 in the United States. £119.95 in the United Kingdom. CAN$249.95 in Canada. £119.95 in the United Kingdom. AUS$399.00 in Australia.

Advantages: Unusually good value. Audio quality clearly tops in size category. Two bandwidths, both well-chosen. Easy to operate and ergonomically superior for advanced-technology radio. A number of helpful tuning features, including keypad, up/down slewing, 40 station presets, "signal seek" frequency scanning and scanning of station presets. Signal-strength indicator. World Time clock with second time zone, any one of which is shown at all times; however, clock displays seconds only when radio is off. Illuminated display.

One that's hard to beat—and sells like it—is the Grundig Yacht Boy 400.

Alarm/sleep features. Demodulates single-sideband signals, used by hams and utility stations, with unusual precision for a portable. Generally superior FM performance. FM in stereo through headphones (not supplied). Longwave. Microprocessor reset control.

Disadvantages: Circuit noise ("hiss") can be slightly intrusive with weak signals. AC adaptor not standard. No tuning knob. At some locations, there can be breakthrough of powerful AM or FM stations. Keypad not in telephone format. No LSB/USB switch.

Bottom Line: This model is overwhelmingly preferred over other compacts by our panelists in Eastern North America and Europe for listening to major world band stations. The Grundig Yacht Boy's audio quality is tops within its size class, even though circuit noise with weak signals could be lower. (It helps if you attach several yards or meters of strung-out doorbell wire to the antenna). Although manufactured in China, the build quality is good.

Retested for 1996 ¢

Passport's Choice

Sony ICF-SW7600G

Price: $239.95 in the United States. CAN$349.00 in Canada. £159.99 in the United Kingdom. AUS$449.00 in Australia.

Advantages: Unusually good value. Far and away the least-costly model available with high-tech synchronous detection coupled to selectable sideband; synchronous detection generally performs very well, reducing adjacent-channel interference and fading distortion on world band, longwave and mediumwave AM signals (see Disadvantages). Single bandwidth, especially when the synchronous-

The lowest-priced radio with fidelity-enhancing synchronous detection is the Sony ICF-SW7600G.

detection feature is used, exceptionally effective at adjacent-channel rejection. Numerous helpful tuning features, including keypad, two-speed up/down slewing, 20 presets (ten for world band) and "signal-seek" scanning. Demodulates single-sideband signals, used by hams and utility stations, with unusual precision for a portable. World Time clock, easy to set. Tape-reel-type outboard passive antenna accessory comes standard. Sleep/timer features. Illuminated display. Travel power lock. FM stereo through earpieces or headphones. Receives longwave and Japanese FM bands. Dead-battery indicator. Comes standard with vinyl carrying case.

Disadvantages: Possible quality control problems, based on the relatively few (three) units tested thus far—on one, synchronous detection alignment drifted somewhat, causing one sideband to have noticeably less high-frequency audio response than the other sideband; the second unit did this to only a minor degree, and was a pleasure to use; the third unit didn't function at all on shortwave. Certain controls, notably for synchronous detection, located unhandily at the side of the cabinet. No tuning knob. Clock not readable when radio is switched on. No meaningful signal-strength indi-

cator. No AC adaptor comes standard, and polarity difference disallows use of customary Sony adaptors. No earphones/earpieces come standard.

Bottom Line: The best compact model available for rejecting adjacent-channel interference and selective fading distortion—a major plus—but audio quality otherwise is *ordinaire*. A worthy value, mainly because it comes with synchronous selectable sideband, but sample-to-sample variations suggest this should be bought on an exchangeable basis.

★ ★ ★

Sony ICF-SW55

Price: $449.95 in the United States. CAN$519.00 in Canada. £249.95 in the United Kingdom. AUS$799.00 in Australia.

Advantages: Although sound emerges through a small port, rather than the usual speaker grille, audio quality is better than most in its size class. Dual bandwidths. Tunes in precise 0.1 kHz increments (displays only in 1 kHz increments). Controls neatly and logically laid out. Innovative tuning system, including factory pre-stored station presets and displayed

Computer-like tuning and good audio quality are hallmarks of Sony's ICF-SW55. It comes with a real tuning knob, too.

Radio Shack/Realistic DX-392
Roberts RC818
Sangean ATS-818CS
Siemens RK 670

Millions do it daily: record television programs on VCRs so they can be enjoyed at a more convenient time. You'd think that with world band radio sales rising for several years now, history would repeat itself, and there would be any number of world band cassette recorders—radios with built-in tape recorders—from which to choose.

Not so. As of when we go to press, there's only one worth considering, the Sangean ATS-818CS, $359.00 in the United States, CAN$399.95 in Canada and AUS$399.95 in Australia. It's single-event, so you can't record more than one time bloc automatically, and even then it can be programmed for only one day. Too, while you can set the recording "on" time, it shuts off automatically only when the tape runs out.

The '818CS is the same as the two-and-a-half-star ATS-818—for performance details, see the review of the '818 elsewhere in this section—but with a cassette deck added. Recording features are bare-bones (no level indicator, no counter, no stereo), but there is a condenser microphone. The fast-forward and rewind controls are inverted from the customary positions, so the indicator arrows are backwards—fast forward points left, rewind points right. Still, recording quality is acceptable, and the limited timing facility works as it should.

Sangean's ATS-818CS allows for one-event world band recording.

Sangean's ATS-818CS is no high-tech wonder, but it is, by default, the best device of its type on the market, and it reportedly is selling very well. It is also available for $259.99 in the United States or AUS$399.95 in Australia as the Radio Shack DX-392, £199.99 in the United Kingdom as the Roberts RC818, and in Germany with factory-preprogrammed stations as the Siemens RK 670.

That's it? Not really. A number of newer models, identified in this section, can be programmed to switch not only themselves on and off, but also a cassette recorder. While that approach is less handy than that of the Sangean offering, the quality of reception—if you use a well-rated radio—can be even better.

Possibly better yet, but a steeper price tag, will be the forthcoming Sony ICF-SW1000T portable, with two-event recording and a variety of advanced-technology features. It will be introduced sometime in the months to come at a list price in the United States of $699.95 (see "Coming Up").

alphabetic identifiers for groups ("pages") of stations. Weak-signal sensitivity a bit better than most. Good single-sideband reception, although reader reports suggest some BFO "pulling" (not found in our unit). Comes complete with carrying case containing reel-in wire antenna, AC adaptor, DC power cord and in-the-ear earpieces. Signal/battery strength indicator. Local and World Time clocks, either (but not both) of which is displayed separately from frequency. Summer time adjustment for local time clock. Sleep/alarm features. Five-event (daily only) timer nominally can automatically turn on/off certain cassette recorders—a plus for VCR-type multiple-event recording. Illuminated display. Receives longwave and Japanese FM bands.

Disadvantages: Tuning system unusually difficult for many people to grasp. Operation sometimes unnecessarily complicated by any yardstick, but especially for listeners in the Americas. Spurious-signal rejection, notably in higher world band segments, not fully commensurate with price class. Wide bandwidth somewhat broad for world band reception. Display illumination dim and uneven. Costly to operate from batteries. Cabinet keeps antenna from tilting fully, a slight disadvantage for reception of some FM signals.

Bottom Line: If the ICF-SW55's operating scheme meets with your approval—for example, if you are comfortable utilizing the more sophisticated features of a typical VCR or computer—and you're looking for a small portable with good audio, this radio is a superior performer in its size class. It can also tape like a VCR, provided you have a suitable recorder to connect to it.

★ ★ ★

Grundig Yacht Boy 500

Price: $299.95 in the United States. CAN$399.95 in Canada. £169.95 in the United Kingdom. AUS$599.00 in Australia.

Advantages: Attractive layout. Audio-boost circuitry for superior volume. 40 presets. Displays operator-assigned alphanumeric names for stations in presets. RDS circuitry for FM. ROM with 90 factory-preassigned world band channels for nine international broadcasters. Two 24-hour clocks, either one of which displays full time. Battery-low indicator. FM in stereo via headphones. Travel power lock. Three-increment signal-strength indicator. Elevation panel. Single-sideband reception via LSB/USB key. Illuminated display. Timer, sleep timer and snooze delay. Comes with worldwide dual-voltage AC adaptor and two types of plugs. Audio quality pretty good. Longwave.

The Grundig Yacht Boy 500 is a nice radio, but slightly outclassed by its sibling Yacht Boy 400.

Disadvantages: Circuit noise relatively high. Lacks tuning knob. Telescopic antenna tends to get in the way of right-handed users. Volume slider fussy to adjust. Keypad not in telephone format. Key design and layout increase likelihood of wrong key being pushed. Owner's manual, although thorough, poor for quick answers. Twenty-four hour clocks display without leading zeroes. Elevation panel flimsy. Socket for AC adaptor appears to be flimsy. Factory-preassigned channels, of use mainly to beginners, relatively complex for beginners to select. AC adaptor lacks UL seal of approval. Relatively high number of spurious "birdie" signals.

Note: Our report covers this model as manufactured after about 11/93. Some earlier units, apparently manufactured in October and November of 1993, reportedly suffered from such problems as audio distortion. These units appear to have virtually disappeared from dealers' shelves since early 1994.

Bottom Line: Exciting design, good performance, with powerful audio and a number of interesting features. Withal, for most users slightly better performance can be had for the same price or less.

★ ★ ★

Price: *RF-B65:* $269.95-279.95 in the United States. CAN$319.00 in Canada. AUS$549.00 in Australia. *RF-B65 and RF-B65D:* £165.95 in the United Kingdom. The equivalent of about US$300-450 elsewhere in the European Union. *RP-65 120 VAC adaptor:* $6.95 in the United States. *RP-38 120/220 VAC*

worldwide adaptor: $14.95 in the United States. (Adaptor prices are as provided by Panasonic; actual selling prices in stores are higher.)

Advantages: Superior overall world band performance for size. Very easy to operate for advanced-technology radio. Pleasant audio. Various helpful tuning features. Signal-strength indicator. World Time clock, plus second time-zone clock. Alarm/sleep features. Demodulates single-sideband signals, used by hams and utility stations. Longwave. Travel power lock. AC adaptor included (outside North America).

Disadvantages: Cumbersome tuning knob inhibits speed. With built-in antenna, weak-signal sensitivity slightly low. Adjacent-channel rejection (selectivity) slightly broad. Clocks not displayed separately from frequency. Display not illuminated. Keypad not in telephone format. AC adaptor extra (North America).

Bottom Line: A very nice, easy-to-use portable, especially if you live in Europe or eastern North America, where world band signals are relatively strong.

Panasonic's RF-B65 is mainly for those living in Europe and eastern North America.

Well-made and fairly priced is the Panasonic RF-B45.

Panasonic RF-B45
(Panasonic RF-B45DL)
(National B45)

Price: *RF-B45:* $189.95-199.95 in the United States. CAN$239.00 in Canada. AUS$399.00 in Australia. *RF-B45DL:* £139.95 in the United Kingdom. The equivalent of US$220-320 in the European Union. *RP-65 120 VAC adaptor:* $6.95 in the United States. *RP-38 120/220 VAC worldwide adaptor:* $14.95 in the United States.

Advantages: Superior performance for price category. Easy to operate for advanced-technology radio. A number of helpful tuning features. Signal-strength indicator. World Time clock. Alarm/sleep features. Demodulates single-sideband signals, used by hams and utility stations. Longwave.

Disadvantages: No tuning knob. Weak-signal sensitivity a bit lacking. Adjacent-channel rejection (selectivity) a bit broad. Clock not displayed separately from frequency. No display illumination. AC adaptor extra.

Bottom Line: A nice little radio, fairly priced, with Panasonic's superior build quality.

Sangean ATS-808
Aiwa WR-D1000
(Roberts R808)
(Siemens RK 661)

Price: *Sangean:* $259.00 in the United States. CAN$249.95 in Canada. AUS$299.00 in Australia. *Aiwa:* $259.95 in the United States. *Siemens:* 399.00 DM in Germany. *Roberts:* £119.99 in the United Kingdom. *ADP-808 120 VAC adaptor:* $9.95 in the United States. CAN$19.95 in Canada.

Advantages: Attractively priced in one version (see Comments). Exceptional simplicity of operation for technology class. Dual bandwidths, unusual in this size radio (see Disadvantages). Various helpful tuning features. Weak-signal sensitivity a bit better than most. Keypad has exceptional feel and tactile response. Longwave. World Time clock, displayed separately from frequency, and local clock. Alarm/sleep features. Signal strength indicator. Travel power lock. Stereo FM via earpieces. Superior FM reception.

Disadvantages: Fast tuning mutes receiver when tuning knob is turned quickly. Narrow bandwidth perfor-

Although somewhat outclassed by newer models, the Sangean ATS-808 can be interesting when it is priced to move.

mance only fair. Spurious-signal ("image") rejection very slightly substandard for class. Pedestrian audio. Display not illuminated. Keypad not in telephone format. No carrying strap or handle. Supplied earpieces inferior to comparable foam-padded headphones. AC adaptor extra.

Comments: ¢ applies to Roberts versions only, or on occasional special sales. *Aiwa:* Cabinet styled differently from the other versions of this model.

Bottom Line: Exceptional simplicity of operation, worthy overall performance and reasonable price. However, mediocre for bandscanning.

New for 1996 is the Grunding Yacht Boy 305, with superior sensitivity to weak signals.

New for 1996   ¢

★ ★ ½   *Passport's Choice*

Grundig Yacht Boy 305

Price: $129.95-149.95 in the United States. CAN$169.95 in Canada.

Advantages: Unusually good value, especially for those in weak-signal parts of the world. Exceptionally sensitive to weak signals for a portable. Above-average selectivity and audio quality. Various helpful tuning features. Travel power lock. Stereo FM via earpieces (not supplied). Microprocessor reset control.

Disadvantages: Spurious-signal ("image") rejection slightly inferior. Tends to overload in the presence of very powerful signals. AC adaptor not standard. No tuning knob.

Note: "PASSPORT'S CHOICE" for the Yacht Boy 305 applies for listening within those parts of the world, such as central and western North America, where signals are usually not strong.

Bottom Line: World band's first true equivalent to the good five-cent cigar. Priced right, exceptionally sensitive to weak signals, with worthy selectivity and audio quality. An outstanding

choice, price or no price, for those in weak-signal parts of the world, such as central and western North America, Australasia, the Caribbean and Pacific islands. Equally, the '305's tendency to overload makes it ill-suited for use in Europe, North Africa and the Near East.

Evaluation of New Model: In the United States, there used to be—maybe still is—a chain called "AtlastA Motel." That's what Grundig ought to call its new Yacht Boy 305, the "AtlastA Radio," because, at last, it's the good performer Americans have been waiting for that's a darned sight cheaper than models just a skootch better.

Americans? You bet, because this radio sniffs out weak signals like a Provencal pig roots out truffles, and North America is full of places where signals arrive weary and beat from long journeys. If you live in someplace like Vancouver or Hilo or Dodge City or Tucson, and don't want to cough up $300 or more for a radio to hear Oslo or Amman or Kiev or even Montreal, then the 305 is for you. For all the fancy things fancy radios do, if they can't suck in the signals you want to hear, the rest is beside the point.

Outside the Americas? The 305's great sensitivity also means it tends to overload in the presence of very strong signals. In the Americas you don't get lots of these, so the problem is minimal. But in Europe, North Africa and such, many signals pound in. Presumably, this is why Grundig is selling the '305 in North America, but plans to offer a "Euro version" for the EU. A very sensible move, long overdue.

Globetrotters still make out, though, because in Europe they can simply collapse the telescopic antenna slightly if they encounter overloading. And there's also a lock button for the power to keep the radio from going on accidentally in your suitcase. But there's no display light to help out in dark hotel rooms or moonlit chaises, nor are there any alarm or sleep facilities. So it's okay for international travel, but nothing more, except for such weak-signal destinations as the Caribbean and Hawaii. Mainly, this is a set for using in the Americas and such, around the house and yard, with occasional duty on trips.

It has the usual tuning aids you expect in better radios, but usually don't find at this price except in radios that perform less well. There are direct-frequency keypad entry, up/down slewing, "signal-seek" scanning and 30 channel presets. Selectors, too, for choosing meter bands—but no tuning knob. It doesn't come with an AC converter, but if you want one call Grundig's toll-free number and they'll tell you how to get it.

Audio quality is something of a Grundig hallmark, and the '305 is no exception. No, it doesn't sound like premium Grundig Satellit radios, but on world band and mediumwave AM it's pretty reasonable. (FM is less so, but improves with headphones.) There is no single-sideband circuitry,

a minus for radio buffs, but arguably a plus for most others because it helps keep things simple. Also simplifying matters, and cost, is that the 305 has only one bandwidth. Although two would be better, that one is well chosen.

The real drawback, though, is that the 305, unlike virtually all models above its price class, has only single-conversion circuitry. This means that stations "repeat" at reduced strength 900 kHz down from where they really are; these "ghost" signals can create what's called "image" interference to the station you're trying to hear. Still, Grundig has managed to keep image interference to a minimum for this type of circuit design. It's good enough for most program listeners in the Americas, but not those in Europe—and certainly not most radio aficionados.

Grundig's Yacht Boy 305 is the best of the "value" models, and generally the best model priced under $350 for American non-aficionados listening west of the East Coast.

★ ★ ½

Sony ICF-SW33

Price: $219.95 in the United States. CAN$269.00 in Canada. £109.95 in the United Kingdom. Not available in Australia.

Advantages: Superior reception quality, with excellent adjacent-channel

The Sony ICF-SW33 performs well, but is not convenient to tune.

rejection (selectivity) and spurious-signal rejection. Weak-signal sensitivity a bit better than most. Easy to operate for advanced-technology radio. Unusual clock gives World Time and local time with local city name displayed. Illuminated display. Audio, although lacking in bass, unusually intelligible. Alarm/sleep features. Travel power lock. FM stereo through headphones (not supplied). Battery-life indicator. Receives Japanese FM band.

Disadvantages: No keypad or tuning knob. Synthesizer chugging and pokey slewing degrade bandscanning. Few (seven) world band station presets. Does not cover two minor world band segments (2 and 3 MHz), the new 19 MHz segment and a scattering of other world band channels. Clock not displayed independent of frequency. Fragile 12/24-hour selector. Clock displays London time and World Time as one and the same, which is true for only part of the year. Radio suddenly goes dead when batteries get weak. No longwave. AC adaptor, much-needed, is extra.

Bottom Line: Attention to detail, but lacking in tuning convenience.

★ ★ ½   ¢

Sony ICF-SW30

Price: $139.95 in the United States. CAN$189.00 in Canada. £89.95 in the United Kingdom. AUS$299.00 in Australia.

Advantages: Excellent value. Superior reception quality, with excellent adjacent-channel rejection (selectivity) and spurious-signal rejection. Weak-signal sensitivity a bit better than most. Easy to operate for advanced-technology radio. World Time and local time clock. Audio, although lacking in bass, unusually intelligible. Alarm/sleep features.

Sony's ICF-SW30 is an excellent value, but inconvenient to tune.

Travel power lock. FM stereo through headphones (not supplied). Battery-life indicator. Receives Japanese FM band.

Disadvantages: No keypad or tuning knob. Synthesizer chugging and pokey slewing degrade bandscanning. Few (seven) world band station presets. Does not cover two minor world band segments (2 and 3 MHz), the new 19 MHz segment and a scattering of other world band channels. Clock not displayed independent of frequency. Radio suddenly goes dead when batteries get weak. No longwave. AC adaptor, much-needed, is extra.

Bottom Line: Among the best-performing radios in the "value" category, and simple to operate, but tuning convenience is pedestrian. An excellent buy if you listen to only a limited number of stations.

★ ★ ½   ¢

Radio Shack/Realistic DX-375

Price: $99.99 in the United States. Not available in Australia.

Advantages: Excellent value. Several handy tuning features. Weak-signal sensitivity a bit above average. Relatively easy to use for digital portable in its price class. Stereo FM

Radio Shack's DX-375 is the best radio in the United States for under $100.

through headphones (not supplied). Travel power lock. Timer. 30-day money-back trial period (in United States).

Disadvantages: Mediocre spurious-signal ("image") rejection. Unusually long pause of silence when tuning from channel to channel. Antenna swivel sometimes needs tightening. AC adaptor plug easy to insert accidentally into headphone socket. Build quality, although adequate, appears to be slightly below average. Static discharges sometimes disable microprocessor (usually remediable if bat-

---

Best Buys if You Live 'Way Out Thar...

Most portables are designed to work well in Europe, where mighty signals can overwhelm radio innards. To get around this, engineers tone down signal sensitivity to make a radio "see" all stations as weaker than they really are.

That's nice for Europeans and residents of Istanbul, Turkey. But it's not very helpful for listeners in Sacramento, Ocho Rios, Honolulu, Thunder Bay, Brisbane or Johannesburg struggling to hear their favorite faraway programs—which are gasping for breath by the time they get there.

Here, then, are PASSPORT's choices for those who live where folks are hardy but signals are weak, listed in the order of their ability to flush out anemic signals. While this ability centers around sensitivity to weak signals, there are other factors, such as the ability to produce intelligible audio at low signal levels. Remember, with any radio, clipping a length of insulated wire or an inverted-L antenna to the telescopic antenna usually helps, especially with lap models. Using an AC adaptor instead of batteries sometimes improves weak-signal reception, too.

- Sony ICF-2010 or ICF-2001D
- Grundig Satellit 700

- Grundig Yacht Boy 305
- Sony ICF-SW77

Also...
- Sangean ATS-808, a/k/a:
  - Aiwa WR-D1000
  - Roberts R808
  - Siemens RK 661
- Sony ICF-SW55
- Sony ICF-SW33
- Sony ICF-SW30

- Sangean ATS-202
- Sangean ATS 800A, a/k/a:
  - Roberts R801
  - Siemens RP 647G4
- Sony ICF-SW7600G
- Grundig Yacht Boy 400

Not good enough? If mobility isn't critical, go for one of the better portatop or tabletop models with a worthy external antenna designed for non-portable receivers, such as those made under the "Eavesdropper" and "Alpha Delta" labels.

The Tesonic R-3000 is poorly made and doesn't cover the entire world band spectrum.

teries are removed for a time, then replaced). No World Time clock. AC adaptor extra. No longwave.

Bottom Line: No Volvo, but if you absolutely don't want to spend more than $100, this is still the way to go.

★ ★ ¢

Tesonic R-3000

Price: ¥620 (about US$71) in China.

Advantages: Least costly portable tested with digital frequency display, keypad and station presets (18 for world band, 18 for FM and mediumwave AM). Up/down slew tuning with "signal-seek" scanning. Slightly better adjacent-channel rejection (selectivity) than usual for price category. World Time and local clocks (see Disadvantages). Alarm/sleep timer. Illuminated display. FM stereo via optional headphones. Selectable 9/10 kHz mediumwave AM increments.

Disadvantages: Mediocre build quality, with one sample having poor sensitivity, another having skewed bandwidth filtering. Inferior dynamic range and spurious-signal rejection. Does not tune 5800-5815, 9300-9495, 11500-11575, 13570-13870, 15000-15095, 18900-19020 kHz and some other useful portions of the world band spectrum. No tuning knob. Tunes world band only in coarse 5 kHz steps. No longwave. No signal-strength indicator. No travel power lock (lock provided serves another function), but power switch not easy to turn on accidental-

ly. No AC adaptor. Clocks do not display independent of frequency. Static discharges occasionally disable microprocessor in high-static environments (usually remediable if batteries are removed for a time, then replaced).

Bottom Line: Made by the Disheng Electronic Cooperative, Ltd., in Guangzhou, China, this bargain-priced model has excellent features, with much-improved performance over in our last test in 1992. However, lacks complete frequency coverage and appears to have unusually high sample-to-sample variations in performance.

Improved for 1996

★ ★

Sangean ATS 800A (Roberts R801) (Siemens RP 647G4)

Price: *Sangean:* $149.00 in the United States. CAN$129.95 in Canada. Not available in Australia. *ADP-808 120 VAC adaptor:* $7.99 in the United States. CAN$14.95 in Canada. *Roberts:* £79.99 in the United Kingdom. *Siemens:* The equivalent of about US$90 in the European Union.

Advantages: Already-pleasant speaker audio improves with headphones.

Sangean's ATS 800A is sensitive to weak signals, but lacks tuning flexibility.

Five station preset buttons retrieve up to ten world band and ten AM/FM stations. Reasonable adjacent-channel rejection (selectivity) for price class. Weak-signal sensitivity a bit better than most. Simple to operate for radio at this technology level. World Time clock. Timer/sleep/alarm features. Travel power lock. Low-battery indicator. Stereo FM via earpieces (supplied in Sangean version).

Disadvantages: Mediocre spurious-signal ("image") rejection. Inferior dynamic range, a drawback for listeners in Europe, North Africa and the Near East. Does not tune such important world band ranges as 7305-7600, 9300-9495 and 21755-21850 kHz. Tunes world band only in coarse 5 kHz steps. No tuning knob; tunes only via multi-speed up/down slewing buttons. No longwave. Signal-strength indicator nigh useless. No display illumination. Clock not displayed separately from frequency. No carrying strap or handle. AC adaptor extra. *Sangean:* Supplied earpieces inferior to comparable foam-padded earphones. FM tuning steps do not conform to channel spacing in much of the world outside the Americas. *Sangean and Siemens:* Do not receive 1635-1705 kHz portion of expanded AM band in Americas.

Comment: Strong signals within the 7305-7595 kHz range can be tuned via the "image" signal 900 kHz down; e.g., 7435 kHz may be heard on 6535 kHz.

Bottom Line: Improved for 1996 by adding a 9/10 kHz channel switch for

---

PORTABLES: WHO'S UP AND WHO'S DOWN

It's been four years since we've taken a look at how the various manufacturers of world band portables are coming along. This year's strokes and pokes...

▲ **GRUNDIG.** For years, manufacturers all but hid their shortwave radios, making them nearly impossible to find. Then they wondered why the market never went anywhere. Grundig's North American operation promoted far and wide—"Look what these little boxes can do!"—then made them available in a myriad of retail and catalog outlets. Now, where they used to sell thousands of radios each year, they now sell hundreds of thousands. Equally important, the quality of their products has improved enormously, giving even mighty Sony a run for its money. *Footnote:* Industry scuttlebutt has it that with Grundig's spectacular success in North America, they're girding their loins to make world band a hot item worldwide.

▲ **SONY.** If not still world band's One and Only, Sony remains the technology leader, with its first-rate synchronous selectable sideband and innovative, if not always successful, attempts to improve upon tuning techniques. The only thing holding Sony back is its sheer mass, which results in world band being given less marketing TLC than at more specialized firms, such as Grundig (which, interestingly, is owned and managed by the giant Philips organization, whose own shortwave operation is a mess).

◆ **RADIO SHACK.** They've never quite understood the dynamics of world band the way Grundig does, but with so many retail outlets they probably don't have to. In North America, they're everywhere, bringing the pleasures of world band to thousands of shopping centers throughout America. And their lineup of models is expanding even further for 1996.

mediumwave AM, but still not competitive within its price class.

★ ★

Bolong HS-490

Price: ¥360 (about US$41) in China.

Advantages: Inexpensive for a model with digital frequency display, ten world band station presets, and ten station presets for mediumwave AM and FM. World Time clock (see Disadvantages). Tape-reel-type outboard passive antenna accessory comes standard. AC adaptor comes standard. Illuminated display. Alarm/sleep timer. FM stereo (see Disadvantages) via earbuds, which come standard.

The Bolong HS-490 is the most popular digital world band radio within China. It's also sold in other parts of the world.

Disadvantages: Requires patience to get a station, as it tunes world band only via 10 station presets and multi-speed up/down slewing/scanning.

Continued

● **CHINESE INDEPENDENT MANUFACTURERS.** The hoped-for move from junkers into higher-quality models hasn't really happened, but production quality is sporadically improving, and some digital models are passable performers.

➤ **SANGEAN.** John Tusa, former head of the BBC World Service, used to say that when you've become an institution, you're already on your way downhill. Still the world's largest manufacturer of world band radios, mainly for other firms, Sangean has been living off its laurels for some time. Bean counters and production types now rule the roost, with neither R&D nor marketing being given more than the most cursory of nods. Nevertheless, their products continue to be superior contenders in the OEM marketplace and, with the long-promised ATS 909 nominally on the horizon, they may yet spring back to life.

➤ **PANASONIC.** Still making at least two nice models, this high-quality producer no longer has a clue as to what the world band market is about. Not quite gone, but almost forgotten.

➤ **PHILIPS.** Yes, Philips world band radios are still out there, but this gargantuan company has slipped from being one of the premier manufacturers (e.g., the former D2999 and D2935 models) to a virtual non-player, seemingly because there is little or no product management for world band. Ironically, their Grundig subsidiary (see above) is a case study in heads-up niche management, leading industry watchers to wonder whether Philips will eventually turn over all its world band production and sales to Grundig.

Tunes world band only in coarse 5 kHz steps. Even-numbered frequencies displayed with final zero omitted; e.g., 5.75 rather than conventional 5.750 or 5750. Poor spurious-signal ("image") rejection. So-so adjacent-channel rejection (selectivity). World Time clock not displayed independent of frequency. Does not receive relatively unimportant 6200-7100 kHz portion of world band spectrum. Does not receive 1615-1705 kHz portion of expanded AM band in the Americas. No signal-strength indicator. No travel power lock. Mediumwave AM tuning increments not switchable, which may make for inexact tuning in some parts of the world other than where the radio was purchased. FM selectivity and capture ratio mediocre. FM stereo did not trigger on our unit.

Bottom Line: Made by a joint venture between Xin Hui Electronics and Shanghai Huaxin Electronic Instruments. No prize, but as good you'll find among the truly cheap, which probably accounts for its being the #1 seller among digital world band radios in China.

★ ★

Lowe SRX-50 (Amsonic AS-908) (Galaxis G 1380/4) (Morphy Richards R191) (Yorx AS-908)

Price: *Lowe:* £39.95 in the United Kingdom. *Galaxis:* About the equivalent of US$33 in the European Union. *Morphy Richards:* £37.00 in the United Kingdom. *Yorx:* CAN$56 in Canada.

Advantages: Inexpensive for a model with digital frequency display, five world band station presets (ten on the Yorx), plus ten station presets for mediumwave AM and FM. Relatively simple to operate for technology

class. Illuminated display. Alarm/sleep timer. FM stereo via headphones. *Except Yorx:* World Time clock. Longwave. *Yorx:* Ten, rather than five, world band station presets. AC adaptor and stereo earpieces come standard. *Galaxis and Lowe:* Headphones come standard.

Disadvantages: Substandard build quality. No tuning knob; tunes only via station presets and multi-speed up/down slewing/scanning. Tunes world band only in coarse 5 kHz steps. Even-numbered frequencies displayed with final zero omitted; e.g., 5.75 rather than conventional 5.750 or 5750. Poor spurious-signal ("image") rejection. Mediocre selectivity. Does not receive 1605-1705 kHz portion of expanded AM band in the Americas. No signal-strength indicator. No travel power lock. Clock not displayed independent of frequency display. Mediumwave AM tuning increments not switchable, which may make for inexact tuning in some parts of the world other than where the radio was purchased. Power switch has no position labeled "off," although "auto radio" power-switch position performs a comparable role. *Except Yorx:* Does not tune important 5800-5895, 17500-

Most low-cost portables under "Western" labels are actually made in China. This, the Lowe SRX-50, is no exception.

17900 and 21750-21850 kHz segments; 15505-15695 kHz tunable only to limited extent. No AC adaptor. *Yorx:* Does not receive 7300-9499 and 21750-21850 kHz portions of the world band spectrum. Clock in 12-hour format.

Comment: Strong signals within the 15505-15800 kHz range can be tuned via the "image" signal 900 kHz down; e.g., 15685 kHz may be heard on 14785 kHz.

Bottom Line: Outclassed by newer value models.

★ ★

Elektro AC 101

Price: $49.95 plus $4 shipping by mail order in the United States. About the equivalent of US$50 in China.

Advantages: One of the least costly portables tested with digital frequency display and presets (ten for world band, ten for AM/FM) and "signal-seek" scan tuning. Slightly more selective than usual for price category. Relatively simple to operate for technology class. World Time clock. Alarm/sleep timer. Illuminated display. FM stereo via optional headphones.

Disadvantages: Mediocre build quality. Relatively lacking in weak-signal sensitivity. No tuning knob; tunes only via presets and multi-speed up/down

Whatever name the Elektro AC 101 appears under, it isn't worth buying.

slewing. Tunes world band only in coarse 5 kHz steps. Mediumwave AM tuning steps do not conform to channel spacing in much of the world outside the Americas. Frequency display in confusing XX.XX/XX.XX5 MHz format. Poor spurious-signal ("image") rejection. Mediocre dynamic range. Does not tune relatively unimportant 6200-7100 and 25600-26100 kHz world band segments. Does not receive longwave band or 1615-1705 kHz portion of expanded AM band in the Americas. No signal-strength indicator. No travel power lock switch. No AC power supply. Antenna swivels, but does not rotate; swivel breaks relatively easily. Limited dealer network.

Bottom Line: Audi cockpit, moped engine. This radio was formerly also available as the DAK MR-101s.

★ ★

Rodelsonic Digital World Band Rodelvox Digital World Band (Amsonic AS-138) (Dick Smith Digitor A-4336) (Scotcade 65B 119 UCY Digital World Band) (Shimasu PLL Digital) (World Wide 4 Band Digital Receiver)

Price: *Rodelvox and Rodelsonic:* $99.95 plus $6.95 shipping in United States. *Amsonic:* ¥265 (about US$31) in China. *Dick Smith Digitor:* AUS$79.95. *Scotcade:* £29.99 plus shipping in the United Kingdom.

Advantages: Relatively inexpensive for a model with digital frequency display and 20 station presets (ten for world band, ten for mediumwave AM and FM). Relatively simple to operate for technology class. Alarm/sleep timer with World Time clock. Illuminated display. FM stereo via optional headphones.

Disadvantages: Poor build quality.

Widely sold, but no bargain, is the Rodelsonic.

Modest weak-signal sensitivity. No tuning knob; tuned only by station presets and multi-speed up/down slewing/scanning. Tunes world band only in coarse 5 kHz steps. Even-numbered frequencies displayed with final zero omitted; e.g., 5.75 rather than conventional 5.750. Poor spurious-signal ("image") rejection. Mediocre dynamic range. Does not receive 1635-1705 kHz portion of expanded AM band in the Americas. No signal-strength indicator. Clock in 12-hour format, not displayed independent of frequency display. No travel power lock. No AC adaptor. Quality of construction appears to be below average. Mediumwave AM tuning increments not switchable, which may make for inexact tuning in some parts of the world other than where the radio was purchased. *Except Scotcade:* Does not tune important 7305-9495 and 21755-21850 kHz segments. No longwave.

Note: The Amsonic is available in at least five versions: AS-138 for China, AS-138-0 for Europe, AS-138-3 for USA/Canada, AS-138-4 for Japan, and AS-138-6 for other countries and Europe. Each version has FM and mediumwave AM ranges and channel spacing appropriate to the market region, plus the Japanese version

replaces coverage of the 21 MHz band with TV audio.

Comment: Strong signals within the 7305-7595 kHz range can be tuned via the "image" signal 900 kHz down; e.g., 7435 kHz may be heard on 6535 kHz.

Bottom Line: Poorly made, and no bargain.

★ ★

Jäger PL-440 (Omega)

Price: *Jäger:* $79.95 plus $6.00 shipping in the United States. *Omega:* 1,500 francs in Belgium.

Advantages: Not costly for a model with digital frequency display. Tuning aids include up/down slewing buttons with "signal-seek" scanning, and 20 station presets (five each for world band, FM, longwave and mediumwave AM). Relatively simple to operate for technology class. World Time clock. Sleep/timer features. Longwave. Antenna rotates and tilts, unusual in price class. Travel power lock.

Disadvantages: Mediocre build quality. Limited coverage of world band spectrum omits important 5800-5945, 15605-15695, 17500-17900 and 21450-21850 kHz ranges, among others. No

The Jäger PL-440 may have a German name, but it's strictly Chinese.

tuning knob; tunes only via station presets and multi-speed up/down slewing/scanning. Tunes world band only in coarse 5 kHz steps. Tortoise-slow band-to-band tuning, remediable by using station presets as band selectors. Slow one-channel-at-a-time slewing is the only means for band-scanning between world band segments. Slightly insensitive to weak signals. Poor adjacent-channel rejection (selectivity). Even-numbered frequencies displayed with final zero omitted; e.g., 5.75 rather than conventional 5.750 or 5750. No signal-strength indicator. Clock not displayed independent of frequency display. Display not illuminated. Not offered with AC adaptor. Does not receive 1605-1705 kHz portion of expanded AM band in the Americas. Lacks selector for 9/10 kHz mediumwave AM steps.

Bottom Line: An Omega not to watch out for.

Revised for 1996

★ ¹/₂

Aroma SEG SED-ECL88C

Price: ¥328 (about US$40) in China.

Advantages: Cheap for a portable with digital frequency display and station presets (five for world band, ten for AM/FM). Slightly more selective and sensitive to weak signals than usual for price category. Relatively simple to operate for technology class. World Time clock. Alarm/sleep timer. Illuminated display. FM stereo via optional headphones.

Disadvantages: Does not tune the most important world band segment, 5730-6250 kHz. Mediocre build quality. No tuning knob; tunes only via station presets and multi-speed up/down slewing. Tunes world band only in coarse 5 kHz steps. Even-numbered frequencies displayed with final zero

omitted; e.g., 7.15 rather than conventional 7.150. Poor spurious-signal ("image") rejection. Mediocre dynamic range. Does not tune relatively unimportant 25600-26100 kHz world band segment. Does not receive longwave or 1603-1705 kHz portion of expanded mediumwave AM band in the Americas. No signal-strength indicator. No travel power lock switch. No AC adaptor. Antenna tilts, but does not rotate; swivel prone to break. Mediumwave AM tuning steps do not conform to channel spacing within the Americas.

Bottom Line: For evening listening, this Aroma smells like something you scraped off the bottom of your shoe. Okay for daytime listening.

Evaluation of Revised Model: Several steps backwards, two steps forward. The earlier version, without the "C" suffix, at least tuned 5730-6250 kHz—the most important band evenings during sunspot minimum—and had ten world band presets, instead of five. Too, it was cheaper, and came with an AC converter and stereo earphones. However, the new version doesn't have to be bandswitched when going from the upper to the lower parts of the world band spectrum, and it's better at picking up weak signals.

★ ¹/₂ **Giros R918, (Digitor Portable A-4336) and Casio PR100.**

LAP PORTABLES

Good for Home, Fair for Travel

If you're looking for a home set, yet one that also can be taken out in the backyard and on the occasional trip, a lap portable is probably your best bet. These are large enough to perform well and can sound pretty good, yet are compact enough to tote in your suitcase now and then. Most take 3-4 "D" (UM-1) cells, plus a couple of "AA" (UM-3) cells for their fancy computer circuits.

How large? Typically just under a foot wide—that's 30 cm—and weighing in around 3-4 pounds, or 1.3-1.8 kg. For air travel, that's okay if you are a dedicated listener, but a bit much otherwise. Too, larger sets with snazzy controls occasionally attract unwanted attention from suspicious customs and airport-security personnel in some parts of the world.

Two stand out for most listeners: the high-tech Sony ICF-2010, also sold as the ICF-2001D; and Grundig's sleek Satellit 700. The mid-priced Sony is the obvious choice for radio enthusiasts, whereas the Grundig should appeal to the larger body of regular listeners to world band, FM and mediumwave AM stations.

The revised Sony ICF-SW77, like opera, is not for everybody. With this high-tech wonder, it's either love or hate—little between.

★ ★ ★ ½   *Passport's Choice*

Sony ICF-2010
Sony ICF-2001D
(Sony ICF-2001DS)

Price: *ICF-2010:* $449.95 in the United States. CAN$519.00 in Canada. *ICF-2001D:* £269.00 in the United Kingdom. The equivalent of about US$500-950 elsewhere in the European Union. No longer available in Australia. *ICF-2001DS:* £279.95 in the United Kingdom.

Advantages: High-tech synchronous detection with selectable sideband; it performs very well, reducing adjacent-channel interference and fading distortion on world band, longwave and mediumwave AM signals. Use of 32 separate station preset buttons in

rows and columns is ergonomically the best to be found on any model, portable or tabletop, at any price; simply pushing one button one time brings in your station, a major convenience. Numerous other helpful tuning features. Two bandwidths offer superior tradeoff between audio fidelity and adjacent-channel rejection (selectivity). Weak-signal sensitivity better than most. Tunes and displays in precise 0.1 kHz increments. Separately displayed World Time clock. Alarm/sleep features, with four-event timer. Illuminated LCD. Travel power lock. Signal-strength indicator. Covers longwave and the Japanese FM band. Some reception of air band signals (most versions). Comes with AC adaptor. In the European Union, sometimes still available for £319.95 in a special "ICF-2001DS" or "kit" version supplied with Sony AN-1 amplified antenna; elsewhere, that antenna may be purchased separately for around $90. *ICF-2001DS:* Reportedly comes standard with Sony AN-1 outboard active antenna.

Disadvantages: Audio quality only average, with mediocre tone control. Controls and high-tech features,

The Babe Ruth and reigning champion of world band portables for aficionados: Sony's ICF-2010, also sold as the Sony ICF-2001D.

although exceptionally handy once you get the hang of them, initially may intimidate or confuse. Station presets and clock/timer features immediately erase whenever computer batteries are replaced, and also sometimes erase when set is jostled. Wide bandwidth quite broad for world band reception. First RF transistor (Q-303) reportedly prone to damage by static electricity, as from nearby lightning strikes, when used with external wire antenna (such antennas should be disconnected with the approach of snow, sand, dry-wind or thunder storms); or when amplified (active) antennas other than Sony AN-1 are used. "Signal-seek" scanning works poorly. Telescopic antenna swivel gets slack with use, requiring periodic adjustment of tension screw. Synchronous detector does not switch off during tuning. Lacks up/down slewing. Keypad not in telephone format. LCD clearly readable only when radio viewed from below. Chugs slightly when tuned. Non-synchronous single-sideband reception can be mistuned by up to 50 Hz. Uninspiring urban FM performance.

Bottom Line: Our panelists, like opinionated Supreme Court justices, usually issue split decisions. But not with this model, which since its introduction has always been, and very much still is, our unanimous favorite among portables. Incredibly, after all these years, this radio is still the Big Enchilada for radiophiles, and fairly priced for all it does so well. Except for pedestrian audio quality and urban FM, plus the learning curve, Sony's high-tech offering remains, for many, the best performing travel-weight portable—regardless of where you live. Its use of separate pushbuttons for each station preset makes station call-up easier than with virtually any other radio tested. Its syn-

chronous detection, which works as it should, not only reduces distortion but also, as one reader puts it, offers the adjacent-channel rejection (selectivity) of a narrow filter with the fidelity of a wide filter.

 An *RDI WHITE PAPER* is available for this model.

Grundig Satellit 700

Price: $499.95-699.95 in the United States. CAN$649.95 in Canada. £369.95 in the United Kingdom. AUS$1,199.00 in Australia.

Advantages: Superior audio quality, aided by separate continuous bass and treble controls. High-tech synchronous detector circuit with selectable sideband reduces adjacent-channel interference and fading distortion on world band, longwave and mediumwave AM signals (see Disadvantages); it also provides superior reception of reduced-carrier single-sideband signals. Two bandwidths offer superior tradeoff between audio fidelity and adjacent-channel rejection (selectivity). Weak-signal sensitivity better than most; to aid in hearing

Grundig's Satellit 700 appeals to exacting listeners who want first-rate audio quality.

weak-signals, if an external antenna is connected to the radio's antenna socket, leave the antenna switch set to "INT," switching over to the "EXT" position only if and when you encounter overloading. 512 station presets standard; up to 2048 station presets optionally available. Schedules for 22 stations stored by factory in memory. Stored station names appear on LCD. Numerous other helpful tuning features. Tunes and displays in precise 0.1 kHz increments in synchronous and single-sideband modes; this, along with a fine-tuning clarifier, produce the best tuning configuration for single sideband in a conventional travel-weight portable. Separately displayed World Time clock. Alarm/sleep features with superior timer that, in principle, can also control a recorder. Superior FM reception. Stereo FM through headphones. Illuminated LCD, which is clearly visible from a variety of angles. Travel power lock. Heavy-duty telescopic antenna. Screw mounts for mobile or maritime operation. Runs off AC power worldwide. Comes with built-in NiCd battery charger. RDS circuitry for European FM station selection—eventually North America, too—by program format. Excellent operator's manuals.

Disadvantages: Chugs when tuned slowly by knob; worse, mutes completely when tuned quickly, making bandscanning unnecessarily difficult. Using station presets relatively complex. Synchronous detection circuit produces minor background rumble and has relatively little sideband separation. Some overall distortion except in AM mode. Wide bandwidth a touch broad for most world band reception. Keypad lacks feel and is not in telephone format. Antenna keels over in certain settings. Location of tuning controls and volume control on separate sides of case tend to

make listening a two-handed affair.

Bottom Line: The favorite model of a broad swathe of regular world band program listeners. Withal, notably for bandscanning, not all it should be. Every time Grundig issues a new Satellit model, it is noticeably better than whatever came earlier, so all eyes are on the forthcoming Satellit 900 (see Coming Up).

★ ★ ★ ½

Sony ICF-SW77
Sony ICF-SW77E

Price: $649.95 in the United States. CAN$699.00 in Canada. £349.95 in the United Kingdom. AUS$1,195.00 in Australia.

Advantages: A rich variety of tuning features, including numerous innovative techniques not found in other world band radios. Synchronous detection, which performs as it should and is exceptionally handy to operate, reduces fading distortion and adjacent-channel interference on world band, longwave and mediumwave AM signals; it also provides superior reception of reduced-carrier single-sideband signals. Two well-chosen bandwidths provide superior adjacent-channel rejection. Weak-signal sensitivity a bit better than most. Tunes in very precise 50 Hz increments; displays in precise 100 Hz

If you like computers, you may wish to consider the sophisticated-to-operate Sony ICF-SW77.

increments. Two illuminated multi-function liquid crystal displays. Preset world band segments. Keypad tuning. Tuning "knob" with two speeds. 162 station presets, including 96 frequencies stored by country or station name. "Signal-seek" scanning. Separately displayed World Time and local time clocks. Station name appears on LCD when station presets used. Signal-strength indicator. Flip-up chart for calculating time differences. VCR-type five-event timer controls radio and recorder alike. Continuous bass and treble tone controls. Superior FM audio quality. Stereo FM through headphones. Receives longwave and Japanese FM. Comes with AC adaptor.

Disadvantages: Excruciatingly complex for many, but not all, to operate. Synthesizer chugging, as bad as we've encountered in our tests, degrades the quality of tuning by knob. Dynamic range only fair. Station presets can't be accessed simply, as they can on most models. Flimsy telescopic antenna. Display illumination does not stay on with AC power. On mediumwave AM band, relatively insensitive, sometimes with spurious sounds during single-side-band reception; this doesn't apply to world band reception, however. Mundane reception of difficult FM signals. Signal-strength indicator over-reads. Reportedly difficult-to-impossible to obtain in many countries where Sony otherwise is well-represented.

Who's On Second? The current, second, version of the Sony ICF-SW77 is definitely the better, and by now is virtually the only one being sold new by dealers—even though old versions are on rare occasion still sold as demos. You can identify the current version by its telescopic antenna, *which has 11 segments*, rather than

the nine found on the original version. Other differences, including those cited here last year and yet others still being offered up by some well-meaning Sony officials, may or may not apply, depending upon what part of the world you live in and other circumstances, so ignore them. However, no rule is immutable. One extremely reputable Midwestern U.S. dealer tells us of how the antenna broke on their new-version showroom demo. They ordered a replacement antenna from Sony Parts, and—you guessed it—it had nine segments. Now, at least we know what Sony did with all those leftover nine-segment antennas!

Bottom Line: The Sony ICF-SW77, a superior performer since it was improved a few years back, uses innovative high technology in an attempt to make listening easier. Results, however, are a mixed bag: What is gained in convenience in some areas is lost in others. The upshot is that whether using the '77 is enjoyable or a hair-pulling exercise comes down to personal taste. In our survey some relish it, most don't.

★ ★ ½

Sangean ATS-818
Radio Shack/Realistic DX-390
Roberts R817

Price: *Sangean:* $299.00 in the United States. CAN$329.95 in Canada. £169.95 in the United Kingdom. AUS$349.00 in Australia. *Radio Shack/Realistic:* $219.99 (as low as $169.99 during special sales) plus #273-1655 AC adaptor at Radio Shack stores in the United States. CAN$299.95 plus #273-1454 AC adaptor in Canada. No longer available in Australia. *Roberts:* £169.95 in the United Kingdom.

Advantages: Superior overall world band performance. Numerous tuning

Sangean's latest and costliest, also sold by Radio Shack, performs poorly for bandscanning.

features, including 18 world band station presets. Two bandwidths for good fidelity/interference tradeoff. Superior spurious-signal ("image") rejection. Illuminated display. Signal-strength indicator. Two 24-hour clocks, one for World Time, with either displayed separately from frequency. Alarm/sleep/timer. Travel power lock. FM stereo through headphones. Longwave. Sangean version supplied with AC adaptor. *Radio Shack/Realistic:* 30-day money-back trial period (in United States).

Disadvantages: Mutes when tuning knob turned quickly, making band-scanning difficult *see Note, below).* Wide bandwidth a bit broad for world band reception. Keypad not in tele-phone format. For single-sideband reception, relies on a touchy variable control instead of separate LSB/USB switch positions. Does not come with tape-recorder jack. Front-end circuitry reportedly unusually susceptible to being damaged by static charges, especially from an external antenna. *Radio Shack/Realistic:* AC adaptor, which some readers complain causes hum and buzz, is extra.

Note: Tuning-knob muting reportedly can be eliminated, albeit with some side effects, by disabling or removing diode D29, according to reader Steven Johnson. We can't vouch for this or any other homebrew modification, but if you are comfortable working with electronic circuitry and wish to take the plunge, you can get further infor-mation by writing him at P.O. Box 80042, Fort Wayne IN 46898 USA. He tells us he will be glad to reply, but please enclose a self-addressed stamped envelope, or outside the United States a self-addressed enve-lope with 3 IRCs or $1, to cover return postage.

Bottom Line: A decent, predictable radio—performance and features, alike—but mediocre for bandscan-ning.

The PASSPORT *portable-radio review team includes regulars Lawrence Magne, Jock Elliott and Tony Jones, with laboratory measurements performed independently by Sherwood Engineering. Additional research this year by Lars Rydén (China), Harlan Seyfer (China) and Craig Tyson (Australia), with a tip of the hat to Paul Donegan and Hugh Waters (Singapore).*

Analog Portables

With digitally tuned portables now commonplace and affordable, there's little reason to purchase an analog, or slide-rule-tuned, model. They lack every tuning aid except a knob, and their coarse indicators make it almost impossible to tell the frequency.

Yet, for the money—nearly all sell for under the equivalent of US$100 or £70—these models sometimes have better weak-signal sensitivity than some of their digital counterparts. However, if you're located where signals are weak, such as western North America, and watching your budget, you'll be far better off with the new digitally tuned Grundig Yacht Boy 305, which costs precious little more.

Listed in order of overall performance.

POCKET ANALOG PORTABLES

★ ★ **Sony ICF-SW22.** Tiny, with superior spurious signal ("image") rejection, but tinny sound and limited frequency coverage.

★ ½ **Grundig Yacht Boy 207, Grundig Yacht Boy 217, Sangean MS-103, Sangean MS-103L, Sangean MS-101, Aiwa WR-A100, Radio Shack/Realistic DX-351, Roberts R101, Sangean SG-789A** and **Sangean SG-789L.**

COMPACT ANALOG PORTABLES

★ ½ **Sangean SG-700L, Radio Shack/Realistic DX-350, Panasonic RF-B20L, Panasonic RF-B20, National B20, Grundig Yacht Boy 230, Amsonic AS-912, Panopus Yacht Boy 230, Sangean SG 621, Sangean SG 631, Siemens RK 710, Sony ICF-SW10, Roberts R621, Elektro AC 100, International AC 100, SoundTronic Multiband Receiver, Pomtrex 120-00300, TEC 235TR, MCE-7760, Pace, SEG Precision World SED 110, Kchibo KK-210B** and **Kchibo KK-168.**

★ **Windsor 2138, Apex 2138, Garrard Shortwave Radio 217, Silver International MT-798, Panashiba FX-928, Shiba Electronics FX-928, Cougar H-88, Cougar RC210, Precision World SED 901, Opal OP-35, Grundig Traveller II** and **Siemens RK 702.**

FULL-SIZED ANALOG PORTABLES

★ **Venturer Multiband, Alconic Series 2959, Dick Smith D-2832, Rhapsody Multiband, Shimasu Multiband, Steepletone MBR-7, Steepletone MBR-8, Radio Shack/Realistic SW-100, Electro Brand SW-2000** and **Electro Brand 2971.**

ANALOG OLDIES

★ ★ **Sony ICF-7601, Sony ICF-SW15, Sony ICF-SW20, Sony ICF-4920, Sony ICF-4900II** and **Sony ICF-5100.**

★ ½ **Magnavox OD1875BK, Philips OD1875BK, Magnavox D1835, Philips D1835, Magnavox AE 3205 GY** and **Philips AE 3205 GY** and **Radio Shack/Realistic DX-342.**

★ **Panasonic RF-B10, National B10** and **Grundig Explorer II.**

Portatop Receivers for 1996

Most of us buy only one world band radio. It has to function not in just a single room, but all over the house—perhaps outdoors, too. That's why portables sell so well.

But this results in some disturbing compromises: Portables, even the very best, usually don't sound as good as some tabletop supersets. Nor can they cut the mustard with really tough signals. The solution: Combine the most desirable characteristics of portables and tabletops into one single receiver.

Two Models

In England, Lowe Electronics offers the HF-150, which stands out from other portatops and most tabletop models because of its top-notch "listenability." Yet, it is somewhat awkward as a portable, and usually requires a separate outboard preselector if used near mediumwave AM or longwave transmitters—a major drawback for listeners in many urban and suburban areas.

The American firm of R.L. Drake now offers a slightly improved version of its own portatop, the SW8, which has FM, but no longwave. Although larger than the HF-150, it is more practical as a portable, and performs much better in the vicinity of mediumwave AM transmitters. Yet, it lacks the quality synchronous selectable sideband and exceptional audio quality found on the '150. Both Drake and Lowe have excellent reputations for service.

Of course, a good portatop model still works best when connected to a worthy external antenna. While

Lowe new offers the new HF-250, in addition to its other models.

115

this is not practical on the fly, a first-rate antenna of this sort should be seriously considered for when the receiver is used in a fixed location.

What Passport's Rating Symbols Mean

Star ratings: ★ ★ ★ ★ ★ is best. We award stars solely for overall performance and meaningful features; price, appearance and the like are not taken into account. To facilitate comparison, the same rating system that is used for portatop models is also used for portable and tabletop models, reviewed elsewhere in this Passport. Whether a radio is portable, a portatop or a tabletop model, a given rating—three stars, say—means largely the same thing. With portatop models, there is roughly equal emphasis on the ability to flush out tough, hard-to-hear signals, and program-listening quality with stronger broadcasts.

Passport's Choice portatop models are our test team's personal picks of the litter—what we would buy for ourselves.

¢: denotes a price-for-performance value.

holds lock well, also allows for either selectable-sideband or double-sideband reception. Synchronous detector switches out automatically during tuning, which aids in bandscanning. Exceptionally rugged cast-aluminum housing of a class normally associated with professional-grade equipment. Mouse keypad, virtually foolproof and a *de rigeur* option, performs superbly for tuning and presets. 60 presets store frequency and mode. Tunes, but does not display, in exacting 8 Hz increments, the most precise found in any model with portable characteristics. Single-sideband reception well above the portable norm. Small footprint saves space and adds to portability. Optional accessory kit, necessary for real portability, provides telescopic antenna, rechargeable nickel-cadmium batteries (four hours per charge) and shoulder strap with built-in antenna. High weak-signal sensitivity with accessory antenna helps make for exceptional portable performance and obviates the need for a large out-

★ ★ ★ ★　　*Passport's Choice*

Lowe HF-150

Price: $699.95 in the United States. CAN$979.00 in Canada. £419.95 in the United Kingdom (add £20.00 for HF-150M marine version, not tested). AUS$995.00 in Australia.

Advantages: Top-notch world band and mediumwave AM audio quality—a treat for the ears—provided a good external speaker or simple headphones are used. High-tech synchronous detection reduces fading distortion on world band, longwave and mediumwave AM signals. Synchronous detection circuit, which

If you don't live near any mediumwave AM stations, the Lowe HF-150 is hard to beat for worthy performance, straightforward operation and outstanding audio.

door antenna. Excellent operating manual. Available with IF-150 optional computer interface.

Disadvantages: Grossly inferior front-end selectivity can result in creation of spurious signals if the radio is connected to a significant external antenna or used near mediumwave AM transmitters. (Lowe's excellent optional PR-150 preselector eliminates this disadvantage, albeit at a hefty cost in treasure, bulk and simplicity of operation.) Requires AK-150 option to be a true portatop. Lacks FM broadcast reception, normally found on portables. Built-in speaker produces only okay audio quality as compared to simple earphones or a good external speaker. No tone control. Frequency displays no finer than 1 kHz resolution. Lacks lock indicator or similar aid (e.g., finer frequency-display resolution) for proper use of synchronous detector, which can result in less-than-optimum detector performance. Bereft of certain features—among them notch filter, adjustable noise blanker and passband tuning—found on premium-priced tabletop models. Lacks signal-strength indicator. Operation of some front-panel button functions tends to be confusing until you get the hang of it. Light weight allows radio to slide on table during operation more than do heavier models. Lacks much-needed elevation feet. Erratic contact on outboard-speaker socket. Display not illuminated. AC power supply via a separate outboard adaptor, rather than inboard. *Portable operation:* Telescopic antenna tilts properly, but is clumsy to rotate. Comes with no convenient way to attach keypad to cabinet (remediable by affixing sticky-backed Velcro). This—plus the use of an outboard AC adaptor, the need for an outboard speaker or headphones for proper fidelity, and no

dial illumination—all conspire to make this model less handy to tote around than a conventional portable.

Bottom Line: Not inexpensive with plenty of options added, but the "sound choice" when used with a worthy external speaker. (Yes, Lowe sells one, but some others also work quite well.) This tough little radio provides superb fidelity on world band, longwave and mediumwave AM—*if* you don't live near any longwave or mediumwave AM transmitters. If audio quality is your primary concern, with portable use being secondary, this is the portatop model to get—indeed, for audiophiles this is arguably the *tabletop* model to get! But beware the possible need at your location for an outboard preselector.

An *RDI WHITE PAPER* is available for this model.

Improved for 1996

★ ★ ★ ★   *Passport's Choice*

Drake SW8

Price: $699.00 in the United States.

Drake has improved its SW8 for 1996, but also raised the price.

CAN$999.95 in Canada. £649.00 in the United Kingdom. AUS$1,599.00 in Australia.

Advantages: Unusually low price for level of performance and features offered; virtually everything you need, except possibly an additional antenna, comes standard with the radio at that price. Portatop design combines virtual tabletop performance with much of the convenience of a portable. Above-average audio quality with internal speaker or headphones. Three bandwidths provide worthy adjacent-channel rejection. Continuous tone control. High-tech synchronous detection reduces fading distortion on world band, longwave and mediumwave AM signals (*see* Disadvantages). Numerous helpful tuning aids, including 70 presets. Helpful (digital) signal-strength indicator. Single-sideband reception well above the portable norm. Weak-signal sensitivity excellent with external antenna. Superior blocking performance aids usable sensitivity. Two timers and 24-hour clocks (*see* Disadvantages). Display illuminated. FM, in mono through speaker, but stereo through headphones, performs well. Covers VHF aeronautical band.

Disadvantages: Synchronous detector lacks selectable sideband and has limited ability to stay locked on frequency. Bereft of certain features—among them notch filter, adjustable noise blanker and passband tuning—found on premium-priced tabletop models. Ergonomics mediocre, including pushbuttons that rock on their centers. Key depressions must each be done within three seconds, lest receiver wind up being mistuned or placed into an unwanted operating mode. Wide bandwidth, nominally 6 kHz, actually 7.8 kHz—wider than it should be for best results. Drake's 120 VAC power supply, via a separate out-board adaptor, emits some hum through headphones. Telescopic antenna doesn't swivel fully for best FM reception. Clocks don't display when frequency is shown. Carrying/elevation handle clunky to adjust, with adjustment stops that can break if handle forced. Optional MS8 outboard speaker not equal to receiver's fidelity potential.

Bottom Line: A clearly superior all-around receiver for use both indoors and out, and a good value. For 1996, Drake has noticeably improved the SW8's sensitivity to weak signals when the telescopic antenna is in use, making it an even better choice. If portability and/or FM reception are important to you, this is the obvious pick of the portatops.

 An *RDI WHITE PAPER* is available for this model.

The PASSPORT *portatop review team includes Jock Elliott, along with Lawrence Magne, Tony Jones and Craig Tyson, with helpful observations by Marie Lamb. Laboratory measurements by Robert Sherwood.*

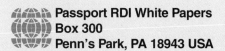

TABLETOP RECEIVERS FOR 1996

More Stations, Better Fidelity

*F*or most, a good portable is adequate to enjoy the offerings found on world band radio. Others, though, aspire to something better.

That "better" is a tabletop or portatop receiver. (Portatops are reported on elsewhere in this edition.) Most excel at flushing out the really tough game—faint stations, or those swamped by interference from competing signals. That's why they are prized by those serious radio aficionados known as "DXers," a term derived from telegraph code meaning "long distance."

International stations beam over great distances, and you can tell it with your ears.

So some models provide enhanced-fidelity reception, welcome relief from the aural gremlins of shortwave.

Helpful in American West and Australasia

Tabletop models, like portatops, can also be especially useful if you live in a part of the world—say, central and western North America or Australasia—where signals tend to be weak and choppy. This is a common problem when world band signals have to follow "high-latitude" paths, those close to or over the geomagnetic North Pole. To find out whether this phenomenon might affect your listening, place a string on a globe (an ordinary map won't do) between where you live and where various signals you like come from. If the string passes near or above latitude 60° N, beware.

Daytime Signals Come in Better

With the end of the Cold War and the worldwide decrease in funding for

Germany's Dieter Reibold, whose expertise in world band listening has earned him a place in the *Guinness Book of Records.* (D. Reibold)

matters related to foreign affairs, certain international stations have compressed their hours of transmission. Yet, at the same time, the proportion of broadcasts in English has actually *increased!* The result is that some excellent English-language programs can be heard now only during the daytime hours.

Thing is, daytime signals tend to be weaker, especially when they're not beamed to your part of the world. However, thanks to the scattering properties of shortwave, you can still eavesdrop on many of these choice "off-beam" signals. But it's harder, so a better radio helps.

A good tabletop model won't guarantee your hearing a favorite daytime or off-beam station, but it will improve the odds—especially if you use a good antenna, which is very important. Tabletop models also do unusually well with non-broadcasting signals, such as "ham" and "utility" stations—many of which use single-sideband and other specialized transmission modes.

Useful for High-Rise Listening

Especially in urban areas, portables can disappoint, and nowhere is this more evident than in high-rise buildings. Signals from local transmitters—ranging from taxicab companies to cellular telephone cells to FM and TV broadcasters—can swamp simpler world band circuits. Too, metal and masonry act like sponges, soaking up signals from afar.

City listeners are almost always at a disadvantage compared to those in less-built-up areas. Yet, with the right equipment, good results can be had. Indeed, the founder of PASSPORT TO WORLD BAND RADIO had his best years DXing rare catches while listening from a high-rise apartment in the middle of Philadelphia, across the street from a 50,000 Watt FM station!

If you live in an apartment, your best bet for bringing in tougher stations is to connect a tabletop or portatop model to an insulated-wire antenna that runs along, or protrudes just outside, a window or balcony. You can also try a passive (unamplified) or, if this is not satisfactory, an active (amplified) whip antenna sticking out, flagpole-style, from a window or balcony ledge. An ordinary car radio antenna will do nicely for a passive whip, but remember that the longer it is, the better. Either way, if your tabletop radio has a built-in preamplifier, use it. With portatop models, the built-in preamplifier can be accessed by connecting your passive antenna to the receiver's whip-antenna input.

Active antennas with the reception elements and amplifiers in separate modules are best; those with the antenna element affixed to the amplifier box should be avoided. Properly made active antennas are found only at world band specialty outlets, but tend to produce false (spurious) signals—although the British-made Datong models are superior in this regard. The quality of performance of active antennas is very location-specific, so try to purchase these only on some sort of money-back basis.

Readily Found in Certain Countries

Tabletop models are readily found in certain countries, such as the United States, Canada, the United Kingdom, Germany and Japan, and almost as easily in places like Australia. At the other extreme, a few countries, such as Saudi Arabia and Singapore, frown upon the importation of tabletop models. That's because tabletops often look like transceivers, which can be used by terrorists and spies. However, when tabletop models are brought in as part of a household's goods, problems are less likely to arise.

Most tabletop and portatop models, unlike portables, are available only from electronics and world band specialty outlets. Firms that sell, distribute or manufacture world band tabletops usually support them with service that is incomparably superior to that for portables, and often continues well after the model has been discontinued. Drake and Lowe—as well as Kenwood, Japan Radio and Yaesu—have particularly good track records in this regard.

Higher Price, but No FM

For the most part, tabletop receivers are pricier than portables. For that extra money you tend to get not only better performance, but also a better-made device. However, what you rarely find in a tabletop is reception of the everyday 87.5-108 MHz FM band, much less FM stereo. That's because most tabletop manufacturers specialize in telecommunications equipment for hams and professionals. They don't have much experience in the consumer market, and thus tend not to realize the importance of FM to that market.

One exception: the Drake SW8 portatop, reviewed elsewhere in this edition. It not only has FM, it works well and is in stereo.

External Antenna Required

Most tabletop models also require an outboard shortwave antenna. Even those radios that don't require an outboard antenna should have one to perform to anything like full advantage.

Indeed, tabletop performance is substantially determined by antenna quality and placement. A first-rate world band outdoor wire antenna, such as the various models manufactured by Antenna Supermarket and Alpha Delta, usually runs from $60 to $80 in the United States—a bit more elsewhere.

These specialized wire antennas are best, and should be used if at all possible. Check with the Radio Database International White Paper, PASSPORT *Evaluation of Popular Outdoor Antennas*, for full details on performance and installation.

While most specialty wire antennas work reasonably well, some models have been getting rave reviews in media where the reviewers reportedly have a vested interest in the product being reviewed. Remember that while some world band specialty wire antennas are better than others, the differences are not profound. Beware of inflated claims.

If you're an apartment dweller with no access to land outdoors, a short amplified antenna is the next-best choice. However, our experience with these antennas has tended to be disappointing, mainly because of spurious signals that can result from their use. Better models, such as those made by Britain's Datong, go for the equivalent of $100-200 in several countries.

Many tabletop and portatop models come equipped with synchronous selectable sideband, which enhances reception not only of world band signals, but also of mediumwave AM stations and longwave. For listening to distant mediumwave AM stations, an outboard specialty antenna, such as that made by Kiwa Electronics, is *de rigeur*.

Virtually Every Model Tested

Models new for 1996 are covered at length in this year's PASSPORT REPORTS. Every receiver, regardless of its introduction year, has been put through the various testing hurdles we established and have honed since 1977, when our firm first started evaluating world band equipment.

Virtually every model available is thoroughly tested in the laboratory, using criteria we developed specially for the strenuous requirements of world band reception. The receiver then undergoes hands-on evaluation, usually for months, before we begin preparing our detailed internal report. That report, in turn, forms the basis for this PASSPORT REPORTS.

The unabridged laboratory and hands-on test results are too exhaustive to reproduce here. However, for many tabletop models they are available as PASSPORT's Radio Database International

Alpha Delta DX-ULTRA Antenna Top-Gun Antenna for Top-Gun Receivers

It seems odd that something so sophisticated as a world band radio should be utterly dependent on a few feet of low-technology wire. Yet, the world's best world band receivers can't perform properly without a good antenna. Indeed, all tabletop receivers reviewed in PASSPORT require an external antenna to receive anything.

As a result, the choice of antenna becomes critical. While a superb antenna won't overcome the shortcomings of a mediocre receiver, a poor antenna can certainly compromise the performance of a top-gun receiver. This subject is covered in the RDI White Paper, PASSPORT *Evaluation of Popular Outdoor Antennas*. Now, another option has appeared on the market, the DX Ultra from Alpha Delta, an established American antenna manufacturer.

Almost a Kit

The 80-foot (24.4 meter) DX-Ultra, alas, does not come fully assembled, as does the Eavesdropper. It consists of a variety of elements on each side of a center connector, and is made of 12-gauge wire and connectors that look like they would support a Bradley Fighting Vehicle.

To put it together, you first unroll one side of the antenna, then carefully straighten out each element, so it has no kinks, by attaching the antenna's center connector to something solid that you can pull against. You thread the lower elements through the spacers, after which you adjust the spacers so they are the proper distance from each other. Finally, you fasten each spacer into place by looping wire around it. There are 18 positions on *each* side of the antenna where spacer and antenna element come together, so you'll get lots of opportunity to perfect your wire-wrapping skills. When you get one side of the antenna completed, you then have to do the other. The whole exercise takes a good hour-and-a-half.

When the antenna is completely assembled, attach a length of coax (which you supply) to the center connector. Then, before you hoist the DX-Ultra into the air, have a cool drink and consider this: *no antenna should ever be erected where it can come into contact with electrical wires, including if the antenna or the electrical lines should fall.*

Before proceeding, make sure the wire is twisted over itself at least half a dozen times after it passes through each end insulator—our DX-Ultra suddenly dropped to the ground while hoisting it because the end connections had been left loose.

White Papers—details on price and availability are elsewhere in this book.

Tips for Using this Section

With tabletop receivers, "list" prices are sometimes quoted by manufacturers, sometimes not. In any event, the spread between "list" and actual selling prices is almost always small except when there are closeouts. Thus, prices given in this section reflect the higher end of actual selling prices. World band tabletop models

---

Continued

How It Performs

How does it perform? We used an Antenna Supermarket Eavesdropper, a popular alternative that scored well in our past tests, as a benchmark. Here are the measured differences:

Segment (MHz)	Eavesdropper	DX-Ultra
21		+1.5-2.5 "S" units
17		+1-3 "S" units
15		+2-4 "S" units
13	+2-4 "S" units	
11	+0.5-3 "S" units	
9	variable, no substantial difference	
7		+4 "S" units
6	no difference	
5	no difference	
4	variable, no substantial difference	
3	variable, no substantial difference	
2	+4 "S" Units	

In some cases, a particular signal would come in stronger on one antenna while another signal within the same segment would be stronger on the other antenna. These results are caused by the unique lobe pattern of each antenna, which makes for stronger reception of certain signals than others. To confuse matters even more, the lobe pattern of the same antenna can change, depending on the height of the antenna's erection.

As a result, it is virtually impossible, without doing exhaustive testing at your particular location, to say for certain that either of these antennas will outperform the other in all cases. The upshot is that most serious DXers will want a choice of antennas to get optimum performance in a variety of listening conditions.

What is certain is that virtually any listener will be well-pleased with the DX-Ultra. It is well-built, and should provide worthy world band performance for many years to come.

— *Jock Elliott*

are virtually unavailable at duty-free shops.

Receivers are listed in order of suitability for listening to difficult-to-hear world band radio broadcasts, with important secondary consideration being given to audio fidelity and ergonomics. Prices are as of when we go to press and are subject to fluctuation.

Unless otherwise stated, all tabletop models have:

- digital frequency synthesis and illuminated display;
- a wide variety of helpful tuning features;
- meaningful signal-strength indication;
- the ability to properly demodulate single-sideband and CW (Morse code); also, with suitable ancillary devices, radio teletype and radio fax;
- full coverage of at least the 155-29999 kHz longwave, mediumwave AM and shortwave spectra—including all world band segments; and
- illuminated display.

Unless otherwise stated, all tabletop models do *not*:

- tune the FM broadcast band (87.5-108 MHz).

What Passport's Rating Symbols Mean

Star ratings: ★ ★ ★ ★ ★ is best. We award stars solely for overall performance and meaningful features; price, appearance and the like are not taken into account. To facilitate comparison, the same rating system is also used for portable and portatop models, reviewed elsewhere in this Passport. Whether a radio is portable, a portatop or a tabletop model, a given rating—three stars, say—means largely the same thing. However, with tabletop models there is a slightly greater emphasis on the ability to flush out tough, hard-to-hear sig-

nals, as this is the primary reason these sets are chosen.

Passport's Choice tabletop models are our test team's personal picks of the litter—serious radios that, funds allowing, we would buy ourselves.

¢: No, this doesn't mean cheap. *None* of these models is cheap! Rather, it denotes a model that costs appreciably less than usual for the level of performance provided.

Models in **(parentheses)** have not been tested by us, but appear to be essentially identical to the model(s) tested.

PROFESSIONAL-GRADE MONITOR RECEIVERS

Get what you pay for? Not necessarily.

Costly professional-grade monitor receivers are designed and made for professional applications, which usually have only some things in common with the needs of world band listening. For that, these receivers usually provide little or no improvement in performance over regular tabletop models costing a fraction as much.

But there is one exception, the improved version of the Watkins-Johnson HF-1000, especially when equipped with the fidelity-enhancing Sherwood SE-3 accessory. But be prepared not only for sticker shock, but also to be exacting in selecting and erecting a suitable antenna if you want it to work properly.

Improved for 1996

★ ★ ★ ★ ★   *Passport's Choice*

Watkins-Johnson HF-1000

Price: $3,995.00 in the United States. CAN$5,400 in Canada. £4,495.00 in the

United Kingdom. Not available in Australia.

Advantages: Generally superior audio quality (see Disadvantages). Unparalleled bandwidth flexibility, with no less than 58 outstandingly high-quality bandwidths. Digital signal processing (DSP). Tunes and displays in extremely precise 1 Hz increments. Extraordinary operational flexibility—virtually every receiver parameter is adjustable. 100 station presets. Synchronous detector reduces distortion with world band, mediumwave AM and longwave signals (see Disadvantages). Built-in preamplifier. Tunable notch filter. Highly adjustable scanning of both frequency ranges and channel presets. Easy-to-read displays. Large tuning knob. Can be fully and effectively computer and remotely controlled. Passband offset (see Disadvantages). Built-in test equipment (BITE) diagnostics.

Disadvantages: Very expensive. Static and modulation splash sound harsher than with most other models. Synchronous detection not sideband-selectable. Requires coaxial antenna feedline to avoid receiver-generated digital noise. Passband offset operates only in CW mode. Jekyll-and-Hyde ergonomics: sometimes wonderful, sometimes awful. Large rack-oriented footprint suboptimal for tabletop use. No traditional cabinet, and front-panel rack "ears" protrude. In principle, mediocre front-end selectivity; however, problems were not apparent during listening; and, if needed (say, if you live very close to a mediumwave AM station), a sub-octave preselector option can be added or installed at factory. Cumbersome operating manual.

Bottom line: With much-improved audio quality and the partial taming of its original digital-hash problems, the Watkins-Johnson HF-1000 assumes

The pricey Watkins-Johnson HF-1000, improved for 1996, is now the best world band radio on the market when it's equipped with Sherwood's SE-3 accessory.

the throne as the king of world band supersets, both for program listening and for DXing. With a final solution to the digital hash problem, and the addition of a tone control, passband tuning, and sideband-selectable synchronous detection, the '1000 could hold its crown even higher. Fortunately, the Sherwood SE-3 remedies all but the hash issue, and improves audio fidelity, to boot. And one of the antennas that we tested with the '1000 eliminates nearly all the hash problem. Thus, the HF-1000 now closely approaches the ideal receiver for demanding aficionados with suitable financial wherewithal—provided you want a high degree of manual control in your receiver. Of course, for around $4,500, with the SE-3 and a suitable speaker, it *should* be nothing short of superb!

Evaluation of Improved Model: The Watkins-Johnson HF-1000 is a professional-grade receiver for DXers and program listeners who prefer to optimize reception manually by carefully adjusting a bank of controls. There are four displays on the face of the receiver, an analog signal-strength meter, and 44 buttons for doing all kinds of good things. This is rounded out by five chunky knobs, plus a huge tuning knob.

Watkins-Johnson, under its own name and various "special" names, is an established supplier of radios to a wide range of government agencies.

Its "spook" heritage clearly shows: The rack-mounted '1000 measures 19 x 19 inches (482 x 482 mm), including handles, and 5 1/4 inches (133 mm) high. No, it doesn't come with or need a cabinet, but something attractive, with proper ventilation, can be made up by your favorite local cabinet maker.

In the arena of world band receivers, the Watkins-Johnson HF-1000 is an anomaly. While plastic portables are punched out by the tens of thousands, and top-ranked tabletop models may see annual production of maybe several thousand, Watkins-Johnson manufactures '1000s at a rate of *less than one per working day*.

In this respect, each HF-1000 is very nearly hand-built, almost a one-of-a-kind. This means that however closely we analyze and dissect, if you choose to buy one it will almost certainly differ in some respects from our findings.

Since we last tested the '1000 for the 1995 edition, there has been one major hardware change—a redesign of the receiver's motherboard and back panel—and a whole series of ROM changes to the all-important software that controls this all-in-one-package computer-*cum*-receiver.

We put two of the latest versions of the '1000 (manufactured in early and late July of 1995) through their paces. We found that the receiver has improved noticeably over the past year or so, now delivering outstanding performance in virtually every yardstick of receiver behavior. Still, even though the two units were manufactured within a few weeks of each other, some lab measurements differed noticeably, suggesting that some unit-to-unit differences can be traced to production, rather than design, variations.

An armada of no less than 58 well-chosen bandwidths, with superb shape factors and excellent ultimate rejection, offer razor-sharp selectivity that's in a league unto itself. Dynamic range is worthy, too, and

Coming Up

Consumer electronic companies have tended to avoid producing world band radios in tabletop format. This is just about to change.

For 1996, Radio Shack is introducing the DX-394, a basic-level tabletop with the usual digital tuning goodies and single-sideband reception. It's scheduled to list at $399.99 in the United States.

Drake also has something in the works, but its development is much more embryonic. It hopes to produce an under-$300 tabletop model for the "For the People" organization (see Disestablishmentarian listing in Addresses PLUS). It would be basic—downright Spartan, really—probably not even demodulating single-sideband signals or otherwise doing many of the things usually associated with tabletop models. Realistically, it would not be surprising if a variant also appeared under the Drake label.

sensitivity to weak signals was unusually good in one unit (less so in the second). In short, our laboratory analysis suggests that this receiver has what it takes for flushing out tough signals, and our hands-on tests confirm this.

Yet curiously, this four-kilobuck receiver omits some goodies found on world band tabletops selling for only a fourth as much. There is no passband tuning (except on CW), no tone control, and the synchronous detection is *still* not sideband selectable. Watkins-Johnson says selectable sideband will eventually be included, but only when their engineers have some "down time" from projects for government clients, who are their bread and butter. For a four kilobuck receiver, this is downright silly, but as we shall see there is an effective solution.

In last year's version, the receiver's sophisticated computer circuitry generated digital hash (RFI) that would interfere with the incoming signal in two ways. First, unshielded antenna feedlines would pick up hash radiating from the receiver. According to industry scuttlebutt, W-J never gave this a second thought when designing the receiver, as their government clients, unlike many shortwave listeners, use heavily shielded antenna feedlines.

Watkins-Johnson has addressed this problem to some extent. Now, using a first-rate passive antenna—the new Alpha Delta "DX-Ultra" fared better than others we used—with a well-shielded coaxial feedline usually eliminates the problem completely. The specialized firms which sell the '1000 can advise you as to the most suitable "coax" for this purpose.

However, our tests also show that active antennas—if you simply *must* use them—need to be chosen with

exceptional care. Even if they have suitable cable and a remote receiving element, their amplifier boxes may not be adequately shielded. As these boxes typically rest close to the receiver, they are likely to pick up radiated hash from the receiver, then feed it back into the radio along with the received signal. So be sure to keep any amplification box and antenna element as far as is practical from the receiver. If this doesn't do the trick, consider using better-shielded coaxial cable than comes with the antenna system.

The second form of intrusive hash is seemingly both generated and then picked up *within* the receiver itself, and thus can't be eliminated by the user. Although somewhat improved over last year's unit, there are still residual traces of this type of internally generated digital noise on a limited number of discrete frequencies, even with a coax-fed antenna. This noise, however, is not enough to affect "DX-ability." While this falls into the category of a now-and-then annoyance, it is astonishing that gear of this caliber has gotten away with this design flaw in the first place.

The exceptionally harsh, tiring audio that plagued last year's sample has been greatly improved. It is now generally pleasant, especially when the synchronous detector is switched in—and provided the dinky built-in speaker isn't used. For serious DXing, the radio as it comes from the factory works commendably, indeed.

No, it won't outperform other DX supersets in each and every instance. It's a rarely mentioned law that even lesser receivers will outperform top-notch sets with at least some signals. Among other things, we found that the weaker of two co-channel signals tended to be harder to make out than on some other tabletop models. Too, the subjective variable of "readability" sometimes gave the edge to some less-exotic models, including some of the larger classic portables no longer manufactured. Still, the '1000 should prevail, as it has in our tests, in the majority of tough-DX situations.

For gilt-eared listening to programs, it fares well, too, but not so well as one might expect from something in this price class. So we connected it to a Sherwood SE-3 Mk III, the latest version of a well-proven fidelity-enhancing accessory that connects simply by plugging a cable into the receiver. The result was excellent, with listener comments ranging from "a definite improvement" to "simply outstanding," and two saying it was the best audio they had heard on a modern shortwave receiver. We found the Radio Shack Optimus 7 that Sherwood recommends to be somewhat bassy, but experimentation with various high-efficiency mini speakers for audiophiles showed that some mate very well with the HF-1000/SE-3 combo. If you go this route, experiment, using speakers obtained locally on a returnable basis. Some high-efficiency speakers have tweeter and other spectrum-discrete gain controls, which should be particularly helpful.

With the SE-3, the synchronous circuit locks as well as it does on the bareback '1000, which also has a top-notch (if double-sideband-only) synchronous detector. Thing is, the SE-3 also offers the ability to offset from the main carrier to avoid adjacent channel interference; that is, continuously tunable selectable sideband. When the SE-3 is shifted thus from the carrier frequency—by using the '1000's tuning knob to choose a shift appropriate to the station being received—the '1000's vast selection of bandwidths allows for selection of the most pleasing tradeoff of audio band-width and interference rejection. Additionally, the SE-3 has a limited tone control.

There is a price to be paid, however, besides the $500, give or take, for the Sherwood enhancement device. To the already vast array of controls on the '1000 are added a half-dozen on the SE-3. However, we found operation of the SE-3 to be largely intuitive, and wound up appreciating its continuation of the spirit of flexibility found on the '1000.

All that having been said, the '1000's state-of-the-art radio performance exacts a price in one aspect of audio fidelity. For one thing, even with the myriad improvements over the past year, the receiver still makes static sound harsher than on other top-quality models. For another, modulation splash from music and voices on adjacent channels tends to come through more disconcertingly than with "normal" receivers.

Although we can't be certain, there appear to be two reasons for this. First, the very nature of digital signal processing tends to give audio "sharp elbows." This would appear to account for the harshness of the static, plus some of the harshness of the modulation splash.

Second, the razor-sharp adjacent-channel rejection sets up something like a "wall" to keep nearby sources of interference at bay. As the high-fidelity experts at McIntosh Laboratories discovered years ago in designing their FM tuners, from the viewpoint of audio fidelity there is definitely such a thing as too much skirt selectivity. For shortwave, with its relatively modest fidelity potential, this is less critical, and thus heretofore has not been noticed as a problem. But it is possible that the '1000 may have crossed the Rubicon in this regard because of its precedent-setting skirt selectivity.

The hypothesis runs along these lines. If you smash your fist into a pond of water, it splashes. But if that pond gets frozen over and you hit it, either you don't penetrate it at all, or if you do the ice breaks with a crash. So it seems to be with the '1000. It keeps much more adjacent-channel interference at bay than does any other receiver we've tested. However, when something does manage to break through, it does so harshly.

A variant hypothesis is that because the '1000 lets through relatively little adjacent-channel interference, the listener notices it more. Perhaps, but there's much more to this phenomenon on the '1000 than those variables of human psychology and aural physiology.

To a very limited extent, these aural annoyances can be softened by judicious use of the AGC controls, which either set to one of three predetermined decay rates, or which can be switched off altogether for manual regulation. This adjustment, of course, also helps reduce the audio-level variations brought about by fading.

The bottom line *for serious DXing* is that the '1000 is almost always as good as, and with some signals better than, any other receiver we've tested. Too, it often does this best without having the SE-3 switched in, as that device has *too* much fidelity for the static and modulation splash typically encountered during DX bandscanning and channel roosting. However, when selectable sideband is needed, you can switch in the SE-3 to reduce interference.

The bottom line for *listening to world band programs* is that the '1000 definitely benefits from the SE-3 and a suitable speaker. The end result is a quality of reception, soup-to-nuts, that all but one of our panelists considers to be the best available.

The Icom IC-R9000 comes complete with a spectrum video display.

★ ★ ★ ★

Icom IC-R9000

Price: $6,389.00 in the United States. CAN$8,199.00 in Canada. £4,080.00 in the United Kingdom. AUS$8,200.00 in Australia.

Advantages: Unusually appropriate for hour-after-hour world band listening. Exceptional tough-signal performance. Flexible, above-average audio for a tabletop model, when used with suitable outboard speaker. Three AM-mode bandwidths. Tunes and displays frequency in precise 0.01 kHz increments. Video display of radio spectrum occupancy. Sophisticated scanner/timer. Extraordinarily broad coverage of radio spectrum. Exceptional assortment of flexible operating controls and sockets. Good ergonomics. Superb reception of utility and ham signals. Two 24-hour clocks.

Disadvantages: Very expensive. No synchronous selectable sideband. Power supply runs hot. Both AM-mode bandwidths too broad for most world band applications. Both single-sideband bandwidths almost identical. Dynamic range merely adequate. Reliability, especially when roughly handled, may be wanting. Front-panel controls of only average construction quality.

Note: The above star rating is contingent upon changing the barn-wide 11.3 kHz AM-mode bandwidth filter to something in the vicinity of 4.5-5.5 kHz. Otherwise, deduct half a star.

Bottom Line: The Icom IC-R9000, with at least one changed AM-mode bandwidth filter—available from some world band specialty firms—is right up there with the best-performing models for DX reception of faint, tough signals. Nevertheless, other models offer virtually the same level of construction and performance, plus synchronous selectable sideband—lacking on the 'R9000—for far less money.

 An *RDI WHITE PAPER* is available for this model.

★ ★ ★ ★

**Lowe HF-235/R
(Lowe HF-235/F)
(Lowe HF-235/H)
(Lowe HF-235)**

Price: Up to $2,700.00 in the United States, depending on configuration. £1,116.00-1,410.00, depending on configuration, in the United Kingdom. Not available in Canada or Australia.

Bottom Line: This radio is essentially similar to the now-discontinued Lowe HF-225, but reconfigured for selected professional applications. For this reason, it offers features some professionals require, but lacks certain niceties for home use and bandscanning. World band listeners and manual-bandscanning professionals are better served by Lowe's other offerings.

 An *RDI WHITE PAPER* is available that covers the Lowe HF-235.

TABLETOP RECEIVERS

If you want a top performer to unearth tough signals, read on. Five-star tabletop models should satisfy even the fussiest, and four-star models are no slouches, either.

The best tabletop models are the Ferraris and Mercedes of the radio world. As with their automotive counterparts, like-ranked receivers may come out of the curve at the same speed, though how they do it can differ greatly from model to model. So if you're thinking of choosing from the top end, study each contender in detail. After all, they're not clones—and they're certainly not cheap!

Too much money? Look into portatop models. Some compromises—but savings, too.

Lowe's non-professional receivers are made to be as tough as most other manufacturers' professional receivers. With the rack-mounted HF-235, Lowe goes one step further and enters the professional market full-bore.

★ ★ ★ ★ ★ *Passport's Choice*

Drake R8A

Still the tabletop champ is the revised version of the Drake R8, the Drake R8A.

Price: $1,099.00 in the United States. CAN$1,559.00 in Canada.

Note: The unit we tested was from an initial small test-production batch. Findings may differ slightly from units from large-scale production (see story).

Advantages: Superior all-round performance for sophisticated listening to world band programs. Above-average audio quality, especially with suitable outboard speaker. High-tech synchronous detection, with selectable sideband, generally performs well—it reduces adjacent-channel interference and fading distortion on world band, longwave and mediumwave AM signals. Five bandwidths, four suitable for world band—among the best configurations of any model tested. Highly flexible performance controls, including variable (albeit AF) notch filter and excellent passband offset. Superior reception of utility, ham and mediumwave AM signals. Tunes in precise 0.01 kHz increments. Displays frequency in 0.01 kHz increments. Superior blocking performance. Slow/fast/off AGC. Sophisticated scan functions. Can access all station presets quickly via tuning knob and slew buttons. Built-in preamplifier. Accepts two antennas. Two 24-hour clocks, with seconds displayed numerically, and timer features.

Disadvantages: Notch filter so fussy to adjust that panelists generally ignored it. Notch depth on our early (test-production) unit was nowhere as deep as manufacturer's specifications would suggest. Synchronous-detector lock on our unit was only fair at hold-

ing lock when passband the offset was tuned well away from the carrier frequency. Most pushbuttons rock on their centers. Ergonomics okay, but not all they could have been. Zero beating on our unit showed the frequency to be consistently around 70 Hz off. Matching optional MS8 outboard speaker not equal to receiver's fidelity potential.

Bottom Line: The best overall performer in or near its price class, with much-improved ergonomics. There is an excellent chance that some oddities we found resulted from the fact that we analyzed a test-production unit, but we won't know for certain until Drake commences regular production. A good speaker is a "must" for the R8A to really shine—but don't bother with Drake's mediocre MS8 offering.

Changes on New Version: In principle, a number of small improvements were made in performance. While these are real, most are virtually undetectable, even during critical use, except for the improved AGC response, which our laboratory summarizes qualitatively as is "Collins-like, rather than Drake-like." On the other hand, the synchronous-detector's lock on our unit, which was from a small initial test-production batch, was only fair in holding lock. Whether this is a sample problem—there were no other units to test before we went to press—or whether this is a side effect of one or more other changes, such as to the AGC, remains to be seen.

What has clearly changed, and much for the better, are the ergonomics. From the elevation system to the display to the operating controls, nearly everything has been re-thought and improved to make operation much handier. While the end result is nowhere near the ergonomic masterpiece that is the Japan Radio NRD-535, it is now quite acceptable.

An *RDI WHITE PAPER* is available for this model in its original incarnation. It will be redone after we have had a chance to exhaustively test the new version after regular production has been underway for a while, probably well into 1996.

★ ★ ★ ★ ★ *Passport's Choice*

Japan Radio NRD-535D

Price: $2,029.00 in the United States. CAN$2,599.00 in Canada. AUS$3,999.95 in Australia.
Evaluation: See below.

The high-water mark of ergonomic excellence is the Japan Radio NRD-535D. It is superb for DXing, and can be equipped for enhanced-fidelity listening.

★ ★ ★ ★

Japan Radio NRD-535

Price: $1,429.00 in the United States. CAN$1,749.00 in Canada. £1,195.00 in the United Kingdom. AUS$3,299.95 in Australia.
Advantages: One of the best and quietest DX receivers ever tested. Top-notch ergonomics, including non-fatiguing display. Construction quality slightly above average. Computer-type modular plug-in circuit boards ease repair. Highly flexible operating controls, including 200 superb station presets, tunable notch filter and passband offset. Superior reception of utility and ham signals. One of the few receivers tested that tunes frequency in exacting 0.001 kHz increments. Displays frequency in precise 0.01 kHz increments. Slow/fast/off AGC. Superior front-end selectivity. Sophisticated scan functions. World Time clock with timer features; displays seconds, albeit only if a wire inside the receiver is cut. Excellent optional NVA-319 outboard speaker. *NRD-535D:* Synchronous detection with selectable sideband for reduced fading and easier rejection of interference. Continuously variable bandwidth in single-sideband (narrow bandwidth) and AM (wide bandwidth) modes.
Disadvantages: Audio quality, although improved over some earlier Japan Radio offerings, still somewhat muddy. Dynamic range and blocking performance adequate, but not fully equal to price class. Excessive beats and birdies. AGC sometimes causes "pop" sounds. Clock shares readout with frequency display. Clock not visible when receiver off. Front feet do not tilt receiver upwards. *NRD-535D:* Synchronous detection circuit locking performance suboptimal, notably with passband offset in use. Variable

bandwidth comes at the expense of deep-skirt selectivity.

Note: Also available in a specially upgraded "NRD-535SE" version for $1,995 from Sherwood Engineering in the United States. More complicated to operate than the regular NRD-535D, but performance, especially fidelity, is exemplary. Informally rated ★ ★ ★ ★ for ergonomics, ★ ★ ★ ★ ★ for performance, in 1994 PASSPORT.

Bottom Line: An exceptional receiver for snaring tough signals, notably in the "D" version, with the best ergonomics we've come across in a tabletop model. Yet, tough-signal performance is a touch shy of what it could have been. Too, it's far from the ideal receiver for armchair listening to everyday world band broadcasts. Superior quality of construction.

An *RDI WHITE PAPER* is available that covers both factory versions of this model.

★ ★ ★ ★

Kenwood R-5000

Price: $1,209.95 in the United States. CAN$1,469.00 in Canada. £999.95 in the United Kingdom. AUS$1,625.00 in Australia.

Advantages: Commendable all-round performance. Good audio, provided a suitable outboard speaker is used. Exceptionally flexible operating controls, including tunable notch filter and passband offset. Tunes and displays frequency in precise 0.01 kHz

Kenwood's only world band receiver is the R-5000.

increments. Excellent reception of utility and ham signals. Superior frequency-of-repair record.

Disadvantages: No synchronous selectable sideband. Ergonomics only fair—especially keypad, which uses an offbeat horizontal format. Mediocre wide bandwidth filter supplied with set; replacement with high-quality YK-88A-1 substitute adds to cost. Audio significantly distorted at tape-recording output.

Note: Some R-5000 units have been found to develop significant hum after use. The manufacturer advises that this is caused by deterioration of the IF board's ground connection to the chassis. The remedy is to clean the IF board foil under the mounting screws, then re-affix those screws snugly.

Bottom Line: The Kenwood R-5000's combination of superior tough-signal performance and good audio quality once made it a top choice for tough-signal DXing, as well as listening to world band programs. Now, it's fast becoming a technological also-ran.

An *RDI WHITE PAPER* is available for this model.

New for 1996
★ ★ ★ ★

Lowe HF-250

Price: $1,489.95 in the United States. £799.00 in the United Kingdom.

Note: The unit we tested was from an initial small test-production batch. The manufacturer suggests, and its track record tends to support, that some improvements will be made once regular production is underway.

Advantages: Top-notch world band and mediumwave AM audio quality, aided by effective tone control—well suited to listening to world band pro-

Lowe's latest is the HF-250, with outstanding audio quality.

grams hour after hour. Clean, simple panel keeps operating controls to a minimum. High-tech synchronous detection reduces fading distortion on world band, longwave and mediumwave AM signals. Synchronous detection circuit also allows for either selectable-sideband or double-sideband reception. Four voice bandwidths. Exceptionally rugged cast-aluminum housing of a class normally associated with professional-grade equipment. Relatively small footprint. Four voice bandwidth filters. Digital display unusually easy to read. World Time clock shows seconds numerically (see Disadvantages).

Disadvantages: Expensive for what it is, based on user comments to date. Synchronous detector only okay in holding lock with signals suffering from flutter fading. Operation of some front-panel button functions tends to be confusing until you get the hang of it. Nonstandard keypad layout. Bereft of certain features—among them notch filter, adjustable AGC and passband tuning—found on some premium-priced models. Occasional minor hum from AC adaptor unless antenna uses coaxial-cable feedline.

Signal-strength indicator has small numbers, hard to read. Clock not displayed when frequency is showing. Minor "braap" chugging within some frequency ranges.

Bottom Line: Think of the Lowe HF-250 as a cleaned-up HF-150 that while generally moving forward, also took a couple of steps backward with the off-beat keypad and "on-during-band-scanning" synchronous detector. It's a hardy, advanced-fidelity receiver for the dedicated listener to world band programs, and in Europe should attract a contingent of exacting customers. But in North America, unless there is steep discounting or a major turnaround in the foreign-exchange market, this model is probably going to gather dust on dealer shelves, which is a pity.

Evaluation of Improved Model:
Here's the radio Lowe watchers have been waiting for: a successor to the venerable HF-225. The new Lowe HF-250 offers both selectable-sideband *and* double-sideband synchronous detection, and comes with 255 tunable channel presets.

The '250 is handily compact for a full tabletop model, partly because it uses an outboard AC adaptor. However, the receiver can occasionally pick up some stray AC hum from that adaptor, although not with an antenna having a coaxial feedline.

The front of the receiver—with few controls, all neatly laid out—is very much in the Lowe tradition. Whether you like this, or prefer the more "stick-shift" approach of most other premium tabletop models, is a matter of personal preference. Our panelists felt it was somewhat counter-intuitive, particularly the admittedly innovative carousel scheme for selecting certain settings.

The LCD is exceptionally easy to read in both daylight and darkness.

There's a genuine analog signal-strength meter, too. Oddly, given the excellent readability of the LCD, the meter's numbers are so small that it is hard to read. The clock, which displays seconds numerically, doesn't display while the received frequency is being shown.

The tuning knob itself is exceptionally smooth—as good as we've come across since the days of the grand old tube-type communications receivers. It works well, too, although during bandscanning there is minor "braap" chugging within some frequency ranges. The built-in speaker works well—it seconds as a handle, even though this may not be the preferred procedure—and it's aided by Lowe's hallmark quality audio, along with a truly effective tone control. Yet, a good external speaker helps even more and is recommended. The end result is what we've come to expect from Lowe: a treat for the ears.

Overall, lab measurements produce good-to-excellent ratings, occasionally superb—particularly in freedom from audio distortion. The receiver comes with fully four bandwidths, which measure 2.5 kHz (nominally 2.2 kHz), 5.7 kHz (4 kHz), 6.7 kHz (7 kHz) and 10 kHz (10 kHz). For world band, the first three are quite useful; for gilt-edged mediumwave AM listening, the 10 kHz setting can sometimes be used.

A real improvement in the '250 over the less-costly Lowe HF-150 is in front-end selectivity. This means the '250 is far less likely to have local mediumwave AM stations leaking in to annoy world band reception.

The '250 comes with a single and slow AGC decay rate. It usually sounds good, but it's a slight disadvantage for DXing during heavy static. Too, the synchronous detector, which is otherwise excellent, sometimes "gurgles" on fluttery signals,

which are more common in North America than in Europe. This might be because the slow AGC decay makes it difficult for the detector to hold lock under these trying conditions. The synchronous detector, unlike that of the '150, stays on when you move the tuning knob, howling as you try to change frequency. The '150's approach is handier.

Instead of a mouse-like external keypad that connects to the receiver via a cable, as is done to excellent effect on other Lowe models, the '250 has a somewhat less-successful wireless remote keypad. The keypad doesn't include a volume control, but it does include a mute button. It also has a non-standard key layout that takes some getting used to, although this may be changed in later production.

The keypad has some other interesting features, even if it has no "cancel" button. For one thing, a key allows you to change bandwidths and slew up and down the bands. But there's a serious problem here. With the keypad, it takes nearly *20 seconds* to move up or down one channel (5 kHz). Fortunately, tuning the receiver "hands on" is nigh flawless.

The Lowe HF-250, although pricey, offers worthy performance in an attractive package. Its front-end performance is especially welcome for those in locations where the '150 is inappropriate.

An *RDI WHITE PAPER* is available for the predecessor to this model, the HF-225, and the Lowe HF-235. A new report will be issued sometime into 1996, only after we have thoroughly tested a unit from a production batch late enough that the various contemplated improvements will have been incorporated.

The AOR AR3030 is one of the most affordable of tabletop models.

★ ★ ★ ★

AOR AR3030

Price: $799.95 in the United States. CAN$1,499.00 in Canada. £699.00 in the United Kingdom. AUS$1,599.00 in Australia.

Advantages: Good-to-excellent in most measurements of receiver performance. Two well-chosen bandwidths. Tunes in 5 Hz increments, displays in 10 Hz increments. Various scanning schemes. Easy-to-use, well-laid-out controls are largely intuitive and easy to operate. Very low audio distortion in single-sideband mode. Synchronous detector reduces distortion with world band, mediumwave AM and longwave signals (see Disadvantages). Weak-signal sensitivity superior within certain world band segments, such as 9 MHz (see Disadvantages). Small. Light. Can be run off batteries for short periods. Easy-to-read display. Can be computer controlled.

Disadvantages: Dynamic range, only fair at 5 kHz spacing, can cause overloading in and around 9 MHz segment. Weak-signal sensitivity only fair within tropical segments. Synchronous detector is not sideband-

selectable, and must be exactly center-tuned; otherwise, with a powerful station, may distort. Lacks some of the exotic controls that DXers love, like a notch filter and passband tuning. Needs an external speaker or headphones to take full advantage of its otherwise-good audio. Tilt bail does not latch properly. Small tuning knob. Non-standard layout for numeric keypad. Runs off external, rather than internal, power supply—albeit one that is approved by Underwriters Laboratories.

Bottom Line: A fine little receiver at a fair price that offers generally pleasant results for program listening.

 An *RDI WHITE PAPER* is available for this model.

★ ★ ★ ★

Icom IC-R71A
(Icom IC-R71E)
(Icom IC-R71D)

Price: *IC-R71A:* $1,440.00 in the United States. CAN$1,649.00 in Canada. No longer available in Australia. *IC-R71E:* £875.00 in the United Kingdom. *IC-R71E and IC-R71D:* $1,000-1,800 in continental Europe.

Advantages: Variable bandwidth. Superb reception of weak, hard-to-hear signals. Reception of faint signals alongside powerful competing ones aided by superb ultimate selectivity, as well as excellent dynamic

Icom's receivers tend to be priced high for what they do, and the IC-R71 is no exception.

range. Flexible operating controls, including tunable notch filter. Excellent reception of utility and ham signals. Tunes in precise 0.01 kHz increments (but displays in 0.1 kHz increments).

Disadvantages: Mediocre audio. No synchronous selectable sideband. Diminutive controls, and otherwise generally substandard ergonomics. Should backup battery die, operating system software erases, requiring reprogramming by Icom service center (expected battery life is in excess of 10 years).

Bottom Line: The venerable Icom IC-R71 was formerly a favorite among those chasing faint, hard-to-hear signals. Now, it is no longer competitive for either program listening or chasing faint DX signals.

 An *RDI WHITE PAPER* is available for this model.

★ ★ ★ ★   ¢

Yaesu FRG-100

Price: $669.00 in the United States. CAN$869.00 in Canada. £599.00 in the United Kingdom. AUS$1,199.00 in Australia.

Advantages: Excellent performance in many respects. Lowest price of any tabletop model tested. Covers 50 Hz to 30 MHz in the LSB, USB, AM and CW modes. Includes three bandwidths, a noise blanker, selectable AGC, two attenuators, the ability to select 16 pre-programmed world band segments, two clocks, on-off timers, 52 tunable station presets that store frequency and mode data, a variety of scanning schemes and an all-mode squelch. A communications-FM module, 500 Hz CW bandwidth and high-stability crystal are optional.

The Yaesu FRG-100 is an excellent buy when it's equipped with an accessory keypad.

Disadvantages: No keypad for direct frequency entry (remediable, see Note, below). No synchronous selectable sideband. Lacks features found in "top-gun" receivers: passband offset, notch filter, adjustable RF gain. Simple controls and display, combined with complex functions, can make certain operations confusing. Dynamic range only fair. Uses AC adaptor instead of built-in power supply.

Note on worthwhile accessories: An outboard accessory keypad is virtually a "must" for the FRG-100, and is a no-brainer to attach. Brodier E.E.I. (3 Place de la Fontaine, F-57420 Curvy, France) makes the best keypad, sold direct for F380 plus shipping, or for $54.95 plus shipping by Universal Radio in Reynoldsburg OH 43068 in the United States. Highly recommended, and the current version also "beeps" when the keys are depressed. Reasonably similar is the QSYer—SWL Version, available for $112 from Stone Mountain Engineering Company in the American city of Stone Mountain GA 30086. These two models we've tested with the FRG-100, but two more have appeared in the United Kingdom since we disposed of our test receiver. These are the model KPAD100 for £38.25 plus shipping from the various Lowe Electronics stores throughout the country (mail orders to Lowe's headquarters in Matlock, Derbyshire DE4 5LE); and the Brodier model KP-100 for £44.95 plus shipping from Martin Lynch, London W13 9SB. Various world band specialty firms in North America and the United Kingdom also install high-quality replacement bandwidth filters, such as those from Kiwa Electronics, for the FRG-100—or you can install them yourself. While these filters are not in the same "must" category as keypads, for some DXers they can be desirable.

Bottom Line: The Yaesu FRG-100, improved shortly after its original incarnation in early 1993, breaks some interesting ground in the price/performance ratio of world band receivers. While this relatively small receiver is sometimes light on features often found in tabletop models, in many respects it succeeds in delivering commendable performance within its price class. Its lack of a keypad for direct frequency entry is now easily remediable (see Note, above).

 An *RDI WHITE PAPER* is available for this model.

The Icom IC-R72 is still available in some parts of the world, but not the United States.

tery—useful during power failure. Novel center-tuning LED for world band and certain other signals. Superb image and IF rejection. Small footprint. Smoothly operating tuning knob. Preamplifier.

Disadvantages: Much too expensive for what it is. Wide bandwidth too broad. Dreadful audio from built-in speaker. Noisy synthesizer. Noise blanker reduces dynamic range. Relatively few features, compared to better models. In our unit, poor low-frequency audio reproduction in upper-sideband.

Bottom Line: Nice, but nothing special and overpriced. Any number of other models offer far better value.

★ ★ ★

Icom IC-R72
(Icom IC-R72A)
(Icom IC-R72E)

Price: CAN$1,499.00 in Canada. £799.95 in United Kingdom. AUS$1,299.00 in Australia. No longer available new in the United States.

Advantages: Pleasant audio with outboard speaker or headphones. Generally superior ergonomics. Tunes and displays frequency in precise 0.01 kHz increments. World clock/timer. Operates for about one hour off built-in rechargeable bat-

The PASSPORT tabletop-model review team: Lawrence Magne, along with Jock Elliott and Tony Jones, with additional observations by George Zeller and laboratory measurements by Robert Sherwood.

Rockwell International

Collins HF Propagation Software

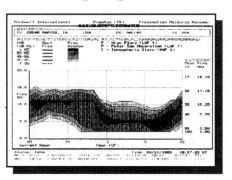

*Typical **PropMan** ™ Screen*

The Collins HF legacy brings you the most comprehensive software propagation prediction tool on the market today

PropMan™ HF propagation prediction made easy at $49.95

(plus tax and shipping)

Propagation made easy

The PropMan™ program is an easy-to-use frequency propagation and management tool, supported by the Collins heritage of quality HF development.

PropMan software offers customization of station parameters, a worldwide station list, software broadcast scheduling and reception, and automatically updated recommendations.

Minimum Hardware Configuration:

- IBM/Compatible, AT 286 (higher speed is recommended)
- 2MB Hard Drive Memory
- Math Coprocessor (highly recommended)
- 490K Conventional Memory
- Color EGA or VGA monitor & graphics card
- DOS 3.2 or higher

Other features include:

- Display of current best frequency and propagating frequency
- 24 hour window of propagation frequency plot, facilitating Automatic Link Establishment (ALE) planning
- Customized channel lists
- Automated IONCAP utilization
- Additional information provided by external sensors is allowed via phone or serial port utilizing SESC data

For information or ordering, please contact:

Rockwell
Collins Avionics & Communications Division
350 Collins Rd. NE
Cedar Rapids, IA 52498-0120

Phone: 319-395-5100 or 800-321-2223
FAX: 319-395-4777

MasterCard, Visa, American Express accepted.

Shipping and Handling:
U.S., Mexico and Canada	+$2.00 USD
Other International	+$7.00 USD
Federal Express (U.S. only)	+$7.00 USD

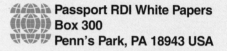

WHERE TO FIND IT:

INDEX TO RADIOS TESTED FOR 1996

*P*ASSPORT *tests nearly every model on the market. Here's your guide to the exact page where each of these reviews can be found. Digital models in bold are new or upgraded for 1996.*

Want even more details? For premium receivers and antennas, there are comprehensive PASSPORT® *Radio Database International White Papers®. These usually run 15-30 pages in length, with one report thoroughly covering a single model or topic. Each RDI White*

Paper®—$5.95 in North America, $7.95 airmail in most other regions—contains virtually all our panel's findings and comments during hands-on testing, as well as laboratory measurements and what these mean to you. They're available from key world band dealers; or, if you prefer, you can contact our 24-hour automated VISA/MC order lines (voice +1 215/794-8252; fax +1 215/794 3396), or write us at PASSPORT *RDI White Papers, Box 300, Penn's Park, PA 18943 USA.*

[1]*Radio Database International White Paper*® available.

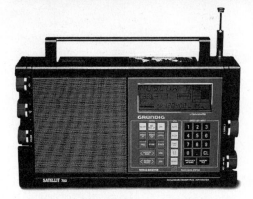
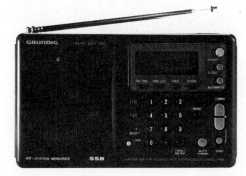

WorldScan®

Musician Ian Anderson hosts the BBC World Service's "Folk Routes." It's one of this year's best shows.   *(BBC)*

WHAT'S ON TONIGHT?

*T*hings ain't what they used to be! Take the BBC World Service, generally considered to be world band's Rock of Gibraltar. Itching for change, it decided to introduce what it calls "streaming"—different programs to different target areas. Nice idea, perhaps, but it's left many of the station's listeners bereft of their favorite programs, or having to listen at inconvenient times.

But, never mind. Gears are churning at the BBC's venerable Bush House headquarters, where remedies are reportedly forthcoming.

In the meantime, here are shows from dozens of nations that you can hear all year long—and where and when to tune. To help you separate the wheat from the chaff, these handy symbols will help you focus on the good stuff:

■ station with superior overall merit
● program of special merit

To be as helpful as possible throughout the year, PASSPORT'S schedules consist not just of observed activity, but also that which we have creatively opined will take place during the forthcoming year. This latter material is original from us, and therefore won't be so exact as factual information.

Key frequencies are given for North America, Western Europe, East Asia and Australasia, plus general coverage of the Mideast. Information on secondary and seasonal channels, as well as channels for other parts of the world, are in "Worldwide Broadcasts in English" and the Blue Pages.

Anushia Sabai and William Teo present news and business reports from Radio Singapore International.   (RSI)

00:00

■**BBC World Service for the Americas.** For many, North America is the only loser to come out of the BBC's decision to divide its programming into separate "streams" for different areas. Indeed, there has been so much negative feedback from North America that the station is considering changes to its programming lineup for later in 1996. In the meantime, this is what you get. The first half hour consists of the comprehensive ●*Newsdesk*, which is then followed by a 15-minute feature and *Britain Today*. Pick of the litter are Tuesday's ●*Folk Routes* (Monday evening, local American date) and Sunday's ●*Letter from America*. On other days you can hear the likes of *Good Books* (Monday), a music feature (Wednesday), *From Our Own Correspondent* (Thursday), *The Farming World* (Friday) and Saturday's *Seven Days*. Audible on 5975, 6175, 7325, 9590 (to 0030) and 9915 kHz.

■**BBC World Service for Asia.** Identical to the service for the Americas, except for some of the features at 0030. Audible in East Asia (till 0030) on 7110, 9580, 11945 and 15280 kHz; and a full hour on 15360 kHz.

Monitor Radio International, USA. North America's number one station for news and in-depth analysis. A one-hour show updated throughout the day and broadcast to different parts of the globe. *News*, then ●*Monitor Radio*—news analysis and news-related features with emphasis on international developments. The final 10 minutes consist of a listener-response program and a religious article from the *Christian Science Monitor* newspaper. To eastern North America and the Caribbean Tuesday through Friday (Monday through Thursday, local American day) on 7535 kHz, and heard throughout much of the United States on 9430 kHz although targeted to Central and South America. On other days, the broadcasts feature Herald of Christian Science and Christian Science Sentinel religious programming (all of it not necessarily in English) or transmissions of the Sunday Service from the Mother Church in Boston.

Radio Bulgaria. Winters only at this time. *News*, then Tuesday through Friday there's 15 minutes of current events in *Today*, replaced Saturday by *Weekly Spotlight*. The remainder of the broadcast is given over to features dealing with Bulgarian life and culture, and includes some lively Balkan folk music. Sixty minutes to eastern North America and Central America on 7205 and 9700 kHz. One hour earlier in summer.

Radio Exterior de España ("Spanish National Radio"). *News*, then Tuesday through Saturday (local weekday evenings in the Americas) it's *Panorama*, which features a recording of popular Spanish music, a commentary or a report, a review of the Spanish press, and weather. The remainder of the program is a mixture of literature, science, music and general programming. Tuesday (Monday evening in North America), there's *Sports Spotlight* and *Cultural Encounters*; Wednesday features *People of Today* and *Entertainment in Spain*; Thursday brings *As Others See Us* and, biweekly,

The Natural World or Science Desk; Friday has *Economic Report* and *Cultural Clippings*; and Saturday offers *Window on Spain* and *Review of the Arts*. The final slot is give over to a language course, *Spanish by Radio*. On the remaining days, you can listen to Sunday's *Hall of Fame*, *Distance Unknown* (for radio enthusiasts) and *Gallery of Spanish Voices*; and Monday's *Visitors' Book*, *Great Figures in Flamenco* and *Radio Club*. Sixty minutes to eastern North America on 9540 kHz.

Radio Norway International. Winter Mondays (Sunday evenings, local American date) only. *Norway Now*. News and features from and about Norway, with the accent often on the lighter side of life. Thirty minutes of friendly programming to the Americas on any two frequencies from 5905, 5910, 6115 and 6120 kHz.

Radio Canada International. Winters only at this time. Tuesday through Saturday (weekday evenings in North America), it's the final hour of the CBC domestic service news program ●*As It Happens*, which features international stories, Canadian news and general human interest features. Weekends, it's *The Inside Track* (sports) and the cultural *Tapestry*, both from the CBC's domestic output. To North America on 5960 and 9755 kHz. One hour earlier in summer.

Voice of Russia World Service. Beamed to eastern North America at this hour. Winters, *news* and opinion take up the first 30 minutes, followed by some excellent musical fare during the second half-hour. Monday and Saturday (Sunday and Friday evenings local American days), there's the incomparable ●*Folk Box*; Thursday brings ●*Music at your Request*; and Wednesday and Friday feature jazz. Summers, it's *News*, followed Tuesday through Saturday by *Focus on Asia and the Pacific* and a

music program. On the remaining days there's a listener-response program, then ●*Audio Book Club* (Sunday) or *Russian by Radio* (Monday). Not the easy catch it used to be, so you have to dial around a bit. Winters, the pickings are slim, indeed; try 7105 and 7165 kHz from 0030 onwards. Failing these, try other frequencies in the 7 MHz segment, or the bottom end of the 6 MHz range (5900-5940 kHz). Best summer options are 9530, 9620, 9720 and 11750 kHz.

Radio Vilnius, Lithuania. Winters only at this time. Tuesday through Saturday (weekday evenings local American date), there's just five minutes of *news* about events in Lithuania. On the remaining days, the broadcast is extended to a full half hour of news and short features about the country. To eastern North America on 7150 kHz. One hour earlier in summer.

Radio Yugoslavia. Summers only at this time. *News*, followed by short features with a strong regional slant. Thirty minutes to eastern North America on 9580 and 11870 kHz. One hour later in winter.

Radio Pyongyang, North Korea. Strictly of curiosity value only, this station continues to occupy the cellar of world band programming. The late Kim Il Sung's shadow still hangs heavily over the station, and although the mantle of "Great Leader" has been passed to his successor, the "Unrivaled Great Man" (as he is now referred to) continues to be the subject of choral and other praises. The last of the old-style communist stations, and unlikely to change, at least for the time being. Fifty minutes to the Americas on 11335, 13760 and 15130 kHz.

Radio Ukraine International. Summers only at this time. An hour's ample coverage of just about everything Ukrainian, including news, sports, politics and culture. Well worth a listen is ●*Music from Ukraine*, which fills most

of the Monday (Sunday evening in the Americas) broadcast. Sixty minutes to Europe and eastern North America on 4825 (to 0030), 6010, 9750, 11780 and 11950 kHz. One hour later in winter.

Radio Australia. Part of a 24-hour service to Asia and the Pacific, but which can also be heard at this time throughout much of North America. Begins with world *news*, then Monday through Friday there's *Network Asia*, replaced Saturday by *Feedback* (a listener-response program) and *Indian Pacific*, and Sunday by *Charting Australia* and *Correspondents Report*. Targeted at Asia and the Pacific on about ten channels, and heard in North America (for 0030, and best during summer) on 15365, 17795 and 17860 kHz. In Southeast Asia, try 9610, 11855, 13745 and 17750 kHz. Also audible in Europe on 15510 kHz, from 0030 onwards.

Radio Prague, Czech Republic. *News* and current events, then one or more features. Wednesday (Tuesday evening in the Americas), it's *Talking Point*; Thursday has *Calling All Listeners*; Friday brings *Economic Report* and *Stamp Corner*; and Saturday there's *I'd Like You to Meet...* and *From the Archives*. Sunday's offerings include a feature on the arts, replaced Monday by music, and Tuesday by a magazine program. Thirty minutes to North America on 5930 and 7345 kHz.

Voice of America. First hour of the VOA's two-hour broadcasts to the Caribbean and Latin America. *News*, followed by split programming Tuesday through Saturday (Monday through Friday evenings in the Americas). Listeners in the Caribbean can tune in to ●*Report to the Caribbean*, followed by *Music USA*. For Latin America there is ●*VOA Business Report* (replaced Saturday be *Newsline*) and Special English news and features. On Sunday, both services carry *Agriculture Today*, followed by *Communications World*

(Caribbean) or the Special English feature ●*American Stories* (Latin America). Monday's programming consists of ●*VOA Business Report* (Caribbean) or ●*Encounter* (Latin America), with the second half-hour's ●*Spotlight* being common to both services. An excellent way to keep in touch with events in the Western Hemisphere. The service to the Caribbean is on 6130, 9455 and 11695 kHz; and the one to the Americas is on 5995, 7405, 9775 and 13740 kHz. The final hour of a separate service to East and Southeast Asia and Australasia (see 2200) can be heard on 7215, 9770, 11760, 15185, 15290, 17735 and 17820 kHz.

Croatian Radio. Eight minutes of *news* from Croatian Radio's Zagreb studio. Best heard in Europe and eastern North America, but also heard elsewhere. Channel usage varies, but try 5895, 7370, 9830, 11635 and 13830 kHz.

Radio Thailand. *Newshour*. Apart from a few items of news and a short feature about Thailand, the rest of the half hour is given over to news which is covered as well, if not better, by several other international broadcasters. Now has considerable transmitter capacity, but seems to have lost a good opportunity to establish itself as an interesting regional broadcaster. To South Asia and East African insomniacs on 9680 (or 9690) kHz, and to Asia on 9655 and 11905 kHz.

China Radio International. *News* and commentary, followed Wednesday through Saturday (Tuesday through Friday evenings in the Americas) by *Current Affairs*. These are followed by various feature programs, such as *Culture in China* (Friday); *Listeners' Letterbox* (Monday and Wednesday); *Press Clippings, Cooking Show, Travel Talk* and ●*Music from China* (Sunday); *Sports Beat, China Scrapbook* and *Music Album* (Monday); *Learn to Speak Chinese* (Tuesday and Thursday); and Saturday's *In the Third World*. Mondays, there is also a biweekly *Business Show* which alternates with *China's Open Windows*. One hour to eastern North America on 9710 and 11715 kHz.

All India Radio. The final 45 minutes of a much larger block of programming targeted at Southeast Asia, and heard well beyond. On 9705, 9950, 11745 and 13750 kHz.

Radio Cairo, Egypt. The final half hour of a 90-minute broadcast to eastern North America on 9900 kHz. See 2300 for specifics.

Radio New Zealand International. A friendly package of *news* and features sometimes replaced by live sports commentary. Part of a much longer broadcast for the South Pacific, but also heard in parts of North America (especially during summer) on 15115 kHz.

FEBC Radio International, Philippines. *Good Morning from Manila*, a potpourri of secular and religious programming targeted at South Asia, but widely heard elsewhere. The first 60 minutes of a two-hour broadcast on 15450 kHz.

WWCR, Nashville, Tennessee. Carries a variety of disestablishmentarian programs at this hour, depending on the day of the week. Winters on 5065 kHz, there's "The Voice of Liberty" and "The Hour of Courage"; in summer it's "Protecting your Wealth", "World of Prophecy" and "Full Disclosure Live." On 7435 kHz, look for "The Baker Report", which is available all year.

WJCR, Upton, Kentucky. Twenty-four hours of gospel music targeted at North America on 7490 and (at this hour) 13595 kHz. Also heard elsewhere, mainly during darkness hours. For more religious broadcasting at this hour, try **WYFR-Family Radio** on 6085 kHz, **KTBN** on (winters) 7510 or (summers) 15590 kHz, and **WHRI-World Harvest Radio** on 5745 kHz. For something a little more controversial, tune to Dr. Gene Scott's University Network, via **WWCR** on 13845 kHz or **KAIJ** on 13815 kHz. Traditional Catholic programming can be heard via **WEWN** on 7425 kHz.

00:30

Radio Nederland. *News*, then Tuesday through Sunday (Monday through Saturday evenings in North America) there's ●*Newsline*, a current affairs program. These are followed by a different feature each day, including the well-produced ●*Research File* (science, Tuesday); *Mirror Images* (arts in Holland, Wednesday); a feature documentary (Thursday) and a media program (Friday). Monday is devoted to *The Happy Station*. Fifty-five minutes to North America on 6020, 6165 and 9845 (or 9840) kHz (may also be available winters on 11655 kHz), and a full hour to South Asia (also widely heard in other parts of the continent, as well as Australasia), winters on 5905 and 7305 kHz, and summers on 9860 and 11655 kHz.

Radio Vlaanderen Internationaal, Belgium. Winters only at this time; Tuesday through Saturday (weekday evenings in North America), there's *News*, *Press Review* and *Belgium Today*, followed by features like *Focus on Europe* (Tuesday), *Living in Belgium* and *Green Society* (Wednesday), *The Arts* and *Around Town* (Thursday), *Economics* and *International Report* (Friday), and *The Arts* and *Tourism* (Saturday). Weekend features include *Music from Flanders* (Sunday) and Monday's *P.O. Box 26* and *Radio World*. Twenty-five minutes to eastern North America on 6030 (or 6035) kHz; also audible on 9925 (or 9930/9935) kHz, though beamed elsewhere. One hour earlier in summer.

Radio Sweden. Tuesday through Saturday (weekday evenings in the Americas), it's *news* and features in

Sixty Degrees North, concentrating heavily on Scandinavian topics. Tuesday's accent is on sports; Wednesday has electronic media news; Thursday brings *Money Matters*; Friday features ecology or science and technology; and Saturday offers a review of the week's news. Sunday, there's *Spectrum* (arts) or *Sweden Today* (current events), while Monday's offering is *In Touch with Stockholm* (a listener-response program) or the musical *Sounds Nordic*. Thirty minutes to South America, also audible in eastern North America. Winters on 6065 and 6200 kHz, and summers on 6065 and 9810 kHz.

Voice of the Islamic Republic of Iran. One hour of *news*, commentary and features with a strong Islamic slant. Targeted at North and Central America winters on 7100, 9022 and 9670 kHz; and summers on 6175, 7180 and 9022.

Radio Thailand. Thirty minutes of *Newshour*; see 0000 for specifics. To North America winters on 11905 kHz, and summers on 15370 kHz. Also available year-round to Asia on 9655 and 11905 kHz.

HCJB—Voice of the Andes, Ecuador. Tuesday through Saturday (weekday evenings in North America), there's the popular *Focus on the Family*, hosted by James Dobson. This is replaced weekends by Sunday's *Musical Mailbag* and Monday's *Mountain Meditations*. To eastern North America on 9745 kHz.

00:50

Radio Roma, Italy. *News* read by an unenthusiastic announcer, with equally uninspiring Italian music making up the remainder of the broadcast. Twenty sleep-inducing minutes to North America on 9645 and 11800 kHz. Better than Valium for those who need it.

01:00

■BBC World Service for the Americas. Starts with the comprehensive ●*Newsdesk*, then it's a 30-minute feature. Choice pickings include Tuesday's ●*Omnibus* (Monday evening, local American date), ●*Andy Kershaw's World of Music* (Wednesday), ●*Focus on Faith* (Friday) and *Network UK* (Saturday). Other offerings include *Composer of the Month* (Monday) and a documentary (Sunday and Thursday). Audible in North America on 5975, 6175, 7325 and 9915 kHz.

■BBC World Service for Asia. Starts with *World News* and *Press Review*, and the rest of the hour is given over to features. Try *From Our Own Correspondent* (0130 Monday), ●*Health Matters* (0145 Tuesday), and ●*Global Concerns* (same time Friday). Audible in East Asia on 15360 kHz.

Monitor Radio International, USA. See 0000 for program details. Tuesday through Saturday (Monday through Friday, local American date) on 7535 kHz, and heard throughout much of the United States on 9430 kHz although targeted at Central and South America. On other days, the broadcasts feature Herald of Christian Science and Christian Science Sentinel religious

Anna Hornsburgh-Porter interviews an elder of the self-sufficient Tibetan community in Ladakh, Kashmir, for the BBC's "The Roof of the World."

programming (all of it not necessarily in English) or transmissions of the Sunday Service from the Mother Church in Boston.

Radio Canada International. Summers only. *News*, followed Tuesday through Saturday (weeknights, local American date) by *Spectrum* (topics in the news), which in turn is replaced Sunday by *Innovation Canada* (science) and ●*Earth Watch*. On Monday (Sunday evening in North America) there's *Arts in Canada* and a listener-response program. Sixty minutes to North America on 6120, 9755 and 13670 kHz, though this last channel is only available for the first 30 minutes Tuesday through Saturday. One hour later in winter.

■**Deutsche Welle,** Germany. *News*, followed Tuesday through Saturday by the comprehensive ●*European Journal*— commentary, interviews, background reports and analysis. This is followed by *German Tribune* (Tuesday and Thursday), *Backdrop* (Wednesday), *Come to Germany* (Friday), or Saturday's *Through German Eyes*. Sunday (Saturday night in North America) is given over to *Inside Europe* and *Religion and Society*; Monday brings *Living in Germany* and *German by Radio*. Fifty minutes of very good reception in North America, winters on 6040, 6085, 6145, 9565, 9670 and 9700 kHz; and summers on 6040, 6085, 6145, 9555, 9640, 11740 and 11865 kHz.

Radio Slovakia International. *Slovakia Today*, a 30-minute window on Slovakian life and culture. Tuesday (Monday evening in the Americas), the accent is on tourism and Slovak personalities; Wednesday has a historical feature; Thursday's slot is devoted to business and economy; and Friday brings a mix of politics, education and science. Weekends, look for Sunday's "best of" series, or Monday's special feature. To eastern North America and Central America on 5930 and 7300 kHz, and to South America on 9440 kHz.

Radio Norway International. Summer Mondays (Sunday evenings, local American date) only. *Norway Now*. Thirty minutes of *news* and chat from and about Norway. To North and Central America on 7480 and 9560 kHz.

Radio Budapest, Hungary. Summers only at this time. *News* and features, some of which are broadcast on a regular basis. These include Monday's *Bookshelf* (local Sunday evening in North America), a press review (Tuesday, Wednesday, Friday and Saturday), *Profiles* (Wednesday), and *Focus on Business* (Thursday). Thirty minutes to North America on 6000, 9835 and 11910 kHz. One hour later in winter.

Radio Prague, Czech Republic. Repeat of the 0000 broadcast. Thirty minutes to North America on 7345 and (summer) 9405 kHz.

Swiss Radio International. *Newsnet*. A workmanlike compilation of news and background reports on world and Swiss events, but dry as a bone and mainly for news hounds. Somewhat lighter fare on Sunday (Saturday evening in North America), when the biweekly *Capital Letters* (a listener-response program) alternates with *Name Game* and *Sounds Good*. A half hour to North America on 5885, 6135, 9885 and 9905 kHz.

Radio Japan. *News*, then Tuesday through Saturday (weekday evenings local American date) there's 10 minutes of *Asian Top News* followed by a half-hour feature. Take your pick from *Profile* (Tuesday), *Enjoy Japanese* (Wednesday, repeated Friday), *History and Classics* (Thursday) and Saturday's *Music and Book Beat*. On the remaining days, look for *Asia Weekly* (Sunday) or Monday's *Let's Learn Japanese*, *Media Roundup* and *Viewpoint*. The broadcasts end with the daily *Tokyo Pop-in*. One hour to eastern North America summers only on 5960 kHz via the powerful relay facilities of Radio Canada International in Sackville, New Brunswick. Also year-round to western North America, winters on 9565 kHz, and summers on 9680 (or 11790) kHz. Also available to Asia on 11840, 11860, 11900, 11910, 17810 and 17845 kHz.

Radio Exterior de España ("Spanish National Radio"). Repeat of the 0000 transmission. To eastern North America on 9540 kHz.

Radio For Peace International, Costa Rica. One of the few remaining places where you can still find the peace and "peoplehood" ideals of the Sixties. This hour is the start of English programming—the initial hour being in Spanish. *FIRE* (Feminist International Radio Endeavour) is one of the better offerings from the mélange of programs that make up RFPI's eight-hour cyclical blocks of predominantly counterculture and New Age programming. Sixty minutes of variable reception in Europe and the Americas on 7385 and 9400 kHz. Some transmissions are in the single-sideband mode, which can be properly processed only on certain radios.

Radio Korea International, South Korea. See 0600 for specifics, although programs are a day later, World Day. Sixty minutes to North America on 7550 (or 11810) and 15575 kHz.

Voice of Vietnam. A relay via the facilities of the Voice of Russia, introduced in 1995 and already rescheduled on two occasions. Begins with *news*, then there's *Commentary* or *Weekly Review*, followed by short features and some pleasant Vietnamese music (especially at weekends). Repeated at 0130, 0200 and 0230 on the same channel. May be one hour later in winter. To eastern North America on 7250 kHz. If not found there, try the 5900-5950 kHz range or other frequencies in the 7100-7400 kHz segment.

Voice of Russia World Service. Continuous programming to North America at this hour. *News*, features and music. Tuesday through Saturday, winters, it's *Focus on Asia and the Pacific*, replaced summers by ●*Commonwealth Update* (Tuesday through Saturday only). The second half hour contains mainly musical fare. In summer, look for Tuesday's ●*Folk Box* (Monday evening local American date), ●*Music at your Request* (Friday), jazz (Thursday and Saturday), and ●*Music and Musicians* (from 0111, Sunday and Monday). Pick of the winter fare is Sunday's ●*Audio Book Club.* Where to tune? In eastern North America winters, shoot for 5940, 7105, 7165 and 7180 kHz. Best bets in summer are likely to be 9530, 9620 and 11750 kHz. If these don't hack it, dial around nearby—the Voice of Russia tends to change its frequencies more often than most other stations. For western North America, it's summers only. Try 12050, 13645, 13665, 15180, 15425 and 15580 kHz.

Radio Habana Cuba. The start of four hours of continuous programming to eastern North America, and made up of *news* and features such as *Latin America Newsline, DXers Unlimited, The Mailbag Show* and ●*The Jazz Place*, interspersed with some good Cuban music. To eastern North America on 6000 kHz. Also available on 9830 kHz upper sideband, though not all radios, unfortunately, can process such signals.

Radio Australia. *World News*, followed Monday through Friday by *Australian News*, a sports bulletin and *Network Asia*. Weekends, there's *Oz Sounds* and *The Australian Scene* (Saturday), and *Book Reading* and *The Europeans* (Sunday). Continuous programming to Asia and the Pacific on about ten channels, and heard in North America (best during summer) on 15240, 15365, 17795 and 17860 kHz. Best for East Asia is 17715 kHz, but listeners in southeastern parts can also tune to 15415, 15425, 15510 and 17750 kHz. In Europe, try 15425 and 15510 kHz. Some channels carry a separate sports service on winter Saturdays.

Radio Yugoslavia. Winters only at this time. *News*, reports and short features, dealing almost exclusively with local and regional topics. Thirty minutes to eastern North America on 6195 or 7115 kHz. One hour earlier in summer.

HCJB—Voice of the Andes, Ecuador. *Studio 9*, featuring nine minutes of world and Latin American *news*, followed Tuesday through Saturday (Monday through Friday, local American day) by 20 minutes of in-depth reporting on Latin America. The final portion of *Studio 9* is given over to one of a variety of 30-minute features—including *You Should Know* (issues and ethics, Tuesday), *El Mundo Futuro* (science, Wednesday), *Ham Radio Today* (Thursday), *What's Cooking in the Andes* (Friday), and the unique ●*Música del Ecuador* (Saturday). On Sunday (Saturday evening in the Americas), news is followed by *DX Partyline*, which in turn is replaced Monday by *Saludos Amigos*—HCJB's international friendship program. Continuous programming to eastern North America on 9745 kHz.

Voice of America. *News*, followed Tuesday through Saturday (Monday through Friday evenings in the target area) by the excellent ●*Report to the Americas*, a series of news features about the United States and other countries in the Western Hemisphere. This is replaced Sunday by *On the Line* and ●*Press Conference U.S.A.*, and Monday by the science program ●*New Horizons* and ●*Issues in the News*. To the Americas on 5995, 6130, 7405, 9455, 9775 and 13740 kHz.

Croatian Radio. Eight minutes of *news* from Croatian Radio's Zagreb studio. Best heard in Europe and eastern North America, but also heard else-

where. Channel usage varies, but try 5895, 7370, 9830, 11635 and 13830 kHz.

WRMI-Radio Miami International, Miami, Florida. Tuesday through Saturday only (local weekday evenings in the Americas). Part of a much longer multilingual transmission to the Caribbean. Thirty minutes of *Viva Miami!*—a potpourri of information, music and entertainment. Also includes regular weather updates during the hurricane season (June-November). Heard in much of the Americas on 9955 kHz. Repeated one hour later during winter.

Radio Ukraine International. Winters only at this time; see 0000 for program details. Sixty minutes of informative programming targeted at eastern North America and European night owls. Try 4780, 7405, 9620, 9810 and 11870 kHz. One hour earlier in summer.

Radio New Zealand International. A package of *news* and features sometimes replaced by live sports commentary. Part of a much longer broadcast for the South Pacific, but also heard in parts of North America (especially during summer) on 15115 kHz.

Radio Tashkent, Uzbekistan. *News* and features reflecting local and regional issues. Thirty minutes to West and South Asia, occasionally heard in North America; winters on 5955, 5975, and 7285 kHz; summers on 7190, 7250, 9715 and 9740 kHz.

FEBC Radio International, Philippines. The final 30 minutes of *Good Morning from Manila* (see 0000 for specifics), followed by a half hour of religious fare. Targeted at South Asia on 15450 kHz, but heard well beyond.

"American Dissident Voices," **WRNO.** This time summers only. Neo-Nazi anti-Israel program, hosted by Kevin Alfred Strom. You have to be a believer to last the course. Thirty minutes Sunday (Saturday evening local

American date) on 7355 kHz; try four hours later on 7395 kHz if preempted by live sports. Targeted at North America, but reaches beyond. Is followed by "Herald of Truth", another disestablishmentarian program of a similar vein.

WWCR, Nashville, Tennessee. Carries a variety of disestablishmentarian programs at this hour, depending on the day of the week. Winters, there's "Protecting your Wealth", "World of Prophecy" and "Full Disclosure Live" on 5065 kHz; and "The Baker Report" (replaced summers by "Protecting Your Wealth") on 7435 kHz.

WJCR, Upton, Kentucky. Continues with country gospel music for North American listeners on 7490 and 13595 kHz. Also with religious programs to North America at this hour are **WYFR-Family Radio** on 6065, 9505 and 15440 kHz, **WWCR** on 13845 kHz, **KTBN** on 7510 kHz, and **WHRI-World Harvest Radio** on 5745 kHz. For traditional Catholic programming, tune to **WEWN** on 7425 kHz.

01:30

Radio Austria International. ●*Report from Austria*, which includes a brief bulletin of *news*, followed by a series of current events and human interest stories. Ample coverage of national and regional issues, and an excellent source for news of Central and Eastern Europe. Thirty minutes to North America on 9655 and 9870 kHz; also audible on 13730 kHz, which is targeted farther south.

Radio Sweden. *News* and features of mainly Scandinavian content; see 0030 for specifics. Thirty minutes to Asia and Australasia on one or more frequencies. Try 9695, 9895 and 11695 kHz.

RDP International—Radio Portugal. Summers only at this time. *News*, which usually takes up at least half the broadcast, followed by features: *Visitor's Notebook* (Tuesday), *Musical*

Kaleidoscope (Wednesday), *Challenge of the 90's* (Thursday), *Spotlight on Portugal* (Friday), and either *Listeners' Mailbag* or *DX Program* and *Collector's Corner* (Saturday). There are no broadcasts on Sunday or Monday (Saturday and Sunday evenings local North American days). Only fair reception in eastern North America—worse to the west—on 6175 (or 9705) and 9570 kHz. One hour later in winter.

Radio Nederland. *News*, followed Tuesday through Saturday by ●*Newsline*, a current affairs program. Then there's a different feature each day, including *Sounds Interesting* (music, Wednesday); a media program (Thursday); ●*Research File* (science, Friday) and a documentary (Saturday). Sunday's *The Happy Station* and a series of Monday features complete the week. One hour to South Asia (also widely heard in other parts of the continent, as well as Australasia); winters on 5905, 7305, 9860 and 11655 kHz; and summers on 9860, 9890 and 11655 kHz.

Voice of Greece. Preceded and followed by programming in Greek. Approximately 10 minutes of English *news*, then Greek music, a short feature about the country, and more music. Resumes programming in Greek at 0200. To North America on any three frequencies from 6260, 7448, 9420, 9935 and 11645 kHz.

01:45

Radio Tirana, Albania. Approximately 10 minutes of *news* and commentary from one of Europe's least known countries. To North America on 6145 and 7160 kHz.

02:00

■**BBC World Service for the Americas.** Thirty minutes of ●*Newsday*, followed on different days

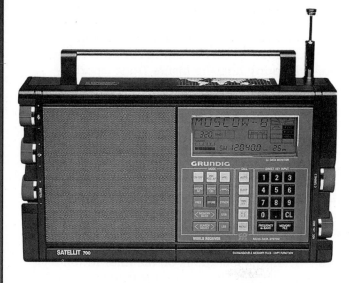

of the week by a variety of features, including a documentary (Wednesday and Friday), classical music (Sunday), the scientific ●*Discovery* (Tuesday), *Thirty-Minute Drama* (Friday), and the arts program *Meridian* on the remaining days. Heard in North America on 5975, 6175, 7325 and 9915 kHz.

■BBC World Service for Asia. ●*Newsday* and a 30-minute feature. Look for some light entertainment at 0230 Tuesday, ●*Andy Kershaw's World of Music* (Wednesday), *Sports International* (Thursday), and Friday's ●*Thirty-Minute Drama*. Continuous to East Asia on 15360 kHz.

Monitor Radio International, USA. See 0000 for program details. To western North America Tuesday through Friday (Monday through Thursday, local American days) on 5850 kHz. Also audible throughout much of North America on 9430 kHz, although not necessarily beamed there. Programming on the remaining days relates to the teachings and experiences of the Christian Science Church.

Radio Cairo, Egypt. Repeat of the 2300 broadcast, and the first hour of a 90-minute potpourri of *news* and features about Egypt and the Arab world. Fair reception and mediocre audio quality to North America on 9475 kHz.

Radio Argentina al Exterior— R.A.E. Tuesday through Saturday only. *News* and short features dealing with aspects of life in Argentina, interspersed with samples of the country's various musical styles, from tango to zamba. Fifty-five minutes to North America on 11710 kHz.

Radio Budapest, Hungary. This time winters only; see 0100 for specifics. Thirty minutes to North America on 6025, 7220 and 9835 kHz. One hour earlier in summer.

Radio Canada International. Starts off with *News*, then Tuesday through Saturday winter (Monday through Friday local American date) it's *Spectrum*. Sunday, there's *Double Exposure* (culture) and *Royal Canadian Air Farce* (self-explanatory), replaced Monday by the unique and popular ●*Quirks and Quarks*. Summers, *News* is followed by features taken from the Canadian Broadcasting Corporation's domestic output. Tuesday through Saturday, there's the *Best of Morningside*; Sunday features *Double Exposure* and *Canadian Air Farce*; and Monday has *The Inside Track* (sports) and a current affairs feature. One hour to North America on 6120, 9755 and 11845 (or 13670) kHz. During summer, 6120 kHz carries a special broadcast Tuesday through Saturday for Canadian peacekeepers in the Caribbean, 30 minutes of which is in French.

Radio Norway International. Winter Mondays (Sunday evenings, local American date) only. *Norway Now*. *News* and features from one of the friendliest stations on the international airwaves. Thirty minutes to western North America on 7450 kHz.

■Deutsche Welle, Germany. *News*, followed Monday through Friday by the highly informative package of ●*Asia Pacific Report* and ●*European Journal*— commentary, interviews, background reports and analysis. These are replaced Saturday by *Commentary*, *The Week in Germany* and *Economic Notebook*. Sunday programming features *Commentary* (or *Sports Report*) and *Mailbag Asia*. Fifty minutes nominally targeted at South Asia, but widely heard elsewhere. Winters on 6035, 6130, 7265, 7285, 7355, 9515, 9615 and 9690 kHz; and summers on 7285, 9615, 9640, 9690, 11945, 11965, 12045 and 15185 kHz.

HCJB—Voice of the Andes, Ecuador. A mixed bag of religious and secular programming, depending on the day of the week. Tuesday (Monday evening in North America) is given over to *Master Control* and *Sounds of Joy;*

Wednesday airs *Unshackled* and the highly enjoyable ●*Blues, Rags and All That Jazz*; and Thursday there's *The Latest Catch* (a feature for radio enthusiasts), *The Book Nook* and *Sounds of Joy*. On other days, you can hear *What's Cooking in the Andes?* (0230 Friday), the Europe-oriented *On-Line* and contemporary Christian music in *On Track* (Saturday), *Solstice* (a youth program, 0230 Sunday), and Monday's *Radio Reading Room* and *HCJB Today*. Continuous to North America on 9745 kHz.

Voice of Free China, Taiwan. *News*, followed by features. The last is *Let's Learn Chinese*, which has a series of segments for beginning, intermediate and advanced learners. Other features include *Jade Bells and Bamboo Pipes* (Monday), *Kaleidoscope* and *Main Roads and Byways* (Tuesday), *Music Box* (Wednesday), *Perspectives* and *Journey into Chinese Culture* (Thursday), *Confrontation* and *New Record Time* (Friday), *Reflections* (Saturday) and *Adventures of Mahlon and Jeanie* and *Mailbag Time* (Sunday). One hour to North and Central America on 5950, 9680 and 11740 kHz; to East Asia on 15345 kHz; to Southeast Asia on 11825 kHz; and to Australasia on 7130 kHz.

Voice of Russia World Service. Continuous to North America at this hour. *News*, features and music to suit all tastes. Winter fare includes ●*Commonwealth Update* (Tuesday through Saturday), ●*Music and Musicians* (Sunday and Monday), and after 0230, ●*Folk Box* (Tuesday), ●*Music at your Request* (Friday), and jazz on Thursday and Saturday. Best in summer is ●*Audio Book Club* at 0231 Tuesday, Thursday and Saturday; though some listeners may prefer *Science and Engineering* (0211 Wednesday) or the business-oriented *Newmarket* (same time, Tuesday). Note that these days are World Time; locally in North America it

will be the previous evening. Winters in eastern North America, try 5940, 7105, 7165 and 7180 kHz; in summer there's just 9530 and 9620 kHz. Failing these, dial around nearby—the Voice of Russia tends to change its frequencies more often than most other stations. Western North America is better served. Winters, choose from 7270, 9825, 9850, 12050, 13640 and 15425 kHz; summers from 12050, 13645, 13665, 15180, 15425 and 15580 kHz.

Radio Habana Cuba. See 0100 for program details. Continues to eastern North America on 6000 and 9820 kHz. Also available on 9830 kHz upper sideband.

Radio Australia. Continuous programming to Asia and the Pacific, but well heard in much of North America. Begins with *World News*, then Monday through Friday there's a summary of the latest sports news followed by *Network Asia*. At 0210 Saturday, there's *Feedback* (a listener-response program) and *Indian Pacific*. These are replaced Sunday by *Charting Australia* and *Correspondents Report*. Targeted at Asia and the Pacific on about ten channels, and heard in North America (best during summer) on 15240, 15365, 17795 and 17860 kHz. For East and Southeast Asia, choose from 15415, 15425, 15510, 17715 and 17750 kHz. European night owls can try 15425 and 15510 kHz. Some of these channels carry a separate sports service on summer weekends and winter Saturdays.

Radio For Peace International, Costa Rica. Part of an eight-hour cyclical block of social-conscience, counter-culture and New Age programming audible in Europe and the Americas on 7385 and 9400 kHz. One of international broadcasting's more unusual features, *The Far Right Radio Review*, can be heard at 0200 Wednesday (Tuesday evening in the Americas). As we go to press, there's a communications feature, *World of Radio*, at the same time

Sunday, but the timing of this program tends to change. Other offerings include *Amnesty International Reports* (0230 Sunday) and *My Green Earth* (a nature program for children, same time Monday). Some transmissions are in the single-sideband mode, which can be properly processed only on some radios.

Croatian Radio. Eight minutes of *news* from Croatian Radio's Zagreb studio. Best heard in Europe and eastern North America, but also heard elsewhere. Channel usage varies, but try 5895, 7370, 9830, 11635 and 13830 kHz.

Voice of Vietnam. A relay to eastern North America via the facilities of the Voice of Russia. See 0100 for further details.

Radio Romania International. *News*, commentary, press review and features on Romania. Regular spots include Wednesday's *Youth Club* (Tuesday evening, local American date), Thursday's *Romanian Musicians*, and Friday's *Listeners' Letterbox* and ●*Skylark* (Romanian folk music). Fifty-five minutes to North America on 5990, 6155, 9510, 9570 and 11940 kHz.

"American Dissident Voices", WRNO. Winter Sundays only (Saturday evenings, local American date) at this time. See 0100 for program details. Thirty minutes to North America and beyond on 7355 kHz; try four hours later on 7395 kHz if preempted by live sports.

WWCR, Nashville, Tennessee. Carries a variety of disestablishmentarian programs at this hour, depending on the day of the week, and whether it is summer or winter. These include "Protecting Your Wealth", "World of Prophecy" and "Radio Free America"; choose between 5065 and 7435 kHz.

WJCR, Upton, Kentucky. Continues with country gospel music for North American listeners on 7490 kHz. Also with religious broadcasts to North America at this hour are **WYFR-Family Radio** on 6065, 9505 and 15440 kHz, **WWCR** on 5935 kHz, **KAIJ on** 5810 kHz, **KTBN** on 7510 kHz, **WHRI-World Harvest Radio** on 5745 kHz. Traditional Catholic programming can be heard via **WEWN** on 7425 kHz.

02:30

Radio Sweden. *News* and features concentrating heavily on Scandinavia. See 0030 for program details. Thirty minutes to North America, winters on 6195 and 7120 kHz, and summers on 7120 and 9850 kHz.

Radyo Pilipinas, Philippines. Monday through Saturday, the broadcast opens with *Voice of Democracy* and closes with *World News*. These are separated by a daily feature: *Save the Earth* (Monday), *The Philippines Today* (Tuesday), *Changing World* (Wednesday), *Business Updates* (Thursday), *Brotherhood of Men* (Friday), and Saturday's *Listeners and Friends*. Sunday fare consists of *Asean Connection, Sports Focus* and *News Roundup*. Approximately one hour to South and East Asia on 17760, 17865 and 21580 kHz.

Radio Budapest, Hungary. Summers only at this time. *News* and features, some of which are broadcast on a regular basis. These include Tuesday's *Musica Hungarica* (local Monday evening in North America), *Focus on Business* and *The Weeklies* (Thursday), *Letter Home* (Friday) and *Profiles* (Sunday). Thirty minutes to North America on 6000, 9835 and 11910 kHz. One hour later in winter.

Radio Nederland. Repeat of the 0030 transmission, except Sunday, when there is a first airing of features from the Monday 0230 broadcast. Fifty-five minutes to South Asia, but heard well beyond, on 9860, 9890 (summers) and 11655 kHz.

Radio Tirana, Albania. Just about the only way to keep up with what is happening in Europe's most obscure backwater, with some pleasantly enjoyable music, to boot. Twenty-five minutes to North America on 6145 and 7160 kHz.

RDP International—Radio Portugal. Winters only at this time. See 0130 for details. Thirty minutes Tuesday through Saturday (weekday evenings local North American days). Fair in eastern North America—worse to the west—on 6175 (or 9705) and 9570 kHz. One hour earlier in summer.

02:50

Vatican Radio. Concentrates heavily, but not exclusively, on issues affecting Catholics around the world. Twenty minutes to eastern North America, winters on 6095 and 7305 kHz, and summers on 7305 and 9605 kHz.

03:00

■BBC World Service for the Americas. Five minutes of world *news*, followed by the best 10 minutes of business and financial reporting you are ever likely to hear. The next quarter-hour is devoted to the highly informative *Sports Roundup*. These are followed Tuesday through Saturday (weekday evenings in the Americas) by ●*The*

Mary Kroszner

The British Empire is gone, and even Greenwich Mean Time isn't called that any more. Yet, Britannia still rules the international airwaves—deservedly so, thanks to the BBC World Service.

World Today. Other offerings at this hour include ●*Brain of Britain* or its substitute (0330 Monday), *From Our Own Correspondent* (same time Sunday), *Development 96* (0345 Tuesday) and the environmental ●*Global Concerns* (0345 Saturday). Audible in North America on 5975, 6175 and (to 0330) 7325 kHz.

■BBC World Service for Europe. Begins with *World News* and *Sports Roundup*, then Monday through Saturday it's ●*Europe Today* (may be replaced winters by features). Sunday fare consists of *From Our Own Correspondent* and *Waveguide*. To Eastern Europe on 6180 (summers) and 6195 kHz, and to the Mideast (different programs at 0330-0400) on 9410 and 11760 kHz.

■BBC World Service for Africa. Identical to the service for Europe until 0330, then there's a daily bulletin of African *news*, followed Monday through Friday by *Network Africa*, a fast-moving breakfast show. On Saturday it's *African Quiz* or *This Week And Africa*, replaced Sunday by *Postmark Africa*. If you are interested in what's happening in Africa, tune in to 3255, 6005, 6190, 9610 and 11730 kHz, some of which are only available from 0330 onwards.

■BBC World Service for Asia. Starts with *World News*, 10 minutes of business and financial reports, and the quarter-hour *Sports Roundup*. Weekdays, the final 30 minutes are taken up by ●*Off the Shelf* and features for students of English. Best of the weekend offerings is Saturday's *The Vintage Chart Show*. Continuous to East Asia till 0330 on 15360 kHz, and thereafter on 11955 and 15280 kHz.

Monitor Radio International, USA. See 0000 for program details. To western North America, Tuesday through Friday (Monday through Thursday, local American days) on 5850 kHz. Also to East Africa (and heard well beyond) on 7535 kHz. Programs on other days are religious in nature.

Voice of Free China, Taiwan. Similar to the 0200 transmission, but with the same programs broadcast one day later. To North and Central America on 5950 and 9680 kHz; to East Asia on 11745 and 15345 kHz; and to Southeast Asia on 11825 kHz.

China Radio International. Repeat of the 0000 transmission. One hour to North America on 9690, 9710 and 11715 kHz.

■Deutsche Welle, Germany. *News,* then Tuesday through Saturday (weekday evenings in North America) it's ●*European Journal*—a comprehensive package of commentary, interviews, background reports and analysis. This is followed by *Economic Notebook* (Tuesday), ●*Insight* (Wednesday), *German by Radio* (Thursday), *Science and Technology* (Friday), and *Through German Eyes* (Saturday). Sunday and Monday, there's a repeat of the 0100 broadcast. Fifty minutes to North America and the Caribbean, winters on 6045, 6085, 6120, 9535, and 9650 kHz; and summers on 6085, 6185, 9535, 9615, 9640 and 11750 kHz.

Voice of America. Three and a half hours (four at weekends) of continuous programming aimed at an African audience. Monday through Friday, there's the informative and entertaining ●*Daybreak Africa,* followed by thirty minutes of features in Special English. Weekend programming consists of *News* and *VOA Saturday/VOA Sunday,* a mixed bag of sports, science, business and other features. Although beamed to Africa, this service is widely heard elsewhere, including many parts of the United States. Try 5980, 6115, 7105, 7280, 7340, 7405, 9575 and 15300 kHz.

Voice of Russia World Service. Continues to North America. *News,* then winters it's a listener-response program (Thursday and Saturday through Monday), the business-oriented *Newmarket* (Tuesday), or *Science and Engineering* (Wednesday). At 0331, there's ●*Audio Book Club* (Tuesday, Thursday and Saturday), *Russian by Radio* (Wednesday and Friday), and music on Sunday and Monday. Note that these days are World Time, so locally in North America it will be the previous evening. In summer, look for *News and Views* followed by a variety of music programs. For eastern North America winters, try 5940, 7105, 7165 and 7180 kHz; summers, it's either 9620 or 9665 kHz. Failing these, try dialing around nearby—the Voice of Russia is not renowned for sticking to its frequencies. Western North America is better served. Good winter bets are 5905, 7175, 7270, 7345, 9825, 9850 and 12050 kHz; in summer, go for 12050, 13645, 13665, 15180 (or 13790), 15425 and 15580 kHz.

Radio Australia. *World News,* followed Monday through Friday by a sports bulletin and *Network Asia.* These are replaced weekends by Saturday's *Soundabout* and Sunday's *Book Reading* and *At Your Request.* Continuous to Asia and the Pacific on about ten channels, and heard in North America (best during summer) on 15240, 15365, 17795 and 17860 kHz. In East and Southeast Asia, pick from 15415, 15425, 15510, 17715 and 17750 kHz. If you're in Europe, and still awake, try 15425 and 15510 kHz. Some of these channels carry a separate sports service at weekends. A popular choice with many listeners.

Radio Habana Cuba. Continuous programming to eastern North America on 6000 and 9820 kHz, and also available on 9830 kHz upper sideband.

Radio Thailand. Thirty minutes of *Newshour;* see 0000 for specifics. To western North America winters on 11890 kHz, and summers on 15370 kHz. Also available to Asia on 9655 and 11905 kHz.

Radio Ukraine International. Summers only at this time. Repeat of the 0000 broadcast (see there for specifics). One hour to Europe and eastern North America on 7405, 9685, 9835 and 9860 kHz. One hour later in winter.

HCJB—Voice of the Andes, Ecuador. Predominantly religious programming at this hour. Try *Joy International*, a selection of Christian music favorites, at 0330 Monday (local Sunday in North America). Continuous to the United States and Canada on 9745 kHz.

Radio Prague, Czech Republic. Repeat of the 0000 broadcast. A half hour to North America on 5930 and 7345 kHz.

Radio Cairo, Egypt. The final half hour of a 90-minute broadcast to North America on 9475 kHz.

Radio Japan. *News*, followed by the weekday *Radio Japan Magazine Hour*. This consists of *Japan Diary*, a feature (two on Tuesday), *Close Up*, *News Commentary*, and a final news bulletin. Monday (Sunday evening in North America), you can hear *Sports Spotlight*, Tuesday features *Japanese Culture* and *Today*, Wednesday has *Asian Report*, Thursday brings *Crosscurrents*, and Friday's offering is *Business Focus*. Weekend fare is made up of Saturday's *This Week* and Sunday's *Hello from Tokyo*. Sixty minutes to western North America winters on 9565 kHz, and summers on 9680 (or 11790) kHz. Available to Asia on 11840 (or 15210) and 17810 kHz. Winters only, can also be heard in eastern North America on 5960 kHz. There is an additional 30-minute year-round version for western North America and Central America on 11885, 11895 and 15230 kHz.

Croatian Radio. Eight minutes of *news* from Croatian Radio's Zagreb studio. Best heard in Europe and eastern North America, but also heard elsewhere. Channel usage varies, but try 5895, 7370, 9830, 11635 and 13830 kHz.

Radio New Zealand International. A friendly broadcasting package targeted at a regional audience. Part of a much longer transmission for the South Pacific, but also heard in parts of North America (especially during summer) on 15115 kHz. Often carries commentaries of local sporting events.

Voice of Turkey. Summers only at this time. Repeat of the 2200 broadcast. *News*, followed by *Review of the Turkish Press* and features (some of them arcane) with a strong local flavor. Selections of Turkish popular and classical music complete the program. Fifty minutes to eastern North America on 9445 kHz. One hour later during winter.

WJCR, Upton, Kentucky. Continues with country gospel music for North American listeners on 7490 kHz. Also with religious programs to North America at this hour are **WYFR-Family Radio** on 6065 and 9505 kHz, **WWCR** on 5935 kHz, **KIAJ** on 5810 kHz and **KTBN** on 7510 kHz. For traditional Catholic fare, try **WEWN** on 7425 kHz.

"For the People," WHRI, Noblesville, Indiana. A two-hour edited repeat of the 1900 (1800 in summer) broadcast. Promotes classic populism— an American political tradition going back to 1891. Suspicious of concentrated wealth and power, *For the People* promotes economic nationalism ("buying foreign amounts to treason"), little-reported health concepts and a sharply progressive income tax, while opposing the "New World Order" and international banking. This two-hour talk show, hosted by former deejay Chuck Harder, can be heard Tuesday-Saturday (Monday through Friday local days) on 5745 kHz. Targeted at North America, but heard beyond.

Radio For Peace International, Costa Rica. Continues with a variety of counterculture and social-conscience features. There is also a listener-response program at 0330 Wednesday

Radio Slovakia International staff celebrates Christmas.

and Sunday (Tuesday and Saturday evenings in the Americas). Audible in Europe and the Americas on 7385 and 9400 kHz. Some transmissions are in the single-sideband mode, which can be properly processed only on some radios.

WWCR, Nashville, Tennessee. "Radio Free America", a populist show hosted by Tom Valentine for two hours Tuesday through Saturday (Monday through Friday evenings, local American date). Winters, starts at this time; summers, it is already at its halfway point. Well heard in North America on 5065 kHz.

03:30

United Arab Emirates Radio, Dubai. *News,* then a feature devoted to Arab and Islamic history or culture. Twenty-five minutes to North America on 11945, 13675, 15400 and 17890 (or 21485) kHz; heard best during the warm-weather months.

Radio Austria International. Winters only at this time. Repeat of the 0130 broadcast. A half hour to North and Central America on 9870 kHz. Also worth a try is 13730 kHz, targeted at South America.

Radio Sweden. Repeat of the 0230 transmission. See 0030 for program details. Thirty minutes to North America, winters on 6200 and 7120 kHz, and summers on 7120 and 9850 kHz.

Radio Prague, Czech Republic. Repeat of the 0000 broadcast. A half hour to the Mideast and beyond. Winters on 7345 kHz, and summers on 9480 kHz.

Radio Budapest, Hungary. This time winters only; see 0230 for specifics. Thirty minutes to North America on 5965, 7220 and 9835 kHz. One hour earlier in summer.

Voice of Greece. Actually starts around 0335. Ten to fifteen minutes of English *news,* preceded by long periods

of Greek music and programming. To North America on any three frequencies from 6260, 7448, 9420, 9935 and 11645 kHz.

04:00

■BBC World Service for the Americas. Starts with the half-hour ●*Newsdesk*, followed Tuesday through Saturday (local weekday evenings in the Americas) by the eclectic and entertaining ●*Outlook*. This is replaced Sunday by ●*Science in Action*, and Monday by ●*The Learning World* and ●*Health Matters*. A full hour of top-notch programming to North America on 5975 kHz. The first 30 minutes are also available winters on 6175 kHz.

■BBC World Service for Europe. The half-hour ●*Newsdesk*, followed Monday through Saturday by ●*Europe Today* (replaced by a variety of features for listeners in the Mideast, where this service is also targeted). Top-notch news reporting. Continuous to Europe on 6180 and 6195 kHz (also on 9410 kHz during summer), and to the Mideast on 9410, 11760, 12095 and 15575 KHz.

■BBC World Service for Africa. ●*Newsdesk*, followed at 0430 by *African News*. Monday through Friday, this is followed by *Network Africa*, Saturday by a repeat of the 0330 feature, and Sunday by *Education Express*. Targeted at African listeners, but also heard elsewhere, on 3255, 6005, 6190, 7160, 9610 and 11730 kHz.

■BBC World Service for Asia. Opens with 10 minutes of *World News* and a five-minute mini-feature, then Tuesday through Saturday it's ●*The World Today*. Pick of the remaining pack includes *A Jolly Good Show* (0415 Sunday), ●*The Learning World* (same time Monday), ●*Brain of Britain* (or its replacement) (0430 Wednesday), ●*Megamix* (0430 Thursday), ●*Folk Routes* (0445 Friday), and ●*Science in Action* (0430 Saturday). Continuous to East Asia on 11955 and 15280 kHz.

Monitor Radio International, USA. See 0000 for program details. Tuesday through Friday to eastern Europe on 7535 kHz, and to central and southern Africa on 9840 kHz. Programming on the remaining days relates to the beliefs and teachings of the Christian Science Church.

Radio Habana Cuba. Continuous programming to eastern North America and the Caribbean on 6180 and 9820 kHz. Also available on 9830 kHz upper sideband.

Swiss Radio International. Repeat of the 0100 broadcast to North America on 6135, 9885 and 9905 kHz. Newsy, but dry. There is an additional 30- minute feature on 9905 kHz which is a simulcast of SRI's satellite programming.

HCJB—Voice of the Andes, Ecuador. Sixty minutes of religious programming. *Afterglow* (0430 Sunday), *Songs in the Night* (0400 Monday) and *Nightsounds* (0430 Tuesday through Saturday) probably offer the most appeal. Continuous to eastern North America on 9745 kHz.

Radio Australia. *World News*, then Monday through Friday it's a short summary of the latest sports news followed by *Pacific Beat* and ●*International Report*. These are replaced Saturday by *Book Reading* and *Indian Pacific*, and Sunday by *Feedback* and *Correspondents Report*. Continuous to Asia and the Pacific on about ten channels, and heard in North America (best during summer) on 15240, 15365, 17795 and 17860 kHz. For East and Southeast Asia, choose from 15415, 15425 (also audible in parts of Europe), 15510, 17715 and 17750 kHz (15510 and 17715 kHz are only available from 0430, Monday through Friday). Some channels carry separate sports programming at weekends.

■Deutsche Welle, Germany.
News, followed Monday through Friday by ●*Africa Report* (*Africa Highlight* on Mondays) and the informative and in-depth ●*European Journal*. Saturday features *Commentary*, *Africa This Week* and ●*Man and Environment*; substituted Sunday by *Sports Report* (or *Commentary*), *International Talking Point* and *People and Places*. A 50-minute broadcast aimed primarily at Africa, but also heard in parts of the Mideast and eastern North America. Winters on 6015, 6045, 6065, 7225, 7265, 9565 and 9765 kHz; and summers on 5990, 6015, 6185, 7150, 7225, 9565, 9765 and 11765 kHz.

Radio Canada International.
News, followed Tuesday through Saturday by the topical *Spectrum*. This is replaced Sunday by the science feature *Innovation Canada*, and Monday by a listener-response program. Thirty minutes to the Mideast, winters on 6150, 9505 and 9670 kHz; summers on 9650, 11835, 11905 and 15275 kHz.

China Radio International.
Repeat of the 0000 transmission. One hour to North America winters on 9730 kHz, and summers on 9560 and 11680 kHz.

Radio Norway International.
Summer Mondays (Sunday evenings in the target area) only. *Norway Now*. A half hour of *news* and human-interest stories targeted at western North America on 7480 kHz.

Radio Bulgaria. Summers only at this time. Starts with 15 minutes of *news*, followed Tuesday through Friday by *Today* (current events), and Saturday by *Weekly Spotlight*, a summary of the major political events of the week. At other times, there are features dealing with multiple aspects of Bulgarian life and culture, including some lively Balkan folk music. To eastern North America and Central America on 9700 and 11720 kHz. One hour later in winter.

Voice of America. Directed to Europe, Africa and the Mideast, but widely heard elsewhere. *News*, followed Monday through Friday by ●*VOA Business Report*. On the half-hour, the African service continues with ●*Daybreak Africa*, replaced to other areas by *Stateside*—a look at issues and personalities in all walks of American life. Weekends, the *news* is followed by 50 minutes of *VOA Saturday/VOA Sunday*. To Europe, North Africa and the Mideast on 3985, 5995, 6010, 6040, 7170 and 7200 kHz, plus 11965 and 15205 kHz in summer. The mainstream African service is available on 5980 (to 0430), 7265, 7280, 7340 (to 0430), 7405, 9575 and 15300 kHz. Reception of some of these channels is also good in North America.

Radio Romania International. An abbreviated version of the 0200 transmission, beginning with national and international *news* and commentary, then the feature program from the first half hour of the 0200 broadcast. Thirty minutes to North America on 5990, 6155, 9510, 9570 and 11940 kHz.

Radio Ukraine International. Winters only at this time. Repeat of the 0100 broadcast (see 0000 for specifics). Sixty minutes to Europe and North America on 4780, 7405, 9810 and 11870 kHz. One hour earlier in summer.

Voice of Turkey. Winters only at this time. Repeat of the 2300 broadcast; see 0300 for specifics. Fifty minutes to eastern North America on 9445 kHz. One hour earlier in summer.

WJCR, Upton, Kentucky. Continues with country gospel music for North American listeners on 7490 kHz. Also with religious programs to North America at this hour are **WYFR-Family Radio** on 6065 and 9505 kHz, **WWCR** on 5935 kHz, **KAIJ** on 5810 kHz and **KTBN** on 7510 kHz. Traditional Catholic programming is available via **WEWN** on 7425 kHz

Kol Israel. Summers only at this time. *News* for 15 minutes from Israel Radio's domestic network. To Europe and

MFJ's high performance *tuned* active antenna rivals long wires hundreds of feet long!

MFJ-1020B
$79⁹⁵

Receive strong clear signals from all over the world with this indoor *tuned* active antenna that rivals the reception of long wires hundreds of feet long!

"World Radio TV Handbook" says MFJ-1020 is a "fine value . . . fair price . . . performs very well indeed!"

Set it on your desktop and listen to the world!

No need to hassle with putting up an outside antenna and then have to disconnect it during storms.

Covers 300 kHz to 30 MHz so you can pick up all of your favorite stations. And discover new ones you couldn't get before. Tuned circuitry minimizes intermodulation, improves selectivity and reduces noise from phantom signals, images and out-of-band signals.

Adjustable telescoping whip gives you maximum signal with minimum noise. Full set of controls for tuning, band selection, gain and On-Off/Bypass. 5x2x6 in.

Doubles as preselector for external antenna. Use 9 volt battery or 110 VAC with MFJ-1312, $12.95.

MFJ *super DSP filter*

MFJ-784B
$239⁹⁵
Super filter uses state-of-the-art *Digital Signal Processing* technology!

It *automatically* searches for and eliminates *multiple* heterodynes.

Tunable, pre-set and programmable "brick wall" filters with *60 dB attenuation just 75 Hz away from cutoff frequency* literally knocks out interference signals.

Adaptive noise reduction reduces random background noise up to 20 dB.

Works with all signals including all voice, CW and data signals. Plugs between radio and speaker or phones.

Dual Tunable Audio Filter

MFJ-752C
$99⁹⁵
Two separately tunable filters let you peak desired signals and notch out interference at the same time. You can peak, notch, low or high pass signals to eliminate heterodynes and interference. Plugs between radio and speaker or phones. 10x2x6 in.

Super Active Antenna

"World Radio TV Handbook" says MFJ-1024 is a "first rate easy-to-operate active antenna . . . quiet . . . excellent dynamic range . . . good gain . . . low noise . . . broad frequency coverage."

Mount it outdoors away from electrical noise for maximum signal, minimum noise. Covers 50 KHz to 30 MHz.

Receives strong, clear signals from all over the world. 20dB attenuator, gain control, ON LED. Switch two receivers and aux. or active antenna. 6x3x5 in. remote has 54 inch whip, 50 ft. coax. 3x2x4 in. 12 VDC or 110 VAC with MFJ-1312, **MFJ-1024** $129⁹⁵ $12.95.

DXers' World Map Clock

Shows time of any DX throughout the world on world map! Displays day/ week/ month/date/year and hour /minute/second in 12 or 24 hour format. Has daylight-savings-time feature.

MFJ-112
$24⁹⁵

Push-buttons let you move a flashing time zone east and west on the map to a major city in every time zone. 4¹/₂x3³/₈x2¹/₄ in.

MFJ Antenna Matcher

MFJ-959B
$99⁹⁵

Matches your antenna to your receiver so you get maximum signal and minimum loss.

Preamp with gain control boosts weak stations 10 times. 20 dB attenuator prevents overload. Pushbuttons let you select 2 antennas and 2 receivers. Covers 1.6-30 MHz. 9x2x6 inches.

SWL's Guide for Apartments

World renowned SWL expert Ed Noll's newest book gives you the key to hearing news as it happens, concerts from Vienna and soccer games from Germany!

MFJ-36
$9⁹⁵

He tells you what shortwave bands to listen to, the best times to tune in, how to DX and QSL, how to send for schedules and construct *indoor* antennas plus many band by band DX tips.

High-Q Passive Preselector

MFJ-956
$39⁹⁵

High-Q passive LC preselector that lets you boost your favorite stations while rejecting images, intermod and other phantom signals. 1.5-30 MHz. Has bypass and receiver grounded position.

High-Gain Preselector

MFJ-1045C
$69⁹⁵

High-gain, high-Q receiver preselector covers 1.8-54 MHz. Boost weak signals 10 times with low noise dual gate MOSFET. Reject out-of-band signals and images with high-Q tuned circuits. Pushbuttons let you select 2 antennas and 2 receivers. Dual coax and phono connectors. Use 9-18 VDC or 110 VAC with MFJ-1312, $129.95.

MFJ-1278B Multimode

MFJ-1278B
$299⁹⁵
Discover a whole new world of communications you never knew existed with this MFJ-1278B, your receiver and computer.

You'll have fun listening to worldwide *packet* networks and watching hams exchange *color SSTV* pictures with their buddies around the world.

You'll marvel at *full color FAX* news photos as they come to life on your screen. You'll see weather changes on highly detailed *weather maps*.

You'll eavesdrop on late breaking news as it happens on *RTTY*. Wanna copy some *CW*? Just watch your screen.

Requires MFJ-1289, $59.95, MultiCom™, software and cables.

Tap into *secret* Shortwave Signals

Turn mysterious signals into exciting text messages with this new MFJ MultiReader™

MFJ-462B

$169⁹⁵

Plug this *MFJ MultiReader™* into your shortwave receiver's earphone jack.

Then *watch* mysterious chirps, whistles and buzzing sounds of RTTY, ASCII, AMTOR and CW turn into exciting text messages as they scroll across your easy-to-read LCD display.

You'll *read* fascinating commerical, military, diplomatic, weather, aeronautical, maritime and amateur traffic from all over the world . . . traffic your friends can't read -- unless they have a decoder.

Eavesdrop on the World

Eavesdrop on the world's press agencies transmitting *unedited* late breaking news in English -- China News in Taiwan, Tanjug Press in Serbia, Iraqui News in Iraq.

Printer monitors 24 hours a day

MFJ's exclusive *TelePrinterPort™* lets you monitor any station 24 hours a day by printing their transmissions on your Epson compatible printer. Printer cable, **MFJ-5412**, $9.95.

MFJ *MessageSaver™*

You can save several pages of text in 8K of memory for re-reading or later review using MFJ's exclusive *MessageSaver™*.

Easy to use, tune and read

It's easy to use -- just push a button to select modes and features from a menu.

It's easy to tune -- a precision tuning indicator makes tuning your receiver fast and easy for best copy.

It's easy to read -- the 2 line 16 character LCD display is mounted on a sloped front panel for easy reading.

Copies most standard shifts and speeds. Has *MFJ AutoTrak™* Morse code speed tracking.

Use 12 VDC or use 110 VAC with MFJ-1312B AC adapter, $12.95. 5¹/₄x2¹/₂x5¹/₄ inches.

Easy-Up Antennas Book

How to build and put up inexpensive, fully tested wire antennas using readily available parts that'll bring signals in like you've never heard before. Covers antennas from 100 KHz to 1000 MHz.

MFJ-38 **$16⁹⁵**

Compact Active Antenna

Plug this new *compact* MFJ all band active antenna into your general coverage receiver and you'll hear strong clear signals from all over the world from 300 KHz to 200 MHz.

MFJ-1022 **$39⁹⁵**

Detachable 20 inch telescoping antenna. 9 volt battery or 110 VAC with MFJ-1312B, $12.95. 3¹/₈x1¹/₄x4 in.

MFJ Antenna Switches

MFJ-1704 **$59⁹⁵**

MFJ-1702B **$21⁹⁵**

MFJ-1704 heavy duty antenna switch lets you select 4 antennas or ground them for static and lightning protection. Unused antennas automatically grounded. Replaceable lightning surge protection device. Good to over 500 MHz. 60 db isolation at 30 MHz.

MFJ-1702B, $21.95, for 2 antennas.

Super *Hi-Q Loop™* Antenna

The MFJ *Super Loop™* is a professional quality remotely tuned 10 to 30 MHz high-Q loop antenna. It's very quiet and has a very narrow bandwidth that reduces receiver overloading and out-of-band interference.

MFJ-1782 **$269⁹⁵**

MFJ 12/24 Hour Clocks

MFJ-107B **$9⁹⁵**

MFJ-108B **$19⁹⁵**

MFJ-105B **$19⁹⁵**

MFJ-108B, *dual* clock displays 24 UTC and 12 hour local time.

MFJ-107B, single clock shows you 24 hour UTC time. *3 star rated* by *Passport to World Band Radio!*

MFJ-105B, accurate 24 hour UTC quartz *wall clock* with huge 10 inch face.

World Band Radio *Kit*

MFJ-8100K **$59⁹⁵** *kit*

MFJ-8100W **$79⁹⁵** *wired*

Build this *regenerative* shortwave receiver *kit* and listen to shortwave signals from all over the world. With just a 10 foot wire antenna.

Has RF stage, vernier reduction drive, smooth regeneration, five bands.

Code Practice Oscillator

MFJ-557 **$24⁹⁵**

Have fun learning Morse code with this MFJ-557 Deluxe Code Practice Oscillator. It's mounted with Morse key and speaker on a heavy steel base so it stays put on your table. Earphone jack, tone, volume controls, adjustable key.

Enjoy *World Bands* in your car

Add *World Band* shortwave reception to your AM car radio and hear late breaking news as it happens from all over the world! Covers 19, 25, 31, 49 Meters. Plugs between radio and antenna.

MFJ-306 **$79⁹⁵**

Personal Morse Code Tutor™

Learn Morse code anywhere with this pocket size battery operated *MFJ Personal Morse Code Tutor™!*

MFJ-411 **$79⁹⁵**

This pocket size tutor takes you from zero code speed with a beginner's course to Extra Class with customized code practice.

Select letters, numbers, punctuations or prosigns or any combination or words or QSOs with normal or Farnsworth spacing. Use earphones or built-in speaker.

Receive FAX, WeFAX, RTTY, ASCII, Morse Code

Use your PC computer

MFJ-1214PC **$149⁹⁵**

and radio to receive and display brilliant *full color* FAX news photos and incredible 16 gray level WeFAX weather maps. Also receives RTTY, ASCII and Morse code.

Animate weather maps. Display 10 global pictures *simultaneously*. Zoom any part of picture or map. Frequency manager lists over 900 FAX stations. Automatic picture capture and save.

Includes interface, software, cables, power supply, manual, Jump-Start™ guide.

North America on 7465 and 9435 kHz. One hour later in winter.

Radio New Zealand Interna-tion-al. Continues with regional programming for the South Pacific. Part of a much longer broadcast, which is also heard in parts of North America (especially during summer) on 15115 kHz. Sometimes carries commentaries of local sporting events.

Radio For Peace International, Costa Rica. Part of an eight-hour cyclical block of social-conscience, counterculture and New Age programming. Some of the offerings at this hour include a women's news-gathering service, *WINGS*, (0430 Friday); a listener-response program (same time Saturday); and *Sound Currents of the Spirit* (0430 Monday). Audible in Europe and the Americas on 7385 and 9400 kHz. Some transmissions are in the single-sideband mode, which can be properly processed only on some radios.

Voice of Russia World Service. Continuous to western North America at this hour. Winters, it's *News and Views*, replaced Tuesday through Saturday summers by the timely ●*Commonwealth Update.* The final half hour is mostly given over to music. Summer pickings include *Jazz Show* (Monday), ●*Music at your Request* (Wednesday), and ●*Folk Box* (Thursday); while the winter offerings are pretty flexible. Best winter bets are 5905, 6065, 7175, 7270, 7345, 9825, 9850 and 11715 kHz; in summer, try 12010, 12050, 13665, 15180 (or 13790), 15425 and 15580 kHz.

"For the People," WHRI, Noblesville, Indiana. See 0300 for specifics. The second half of a two-hour broadcast targeted weeknights to North America on 5745 kHz.

Croatian Radio. Eight minutes of *news* from Croatian Radio's Zagreb studio. Best heard in Europe and eastern North America, but also heard elsewhere. Channel usage varies, but try 5895, 7370, 9830, 11635 and 13830 kHz.

Radio Pyongyang, North Korea. Fifty soporific minutes of old-fashioned communist propaganda. To Southeast Asia on 15180, 15230 and 17765 kHz.

WWCR, Nashville, Tennessee. Carries a variety of disestablishmentarian programs at this hour, depending on the day of the week, and whether it is summer or winter. These include "America First Radio", "Hour of the Time", "Duncan Long Show" and "Radio Free America"; choose between 5065 and 7435 kHz.

04:30

Radio Yugoslavia. Summers only at this time. Repeat of the 0000 broadcast. Thirty minutes to western North America on 9580 and 11870 kHz. One hour later in winter.

Radio Nederland. Repeat of the 0030 transmission. Fifty-five minutes to western North America on 5995 (winter), 6165 and (summer) 9590 kHz.

Radio Finland. Summers only at this time. Starts with *Compass North*, a compendium of Finnish and other Scandinavian stories, followed Tuesday through Friday by a press review and, later in the broadcast, *Northern Lights.* The remaining time is taken up by one or more short features. The week starts off with *Focus* and *Nuntii Latini* (news in Latin)—one of the curiosities of world band radio. Monday brings *Economic Roundup*, Tuesday has sports, Wednesday features *Environment Report*, Thursday has *Finnish History*, Friday's presentation is *Culture Closeup*, and the Saturday offerings are *Starting Finnish* and *Capital Coffee-break.* Thirty minutes to the Mideast on 15440 kHz. One hour later in winter.

05:00

■**BBC World Service for the Americas.** Thirty minutes of ●*Newsday*, followed most days by programming aimed at younger listeners. Take you choice from *Multitrack* (Tuesday, Thursday and Saturday), ●*Megamix* (Wednesday) and *John Peel* (Sunday). These are replaced Friday by the excellent *Andy Kershaw's World of Music*, and Monday by a documentary. Audible in North America (better to the west) on 5975 and 9640 kHz.

■BBC World Service for Europe. ●*Newsday*, followed on the half-hour by ●*Anything Goes* (Monday), ●*Omnibus* (Wednesday), ●*The Learning World* (Thursday) and ●*Andy Kershaw's World of Music* (Friday). Quality programming. At the same time weekends, Saturday airs popular music, and Sunday features *In Praise of God*. This programming may be replaced Monday through Saturday winters by ●*Europe Today*. Continuous to Europe on 3955 (winter), 6180, 6195 and 9410 kHz; and to the Mideast on 9410, 11760, 12095 and 15575 kHz.

■BBC World Service for Africa. Thirty minutes of ●*Newsday*, then weekdays it's a continuation of *Network Africa*. Weekends, there's a repeat of the 0330 features. Continuous programming on 3255, 6005, 6190, 7160, 15400, 15420 and 17885 kHz.

■BBC World Service for Asia and the Pacific. ●*Newsday* and a variety of features. These include ●*Anything Goes* (Sunday), ●*Development 96* and ●*Short Story* (Monday), ●*Discovery* (Tuesday), ●*Omnibus* (Wednesday), ●*Focus on Faith* (Friday), and the classical *Composer of the Month* (Saturday). Continuous to East Asia on 11955, 15280 and 15360 kHz; and to Australasia on 11955 and 15360 kHz.

Monitor Radio International, USA. See 0000 for program details. Tuesday through Friday to Europe on 7535 kHz. On other days, programs are of a religious nature.

■Deutsche Welle, Germany. Repeat of the 50-minute 0100 transmission to

North America, winters on 5960, 6045, 6120 and 6185 kHz; and summers on 5960, 6175, 6185, 9515 and 11705 kHz. This slot is by far the best for western North America.

Radio Exterior de España ("Spanish National Radio"). Repeat of the 0000 and 0100 transmissions to North America, on 9540 kHz.

Swiss Radio International. Summers only at this time. Fifteen minutes of *news* to Europe on 6165 and 9535 kHz. One hour later in winter.

Radio Canada International. Summer weekdays only. See 0600 for program details. To Europe, Africa and the Mideast on 6050, 6150, 7295, 15430 and 17840 kHz. One hour later during winter.

Vatican Radio. Summers only at this time. Twenty minutes of programming oriented to Catholics. To Europe on 4005 and 5860 kHz. Frequencies may vary slightly. One hour later in winter.

China Radio International. This time winters only. Repeat of the 0000 broadcast; one hour to North America on 9595 kHz.

HCJB—Voice of the Andes, Ecuador. Repeat of the 0100 transmission. To western North America on 9745 kHz.

Voice of America. Continues with the morning broadcast to Europe, Africa and the Mideast. Starts with *News*, followed weekdays by *VOA Today*—a conglomeration of business, sports, science, entertainment and virtually anything else that may be newsworthy. On weekends, the news is followed by an extended version of *VOA Saturday/VOA Sunday*. To Europe, the Mideast and North Africa on 3985, 5995, 6040, 6140, 7170, 7200, 11965 (summer) and 15205 kHz; and to the rest of Africa on 6035, 7405, 9630 and 12080 kHz. Several of these channels provide good reception in North America.

Radio Norway International. Winter Mondays (Sunday evenings in the target area) only. *Norway Now.* A half hour of *news* and human-interest stories targeted at western North America on 5905 (or 5910) kHz.

Radio Bulgaria. Winters only at this time; see 0400 for specifics. A distinctly Bulgarian mix of news, commentary, interviews and features, plus a fair amount of music. Sixty minutes to eastern North America and Central America on 7335 and 9700 kHz. One hour earlier in summer.

Radio Habana Cuba. Repeat of the 0100 transmission. To western North America on 9820 kHz.

Channel Africa, South Africa. Although now broadcasting only to an African audience, this station can still be heard in Europe and eastern North America. One of the best opportunities is during this time slot, when the station broadcasts to West Africa. One hour winters on 11900 kHz, and summers on 9695 kHz.

Voice of Nigeria. Targeted at West Africa, but also audible in parts of Europe and North America, especially during winter. Monday through Friday, opens with the lively *Wave Train* followed by *VON Scope*, a half hour of *news* and press comment. Pick of the weekend programs is ●*African Safari*, a musical journey around the African continent, which can be heard Saturdays at 0500. This is replaced Sunday by five minutes of *Reflections* and 25 minutes of music in *VON Link-Up*, with the second half hour taken up by *News*. The first 60 minutes of a daily two-hour broadcast on 7255 kHz.

Radio New Zealand International. Continues with regional programming for the South Pacific. Part of a much longer broadcast, which is also heard in parts of North America (especially during summer) on 9570 or 15115 kHz.

Radio Australia. *World News*, then Monday through Friday there's *Australian News*, a sports bulletin and a feature for listeners in the Pacific.

Weekends, look for Saturday's *Oz Sounds* and *One World*, or Sunday's *Beat of the Pacific* and *Australian Music Show*. Continuous to Asia and the Pacific on about ten channels, and heard in North America (best during summer) on 15240, 15365, 17795 and 17860 kHz. For East Asia and Southeast Asia, choose from 15415, 15425 and 17715 kHz. Early risers in Europe can try 15425 kHz. Some channels carry alternative sports programming at weekends.

Voice of Russia World Service. Continues to western North America. Tuesday through Saturday, winters, the first half hour features *News* and ●*Commonwealth Update*, the latter replaced summers by *Focus on Asia and the Pacific*. Sunday's winter fare is *Top Priority*, replaced summer by *Science and Engineering*. At 0531 winters, look for some interesting musical shows, including ●*Music at your Request* (Wednesday), ●*Folk Box* (Thursday), and Monday's jazz feature. Summers, this slot is given over to a variety of musical styles. Winters on 5905, 6065, 7175, 7270, 7345, 9825, 9850 and 11710 kHz; and summers on 12010, 12040, 12050, 13665, 15425 and 15580 kHz.

Radio For Peace International, Costa Rica. Continues at this hour with a potpourri of United Nations, counter-culture and other programs. These include *WINGS* (news for and of women, 0530 Wednesday), *Vietnam Veterans Radio Network* (0530 Thursday) and *Focus on Haiti* (0500 Sunday). Audible in Europe and the Americas on 7385 and 9400 kHz. Some transmissions are in the single-sideband mode, which can be properly processed only on some radios.

Kol Israel. Winters only at this time. *News* for 15 minutes from Israel Radio's domestic network. To Europe and eastern North America on 7465 and 9435 kHz. One hour earlier in summer.

Radio Japan. Repeat of the 0300 broadcast, except that Sunday's *Hello from Tokyo* is replaced by *Let's Learn*

Radio Japan's "Media Roundup" host, Mari Kishi, with listeners' letters. The athletic Ms. Kishi relates well to her American audience, as she lived in Hawaii for five years until she was 15.

Japanese, Media Roundup and *Viewpoint.* Sixty minutes to Europe on 5975 and 7230 kHz; to East and Southeast Asia on 11725 (or 11955), 11740 and 17810 kHz; and to western North America winters on 6025, 9565 and 11885 kHz; summers on 6110, 9680 (or 11790) and 11885 kHz.

Croatian Radio. Winters only at this time. Eight minutes of *news* from Croatian Radio's Zagreb studio. Best heard in Europe and eastern North America, but also heard elsewhere. Channel usage varies, but try 5895, 7370, 9830, 11635 and 13830 kHz. One hour earlier in summer.

WWCR, Nashville, Tennessee. Carries a variety of disestablishmentarian programs at this hour, depending on the day of the week, and whether it is summer or winter. These include winter's "America First Radio", "Hour of the Time" and "Duncan Long Show"; and summer's "Herald of Truth", "The Hour of Courage" and "Seventieth Week Magazine." On 5065 and 7435 kHz.

WJCR, Upton, Kentucky. Continues with country gospel music for North American listeners on 7490 kHz. Also with religious programs to North America at this hour are **WYFR-Family Radio** on 5985 kHz, **WWCR** on 5935 kHz, **KAIJ** on 5810 kHz and **KTBN** on 7510 kHz. For traditional Catholic programming (some of which may be in Spanish), tune to **WEWN** on 7425 kHz.

05:30

Radio Austria International. ●*Report from Austria;* see 0130 for more details. Year-round to North America on 6015 kHz, and winters only to Europe and the Mideast on 6155, 13730, 15410 and 17870 kHz.

Radio Finland. Winters only at this time; see 0430 for specifics. Thirty minutes to the Mideast on 9635 kHz. One hour earlier in summer.

United Arab Emirates Radio, Dubai. See 0330 for program details. To East Asia and Australasia on 15435, 17830 and 21700 kHz.

Radio Yugoslavia. Winters only at this time. Repeat of the 0100 broadcast. Thirty minutes to western North America on 6190 or 6195 kHz. One hour earlier in summer.

Radio Romania International. *News,* commentary, a press review, and one or more short features. Thirty minutes to southern Africa (and heard elsewhere) on 11810 (or 11940), 15250, 15340 (or 15380), 17720, 17745 and 17790 kHz.

06:00

■BBC World Service for the Americas. *World News,* followed Tuesday through Friday by a 15- or 45-minute popular music feature. Pick of the remaining programs is ●*Concert Hall* (or its substitute) at 0615 Monday. Continuous to North America (better to the west) on 9640 kHz.

■BBC World Service for Europe. *World News,* followed Tuesday through Saturday by ●*The World Today.* Pick of the remaining programs includes ●*Megamix* (Wednesday), *Sports International* (Thursday), ●*Focus on Faith* (Saturday), and Sunday's ●*Letter from America* and *Jazz for the Asking.* Continuous to Europe on 3955 (winter), 6180, 6195, 9410, 11780 (winter) 12095, 15070 and (summer) 15575 kHz; and to the Mideast on 9410, 11760, 12095, 15070 and 15575 kHz.

■BBC World Service for Africa. Opens with 15 minutes of *World News,* then Monday through Friday it's the breakfast show *Network Africa.* Saturdays, there's *From the Weeklies* and *Talkabout Africa,* replaced Sunday by ●*Letter from America* and *African Perspective.* One hour to Africa (and heard well beyond) on 6005, 6190, 7160, 11940, 15400, 15420 and 17885 kHz.

■BBC World Service for Asia and the Pacific. *World News,* then it's very much take-your-pick from a variety of offerings. Try the arts show *Meridian* (0630 Wednesday, Friday and Saturday), Sunday's ●*Letter from America* and *Jazz for the Asking,* Tuesday's ●*Health Matters,* or Thursday's *Sports*

International. Continuous to East Asia on 11955, 15280 and 15360 kHz; and to Australasia on 11955 and 15360 kHz.

Monitor Radio International, USA. See 0000 for program details. Tuesday through Friday to western Europe on 7535 kHz. Weekend programs deal with various aspects of the Christian Science faith.

Radio Habana Cuba. Repeat of the 0200 transmission. To western North America on 9820 kHz.

Croatian Radio. Monday through Saturday, summers only at this time; actually starts at 0603. Ten minutes of on-the-spot *news* from one of Europe's most troubled areas. Intended mainly for Europe and Australasia at this hour, but also heard elsewhere. Frequencies vary, but try 5895, 5920, 7370, 9830 and 13830 kHz. Although not available at this time Sunday, there is a short summary of news at 0703 for those who have an interest in the region. One hour later during winter.

Radio Norway International. Summer Sundays only. *Norway Now.* Thirty minutes of *news* and human-interest stories to Australasia on 7295 (or 15175) kHz.

Swiss Radio International. *News* and news-related fare. Year-round, but reduced from 30 to 15 minutes in winter. To Europe on 6165 and 9535 kHz. The latter channel may be changed to 3985 kHz during winter. There is also a year-round broadcast to Africa on 9885, 13635 and 15340 kHz.

Radio Canada International. Winter weekdays only. Thirty minutes targeted at Canadian peacekeepers overseas. To Europe, Africa and the

Mideast on 6050, 6150, 9740, 9760 and 11905 kHz. One hour earlier in summer.

Voice of America. Final segment of the transmission to Europe, Africa and the Mideast. Monday through Friday, the mainstream African service carries just 30 minutes of ●*Daybreak Africa*, with other channels carrying a full hour of *news* and *VOA Today*—a mixed bag of popular music, interviews, human interest stories, science digest and sports news. Weekend programming is the same to all areas—a bulletin of *news* followed by 50 minutes of *VOA Saturday*/*VOA Sunday*. To Europe, North Africa and the Mideast on 3985, 5995, 6040, 6060, 6140, 7170, 7325, 11805, 11965 (summer) and 15205 kHz; and to mainstream Africa on 6035, 7405, 9630, 11950, 12035 (to 0630) and 12080 kHz. Several of these channels provide good reception in North America.

Radio Australia. *World News*, then Monday through Friday it's the latest sports headlines, *Pacific Beat* and a regional weather report for the South Pacific. These are followed on the half-hour by ●*International Report*. Weekends, there's *Book Reading* and *Indian Pacific* (Saturday), and *Feedback* and *Correspondents Report* (Sunday). Continuous to Asia and the Pacific on about ten channels, and heard in North America (best during summer) on 15240 and 17795 kHz (replaced by 9580 and 9860 kHz at 0630). Listeners in East and Southeast Asia can choose from 15415, 15425, 15510 and 17715 kHz. In Europe, try 15425 and 15510 kHz. Some channels carry an alternative sports program until 0630 at weekends (0730 in summer).

Voice of Nigeria. The second (and final) hour of a daily broadcast intended for listeners in West Africa, but also heard in parts of Europe and North America (especially during winter). Features vary from day to day, but are predominantly concerned with Nigerian and West African affairs. There is a lis-

tener-response program at 0600 Friday and 0615 Sunday, and other slots include *Across the Ages* and *Nigeria and Politics* (Monday), *Southern Connection* and *Nigerian Scene* (Tuesday), *West African Scene* (0600 Thursday) and *Images of Nigeria* (0615 Friday). There is a weekday 25-minute program of *news* and commentary on the half-hour, replaced weekends by the more in-depth *Weekly Analysis*. To 0657 on 7255 kHz.

Voice of the Mediterranean, Malta. More culture-oriented than most other stations. Try *Maltese Heritage* (Monday) or Saturday's *Study in Maltese Folklore* for a taste of what's on offer. Sixty minutes (except for 0635-0700 Sunday) to Europe, North Africa and the Mideast on 9765 KHZ.

Radio New Zealand International. Continues with regional programming for the South Pacific. Part of a much longer broadcast, which is also heard in parts of North America (especially during summer) on 9570, 9700 or 15115 kHz.

Voice of Russia World Service. *News*, then winters it's *Focus on Asia and the Pacific* (Tuesday through Saturday), *Science and Engineering* (Sunday), and *Mailbag* (Monday). In summer, the news is followed by *Science and Engineering* (Monday and Friday), *This is Russia* (Saturday), the business-oriented *Newmarket* (Thursday), and a listener-response program on Tuesday and Sunday. The second half hour mainly consists of a wide variety of music programs. Exceptions include *Moscow Yesterday and Today* (winter Mondays) and *Russian by Radio* (summer weekends). Continuous to western North America winters on 5905, 5930, 6065, 7175, 7270, 7345, 9850 and 11710 kHz; and summers on 12010, 12040, 12050, 13665, 15425 and 15580 kHz. Also available to Australasia at this time—try 15560, 17570, 17590 and 17870 kHz.

Radio For Peace International, Costa Rica. Continues with counterculture and social-conscience programs ranging from *Peace Forum* (0600 Wednesday and Saturday) to *The Far Right Radio Review* (same time Monday). *My Green Earth*, a nature program for children, is aired at 0600 Friday. Audible in Europe and the Americas on 7385 and 9400 kHz. Some transmissions are in the single-sideband mode, which can be properly processed only on some radios.

Radio Prague, Czech Republic. Summers only at this time. *News* and features with a distinct Central European flavor. These include *Talking Point* and *The Arts* (Tuesday), *From the Archives* (Thursday), *Economic Report* and a guest interview (Friday), and musical features on Sunday and Monday. Thirty minutes to Europe on 7345 kHz, and to South Asia and Australasia on 15640 kHz. One hour later in winter.

Radio Pyongyang, North Korea. See 1100 for specifics. Fifty minutes to Southeast Asia on 15180 and 15230 kHz.

Vatican Radio. Winters only at this time. Twenty minutes with a heavy Catholic slant. To Europe on 4010 and 5860 (or 6245) kHz. One hour earlier in summer. Frequencies may vary slightly.

Radio Korea International, South Korea. The hour-long broadcast opens with *news* and commentary, followed Monday through Wednesday by *Seoul Calling*. Weekly features include *Echoes of Korean Music* and *Shortwave Feedback* (Sunday), *Tales from Korea's Past* (Monday), *Korean Cultural Trails* (Tuesday), *Pulse of Korea* (Wednesday), *From Us to You* (a listener-response program) and *Let's Learn Korean* (Thursday), *Let's Sing Together* and *Korea Through Foreigners' Eyes* (Friday), and Saturday's *Discovering Korea*, *Korean Literary Corner* and *Weekly News Focus*. To eastern North America on 7205 kHz.

WJCR, Upton, Kentucky. Continues with country gospel music to North America on 7490 kHz. Also with religious programs for North American listeners at this hour are **WYFR-Family Radio** on 5985 kHz, **WWCR** on 5935 kHz, **KAIJ** on 5810 kHz, **KTBN** on 7510 kHz, and **WHRI-World Harvest Radio** on 5745 and 9495 kHz. Traditional Catholic fare (some of it may be in Spanish) is available on 7425 kHz.

Voice of Malaysia. Actually starts at 0555 with opening announcements and program summary, followed by *News*. Then comes *This is the Voice of Malaysia*, a potpourri of news, interviews, reports and music. The hour is rounded off with *Personality Column*. Part of a 150-minute broadcast to Southeast Asia and Australia on 6175, 9750 and 15295 kHz.

Radio Japan. Repeat of the 0300 transmission, except that the end-of-broadcast news is replaced Saturdays by *News Desk* and Sundays by *Tokyo Pop-in*. Sixty minutes to East and Southeast Asia on 11725 (or 11955), 11860 and 17810 kHz.

HCJB—Voice of the Andes, Ecuador. Tuesday through Saturday, a repeat of the 0200 broadcast (don't miss Wednesday's ●*Blues, Rags, and All That Jazz*). Pick of the remaining fare is *Musical Mailbag* (0630 Sunday) and *Radio Reading Room* (0600 Monday). One hour of predominantly religious programming. To western North America on 9745 kHz.

06:30

Radio Austria International. ●*Report from Austria* (see 0130). A half hour via the Canadian relay, aimed primarily at western North America on 6015 kHz.

Radio Vlaanderen Internationaal, Belgium. Summers only at this time. *News*, then *Press Review* (except

Sunday), followed Tuesday through Friday by *Belgium Today* (various topics) and features like *Focus on Europe* (Tuesday), *Living in Belgium* and *Green Society* (Wednesday), *The Arts* and *Around Town* (Thursday), and *Economics* and *International Report*(Friday). Weekend features consist of Saturday's *Music from Flanders* and Sunday's *P.O. Box 26* (a listener-response program) and *Radio World*. Twenty-five minutes to Europe on 6015 (or 5910) and 9925 kHz; and to Australasia on 9925 kHz. One hour later in winter.

Radio Romania International. Actually starts at 0631. A nine-minute news broadcast to Europe winters on 7105, 7175, 9665 and 11775 kHz; and summers on 7225, 9550, 9665 and 11810 kHz.

06:45

Radio Finland. Summers only at this time. See 0745 winter transmission for program details. Fifteen minutes to Europe on 6120, 9560 and 11755 kHz.

Radio Romania International. *News*, commentary, a press review and short features, with interludes of lively Romanian folk music. To Australasia for 55 minutes Monday through Saturday on 15250, 17720 and 17805 kHz; and 30 minutes Sunday on 11775 and 15335 kHz.

07:00

■BBC World Service for the Americas. Fifteen minutes of *World News*, then it's a mixed bag. Choice pickings include ●*The Greenfield Collection* (classical music, Tuesday), ●*Health Matters* and ●*Anything Goes* (Wednesday), ●*Network UK* (Thursday), and ●*Global Concerns* and *Jazz for the Asking* (Sunday). Continuous to North America (and better to the west) on 9640 kHz.

■BBC World Service for Europe. *World News* followed by features, some of which are amongst the BBC's best. Try ●*Development 96* (0715 Monday), ●*Health Matters* (same time Tuesday), ●*Discovery* (0730 Wednesday), *The Farming World* and ●*Network UK* (Thursday), ●*Science in Action* (0730 Friday), and Sunday's ●*Global Concerns*, *From Our Own Correspondent* and *Write On*. Continuous to Europe on 3955 (winter), 6195, 7325 (winter), 9410, 12095 and 15070 kHz; and to the Mideast on 9410, 11760, 15070 and 15575 kHz.

■BBC World Service for Asia and the Pacific. *World News*, then Monday through Fridays there's ●*Off the Shelf* (readings from world literature). Best of the remaining offerings are Wednesday's ●*Andy Kershaw's World of Music*, Thursday's ●*Network UK* and Saturday's ●*People and Politics*. Continuous to East Asia on 11955, 15280 and 15360 kHz; and to Australasia on 11955 and 15360 kHz.

Monitor Radio International, USA. See 0000 for program details. Monday through Friday to western Europe on 7535 kHz. Weekends are given over to nonsecular programming, mainly of interest to members of, and others interested in, the Christian Science Church.

Voice of Malaysia. First, there is a daily feature with a Malaysian theme (except for Thursday, when *Talk on Islam* is aired), then comes a half hour of *This is the Voice of Malaysia* (see 0600), followed by 15 minutes of *Beautiful Malaysia*. Not much doubt about where the broadcast originates! Continuous to Southeast Asia and Australia on 6175, 9750 and 15295 kHz.

Swiss Radio International. Winters only at this time. Thirty minutes of *news* and background reports from SRI's satellite service. To Europe on 3985 (or 9535) and 6165 kHz. One hour earlier in summer.

Radio Prague, Czech Republic. Winters only at this time. Thirty minutes of *news* and features; see 0600 for specifics. To Europe on 7345 kHz, and to South Asia and Australasia on 15640 or 17485 kHz.

Radio Australia. *World News*, followed Monday through Friday by news and features for listeners in the Pacific. Saturday, look for *Ockham's Razor* (science) and the environmental *One World*, replaced Sunday by *Australiana* and *At Your Request*. Continuous to Asia and the Pacific on about ten channels, and heard in North America (best during summer) on 9580 and 9860 kHz. In East and Southeast Asia, take your pick from 9710 (from 0730), 15425, 15530 and 17715 kHz. European listeners can try 15425 kHz.

Radio For Peace International, Costa Rica. The final 60 minutes of an eight-hour cyclical block of United Nations, counterculture, social-conscience and New Age programming. Audible in Europe and the Americas on 7385 and 9400 kHz. Some transmissions are in the single-sideband mode, which can be properly processed only on some radios.

Voice of Russia World Service. *News*, followed Tuesday through Saturday, summers, by the informative ●*Commonwealth Update*. Then comes ●*Audio Book Club* (Tuesday, Thursday and Saturday) or *Russian by Radio* (Wednesday and Friday). At 0711 Saturday, listen to the sounds of ●*Music and Musicians*. Winter's offerings are a mixed bag, with *Science and Engineering* (0711 Monday and Friday) and *This is Russia* (same time, Saturday) probably the most interesting. There is also a listener-response program at this time Sunday and Tuesday. Winters, the final 60 minutes of a six-hour block of programming to western North America on 5905, 5930, 6065, 7270, 7345, 9850 and 11710 kHz. Also year-round to Australasia, winters

on 15230, 17840, 17860 and 21790 kHz; and summers on 15560, 17570, 17590, 17690 and 17870 kHz.

WJCR, Upton, Kentucky. Continues with country gospel music for North American listeners on 7490 kHz. Also with religious programs to North America at this hour are **WWCR** on 5935 kHz, **KAIJ** on 5810 kHz, **KTBN** on 7510 kHz, and **WHRI-World Harvest Radio** on 5745 and 9495 kHz. For traditional Catholic programming, tune **WEWN** on 7425 kHz.

Radio Pyongyang, North Korea. See 1100 for specifics. Fifty minutes from the last of the old-time communist stations. To Southeast Asia on 15340 and 17765 kHz.

Croatian Radio. Monday through Saturday, winters only at this time; actually starts at 0703 (Sunday, there is a brief summary at 0803). Ten minutes of English *news* from one of Croatian Radio's domestic networks. In times of crisis, one of the few sources of up-to-date news on what is actually happening in the region. Frequency usage varies, but try 5985, 5920, 7370, 9830 and 13830 kHz. One hour earlier in summer.

Radio New Zealand International. Continues with regional programming for the South Pacific. Part of a much longer broadcast, which is also heard in parts of North America (especially during summer) on 6100, 9570 or 9700 kHz.

Voice of Free China, Taiwan. Repeat of the 0200 transmission. Best heard in southern and western parts of the United States on 5950 kHz.

Radio Japan. Monday through Friday, it's *Radio Japan News Round* followed by *Radio Japan Magazine Hour*, which consists of a feature (two on Tuesday) and *News Commentary*. On Monday you can hear *Sports Spotlight*, Tuesday has *Japanese Culture* and *Today*, Wednesday features *Asian Report*, Thursday brings *Crosscurrents*, and Friday's offering is *Business Focus*. Weekend fare is made up of a bulletin of

NHK

Shiro Akiyama and Katsue Suma host "Radio Japan Saturday Wide" over Radio Japan on...you guessed it, Saturdays.

news, followed by Saturday's *This Week* or Sunday's *Let's Learn Japanese*, *Media Roundup* and *Viewpoint*. The broadcast ends with a daily *news* summary. Sixty minutes to Europe on 5975, 7230 and 15335 kHz; to the Mideast on 15335 kHz; to Africa on 15335 and 17815 kHz; to East and Southeast Asia on 11725 (or 11955), 11740, 17810 and 21610 kHz; and to Australasia on 11850 (or 15270) kHz.

HCJB—Voice of the Andes, Ecuador. Opens with 30 minutes of religious programming—except for Saturday, when *Musical Mailbag* is on the air. Then comes *Studio 9* (see 0030 for more details, except that all features are one day earlier), replaced Saturday by *DX Partyline*. Sunday is given over to *Saludos Amigos*—the HCJB international friendship program. To Europe winters on 6205 kHz, and summers on 11615 kHz. A separate block of religious programming is broadcast to Australasia on 5900 (or 6135) kHz.

07:30

Radio Nederland. *News*, then Monday through Saturday it's ●*Newsline* followed by a feature. Pick

of the pack is undoubtedly Monday's ●*Research File*. Other offerings include *Mirror Images* (Tuesday), a documentary (Wednesday), *Media Network* (Thursday) and Saturday's *Sounds Interesting*. Sunday is given over to the long-running *Happy Station*. To Australasia on 9700 (summer), 9720 and (winter) 11895 kHz. Worth a listen.

Radio Austria International. Summers only at this time. ●*Report from Austria*, which includes a short bulletin of *news* followed by a series of current events and human interest stories. Ample coverage of national and regional issues, and a valuable source of news from Central and Eastern Europe. Thirty minutes to Europe on 6155 and 13730 kHz, and to the Mideast on 15410 and 17870 kHz.

Radio Prague, Czech Republic. Thirty minutes of *news* and features; see 0600 for specifics. To Africa and beyond on 15640 or 17485 kHz. There may also be an additional winter channel for Southeast Asia and Australasia — try 21705 kHz.

Radio Vlaanderen Internationaal, Belgium. Winters only at this time. See 0630 for program details. To Europe on 5985 (or 5910) and 9925 (or 9905) kHz, with the latter channel also available for Australasia. One hour earlier in summer.

Voice of Greece. Actually starts around 0740. Ten minutes of English news from and about Greece. Part of a longer broadcast of predominantly Greek programming. To Europe and Australasia on 9425, 9375 (or 9935) and 11645 kHz.

07:45

Radio Finland. Winters only at this time. *Compass North*, a compilation of Finnish and other Nordic stories. Fifteen minutes targeted at Europe on 6120, 9560 and 11755 kHz. One hour earlier in summer.

■BBC World Service for Europe.
News, then the religious *Words of Faith*,
followed by a wide variety of programming, depending on the day of the
week. Choice programs include ●*The
Greenfield Collection* (Sunday),
●*Concert Hall* (alternating periodically
with ●*International Recital* or ●*From
the Proms*) (Tuesday), ●*Thirty-Minute
Drama* (Wednesday), *Composer of the
Month* and *Good Books* (Thursday), classical music (Friday) and *A Jolly Good
Show* (Saturday). Continuous to Europe
on 6195 (winter), 7325 (winter), 9410,
12095, 15070 and 17640 kHz; and to the
Mideast on 9410 and 11760 kHz.

**■BBC World Service for Asia
and the Pacific.** Begins with *World
News*, and unlike the service for Europe,
ends with *Words of Faith*. Between the
two extremes there is classical music
on Sunday, Monday, Tuesday and
Friday; the youth-oriented ●*Megamix*
(Wednesday), *Good Books* and *John Peel*
(Thursday), and *A Jolly Good Show*
(Saturday). Continuous to East Asia on
11955 and 15280 kHz, and to Australasia
on 11955 kHz.

Monitor Radio International,
USA. See 0000 for program details.
Tuesday through Friday to Europe on
7535 or 15665 kHz, and to Australasia on
13615 (or 9425) kHz. Weekend programs
are devoted to the teachings and beliefs
of the Christian Science Church.

HCJB—Voice of the Andes,
Ecuador. Continuous programming to
Europe and Australasia. For Europe
there's the final 30 minutes of *Studio 9*
(or weekend variations), while
Australasia gets a full hour's serving of
predominantly religious fare. To Europe
winters on 6205 kHz, and summers on
11625 kHz; and to Australasia on 5900 (or
6135) kHz.

Voice of Malaysia. *News* and commentary, followed Monday through
Friday by *Instrumentalia*, which is
replaced weekends by *This is the Voice
of Malaysia* (see 0600). The final 25 minutes of a much longer transmission targeted at Southeast Asia and Australia
on 6175, 9750 and 15295 kHz.

Croatian Radio. Monday through
Saturday, summers only at this time;
actually starts at 0803. Ten minutes of
English *news* from one of the domestic
networks (replaced Sunday by a brief
summary at 0903). A good way to keep
abreast of events in one of Europe's most
unstable regions. Frequency usage
varies, but try 5985, 5920, 7370, 9830 and
13830 kHz. One hour later in winter.

Radio Norway International.
Sunday only. *Norway Now*. A pleasant
half hour of *news* and human-interest
stories from and about Norway. To East
Asia and Australasia winters on 9590 (or
15175) kHz, and to the Mideast summers
on 15220 kHz.

Radio Pakistan. Opens with a brief
bulletin of *news* followed by recitations
from the Koran (with English translation). This in turn is followed by a press
review and a ten-minute interlude of
Pakistani music. On the half-hour
there's a feature on Pakistan or Islam,
which then gives way to extracts from
Pakistani concert recordings. Fifty minutes to Europe on 15625 and 17900 kHz.

Radio Australia. Part of a 24-hour
service to Asia and the Pacific, but
which can also be heard at this time

Children gather near electrical facility for Radio
Pakistan transmitters.

throughout much of North America. Begins with *World News*, then Monday through Friday there's a sports bulletin, ●*International Report* and *Stock Exchange Report*. Weekends, it's *Oz Sounds* (Saturday) or *Feedback* (Sunday), followed by a sport bulletin on the half-hour. To Asia and the Pacific on a variety of channels, and audible in North America on 9580 and 9860 kHz. Best bets for East Asia are 9710 and 17715 kHz, with 15530 kHz also available in the southeast. In Europe and the Mideast, try 21725 kHz.

WJCR, Upton, Kentucky. Continues with country gospel music to North America on 7490 kHz. Other U.S. religious broadcasters operating at this hour include **WWCR** on 5935 kHz, **KAIJ** on 5810 kHz, **KTBN** on 7510 kHz, and **WHRI-World Harvest Radio** on 5745 and 9495 kHz. Traditional Catholic programming can be heard via **WEWN** on 7425 kHz.

Radio Pyongyang, North Korea. See 1100 for specifics. Fifty minutes of monolithic mediocrity to Southeast Asia on 15180 and 15230 kHz.

Radio Finland. Summers only at this time. Starts with *Compass North*, a compilation of Finnish and other Scandinavian stories, followed Tuesday through Friday by a press review and, later in the broadcast, *Northern Lights*. The remaining time is taken up by one or more short features. The week starts off with *Focus* and *Nuntii Latini* (news in Latin)—one of the more unusual offerings of world band radio. Monday brings *Economic Roundup*, Tuesday has sports, Wednesday features *Environment Report*, Thursday has *Finnish History*, Friday's presentation is *Culture Closeup*, and the Saturday offerings are *Starting Finnish* and *Capital Coffee-break*. Thirty minutes to Southeast Asia and Australasia on 15115 (or 15330) and 17800 (or 17820) kHz. One hour later in winter.

Voice of Russia World Service. *News*, then Tuesday through Saturday, winters, it's ●*Commonwealth Update* followed by ●*Audio Book Club* or *Russian by Radio*. Pick of the remaining days is Sunday's ●*Music and Musicians*, which follows the news. In summer, the *news* is followed Tuesday through Saturday by *Focus on Asia and the Pacific*. This in turn gives way, on the half-hour, to some entertaining musical fare—●*Folk Box* (Wednesday and Saturday), *Yours for the Asking* (Monday), ●*Music at your Request* (Tuesday), and Friday's *Jazz Show*. Continuous to East and Southeast Asia, winters on 11675, 15230, 17840 and 17860 kHz; and summers on 11900, 15560, 17590 and 17695 kHz. Also available to Australasia winters on 15230, 17840 and 17860 kHz; and summers on 9835, 11800, 11900, 15560, 17590, 17695, 17765 and 17870 kHz.

KTWR-Trans World Radio, Guam. Actually starts at 0755. Eighty minutes of evangelical programming targeted at East Asia on 15200 kHz.

Radio New Zealand International. *News* and features, music or special programs for the South Sea Islands, all with a distinctly Pacific flavor. Sometimes includes relays from the domestic National Radio. Part of a much longer broadcast for the South Pacific, but well heard in North America winters on 9700, and summers on 6100 kHz.

Radio Korea International, South Korea. See 0600 for program details. Sixty minutes to Europe on 7550 and 13670 kHz.

08:30

Radio Austria International. The comprehensive ●*Report from Austria*; see 0130 for more details. To Australia and the Pacific (year-round) on 15450 and 17870 kHz, and to Europe (winters only) on 6155 and 13730 kHz.

Radio Slovakia International. *Slovakia Today*, a package of *news* and features with the accent on Slovak life and culture. Thirty minutes to Australasia (and widely heard elsewhere) on 11990, 15640 and 17485 kHz.

Radio Nederland. The second of three hours aimed at Australasia. *News*, followed Monday through Saturday by ●*Newsline*, then a feature program. Best pickings are probably *Sounds Interesting* (Wednesday), ●*Research File* (Thursday) and Friday's documentary. Monday through Friday, there is also a daily *Press Review*. On 9720 and (winter) 13700 kHz.

Voice of Armenia. Summer Sundays only. Mainly of interest to Armenians abroad. Thirty minutes of Armenian *news* and culture. To Europe on 15170 and 15270 kHz. One hour later in winter.

09:00

■BBC World Service for Europe. Starts with *News* and ●*World Business Report/Review*, and ends with *Sports Roundup*. The remaining time is taken up by a series of 30-minute features, the pick of which are ●*Andy Kershaw's World of Music* (Wednesday), *Sports International* (Thursday) and *The Vintage Chart Show* (Saturday). Continuous to Europe on 9410, 12095, 15070 and 17640 kHz; and to the Mideast on 9410, 11760 and 15575 kHz.

■BBC World Service for Asia and the Pacific. Starts and ends like the service for Europe, but the features are different. Choice offerings include ●*Science in Action* (0915 Sunday), ●*Health Matters* (0930 Monday), *From Our Own Correspondent* and *The Farming World* (Thursday), ●*Global Concerns* (0915 Friday) and ●*Development 96* (0930 Saturday). Continuous to East Asia on 9740, 15280 and 17830 kHz; and to Australasia on 15280 kHz.

Monitor Radio International, USA. See 0000 for program details. Tuesday through Friday (Monday through Friday in summer), to Europe on 7535 or 9840 kHz, to East Asia on 9430 kHz, and to Australasia on 13615 kHz. Also audible in parts of North America on 7395 kHz, though targeted farther south. Weekend programs are of a religious nature and are mainly of interest to members of, and others interested in, the Christian Science faith.

■Deutsche Welle, Germany. *News*, followed Monday through Friday by ●*Newsline Cologne* and a feature: *Science and Technology* (Monday), ●*Man and Environment* (Tuesday), ●*Insight* (Wednesday), *Living in Germany* (Thursday) and *Spotlight on Sport* (Friday). These are replaced Saturday by *International Talking Point*, *Development Forum* and *Religion and Society*; and Sunday by *Arts on the Air* and *German by Radio*. Fifty minutes to Asia and Australasia winters on 6160, 9875, 11715, 17780, 17820, 21650 and 21680 kHz; and summers on 6160, 11730, 12055, 15245, 17715 and 21680 kHz.

Radio New Zealand International. Continuous programming for the islands of the South Pacific, where the broadcasts are targeted. Summers on 6100 kHz, and winters on 9700 kHz. Audible in much of North America.

Radio Vlaanderen Internationaal, Belgium. Monday through Saturday, summers only at this time. *News* and *Press Review*, followed Tuesday through Friday by *Belgium Today* (various topics) and features like *Focus on Europe* (Tuesday), *Living in Belgium* and *Green Society* (Wednesday), *The Arts* and *Around Town* (Thursday), and *Economics* and *International Report* (Friday). Other offerings include *The Arts* and *Tourism* (Monday), and Saturday's *Music from Flanders*.

Twenty-five minutes to Europe on 6035 (or 5910) kHz, and to Africa on 15545 and 17595 kHz. One hour later in winter.

Croatian Radio. Monday through Saturday, winters only at this time; actually starts at 0903 (Sunday, there is only a brief summary at 1003). Ten minutes of on-the-spot *news* from the Balkans. Frequencies vary, but try 5895, 5920, 7370, 9830 and 13830 kHz. One hour earlier during summer.

HCJB—Voice of the Andes, Ecuador. Sixty minutes of religious and secular programming to Australasia. See 0200 for program specifics, except that features are one day earlier, and not necessarily in the same order. Pick of the pack is *Blues, Rags and All That Jazz* at 0900 Tuesday. On 5900 (or 6135) kHz.

China Radio International. *News* and commentary, followed Tuesday through Friday by *Current Affairs.* These are followed by various feature programs, such as *Culture in China* (Thursday); *Listeners' Letterbox* (Sunday and Tuesday); *Press Clippings, Cooking Show, Travel Talk* and ●*Music from China* (Saturday); *Sports Beat, China Scrapbook* and *Music Album* (Sunday); *Learn to Speak Chinese* (Monday and Wednesday); and Friday's *In the Third World.* Sundays, there is also a biweekly *Business Show* which alternates with *China's Open Windows.* One hour to Australasia on 11755 and 15440 kHz.

Voice of Russia World Service. Tuesday through Saturday, winters, *News* is followed by *Focus on Asia and the Pacific.* This is replaced summers by a variety of features—Wednesday and Sunday offer the business-oriented *Newmarket,* Thursday features *Science and Engineering,* Monday has *This is Russia,* and there's a listener-response program on Friday. Year-round, the second half hour concentrates mainly on music, with the main winter attractions

being ●*Folk Box* (Wednesday and Saturday), ●*Music at your Request* (Tuesday), and Friday's *Jazz Show.* Sixty minutes of continuous programming beamed to Asia and the Pacific. For East and Southeast Asia winters, try 9480, 11675, 12015, 17765, 17840 and 17860 kHz; and summers on 11900, 17590, 17695 and 17765 kHz. Best winter bets for Australasia are 9550, 9800, 11710, 12015, 17840 and 17860 kHz; in summer, go for 9835, 11800, 11900, 17590, 17695, 17765 and 17870 kHz.

Swiss Radio International. Thirty minutes of *news* and background reports. There's a little light relief on Saturday, with *Capital Letters* (a biweekly listener-response program) alternating with *Name Game* and *Sounds Good.* To Australasia on 9885, 13685 and 17515 kHz.

Radio Australia. *World News,* followed Monday through Friday by *Australian News* and *Countrywide* (rural issues). These are replaced weekends by Saturday's *Science Show* or Sunday's *Soundabout.* Continuous to Asia and the Pacific on a number of channels, and heard in North America on 9580 and 9860 kHz. In Europe and the Mideast, try 21725 kHz, while listeners in East and Southeast Asia can choose from 7240, 9510 and 13605 kHz.

Radio For Peace International, Costa Rica. *FIRE* (Feminist International Radio Endeavour). Repeat of the 0100 broadcast. To the Americas on 9400 kHz in single-sideband mode, which can only be received on superior world band radios.

KTWR-Trans World Radio, Guam. Actually starts at 0855. Evangelical programming to Australasia on 11830 kHz.

WJCR, Upton, Kentucky. Continues with country gospel music to North America on 7490 kHz. Other U.S. religious broadcasters operating at this hour include **WWCR** on 5935, **KAIJ** on

5810, **KTBN** on 7510 kHz, and **WHRI-World Harvest Radio** on 5745 and 9495 kHz. Traditional Catholic programming is aired via **WEWN** on 7425 kHz.

Radio Japan. Repeat of the 0300 broadcast; see there for specifics. Up-to-the-minute news from and about the Far East. Sixty minutes to East and Southeast Asia on 9610 and 15190 kHz; and to Australasia on 11850 (or 15270) kHz.

Radio Finland. Winters only at this time; see 0800 for specifics. Thirty minutes to Southeast Asia and Australasia on 15115 (or 15330) and 17800 (or 17820) kHz. One hour earlier in summer.

09:30

Radio Nederland. Repeat of the 0730 broadcast. Fifty-five minutes to Australasia on 9720 kHz; and a full hour to East and Southeast Asia winters on 7260 and 9810 kHz, and summers on 12065 and 13705 kHz.

FEBC Radio International, Philippines. Opens with *World News Update* and *Computer Corner*, followed by a 15-minute feature (try Friday's *Far East Forum* or Saturday's *Mailbag*). The first half hour of a 90-minute predominantly religious broadcast targeted at East and Southeast Asia on 11690 kHz.

Voice of Armenia. Winter Sundays only. Mainly of interest to Armenians abroad. Thirty minutes of Armenian *news* and culture. To Europe on 15275 and 15370 kHz. One hour earlier in summer.

10:00

■**BBC World Service for Europe.** ●*Newsdesk*, followed on the half-hour by 15 minutes of programming for students of English (alternative features are carried on channels for the Mideast, where this service is also targeted). At 1045 Monday through Saturday, you can enjoy ●*Off the Shelf*, serialized readings of world literature. This is replaced weekends by Alistair Cooke's ●*Letter from America* (Saturday), and Sunday's ●*Short Story*. Continuous to Europe on 9410, 12095, 15070 and 17640 kHz; and to the Mideast on 11760 and 15575 kHz.

■**BBC World Service for Asia and the Pacific.** Thirty minutes of ●*Newsdesk*, then features. Try ●*Anything Goes* (Monday), *Jazz for the Asking* (Wednesday), Thursday's ●*Brain of Britain* (or replacement quiz), and Friday's *The Vintage Chart Show*. Continuous to East Asia on 3910, 9740, 15280 and 17830 kHz; and to Australasia on 15280 kHz. Some of these channels close at 1030, but others are available for the full hour.

Monitor Radio International, USA. See 0000 for program details. Monday through Friday to eastern North America and the Caribbean on 6095 kHz, to South America (and audible in parts of North America) on 7395 kHz, to East Asia on 9430 kHz, and to Southeast Asia on 13625 kHz. Weekend programming is nonsecular, and is devoted to the teachings and beliefs of the Christian Science Church.

Radio Australia. *World News*, then weekdays it's *Asia Focus*, ●*International Report* and *Stock Exchange Report*. Saturday brings *Ockham's Razor* (science) and *Background Report*, replaced Sunday by *Charting Australia* and *Report from Asia*. Continuous to Asia and the Pacific, and heard in North America on 9580 and 9860 kHz. In Europe and the Mideast, try 21725 kHz. Listeners in East and Southeast Asia can opt for 7240, 9510 or 13605 kHz, although the last two frequencies are only available until 1030.

Swiss Radio International. Summers only at this time. Repeat of the 0600 transmission. Thirty minutes of news-related fare to Europe on 6165 and 9535 kHz. One hour later in winter.

Radio New Zealand International.
A mixed bag of Pacific regional *news*,
features, and relays of the domestic
National Radio network. Continuous to
the Pacific; summers on 6100 kHz, and
winters on 9700 kHz. Easily audible in
much of North America.

Voice of Vietnam. Begins with
news, then there's *Commentary* or
Weekly Review, followed by short features and some pleasant Vietnamese
music (especially at weekends). Heard
extensively on 9840 and (winters) 12019
or (summers) 15009 kHz. Targeted to
Asia at this hour.

Radio Vlaanderen Internationaal,
Belgium. Monday through Saturday,
winters only at this time. See 0900 for
program details. Twenty-five minutes to
Europe on 6035 kHz; may also use 5910
(or 5900) kHz. Elsewhere, try 15510 and
17595 kHz, targeted at Africa. One hour
earlier in summer.

Voice of America. The start of
VOA's daily broadcasts to the
Caribbean. *News*, followed Monday
through Friday by *VOA Today*—a compendium of news, sports, science, business and other features. Replaced
weekends by *VOA Saturday/VOA
Sunday*, which have less accent on
news, and more on features. On 6165,
7405 and 9590 kHz. For a separate service to Australasia, see the next item.

Voice of America. *News*, followed
Monday through Friday by *Stateside*, a
look at issues and personalities in different walks of American life. This is
replaced Saturday by ●*Encounter* and
Communications World, and Sunday by
Critic's Choice and a feature in slow-
speed English. To Australasia on 5985,
11720, and 15425 kHz.

Radio For Peace International,
Costa Rica. Another hour of countercul-
ture and social-conscience programs.
Offerings at this hour include *The Far
Right Radio Review* (1000 Wednesday),
Amnesty International Reports (1030

Sunday) and *My Green Earth* (a nature
program for children, same time
Monday). Continuous to North America
on 9400 kHz in the single-sideband
mode, which can be properly processed
only on some radios.

China Radio International.
Repeat of the 0900 broadcast. One hour
to Australasia on 11755 and 15440 kHz.

FEBC Radio International,
Philippines. The final hour of a 90-
minute mix of religious and secular programming for East and Southeast Asia.
Monday through Friday, it's *Focus on the
Family*, then a 15-minute religious feature, *Asian News Update* (on the half-
hour) and *In Touch*. All weekend offerings are religious in nature. On 11690
kHz.

All India Radio. *News*, then a com-
posite program of commentary, press
review and features, interspersed with
ample servings of enjoyable Indian
music. To East Asia on 15050, 15180 and
17895 kHz; and to Australasia on 15050
and 17387 kHz.

WJCR, Upton, Kentucky. Continues
with country gospel music to North
America on 7490 kHz. Other U.S. reli-
gious broadcasters operating at this
hour include **WWCR** on 5935 kHz,
KTBN on 7510 kHz, **WYFR-Family
Radio** on 5950 kHz, and **WHRI-World
Harvest Radio** on 6040 and 9850 kHz.
For traditional Catholic programming,
try **WEWN** on 7425 kHz.

Voice of Russia World Service.
News, followed winters by a variety of
features. Sunday and Wednesday it's
business in *Newmarket*, Monday features *This is Russia*, Thursday has
Science and Engineering, and there's a
listener-response program on Friday.
The second half hour consists mainly
of music, though noteworthy exceptions are Monday's ●*Audio Book Club*
and Saturday's potpourri,
Kaleidoscope. In summers, the news is
followed Tuesday through Saturday by

the timely ●*Commonwealth Update*, replaced Sunday by *This is Russia* and Monday by *Science and Engineering*. These, in turn, are followed by ●*Audio Book Club* (Sunday, Wednesday and Friday), *Russian by Radio* (Tuesday and Thursday) or music. Continuous to East and Southeast Asia and the Pacific. For Asia, try the winter channels of 9480, 11675, 12015, 17710 and 17860 kHz; and summer, choose from 11900, 15405, 17590, 17765, 17775 and 17860 kHz. Winters (local summers) in Australasia, go for 9550, 9800, 11710, 12015 and 17860 kHz; midyear, choose from 9835, 11800, 11900, 17590, 17765 and 17870 kHz.

HCJB—Voice of the Andes, Ecuador. Monday through Friday it's *Studio 9*. As 0100, but one day earlier. Saturdays feature *DX Partyline*, while Sundays are given over to *Saludos Amigos*. To Australasia on 5900 (or 6135) kHz.

Radio Korea International, South Korea. Summers only at this time. Starts off with *News*, followed Monday through Wednesday by *Economic News Briefs*. The remainder of the 30-minute broadcast is taken up by a feature: *Shortwave Feedback* (Sunday), *Seoul Calling* (Monday and Tuesday), *Pulse of Korea* (Wednesday), *From Us to You* (Thursday), *Let's Sing Together* (Friday) and *Weekly News Focus* (Saturday). On 11715 kHz via their Canadian relay, so this is the best chance for North Americans to hear the station. One hour later in winter.

Radio Prague, Czech Republic. This time summers only. Repeat of the 0600 broadcast. A half hour to Europe on 7345 and 9505 kHz. One hour later during winter.

Radio Nederland. Repeat of the 0830 transmission (except Tuesday, when *Mirror Images* is aired). Too, there's no

press review. Fifty-five minutes to East and Southeast Asia winters on 7260 and 9810 kHz, and summers on 12065 kHz. Also available, summers only, to Australasia on 9820 and 12065 kHz, and to Western Europe on 6045 and 9650 kHz.

Radio Austria International. ●*Report from Austria* (see 0730). Year-round to Australasia on 15450 and 17870 kHz, and winters only to Europe on 6155 and 13730 kHz.

United Arab Emirates Radio, Dubai. *News*, then a feature dealing with one or more aspects of Arab life and culture. Weekends, there are replies to listeners' letters. To Europe on 13675, 15395, 17825 (or 15320) and 21605 kHz.

■**BBC World Service for the Americas.** ●*Newsdesk*, followed on the half-hour by a mixed bag of features. Choice pickings include ●*Thirty-Minute Drama* (Tuesday), ●*Folk Routes* (Wednesday), ●*The Learning World* (1145 Thursday) and ●*Focus on Faith* (Friday). To eastern North America on 5965, 6195 and 9515 kHz.

■**BBC World Service for Europe.** Thirty minutes of the comprehensive ●*Newsdesk*, then a feature. Wednesday, Friday and Saturday bring *Meridian* (the arts), Monday has ●*Omnibus*, Tuesday airs the excellent ●*Thirty-Minute Drama*, Thursday's fare is *Rock Salad* (good, but not for all tastes), and Saturday swings to *Jazz for the Asking*. Continuous to Europe on 9410, 12095, 15070 and 17640 kHz; and to the Mideast on 11760 and 15575 kHz.

■**BBC World Service for Asia and the Pacific.** Identical to the service for Europe, except for Thursday (*Pick of the World*) and Saturday (first part of ●*Play of the Week*). Continuous to Asia on 3910, 9575, 9740, 11765, 11955 and 15360 kHz. The first half hour is available to Australasia via Radio New

Zealand International on 9700 (or 6100) kHz, but then the service is resumed via the BBC's own facilities on 9740 kHz.

Monitor Radio International, USA. See 0000 for program details. Audible Monday through Friday in eastern North America and the Caribbean on 6095 kHz, in Central and South America on 7395 kHz, in East Asia on 9355 kHz, and in Australasia on 9425 kHz. Weekends are given over to programming of a religious nature, not all of it necessarily in English.

Voice of Asia, Taiwan. One of the few stations to open with a feature: *Asian Culture* (Monday), *Touring Asia* (Tuesday), *World of Science* (Wednesday), *World Economy* (Thursday), and music on the remaining days. There is also a listener-response program on Saturday. After the feature there's a bulletin of news, and no matter what comes next, the broadcast always ends with *Let's Learn Chinese.* One hour to Southeast Asia on 7445 kHz.

Radio Australia. The first half hour consists of world and Australian *news* followed by a sports bulletin. Then comes a feature. Choose from *Innovations* (Monday), *Arts Australia* (Tuesday), *Science File* (Wednesday), *Book Talk* (Thursday), *The Parliament Program* (Friday), *Business Weekly* (Saturday) and *Fine Music Australia* (Sunday). Continuous to Asia and the Pacific on several channels, and easily heard in most of North America on 9580 and 9860 kHz. Beamed to Southeast Asia on 7240 (moves to 9560 at 1130), 9615 and 15530 kHz. This last frequency is also audible in Europe and the Mideast.

HCJB—Voice of the Andes, Ecuador. Thirty minutes of religious programming to Australasia on 5900 (or 6135) kHz. For a separate service to the Americas, see the next item.

HCJB—Voice of the Andes, Ecuador. First 60 minutes of a four-hour block of religious programming to the Americas on 12005 and (from 1130) 15115 kHz.

Voice of America. The second, and final, hour of the morning broadcast to the Caribbean. *News,* followed Monday through Friday by *Stateside,* a look at issues and personalities in the United States. Weekend fare consists of *Agriculture Today* and *Music U.S.A.* (Saturday), and *Critic's Choice* and *Studio One* (Sunday). On 6165, 7405 and 9590 kHz. For a separate service to Asia and Australasia, see the next item.

Voice of America. These programs are, in the main, different from those to the Caribbean. *News,* then Saturday it's *Agriculture Today* and ●*Press Conference U.S.A.;* Sunday there's ●*New Horizons* and ●*Issues in the News;* and weekdays have features in Special English followed by *Music U.S.A.* To East Asia on 6110, 9760 and 15160 kHz, and to Australasia on 5985, 9645, 11720 and 15425 kHz.

Radio Jordan. Summers only at this time. A 60-minute partial relay of the station's domestic broadcasts, beamed to Europe and eastern North America on 15170 kHz. One hour later in winter.

Voice of Russia World Service. Continuous programming to Asia at this hour. Starts off with *News,* then Tuesday through Saturday, winters, it's the informative ●*Commonwealth Update,* replaced Sunday by *This is Russia,* and Monday by *Science and Engineering.* Summers at this time, there's *News and Views,* with the second half-hour mostly given over to a variety of musical styles, including the top-rated ●*Folk Box* (Tuesday) and ●*Music at your Request* (Monday and Saturday). Winters at 1131, it's the literary ●*Audio Book Club* (alternating with *Russian by Radio* or a music program). Winters on 7205, 11675, 11835, 12015, 15150, 17680, 17755, 17765 and 17860 kHz; summers on 11900, 15110, 15405 and 15510 kHz, plus several channels between 17560 and 17870 kHz.

Winter reception is also possible in parts of Australasia on 9550, 9800, 11710 and 12015 kHz.

Voice of Vietnam. Repeat of the 1000 broadcast. A half hour to Asia on 7285 and 9730 kHz. Both frequencies vary somewhat.

Radio Singapore International. A three-hour package for Southeast Asia, and widely heard elsewhere. Starts with a summary of *news* and weather conditions in Asia and the Pacific, followed by a wide variety of short features, depending on the day of the week. These include Monday's eclectic *Frontiers*, Tuesday's *Kaleidoscope*, the literary *Bookmark* (Friday), and *Dateline RSI* (a listener-participation program, Sunday). At 1120 Monday through Friday, it's the *Business and Market Report*. There's *news* on the half-hour, then weekdays there's a brief press review, music, and either *Newsline* (1145 Monday, Wednesday and Friday) or *Business World* (same time, Tuesday and Thursday). Weekends, it's *The Week Ahead* (1133 Saturday and Sunday), *Regional Press Review* and *Newsline* (Saturday) or *The Sunday Interview*. On 9530 kHz.

CBC North-Québec, Canada. Summers only at this time; see 1200 for specifics. Intended for a domestic audience, but also heard in the northeastern United States on 9625 kHz.

Swiss Radio International. Thirty minutes of world and Swiss *news* and background reports. To Europe on 6165 and 9535 kHz, and to East Asia and Australasia on 9885 and 11640 (winter), 13635 and (summer) 15545 and 17515 kHz.

Radio Japan. On weekdays, opens with *Radio Japan News Round*, with news oriented to Japanese and Asian affairs. This is followed by *Radio Japan Magazine Hour*, which includes features like *Sports Spotlight* (Monday), *Japanese Culture* and *Today* (Tuesday), *Asian Report* (Wednesday), *Crosscurrents*

(Thursday) and *Business Focus* (Friday). *Commentary* and *News* round off the hour. These are replaced Saturday by *This Week*, and Sunday by *Hello from Tokyo*. One hour to North America on 6120 kHz, and to East and Southeast Asia on 9610 and 15295 (or 15350) kHz.

Radio For Peace International, Costa Rica. Continues with a variety of counterculture and social-conscience features. There is also a listener-response program at 1130 Wednesday and Sunday. To North America on 9400 kHz in the single-sideband mode, which can be properly processed only on superior world band radios.

Radio Pyongyang, North Korea. One of the last of the old-time communist stations, with quaint terms like "Great Leader" and "Beloved Comrade" being the order of the day. Starts with "*news*", with much of the remainder of the broadcast devoted to revering the memory of Kim Il Sung ("The Unrivaled Great Man"). Abominably bad programs, but worth the occasional listen just to hear how really awful they are. Fifty minutes to North America on 6576, 9977 and 11335 kHz.

WJCR, Upton, Kentucky. Continues with country gospel music to North America on 7490 kHz. Other U.S. religious broadcasters operating at this hour include **WWCR** on 5935 (or 15685) kHz, **KTBN** on 7510 kHz, **WYFR-Family Radio** on 5950 and 7355 (or 11830) kHz, and **WHRI-World Harvest Radio** on 6040 and 9850 kHz. Traditional Catholic programming (some of which may be in Spanish) can be found on **WEWN** on 7425 kHz.

11:30

Radio Finland. Summers only at this time. *Compass North*, a compilation of Finnish and other Scandinavian stories, followed Tuesday through Friday by a press review and, later in the broadcast,

Northern Lights. The remaining time is taken up by one or more short features. Sunday, there's *Focus* and *Nuntii Latini* (news in Latin), Monday brings *Economic Roundup,* Tuesday has sports, Wednesday features *Environment Report,* Thursday has *Finnish History,* Friday's presentation is *Culture Closeup,* and the Saturday offerings are *Starting Finnish* and *Capital Coffeebreak.* Thirty minutes to North America on 11900 and 15400 kHz. One hour later in winter.

Radio Korea International, South Korea. Winters only at this time. See 1030 for program details. A half hour on 9650 kHz via their Canadian relay, so a good chance for North Americans to hear the station. One hour earlier in summer.

Radio Nederland. Repeat of the 0730 broadcast, except that an additional *Press Review* is included. One hour to Western Europe on 6045 and (winter) 7130 or (summer) 9650 kHz.

Radio Austria International. Summers only at this time. ●*Report from Austria* (see 0730 for further details). Thirty minutes to Europe on 6155 and 13730 kHz, and to North America on 13730 kHz.

Radio Prague, Czech Republic. Winters only at this time. Repeat of the 0700 transmission (see 0600 for specifics). A half hour to Europe on 7345 and 9505 kHz. One hour earlier in summer.

Radio Sweden. Summers only at this time; see 1230 for program details. To Asia and Australasia on 13740, 15120 and 15240 kHz. One hour later during winter.

Radio Bulgaria. Summers only at this time. *News,* then Monday through Thursday there's 15 minutes of current events in *Today.* This is replaced Friday by *Weekly Spotlight,* a summary of the week's major political events. The remainder of the broadcast is given over to features dealing with Bulgaria and its people, plus some lively folk music. Sixty minutes to South and East Asia on 15635 and 17625 kHz. One hour later during winter.

Voice of the Islamic Republic of Iran. Sixty minutes of *news,* commentary and features, much of it reflecting the Islamic point of view. Targeted at the Mideast and South and Southeast Asia on 11745, 11790, 11875 (summer), 11930, 15260 and 11930 kHz.

12:00

■BBC World Service for the Americas. *World News*, then it's 10 minutes of specialized business and financial reporting. Next come one or more features, the best of which are ●*Anything Goes* (1215 Monday) and *The Vintage Chart Show* (same time Thursday). *Sports Roundup* follows at 45 minutes past the hour, except for Saturday, when it is replaced by the final quarter-hour of the popular *A Jolly Good Show*. Continuous to North America on 6195, 9515 and 11865 kHz.

■BBC World Service for Europe. *World News*, ●*World Business Report/Review/Brief* (easily the best program of its kind) and *Britain Today*. On the half-hour, it's classical music (Monday and Wednesday), a documentary (Tuesday and Thursday), ●*Science in Action* (Friday), popular music (Sunday), and ●*Brain of Britain* (or its substitute) on Saturday.

Continuous to Europe on 9410, 12095, 15070 and 17640 kHz; and to the Mideast on 11760 and 15575 kHz.

■BBC World Service for Asia and the Pacific. Monday through Saturday, opens with *World News* and ●*World Business Report/Review*. These are followed by a series of shows (mainly rock or popular music) geared to a youthful audience. Weekdays, the hour is rounded off with *Sports Roundup*, replaced Saturday by Alistair Cooke's ●*Letter from America*. Sunday is given over to the second half of ●*Play of the Week*, followed by ●*Andy Kershaw's World of Music*. Continuous to East Asia on 3915, 9575, 9740, 11765, 11955 and

15360 kHz; and to Australasia on 9740 kHz.

Monitor Radio International, USA. See 0000 for program details. Monday through Friday to eastern North America on 6095 kHz, to Central and South America on 9455 kHz, to Australasia on 9425 kHz, and to Southeast Asia on 9355 kHz. Weekends, the news-oriented fare gives way to religious programming.

Radio Canada International. Summer weekdays only. Tuesday through Friday, it's a shortened version of the Canadian Broadcasting Corporation's domestic *news* program ●*As It Happens*, which is replaced Monday by *Double Exposure* and *Royal Canadian Air Farce*. Sixty minutes to North America and the Caribbean on 9635, 11855 and 13650 kHz. One hour later in winter.

Radio Tashkent, Uzbekistan. *News* and commentary, followed by features such as *Life in the Village* (Wednesday), a listeners' request program (Monday), and local music (Thursday). Heard better in Asia, Australasia and Europe than in North America. Thirty minutes winters on 6025, 9715 and 13785 kHz; and summers on 7285, 9715, 15295 and 17815 kHz.

■Radio France Internationale. The first 30 minutes consist of *news* and correspondents' reports, with a review of the French press rounding off the half hour. The next 25 minutes are given over to a series of short features, including Sunday's *Paris Promenade* and *Club 9516* (a listener-response program); the weekday *RFI Europe*; sports (Monday and Thursday); *Arts in France, Books* and *Science Probe* (Tuesday); *Bottom Line* (business and finance) and *Land of France* (Wednesday); the biweekly *North/South* (or *Planet Earth*) and t*The Americas* (Thursday); *Film Reel* and *Made in France* (Friday); and Saturday's *Focus on France, Spotlight on Africa* and *Counterpoint* (human rights) or *Echoes from Africa*. A fast-moving information-packed 55 minutes to Europe on 9805, 15155 and 15195 kHz; and to North America on 11615 (15530 in summer) and 13625 kHz. In eastern North America, you can also try 15325 kHz, targeted at West Africa.

Polish Radio Warsaw, Poland. This time summers only. Fifty-five minutes of news, commentary, features and music—all with a Polish accent. Monday through Friday, it's *News from Poland*—a potpourri of news, reports and interviews. This is followed by *Jazz, Folk, Rock and Pop from Poland* (Monday), *Request Concert* and *A Day in the Life of...* (Tuesday), classical music and the historical *Flashback* (Wednesday), a communications feature and *Letter from Poland* (Thursday), and a Friday feature followed by *Business Week*. The Saturday broadcast begins with a bulletin of *news*, then there's *Weekend Papers* (a press review), *What We Said* (a summary of the station's output during the previous week) and an arts magazine, *Focus*. Sundays, you can hear *Weekend Commentary, Panorama* (a window on day-to-day life in Poland) and *Postbag*, a listener-response program. To Europe on 6135, 7145, 7270, 9525 and 11815 kHz. One hour later in winter.

Radio Australia. *World News*, then a feature. Saturday, there's *Ockham's Razor* (science), Wednesday and Sunday bring *Charting Australia*, and *Australiana* is broadcast on the remaining days. Weekdays on the half-hour, it's ●*International Report*, which is replaced Saturday by *Background Report*, and Sunday by *Report on Asia*. Not the most original of titles, but not much doubt about the content. Continuous to Asia and the Pacific, and well heard in North America on 5995 and 11800 kHz. In Southeast Asia, tune to 9560, 9615 or 15530 kHz. This last channel can also be heard in Europe and the Mideast.

Radio Jordan. Winters only at this time. A 60-minute partial relay of the station's domestic broadcasts, beamed to Europe and eastern North America on 15170 (or 9560) kHz. One hour earlier in summer.

Croatian Radio. Summers only at this time; actually starts at 1203. Ten minutes of English *news* from one of the domestic networks. A valuable source of up-to-the-minute information from the region. Heard best in Europe at this hour, but also audible in eastern North America. Channel usage varies, but try 5895, 5920, 7370, 9830 and 13830 kHz. One hour later in winter.

Swiss Radio International. Winters only at this time. Thirty minutes of *news* and background reports to Europe on 6165 and 9535 kHz. One hour earlier in summer.

Radio Korea International, South Korea. Opens with *news* and commentary, followed Monday through Wednesday by *Seoul Calling*. Weekly features include *Echoes of Korean Music* and *Shortwave Feedback* (Sunday), *Tales from Korea's Past* (Monday), *Korean Cultural Trails* (Tuesday), *Pulse of Korea* (Wednesday), *From Us to You* (a listener-response program) and *Let's Learn Korean* (Thursday), *Let's Sing Together* and *Korea Through Foreigners' Eyes* (Friday), and Saturday's *Discovering Korea, Korean Literary Corner* and *Weekly News Focus*. Sixty minutes to East Asia on 7180 (or 7285) kHz. For a separate (and shorter) service to Southeast Asia, see the following item.

Radio Korea International, South Korea. Starts off with *news*, followed Monday through Wednesday by *Economic News Briefs*. The remainder of the broadcast is taken up by a feature: *Shortwave Feedback* (Sunday), *Seoul Calling* (Monday and Tuesday), *Pulse of Korea* (Wednesday), *From Us to You* (Thursday), *Let's Sing Together* (Friday) and *Weekly News Focus* (Saturday). Thirty minutes to Southeast Asia on 9570 and 9640 kHz.

CBC North-Québec, Canada. Part of an 18-hour multilingual broadcast for a domestic audience, but which is also heard in the northeastern United States. Weekend programming at this hour is in English, and features *news* followed by the enjoyably eclectic ●*Good Morning Québec* (Saturday) or *Fresh Air* (Sunday). Starts at this time winters, but summers it is already into the second hour. On 9625 kHz.

HCJB—Voice of the Andes, Ecuador. Continuous religious programming to North America on 12005 and 15115 kHz.

Radio Norway International. Sunday only. *Norway Now*, a friendly 30-minute package of *news* and features targeted at Asia and Australasia, winters on 11850 and 15165 kHz, and summers on 13800 and 15170 kHz.

Radio Singapore International. Continuous programming to Southeast Asia and beyond. Starts with a brief summary of *news*, then the musical *E-Z Beat*. This is followed weekdays by the *Business and Market Report*, *news* on the half-hour, and then a feature. Monday, it's *Bookmark*, replaced Tuesday by *Reflections*, and Wednesday by *Frontiers*. Thursday brings *Snapshots*, and Friday has a listener-participation program, *Dateline RSI*. These are replaced Saturday by *Snapshots*, *Asean Notes* and *Arts Arena*, and Sunday by *Frontiers* and *Kaleidoscope*. On 9630 kHz.

Voice of Free China, Taiwan. *News*, followed by features. The last is *Let's Learn Chinese*, which has a series of segments for beginning, intermediate and advanced learners. Other features include *Jade Bells and Bamboo Pipes* (Monday), *Kaleidoscope* and *Main Roads and Byways* (Tuesday), *Music Box* (Wednesday), *Perspectives* and *Journey into Chinese Culture* (Thursday), *Confrontation* and *New Record Time* (Friday), *Reflections* (Saturday) and *Adventures of Mahlon and Jeanie* and *Mailbag Time* (Sunday). One hour to East Asia on 7130 kHz, and to Australasia on 9610 kHz.

Voice of America. *News*, followed Monday through Friday by *Stateside*. End-of-week programming consists of Saturday's *On the Line* and *Communications World*, and Sunday's ●*Encounter* and *Studio One*. To East Asia on 6110, 9760, 11715 and 15160 kHz; and to Australasia on 9645, 11715 and 15425 kHz.

China Radio International. *News* and a variety of features—see 0900 for specifics. One hour to Southeast Asia on 9715 and 11660 kHz; and to Australasia on 11795 and 15440 kHz.

Radio Nacional do Brasil (Radiobras), Brazil. Monday through Saturday, you can hear *Life in Brazil* or *Brazilian Panorama*, a potpourri of news, facts and figures about this fascinating land, interspersed with examples of the country's various unique musical styles. The *Sunday Special*, on the other hand, is devoted to one particular theme, and often contains lots of exotic Brazilian music. Eighty minutes to North America on 15445 kHz.

Radio For Peace International, Costa Rica. Part of an eight-hour cyclical block of counterculture, social-conscience and New Age programming. Some of the offerings at this hour include *WINGS* (news for and of women, 1230 Friday), a listener-response program (same time Saturday),; and *Sound*

Currents of the Spirit (1230 Monday). To North America and beyond on 9400 and 15050 kHz. Some transmissions are in the single-sideband mode, which can be properly processed only on some radios.

Voice of Russia World Service. Continuous programming to Asia at this hour. Winters, it's *News and Views*, then twenty-five minutes of entertainment. Monday's and Saturday's ●*Music at your Request* and Tuesday's ●*Folk Box* alternate with *Kaleidoscope* (Sunday), *Jazz Show* (Thursday) and music on the remaining days. Tuesday through Saturday, summers, there's *Focus on Asia and the Pacific*, then music of various styles. Pick of the weekend's programs is ●*Music and Musicians* at 1311 Sunday. Winters to East Asia on 5960, 6000, 7160 and 7205 kHz; and to the rest of continent on 4740, 4975, 9540, 11655, 11675 and 11760 kHz. Good summer bets are 5960, 7150, 9800 and 9895 kHz for East Asia; and 11820, 11880, 11940, 15350, 15405, 15510, 17590, 17645, 17775, 17835 and 17870 kHz for South and Southeast Asia (several of which are also audible in western parts of Australia).

WJCR, Upton, Kentucky. Continues with country gospel music to North America on 7490 kHz. Other U.S. religious broadcasters operating at this hour include **WWCR** on 5935 (or 13845) and 15685 kHz, **KTBN** on 7510 kHz, **WYFR-Family Radio** on 5950, 6015 (or 7355), 11830 and 11970 (or 17750) kHz, and **WHRI-World Harvest Radio** on 6040 and 9850 kHz. For traditional Catholic programming, tune **WEWN** on 7425 kHz.

12:15

Radio Cairo, Egypt. The start of a 75-minute package of news, religion, culture and entertainment. The initial quarter-hour consists of virtually anything, from quizzes to Islamic religious talks, then there's *news* and commen-

tary, which in turn give way to political and cultural items. To Asia on 17595 kHz.

12:30

Radio Bangladesh. *News*, followed by Islamic and general interest features, not to mention some very pleasant Bengali music. Thirty minutes to Southeast Asia, also heard in Europe, on 9548 (variable) and 13615 kHz.

Radio Canada International. *News*, followed Monday through Friday by *Spectrum* (topical events). The scientific *Innovation Canada* airs on winter Saturdays (replaced by *Earth Watch* during summer), and a year-round listener-response program occupies Sunday's slot. Thirty minutes to East and Southeast Asia, winters on 6150 and 11730 kHz, and summers on 9660 and 15195 kHz.

Radio Nederland. Repeat of the 0830 broadcast (see there for specifics), except for the press review. Fifty-five minutes to Europe winters on 6045 and 7130 kHz.

Swiss Radio International. Summers only at this time. Thirty minutes of news-related fare from SRI's satellite service. To Europe on 6165 and 9535 kHz. One hour later during winter.

Radio Finland. See 1130 for program specifics. Thirty minutes to North America on 11735 (winter), 11900 (summer) and 15400 kHz.

Voice of Vietnam. Repeat of the 1000 transmission. A half hour to Asia on 9840 and 12020 (or 15009) kHz. Frequencies may vary slightly.

Radio Austria International. Winters only at this time. ●*Report from Austria* (see 0730 for further details). Thirty minutes to Europe on 6155 and 13730 kHz, to North America on 13730 kHz, and to East Asia on 15450 kHz.

Voice of Turkey. This time summers only. Thirty minutes of *news*, fea-

Radio Sweden's English Service. Front: Bill Schiller (beard), Sarah Roxström, Jim Downing, Greta Grandin and James Proctor. Standing: Azariah Kiros, Al Simon, George Wood, Keith Foster and Mark Cummins.

tures and Turkish music targeted at the Mideast and Southwest Asia on 9675 kHz. One hour later in winter.

Radio Sweden. Monday through Friday, it's *news* and features in *Sixty Degrees North*, concentrating heavily on Scandinavian topics. Monday's accent is on sports; Tuesday has electronic media news; Wednesday brings *Money Matters*; Thursday features ecology or science and technology; and Friday offers a review of the week's news. Saturday's slot is filled by *Spectrum* (arts) or *Sweden Today*, and Sunday fare consists of *In Touch with Stockholm* (a listener-response program) or the musical *Sounds Nordic*. A half hour winters to Asia and Australasia on 13775, 15120 and 15240 kHz; and summers to North America on 11650 and 15240 kHz.

Radio Vlaanderen Internationaal, Belgium. Summer Sundays only at this time. *News, P.O. Box 26* (a listener-response program) and *Radio World*. Twenty-five minutes to eastern North America on 13670 kHz. One hour earlier in summer.

Radio Bulgaria. Winters only at this time. See 1230 for specifics. Sixty minutes to South and East Asia on 9770 and 11740 kHz. One hour earlier during summer.

13:00

■**BBC World Service for the Americas.** ●*Newshour*—the *crème de la crème* of all news shows. Sixty minutes to North America on 6195, 9515 and 11865 kHz.

■**BBC World Service for Europe.** Same as for the Americas. Sixty minutes of quality news reporting to Europe on 9410, 12095, 15070 and 17640 KHz; and to the Mideast on 11760 and 15575 kHz.

■**BBC World Service for Asia and the Pacific.** Same as for Europe and the Americas. Broadcast worldwide at this hour, it's too good to miss. Continuous to East Asia on 3915, 9740, 11955 and 15360 kHz; and to Australasia on 9740 kHz.

Monitor Radio International, USA. See 0000 for program details. Monday through Friday to North America on 6095 and 9455 kHz, to South Asia on 9355 kHz, and to Southeast Asia on 13625 kHz. Weekends are given over to religious offerings from and about the Christian Science Church.

Radio Canada International. Winter weekdays only. Tuesday through Friday, it's a shortened version of the Canadian Broadcasting Corporation's domestic *news* program ●*As It Happens*, while Monday's offerings are a listener-response program and *Innovation Canada*. Sixty minutes to North America and the Caribbean on 11855 and 17820 (or 13650) kHz. One hour earlier in summer. For an additional service, see the next item.

Radio Canada International. Summers only at this time; see 1400 for program details. Sunday only to North America and the Caribbean on 11955 and 17820 kHz.

Radio Pyongyang, North Korea. Repeat of the 1100 transmission. Fifty minutes to Europe on 9345 and 11740 kHz, to North America on 13760 and 15230 kHz, and to South and Southeast Asia on 9640 and 15230 kHz.

Swiss Radio International. Repeat of the 1100 broadcast. Strictly for news hounds. Thirty minutes to East and Southeast Asia on 7230 (or 7250), 7480, 11640 (winter), 13635 and (summer) 15460 (or 15545) kHz.

Radio Norway International. Summer Sundays only. Repeat of the 1200 transmission. A half hour of *news* and features targeted at Europe on 9590 kHz, and at North America on 11850 (or 15340) kHz.

Radio Nacional do Brasil (Radiobras), Brazil. The final 20 minutes of the broadcast beamed to North America on 15445 kHz.

Radio Vlaanderen Internationaal, Belgium. Monday through Saturday, summers only at this time. Repeat of the 0900 broadcast; see there for program details. Twenty-five minutes to eastern North America on 13670 kHz. One hour later in winter.

China Radio International. See 0900 for specifics. One hour to western North America summers on 7405 kHz, and year-round to Southeast Asia on 9715 and 11660 kHz, and to Australasia on 15440 kHz.

Polish Radio Warsaw, Poland. This time winters only. *News,* commentary, music and a variety of features. See 1200 for specifics. Fifty-five minutes to Europe on 6135, 7145, 7270, 9525 and 11815 kHz. One hour earlier during summer.

Radio Cairo, Egypt. The final half hour of the 1215 broadcast, consisting of listener participation programs, Arabic language lessons and a summary of the latest news. To Asia on 17595 kHz.

CBC North-Québec, Canada. Continues with multilingual program-ming for a domestic audience. *News,* then winter Saturdays it's the second hour of ●*Good Morning Québec,* replaced Sunday by *Fresh Air.* In summer, the news is followed by *The House* (Canadian politics, Saturday) or the highly professional ●*Sunday Morning.* Weekday programs are mainly in languages other than English. Audible in the northeastern United States on 9625 kHz.

Radio Romania International. First afternoon broadcast for European listeners. *News,* commentary, press review, and features about Romanian life and culture, interspersed with some lively Romanian folk music. Fifty-five minutes winters on 9690, 11790 and 11940 kHz; summers on 11940, 15365 and 17720 kHz.

Croatian Radio. Winters only at this time; actually starts at 1303. Ten minutes of on-the-spot *news* from one of Europe's political volcanoes. Best heard in Europe at this hour, but also audible in eastern North America. Frequency usage varies, but try 5985, 5920, 7370, 9830 and 13830 kHz. One hour earlier during summer.

Radio Australia. *World News,* then Monday through Friday it's *Asia Focus,* replaced Saturday by *Business Weekly,* and Sunday by *Oz Sounds.* On the half-hour, choose from *The Europeans* (Sunday), *The Australian Music Show* (Monday), *Jazz Notes* (Tuesday), ●*Blacktracker* (Wednesday), *Australian Country Style* (Thursday), ●*Music Deli* (Friday), and Saturday's *The Australian Scene.* Continuous to Asia and the Pacific on a number of frequencies, and tends to be easily audible in much of North America on 5995 and 11800 kHz. Available to East Asia (till 1330) on 9510 kHz, and to Southeast Asia on 9560 and 9615 kHz.

Radio For Peace International, Costa Rica. Continues at this hour with a potpourri of United Nations, counterculture and other programs. These include *WINGS* (news for and of women, 1330 Wednesday), *Vietnam Veterans Radio Network* (1330 Thursday) and *Focus on Haiti* (1300 Sunday). To North America on 9400 and 15050 kHz. Some transmissions are in the single-side-band mode, which can be properly processed only on some radios.

Radio Singapore International. The third and final hour of a daily broadcasting package to Southeast Asia and beyond. Starts with a summary of the latest *news*, then it's pop music. On the half-hour, there's a 10-minute *news* bulletin (replaced by a short summary at weekends), followed by *Newsline* (Monday, Wednesday and Friday), *Business World* (Tuesday and Thursday), *Regional Press Review* (Saturday), or *The Sunday Interview*. On 9630 kHz.

WJCR, Upton, Kentucky. Continues with country gospel music to North America on 7490 kHz. Other U.S. religious broadcasters operating at this hour include **WWCR** on 5935 (or 13845) and 15685 kHz, **KTBN** 7510 kHz, **WYFR-Family Radio** on 5950, 6015 (or 9705), 11830 and 11970 (or 17750) kHz, and **WHRI-World Harvest Radio** on 6040 and 15105 kHz. Traditional Catholic programming is available via **WEWN** on 7425 kHz.

Voice of Russia World Service. Continues to most of Asia. *News*, then very much a mixed bag depending on the day and season. Winter programming includes *Focus on Asia and the Pacific* (Tuesday through Saturday) and Sunday's ●*Music and Musicians*, both of which start at 1311. At the same time summer there's the business feature *Newmarket* (Tuesday and Saturday), *This is Russia* (Thursday), *Science and Engineering* (Sunday), and a listener-response program on Wednesday. ●*Audio Book Club* (Monday, Thursday and Saturday) is the obvious choice

from 1330 onwards, and alternates with *Russian by Radio* or a music program. Winters to East Asia on 6000, 7205 and 9540 kHz; and summers on 9800, 9895 and 11940 kHz. For the rest of Asia, try winters on 4740, 4975, 7295, 7350, 15150, 15460 and 15470 kHz; and summers on 11800, 17675, 17685, 17755, 17795 and 17835 kHz.

HCJB—Voice of the Andes, Ecuador. Sixty minutes of religious broadcasting. Continuous to the Americas on 12005 and 15115 kHz.

FEBC Radio International, Philippines. The first 60 minutes of a three-hour (mostly religious) package to South and Southeast Asia. Weekdays, starts with *Good Evening Asia*, which includes *News Insight* and a number of five-minute features (world band enthusiasts should look for Wednesday's *DX Dial*, also aired at 1330 Sunday). Other offerings include *World News Update* (1330 Monday through Saturday) and *Mailbag* (a listener-response program, 1340 Sunday). Most of the remaining features are religious in nature. On 11995 kHz.

Voice of America. *News*, then it's *Business and Finance* (Monday), *Inside USA* (Tuesday), *International Focus* (Wednesday), *Reporters Notebook* (Thursday), *Perspectives* (Friday and Saturday), and *Critic's Choice* (Sunday). The second half hour has features in Special English. To East Asia on 6110, 9760 and 15160 kHz; and to Australasia on 9645 and 15425 kHz. Both areas are also served by 11715 kHz until 1330.

13:30

United Arab Emirates Radio, Dubai. *News*, then a feature devoted to Arab and Islamic history and culture. Twenty-five minutes to Europe (also audible in eastern North America) on 13675, 15395, 17825 (or 15320) and 21605 kHz.

Radio Austria International.
●*Report from Austria* (see 0730 for more details). To East Asia on 15450 kHz.

Radio Vlaanderen Internationaal, Belgium. Winter Sundays only at this time. *News, P.O. Box 26* (a listener-response program) and *Radio World.* Twenty-five minutes to eastern North America on 13670 kHz. One hour later in winter.

Voice of Turkey. This time winters only. A reduced version of the normal 50-minute broadcast (see 2000). A half hour of *news* and features targeted at the Mideast and Southwest Asia on 9675 kHz. One hour earlier in summer.

Radio Finland. Repeat of the 1230 broadcast; see 1130 for program specifics. To North America on 11900 (summer), 17740 (winter) and 15400 kHz.

Radio Canada International. *News,* followed Monday through Friday by *Spectrum* (topical events), Saturday by *Innovation Canada,* and Sunday by a listener-response program (replaced winter by *Arts in Canada* for Asian listeners). To East Asia on 6150 (winter), 11795 (summer) and 9535 kHz. Also to Europe, the Mideast and Africa, summers only, on 15315, 15325, 17820, 17895 and 21455 kHz. The frequencies of 15315, 17820 and 17895 kHz are not available on Sundays.

RDP International—Radio Portugal. Monday through Friday, summers only, at this time. See 1900 for program details. Thirty minutes to the Mideast and South Asia on 21515 kHz. One hour later during winter.

Swiss Radio International. Winters only at this time. Repeat of the 1200 broadcast. *News,* reports and not much else. Thirty minutes to Europe on 6165 and 9535 kHz. One hour earlier in summer.

Radio Nederland. Repeat of the 0730 broadcast. Beamed to South Asia on 9890 (or 9895), 13700 and 15150 kHz. Also heard in the Mideast, especially on 13700 kHz.

Radio Sweden. See 1230 for program details. Thirty minutes to North America on 11650 and 15240 kHz.

Voice of Vietnam. Repeat of the 1000 transmission. A half hour to East Asia on 9840 and 12020 (or 15009) kHz. Also audible in parts of North America, especially during summer.

Voice of Greece. Summers only at this time, and actually starts around 1335. Several minutes of English news, preceded by a lengthy period of Greek music and programming. To North America on 15630 and 17525 kHz. One hour later during winter.

All India Radio. The first half hour of a 90-minute package of exotic Indian music, regional and international *news,* commentary, and a variety of talks and features of general interest. To Southeast Asia and beyond on 13732 and 15120 kHz.

Radio Tashkent, Uzbekistan. *News* and commentary, then features. Look for an information and music program on Tuesdays, with more music on Sundays. Apart from Wednesday's *Business Club,* most other features are broadcast on a non-weekly basis. Heard in Asia, Australasia, Europe and occasionally in North America; winters on 6025, 9715 and 13785 kHz; and summers on 7285, 9715, 15295 and 17815 kHz.

13:45

Vatican Radio. Twenty minutes of religious and secular programming to Southeast Asia and Australasia on 11625 and 15585 kHz.

14:00

■**BBC World Service for the Americas.** *World News,* then Monday through Friday it's the long-running and eclectic ●*Outlook,* followed by one or more interesting features. These include ●*Omnibus* (Monday), ●*Health Matters* (Tuesday), *Country Style* and *Good Books* (Wednesday), ●*Network UK* (Thursday), and *The Farming World* (1445 Friday). Weekend programming consists of Saturday's *Sportsworld* (winters from 1430), and a Sunday feature followed by *Music Review*. Continuous to North America on 9515 and 11865 kHz.

■**BBC World Service for Europe.** Weekdays until 1430 it's the same as for the Americas, then a different set of features, aimed at a younger audience. Pick of the pack is Wednesday's ●*Megamix*. Saturday's offerings are a mixed bag, while Sunday airs the exceptional ●*Play of the Week* (world theater). Continuous to Europe on 9410, 12095, 15070 and 17640 KHz; and to the Mideast on 12095 and 15575 kHz.

■**BBC World Service for South Asia.** Similar to the service for the rest of Asia (see below), except for the second half hour, when the features are different. Try ●*Development 96* (1445 Monday), ●*Health Matters* (same time Tuesday), *Sports International* (1430 Thursday) and ●*Global Concerns* (1445 Friday). On 11750 and 15310 kHz. Part of an 18-hour continuous block of programming, and a valid alternative for western North America on 11750 kHz at this hour.

■**BBC World Service for Asia and the Pacific.** Five minutes of *World News*, then Monday through Friday it's the popular magazine program ●*Outlook*. Choice plums during the second half hour include ●*Health Matters* (Monday), ●*Discovery* (Tuesday) and ●*Omnibus* (Wednesday). Saturday is given over to *Sportsworld*, and Sunday features *Write On* and ●*Concert Hall*. Continuous to East Asia on 3915, 7180 and 9740 kHz; and to Australasia on 9740 kHz. Also audible in western North America on 9740 kHz.

Monitor Radio International, USA. See 0000 for program details. Monday through Friday to East and South Asia on 9355 kHz. All weekend programs are nonsecular.

Radio Japan. Repeat of the 0600 broadcast; see there for specifics. One hour to western North America on 9535 and 11705 kHz, and to Asia on 9610, 11840 (or 11895) and 11915 kHz.

■Radio France Internationale. *News*, press reviews and correspondents' reports, with emphasis on events in Asia and the Mideast. These are followed, on the half-hour, by two or more short features (see the 1200 broadcast for specifics, although there may be one or two minor alterations). Fifty-five minutes of interesting and well-produced programming to the Mideast and beyond on 17560 kHz.

Voice of Russia World Service. Winters, it's *News* and a variety of features (see 1300 summer programs), followed on the half-hour by ●*Audio Book Club* (Monday, Thursday and Saturday), *Russian by Radio* or a music program. Summer offerings include the daily *News and Views* followed by some of the station's better entertainment features. Try Monday's ●*Folk Box* and Friday's ●*Music at your Request*, both of which should please. For different tastes, there's also *Jazz Show* (Wednesday) and *Yours for the Asking* (Thursday). Mainly to the Mideast and West Asia at this hour. Winters, try 4740, 4975, 6060, 7165, 9635, 12015 and 15320 kHz; in summer, check out 4740, 4975, 9595, 11835, 11910, 11935, 11945, 11985, 15320, 15480 and 15540 kHz.

Radio Australia. Begins with *World News* and a sports bulletin, then weekdays on the half-hour there's ●*International Report* followed, at 1450, by *Stock Exchange Report*. This is replaced Saturday by *Background Report*, and Sunday by *Report from Asia*. Continuous to Asia and the Pacific

on a number of frequencies, and also audible in western North America on 5995, 6060 (from 1430) and 11800 kHz. For East Asia (from 1430), try 9710 kHz, while listeners in Europe and the Mideast can shoot for 7260 (or 9615), 9770 and 11660 kHz. All three channels are available from 1430 onwards.

Voice of the Mediterranean, Malta. An unusual broadcasting package which leans less towards news, and more towards cultural topics. Sixty minutes (except for 1435-1500 Sunday) to Europe, North Africa and the Mideast on 11925 kHz.

China Radio International. See 0900 for specifics. One hour to western North America on 7405 kHz.

Radio Vlaanderen Internationaal, Belgium. Monday through Saturday, winters only at this time. Repeat of the 1000 broadcast; see 0900 for program details. Twenty-five minutes to eastern North America on 13670 kHz.

All India Radio. The final hour of a 90-minute package of regional and international *news*, commentary, features and exotic Subcontinental music. To Southeast Asia and beyond on 13732 kHz.

Radio Canada International. *News* and the Canadian Broadcasting Corporation's popular ●*Sunday Morning*. A three-hour broadcast starting at 1400 winters, and 1300 summers. Sunday only to North America and the Caribbean on 11955 and 17820 kHz.

HCJB—Voice of the Andes, Ecuador. Another hour of religious fare to the Americas on 12005 and (till 1430) 15115 kHz.

CBC North-Québec, Canada. Continues with multilingual programming for a domestic audience. *News*, followed winter Saturdays by *The House* (Canadian politics). In summer, it's *The Great Eastern*, a magazine for Newfoundlanders. Sundays, there's the excellent ●*Sunday Morning*. Weekday programs are in languages other than English. Audible in the northeastern United States on 9625 kHz.

Radio For Peace International, Costa Rica. Continues with counterculture and social-conscience programs ranging from *Peace Forum* (1400 Wednesday and Saturday, and 1430 Monday) to *The Far Right Radio Review* (1400 Monday). *My Green Earth*, a nature program for children, is aired at 1400 Friday. To North America and beyond on 9400 and 15050 kHz. Some transmissions are in the single-sideband mode, which can be properly processed only on some radios.

Radio Jordan. Summers only at this time. A partial relay of the station's domestic broadcasts, beamed to Europe on 15270 kHz. Continuous till 1630, and one hour later in winter.

Voice of America. *News*, followed weekdays by *Asia Report*. On Saturday there's jazz, and Sunday is given over to classical music. At 1455, there's a daily editorial. To East Asia on 6110, 9760 and 15160 kHz; and to Australasia on 15425 kHz.

FEBC Radio International, Philippines. Continues with mostly religious programming for South and Southeast Asia. For some secular fare, try *World News Update* (1430 Monday through Saturday) and *News from the Philippines* (1440 Monday through Friday). On 11995 kHz, and widely heard beyond the target areas.

WJCR, Upton, Kentucky. Continues with country gospel music to North America on 7490 kHz. Other U.S. religious broadcasters operating at this hour include **WWCR** on 13845 and 15685 kHz, **KTBN** on 7510 kHz, **WYFR-Family Radio** on 6015 (or 9705), 11830 and 17750 (or 17760) kHz, and **WHRI-World Harvest Radio** on 6040 and 15105 kHz. For traditional Catholic fare, try **WEWN** on 7425 kHz.

CFRX-CFRB, Toronto, Canada.

Audible throughout much of the northeastern United States and southeastern Canada during the hours of daylight with a modest, but clear, signal on 6070 kHz. This pleasant, friendly station carries news, sports, weather and traffic reports—most of it intended for a local audience. Call in if you'd like at +1 (514) 790-0600—comments from outside Ontario are welcomed.

14:30

Radio Nederland. Basically a repeat of the 0830 transmission, except for Saturday, when *Sounds Interesting* gets a second airing. Beamed to South Asia, and heard well beyond; winters on 9895, 13700 and 15150 kHz; summers on 9890 and 15150 kHz.

Radio Canada International. This time winters only. *News*, followed Monday through Friday by *Spectrum* (current events), Saturday by *Innovation Canada* (science), and Sunday by *The Mailbag* (a listener-response program). Thirty minutes to Europe, the Mideast and Africa on 9555, 11915, 11935, 15315, 15325 and 17820 kHz. The frequencies of 15315 and 17820 kHz are not available on Sundays. One hour earlier in summer.

Radio Romania International. Fifty-five minutes of *news*, commentary, features and some enjoyable Romanian folk music. Targeted at the Mideast and South Asia on 11740 (winter), 11775 (summer), 11810 (winter), 15335 and 17720 kHz.

Radio Sweden. Winters only at this time. Repeat of the 1330 broadcast; see 1230 for program specifics. *News* and features (sometimes on controversial subjects not often discussed on radio), with the accent strongly on Scandinavia. Thirty minutes to North America on 11650 and 15240 kHz.

Voice of Greece. Winters only at this time, and actually starts around 1435. Several minutes of English news, preceded by a lengthy period of Greek music and programming. To North America on 15630 (or 15650) and 17520 (or 17525) kHz. One hour earlier during summer.

Radio Finland. Winters only at this time. Starts with *Compass North*, a compilation of Finnish and other Scandinavian stories, followed Tuesday through Friday by a press review and, later in the broadcast, *Northern Lights*. The remaining time is taken up by one or more short features. The week starts off with *Focus* and *Nuntii Latini* (news in Latin)—one of the curiosities of world band radio. Monday features *Economic Roundup*, Tuesday has sports, Wednesday's slot is given over to *Environment Report*, Thursday has *Finnish History*, Friday's presentation is *Culture Closeup*, and the Saturday offerings are *Starting Finnish* and *Capital Coffee-break*. Thirty minutes to North America on 15400 and 17740 kHz. One hour earlier in summer.

RDP International—Radio Portugal. Monday through Friday, winters only, at this time. See 1900 for program details. Thirty minutes to the Mideast and South Asia on 21515 kHz. One hour earlier in summer.

Radio Austria International. Summers only at this time. ●*Report from Austria*; see 0730 for more details. To Europe on 6155 and 13730 kHz; to East Asia on 15450 kHz; and to West Africa (also heard in parts of Europe) on 9870 kHz.

15:00

■BBC World Service for the Americas. *News*, then a thoroughly mixed bag of programs, depending on the day of the week. Try Thursday's ●*The Learning World* and youth-oriented ●*Megamix*, Friday's ●*Concert Hall* (or its substitute), Saturday's *Sportsworld* and Sunday's *From Our*

Own Correspondent. Continuous to North America on 9515, 11775 and 11865 kHz.

■BBC World Service for Europe. Sunday through Friday, the first half hour consists of *World News*, *Sports Roundup* and a feature for students of English. The next 30 minutes feature some of the best of the BBC's output, including ●*Global Concerns* (Monday), ●*Development 96* and ●*Health Matters* (Tuesday), ●*Discovery* (Wednesday), ●*Network UK* (Thursday), and Friday's ●

Focus on Faith. Saturday airs five minutes of *news* followed by *Sportsworld*. Continuous to Europe on 6195 (winter), 9410, 12095 and 15070 kHz; and to the Mideast on 9410, 12095 and 15070 kHz.

■BBC World Service for South Asia. *World news*, then weekdays it's *Sports Roundup*. A mixed bag of features follow on the half-hour. Weekends, there's Saturday's live *Sportsworld*, and Sunday's excellent ●*Play of the Week*. On 5975 and 11750 kHz. Part of an 18-hour continuous block of programming, and a valid alternative for parts of western North America on 11750 kHz.

■BBC World Service for Asia and the Pacific. Monday through Friday, opens with *East Asia Today* and closes with *Sports Roundup*. Holding the middle ground are ●*Development 96* (Monday), *On Screen* (Tuesday), ●*The Learning World* (Wednesday), *From Our Own Correspondent* (Thursday), and Friday's ●*Global Concerns*. Weekends, there's Saturday's *Sportsworld* and Sunday's popular music and ●*Short Story* (sometimes preempted by live sports). Continuous to East Asia on 3915, 7180 and 9740 kHz; and to Australasia on 9740 kHz. Also audible in western North America on 9740 kHz.

Monitor Radio International, USA. See 0000 for program details. Monday through Friday to East and

A whole world of listening SANGEAN

Sangean ATS818 FM Stereo/MW/LW/SW PLL Synthesized Receiver

Continuous AM coverage from 150KHz to 29.999 MHz plus Broadcast FM reception from 87.5 to 108MHz. F ive different tuning methods: Direct frequency input, auto scanning, manual scanning, memory recall or conventional rotary (VFO) tuning. 45 memory preset with 9 presets each on FM, LW, MW (broadcast AM) and 18 presets on SW (shortwave) BFO (Beat Frequency Oscillator) for reception of LSB/USB (sideband) and CW (morse code) transmissions. Hi/Low tone control, standby timer alarm clock function and key -lock function Supplied with AC adaptor, external antenna adaptor,& shortwave handbook. .8W audio to 3" 4 ohm speaker. Size: 7.5"W x 5"H x 1.75"D. Wt. 4.5lbs. Requires 7 AA for portable power.

Sangean ATS818CS FM Stereo/MW/LW/SW PLL Synthesized Receiver

This is the same receiver as the 818 above , but with the addition of a built in cassette recorder which can be set to turn on and tape a program at a preset time. Like the ATS818 above, it offers FM stereo reception is available through the headphone jack. Dual time display clock for tracking Greenwich time and local time & sleep timer. Signal strength and battery strength indicators in LCD indicator. AM wide/narrow filter and RF gain to increase selectivity and prevent receiver overloading of this dual conversion design.

Sangean ATS808 FM Stereo/MW/LW/SW PLL Synthesized Receiver

Continuous 150 to 29999KHz shortwave plus FM coverage with five different tuning methods. 45 memory presets with 18 available for shortwave bands. Dual time display with alarm clock funtions and sleep timer. Supplied with suede pouch, stereo headphones, shortwave hand book, ext. antenna adaptor. Size: 8W x 4 1/2"H x 11/2"D.

South Asia on 9355 kHz. Weekends are devoted to the beliefs and teachings of the Christian Science Church.

China Radio International. See 0900 for program details. One hour to western North America winters on 7405 kHz. One hour earlier during summer.

Radio Australia. *World News*, followed Monday through Friday by *Asia Focus*, and weekends by *Oz Sounds*. On the half-hour there is a repeat of the 1130 features (see 1100 for specifics). Continuous to Asia and the Pacific, and also audible in western North America on 5995, 6060 and 11800 kHz. East Asia is best served by 9710 kHz, with 6080 and 11695 kHz available for southeastern parts. In Europe and the Mideast, try 7260 (or 9615), 9770 and 11660 kHz.

Radio Pyongyang, North Korea. See 1100 for program details. Fifty minutes to Europe, the Mideast and beyond on 9325, 9640, 9977 and 13785 kHz.

Voice of America. The first of several hours of continuous programming to the Mideast. *News*, then Monday through Friday there's *Newsline*, replaced Saturday by *Inside USA*, and Sunday by the science program ●*New Horizons*. On the half-hour, it's *Music USA* (weekdays), *Press Conference USA* (Saturday) and *Studio One* (Sunday). On 9700, 15205 (also heard in Europe) and 15255 kHz.

Radio Norway International. Winter Sundays only. *Norway Today*. *News* and features from and about Norway. A pleasant thirty minutes to the Mideast on 9480 kHz.

Radio Canada International. Continuation of the CBC domestic program ●*Sunday Morning*. Sunday only to North America and the Caribbean on 11955 and 17820 kHz.

Radio Japan. *News*, then weekdays there's 10 minutes of *Asian Top News* followed by a half-hour feature. Take your pick from *Profile* (Monday), *Enjoy Japanese* (Tuesday, repeated Thursday),

History and Classics (Wednesday) and Friday's *Music and Book Beat*. Weekends, look for *Asia Weekly* (Saturday) or Sunday's *Hello from Tokyo*. The broadcasts end with the daily *Pop-in*. One hour to western North America on 9535 kHz, to southern Africa on 15355 kHz, and to South Asia on 11955 kHz.

Voice of Russia World Service. Predominantly news-related fare for the first half hour, then a mixed bag, depending on the day and season. Best pickings are at 1531 winter, including ●*Folk Box* (Monday), *Jazz Show* (Wednesday), *Yours for the Asking* (Thursday), and ●*Music at your Request* (Friday). Summers, try *This is Russia* (1511 Monday), and *Moscow Yesterday and Today* (1531 Sunday). Continuous to the Mideast winters on 6035, 7165, 11910, 12015 and 15320 kHz; and summers on 4740, 8940, 4975, 9595, 11775, 11910, 11945, 15320 and 15540 kHz.

FEBC Radio International, Philippines. The final 60 minutes of a three-hour (mostly religious) broadcast to South and Southeast Asia. For secular programming, try the 10-minute news package at 1530 Monday through Saturday, and a listener-response feature at 1540 Saturday. On 11995 kHz, and often heard outside the target area.

WJCR, Upton, Kentucky. Continues with country gospel music to North America on 7490 and 13595 kHz. Other U.S. religious broadcasters operating at this hour include **WWCR** on 13845 and 15685 kHz, **KTBN** on 7510 (or 15590) kHz, and **WYFR-Family Radio** on 11705 (or 15215), 11830 and 17750 (or 17760) kHz. Traditional Catholic programming is available from **WEWN** on 7425 kHz.

Radio For Peace International, Costa Rica. The final 60 minutes of an eight-hour cyclical block of United Nations, counterculture, social-conscience and New Age programming. Not for every taste, but one of the very few world band stations to provide this type of programming. To North America and beyond on 9400 and 15050 kHz. Some transmissions are in the single-side-band mode, which can be properly processed only on some radios.

Radio Jordan. A partial relay of the station's domestic broadcasts, beamed to Europe on 15270 (or 9560) kHz. Continuous till 1730, and one hour earlier in summer.

CFRX-CFRB, Toronto, Canada. See 1400.

15:30

Radio Nederland. A repeat of the 0730 broadcast except for Saturday, when a sports program replaces *Sounds Interesting*. Fifty-five minutes to South Asia and beyond on 9890 (or 9895) and 15150 kHz.

Radio Austria International. ●*Report from Austria*, a half hour of news and human interest stories. Ample coverage of national and regional issues, and a valuable source of news about Central and Eastern Europe. Winters only to Europe on 6155 and 13730 kHz, and to the Mideast on 9880 kHz. Available year round to South and Southeast Asia on 11780 kHz.

Radio Finland. Summers only at this time. See 1430 winter broadcast for program details. Thirty minutes to North America on 11900 and 15400 kHz. One hour later in winter.

Voice of the Islamic Republic of Iran. Sixty minutes of *news*, commentary and features, most of it reflecting the Islamic point of view. To South and Southeast Asia (and also heard elsewhere) on 9575 (winter), 11790 (winter), 11875 (summer), 15260 and 17750 kHz.

16:00

■BBC World Service for the Americas. *World News*, then it's predominantly arts or sports. *Meridian* (an arts magazine) is aired Wednesday, Friday and (when live sports don't preempt it) Sunday. Sports fans come into their own on Saturday (*Sportsworld*) and Thursday (*Sports International*). On other days, it's a documentary or general feature. The hour is rounded off with the 15-minute *Britain Today*, except when there are live sports programs. Continuous to North America on 9515, 11775 and 11865 kHz.

■BBC World Service for Europe. Fifteen minutes of *World News*, then Sunday, Tuesday and Friday there's classical music (except when Sunday's ●*The Greenfield Collection* is preempted by live sports coverage). Choice plum from the remaining days is ●*Folk Routes* at 1645 Wednesday. Continuous to Europe on 6195 (winters), 9410, 12095 and 15070 kHz; and to the Mideast on 9410, 12095 and 15070 kHz.

Monitor Radio International, USA. A one-hour show updated throughout the day and broadcast to different parts of the globe. *News*, then ●*Monitor Radio*—news analysis and news-related features with emphasis on international developments. The final 10 minutes consist of a listener-response program and a religious article from the *Christian Science Monitor* newspaper. Available Monday through Friday to Africa and beyond on 9355 and 21640 kHz. Weekends, this news programming is replaced by religious offerings from and about the Christian Science Church, not necessarily all in English.

■Radio France Internationale. *News*, press reviews and correspondents' reports, with particular attention paid to events in Africa. These are followed by two or more short features (basically a repeat of the 1200 broadcast, except for weekends when there is more emphasis on African themes). A fast-moving fifty-five minutes to Africa on 11615 (winter), 11700, 12015, 15210 (or 17795), 15460 and 15530 kHz. Available in

Europe on 6175 kHz, and in parts of the Mideast on 15460 kHz. Some of these frequencies are also audible, to a varying degree, in eastern North America. Best bet is 11700 kHz, but 15210 (or 17795) kHz is another possibility.

United Arab Emirates Radio, Dubai. Starts with a feature on Arab history or culture, then music, and a bulletin of *news* at 1630. Answers listeners' letters at weekends. Forty minutes to Europe (also heard in eastern North America) on 13675, 15395, 17825 (or 15320) and 21605 (or 11795) kHz.

■**Deutsche Welle,** Germany. *News*, followed Monday through Friday by ●*Newsline Cologne*, *African News* and a feature. Weekends, the news is followed by *Africa in the German Press*, *Focus on Development* (or *Women on the Move*) and *Economic Notebook* (Saturday), and *The Week in Germany*, *Religion and Society* and *Through German Eyes* (Sunday). A 50-minute broadcast aimed primarily at Africa, but also audible in the Mideast. Try 7185 (or 7195), 9735, 11965, 15145 (winters) and 17800 kHz.

Radio Korea International, South Korea. Opens with *news* and commentary, followed Monday through Wednesday by *Seoul Calling*. Weekly features include *Echoes of Korean Music* and *Shortwave Feedback* (Sunday), *Tales from Korea's Past* (Monday), *Korean Cultural Trails* (Tuesday), *Pulse of Korea* (Wednesday), *From Us to You* (a listener-response program) and *Let's Learn Korean* (Thursday), *Let's Sing Together* and *Korea Through Foreigners' Eyes* (Friday), and Saturday's *Discovering Korea*, *Korean Literary Corner* and *Weekly News Focus*. One hour to East Asia on 5975 kHz, to Europe on 6480 kHz, and to the Mideast and beyond on 9515 and 9870 kHz.

Radio Norway International. Summer Sundays only. *Norway Today*. A half hour of *news* and features targeted

at western North America on 11850 kHz.

Radio Pakistan. Fifteen minutes of *news* from the Pakistan Broadcasting Corporation's domestic service, followed by a similar period at dictation speed. Intended for the Mideast and Africa, but heard well beyond on several channels. Choose from 7425 (or 9435), 9470 (or 9485), 11570, 11710 (or 17660), 13590, 15555, 15675 and 17660 kHz.

Radio Prague, Czech Republic. Summers only at this time. *News* and features with a distinctly Czech slant, including *Talking Point* (Tuesday), *Calling All Listeners* (Wednesday), *Economic Report* and *Stamp Corner* (Thursday), *I'd Like you to Meet...* and *From the Archives* (Friday), and *The Arts* on Saturday. There is also a Sunday musical feature, replaced Monday by a magazine program. A half hour to Europe on 5930 kHz, and to East Africa and the Mideast on 17485 kHz. One hour later in winter.

Voice of Vietnam. Repeat of the 1000 transmission. A half hour to Africa (and heard well beyond) on 9840 and 12020 (or 15009) kHz.

Radio Australia. *World News*, then Monday through Friday it's *Australiana*, replaced Saturday by *Asia Focus*, and Sunday by *Background Report*. Weekdays on the half-hour there's ●*International Report*, replaced weekends by *Business Weekly* (Saturday), and *Report from Asia* (Sunday). Continuous to Asia and the Pacific on a number of frequencies, and also audible in Europe and the Mideast on 6080 (from 1630), 7260 (or 9615), 9770 (to 1630) and 11660 kHz. In East Asia, tune to 9710 kHz, with 11695 kHz also available for the southeastern part of the continent. Western North America is served by 5995 (to 1630), 6060, 9860 (from 1630) and 11800 kHz.

Channel Africa, South Africa. Broadcasts to the African continent at this hour, but can also be heard winters in Europe and eastern North America on 15240 kHz.

Radio Tirana, Albania. Summers only at this time. Approximately 10 minutes of *news* and commentary from and about Albania. To Europe on 7155 and 9760 kHz. One hour later during winter.

Radio Jordan. A partial relay of the station's domestic broadcasts, beamed to Europe on 15270 (or 9560) kHz. Continuous till 1730 (1630 during winter).

Voice of Russia World Service. *News*, then very much a mixed bag, depending on the day and season. Winters, there's *Focus on Asia and the Pacific* (Tuesday through Saturday) and *This is Russia* (Sunday), followed on the half-hour by a variety of musical styles. Pick of the summer programming is ●*Music and Musicians* (1611 Saturday) and ●*Audio Book Club* (1631 Monday and Friday). Other options (all at 1611) include *Science and Engineering* (Tuesday), *This is Russia* (Wednesday and Sunday), and the business-oriented *Newmarket* (Monday and Friday). Continuous to the Mideast winters on 4740, 4940, 4975, 6035, 7210, 9830, 11910 and 12015 kHz; and summers on 11715, 11910, 15480 and 15540 kHz. Also available summers to Europe on 7350, 9480, 9820, 9880, 11630, 11675 and 15105 kHz.

Radio Canada International. Winters only. Final hour of CBC's ●*Sunday Morning.* Sunday only to North America and the Caribbean on 11955 and 17820 kHz.

"Rush Limbaugh Show," WRNO, New Orleans, Louisiana. Summer weekdays only at this time. The first sixty minutes of a three-hour live package. Arguably of little interest to most listeners outside North America, but popular and controversial within the United States. To North America, the Caribbean and beyond on 15420 kHz.

Voice of America. Several hours of continuous programming aimed at an African audience. Monday through Friday, starts at 1630 with *Africa World Tonight*. This is replaced weekends by a full hour (from 1600) of *Nightline Africa*—special news and features on African affairs. Heard well beyond the target area—including North America—on a number of frequencies. Try 11920, 12040, 13710, 15225, 15410, 15445 and 17895 kHz. For a separate service to the Mideast, see the next item.

Voice of America. *News*, then a weekly feature: *Business and Finance* (Monday), *Inside USA* (Tuesday), *International Focus* (Wednesday), *Reporter's Notebook* (Thursday), *Perspectives* (Friday), *On the Line* (Saturday) or ●*Encounter* (Sunday). There is a daily program in Special English on the half-hour. To the Mideast on 9700, 15205 (also heard in Europe) and 15255 kHz.

WJCR, Upton, Kentucky. Continues with country gospel music to North America on 7490 and 13595 kHz. Other U.S. religious broadcasters operating at this hour include **WWCR** on 13845 and 17535 kHz, **KTBN** on 15590 kHz, and **WYFR-Family Radio** on 11705 (or 15215), 11830, 15355, 21525 and 21615 kHz. Traditional Catholic programming can be heard via **WEWN** on 7425 kHz.

CFRX-CFRB, Toronto, Canada. See 1400.

16:15

Radio Sweden. Summers only at this time. See 2030 for specifics. Thirty minutes to Europe on 6065 kHz. One hour later in winter.

16:30

Radio Canada International. *News*, then Monday through Friday it's *Spectrum* (current events). *Innovation Canada* airs on Saturday, and a listener-response program occupies Sunday's slot. Thirty minutes to Asia on 7150 and 9550 kHz.

Radio Finland. Winters only at this time. Repeat of the 1430 broadcast; see there for program details. Thirty minutes to North America on 13645 and 15400 kHz. One hour earlier in summer.

Radio Cairo, Egypt. The first 30 minutes of a two-hour package of Arab music and features reflecting Egyptian life and culture, with *news* and commentary about events in Egypt and the Arab world. There are also quizzes, mailbag shows, and answers to listeners' questions. Mediocre audio quality often spoils what otherwise could be an interesting broadcast. To southern Africa on 15255 kHz.

16:45

Radio Canada International. Summers only at this time. Fifteen minutes of news for Europe and the Mideast on 9555, 11935, 15325 and 17820 kHz. One hour later in winter.

17:00

■**BBC World Service for the Americas.** *World News,* followed by ten informative minutes of specialized business and financial reporting. The final quarter-hour of a continuous block of programming to the Americas on 9515, 11775 and 11865 kHz.

■**BBC World Service for Europe.** Opens with the same 15 minutes as on the Americas service (see above), and continues with a veritable mixed bag of features, the best of which is Wednesday's *From Our Own Correspondent.* The final half hour consists of the weekday ●*The World Today* (replaced Saturday by *From the Weeklies*) and the daily *Sports Roundup.* Continuous to Europe on 3955 (winters), 6180, 6195, 9410, 12095 and (summers) 15070 kHz; and to the Mideast on 9410,

12095 and 15070 kHz. Some of these channels are well heard in eastern North America.

■**BBC World Service for Africa.** *World News, Focus on Africa, African News* and *Sports Roundup.* Part of a 20-hour daily service to the African continent on a variety of channels. Best reception outside Africa at this hour (including parts of North America) is on 15400 and 17830 kHz.

Monitor Radio International, USA. See 1600 for program details. Available Monday through Friday to Africa and beyond on 9355 and 21640 kHz. Weekend programming at this and other times is of a religious nature, and may be in languages other than English.

Radio Pakistan. Opens with 15 minutes of *news* and commentary. The remainder of the broadcast is taken up by a repeat of the features from the 0800 transmission (see there for specifics). Fifty minutes to Europe on 7485 and 11570 (or 9855) kHz.

Radio Prague, Czech Republic. See 1600 for specifics. A half hour of *news* and features beamed to Europe on 5930 kHz; also winters to the Mideast on 9420 kHz, and summers to southwestern Europe and West Africa on 15640 kHz.

Radio Australia. Begins with world and Australian *news,* followed by a sports bulletin. Weekdays on the half-hour there's a repeat of the 1330 feature (see 1300 for specifics). Weekend offerings consist of Saturday's *One World* (the environment) and Sunday's *The Australian Scene.* Continuous to southern Asia and the Pacific on a number of channels, and audible in Europe and the Mideast on 6080, 7260 (or 9615) and 11660 kHz. Also heard in western North America on 6060, 9580, 9860 and 11695 kHz.

Swiss Radio International. World and Swiss *news* and background reports. Information at the expense of entertainment. Thirty minutes to the Mideast and East Africa on 6205 (winter), 9885, 12075 (summer) and 13635 kHz.

Polish Radio Warsaw, Poland. This time summers only. Monday through Friday, it's *News from Poland*—a compendium of news, reports and interviews. This is followed by *Request Concert* and *A Day in the Life of...* (Monday), classical music and the historical *Flashback* (Tuesday), a communications feature and *Letter from Poland* (Wednesday), a feature and a talk or special report (Thursday), and Friday's *Focus* (the arts in Poland) followed by *Business Week*. The Saturday broadcast begins with a bulletin of *news*, then there's *Weekend Papers* (a press review), *Panorama* (a window on day-to-day life in Poland) and a listener-response program, *Postbag*. Sundays, you can hear *What We Said* (a summary of the station's output during the previous week) and *Jazz, Folk, Rock and Pop from Poland*. Fifty-five minutes to Europe on

5995, 7270 and 7285 kHz. One hour later during winter.

Radio Jordan. Winters only at this time. The last 30 minutes of a partial relay of the station's domestic broadcasts, beamed to Europe on 15270 (or 9560) kHz.

Voice of Russia World Service. The initial half hour is taken up winters by *News* and features (see 1600 summer programs), with the choice plum being Saturday's ●*Music and Musicians*. Summers, there's the daily *News and Views*. Pick of the final 30 minutes include ●*Audio Book Club* (Monday and Friday, winter), and the summer offerings of *Kaleidoscope* (Sunday), *Jazz Show* (Tuesday), ●*Music at your Request* (Thursday) and Friday's ●*Folk Box*. Continuous to Europe winters on 7115, 7170, 7180, 7205, 7330 and 9890 kHz; and summers on 9480, 9880, 11630 and 15105 kHz. Also to the Mideast winters on 9575 and 9860 kHz, and summers on 11960, 12065 and 15480 kHz.

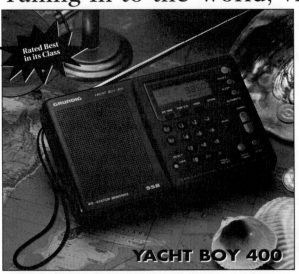

Radio For Peace International, Costa Rica. The first daily edition of *FIRE* (Feminist International Radio Endeavour), and the start of the English portion of an eight-hour cyclical block of predominantly social-conscience and counterculture programming. Audible in North America and elsewhere on 9400 and 15050 kHz. Some transmissions are in the single-sideband mode, which can be properly processed only on some radios.

Radio Japan. Repeat of the 1500 broadcast, except that Sunday's *Hello from Tokyo* is replaced by *Let's Learn Japanese*, *Media Roundup* and *Viewpoint*. One hour to the Mideast on 11930 kHz, to western North America on 9535 kHz, and to Asia on 6150, 9570 (or 11840) and 9580 kHz.

HCJB—Voice of the Andes, Ecuador. The first of three hours of religious and secular programming targeted at Europe. Monday through Friday it's *Studio 9*. As 0100, but one day earlier. Saturdays feature *DX Partyline*, while Sundays are given over to *Saludos Amigos*. On 15490 (or 15350) kHz.

Radio Tirana, Albania. Winters only at this time. Approximately 10 minutes of *news* and commentary from and about Albania. To Europe on 7155 and 9760 kHz. One hour earlier during summer.

Radio Pyongyang, North Korea. Repeat of the 1100 transmission. Fifty minutes to Europe, the Mideast and beyond on 9325, 9640, 9977 and 13785 kHz.

Voice of America. *News*, then Monday through Friday it's the interactive *Talk to America*. Weekend programming consists of *Reporter's Notebook* and *Communications World* (Saturday), and Sunday's *Critic's Choice* and ●*Issues in the News*. To Europe on 6040, 9760 and 15205 kHz; and to the Mideast on 9700 and 15255 kHz. For a separate service to Africa, see the next item.

Voice of America. Programs for Africa. Monday through Saturday, identical to the service for Europe and the Mideast (see previous item). On Sunday, opens with *News*, then it's *Voices of Africa* and ●*Music Time in Africa*. Audible well beyond where it is targeted. On 11920, 12040, 13710, 15410, 15445 and 17895 kHz. For yet another service (to East Asia and the Pacific), see the next item.

Voice of America. Monday through Friday only. *News*, followed by the interactive *Talk to America*. Sixty minutes to East and Southeast Asia on 5990, 6045, 7170, 9550, 9770 and 11870 kHz; and to Australasia on 7150 kHz.

■**Radio France Internationale.** An additional half hour (see 1600) of predominantly African fare. To East Africa on 15210 (or 17795) and 15460 kHz. The latter frequency is also available to parts of the Mideast, while the remaining channel can sometimes be heard in eastern North America.

Radio Cairo, Egypt. See 1630 for specifics. Continues with a broadcast to southern Africa on 15255 kHz.

"Rush Limbaugh Show," WRNO, New Orleans, Louisiana. Monday through Friday only; see 1600 for specifics. Starts at this time winters; summers, it's already into the second hour. Continuous to North America, the Caribbean and beyond on 15420 kHz.

WJCR, Upton, Kentucky. Continues with country gospel music to North America on 7490 and 13595 kHz. Other U.S. religious broadcasters operating at this hour include **WWCR** on 13845 and 15685 kHz, **KTBN** on 15590 kHz, and **WHRI-World Harvest Radio** on 13760 and 15105 kHz.

WWCR, Nashville, Tennessee. Summer weekdays, carries the disestablishmentarian "Preparedness Hour" on 12160 kHz.

CFRX-CFRB, Toronto, Canada. See 1400.

17:15

Radio Sweden. Winters only at this time. See 2030 for program details. Thirty minutes to Europe on 6065 kHz. One hour earlier in summer.

17:30

Radio Nederland. Targeted at Africa, but heard well beyond. *News*, followed Monday through Saturday by *Newsline* and a feature. Monday's science program ●*Research File* is undoubtedly the pick of the week, but there is other interesting fare on offer—try *Mirror Images* (Tuesday) or Wednesday's documentaries, some of which are excellent. Other programs include *Media Network* (Thursday), a sports feature (Friday), *Sounds Interesting* (Saturday), and Sunday's *Happy Station*. Monday through Friday there is also a *Press Review*. One hour on 6020, 7120 (summer), 9605 (winter) and 11655 kHz.

Radio Sweden. Summers only at this time. See 2030 for program details. Thirty minutes to Europe, the Mideast and Africa on 6065, 13605 (or 13690) and 15600 kHz. One hour later in winter.

Radio Romania International. *News*, commentary, a press review, and one or more short features. Thirty minutes to eastern and southern Africa (and also heard elsewhere). Winters on 9510, 9750, 11740 and 11940 kHz; and summers on 15340, 15365 and 17805 kHz.

Radio Almaty, Kazakhstan. Summers only at this time. See 1830 for further details. One hour later during winter.

17:45

All India Radio. The first 15 minutes of a two-hour broadcast to Europe, the Mideast and Africa, consisting of regional and international *news*, commentary, a variety of talks and features, press review and enjoyably exotic Indian music. Continuous till 1945. To Europe on 7412, 9650, 11620 and 13750 kHz; and on 9950, 11935 and 15075 to the remaining areas.

Radio Canada International. Winters only at this time. Fifteen minutes of news for Europe and the Mideast on 5995, 11935, 13610, 15325 and 17820 kHz. One hour later in winter.

Voice of Armenia. Monday through Friday only. Mainly of interest to Armenians abroad. Fifteen minutes of *news* from and about Armenia. To the Mideast on 4810, 4990 (winter), 7480 and (summer) 9675 and 11960 kHz.

1800-2359
Europe & Mideast—Evening Prime Time
East Asia—Early Morning
Australasia—Morning
Eastern North America—Afternoon
Western North America—Midday

18:00

■BBC World Service for Europe.
Thirty minutes of ●*Newsdesk*, with the
next half hour containing some varied
and interesting fare. Monday's
●*Omnibus* is substituted Tuesday by
light entertainment (often humorous);
Wednesday has classical music;
Thursday and Friday feature documentaries; and Saturday airs the highly
informative ●*Science in Action*.
Continuous to Europe on 3955 (winter),
6180, 6195, 9410, 12095 and (summer)
15070 kHz; and to the Mideast on 9410,
12095 and 15070 kHz. Some of these
channels provide good reception in
eastern North America.

■BBC World Service for Africa.
●*Newsdesk*, then Monday through
Friday it's *Focus on Africa*. This is
replaced Saturday by *Education
Express*, with Sunday featuring the discussion program *African Perspective*.
Continuous programming to the African
continent (and heard beyond) on 6005
(from 1830), 6190, 9630 (from 1830), 15400
and 17830 kHz. The last two channels
are audible in parts of North America.

**■BBC World Service for the
Pacific.** Identical to the service for
Europe at this hour. To Australasia on
9740 (from 1830) and 11955 kHz.

Monitor Radio International,
USA. See 1600 for program details.
Monday through Friday to Eastern
Europe on any one channel from 9370,
13770 and 15665 kHz; to Europe and the
Mideast on 9355 kHz; to South Africa on
17510 kHz; and to Australasia on 9355

kHz. Weekends are given over to
Christian Science religious programming.

Radio Kuwait. The start of a three-
hour package of *news*, Islamic-oriented
features and western popular music.
Some interesting features, even if you
don't particularly like the music. There
is a full program summary at the beginning of each transmission, to enable you
to pick and choose. To Europe and eastern North America on 11990 kHz.

Voice of Vietnam. Repeat of the
1000 transmission. A half hour to Europe
on 9840 and 12020 (or 15009) kHz.

Radio For Peace International,
Costa Rica. Part of a continuous eight-
hour cyclical block of social-conscience,
counterculture and New Age programming. One of international broadcasting's more unusual features, *The Far
Right Radio Review*, can be heard at
1800 Tuesday. Other offerings include
Amnesty International Reports (1830
Saturday) and *My Green Earth* (a nature
program for children, same time
Monday). To North America and beyond
on 9400 and 15050 kHz. Some transmissions are in the single-sideband mode,
which can be properly processed only
on some radios.

Radio Vlaanderen Internationaal,
Belgium. Summers only at this time. See
1900 for program details. Twenty-five
minutes to Europe on 5910 kHz, and to
Africa on 13685 kHz. One hour later in
winter.

All India Radio. Continuation of
the transmission to Europe, the Mideast
and beyond (see 1745). *News* and com-

mentary, followed by programming of a more general nature. To Europe on 7412, 9650, 11620 and 113750 kHz; and to the Mideast and Africa on 9950, 11935 and 15075 kHz.

Radio Prague, Czech Republic. Winters only at this time. Repeat of the 1700 broadcast (see 1600 for program details). A half hour to Europe on 5930 kHz, and to East Africa and the Mideast on 9420 kHz. One hour earlier in summer.

Radio Norway International. Sunday only. *Norway Now.* Repeat of the 1200 transmission. Thirty minutes of Norwegian hospitality targeted at Europe, the Mideast and Africa, winters on 7120 and 11930 kHz, and summers on 5960, 13805 and 15220 kHz.

HCJB—Voice of the Andes, Ecuador. Continues with a three-hour block of religious and secular programming to Europe. Monday through Friday it's the same features as 0200 (see there for specifics), but one day earlier. Weekend programs are mainly of a religious nature. On 15490 (or 15350) kHz.

Radio Australia. *World News,* followed Monday through Friday by *Asia Focus* and ●*International Report.* Saturday, it's *Pacific Religion* and *Background Report,* replaced Sunday by *Pacific Women* and *Report from Asia.* Continuous to Asia and the Pacific on a number of channels, and also audible in Europe and the Mideast on 7260 kHz. For East Asia, try 11660 kHz; and in western North America, tune to 9580, 9860 or 11695 kHz.

Radio Nacional do Brasil (Radiobras), Brazil. A repeat of the 1200 broadcast. Eighty minutes to Europe on 15265 kHz.

Polish Radio Warsaw, Poland. This time winters only. See 1700 for program specifics. *News,* music and features, covering multiple aspects of Polish life and culture. Fifty-five minutes to Europe on 5995, 7270 and 7285 kHz. One hour earlier in summer.

"World Wide Country Radio," WWCR, Nashville, Tennessee. Summers only at this time (one hour later in winter). A country package of music, information, contests and more. Part of a much longer broadcast to Europe and eastern North America, Monday through Friday, on 12160 kHz. Winter weekdays, this channel carries the disestablishmentarian "Preparedness Hour."

Voice of Russia World Service. Predominantly news-related fare during the initial half hour, with *News and Views* the daily winter offering. In summer, it's ●*Commonwealth Update* Monday through Friday, and *Top Priority* on Saturday. At 1830, winter features include Tuesday's *Jazz Show,* Wednesday's *Yours for the Asking,* ●*Music at your Request* (Thursday), and Friday's exotic ●*Folk Box.* In summer, look for some interesting musical selections, replaced Sunday by *Moscow Yesterday and Today.* Continuous to Europe winters on 7105, 7170, 7180, 7205 and 7340 kHz; and summers on 7350, 9480, 9880, 11630, 11675 and 15105 kHz. Also to the Mideast, winters on 9530, 9575 and 11945 kHz; summers on 11910, 11945, 11960 and 15480 kHz.

Voice of America. *News,* then a weekly feature: *Business and Finance* (Monday), *Inside USA* (Tuesday), *International Focus* (Wednesday), *Reporter's Notebook* (Thursday), *Perspectives* (Friday), *Agriculture Today* (Saturday) or ●*Encounter* (Sunday). There is a daily program in Special (slow-speed) English on the half-hour. To Europe on 3980, 6040, 9760 and 15205 kHz; and to the Mideast on 9770 (or 9700) kHz. For a separate service to Africa, see the next item.

Voice of America. Monday through Friday, it's 60 minutes of *Africa World Tonight,* with weekend programs identical to those for Europe and the Mideast (see above). To Africa, but heard well beyond, on 4975 (Monday through

Friday), 11920, 12040, 13710, 15410, 15580 and 17895 kHz.

Radio Algiers, Algeria. *News*, then rock and popular music, with an occasional brief feature also thrown in. One hour of so-so reception in Europe on 11715 kHz, and occasionally heard in eastern North America. Sometimes heard irregularly on 17745 kHz.

Radio Cairo, Egypt. See 1630 for specifics. The final 30 minutes of a two-hour broadcast to southern Africa on 15255 kHz.

Radio Omdurman, Sudan. A one-hour package of *news* and features (often from a pro-government viewpoint), plus a little ethnic Sudanese music. Better heard in Europe than in North America, but occasionally audible in the eastern United States. On 9200 kHz.

"Rush Limbaugh Show," WRNO, New Orleans, Louisiana. Monday through Friday only; see 1600 for specifics. Continuous to North America, the Caribbean and beyond on 15420 kHz.

"For the People," WHRI, Noblesville, Indiana. Summers only at this time; see 0300 for specifics. Three hours of live populist programming targeted at North America on 9495 kHz. One hour later in winter.

WJCR, Upton, Kentucky. Continues with country gospel music to North America on 7490 and 13595 kHz. Other U.S. religious broadcasters operating at this time include **WWCR** on 13845 and 15685 kHz, **KTBN** on 15590 kHz, and **WHRI-World Harvest Radio** on 13760 and 15105 kHz. For traditional Catholic programming, tune **WEWN** on 7425 kHz.

CFRX-CFRB, Toronto, Canada. See 1400.

18:15

Radio Bangladesh. *News*, followed by Islamic and general interest features. Thirty minutes to Europe on 7190

and 9685 kHz. Frequencies may be slightly variable.

18:30

Radio Nederland. Well heard in parts of North America, despite being targeted at Africa. *News*, followed Monday through Saturday by *Newsline* and a feature. These include the music program *Sounds Interesting* (Wednesday), ●*Research File* (Thursday) and an often excellent documentary (Friday). Sixty minutes on 6015 (winter), 6020, 7120 (summer), 9605 (winter), 9860, 9895, 11655, 13700 (summer), 15315 and 17605 kHz. The last two frequencies, via the relay in the Netherlands Antilles, are best for North American listeners.

Radio Austria International. Summers only at this time; the informative ●*Report from Austria*. A half hour to Europe, the Mideast and Africa on 5945, 6155, 9880 and 13730 kHz. One hour later during winter.

Radio Slovakia International. Summers only at this time. *Slovakia Today*, consisting of *news* and features dealing with multiple aspects of Slovak life and culture. Try a feature on tourism (Monday); history, sport and culture (Tuesday); business and economic matters (Wednesday), politics and science (Thursday), and culture on Friday. Saturday's "Best of" series is replaced Sunday by *Listeners' Tribune* and special features. Thirty minutes to Western Europe on 5915, 6055 and 7345 kHz. One hour later in winter.

Radio Sweden. Winters only at this time. See 2030 for program details. Thirty minutes to Europe, Africa and the Mideast on 6065, 9655 and 13690 kHz. One hour earlier in summer.

Radio Tirana, Albania. Summers only at this time. *News*, commentary and short features about events in Europe's most obscure backwater. Complemented with some pleasant

Albanian music. Thirty minutes to Europe on 7155 and 9760 kHz. One hour later during winter.

Radio Yugoslavia. Summers only at this time. *News* and short features with a strong regional slant. Thirty minutes to Europe on 6100 kHz, and to Africa on 9720 kHz. One hour later during winter.

Radio Almaty, Kazakhstan. Winters only at this time. Thirty minutes of *news* and features, consisting of a variety of topics, depending on which day you listen. Offerings include programs with an Islamic slant, readings from Kazakh literature, features on the country's history and people, and a mailbag program. Saturdays and Sundays are given over to recordings of the country's music, ranging from rarely heard folk songs to even rarer Kazakh opera. One of the most exotic stations to be found on the world bands, so give it a try. These broadcasts are not targeted at any particular part of the world, since most of the transmitters use only a modest 20 to 50 kilowatts, and the antennas are, in the main, omnidirectional. No matter where you are, try 5035, 5260, 5960, 5970, 9505, 11825, 15215, 15250, 15270, 15315, 15360, 15385, 17605, 17715, 17730, 17765 and 21490 kHz. One hour earlier in summer.

19:00

■**BBC World Service for Europe.** ●*Newshour*, the standard for all in-depth news shows from international broadcasters. Sixty fully packed minutes to Europe on 3955 (winters), 6180, 6195, 9410 and (summers) 12095 and 15070 kHz; and to the Mideast on 9410 kHz, 12095 and 15075 kHz. Some of these

channels are also easily heard in eastern North America.

■BBC World Service for the Pacific. ●*Newshour*. The best. To Australasia on 9740 and 11955 kHz.

■BBC World Service for Africa. A series of features aimed at the African continent, but worth a listen even if you live farther afield. The list includes *Fast Track* (Sports, Monday), *Money Focus* (Tuesday), *Talkabout Africa* (discussion, Wednesday), *Education Express* (Thursday), *African Quiz* or *African Perspective* (Friday), ●*The Jive Zone* (music and musicians, Saturday), and *Postmark Africa* (Sunday). Continuous programming to the African continent (and heard beyond) on 6005, 6190, 9630, 15400 and 17830 kHz. The last two channels are audible in parts of North America.

Monitor Radio International, USA. See 1600 for program details. Monday through Friday to Europe and the Mideast on 9355 kHz; to Eastern Europe on any one channel from 9370, 13770 and 15665 kHz; and to West Africa on 17510 kHz. This news-oriented programming is replaced weekends by nonsecular offerings from and about Christian Scientists.

Radio Nacional do Brasil (Radiobras), Brazil. Final 20 minutes of the 1800 broadcast to Europe on 15265 kHz.

Radio Vlaanderen Internationaal, Belgium. Winters only at this time. Weekdays, there's *News, Press Review* and *Belgium Today*, followed by features like *Focus on Europe* (Monday), *Living in Belgium* and *Green Society* (Tuesday), *The Arts* and *Around Town* (Wednesday), *Economics* and *International Report* (Thursday), and *The Arts* and *Tourism* (Friday). Weekend features include *Music from Flanders* (Saturday) and Sunday's *P.O. Box 26* (a listener-response program) and *Radio World*. Twenty-five minutes to Europe on 5910 kHz; also to Africa (and heard elsewhere) on 9925 kHz. One hour earlier in summer.

Radio Australia. Begins with *World News, Pacific News* (Monday through Friday) and *Sports Report*. These are followed, on the half-hour, by a feature. Choose from *Innovations* (Monday), *Arts Australia* (Tuesday), *Science File* (Wednesday), *Book Talk* (Thursday), *The Parliament Program* (Friday), *One World* (the environment, Saturday) and *Business Weekly* (Sunday). Continuous to Asia and the Pacific on a number of channels, and also audible in Europe and the Mideast on 7260 kHz. To East and Southeast Asia on 6150 and 11660 kHz, and heard in western North America on 9580, 9860 and 11695 kHz.

Radio Norway International. Winter Sundays only. *Norway Now. News* and features from and about Norway. Thirty minutes to Europe and Africa on 5960 and 9590 kHz, and to Australasia on 7215 kHz.

Radio Vilnius, Lithuania. Summers only at this time. A 30-minute window on Lithuanian life. To Europe on 9710 kHz. One hour later in winter.

Radio Kuwait. See 1800; continuous to Europe and eastern North America on 11990 kHz.

Kol Israel. Summers only at this time. ●*Israel News Magazine*. Thirty minutes of even-handed and comprehensive news reporting from and about Israel. To Europe and eastern North America on 7465, 9435, 11603 and 11685 kHz; and to Central and South America on 15640 kHz. One hour later in winter.

All India Radio. The final 45 minutes of a two-hour broadcast to Europe, the Mideast and Africa (see 1745). Starts off with *news*, then continues with a mixed bag of features and Indian music. To Europe on 7412, 9650, 11620 and 13750 kHz; and to the Mideast and Africa on 9950, 11935 and 15075 kHz.

Radio Bulgaria. Summers only at this time. *News*, then Monday through Thursday there's 15 minutes of current events in *Today*, replaced Friday by *Weekly Spotlight*, a summary of the week's major political stories. The remainder of the broadcast is given over to features dealing with Bulgaria and Bulgarians, and includes some lively ethnic music. To Europe, also audible in eastern North America, on 9700 and 11720 kHz. One hour later during winter.

HCJB—Voice of the Andes, Ecuador. The final sixty minutes of a three-hour block of predominantly religious programming to Europe on 15490 (or 15350) kHz.

Radio Budapest, Hungary. Summers only at this time. *News* and features, some of which are broadcast on a regular basis. These include Sunday's *Bookshelf* a press review (Monday, Tuesday, Thursday and Friday), *Profiles* (Tuesday), and *Focus on Business* (Wednesday). Thirty minutes to Europe on 3955, 6140, 7130 and 9835 kHz. One hour later in winter.

"World Wide Country Radio," **WWCR,** Nashville, Tennessee. Continuous programming targeted at fans of country music. To Europe and eastern North America, Monday through Friday, on 12160 kHz.

■**Deutsche Welle,** Germany. Repeat of the 1500 broadcast. Fifty minutes to Africa and the Mideast, and heard well beyond. Winters, try 9670, 9765, 11785, 11810, 11865, 13790, 15145 and 15425 kHz; in summer, go for 7170, 9670, 9735, 11740, 11785, 13690 and 13790 kHz.

Radio Finland. Summers only at this time; see 2000 for specifics. Thirty minutes to Europe on 9730 and 15440 kHz. One hour later in winter.

Radio Romania International. *News*, commentary, press review and features. Regular spots include *Youth Club* (Tuesday), *Romanian Musicians* (Wednesday), and Thursday's *Listeners'*

Letterbox and ●*Skylark* (Romanian folk music). Fifty-five minutes to Europe; winters on 5955, 6105, 6190 and 7195 kHz; and summers on 9550, 9690, 11810 and 11940 kHz. Also audible in eastern North America.

Radio Japan. Repeat of the 1500 transmission; see there for specifics. One hour to East and Southeast Asia on 6150 and 9580 kHz, to Australasia on 7140 and 11850 kHz, and to western North America on 9535 kHz.

Voice of Russia World Service. *News*, followed winter weekdays by ●*Commonwealth Update*, and Saturday by *Top Priority*. Summers, it's the daily *News and Views*. The second half hour consists of a variety of musical styles, except for *Moscow Yesterday and Today* (winter Sundays, 1831). To Europe winters on 5995, 6055, 6110, 7105, 7170, 7180, 7205, 7340 and 9890 kHz; and summers on 7230, 7350, 9480, 9865, 9880, 11630, 11675 and 15105 kHz. Some of these channels are audible in eastern North America. Also available winters to the Mideast on 7210, 7275, 9530 and 9575 kHz.

Voice of Greece. Winters only at this time, and actually starts about three minutes into the broadcast, following some Greek announcements. Approximately ten minutes of *news* from and about Greece. To Europe on 6260 and 9380 kHz.

RDP International—Radio Portugal. Monday through Friday, summers only, at this time. *News*, then features: *Visitor's Notebook* (Monday), *Musical Kaleidoscope* (Tuesday), *Challenge of the 90's* (Wednesday), *Spotlight on Portugal* (Thursday), and either *Listeners' Mailbag* or *DX Program* and *Collector's Corner* (Friday). Thirty minutes to Europe on 6130, 9780 and 9815 kHz, and to Africa on 15515 kHz. One hour later in winter.

Radio Thailand. A 60-minute package of *news*, features and (if you're lucky) enjoyable Thai music. To Northern Europe winters on 11855 kHz, and summers on 7200 kHz. Also available to Asia on 9655 and 11905 kHz.

Radio For Peace International, Costa Rica. Continues with a variety of counterculture and social-conscience features. There is also a listener-response program at 1930 Tuesday and Saturday. Audible in Europe and North America on 9400 and 15050 kHz. Some transmissions are in the single-side-band mode, which can be properly processed only on some radios.

Swiss Radio International. This time summers only. World and Swiss *news* and background reports for a European audience. Thirty minutes on 6165 kHz. One hour later during winter.

Voice of Vietnam. Repeat of the 1800 transmission (see 1000 for program specifics). A half hour to Europe on 9840 and 12020 (or 15009) kHz.

Voice of America. Continuous programming to Europe, Africa and the Mideast. *News,* followed Monday through Saturday by *Newsline.* Sunday has *International Focus* to Europe, North Africa and the Mideast, and *Voices of Africa* to the rest of Africa. On the half-hour, the African service carries an editorial and *World of Music* (weekdays), ●*Press Conference U.S.A.* (Saturday), and ●*Music Time in Africa* (Sunday). For the rest of Africa, Europe and the Mideast, there's *Music USA* (Monday through Saturday) and Sunday's ●*Press Conference USA.* The European transmission is on 3980, 6040, 9760 and 15205 kHz (available to the Mideast on 9700 or 9770 kHz), and the African service (also heard in North America) goes out on 7375, 7415, 11920, 12040, 15410, 15445 and 15580 kHz. For a separate service to Australasia, see the following item.

Voice of America. *News,* then Sunday through Friday there's *Newsline* and *Music USA,* replaced Saturday by *International Focus* and *Press*

Conference USA. One hour to Australasia on 9525, 11870 and 15180 kHz.

"Rush Limbaugh Show," WRNO, New Orleans, Louisiana. See 1600 for specifics. Winters only at this time. The final sixty minutes of a three-hour presentation. Popular and controversial within the United States, but of little interest to most other listeners. To North America, the Caribbean and beyond on 15420 kHz.

Radio Korea International, South Korea. Repeat of the 1600 broadcast. one hour to Europe on 6480 kHz, and to East Asia on 5975 and 7275 kHz.

Radio Argentina al Exterior— R.A.E. Monday through Friday only. *News* and short features dealing with Argentinian life and culture, interspersed with fine examples of the country's various musical styles, from chamamé to zamba. Fifty-five minutes to Europe on 15345 kHz.

"For the People," WHRI, Noblesville, Indiana. See 0300 for specifics. Monday through Friday only. A three-hour populist package broadcast live to North America on 9495 kHz.

WJCR, Upton, Kentucky. Continues with country gospel music to North America on 7490 and 13595 kHz. Other U.S. religious broadcasters operating at this time include **WWCR** on 13845 and 15685 kHz, **KTBN** on 15590 kHz, and **WHRI-World Harvest Radio** on 13760 kHz. For traditional Catholic programming, try **WEWN** on 7425 kHz.

CFRX-CFRB, Toronto, Canada. See 1400.

19:30

Polish Radio Warsaw, Poland. Summers only at this time. Weekdays, it's *News from Poland*— news, reports and interviews on the latest events in the country. This is followed by classical music and the historical *Flashback*

(Monday), *DX-Club* and *Letter from Poland* (Tuesday), a feature and a talk or special report (Wednesday), *Focus* (the arts in Poland) and *A Day in the Life of...* (Thursday), and *Postbag* (a listener-response program) followed by *Business Week* (Friday). The Saturday transmission begins with a bulletin of *news*, then there's *Weekend Papers* (a press review) and, later in the broadcast, *Jazz, Folk, Rock and Pop from Poland*. Sundays, you can hear *Panorama* (a window on day-to-day life in Poland) and *Request Concert*. Fifty-five minutes to Europe on 5995, 6135 and 7285 kHz. One hour later during winter.

Radio Slovakia International. Winters only at this time. *News* and features with a strong Slovak accent. See 1930 for specifics. Thirty minutes to Western Europe on 5915, 6055 and 7345 kHz. One hour earlier in summer.

Voice of the Islamic Republic of Iran. Sixty minutes of *news*, commentary and features with a strong Islamic slant. Not the lightest of programming fare, but reflects a point of view not often heard in western countries. To Europe on 7260 and 9022 kHz.

Radio Yugoslavia. Winters only at this time; see 1830 for specifics. Thirty minutes to Europe on 6100 kHz, and to Africa on 9720 kHz. One hour earlier in summer.

Radio Austria International. Winters only at this time. News and human-interest stories in ●*Report from Austria*. A half hour to Europe, the Mideast and Africa on 5945, 6155, 9880 and 13730 kHz. One hour earlier in summer.

Radio Tirana, Albania. Winters only at this time. A thoroughly Albanian package of *news*, commentary, short features and pleasant music. Thirty minutes to Europe on 7260 and 9730 kHz. One hour earlier during summer.

Radio Nederland. Repeat of the 1730 transmission; see there for specifics. Fifty-five minutes to Africa on 6020 (winter), 7120 and 7305 (summer), 9605 (winter), 9860, 9895, 11655, 13700 (summer), 15315 and 17605 kHz. The last two frequencies are heard well in many parts of North America.

Radio Roma, Italy. Actually starts at 1935. Approximately 12 minutes of *news*, then music. Twenty sleep-inducing minutes, best given a miss unless you suffer from insomnia. To western Europe on 7275, 9575 and 11905 kHz.

19:50

Vatican Radio. Summers only at this time. Twenty minutes of programming oriented to Catholics. To Europe on 4005, 5882 and 7250 kHz. One hour later in winter.

20:00

■**BBC World Service for Europe.** Sunday through Friday, there's 30 minutes of the latest news, comment and analysis in *Europe Today* (may be broadcast one hour later in winter). This is followed weekdays by the popular magazine program ●*Outlook*. Pick of the weekend offerings include Saturday's *Write On, From the Weeklies* and *From Our Own Correspondent*; and Sunday's ●*Folk Routes* (2030). Continuous programming on 3955 (winter), 6180, 6195, 7325 and 9410 kHz. Some of these channels are also well heard in eastern North America.

■**BBC World Service for the Pacific.** Identical to the service for Europe at this hour. To Australasia on 9740 and 11955 kHz.

Monitor Radio International, USA. See 1600 for program details. Monday through Friday to Europe on any two frequencies from 7510, 9355, 11645 and 13770 kHz. Replaced weekends by programs devoted to the beliefs and teachings of the Christian Science Church.

■Deutsche Welle, Germany. *News*, followed Monday, Wednesday and Friday by *Germany Today*, and Tuesday and Thursday by ●*European Journal*. Then comes a feature: *Come to Germany* (Monday), *Backdrop* (Tuesday), *Science and Technology* (Wednesday), *Living in Germany* (Thursday) and *German by Radio* (Friday). Weekend fare consists of Saturday's *Sports Report*, *The Week in Germany* and *Weekend*; replaced Sunday by *Through German Eyes* and a music feature. Fifty minutes to Europe winters on 5960 and 7285 kHz, and summers on 7170 and 9615 kHz.

Radio Canada International. Summers only at this time. The first hour of a 90-minute broadcast to Europe and beyond. *News*, followed Monday through Friday by *Spectrum* (current events), which is replaced Saturday by *Innovation Canada* and ●*Earth Watch*, and Sunday by *Arts in Canada* and a listener-response program. To Europe and Africa on 5995 (also available in the Mideast), 7235, 11985, 13650, 13670, 15150, 15325 and 17820 kHz. Some of these are audible in parts of North America. One hour later during winter.

Radio Habana Cuba. Sixty minutes of *news* and features, with a strong emphasis on Cuba and its people. Some lively Cuban music, too. To Europe winters on 11720 kHz, and summers on 11705 kHz. Also audible in eastern North America.

Radio Damascus, Syria. Actually starts at 2005. *News*, a daily press review, and different features for each day of the week. These can be heard at approximately 2030 and 2045, and include *Arab Profile* and *Palestine Talk* (Monday), *Syria and the World* and *Listeners Overseas* (Tuesday), *Around the World* and *Selected Readings* (Wednesday), *From the World Press* and *Reflections* (Thursday), *Arab Newsweek* and *Cultural Magazine* (Friday),

Welcome to Syria and *Arab Civilization* (Saturday), and *From Our Literature* and *Music from the Orient* (Sunday). Most of the transmission, however, is given over to Syrian and some western popular music. One hour to Europe, often audible in eastern North America, on 12085 and 15095 kHz.

Radio Vilnius, Lithuania. Winters only at this time. *News* and features reflecting events in Lithuania. Thirty minutes to Europe on 9710 (or 6100) kHz. One hour earlier in summer.

Swiss Radio International. This time winters only. Thirty minutes of *news* and background reports for Europe and North Africa on 6165 kHz. One hour earlier in summer. There is an additional year-round broadcast for central and southern Africa (also audible in eastern North America) on 9770, 9885, 11640 and 13635 kHz.

Radio Australia. Starts with world *news*, then Monday through Thursday it's *Australiana*, with features for listeners in the South Pacific on the remaining days. Weekdays on the half-hour, look for ●*International Report*, replaced Saturday by *Background Report*, and Sunday by *Report from Asia*. Continuous to Asia and the Pacific on several channels, and also heard in Europe and the Mideast on 7260 kHz. Available to East Asia on 11660 kHz, to Southeast Asia on 6150 kHz, and to western North America on 9580, 9860 and (till 2030) 11695 kHz.

Voice of Russia World Service. *News*, then winters it's more of the same in *News and Views*, replaced summer by a series of features. These include *Science and Engineering* (Thursday), the business-oriented *Newmarket* (Wednesday and Sunday), and Friday's *This is Russia*. On the half-hour, there's music during winter, and a variety of features in summer. Choose from *Jazz Show* (Monday and Friday), *Yours for the*

Asking (Tuesday), ●*Music at your Request* (Wednesday), ●*Folk Box* (Thursday), and Saturday's *Kaleidoscope*. To Europe winters on 4860, 5905, 5920, 5995, 6055, 6110, 7170, 7180, 7205, 7230, 7400 and 9890 kHz; and summers on 7350, 9480, 9880, 11630, 11675 and 11730 kHz. Some of these channels are also audible in eastern North America.

Radio Kuwait. The final sixty minutes of a three-hour broadcast to Europe and eastern North America (see 1800). Regular features at this time include *Theater in Kuwait* (2000), *Saheeh Muslim* (2030) and *News in Brief* at 2057. On 11990 kHz.

Radio Bulgaria. This time winters only; see 1900 for specifics. Sixty minutes of *news* and entertainment, including lively Bulgarian folk rhythms. To Europe, also heard in eastern North America, on 7305 and 9700 kHz. One hour earlier during summer.

"World Wide Country Radio," **WWCR,** Nashville, Tennessee. Continues with programming oriented to country music fans. To Europe and eastern North America, Monday through Friday, on 12160 kHz.

Voice of Greece. Summers only at this time and actually starts about three minutes into the broadcast, after a little bit of Greek. Approximately ten minutes of *news* from and about Greece. To Europe on 9375 kHz.

Radio Budapest, Hungary. Winters only at this time; see 2100 for specifics. Thirty minutes to Europe on 3975, 6110 and 7220 kHz. One hour earlier in summer.

China Radio International. *News* and commentary, followed Tuesday through Friday by *Current Affairs*. These are followed by various feature programs, such as *Culture in China* (Thursday); *Listeners' Letterbox* (Sunday and Tuesday); *Press Clippings*, *Cooking Show*, *Travel Talk* and ●*Music from*

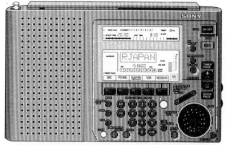

China (Saturday); *Sports Beat*, *China Scrapbook* and *Music Album* (Sunday); *Learn to Speak Chinese* (Monday and Wednesday); and Friday's *In the Third World*. Sundays, there is also a biweekly *Business Show* which alternates with *China's Open Windows*. One hour to Europe on 6950 and 9920 kHz.

Voice of Turkey. Summers only at this time. *News*, followed by *Review of the Turkish Press*, then features on Turkish history, culture and international relations, interspersed with enjoyable selections of the country's popular and classical music. Fifty minutes to Western Europe on 9400 or 9445 kHz. One hour later in winter.

Radio Pyongyang, North Korea. Repeat of the 1100 broadcast. To Europe, the Mideast and beyond on 6576, 9345, 9640 and 9977 kHz.

RDP International—Radio Portugal. Winter weekdays only. *News*, followed by a feature about Portugal; see 1900 for more details. Thirty minutes to Europe on 6130, 9780 and 9815 kHz, and to Africa on 15515 kHz. One hour earlier in summer.

"For the People," WHRI, Noblesville, Indiana. Monday through Friday only; see 0300 for specifics. Part of a three-hour populist package broadcast live to North America on 9495 kHz.

Kol Israel. Winters only at this time. Thirty minutes of *news* and in-depth reporting from and about Israel. To Europe and eastern North America on 7405, 7465, 9435 and 11603 kHz; and to Central and South America on 15640 kHz.

Radio Finland. Winters only at this time. *Compass North*, a compilation of Finnish and other Scandinavian stories, followed Tuesday through Friday by a press review and, later in the broadcast, *Northern Lights*. The remaining time is taken up by one or more short features. Sunday, there's

Focus and *Nuntii Latini* (news in Latin), Monday brings *Economic Roundup*, Tuesday has sports, Wednesday features *Environment Report*, Thursday has *Finnish History*, Friday's presentation is *Culture Closeup*, and the Saturday offerings are *Starting Finnish* and *Capital Coffee-break*. Thirty minutes to Europe on 9730 kHz. One hour earlier in summer.

Voice of America. *News*. Listeners in Europe can then hear ●*Music U.S.A. (Jazz)*—replaced Sunday by *The Concert Hall*—on 6040, 9760 and (summers) 15205 kHz; also available to the Mideast on 9700 (or 9770) kHz. For African listeners there's the weekday *Africa World Tonight*, replaced weekends by *Nightline Africa*, on 7375, 7415, 11855 (to 2030), 15410, 15445, 15580, 17725 and 17755 kHz. Both transmissions are also audible elsewhere, including parts of North America.

Radio For Peace International, Costa Rica. Part of an eight-hour cyclical block of social-conscience, counter-culture and New Age programming. Some of the offerings at this hour include a women's news-gathering service, *WINGS*, (2030 Thursday); a listener-response program (same time Friday); and *Sound Currents of the Spirit* (2030 Sunday). Audible in Europe and North America on 9400 and 15050 kHz. Some transmissions are in the single-side-band mode, which can be properly processed only on some radios.

WJCR, Upton, Kentucky. Continues with country gospel music to North America on 7490 and 13595 kHz. Other U.S. religious broadcasters which operate at this time include **WWCR** on 13845 and 15685 kHz, **KTBN** on 15590 kHz, and **WHRI-World Harvest Radio** on 13760 kHz. For traditional Catholic programming, tune **WEWN** on 7425 kHz.

Radio Prague, Czech Republic. Summers only at this time. Repeat of the 1600 broadcast. Thirty minutes to

Europe on 5930 and 9420 kHz.

CFRX-CFRB, Toronto, Canada. See 1400.

20:30

Radio Sweden. Summers only at this time. Monday through Friday, it's *news* and features in *Sixty Degrees North*, concentrating heavily on Scandinavian topics. Monday's accent is on sports; Tuesday has electronic media news; Wednesday brings *Money Matters*; Thursday features ecology or science and technology; and Friday offers a review of the week's news. Saturday, there's *Spectrum* (arts) or *Sweden Today* (current events). Sunday fare consists of *In Touch with Stockholm* (a listener response program) or the musical *Sounds Nordic*. Thirty minutes to Europe, Africa and the Mideast on 6065 and 9655 kHz.

Voice of Vietnam. Repeat of the 1800 transmission (see 1000 for program specifics). A half hour to Europe on 9840 and 12020 (or 15009) kHz.

Radio Thailand. Fifteen minutes of *news* targeted at Europe. Winters on 11835 kHz, and summers on 9555 kHz. Also available to Asia on 9655 and 11905 kHz.

Radio Dniester International, Moldova. Saturday through Thursday, summers only at this time. A 30-minute broadcast from the Russian separatists in the Pridnestrovye region of the country. See 2130 for specifics. To Europe (and audible in eastern North America) on 11750 kHz. One hour later in winter.

Polish Radio Warsaw, Poland. Winters only at this time. See 1930 for program specifics. Fifty-five minutes of *news*, music and features spotlighting Poland past and present. To Europe on 5995, 6135 and 7285 kHz. One hour earlier during summer.

Voice of Armenia. Mainly of interest to Armenians abroad. Thirty minutes of Armenian *news* and culture. To

Europe summers on 11920 kHz (and occasionally on 11960 kHz). Sometimes audible in eastern North America. One hour later in winter.

Radio Nederland. Repeat of the 1830 broadcast. Fifty-five minutes to Africa (and heard well beyond) on 9860, 9895 and (summers) 11655 kHz.

Radio Roma, Italy. Actually starts at 2025. Twenty soporific minutes of *news* and music targeted at the Mideast on 7235, 9710 and 11800 kHz.

20:45

All India Radio. The first 15 minutes of a much longer broadcast, consisting of a press review, Indian music, regional and international *news*, commentary, and a variety of talks and features of general interest. Continuous till 2230. To Western Europe on 7412, 9950 and 11620 kHz; and to Australasia on 9910, 11715 and 15225 (or 15265) kHz.

Vatican Radio. Winters only at this time, and actually starts at 2050. Twenty minutes of predominantly Catholic fare. To Europe on 3945 and 5882 kHz. One hour earlier in summer.

21:00

■**BBC World Service for the Americas.** *World News*, then ten minutes of specialized business and financial reports. Monday through Friday, these are followed by ●*Caribbean Report* (see 2115 for specifics). On the half-hour, look for the weekday ●*Off the Shelf* (literature), followed by a 15-minute feature. Best of these are Thursday's *From Our Own Correspondent* and Friday's *The Farming World*. On Saturdays you can hear *On Screen,* ●*Global Concerns* and the inimitable ●*Letter from America.* Sunday, there's ●*Concert Hall* or its substitute. To eastern North America and the Caribbean on 5975 kHz.

■BBC World Service for Europe. Opens with the same 15 minutes as on the Americas service (see above), and then it's *Britain Today*. On the half-hour, look for *Meridian* (Tuesday, Thursday and Saturday), *Multitrack* (Monday, Wednesday and Friday), and Sunday's ●*Brain of Britain* (or its substitute). Continuous on 3955 (winters), 6180, 6195, 7325, 9410 and (summers) 12095 kHz. Also audible in eastern North America.

■BBC World Service for Asia and the Pacific. Opens with *World News* and a business report, and closes the hour with 15 minutes of slow-speed *news* for listeners whose first language is other than English. The remaining half hour is taken up by one or more features, including ●*Brain of Britain* or its replacement (Sunday), *The Vintage Chart Show* (Monday), ●*Discovery* (Tuesday), classical music (Wednesday and Friday), and Thursday's ●*Network UK*. Continuous to East Asia on 3915, 6195, 9580 and 11945 kHz; and to Australasia on 9740 and 11955 khz.

Monitor Radio International, USA. See 1600 for program details. Monday through Friday to North America on 9355 or 11645 kHz, to Western Europe on 7510 or 13770 kHz, and to Australasia on 13840 kHz. Weekend programming is nonsecular, and mainly of interest to Christian Scientists.

Radio Exterior de España ("Spanish National Radio"). *News*, followed Monday through Friday by *Panorama* (Spanish popular music, commentary, press review and weather), then a couple of features: *Sports Spotlight* and *Cultural Encounters* (Monday); *People of Today* and *Entertainment in Spain* (Tuesday); *As Others See Us* and, biweekly, *The Natural World* or *Science Desk* (Wednesday); *Economic Report* and

Cultural Clippings (Thursday); and *Window on Spain* and *Review of the Arts* (Friday). The broadcast ends with a language course, *Spanish by Radio*. On weekends, there's Saturday's *Hall of Fame*, *Distance Unknown* (for radio enthusiasts) and *Gallery of Spanish Voices*; replaced Sunday by *Visitors' Book*, *Great Figures in Flamenco* and *Radio Club*. One hour to Europe on 6125 kHz.

Radio Ukraine International. Summers only at this time. *News*, commentary, reports and interviews, covering virtually every aspect of Ukrainian life. Saturdays feature a listener-response program, and most of Sunday's broadcast is a showpiece for Ukrainian music. Sixty minutes to Europe, Africa and beyond on 4825, 5905, 6010, 6090, 7240, 7285, 9560, 9750, 11780, 11875 and 11950 kHz. Also audible in parts of eastern North America. One hour later in winter.

Radio Canada International. Winters, the first hour of a 90-minute broadcast; summers, the last half hour of the same. Winters, there's *News*, followed Monday through Friday by *Spectrum* (current events), which is replaced Saturday by *Innovation Canada* and ●*Earth Watch*, and Sunday by *Arts in Canada* and a listener-response program. Summer weekdays, it's the CBC domestic service's *The World at Six*, with weekend fare consisting of *Royal Canadian Air Farce* (Saturday), and Sunday's *The Inside Track*. To Europe and Africa winters on 5995, 7260, 9725, 11945, 13650, 13690, 15140 and 17820 kHz; and summers on 5995 (also to the Mideast), 7235, 11690, 13650, 13670, 15150, 15325 and 17820 kHz. Some of these are also audible in parts of North America.

Radio Vlaanderen Internationaal, Belgium. Summers only at this time. Repeat of the 1800 transmission (see 1900 for program details); 25 minutes daily to Europe on 5910 kHz. One hour later in winter.

Radio Prague, Czech Republic. See 1600 for program details. *News* and features dealing with Czech life and culture. A half hour to Europe on 5930 and 7345 kHz.

Radio Bulgaria. This time summers only; see 1900 for specifics. *News*, features and some entertaining folk music. To Europe and eastern North America on 9700 and 11720 kHz. One hour later during winter.

China Radio International. Repeat of the 2000 transmission. One hour to Europe on 6950 and 9920 kHz. A 30-minute shortened version is also available summers (2100-2130) on 6165 kHz.

Voice of Russia World Service. Winters, it's *news* and a choice of features: *Science and Engineering* (Thursday), *This is Russia* (Friday), *Newmarket* (Wednesday and Sunday), and listener-response programs on Saturday and Monday. These are followed on the half-hour by *Yours for the Asking* (Tuesday), *Jazz Show* (Monday and Friday), ●*Music at your Request* (Wednesday), ●*Folk Box* (Thursday), and *Kaleidoscope* (Saturday). Summer weekdays, *Focus on Asia and the Pacific* is followed by *Science and Engineering* (Monday and Friday), *This is Russia* (Tuesday), and a listener-response program on Thursday. Pick of the weekend programs is ●*Music and Musicians* at 2111 Saturday, with Sunday's *Mailbag* and *Kaleidoscope* completing the roster. Continuous to Europe winters on 5905, 5920, 5965, 5975, 5995, 6055, 7170, 7180, 7205, 7230, 7300, 7330, 7350, 7380 and 9890 kHz; and summers on 7350, 9480, 9880, 11630, 11675, 11730, 11750, 11980 and 12070 khz. Several of these channels are also audible in eastern North America.

Radio Budapest, Hungary. Summers only at this time. *News* and features, some of which are broadcast on a regular basis. These include Monday's *Musica Hungarica*, *Focus on Business* and *The Weeklies* (Wednesday), *Letter Home* (Thursday) and *Profiles* (Saturday). Thirty minutes to Europe on 3955, 5935, 7250 and 9835 kHz. One hour later in winter.

Radio Australia. *World news*, then Monday through Friday it's discussion in *Australia Talks Back*. Saturday brings *That's History*, and *Science Show* is aired on Sunday. Continuous to Asia and the Pacific on a number of frequencies. To East Asia on 11660 (or 11855) kHz, and to Southeast Asia on 9645 and 11695 kHz. Also audible in western North America (from 2130) on 15365 and 17860 kHz.

■**Deutsche Welle,** Germany. *News*, followed Sunday through Thursday by ●*European Journal* and ●*Asia and Pacific Report*. The remaining days' programs include *The Week in Germany* and *Economic Notebook* (Friday), and Saturday's *Mailbag Asia*. Fifty minutes to Asia and Australasia on 6185 (winter), 9670, 9765 and 11785 kHz.

Radio Japan. Repeat of the 1700 transmission; see there for specifics. One hour to Europe and North Africa on 11865 (or 11925) kHz; to East and Southeast Asia on 6035, 7140 and 9580 (or 9675) kHz; and to Australasia on 11850 kHz. There is also a separate 15-minute *news* broadcast to Southeast Asia on 9660 and 11915 kHz.

Radio Yugoslavia. This time summers only. *News*, reports and features, mostly about Yugoslavia. Thirty minutes to Europe on 6100 and 6185 kHz. One hour later in winter.

Radio Romania International. *News*, commentary and features (see 1900), interspersed with some thoroughly enjoyable Romanian folk music. One hour to Europe winters on 5990, 6105, 6190, 7105 and 7195 kHz; summers on 9550, 9690 and 11940 kHz. Also audible in eastern North America.

Radio Korea International, South Korea. Repeat of the 1900 broadcast; see 1600 for program details. One hour to Europe on 6480 and 15575 kHz.

Radio For Peace International, Costa Rica. Continues at this hour with a potpourri of United Nations, counterculture and other programs. These include *WINGS* (news for and of women, 2130 Tuesday), *Vietnam Veterans Radio Network* (2130 Wednesday) and *Focus on Haiti* (2100 Saturday). Audible in Europe and North America on 9400 and 15050 kHz. Some transmissions are in the single-sideband mode, which can be properly processed only on some radios.

"World Wide Country Radio," WWCR, Nashville, Tennessee. Winters only at this time. Continues with live programming for country music fans. To Europe and eastern North America, Monday through Friday, on 12160 kHz. One hour earlier in summer.

Voice of Turkey. Winters only at this time. See 2000 for program details. Some rather unusual programming and friendly presentation make this station worth a listen. To Western Europe on 9445 (or 9400) kHz. One hour earlier in summer.

Voice of America. Monday through Friday, it's one hour of *World Report*. Weekends, there's *News* and a variety of features, depending on the area served. Pick of the litter is the science program ●*New Horizons* (Africa, Europe and the Mideast at 2110 Sunday). Other offerings include *VOA Pacific* (Australasia, same time Sunday), ●*Issues in the News* (Africa, 2130 Sunday; Australasia, 2130 Saturday), *Studio One* (Europe and Mideast, 2130 Sun) and *On the Line* (Europe, Africa and the Mideast at 2110 Saturday). To Europe on 6040, 9760 and (summers) 9535 and 15205 kHz; to the Mideast on 6160 kHz; to Africa, and

often heard elsewhere, on 7375, 7415, 15410, 15445, 15580 and 17725 kHz; and to Southeast Asia and the Pacific on 11870, 15185 and 17735 kHz.

All India Radio. Continues to Western Europe on 7412, 9950 and 11620 kHz; and to Australasia on 9910, 11715 and 15225 (or 15265) kHz. Look for some authentic Indian music from 2115 onwards. Also audible in parts of eastern North America on 9950 and 11620 kHz.

"For the People," WHRI, Noblesville, Indiana. winters only at this time. Monday through Friday only; see 0300 for specifics. The final hour of a three-hour populist package broadcast live to North America on 9495 kHz. One hour earlier in summer.

WWCR, Nashville, Tennessee. Carries a mixture of religious and disestablishmentarian programs on 12160 kHz at this hour, depending on the day of the week, and whether it is summer or winter. The latter category includes "The Hour of Courage" and the strangely titled "Executive Intelligence Review Talks."

CFRX-CFRB, Toronto, Canada. See 1400. Summers at this time, you can hear ●*The World Today*, 90 minutes of news, interviews, sports and commentary. On 6070 kHz.

21:15

Radio Damascus, Syria. Actually starts at 2110. *News*, a daily press review, and a variety of features (depending on the day of the week) at approximately 2130 and 2145. These include *Arab Profile* and *Economic Affairs* (Sunday), *Camera and Masks* and *Selected Readings* (Monday), *Reflections* and *Back on the Stage* (Tuesday), *Listeners Overseas* and *Palestine Talking* (Wednesday), *From the World Press* and *Arab Women in*

Focus (Thursday), *Arab Newsweek* and *From Our Literature* (Friday), and *Human Rights* and *Syria and the World* (Saturday). The transmission also contains Syrian and some western popular music. Sixty minutes to North America and Australasia on 12085 and 15095 kHz.

■BBC World Service for the Caribbean. ●*Caribbean Report*, although intended for listeners in the area, can also be clearly heard throughout much of eastern North America. This brief, 15-minute program provides comprehensive coverage of Caribbean economic and political affairs, both within and outside the region. Monday through Friday only, on 6110, 15390 and 17715 kHz.

Radio Cairo, Egypt. The start of a 90-minute broadcast devoted to Arab and Egyptian life and culture. The initial quarter-hour of general programming is followed by *news*, commentary and political items. This in turn is followed by a cultural program until 2215, when the station again reverts to more general fare. A Middle Eastern cocktail, including exotic Arab music, beamed to Europe on 9900 kHz.

WJCR, Upton, Kentucky. Continuous gospel music to North America on 7490 and 13595 kHz. Other U.S. religious broadcasters operating at this hour include **WWCR** on 13845 and 15685 kHz, **KTBN** on 15590 kHz, and **WHRI-World Harvest Radio** on 13760 kHz. Traditional Catholic programming is available from **WEWN** on 7425 kHz.

21:30

BBC World Service for the Falkland Islands. *Calling the Falklands* is one of the curiosities of international broadcasting, and consists of news and features for this small community in the South Atlantic. It also

provides some insight into Argentinian politics. Fifteen minutes Tuesdays and Fridays on 11680 (or 13660 kHz)—easily heard in eastern North America.

Radio Finland. Summers only at this time. Repeat of the 1900 transmission; see the 2000 winter broadcast for program details. Thirty minutes to Europe and West Africa on 6120, 9730, 11755 and 15440 kHz.

Radio Vilnius, Lithuania. Summers only at this time. Repeat of the 1900 broadcast. Thirty minutes to Europe on 9710 kHz. One hour later in winter.

Radio Dniester International, Moldova. Saturday through Thursday, winters only at this time. A 30-minute broadcast from the Russian-separatists in the Pridnestrovye region of the country. Starts with *News Magazine*, then there is a translated interview or speech on a local topic. The musical *Juke Box* and a press review make up the rest of the broadcast. Original programming is aired on Monday, Wednesday and Saturday, and repeated on the following day. To Europe (also audible in eastern North America) on 9620 kHz. One hour earlier in summer.

Voice of the Islamic Republic of Iran. A recently-introduced service to Australasia. Sixty minutes of *news*, commentary and features with a strong Islamic slant. On 6175 and 9670 kHz, but may be subject to change.

Voice of Armenia. Mainly of interest to Armenians abroad. Thirty minutes of Armenian *news* and culture. To Europe winters on 9480 kHz, and sometimes audible in eastern North America. One hour earlier in summer.

Radio Austria International. Summers only at this time. The informative and well-presented ●*Report from Austria.* A half hour to Europe and Africa on 5945, 6155, 9880 and 13730 kHz.

Radio Sweden. Thirty minutes of predominantly Scandinavian fare (see 2030 for specifics). Year-round to Europe on 6065 kHz, and summer to Africa and the Mideast on 6065 and 9655 kHz.

22:00

■BBC World Service for the Americas. Thirty minutes of the comprehensive ●*Newsdesk*, followed Monday, Wednesday and Friday by *Multitrack*, Tuesday by the youth-oriented ●*Megamix*, and Thursday by *Sports International*. At the same time Saturday, look for the first part of ●*Play of the Week*, a *tour de force* of world theater. Sunday has the religious *In Praise of God*. Audible in North America on 5975 and 9590 kHz. As we go to press, the BBC has announced that it will be making adjustments to its programming lineup, and that a 2245 edition of *Sports Roundup* is to be introduced.

■BBC World Service for Europe. Thirty minutes of ●*Newsdesk*. The next half hour is only available during winter, with weekday fare consisting of ●*The World Today* followed by a 15-minute feature. Pick of the weekend programming is Sunday's ●*Network UK*. It is possible that this lineup will be changed in the near future, so as to include a daily edition of *Sports Roundup*. On 3955 (winters), 6180, 6195, 9410 and (summers) 12095 kHz. Also audible in eastern North America.

■BBC World Service for Asia and the Pacific. Thirty minutes of ●*Newsdesk*, then Sunday through Friday there's a feature for students of English, replaced Saturday by ●*Development 96*. The final quarter-hour is taken up by a short feature and *What's On?* Continuous to East Asia on 6195, 7110 and (summers only?) 9890 kHz; and to Australasia on 11695 and 11955 kHz.

Monitor Radio International, USA. See 1600 for program details. Monday through Friday to Western Europe (and audible in eastern North America) on 7510 kHz, to South America on 13770 kHz, and to East Asia on 9430 (or 15405) and 13625 kHz. Weekend programming concentrates on Christian Science beliefs and teachings.

Radio Bulgaria. Winters only at this time; see 1900 for specifics. Sixty minutes of *news* and features from and about Bulgaria, interspersed with lively Bulgarian folk music. To Europe and eastern North America on 7105 and 9700 kHz. One hour earlier in summer.

Radio Cairo, Egypt. The second half of a 90-minute broadcast to Europe on 9900 kHz; see 2115 for program details.

Voice of America. The beginning of a three-hour block of programs to East and Southeast Asia and the Pacific. *News*, followed Sunday through Thursday (Monday through Friday in the target areas) by *VOA Today*, interrupted on the half-hour for 10 minutes of news in slow-speed English. Friday's post-news offering is *Newsline*, replaced Saturday by *VOA Sunday*. These are followed on the half-hour by features in Special English. To East and Southeast Asia on 7215, 9705, 9770, 11760, 15185, 15290, 15305, 17735 and 17820 kHz; and to Australasia on 15185, 15305 and 17735 kHz. There is a separate 30-minute week night service to Africa which features *Music USA* on 7340, 7375 and 7415 kHz.

Radio Korea International, South Korea. Starts off with *news*, followed Monday through Wednesday by *Economic News Briefs*. The remainder of the broadcast is taken up by a feature: *Shortwave Feedback* (Sunday), *Seoul Calling* (Monday and Tuesday), *Pulse of Korea* (Wednesday), *From Us to You* (Thursday), *Let's Sing Together* (Friday) and *Weekly News Focus* (Saturday). Thirty minutes to Europe, winters on 3975 kHz, and summers on 5965 kHz.

Radio Australia. *World News*, then Monday through Thursday it's *Network Asia*. Other offerings include *Feedback* and *Business Weekly* (Friday), and Saturday's *Australia All Over*. Continuous to Asia and the Pacific on several frequencies. To East Asia on 11660 (or 11855) kHz, and to Southeast Asia on 9610 (or 11855) and 9645 kHz. Also audible in western North America on 15365, 17795 and 17860 kHz.

Voice of Russia World Service. *News*, then Monday through Friday winters, it's *Focus on Asia and the Pacific* followed by a feature (see 2100 summer programs). Saturday's spot is given over to the excellent ●*Music and Musicians*, and Sunday airs *Mailbag* and *Kaleidoscope*. Summers, there's the weekday ●*Commonwealth Update*, replaced Sunday by *Top Priority*. On the half-hour, ●*Audio Book Club* (Tuesday, Thursday and Sunday), alternates with *Russian by Radio* or a music program. Winters to Europe on 5905, 5975, 5995, 6055, 7150, 7180, 7350, 9620 and 9750 kHz (several of which are audible in eastern North America); and summers to eastern North America on 9530, 11730 and 11750 kHz.

Voice of Free China, Taiwan. *News*, then features. The last is *Let's Learn Chinese*, which has a series of segments for beginning, intermediate and advanced learners. Other features include *Jade Bells and Bamboo Pipes* (Monday), *Kaleidoscope* and *Main Roads and Byways* (Tuesday), *Music Box* (Wednesday), *Perspectives* and *Journey into Chinese Culture* (Thursday), *Confrontation* and *New Record Time* (Friday), *Reflections* (Saturday) and *Adventures of Mahlon and Jeanie* and *Mailbag Time* (Sunday). Sixty minutes to Western Europe, winters on 5810 and 9850 kHz, and summers on 17750 and 21720 kHz.

Croatian Radio. Summers only at this time. Eight minutes of on-the-spot *news* from one of Europe's most volatile regions. Best heard in Europe and eastern North America at this hour, but also

heard elsewhere. Channel usage varies, but try 5895, 7370, 9830, 11635 and 13830 kHz. One hour later during winter.

Radio Habana Cuba. Sixty minutes of *news* (mainly about Cuba and Latin America), features about the island and its inhabitants, and some thoroughly enjoyable Cuban music. To the Caribbean and southern United States on 6180 kHz, and to eastern North America and Europe on 11960 kHz upper sideband.

Radio Budapest, Hungary. Winters only at this time; see 2100 for specifics. Thirty minutes to Europe on 3955, 6110 and 7220 kHz. One hour earlier in summer.

Voice of Turkey. Summers only at this time. See 2000 for program details. Fifty minutes to Europe on 11710 kHz, to eastern North America on 9445 kHz, and for late-night listeners in the Mideast on 7185 kHz. One hour later in winter.

Radio Yugoslavia. Winters only at this time. Repeat of the 1930 broadcast. Thirty minutes to Europe on 6100 and 6185 kHz. One hour earlier in summer.

China Radio International. Repeat of the 2000 broadcast. One hour to Europe winters on 7170 kHz, summers on 9880 kHz. a shortened version is also available winters at 2200-2230 on 3985 kHz.

Radio Vlaanderen Internationaal, Belgium. Winters only at this time. Repeat of the 1900 broadcast; see there for program details. Twenty-five minutes to Europe on 5910 kHz, also audible in parts of eastern North America. One hour earlier in summer.

Radio Canada International. This time winters only. The final half hour of a 90-minute broadcast. Monday through Friday, it's the CBC domestic service's *The World at Six*, with weekend fare consisting of *Innovation Canada* (Saturday), and Sunday's *Arts in Canada*. To Europe and Africa on 5995, 7260, 11945, 13650, 13690, 15140 and

17820 kHz. For a separate summer service, see the following item.

Radio Canada International.
Summers only; a relay of CBC domestic programming, except for the final 30 minutes weekends. Monday through Friday, there's ● *The World at Six*; Saturday and Sunday, *The World This Weekend*. On the half-hour, the weekday ●*As It Happens* is replaced Saturday by ●*Earth Watch*, and Sunday by a listener-response program. Sixty minutes to North America on 5960, 9755, 11895 (to 2230) and 13670 kHz. One hour later in winter. For a separate year-round service to Asia, see the next item.

Radio Canada International.
Monday through Friday, it's ●*The World At Six*; Saturday and Sunday, *The World This Weekend* (may be replaced winters by Saturday's *Innovation Canada* and Sunday's *Arts in Canada*).Thirty minutes to Southeast Asia on 11705 kHz.

Radio Roma, Italy. Approximately ten minutes of *news* followed by a quarter-hour feature (usually music). Arguably, the best parts of the broadcast are the periods of dead air between records. Twenty-five lethargic minutes to East Asia on 5990 (or 15330), 9710 and 11800 kHz.

Radio Ukraine International.
Winters only at this time. a potpourri of all things Ukrainian, with the Sunday broadcast often featuring some excellent music. Sixty minutes to Europe, Africa and beyond on 4780, 4820, 5940, 6020, 7240, 7405, 9560, 9610, 9620, 9810 and 11870 kHz. Also audible in parts of eastern North America. One hour earlier in summer.

United Arab Emirates Radio,
Abu Dhabi. Begins with *Readings from the Holy Koran*, in which verses are chanted in Arabic, then translated into English. This is followed by an Arab cultural feature. The last half hour is a relay of Capital Radio in Abu Dhabi, complete with pop music and local contests. To eastern North America winters on 9605, 9770 and 11885 (or 7215) kHz; and summers on 11885, 11970 and 13605 kHz.

Radio Exterior de España ("Spanish National Radio"). *News* and features (see 2100 for details). To Africa, and heard well beyond, on 9675 kHz.

Radio For Peace International,
Costa Rica. Continues with counterculture and social-conscience programs ranging from *Peace Forum* (2200 Tuesday and Friday) to *The Far Right Radio Review* (same time Sunday). *My Green Earth*, a nature program for children, is aired at 2200 Thursday. Audible in Europe and North America on 7385, 9400 and 15050 kHz. Some transmissions are in the single-sideband mode, which can be properly processed only on some radios.

All India Radio. The final half hour of a transmission to Europe and Australasia, consisting mainly of news-related fare. To Europe on 7412, 9950 and 11620 kHz; and to Australasia on 9910, 11715 and 15225 (or 15265) kHz. Also sometimes audible in eastern North America on 11620 kHz.

WWCR, Nashville, Tennessee. Carries a variety of disestablishmentarian programs at this hour, depending on the day of the week, and whether it is summer or winter. These include winter's "The Hour of Courage" and "Executive Intelligence Review Talks"; and summer's "Norman Resnick Show." On 12160 kHz.

WJCR, Upton, Kentucky. Continues with country gospel music to North America on 7490 and 13595 kHz. Other U.S. religious broadcasters heard at this hour include **WWCR** on 13845 kHz, **KAIJ** on 13815 kHz, **KTBN** on 15590 kHz, and **WHRI-World Harvest Radio** on 5745 (or 13760) kHz. For traditional Catholic programming, try **WEWN** on 7425 kHz.

CFRX-CFRB, Toronto, Canada. If you live in the northeastern United States or southeastern Canada, try this pleasant little local station, usually audible for hundreds of miles/kilometers during daylight hours on 6070 kHz. At this time, you can hear ●*The World Today* (summers, starts at 2100)—90 minutes of news, sport and interviews.

22:30

Radio Vilnius, Lithuania. Winters only at this time. Repeat of the 2000 broadcast. Thirty minutes to Europe on 9710 (or 6100) kHz. One hour earlier during summer.

Radio Finland. Summers only at this time. Starts with *Compass North*, a compilation of Finnish and other Scandinavian stories, followed Tuesday through Friday by a press review and, later in the broadcast, *Northern Lights*. The remaining time is taken up by one or more short features. The week starts off with *Focus* and *Nuntii Latini* (news in Latin). Monday features *Economic Roundup*, Tuesday has sports, Wednesday's slot is given over to *Environment Report*, Thursday has *Finnish History*, Friday's presentation is *Culture Closeup*, and the Saturday offerings are *Starting Finnish* and *Capital Coffee-break*. Thirty minutes to East and Southeast Asia on 9665 kHz, and to South America (and heard elsewhere) on 9650 and 11845 kHz. One hour later during winter.

Radio Sweden. Winters only at this time. Repeat of the 2130 broadcast (see 2030 for program details). Thirty minutes of *news* and features, with the accent heavily on Scandinavian topics. To Europe on 6065 kHz.

Voice of Greece. Actually starts around 2235. Fifteen minutes of English news from and about Greece. Part of a much longer, predominantly Greek,

broadcast. To Australasia on 6260 (or 9425) and 9375 kHz.

22:45

All India Radio. The first 15 minutes of a much longer broadcast, consisting of Indian music, regional and international *news*, commentary, and a variety of talks and features of general interest. Continuous till 0045. To Southeast Asia (and heard beyond) on 9705, 9950, 11745 and 13750 kHz.

Vatican Radio. Twenty minutes of religious and secular programming to East and Southeast Asia and Australasia on 6150, 7305, 9600 and 11830 kHz.

23:00

■**BBC World Service for the Americas.** Sunday through Friday, opens with *news* and *East Asia Today*, replaced Saturday by a continuation of ●*Play of the Week* (world theater). Weekdays on the half-hour there's ●*Outlook*, and Sunday's offerings include ●*Short Story* and *Write On* (a listener-response program). Continuous to North America on 5975, 6175, 7325 and 9590 kHz.

■**BBC World Service for Asia and the Pacific.** *World News*, then Sunday through Friday there's *East Asia Today*. This is followed Monday through Friday by ●*The World Today*, replaced Sunday by the popular ●*Letter from America*. Saturday's offerings are *Pick of the World* and *Book Choice*. The hour is rounded off by the daily *Sports Roundup*. Continuous to East Asia on 7250, 9580, 11945 and 11955 kHz; and to Australasia on 11955 kHz.

Monitor Radio International, USA. See 1600 for program details. Monday through Friday to southern Europe and West Africa on 7510 kHz; to South America on 13770 kHz, to East

Asia on 9430 or 15405 kHz, and to Australasia on 13625 kHz. Weekends, news-oriented fare is replaced by Christian Science religious programming.

Voice of Turkey. Winters only at this hour. See 2000 for program details. Fifty minutes to Europe on 11710 kHz, to eastern North America on 9445 kHz, and to Middle Eastern night owls on 7185 kHz. One hour earlier in summer.

Radio Vilnius, Lithuania. Summers only at this time. Monday through Friday, there's just five minutes of *news* about events in Lithuania. On weekends, the broadcast is extended to a full half hour of news and short features about the country. To eastern North America on 9530 (or 11805) kHz. One hour later in winter.

■Deutsche Welle, Germany. Repeat of the 2100 broadcast, except that ●*European Journal* is preceded by *Asia Pacific Report.* Fifty minutes to East and Southeast Asia on 6000 (winter), 7235, and (summer) 11705 kHz.

Radio Japan. Repeat of the 1500 transmission; see there for specifics. One hour to Europe on 5965 (or 6055) and 6155 kHz; to East and Southeast Asia on 7140 and 9580 (or 9675) kHz; and to Australasia on 11850 kHz.

Radio Australia. *World News*, then Sunday through Thursday it's a sports bulletin followed by *Network Asia.* These are replaced Friday by *Asia Focus* and *At Your Request*, and Saturday by *Australia All Over.* Continuous to Asia and the Pacific on a number of channels. To East Asia on 11660 (or 11855) and (from 2330) 13605 kHz, and to Southeast Asia on 9610 (or 11855) and (from 2330) 9645 and 9850 kHz. Also audible in western North America on 15365, 17795 and 17860 kHz.

Radio Canada International. Summer weekdays, the final hour of ●*As It Happens*; winters, the first 30 minutes of the same, preceded by the up-to-the-minute *news* program ●*World at Six.* Summer weekends, look for ●*Quirks and Quarks* (Saturday, science) and *Tapestry* (Sunday, culture). These are replaced winter Saturdays by *Innovation Canada* and ●*Earth Watch*, followed the next day by *Arts in Canada* and a listener-response program. To eastern North America on 5960 and 9755 kHz, with 13670 kHz also available in summer.

Croatian Radio. Eight minutes of on-the-spot *news* from Croatian Radio's Zagreb studio. Best heard in Europe and eastern North America, but also heard elsewhere. Channel usage varies, but try 5895, 7370, 9830 11635 and 13830 kHz.

Radio Pyongyang, North Korea. Fifty minutes of old-time communist propaganda. To the Americas on 11700 and 13650 kHz.

Radio For Peace International, Costa Rica. The final 60 minutes of a continuous eight-hour cyclical block of United Nations, counterculture, social-

conscience and New Age programming. Audible in Europe and the Americas on 7385, 9400 and 15050 kHz. Audible in Europe and the Americas on 7385, 9400 and 15050 kHz. Some transmissions are in the single-sideband mode, which can be properly processed only on some radios.

Radio Cairo, Egypt. The first hour of a 90-minute potpourri of exotic Arab music and features reflecting Egyptian life and culture, with *news* and commentary about events in Egypt and the Arab world. There are also quizzes, mailbag shows, and answers to listeners' questions. Fair reception and mediocre audio quality to North America on 9900 kHz.

WRMI-Radio Miami International, Miami, Florida. Part of a much longer multilingual transmission to the Caribbean. Summer weekdays at this time, you can hear 30 minutes of *Viva Miami!*—a potpourri of information, music and entertainment. Also includes regular weather updates during the hurricane season (June-November). Heard in much of the Americas on 9955 kHz. One hour later in winter.

Radio Bulgaria. Summers only at this time; see 1900 for specifics. a potpourri of *news* and features with a strong Bulgarian flavor. Sixty minutes to eastern North America on 9700 and 11720 kHz. One hour later during winter.

Voice of Russia World Service. *News*, then winter weekdays, try the informative ●*Commonwealth Update*, with the pick of the second half hour being ●*Audio Book Club* (Tuesday, Thursday and Sunday). Summers, there's the daily *News and Views*, followed by *Yours for the Asking* (Monday), *Jazz Show* (Tuesday and Thursday), ●*Music at your Request* (Wednesday), ●*Folk Box* (Friday and Sunday), and *Kaleidoscope* (Saturday). To eastern North America winters on 7150, 9620 and

9750 kHz; and summers on 9720, 11730 and 11750 kHz.

United Arab Emirates Radio, Abu Dhabi. The second part of a two-hour broadcast to eastern North America. Opens with 15-20 minutes of extracts from the Arab press, then the Islamic *Studies in the Mosque*, an editorial, and an Arab cultural feature. Heard in eastern North America winters on 9605, 9770 and 11885 (or 7215) kHz; and summers on 11885, 11970 and 13605 kHz.

Voice of America. *News*, then Sunday through Thursday (Monday through Friday in the target area) there's *VOA Today*. On the remaining days, there's *VOA Saturday* and *VOA Sunday*. Not very original, but helpful if you have lost your calendar. Continuous programming to East Asia and the Pacific on the same frequencies as at 2200.

WWCR, Nashville, Tennessee. Carries a variety of disestablishmentarian programs at this hour, depending on the day of the week, and whether it is summer or winter. These include winter's "Norman Resnick Show" and summer's "The Hour of Courage" and "The Voice of Liberty." On 12160 kHz.

WJCR, Upton, Kentucky. Continuous country gospel music to North America on 7490 and 13595 kHz. Other U.S. religious broadcasters heard at this time include **WWCR** on 13845 kHz, **KAIJ** on 13815 kHz, **KTBN** on 15590 kHz, and **WHRI-World Harvest Radio** on 5745 kHz. For traditional Catholic programming, tune **WEWN** on 7425 kHz.

CFRX-CFRB, Toronto, Canada. See 2200.

23:30

Radio Vlaanderen Internationaal, Belgium. Summers only at this time. Weekdays, there's *News*, *Press Review* and *Belgium Today*, followed by features like *Focus on Europe* (Monday), *Living in*

Belgium and *Green Society* (Tuesday), *The Arts* and *Around Town* (Wednesday), *Economics* and *International Report* (Thursday), and *The Arts* and *Tourism* (Friday). Weekend features include *Music from Flanders* (Saturday) and Sunday's *P.O. Box 26* (a listener-response program) and *Radio World*. Twenty-five minutes to eastern North America on 9925 kHz; also audible on 13800 kHz, targeted at South America.

Radio Finland. Winters only at this time. See 2230 for program details. Thirty minutes to East and Southeast Asia on 5990 kHz, and to South America (and heard elsewhere) on 6015 and 9680 kHz. One hour earlier in summer.

Radio Nederland. *News*, followed Monday through Saturday by ●*Newsline*, then a feature program. Best of the pack are *Sounds Interesting* (Wednesday), ●*Research File* (Thursday) and Friday's documentary. One hour to North America on 6020 and 6165 kHz. Also available summers (and possibly winters too) on 9845 (or 9840) kHz.

All India Radio. Continuous programming to Southeast Asia. a potpourri of *news*, commentary, features and exotic Indian music. On 9705, 9950, 11745 and 13750 kHz.

Voice of Vietnam. Repeat of the 1000 transmission (see there for program specifics). a half hour to Asia (also heard in Europe) on 9840 and 12020 (or 15009) kHz.

Radio Austria International. Winters only at this time. News and human-interest stories in ●*Report from Austria*. a half hour targeted at South America on 9870 and 13730 kHz, and also audible in parts of eastern North America.

Voice of Greece. Actually starts around 2335. Ten minutes of English news from and about Greece. Part of a much longer, multilingual, broadcast. To Central America (and well heard in eastern North America) on any two (sometimes three) frequencies from 9375, 9425, 11595 and 11645 kHz.

Prepared by Don Swampo and the staff of Passport to World Band Radio.

Worldwide Broadcasts in English—1996

Country-by-Country Guide to Best-Heard Stations

Dozens of countries reach out to us in English over world band radio. This section of PASSPORT gives the times and frequencies (channels) where you're most likely to hear the country you want. Once you know this, you can also peruse the "What's On Tonight" section for descriptions of the shows.

No Wasted Time

Here are some tips so that you don't waste your time tuning in dead air:

- **Best times and frequencies:** In general, listen during the late afternoon and evening, when most programs are beamed your way. Tune the world band segments within the 5800-7600 kHz range (5800-15800 kHz midyear). Around breakfast, you can also tune segments within the 5800-17900 kHz range for a smaller, but interesting, range of selections. "Best Times and Frequencies," at the end of this book, tells you where each world band segment is found, and gives helpful specifics as to when and where to tune.
- **Strongest frequencies:** Frequencies shown in italics—say, *6175* kHz—tend to be the best, as they are from transmitters that may be located near you.

World Time Standard

Times and days of the week are in World Time, explained in the Glossary. World Time—a handy concept also known as Coordinated Universal Time (UTC) and Greenwich Mean Time (GMT)—is used to avoid the complication of so many time zones throughout the world. It treats the entire planet as a single time zone, and is announced on the hour by many world band stations.

For example, if you're in New York and it's 6:00 AM EST, you will hear World Time announced as "11 hours." A glance at your watch shows that this is five hours ahead of local time. You can either keep this figure in your head or, better, use a special World Time

Matthew Wattis, Jack Malembeka and Andrew Flynn install antennas for Zambia's new Christian Voice station.   *(Christian Voice)*

clock. A growing number of radios come with this type of clock built in, and separate 24-hour clocks are also widely available.

Some Programs Change Times Midyear

Some stations shift broadcast times by one hour midyear. These are indicated by ⬅ (one hour earlier) and ➡ (one hour later). Stations may also extend their hours of transmission, or air special programs, during national holidays or sports events.

Eavesdropping on World Music

Broadcasts in other than English? Turn to the next section, "Voices from Home," or the Blue Pages. Keep in mind that stations for kinsfolk abroad sometimes carry delightful chunks of indigenous music. It makes for exceptional listening, regardless of language.

Schedules Prepared for Entire Year

To be as helpful as possible throughout the year, PASSPORT'S schedules consist not just of observed activity, but also that which we have creatively opined will take place during the forthcoming year. This material is original from us, and therefore will not be so exact as factual information.

Most frequencies are used year round. Those that are used only seasonally are labeled **S** for summer (midyear), and **W** for winter.

ALBANIA
RADIO TIRANA
North America and Caribbean
0145-0200 &
0230-0300   6145 & 7160 (E North Am)
Europe and North Africa
1700-1715 ⬅ 7155 & 9760 (W Europe)
1930-2000 ⬅ 7260 & 9730 (Europe)
ALGERIA

RTV ALGERIENNE
Europe and North Africa
1500-1600   11715 (Europe)
1800-1900   11715 & 15160 (Europe)
2000-2100   15160 (Europe)
Other World Zones
1800-1900   15205/7145 (Mideast)
ANGOLA
RADIO NACIONAL—(S Africa)
2000-2100   3354 (Irr) & 9535
ARGENTINA
RADIO ARGENTINA-RAE
North America and Caribbean
0100-0200   Tu-Sa 11710 (Americas)
Europe and North Africa
1900-2000   M-F 15345 (Europe & N Africa)
ARMENIA
VOICE OF ARMENIA
North America and Caribbean
2030-2100   **S** 11920 (C America)
2130-2200   **W** 9480 (C America)
Europe and North Africa
0830-0900   **S** Su 15170 & **S** Su 15270 (Europe)
0930-1000   **W** Su 15275 & **W** Su 15370 (Europe)
1745-1800   M-F 4810 & M-F 7480 (E Europe)
2030-2100   **S** 11920 (W Europe)
2130-2200   **W** 9480 (Europe)
Other World Zones
1745-1800   M-F 4810, **W** M-F 4990, M-F 7480, **S** M-F 9675 & **S** M-F 11960 (Mideast)

AUSTRALIA
ABC/CAAMA RADIO—(Australasia)
2130-0830   4835 & 4910
ABC/RADIO RUM JUNGLE—(Australasia)
2130-0830   5025
ARMED FORCES RADIO
0100-0300,
0430-0630 &
1000-1200   13525 USB (SE Asia)
1400-1600   5791 USB (SE Asia), 8743 USB (E Africa)
RADIO AUSTRALIA
North America and Caribbean
1200-1630   5995 (W North Am)
1430-2130   6060 (W North Am)
1630-2100   9860 (W North Am)
1700-2030   11695 (W North Am)
1700-2100   9580 (W North Am)
Europe and North Africa
0030-0400   15510 (Europe)
0100-0800   15425 (Europe)
0600-0700   15510 (Europe)
0800-1100   21725 (Europe)
1100-1300   15530 (Europe)
1430-1630   9770 (Europe)
1430-1800   **W** 7260, **S** 9615 & 11660 (Europe)
1630-1900   6090/6080 (Europe)
1800-2100   7260 (Europe)
Other World Zones
0000-0100   **W** 9610, **S** 11855 & 13745 (SE Asia)
0000-0500   17750 (SE Asia)
0030-0100   13755 (Pacific), 15240 (SE Asia)
0030-0400   15510 (SE Asia)
0030-0600   15365 & 17860 (Pacific)
0030-0630   9660 & 17795 (Pacific)

0030-0730	15415 (SE Asia)
0100-0400	17715 (E Asia)
0100-0630	15240 (Pacific), Sa/Su 17880 (S Asia)
0100-0800	15425 (SE Asia)
0400-0430	Sa/Su 15510 & Sa/Su 17715 (E Asia)
0430-0500	15510 (E Asia)
0430-0900	17715 (E Asia)
0600-0700	15510 (SE Asia)
0600-0900	15530 (SE Asia)
0630-0900	5995, 6020 & 6080 (Pacific)
0630-1200	9580 & 9860 (Pacific)
0730-0900	9710 (Pacific & E Asia)
0800-1100	21725 (S Asia & Mideast)
0900-1030	9510 (E Asia & SE Asia), 13605 (E Asia)
0900-1130	7240 (SE Asia)
1100-1300	15530 (SE Asia & Mideast)
1100-1430	9615 (SE Asia)
1130-1430	9560 (SE Asia)
1200-1630	5995 & 11800 (Pacific)
1300-1330	9510 (E Asia & SE Asia)
1430-1630	6080 (Pacific & SE Asia), 9770 (S Asia & Mideast)
1430-1700	9710 (Pacific & E Asia), 11695 (SE Asia)
1430-1800	Ⓦ 7260, Ⓢ 9615 & 11660 (S Asia & Mideast)
1430-2130	6060 (Pacific)
1630-1900	6090/6080 (S Asia)
1630-2100	9860 (Pacific)
1630-2130	6080 (Pacific)
1700-2030	11695 (Pacific)
1700-2100	9580 (Pacific)
1800-2100	7260 (S Asia & Mideast), 11660 (Pacific & E Asia)
1900-2100	6150 (SE Asia)
2100-2200	11695 (SE Asia)
2100-2300	9645 (SE Asia)
2100-2400	9660 (Pacific), Ⓢ 11660 & Ⓦ 11855 (Pacific & E Asia)
2130-2400	15365 & 17860 (Pacific)
2200-2400	Ⓦ 9610 & Ⓢ 11855 (SE Asia), 13755 & 17795 (Pacific)
2300-2400	11695 (SE Asia)
2330-2400	9645 & 9850 (SE Asia), 13605 (E Asia), 15240 (SE Asia)

AUSTRIA
RADIO AUSTRIA INTERNATIONAL
North America and Caribbean
0130-0200	9655 (E North Am)
0230-0300	9655 (E North Am), 9870 (C America)
1130-1200	Ⓢ M-Sa 13730 (E North Am)
1230-1300	Ⓦ M-Sa 13730 (E North Am)

Europe and North Africa
0530-0600	Ⓦ 6155 & Ⓦ 13730 (Europe)
0730-0800	Ⓢ 6155 & Ⓢ 13730 (Europe)
0830-0900	Ⓦ 6155 & Ⓦ 13730 (Europe)
0930-1000	Ⓢ M-Sa 6155 & Ⓢ M-Sa 13730 (Europe)
1030-1100	Ⓦ M-Sa 6155 & Ⓦ M-Sa 13730 (Europe)
1130-1200	Ⓢ M-Sa 13730 (W Europe)
1230-1300	Ⓦ M-Sa 6155 (Europe), Ⓦ M-Sa 13730 (W Europe)
1330-1400	Ⓢ 6155 & Ⓢ 13730 (Europe)
1430-1500	Ⓢ 13730 (Europe)
1530-1600	Ⓦ 6155 & Ⓦ 13730 (Europe)

1930-2000	5945 & 6155 (Europe)

Other World Zones
0530-0600	Ⓦ 15410 & Ⓦ 17870 (Mideast)
0730-0800	Ⓢ M-Sa 15410 & M-Sa 17870 (Mideast)
0930-1000	Ⓢ M-Sa 17870 & Ⓦ 17870 (Australasia)
1030-1100	Ⓢ 17870 & Ⓦ M-Sa 17870 (Australasia)
1230-1300	Ⓦ 15450 (E Asia)
1330-1400	15450 (E Asia)
1530-1600	Ⓦ 9665/9880 (Mideast), 11780 (S Asia & SE Asia)
1630-1700	Ⓦ 11780 (S Asia & SE Asia)
1730-1800	Ⓢ 9665/9880 (Mideast), Ⓢ 11780 (S Asia & SE Asia)
1930-2000	M-Sa 9665/9880 (Mideast), 13730 (S Africa)

BANGLADESH
RADIO BANGLADESH
Europe and North Africa
1745-1815 &	
1815-1900	7190 & 9650 (Europe)

Other World Zones
1230-1300	7185 & 9650 (SE Asia)

BELGIUM
RADIO VLAANDEREN INTERNATIONAAL
North America and Caribbean
0030-0100	⏴ 6030 (E North Am)
1330-1400	⏴ Su 13670 (E North Am)
1330-1400	Ⓦ Su 17590/17555 (E North Am)
1400-1430	⏴ M-Sa 13670 (E North Am)
1400-1430	Ⓦ M-Sa 17590/17555 (E North Am)

Europe and North Africa
0730-0800	Ⓦ 5985 (Europe)
1000-1030	⏴ M-Sa 5910/6035 (Europe)
1900-1930 &	
2200-2230	⏴ 5910 (Europe)

Other World Zones
0730-0755	⏴ M-Sa 9925 (Australasia)
1000-1030	⏴ M-Sa 15545/15510 & M-Sa 17595 (Africa)
1800-1830	Ⓢ 13685 (Africa)
1900-1930	⏴ 9925 (Africa)

BRAZIL
RADIO NACIONAL
North America and Caribbean
1200-1320	15445 (C America)

Europe and North Africa
1800-1920	15265 (Europe)

Other World Zones
1800-1920	15265 (W Africa)

BULGARIA
RADIO BULGARIA
North America and Caribbean
0000-0100	⏴ 9700 (E North Am & C America)
0000-0100	Ⓦ 7205 (E North Am)
0400-0500	Ⓢ 11720 (E North Am)
0500-0600	⏴ 9700 (E North Am & C America)
0500-0600	Ⓦ 7335 (E North Am)
2300-2400	Ⓢ 11720 (E North Am)

Europe and North Africa
1900-2000	Ⓢ 11720 (Europe)
2000-2100	⏴ 9700 (Europe)
2000-2100	Ⓦ 7305 (Europe)

2100-2200　🅂 11720 (Europe)
2200-2300　◄ 9700 (Europe)
2200-2300　🅦 7105 (Europe)
Other World Zones
1130-1230　🅂 15635 (S Asia & E Asia), 🅂 17625 (E Asia)
1230-1330　🅦 9770 (E Asia), 🅦 11740 (S Asia & E Asia)

CAMBODIA
NATIONAL VOICE OF CAMBODIA—(SE Asia)
0000-0015 &
1200-1215　11940

CANADA
CANADIAN BROADCASTING CORPORATION—(Northern Quebec)
0000-0300　◄ Su 9625
0200-0300　◄ Tu-Sa 9625
0300-0310 &
0330-0609　◄ M 9625
0400-0609　◄ Su 9625
0500-0609　◄ Tu-Sa 9625
1200-1255　◄ M-F 9625
1200-1505　◄ Sa 9625
1200-1700　◄ Su 9625
1600-1615 &
1700-1805　◄ Sa 9625
1800-2400　◄ Su 9625
1945-2015,
2200-2225 &
2240-2330　◄ M-F 9625
CFCX, MONTREAL—(E North Am)
24 Hr　　　6005
CFRX-CFRB, TORONTO—(E North Am)
24 Hr　　　6070
CFVP-CKMX, CALGARY—(W North Am)
24 Hr　　　6030
CHNX-CHNS, HALIFAX—(E North Am)
24 Hr　　　6130
CKFX-CKWX, VANCOUVER—(W North Am)
24 Hr　　　6080
CKZN-CBN, ST. JOHN'S NF—(E North Am)
0930-0500　◄ 6160
CKZU-CBU, VANCOUVER—(W North Am)
24 Hr　　　6160
RADIO CANADA INTERNATIONAL
North America and Caribbean
0000-0100　◄ 9755 (E North Am)
0000-0100　🅦 5960 (E North Am)
0100-0130　🅂 9535 & 🅂 11940 (C America)
0100-0200　🅂 6120 (E North Am & C America)
0130-0200　🅂 Su/M 9535 & 🅂 Su/M 11940 (C America)
0200-0230　🅂 6120 (E North Am & C America), 9535 & 🅂 11940 (C America)
0200-0300　◄ 9755 (E North Am)
0200-0300　🅦 6120 (W North Am), 🅂 9755 (E North Am & C America), 🅦 11845 (C America)
0230-0300　🅂 Su/M 6120 (E North Am & C America), 🅂 Su/M 9535, 🅦 9535 & 🅂 Su/M 11940 (C America)
0300-0330　🅦 6000, 🅦 9725 & 🅦 9755 (C America)
0330-0400　🅦 Su/M 6000, 🅦 Su/M 9725 & 🅦 Su/M 9755 (C America)
1200-1300　🅂 M-F 9635 (E North Am)

1300-1400　◄ M-F 11855 (E North Am), M-F 13650 (E North Am & C America)
1400-1700　◄ Su 11955 (E North Am), Su 17820 (C America)
2200-2230　🅂 11895 (E North Am), 🅂 13740 & 🅂 15305 (C America)
2200-2300　🅂 5960 (E North Am)
2200-2400　🅂 13670 (C America)
2300-2330　🅦 9535, 🅦 11845, 11940 & 🅂 15305 (C America)
2300-2400　◄ 9755 (E North Am)
2300-2400　5960 (E North Am)
2330-2400　🅦 Sa/Su 9535, 🅦 Sa/Su 11845, Sa/Su 11940 & 🅂 Sa/Su 15305 (C America)
Europe and North Africa
0000-0100　◄ 5995 (Europe)
0000-0100　🅦 7250 (N Africa)
0500-0530　🅂 M-F 7295 (W Europe & N Africa)
0600-0630　◄ M-F 6050 (Europe)
0600-0630　🅦 M-F 6150 & 🅦 M-F 9760 (Europe)
1330-1400　🅂 M-Sa 15315 (Europe), 🅂 21455 (E Europe)
1430-1500　◄ 15325 & M-Sa 17820 (Europe)
1430-1500　🅦 9555, 🅦 11915 & 🅦 11935 (Europe)
1645-1700　🅂 M-F 9555 (Europe)
1745-1800　◄ M-F 11935, M-F 15325 & M-F 17820 (Europe)
1745-1800　🅦 M-F 9555 & 🅦 13610 (Europe)
2000-2100　🅂 11985 (Europe)
2000-2130　🅂 5995, 🅂 7235, 🅂 13650 & 🅂 15325 (Europe)
2100-2130　🅂 11690 (Europe)
2100-2200　🅦 9725 (Europe)
2100-2230　🅦 5995 (Europe & N Africa), 🅦 7260 (W Europe), 🅦 11945 & 🅦 13650 (Europe)
2300-2400　◄ 5995 (Europe)
2300-2400　🅦 7250 (N Africa)
Other World Zones
0000-0100　◄ 5995 (Africa)
0000-0100　🅦 7250 (W Africa)
0400-0430　🅦 6150, 🅦 9505, 🅂 9650, 🅦 9670, 🅂 11835, 🅂 11905 & 🅂 15275 (Mideast)
0500-0530　🅂 M-F 15430 (Africa)
0600-0630　🅦 M-F 9740 (Africa), 🅦 M-F 11905 (Mideast)
1230-1300　🅦 6150 & 🅂 9660 (E Asia), 🅦 11730 & 🅂 15195 (SE Asia)
1330-1357　9535 (E Asia)
1330-1400　🅦 6150 & 🅂 11795 (E Asia), 🅂 M-Sa 17895 (Africa), 🅂 21455 (Mideast)
1430-1500　🅦 9555 (Mideast)
1630-1657　6550 (E Asia), 7150 & 9550 (S Asia)
2000-2130　🅂 5995 (Mideast), 🅂 13670 & 🅂 15150 (Africa)
2100-2230　◄ 17820 (Africa)
2100-2230　🅦 13690 & 🅦 15140 (Africa)
2200-2230　11705 (SE Asia)
2300-2400　◄ 5995 (Africa)
2300-2400　🅦 7250 (W Africa)

CHINA
CHINA RADIO INTERNATIONAL
North America and Caribbean
0300-0400　9690 (C America)
0400-0500　🅦 9730 & 🅂 11680 (W North Am)
1200-1300　9655 (E North Am)

1300-1400   **[S]** 7405 (W North Am)
1400-1500   7405 (W North Am)
1500-1600   **[W]** 7405 (W North Am)

Europe and North Africa
1900-2000   **[S]** 11515 (N Africa)
1900-2100   9440 (N Africa)
2000-2200   6950 & 9920 (Europe)
2200-2230   *3985* (Europe)
2200-2300   **[W]** *7170* & **[S]** *9880* (Europe)

Other World Zones
0900-1100   **[W]** 8260 & 8450 (E Asia), 11755, 15440 & 17710 (Australasia)
1140-1155   8660 (E Asia), 11445 & 15135 (SE Asia)
1200-1300   8425 (E Asia), 11795 (Australasia)
1200-1400   9715 & 11660 (SE Asia), 15440 (Australasia)
1210-1225   8660 (E Asia), 11445, 12110 & 15135 (SE Asia)
1400-1600   4200 (E Asia), 9785 & 11815 (S Asia)
1440-1455   8660 (E Asia), 11445 & 15135 (SE Asia)
1600-1700   *15110* (C Africa & S Africa), *15130* (S Africa)
1600-1755   4130 (E Asia)
1600-1800   11575 (E Africa & S Africa)
1700-1800   7405 (Africa), 9570 (E Africa & S Africa)
1900-2000   **[W]** 6955 (W Africa), **[S]** 11515 (Mideast)
1900-2100   9440 (W Africa)
2000-2130   *11715* (S Africa), *15110* (C Africa & S Africa)
2000-2155   4130 (E Asia)
2100-2130   *11790* (C Africa & E Africa)

CHINA (TAIWAN)

VOICE OF FREE CHINA
North America and Caribbean
0200-0300   *5950* (E North Am), *11740* (C America)
0200-0400   *9680* (W North Am)
0300-0400   *5950* (E North Am & C America)
0700-0800   *5950* (C America)
Europe and North Africa
2200-2300   **[W]** *5810*, **[W]** *9850*, **[S]** *17750* & **[S]** *21720* (Europe)
Other World Zones
0200-0300   7130 (Australasia), 11825 (SE Asia)
0200-0400   15345 (E Asia)
0300-0400   11745 & 11825 (SE Asia)
1200-1300   7130 (E Asia), 9610 (SE Asia)
VOICE OF ASIA—(SE Asia)
1100-1200   7445

COSTA RICA

ADVENTIST WORLD RADIO—(C America)
0000-0100   5030, 6150, 7375, 9725 & 13750
1100-1200   7375
1100-1300   5030, 9725 & 13750
1200-1300   6150
1700-1800   Sa/Su 13750 & Sa/Su 15460
1900-2000   13750 & 15460
2300-2400   5030, 6150, 7375, 9725 & 13750

RADIO FOR PEACE INTERNATIONAL
North America and Caribbean
0100-0630   7385 (C America), 9400 USB (Americas)

0630-0700   Su-F 7385 (C America), Su-F 9400 USB (Americas)
0700-0800   7385 (C America), 9400 USB (Americas)
0900-1430   9400 USB (C America)
1200-1230   6200 (C America)
1430-1500   Su-F 9400 USB (C America)
1500-1600   9400 USB (C America)
1700-2230   6200 & 9400 USB (C America)
2230-2300   Sa-Th 6200 & Sa-Th 9400 USB (C America)
2300-2400   6200 (C America), 9400 USB (Americas)

CROATIA

CROATIAN RADIO
North America and Caribbean
0000-0008 &
0100-0108 ◀ 7370 (E North Am)
0200-0208,
0300-0308,
0400-0408 &
0500-0508 ◀ 5895 (E North Am)
1303-1313 ◀ 13830 (E North Am)
2300-2308 ◀ 7370/11635 (E North Am)
Europe and North Africa
0000-0008,
0100-0108,
0200-0208,
0300-0308,
0400-0408 &
0500-0508 ◀ 5895 (Europe)
0703-0713 &
0903-0913 ◀ M-Sa 5920, M-Sa 7370 & M-Sa 9830 (Europe)
1303-1313 ◀ 5920 & 7370 (Europe)
2300-2308 ◀ 5895 (Europe)
Other World Zones
0703-0713 ◀ M-Sa 7370 & M-Sa 13830 (Australasia)

CUBA

RADIO HABANA CUBA
North America and Caribbean
0100-0400   6000 (E North Am)
0100-0500   9830 USB (E North Am)
0400-0500   6180 (C America)
0500-0700   9820 (W North Am)
2100-2200   **[S]** 11705 & **[W]** 11720 (E North Am)
2200-2300   6180 (C America), 11960 USB (E North Am)
Europe and North Africa
2100-2200   **[S]** 11705 & **[W]** 11720 (Europe)
2200-2300   11960 USB (Europe)

CZECH REPUBLIC

RADIO PRAGUE
North America and Caribbean
0000-0030   5930 & 7345 (E North Am)
0100-0130   7345 & **[S]** 9405 (E North Am)
0300-0330   5930 & 7345 (E North Am)
Europe and North Africa
0700-0730 ◀ 7345 (W Europe)
1130-1200 ◀ 7345 & 9505 (W Europe)
1700-1730 &
1800-1830 ◀ 5930 (W Europe)
2000-2030   **[S]** 11640 (W Europe)
2100-2130 ◀ 5930 (W Europe)
2100-2130   **[W]** 7345 (W Europe)

Other World Zones

0330-0400	[W] 7345 (Mideast & E Africa), [S] 9480 (Mideast & S Asia)
0600-0630	[S] 15640 (S Asia & Australasia)
0700-0730	[W] 17485 (S Asia & Australasia)
0730-0800	[S] 15640 (W Africa & E Africa), [W] 17485 (E Africa & S Asia), [W] 21705 (SE Asia & Australasia)
1600-1630	[S] 17485 (E Africa & Mideast)
1700-1730	[W] 9420 (Mideast & S Asia), [S] 15640 (W Africa)
1800-1830	[W] 9420 (E Africa & Mideast)

ECUADOR

HCJB-VOICE OF THE ANDES
North America and Caribbean

0030-0500	9745 (E North Am)
0500-0700	9745 (W North Am)
1100-1500	12005 (C America)

Europe and North Africa

0700-0830	[W] 6205 & [S] 11615 (Europe)
1700-2000	15490/15350 (Europe)

Other World Zones

0700-1130	5900 (Australasia)

EGYPT

RADIO CAIRO
North America and Caribbean

0000-0030 &	
2300-2400	9900 (E North Am)

Europe and North Africa

2115-2245	9900 (Europe)

Other World Zones

1215-1330	17595 (S Asia)
1630-1830	15255 (C Africa & S Africa)
2030-2200	15375 (W Africa)

EQUATORIAL GUINEA

RADIO AFRICA—(W Africa)

1700-2300	7190/15186

RADIO EAST AFRICA—(E Africa)

0500-1400	7190/15186

ETHIOPIA

RADIO ETHIOPIA—(E Africa)

1600-1700	7165 & 9560

FINLAND

RADIO FINLAND
Europe and North Africa

0745-0800	⏴ 6120, 9560 & 11755 (Europe)
1900-1930	[S] 15440 (Europe)
2000-2030	⏴ 9730 (Europe)
2130-2200	[S] 6120, [S] 9730, [S] 11755 & [S] 15440 (Europe)

Other World Zones

0430-0500	[S] 15440 (Mideast)
0530-0600	[W] 9635 (Mideast)
0800-0830	[S] 17820 USB (SE Asia & Australasia)
0900-0930	⏴ 15330/15115 (SE Asia & Australasia)
0900-0930	[W] 9760 (SE Asia & Australasia)
2000-2030	⏴ 9730 (W Africa)
2130-2200	[S] 9730 (W Africa)
2230-2300	[S] 9665 (E Asia & SE Asia)
2330-2400	[W] 5990 (E Asia & SE Asia)

FRANCE

RADIO FRANCE INTERNATIONALE
North America and Caribbean

1200-1300	[W] 11615 (E North Am), 13625 (C

America), [S] 15365 (E North Am), [W] 15365 & [S] 15530 (C America)

Europe and North Africa

1200-1300	9805, 15155 & 15195 (E Europe)
1600-1700	6175 (Europe & N Africa), 11615 (N Africa)

Other World Zones

1200-1300	[S] 11615 (SE Asia)
1400-1455	[W] 4130 (E Asia)
1400-1500	7110 (S Asia), [W] 12030 & [S] 15405 (S Asia & SE Asia), 17560 (Mideast)
1600-1700	[S] 11615 (Mideast), 11700 (W Africa), 12015 & 15530 (S Africa)
1600-1730	[W] 9485/11975 (Mideast & E Africa), [S] 15210 & [S] 15460 (E Africa)

GEORGIA

RADIO GEORGIA—(Europe)

0700-0730	[W] 11805
0900-0930	[S] 11910
1100-1130	[W] 11815

GERMANY

DEUTSCHE WELLE-VOICE OF GERMANY
North America and Caribbean

0100-0150	6085, 6145, [W] 9555, [S] 9640, [W] 9670 & [S] 11740 (C America)
0200-0250	[S] 9640 (C America)
0300-0350	[W] 6040, 6085, [W] 6120, [S] 6185 & [S] 9640 (C America)
0500-0550	[W] 6045 & [S] 6175 (C America), [W] 6185 (W North Am)
2100-2150	[W] 15270 (Americas)

Europe and North Africa

0700-0750	[S] 6015 & [S] 9565 (Europe)
2000-2050	[W] 5960, [S] 7170, [W] 7285 & [S] 9615 (Europe)

Other World Zones

0200-0250	[W] 6035 (S Asia & SE Asia), [W] 6130 (S Asia), 7285 (S Asia & SE Asia), [W] 7355, 9615, [S] 9690, [S] 11945, [S] 11965 & [S] 12045 (S Asia)
0400-0450	6015 (C Africa & E Africa), [W] 6065 (Africa), [S] 7150 (Mideast & Africa), [W] 7225 (C Africa & S Africa), [W] 9565 (S Africa), [S] 11765 (Africa)
0600-0650	[W] 6100, [W] 9565, [W] 11765, [S] 11915, 13790, 15185 & [S] 15225 (W Africa), 17820 (E Asia), [S] 17875 (Africa), [S] 21680 (Mideast), [W] 21705 (W Africa)
0900-0950	6160 (Australasia), [W] 9565 (C Africa & E Africa), [W] 9875 (E Asia), [W] 11715 (S Asia), [W] 11725 (S Africa), [S] 11730 (SE Asia & Australasia), [S] 12055 (E Asia), [W] 15145 & [W] 15410 (S Africa), [S] 17715 (SE Asia & Australasia), 17780 (Australasia), [W] 17800 (W Africa), [W] 17820 (SE Asia & Australasia), 21600 (Africa), 21680 (SE Asia & Australasia)
1100-1150	[W] 15370 (S Africa), [W] 15410, [S] 17715, 17765, [W] 17800 & [S] 17860 (W Africa), [S] 21600 (Africa)
1600-1650	6170 (S Asia), [W] 7195 (S Africa), 7225, [W] 7305 & [W] 9585 (S Asia), [W] 9735 (C Africa & E Africa), [S] 9875 (S Asia), [W] 11965 (S Africa), [S] 13690 (S

Asia), W 15145 (E Africa & S Africa), S 15595 (S Asia), S 17800 (Africa)

1900-1950	W 7110 (W Africa), S *7170* & S *9670* (Africa), W *9670* (W Africa), W *9765* (Africa), W 11785 (W Africa & S Africa), S *11785* (W Africa), W *11810* (Africa), W *11865* (W Africa), S 13690 (Mideast), S 13790 (W Africa), W *13790* (Mideast), W *15425* (W Africa)
2100-2150	W 6185 (S Asia & SE Asia), S 7115 (E Asia), W 7225 & W *9615* (W Africa), *9670* (SE Asia & Australasia), W 9690 (W Africa), 9765 (SE Asia & Australasia), S 11765 (W Africa), *11785* (SE Asia & Australasia), W 11810 & W *15270* (W Africa)
2300-2350	S *5980* (S Asia & SE Asia), W 6000 (SE Asia), W *6160* (S Asia & E Asia), S *7235* (E Asia), W *7235* (SE Asia), S 9690 (E Asia)

GREECE
FONI TIS HELLADAS-VOICE OF GREECE
North America and Caribbean
| 2335-2350 | 9375 & W 9425 (C America) |

Europe and North Africa
0735-0745	W 9935 & 11645 (Europe)
0735-0750	9425 (Europe)
1840-1855	S 11645 (E Europe)
1900-1910	W 6260 & W 9380 (Europe)
2000-2010	S 9375 (Europe)

Other World Zones
0735-0745	S 9375 (Australasia)
0935-0950	W 15650 & W 17525 (Australasia)
1840-1855	S 15650 (C Africa & S Africa)
2235-2245	S 6260, 9375 & W 9425 (Australasia)

GUAM
ADVENTIST WORLD RADIO
0900-1000	9530 (E Asia)
1600-1700	9370 (S Asia)
2300-2400	11980 (SE Asia)

KTWR-TRANS WORLD RADIO
0745-0915	15200 (SE Asia)
0845-1000	11830 (Australasia)
1500-1615	11580 (S Asia & SE Asia)
1615-1630	W-Su 11580 (S Asia & SE Asia)

HOLLAND
RADIO NEDERLAND WERELDOMROEP
North America and Caribbean
0000-0125	6020 & S *9845/9840* (E North Am)
0030-0125	W *9845/9840* & W *11655* (C America)
0430-0525	W *5995* (C America), *6165* & S *9590* (W North Am)
2330-2400	6020 & S *9845/9840* (E North Am)

Europe and North Africa
1030-1225	S *9650* (W Europe)
1130-1325	← *6045* (W Europe)
1130-1325	W *7130* (W Europe)
1930-2025	W 6020 (N Africa)

Other World Zones
0030-0225	W *7305* & S *11655* (S Asia)
0030-0230	W *5905* (S Asia)
0030-0325	S *9860* (S Asia)
0130-0230	W *11655* (S Asia)
0130-0325	W *9860* & S *9890* (S Asia)

0230-0325	*11655* (S Asia)
0730-0825	S *9700* & W *11895* (Australasia)
0730-1025	*9720* (Australasia)
0830-0925	W *13700* (Australasia)
0930-1125	W *7260* (E Asia), W *9810* (E Asia & SE Asia), S *12065* & S *13705* (E Asia & Australasia)
1030-1125	S *9820* (Australasia)
1330-1425	13700 (Mideast & S Asia)
1330-1625	S *9890* & W *9895* (S Asia), *15150* (S Asia & E Asia)
1430-1525	W 13700 (S Asia)
1730-1925	*6020* (S Africa), 11655 (W Africa)
1730-2025	S *7120* & W *9605* (E Africa)
1830-1925	W 6015 & S 13700 (W Africa)
1830-2025	*15315* & *17605* (W Africa)
1830-2125	S 9860 (E Africa), W 9860 & 9895 (W Africa)
1925-2125	S 11655 (W Africa)
1930-2025	W 6020 (W Africa), S *7305/7205* (C Africa & W Africa), W *11655* (W Africa & C Africa)

HUNGARY
RADIO BUDAPEST
Europe and North Africa
1900-1930	S 3955 (Europe), S 7130 (W Europe)
2000-2030	W 3975 (Europe), W 6110 & W 7220 (W Europe)
2100-2130	S 7250 & S 9835 (W Europe)
2200-2230	← 3955 (Europe)
2200-2230	W 6110 & W 7220 (W Europe)

INDIA
ALL INDIA RADIO
Europe and North Africa
| 1745-1945 | 9650 (N Africa), 9950 (W Europe), 13750 (N Africa) |
| 2045-2230 | 7412, 9950 & 11620 (W Europe) |

Other World Zones
0000-0045	9705 & 9950 (SE Asia), 13700 (E Asia), 15145 (SE Asia)
1000-1100	15050 (E Asia & Australasia), 15180 & 17387 (Australasia), 17890 (E Asia)
1115-1215	15770 & 17865 (SE Asia)
1130-1140	11620 (S Asia)
1330-1500	11620 & 13750 (SE Asia)
1530-1545	7412, 9630 & 9910 (SE Asia)
1745-1945	11935 & 15075 (E Africa)
2045-2230	9910, 11715 & 15225 (Australasia)
2245-2400	9705 & 9950 (SE Asia), 13700 (E Asia), 15145 (SE Asia)

IRAN
VOICE OF THE ISLAMIC REPUBLIC OF IRAN
North America and Caribbean
| 0030-0130 | S 6175 & S 7180 (C America), S 7260 & W 9670 (E North Am) |

Europe and North Africa
| 1930-2030 | 7260 & 9022 (Europe) |

Other World Zones
| 1130-1230 | 11745 (Mideast), W 11790 (S Asia & SE Asia), S 11875 (S Asia), 11930 (Mideast), 15260 & 17750 (S Asia & SE Asia) |
| 1530-1630 | W 9575 (S Asia), W 11790 (S Asia & SE Asia), S 11875 (S Asia), 15260 & 17750 (S Asia & SE Asia) |

2130-2230	**S** 6175 & **S** 9670 (Australasia)

IRAQ
RADIO IRAQ INTERNATIONAL—(S Asia)
0900-1300 ◧ 13680 (Irr)

ISRAEL
KOL ISRAEL
North America and Caribbean
0500-0515 ◧ 7465 & 9435 (E North Am)
2000-2030 ◧ 9435 & 11603 (E North Am)
Europe and North Africa
0500-0515 ◧ 7465 & 9435 (W Europe)
1900-1930 **S** 11685 (E Europe)
2000-2030 ◧ 7465, 9435 & 11603 (W Europe)
2000-2030 **W** 7405 (E Europe)

ITALY
ADVENTIST WORLD RADIO—(Europe)
1500-1600 7230
EUROPEAN CHRISTIAN RADIO—(Europe)
0700-0715 &
0745-0800 Su 6220/6210
ITALIAN RADIO RELAY—(Europe)
0000-0030 ◧ Sa 7125
0600-0615 ◧ Su-F 7125
0615-2100 ◧ 7125
2100-2300 ◧ F-Su 7125
2300-2315 ◧ F/Sa 7125
2315-2400 ◧ F 7125
RADIO ROMA
North America and Caribbean
0050-0110 9545 (E North Am & C America),
11800 (C America)
Europe and North Africa
0425-0440 **W** 5975 & 7275 (Europe & N Africa)
1935-1955 7275 & 9575 (W Europe)
2025-2045 7235 & **S** 9710 (E Europe)
Other World Zones
0425-0440 **W** 5975 & 7275 (Mideast)
2025-2045 7235, **S** 9710 & 11800 (Mideast)
2200-2225 **W** 5990, 9710, 11800 & **S** 15330 (E
Asia)
RAI-RTV ITALIANA
Europe and North Africa
0003-0012,
0103-0112,
0203-0212,
0303-0312 &
0403-0412 6060 (Europe & N Africa)
Other World Zones
0003-0012,
0103-0112,
0203-0212,
0303-0312 &
0403-0412 6060 (Mideast)

JAPAN
RADIO JAPAN/NHK
North America and Caribbean
0100-0200 **S** 5960 (E North Am), **W** 9565 & **S**
11790/9680 (W North Am)
0300-0330 11885 (W North Am), 11895 (C America), 15230 (W North Am)
0300-0400 **W** 5960 (E North Am), **W** 9565 & **S**
11790/9680 (W North Am)
0500-0600 **W** 6025 & **S** 6110 (W North Am & C
America), **W** 9565, **S** 11790/9680 &
11885 (W North Am)

1400-1500	11705 (W North Am)
1400-1600,	
1700-1800 &	
1900-2000	9535 (W North Am)

Europe and North Africa
0500-0600 5975 & 7230 (Europe)
0700-0800 5975 & 7230 (Europe), 15335 (Europe
& N Africa)
1700-1800 11930 (N Africa)
2100-2200 11865/11925 (Europe & N Africa)
2300-2400 **S** 5965, **W** 6055 & 6155 (Europe)
Other World Zones
0100-0200 11840 (E Asia), 11860 (SE Asia),
11900 (S Asia), 11910 (E Asia), 17810
(SE Asia), 17845 (S Asia)
0300-0400 11840/15210 (E Asia), 17810 (SE
Asia)
0500-0600 11740 (SE Asia)
0500-0800 11955/11725 (E Asia), 17810 (SE
Asia)
0600-0700 **S** 11860 (E Asia)
0700-0800 11740 (SE Asia), 11850/15270 (Australasia), 15335 (Mideast), 17815 (C
Africa), 21610 (SE Asia)
0900-1000 9610 (E Asia), 11850/15270 (Australasia), 15190 (SE Asia)
1100-1200 9610 (E Asia), 15350/15295 (SE Asia)
1400-1500 9610 (E Asia), 11895/11840 (S Asia)
1400-1600 11915 (SE Asia)
1500-1600 11955 (S Asia), 15355 (S Africa)
1700-1800 6150 (E Asia), 9580 (SE Asia),
11840/9570 (S Asia), 11930 (Mideast)
1900-2000 6150 (E Asia), 7140 (Australasia),
9580 (SE Asia), 11850 (Australasia)
2100-2115 9660 & 11915 (SE Asia)
2100-2200 6035 (SE Asia), 7140 (E Asia),
9675/9580 (SE Asia), 11850 (Australasia)
2300-2400 7140 (E Asia), 9675/9580 (SE Asia),
11850 (Australasia)

JORDAN
RADIO JORDAN
North America and Caribbean
1200-1300 ◧ 11970/15170 (E North Am)
1500-1730 ◧ 11970/15270 (E North Am)
Europe and North Africa
1200-1300 ◧ 11970/15170 (W Europe)
1500-1730 ◧ 11970/15270 (W Europe)

KOREA (DPR)
RADIO PYONGYANG
North America and Caribbean
0000-0050 11335, 13760 & 15130 (Americas)
1100-1150 6576, 9977 & 11335 (Americas)
1300-1350 13760 (Americas)
2300-2350 **W** 11700 (C America), 13650 (Americas)
Europe and North Africa
1300-1350 9345 & 11740 (Europe)
1500-1550 &
1700-1750 9325 & 13785 (Europe)
2000-2050 6576 & 9345 (Europe)
Other World Zones
0400-0450 15180, 15230 & 17765 (SE Asia)
0600-0650 15180 & 15230 (SE Asia)
0700-0750 15340 (E Asia & S Asia), 17765 (SE
Asia)

0800-0850	15180 & 15230 (SE Asia)
1300-1350	9640 (S Asia), 15230 (SE Asia)
1500-1550,	
1700-1750 &	
2000-2050	9640 (Mideast & Africa), 9977 (Africa)

KOREA (REPUBLIC)
RADIO KOREA INTERNATIONAL
North America and Caribbean

0600-0700	7205 (E North Am)
1030-1100	[S] 11715 (E North Am)
1130-1200	[W] 9650 (E North Am)

Europe and North Africa

0800-0900	7550 & 13670 (Europe)
1600-1700 &	
1900-2000	6480 (Europe)
2100-2200	6480 & 15575 (Europe)
2200-2230	[W] 3975 (Europe), [S] 5965 (W Europe)

Other World Zones

1200-1300	7285/7180 (E Asia)
1230-1300	9570 (SE Asia), 9640 (E Asia), 13670 (SE Asia)
1600-1700	5975 (E Asia), 9515 & 9870 (Mideast & Africa)
1900-2000	5975 & 7275 (E Asia)

KUWAIT
RADIO KUWAIT
North America and Caribbean

1800-2100	11990 (E North Am)

Europe and North Africa

1800-2100	11990 (Europe)

LEBANON
VOICE OF HOPE
Europe and North Africa

0000-0100	6280 (E Europe)
0000-0200 &	
0400-1100	9960 (E Europe)
0800-1100	6280 (E Europe)
1300-1500 &	
1530-1630	9960 (E Europe)
1600-1900	6280 (E Europe)
1900-2400	9960 (E Europe)
2100-2400	6280 (E Europe)

Other World Zones

0000-0100	6280 (Mideast)
0000-0200 &	
0400-1100	9960 (Mideast)
0800-1100	6280 (Mideast)
1300-1500 &	
1530-1630	9960 (Mideast)
1600-1900	6280 (Mideast)
1900-2400	9960 (Mideast)
2100-2400	6280 (Mideast)

LITHUANIA
RADIO VILNIUS
North America and Caribbean

0000-0008	[W] Tu-Sa 7150 (E North Am)
0000-0030	[W] Su/M 7150 (E North Am)
2300-2308	[S] M-F 9530/7360 (E North Am)
2300-2330	[S] Sa/Su 9530/7360 (E North Am)

Europe and North Africa

2000-2030 &	
2230-2300	[←] 9710 (Europe)

MALAYSIA
VOICE OF MALAYSIA

0555-0825	6175 (SE Asia), 9750 (SE Asia & Aus-

tralasia), 15295 (Australasia)

MALTA
VOICE OF MEDITERRANEAN
Europe, North Africa and Mideast

0600-0635	9765 (Europe, N Af & ME)
0635-0700	M-Sa 9765 (Europe, N Af & ME)
1400-1435	11925 (Europe, N Af & ME)
1435-1500	M-Sa 11925 (Europe, N Af & ME)

MOLDOVA
RADIO DNIESTER INTERNATIONAL
Europe, North America and Caribbean

2030-2100	[S] Sa-Th 11750 (E North Am)
2130-2200	[W] Sa-Th 9620 (E North Am)

RADIO MOLDOVA INTERNATIONAL
North America and Caribbean

0100-0125	[S] Tu-Su 9540 (E North Am)
0200-0225	[W] Tu-Su 7190 (E North Am)
1330-1355	[←] M-Sa 15315/15390 (E North Am)

Europe and North Africa

1400-1425	[S] M-Sa 11580 (Europe)
1500-1525	[W] M-Sa 11775 (Europe)
1930-1955	[S] M-Sa 11580 (Europe)
2030-2055	[W] M-Sa 7235 (Europe)

MONACO
TRANS WORLD RADIO—(W Europe)

0740-0905	[←] 7115/7110
0905-0920	[←] Su-F 7115/7110
1230-1255	[←] Sa/Su 7115/7110

MONGOLIA
RADIO ULAANBAATAR
North America and Caribbean

0300-0330	9960 & 12000 (W North Am)

Europe and North Africa

1930-2000	4081 (E Europe), 7530 (Europe)

Other World Zones

0910-0940	9960 & 12000 (Australasia)
1445-1515	7293 & 9950 (SE Asia)
1930-2000	4081 & 7530 (Mideast)

MOROCCO
RTV MAROCAINE
Europe, North Africa & West Africa

1400-1500	Su 17595 (Europe)

NEW ZEALAND
RADIO NEW ZEALAND INTERNATIONAL—(Pacific)

0000-0458	15115
0458-0542	[W] 15115
0459-0716	[S] 9570
0542-0600	[W] Su-F 15115
0543-0601	[W] Sa 9700
0600-0716	[W] M-F 15115
0601-0717	[W] Sa/Su 9700
0716-0758	[S] Sa/Su 9570
0717-0759	[S] M-F 6100
0717-1130	[W] 9700
0759-1130	[S] 6100
1130-1206	[S] Th-Tu 6100 & [W] Th-Tu 9700
1207-1649	[S] 6100 (Irr) & [W] 9655 (Irr)
1650-1849	[W] M-F 9655
1650-1930	[S] M-F 6145
1850-2050	[W] 11735
1926-1946	[S] F/Sa 11910
1946-2200	[S] 11910
2051-2206	[W] 15115
2206-2400	15115

NIGERIA
VOICE OF NIGERIA—(Africa)
0455-0700,
1000-1100,
1500-1700 &
1900-2100   7255

NORTHERN MARIANA IS
KFBS-FAR EAST BROADCASTING—(E Europe)
1830-1900   W/Sa 9465/5810

NORWAY
RADIO NORWAY INTERNATIONAL
North America and Caribbean
0100-0130   [S] M 7480 (E North Am & C America)
0200-0230   [W] M 7450 (W North Am)
0400-0430   [S] M 7480 (W North Am)
0500-0530   [W] M 5910/5905 (W North Am)
1600-1630   [S] Su 11850 (W North Am)
Europe and North Africa
1300-1330   [S] Su 9590 (Europe)
1800-1830   [S] Su 5960 (W Europe), [W] Su 7120 (E
Europe)
1900-1930   [W] Su 9590 (Europe)
Other World Zones
0600-0630   [S] Su 7295/15175 (Australasia)
0800-0830   [W] Su 9590/15175 (E Asia & Australasia), [S] Su 15220 (Mideast)
1200-1230   [W] Su 11850 (Australasia), [S] Su
13800 & [W] Su 15165 (SE Asia & Australasia), [S] Su 15170 (E Asia)
1500-1530   [W] 9480 (Mideast)
1800-1830   [W] Su 7120 (Mideast & E Africa), [W]
Su 11930 (Africa), [S] Su 13805 (W
Africa), [S] Su 15220 (C Africa & S
Africa)
1900-1930   [W] Su 5960 (W Africa), [W] Su 7215
(Australasia), [W] Su 9590 (Africa)

PAKISTAN
RADIO PAKISTAN
Europe and North Africa
0800-0845 &
1100-1120   17900 & 21520 (Europe)
1600-1630   11570 & 17660 (N Africa)
1700-1800   7485, [W] 9865 & [S] 11570/9855 (Europe)
Other World Zones
0230-0245   7290 (S Asia), [W] 15190 (S Asia & SE
Asia), 17705 (SE Asia), 17725 (E Af-
rica), 21730 (S Asia & SE Asia)
1600-1630   [S] 7290 (S Asia), 9470, 11570, 13590,
15555, 15675 & 17660 (Mideast)

PALAU
KHBN-VOICE OF HOPE
0000-0100   15140 (E Asia & SE Asia)
0800-0830   9965/9830 (E Asia & SE Asia)
0800-1200   15395 (SE Asia)
0930-1000 &
1530-1930   9965/9830 (E Asia & SE Asia)
2330-2400   15140 (E Asia & SE Asia)

PHILIPPINES
FEBC RADIO INTERNATIONAL
0000-0200   15450 (S Asia & SE Asia)
0930-1100   11690/11635 (E Asia & Australasia)
1300-1600   11995 (S Asia & SE Asia)
RADIO VERITAS ASIA—(Mideast)

1515-1525   11850/11715
1525-1555   Sa-M 11850/11715
RADYO PILIPINAS
0230-0330   17760 & 17865/17840 (S Asia), 21580
(E Asia)

PIRATE (PACIFIC)
"KIWI RADIO, NEW ZEALAND"—(Pacific)
0600-0830   5850 (Irr)
0600-0850   7445 (Irr)
0850-1000   7445/7455 (Irr)

POLAND
POLISH RADIO—(W Europe)
1300-1355   ◄ 6135, 7145, 7270, 9525 & 11815
1800-1855   ◄ 6000/6095 & 7270
2030-2125   ◄ 6000/6095, 6135 & 7285

PORTUGAL
RDP INTERNATIONAL
North America and Caribbean
0230-0300   ◄ Tu-Sa 9570 (E North Am)
Europe and North Africa
2000-2030   ◄ M-F 6130, M-F 9780 & M-F 9815 (Europe)
Other World Zones
1430-1500   ◄ M-F 21515 (Mideast & S Asia)
2000-2030   ◄ M-F 15515 (E Africa & S Africa)

ROMANIA
RADIO ROMANIA INTERNATIONAL
North America and Caribbean
0200-0300 &
0400-0430   5990 (E North Am)
Europe and North Africa
0632-0641   [W] 7105, [W] 7175, [S] 7225, [S] 9550,
9665, [W] 11775 & [S] 11810 (Europe)
1300-1400   [W] 9690, [W] 11790 & 11940 (Europe),
[S] 15365 & [S] 17720 (W Europe)
1730-1800   [W] 11940 & [S] 15340 (N Africa)
1900-2000   [W] 5955, [W] 5995, [W] 6105, [W] 6190, [W]
7195, [S] 9550, [S] 9690, [S] 11810 & [S]
11940 (Europe)
2100-2200   [W] 5990, [W] 6105, [W] 6190, [W] 7105,
7195, [S] 9550, [S] 9690 & [S] 11940
(Europe)
Other World Zones
0530-0600   [S] 11810, [W] 11940, 15250, [S] 15340 &
[W] 15380 (C Africa & S Africa), [W]
17720 (Africa), 17745 & 17790 (C Africa & S Africa)
0645-0715   Su 11775 & Su 15335 (Australasia)
0645-0745   M-Sa 15250, M-Sa 17720 & M-Sa
17805 (Australasia)
1430-1530   [W] 11740 & [S] 11775 (S Asia), [W]
11810 & 15335 (Mideast & S Asia),
17720 (S Asia & SE Asia)
1730-1800   [W] 9510 (Africa), [W] 9750 & [W] 11740
(S Africa), [W] 11940 & [S] 15340 (C
Africa), 15365 (C Africa & S Africa),
[S] 17805 (E Africa)

RUSSIA
ADVENTIST WORLD RADIO—(Mideast)
0500-0600   [W] 9885 & [S] 9895/13645
TRANS WORLD RADIO—(S Asia)
1530-1600   [W] 7420 & [S] 12005
VOICE OF RUSSIA
North America and Caribbean
0000-0100   [S] 9720 (E North Am)

0000-0200	S *11750* (E North Am)	
0000-0300	S 9530 (E North Am)	
0030-0400	W *7105* & W 7165 (E North Am)	
0030-0500	S 9620 (C America)	
0100-0200	S 12050 & S 15425 (W North Am)	
0100-0400	W 7180 (E North Am)	
0100-0500	S 15180 (W North Am)	
0100-0700	S 13665 & S 15580 (W North Am)	
0130-0400	W 5940 (E North Am), S 13645 (W North Am)	
0200-0300	12050, W 13640 & 15425 (W North Am)	
0200-0500	W 9825 (W North Am)	
0200-0800	W 9850 (W North Am)	
0230-0800	W 7270 (W North Am)	
0300-0500	S *9665* (E North Am & C America)	
0300-0700	S 12050 & S 15425 (W North Am)	
0330-0800	W 5905, W 7175 & W 7345 (W North Am)	
0400-0800	W 6065 (W North Am)	
0430-0700	S 12010 (W North Am)	
0430-0800	W 11710 (W North Am)	
0530-0700	S 12040 (W North Am)	
0530-0800	W 5930 (W North Am)	
1600-2000	S *15105* (E North Am)	
1700-2300	W 7180 (E North Am)	
2030-2100	W 6185 (C America)	
2030-2200	S 12070 (C America)	
2030-2400	S *11730* (E North Am & C America)	
2100-2400	S *11750* (E North Am)	
2130-2300	W 7400 (C America), S 9530/7360 (E North Am)	
2130-2400	W 7150 & W 9750 (E North Am)	
2200-2400	W *9620* (E North Am)	
2230-2300	W 7300 (C America)	
2230-2400	S 9720 (E North Am)	

Europe and North Africa

0030-0400	W *7105* (Europe)	
0900-1000	W 13370 USB (Europe)	
1000-1100	S 13370 USB (Europe)	
1100-1500	13370 USB (Europe)	
1230-1500	W *6060* (E Europe)	
1430-1800	W 7115 (Europe)	
1500-1700	W 6035 (E Europe)	
1500-2000	S 11890 (W Europe)	
1530-1600	W 5920 (Europe)	
1530-1800	W 7330 (Europe)	
1530-2200	W 7205 (Europe)	
1600-1700	W 6000 (N Africa)	
1600-1800	W 7120 (N Africa)	
1600-2000	S 11630 & S *15105* (W Europe)	
1600-2100	W 7210 (N Africa)	
1600-2200	W 7170, S 9880 & W 9890 (Europe)	
1630-1700	W 7150 (Europe)	
1730-2000	W *7105* (W Europe), W 7340 (Europe)	
1900-2200	S 9640 (Europe)	
1900-2300	W 5975 (Europe)	
2000-2100	W 4860 (Europe), W 6085 (N Africa), S 7230 & W 7400 (Europe)	
2000-2200	W 5905, W 7230 & S 11630 (Europe)	
2000-2300	W 5920 (Europe)	
2030-2100	W 6185 (Europe)	
2030-2200	S 12070 (W Europe)	
2100-2200	W 5965, W 7330, S 9710 & S 11980 (Europe)	
2200-2300	W 6000 (N Africa), W 7215 (Europe)	
2200-2400	W *9620* (W Europe)	

Other World Zones

0600-0800	17570 & W 17610 (Australasia), W 21790 (E Asia & Australasia)	
0600-0900	S 15560 (SE Asia & Australasia)	
0700-0900	W 11675 (E Asia), W *15230* (SE Asia & Australasia)	
0700-1000	S 17695 & W *17840* (SE Asia & Australasia)	
0700-1200	W 17860 (S Asia, SE Asia & Australasia)	
0700-1300	S 17590 (SE Asia & Australasia), S 17870 (S Asia, SE Asia & Australasia)	
0800-1200	S 17765 (S Asia, SE Asia & Australasia)	
0830-1100	S 9835 (Australasia)	
0830-1200	S 11900 (E Asia, SE Asia & Australasia)	
0830-1400	W 11710 (Australasia)	
0900-1200	W 9480 (E Asia), W 17765 (SE Asia)	
0900-1500	W 9550 (Australasia)	
0930-1300	W 11675 (E Asia & SE Asia), W 12015 (E Asia & Australasia)	
0930-1400	W 9800 (Australasia)	
1000-1200	S 17560 (Australasia)	
1000-1300	S 15110 (S Asia), S *15405* (S Asia & SE Asia), S 15510 (S Asia), W *17755* (SE Asia), S *17775* (S Asia & SE Asia)	
1100-1200	W *11760* (SE Asia), W 11835 & W *15150* (S Asia), W *15230* (SE Asia), W 15560 (S Asia & SE Asia), S 17675 (SE Asia)	
1100-1400	S 11940 (E Asia & SE Asia), S *17755* & S *17835* (S Asia & SE Asia)	
1100-1500	W 7205 (E Asia & SE Asia)	
1200-1300	5960, S 7150 & W 7160 (E Asia), W 11655, S *11820* & S *11880* (S Asia), S *15350*, S 15560 & S 15570 & S 17645 (S Asia & SE Asia)	
1200-1400	⬅ *4740* & *4975* (S Asia)	
1200-1400	9540 (E Asia & SE Asia), S 9800 & S 9895 (E Asia)	
1200-1500	S *17780* (W Africa)	
1230-1300	S 15435 (S Asia), S 17600 (S Asia & SE Asia)	
1230-1400	W 15460 (SE Asia), W 15470 (S Asia)	
1230-1500	W 6000 (E Asia), W *6060* (Mideast)	
1300-1400	W 7295 & W *15150* (S Asia), S 17675 (SE Asia), S 17685 & W *17775* (S Asia)	
1300-1500	W 9810 (S Asia), W 9830 (Mideast), W *11760* & W *15230* (SE Asia), W 15480 (Mideast), W 15560 (S Asia & SE Asia)	
1330-1600	W 7165 (Mideast), S 17710 (E Africa & S Africa)	
1330-1700	W 12015 (Mideast)	
1400-1500	W 7135 & W 7160 (E Asia), W 7350 (S Asia), S *11835* & S 15425 (Mideast)	
1400-1600	W *9635* & S 15540 (Mideast)	
1400-1700	S 11910 & S *11945* (Mideast & E Africa), S 12025 (S Asia)	
1400-1800	S *17570* (C Africa)	
1400-2100	W *15205* (E Africa & S Africa)	
1500-1600	W 7295 (S Asia)	
1500-1700	⬅ *4940* & *4975* (S Asia), 15320 (Mideast)	
1500-1700	W 6035 (Mideast)	

1500-2000	**S** 15480 (Mideast)
1530-1600	**W** 6005, **W** 7130 & **W** *11765* (Mideast)
1530-1700	**S** 11775 (E Africa)
1530-2000	**W** 9775 (E Africa & S Africa)
1600-1700	◄ *4740* (S Asia)
1600-1700	**W** 9830 (Mideast)
1600-1800	**W** 7120 (W Africa)
1600-1900	**S** *21740* (E Africa & S Africa)
1600-2100	**W** 7210 (Mideast & E Africa), **W** 9515 (W Africa & C Africa), **W** 9860 (E Africa & S Africa)
1630-1800	**S** *17875* (W Africa)
1630-1900	**S** 11715 (Mideast & E Africa)
1630-2000	**W** *9575* (Mideast, E Africa & S Africa)
1630-2100	**W** *9800* (E Africa & S Africa)
1700-2000	**W** *9505* & **W** 11825 (S Africa)
1730-1800	**S** 12065 (Mideast)
1730-2000	**W** *7105* (W Africa)
1730-2200	**W** *13670* (W Africa)
1800-2000	**S** 11775 (E Africa), **S** 11910 & **S** *11945* (Mideast & E Africa)
1800-2100	**W** 9530 (E Africa), **W** *11945* (Mideast & C Africa), **W** *15385* (W Africa)
1900-2000	**S** *17570* (C Africa), **S** *17875* (W Africa)
1900-2100	**W** 7275 (Mideast)
1930-2000	**W** 7200 (Mideast & E Africa)
2000-2100	**W** 6085 (W Africa)
2100-2200	**S** 9710 (W Africa)
2200-2300	**W** 7215 (W Africa)

SEYCHELLES
FAR EAST BROADCASTING ASSOCIATION
0500-0545	F 15555 (E Africa & Mideast)
1500-1530	12090/11870 (S Asia)
1500-1600	M-Sa 9810 (S Asia)
1530-1545	Sa-M 12090/11870 (S Asia)

SINGAPORE
RADIO SINGAPORE INTERNATIONAL—(SE Asia)
| 1100-1400 | 9530 |

SLOVAKIA
ADVENTIST WORLD RADIO
Europe and North Africa
| 2100-2200 | **S** 6055 (W Europe) |
| 2200-2300 | **S** 11610 (N Africa) |

Other World Zones
0100-0200	**W** 7150/7270 & **S** 9465 (S Asia)
0400-0500	**S** 9455 (E Africa), **W** 9465 (S Asia)
0600-0700	13715 (W Africa)
1400-1500	**W** 9450, **S** 13595 & 13790 (S Asia)
1500-1600	**W** 9455/9450 (S Asia)
1500-1700	**W** 9450 (S Asia)
1700-1800	**S** 13595 (Mideast & S Asia)
2200-2300	**S** 11610 (W Africa)

RADIO SLOVAKIA INTERNATIONAL
North America and Caribbean
| 0100-0130 | 5930 (E North Am & C America), 7300 (E North Am) |

Europe and North Africa
| 1930-2000 | ◄ 5915, 6055 & 7345 (W Europe) |

Other World Zones
| 0830-0900 | 11990, 15640 & 17485 (Australasia) |

SOUTH AFRICA
CHANNEL AFRICA
0300-0500	**S** 3220 (S Africa), 5955 & **W** 9585 (E Africa & C Africa)
0500-0600	**S** 9695 & **W** 11900 (W Africa)
0500-0700	**S** 5955 & **W** 7185 (S Africa)
1500-1800	**S** 3220 (S Africa), **W** 7225 & **S** 7240 (S Africa & C Africa)
1600-1700	**S** 9695 & **W** 15240 (W Africa)

SOUTH AFRICAN BROADCASTING CORP—(S Africa)
0000-0300	**S** 3320 & **W** 4810
0450-1555	**W** 7270
0555-1525	**S** 5965
2300-2400	**S** 3320 & **W** 4810

TRANS WORLD RADIO—(W Africa)
| 0600-0657 | 11730 |

SPAIN
RADIO EXTERIOR ESPANA
North America and Caribbean
| 0000-0200 & | |
| 0500-0600 | 9540 (C America) |

Europe and North Africa
| 2100-2200 | 6125 (Europe) |

Other World Zones
| 2200-2300 | 9675 (W Africa) |

SRI LANKA
SRI LANKA BROADCASTING CORPORATION
0030-0230	6005 (S Asia)
0030-0430	9720 & 15425 (S Asia)
1030-1130	11835 (SE Asia & Australasia), 17850 (SE Asia)
1230-1730	6075, 9720 & 15425 (S Asia)
2000-2130	9720 (E Asia)

SUDAN
RADIO OMDURMAN
Europe, Africa and Mideast
| 1800-1900 | 9200 (Europe) |

SWAZILAND
SWAZI RADIO—(S Africa)
1200-1600	Sa 6155
1800-2000	6155
2000-2030	Su-F 6155
2030-2045	Su 6155

TRANS WORLD RADIO
0430-0600	3200 (S Africa)
0430-0805	5055 & 6070 (S Africa)
0505-0805	9500 (S Africa)
0605-0805	9650 (S Africa)
0805-0835	M-F 5055, M-F 6070, M-F 9500 & M-F 9650 (S Africa)
1600-1830	9500 (E Africa)
1745-1800	M-F 3200 (S Africa)
1800-2015	**S** 3200 (S Africa)
2015-2045	Su 3200 (S Africa)

SWEDEN
RADIO SWEDEN
North America and Caribbean
0230-0300	**W** 6195 (E North Am & C America)
0330-0400	**W** 6200 (E North Am & C America)
1230-1300	**S** 15240 (E North Am)
1330-1400	15240 (E North Am)
1430-1500	**W** 15240 (E North Am)

Europe and North Africa
1715-1745	◄ 6065 (Europe)
1730-1800	**S** 15600 (Europe)
1830-1900	◄ 6065 (Europe)
1830-1900	**W** 9655 (Europe & N Africa)
2130-2200	◄ 6065 & 9655 (Europe)

2230-2300 ◼ 6065 (Europe)
Other World Zones
0130-0200 9695/9895 (SE Asia & Australasia), **W** 11695 (S Asia)
1130-1200 **S** 13740 & **S** 15120 (E Asia & Australasia), **S** 15240 (S Asia)
1230-1300 **W** 13775 & **W** 15120 (E Asia & Australasia), **W** 15240 (S Asia)
1730-1800 **S** 15600 (Africa)
1830-1900 ◼ 6065 & 13690/13605 (Mideast)
2130-2200 ◼ 6065 (Mideast), 9655 (Africa)

SWITZERLAND
SWISS RADIO INTERNATIONAL
North America and Caribbean
0100-0130 *5885/5888* (C America & W North Am), 6135 & 9885 (E North Am & C America), *9905* (C America)
0400-0430 6135 (W North Am)
0400-0500 *9905* (C America)
Europe and North Africa
0600-0615 ◼ 6165 (Europe & N Africa), 9535 (E Europe)
0600-0630 13635 (N Africa)
0700-0730 ◼ 6165 (Europe & N Africa), 9535 (E Europe)
1100-1130,
1200-1230 &
1330-1400 ◼ 6165 (Europe & N Africa), 9535 (W Europe)
1630-1645 ◼ M-F 6165 (Europe & N Africa)
2000-2030 ◼ 6165 (Europe & N Africa)
Other World Zones
0600-0630 9885 & 13635 (W Africa), 15340 (C Africa & S Africa)
0900-0930 *9885*, 13685 & 17515 (Australasia)
1100-1130 **W** 9885 & **W** 11640 (E Asia), 13635 (E Asia & SE Asia), **S** 15545 & **S** 17515 (E Asia)
1300-1330 *7230/7250* (SE Asia), *7480* (E Asia), **W** 11640, 13635 & **S** 15545/15460 (SE Asia)
1500-1530 **W** 9885, 12075, 13635 & **S** 15545/15490 (S Asia)
1700-1730 **W** 6205, 9885 & **S** 12075 (Mideast), 13635 (E Africa)
2000-2030 *9770* (S Africa), 9885 (C Africa & S Africa), **S** 11640 (E Africa), **W** 11640 & **S** 13635 (S Africa), **W** 13635 (E Africa)

SYRIA
RADIO DAMASCUS
Europe and North Africa
2005-2105 12085 & 15095 (Europe)
Other World Zones
2110-2210 15095 (Australasia)

TANZANIA
RADIO TANZANIA—(E Africa)
0330-0430 &
0900-1030 5050
1030-1530 Sa/Su 5050
1530-1915 5050

THAILAND
RADIO THAILAND
North America and Caribbean
0300-0330 **W** 11890 & **S** 15370 (W North Am)

Europe and North Africa
2030-2045 **S** 9555 & **W** 11835 (Europe)
Other World Zones
0000-0030 **W** 9680 & **S** 9690 (S Asia & E Africa)
0000-0100,
0300-0330,
1900-2000 &
2030-2045 9655 & 11905 (Asia)

TURKEY
VOICE OF TURKEY
North America and Caribbean
0400-0450 &
2300-2350 ◼ 9445 (E North Am)
Europe and North Africa
0400-0450 ◼ 9445 (Europe)
2100-2150 ◼ 9445/9400 (Europe)
2300-2350 ◼ 9445 & 11710 (Europe)
Other World Zones
2300-2350 ◼ 7185 (Mideast)

UKRAINE
RADIO UKRAINE
North America and Caribbean
0000-0100 **S** 11780 & **S** 11950 (E North Am)
0100-0200 **W** 9810 (E North Am)
0300-0400 **S** 9685 (E North Am), **S** 9835 (C America), **S** 9860 (E North Am)
0400-0500 **W** 9810 (E North Am)
2100-2200 **S** 11780 & **S** 11950 (E North Am)
2200-2300 **W** 9810 (E North Am)
Europe and North Africa
0000-0100 **S** 6010 (N Africa), **S** 11780 & **S** 11950 (W Europe)
0100-0200 **W** 7405 (Europe), **W** 9810 (W Europe)
0300-0400 **S** 9685 & **S** 9860 (W Europe)
0400-0500 **W** 7405 (Europe), **W** 9810 (W Europe)
2100-2200 **S** 5905 (Europe), **S** 6010 (N Africa), **S** 7240 (Europe & N Africa), **S** 9560 (N Africa), **S** 11780 & **S** 11950 (W Europe)
2200-2300 **W** 4820 & **W** 5940 (Europe), **W** 7240 (W Europe), **W** 7405 & **W** 9610 (Europe), **W** 9810 (W Europe)
Other World Zones
0100-0200 **W** 9620 & **W** 11870 (W Africa)
0400-0500 **W** 11870 (W Africa)
2100-2200 **S** 11875 (S Africa)
2200-2300 **W** 9620 & **W** 11870 (W Africa)

UNITED ARAB EMIRATES
UAE RADIO FROM ABU DHABI
North America and Caribbean
2200-2400 **W** 7215, 9605, **W** 9770/11885, **S** 11970, **S** 13605 (E North Am)
UAE RADIO IN DUBAI
North America and Caribbean
0330-0355 17890 (E North Am)
0330-0400 11945 & 13675 (E North Am & C America), 15400 (E North Am)
Europe and North Africa
1030-1110 13675 & 15395 (Europe), 17825/15320 (N Africa), 21605 (Europe)
1330-1400 13675 & 15395 (Europe), 17835/15320 (N Africa), 21605 (Europe)
1600-1640 13675 & 15395 (Europe), 17825/15320 (N Africa), 21605 (Europe)
Other World Zones
0530-0600 15435 (Australasia), 17830 (E Asia)

and 21700 (Australasia)

UNITED KINGDOM
BBC WORLD SERVICE
North America and Caribbean

0000-0330	*5970* (C America), 7325 (Americas)
0000-0430	*5975* (C America)
0030-0230	*9590* (C America)
0430-0800	*5975* (C America & W North Am)
1000-1400	*6195* (C America)
1100-1200	*5965* (E North Am)
1100-1300	S *9515* (E North Am)
1200-1400	W *5965* (E North Am)
1300-1600	*9515* (E North Am)
1600-1715	Sa *9515* (E North Am)
2100-2400	*5975* (C America)
2115-2130	M-F *15390* & M-F *17715* (C America)
2130-2145	Tu/F *13660* (Atlantic)
2300-2400	7325 (Americas)

Europe and North Africa

0300-0815	W *3955* (Europe)
0300-0830	⬅ 6195 (Europe)
0300-2230	9410 (Europe)
0330-0400	S M-Sa *11710* (E Europe)
0400-0500	S *12095* (Europe)
0400-0730	*6180* (Europe)
0500-0730	S *15400* (W Europe)
0500-2000	12095 (Europe)
0600-0730	W *11780* (Europe & N Africa), S *15575* (E Europe), W *15575* (N Africa)
0600-0800	W *15070* (Europe)
0700-0800	W *7325* (Europe)
0800-0915	W *7325* (Europe)
0800-1500	17640 (Europe & N Africa)
0800-2000	15070 (Europe & N Africa)
0830-0915	W *6195* (Europe)
0900-1615	17705 (N Africa)
1500-1700	S *6195* (Europe)
1530-1615	W Su *5875* (Europe)
1700-2330	W *3955* (Europe)
1715-2200	*6180* (Europe)
1800-2330	⬅ 6195 (Europe)
2000-2030	S *15070* (W Europe & N Africa)
2000-2100	W *12095* (Atlantic)
2000-2200	7325 (Europe)
2000-2230	S *12095* (Europe)
2200-2230	S *7325* (Europe)
2230-2300	W *9410* (Europe)

Other World Zones

0000-0030	W *9525*, S *11945*, W *15280* & S *15360* (E Asia)
0000-0045	W *7110* (SE Asia)
0000-0100	*5965* (S Asia), W *9580* (E Asia)
0000-0200	*6195* (SE Asia), W *7265* & S *9410* (S Asia)
0000-0300	W *9410* (E Asia), *11955* (S Asia)
0100-0200	W *5965* (S Asia)
0100-0300	S *9605* (S Asia), *17790* (E Asia)
0100-0330	*15360* (SE Asia)
0200-0300	W *9605* (S Asia)
0200-0330	*6135* (E Africa), W *7235* (S Asia)
0300-0400	*6005* (W Africa & S Africa), W *9605* (S Asia), *12095* (E Africa)
0300-0430	S *9605* (S Asia)
0300-0500	*11955* (E Asia)
0300-0600	*3255* (S Africa)
0300-0800	*9600* (S Africa)

0300-0815	*6190* (S Africa)
0300-0900	*15280* (E Asia)
0300-0915	*11760* (Mideast), *15310* (S Asia)
0330-0409	S *9615* (E Africa)
0330-0410	W *9610* (E Africa)
0330-0430	9610 (E Africa)
0330-0500	*11730* (E Africa), W *17790* & S *21715* (E Asia)
0330-0700	W *15575* (E Africa)
0330-0915	W *15360* (E Asia)
0400-0500	W *12095* (E Africa)
0400-0715	*7160* (W Africa & C Africa)
0400-0730	*6005* (W Africa)
0430-0630	*15420* (E Africa)
0500-0630	*17885* (E Africa)
0500-0915	*11955* (SE Asia & Australasia), S *15360* (SE Asia)
0500-1030	S *17830* (SE Asia & Australasia)
0500-1130	*9740* (SE Asia)
0600-0810	W *7145* (Australasia)
0600-0815	*11940* (S Africa), *17790* (S Asia)
0630-0700	15420 & M-F *17885* (E Africa)
0630-0900	Sa/Su *17885* (E Africa)
0700-0730	W *9610* (W Africa), *17830* (Africa)
0730-0815	*15400* (W Africa & S Africa), *17830* (C Africa)
0730-0900	W Sa/Su *15575* (Mideast)
0815-0900	Sa/Su *15400* (W Africa), Sa/Su *17830* (C Africa)
0815-1000	Sa/Su *6190* & Sa/Su *11940* (S Africa)
0900-0930	*15575* (Mideast)
0900-1000	W *7180*, S *9580* & S *11765* (E Asia)
0900-1030	*15280* (E Asia & Australasia), W *17830* (SE Asia), S *21715* (E Asia)
0900-1100	*17790* (S Asia)
0900-1130	*15400* (W Africa)
0900-1400	*17885* (E Africa)
0900-1615	*6195* (SE Asia), 17705 (W Africa)
0900-1815	*11750* (S Asia)
0900-2030	*17830* (C Africa)
0930-1400	*15575* (Mideast)
1000-1400	*11760* (Mideast), *15310* (S Asia)
1000-1615	*11940* (S Africa)
1000-2200	*6190* (S Africa)
1100-1300	W *6065*, W *7180*, 9580, S *11765* & *11955* (E Asia)
1100-1700	21660 (S Africa)
1130-1615	9740 (SE Asia & Australasia)
1300-1430	*15420* (E Africa)
1300-1615	W *5990* & S *7180* (E Asia)
1400-1500	*15310* (S Asia), *15575* (Mideast)
1400-1615	21470 (E Africa)
1400-1700	W *7205* (S Asia)
1500-1515	Sa/Su *11860* (E Africa), Sa/Su *21490* (C Africa & E Africa)
1500-1530	*15420* (E Africa), *17790* (C Africa)
1500-1700	S *5975* (S Asia), *15400* (W Africa)
1515-1530	*11860* (E Africa), *21490* (C Africa & E Africa)
1530-1615	W M-F *7180* (E Asia)
1600-1745	*3915* & W *7135* (SE Asia)
1615-1745	S *7180* (SE Asia)
1615-1800	S *3255* (S Africa), W *9510* (S Asia), W *11940* (S Africa)
1615-1830	S *9510* & 9740 (S Asia)
1630-1700	*15420* (E Africa)

1700-1745	[S] *6005* & *9630* (E Africa)
1700-1900	*15420* (E Africa)
1700-2100	*15400* (W Africa & S Africa)
1715-1830	*5975* (S Asia), *7160* (Mideast)
1800-2000	[S] *11955* (Australasia)
1800-2200	*3255* (S Africa)
1830-2130	*9630* (E Africa)
1830-2200	*6005* (E Africa), *9740* (Australasia)
1900-2000	[S] *7160* (Mideast)
2000-2100	*11955* (Australasia)
2100-2200	*3915* (SE Asia), [W] *5990*, [W] *6120* & [S] *15360* (E Asia), [S] *15400* (S Africa)
2100-2300	*15400* (W Africa)
2100-2400	*6195* (SE Asia), *11955* (SE Asia & Australasia)
2145-2200	*9580* (E Asia)
2200-2300	[W] *5905* & [S] *9890* (E Asia), *11695* (SE Asia)
2200-2400	[W] *7110* & [S] *9570* (SE Asia)
2300-2400	[W] *7180*, [S] *7250*, [W] *9525*, [W] *9580*, [S] *11945* & [S] *15360* (E Asia), [W] *15380* (Australasia)

USA

FAMILY RADIO—(S Asia)

1302-1502	*11550*

KJES, MESQUITE NM

North America and Caribbean

1300-1400	11715 (E North Am)
1400-1500	11715 (W North Am)

Other World Zones

1800-1900	[W] 9510 & [S] 15385 (Australasia)

KNLS-NEW LIFE STN—(E Asia)

0800-0900	[W] 7365 & [S] 9615
1300-1400	7365

KTBN, SALT LAKE CITY UT—(E North Am)

0000-0100	[W] 7510 & [S] 15590
0100-1500	7510
1500-1600	[W] 7510 & [S] 15590
1600-2400	15590

KVOH-VO HOPE—(W North Am & C America)

0000-0330	Tu-Sa 17775
0400-0800	7415 & 9785
1800-1900	Su 17775
1900-2100	Sa/Su 17775
2100-2200	Su 17775

KWHR, BIG ISLAND, HAWAII

0000-0200	17510 (Australasia)
0200-0400	17510 (E Asia)
0400-0800	[W] 9930 & [S] 17880 (E Asia)
0800-1300	9930 (E Asia)
1430-1600	9930 (SE Asia)
1600-1800	[W] 6120 & [S] 7425 (Australasia)
1800-2000	13625 (Australasia)
2000-2200	[W] 11980, [S] 13720 & 15405 (E Asia)
2200-2400	17510 (E Asia)

MONITOR RADIO INTERNATIONAL

North America and Caribbean

0000-0057	M-Sa 7535 (E North Am), M-Sa 9430 (C America)
0100-0157	M-Sa 9430 (C America)
0200-0257	5850 (W North Am), M-F 9430 (W North Am & C America)
0300-0357	5850 (W North Am)
1000-1057	M-F 6095 (E North Am)
1100-1157	6095 (E North Am), 7395 (C America)
1200-1257	M-F 6095 (E North Am), M-F 9455 (C America)
1300-1357	M-F 9455 (W North Am & C America)
2100-2157	[W] 9355 & [S] 11645 (E North Am)

Europe and North Africa

0400-0457	M-F 7535 (Europe)
0500-0557	Tu-F 7535 (Europe)
0600-0657 &	
0700-0757	Tu-F 7535 (W Europe)
0800-0857	Tu-Su 7535 (Europe), Tu-Su *15665* (E Europe)
0900-0957	M-F 7535 (Europe)
1800-1857	*9355* (Europe), [W] M-F 9370/13770 & [S] M-F 15665 (E Europe)
1900-1957	M-Sa *9355* (Europe), [W] M-F 9370/13770 & [S] M-F 15665 (E Europe)
2000-2057	[W] M-F 7510, [W] 9355 & [S] 11645 (Europe), [S] M-F 13770 (W Europe)
2100-2157	[W] 7510 (Europe), [S] 13770 (W Europe)
2200-2257	Su-F 7510 (Europe)

Other World Zones

0300-0357	[W] M-F 7535 & [S] M-F 9840 (E Africa)
0400-0457	M-F 9840 (C Africa & S Africa)
0800-0857	[S] *9425* & [W] *13615* (Australasia)
0900-0957	[S] M *9430* & Tu-F *9430* (E Asia), *13615* (Australasia)
1000-1057	*9430* (E Asia), *13625* (SE Asia)
1100-1157	M-Sa *9355* (E Asia), *9425* (Australasia)
1200-1257	M-F *9355* (SE Asia), *9425* (Australasia)
1300-1357	*9355* (S Asia), *13625* (SE Asia)
1400-1457 &	
1500-1557	*9355* (E Asia & S Asia)
1600-1657	*9355* (S Africa), M-Sa 21640 (E Africa)
1700-1757	M-Sa *9355* (E Africa)
1700-1800	[W] 21640 (C Africa)
1800-1857	*9355* (Mideast & Australasia), 17510 (S Africa)
1900-1957	M-Sa *9355* (Mideast), M-F 17510 (W Africa)
2100-2157	*13840* (Australasia)
2200-2257	[W] *9430*, Su-F *13625* & [S] *15405* (E Asia)
2300-2357	M-F 7510 (W Africa), [W] *9430* (E Asia), *13625* (SE Asia), [S] *15405* (E Asia)

UNIVERSITY NETWORK—(S Asia)

0300-0700	[S] *17655*
0400-0800	[W] *21845*
0700-1600	[S] *15500*
0800-1300	[W] *17600*
1330-1700	[W] *9835*

VOA-VOICE OF AMERICA

North America and Caribbean

0000-0100	11695 (C America)
0000-0200	5995, 6130, 7405, 9455, 9775 & 13740 (C America)
1000-1200	6165, 7405 & 9590 (C America)

Europe and North Africa

0100-0300	7651 ISU (Europe)
0400-0500	[S] *6010* (E Europe), [W] *6140* (Europe)
0400-0600	[S] *7200* (Europe)
0400-0700	[S] *3985* & *5995* (E Europe), *6040* (Europe), [S] 6873 ISL, [W] 6873 ISU & *7170* (N Africa), [S] *11965* (E Europe)
0500-0600	*6140* (Europe), [W] *9700* (N Africa)

0600-0700 6060 (E Europe), 6140 (N Africa), 7325 (Europe), 11805 (N Africa)
1500-1700 [S] 15205 (Europe & N Africa)
1500-2200 19379 ISL (Europe)
1630-1700 [W] 9760 & [W] 11805 (E Europe), 15245 (Europe), [S] 17735 (E Europe)
1630-2200 6040 (Europe)
1700-2100 9760 (E Europe)
1700-2200 [S] 15205 (Europe)
1800-2000 [S] 3980 (E Europe)
1800-2100 [S] 9770 (N Africa)
2100-2200 [S] 9535 (Europe & N Africa), 9760 (E Europe)
2100-2400 [W] 18275 ISU (N Africa)

Other World Zones
0000-0100 7215, [S] 9770, [W] 9890 & 11760 (SE Asia), 15185 (Pacific & SE Asia), 15290 (E Asia), 17735 (E Asia & Australasia), 17820 (E Asia)
0100-0300 7115, 7205, [W] 7215 & [S] 9635 (S Asia), [W] 9740 (Mideast & S Asia), 11705, [S] 11725, [S] 15170, 15250, [W] 15370, 17740 & [W] 21550 (S Asia)
0300-0400 [W] 6035 (E Africa), [S] 6115 (Africa), 7105 (S Africa)
0300-0430 [S] 5980 & 7340 (Africa), [W] 9885 (E Africa)
0300-0500 7280 (Africa), [W] 7405 & 9575 (W Africa & S Africa), [S] 15300 (E Africa)
0300-0630 [S] 7405 (Africa)
0400-0500 [W] 6035 (W Africa & S Africa), [S] 7265 (Africa)
0400-0600 [W] 9630 (E Africa)
0400-0700 [S] 11965 (Mideast)
0500-0600 [W] 7130 & [W] 9700 (W Africa)
0500-0630 6035 (W Africa & S Africa), [S] 9630 & 12080 (Africa)
0500-0700 ← 15205 (Mideast & S Asia)
0500-0700 [W] 11825 (Mideast)
0530-0630 [W] M-F 13710 (Africa)
0600-0630 [W] 7115 (W Africa), 11950 (E Africa), [S] 12035 & [W] 15080 (W Africa), [W] 15600 (C Africa & E Africa)
0600-0700 6140 (Mideast), 11805 (W Africa)
0630-0700 Sa/Su 6035 (W Africa & S Africa), [W] Sa/Su 7115 (W Africa), [S] Sa/Su 7405 & [S] Sa/Su 9630 (Africa), Sa/Su 11950 (E Africa), Sa/Su 12080 (Africa), [W] Sa/Su 15600 (C Africa & E Africa)
1000-1200 5985 (Pacific & Australasia), 11720 (E Asia & Australasia)
1000-1500 15425 (SE Asia & Pacific)
1100-1300 6110 (SE Asia)
1100-1400 9645 (SE Asia & Australasia)
1100-1500 9760 (E Asia, S Asia & SE Asia), 15160 (E Asia)
1200-1330 11715 (E Asia & Australasia)
1300-1800 6110 (S Asia & SE Asia)
1400-1800 7125, 7215 & 9645 (S Asia), [W] 15205 (Mideast & S Asia), [S] 15255 (Mideast), 15395 (S Asia)
1500-1700 9760 (S Asia & SE Asia), [S] 15205 (Mideast)
1500-1800 9700 (Mideast)
1600-1630 Sa/Su 11920 & Sa/Su 12040 (E Africa), Sa/Su 13710 (Africa), Sa/Su 15225 (S Africa), Sa/Su 15445 (C Africa & E Africa), Sa/Su 17895 (W Africa)
1600-1700 Sa/Su 3970 (S Africa)
1630-1700 15225 (S Africa), Sa/Su 15410 (Africa)
1630-1800 15445 (C Africa & E Africa), 17895 (W Africa)
1630-1900 13710 (Africa)
1630-2000 11920 & 12040 (E Africa)
1700-1800 M-F 5990 & M-F 6045 (E Asia), [S] 7150 (SE Asia), [S] 7170 (E Asia & Australasia), [W] M-F 9525 (E Asia & SE Asia), [S] M-F 9550 & [W] M-F 9670 (SE Asia), M-F 9770 (E Asia, S Asia & SE Asia), [W] M-F 11895 (SE Asia), [W] M-F 11945 & [W] M-F 15255 (E Asia & Australasia), 15410 (Africa)
1800-1900 M-F 4875 (S Africa), [W] 9700 (Mideast), [S] 17895 (W Africa)
1800-2100 [S] 9770 (Mideast)
1800-2130 [S] 15410 (Africa), [W] 15410 (W Africa & S Africa), 15580 (W Africa)
1900-2000 9525 & 11870 (E Asia & Australasia), 15180 (Pacific)
1900-2100 [W] 9585 (Mideast)
1900-2130 [S] 7375, 7415, [W] 13710 & [S] 15445 (Africa)
2000-2030 11855 (W Africa)
2000-2100 17755 (W Africa & C Africa)
2000-2130 17725 (W Africa)
2000-2200 [W] 15205 (Mideast & S Asia)
2100-2130 [W] 15445 (C Africa)
2100-2200 [W] 6070, [S] 6160 & [W] 9595 (Mideast), 11870 (E Asia & Australasia)
2100-2400 15185 (Pacific & SE Asia), 17735 (E Asia & Australasia)
2123-2200 Su-F 15580 (W Africa)
2130-2200 [S] Su-F 7375, Su-F 7415, [W] Su-F 13710 & [S] Su-F 15410 (Africa), [W] Su-F 15410 (W Africa & S Africa), [S] Su-F 15445 (Africa), [W] Su-F 15445 (C Africa), Su-F 17725 (W Africa)
2200-2230 [S] M-F 7340, [S] M-F 7375, M-F 7415, [W] M-F 12080 & [W] M-F 13710 (Africa)
2200-2400 [W] 6035 (S Asia & SE Asia), 7215 (SE Asia), [S] 9705 (SE Asia & Australasia), [S] 9770 (SE Asia), [W] 9770 (SE Asia & Australasia), [W] 9890 & 11760 (SE Asia), 15290 (E Asia), 15305 (E Asia & Australasia), 17820 (E Asia)
2330-2400 6185 (SE Asia)

WEWN, BIRMINGHAM AL
North America and Caribbean
0800-0900 [W] F 9350 (W North Am)
0800-1000 Sa-Th 9350 (W North Am)
0900-1000 [S] F 9350 (W North Am)
1000-1100 [W] 9350 (W North Am)
1100-1400 [S] 9350 (W North Am)
1200-1500 [W] 7425 (W North Am)
1400-1500 [S] M-Sa 9350 (W North Am)
1500-1600 [W] M-Sa 7425 & [S] 9350 (W North Am)
Europe and North Africa
0000-0100 [S] 9410 (Europe)
0000-0200 [W] 5825 (Europe)
0800-1000 [S] 12160 (Europe)
0900-1100 [W] 7465 (Europe)

1200-1300 &
1700-1800   **S** 15695 (Europe)
1800-1900   15695 (Europe)
1900-2000   **W** 9985 (Europe)
2300-2400   **S** 9985 (Europe)
Other World Zones
0100-0200   **S** 13710 (Mideast)
0200-0300   **W** 9410 (Mideast)
0800-0900   **W** F 9350 (Australasia)
0800-1000   Sa-Th 9350 (Australasia)
0900-1000   **S** F 9350 (Australasia)
1000-1100   **W** 9350 (Australasia)
1000-1200   **S** 9370 (E Asia)
1100-1300   **W** 7465 (E Asia)
1500-1600   17510 (Mideast)

WINB-WORLD INTERNATIONAL BROADCASTING
(Temporarily Inactive)
North America and Caribbean
0000-0530   11950 (W North Am & C America)
0530-0600   Su-F 11950 (W North Am & C America)
0600-0800   11950 (W North Am & C America)
0800-0815   W-M 11950 (W North Am & C America)
0815-1100   11950 (W North Am & C America)
Europe and North Africa
1600-1730   15715 (Europe & N Africa)
1730-1800   Su-F 15715 (Europe & N Africa)
1800-1900   15715 (Europe & N Africa)
1900-2100   **W** 12160 (Europe & N Africa)
1900-2300   **S** 15715 (Europe & N Africa)
2100-2300   **W** 11915 (Europe & N Africa)
2330-2345   **W** Th/Sa-Tu 11915 & **S** Th/Sa-Tu 15715 (Europe & N Africa)
2345-2400   **W** 11915 & **S** 15715 (Europe & N Africa)

WJCR, UPTON KY
North America and Caribbean
24 Hr   7490 (E North Am)
1500-0300   13595 (W North Am)
Other World Zones
1500-0300   13595 (E Asia)

WMLK, BETHEL PA
Europe and North Africa
0400-0900 &
1700-2200   Su-F 9465 (Europe)
Other World Zones
0400-0900 &
1700-2200   Su-F 9465 (Mideast)

WORLD HARVEST RADIO
North America and Caribbean
0000-0500   M 9495 (Americas)
0000-1000   5745 (E North Am)
0500-0800   9495 (Americas)
0500-1300   7315 (E North Am)
0800-0900   Sa/Su 9495 (C America)
0900-1000   9495 (C America)
1000-1100   Su 9495 (C America)
1000-1500   6040 (E North Am)
1300-1500   7315/9465 (E North Am)
1300-1800   15105 (C America)
1500-2200   13760 (E North Am)
1800-2100   9495/9485 (C America)
2100-2300   Sa/Su 9495/15545 (C America)
2200-2400   5745 (E North Am)
2300-2400   Su 9495 (Americas)
Europe and North Africa

1500-2200   13760 (W Europe)
WRMI-RADIO MIAMI INTERNACIONAL—(C America)
0000-0200   ◄ 9955
1230-1500   ◄ Su 9955
1500-2200 &
2200-2400   ◄ Sa/Su 9955
WRNO WORLDWIDE—(E North Am)
0000-0300   7355
0300-0400   **S** 7395
0400-0600   7395
0600-0700   **W** 7395
1400-1500   Su 15420
1500-1600   **S** 15420 & **W** Su 15420
1600-2300   15420
2300-2400   7355
WVHA, OLAMON ME
Europe and North Africa
0000-0400   **W** 7465 & **S** 9855 (N Africa)
0400-1100   **W** 5850 (Europe)
1100-1600   11695/11745 (Europe)
1300-1800   15665 (Europe)
1800-2000   **W** 9930 (Europe)
2000-2300   **W** 5850 (Europe)
2300-2400   **W** 7465 & **S** 9855 (N Africa)
Other World Zones
1500-1700   21670 (E Africa)
1700-2000   17613 (Africa)
2000-2300   11695 (Africa)
WWCR, NASHVILLE TN
North America and Caribbean
0000-0100   13845 (W North Am)
0000-0300   5065 (E North Am)
0000-0700   ◄ 7435 (E North Am)
0100-0200   **W** 5935 (E North Am), **S** 13845 (W North Am)
0200-1100   5935 (E North Am)
0300-0400   Tu-Su 5065 (E North Am)
0400-1500   5065 (E North Am)
1100-1400   **W** 5935 (E North Am), **S** 13845 (W North Am)
1145-1200   ◄ Sa 15685 (E North Am)
1200-1700   ◄ 15685 (E North Am)
1400-2400   13845 (W North Am)
1500-1900   12160 (E North Am)
1700-1815   ◄ M-Sa 15685 (E North Am)
1815-2215   ◄ 15685 (E North Am)
1900-2100   11970 (E North Am)
2100-2300   12160 (E North Am)
2215-2245   ◄ F-Tu 15685 (E North Am)
2245-2400   ◄ Sa/Su 15685 (E North Am)
2300-2400   5065 (E North Am)
Europe and North Africa
0000-0300   5065 (Europe)
0000-0700   ◄ 7435 (Europe)
0100-0200   **W** 5935 (Europe)
0200-1100   5935 (Europe)
0300-0400   Tu-Su 5065 (Europe)
0400-1500   5065 (Europe)
1100-1400   **W** 5935 (Europe)
1145-1200   ◄ Sa 15685 (Europe)
1200-1700   ◄ 15685 (Europe)
1500-1900   12160 (Europe)
1700-1815   ◄ M-Sa 15685 (Europe)
1815-2215   ◄ 15685 (Europe)
1900-2100   11970 (Europe)
2100-2300   12160 (Europe)

2215-2245 ⬅ F-Tu 15685 (Europe)
2245-2400 ⬅ Sa/Su 15685 (Europe)
2300-2400 5065 (Europe)

WYFR-FAMILY RADIO

North America and Caribbean

0000-0045 6085 (E North Am)
0100-0245 15440 (C America)
0100-0445 6065 (E North Am), 9505 (W North Am)
0500-0700 5985 (W North Am)
1000-1400 5950 (E North Am)
1100-1200 [S] 11830 (W North Am)
1100-1245 [W] 7355 (W North Am)
1200-1345 [W] 11970 (C America)
1200-1445 [S] 6015 (W North Am)
1200-1700 11830 (W North Am), [S] 17750 (C America)
1300-1400 13695 (E North Am)
1300-1445 [W] 9705 (W North Am)
1400-1700 [W] 17760 (C America)
1500-1700 [S] 11705 & [W] 15215 (W North Am)

Europe and North Africa

0400-0445 [W] 11825 (Europe)
0400-0500 [S] 9370 & [W] 9770 (Europe)
0500-0600 [W] 9850 & [S] 11580 (Europe)
0500-0745 [S] 9985 & [S] 11725 (Europe)
0600-0745 7355 & [W] 9680 (Europe)
1600-1700 15355 & 21615 (Europe)
1700-1845 21500 (Europe)
1845-1900 [S] 21500 (Europe)
1900-1945 15355 & 21615 (Europe)
1945-2045 [S] 15355 (Europe)
1945-2145 [S] 21615 (Europe)
2000-2100 [W] 15566 (Europe)
2000-2200 [W] 7355 (Europe)
2100-2145 15566 (Europe)
2145-2200 [S] 15566 (Europe)

Other World Zones

0500-0800 [W] 11580 & [S] 13695 (W Africa)
1600-1700 21525 (C Africa & S Africa)
2000-2245 [S] 17613 & [W] 17750 (W Africa), 21525 (C Africa & S Africa)

UZBEKISTAN

RADIO TASHKENT

0100-0130 [W] 5955 (S Asia), [W] 5975 & [S] 7190 (Mideast), [S] 7250 (S Asia), [W] 7285 & [S] 9715 (Mideast)
1200-1230 &
1330-1400 [W] 6025, [S] 7285 & 9715 (S Asia), [W] 13785 & [S] 17815 (S Asia & SE Asia)

VATICAN STATE

VATICAN RADIO

North America and Caribbean

0250-0310 [W] 6095 & 7305 (E North Am), [S] 9605 (E North Am & C America)

Europe and North Africa

0600-0620 ⬅ 4010/4005 (Europe), 6245/5860 (W Europe)
0730-0745 ⬅ M-Sa 4010/4005 (Europe), M-Sa 6245/5860 (W Europe), M-Sa 7250 & M-Sa 9645 (Europe), M-Sa 11740 (W Europe & N Africa)
1120-1130 ⬅ M-Sa 6245 & M-Sa 7250 (Europe), M-Sa 11740 (W Europe)
1715-1730 ⬅ 6245 (Europe), 9645 (W Europe)
2050-2110 ⬅ 3945/4005 (Europe), 5882/5885 (W Europe)

Other World Zones

0140-0200 5980, [W] 7335, [S] 9650 & [S] 11935 (S Asia)
0320-0350 7360 & 9660/5865 (E Africa)
0500-0530 [W] 7360 (E Africa), 9660 (Africa), 11625 & [S] 13765 (E Africa)
0630-0700 [W] 7360 (W Africa), [W] 9660 (Africa), [S] 11625 (W Africa), [W] 11625 (Africa), [S] 13765 (W Africa), [S] 15570 (Africa)
0730-0745 ⬅ M-Sa 15210/15215 (Mideast)
1020-1030 M-Sa 17550 (Africa)
1120-1130 ⬅ M-Sa 15210 (Mideast)
1120-1130 [W] 17585 (Africa)
1345-1405 [W] 9500, 11625 & [S] 13765 (Australasia), 15585 (SE Asia)
1545-1600 [W] 9500, 11640 & [S] 15585 (S Asia)
1600-1630 [W] Sa 9500, Sa 11640 & Sa 15585 (S Asia)
1600-1635 [W] Sa 9660 (E Africa)
1615-1630 [S] 11810 (Mideast)
1715-1730 [W] 7250 (Mideast)
1730-1800 [W] 7305 & [W] 9660 (E Africa), 11625 (E Africa & S Africa), [S] 13765 (E Africa), [S] 15570 (Africa)
2000-2030 [W] 7355 & 9645 (Africa), 11625 & [S] 13765 (W Africa)
2245-2305 [W] 6150 (SE Asia), [W] 7305 (E Asia), 9600 & 11830 (Australasia)

VIETNAM

VOICE OF VIETNAM

North America and Caribbean

0100-0300 [S] *7250* (E North Am)
1230-1300 &
2330-2400 9840, [W] 12020 & [S] 15009 (Americas)

Europe and North Africa

1800-1830,
1900-1930 &
2030-2100 9840, [W] 12020 & [S] 15009 (Europe)

Other World Zones

1000-1030 9840, [W] 12020 & [S] 15009 (SE Asia)
1100-1130 7285 & 9730 (SE Asia)
1230-1300 9840, [W] 12020 & [S] 15009 (E Asia)
1330-1400 9840, [W] 12020 & [S] 15009 (SE Asia)
1600-1630 9840, [W] 12020 & [S] 15009 (Africa)
2330-2400 9840, [W] 12020 & [S] 15009 (E Asia)

YEMEN

REPUBLIC OF YEMEN RADIO

0600-0700 9780 (Mideast & E Africa)
1600-1630 5970 (Mideast)
1800-1900 9780 (Mideast & E Africa)

YUGOSLAVIA

RADIO YUGOSLAVIA

North America and Caribbean

0000-0030 [S] 9580 & [S] 11870 (E North Am)
0100-0130 [W] 6195/7115 (E North Am)
0430-0500 [S] 9580 & [S] 11870 (W North Am)
0530-0600 [W] 6195/6190 (W North Am)

Europe and North Africa

1930-2000 ⬅ 6100 (W Europe)
2200-2230 ⬅ 6100 & 6185 (W Europe)

Other World Zones

1930-2000 ⬅ 9720 (S Africa)

ZAMBIA

CHRISTIAN VOICE—(S Africa)

1300-1500 6065
1500-2030 4965

YACHT BOY 305

GRUNDIG'S ALL NEW DIGITAL WORLD RECEIVER

GRUNDIG
made for you

Grundig announces another breakthrough in shortwave radio technology. Finally, a well-built, high-quality, inexpensive digital radio. You no longer have to sacrifice audio quality or memory. The YB-305 features a large cavity speaker enclosure for true rich sound. And with 30-memories, you can build your own listening library. Best of all, the YB-305 is easy to use, with an array of tuning features including: direct entry digital tuning, auto-scan and up or down slewing. Couple that with continuous shortwave coverage from 2.30-21.85 MHz, and you truly have an affordable portable shortwave radio that even the critics will love.

With the YB-305, it's easy to listen to broadcasts from around the world. It even has direct access to the twelve most important bands designated for international broadcasting: the 13, 16, 19, 22, 25, 31, 41, 49, 60, 75, 90 and 120 meter bands. And tuning around in the shortwave bands is as easy as tuning around in the AM and FM bands everyone is familiar with. Imagine, in the comfort of your home or apartment, listening to stations from England, Germany, Holland, Russia and China, all broadcasting in both English and their native languages. News, insightful commentary and culturally oriented programming very different from what is heard from domestic sources.

Multi-Function Liquid Crystal Display: The LCD displays frequency, band, memory and sleep timer.

The Digital Key Pad: The key pad itself is a marvel of performance. It's intelligently designed and easy to use with direct frequency access and 30 memories.

Voices From Home—1996

Country-by Country Guide to Native Broadcasts

For some, English offerings are merely icing on the cake. Their real interest is in eavesdropping on broadcasts for natives. These can be enjoyable regardless of language, and include delightful and exotic music.

Some you'll hear, many you won't—depending in part upon your location and receiving equipment. Keep in mind that native-language broadcasts tend to be weaker than those in English, so you'll need more patience and better hardware.

When to Tune

Some broadcasts come in best during the day within world band segments between 11550-17900 kHz. However, those from Latin America and Africa peak near or during darkness, especially between 4750-5075 kHz. See "Best Times and Frequencies" at the end of this book for tuning tips.

Times and days of the week are given in World Time, explained in the Glossary; for local times, see "Addresses PLUS." Midyear, some stations are an hour earlier (◄■) or later (■►) for summer savings time. Stations may also extend their hours, or air special programs, during holidays or sports events.

Frequencies in *italics* may be best, as they come from relay transmitters that might be near you.

Schedules Prepared for Entire Year

To be as helpful as possible throughout the year, PASSPORT'S schedules consist not just of observed activity and other factual data, but also that which we have creatively opined will take place. This latter material is original from us, and therefore will not be so exact as factual information.

Most frequencies are used year round. Those used only parttime are labeled **S** for summer (midyear), and **W** for winter.

A Kazakh herdsman plays the Dombria during an interview with China Radio International *(CRI)*

ALGERIA
"VOICE OF FREE SAHARA"—(W Africa & S America)
Arabic

2200-2300	15215

RTV ALGERIENNE
Arabic

1300-1500	[W] 15205 (Mideast)
1600-1800	[S] 15205 (Mideast)
1600-1900	17745 (E Africa)
2000-2200	15215 (W Africa & S America)

French

1700-1800	11715 (Europe)
1800-1900	9535 (Mideast)

ARGENTINA—Spanish
RADIO ARGENTINA-RAE

0000-0200	Tu-Sa 15345 (Americas)
1100-1300	M-F 11710 (S America)
1800-1900	M-F 15345 (Europe & N Africa)
2300-2400	M-F 15345 (Mideast & N Africa)

RADIO NACIONAL

24 Hr	6180 (Irr)
0100-1400	6060 (S America)
0900-1000	Sa/Su 15345 (S America)
0900-1400	Sa/Su 11710 (S America & Antarctica)
1000-1400	15345 (S America)
1400-1700	11710 (S America & Antarctica)
1700-2200	Su 6060 (S America), Su 11710 (S America & Antarctica)
2100-2200	M-F 6060 (S America)

ARMENIA—Armenian
ARMENIAN RADIO

0200-0400, 0415-0630, 0700-1200 & 1215-1330	4040, 4810, 6065
1415-1500	4810
1415-1800 & 1815-2000	4040, 6065

VOICE OF ARMENIA

0100-0130	[W] 9685, [S] 11920, [S] 11945 & [W] 11970 (S America)
1800-1900 & 2000-2200	4810 (E Europe, Mideast & W Asia), [W] 4990 (Mideast), 7480 (E Europe, Mideast & W Asia), [S] 9675 & [S] 11960 (Mideast)

AUSTRIA—German
RADIO AUSTRIA INTERNATIONAL

0000-0030 & 0100-0130	9655 (E North Am), 9870 & 13730 (S America)
0200-0230	9655 (E North Am), 9870 (C America), 13730 (S America)
0300-0330	9870 (C America), 13730 (S America)
0400-0430	6155 & 13730 (Europe)
0430-0455	M-Sa 6155 & M-Sa 13730 (Europe)
0455-0530	6155 & 13730 (Europe)
0500-0530	*6015* (N America), 15410 & 17870 (Mideast)
0530-0600	[S] 6155 & [S] 13730 (Europe), [S] 15410 & [S] 17870 (Mideast)
0600-0630	*6015* (N America), 6155 & 13730 (Europe), 15410 & 17870 (Mideast)
0630-0700	[W] 6155 & [W] 13730 (Europe), [W] 15410 & [W] 17870 (Mideast)
0700-0730	6155 & 13730 (Europe), 15410 & 17870 (Mideast)
0800-0830	6155 & 13730 (Europe)
0800-0930	17870 (Australasia)
0830-0900	[S] 6155 & [S] 13730 (Europe)
0900-0930	6155 & 13730 (Europe)
0930-1000	[S] Su 6155, [W] 6155, [S] Su 13730 & [W] 13730 (Europe), [S] Su 17870 (Australasia)
1000-1030	6155 & 13730 (Europe), 17870 (Australasia)
1030-1100	[W] Su 6155 & [W] Su 13730 (Europe), [W] Su 17870 (Australasia)
1100-1130	6155 (Europe), 13730 (W Europe & E North Am)
1130-1200	[S] 6155 (Europe)
1200-1230	6155 (Europe), 13730 (W Europe & E North Am), 15450 (E Asia)
1230-1300	[S] 15450 (E Asia)
1300-1330	6155 & 13730 (Europe), 15450 (E Asia)
1400-1430	13730 (Europe)
1400-1500	15450 (E Asia)
1400-1530	6155 (Europe)
1430-1530	13730 (Europe)
1500-1530	9665/9880 (Mideast), 11780 (S Asia & SE Asia)
1530-1600	[S] 6155 (Europe), [S] 9665/9880 (Mideast), [S] 13730 (Europe)
1600-1630	6155 (Europe), 9665/9880 (Mideast), 11780 (S Asia & SE Asia), 13730 (Europe)
1630-1700	[W] 6155 (Europe), [W] 9665/9880 (Mideast), [W] 13730 (Europe)
1700-1730	6155 (Europe), 9665/9880 (Mideast), 11780 (S Asia & SE Asia), 13730 (Europe)
1730-1800	[S] 6155 & [S] 13730 (Europe)
1800-1930	5945 & 6155 (Europe), 9665/9880 (Mideast)
1900-1930 2000-2030 &	13730 (S Africa)
2100-2130	5945 & 6155 (Europe), 9880 (W Europe & W Africa), 13730 (S Africa)
2200-2230	5945 & 6155 (Europe), 9870 (S America)
2300-2330	9870 (S America)

BAHRAIN—Arabic
RADIO BAHRAIN

0300-2115	9745

BANGLADESH—Bangla
RADIO BANGLADESH

0030-0305, 0315-0415 & 1150-1250	4880
1230-1250	15520
1300-1315	4880
1300-1430	15520
1345-1530	4880
1430-1530	15520
1545-1600	4880
1545-1705	15520
1630-1730	9650 & 13615 (Mideast)
1715-1730	15520

1915-2000 ■→ 7190 & 9650 (Europe)

BELGIUM
RADIO VLAANDEREN INTERNATIONAAL
Dutch

0500-0600	11640/9925 (Africa)
0600-0700	W 5985 (Europe)
0700-0730	M-Sa 9925 (Australasia)
0700-0730	W 5985 (Europe)
0730-0830	S M-Sa 7120 (Europe)
0830-0900	■ M-Sa 5910/6035 (Europe)
0830-0930	■ M-Sa 9925/9905 (Europe)
0900-0930	■ 5910/6035 (Europe)
0900-1100	■ Su 17595 (Africa)
0930-1100	■ Su 5910/6035 (Europe)
1100-1200	■ 15545/15510 & 17595 (Africa)
1100-1230	■ M-Sa 5910/6035 (Europe)
1200-1230	■ 17595 (Africa)
1300-1330	13670 (E North Am)
1330-1400	M-Sa 13670 (E North Am)
1400-1500	■ Su 9925 (Europe)
1400-1700	■ Su 17690/15505 (Africa)
1500-1700	9925 (Europe)
1600-1630	&
1630-1700	S 17640 (Africa)
1700-1730	9925 (Mideast)
1700-1730	W 11765 & W 17515 (Africa)
1800-1830	5910 (Europe), 9925 (W Europe & W Africa)
1800-2015	S W/Sa 13645 (Africa)
1900-1955	S 13685 (Africa)
1900-2115	W W/Sa 9940 (Africa)
2000-2100	■ 9925 (Africa)
2000-2130	■ 5910 (Europe)
2100-2130	Su 9925 (Africa)
2200-2300	S 13800 (S America)
2300-2400	6030 (E North Am)
2300-2400	W 9925 (S America)

French

0800-0830	■ 5910/6035 & M-Sa 9925/9905 (Europe), 15545 (Africa)
1030-1100	■ M-Sa 5910/6035 (Europe), M-Sa 15545/15510 & M-Sa 17595 (Africa)
1430-1500	M-Sa 13670 (E North Am)
1830-1855	S 13685 (Africa)
1930-2000	5910 (Europe), 9925 (Africa)
2130-2200	S 13800 (S America)
2230-2300	6030 (E North Am)
2230-2300	W 9925 (S America)

BOSNIA HERCEGOVINA
Various Languages
RADIO BOSNIA HERCEGOVINA

24 Hr	7108 USB
0715-2200	7105

BRAZIL—Portuguese
RADIO NACIONAL DA AMAZONIA

0800-2200	→■ 6180/6183, 11780
2200-2400	M-F 11780

RADIO BANDEIRANTES

24 Hr →■	6090, 9645

RADIO CULTURA

0700-0210 →■	9615, 17815

RADIO NACIONAL

1630-1750	15265 (Europe & W Africa)
1800-1920	17750 (Africa)

CANADA—French

CANADIAN BROADCASTING CORPORA-TION—(Northern Quebec)

0100-0300	■ M 9625
0300-0400	■ Su 9625 & Tu-Sa 9625
1300-1310	&
1500-1555	■ M-F 9625
1700-1715	■ Su 9625
1900-1945	■ M-F 9625
1900-2310	Sa 9625

CFCX, MONTREAL—(E North Am)

24 Hr	6005 (Irr)

RADIO CANADA INTERNATIONAL

0000-0030	S Tu-Sa 9535 & S Tu-Sa 11940 (C America & S America), S Tu-Sa 13670 (S America)
0000-0100	S 5960 (E North Am)
0100-0130	W 9535 (C America & S America), W 11725 (S America), W 11845 (C America)
0100-0200	9755 (E North Am)
0100-0200	W 5960 (E North Am), W 13670/13720 (S America)
0130-0200	W Su/M 9535 (C America & S America), W Su/M 11725 (S America), W Su/M 11845 (C America)
0230-0300	S Tu-Sa 6120 (E North Am & C America), S Tu-Sa 9535 & S Tu-Sa 11940 (C America & S America)
0300-0330	W 6025, W 9505, S 9650/11970 & S 11835 (Mideast)
0330-0400	W Tu-Sa 6000, W Tu-Sa 9725 & W Tu-Sa 9755 (C America)
0530-0600	S M-F 7295 (W Europe & N Africa), S M-F 15430 (Africa), S M-F 17840 (Africa & Mideast)
0630-0700	M-F 6050 (Europe)
0630-0700	W M-F 6150 (Europe), W M-F 9740 (Africa), W M-F 9760 (Europe), W M-F 11905 (Mideast)
1200-1230	W 6150 & S 9660 (E Asia), W 11730 & S 15195 (SE Asia)
1300-1400	M-F 9650 (E North Am), M-F 15425 (C America)
1400-1500	S M-Sa 15305 & S 15325 (Europe), S M-Sa 17895 (Africa)
1400-1700	Su 11855 (E North Am)
1500-1530	W 11915 (E Europe)
1500-1600	11935 & M-Sa 17820 (Europe)
1500-1600	W 9555 (Europe & Mideast), W M-Sa 15325 (Europe)
1845-1900	S M-F 7235, S M-F 11905 & S M-F 13670 (Europe)
1900-2000	S 5995 (Europe & Mideast), S 7235, S 11985 & S 13650 (Europe), S 13670 & S 15150 (Africa), S 15325 (Europe)
1945-2000	M-F 15325 & M-F 17820 (Europe)
1945-2000	W M-F 7200, W M-F 7235, W M-F 11945 & W M-F 13650 (Europe)
2000-2100	17820 (Africa)
2000-2100	S 5995 (Europe & Mideast), W 7235, W 9725, W 11945 & W 13650 (Europe), W 13690 & W 15140 (Africa)
2130-2140	S 13740 & S 15305 (C America)
2130-2200	S 5995 (Europe & Mideast), S 7235, S 11690 & S 13650 (Europe), S 13670 (Africa)

2140-2200	**S** Sa/Su 13740 & **S** Sa/Su 15305 (C America)
2230-2240	9755 (E North Am & C America)
2230-2240	**W** 5960 (E North Am), **W** 11885 (C America)
2230-2300	17820 (Africa)
2230-2300	**W** *5995* & **W** *7230* (Europe & N Africa), *11705* (SE Asia), **S** 11895 (E North Am), **W** 11945 (Europe), **W** 13690 (Africa), **S** 13740 (C America), **S** 15305 (C America & S America)
2240-2300	Sa/Su 9755 (E North Am & C America)
2240-2300	**W** Sa/Su 5960 (E North Am), **W** Sa/Su 11885 (C America)

CHINA

CENTRAL PEOPLE'S BROADCASTING SERVICE

Chinese

0000-0004	3815, **S** 9380, **S** 9455, 11100, 11935
0000-0100	5880, 5915, 5955, 6125, 6750
0000-0104	9170, 11000
0000-0200	4800, 9755, 9775
0000-0515	11040, 15500
0000-0600	6840, 7504, 9064, 9290, 11610, 11800, 12120, 15390, 15550
0003-0515	17700
0003-0600	17605
0055-0610	11100, 11935, 15710
0355-0604	11000, 15880
0515-0600	W-M 11040, W-M 15500, W-M 17700
0600-0853	W-M 15550
0600-0855	W-M 6840, W-M 7504, W-M 9290, W-M 12120, W-M 15390, W-M 17605
0600-0900	Th/Sa-M 11040, Th/Sa-M 15500, Th/Sa-M 17700
0600-0953	W-M 11800
0600-0955	Th/Sa-Tu 9064, Th/Sa-Tu 11610
0604-0955	W-M 11000, W-M 15880
0855-1230	17605
0855-1330	15550
0855-1400	12120
0855-1410	15390
0855-1735	6840, 7504, 9290
0900-0955	Th/Sa-Tu 11040, Th/Sa-Tu 15500, Th/Sa-Tu 17700
0955-1045	15880
0955-1100	11000, 11040, 11935
0955-1130	11100
0955-1230	4800
0955-1240	17700
0955-1315	**S** 15710
0955-1330	15500
0955-1600	9064
0955-1733	11800
0955-1804	6095
0955-2400	3815, **S** 9455
1000-1315	**W** 9380
1000-1600	9755, 11610
1030-1200	9775
1045-1615	**S** 15880
1100-1240	11630
1100-1600	7440, 7516
1100-1615	**W** 9170
1100-1735	5880, 6125, 6750, 9800
1100-1800	**W** 6790
1100-1804	**S** 11000
1100-2230	7620

1100-2330	**S** 11935
1103-1600	6890
1130-2230	6015, **S** 11100
1200-1330	10260
1233-1415	**W** 7935
1240-1430	**S** 17700
1243-1600	11740
1300-1600	4800, 9775
1315-2245	5125
1315-2400	**S** 9380
1330-1600	11630, **S** 15500
1333-1600	7770
1333-1735	5320
1403-1733	4460
1410-1735	**S** 15390
1413-1735	**W** 9080
1415-1735	7935
1515-1804	**S** 9170
2000-2220	9080
2000-2300	4460
2000-2315	5320
2000-2400	5880, 5915, 5955, 6125, 6750, 6840, 7504, 7935, 9290
2055-2300	**W** 5090, **W** 6790, **S** 11000
2055-2315	**S** 9170
2100-2330	4905, 6890, 7516
2100-2340	5163, 7770, 11630
2100-2400	9064, 10260, 11610, 11740
2223-2400	15390
2230-2330	**W** 7620
2230-2400	4800, 9775, 11100
2300-2400	11000, 11800
2303-2400	12120
2315-2400	9170
2318-2400	15550
2330-2400	11040, 11935
2343-2400	9755, 15500

CHINA RADIO INTERNATIONAL

Chinese

0200-0300	*9690* (N America & C America), *9710* & *11715* (N America), 12055 & 15435 (S America)
0300-0400	**W** *9730* & **S** *11680* (W North Am)
0400-0500	*9710* & *11715* (N America)
0900-1000	9480 (E Asia), 9945 (SE Asia), 11695 (Australasia), 11945 & 12015 (SE Asia), 15100 & 15180 (E Asia), 15205 & 15260 (SE Asia)
1300-1400	11945, 12015, 15205 & 15260 (SE Asia)
1500-1600	4020 (E Asia), 9457 (S Asia), 11910 (S Asia & E Africa), **S** 15455 (S Asia)
1730-1830	4020 (E Asia), 7335 & 7350 (Europe & N Africa), **W** 7700 (N Africa & W Africa), 7800 (Europe & N Africa), **S** 9820 (N Africa & W Africa)
2000-2100	4620 & 5220 (E Asia), 7125, **W** 7435 & 7660 (E Europe), 7780 (W Africa), **S** 8345 (E Asia), 9620 (E Africa), 11445 (Africa), **S** 11650 (E Europe), *11790* (C Africa & E Africa)
2100-2130	*6165* (Europe)
2230-2300	*11790* (C Africa & E Africa), *15110* (C Africa & S Africa)
2230-2330	5220 (E Asia), 6140 & 7190 (SE Asia), 8260 (E Asia), 9440 (SE Asia), 9535 (E Asia), 11685, 12015 & 15400 (SE Asia)

Cantonese

0100-0200	*9710* & *11715* (N America), 12055 (S America)
1000-1100	9945 (SE Asia), 15100 (E Asia)
1100-1200	11945, 12015, 15205 & 15260 (SE Asia)
1700-1800	9900 (S Asia & E Africa)
1900-2000	7780 (W Africa)

CHINA (TAIWAN)

BROADCASTING CORPORATION CHINA

Chinese

0000-0100	*5950* (E North Am), *11740* (C America), *11855* (W North Am), 15270, *15440* (C America)
0000-0700	9280 (E Asia)
0000-1700	11725, 11885, 15125
0100-0400	7295
2100-2400	11725, 15270
2155-2400	11885, 15125
2200-2400	*5950* (E North Am), *11740* (C America), *11855* (W North Am), *15440* (C America)

VOICE OF FREE CHINA

Chinese

0000-0100	[W] *9690*, [W] *11720*, [S] *15130* & [S] *17805* (S America)
0100-0200	[W] *11825*, *15215* & [S] *17845* (S America)
0400-0500	*5950* (E North Am & C America), 7130 (SE Asia), *9680* (W North Am), 11825, 15270 & 15345 (SE Asia)
0700-0800	7130 (SE Asia)
0900-1000	7445 (SE Asia), 9610 (Australasia), 11745 (E Asia), 11915, 15270 & 15345 (SE Asia)
1200-1300	11745 (E Asia), 15270 (SE Asia)
1900-2000	[W] *9850* (Europe), 9955 (Mideast & N Africa), *17750* & [S] *21720* (Europe)

Cantonese

0100-0200	*5950* (E North Am)
0300-0400	*11740* (C America)
0500-0600	*5950* (E North Am & C America), *9680* (W North Am), 11825, 11915, 15270 & 15345 (SE Asia)
1000-1100	7285, 7445 & 11915 (SE Asia)
1100-1200	9610 & 15270 (SE Asia)
1300-1400	11915/9610 & 15345 (SE Asia)

CLANDESTINE (CENTRAL AMERICA)—Spanish

"LA VOZ DEL CID"—(C America)

0400-1200	6306
1200-0400	9941

CLANDESTINE (MIDEAST)—Persian

"VOICE OF HUMAN RIGHTS"—(Mideast)

0230-0425	9350, 11470 & 15100
0645-0730	11470, 15100 & 15640
1400-1445	9350 & 15100
1630-1825	[W] 9350, 11470, 15100 & 15670

COLOMBIA—Spanish

CARACOL COLOMBIA

24 Hr	6150
2100-1200	5075

ECOS DEL ATRATO

1000-0400	5020 (Irr)

LA VOZ DE YOPAL

24 Hr	5040

RADIO NACIONAL

1100-0400	4955

CROATIA—Other

CROATIAN RADIO

0008-0100	&
0108-0200	[→] 5895 (Europe), 7370 (E North Am)
0208-0300,	
0308-0400,	
0408-0500	&
0508-0600	[→] 5895 (Europe & E North Am)
0600-0700	[→] 5895 (Europe)
0600-0703	[→] 7370 (Europe & Australasia), 13830 (Australasia)
0630-0703	[→] 9830 (Europe)
0703-0713	[→] Su 5920 (Europe), Su 7370 (Europe & Australasia), Su 9830 (Europe), Su 13830 (Australasia)
0713-0900	[→] 7370 (Europe & Australasia), 13830 (Australasia)
0713-0903	[→] 5920 & 9830 (Europe)
0903-0913	[→] Su 5920, Su 7370 & Su 9830 (Europe)
0913-1230	[→] 9830 (Europe)
0913-1303	[→] 5920 & 7370 (Europe)
1230-1303	&
1308-2200	[→] 13830 (E North Am)
1313-1430	[→] 5920 (Europe)
1313-2000	[→] 7370 (Europe)
1430-2300	[→] 5895 (Europe)
2308-2400	5895 (Europe), 7370/11635 (E North Am)

CUBA—Spanish

RADIO HABANA CUBA

0000-0200	6180 (C America), 9820 (N America)
0000-0400	11970 (S America)
0000-0500	5965/6060, 9505, 9550 & 11760 (C America), 11875 & [S] 15230 (S America)
1100-1300	11860/11875 (S America)
1100-1400	9550 (C America & N America)
1100-1500	6000 & 11760 (C America)
1200-1500	9505 (C America)
2100-2300	9820 USB (E North Am), [W] 11740 & [S] 11760 (Europe & N Africa), 15220/17705 (Europe)

RADIO REBELDE

1030-0500	5025

CYPRUS

CYPRUS BROADCASTING CORPORA-TION—(Europe)

Greek

2215-2245	F-Su 6180, [W] F-Su 7125, [S] F-Su 7205, [W] F-Su 9635 & [S] F-Su 9760

RADIO MONTE CARLO—(N America)

Arabic

0400-0420	*5960* & *9755*

CZECH REPUBLIC—Czech

RADIO PRAGUE

0130-0200	[S] 7345 (E North Am), [W] 7345 (E North Am & S America), [S] 9405 (S America)
0230-0300	5930 & 7345 (E North Am)
0800-0830	[W] 17485 (E Africa & S Asia), [W] 21705 (SE Asia & Australasia)
1230-1300	[S] 15640 (S Asia & E Asia)

1330-1400	6055 (Europe)
1330-1400	**W** 7345 (W Europe)
1400-1430	**S** 13580 (S Asia & E Asia)
1500-1530	5930 (W Europe)
1500-1530	**W** 13580 (C Africa & E Africa)
1530-1600	**S** 17485 (E Africa)
1630-1700	5930 (W Europe)
1630-1700	**W** 9420 (Mideast & S Asia)
1730-1800	**S** 15640 (W Africa)
1830-1900	5930 (W Europe)
1830-1900	**W** 9420 (E Africa & Mideast)
2330-2400	**W** 5930, 7345 & **S** 9405 (E North Am)

DENMARK—Danish

RADIO DANMARK

0030-0055	**W** 5905/6115 (S America), **W** 5910/6120 (N America), **S** 7135 (SE Asia), **S** 7275 (SE Asia & Australasia), **S** 7445 (S America), **S** 7480 (E North Am & C America)
0130-0155	**W** 5910 (C America & S America), **S** 7480 (E North Am & C America), **S** 9560 (N America)
0230-0255	**W** 5910/5905 (E North Am & C America), **W** 7450 (W North Am), **S** 9560 (N America)
0330-0355	**S** 7165 (Mideast), **W** 7215 (E Africa), **S** 7480 (W North Am), **W** 9560 (N America), **S** 9565 (Mideast), **W** 9590 (E Africa)
0430-0455	**W** 7165 (Mideast & E Africa), **S** 7480 (W North Am), **S** 9480 (E Europe), **S** 9565, **W** 9590 & **S** 9595 (Mideast)
0530-0555	**W** 5910/5905 (W North Am), **W** 7165 (E Africa), **S** 9480 (E Europe), **W** 9590 (Mideast), **S** 13800 (E Africa)
0630-0655	**W** 5965 (W Europe), 7180 (Europe), **S** 7295/15175 (Australasia), **W** 9590 (E Europe & Mideast), **W** 11735 (Mideast), **S** 11850 (W Africa), **S** 13800 (E Africa)
0730-0755	**W** 5965 (W Europe), 7180 (Europe), **S** 7295/15175 (Australasia), 9590 (Europe), **S** 13800 (W Africa), **W** 15175 (S Europe & Africa)
0830-0855	**W** 9590/15175 & **W** 11735 (E Asia & Australasia), **S** 15220 (Mideast), **S** 21705 (Australasia)
0930-0955	**S** 15220 (Mideast), 17740/17730 (SE Asia & Australasia), **W** 17840 (Mideast)
1030-1055	**W** 11860 (S Europe), **S** 13800 (Atlantic), **W** 15165 (S Europe & W Africa), **S** 17840 (S America)
1130-1155	**S** 7295 (Europe), **W** 11850/9590 (Atlantic & E North Am), **S** 15345 (E North Am)
1230-1255	**S** 9590 (Europe), **W** 11850 (Australasia), **S** 13800 & **W** 15165 (SE Asia & Australasia), **S** 15170 (E Asia), **W** 15175 (E North Am & C America), **S** 15345 (E North Am), **W** 17810 (S America)
1330-1355	9590 (Europe), 13800/11730 (SE Asia & Australasia), **S** 15170 (E Asia), **W** 15335 (E North Am & C America), **S** 15340/11850 (N America), **W** 15605 (S

Asia & SE Asia)
1430-1455	**S** 11850 (SE Asia), **W** 11870 (SE Asia & Australasia), **W** 13800 (N America), **W** 15335 (E North Am & C America), **S** 15340 (N America), **S** 15620 (S Asia)
1530-1555	**W** 9480 (Mideast), **W** 9550 & 11850/11840 (W North Am), **S** 13805 & **S** 15230 (Mideast), **W** 15230 (E Africa)
1630-1655	**W** 9550 (W North Am), **S** 9590 (E Europe), **W** 9590 (E Africa), **W** 11825 (Mideast), 11850 (W North Am), **S** 13800 (E Africa)
1730-1755	**W** 7120 (S Europe & W Africa), **S** 7485 (E Europe), 9590 (W Europe), **W** 11850 (W North Am), **S** 15220 (E Africa), **W** 15220 (Africa)
1830-1855	**S** 5960 (W Europe), **W** 5960 (Europe), **W** 7120 (E Europe, Mideast & E Africa), **W** 9590 (Europe & Africa), **W** 11930 (S Europe & Africa), **S** 13805 (W Africa), **S** 15220 (C Africa & S Africa)
1930-1955	**W** 5960 (S Europe & W Africa), **W** 7215 (Australasia), **S** 7485 (Europe), **S** 9590 (Australasia), **W** 9590 (Europe & Africa), **S** 13805 (W Africa), **S** 15220 (C Africa & S Africa)
2030-2055	**S** 7305/7315 (Australasia), **S** 7485 (Europe), **W** 9590 (Europe, W Africa & N America)
2130-2155	**S** 7135 (Australasia), **S** 7305/7315 (E Asia), 9590 (Atlantic & N America), **W** 9600 (S America)
2230-2255	**W** 5905/6120 (S America), **S** 9480/9490 (E Asia), **S** 9485 (E North Am), **W** 9590 (S America), **S** 9635 (Australasia)
2330-2355	**W** 6030/6120 (SE Asia), **W** 6060 (S America), 7275 (SE Asia & Australasia), **S** 9485 (E North Am)
2330-2400	**S** 7445 (S America)

ECUADOR—Spanish

HCJB-VOICE OF THE ANDES

0000-0500	6050 (S America), 15140 (N America & S America)
1030-1500	11960 (N America & S America)
1030-2400	6050 (S America)
1200-1300	9415 (N America & S America)
1500-2400	15140 (N America & S America)
2200-2300	**W** 11835 & **S** 15520 (Europe)

EGYPT—Arabic

RADIO CAIRO

0000-0045	15220 (C America & S America), 17770 (S America)
0030-0330	9900 (E North Am)
0330-0430	9900 (W North Am)
1015-1215	17745 (Mideast & S Asia)
1100-1130	17800 (C Africa & S Africa)
1400-1700	15220 (C Africa)
2000-2200	11990 (Australasia)
2345-2400	15220 (C America & S America), 17770 (S America)

REPUBLIC OF EGYPT RADIO

0000-0030 ◄ 9700 (N Africa), 11665 (C Africa & E Africa), 15285 (Mideast)
0200-0700 ◄ 12050 (Europe & E North Am)
0200-2200 ◄ 9755 (N Africa & Mideast)
0300-0600 ◄ 9850 (N Africa & Mideast)
0300-2400 ◄ 15285 (Mideast)
0350-0700 ◄ 9620 & 9770 (N Africa)
0350-1800 ◄ 11665 (Mideast)
0350-2400 ◄ 9800 (Mideast)
0600-1400 ◄ 11980 (N Africa & Mideast)
0700-1100 ◄ 15115 (W Africa)
0700-1500 ◄ 11785 (N Africa)
0700-1530 ◄ 12050 (Europe, E North Am & E Africa)
1100-2400 ◄ 9850 (N Africa)
1300-1900 ◄ 17670 (N Africa)
1530-2400 ◄ 12050 (Europe & N America)
1800-2400 ◄ 9700 (N Africa)
1900-2400   11665 (C Africa & E Africa)

FINLAND—Finnish & Swedish
RADIO FINLAND
0000-0100   [W] 5990 (E Asia & SE Asia), [W] 6015 & [W] 9680 (S America)
0300-0330   [S] 9655 (E Europe)
0330-0430   [S] 15440 (Mideast)
0355-0530   [S] 9655 (E Europe)
0400-0430   6120 (Europe)
0400-0430   [W] 6070 (E Europe)
0430-0530   [W] 9635 (Mideast)
0430-0630 ◄ 11755 (Mideast & E Africa)
0455-0630   6120 (Europe)
0455-0630   [W] 6070 (E Europe)
0500-0530   [S] 15440 (Mideast)
0600-0630   [W] 9635 (Mideast)
0700-0730   6120, 9560 & 11755 (Europe)
0700-0800   [S] 17820 USB (SE Asia & Australasia)
0800-0900   15330/15115 (SE Asia & Australasia)
0800-0900   [W] 9760 (SE Asia & Australasia)
0800-0930   6120 & 11755 (Europe)
0900-1000   [S] 13750 USB (E Asia)
1000-1015 ◄ 11755 (Europe)
1000-1100   15240 (E Asia & SE Asia)
1000-1100   [W] 13770 USB (E Asia)
1000-2030   6120 (Europe)
1100-1130   [S] 11900 (N America)
1100-1200 ◄ 15240 & 17800/17820 USB (SE Asia & Australasia)
1100-2030 ◄ 11755 (Europe)
1200-1230   15400 (N America)
1200-1230   [W] 11735 & [S] 11900 (N America)
1300-1330   15400 (N America)
1300-1330   [S] 11900 & [W] 17740 (N America)
1400-1430   15400 (N America)
1400-1430   [W] 17740 (N America)
1400-1530   [S] 11900 (N America)
1500-1630   15400 (N America)
1500-1630   [W] 11785 & [W] 13645 (N America)
1530-1700   [W] 6070 & [W] 9670 (E Europe)
1600-1800   [S] 13750 & [S] 15120 (Mideast)
1700-1900   [W] 6070 (W Europe), 9730 (Europe & W Africa), [W] 11755 & [W] 15440 (Mideast)
1800-1900   [S] 15440 (Europe)
1900-2000   9730 (Europe & W Africa)
2000-2130   [S] 11755 & [S] 15440 (Europe)
2015-2130   [S] 6120 (Europe)
2100-2130   [S] 9730 (Europe & W Africa)

2115-2200   9730 (Europe & W Africa)
2300-2400   [S] 9650 (S America), [S] 9665 (E Asia & SE Asia), [S] 11845 (S America)

FRANCE—French
RADIO FRANCE INTERNATIONALE
0000-0030   [S] *15440* (SE Asia)
0000-0100   [W] 5920 (C America), [W] 7120 (S Asia & SE Asia), 9800 (S America), [W] *9800* (N America), [S] 9805 (S Asia & SE Asia), [S] 11670 (C America), [S] *12025* (SE Asia), [W] *12045* (E Asia & SE Asia)
0000-0200   *9715* (S America), 9790 (C America)
0000-0300   5945 & [S] 9790 (E North Am)
0000-0900   3965 (Europe)
0100-0200   [W] *11600* & [S] *15440* (S Asia)
0200-0300   5920 (C America), 9715 (S America), *9800* (N America & C America)
0300-0400   5945 (E Africa & Mideast), 7315 (Mideast)
0300-0445   5990 (E Europe)
0300-0500   [S] *6175* (S Africa), [S] 9550 (Mideast), *9800* (C America)
0300-0600   6045 (E Europe)
0300-0700   9790 (Africa)
0300-0800   7135 (Africa), 7280 (E Europe)
0400-0500   *5920* (C America), 5925 (N Africa), [W] 5945 (E Africa & Mideast), [W] 7315 & [S] 11685 (Mideast), [S] 11700 (E Africa)
0400-0600   9805 (E Africa)
0400-0600   *4890* (C Africa), [S] 9745 (E Europe), [W] 9805 (E Africa & Mideast)
0445-0545   [W] 5990 (E Europe)
0500-0600   [S] 9805 (E Europe), 11685 (Mideast), 11700 (E Africa), [S] 15135 (Mideast & E Africa), [S] 15155 (E Africa)
0500-0700   11995 (E Africa)
0500-0700   [W] 5925 & [S] 7305 (N Africa), [W] 9550 (Mideast), [S] 11790 (E Europe), [S] 15485 (Mideast)
0500-1600   6175 (Europe & N Africa)
0600-0700   [W] 5990 & [W] 6045 (E Europe), *9845* (W Africa), 15135 & 15155 (E Africa), [S] 15315 (W Africa), [S] 17800 (E Africa)
0600-0800   [W] 9745 (E Europe), [W] 11685 (Mideast), 11700 (Africa)
0600-1200   9805 (E Europe)
0700-0800   [W] 7305 & [S] 9845 (N Africa), [S] 15605 (Mideast), [S] 17620 & 17800 (E Africa)
0700-0900   9790 (N Africa), 11790 & [W] 15155 (E Europe), 15300 (Africa), 15315 (W Africa)
0700-1000   [W] 15155 (Mideast), [W] 21620 (E Africa)
0700-1300   11670 (E Europe)
0800-0900   [S] 17800 (E Africa)
0800-1000   [W] 17650 (Mideast)
0800-1100   17620 (E Africa), [W] 17620 (W Africa)
0800-1200   15195 (E Europe), 15605 (Mideast & S Asia)
0800-1600   11845 (N Africa), 17850 (Africa)
0805-0835   M 11660 (Antarctica)
0900-1200   15155 (E Europe), [W] 21580 (C Africa & S Africa)

0900-1600	15315 (N Africa & W Africa)
0900-1700	15300 (N Africa & W Africa)
1000-1300	21620 (E Africa)
1000-1400	17650 (Mideast)
1030-1130	**S** *9715* (S America), *9790* (C America), *11670* (S America), *11700* (Australasia), **W** *13625* (S America)
1030-1200	**W** *7140* & **S** *9650* (E Asia), **W** *9650* & **S** *11715* (SE Asia), **S** 15530 (C America)
1100-1200	**S** *11890* (SE Asia), **S** *17795* & **W** *21520* (S Africa)
1100-1500	17620 (Africa)
1130-1200	**S** 15365 (E North Am), **W** 15365 (C America)
1130-1300	11700 (E North Am)
1200-1300	*11670* (C America), **S** *13640* (C America), **S** *15325* (W Africa), **W** *15435* (S America), **W** *15515* (C America)
1200-1400	*9790* (C Africa), **W** 21685 (W Africa)
1200-1500	21580 (C Africa & S Africa)
1300-1400	9805 & **W** 11670 (E Europe), *13625* (C America), **S** *13625* (N America), **W** 15155 (E Europe), **S** 17795 (E Africa)
1300-1500	15195 (E Europe)
1300-1600	15365 (E North Am), **W** 21620 (E Africa)
1330-1400	**S** M-Sa *13640* (C America), *15435* (S America), **S** M-Sa *15515* & **W** *15515* (C America), **W** *17560* (S America), **W** *17860* (C America)
1400-1500	11615 & **S** 15155 (E Europe), 15605 (Mideast)
1400-1600	**S** *13640* (C America), **S** *15525* (N America), **W** *17575* (N America & C America), 17795 (E Africa)
1430-1500	**W** M-Sa *17860* & **W** M-Sa *21645* (C America)
1430-1600	**S** *15515* (C America)
1500-1600	11615 (Mideast), **S** 11615 & **S** 15195 (E Europe), **S** 15405 (S Asia & SE Asia), **W** 15460 (E Africa), **S** 15605 (Mideast), **W** *17860* (C America), **S** 21580 (C Africa & S Africa), **W** *21645* (C America)
1500-1700	**W** 9790 (S Asia & SE Asia)
1500-1800	**W** 9495 & **W** 9605 (E Europe), **W** 11995 (E Africa), 17620 (W Africa), **S** 17620 (E Africa)
1600-1700	**S** 12030 (S Asia & SE Asia)
1600-1800	9790 (N Africa), **S** 11670 (E Europe), **W** 11965 (W Africa)
1600-1900	**S** 11995 (E Europe), **S** *15525* & **W** *17630* (S America)
1600-2400	3965 (Europe)
1700-1800	**W** 9790 (Africa), **S** 9805 (E Europe)
1700-2000	11705 (Africa)
1700-2200	6175 (Europe & N Africa), 15300 (Africa)
1730-1800	**S** 15210 (E Africa)
1730-1900	**W** 9485 & **S** 15460 (E Africa)
1800-1900	**W** 5900 (E Europe), **W** 7160 (N Africa), 9605 (E Europe)
1800-2000	**W** 7135 (E Europe), **W** 7315 (E Africa), 11965 & **S** 17620 (W Africa)
1800-2100	**S** 11995 (E Africa)
1800-2200	*7160* (C Africa), **S** 9495 (E Europe), 9790 (Africa)
1900-2100	**S** 9605 (E Europe)
1900-2200	**W** 5945 (E Africa & Mideast), 7160 (N Africa & W Africa), 9485 (E Africa), **S** *17630* & **W** *21765* (S America)
2000-2100	5915 (E Europe), **S** 11965 (W Africa)
2000-2200	7315 & **S** 11705 (Africa)
2100-2200	**S** 5900 & **W** 5915 (E Europe)
2200-2300	**W** 5920 (C America), **W** 5945 (E North Am), 9715 (S America), **W** 9790 (C Africa), 9800 (S America), **S** 11670 (C America), *13640/15190* (N America)
2200-2400	9790 (C America), **S** 9790 (E North Am)
2300-2400	5945 (E North Am), **W** 7120 (S Asia & SE Asia), **W** 9565 (SE Asia), *9715* (S America), **S** 9805 (S Asia & SE Asia), **S** *12025* (SE Asia), **W** *12045* (E Asia & SE Asia), **S** *15440* (SE Asia)

FRENCH POLYNESIA—French & Tahitian
RFO-TAHITI—(Pacific)

24 Hr	11827 & 15168

GABON—French & Arabic
AFRIQUE NUMERO UN

0500-2300	9580 (C Africa)
0800-1600	17630 (W Africa)
1600-1900	15475 (W Africa & E North Am)

GERMANY—German
BAYERISCHER RUNDFUNK

24 Hr	6085

DEUTSCHE WELLE

0000-0150	**S** 9730 (E North Am & C America), **S** *15410* (S America)
0000-0155	**W** 6180 (S Asia & SE Asia), 7130 (S Europe, N Africa & S America), **W** 7235 (E Asia & S Asia), **S** 7275 (N Europe), **S** 9680 (S Asia), **S** *11785*, **W** *11795* & *13780* (S America), **W** *15270* (C America)
0000-0200	**W** *7225* (S Asia), 9545 (C America & S America), 9765 (S America), **W** *9765* (C America), **S** 11795 (S Asia)
0000-0255	**W** *9690* (S Asia & SE Asia)
0000-0300	**S** *9525* (S Asia)
0000-0355	**W** *11785* (W Africa & Americas)
0000-0400	6100 (N America & C America)
0000-0555	3995 (Europe), **W** 6075 (E North Am)
0000-1800	6075 (Europe)
0100-0300	**W** 9515 (S Asia)
0200-0350	**S** 7175 (E Africa)
0200-0355	**W** 6145 (E Europe & C America), **W** 7130 (S Europe, N Africa & S America), **W** *7250* (Mideast)
0200-0400	**W** *7105* (Mideast), **S** 9735 (N America & C America)
0200-0555	*6075* & **S** 6145 (N America)
0200-0600	**S** 9545 (E Europe & W Asia), **W** 9545 (Africa)
0400-0555	**W** 7105 (Mideast), *9535* & **S** 9735 (N America), **W** 9735 (Mideast & Africa), **S** 11795 (Africa & Australasia)
0400-0600	*6085* (N America & C America), 6100

	(N America), ⬛W 7195 (Africa), ⬛S *9545* (W Europe), ⬛S 13780 (Mideast)
0500-0600	⬛S 9735 (Australasia)
0600-0800	⬛W *6185* (Australasia), ⬛W 15105 (SE Asia & Australasia), 15275 (Mideast & Africa)
0600-0955	⬛W 7200 (Australasia), ⬛W 9670 (E Europe & W Asia), *9690*, 9735, 11795 & ⬛S *21640* (Australasia)
0600-1000	⬛S 11865 (Europe), 17845 (SE Asia & Australasia)
0600-1350	⬛S 17845 (Mideast)
0600-1755	13780 (S Europe & Mideast)
0600-2200	9545 (Europe)
0700-1700	6140 (Europe)
0800-0955	⬛W 15105 (E Asia)
0800-1000	⬛S 15275 (Mideast), ⬛W 15275 (Mideast & Africa)
0800-1100	⬛S 17560 (W Africa)
0800-1355	⬛S 13780 (E Asia)
0800-1800	⬛W 13690 (W Europe)
1000-1355	⬛W 9680 (E Asia), ⬛S 15275 (E Europe & W Asia), ⬛W 17845 (SE Asia & Australasia), 21560 (Mideast)
1000-1400	⬛W *7340*, ⬛W *11865* & ⬛S *12000* (E Asia), ⬛W 15275 (Mideast), ⬛W 17560 (S Asia & SE Asia), ⬛S *21640* (E Asia)
1000-1555	⬛S 17845 (S Asia & SE Asia)
1000-1600	⬛W 7175 (E Europe & W Asia)
1100-1300	⬛S *11765* (Europe)
1100-1400	⬛S 17560 (Africa)
1200-1355	⬛W 7285 (E Asia), ⬛S 11785 & ⬛W *11925* (Europe), ⬛S *15275* (S America), ⬛W *15275* (N America & C America)
1200-1400	⬛S *17765* (S America)
1400-1555	⬛W 9595 (S Asia), ⬛S 15350 (W Africa)
1400-1600	⬛W 7185 (E Europe), ⬛W 9545 (S Asia), *13790* (N America), ⬛W 15275 (Mideast & W Africa)
1400-1700	*17715* (N America), ⬛W *17765* (S America)
1400-1755	⬛W *9620*, ⬛W 9650 & ⬛S *9655* (S Asia), ⬛S 11795 (Europe & S Asia), ⬛S 15275 (S Asia)
1400-1800	⬛W *7315* & ⬛S *12055* (S Asia), ⬛S 17560 (W Africa)
1400-1955	⬛S 15275 (E Africa)
1600-1755	⬛W 7175 (W Asia & S Asia), ⬛S 13780 (S Asia & SE Asia)
1600-1800	⬛W 9545 & ⬛W 15275 (Africa)
1800-1955	⬛S 13610 (Africa)
1800-2000	⬛W 3995 (Europe), ⬛W 9545 (Africa)
1800-2155	⬛W 7215 (Africa), ⬛S *9655* (SE Asia & Australasia), ⬛W *9735* (S Africa), ⬛S 13780 (C Africa & E Africa), ⬛S 15275 (W Africa & S America), ⬛W *17860* (W Africa & Americas)
1800-2200	6075 (Europe & Africa), ⬛W 6100 (Africa), ⬛W *11765* (SE Asia & Australasia), ⬛S 11795 (Africa), ⬛W 11795 (W Africa & S America)
2000-2120	*17810* (Americas)
2000-2200	9545 (Africa)
2000-2400	3995 (Europe)
2120-2255	*17810* (S America)
2200-2355	⬛W *7140* (E Europe)
2200-2400	⬛W *5925* (E Asia), ⬛W 6010 (S Asia & E

	Asia), 6075 (Europe), ⬛W 6075 (E North Am), 6100 (N America & C America), 9545 (C America & S America), ⬛S 9680 (S Asia), ⬛W *9690* (S Asia & SE Asia), *9715* (E Asia), ⬛S 9730 (E North Am & C America), 9765 (S America), ⬛W *9765* (C America), ⬛S 11785 (S America), ⬛W *11785* (W Africa & Americas), ⬛S *11795* (E Asia), ⬛W 11795 & *13780* (S America), ⬛W *15270* (C America), ⬛S *15410* (S America)

DEUTSCHLAND RADIO—(Europe)
24 Hr	6005

RADIO BREMEN—(Europe)
24 Hr ⬅	6190

RADIOROPA-INFO—(Europe)
0400-1600 ⬅	*5980*
1600-2200 ⬅	*5980/5975*

SUDDEUTSCHER RUNDFUNK—(Europe)
0455-2305	6030

SUDWESTFUNK—(Europe)
24 Hr	7265

GREECE—Greek

FONI TIS HELLADAS
0000-0130 &	
0200-0335	6260, ⬛W 7448, ⬛W 9420, 9935 & ⬛S 11645 (N America)
0400-0530	⬛W 7450, 9425 & 21465/11645 (Mideast)
0600-0735	9425, ⬛W 9935 & 11645 (Europe)
0745-0800	⬛S 9375 (Australasia)
0800-0935	⬛W 15650 & ⬛W 17525 (Australasia)
0900-0950 ⬅	11645 (Europe)
1000-1050	15650 (E Asia)
1000-1050	⬛W 17525 (E Asia)
1000-1130	9425 & 9825 (Mideast)
1200-1230	⬛W 9935 (E Africa), ⬛W 11645 (Africa)
1200-1235	15650 (Africa)
1200-1335	⬛S 15630 (N America)
1300-1435	17525/17520 (N America)
1400-1430	⬛S 9425 (Mideast)
1400-1435	11645, ⬛S 11645 & ⬛S 15650 (Mideast), ⬛W 15650 (N America)
1435-1450	17525/17520 (N America)
1500-1600	⬛W 7450 (Europe), 9425/9420 (E Europe), 9935 (Europe)
1710-1725	9425, 9935 & 11645 (E Europe)
1800-1825	⬛S 11645 (E Europe), ⬛S 15650 (C Africa & S Africa)
1800-2150	⬛S 9425 (Europe)
1800-2200	7450/7448 (Europe)
2000-2150	6260 (Europe)
2100-2235	⬛S 6260, 9375 & ⬛W 9425 (Australasia)
2200-2305 ⬅	11595 (S America)

RADIOSTANTSIYA MAKEDONIAS
0600-1800 ⬅	11595 (Europe)
0600-2300 ⬅	9395 (Mideast)
1400-2300 ⬅	7430 (Europe)
1800-2300	7500 (Mideast)

HOLLAND—Dutch

RADIO NEDERLAND WERELDOMROEP
0000-0025	*7285*, 9590, ⬛W *11660/13700* & ⬛S *13695* (SE Asia)
0130-0225	6020 (E North Am), *6165* (N America), ⬛S 9895 (E North Am), *15315* (S America)

0330-0425	**S** *7310* & **W** *9860* (E Africa), *11655* (Mideast)
0530-0625	**W** *5995, 6165* & **S** *9715* (W North Am)
0530-0630	**S** 5945 (W Europe), **S** 7130/7240 & **S** 9895 (Europe), **S** 11655 (E Europe & Mideast)
0530-0730	**S** *7395* (W Europe)
0630-0725	**W** 6020 (S Europe), **W** 7130 (Europe), **S** *9615/9815, 9715/9720* & **W** *11655* (Australasia)
0630-0730	**S** *7130/7240* (W Europe)
0630-0830	**S** 11935 (W Europe)
0630-0855	**W** *9470* (Europe)
0630-1725	5955 & 9895 (Europe)
0730-0830	7130 (W Europe)
0730-0855	**W** 11935 (E Europe)
0830-0855	**W** 7130 (W Europe)
0830-0955	**S** Sa 9590, **W** Sa 9860 & **S** Sa 11935 (Europe), **S** Su-F 11935 (W Europe)
0930-0955	*6020* (C America)
0930-1025	**W** Su-F 21505 (Asia & Australasia)
1000-1155	**S** 13700 (S Europe)
1030-1125	*9720,* **S** *9810* & **W** *11895* (Australasia), *17580* (SE Asia), *21480* (E Asia), **W** 21505 (Asia & Australasia)
1130-1225	**W** 11900 (W Europe)
1330-1425	*7260* (E Asia), **W** *7400/9860* (E Asia & SE Asia), **S** *12065* (SE Asia), **W** 13770 (S Asia), **S** 15530 (SE Asia)
1430-1525	*7365,* **S** *7400* & **W** 13770 (S Asia)
1500-1725	**S** *7310* (W Europe), **S** 13700 (S Europe)
1530-1625	**W** 9860 & **W** 13770 (Mideast)
1630-1725	**W** 6015 (W Europe), *6020* (S Africa), **W** *7300* (Irr) (Europe), **W** 9860 (S Europe), *11655* (E Africa), Su *15120* (C America), Su *17605* (E North Am)
1730-1825	**W** 6015 (S Europe & W Africa), 9860 (Mideast), **W** 9895 (E Africa), **S** 13700 (Mideast), **S** 15560 (S Africa & E Africa), *17605* & *21515/21590* (W Africa)
1930-2025	**S** 6020 (W Europe & N Africa)
2030-2125	*6015* (S Africa), **S** *7120* (C Africa & S Africa), **W** *11655* (W Africa & C Africa), *15315* & *17605* (W Africa)
2030-2225	6020 (N Africa & W Africa)
2130-2225	**S** 6020 (N Africa & W Africa), **W** 6020 & **S** 9895 (C America), **W** *11730* (E North Am), **S** 11950 (C America), **S** 13700 (S America), **S** *15155* (E North Am), *15315* (S America)
2330-2400	*7285,* 9590, **W** *11660/13700* & **S** *13695* (SE Asia)

HUNGARY—Hungarian
RADIO BUDAPEST
0000-0100	M 9835 (S America)
0000-0100	**W** M 5970 (S America), **S** 6000 (N America), **W** M 7220 (S America), **S** 11910 (N America)
0100-0200	9835 (N America)
0100-0200	**W** 6025 & **W** 7220 (N America)
0130-0230	**S** 6000 & **S** 11910 (N America)
0230-0330	9835 (N America)
0230-0330	**W** 5965 & **W** 7220 (N America)
0900-1000	**S** 17750 (Australasia)

1000-1100	13695 & 15220/15160 (Australasia)
1000-1100	**W** 11910 & **S** Su 17750 (Australasia)
1100-1200	Su 13695 & Su 15220/15160 (Australasia)
1100-1200	**S** Su 7215 & **S** Su 11905 (N Europe), **W** Su 11910 (Australasia)
1200-1300	Su 5970 (W Europe), Su 9835 (Europe)
1200-1300	**W** Su 7220 (W Europe)
1300-1400	**S** Su 7215 & **S** Su 11905 (N Europe)
1400-1500	Su 5970 (W Europe), Su 9835 (N Europe)
1400-1500	**W** Su 7220 (Europe)
1800-1900	**S** 3955 (Europe), **S** 5975 (N Europe), **S** 7130 (W Europe)
1900-1930	**S** 9835 (W Europe)
1900-2000	9835 (W Europe)
1900-2000	**W** 4010 (Europe), **W** 5970 & **W** 7220 (W Europe)
2000-2100	**S** 3955 (Europe), **S** 6140 (N Europe), **S** 7130 (W Europe)
2100-2200	9835 (W Europe)
2100-2200	**W** 4010 (Europe), **W** 5970 (W Europe), **W** 7220 (Europe)
2200-2300	**S** 6010 & **S** 11910 (S America)
2300-2400	9835 (S America)
2300-2400	**W** 5970, **S** Su 6010, **W** 7220 & **S** Su 11910 (S America)

IRAN—Persian
VOICE OF THE ISLAMIC REPUBLIC OF IRAN
0000-0030	**W** 7100 & **S** 7130 (Mideast & Europe)
24 Hr	15084
0130-1330	15365 (W Asia & S Asia)
1630-1930	6175/6005 & **W** 7180 (W Asia)
1630-2400	**W** 7100 & **S** 7130 (Mideast & Europe)

IRAQ—Arabic
RADIO IRAQ INTERNATIONAL
1000-1400	◄ 13650 (Irr)
2100-2315	◄ 11749 (Irr), 13650/9745 (Irr)

REPUBLIC OF IRAQ RADIO
0300-0025	◄ 4615
0700-1100	◄ 17740 (Irr) (Mideast)

ISRAEL
GALEI ZAHAL—(Europe)
Hebrew
1900-0900	◄ 8127 (Irr) USB

KOL ISRAEL
Arabic
0400-2220	◄ 5900, 5915, 9815 & 15480 (Mideast)

Hebrew
1725-1745	◄ 11685 (E Europe)

Yiddish
1700-1725 &	
1800-1830	7465 (E Europe), 9435 (Europe), 9845, 11603 & 11685 (E Europe)

RESHET BET
Hebrew
0000-0600	**S** 9385 (W Europe & E North Am)
0000-0800	**W** 7490/7495 (W Europe & E North Am)
0400-0700	◄ 11590 (W Europe & E North Am)
0400-2000	13750/13755 (N Europe & E Europe), 15615 (W Europe & E North Am)
0600-0800	**S** 17545 (W Europe)
0700-0800	**W** 11590 (W Europe & E North Am)
0800-1700	17545 (W Europe)

1700-1830	**S** 17545 (W Europe)
1700-2300	11588 (W Europe & E North Am)
1700-2300	**W** 9388 (W Europe & E North Am)
1800-2400	**W** 7490/7495 (W Europe & E North Am)
1900-2400	**S** 9385 (W Europe & E North Am)
2000-2200	**S** 13750 (N Europe & E Europe), **S** 15615 (W Europe & E North Am)

ITALY—Italian
RADIO ROMA

0000-0050	9575 (S America), 9645 (E North Am & C America), 11800 (N America & C America), 11880 (S America)
0130-0230	*6110 & 11765 (Americas)*
0130-0305	9575 (S America), 9645 (N America & C America), 11800 (E North Am & C America), 11880 (S America)
0415-0425	**W** 5975 & 7275 (Europe, N Africa & Mideast)
0435-0510	**W** 9680, **S** 11745/11910, 15245 & **S** 17795 (E Africa)
0700-1400	21775 (Australasia)
1000-1100	*11850/11925 (Australasia)*
1330-1630	Su 9855 (Europe), Su 21520 (E Africa), Su 21535 (S America), Su 21710 (S Africa)
1400-1425	15125 & 17780 (E North Am)
1425-1630	Su 17780 (E North Am)
1430-1455	7235 & **S** 9710 (N Africa)
1555-1635	**W** 5990 (Europe), 7110 (Europe, N Africa & Mideast), 7290 (W Europe), 9755 (Europe)
1700-1745	7235, **S** 9680 & **W** 9710 (N Africa), 15230 (Africa), 17870 (E Africa), 21710 (S Africa)
1830-1905	15225 & 17780 (E North Am)
2230-2400	9575 (S America), 9645 (E North Am & C America), 11800 (N America & C America), 11880 (S America)

RAI-RTV ITALIANA

0000-0003,	
0012-0103,	
0112-0203,	
0212-0303,	
0312-0403 &	
0412-0500	6060 (Europe, Mideast & N Africa)
0500-1430	6060 & 9515 (Europe, N Africa & Mideast)
0500-2230	7175 (Europe, Mideast & N Africa)
1430-1445	Su 6060 & Su 9515 (Europe, N Africa & Mideast)
1445-2230	6060 & 9515 (Europe, N Africa & Mideast)
2230-2400	6060 (Europe, Mideast & N Africa)

JAPAN—Japanese
RADIO JAPAN/NHK

0000-0030	7140 & 9560 (E Asia), 9660 (SE Asia), 11850 (Australasia), 11875/11800 (SE Asia), 17845 (S Asia)
0000-0100	**W** 6055, *6155* & **S** *6180* (Europe)
0200-0300	*5960* (E North Am), **W** 9565 & **S** 9680/11790 (W North Am), 11840 (E Asia), *11860* (SE Asia), 11885 (W North Am), *11895* (C America), 11910 (E Asia), *11950/15350* (S America), 15230 (W North Am), 17810 (SE Asia)
0400-0500	*5960* (Europe), **W** *6025* (W North Am & C America), **W** *6095* (Europe), **S** *6110* (W North Am & C America), **S** *7230* (Europe), **W** 9565 & **S** 11790/9680 (W North Am), 11840/15210 (E Asia), 11885 (W North Am), 17810 (SE Asia), *17820* (Mideast & N Africa)
0600-0700	5975 & 7230 (Europe), **W** 9565 (W North Am), *11740* (SE Asia), **S** 11790/9680 (W North Am), 11850/15270 (Australasia), 11885 (W North Am), 21610 (SE Asia)
0800-0900	**S** *6070* (S America), 9610 (E Asia), **W** 9675 & 9685 (S America), *11740* (SE Asia), 11850/15270 (Australasia), *15135* (W Africa), 15190 (SE Asia), *15335* & *17760/21640* (Europe, N Africa & Mideast), 17810 (SE Asia), *17815* (C Africa), 21610 (SE Asia)
0800-1400	9750 (E Asia)
0900-1400	11815 (SE Asia)
1000-1100	**S** *6120* (N America), 9610 (E Asia), *11785* (S Africa), 11850/15270 (Australasia), *11895/15350* (S America), 15190 (SE Asia)
1200-1300	**W** *6120* (N America), 7125 & 9610 (E Asia), **S** 15350/15295 (SE Asia)
1300-1400	9535 & *11705* (W North Am), *11895/11840* (S Asia), *15400/15150* (W Africa), *21490* (C Africa)
1600-1700	6150 (E Asia), 9535 (W North Am), 9580 (SE Asia), 11955 (S Asia), *21700* (Europe)
1800-1900	6150 (E Asia), 7140 (Australasia), 9535 (W North Am), 9580 (SE Asia), *11840/9570* (S Asia), 11850 (Australasia), *11930* (Mideast & N Africa)
2000-2100	**W** *6085* (Europe), **W** *7140* (Australasia), **S** *7255* (Europe), 9535 (W North Am), 11850 (Australasia)
2000-2400	9560 (E Asia), 11875/11800 (SE Asia)
2200-2300	*6055* & *6165/6140* (Europe), 7140 (E Asia), 9675/9580 (SE Asia), *9685* (S America), 11850 (Australasia)

RADIO TAMPA

0000-0800	3925, 9760
0000-1000	6115
0000-1300	3945
0000-1730	6055, 9595
0800-1730 &	
2020-2300	3925
2020-2400	6055, 9595
2300-2400	3925, 3945, 6115, 9760

JORDAN—Arabic
RADIO JORDAN

0000-0210	[←] 7180 (Mideast, SE Asia & Australasia), 11805 (S America), 11935 (W Europe & E North Am)
0400-0600	9630 (N Africa & E Africa)
0400-0815	[←] 11810 (Mideast, SE Asia & Australasia)
0400-0900	[←] 15290 (W Europe)
0600-0900	11835 (E Europe)
0830-1130	[←] 11810 (Mideast, SE Asia & Australasia)

1100-1300 ◀	15355 (N Africa & C America)
1200-1515 ◀	15215 (Mideast, SE Asia & Australasia)
1300-1500 ◀	17800 (W Europe)
1300-1630	11705 (N Africa & E Africa)
1600-2100 ◀	9610 (Mideast, SE Asia & Australasia)
1630-1800 ◀	11945 (E Europe)
1800-2200 ◀	9830 (W Europe)
1900-2200 ◀	11740 (E Europe)
2100-2400 ◀	7180 (Mideast, SE Asia & Australasia)
2200-2400	11805 (S America), 11935 (W Europe & E North Am)

KOREA (DPR)—Korean
RADIO PYONGYANG

0000-2030	6250 (E Asia)
0400-0550	7200 & 9345 (E Asia)
0500-0550	15180, 15230 & 17765 (SE Asia)
0800-0850	7250 & 9505 (E Asia)
1000-1050	6576 & 9977 (Americas)
1200-1250	4780, 6125 & 7200 (E Asia), 9345 (Asia)
1400-1450	9640 (S Asia), 9977 (SE Asia), 15230 (SE Asia & N America)
1600-1650	6520/6540 (Mideast & N Africa), 9600 & 11905 (N Africa)
1700-1750	6576 & 9345 (Europe)
1800-1850	9325 (Europe), 9640 (Mideast & Africa), 9977 (Africa), 13785 (Europe)
1900-1950	6520/6540 (Mideast & N Africa), 9600 & 11905 (N Africa)
2100-2400	6250 (E Asia)
2200-2250	11335 (Americas), Ⓦ 11700 (C America), 13650, 13760 & 15130 (Americas), 15230 (SE Asia)
2300-2350	7200 & 9345 (E Asia)

KOREA (REPUBLIC)—Korean
KOREAN BROADCASTING SYSTEM

0000-0400	9580 (N America)
24 Hr	3930
0400-2100	6015 (E Asia)
1400-2400	6135 (E Asia)
2200-2400	9580 (N America)

RADIO KOREA INTERNATIONAL

0000-0100	5975 (E Asia)
0100-0200	7275 (E Asia)
0300-0400	7275 (E Asia), Ⓦ 7550 & Ⓢ 11810 (N America), 15575 (S America)
0700-0800	Ⓦ 3975 (Europe), Ⓦ 7105 (W Europe), 7205 (E North Am), Ⓢ 9510 (W Europe), 15575 (Mideast & Africa)
0900-1100	7275 (E Asia), 9570 (Australasia), 13670 (Europe)
1000-1100	5975 & 6135 (E Asia)
1100-1130	6145 (E North Am), 9580 (S America), 9640 (E Asia), 9650 (E North Am)
1300-1400	9570 (SE Asia), 9640 (E Asia), 13670 (SE Asia)
1700-1900	5975 (E Asia), 7550 & 15575 (Europe)
2100-2200	5975 & 7275 (E Asia), 9640 (SE Asia)
2300-2400	5975 (E Asia)

KUWAIT—Arabic
RADIO KUWAIT

0000-0530	9840 (W North Am)
0200-1305	6055 (Mideast), 15495 (N Africa)

0400-0805	15505 (E Europe & W Asia)
0815-1740	15505 (W Africa & C Africa)
0900-1305	17885 (E Asia)
1315-1600	13620 (Europe & E North Am)
1315-1730	15110 (S Asia)
1315-1745	9880 (N Africa)
1615-1800	11990 (Europe & E North Am)
1745-2300	15505 (Europe & E North Am)
1800-2400	9840 (Europe & E North Am), 15495 (W Africa & C Africa)

LEBANON
VOICE OF LEBANON
Arabic

0000-0025,	
0355-0800,	
0808-0900,	
0915-1300,	
1330-1615,	
1630-1800 &	
1830-2400 ◀	6550

French

0800-0808,	
1300-1315,	
1615-1630 &	
1815-1830	6550

LIBYA—Arabic
RADIO JAMAHIRIYA

1015-0345	15235 (W Africa & S America), 15415 (Europe), 15435 (N Africa & Mideast)

LITHUANIA—Lithuanian
LITHUANIAN RADIO

0400-1300,	
1400-1600,	
1630-1700,	
1700-1905,	
1915-2000 &	
2030-2200	9710

RADIO VILNIUS

0008-0030	Ⓦ Tu-Sa 7150 (E North Am)
2200-2230	9710 (Europe)
2308-2330	Ⓢ M-F 9530/7360 (E North Am)

MEXICO—Spanish
RADIO EDUCACION

0000-1200	6185

MOROCCO
RADIO MEDI UN—(Europe & N Africa)
French

0500-0100	9575

RTV MAROCAINE
Arabic

0000-0500	11920 (N Africa & Mideast)
0945-2100	15345 (N Africa)
1100-1400	17815 (N Africa & Mideast)
1100-1500 &	
2200-2400	15335 (Europe)

French

1400-1500	M-Sa 17595 (Europe & W Africa)
1500-1700	17595 (Europe & W Africa)

NORWAY—Norwegian
RADIO NORWAY INTERNATIONAL

0000-0030	Ⓦ Tu-Su 5905/6115 (S America), Ⓦ Tu-Su 5910/6120 (N America), Ⓢ 7135 (SE Asia), Ⓢ 7275 (SE Asia & Australasia), Ⓢ 7445 (S America), Ⓢ

0100-0130	7480 (E North Am & C America)
	W 5910 (C America & S America), W 5910 (S America), S Tu-Su 7480 (E North Am & C America), S Tu-Su 9560 (N America)
0200-0230	W 5910/5905 (E North Am & C America), W Tu-Su 7450 (W North Am), S 9560 (N America)
0300-0330	S 7165 (Mideast), W 7215 (E Africa), S 7480 (W North Am), W 9560 (N America), S 9565 (Mideast), W 9590 (E Africa)
0400-0430	W 7165 (Mideast & E Africa), S Tu-Su 7480 (W North Am), S 9480 (E Europe), S 9565, W 9590 & S 9595 (Mideast)
0500-0530	W Tu-Su 5910/5905 (W North Am), W 7165 (E Africa), S 9480 (E Europe), W 9590 (Mideast), S 13800 (E Africa)
0600-0630	W 5965 (W Europe), 7180 (Europe), S M-Sa 7295/15175 (Australasia), W 9590 (E Europe & Mideast), W 11735 (Mideast), S 11850 (W Africa), S 13800 (E Africa)
0700-0730	W 5965 (W Europe), 7180 (Europe), S 7295/15175 (Australasia), 9590 (Europe), S 13800 (W Africa), W 15175 (S Europe & Africa)
0800-0830	W M-Sa 9590/15175 & W 11735 (E Asia & Australasia), S M-Sa 15220 (Mideast), S 21705 (Australasia)
0900-0930	S 15220 (Mideast), 17740/17730 (SE Asia & Australasia), W 17840 (Mideast)
1000-1030	W 11860 (S Europe), S 13800 (Atlantic), W 15165 (S Europe & W Africa), S 17840 (S America)
1100-1130	S 7295 (Europe), W 11850/9590 (Atlantic & E North Am), S 15345 (E North Am)
1200-1230	S 9590 (Europe), W M-Sa 11850 (Australasia), S M-Sa 13800 & W M-Sa 15165 (SE Asia & Australasia), S M-Sa 15170 (E Asia), W 15175 (E North Am & C America), S 15345 (E North Am), W 17810 (S America)
1300-1330	W Su 9590 & M-Sa 9590 (Europe), 13800/11730 (SE Asia & Australasia), S 15170 (E Asia), W 15335 (E North Am & C America), S M-Sa 15340/11850 (N America), W 15605 (S Asia & SE Asia)
1400-1430	S 11850 (SE Asia), W 11870 (SE Asia & Australasia), W 13800 (N America), W 15335 (E North Am & C America), S 15340 (N America), S 15620 (S Asia)
1500-1530	W 9550 & 11850/11840 (W North Am), S 13805 & S 15230 (Mideast), W 15230 (E Africa)
1600-1630	W 9550 (W North Am), S 9590 (E Europe), W 9590 (E Africa), W 11825 (Mideast), W Su 11850 & M-Sa 11850 (W North Am), S 13800 (E Africa)
1700-1730	W 7120 (S Europe & W Africa), S 7485 (E Europe), 9590 (W Europe), W 11850 (W North Am), S 15220 (E Af-

	rica), W 15220 (Africa)
1800-1830	S M-Sa 5960 (W Europe), W 5960 (Europe), W M-Sa 7120 (E Europe, Mideast & E Africa), W 9590 (Europe & Africa), W M-Sa 11930 (S Europe & Africa), S M-Sa 13805 (W Africa), S M-Sa 15220 (C Africa & S Africa)
1900-1930	W M-Sa 5960 (S Europe & W Africa), W M-Sa 7215 (Australasia), S 7485 (Europe), S 9590 (Australasia), W M-Sa 9590 (Europe & Africa), S 13805 (W Africa), S 15220 (C Africa & S Africa)
2000-2030	S 7305/7315 (Australasia), S 7485 (Europe), W 9590 (Europe, W Africa & N America)
2100-2130	S 7135 (Australasia), S 7305/7315 (E Asia), 9590 (Atlantic & N America), W 9600 (S America)
2200-2230	W 5905/6120 (S America), S 9480/9490 (E Asia), S 9485 (E North Am), W 9590 (S America), S 9635 (Australasia)
2300-2330	W 6030/6120 (SE Asia), W 6060 (S America), 7275 (SE Asia & Australasia), S 7445 (S America), S 9485 (E North Am)

OMAN—Arabic
RADIO OMAN
0200-0400	6085 (E Africa), 6120 (Mideast), 7230 (Mideast & N Africa)
0200-0600	S 7270 (Mideast)
0400-0800	9735 (Mideast)
0800-1400	15375 (Mideast)
0800-1600	11890 (Mideast)
1000-2145	7230 (Mideast & N Africa)
1500-2145	7170 (Mideast)
1600-1800	W 6085 (Mideast)
1600-2145	9735 (Mideast)
1800-2145	6085 (Mideast)
2145-2400	➡ 6085 (Irr) (Mideast), 7230 (Irr) (Mideast & N Africa), 9735 (Irr) (Mideast)

PARAGUAY—Spanish
RADIO ENCARNACION
0700-0300	➡ 11939

RADIO NACIONAL
0700-1700	➡ 9735 (S America & E North Am)
1700-2000	➡ 9735 (Irr) (S America)
2000-0300	9735 (S America & E North Am)

PERU—Spanish
RADIO CORA
0930-1030	M-Sa 4915
1030-1500 &	
2300-0500	4915

RADIO UNION
1100-1200	M-Sa 6115
1200-1000	6115

POLAND—Polish
POLISH RADIO
0630-0755	⬅ 5995 (W Europe), 6035 (E Europe), 6095 (W Europe), 7285 (E Europe)
1630-1725	⬅ 6035/7145 & 6135 (W Europe)
2200-2255	⬅ 6135 (E Europe)

PORTUGAL—Portuguese
RDP INTERNATIONAL

0000-0230 ⬅ 6175/9705 (N America), 9570 (E North Am), 9635 (C America & S America), 11840 (S America)

0015-0230 ⬅ 9555 (S America)

0230-0300 ⬅ Su/M 6175/9705 (N America), Su/M 9555 (S America), Su/M 9570 (E North Am), Su/M 11840 (S America)

0500-0700 ⬅ M-F 6130 (Europe)

0600-0700 ⬅ M-F 9780 (Europe)

0645-0800 ⬅ M-F 9630 (Europe)

0700-0900 ⬅ Sa/Su 17595 (SE Asia)

0700-1000 ⬅ Sa/Su 17685 (E Africa & S Africa), Sa/Su 21655 (W Africa & S America)

0700-1300 ⬅ 6130 & 9780 (Europe)

0800-0930 ⬅ Sa/Su 9615 (Europe)

1000-1100 ⬅ M-F 17595 (SE Asia)

1000-1200 ⬅ 17685 (E Africa & S Africa), 21655 (W Africa & S America), M-F 21720 (E Africa & S Africa)

1200-1600 ⬅ Sa/Su 21655 (W Africa & S America)

1200-1700 ⬅ Sa/Su 17685 (E Africa & S Africa)

1200-2000 ⬅ Sa/Su 15200 (E North Am), Sa/Su 17745 (C America)

1300-1430 ⬅ M-F 21515 (Mideast & S Asia)

1300-1700 ⬅ Sa/Su 6130 & Sa/Su 9780 (Europe)

1500-1800 ⬅ Sa/Su 21515 (Mideast & S Asia)

1700-1800 ⬅ Sa/Su 17685 (Irr) (E Africa & S Africa)

1700-2000 ⬅ 6130, 9780 & M-F 9815 (Europe), 15515 (E Africa & S Africa), 21655 (W Africa & S America)

2000-2200 ⬅ 9780 (Irr) (Europe), 21655 (Irr) (W Africa & S America)

2200-2400 6175/9705 (N America), 9570 (E North Am), 9600 (S America), 9635 (C America & S America), 11840 (S America)

QATAR—Arabic
QATAR BROADCASTING SERVICE
0245-0708 [W] 7170 & [S] 11785 (Mideast & N Africa)

0715-1308 [W] 11820 & [S] 15345 (Mideast & N Africa)

1315-1708 [W] 11750/9535 & [S] 15345 (Europe)

1715-2130 [W] 7170 & [S] 11785 (Europe)

ROMANIA—Romanian
RADIO ROMANIA
0500-0800 9570 & [W] 11970 (Europe)

0600-0800 [S] 11940 (Europe)

0800-1500 15105 (Europe, N Africa & Mideast), [W] 17850 (Europe)

0800-1700 [S] 11790 (Europe)

RADIO ROMANIA INTERNATIONAL
0130-0200 5990 (E North Am), 6155, 9510, 9570 & 11940 (N America)

0600-0614 [S] 9550, 9665, [W] 11775 & [S] 11810 (Europe)

0715-0815 Su 15335 (S Asia & SE Asia), Su 15370 & Su 17790 (Mideast & S Asia)

0815-0915 Su 15335 (W Africa), Su 15380 & [S] Su 17720 (S Africa), Su 17790 (W Africa)

0915-1015 Su 9570 (Europe), Su 9590 & Su 9665 (W Europe), [S] Su 11775 & [S] Su 11810 (Europe & Atlantic), [W] Su 11940 (Europe), [S] Su 11970 (Europe & Atlantic)

1300-1330 [S] 9510, [S] 11775, [W] 15335 & [W] 17790 (Australasia)

1630-1700 [W] 7105, [W] 7195, [S] 9510, [W] 9665 & [S] 11775 (Mideast)

1730-1800 [W] 5990, [W] 7195, [S] 9510, [W] 9690 & [S] 11830 (Europe), [S] 11840 (N Europe)

2000-2030 [W] 6080 & [W] 7175 (Europe), [S] 9510 & [S] 11790 (W Europe)

2230-2300 9570, [W] 9580, [S] 11775 & [S] 11830 (S America)

2300-2400 [W] 5990 (C America), [W] 7175 (Australasia), 9570 (E North Am), 9750/9550 & [S] 11810 (Australasia), [S] 11830 & 11940 (N America)

RUSSIA—Russian
GOLOS ROSSII
0100-0200 [S] 11830, [S] 13605 (W North Am), [S] 15350 (Mideast), [S] 15435

0100-0300 [S] 15545 (Australasia), [S] 21845 (S Asia & SE Asia)

0100-0400 [S] 9830 (S America)

0100-0500 [S] 9720 (E North Am), [S] 11900 (S America), [S] 12005 (Mideast & E Africa), [S] 12055 (Mideast), [S] 12065 (S Asia & SE Asia)

0100-0700 [S] 11660 (W North Am), [S] 11850 (Europe & S America), [S] 12000 & [S] 15455 (W North Am), [S] 17580 (S Asia & E Africa)

0200-0300 [W] 15160 (E Asia)

0200-0400 [W] 12000 (W North Am), [W] 21635 (S Asia & SE Asia), [W] 21750 (Australasia)

0200-0500 13605 & [W] 17700 (W North Am)

0200-0600 [W] 7125 (N Europe & W Europe), [W] 9650 (W Africa & S America), [W] 9715 (Mideast & W Asia), [W] 9835 (W Asia & S Asia), [W] 15220 (S Asia)

0200-0800 [W] 7350, [W] 9710 (W Africa & S America)

0300-0700 [S] 9630 (Europe & W Africa), [S] 11890 (Mideast), [S] 11930 (N Africa & W Africa), [S] 12015 (E Africa), [S] 15110 (Mideast & E Africa)

0400-0700 [S] 9450 (Europe), [W] 12025 (E Africa)

0400-0800 [W] 9820 (N Africa & W Africa), [W] 11810 (Mideast & E Africa)

0430-0700 [S] 11690 (Europe)

0430-0800 [W] 9580 (Europe)

0500-0700 [S] 13605 (W North Am)

0500-0800 [W] 7440 (Europe), [W] 9800 (E Africa)

0530-0700 [S] 13680 (W Europe & Atlantic)

0530-0800 [W] 7300 (W North Am)

0600-0800 [W] 7250 (N Europe)

0630-0800 [W] 13650 (W Europe & Atlantic)

1000-1100 [S] 17620 (S Asia & SE Asia)

1000-1200 [S] 11915 (E Asia), [S] 15435

1000-1300 [S] 15395 (W Asia & S Asia), [S] 17840 (Mideast & N Africa)

1000-1400 [S] 9565 & [S] 11675 (E Asia), [S] 13680 (W Europe & Atlantic), [S] 15475 (Europe, Atlantic & S America), [S] 15550 (S Asia & SE Asia), [S] 17745 (Europe & W Africa)

1000-1500 [S] 12035 & [S] 13625 (E Asia)

1000-1600 [S] 11730 (E Asia), [S] 15140 (S Asia,

SE Asia & Australasia), **S** 15220 (S Asia & SE Asia)

1000-1700	**S** 9540, **S** *21845* (S Asia & SE Asia)
1000-1800	**S** *15430* (W Europe & E North Am)
1100-1200	**S** 6080 (E Asia), **S** 15500 (W Asia & S Asia), **W** *17725* (C Africa & S Africa)
1100-1300	**W** 15200 (S Asia), **W** 17795 (S Asia & SE Asia)
1100-1400	**W** 7170 (E Asia & SE Asia), **W** 9895 (E Asia), **W** 15220 (S Asia), **W** 15305 (Europe & Atlantic)
1100-1500	**S** 5905, **W** 9625 (E Asia & Australasia), **W** 13650 (W Europe & Atlantic), **W** 17680 (W Africa & S America)
1100-1600	**W** 4810 & **W** 9845 (E Asia), **W** *17670* (Europe)
1100-1800	**W** 9780 (Australasia)
1100-2300	**W** 7245 (SE Asia)
1200-1300	**S** 15525 (Mideast & W Asia), **W** 17860 (S Asia, SE Asia & Australasia)
1200-1400	**S** 11685 (E Asia)
1230-1500	**W** 17605
1230-1600	**S** 11860 (E Asia & SE Asia)
1230-1700	**S** 15450 (S Asia & SE Asia)
1300-1400	**S** 13650 (Europe & W Africa), **S** 13790, **S** 17885 (N Africa)
1300-1500	**S** *11765* (Mideast & N Africa), **W** 17530
1300-2300	**W** 7220 (E Asia & SE Asia)
1330-1700	**W** 11860 (S Asia & SE Asia)
1330-2300	**W** 7235 (E Africa)
1400-1500	**S** 11705 (Europe & Atlantic)
1400-2000	**S** *11900* (Mideast & W Africa)
1400-2200	**S** 9610 (W Europe), **S** 11725 (E Africa)
1430-1800	**W** *11820* (SE Asia), **S** 11975 (Mideast)
1430-1900	**S** 12060 (W North Am)
1430-2000	**S** 11685 (S Asia & E Africa)
1430-2100	**S** 12040 (Europe & Atlantic)
1430-2200	**W** 7310 (Europe), **S** 15465 (Europe & W Africa)
1500-1600	**S** 9480 (E Asia), **S** 15435
1500-1700	**S** 15190
1500-1900	**S** 9795 (W North Am)
1500-2200	**S** 11765 (Mideast & C Africa), **S** 11800 (N Africa & W Africa), **S** 11970 (W Africa), **S** 15130 (Mideast & E Africa)
1500-2300	**W** 9775 (Europe & W Africa)
1530-1900	**S** 11660 (W North Am)
1530-2300	**W** 6045 (Europe & Atlantic)
1600-1900	**W** 9600 (Europe & W Africa)
1600-2200	**W** 9800
1600-2300	9450 (Europe)
1600-2300	**W** 7440 (Europe), **W** 9560 (Mideast), **W** 9820 (N Africa & W Africa)
1630-2200	**S** 11850 (Europe & S America)
1700-2000	**S** 13605 (W North Am)
1700-2300	**W** *9765* (E North Am)
1800-2300	**W** 9730 (E Africa)
1830-2200	**S** *11840* (W Europe & E North Am), **S** 12045 (Mideast)
1900-2200	**S** 9685 (S Europe), **S** 11930 (Europe & W Africa)
1930-2300	**W** 7120 (Mideast & E Africa)

2000-2200	**S** 7255 (E Asia), **S** 7390 (W Europe & N Africa), **S** 9735, **S** 11755 (SE Asia), **S** 12035 (E Asia)
2000-2300	**W** 7160 (N Europe), **W** 9865
2100-2200	**S** 12005 (E Asia & SE Asia), **S** 13720 (S Asia)
2100-2300	**W** 7185 & **W** 12005 (E Asia & SE Asia)

MAYAK

0000-0200	**S** 7320
0000-0300	**S** 7400
0000-0400	**W** 9670
0000-0430	**S** 9875 (E Europe)
0000-2200	*4825*
24 Hr	4930
0100-0400	**S** 7440
0200-1300	9545
0330-0500	**S** 12060
0430-0630	**S** *9470*
0500-1030	12060
0500-1230	**S** 11985
0630-1130	**S** 9670
0930-1500	5970 USB
1000-1100	**S** 9765 (N Asia)
1030-1500	**W** 12060
1300-1600	7330
1300-1730	**S** 9885
1330-1800	**W** 3995
1430-1700	**W** 6040
1630-2400	**S** 7400
1700-1730	**S** Tu-Th/Sa/Su 7305 (Mideast & W Asia)
1730-1800	**S** Tu/Th/Sa 7305 (Mideast & W Asia)
1800-1830	**W** Tu-Th/Sa/Su 5935 (Mideast & W Asia)
1830-1900	**W** Tu/Th/Sa 5935 (Mideast & W Asia)
1900-2300	**S** 9885
2330-2400	**S** 7320

RADIO TIKHIY OKEAN

0715-0800	**S** 7185 (E Asia & N Pacific), **S** 9670, **S** 12040 (W North Am), **S** 12065 (E Asia & SE Asia), **S** 15435 (Australasia), **S** 15490 (E Asia & N Pacific), **S** 17805 (E Asia)
0815-0900	4050 & 5015 (E Asia), 6065 USB (N Pacific & W North Am), 7210, 10344 USB & 11840 (E Asia)
0815-0900	**W** 4810 (E Asia), **W** 5920 (N Pacific & W North Am), **W** 7175 (W North Am), 9530 (N Pacific), **W** 17560 (SE Asia), **W** 17570 (Australasia)
1215-1300	5015 (E Asia)
1800-1845	**S** 5960 & **S** 7240 (E Asia & N Pacific), **S** 9510 (E Asia), **S** 9735 (E Asia & SE Asia), **S** 11655 (E Asia & Australasia), **S** 11860 (E Asia & SE Asia), **S** 15470 (N Pacific)
1900-1945	5015 (E Asia)
1900-1945	**W** 4810 (E Asia), **W** 7135 & **W** 7185 (E Asia & SE Asia), **W** 7195 (SE Asia), **W** 7420 (E Asia & Australasia), **W** 9850 (N Pacific), **W** 12015 (Australasia)

RADIO PAMYAT

1400-1600	**S** 12060
1500-1700	**W** 7380

RADIO ROSSII

0000-0100	**W** 5980 (N Europe & E Europe)
0000-0300	**S** 9525 (W Asia)

0000-0400	[W] 6090 (W Asia)
0000-2000	7145 (N Asia)
0100-0300	[S] 5995 (N Europe), [S] 6030 (Europe)
0100-0500	[S] 7390 (Europe), [S] 12175 USB
0100-0600	[S] 9845
0100-1300	[S] 11750 (W Asia)
0200-0500	[W] 5910 (Arctic), [S] 7305 & [W] 7325 (W Asia)
0200-0600	[W] 6110 (Europe), [W] 7970 USB
0200-0700	[W] 6805 USB, [W] 7265 (W Asia)
0200-1300	[W] 11990 (W Asia)
0330-1400	[S] 15330 (W Asia)
0330-1500	[S] 7105 (N Europe)
0430-0530	[S] 11720 (W Asia)
0430-1400	[W] 11905 (W Asia)
0500-1800	[S] 16300 USB
0530-1200	11720 (W Asia)
0530-1400	9720 (Europe)
0530-1500	[W] 7250 (N Europe)
0630-0730	[S] 12045 (E Europe & W Asia)
0700-1400	[W] 12175 USB, 18870 USB
0700-1500	18870 USB (W Africa & Atlantic)
0730-1400	12045 (E Europe & W Asia)
0800-1900	7345
0930-1030	[W] 7120
1200-1500	[S] 11720 (W Asia)
1230-1600	[W] 7145 (W Asia)
1330-2300	[S] 7355
1330-2400	[W] 6125 (W Asia)
1400-1500	[W] 9720 (Europe)
1400-1900	[W] 8005 USB
1430-1800	[W] 7390
1430-2000	[W] 7340 (E Europe & Mideast), [S] 9840 (E Europe & W Asia)
1430-2100	[S] 9525 (W Asia)
1430-2200	[W] 5995 (W Asia)
1430-2300	[S] 6030 (Europe)
1500-1800	[W] 5920
1500-1900	[W] 11575 USB
1530-2300	[S] 5995 (N Europe), [S] 9560 (Europe)
1530-2400	[W] 5910 (Arctic), [W] 6060 (Europe)
1630-2400	[W] 5980 (N Europe & E Europe)
1822-2300	[S] 12175 USB
1900-2400	[W] 6805 USB, [W] 7970 USB
2030-2300	[S] 9845
2030-2400	[W] 7335 (E Europe & W Asia)
2100-1600	⬅ 4395
2200-2400	7145 (N Asia)
2300-2400	[S] 9525 (W Asia)

SAUDI ARABIA—Arabic
BROADCASTING SERVICE OF THE KINGDOM

0300-0600	9555 (Mideast), 9720 (W Asia), 9885 (N Africa), 11740/11935 & 17745/17895 (C Asia)
0300-1700	9580 (Mideast & E Africa)
0300-2100	10990 (Irr) ISL & 10990 (Irr) ISU (Mideast)
0600-0900	11710 (N Africa), 11950 (W Asia)
0600-1200	11820 (Mideast)
0900-1200	17880 (S Asia & SE Asia), 21495 (E Asia & SE Asia)
0900-1500	15060 (N Africa)
1200-1500	15175 (W Europe), 15380 (W Asia)
1200-1600	15165 (N Africa), 15280 (Mideast)
1500-1800	11780 (N Africa), 11910/11965 (W Europe), 11950 (W Asia)
1600-1800	9730 (C Africa), 11710 (N Africa),

	11835 (Mideast)
1700-2100	6020 (Mideast & E Africa)
1800-2100	9705 (W Asia), 11935 (N Africa)
1800-2300	9555 (N Africa); 9870 (W Europe)

SINGAPORE—Chinese
RADIO SINGAPORE INTERNATIONAL—(SE Asia)

1100-1400	9590

RADIO CORPORATION OF SINGAPORE

2200-1600	6000

SLOVAKIA—Slovak
RADIO SLOVAKIA INTERNATIONAL

0130-0200	5930 (E North Am & C America), 7300 (E North Am), 9440 (S America)
0900-0930	11990, 15640 & 17485 (Australasia)
1630-1730	[S] 9485 (W Europe)
1730-1830	5915 & 6055 (W Europe)
1730-1830	[W] 7150 (W Europe)
2000-2030	5915, 6055 & 7345 (W Europe)

SPAIN—Spanish
RADIO EXTERIOR DE ESPANA

0000-0100	Su/M *5970* (C America), Su/M *11815* (N America), Su/M *17870* (S America)
0000-0200	11945 (S America)
0000-0500	6055 (N America & C America), 6125 & 9620 (S America)
0100-0400	Tu-Su *5970* (C America), Tu-Su *9630* (N America), Tu-Su *11815* (S America)
0200-0500	9540 (N America & C America)
0500-0700	9650 (Australasia), 9685 (Europe), 9760 (Australasia), 11890 (Mideast), 11920 (Europe)
0600-0910	12035 (Europe)
0900-0910	17715 (S America)
0900-1200	Su 9620 (W Europe)
0900-1700	15110 (Mideast), 17755 (W Africa & S Africa)
0910-0940	Su-F *12035* (Europe), Su-F *17715* (S America)
0940-1515	12035 (Europe)
0940-1900	17715 (S America)
1000-1200	*9620* (E Asia)
1100-1400	M-F *5970* (C America), M-F *9630* (N America), M-F *11815* (S America)
1200-1400	[W] *4130* (E Asia), *11910* (SE Asia)
1200-1515	9620 (W Europe)
1200-1800	17845 (C America & S America)
1300-1800	Sa/Su *11815* (N America)
1400-1800	Sa/Su *5970* (C America), Sa/Su *17870* (S America)
1515-1600	Sa/Su 9620 (W Europe), Sa/Su 12035 (Europe)
1600-1700	9620 (W Europe)
1600-1900	12035 (Europe)
1700-1900	[W] 11890 & [S] 17755 (W Africa & S Africa)
1700-2000	Sa/Su 9620 (W Europe)
1800-2000	[W] Sa/Su 9745 & [S] Sa/Su 17845 (C America & S America)
1800-2235	*5970* (C America), *11815* (N America), *17870* (S America)
1900-2235	7275 (Europe), [W] 11880 & [S] 15110 (E North Am & C America)
2000-2100	Sa 9620 (W Europe), [W] Sa 9745 & [S] Sa 17845 (C America & S America)
2200-2235	6125 (S America)

2200-2300	6130/9580 (Mideast), 9875 (N Africa & W Africa)
2235-2255	Su *5970* (C America), Su 6125 (S America), Su *11815* (N America), [W] Su 11880 & [S] Su 15110 (E North Am & C America), Su *17870* (S America)
2235-2300	Su 7275 (Europe)
2255-2400	*5970* (C America), 6125 (S America), *11815* (N America), [W] 11880 & [S] 15110 (E North Am & C America), *17870* (S America)
2300-2400	9620 & 11945 (S America)

SUDAN—Arabic
REPUBLIC OF SUDAN RADIO

0300-0830	7200
0300-1015	9200
1200-2300	7200
1600-2300	4994
1900-2300	9200

SWEDEN—Swedish
RADIO SWEDEN

0000-0030	6065, [W] 6200 & [S] 9810 (S America)
0100-0130	9695/9895 (SE Asia & Australasia), [W] 11695 (S Asia)
0200-0230	[W] 6195 (E North Am & C America), 7120 & [S] 9850 (N America)
0300-0330	[W] 6200 (E North Am & C America), 7120 & [S] 9850 (N America)
0400-0615	[S] M-F 9730 (Europe & N Africa)
0500-0715	M-F 6065 (Europe)
0500-0715	[W] M-F 9860 (Europe & N Africa)
0600-0800	[S] Sa 13625 (Africa)
0700-0900	Sa 6065 (Europe)
0700-0900	[W] Sa 9860 (Europe & N Africa), [S] Su 13625 & [W] Sa 15390 (Africa)
0800-1000	Su 6065 (Europe)
0800-1000	[W] Su 9860 (Europe & N Africa), [W] Su 15390 (Africa)
1030-1100	[S] 15230 (Europe & N Africa)
1100-1130	Sa/Su 6065 (Europe)
1100-1130	[S] 13740 (E Asia & Australasia), [W] 13775 (SE Asia & Australasia), 15120 (E Asia & Australasia), [S] 15240 (S Asia)
1130-1200	6065 (Europe), 11650 (E North Am)
1130-1200	[W] 9860 (Europe & N Africa)
1200-1230	[S] 13740, [W] 13775 & 15120 (E Asia & Australasia), 15240 (S Asia)
1300-1330	[W] 13775 (E Asia & Australasia), [W] 15120 (E Asia), [W] 15240 (S Asia)
1400-1430	[S] 15240 (E North Am)
1500-1530	11650 (N America)
1500-1530	[W] 15240 (E North Am)
1545-1600	6000 (E Europe), 6065 (Europe), 11650 (N America)
1545-1600	[S] 13765 (Mideast)
1545-1605	[S] 11650 (Europe & Africa)
1600-1645	Sa/Su 6065 (Europe)
1605-1615	[S] M-F 11650 (Europe & Africa), [S] M-F 13765 (Mideast)
1645-1705	6065 (Europe)
1645-1705	[W] 9670 (Europe & Africa), [W] 13700 (Mideast)
1705-1715	M-F 6065 (Europe)
1705-1715	[W] M-F 9670 (Europe & Africa), [W] M-F 13700 (Mideast)

1800-1830	[S] 15600 (Europe & Africa)
1900-1930	6065 (Europe & Mideast), 13690/13605 (Mideast)
1900-1930	[W] 9655 (Europe & N Africa)
1930-2000	[W] M-F 9655 (Europe & N Africa)
2000-2030	[←] M-F 6065 (Europe)
2100-2130	[←] 6065 (Europe & Mideast), 9655 (Europe & Africa)
2200-2230	6065 (Europe), 9655 (Europe & Africa)

SWITZERLAND
SWISS RADIO INTERNATIONAL
French

0200-0230	*5885/5888* (C America & W North Am), 6135 & 9885 (E North Am & C America), *9905* (N America & C America)
0430-0500	[←] 6135 (W North Am), 9885 (N America)
0500-0545 &	
0630-0645	6165 (Europe & N Africa), 9535 (S Europe & E Europe)
0630-0700	[←] 9885 (W Africa), 13635 (N Africa & W Africa), 15340 (C Africa & S Africa)
0730-0800	[←] 6165 (Europe & N Africa), 9535 (S Europe & E Europe)
0800-1100	6165 (Europe & N Africa)
0930-1000	*9885*, 13685 & 17515 (Australasia)
1130-1200	[W] 9885 & [W] 11640 (E Asia), 13635 (E Asia & SE Asia), [S] 15545 & [S] 17515 (E Asia)
1230-1300	6165 (Europe & N Africa), 9535 (S Europe & W Europe)
1330-1400	*7230/7250* (SE Asia), *7480* (E Asia), [W] 11640, 13635 & [S] 15545/15460 (SE Asia)
1530-1600	[W] 9885 & 12075 (C Asia & S Asia), 13635 (W Asia & S Asia), [S] 15545/15490 (C Asia & S Asia)
1830-1845	[W] 6205 & 9885 (Mideast), [S] 9905 (N Europe), [S] 12075 (Mideast), 13635 (E Africa)
1930-1945	[W] 3985 (N Europe)
1930-2000	6165 (Europe & N Africa)
2030-2100	*9770* (S Africa), 9885 (C Africa & S Africa), [S] 11640 (E Africa), [W] 11640 & [S] 13635 (S Africa), [W] 13635 (E Africa)
2215-2230	[W] 6205 (S America), 9885 (C America & S America), [S] 9905 & *11650* (S America)

German

0030-0100	*5885/5888* (C America & W North Am), 6135 & 9885 (E North Am & C America), *9905* (N America & C America)
0330-0400	6135 (W North Am), 9885 (N America), *9905* (N America & C America)
0615-0630	6165 (Europe & N Africa), 9535 (S Europe & E Europe)
0730-0800	9885 (W Africa), 13635 (N Africa & W Africa), 15340 (C Africa & S Africa)
1000-1030	*9885*, 13685 & 17515 (Australasia)
1130-1200	6165 (Europe & N Africa), 9535 (S Europe & W Europe)
1200-1230	[W] 9885 & [W] 11640 (E Asia), 13635 (E Asia & SE Asia), [S] 15545 & [S] 17515 (E Asia)
1430-1445	*7230/7250* (SE Asia), *7480* (E Asia),

[W] 11640, 13635 & [S] 15545/15460 (SE Asia)

1600-1630	6165 (Europe & N Africa)
1600-1630	[W] 9885 & 12075 (C Asia & S Asia), 13635 (W Asia & S Asia), [S] 15545/15490 (C Asia & S Asia)
1630-1645	[←] Sa/Su 6165 (Europe & N Africa)
1645-1900	6165 (Europe & N Africa)
1700-1800	[S] 9905 (N Europe)
1730-1800	[W] 6205, 9885 & [S] 12075 (Mideast), 13635 (E Africa)
1800-1900	[W] 3985 (N Europe)
2130-2200	9885 (C Africa & S Africa), [S] 11640 (E Africa), [W] 11640 & [S] 13635 (S Africa), [W] 13635 (E Africa)
2230-2300	[W] 6205 (S America), 9885 (C America & S America), [S] 9905 & *11650* (S America)

Italian

0300-0315	*5885/5888* (C America & W North Am), 6135 & 9885 (E North Am & C America), *9905* (N America & C America)
0500-0530	6135 (W North Am), 9885 (N America), *9905* (N America & C America)
0545-0600 &	
0645-0700	6165 (Europe & N Africa), 9535 (S Europe & E Europe)
0700-0730	9885 (W Africa), 13635 (N Africa & W Africa), 15340 (C Africa & S Africa)
0830-0900	*9885*, 13685 & 17515 (Australasia)
1230-1245	[W] 9885 & [W] 11640 (E Asia), 13635 (E Asia & SE Asia), [S] 15545 & [S] 17515 (E Asia)
1300-1330	6165 (Europe & N Africa), 9535 (S Europe & W Europe)
1400-1430	*7230/7250* (SE Asia), *7480* (E Asia), [W] 11640, 13635 & [S] 15545/15460 (SE Asia)
1400-1600	6165 (Europe & N Africa)
1630-1645	[W] 9885 & 12075 (C Asia & S Asia), 13635 (W Asia & S Asia), [S] 15545/15490 (C Asia & S Asia)
1800-1830	[W] 6205 & 9885 (Mideast), [S] 9905 (N Europe), [S] 12075 (Mideast), 13635 (E Africa)
1900-1930	6165 (Europe & N Africa)
1900-1930	[W] 3985 (N Europe)
2100-2130	9885 (C Africa & S Africa), [S] 11640 (E Africa), [W] 11640 & [S] 13635 (S Africa), [W] 13635 (E Africa)
2300-2330	[W] 6205 (S America), 9885 (C America & S America), [S] 9905 & *11650* (S America)

SYRIA—Arabic
RADIO DAMASCUS
0400-0600 &	
1700-1900	9995 (Mideast)
2215-2315	12085 & 15095 (S America)

SYRIAN BROADCASTING SERVICE
| 0315-0600 | 9950/9955 |
| 0600-1700 | 12085, 15095 |

THAILAND—Thai
RADIO THAILAND
| 0100-0200 | 9655 & 11905 (Asia), [S] 15370 (N America) |

0330-0430	9655 (Asia), [W] 11890 (W North Am), 11905 (Asia), [S] 15370 (W North Am)
1330-1400	[W] 7145 (E Asia), 9655 & 11905 (Asia), [S] 11955 (E Asia)
1800-1900	9655 (Asia), [S] 9690 & [W] 11855 (Mideast), 11905 (Asia)
2045-2115	9655 (Asia), [S] 9755 & [W] 11835 (Europe), 11905 (Asia)

TUNISIA—Arabic
RTV TUNISIENNE
0400-0600	7475 (Europe), 12006 (N Africa & Mideast)
0500-1700	15450 (N Africa & Mideast)
0600-1700	11730 (Europe), 17500 (N Africa & Mideast)
1700-2330	7280 (N Africa & Mideast), 7475 (Europe), 12006 (N Africa & Mideast)

TURKEY—Turkish
VOICE OF TURKEY
0000-0400	[←] 9445 (Europe & E North Am), 9560 (Australasia), 11710 (Europe)
0400-0600	[←] 6140 (E Europe)
0500-1000	[←] 9460 (Europe & E North Am), 11925 & 15145 (W Asia), 15385 (Europe)
1000-1700	[←] 15350 (Europe)
1000-2400	[←] 9460 (Europe)
1100-1600	[←] 11955 (Mideast), F 15430 (N Africa)
1700-2300	[←] 9685 (Europe), 11945 (N Africa)
1800-2200	5980 (E Europe)

UKRAINE—Ukrainian
RADIO UKRAINE
0000-0200	[S] 6090 (W Asia)
0000-0300	[S] 9560 (N Africa), [S] 11875 (S Africa)
0000-0330	[S] 5960 (W Asia), [S] 7240 (Europe & N Africa), [S] 7285 (W Asia)
0000-0700	[W] 9610 (Europe)
0100-0200	[S] 9750 (S America)
0100-0300	6020 (N Europe)
0100-0300	[S] 6010 (N Africa), [W] 7240 (W Europe), [S] 7405 (N Europe)
0100-0700	[W] 4820 & [W] 5915 (Europe)
0130-0300	[S] 9685 (W Europe & E North Am)
0200-0330	[W] 9620 (W Africa & S America)
0200-0400	[W] 4780 (N Europe), [W] 7405 (Europe), [W] 9810 (W Europe & E North Am), [W] 11870 (W Africa & S America)
0200-0500	[S] 6020 (E Europe)
0230-0300	[S] 9835 (C America), [S] 9860 (W Europe & E North Am)
0230-1030	[S] 11590 (Europe)
0300-0330	[W] 6020 (N Europe)
0300-1700	[S] 9640 (W Asia)
0330-0730	[S] 13720 (N Africa)
0330-1500	[S] 11825 (W Asia)
0330-1700	[S] 11980 (W Asia)
0400-0730	[S] 9835 (C America)
0400-0800	[S] 21800 (S Africa)
0400-0900	[S] 11705 (W Europe)
0400-1000	[S] 9685 & [S] 9860 (W Europe & E North Am)
0400-1700	[S] 7405 (N Europe), [S] 13690 (W Europe)
0500-0700	[W] 4780 & [W] 6055 (N Europe), [W] 7405 (Europe), [W] 9810 (W Europe & E North Am)
0500-0900	[W] 11870 (W Africa & S America)

0500-1100	[S]9620 (S Europe)
0500-1200	6020 (E Europe)
0530-0830	[W]6010 (W Europe)
0600-1130	[S]11720 (Europe)
0730-1700	13720 (N Africa)
0800-1130	[S]17655
0800-1600	[W]13600 (W Europe & E North Am)
0800-1700	[W]7240 (Europe & N Africa)
0800-1800	[W]12030 (N Europe & W Europe)
0830-1500	[W]15525 (Europe)
0900-1700	11705 (W Europe), [W]13680 (W Asia), [S]21800 (S America), [W]21800 (C Africa & S Africa)
1000-1800	[W]7290 (S Europe & W Africa)
1030-1700	[S]15135 & [S]15265 (W Europe & E North Am)
1130-1630	[S]9620 (W Asia)
1300-1700	6020 (E Europe)
1400-1700	[S]15550
1500-1530	[S]7205 (N Africa)
1600-1700	[S]4920 & [S]11840 (Europe), [S]15380 (E North Am)
1600-1800	[W]4820 (Europe), [W]9610 (W Europe & E North Am)
1700-1800	[W]4780 (N Europe), [W]6020 (E Europe), [W]9640 (W Asia), [W]11705 (W Europe), [W]13720 (N Africa)
1800-1830	[S]11980 (W Asia), [S]13690 (W Europe)
1800-1900	[S]7405 (N Europe), [S]9640 (W Asia), [S]11705 (W Europe), [S]13720 (N Africa), [S]15550
1800-2000	[S]4920 (Europe), [S]6010 (N Africa), [S]6130 & [S]15135 & [S]15265 (W Europe & E North Am)
1900-2000	[S]5905 (Europe), [S]6090 (W Asia), [S]11840 (Europe), [S]11875 (S Africa), 13720 (N Africa)
1900-2100	[W]4780 (N Europe), [W]4820 (Europe), [W]6020 (N Europe), [W]6130 (Europe & N Africa), [W]7240 (W Europe), [W]7290 (S Europe & W Africa), [W]9610 (Europe), [W]9640 (W Asia), [W]9810 (W Europe & E North Am)
1930-2000	[S]11780 & [S]11950 (W Europe & E North Am)
2000-2100	[W]5940 & [W]7405 (Europe), [W]13720 (N Africa)
2200-2300	[S]4825 (N Europe), [S]6010 (N Africa), [S]6090 (W Asia), [S]7240 (Europe & N Africa), [S]7285 (W Asia), [S]9560 (N Africa), [S]9750 (S America), [S]11780 (W Europe & E North Am), [S]11875 (S Africa), [S]11950 (W Europe & E North Am)
2300-2400	6020 (N Europe)
2300-2400	[W]4780 (N Europe), [W]4820 & [W]5940 (Europe), [W]7240 (W Europe), [W]7405 & [W]9610 (Europe), [W]9620 (W Africa & S America), [W]9810 (W Europe & E North Am), [W]11870 (W Africa & S America)
2330-2400	[W]5915 (Europe)

UNITED ARAB EMIRATES—Arabic
UAE RADIO FROM ABU DHABI

0000-0200	[W]7215 & [S]9770 (E North Am), 9770 (Irr) (Europe), [S]11885, [S]13605, [S]
	15305 & [S]15315 (E North Am)
0200-0400	[W]6180 & [S]7215 (N Africa & Mideast)
0200-0630	9695 (Mideast & S Asia)
0300-0500	[S]11885 (N Africa & Mideast)
0300-0600	[S]11710 (N Africa & Mideast)
0400-0600	7215 & [W]9770 (N Africa & Mideast)
0600-0800	[W]13605 (Europe)
0600-0900	17855 & 21735 (Europe)
0900-1200	21735 (E Asia)
0900-1300	17855 (E Asia), 21570/21630 (Europe)
1000-1100	[W]21510 (E Asia)
1100-1200	[W]15315 (E Asia)
1100-1300	[W]13605 (E Asia)
1300-1600	[S]17645 (E Asia)
1300-1700	17855 (Europe)
1500-1700	[S]9770 (N Africa & Mideast)
1500-1900	[S]13605 (N Africa & Mideast)
1600-1800	[S]21735 (Europe)
1600-1900	[S]15315 (Europe)
1600-2000	9695 (Mideast & S Asia)
1600-2130	[W]6180 (N Africa & Mideast), 11970 (Europe)
1700-1800	[S]17855 (Europe)
1700-1900	[S]7215 (N Africa & Mideast)
1700-2130	[S]11885 (N Africa)
1800-2125	[W]9770 (Europe)
2000-2130	[W]7215 (N Africa & Mideast)
2125-2400	9770 (Irr) (Europe)

UAE RADIO IN DUBAI

0230-0330	11945 & 13675 (E North Am & C America), 15400 & 17890 (E North Am)
0400-0500	[W]15265 (Mideast)
0415-0530	15435 (Australasia), 17830 (E Asia) & 21700 (Australasia)
0600-1030	15395 (Europe)
0615-1030	13675 & 21605 (Europe)
1110-1330	13675 & 15395 (Europe), 17825/15320 (N Africa), 21605 (Europe)
1400-1600	13675 & 15395 (Europe), 17835/15320 (N Africa), 21605 (Europe)
1640-2100	11795, 13675 & 15395 (Europe), 17825/15320 (N Africa)
2050-2400	13675 (Irr) (Europe)

UNITED KINGDOM
BBC WORLD SERVICE
Arabic

0330-0445	11740 (Mideast)
0330-0600	7140 (Mideast & E Africa), 9760, [W]9825 & 15235 (Mideast)
0445-0600	[W]6110, 7325 & 9825 (N Africa)
0645-0715	7150 & [S]13660 (N Africa)
1225-1255	[W]M-F 11730 (Mideast), M-Sa 13660 & M-Sa 15180 (N Africa)
1225-1630	7140 (Mideast & E Africa), [W]7325 (Mideast), [S]17715 (N Africa & W Africa)
1255-1630	[W]11730 & [S]15590 (Mideast)
1255-1800	13660 & 15180 (N Africa)
1630-2100	11730 (N Africa & Mideast)
1630-2115	6030, [S]6030 & 7140 (Mideast)
1800-2100	[W]11680, [S]13660 & [S]15180 (N Africa)
1800-2115	[W]6110 (N Africa)

Persian

0230-0330	[W]6095, [W]7135, [W]9585 & [S]9595 (W Asia)

0230-0530	**S** 7235 (W Asia)
0945-1200	Th/F *15590* (W Asia)
1615-1715	7160 (W Asia)
1830-1900	⬅ *5975 & 9915* (W Asia)

USA—Creole

WRMI-RADIO MIAMI INTERNACIONAL—(C Amer)

| 2200-2400 | M-F 9955 |

VENEZUELA—Spanish

ECOS DEL TORBES

| 0850-0400 | 4980 |
| 1300-1900 | 9640 |

RADIO RUMBOS

0000-0400 &	
1000-1400	4970, 9659
1400-2100	Sa/Su 4970, Sa/Su 9659
2100-2400	4970, 9659

RADIO TACHIRA

0130-0400	4830 (Irr)
1000-1300 &	
2000-0130	4830

VIETNAM—Vietnamese

VOICE OF VIETNAM

| 0000-0100 | 9840 & **S** 15009 (E Asia & Americas) |

0000-1700	12035
0300-0900	4960, 5924, 10059, **W** 12020
0700-0800	**S** *12010* (W North Am)
0800-0900	**S** *7270* (W North Am)
1100-1600	4960, 5924, 10059
1700-1800	9840, **W** 12020 & **S** 15009 (Europe)
2100-2300	4960, 5924, 10059
2200-2400	12035

YUGOSLAVIA—Serbian

RADIO YUGOSLAVIA

0030-0100	**W** 6195/7115, **S** 9580 & **S** 11870 (E North Am)
0130-0200	**W** 6195/7115 (E North Am)
1800-1900	6100 (E Europe)
1930-2000	**S** M-F 7230 (Australasia)
2030-2100	M-F 6100 (W Europe)
2030-2100	**W** M-F 9595 (Australasia)
2330-2400	**S** 9580 & **S** 11870 (E North Am)

RTV SRBIJE—(Europe, N Africa & Mideast)

| 0600-2308 | ⬅ 7200 |

Jin Meifen, of China Radio International's English Service, on assignment in New Delhi.

ADDRESSES PLUS—1996

Station Addresses...PLUS Local Times in Each Country, Station Personnel, Phone and Fax Numbers, E-mail, Gifts, Items for Sale, News Bureaus and Future Plans.

*L*etters, faxes and e-mail are a station's prized links with listeners. Most are eager to hear from you—and sometimes be generous in return.

"Applause" Correspondence Welcomed (Boos, too)

When radio was in its infancy, stations were anxious for feedback on how well their signals were being received. Listeners sent in "applause" cards not only to let stations know about reception quality, but also how much their shows were—or were not—being appreciated. By way of saying "thanks," stations would reply with a letter or attractive card verifying ("QSLing" in radio lingo) that the station the listener reported hearing was, in fact, theirs.

A number of broadcasters still seek out information on reception quality, but most are chiefly interested in knowing whether you like their programs. Polling organizations let local broadcasters know exactly how they are faring, but this is rarely feasible with world band. So with listeners scattered throughout the world, most stations can't know how well they're doing—unless they hear from you.

Uncommon Freebies

How? For starters, nearly all stations give away program schedules. But some go further. They hand out free souvenirs: colorful pennants, stickers, brochures on local history, exotic calendars, offbeat periodicals, language-learning aids, attractive verification postcards, lapel pins and key chains.

Electronic Bazaar

You can buy stuff, too. Besides the obvious, such as world band radios, various stations peddle native recordings, books, magazines, station T-shirts, ties, tote bags, aprons, caps, watches, clocks, pens, knives, letter openers, lighters, refrigerator magnets, keyrings and other collectables. One Honduran station will even sell you airtime for a buck a minute!

Travel Tips Not in Your Baedeker

Here's a little-known secret: World band stations will sometimes provide helpful information to adventurous would-be visitors. When writing, especially to smaller stations, appeal to their civic pride and treat them like kindly aunts or uncles you're seeking a favor from. After all, they don't *have* to help you.

Paying the Postman

Most major stations that reply do so for free. Yet, smaller organizations often expect, or at least hope for, reimbursement for postage costs. Most effective, especially for Latin American and Indonesian stations, is to enclose return postage; that is, unused (mint) stamps from the *station's* country. These are available from the long-established Plum's Airmail Postage, 12 Glenn Road, Flemington NJ 08822 USA, phone +1 (908) 788-1020, fax +1 (908) 782-2612 (minimum VISA/MC/AX/Discover order $15, but no minimum order by check; also, sells lightweight airmail envelopes and special QSL-card albums). Too, you can try DX Stamp Service, 7661 Roder Parkway, Ontario NY 14519 USA (send $1 or SASE for details); or DX-QSL Associates, 434 Blair Road NW, Vienna VA 22180 USA (ditto); and some local private stamp dealers. Unused Brazilian international reply stamps are also available (one stamp $1 or 6 IRCs) from Antonio Ribeiro da Motta, Caixa Postal 949, 12201-970 São José dos Campos—SP, Brazil.

One way to help ensure your return postage will be used for your intended purpose is to affix it onto a pre-addressed return airmail envelope (self-addressed stamped envelope, or SASE). However, if the envelope is too small, the contents may have to be folded to fit in.

You can also prompt reluctant stations by donating one U.S. dollar, preferably hidden from prying eyes by a piece of foil-covered carbon paper or the like. Registration helps, too, as cash tends to get stolen. Additionally, International Reply Coupons (IRCs), which recipients may exchange locally for air or surface stamps, are available at many post offices worldwide. Thing is, they're relatively costly, are not all that effective, and aren't accepted by postal authorities in all countries.

Tips for Effective Correspondence

Write to be read. When writing, remember to make your letter interesting and helpful from the recipient's point of view, and friendly without being excessively personal or forward. Well-thought-out comments on specific programs are almost always appreciated. If you must use a foreign-language form letter as the basis for your communication, individualize it for each occasion either by writing or typing it out, or by making use of a word processor.

Incorporate language courtesies. Writing in the broadcaster's tongue is always a plus—this section of PASSPORT indicates when it is a requirement—but English is usually the next-best bet. In addition, when writing in any language to Spanish-speaking countries, remember that what gringos think of as the "last name" is actually written as the penultimate name. Thus Juan Antonio Vargas García, which can also be written as Juan Antonio Vargas G., refers to Sr. Vargas; so your salutation should read, *Estimado Sr. Vargas*.

What's that "García" doing there, then? That's *mamita's* father's family name. Latinos more or less solved the problem of gender fairness in names long before the Anglos.

But, wait—what about Portuguese, used by all those stations in Brazil?

Same concept, but in reverse. *Mamá's* father's family name is penultimate, and the "real" last name is where English-speakers are used to it, at the end.

In Chinese, the "last" name comes first. However, when writing in English, Chinese names are sometimes reversed for the benefit of *weiguoren*—foreigners. Use your judgement. For example, "Li" is a common Chinese last name, so if you see "Li Dan," it's "Mr. Li." But if it's "Dan Li," he's already one step ahead of you, and it's still "Mr. Li." Less widely known is that the same can also occur in Hungarian. For example, "Bartók Béla" for Béla Bartók.

If in doubt, fall back on the ever-safe "Dear Sir" or "Dear Madam." And be patient—replies usually take weeks, sometimes months. Slow responders, those that tend to take six months or more to reply, are cited in this section, as are erratic repliers.

Local Time Given for Each Country

Local times are given in terms of hours' difference from World Time, also known as Coordinated Universal Time (UTC), Greenwich Mean Time (GMT) and Zulu time (Z).

For example, Algeria is World Time +1; that is, one hour ahead of World Time. So, if World Time is 1200, the local time in Algeria is 1300 (1:00 PM). On the other hand, México City is World Time - 6; that is, six hours behind World Time. If World Time is 1200, in México City it's 6:00 AM. And so it goes for each country in this section. Times in (parentheses) are for the middle of the year—roughly April-October.

These nominal times are almost always the actual times, as well. Yet, there are a very few exceptions. For example, in China the actual time nationwide is World Time +8 ("Beijing Time"); yet, in one region, Xinjiang, it's officially +6 ("Urümqi Time"), even though nobody observes that time. These rare exceptions are explained in this section.

The times in this section are based on the *local-time* difference from World Time. This is handy, because once you have your World Time clock set, you can use it to determine the local time in any part of the world where you might be hearing a station. But if you want to figure out what World Time is, rather than use World Time to figure out some local time, you should add where it says subtract, and subtract where it says add. So, say you're in San Francisco, and want to know the World Time. Under "USA" you see that local time is -8 hours from World Time, so to find the opposite you would *add* eight hours to local time to get World Time.

Confusing? You bet, but with a World Time clock you only have to suffer through this once, then set your clock and forget it. (Even easier, just listen to the BBC World Service or some other major station. Most give World Time on the hour.) There's even more information on World Time in the Glossary and the "Compleat Idiot's Guide to Getting Started."

Spotted Something New?

PASSPORT folks, scattered about the globe, strive year-round to gather and prepare material to make this book more accurate. In addition to having unearthed and sifted through tens of thousands of items of data, they have made countless judgement calls based on years of specialized experience. Still, we don't uncover everything, we don't always call it right, and the passage of time diminishes the accuracy of what's on the page.

Has something changed since we went to press? A missing detail? Please let us know. Your update information, especially photocopies of material received from stations, is very much welcomed and appreciated. Write to any of us at the IBS Editorial Office, Box 300, Penn's Park, PA 18943 USA, fax +1 (215) 598 3794.

Special thanks to John Herkimer, Editor-Publisher, and Don Jensen, Editor Emeritus, of *Número Uno*; Tetsuya Hirahara, Overseas Charge Secretary of *Radio Nuevo Mundo*; and the members of both organizations—as well as *Ask-DX* editor Anatoly Klepov and *India Broadbase* editor Manosij Guha—for their kind cooperation in the preparation of this section.

Using Passport's Addresses PLUS Section

- All stations known to reply, however erratically, or new stations which possibly may reply, to correspondence from listeners are included.
- Giveaways are often available only until supplies run out.
- Mailing addresses are given. These sometimes differ from the physical locations given in the Blue Pages.
- Private non-political organizations that lease air time, but which possess no world band transmitters of their own, are not necessarily listed. However, they may be reached via the stations over which they are heard.
- Unless otherwise indicated, stations:
  — Reply regularly within six months to most listeners' letters in English.
  — Provide, upon request, free station schedules and verification ("QSL") postcards or letters. We specify when other items are available for free or for purchase.
  — Do not require compensation for postage costs incurred in replying to you. Where compensation is required, details are provided as to what to send.
- Local times are given in difference

from World Time (UTC). For example, "World Time -5" means that if you subtract five hours from UTC, you'll get the local time in that country; so if it were 1100 World Time, it would be 0600 local time in that country. Times in (parentheses) are for the middle of the year—roughly April-October.

- To help avoid confusion, fax numbers are given without hyphens, telephone numbers with hyphens, and are configured for international dialing once you add your country's international access code (011 in the United States and Canada, 010 in the United Kingdom, and so on). For domestic dialing within countries outside the United States, Canada and the Caribbean, replace the country code (1-3 digits preceded by a "+") by a zero.
- E-mail numbers are given in Internet format. CompuServe users wishing to communicate with CompuServe addresses (those ending with @compuserve.com) should simply use the numeric address, replacing the dot with a comma. Thus, 74434.3020@compuserve.com (Internet format) becomes 74434,3020 (CompuServe format). As is the custom, World Wide Web addresses are prefaced http://. Remember that e-mail is not 100% reliable, especially via the Internet. Too, periods, commas and semicolons at the end of an address are normal sentence punctuation, *not* part of that address.

AFGHANISTAN World Time +4:30
Note: Postal service to this country is occasionally suspended.
Radio Afghanistan (if reactivated), P.O. Box 544, Kabul, Afghanistan. Rarely replies.

ALBANIA World Time +1 (+2 midyear)
Radio Tirana, Radiotelevisione Shqiptar, International Service, Rruga Ismail Qemali, Tirana, Albania. Phone: +355 (42) 23-239. Fax: +355 (42) 23 650. Contact: Bardhyl Pollo, Director of External Services; Adriana Bisha; or Diana Koci. Recent budget cutbacks have caused the once-vigorous Correspondence Section to be completely eliminated, so getting any sort of reply is unlikely. For example, staffers are now too few to fill the little remaining airtime with programs (music filler is used instead),

even though they reportedly work seven days a week (and are paid only around $60 per month).

ALGERIA World Time +1 (+2 midyear)

Radio Algiers International—same details as "Radiodiffusion-Télévision Algerienne," below.

Radiodiffusion-Télévision Algerienne (ENRS)
Nontechnical and General Technical: 21 Boulevard el Chouhada, Algiers, Algeria. Phone: +213 (2) 594-266. Fax: +213 (2) 605 814. Contact: (nontechnical) L. Zaghlami; or Chaabane Lounakil, Head of International Arabic Section; Yahi Zéhira, Head of International Relations; or Relations Extérieures; (general technical) Direction Technique. Replies irregularly. French or Arabic preferred, but English accepted.
Frequency Management Office: Télédiffusion d'Algérie, route de Bainem, B.P. 50, Bouzareah, Algeria. Fax: +213 (2) 797 390 or +213 (2) 941 390. Contact: Mouloud Lahlou, Director General.

ANGOLA World Time +1

Note: Because of the unsettled conditions prevalent in Angola, except for the first three stations given below, none of the former stations have been active in recent years. Whether they will eventually be reactivated is unknown at this time.

A Voz da Resistência do Galo Negro (Voice of the Resistance of the Black Cockerel), Free Angola Information Service, P.O. Box 65463, Washington DC 20035 USA (physical address is 1350 Connecticut Avenue NW, Suite 907, Washington DC 20036); Contact: Jaime de Azevedo Vila Santa, Director of Information. Pro-UNITA—once a rebel organization, but which is now considered to be part of the legitimate Angolan political structure.

Rádio Nacional de Angola, Cx. Postal 1329, Luanda, Angola. Fax: +244 (2) 391 234. Contact: Bernardino Costa, Public Opinion Office; Sra. Luiza Fancony, Diretora de Programas; Lourdes de Almeida, Chefe de Seção; or Cesar A.B. da Silva, Diretor Geral. Replies occasionally to correspondence, preferably in Portuguese. $1, return postage or 2 IRCs most helpful.

Emissora Provincial de Benguela, Cx. Postal 19, Benguela, Angola. Contact: Simão Martins Cuto, Responsável Administrativo; Carlos A.A. Gregório, Diretor; or José Cabral Sande. $1 or return postage required. Replies irregularly.

Emissora Provincial de Bié (if reactivated), C.P. 33, Kuito, Bié, Angola. Contact: José Cordeiro Chimo, O Diretor. Replies occasionally to correspondence in Portuguese.

Emissora Provincial de Moxico (if reactivated), Cx. Postal 74, Luena, Angola. Contact: Paulo Cahilo, Diretor. $1 or return postage required. Replies to correspondence in Portuguese.

Other **Emissora Provincial** stations (if reactivated)—same address, etc., as Rádio Nacional, above.

ANTARCTICA World Time -2 (-3 midyear) Base Antárctica Esperanza; +13 McMurdo

Radio Nacional Arcángel San Gabriel—LRA 36 (when operating), Base Antárctica Esperanza (Tierra de San Martín), 9411 Territorio Antárctico Argentino, Argentina. Contact: (general) Elizabeth Beltrán de Gallegos, Programación y Locución; (technical) Cristian Omar Guida. Return postage required. Replies irregularly to correspondence in Spanish. If no reply, try sending your correspondence (but don't write the station's name on your envelope) and 2 IRCs via the helpful Gabriel Iván Barrera, Casilla 2868, 1000-Buenos Aires, Argentina; fax +54 (1) 322 3351.

ANTIGUA World Time -4

BBC World Service—Caribbean Relay Station, P.O. Box 1203, St. John's, Antigua. Phone: +1 (809) 462-0994. Fax: +1 (809) 462 0436. Contact: (technical) G. Hoef, Manager; Roy Fleet; or R. Pratt, Company Engineer.

Nontechnical correspondence should be sent to the BBC World Service in London (see).

Deutsche Welle—Relay Station Antigua—same address and contact as BBC World Service, above. Nontechnical correspondence should be sent to the Deutsche Welle in Germany (see).

ARGENTINA World Time -3 Buenos Aires and eastern provinces; -4 in some western provinces.

Radiodifusión Argentina al Exterior—RAE, C.C. 555 Correo Central, 1000-Buenos Aires, Argentina. Fax: +54 (1) 325 9433. Contact: (general) Paul F. Allen, Announcer, English Team; John Anthony Middleton, Head of the English Team; María Dolores López; Rodrigo Calderan; or Sandro Cenci, Chief, Italian Section; (head of administration) Marcela G.R. Campos, Directora; (technical) Gabriel Iván Barrera, DX Editor; or Patricia Menéndez. Free paper pennant and tourist literature. Return postage or $1 appreciated.

Radio Continental, Rivadavia 835, 1002-Buenos Aires, Argentina. Fax: +54 (1) 345 1845/6. Contact: Julio A. Valles. Stickers and tourist literature; $1 or return postage required. Replies to correspondence in Spanish.

Radio Malargüe, Esq. Aldao 350, 5613-Malargüe, Argentina. Contact: Eduardo Vicente Lucero, Jefe Técnico; Nolasco H. Barrera, Interventor; or José Pandolfo, Departamento Administración. Free pennants. Return postage necessary. Prefers correspondence in Spanish.

Radio Nacional Buenos Aires, Maipú 555, 1000-Buenos Aires, Argentina.

Radio Nacional Mendoza, Emilio Civit 460, 5500-Mendoza, Argentina. Phone: +54 (61) 257-931. Fax: +54 (61) 380 596. Contact: (general) Lic. Jorge Horacio Parvanoff, Director; (technical) Juan Carlos Fernández, Jefe del Departamento Técnico. Free stickers. Replies to correspondence, preferably in Spanish, but English also accepted. Replacement shortwave transmitter to be put into service during 1996.

Radio Rivadavia (when operating to Antarctica), Arenales 2467, 1124-Buenos Aires, Argentina. Fax: +54 (1) 824 6927.

ARMENIA World Time usually +4 year around (some years +3 winter)

Armenian Radio—see Voice of Armenia for details.

Lutherische Stunde (religious program aired over Radio Intercontinental), Postfach 1162, D-27363 Sottrum, Germany.

Mitternachtsruf (religious program aired via Radio Intercontinental), P.O. Box 62, 79807 Lottstetten, Germany; Postfach 290, Eicholzstrasse 38, CH-8330 Pfaffikon, Switzerland; or P.O. Box 4389, W. Columbia, SC 29171 USA. Contact: Jonathan Malgo. Free stickers and promotional material.

Radio Intercontinental—see Voice of Armenia, below, for details.

Voice of Armenia, Radio Agency, Alek Manoukyan Street 5, 375025 Yerevan, Armenia. Phone: +7 (8852) 558-010. Fax: +7 (8852) 551 513. Contact: V. Voskanian, Deputy Editor-in-Chief; R. Abalian, Editor-in-Chief; or Levon Amamikian. Free postcards and stamps. Replies slowly.

ASCENSION World Time exactly

BBC World Service—Atlantic Relay Station, English Bay, Ascension (South Atlantic Ocean). Fax: +247 6117. Contact: (technical) Jeff Cant, Staff Manager; M.R. Watkins, A/Assistant Resident Engineer; or Nicola Nicholls, Transmitter Engineer. Nontechnical correspondence should be sent to the BBC World Service in London (see).

Radio Japan, Radio Roma and Voice of America—via BBC Ascension Relay Station—All correspondence should be directed to the regular addresses in Japan, Italy and the USA (see).

Voice of America—Ascension Relay Station—same details as "BBC World Service," above. Nontechnical correspondence should be directed to the regular VOA address (see USA).

AUSTRALIA World Time +11 (+10 midyear) Victoria (VIC), New South Wales (NSW), Australian Capital Territory (ACT) and Tasmania (TAS); +10:30 (+9:30 midyear) South Australia (SA); +10 Queensland (QLD); +9:30 Northern Territory (NT); +8 Western Australia (WA)

Australian Defense Forces Radio, Department of Defense, EMU (Electronic Media Unit) ANZAC Park West, APW 1-B-07, Reid, Canberra, ACT 2600, Australia. Phone: +61 (6) 266-6669. Fax: +61 (6) 266 6565. Contact: (general) Adam Iffland, Presenter; (technical) Hugh Mackenzie, Managing Presenter; or Brian Langshaw. SAE and 2 IRCs needed for a reply. Station replies to verification inquiries only.

Australian Broadcasting Corporation—ABC Darwin, Administrative Center for the Northern Territory Shortwave Service, ABC Box 9994, GPO Darwin NT 0801, Australia. Phone: +61 (89) 433-230. Fax: +61 (89) 433 235. Contact: (general) Sue Camilleri, Broadcaster and Community Liaison Officer; or Fred McCue, Producer, "Mornings with Michael Mackenzie"; (technical) Peter Camilleri. Free stickers. Free "Travellers Guide to ABC Radio." T-shirts US$20. Cyclone Tracy 20th anniversary cassette recording US$12. Three IRCs or return postage helpful.

CAAMA Radio—ABC, Central Australian Aboriginal Media Association, Bush Radio Service, P.O. Box 2924, Alice Springs NT 0871, Australia. Phone: +61 (89) 529-204. Fax: +61 (89) 529 214. Contact: Merridie Satoar, Department Manager; Mark Lillyman, News Director; or Owen Cole, CAAMA General Manager; (head of administration) Graham Archer, Station Manager; (technical) Warren Huck, Technician. Free stickers. Two IRCs or return postage helpful.

Radio Australia—ABC
Studios and Main Offices: GPO Box 428 G, Melbourne VIC 3001, Australia. Phone: ("Openline" voice mail for listeners' messages and requests) +61 (3) 9626-1825; (general) +61 (3) 9616-1800; (management) +61 (3) 9626-1901; (technical) +61 (3) 9626 1912/3/4; (ABC programs) +61 (3) 9626-1916. Fax: (general) +61 (3) 9626 1899; (management) +61 (3) 9626 1903; (technical) +61 (3) 9626 1917. E-mail: raust3@ozemail.com.au. Contact: (general) Susan Jenkins, Correspondence Officer; Roger Broadbent, Head, English Language Programming; Judi Cooper, Business Development Manager; Derek White, General Manager, International Broadcasting; Ms. Lisa T. Breeze, Publicist; or Denis Gibbons, Producer, "Feedback." Contact: (technical) Nigel Holmes, Transmission Manager, Transmission Management Unit, Arie Schellaars, Asst. Transmission Manager, Master Control; or Neil Deer, Controller, Resources & Distribution.
New York Bureau, Nontechnical: 1 Rockefeller Plaza, Suite 1700, New York NY 10020 USA. Phone: +1 (212) 332-2540. Fax: +1 (212) 332 2546. Contact: Maggie Jones, North American Representative.
London Bureau, Nontechnical: 54 Portland Place, London W1N 4DY, United Kingdom. Phone: +44 (171) 631-4456. Fax: (administration) +44 (171) 323 0059, (news) +44 (171) 323 1125. Contact: Robert Bolton, Manager.
Bangkok Bureau, Nontechnical: 209 Soi Hutayana off Soi Suanplu, South Sathorn Road, Bangkok 10120, Thailand. Fax: +66 (2) 287 2040. Contact: Nicholas Stuart.

Radio Rum Jungle—ABC (program studios), Top Aboriginal Bush Association, Corner Speed Street & Gap Road, Batchelor NT 0870, Australia. Phone: +61 (89) 523-433. Fax: +61 (89) 522 093. Contact: Mae-Mae Morrison, Announcer; Andrew Joshua, Chairman; or George Butler. Three IRCs or return postage helpful. May send free posters.

VNG (official time station)
Primary Address: National Standards Commission, P.O. Box 282, North Ryde, NSW 2113, Australia. Phone: +61 (2) 888-3922. Fax: +61 (2) 888 3033. Contact: Dr. Richard Brittain. Station offers a free 16-page booklet about VNG and free promotional material. Free stickers and postcards. Three IRCs helpful.
Alternative Address: VNG Users Consortium, GPO Box 1090, Canberra ACT 2601, Australia. Fax: +61 (6) 249 9969. Contact: Dr. Marion Leiba, Honorary Secretary. Three IRCs required.

AUSTRIA World Time +1 (+2 midyear)
Radio Austria International
Main Office: Würzburggasse 30, A-1136 Vienna, Austria. Phone: (general) +43 (1) 87878-2130; (voice mail) +43 (1) 87878-3636; (technical) +43 (1) 87878-2629. Fax: (general) +43 (1) 87878 4404; (technical) +43 (1) 87878 2773. E-mail: kwp@rai.ping.at. World Wide Web: http://www.apa.co.at/orf/teletext/598.html. Contact: (general) Vera Bock, Listener's Service; ("Kurzwellen Panorama") Wolf Harranth, Editor; (heads of administration) Prof. Paul Lendvai, Director; Dr. Edgar Sterbenz, Deputy Director; (technical) Franz Rymes, Frequency Management Department. Free stickers and program schedule twice a year. Mr. Harranth seeks collections of old verification cards and letters for the highly organized historical archives he is maintaining.
Washington News Bureau: 1206 Eaton Ct. NW, Washington DC 20007 USA. Phone: +1 (202) 822-9570. Contact: Franz R. Kössler.

AZERBAIJAN World Time +3
Azerbaijani Radio—see Radio Dada Gorgud for details.
Radio Dada Gorgud (Voice of Azerbaijan), ul. M. Guzeina 1, 370011 Baku, Azerbaijan. Contact: Mrs. Tamam Bayatli-Öner, Director. Free postcards. $1 or return postage helpful. Replies occasionally to correspondence in English.

BAHRAIN World Time +3
Radio Bahrain, Broadcasting & Television, Ministry of Information, P.O. Box 702, Al Manamah, Bahrain. Phone: (Arabic Service) +973 781-888; (English Service) +973 629-085. Fax: (Arabic Service) +973 681 544; (English Service) +973 780 911. Contact: A. Suliman (for Director of Broadcasting). $1 or IRC required. Replies irregularly.

BANGLADESH World Time +6
Radio Bangladesh
Nontechnical correspondence: External Services, Shahbagh Post Box No. 2204, Dhaka 1000, Bangladesh. Phone: +880 (2) 504-348 or +880 (2) 503-688. Contact: Masudul Hasan, Deputy Director; Syed Zaman; Ashraf ul-Alam, Assistant for Director; or Mobarak Hossain Khan, Director.
Technical correspondence: National Broadcasting Authority, NBA House, 121 Kazi Nazrul Islam Avenue, Dhaka 1000, Bangladesh. Contact: Mohammed Romizuddin Bhuiya, Senior Engineer (Research Wing). Verifications not common.

BELARUS World Time +2 (+3 midyear)
Belarussian Radio—see Radio Belarus for details.
Die Antwort (religious program aired over Radio Minsk), Postfach 767, CH-1701 Freiburg, Switzerland. Phone: +41 (37) 281-717. Fax: +41 (37) 281 752. Contact: Rev. Hermann A. Parli, Director of Claropa Radio Center. *Die Antwort* quarterly newsletter for SF5.00 or DM6.00 per year. Calendar for SF10.00 or DM12.00.
Grodno Radio—see Radio Belarus for details.
Mogilev Radio—see Radio Belarus for details.
Radio Belarus, ul. Krasnaya 4, 220807 Minsk, Belarus. Phone: +7 (0172) 338-875 or +7 (0172) 334-039. Fax: +7 (0172) 366 643 or +7 (0172) 648 182. Contact: Michail Tondel, Chief

Editor; or Jürgen Eberhardt. Free Belarus stamps.
Radio Minsk—*see* Radio Belarus for details.
Voice of Orthodoxy (program)
Minsk Office: V. Pristavko, P.O. Box 17, 220012 Minsk, Belarus. Aired via transmission facilities of Radio Trans Europe, Portugal, and the Voice of Hope, Lebanon. Correspondence and reception reports welcomed.
Paris Office: B.P. 416-08, F-75366 Paris Cedex 08, France. Contact: Valentin Korelsky, General Secretary.

BELGIUM World Time +1 (+2 midyear)
Radio Vlaanderen Internationaal
Note: According to a spokesperson for RVI, as of mid-1995 the station expects to make no further investment in short-wave equipment, as it considers it to be an "old, obsolete medium." However, discussions with RVI suggest that they may not be fully aware of certain variables for successful-ly reaching audiences—notably, the growth since the late Eighties in world band listening in such places as North America, where advanced-technology broadcasting and narrowcasting options are greater than anyplace else; and, at the other end of the economic-technological con-tinuum, the paucity of affordable advanced-technology options in key parts of the world to which RVI transmits. Taken together, these suggest that this course of action may be reconsidered in due course if the station is to remain viable.
Nontechnical and General Technical: (English Department) Brussels Calling, P.O. Box 26, B-1000 Brussels, Belgium; (other departments) Belgische Radio en Televisie, Postbus 26, B-1000 Brussels, Belgium. Phone: +32 (2) 741-3802. Fax: +32 (2) 732 6295 or +32 (2) 734 7804. E-mail: rvi@brtn.be. World Wide Web: http://www.brtn.be/rvi/. Contact: (general) Monique Delvaux, Editor-in-Chief; Liz Sanderson, Head, English Service; Maryse Jacob, Head, French Service; Martina Luxen, Head, German Service; Ximena Prieto, Head, Spanish Service; (head of administration) Jacques Vandersichel, Director; (general technical) Frans Vossen, Producer, "Radio World." For members of their Listeners' Club, there are free stickers, key rings, ballpoint pens and *Club Echo* Listeners' Club magazine—plus Club members can receive genuine QSL cards.
Frequency Management Office: BRTN, Ave. Reyerslaan 52, B-1043 Brussels, Belgium. Phone: +32 (2) 741-5571. Fax: +32 (2) 741 5567. Contact: Hugo Gauderis or Willy Devos.

BENIN World Time +1
Office de Radiodiffusion et Télévision du Benin, La Voix de la Révolution, B.P. 366, Cotonou, Bénin; this address is for Cotonou and Parakou stations, alike. Contact: (Cotonou) Damien Zinsou Ala Hassa; or Leonce Goohouede; (technical) Anastase Adjoko, Chef de Service Technique; (Radio Parakou, general) J. de Matha, Le Chef de la Station, or (Radio Parakou, technical) Léon Donou, Le Chef des Services Techniques. Return postage, $1 or IRC required. Replies irregularly and slowly to correspon-dence in French.

BHUTAN World Time +6
Bhutan Broadcasting Service
Station: Department of Information and Broadcasting, Ministry of Communications, P.O. Box 101, Thimphu, Bhutan. Phone: +975 23-070. Fax: +975 23 073. Contact: (general) Ashi Renchen Chhoden, News and Current Affairs; or Narda Gautam; (technical) C. Proden, Station Engineer. Two IRCs, return postage or $1 required. Replies extreme-ly irregularly; correspondence to the U.N. Mission (*see* following) may be more fruitful.
United Nations Mission: Permanent Mission of the Kingdom of Bhutan to the United Nations, Two United Nations Plaza, 27th Floor, New York NY 10017 USA. Fax: +1 (212) 826 2998. Contact: Mrs. Kunzang C. Namgyel, Third Secretary; Mrs. Sonam Yangchen, Attaché; Ms. Leki Wangmo, Second Secretary; Thinley Dorrji, Second

Secretary; or Hari K. Chhetri, Second Secretary. Free news-papers and booklet on the history of Bhutan.

BOLIVIA World Time -4
Note on Station Identifications: Many Bolivian stations listed as "Radio..." may also announce as "Radio Emisora..." or "Radiodifusora..."
Galaxia Radiodifusión—*see* Radio Galaxia, below.
Hitachi Radiodifusión—*see* Radio Hitachi, below.
Paititi Radiodifusión—*see* Radio Paititi, below.
La Voz del Trópico (when operating), "Radiodifusora CVU," Casilla 2494, Cochabamba, Bolivia. Contact: Eduardo Avila Alberdi, Director; or Carlos Pocho Hochmann, Locutor. Return postage or $1 required. Replies occasionally to correspondence in Spanish.
Radio Abaroa, Calle Nicanor Gonzalo Salvatierra 249, Riberalta, Beni, Bolivia. Contact: René Arias Pacheco, Director. Return postage or $1 required. Replies rarely to correspondence in Spanish.
Radio Animas, Chocaya, Animas, Potosí, Bolivia. Return postage or $1 required. Replies irregularly to correspon-dence in Spanish.
Radio Camargo—*see* Radio Emisoras Camargo, below.
Radio Centenario "La Nueva"
Main Office: Casilla 818, Santa Cruz de la Sierra, Bolivia. Phone: +591 (3) 529-265. Fax: +591 (3) 524 747. Contact: Napoleón Ardaya Borja, Director. May send a calendar. Free stickers. Return postage or $1 required. Audio cas-settes of contemporary Christian music and Bolivian folk music $10, including postage; CDs of Christian folk music $15, including postage. Replies to correspondence in English and Spanish. Possible addition of new transmitter in 1996.
U.S. Branch Office: LATCOM, 1218 Croton Avenue, New

Castle PA 16101 USA. Phone: +1 (412) 652-0101. Fax: +1 (412) 652-4654. Contact: Hope Cummins.

Radio Cosmos (when operating), Casilla 1092, Cochabamba, Bolivia. Phone: +591 (42) 50-423. Fax: +591 (42) 51 173. Contact: Laureano Rojas, Jr. $1 or return postage required. Replies to correspondence in Spanish.

Radiodifusora CVU—see La Voz del Trópico, above.

Radiodifusoras Integración—see Radio Integración, below.

Radiodifusoras Minería—see Radio Minería, below.

Radio Dos de Febrero, Vaca Diez 400, Rurrenabaque, Beni, Bolivia. Contact: John Arce. Replies occasionally to correspondence in Spanish.

Radio Eco
Main Address: Correo Central, Reyes, Bellivián, Beni, Bolivia. Contact: Gonzalo Espinoza Cortés, Director. Free station literature. $1 or return postage required. Replies to correspondence in Spanish.
Alternative Address: Rolman Medina Méndez, Correo Central, Reyes, Bellivián, Bolivia.

Radio Eco San Borja (San Borja la Radio), Correo Central, San Borja, Ballivián, Beni, Bolivia. Contact: Gonzalo Espinoza Cortés, Director. Free station poster promised to correspondents. Return postage appreciated.

Radio Ecología Internacional (when operating), Calle Bolívar 30, San Matías, Angel Sandoval, Santa Cruz, Bolivia. Contact: José Vaca Diez Justiniano, Director-Propietario. Replies to correspondence in Spanish.

Radio El Mundo, Casilla 1984, Santa Cruz de la Sierra, Bolivia. Phone: +591 (3) 464-646. Fax: +591 (3) 465 057. Contact: Freddy Banegas Carrasco, Gerente; or Lic. Juan Pablo Sainz, Gerente General. Free stickers and pennants. $1 or return postage required. Replies irregularly to correspondence in Spanish.

Radio Emisora Dos de Febrero—see Radio Dos de Febrero, above.

Radio Emisora Galaxia—see Radio Galaxia, below.

Radio Emisora Padilla—see Radio Padilla, below.

Radio Emisora San Ignacio, Calle Ballivián s/n, San Ignacio de Moxos, Beni, Bolivia. Contact: Carlos Salvatierra Rivero, Gerente y Director. $1 or return postage necessary.

Radio Emisora Villamontes—see Radio Vilamontes, below.

Radio Emisoras Camargo, Casilla 09, Camargo, Pcia. Nor Cinti, Bolivia. Contact: Pablo García B., Gerente Propietario. Return postage or $1 required. Replies slowly to correspondence in Spanish.

Radio Estación Frontera—see Radio Frontera, below.

Radio Fides, Casilla 9143, La Paz, Bolivia. Fax: +591 (2) 379 030. Contact: Pedro Eduardo Pérez, Director; Felicia de Rojas, Secretaria; or Roxana Beltrán C. Replies occasionally to correspondence in Spanish.

Radio Frontera, Casilla 179, Cobija, Pando, Bolivia. Contact: Lino Miahuchi von Ancken, CP9AR. Free pennants. $1 or return postage necessary. Replies to correspondence in Spanish.

Radio Galaxia, Calle Beni s/n casi esquina Udarico Rosales, Guayaramerín, Beni, Bolivia. Contact: Dorián Arias, Gerente; Jeber Hitachi Banegas, Director; or Carlos Arteaga Tacaná, Director-Dueño. Return postage or $1 required. Replies to correspondence in Spanish.

Radio Grigotá, Casilla 203, Santa Cruz, Bolivia. Contact: Víctor Hugo Arteaga, Director General. $1 or return postage required. Replies occasionally to correspondence in Spanish.

Radio Hitachi (Hitachi Radiodifusión), Calle Sucre 20, Guayaramerín, Beni, Bolivia. Contact: Héber Hitachi Vanegas, Director. Return postage of $1 required.

Radio Illimani, Casilla 1042, La Paz, Bolivia. Phone: +591 (2) 376-364. Contact: Sra. Gladys de Zamora, Administradora. $1 required, and your letter should be registered and include a tourist brochure or postcard from where you live. Replies irregularly to friendly correspondence in Spanish.

Radio Integración, Casilla 7902, La Paz, Bolivia. Contact: Benjamín Juan Carlos Blanco, Director Ejecutivo; Andres A. Quiroga V., Gerente General; or Carmelo de la Cruz Huanca, Comunicador Social. Free pennants. Return postage required.

Radio Juan XXIII (Veintitrés), Avenida Santa Cruz al frente de la plaza principal, San Ignacio de Velasco, Santa Cruz, Bolivia. Phone: +591 (962) 2188. Contact: Fernando Manuel Picazo Torres, Director; or Pbro. Elías Cortezon, Director. Return postage or $1 required. Replies occasionally to correspondence in Spanish.

Radio La Cruz del Sur, Casilla 1408, La Paz, Bolivia. Contact: Pastor Rodolfo Moya Jiménez, Director. Pennant $1 or return postage. Replies slowly to correspondence in Spanish.

Radio La Palabra, Parroquia de Santa Ana de Yacuma, Beni, Bolivia. Phone: +591 (848) 2117. Contact: Padre Yosu Arketa, Director. Return postage necessary. Replies to correspondence in Spanish.

Radio La Plata, Casilla 276, Sucre, Bolivia. Phone: +591 (64) 31-616. Fax: +591 (64) 41 400. Contact: Freddy Donoso Bleichner.

Radio Libertad, Casilla 5324, La Paz, Bolivia. Phone: +591 (2) 365-154. Fax: +591 (2) 363 069. Contact: Lic. Teresa Sanjinés Lora, Directora. Depending upon what's on hand, free buttons, key rings, lighters, match books, notebooks, purses, pennants and stickers. Return postage or $1 required. T-shirts $5 plus postage. Upon request, they will record for listeners any type of Bolivian music they have on hand, and send it to that listener for the cost of the cassette and postage; or, if the listener sends a cassette, for the cost of postage. Replies fairly regularly to correspondence in English and Spanish. Intends changing hours of transmission during 1996.

Radio Loyola, Casilla 40, Sucre, Bolivia. Phone: +591 (64) 30-222. Contact: José Cabanach, Director de Programs. Replies occasionally to correspondence in Spanish.

Radio Mauro Núñez, Centro de Estudios para el Desarrollo de Chuquisaca (CEDEC), Casilla 196, Sucre, Bolivia. Contact: Dr. Vladimir Gutiérrez P., Director.

Radio Metropolitana, Casilla de Correo 8704, La Paz, Bolivia. Phone: +591 (2) 358-832. Contact: Rodolfo Beltrán Rosales, Jefe de Prensa de "El Metropolicial"; or Carlos Palenque Avilés, Presidente Ejecutivo RTP. Free postcards and pennants. $1 or return postage necessary.

Radio Minería, Casilla de Correo 247, Oruro, Bolivia. Phone: +591 (52) 52-736. Contact: Dr. José Carlos Gómez Espinoza, Gerente y Director General; or Srta. Costa Colque Flores., Responsable del programa "Minería Cultural." Free pennants. Replies to correspondence in Spanish.

Radio Movima, Calle Baptista No. 24, Santa Ana de Yacuma, Beni, Bolivia. Contact: Rubén Serrano López, Director; Javier Roca Díaz, Director Gerente; or Mavis Serrano, Directora. Return postage or $1 required. Replies irregularly to correspondence in Spanish.

Radio Nacional de Huanuni, Casilla 681, Oruro, Bolivia. Contact: Rafael Linneo Morales, Director General; or Alfredo Murillo, Director. Return postage or $1 required. Replies irregularly to correspondence in Spanish.

Radio 9 (Nueve) de Abril (when operating), Planta Industrial de Pulacayo, Pcia. Quijarro, Potosí, Bolivia. Contact: Antonio Lafuente Azurduy, Presidente & Director; Bruno Condori Sinani, Secretario de Relaciones; David Bustillos Arécalo, Secretario de Hacienda; or Julián García Pérez, Secretario de Prensa y Propaganda. $1 or return postage necessary. Replies slowly to correspondence in Spanish.

Radio Norte, Calle Warnes 195, 2do piso del Cine Escorpio, Montero, Santa Cruz, Bolivia. Phone: +591 (92) 20-970. Contact: Leonardo Arteaga Ríos, Director.

Radio Padilla, Padilla, Chuquisaca, Bolivia. Contact: Moisés Palma Salazar, Director. Return postage or $1 required. Replies to correspondence in Spanish.

Radio Paitití, Casilla 172, Guayaramerín, Beni, Bolivia. Contact: Armando Mollinedo Bacarreza, Director; Luis Carlos Santa Cruz Cuéllar, Director Gerente; or Ancir Vaca Cuéllar, Gerente-Propietario. Free pennants. Return postage or $3 required. Replies irregularly to correspondence in Spanish.

Radio Panamericana, Casilla 5263, La Paz, Bolivia. Contact: Daniel Sánchez Rocha, Director. Replies irregularly, with correspondence in Spanish preferred. $1 or 2 IRCs helpful.

Radio Perla del Acre, Casilla 7, Cobija, Departamento de Pando, Bolivia. Return postage or $1 required. Replies irregularly to correspondence in Spanish.

Radio Pío XII (Doce), Casilla 434, Oruro, Bolivia. Phone: +591 (52) 53-168. Contact: Pbro. Roberto Durette, OMI, Director General. Return postage necessary. Replies occasionally to correspondence in Spanish.

Radio San Gabriel, Casilla 4792, La Paz, Bolivia. Phone: +591 (2) 355-371. Fax/phone: +591 (2) 321 174. Contact: Hno. José Canut Saurat, Director General; or Sra. Martha Portugal, Dpto. de Publicidad. $1 or return postage helpful. Free book on station, Aymara calendars and *La Voz del Pueblo Aymara* magazine. Replies fairly regularly to correspondence in Spanish. Station of the Hermanos de la Salle Catholic religious order.

Radio San Miguel, Casilla 102, Riberalta, Beni, Bolivia. Phone: +591 (852) 8268. Contact: Félix Alberto Rada Q., Director. Free stickers and pennants. Return postage or $1 required. Replies irregularly to correspondence in Spanish. Feedback on program "Bolivia al Mundo" (aired 0200-0300 World Time) especially appreciated.

Radio Santa Ana, Calle Sucre No. 250, Santa Ana de Yacuma, Beni, Bolivia. Contact: Mario Roberto Suárez, Director; or Mariano Verdugo. Return postage or $1 required. Replies irregularly to correspondence in Spanish.

Radio Santa Cruz, Emisora del Instituto Radiofónico Fé y Alegría (IRFA), Casilla 672, Santa Cruz, Bolivia. Phone: +591 (3) 531-817. Fax: +591 (3) 532 257. Contact: Padre Francisco Flores, S.J., Director de Programas; Srta. María Yolanda Marco, Secretaria; or Padre Victor Blajot, S.J., Director General. Free stickers, pennants and pins. *Araqua* book of tales and legends $3 plus postage, and *Panorama de la Historia de Bolivia* $4 plus postage. Return postage required. Replies to correspondence in Spanish, French and Italian.

Radio Sararenda, Casilla 7, Camiri, Santa Cruz, Bolivia. Phone: +595 (952) 2469. Contact: Freddy Lara Aguilar, Director.

Radio 27 (Veintisiete) de Diciembre (when operating), Calle Méndez Arcos No. 171, Villamontes, Tarija, Bolivia. Contact: José Maldonado Terán, Director-Dueño. Return postage necessary.

Radio Villamontes, Avenida Méndez Arcos No. 156, Villamontes, Departamento de Tarija, Bolivia. Contact: Gerardo Rocabado Galarza, Director. $1 or return postage required.

BOSNIA-HERCEGOVINA **World Time +1 (+2 midyear)**

Radio Bosnia-Hercegovina, 71000 Sarajevo, Bosnia-Hercegovina. Fax: +387 (71) 645 142 (when circuits are open). Contact: Milenko Vockic, Director; or Mr. N. Dizdarevic. Because of wartime conditions at press time, mail service to or from this station has been virtually nonexistent. However, some fax contact has been reported when circuits have been open.

Radio UNPROFOR (when operating via facilities of Radio Bosnia-Hercegovina), UNPROFOR THQ, Division of Information, Ilica 207, 41001 Zagreb, Croatia. Contact: Jeffrey Heyman, Head, Radio Broadcasting Unit, Radio Projects Manager.

BOTSWANA World Time +2

Radio Botswana, Private Bag 0060, Gaborone, Botswana. Phone: +267 352-541. Phone: +267 352-541. Fax: +267 371 588 or +267 357 138. Contact: (general) Ted Makgekgenene, Director; or Monica Mphusu, Producer, "Maokaneng/Pleasure Mix"; (technical) Kingsley Reebang. Free stickers, pennants and pins. Return postage, $1 or 2 IRCs required. Replies slowly and irregularly.

Voice of America—Botswana Relay Station

Transmitter Site: Voice of America, Botswana Relay Station, Moepeng Hill, Selebi-Phikwe, Botswana. Phone: +267 810-932. Fax: +267 810 252. Contact: Dennis G. Brewer, Station Manager. This address for specialized technical correspondence only. All other correspondence should be directed to the regular VOA address (*see USA*).

Frequency and Monitoring Office: Voice of America, 330 Independence Avenue, S.W., Washington DC 20540 USA. Phone: +1 (202) 619-1669. Fax: +1 (202) 619 1781. E-mail: ferguson@beng.voa.gov. Contact: Daniel Ferguson, Botswana QSL Desk, VOA/EOFF:Frequency Management & Monitoring Division. The Botswana Desk is for technical correspondence only. Nontechnical correspondence should be directed to the regular VOA address (*see USA*).

BRAZIL World Time -1 (-2 midyear) Atlantic Islands; -2 (-3 midyear) Eastern, including Brasília and Rio de Janeiro, plus the town of Barra do Garças; -3 (-4 midyear) Western; -4 (-5 midyear) Acre. Some northern states keep midyear time year round.

Note 1: Postal authorities recommend that, because of the level of theft in the Brazilian postal system, correspondence to Brazil be sent only via registered mail.

Note 2: For Brazilian return postage, see the introduction to this section.

Emissora Rural A Voz do São Francisco, C.P. 8, 56301 Petrolina, Pernambuco, Brazil. Contact: Maria Letecia de Andrade Nunes. Return postage necessary. Replies to correspondence in Portuguese.

Rádio Alvorada (Londrina), Rua Sen. Souza Naves 9, 9 Andar, 86015 Londrina, Paraná, Brazil. Contact: Padre José Guidoreni, Diretor. Pennants $1 or return postage. Replies to correspondence in Portuguese.

Rádio Alvorada (Parintins), Travessa Leopoldo Neves 503, 69150 Parintins, Amazônas, Brazil. Contact: Raimunda Ribeira da Motta, Diretora. Return postage required. Replies occasionally to correspondence in Portuguese.

Rádio Anhanguera, C.P. 13, 74001 Goiânia, Goiás, Brazil. Contact: Rossana F. da Silva. Return postage required. Replies to correspondence in Portuguese.

Rádio Aparecida, C.P. 14664, 03698 São Paulo SP, Brazil. Contact: Padre Cabral; Cassiano Macedo, Producer, "Encontro DX"; or Antonio C. Moreira, Diretor Geral. Return postage or $1 required. Replies occasionally to correspondence in Portuguese.

Rádio Bandeirantes, C.P. 372, Rua Radiantes 13, Morumbí, 01059-970 São Paulo SP, Brazil. Fax: +55 (11) 843 5391. Contact: Samir Razuk, Diretor Geral; Carlos Newton; or Salomão Esper, Superintendente. Free stickers, pennants and canceled Brazilian stamps. $1 or return postage required.

Rádio Baré, Avenida Santa Cruz Machado 170 A, 69010-070 Manaus, Amazônas, Brazil. Contact: Fernando A.B. Andrade, Diretor Programação e Produção. The Diretor is looking for radio catalogs.

Radiobrás—see Rádio Nacional do Brasil.

Rádio Brasil, C.P. 625, 13101 Campinas, São Paulo SP, Brazil. Contact: Wilson Roberto Correa Viana, Gerente. Return postage required. Replies to correspondence in Portuguese.

Rádio Brasil Central, C.P. 330, 74001-970 Goiânia, Goiás, Brazil. Contact: Ney Raymundo Fernández,

Coordinador Executivo; or Arizio Pedro Soarez, Diretor Gerente. Free stickers. $1 or return postage required. Replies to correspondence in Portuguese.

Rádio Brasil Tropical, C.P. 405, 78005-970 Cuiabá, Mato Grosso, Brazil. Contact: Klecius Santos. Free stickers. $1 required. Replies to correspondence in Portuguese.

Rádio Cabocla, Rua 4 Casa 9, Conjunto dos Secretarios, 69000 Manaus, Amazônas, Brazil. Contact: Francisco Puga, Diretor Geral. Return postage required. Replies occasionally to correspondence in Portuguese.

Rádio Caiari, C.P. 104, 78901 Pôrto Velho, Rondônia, Brazil. Contact: Carlos Alberto Diniz Martins, Diretor Geral. Free stickers. Return postage helpful. Replies irregularly to correspondence in Portuguese.

Rádio Canção Nova, C.P. 15, 12630 Cachoeira Paulista, São Paulo SP, Brazil. Contact: Benedita Luiza Rodrigues; or Valera Guimarães Massafera, Secretária. Free stickers, pennants and station brochure sometimes given upon request. $1 helpful.

Rádio Capixaba, C.P. 509, 29001 Vitória, Espírito Santo, Brazil. Contact: Jairo Gouvea Maia, Diretor; or Sofrage do Benil. Replies occasionally to correspondence in Portuguese.

Rádio Carajá, C.P. 520, 75001-970 Anápolis, Goiás, Brazil. Contact: Nilson Silva Rosa, Diretor Geral. Return postage helpful. Replies to correspondence in Portuguese.

Rádio Clube do Pará, C.P. 533, 66001 Belém, Pará, Brazil. Contact: Edyr Paiva Proença, Diretor Geral. Return postage required. Replies irregularly to correspondence in Portuguese.

Rádio Clube Marilia (when operating), C.P. 325, Marilia, 17500 São Paulo SP, Brazil. Contact: Antonio Carlos Nasser. Return postage required. Replies to correspondence in Portuguese.

Rádio Clube de Rondonópolis, C.P. 190, Rondonópolis, Mato Grosso, Brazil. Contact: Canário Silpa, Departamento Comercial; or Saúl Feliz, Gerente-Geral. Return postage helpful. Replies to correspondence in Portuguese.

Rádio Clube Varginha, C.P. 102, 37101 Varginha, Minas Gerais, Brazil. Contact: Juraci Viana. Return postage necessary. Replies slowly to correspondence in Portuguese.

Rádio Cultura, C.P. 79, 28100-970 Campos, Rio de Janeiro, Brazil. $1 or return postage necessary. Replies to correspondence in Portuguese.

Rádio Cultura de Araraquara, Avenida Espanha 284, Araraquara 14800, São Paulo SP, Brazil. Contact: Antonio Carlos Rodrigues dos Santos. Return postage required. Replies slowly to correspondence in Portuguese.

Rádio Cultura do Pará, Avenida Almirante Barroso 735, 66065 Belém, Pará, Brazil. Contact: Ronald Pastor; or Augusto Proença, Diretor. Return postage required. Replies irregularly to correspondence in Portuguese.

Rádio Cultura Foz do Iguaçu, C.P 312, 85890 Foz do Iguaçu, Paraná, Brazil. Contact: Ennes Mendes da Rocha, Gerente-Geral. Return postage necessary. Replies to correspondence in Portuguese.

Rádio Cultura Ondas Tropicais, Rua Barcelos s/n esquina com Major Gabriel, 69020-060 Manaus, Brazil. Contact: Luíz Fernando de Souza Ferreira.

Rádio Cultura São Paulo, Rua Cenno Sbrighi 378, 05099 São Paulo SP, Brazil. Contact: Thais de Almeida Dias, Chefe de Produção e Programação; Sra. Maria Luíza Amaral Kfouri, Chefe de Produção; or José Munhoz, Coordenador. $1 or return postage required. Replies slowly to correspondence in Portuguese.

Rádio Difusora Cáceres, C.P. 297, 78200-000 Cáceres, Mato Grosso, Brazil. Contact: Sra. Maridalva Amaral Vignardi. $1 or return postage required. Replies occasionally to correspondence in Portuguese.

Rádio Difusora de Aquidauana, C.P. 18, 79200-000 Aquidauana, Mato Grosso do Sul, Brazil. Phone: +55 (67) 241-3956 or +55 (67) 241-3957. Contact: Primaz Aldo Bertoni,

Diretor. Free tourist literature and used Brazilian stamps. $1 or return postage required. This station sometimes identifies during the program day as "Nova Difusora," but its sign-off announcement gives the official name as "Rádio Difusora, Aquidauana."

Rádio Difusora de Londrina, C.P. 1870, 86010 Londrina, Paraná, Brazil. Contact: Walter Roberto Manganoli, Gerente. Free tourist brochure, which sometimes seconds as a verification. $1 or return postage helpful. Replies irregularly to correspondence in Portuguese.

Rádio Difusora do Amazônas, C.P. 311, 69001 Manaus, Amazônas, Brazil. Contact: J. Joaquim Marinho, Diretor. Joaquim Marinho is a keen stamp collector and especially interested in Duck Hunting Permit Stamps. Will reply to correspondence in Portuguese or English. $1 or return postage helpful.

Rádio Difusora do Maranhão, C.P. 152, 65001 São Luíz, Maranhão, Brazil. Contact: Alonso Augusto Duque, BA, Presidente; José de Arimatéla Araújo, Diretor; or Fernando Souza, Gerente. Free tourist literature. Return postage required. Replies occasionally to correspondence in Portuguese.

Rádio Difusora Jataí, C.P. 33 (or Rua de José Carvalhos Bastos 542), 76801 Jataí, Goiás, Brazil. Contact: Zacarías Faleiros, Diretor Gerente.

Rádio Difusora Macapá (when operating), C.P. 2929, 68901 Macapá, Amapá, Brazil. Contact: Francisco de Paulo Silva Santos or Rui Lobato. $1 or return postage required. Replies irregularly to correspondence in Portuguese.

Rádio Difusora Poços de Caldas, C.P. 937, 37701-970 Poços de Caldas, Mínas Gerais, Brazil. Contact: Marco Aurelio C. Mendoça, Diretor. $1 or return postage required. Replies to correspondence in Portuguese.

Rádio Difusora Roraima, Rua Capitão Ene Garcez 830, 69300 Boa Vista, Roraima, Brazil. Contact: Geraldo França, Diretor Geral; Angelo F. Sant'Anna, Diretor; or Francisco Alves Vieira. Return postage required. Replies occasionally to correspondence in Portuguese.

Rádio Educação Rural—Campo Grande, C.P. 261, 79002-233 Campo Grande, Mato Grosso do Sul, Brazil. Phone: +55 (67) 384-3164, +55 (67) 382-2238 or +55 (67) 384-3345. Contact: Ailton Guerra, Gerente-Geral; Angelo Venturelli, Director; or Diácono Tomás Schwamborn. $1 or return postage required. Replies to correspondence in Portuguese.

Rádio Educação Rural—Coari, Praça São Sebastião 228, 69460 Coari, Amazônas, Brazil. Contact: Joaquim Florencio Coelho, Diretor Administrador da Comunidad Salgueiro; or Elijane Martins Correa. $1 or return postage helpful. Replies irregularly to correspondence in Portuguese.

Rádio Educadora Cariri, C.P. 57, 63101 Crato, Ceará, Brazil. Contact: Padre Gonçalo Farias Filho, Diretor Gerente. Return postage or $1 helpful. Replies irregularly to correspondence in Portuguese.

Rádio Educadora da Bahia, Centro de Rádio, Rua Pedro Gama 413/E, Alto Sobradinho Federação, 40000 Salvador, Bahia, Brazil. Contact: Antonio Luís Almada, Gerente Geral da Rádio; Elza Correa Ramos; or Walter Sequieros R. Tanure. $1 or return postage required. Replies irregularly to correspondence in Portuguese.

Rádio Educadora de Bragança (when operating), Rua Barão do Rio Branco 1151, 68600 Bragança, Brazil. Contact: José Rosendo de S. Neto. $1 or return postage required. Replies to correspondence in Portuguese.

Rádio Educadora de Guajará Mirim, Praça Mario Correa No.90, CEP78957-000 Guajará Mirim, Estado de Rondônia, Brazil. Contact: Padre Isidoro José Moro. Return postage helpful. Replies to correspondence in Portuguese.

Rádio Gaúcha, Avenida Ipiranga 1075 2do andar, Azenha, 90060 Pôrto Alegre, Rio Grande do Sul, Brazil. Phone: +55 (51) 223-6600. Contact: Alexandre Amaral de Aguiar, News Editor; Almind Antônio Ranzlun, Diretor

Gerente; or Geraldo Canali. Replies occasionally to correspondence, preferably in Portuguese.

Rádio Gazeta, Avenida Paulista 900, 01310 São Paulo SP, Brazil. Fax: +55 (11) 285 4895. Contact: Shakespeare Ettinger, Superv. Geral de Operação; Bernardo Leite da Costa; or Ing. Aníbal Horta Figueiredo. Free stickers. $1 or return postage necessary. Replies to correspondence in Portuguese.

Rádio Globo, Rua das Palmeiras 315, 01226 São Paulo SP, Brazil. Contact: Ademar Dutra, Locutor, "Programa Ademar Dutra"; or José Marques. Replies to correspondence, preferably in Portuguese.

Rádio Guaíba, Rua Caldas Junior 219, 90010-260 Pôrto Alegre, Rio Grande do Sul, Brazil. Return postage may be helpful.

Radio Guaraní, Avenida Assis Chateaubriand 499, Floresta, 30150-101 Belo Horizonte, Minas Gerais, Brazil. Contact: Junara Belo, Setor de Comunicaçoes. Replies slowly to correspondence in Portuguese. Return postage helpful.

Rádio Guarujá
Station: C.P. 45, 88001 Florianópolis, Santa Catarina, Brazil. Contact: Acy Cabral Tieve, Diretor; Joana Sempre Bom Braz, Assessora de Marketing e Comunicação; or Rosa Michels de Souza. Return postage required. Replies irregularly to correspondence in Portuguese.
New York Office: 45 West 46 Street, 5th Floor, Manhattan, NY 10036 USA.

Rádio Inconfidência, C.P. 1027, 30001 Belo Horizonte, Minas Gerais, Brazil. Fax:+55 (31) 296 3070. Contact: Isaias Lansky, Diretor; Manuel Emilio de Lima Torres, Diretor Superintendente; Jairo Antolio Lima, Diretor Artístico; or Eugenio Silva. Free stickers and postcards. $1 or return postage helpful.

Rádio Integração, Rua Alagoas 270, lotes 8 e 9, 69980 Cruzeiro do Sul, Acre, Brazil. Contact: Claudio Onofre Ferreiro. Return postage required. Replies to correspondence in Portuguese.

Rádio IPB AM, Rua Itajaí 473, Bairro Antonio Vendas, 79050 Campo Grande, Mato Grosso do Sul, Brazil. Contact: Iván Páez Barboza, Diretor Geral (hence, the station's name, "IPB"); Pastor Laercio Paula das Neves, Dirigente Estadual; Agenor Patrocinio S., Locutor; or Kelly Cristina Rodrigues da Silva, Secretária. Return postage required. Replies to correspondence in Portuguese.

Rádio Itatiaia, Rua Itatiaia 117, 31210-170 Belo Horizonte, Minas Gerais, Brazil. Fax: +55 (31) 446 2900. Contact: Lúcia Araújo Bessa, Assistente da Diretória.

Rádio Marajoara, Travessa Campos Sales 370, Centro, 66015 Belém, Pará, Brazil. Contact: Elizete Maria dos Santos Pamplona, Diretora Geral; or Sra. Neide Carvalho, Secretária da Diretoria Executiva. Return postage required. Replies irregularly to correspondence in Portuguese.

Rádio Marumbí, C.P. 62 (C.P. 296 is the alternative box), 88010-970 Florianópolis, Santa Catarina, Brazil. Contact: Davi Campos, Diretor Artístico. $1 or return postage required. Replies to correspondence in Portuguese.

Rádio Meteorologia Paulista, C.P. 91, 14940-970 Ibitinga, São Paulo SP, Brazil. Contact: Roque de Rosa, Diretora. Replies to correspondence in Portuguese. $1 or return postage required.

Rádio Mundial, Rua da Consolação 2608, 1º Andar, CJ. 11, 01416-000 Consolação, São Paulo SP, Brazil. Fax: +55 (11) 258 5838 or +55 (11) 258 0152. Also, *see* Rádio Nikkei, Brazil.

Rádio Nacional da Amazônia, Radiobrás, SCRN 702/3 Bloco B, Ed. Radiobrás, Brasília DF, Brazil. Fax: +55 (61) 321 7602. Contact: (general) Luíz Otavio de Castro Souza, Diretor; Fernando Gómez da Camara, Gerente de Escritório; or Januario Procopio Toledo, Diretor. Free stickers, but no verifications. Also, *see* Radiobrás, above.

Rádio Nacional do Brasil—Radiobrás, External Service, C.P. 08840, CEP 70912-790, Brasília DF, Brazil. Fax:

+55 (61) 321 7602. Contact: Renato Geraldo de Lima, Manager; Michael Brown, Announcer; or Gaby Hertha Einstoss, Correspondence Service. Free stickers. Also, *see* Rádio Nacional da Amazônia, below.

Rádio Nacional São Gabriel da Cachoeira, Avenida Alvaro Maia s/n, 69750-000 São Gabriel da Cachoeira, Amazônas, Brazil. Contact: Luíz dos Santos Franca, Gerente; or Valdir de Souza Marques. Return postage necessary. Replies to correspondence in Portuguese.

Rádio Nikkei, Rua Grumixamas 843, 04349 Jabaquara, São Paulo SP, Brazil. Contact: Paulo N. Miyagui, Presidente. This Japanese-language program is aired over the facilities of Rádio Mundial, Brazil (*see*).

Rádio Novas de Paz, C.P. 22, 80001 Curitiba, Paraná, Brazil. Contact: João Falavinha Ienzen, Gerente. $1 or return postage required. Replies irregularly to correspondence in Portuguese.

Rádio Nova Visão
Studios: C.P. 551, 97100 Santa Maria, Rio Grande do Sul, Brazil; or C.P. 6084, 90031 Pôrto Alegre, Rio Grande do Sul, Brazil. Contact: Rev. Iván Nunes; or Marlene P. Nunes, Secretária. Return postage required. Replies to correspondence in Portuguese. Free stickers and non-data verifications.
Transmitter: Rua do Manifesto 1373, 04209-001 São Paulo, Brazil. Reportedly issues full-data verifications, upon request, from this location. If no luck, try writing, in English or Dutch, to Tom van Ewijck in Holland, who is in contact with the transmitter site, via e-mail at egiaroll@cat.cce.usp.br.

Rádio Oito de Setembro, C.P. 8, 13691 Descalvado, São Paulo SP, Brazil. Contact: Adonias Gomes. Replies to correspondence in Portuguese.

Rádio Pioneira de Teresina, Rua 24 de Janeiro, 150 sul/centro Teresina 64001-230, Piauí, Brazil. Contact: Luíz Eduardo Bastos; or Padre Tony Batista, Diretor. $1 or return postage required. Replies slowly to correspondence in Portuguese.

Rádio Portal da Amazônia (when operating), Rua Dom Antônio Malan 674, 78010 Cuiabá, Mato Grosso, Brazil; also, C.P. 277, 78001 Cuiabá, Mato Grosso, Brazil. Contact: Celso Castilho, Gerente Geral; or Arnaldo Medina. Return postage required. Replies occasionally to correspondence in Portuguese.

Rádio Potí, C.P. 145, 59001-970 Natal, Rio Grande do Norte, Brazil. Contact: Cid Lobo. Return postage helpful. Replies slowly to correspondence in Portuguese.

Rádio Progresso, Estrada do Belmont s/n, Bº Nacional, 78000 Pôrto Velho, Rondônia, Brazil. Return postage required. Replies occasionally to correspondence in Portuguese.

Rádio Record
Station: C.P. 7920, 04084-002 São Paulo SP, Brazil. Contact: Mário Luíz Catto, Diretor Geral. Free stickers. Return postage or $1 required. Replies occasionally to correspondence in Portuguese.
New York Office: 630 Fifth Avenue, Room 2607, New York NY 10111 USA.

Rádio Ribeirão Preto, C.P 814, 14001-970 Ribeirão Preto, São Paulo SP, Brazil. Contact: Lucinda de Oliveira, Secretária; or Paulo Henríque Rocha da Silva. Replies to correspondence in Portuguese.

Rádio Rio Mar, Rua José Clemente 500, Manaus, Amazonas, Brazil. Replies to correspondence in Portuguese. $1 or return postage necessary.

Rádio Rural Santarém, Rua Floriano Peixoto 632, 68005-060 Santarém, Pará, Brazil. Contact: João Elias B. Bentes, Gerente Geral. Replies slowly to correspondence in Portuguese. Free stickers. Return postage or $1 required.

Rádio Sentinela, Travessa Ruy Barbosa 142, 68250 Obidos, Pará, Brazil. Contact: Max Hamoy or Maristela

Hamoy. Return postage required. Replies occasionally to correspondence in Portuguese.

Radio Timbira, Rua do Correio, s/n Bairro de Fátima, 65050 São Luís, Maranhão, Brazil. Contact: Sandoval Pimentel Silva, Diretor Geral. Free picture postcards. $1 helpful. Replies occasionally to correspondence in Portuguese; persist.

Rádio Tropical, C.P. 23, 78600-000 Barra do Garças, Mato Grosso, Brazil. Contact: Alacir Viera Cándido, Diretor e Presidente; or Walter Francisco Dorados, Diretor Artístico. $1 or return postage required. Replies slowly and rarely to correspondence in Portuguese.

Rádio Tupí, Rua Nadir Dias Figueiredo 1329, 02110 São Paulo SP, Brazil. Contact: Alfredo Raymundo Filho, Diretor Geral; Celso Rodrigues de Oliveira, Asesor Internacional da Presidencia; or Elia Soares. Free stickers. Return postage required. Replies occasionally to correspondence in Portuguese.

Rádio Universo, C.P. 7133, 80001 Curitiba, Paraná, Brazil. Contact: Luíz Andreu Rúbio, Diretor. Replies occasionally to correspondence in Portuguese.

Rádio Verdes Florestas, C.P. 53, 69981-970 Cruzeiro do Sul, Acre, Brazil. Contact: Marlene Valente de Andrade. Return postage required. Replies occasionally to correspondence in Portuguese.

BULGARIA   World Time +2 (+3 midyear)

Radio Horizont, Bulgarian Radio, 4 Dragan Tsankov Blvd., 1040 Sofia, Bulgaria. Fax: (weekdays) +359 (2) 657 230. Contact: Borislav Djamdjiev, Director; or Iassen Indjev, Executive Director; Martin Minkov, Editor-in-Chief.

Radio Bulgaria

Nontechnical and Technical: 4 Dragan Tsankov Blvd., 1040 Sofia, Bulgaria. Phone: +359 (2) 66-19-54. Fax: (general, usually weekdays only) +359 (2) 87 10 60, +359 (2) 87 10 61, +359 (2) 65 05 60; (Managing Director) +359 (2) 66 22 15. Contact: (general) Mrs. Iva Delcheva, English Section; Kristina Mihailova, In Charge of Listeners' Letters, English Section; Svilen Stoicheff, Head of English Section; (administration and technical) Anguel H. Nedyalkov, Managing Director. Free tourist literature, postcards, stickers, T-shirts, bookmarks and pennants. Gold, silver and bronze diplomas for correspondents meeting certain requirements. Free sample copies of *Bulgaria* magazine. Replies regularly, but sometimes slowly. For concerns about frequency usage, contact BTC, below, with a copy to Mr. Nedyalkov of Radio Bulgaria.

Frequency Management and Transmission Operations: Bulgarian Telecommunications Company (BTC), Ltd., 8 Totleben Blvd., 1606 Sofia, Bulgaria. Phone: +359 (2) 88-00-75. Fax: +359 (2) 87 58 85 or +359 (2) 80 25 80. Contact: Roumen Petkov, Frequency Manager; or Mrs. Margarita Krasteva, Radio Regulatory Department.

Radio Varna, 22 Primorski Boulevard, Varna 9000, Bulgaria. Contact: Emma Gilena, English Section. Free postcards and calendars.

BURKINA FASO   World Time exactly

Radiodiffusion-Télévision Burkina, B.P. 7029, Ouagadougou, Burkina Faso. Contact: Raphael L. Onadia or M. Pierre Tassembedo. Replies irregularly to correspondence in French. IRC or return postage helpful.

BURMA—see MYANMAR.

BURUNDI   World Time +2

La Voix de la Révolution, B.P. 1900, Bujumbura, Burundi. Phone: +257 22-37-42. Fax: +257 22 65 47 or +257 22 66 13. Contact: (general) Grégoire Barampumba, Head of News Section; Frederic Havugiyaremye; Journalist; (heads of administration) Gérard Mfuranzima, Le Directeur de la Radio; Didace Barandereste, Directeur Général de la Radio; (technical) Abraham Makuza, Le Directeur Technique. $1 required.

CAMBODIA   World Time +7
National Radio of Cambodia

Station Address: Preah Meha Keatreyany Kessamak, Phnom Penh, Cambodia. Fax: + 855 (23) 27319. Contact: (general) Miss Hem Bory, English Announcer; Kem Yan, Chief of External Relations; Touch Chhatha, Producer, Art Department; (heads of administration) In Chhay, Chief of Overseas Service; Som Sarun, Chief of Home Service; Van Sunheng, Deputy Director General, Cambodian National Radio and Television; (technical) Oum Phin, Chief of Technical Department. Free programme schedule. Replies irregularly and slowly. Do not include stamps, currency, IRCs or dutiable items in envelope. Registered letters stand a much better chance of getting through.

CAMEROON   World Time +1

Note: Any CRTV outlet is likely to be verified by contacting via registered mail, in English or French with $2 enclosed, James Achanyi-Fontem, Head of Programming, CRTV, B.P. 986, Douala, Cameroon.

Cameroon Radio Television Corporation (CRTV)—Bafoussam (when operating), B.P. 970, Bafoussam (Ouest), Cameroon. Contact: (general) Boten Celestin; (technical) Ndam Seidou, Chef Service Technique. IRC or return postage required. Replies irregularly in French to correspondence in English or French.

Cameroon Radio Television Corporation (CRTV)—Bertoua (when operating), B.P. 230, Bertoua (Eastern), Cameroon. Rarely replies to correspondence, preferably in French. $1 required.

Cameroon Radio Television Corporation (CRTV)—Buea (when operating), P.M.B., Buea (Sud-Ouest), Cameroon. Contact: Ononino Oli Isidore, Chef Service Technique. Three IRCs, $1 or return postage required.

Cameroon Radio Television Corporation (CRTV)—Douala, B.P. 986, Douala (Littoral), Cameroon. Contact: (technical) Emmanuel Ekite, Technicien. Free pennants. Three IRCs or $1 required.

Cameroon Radio Television Corporation (CRTV)—Garoua, B.P. 103, Garoua (Nord/Adamawa), Cameroon. Contact: Kadeche Manguele. Free cloth pennants. Three IRCs or return postage required. Replies irregularly and slowly to correspondence in French.

Cameroon Radio Television Corporation (CRTV)—Yaoundé, B.P. 1634, Yaoundé (Centre-Sud), Cameroon. Phone: +237-21-40-77. Fax: +237 20 43 40. Contact: (technical or non technical) Gervais Mendo Ze, Le Directeur-Général; (technical) Francis Achu Samba, Le Directeur Technique. $1 required. Recorded musical cassettes 60 francs. Replies slowly to correspondence in French.

CANADA   World Time   -3:30   (-2:30 midyear) Newfoundland; -4 (-3 midyear) Atlantic; -5 (-4 midyear) Eastern, including Quebec and Ontario; -6 (-5 midyear) Central; -7 (-6 midyear) Mountain; -8 (-7 midyear) Pacific, including Yukon

Canadian Forces Network Radio—see Radio Canada International, below.

CBC Northern Quebec Shortwave Service—see Radio Canada International, below.

CFCX-CIQC/CKOI

Transmitter (CFCX); also, Studios for CIQC English-Language Programs: CFCX-CIQC, Radio Montréal, Mount Royal Broadcasting, Inc., 1200 McGill College Avenue, Suite 300, Montréal PQ, H3B 4G7 Canada. Phone: +1 (514) 766-2311, then press keys for appropriate department. Fax: +1 (514) 393 4659. Contact: Ted Silver, Program Director; (technical) Kim Bickerdike, Technical Director. Correspondence welcomed in English or French.

French-Language Program Studios: CKOI, 211 Gordon Avenue, Verdun PQ, H4G 2R2 Canada. Fax: (CKOI— Programming Dept.) +1 (514) 766 2474; (sister station CKVL)

+1 (514) 761 0136. Correspondence in French preferred, but English and Spanish accepted.

CFRX-CFRB

Main Address: 2 St. Clair Avenue West, Toronto ON, M4V 1L6 Canada. Phone: (talkshow) +1 (416) 872-1010; (general) +1 (416) 924-5711. Fax: +1 (416) 924 9685. Contact: Rob Mise, Operations Manager; or Nathalie Chamberland; (technical) David Simon, Engineer; or Ian Sharp. Free station history sheet. Reception reports should be sent to verification address, below.

Verification Address: ODXA, P.O. Box 161, Station A, Willowdale ON, M2N 5S8 Canada. Phone/fax: +1 (905) 853 3169. E-mail: 73737.3453@compuserve.com. Contact: Stephen Canney, VA3ID. Free program schedules and ODXA information sheets. Reception reports are processed quickly if sent to this address, rather than to the station itself.

CFVP-CFCN, P.O. Box 2750, Stn. M, Calgary AB, T2P 4P8 Canada. Phone: (general and technical) +1 (403) 240-5600; (news) +1 (403) 240-5844. Fax: (general and technical) +1 (403) 240 5801; (news) +1 (403) 246 7099. Contact: (general) Ken O'Neil; (technical) Ken Pasolli, Technical Director.

CHNX-CHNS, P.O. Box 400, Halifax NS, B3J 2R2 Canada. Phone: +1 (902) 422-1651. Fax: +1 (902) 422 5330. Contact: (general) Troy Michaels, Operations Manager; or Morrisey Dunn, Host; (technical) Kurt J. Arsenault, Chief Engineer; or Wayne Harvey, Engineer. Return postage or $1 helpful. Replies irregularly.

CHU (official time and frequency station), Time and Frequency Standards, Bldg. M-36, National Research Council, Ottawa ON, K1A 0R6 Canada. Phone: (general) +1 (613) 993-5186; (administration) +1 (613) 993-1003 or +1 (613) 993-2704. Fax: +1 (613) 993 1394. Contact: Dr. R.J. Douglas, Group Leader. Official standard frequency and World Time station for Canada on 3330, 7335 and 14670 kHz. Brochure available upon request. Those with a personal computer, Bell 103 standard and appropriate software can get the exact time, via CHU's cesium clock, off the air from their computer; details available upon request.

CKFX-CKWX, 2440 Ash Street, Vancouver BC, V5Z 4J6 Canada. Phone: +1 (604) 873-2599. Fax: +1 (604) 873 0877. Contact: (general) Sandra Gilmore; (technical) Vijay Chanbra, Engineer; or Jack Wiebe, Chief Engineer. Free stickers.

CKOI (when being aired), Metromedia CMR, Inc., 211 Ave. Gordon, Montreal, PQ H4G 2R2 Canada. Free stickers and possibly T-shirts. This station has had programs aired over CFCX (see above).

CKZN-CBN, CBC, P.O. Box 12010, Station "A", St. John's NF, A1B 3T8 Canada. Phone: +1 (709) 576-5000. Fax: +1 (709) 576 5099. Contact: (general) John O'Mara, Manager of Communications; (technical) Elaine Janes, Engineering Assistant; or Shawn R. Williams, Manager, Regional Engineering, Newfoundland Region. Free CBC sticker. Free folder on Newfoundland's history.

CKZU-CBU, CBC, P.O. Box 4600, Vancouver BC, V6B 4A2 Canada. Phone: +1 (604) 662-6000. Fax: +1 (604) 662 6350. Contact: (general) Public Relations; (technical) Dave Newbury, Transmission Engineer.

Radio Canada International

Note: The following RCI address, fax and e-mail information for the Main Office and Transmission Office is also valid for the Canadian Forces Network Radio and CBC Northern Quebec Shortwave Service.

Main Office: P.O. Box 6000, Montréal PQ, H3C 3A8 Canada. Phone: (general) +1 (514) 597-7555; (English and French Programming) +1 (514) 597-7551; (Russian Programming) +1 (514) 597-6866; (CBC's 'As It Happens' Talkback Machine") +1 (416) 205-3331. Fax: (general) +1 (514) 284 0891; (Canadian Forces Network) +1 (514) 597 7893. E-mail: (Audience Relations) to be activated shortly. World Wide Web: http://radioworks.cbc.ca or http://www.cbc.ca. Contact: (general) Maggy Akerblom, Director of Audience Relations; Ousseynou Diop, Manager,

English and French Programming; or André Courey, Producer/Host, the "Mailbag"; (head of administration) Terry Hargreaves, Executive Director; (technical—verifications) Bill Westenhaver, CIDX. Free stickers and other small station souvenirs. 50th Anniversary T-shirts, sweatshirts, watches, lapel pins and tote bags available for sale; write to the above address for a free illustrated flyer giving prices and ordering information.

CBC Record Sales: Various CBC items available in the United States from CBC Radio Works at toll-free telephone (800) 363-1530 (VISA/MC). Canadian CDs sold worldwide except North America, from International Sales, CBC Records, P.O. Box 500, Station "A", Toronto ON, M5W 1E6 Canada (VISA/MC), fax +1 (416) 975 3482; and within the United States from CBC/Allegro, 3434 SE Milwaukie Avenue, Portland OR 97202 USA, toll-free telephone (800) 288-2007, fax (503) 232 9504 (VISA/MC).

Transmission Office: P.O. Box 6000, Montréal PQ, H3C 3A8 Canada. Phone: +1 (514) 597-7616/17/18/19/20. Fax: +1 (514) 284 9550 or +1 (514) 284 2052. Contact: (general) Gérald Théorêt, Frequency Manager; or Mrs. Maya Wegrowicz; (head of administration) Jacques Bouliane, Chief Engineer. This office only for informing about transmitter-related problems (interference, modulation quality, etc.), especially by fax. Verifications not given out at this office; requests for verification should be sent to the main office, above.

Washington News Bureau: CBC, National Press Building, Suite 500, 529 14th Street NW, Washington DC 20045 USA. Phone: +1 (202) 638-3286. Fax: +1 (202) 783 9321. Contact: Jean-Louis Arcand, David Hall or Susan Murray.

London News Bureau: CBC, 43-51 Great Titchfield Street, London W1P 8DD, England. Phone: +44 (171) 412-9200. Fax: +44 (171) 631 3095.

Paris News Bureau: CBC, 17 avenue Matignon, F-75008 Paris, France. Phone: +33 (1) 43-59-11-85. Fax: +33 (1) 44 21 15 14.

Radio Monte-Carlo Middle East (via Radio Canada International)—see Cyprus.

Shortwave Classroom: Naismith Memorial Public School, P.O. Box 280, Almonte ON, K0A 1A0 Canada. Phone: (weekdays during school season) +1 (613) 256-3773; (other times) +1 (613) 256-2018. Fax: (during school season) +1 (613) 256 3825. E-mail: as167@freenet.carleton.ca. Contact: Neil Carleton, Organizer. *The Shortwave Classroom* newsletter, three times per year, for "$10 and an accompanying feature to share with teachers in the newsletter." Ongoing nonprofit volunteer project of teachers and others to use shortwave listening in the classroom to teach about global perspectives, media studies, world geography, languages, social studies and other subjects. Interested teachers and parents worldwide are invited to make contact.

CENTRAL AFRICAN REPUBLIC World Time +1

Radiodiffusion-Télévision Centrafricaine, B.P. 940, Bangui, Central African Republic. Contact: (technical) Jacques Mbilo, Le Directeur des Services Techniques; or Michèl Bata, Services Techniques. Replies on rare occasion to correspondence in French; return postage required.

CHAD World Time +1

Radiodiffusion Nationale Tchadienne—N'djamena, B.P. 892, N'Djamena, Chad. Contact: Djimadoum Ngoka Kilamian. Two IRCs or return postage required. Replies slowly to correspondence in French.

Radio Diffusion Nationale Tchadienne—Radio Abéché, B.P. 105, Abéché, Ouaddai, Chad. Return postage helpful. Replies rarely to correspondence in French.

Radiodiffusion Nationale Tchadienne—Radio Moundou, B.P. 122, Moundou, Logone, Chad. Contact: Dingantoudji N'Gana Esaie.

CHILE World Time -3 (-4 midyear)

Radio Esperanza, Casilla 830, Temuco, Chile. Fax: +56 (45) 236 179. Contact: (general) Eleazar Jara, Dpto. de Programación; Ramón Woerner, Publicidad; or Alberto Higueras Martínez, Locutor; (technical) Juan Luis Puentes, Dpto. Técnico. Free pennants, stickers, bookmarks and tourist information. Two IRCs or 2 U.S. stamps appreciated. Replies, usually quite slowly, to correspondence in Spanish or English.

Radio Santa María, Apartado 1, Coyhaique, Chile. Fax: +56 (67) 23 13 06. Contact: Pedro Andrade Vera, Coordinador. $1 or return postage required. May send free tourist litertature. Replies to correspondence in Spanish and Italian.

Radio Triunfal Evangélica, Costanera Sur 7209, Comuna de Cerro Navia, Santiago, Chile. Contact: Fernando González Segura, Obispo de la Misión Pentecostal Fundamentalista. Two IRCs required. Replies to correspondence in Spanish.

CHINA World Time +8; still nominally +6 ("Urümqi Time") in the Xinjiang Uighur Autonomous Region, but in practice +8 is observed there, as well.

Note: China Radio International, the Central People's Broadcasting Station and certain regional outlets reply regularly to listeners' letters in a variety of languages. If a Chinese regional station does not respond to your correspondence within four months—and many will not, unless your letter is in Chinese or the regional dialect—try writing them c/o China Radio International.

Central People's Broadcasting Station/CPBS (China National Radio), Zhongyang Renmin Guangbo Diantai, P.O. Box 4501, Beijing, China. Phone: +86 (10) 609-2008. Fax: +86 (10) 851 6630. Contact: Wang Changquan, Audience Department, China National Radio. Tape recordings of music and news $5 plus postage. CPBS T-shirts $10 plus postage; also sells ties and other items with CPBS logo. No credit cards. Free stickers, pennants and other small souvenirs. Return postage helpful. Responds regularly to correspondence in English and Standard Chinese (Mandarin). Although in recent years this station has consistently stated to English-speaking correspondents that it is officially called "China National Radio," perhaps to reflect the spirit of reduced communist orthodoxy, all on-air identifications continue to be "Zhongyang Renmin Guangbo Diantai" (Central People's Broadcasting Station).

China Huayi Broadcasting Company, P.O. Box 251, Fuzhou City, Fujian 350001, China. Contact: Lin Hai Chun. Replies to correspondence in English.

China National Radio—see Central People's Broadcasting Station/CPBS.

China Radio International

Main Office, Non-Chinese Languages Service: 2 Fuxingmenwaidajie Street, Beijing 100866, China. Phone: (general) +86 (10) 609-2274; (English Dept.) +86 (10) 609-2760; (English News) +86 (10) 862-691; (Current Affairs) +86 (10) 801-3134; (administration) +86 (10) 851-3135. Fax: (Audience Relations) +86 (1) 851 3175 or (administration) +86 (1) 851 3174. Contact: (general) Yanling Zhang, Head of Audience Relations; Ms. Chen Lifang, Mrs. Fan Fuguang, Ms. Qi Guilin, Audience Relations, English Department; Zhang Hong Quan, Reporter, General Editor's Office; Dai Mirong and Qui Mei, "Listeners' Letterbox"; Zang Guohua, or Deputy Director of English Service; (technical) Liu Yuzhou, Technical Director; or Ge Hongzhang, Frequency Manager; (research) Ms. Zhang Yanling; (head of administration) Zhang Zhenhua, Director General, China Radio International; Wang Guoqing, Assistant Director, China Radio International;. Free bi-monthly *The Messenger* magazine, pennants, stickers, desk calendars, pins, hair ornaments and such small souvenirs as handmade papercuts. T-shirts $5 and CDs $15. Two-volume, 820-page set of *Day-to-Day Chinese* language-lesson books $15, including

postage worldwide; contact Li Yi, English Department. Various other Chinese books (on arts, medicine, etc.) in English available from Chen Denong, CIBTC, P.O. Box 399, Beijing, China; fax +86 (10) 841 2023. To remain on *The Messenger* magazine mailing list, listeners should write to the station at least once a year. CRI is also relayed via shortwave transmitters in Brazil, Canada, France, French Guiana, Mali, Russia, Spain and Switzerland.

Main Office, Chinese Languages Service: Box 565, Beijing, China. Prefers correspondence in Chinese (Mandarin), Cantonese, Hakka, Chaozhou or Amoy.

Bonn News Bureau: Am Buchel 81, D-53173 Bonn, Germany. Contact: Ma Xuming.

Hong Kong News Bureau: 387 Queen's Road East, Hong Kong. Contact: Zang Daolin, Bureau Chief; Zhang Xiujuan; or Zhang Jiaping.

Washington News Bureau: 2401 Calvert Street NW, Suite 1012, Washington DC 20008 USA. Phone: +1 (202) 387-6860. Fax/phone: +1 (202) 387 0459, but first call +1 (202) 387-6860 so fax can be switched on. Contact: Tang Minguo, Bureau Chief; Luo Qiao; or Dai Hongfeng.

New York News Bureau: 630 First Avenue #35K, New York NY 10016 USA. Fax: +1 (212) 889 2076. Contact: Liu Hui, Bureau Chief.

Paris News Bureau: 7 rue Charles Lecocq, F-75015 Paris, France. Contact: Huang Liangde, Chef de Bureau; Jia Yanjing; or Xiong Wei.

Sydney News Bureau: 121/226 Sussex Street, Sydney NSW 2000, Australia. Contact: Xu Rongmao, Bureau Chief; or Shi Chungyong.

Tokyo News Bureau: Meith Fuyoku Nakameguro 2F3-10-3 Kamimeguro, Megoro-ku, Tokyo 153, Japan. Phone/fax: +81 (3) 3719 8414. Contact: Zhang Guo-qing, Bureau Chief.

Fujian People's Broadcasting Station, Fuzhou, Fujian, China. $1 helpful. Replies occasionally and usually slowly.

Gansu People's Broadcasting Station, Lanzhou, China. Contact: Li Mei. IRC helpful.

Guangxi People's Broadcasting Station, No. 12 Min Zu Avenue, Nanning, Guangxi 530022, China. Contact: Song Yue, Staffer; or Li Hai Li, Staffer. Free stickers and handmade papercuts. IRC helpful. Replies irregularly.

Heilongjiang People's Broadcasting Station, No. 115 Zhongshan Road, Harbin City, Heilongjiang, China. $1 or return postage helpful.

Honghe People's Broadcasting Station, Jianshe Donglu 32, Geji City 661400, Yunnan, China. Contact: Shen De-chun, Head of Station; or Mrs. Cheng Lin, Editor-in-Chief. Free travel brochures.

Hubei People's Broadcasting Station, No. 563 Jie Fang Avenue, Wuhan, Hubei, China.

Jiangxi People's Broadcasting Station, Nanchang, Jiangxi, China. Contact: Tang Ji Sheng, Editor, Chief Editor's Office. Free gold/red pins. Replies irregularly. Mr. Tang enjoys music, literature and stamps, so enclosing a small memento along these lines should help assure a speedy reply.

Nei Monggol (Inner Mongolia) People's Broadcasting Station, Hohhot, Nei Monggol Zizhiqu, China. Contact: Zhang Xiang-Quen, Secretary; or Liang Yan. Replies irregularly.

Qinghai People's Broadcasting Station, Xining, Qinghai, China. $1 helpful.

Sichuan People's Broadcasting Station, Chengdu, Sichuan, China. Replies occasionally.

Voice of Jinling, P.O. Box 268, Nanjing, Jiangsu 210002, China. Fax: +86 (25) 413 235. Contact: Strong Lee, Producer/Host, "Window of Taiwan." Free stickers and calendars, plus Chinese-language color station brochure and information on the Nanjing Technology Import & Export Corporation. Replies to correspondence in Chinese and to simple correspondence in English. $1 or return postage helpful.

Voice of Pujiang, P.O. Box 3064, Shanghai 200002, China. Contact: Jiang Bimiao, Editor & Reporter.

Voice of the Strait, People's Liberation Army Broadcasting Centre, P.O. Box 187, Fuzhou, Fujian, China. Replies very irregularly.

Wenzhou People's Broadcasting Station, Wenzhou, China.

Xilingol People's Broadcasting Station, Xilinhot, Xilingol, China.

Xinjiang People's Broadcasting Station, No. 84 Tuanjie Lu (United Road), Urümqi, Xinjiang 830044, China. Contact: Zhao Ji-shu. Free tourist booklet, postcards and used Chinese stamps.

Xizang People's Broadcasting Station, Lhasa, Xizang (Tibet), China. Contact: Lobsang Chonphel, Announcer. Free stickers and brochures.

Yunnan People's Broadcasting Station, No 73 Renmin Road (W), Central Building of Broadcasting & TV, Kunming, Yunnan 650031, China. Contact: Sheng Hongpeng or F.K. Fan. Free Chinese-language brochure on Yunnan Province, but no QSL cards. $1 or return postage helpful. Replies occasionally.

CHINA (TAIWAN)   World Time +8

Central Broadcasting System (CBS), 55 Pei An Road, Taipei, Taiwan. Contact: Lee Ming, Deputy Director. Free stickers.

Voice of Asia, P.O. Box 24-777, Taipei, Taiwan. Phone: +886 (2) 771-0151, X-2431. Fax: +886 (2) 751 9277. Contact: (general) Vivian Pu, Co-Producer, with Isaac Guo of "Letterbox"; or Ms. Chao Mei-Yi, Deputy Chief; (technical) Engineering Department. Free shopping bags, inflatable globes, coasters, calendars, stickers and booklets. T-shirts $5.

Voice of Free China, P.O. Box 24-38, Taipei 106, Taiwan. Phone: +886 (2) 752-2825 or +886 (2) 771-0151. Fax: +886 (2) 751 9277. Contact: (general) Daniel Dong, Chief, Listeners' Service Section; Paula Chao, Producer, "Mailbag Time";Yea-Wen Wang; Phillip Wong, "Perspectives"; (heads of administration) John C.T. Feng, Director; Dong Yu-Ching, Deputy Director; (technical) Wen-Bin Tsai, Engineer, Engineering Department; Tai-Lau Ying, Engineering Department; Tien-Shen Kao; or Huang Shuh-shyun, Director, Engineering Department. Free stickers, caps, shopping bags, *Voice of Free China Journal*, annual diary, "Let's Learn Chinese" language-learning course materials, booklets and other publications, and Taiwanese stamps. Station offers listeners a free Frisbee-type saucer if they return the "Request Card" sent to them by the station. T-shirts $5.
Osaka News Bureau: C.P.O. Box 180, Osaka Central Post Office, Osaka 530-91, Japan.
Tokyo News Bureau: P.O Box 21, Azubu Post Office, Tokyo 106, Japan.
San Francisco News Bureau, Nontechnical: P.O. Box 192793, San Francisco CA 94119-2793 USA.

CLANDESTINE—see DISESTABLISHMENTARI-AN.

COLOMBIA   World Time -5
Note: Colombia, the country, is always spelled with two o's. It is never written as "Columbia."
Armonías del Caquetá, Apartado Aéreo 71, Florencia, Caquetá, Colombia. Phone: 57 (88) 352-080. Contact: Padre Alvaro Serna Alzate, Director. Replies rarely to correspondence in Spanish. Return postage required.
Caracol Bucaramanga (when operating), Calle 35 No. 16-24 P. 8, Bucaramanga, Colombia. Phone: +57 (76) 425-600. Contact: Germán Gómez Vahos, Gerente.
Caracol Colombia
Main Office: Apartado Aéreo 9291, Santafé de Bogotá, D.C., Colombia. Phone: +57 (1) 337-8866. Fax: +57 (1) 337 7126. Contact: Hernán Peláez Restrepo, Jefe Cadena Básica.

Free stickers. Replies to correspondence in Spanish and English.
Miami Office: 2100 Coral Way, Miami FL 33145 USA. Phone: +1 (305) 285-2477 or +1 (305) 285-1260. Fax: +1 (305) 858 5907.
Caracol Villavicencio—see La Voz de los Centauros.
Ecos del Atrato, Apartado Aéreo 196, Quibdó, Chocó, Colombia. Phone: +57 (49) 711-450. Contact: Absalón Palacios Agualimpia, Administrador. Free pennants. Replies to correspondence in Spanish.
La Voz de la Selva, Apartado Aéreo 465, Florencia, Caquetá, Colombia. Contact: Alonso Orozco, Gerente. Replies occaisonaly to correspondence in Spanish. Return postage helpful.
La Voz de los Centauros (Caracol Villavicencio), Cra. 31 No. 37-71 Of. 1001, Villavicencio, Meta, Colombia. Phone: +57 (86) 214-995. Fax: +57 (86) 623-954. Contact: Carlos Torres Leyva, Gerencia; or Cielo de Corredor, Administradora. Replies to correspondence in Spanish.
La Voz del Cinaruco, Calle 19 No. 19-62, Arauca, Colombia. Contact: Efrahim Valera, Director. Pennants for return postage. Replies rarely to correspondence in Spanish; return postage required.
La Voz del Guainía, Calle 6 con Carrera 3, Puerto Inírida, Guainía, Colombia. Contact: Luis Fernando Román Robayo, Director. Replies occasionally to correspondence in Spanish.
La Voz del Guaviare, Carrera 3 con Calle 2, San José del Guaviare, Colombia. Contact: Jairo Hernán Benjumea, Gerente. Replies slowly to correspondence in Spanish.
La Voz del Llano, Calle 38 No. 30A-106, Villavicencio, Meta, Colombia. Phone: +57 (86) 624-102. Fax: +57 (86) 625 045. Contact: Alcides Antonio Jáuregui B., Director. Replies occasionally to correspondence in Spanish. $1 or return postage necessary.
La Voz del Río Arauca
Station: Carrera 20 No. 19-09, Arauca, Colombia. Phone: +57 (818) 52-910. Contact: Jorge Flórez Rojas, Gerente; Luis Alfonso Riaño, Locutor; or Mario Falla, Periodista. $1 or return postage required. Replies occasionally to correspondence in Spanish; persist.
Bogotá Office: Cra. 10 No. 14-56, Of. 309/310, Santafé de Bogotá, D.C., Colombia.
La Voz del Yopal, Calle 9 No. 22-63, Yopal, Casanare, Colombia. Phone: +57 (87) 558-382. Fax: +57 (87) 557 054. Contact: Pedro Antonio Socha Pérez, Gerente; or Marta Cecilia Socha Pérez, Subgerente. Return postage necessary. Replies to correspondence in Spanish.
Ondas del Meta, Calle 38 No. 30A-106, Villavicencio, Meta, Colombia. Phone: +57 (86) 626-783. Fax: +57 (86) 625 045. Contact: Yolanda Plazas Agredo, Administradora. Free tourist literature. Return postage required. Replies irregularly and slowly to correspondence in Spanish.
Ondas del Orteguaza, Calle 16, No. 12-48, piso 2, Florencia, Caquetá, Colombia. Contact: Sra. Dani Yasmín Anturi Durán, Secretaria; Yolanda Plazas Agredo, Administradora; Jorge Daniel Santos Calderón, Gerente; or C.P. Norberto Plaza Vargas, Subgerente. Free stickers. IRC, return postage or $1 required. Replies occasionally to correspondence in Spanish.
Radio Buenaventura (when operating), Calle 1a. No. 2-39, piso 2, Buenaventura, Colombia. Phone: +57 (32) 24-387. Contact: Mauricio Castaño Angulo, Gerente; or María Herlinda López Meza, Secretaria. Free stickers. Return postage or $1 required. Replies to correspondence in Spanish.
Radio Católica Nacional, Primer Sector Vereda San Carlos, Cuatro Esquinas, Túquerres, Nariño, Colombia. Contact: José Celio Díaz. Sr. Díaz, the station operator, is a botanist by profession. Married to an Ecuadorian woman, he loves to play Ecuadorian music on his station, which is a hobby operation. Correspondence in Spanish is traditionally answered on the air, but thus far no written replies to correspondence are known to exist, nor is there any

phone or fax over which you can exercise your persuasive talents.

Radiodifusora Nacional de Colombia

Main Address: Edificio Inravisión, CAN, Av. Eldorado, Santafé de Bogotá, D.C., Colombia. Phone: +57 (1) 222-0415. Fax: +57 (1) 222 0409 or +57 (1) 222 8000. Contact: Jimmy García Camargo, Director; or Rubén Darío Acero. Tends to reply slowly.

Canal Internacional: Apartado Aéreo 93994, Santafé de Bogotá, D.C., Colombia. Contact: Jesús Valencia Sánchez.

Radio Macarena, Calle 38 No. 32-41, P. 7, Edif. Santander, Villavicencio, Meta, Colombia. Phone: +57 (86) 626-780. Contact: Carlos Alberto Pimienta, Gerente. Return postage required. Replies slowly to correspondence in Spanish.

Radio Melodía (when active), Apartado Aéreo 58721, Santafé de Bogotá, D.C., Colombia. Contact: Gerardo Páez Mejía, Vicepresidente; Elvira Mejía de Pérez, Gerente General; or Gracilla Rodríguez, Asistente Gerencia. Stickers and pennants $1 or return postage.

Radio Mira (when active), Apartado Aéreo 165, Tumaco, Nariño, Colombia. Phone: +57 (27) 272-452. Contact: Padre Julio Arturo Ochoa Zea. Return postage required.

Radio Nueva Vida (if active), Apartado Aéreo 3068, Bucaramanga, Colombia. Phone: +57 (76) 443-195. Contact: Marco Antonio Caicedo, Director. Cassettes with biblical studies $3 each. Return postage. Replies to correspondence in Spanish.

Radio Santa Fé (if reactivated), Apartado Aéreo 9339, Santafé de Bogotá, D.C., Colombia. Phone: +57 (1) 345-6770. Fax: +57 (1) 249 6095. Contact: (general) César Augusto Duque; or Adolfo Bernal Mahé, Gerente Administrativo; (technical) Sra. María Luisa Mahé Vda. de Bernal, Gerente. Return postage appreciated. Replies slowly to correspondence in Spanish.

Radio Super (Bogotá), Calle 39A No. 18-12, Santafé de Bogotá, D.C., Colombia. Phone: +57 (1) 338-2166. Fax: +57 (1) 287 8678. Contact: Henry Pava Camelo, Director Gerente. Free posters. Return postage required.

Radio Super (Ibagué), Parque Murillo Toro 3-31, P. 3, Ibagué, Tolima, Colombia. Contact: Fidelina Caycedo Hernández; or Germán Acosta Ramos, Locutor Control. Free stickers. Return postage or $1 helpful. Replies irregularly to correspondence in Spanish.

CONGO World Time +1

Radio Congo, Radiodiffusion-Télévision Congolaise, B.P. 2241, Brazzaville, Congo. Contact: (general) Antoine Ngongo, Rédacteur en chef; (head of administration) Albert Fayette Mikano, Directeur. $1 required. Replies irregularly to letters in French sent via registered mail.

COSTA RICA World Time -6

Adventist World Radio, the Voice of Hope, Radio Lira Internacional, Apartado 1177, 4050 Alajuela, Costa Rica. Phone +506 443-0560. Fax +506 (441) 1282. E-mail: 74617.1577@compuserve.com. Contact: David L. Gregory, General Manager. Free stickers, calendars, Costa Rican stamps, pennants and religious printed matter. $1, IRC or return postage helpful, with $0.50 in unused U.S. stamps also being acceptable. Also, *see* USA.

Faro del Caribe—TIFC

Main Office: Apartado 2710, 1000 San José, Costa Rica. Fax: +506 (227) 1725. Contact: Juan Francisco Ochoa, Director; Pedro Jiménez Mora, Director Administrativo; or Jacinto Ochoa A., Administrador. Free stickers and pennants. $1 or IRCs helpful.

U.S. Office, Nontechnical: P.O. Box 620485, Orlando FL 32862 USA. Contact: Lim Ortiz.

Radio Casino, Apartado 287, 7301 Puerto Limón, Costa Rica. Contact: Max DeLeo, Announcer; Luis Grau Villalobos, Gerente; (technical) Ing. Jorge Pardo, Director Técnico; or Luis Muir, Técnico.

Radio Exterior de España—Cariari Relay

Station, Cariari de Pococí, Costa Rica. Phone: +506 767-7308. Fax: +506 767 7311.

Radio For Peace International (RFPI)

Main Office: Apartado 88, Santa Ana, Costa Rica. Phone: +506 249-1821. Fax: +506 249 1925. E-mail: rfpicr@sol.racsa.co.cr. Contact: (general) Debra Latham, General Manager; (nontechnical or technical) James L. Latham, Station Manager; Joe Bernard, Program Coordinator; Willie Barrantes, Director, Spanish Department; María Suárez, Katerina Anfossi and Nancy Vargas, FIRE, Women's Programming. Replies sometimes slow in coming because of the mail. Audio cassette presentations, in English or Spanish, from women's perspectives welcomed for replay over "FIRE" program. Quarterly *Vista* newsletter, which includes schedules and program information, $35 annual membership ($50 family/organization) in "Friends of Radio for Peace International"; station commemorative T-shirts and rainforest T-shirts $15; thermo mugs $10 (VISA/MC). Actively solicits listener contributions—directly and through "PeaceCOM" long distance telephone service or designated purchases from Grove Enterprises—for operating expenses. $1 or 3 IRCs appreciated. Limited number of places available for volunteer broadcasting and journalism interns; those interested should send resume. If funding can be worked out, hopes to add a world band transmission facility in Salmon Arm, British Columbia, Canada.

U.S. Office, Nontechnical: P.O. Box 20728, Portland OR 97294 USA. Phone: +1 (503) 252-3639. Fax: +1 (503) 255 5216. Contact: Dr. Richard Schneider, Chancellor CEO, University of Global Education (formerly World Peace University). Newsletter, T-shirts and so forth, as above. University of the Air courses ("Global Spirituality" and "History of the U.N.") $25 each, or on audio cassette (ditto, plus "The World Is My Body") $75 each (VISA/MC).

Radio Reloj, Sistema Radiofónico H.B., Apartado 4334, 1000 San José, Costa Rica. Contact: Roger Barahona, Gerente; or Francisco Barahona Gómez. $1 required.

Radio Universidad de Costa Rica, San Pedro de Montes de Oca, 1000 San José, Costa Rica. Contact: Marco González; or Nora Garita B., Directora. Free postcards and stickers. Replies slowly to correspondence in Spanish or English. $1 or return postage required.

CROATIA World Time +1 (+2 midyear)

Croatian Radio

Main Office: Hrvatska Radio-Televizija (HRT), Prisavlje 3, 41000 Zagreb, Croatia. Phone: (technical) +385 (1) 66-33-55. Fax: (technical) +385 (1) 66 33 47. World Wide Web: (general) http://hrt.com.hr; (technical) zklasan@bourbon.hrt.com.hr. Contact: Darko Kragovic. Free Croatian stamps. Subscriptions to *Croatian Voice*. $1 helpful. Replies regularly, although sometimes slowly.

Washington News Bureau: Croatian-American Association, 1912 Sunderland Place NW, Washington DC 20036 USA. Phone: +1 (202) 429-5543. Fax: +1 (202) 429 5545. Contact: Bob Schneider, Director.

Hrvatska Radio-Televizija—see Croatian Radio, Studio Zagreb, above, for details.

CUBA World Time -5 (-4 midyear)

Radio Habana Cuba, (general) P.O. Box 7026, Havana, Cuba; (technical) P.O. Box 6240, Havana 10600, Cuba. Fax: +53 (7) 795 007. E-mail: (general) radiohc@tinored.cu; ("DXers Unlimited") acoro@tinored.cu. Contact: (general) Rolando Peláez, Head of Correspondence; Jorge Miyares, English Service; or Mike La Guardia, Senior Editor; (head of administration) Ms. Milagro Hernández Cuba, General Director; (technical) Arnie Coro, Producer, "DXers Unlimited"; or Luis Pruna Amer, Director Técnico. Free wallet and wall calendars, pennants, stickers, keychains and pins. DX Listeners' Club. Thirty-fifth anniversary contest for five free trips to Cuba; entries no later than March 31, 1996, to the Box 6240 address.

Radio Rebelde, Departamento de Relaciones Públicas, Apartado 6277, Havana 10600, Cuba. Contact: Noemí Cairo Marín, Secretaria, Relaciones Públicas; Iberlise González Padua, Relaciones Públicas; or Jorge Luís Más Zabala, Director, Relaciones Públicas. Replies very slowly, with correspondence in Spanish preferred.

CYPRUS   World Time +2 (+3 midyear)

BBC World Service—East Mediterranean Relay, P.O. Box 219, Limassol, Cyprus. Nontechnical correspondence should be sent to the BBC World Service in London (see).

Cyprus Broadcasting Corporation, Broadcasting House, P.O. Box 4824, Nicosia, Cyprus. Phone: +357 (2) 422-231. Fax: +357 (2) 314 050. Contact: Dimitris Kiprianou, Director General. Free stickers. Replies occasionally, sometimes slowly. IRC or $1 helpful.

Radio Monte-Carlo Middle East, P.O. Box 2026, Nicosia, Cyprus. Contact: M. Pavlides, Chef de Station. This address for listeners to the RMC Arabic Service, which prepares its world band programs in Cyprus, but transmits them via facilities of Radio Canada International in Canada. For details of Radio Monte-Carlo's headquarters and other branch offices, see Monaco.

CZECH REPUBLIC   World Time +1 (+2 midyear)

Radio Prague, Czech Radio, Vinohradská 12, 120 99 Prague, Czech Republic. Phone: +42 (2) 25-06-16 or +42 (2) 25-79-22. Fax: (general) +42 (2) 242 22236 (general, external programs) +42 (2) 242 18239 or +42 (2) 235 4760 or (technical, external programs and domestic programs) +42 (2) 232 1020 or +42 (2) 25 38 43. E-mail: (general) cr@radio.cz; (reception reports, Nora Mikes) nora@werich.radio.cz. World Wide Web: http://town.hall.org/archives/radio/mirrors/prague/. Contact: (general) Markéta Albrechtová or Lenka Adamová, "Mailbag"; Zdenek Dohnal; Nora Mikes, Listener Relations; L. Kubik; or Jan Valeška, Head of English Section; (head of administration) Dr. Richard Seeman, Director, Foreign Broadcasts; (technical, all programs) Oldrich Čip, Chief Engineer. Free stickers, key chains, and calendars; free Radio Prague Monitor Club "DX Diploma" for regular correspondents. Free books available for Czech-language course called "Check out Czech." Samples of Welcome to the Czech Republic and Czech Life available upon request from Orbis, Vinohradská 46, 120 41 Prague, Czech Republic.

RadioRopa Info—see Germany.

RFE-RL—see USA.

DENMARK   World Time +1 (+2 midyear)

Radio Danmark
Main Office, Nontechnical: Rosenørns Allé 22, DK-1999 Frederiksberg C, Denmark. Phone: (Danish-language 24-hour telephone tape recording for schedule information) +45 35-20-57-96 for Europe/Africa, +45 35-20-57-97 for Eastern Hemisphere, +45 35-20-57-98 for Western Hemisphere; (general) +45 35-20-57-85; (voice mail) +45 35-20-57-91; (technical) +45 35-20-66-90 or +45 35-20-57-86. Fax: (nontechnical and technical) + 45 35 20 57 81; (technical) +45 35 20 58 76 or +45 33 12 28 59. E-mail: (technical) rdk.ek@login.dknet.dk. Contact: (general) Lulu Vittrup, Audience Communications; or "Tune In" bi-weekly Saturday letterbox program; (technical) Erik Køie or Bjorn Schionning. Replies to correspondence in English or Danish. Will verify all correct reception reports if $1 or IRC is enclosed for return postage. Transmits via facilities of Radio Norway. All transmissions are in Danish, but Radio Denmark is seriously considering adding, by January, 1996, a 15-minute English report, covering mainly cultural events in Denmark, the first Sunday of each month. Should that prove to be popular, they may increase the number of such newscasts. Additionally, Radio Danmark is looking into the possibility of broadcasting via relay facilities in the Americas, such as those of Radio Nederland Wereldomroep in the Netherlands Antilles, to improve reception quality in the Western Hemisphere.
Transmission Management Authority: Telecom Denmark, Telegade 2, DK-2630 Taastrup, Denmark. Phone: +45 42-52-91-11, Ext. 5746. Fax: +45 43 71 11 43. Contact: Ib H. Lavrsen, Senior Engineer.
Norwegian Office, Technical: Details of reception quality may also be sent to the Engineering Department of Radio Norway International (see), which operates the transmitters currently used for Radio Denmark.
Washington News Bureau: 3001 Q Street NW, Washington DC 20007 USA. Phone: +1 (202) 463-7518 or +1 (202) 342-2454. Fax: +1 (202) 342 2463. Contact: Frank Esman.

DISESTABLISHMENTARIAN

Note on Stations within the United States and Costa Rica: In the United States and Costa Rica, disestablishmentarian programs are aired within the provisions of national law, and thus usually welcome correspondence and requests for free or paid materials. Virtually all such programs in the United States are aired over powerful private stations—notably WWCR in Nashville, WRNO near New Orleans, WHRI in Noblesville, Indiana and, more recently, KVOH in Los Angeles—which sell airtime to nearly all comers. (WINB and WRMI no longer carry such programs, at least in English.) The programs usually refer to themselves as "patriotic," and include such traditional and relatively benign ideologies as populism and politically conservative evangelism. Among these categories, some go out of their way to disassociate themselves from bigotry. However, other programs, with tiny but dedicated audiences, are survivalist, antisemitic, neo-fascist, ultranationalist or otherwise on the fringes of the political "right," including the much-publicized militia movement. Perhaps surprisingly, few are overtly racist, although racism is often implied. These programs reflect the American climate of unfettered freedom of speech, as well as, in some cases, the more cynical American tradition of profiting from proselytization. ("Our society is about to be conquered by alien or internationalist forces. To cope with this, you'll need certain things, which I sell.") Thus, American disestablishmentarian programs often differ greatly from the sorts of broadcasting discourse allowed within the laws and traditions of most other countries.
Well removed from this genre is the relatively low-powered voice of Radio For Peace International (see), a largely American-staffed station in Costa Rica. RFPI airs disestablishmentarian-cum-social-conscience programs from the relatively internationalistic perspective of the political "new left" that grew into prominence in North America and Europe during the late Sixties. It also regularly follows and reports on the aforementioned disestablishmentarian programs aired over stations within the United States.
Note on Stations Outside the United States and Costa Rica: Outside the United States and Costa Rica, disestablishmentarian broadcasting activities, some of which are actually clandestine, are unusually subject to abrupt change or termination. Being operated by anti-establishment political and/or military organizations, these groups tend to be suspicious of outsiders' motives. Thus, they are most likely to reply to contacts from those who communicate in the station's native tongue, and who are perceived to be at least somewhat favorably disposed to their cause. Most will provide, upon request, printed matter in their native tongue on their cause. For more detailed information on clandestine (but not disestablishmentarian) stations, refer to the annual publication, Clandestine Stations List, about $10 or 10 IRCs postpaid by air, published by the Danish Shortwave Clubs International, Tavleager 31, DK-2670 Greve, Denmark; phone (Denmark) +45 4290-2900; fax (via Germany) +49 6371 71790; e-mail 100413.2375@com-

puserve.com. For CIA media contact information, *see* USA.

"Along the Color Line," Department of History, Columbia University, 611 Fayerweather Hall, New York NY 10027 USA. Phone: +1 (212) 854-7080. Fax: +1 (212) 854 7060. Contact: Dr. Manning Marable, Director of the Institute for Research in African-American Studies. Critiques a wide variety of domestic and international issues relevant to African-Americans.

"Alternative Radio," P.O. Box 551, Boulder CO 80306 USA. Phone: +1 (303) 444-8788. Contact: David Barsamian. Critiques such issues as multiculturalism, the environment, racism, American foreign policy, the media and the rights of indigenous peoples. Via RFPI, Costa Rica.

"America First Radio," P.O. Box 15499, Pittsburgh PA 15237 USA. Phone: (talk show, toll-free within United States) (800) 518-5979; (Populist Party, toll-free within the United States) (800) 998-4451. Fax: +1 (412) 443-4240. Contact: Harry Bertram. Monthly *Populist Observer* newspaper $30/yr, or $19 for introductory subscription. Populist Party talk show, reflecting American nationalist and populist perspective. Via WWCR, USA.

"American Dissident Voices," P.O. Box 90, Hillsboro WV 24946 USA; or P.O. Box 596, Boring OR 97009 USA. Contact: Kevin Alfred Strom, Producer. E-mail: triton@abzolute.org. FTP: (program transcripts and related matter) ftp://ftp.netcom.com/pub/na/na/. $12 for audio cassette of any given program. $55 for latest book from Canadian neo-nazi Ernst Zündel. *Free Speech* publication $40 per year. $1 for catalog of books and tapes. Free bumper stickers and sample copies of *Patriot Review* newsletter. Program of the neo-nazi National Alliance organization, which in its publicity claims to support "ordinary straight White Americans." Via WRNO, and before that believed to be behind the U.S. clandestine station, "Voice of To-morrow," which became inactive not long before "American Dissident Voices" came on the air.

"Amnesty International Reports," KCRW Radio, 1990 Pico Boulevard, Santa Monica CA 90405 USA. Phone: +1 (310) 450-5183. Fax: +1 (310) 450 7172. Each month, this program reports on Amnesty International's human-rights findings within three countries. Via RFPI, Costa Rica.

"A Voz da Resistencia do Galo Negro" (Voice of the Resistence of the Black Cockerel)—*see* Angola.

"Baker Report," 2083 Springwood Road #300, York PA 17403 USA. Phone: (show, toll-free in United States) (800) 482-5560; (orders, toll-free in United States) (800) 782-4843; (general number/voice mail) +1 (717) 244-1110. Contact: Jeff Baker. Three months of *The Baker Report* periodical $24.95; also sells audio tapes of programs and other items. Anti-"New World Order," and distrustful of official versions of various events, including the Oklahoma City bombing. Via WWCR, USA.

"Battle Cry Sounding"

Headquarters: Command Post, ACMTC, P.O. Box 90, Berino NM 88024 USA. Fax: +1 (505) 882 7325. Contact: General James M. Green. Voice of the Aggressive Christianity Missions Training Corps, which seeks to eliminate churches, synagogues, mosques and central governments, thence to replace them with fundamentalist "warrior tribes"; also, operates Women's International Mobilization Movement. Publishes *Wisdom's Cry*, *Words of the Spirit* and *Battle Cry Sounding* periodicals, and offers various other publications, as well as video and audio tapes. Via facilities of WWCR, USA.

African Office: P.O. Box 2686, Jos North, Plateau State, Nigeria. Contact: Colonel Simon Agwale, Adjutant.

"CCC Radio" (when active), Conservative Consolidated Confederacy, P.O. Box 5635, Longview TX 75608 USA. Contact: Tim Harper. Free Ku Klux Klan printed matter.

"Contacto con Cuba"—*see* Radio Miami Internacional, USA, for address. Contact: Carlos Pacheco. Cuban exile program.

"CounterSpin," Fairness and Accuracy in Reporting, 130

W. 25th Street, New York NY 10001 USA. Phone: +1 (212) 633-6700. Media watchdog organization that reports on what it feels are propaganda, disinformation and other abuses of the media, as well as citing instances of "hard-hitting, independent reporting that cuts against the prevailing media grain." Via RFPI, Costa Rica.

"Democratic Voice of Burma" ("Democratic Myanmar α-Than"), P.O. Box 6720, St. Olavs Plass, N-0130 Oslo, Norway. Phone: +47 (22) 200-021. Fax: +47 (22) 114 988. Contact: Maung Maung Myint or Khin Maung Win. Programs produced by four expatriate Burmese students belonging to a jungle-based revolutionary student organization called "All Burma Students' Democratic Front." Anti-Myanmar government. Transmits via the facilities of Radio Norway International.

"Duncan Long Show," USA Patriot Network, P.O. Box 430, Johnstown CO 80534 USA. Phone: (talk show, toll-free within U.S.) (800) 607-8255; (elsewhere) +1 (970) 587-5171; (order line, toll-free within U.S.) (800) 205-6245. Fax: +1 (970) 587 5450. Contact: Duncan Long, Host; or "Don W." Network Manager. Free sample of *USA Patriot News* monthly newspaper/catalog, otherwise $16/six months. Sells survival gear, night-vision goggles, Sangean shortwave radios, books and NTSC videos. VISA/MC/AX. Survivalist/militia how-to show, detailing such things as how and where to obtain, modify and use firearms and other military-type gear for various types of situations, including conventional, guerilla/special, biological and chemical combat, as well as "target shooting." Via WWCR, USA.

"Executive Intelligence Review Talks," EIR News Service, P.O. Box 17390, Washington DC 20041 USA. Phone: (Executive Intelligence Review) +1 (202) 544-7010; (Schiller Institute) +1 (202) 544-7018; (21st Century Institute, general information) +1 (202) 639-6821; (21st Century Institute, subscription information) +1 (703) 777-9451; (Ben Franklin Bookstore for LaRouche publications) toll-free daytimes only within United States (800) 453-4108, elswhere +1 (703) 777-3661. Fax: +1 (202) 544 7105. E-mail: (technical) ralphgib@aol.com. Contact: (general) Mel Kanovsky or Frank Bell; or, asking correspondence to be forwarded to the Federal penitentiary where he currently resides, Lyndon LaRouche; (technical) Ralph Gibbons. Publishes *Executive Intelligence Review* newsletter, $896/year, and a wide variety of other periodicals and books. Supports former U.S. presidential candidate Lyndon LaRouche's populist political organization worldwide, including the Schiller Institute and 21st Century Institute of Political Action. Via WWCR, USA.

"Far Right Radio Review"—*see* RFPI, Costa Rica, for contact information. Critiques populist and politically rightist programs emanating from various privately owned world band stations in the United States.

"FIRE"—*see* RFPI, Costa Rica, for contact information. Award-winning multilingual (English and Spanish) feminist program produced by the Feminist International Radio Endeavour staff at RFPI, led by María Suárez. Financially supported by the Foundation for a Compassionate Society.

"Focus on Haiti"—*see* Haiti.

"Food Not Bombs Radio Network"

Production Facility: 350 7th Avenue #35, San Francisco CA 94118 USA. Phone: +1 (415) 330-5030. Contact: Richard Edmondson, Producer. Via RFPI, Costa Rica.

Organizational Address: Food Not Bombs, 3145 Gary Blvd. #12, San Francisco CA 94118 USA; also, temporarily can be reached at 25 Taylor Avenue, San Francisco CA 94118 USA. Phone: +1 (415) 351-1672. Food Not Bombs is a political activist group concerned with American homeless people, with the radio program focusing on what it views as "oppressive local, state and federal policies." The producer is a former homeless person.

"For the People," People's Network, Inc., Telford Hotel, 3 River Street, White Springs FL 32096 USA. Phone: (24-hour toll-free order line, within U.S. only) (800) 888-9999; (toll-free within U.S. for other contacts) (800) 825-5937; (elsewhere) +1 (904) 397-4145 or +1 (904) 397-4288; (station affiliate contact) +1 (904) 397-4300; (front desk) +1 (904) 397-1000. Fax: +1 (904) 397 4149. Contact: Kent Phillips, Producer; Chuck Harder, Host; or Dianne Harder, Administrator. Free monthly *Station Listing & Program Guide* Flyer. Annual membership, including quarterly *For the People Magazine* and *Lemons* book $15. Bi-weekly *News Reporter* newspaper $19/year. NTSC videos of past FTP broadcasts $23.95. T-shirts and golf shirts $9.95-21.95 plus shipping. Sells a wide variety of books from its "For the People Bookstore"; free catalog upon request. Currently sells two models of Chinese-made analog shortwave radios, but has announced that by 1996 it will be offering a special simplified version of an American-made Drake world band receiver, which FTP hopes to sell for under $300. VISA/MC. This talk show espouses American populism, a philosophy going back to 1891. FTP's governing non-profit organization supports trade restrictions, freedom of health-care choice and progressive taxes on high incomes, while opposing racism and antisemitism. Live afternoons and on tape evenings (local time) via WHRI, USA. A non-talk-show version of FTP is now on television Stateside. FTP is currently researching the feasibility of setting up one or two of its own 50 kW shortwave transmitters within the United States, although no application has as yet been filed with the Federal Communications Commission.

"Forum for Democracy"—see Radio Miami Internacional, USA, for address. Program of the Vietnam Restoration Party, based in California. Aired via KWHR, Hawaii, USA.

"Full Disclosure Live," Studio 303, The Superior Broadcasting Company, P.O. Box 1533, Oil City PA 16301 USA. Phone: (toll-free within the United States) (800) 825-5303; (elsewhere) +1 (814) 678-8801. World Wide Web: http://ripco.com:8080/~glr/glr.html. Contact: Glen Roberts. Free sample newsletter and catalog. Offers a variety of electronics and related publications. Conservative talk show concerning such topics as militias, political broadcasts and related communications, and eavesdropping. Via WWCR, USA.

"Herald of Truth," P.O. Box 1021, Harrison AK 72602 USA. Phone: +1 (501) 741-1119. Contact: Pastor Bob Hallstrom. Free copies of broadcast transcripts and packet of information. Program of the Kingdom Identity Ministries. Opposes to what it calls "Jews, queers, aliens and minorities," and supports "white Christians." Also opposes a seemingly endless roster of political leaders, including conservatives Rush Limbaugh and U.S. House Speaker Newt Gingrich, and claims the late U.S. President Franklin Roosevelt was a Jewish communist. Via WWCR, USA; Kingdom Identity Ministries programs are also aired over other American world band stations, such as WRNO, but no longer via WINB. Sells various books and audio cassettes.

"Hightower Radio," Saddle Burr Productions, P.O. Box 13516, Austin TX 78711 USA. Phone: +1 (512) 477-5588. Fax: +1 (512) 478 8536. Contact: Jim Hightower. The term "maverick" comes from the contrarian way Texas pioneer Samuel Maverick and certain of his descendants handled cattle and other matters. Hightower Radio is considered to be heir to that spirit, featuring former Texas Agriculture Commissioner Jim Hightower, something of an establishment Texas disestablishmentarian and a gen-yew-wine Lone Star liberal. Via RFPI, Costa Rica.

"Holy Medina Radio" (when operating)—see Radio Iraq International for contact information. Opposes the Saudi government.

"Hour of Courage," International Commerce Corporation, 135 S. Main Street, 7th Floor, Greenville SC 29601 USA. Phone: (toll-free within United States) (800) 327-8606. Fax: +1 (803) 232 9309. Contact: Ron Wilson. *Creatures* *from Jeckyl Island* book $25. Forsees a conspiracy to take over the United States, opposes gun control, and is distrustful of official versions of various events, such as Waco. Also predicts the coming of a "greatest financial catastrophe in the world," and suggests that to protect against its consequences that listeners purchase precious metals from its sponsoring organization, Atlantic Bullion and Coin. Theme song: "Dixie." Via WWCR, USA.

"Hour of the Time"
Program and "Center" Headquarters: CAJI, P.O. Box 1420, Show Low AZ 85901 USA. Phone: (general) +1 (602) 337-2562; (sponsoring organization, toll-free in United States) (800) 289-2646. Contact: William Cooper. Opposes "New World Order," the United Nations and the Federal Reserve; favors militias to resist potentially oppressive government. Predicts financial catastrophe, and as protection suggests that listeners purchase gold and silver from its sponsoring organization, Swiss-America Trading. *Behold a Pale Horse* (Light Technology Publishing), a 1991 book on Cooper's life, covers his many claims, including about alien space invaders: "1 in 40 humans have been implanted with devices... aliens are building an army of implanted humans who can be activated and turned on us." Via WWCR, USA.
Newspaper: Veritas, P.O. Box 3390, St. John's AZ 85936 USA. Phone: +1 (520) 337-2878. Prices range from $15 for six issues to $50 for 24 issues.

"Insight," The Progressive, 409 East Main Street, Madison WI 53703 USA. Phone: +1 (608) 257-4626. Fax: +1 (608) 2573373. E-mail: progressive@peacenet.org. Contact: Matthew Rothschild, Editor. Radio outlet for *The Progressive* magazine, a disestablishmentarian publication founded in 1909. Via RFPI, Costa Rica.

"Junta Patriótica Cubana"—see "Puerto Libre," below.

"La Voz de Alpha 66"—see Radio Miami Internacional, USA, for address. Contact: Diego Medina, Producer. Anti-Castro, anti-communist; privately supported by the Alpha 66 organization. Aired via private American stations.

"La Voz de Cuba 21"—see Radio Miami Internacional, USA, for address. Contact: Sergio Ramos. Program of the Movimiento Cuba 21 in Puerto Rico.

"La Voz de la Fundación," P.O. Box 440069, Miami FL 33144 USA. Contact: Ninoska Pérez Castellón, Executive Producer; (technical) Mariela Ferretti. Free stickers. Anti-Castro, anti-communist; privately supported by the Cuban American National Foundation. Via Radio Miami Internacional and WHRI.

"La Voz del CID," 10021 SW 37th Terrace, Miami FL 33165 USA; if no result, try AFINSA Portugal, R Ricardo Jorge 53, 4000 Oporto, Portugal. Fax: +351 (2) 41 49 94; Apartado de Correo 8130, 1000 San José, Costa Rica; or Apartado Postal 51403, Sabana Grande 1050, Caracas, Venezuela. Phone: (U.S.) +1 (305) 551-8484. Fax: (U.S.) +1 (305) 559 9365. Contact: Alfredo Aspitia, Asistente de Prensa e Información; or Francisco Fernández. Anti-Castro, anti-communist; privately supported by Cuba Independiente y Democrática. Free political literature. Via their own clandestine transmitters in Central America, possibly Guatemala.

"La Voz del Veterano"—see Radio Copán International, Honduras, for address. Contact: Frank Hernández. Program of the Cuban-American Veterans Association.

"La Voz Popular," Fernando García, Centro de Promoción Popular, Apartado 20-668, México D.F, Mexico; Arcoios, P.O. Box 835, Seattle WA 98111 USA; or Network in Solidarity with the People of Guatemala, 930 F Street NW, Suite 720, Washington DC 20004 USA. Contact: Julia Batres Lemus. Station of anti-Guatamalan-government rebels, which operate in the mountains.

"Making Contact," *Production Office:* David Barsamian,

P.O. Box 551, Boulder CO 80306 USA. Phone: +1 (303) 444-8788. Via RFPI, Costa Rica.

Organization Office: National Radio Project, 830 Los Trancos Road, Portola Valley CA 94028 USA. Phone: +1 (415) 851-7256. Focuses on social and political problems and solutions within the United States and beyond.

"National Radio of the Saharan Arab Democratic Republic,"— *see* "Voice of the Free Sahara," below, which is operated by the same group, the Frente Polisario.

"National Unity Radio"—*see* Sudan National Broadcasting Corporation for contact information.

"Norman Resnick Show," USA Patriot Network, P.O. Box 430, Johnstown CO 80534 USA. Phone: (talk show, toll-free within U.S.) (800) 607-8255; (elsewhere) +1 (970) 587-5171; (order line, toll-free within U.S.) (800) 205-6245. Fax: +1 (970) 587 5450. Contact: Norman Resnick, Host; or "Don W.", Network Manager. Free sample of *USA Patriot News* monthly newspaper/catalog, otherwise $16/six months. Sells survival gear, night-vision goggles, Sangean short-wave radios, books and NTSC videos. VISA/MC/AX. Former professor Resnick is considered to be an anti-semite by various analysts in the media; however, he states that he is "an observant, kosher Jew." He describes his program as discussing "educational, social, political and economic issues from a Constitutional perspective," with emphasis on the activities on the U.S. Bureau of Alcohol, Tobacco and Firearms. Via WWCR, USA.

"Officer Jack Program," P.O. Box 8712, Phoenix AZ 85066 USA. Phone: (toll-free within the United States) (800) 289-2646. Program and sister organization, "Police Against the New World Order," support activities to convert American police officers and military personnel over to view and act favorably towards militias, as well as similar groups and armed individuals. Sells *The Waco Whitewash* and other books. Via WHRI, USA.

"Overcomer" ("Voice of the Last Day Prophet of God"), P.O. Box 691, Walterboro SC 29488 USA. Contact: Brother Stair. Primarily a fundamentalist Christian program from an exceptionally pleasant Southern town, but disestablishmentarian in such things as its characterizations of homosexuals in general, as well as the supposed homosexual and heterosexual activities of priests and nuns within the Roman Catholic Church. Also opposes Freemasonry and reported abuses of powers of U.S. Federal Authorities. Invites listeners to write in, giving the name of the station over which "The Overcomer" was heard and the quality of reception. States that the program spends $55,000 per month on renting airtime over world band, satellite and local stations; at one point, tried in vain to go on the air via oceangoing craft. Via WRNO, USA.

"Preparedness Hour," USA Patriot Network, P.O. Box 430, Johnstown CO 80534 USA. Phone: (talk show, toll-free within U.S.) (800) 607-8255; (elsewhere) +1 (970) 587-5171; (order line, toll-free within U.S.) (800) 205-6245. Fax: +1 (970) 587 5450. Contact: (general) Bob Speer, Host; or "Don W.", Network Manager; (sponsor) Jim Cedarstrom. Free sample of *USA Patriot News* monthly newspaper/catalog, $16/six months. Sells survival gear, night-vision goggles, Sangean shortwave radios, books and NTSC videos. VISA/MC/AX. Program concentrates on such survivalist skills as growing food, making soap and cheese, home childbirth and how to obtain and train mules or donkeys. Speer is described by his associates as a "spike trainer" for retired U.S. General Bo Gritz. Sponsored by Discount Gold, which urges listeners to invest in precious metals as an alternative to holding paper money or investments. Via WWCR, USA.

"Prophecy Club," P.O. Box 750234, Topeka KS 66675 USA. Phone/fax: (club) +1 (913) 478-1112; (sponsor, toll-free in U.S. only) (800) 525-9556. Contact: Stan Johnson, Director. Club, which takes no cards or phone orders, offers free sample newsletter and catalog; also sells newsletter sub-

scriptions, as well as videos in NTSC format for $28.75 within the United States and $30 elsewhere, including shipping. Also offers audio cassettes for $5.75 (U.S.) or $6 (elsewhere). Sponsor accepts cards and sells similar items. Organization states that it is devoted to study and research on Bible prophecy. Programs oppose, *i.a.*, the "New World Order" and Freemasonry. Via WHRI, USA, as well as within the United States, on AM, FM and television stations.

"Protecting Your Wealth," 9188 E. San Salvador Drive #203, Scottsdale AZ 85258 USA. Phone: (program, toll-free within United States) (800) 598-1500; (sponsoring organization, toll-free within the United States) (800) 451-4452; (elsewhere) +1 (602) 451-0575. Fax: +1 (602) 451 4394. Contact: Mike Callahan or Eric Cedarstrom. Opposed to the "New World Order" and groups involved in paper-based financial markets. Supports rural-based survivalism, and claims that the purpose of anti-terrorism and related American legislation is to extend government control over people so as to strip them of their assets. Alleges that paper money, bonds and securities are controlled by an elite that is about to create a second Great Depression, rendering those assets worthless. As an alternative, urges people to invest in the precious metals sold by their sponsoring organization, Viking International Trading, as well as to move to the countryside with their shortwave radios and to purchase hoardable foods sold by a sister firm. Via WWCR, USA.

"Pueblo Libre"—*see* Radio Copán International, Honduras, for address. Anti-Castro, anti-communist; privately supported by the Junta Patriótica Cubana.

"Radio Amahoro" ("Radio Voice of Peace for Rwanda") *Station Office:* Inter-Africa Group, P.O. Box 1631, Addis Ababa, Ethiopia.
Sponsoring Organization: Centre Amani/Europep, rue du Noyer 322, B-1040 Brussels, Belgium. Fax: +32 (2) 735 3916. Contact: Tatien Musabyimana, Director; or Guy Theunis, Administrateur. Free stickers. Christian humanitarian organization seeking peace and reconciliation among Rwandan tribes and refugees. Via Afrique Numéro Un (*see* Gabon) and the Voice of Ethiopia (*see*).

"Radio Conciencia" (when operating)—*see* Radio Miami Internacional, USA, for address. Contact: Ramón Sánchez, Director. Anti-Castro, anti-communist; privately supported by the Comisión Nacional Cubana.

"Radio Dniester International"—*see* "Moldavian Republic of Pridnestrovye."

"Radio Free America"
Network: Sun Radio Network, 2857 Executive Drive, Clearwater FL 34622 USA. Phone: (call-in show, toll-free within U.S.) (800) 878-8255; (general) +1 (813) 572-9209. Contact: Tom Valentine, Host. Succeeds *Liberty Lobby* program aired two decades ago. Via WWCR, USA.
Sponsoring Organization: Liberty Lobby, 300 Independence Avenue SE, Washington DC 20003 USA. Phone: (executive offices) +1 (202) 546-5611; (newspaper) +1 (202) 544-1794; (video sales, toll-free within U.S.) (800) 596-4465; (book and newspaper sales, toll-free within U.S.) (800) 522-6292; (publication/video sales to other countries) +1 (941) 263-4101. Fax: +1 (202) 546 3626. Contact: Don Markey, Public Affairs Associate or Ted Gunderson, spokesman. *Spotlight* newspaper nominally $38/year, but sometimes offered over the air for less; sells books at various prices and NTSC videos $23.95, including shipping. Tapes of past broadcasts $9. VISA/MC. Opposes the "New World Order" and various activities of the Bilderberg gathering, Trilateral Commission, U.S. Federal Reserve, Israeli government and Anti-Defamation League of the B'Nai B'Rith. Expresses occasional interest in unorthodox medical treatments and UFOs; but primarily describes itself as populist, eschewing the rubric "antisemitic" that is frequently attached to Liberty Lobby activities by the media. Supports the political aspirations of such conservative figures as Pat Buchanan, but also expresses skepticism

Australian Sam Voron (standing, right) and volunteers man "Radio Free Somalia" rebel station, whose low-powered transmitter is to the right.

towards capitalism. Keeps close watch, with occasional live coverage, on sieges and other activities of such law-enforcement agencies as the U.S. Bureau of Alcohol, Tobacco and Firearms. How far this program can go concerning issues related to Israel, and still remain on the air, may be open to question. For example, on June 26, 1995, a caller named "Willis," obviously known to host Tom Valentine ("Why, Willis, what a surprise!"), and thus presumably Liberty Lobby leader Willis Carto, stated that Israel is not a legitimate country, "is a phoney state," and that the American people have been deceived about Israel by what was implied as inordinate Jewish influence over the media. At that point, "Radio Free America" was abruptly replaced in mid-program by an NPR show on rebuilding old cars. Whether this switchover took place at WWCR or in the feed to the station was not apparent.

"Radio Free Bougainville"
Main Address: 2 Griffith Avenue, Roseville NSW 2069, Australia. Phone/fax: +61 (2) 417 1066. Contact: Sam Voron, Australian Director. $5, AUS$5 or 5 IRCs required. Station's continued operation is totally dependent on the availability of local coconuts for power generation, currently the only form of power available for those living in the blockaded areas of the island of Bougainville. Station is opposed to the Papua New Guinea government, and supports armed struggle for complete independence and the "Bougainville Interim Government."
Alternative Address: P.O. Box 1203, Honiara, Solomon Islands. Contact: Martin R. Miriori, Humanitarian Aid Coordinator. $1, AUS$2 or 3 IRCs required. No verification data issued from this address.
"Radio Free Somalia," 2 Griffith Avenue, Roseville NSW 2069, Australia. Phone/fax: +61 (2) 417 1066. Contact: Sam Voron, Australian Director. $5, AUS$5 or 5 IRCs required. Operated by the Somali International Amateur Radio Club. Seeks volunteers and donations of radio equipment and airline tickets.

"Radio Liberty"—proposed American talk show which says it is concerned with "the battle for the survival of Western civilization" and supposed censorship of newscasts by "someone." Via KVOH.
"Radio Message of Freedom" ("Radyo Pyam-e Azadi"), GPO Box 857, University Town, Peshawar, Pakistan. Contact: Qaribur Rehman Saeed, Director of Radio. Sponsored by the Islamic Party of Afghanistan rebel organization, headed by Golboddin Hekmatyar. Via its own transmitting facilities, once and possibly still located in Afghanistan.
"Radio Newyork International" (if reactivated), 97 High Street, Kennebunk ME 04043 USA. Phone: +1 (207) 985-7547. E-mail: 74434.3020@compuserve.com. Contact: Alan Weiner or Anita McCormick. Two "RNI the Video" NTSC cassettes $24.95 each; two "Best of Voyages Broadcast Services" audio cassettes $14.95 each, or both $24.95. Last heard as an entertainment program, rather than the original disestablishmentarian offshore exercise.
"Radio of the Provisional Government for National Solidarity and the National Salvation of Kampuchea," 212 E. 47th Street #24G, New York NY 10017 USA; or Permanent Mission of Democratic Kampuchea to the United Nations, 747 3rd Avenue, 8th Floor, New York NY 10017 USA. Contact: Phobel Cheng, First Secretary, Permanent Mission of Cambodia to the United Nations. Khmer Rouge station.
"Radio of the Saudi Opposition from Najd and Hijaz" ("Idha'at al-Mu'aradah al-Sa'udiyah fi Najd wa al-Hijaz")—see Radio Iraq International for contact information. Opposes the Saudi government.
"Radio Periódico Panamericano" (when operating)—see Radio Miami Internacional, USA for address. Contact: René L. Díaz, Program Director. Moderately anti-Castro and anti-communist; privately supported by Caribe Infopress and allied with the Plataforma Democrática Cubana.

"Radio Periódico Semanal de los Coordinadores Social Demócrata de Cuba"—see "Un Solo Pueblo," below.

"Radio Pridnestrovye"—see "Moldavian Republic of Pridnestrovye."

"Radio Roquero"—see Radio Copán International, Honduras, for address. Contact: García Rivera, Host. Music and political comment from the Cuban exile community.

"Radiostantsiya Pamyat"—see Russia.

"Radio Voice of Peace for Rwanda"—see "Radio Amahoro," above.

"Radio Voice of the Mojahed"—see "Voice of the Mojahed," below.

"Republic of Iraq Radio, Voice of the Iraqi People" ("Idha'at al-Jamahiriya al-Iraqiya, Saut al-Sha'b al-Iraqi"), Broadcasting Service of the Kingdom of Saudi Arabia, P.O. Box 61718, Riyadh 11575, Saudi Arabia. Phone: +966 (1) 442-5170. Fax: +966 (1) 402 8177. Contact: Suliman A. Al-Samnan, Director of Frequency Management. Anti-Saddam Hussein "black" clandestine supported by CIA, British intelligence, the Gulf Cooperation Council and Saudi Arabia. The name of this station has changed periodically since its inception during the Gulf crisis. Via transmitters in Saudi Arabia.

"RFPI Reports"—see RFPI, Costa Rica, for contact information. News about human rights, social justice and the environment, mainly from Latin America and the Caribbean.

"Rush Limbaugh Show," EIB World Band, WABC, #2 Pennsylvania Avenue, New York NY 10121 USA; telephone (toll-free, USA only) (800) 282-2882, (elsewhere) +1 (212) 613-3800; fax (during working hours) +1 (212) 563 9166. E-mail 70277.2502@compuserve.com. Via WRNO, USA. Reception reports concerning this program can also be sent with 2 IRCs or an SASE directly to WRNO, which may verify with a special Rush Limbaugh QSL card.

"Scriptures for America," P.O. Box 766, Laporte CO 80535 USA. Phone: +1 (307) 745-5913. Fax: +1 (307) 745 5914. Contact: Pastor Pete Peters. "Introductory Packet" $2. Opposes, *inter alia*, the Anti-Defamation League of the B'Nai B'Rith and various other Jewish organizations, as well as international banking institutions and homosexuals. Also expresses suspicion of official and media responses to such events as the Oklahoma City bombing. Via WHRI, USA.

"Second Opinion"—see "Insight," above, for contact information. Various thinkers propose solutions to world problems. Via Radio for Peace International, Costa Rica.

"Seventieth Week Magazine," P.O. Box 771, Gladewater TX 75647 USA. Contact: Ben McKnight. Free "Flash Bulletins" booklets. Opposes "New World Order," believes United Nations and UFOs are plotting to take over the United States and commit genocide against Christians and patriots, and distrusts official versions of various events, such as the Oklahoma City bombing. Via WWCR, USA.

"Steppin' Out of Babylon," 2804 Piedmont Avenue, Berkeley CA 94705 USA. Phone: +1 (510) 540-8850. Contact: Sue Supriano, Producer. Interviews with those protesting various conditions, including war, poverty and human-rights abuses. Via RFPI.

"This Way Out," Overnight Productions, P.O. Box 38327, Los Angeles CA 90038 USA. News, music, interviews and features from and about lesbians and gays, mainly but not exclusively within the United States. Via RFPI.

"Un Solo Pueblo"—see Radio Copán International, Honduras, for address; or write directly to the sponsoring organization at 8561 NW South River Drive, Suite 201, Medley FL 33166 USA; also, Organo del Centro de la Democracia Cubana, P.O. Box 161742, Miami FL 33116 USA. Anti-Castro, anti-communist; privately supported by the Coordinadora Social Demócrata Cubana.

"Vietnam Veterans Radio Network," 7807 N. Avalon, Kansas City MO 64152 USA. Contact: John ("Doc") Upton. This radio voice of the Vietnam Veterans Against the War mixes music, commentaries and sound bites concerning some of the more difficult aspects of the Vietnam War experience. Via RFPI.

"Voice of Arab Syria"—see Radio Iraq International for contact information.

"Voice of China" ("Zhongguo Zhi Yin Guangbo Diantai"), Democratization of China, P.O. Box 11663, Berkeley CA 94701 USA; Foundation for China in the 21st Century, P.O. Box 11696, Berkeley CA 94701 USA; or P.O. Box 79218, Monkok, Hong Kong. Phone: +1 (510) 2843-5025. Fax: +1 (510) 2843 4370. Contact: Bang Tai Xu, Director. Mainly "overseas Chinese students" interested in the democratization of China. Financial support from the Foundation for China in the 21st Century. Have "picked up the mission" of the earlier Voice of June 4th, but have no organizational relationship with it. Transmits via facilities of the Central Broadcasting System, Taiwan (see).

"Voice of Eritrea"—see Radio Iraq International, Iraq, for contact information.

"Voice of Freedom" (if reactivated), 206 Carlton St., Toronto ON, Canada. Contact: Ernst Zündel. Neo-nazi. Although Zündel's program is currently not aired over world band, he is sometimes heard over "American Dissident Voices" (see).

"Voice of Human Rights and Freedom for Iran" ("Seda-ye Hoquq-e Bashar va Aazadiha-ye Iran"), Organization for Human Rights and Fundamental Freedoms for Iran, 18 bis rue Violet, F-75017 Paris, France; Reza Ferhadi, P.O. Box 19740-187, Irvine CA 92740 USA; P.L.K. 00559 B, D-22391 Hamburg, Germany; or Postfach 102824, D-44028 Dortmund, Germany. Phone: (France) +33 (1) 46-03-06-42. Fax: (France) +33 (1) 46 03 49 74 or +33 (1) 48 25 81 78. Contact: Manouchehr Ganji, Secretary-General; or Mina Alborzi; both are known to reply regularly to correspondence in English, French or Persian. Anti-Iranian government. Transmits via the facilities of Radio Cairo. Supported by the CIA and the Egyptian government, and nominally operated by the Organization of Human Rights and Freedom for Iran. Claims to be affiliated with the Association for the Advancement of Education in Iran, Flag of Freedom Society, Iranian Students' Association, Iranian Youth Solidarity, and League of Iranian Women.

"Voice of Iraq"—see Radio Damascus for contact information.

"Voice of Iraqi Kurdistan" ("Aira dangi Kurdestana Iraqa") (when active), P.O. Box 2443, Merrifield VA 22116 USA; P.O. Box 1504, London W7 3LX, United Kingdom; Kurdiska Riksförbundet, Hornsgatan 80, S-117 21 Stockholm, Sweden; or Kurdistan Press, Örnsvägen 6C, S-172 Sundbyberg, Sweden. Phone: (Stockholm) +46 (8) 668-6060 or +46 (8) 668-66088; (Sundbyberg) +46 (8) 298-332. Sponsored by the Kurdistan Democratic Party, led by Masoud Barzani, and the National Democratic Iraqi Front. From its own transmitting facilities, reportedly once located in the Kurdish section of Iraq.

"Voice of Kashmir Freedom" ("Sada-i Hurriyat-i Kashmir"), P.O. Box 102, Muzaffarabad, Azad Kashmir, Pakistan. Favors Azad Kashmiri independence from India; pro-Moslem, sponsored by the Kashmiri Mojahadin organization. From transmission facilities believed to be in Pakistan.

"Voice of Liberty," Box 1776, Liberty KY 42539 USA; or Box 3987, Rex GA 32073 USA. Phone: (call-in) toll-free in United States (800) 526-1776, or elsewhere +1 (404) 968-8865; (voice mail) +1 (404) 968-0330. Contact: Paul Parsons or Rick Tyler. Sells various audio cassettes, $50 starter kit and *News Front* newspaper. Opposed to certain practices of the Bureau of Alcohol, Tobacco and Firearms and various other law-enforcement organizations in the United States, abortion, and restrictions on firearms and Christian prayer. Via WWCR, USA.

"Voice of National Salvation" ("Gugugui Sori Pangsong")—former address in Japan no longer valid for this station. Pro-North Korea, pro-Korean unification; supported by North Korean government. On the air since 1967, but not always under the same name. Via North Korean transmitters located in Pyongyang, Haeju and Wongsan.

"Voice of Peace," Inter-Africa Group, P.O. Box 1631, Addis Ababa, Ethiopia. Humanitarian organization, partially funded by UNICEF, seeking peace and reconciliation among warring factions in Somalia. Via the Voice of Ethiopia (see).

"Voice of Rebellious Iraq" ("Saut al-Iraq al-Tha'ir"), P.O. Box 11365/738, Tehran, Iran; P.O. Box 37155/146, Qom, Iran; or P.O. Box 36802, Damascus, Syria. Anti-Iraqi regime, supported by the Shi'ite-oriented Supreme Assembly of the Islamic Revolution of Iraq, led by Mohammed Baqir al-Hakim. Supported by the Iranian government.

"Voice of the Communist Party of Iran" ("Seda-ye Hezb-e Komunist-e Iran"), B.M. Box 2123, London WC1N 3XX, United Kingdom; or O.I.S., Box 50040, S-104 05 Stockholm, Sweden. Sponsored by the Communist Party of Iran (KOMALA, formerly Tudeh).

"Voice of the Crusader"—see "Voice of the Mojahed," below.

"Voice of the Free Sahara" ("La Voz del Sahara Libre, La Vox del Pueblo Sahel"), Sahara Libre, Frente Polisario, B.P. 10, El-Mouradia, 16000 Algiers, Algeria; Sahara Libre, Ambassade de la République Arabe Saharaui Démocratique, 1 Av. Franklin Roosevelt, 16000 Algiers, Algeria; or B.P. 10, Al-Mouradia, Algiers, Algeria. Fax: +213 747 933. Contact: Mohamed Lamin Abdesalem; Mahafud Zein; or Sneiba Lehbib. Free stickers, booklets, cards, maps, paper flags and calendars. Two IRCs helpful. Pro-Polisario Front; supported by Algerian government and aired via the facilities of Radiodiffusion-Télévision Algerienne.

"Voice of the Iranian Revolution" ("Aira dangi Shurashi Irana")—see "Voice of the Communist Party of Iran," above, for details.

"Voice of the Iraqi People"—see "Radio of the Iraqi Republic from Baghdad, Voice of the Iraqi People," above.

"Voice of the Islamic Revolution in Iraq"—see "Voice of Rebellious Iraq," above, for contact information. Affiliated with the Shi'ite-oriented Supreme Assembly of the Islamic Revolution of Iraq, led by Mohammed Baqir al-Hakim.

"Voice of the Martyrs" ("Radioemission der Hilfsaktion Martyrerkirche"), Postfach 5540, 78434 Konstanz, Germany. Possibly linked with Internationale Radioarbeits-Gemeinschaft fur die Martyrerkirche, which previously broadcast via Radio Trans-Europe, Portugal, as Radio Stephanusbotschaft. Sometimes uses facilities of Radio Intercontinental, Armenia.

"Voice of the Mojahed" ("Seda-ye Mojahed ast"), M.I.S.S., B.M. Box 9720, London WC1N 3XX, United Kingdom; P.O. Box 951, London NW11 9EL, United Kingdom; or P.O. Box 3133, Baghdad, Iraq. Contact: A. Hossein. Sponsored by the People's Mojahedin Organization of Iran (OMPI) and the National Liberation Army of Iran.

"Wings," P.O. Box 33220, Austin TX 78764 USA. Fax: +1 (512) 416-9000. E-mail: wings@igc.apc.org. Contact: Frieda Werden, Producer. News program of the Women's International News Gathering Service, covering such issues as women's rights, women activists and movements for sociopolitical change. Via RFPI, Costa Rica.

"World of Prophecy," 1708 Patterson Road, Austin TX 78733 USA. Contact: Texe Marrs. Conservative Christian program opposing various forms of government regulation and control, such as of the environment. Via WWCR and WHRI, USA.

"World Voice of Historic Adventism"—see WVHA, for details.

DJIBOUTI World Time +3

Radiodiffusion-Télévision de Djibouti (if reactivated), B.P. 97, Djibouti. Return postage helpful. Correspondence in French preferred. This station is currently off the air due to transmitter failure. It is unlikely to come back on the air in the forseeable future, unless the French resuscitate the failed transmitter as part of the proposed, but as yet not approved, effort to install a Radio France Internationale relay in Djibouti.

DOMINICAN REPUBLIC World Time -4

Emisora Onda Musical (when operating), Palo Hincado 204 Altos, Apartado Postal 860, Santo Domingo, Dominican Republic. Contact: Mario Báez Asunción, Director. Replies occasionally to correspondence in Spanish.

La N-103/Radio Norte (when operating), Apartado Postal 320, Santiago, Dominican Republic. Contact: José Darío Pérez Díaz, Director; or Héctor Castillo, Gerente.

Radio Amanecer Internacional, Apartado Postal 1500, Santo Domingo, Dominican Republic. Contact: (general) Señora Ramona C. de Subervi, Directora; (technical) Ing. Sócrates Domínguez. $1 or return postage required. Replies slowly to correspondence in Spanish.

Radio Barahona (when operating), Apartado 201, Barahona, Dominican Republic; or Gustavo Mejía Ricart No. 293, Apto. 2-B, Ens. Quisqueya, Santo Domingo, Dominican Republic. Contact: (general) Rodolfo Z. Lama Jaar, Administrador; (technical) Ing. Roberto Lama Sajour, Administrador General. Free stickers. Letters should be sent via registered mail. $1 or return postage helpful. Replies to correspondence in Spanish.

Radio Cima (when operating), Apartado 804, Santo Domingo, Dominican Republic. Fax: +1 (809) 541 1088. Contact: Roberto Vargas, Director. Free pennants, postcards, coins and taped music. Roberto likes collecting stamps and coins.

Radio Quisqueya (when operating), Apartado Postal 135-2, Santo Domingo, Dominican Republic. Contact: Lic. Gregory Castellanos Ruano, Director. Replies occasionally to correspondence in Spanish.

Radio Santiago (when operating), Apartado 282, Santiago, Dominican Republic. Contact: Luis Felipe Moscos Finke, Gerente; Luis Felipe Moscos Cordero, Jefe Ingeniero; or Carlos Benoit, Announcer & Program Manager.

ECUADOR World Time -5 (-4 sometimes, in times of drought); -6 Galapagos

Note: According to HCJB's excellent "DX Party Line," during periods of drought, such as caused by "El Niño," electricity rationing causes periods in which transmitters cannot operate because of inadequate hydroelectric power, as well as spikes which occasionally damage transmitters. Accordingly, many Ecuadorian stations tend to be irregular, or even entirely off the air, during drought conditions.

Ecos del Oriente (when operating), Sucre y 12 de Febrero, Lago Agrio, Sucumbíos, Ecuador. Phone: +593 (6) 830-141. Contact: Elsa Irene Velástegui, Secretaria. Sometimes includes free 20 sucre note (Ecuadorian currency) with reply. $1 or return postage required. Replies, often slowly, to correspondence in Spanish.

Emisoras Gran Colombia (if reactivated), Casilla 17-01-2246, Quito, Ecuador (new physical address: Vasco de Contreras 689 y Pasaje "A", Quito, Ecuador). Phone: +593 (2) 443-147. Fax/phone: +593 (2) 442 951. Contact: Nancy Cevallos Castro, Gerente General. Return postage required. Replies to correspondence in Spanish. Their shortwave transmitter is out of order. While they would like to repair or replace it, for the time being they don't have the funds to do so, as they have just spent what extra money they had on new premises.

Emisoras Jesús del Gran Poder, Casilla 17-01-133, Quito, Ecuador. Phone: +593 (2) 513-077.

Emisoras Luz y Vida, Casilla 11-01-222, Loja, Ecuador. Phone: +593 (7) 570-426. Contact: Hermana (Sister) Ana Maza Reyes, Directora; or Lic. Guido Carrión H., Directora de Programas. Return postage required. Replies irregularly to correspondence in Spanish.

Escuelas Radiofónicas Populares del Ecuador, Casilla 06-01-693, Riobamba, Ecuador. Fax: +593 (3) 961 625. Contact: Juan Pérez Sarmiento, Director Ejecutivo; or María Ercilia López, Secretaria. Free pennants and key rings. "Chimborazo" cassette of Ecuadorian music for 10,000 sucres plus postage; T-shirts for 12,000 sucres plus postage; and caps with station logo for 8,000 sucres plus postage. Return postage helpful. Replies to correspondence in Spanish.

Estéreo Carrizal, Avenida Estudiantil, Quinta Velásquez, Calceta, Ecuador. Phone: +593 (5) 685-5470. Contact: Ovidio Velásquez Alcundia, Gerente General. Free book of Spanish-language poetry by owner. Replies to correspondence in Spanish.

HCJB, Voice of the Andes

Main Office: Casilla 17-17-691, Villalengua 884, Quito, Pichincha, Ecuador. Phone: +593 (2) 466-808. Fax: +593 (2) 447 263. E-mail: (English Dept.) english@mhs.hcjb.com.ec; (Spanish Dept.) spanish@mhs.hcjb.com.ec; (Japanese Dept.) japanese@mhs.hcjb.com.ec. FTP: nw311.hcjb.com. ec. Contact: (general) Ken MacHarg, Host, Saludos Amigos—letterbox; (head of administration) Glen Volkhardt, Director of Broadcasting; Mark Irwin, Director Radio (technical) Richard McVicar, Frequency Manager; or Karen Schmidt. Free religious brochures, calendars and pennants. ANDEX International listeners' club bulletin. *Catch the Vision* book $8, postpaid. IRC or unused U.S., Canadian or Ecuadorian stamps required for airmail reply.

U.S. Main Office: International Headquarters, World Radio Missionary Fellowship, Inc., P.O. Box 39800, Colorado Springs CO 80949 USA. Phone: +1 (719) 590-9800. Fax: +1 (719) 590 9801. Contact: Andrew Braio, Public Information; (head of administration) Richard D. Jacquin, Director, International Operations. Various items sold via U.S. address—catalog available.

U.S. Engineering Center: 1718 W. Mishawaka Road, Elkhart IN 46517 USA. Phone: +1 (219) 294-8201. Fax: +1 (219) 294 8329. Contact: Dave Pasechnik, Project Manager; or Bob Moore, Engineering. This address concerned only with the design and manufacture of transmitter and antenna equipment.

U.S. Consulting Office: 267 N. Bobwhite, Orange CA 92669 USA. Phone/fax: +1 (714) 771-1843. Contact: William E. Haney, Broadcasting Consultant.

Canadian Office: 6981 Millcreek Drive, Unit 23, Mississauga ON, L5N 6B8 Canada.

U.K. Office: HCJB-Europa, 131 Grattan Road, Bradford, West Yorkshire BD1 2HS, United Kingdom. Fax: +44 (1274) 741 302. Contact: Andrew Steele, Director.

Australian Office and Studios: P.O. Box 291, Kilsyth, VIC 3137, Australia. Phone: +61 (3) 9761-4844. Fax: +61 (3) 9761 4061. E-mail: office@hcjbaus.dialix.oz.au. Contact: David C. Maindonald, Australian Director; or Greg Pretty, Studio Director. Foundation story of HCJB, *Come up to the Mountain*, US$9, including postage.

La Voz de los Caras (when not off during drought), Casilla 13-01-629, Bahía de Caráquez, Manabí, Ecuador. Fax: +593 (5) 690 305. Contact: (general) Alejandro Nevárez Pinto, Gerente; (technical) Ing. Marcelo Nevárez Feggioni, Director. $1 or return postage required. Replies occasionally and slowly to correspondence in Spanish.

La Voz de Saquisilí—Radio Libertador (when not off during drought), Casilla 669, Saquisilí, Ecuador; or Calle 24 de Mayo, Saquisilí, Cotopaxi, Ecuador. Phone: +593 (3) 721-035. Contact: Eddy Roger Velástegui Mena, Director de Relaciones Públicas; Srta. Carmen Mena Corrales; or Arturo Mena Herrera, Gerente-Propietario. $1

or mint Ecuadorian stamps for return postage; IRCs difficult to exchange. Eddy Velástegui M. is the only reliable responder at this station; but, as he is away at college most of the time, replies to correspondence tend to be slow and irregular. Spanish strongly preferred.

La Voz del Napo, Misión Josefina, Tena, Napo, Ecuador. Phone: +593 (6) 886-422. Contact: Ramiro Cabrera, Director. Free pennants and stickers. $1 or return postage required. Replies occasionally to correspondence in Spanish.

La Voz del Río Tarqui (if operating), Casilla 01-01-877, Cuenca, Ecuador. Phone: +593 (7) 823-198. Contact: Sra. Alicia Pulla Célleri, Administración; or Prof. Manuel Pulla Cornejo. Replies irregularly to correspondence in Spanish. May or may not continue operation on shortwave.

La Voz del Upano, Vicariato Apostólico de Méndez, Misión Salesiana, 10 de Agosto s/n, Macas, Ecuador. Phone: +593 (7) 700 186. Contact: Sor Luz Benigna Torres, Directora; or P. Domingo Barrueco C., Director. Free stickers, pennants and calendars. On one occasion, not necessarily to be repeated, sent tape of Ecuadorian folk music $2. Otherwise, $1 required. Replies to correspondence in Spanish.

Ondas Quevedeñas (when operating), Décima Segunda Calle 207, Quevedo, Ecuador. Phone: +593 (5) 750-330. Fax: +593 (5) 753 854. Contact: Sra. Maruja Jaramillo, Gerente; or Humberto Alvarado P., Director Propietario. Return postage required. Replies irregularly to correspondence in Spanish.

Radio Bahá'í, "La Emisora de la Familia," Casilla 10-02-1464, Otavalo, Imbabura, Ecuador. Phone: +593 (6) 920-245. Fax: +593 (6) 922 504. Contact: (general) William Rodríguez Barreiro, Gerente; (technical) Ing. Tom Dopps. Free information about the Bahá'í faith, which teaches the unity of all the races, nations and religions, and that the Earth is one country and mankind its citizens. Free pennants. Return postage appreciated. Replies regularly to correspondence in English or Spanish. Station is property of the Instituto Nacional de Enseñanza de la Fe Bahá'í (National Spiritual Assembly of the Bahá'ís of Ecuador). Although there are many Bahá'í radio stations around the world, Radio Bahá'í in Ecuador is the only one on shortwave.

Radio Buen Pastor, Asociación Christiana de Indígenas Saragusos (ACIS), Reino de Quito y Azuay, Saraguro, Loja, Ecuador. Contact: Segundo Poma, Director; or Zoila Vacacela, Secretaria. $1 or return postage in the form of mint Ecuadorian stamps required, as IRCs are difficult to exchange in Ecuador. Station is keen to receive reception reports; may respond to English, but correspondence in Spanish preferred.

Radio Católica Nacional del Ecuador, Av. América 1830 y Mercadillo (Apartado 540A), Quito, Ecuador. Phone: +593 (2) 545-770. Contact: John Sigüenza, Director; Sra. Yolanda de Suquitana, Secretaria; (technical) Sra. Gloria Cardozo, Technical Director. Free stickers. Return postage required. Replies to correspondence in Spanish.

Radio Católica Santo Domingo (when operating), Apartado Postal 17-24-0006, Santo Domingo de los Colorados, Pichincha, Ecuador. Contact: Nancy Moncada, Secretaria; Pedro Figueroa, Director de Programas; or Padre Gualberto Pérez Paredas, Director. Free pennants. Return postage or $1 helpful. Replies to correspondence in Spanish.

Radio Centro, Casilla 18-01-574, Ambato, Ecuador. Phone: +593 (3) 822-240 or +593 (3) 841-126. Fax: +593 (3) 829 824. Contact: Luis Alberto Gamboa Tello, Director Gerente; Lic. María Elena de López. Free stickers. Return postage appreciated. Replies to correspondence in Spanish.

Radio Centinela del Sur (C.D.S. Internacional), Casilla 11-01-106, Loja, Ecuador. Fax: +593 (7) 562-270. Contact: (general) Marcos G. Coronel V., Director de Programas; (technical) José Coronel Illescas, Director Propietario. Return postage required. Replies rarely to correspondence in Spanish.

Radio Cumandá (if reactivated)

Station: Principal y Espejo, Coca, Napo, Ecuador. Phone: +593 (6) 315-089. Contact: Angel Bonilla, Director.

Owner: Luís Cordero 226, Machachi, Pichincha, Ecuador. Contact: José J. Quinga, Propietario.

Radiodifusora Cultural Católica La Voz del Upano—see La Voz del Upano, above.

Radiodifusora Cultural, La Voz del Napo—see La Voz del Napo, above.

Radio Federación Shuar (Shuara Tuntuiri), Casilla 17-01-1422, Quito, Ecuador. Phone/fax: +593 (2) 504-264. Contact: Manuel Jesús Vinza Chacucuy, Director; or Prof. Albino M. Utitiaj P., Director de Medios. Return postage or $1 required. Replies irregularly to correspondence in Spanish.

Radio Interoceánica (if reactivated), Santa Rosa de Quijos, Cantón El Chaco, Provincia de Napo, Ecuador. Contact: Byron Medina, Gerente; or Ing. Olaf Hegmuir. $1 or return postage required, and donations appreciated (station owned by Swedish Covenant Church). Replies slowly to correspondence in Spanish or Swedish. Station's shortwave transmitter needs repair, but funds are not forthcoming, so it's anybody's guess if it will ever return to the air.

Radio Jesús del Gran Poder—see Emisoras Jesús del Gran Poder, above.

Radio Luz y Vida—see Emisoras Luz y Vida, above.

Radio Municipal (when activated), Alcaldía Municipal de Quito, García Moreno 887 y Espejo, Quito, Ecuador. Contact: Miguel Arízaga Q., Director. Currently not on shortwave, but plans to activate a 2 kW shortwave transmitter—its old mediumwave AM transmitter modified for shortwave—on 4750 kHz once the legalities are completed. Expected to welcome correspondence from abroad, especially in Spanish.

Radio Nacional Espejo, Casilla 17-01-352, Quito, Ecuador. Phone: +593 (2) 21-366. Contact: Marco Caceido, Gerente; or Mercedes B. de Caceido, Secretaria. Replies irregularly to correspondence in English and Spanish.

Radio Nacional Progreso, Casilla V, Loja, Ecuador. Contact: José A. Guamán Guajala, Director del programa "Círculo Dominical." Replies irregularly to correspondence in Spanish, particularly for feedback on "Círculo Dominical" program aired Sundays from 1100 to 1300. Return postage required.

Radio Oriental, Casilla 260, Tena, Napo, Ecuador. Phone: +593 (6) 886-033. Contact: Luis Enrique Espín Espinosa, Gerente General. $1 or return postage helpful. Reception reports welcome. Station, which recently revived its shortwave facility after an animal caused it to catch fire, especially appreciates being told if the transmitter is drifting significantly off its frequency of 4779.8 kHz.

Radio Popular de Cuenca (if active), Av. Loja 2408, Cuenca, Ecuador. Phone: +593 (7) 810-131. Contact: Sra. Manena Escondón Vda. de Villavicencio, Directora y Propietaria. Return postage or $1 required. Replies rarely to correspondence in Spanish.

Radio Quito, Casilla 17-21-1971, Quito, Ecuador. Phone/fax: +593 (2) 508-301. Contact: Xavier Almeida, Gerente General; or José Almeida, Subgerente. Return postage required. Replies slowly, but regularly.

Sistema de Emisoras Progreso—see Radio Nacional Progreso, above.

EGYPT World Time +2 (+3 midyear)

Radio Cairo

Nontechnical: P.O. Box 566, Cairo, Egypt. Contact: Mrs. Sahar Kalil, Director of English Service to North America & Producer, "Questions and Answers"; or Mrs. Magda Hamman, Secretary. Free stickers, postcards, stamps, maps, papyrus souvenirs, calendars and *External Services of Radio Cairo* book. Free booklet and individually tutored Arabic-language lessons with loaned textbooks from Kamila Abdullah, Director General, Arabic by Radio, Radio Cairo, P.O. Box 325, Cairo, Egypt. Arabic-language religious, cultural and language-learning audio and video tapes from the Egyptian Radio and Television Union sold via Sono Cairo Audio-Video, P.O. Box 2017, Cairo, Egypt; when ordering video tapes, inquire to ensure they function on the television standard (NTSC, PAL or SECAM) in your country. Replies regularly, but sometimes slowly; for concerns about audio quality, *see Technical*, below.

Nontechnical, Holy Koran Radio: P.O. Box 1186, Cairo, Egypt. Contact: Abd al-Samad al Disuqi, Director. Operates only on 9755 kHz.

Technical: Broadcast Engineering Department, 24th Floor—TV Building (Maspiro), Egyptian Radio and Television Union, P.O. Box 1186/11151, Cairo, Egypt. Phone/fax: (Propagation and Monitoring Office, set to automatically receive faxes outside normal working hours; otherwise, be prepared to request a switchover from voice to fax) +20 (2) 578-9491. Fax: (ERTU Projects) +20 (2) 766 909. E-mail: to be inaugurated shortly. Contact: Dr. Eng. Abdoh Fayoumi, Head of Propagation and Monitoring; or Nivene W. Laurence, Engineer. Comments and suggestions on audio quality and level especially welcomed.

ENGLAND—see UNITED KINGDOM.

EQUATORIAL GUINEA World Time +1

Radio Africa

Transmission Office: Apartado 851, Malabo, Isla Bioko, Equatorial Guinea.

U.S. Office for Correspondence and Verifications: Pan American Broadcasting, 20410 Town Center Lane #200, Cupertino CA 95014 USA. Phone: +1 (408) 996-2033. Fax: +1 (408) 252 6855. Contact: Carmen Jung, Terry Kraemer or James Manero. $1 or return postage required.

Radio East Africa—same details as "Radio Africa," above.

Radio Nacional de Guinea Ecuatorial—Bata (Radio Bata), Apartado 749, Bata, Río Muni, Equatorial Guinea. Phone: +240 08-382. Contact: José Mba Obama, Director. If no response try sending your letter c/o Spanish Embassy, Bata, enclosing $1 for return postage. Spanish preferred.

Radio Nacional de Guinea Ecuatorial—Malabo (Radio Malabo), Apartado 195, Malabo, Isla Bioko, Equatorial Guinea. Phone: +240 92-260. Fax: +240 92 097. Contact: (general) Román Manuel Mané-Abaga, Jefe de Programación; or Ciprano Somon Suakin; or Manuel Chema Lobede; (technical) Hermenegildo Moliko Chele, Jefe Servicios Técnicos de Radio y Televisión. $1 or return postage required. Replies irregularly to correspondence in Spanish.

ERITREA World Time +3

Voice of the Broad Masses of Eritrea (Dimisi Hafash), EPLF National Guidance, Information Department, Radio Branch, P.O. Box 872, Asmara, Eritrea; Ministry of Information and Culture, Technical Branch, P.O. Box 243, Asmara, Eritrea; EPLF National Guidance, Information Department, Radio Branch, P.O. Box 2571, Addis Ababa, Ethiopia; Eritrean Relief Committee, 475 Riverside Drive, Suite 907, New York NY 10015 USA; EPLF National Guidance, Information Department, Radio Branch, Sahel Eritrea, P.O. Box 891, Port Sudan, Sudan; or EPLF Desk for Nordic Countries, Torsplan 3, 1 tr, S-113 64 Stockholm, Sweden. Fax (Stockholm) +46 (8) 322 337. Contact: (Eritrea) Ghebreab Ghebremedhin; (Ethiopia and Sudan) Mehreteab Tesfa Giorgis. Return postage or $1 helpful. Free information on history of station, Ethiopian People's Liberation Front and Eritrea.

ESTONIA World Time +2 (+3 midyear)

Estonian Radio (Eesti Raadio)—same details as "Radio

Estonia," below, except replace "Radio Estonia, External Service, The Estonian Broadcasting Company" with "Eesti Raadio."

Radio Estonia, External Service, The Estonian Broadcasting Company, 21 Gonsiori Street, EE-0100 Tallinn, Estonia. Phone: +372 (2) 43-41-15. Fax: +372 (2) 43 44 57. World Wide Web: http://www.online.ee/er/er. Contact: (general) Silja Orusalu, Editor, I.C.A. Department; Harry Tiido; Mrs. Tiina Sillam, Head of English Service; Mrs. Kai Siidiratsep, Head of German Service; Enno Turmen, Head of Swedish Service; Juri Vilosius, Head of Finnish Service; Mrs. Mari Maasik, Finnish Service; or Elena Rogova; (head of administration) Kusta Reinsoo, Deputy Head of External Service. Free pennants. $1 required. Replies occasionally.

ETHIOPIA   World Time +3
"Radio Amahoro"—see Disestablishmentarian listing earlier in this section.

Radio Ethiopia: (External Service) P.O. Box 654; (Domestic Service) P.O. Box 1020—both in Addis Ababa, Ethiopia. Contact: (External Service) Kahsai Tewoldemedhin, Program Director; Ms. Ellene Mocria, Head of Audience Relations; or Yohaness Rufael, Producer, "Contact"; (head of administration) Kasa Miliko, Head of Station; (technical) Terefe Ghebre Medhin. Free stickers. Very poor replier.

Radio Fana, Addis Ababa, Ethiopia. No further details available.

"Voice of Peace"—see Disestablishmentarian listing earlier in this section.

FINLAND   World Time +2 (+3 midyear)
YLE/Radio Finland
Main Office: P.O. Box 78, FIN-00024 Helsinki, Finland. Phone: (general) +358 (0) 148-01; (administration) +358 (0) 148-04316. Fax: +358 (0) 148 1169; (International Information) +358 (0) 148 03390; or (Technical Affairs) +358 (0) 148 035 88. E-mail: rfinland@yle.mailnet.fi. Contact: (general) Mrs. Riitta Raukko, International Information; Ms. Salli Korpela, International Relations/Radio; Christine Rockstroh; or Kate Moore, Producer, "Airmail"; (head of administration) Juhani Niinistö, Head of External Broadcasting; (technical) Mr. Kari Llmonen, Technical Affairs. Free stickers, tourist and other magazines. *Finnish by Radio* and *Nuntii Latini* textbooks available. Replies to correspondence, but doesn't provide verification data.
Transmission Authority: Yleisradio, P.O. Box 20, FIN-00024 Helsinki, Finland. Phone: +358 (0) 1480-6287. Fax: +358 (0) 148 5260. Contact: Esko Huuhka.
Measuring Station: Yleisradio, FIN-05400 Jokela, Finland. Phone: +358 (0) 282-006. Fax: +358 (14) 472 410. Contact: Ing. Kari Hautala.
U.S. Office: P.O. Box 462, Windsor CT 06095 USA. Phone/fax: (24-hour toll-free within U.S. for recorded schedule and voice mail) (800) 221-9539. A verification may be received from this office by enclosing $1 with your report. Address your letters to: QSL Manager, Radio Finland North American Service, c/o the Windsor address.

FRANCE   World Time +1 (+2 midyear)
Radio France Internationale (RFI)
Main Office: B.P. 9516, F-75016 Paris Cedex 16, France. Phone: (general) +33 (1) 42-30-22-22; (Service de la communication) +33 (1) 42-30-29-51; (Audience Relations) +33 (1) 44-30-89-69/70/71; (media relations) +33 (1) 42-30-29-85; (*Fréquence* **Monde**) +33 (1) 42-30-10-86. Fax: (general) +33 (1) 42 30 30 71; (Audience Relations) +33 (1) 44 30 89 99; (other nontechnical) +33 (1) 42 30 44 81. World Wide Web: http://town.hall.org/travel/france/rfi.html. Contact: (English programs) Simson Najovits, Chief, English Department; (other programs) J.P. Charbonnier, Producer, "Lettres des Auditeurs"; Daniel Ollivier, Directeur du développement et de la communication; Nicolas Levkov, Rédactions en Langues Etrangères; Daniel Franco, Rédaction en

français; Mme. Anne Toulouse, Rédacteur en chef du Service Mondiale en français; Christine Berbudeau, Rédacteur en chef, *Fréquence* **Monde**; or Marc Verney, Attaché de Presse; (head of administration) André Larquié, Président-Directeur Général; (technical) M. Raymond Pincon, Producer, "Le Courrier Technique." Free *Fréquence* **Monde** bi monthly magazine in French upon request. Free souvenir keychains, pins, lighters, pencils, T-shirts and stickers have been received by some—especially when visiting the headquarters at 116 avenue du Président Kennedy, in the chichi 16th Arrondissement. Can provide supplementary materials for "Dites-moi tout" French-language course; write to the attention of Mme. Chantal de Grandpre, "Dites-moi tout." "Le Club des Auditeurs" French-language listener's club ("Club 9516" for English-language listeners); applicants must provide name, address and two passport-type photos, whereupon they will receive a membership card and the club bulletin. RFI hopes to install a shortwave broadcasting center in Djibouti, which if approved could be operational in two or three years' time.
Transmission Office, Technical: Direction de l'Equipment et de la Production, TDF—Groupe France Telecom, Ondes décamétriques, F-92542 Montrouge Cedex, France. Phone: +33 (1) 46-57-77-83 or +33 (1) 49-65-11-61. Fax: +33 (1) 49 65 19 11 or +33 (1) 49 65 21 37. Contact: Daniel Bochent, Chef du service ondes décamétriques; Alain Meunier; Mme. Annick Tusseau; Mme. Christiane Bouvet; or M. Michel Azibert, chef internationale. This office only for informing about transmitter-related problems (interference, modulation quality, etc.), especially by fax. Verifications not given out at this office; requests for verification should be sent to the main office, above.
New York News Bureau, Nontechnical: 1290 Avenue of the Americas, New York NY 10019 USA. Phone: +1 (212) 581-1771. Fax: +1 (212) 541 4309. Contact: Ms. Auberi Edler, reporter; or Bruno Albin, reporter.
Washington News Bureau: 529 14th Street NW, Suite 1126, Washington DC 20045 USA. Phone: +1 (202) 879-6706. Contact: Pierre J. Cayrol.
San Francisco Office, Schedules: 2654 17th Avenue, San Francisco CA 94116 USA. Phone: +1 (415) 564-9968. Contact: George Poppin. Self-addressed stamped envelope or IRC required for reply. This address, a volunteer office, only provides RFI schedules to listeners. All other correspondence should be sent directly to Paris.
Voice of Orthodoxy—see Belarus.

FRENCH GUIANA   World Time -3
Radio France Internationale/Swiss Radio International—Guyane Relay Station, TDF, Montsinéry, French Guiana. Contact: (technical) Chef des Services Techniques, RFI Guyane. All correspondence concerning non-technical matters should be sent directly to the main addresses (see) for Radio France International in France and Swiss Radio International in Berne. Can consider replies only to technical correspondence in French.

RFO Guyane, Cayenne, French Guiana. Fax: +594 30 26 49. Free stickers. Replies occasionally and sometimes slowly; correspondence in French preferred, but English often okay.

FRENCH POLYNESIA   World Time -10 Tahiti
RFO Tahiti—Radio Tahiti, B.P. 125, Papeete, Tahiti, French Polynesia. Fax: +689 413 155 or +689 425 041. Contact: (general) J.R. Bodin; (technical) León Siquin, Services Techniques. Free stickers, tourist brochures and broadcast-coverage map. Three IRCs, return postage, 5 francs or $1 helpful, but not mandatory. M. Siquin and his teenage sons Xavier and Philippe, all friendly and fluent in English, collect pins from radio/TV stations, memorabilia from the Chicago Bulls basketball team and other souvenirs of American pop culture; these make more appro-

priate enclosures than the usual postage-reimbursement items. Station once hoped to obtain new studios and transmitters, but nothing seems to have come of this. In the meantime, only one of their three ancient world band transmitters continues to function regularly, and its charming island programming of yore has become more European and prosaic.

GABON   World Time +1
Afrique Numéro Un, B.P. 1, Libreville, Gabon. Fax: +241 742 133. Contact: (general) Gaston Didace Singangoye; or A. Letamba, Le Directeur des Programmes; (technical) Mme. Marguerite Bayimbi, Le Directeur [sic] Technique. Free calendars and bumper stickers. $1, 2 IRCs or return postage helpful. Replies very slowly.
RTV Gabonaise, B.P. 10150, Libreville, Gabon. Contact: André Ranaud-Renombo, Le Directeur Technique, Adjoint Radio. Free stickers. $1 required. Replies occasionally, but slowly, to correspondence in French.

GEORGIA   World Time +4
Georgian Radio, TV-Radio Tbilisi, ul. M. Kostava 68, 380071 Tbilisi, Republic of Georgia. Contact: (External Service) Helena Apkhadze, Foreign Editor; Tamar Shengelia; Mrs. Natia Datuaschwili, Secretary; or Maya Chihradze; (Domestic Service) Lia Uumlaelsa, Manager; or V. Khundadze, Acting Director of Television and Radio Department. Replies occasionally and slowly.

GERMANY   World Time +1 (+2 midyear)
Adventist World Radio, the Voice of Hope, P.O. Box 100252, D-64202 Darmstadt, Germany. Phone: +49 (6151) 390-90 Fax: +49 (6151) 390 913. Contact: Iris Manuela Brandl, Listener Mail Services. Free religious printed matter, quarterly *AWR Current* newsletter, pennants, stickers and other small souvenirs. Transmitters are located in Costa Rica, Guam, Guatemala, Italy, Slovakia and Russia; this office will verify reports for AWR broadcasts from Italy, Russia and Slovakia. (Additionally, non-affiliated local Adventist stations are found in the Dominican Republic and Perú.) Also, *see* USA. Drop-mailing address include:
Africa Address: AWR, B.P. 1751, Abidjan 08, Côte d'Ivoire. Fax: +225 442 341 or +225 445 118. Contact: Daniel B. Grisier, Director; Julien M. Thiombiano, Program Director; or "Listener Mailbox."
London Address: AWR, 39 Brendon Street, London W1, United Kingdom.
Bayerischer Rundfunk, Rundfunkplatz 1, D-80300 Munich, Germany. Fax: +49 (89) 5900 2375. Contact: Dr. Gualtiero Guidi; or Jutta Paue, Engineering Adviser. Free stickers and 250-page program schedule book.
Canadian Forces Network Radio—*see* CANADA.
Deutsche Welle, Radio and TV International
Note for European Listeners: At a convention in Europe in June, 1995, Deutsche Welle announced that in the interests of Germany's being seen as a pioneer in advanced technology, and presumably to further Germany's own interest in the proposed Eureka system of satellite broadcasting, it is terminating all shortwave operations to Europe in 1996 and relying, instead, on satellite distribution and program placement. It recommends that its European listeners obtain the appropriate satellite hardware if they wish to tune in thereafter. A more feasible solution for most Europeans would be to try Deutsche Welle's world band transmissions beamed to other parts of the world.
Main Office: Postfach 10 04 44, D-50588 Cologne, Germany. Phone: (general) +49 (221) 389-2001/2; (Program Distribution) +49 (221) 389-2731; (technical) +49 (221) 389-3221 or +49 (221) 389-3228. Fax: (general) +49 (221) 389 4155 , +49 (221) 389 2080 or +49 (221) 389 3000; (English Service, general) +49 (221) 389 4599; (English Service, Current Affairs) +49 (221) 389 4554; (Public Relations) +49 (221) 389 2047; (Program Distribution) +49 (221) 389 2777; (technical)

+49 (221) 389 3200. E-mail: (general) deutsche.welle@ dw.gmd.de; (schedule information) 100144.2133@compuserve.com; (specific individuals or programs) format is firstname.lastname@dw.gmd.de, so to reach, say, Harald Schuetz, it would be harald.schuetz@dw.gmd.de; (Program Distribution) 100302.2003@compuserve.com. World Wide Web: http://www-dw.gmd.de/. Contact: (general) Ursula Fleck-Jerwin, Audience Mail Department; Ernst Peterssen, Head of Audience Research and Listeners' Mail; Dr. Wilhelm Nobel, Director of Public Relations; or Dr. Burkhard Nowotny, Director of Media Department; (listener questions and comments) Harald Schuetz; ("German by Radio" language course) Herrad Meese; (head of administration) DieterWeirich, Director General; (technical— Radio Frequency Department) Peter Pischalka or Horst Scholz. Free pennants, stickers, key chains, pens, *Deutsch—warum nicht?* language-course book, *Germany—A European Country and its People* book, and the excellent *tune-in* magazine. Local Deutsche Welle Listeners' Clubs in selected countries. Operates via world band transmitters in Germany, Antigua, Canada, Madagascar, Malta, Portugal, Russia, Rwanda and Sri Lanka.
Electronic Transmission Office for Program Previews: Infomedia, 25 rue du Lac, L-8808 Arsdorf, Luxembourg. Phone : +352 649-270. Fax: +352 649 271. This office will electronically transmit Deutsche Welle program previews to you upon request; be sure to provide either a dedicated fax number or an e-mail address so they can reply to you.
Brussels News Bureau: International Press Center, 1 Boulevard Charlemagne, B-1040 Brussels, Belgium.
U.S./Canadian Listener Contact Office: P.O. Box 50641, Washington DC 20091 USA.
Russian Listener Contact Office: Nemezkaja Wolna, Abonentnyj jaschtschik 596, Glawpotschtamt, 190000 St. Petersburg, Russia.
Tokyo News Bureau: C.P.O. Box 132, Tokyo 100-91, Japan.
Washington News Bureau: P.O. Box 14163, Washington DC 20004 USA. Fax: +1 (202) 526 2255. Contact: Adnan Al-Katib, Correspondent.
DeutschlandRadio-Berlin, Hans-Rosenthal-Platz 1, D-10825 Berlin Schönberg, Germany. Fax: +49 (30) 850 3390. Contact: Gerda Holunder. $1 or return postage required. Free stickers and postcards.
Radio Bremen, Heinrich Hertzstr. 13, D-28329 Bremen, Germany. Fax: +49 (421) 246 1010. Contact: Jim Senberg. Free stickers and shortwave guidebook.
RadioRopa Info, Technic Park, Postfach 549, D-54550 Daun, Germany. Fax: +49 (6592) 203 537. E-mail: ("DX-Report") dx-report@ng-box.wwb.sub.de. Contact: Sabine K. Thome. Free stickers and booklets. Transmits via the facilities of Radio Prague.
Süddeutscher Rundfunk, Neckarstr. 230, D-70049 Stuttgart, Germany. Fax: +49 (711) 929 2600. Free stickers.
Südwestfunk, Hans Bredowstr., D-76530 Baden-Baden, Germany. Fax: +49 (722) 192 2010. Contact: (technical) Prof. Dr. Hans Krankl, Chief Engineer.
Universell Leben (Universal Life), P.O. Box 5643, D-97006 Würzburg, Germany. Transmits "The Word" via the Voice of Russia, WWCR (USA) and various other world band stations, as well as "Viva Universal" via Radio Miami Internacional in the United States. Replies to correspondence in English, German or Spanish.

GHANA   World Time exactly
Warning—Confidence Artists: Attempted correspondence with Radio Ghana may result in requests, perhaps resulting from mail theft, from skilled confidence artists for money, free electronic or other products, publications or immigration sponsorship. To help avoid this, correspondence to Radio Ghana should be sent via registered mail.
Radio Ghana, Ghana Broadcasting Corporation, P.O. Box 1633, Accra, Ghana. Fax: +233 (21) 773 227. Contact:

(general) Maud Blankson-Mills, Head, Audience Research; Robinson Aryee, Head, English Section; Emmanuel Felli, Head, French Section; or Victor Markin, Producer, English Section; (head of administration) Mrs. Anna Sai, Assistant Director of Radio; (technical) E. Heneath, Propagation Department. Mr. Markin states that he is interested in reception reports, as well as feedback on the program he produces, "Health Update," so directing your correspondence to him may be the best bet. Otherwise, replies are increasingly scarce, but whomever you send your correspondence to, you should register it, and enclose an IRC, return postage or $1.

GREECE World Time +2 (+3 midyear)

Foni Tis Helladas

Nontechnical: ERT A.E., ERA-5 Program, Voice of Greece, Messoghion 432 Av., Aghia Paraskevi, GR-153 42 Athens, Greece. Phone: +30 (1) 639-6762 or +30 (1) 686-8305. Fax: (specify "5th Program" on cover sheet) +30 (1) 639 7375 or +30 (1) 655 0943. E-mail: daggel@leon.nrcps.ariadne-t.gr. Contact: Kosta Valetas, Director, Programs for Abroad. Free tourist literature.

Technical: ERT 5th Program, Direction of Engineering and Developement, P.O. Box 60019, 432 Aghia Paraskevi Attikis, GR-15342 Athens, Greece. Phone: +30 (1) 601-4700 or +30 (1) 639-6762. Fax: +30 (1) 639 7375, +30 (1) 639 0652 or +30 (1) 600 9608. Contact: Demetri H. Vafeas, Chief Engineer; or Ing. Filotas Gianotas.

Radiophonikos Stathmos Makedonias

Nontechnical: Odos Yeorghikis Scholis 129, GR-546 39 Thessaloniki, Greece.

Contact: Mrs. Tatiana Tsioli.

Technical: ERT S.A., Subdirection of Technical Support, P.O. Box 11312, GR-541 10 Thessaloniki, Greece. Contact: Tassos A. Glias, Telecommunications Engineer; or Dimitrios Keramides, Engineer. Free stickers and booklets.

Voice of America—Kaválla Relay Station. Phone: +30 (5) 912-2855. Fax: +30 (5) 913 1310. Contact: Michael Nardi, Relay Station Manager. These numbers for urgent technical matters only. Otherwise, does not welcome direct correspondence; *see* USA for acceptable VOA Washington address and related information.

Voice of America—Rhodes Relay Station. Phone: +30 (241) 24-731. Fax: +30 (241) 27 522. Contact: Wesley Robinson, Relay Station Manager. These numbers for urgent technical matters only. Otherwise, does not welcome direct correspondence; *see* USA for acceptable VOA Washington address and related information.

GUAM World Time +10

Adventist World Radio, the Voice of Hope—KSDA

Main Office, General Programs: P.O. Box 7468, Agat, Guam 96928 USA. Phone: +671 585-2000. Fax: +671 565 2983. E-mail: 70673.2552@compuserve.com. Contact: (general) Lolita Colegado, Listener Mail Services; (technical) Elvin Vence, Engineer. Free pennants, stickers, postcards, quarterly *AWR Current* newsletter and religious printed matter. A fourth shortwave transmitter, of 100 kW, is planned to be on the air by early 1996. Also, *see* USA.

Hong Kong Address: AWR-Asia, P.O Box 310, Hong Kong.

India Address: P.O. Box 17, Poona-411 001, India.

"Wavescan" DX Program: P.O. Box 29235, Indianapolis IN 46229 USA.

Yokohama Address: 846 Kami Kawai-cho, Asahi-ku, Yokohama-city, Kanagawa 241, Japan. Fax: +81 (45) 921 2319.

Trans World Radio—KTWR

Main Office, Nontechnical: P.O. Box CC, Agana, Guam 96910 USA. Phone: +671 828-8637. Fax: +671 477 2838. Contact: (general) Ed. Stortro; (listeners' questions program) Jim Elliott, Producer, "Friends in Focus"; Wayne T. Frost, Program Director & Producer, "Pacific DX Report"; Kathy Gregowski; Karen Zeck; or Judy C. Speck; (technical) Kevin Mayer or George Ross. Also, *see* USA. Free stickers,

AWR-Asia's modern facility at Facpi Point, Guam.

pennants and wall calendars. Plans to install an additional (fourth) 100 kW transmitter by early 1996.

Frequency Coordination Office: 1868 Halsey Drive, Asan, Guam 96922 USA. Phone: +671 828-8637. Fax: +671 828 8636. Contact: Wayne Frost.

Australian Office: G.P.O. Box 602D, Melbourne 3001, Australia. Phone: +61 (3) 9872-4606. Fax: +61 (3) 9874 8890. Contact: John Reeder, Director.

India Office: P.O. Box 4310, New Delhi-110 019, India. Contact: N. Emil Jebasingh, Vishwa Vani.

Singapore Bureau, Nontechnical: 273 Thomson Road, 03-03 Novena Gardens, Singapore 1130, Singapore.

Tokyo Office: C.P.O. Box 1000, Tokyo Central Post Office, Tokyo 100-91, Japan. Fax: +81 (3) 3233 2650.

GUATEMALA World Time -6

Adventist World Radio, the Voice of Hope—Unión Radio, Apartado de Correo 35-C, Guatemala City, Guatemala. Fax: +502 (2) 691 330. Contact: Rolando García, Gerente General. Free tourist and religious literature, and Guatemalan stamps. Return postage, 3 IRCs or $1 helpful. Correspondence in Spanish preferred. Also, *see* USA.

Radio Cultural—TGNA, Apartado de Correo 601, Guatemala City, Guatemala. Phone: +502 (2) 427-45 or +502 (2) 443-78. Contact: Mariella Posadas, QSL Secretary; or Wayne Berger, Chief Engineer. Free religious printed matter. Return postage or $1 appreciated.

La Voz de Atitlán—TGDS, Santiago Atitlán, Guatemala. Contact: Juan Ajtzip Alvarado, Director; José Miguel Pop Tziná; or Esteban Ajtzip Tziná, Director Ejecutivo. Return postage required. Replies to correspondence in Spanish.

La Voz de Nahualá, Nahualá, Sololá, Guatemala. Contact: (technical) Juan Fidel Lepe Juárez, Técnico Auxiliar; or F. Manuel Esquipulas Carrillo Tzep. Return postage required. Correspondence in Spanish preferred.

Radio Buenas Nuevas, 13020 San Sebastián, Huehuetenango, Guatemala. Contact: Israel Rodas Mérida, Gerente; Roberto Rice, Technician; or Andrés Maldonado López, Julián Pérez Megía, and Israel Maldonado, Locutores. $1 or return postage helpful. Free religious and station information in Spanish. Replies to correspondence in Spanish.

Radio Coatán, San Sebástian Coatán, Huehuetenango, Guatemala. Contact: Domingo Hernández, Director; or Virgilio José, Locutor.

Radio Chortís, Centro Social, 20004 Jocotán, Chiquimula, Guatemala. Contact: Padre Juan María Boxus, Director. $1 or return postage required. Replies irregularly to correspondence in Spanish.

Radio K'ekchi—TGVC, K'ekchi Baptist Association, 16015 Fray Bartolomé de las Casas, Alta Verapaz, Guatemala. Contact: Gilberto Sun Xicol, Gerente; Carlos Díaz Araújo, Director; Ancelmo Cuc Chub, Locutor y Director; or David Daniel, Media Consultant. Free paper pennant. $1 or return postage required. Replies to correspondence in Spanish.

Radio Mam, Acu'Mam, Cabricán, Quetzaltenango, Guatemala. Contact: Porfirio Pérez, Director. Free stickers and pennants. $1 or return postage required. Replies irregularly to correspondence in Spanish. Donations permitting (the station is religious), they would like to get a new transmitter to replace the current unit, which is failing.

Radio Maya de Barillas—TGBA, 13026 Villa de Barillas, Huehuetenango, Guatemala. Contact: José Castañeda, Pastor Evangélico y Gerente. Free pennants and pins. $1 or return postage required. Replies occasionally to correspondence in Spanish and Indian languages.

Radio Tezulutlán, Apartado de Correo 19, 16901 Cobán, Guatemala. Contact: Alberto P.A. Macz, Director; or Hno. Antonio Jacobs, Director Ejecutivo. $1 or return postage required. Replies to correspondence in Spanish.

GUINEA   World Time exactly

Radiodiffusion-Télévision Guinéenne, B.P. 391, Conakry, Guinea. Contact: (general) Yaoussou Diaby, Journaliste Sportif; (head of administration) Alpha Sylla, Directeur, Sofoniya I Centre de Transmission; (technical, studio) Mbaye Gagne, Chef de Studio; (technical, overall) Direction des Services Techniques. Return postage or $1 required. Replies very irregularly to correspondence in French.

GUYANA   World Time -3

Voice of Guyana (when operating), Guyana Broadcasting Corporation, P.O. Box 10760, Georgetown, Guyana. Contact: (technical) Roy Marshall, Senior Technician; or S. Goodman, Chief Engineer. $1 or IRC helpful. Sending a spare sticker from another station helps assure a reply.

HAITI   World Time -5 (-4 midyear)

Note: Although no world band station currently operates from Haitian soil, the following function as de facto official broadcasts to Haitians abroad:

Focus on Haiti, P.O. Box 525, Monset NY 10952 USA. Contact: "Jean-Pierre." Focuses on progress of government of Jean-Pierre Aristide. Via Radio for Peace International, Costa Rica.

Radio 16th December (Radio 16 de Sanm)—*see* Radio Miami Internacional, USA, for the best address; or you can also try via the Embassy of Haiti, 2311 Massachusetts Avenue NW, Washington DC 20008 USA. Phone: +1 (202) 332-4090. Contact: Emmanuel Cantave. Supports Aristide government activities in Haiti.

HOLLAND (THE NETHERLANDS)   World Time +1 (+2 midyear)

Radio Nederland Wereldomroep (Radio Netherlands)

Main Office: P.O. Box 222, 1200 JG Hilversum, The Netherlands. Phone: (English Department) +31 (35) 672-4242; (Answerline) +31 (35) 672-4222. Fax: (general) +31 (35) 672 4352, but indicate destination department on fax cover sheet; (English Department) +31 (35) 672 4239; (Distribution & Frequency Planning Department) +31 (35) 672 4429. E-mail: letters@rnw.nl. World Wide Web: http://www.rnw.nl/rnw. Contact: (general) Jonathan Marks, Director of Programs; Rina Miller, Head English Department; Mike Shea, Network Manager English; Iris Walstra, English Correspondence; Diana Janssen, Producer, Media Network; or Robert Chesal, Host, "Sounds Interesting" (include your telephone number); (head of administration) Lodewijk Bouwens, Director General; (technical, including for full-data verifications) Jan-Willem Drexhage, Head of Distribution and Frequency Planning (full-data QSL card if the report follows guidelines issued in the RNW publication "Writing Useful Reception Reports," available free upon request). Semi-annual *On Target* newsletter also free upon request, as are stickers and booklets. The Radio Netherlands "GOLD" label, with the best of their English-language programs, will be released in early 1996; RNW also produces around 24 CDs per year, mainly of classical and world music, under the label "NM Classics." Future plans include the further development of placement programs in North America, in co-operation with Public Radio International. Sometimes hosts international broadcasting conventions.

Washington News Bureau: 1773 Lanier Place, Apt. 1, Washington DC 20009 USA. Phone: +1 (202) 265-9530. Contact: Arnoud Hekkens.

Guatemala's Radio Maya broadcasts to the Indian population, largely in their own languages.

Latin American Office: (local correspondence only) Apartado 880-1007, Ventro Colón, Costa Rica. This address only for correspondence to RNW's Costa Rican employees, who speak only Spanish. All other correspondence should be sent directly to Holland.

New Delhi Office: (local correspondence only) P.O. Box 5257, Chanakya Puri Post Office, New Delhi-110 021, India. All non-local correspondence should be sent directly to Holland.

HONDURAS World Time -6

La Voz de la Mosquitia

Station: Puerto Lempira, Región Mosquitia, Honduras. Contact: Sammy Simpson, Director; Sra. Wilkinson; or Larry Sexton. Free pennants.

U.S. Office: Global Outreach, Box 1, Tupelo MS 38802 USA. Phone: +1 (601) 842-4615.

La Voz Evangélica—HRVC

Main Office: Apartado Postal 3252, Tegucigalpa, M.D.C., Honduras. Phone: +504 34-3468/69/70. Fax: +504 33 3933. Contact: (general) Srta. Orfa Esther Durón Mendoza, Secretaria; Tereso Ramos, Director de Programación; or Modesto Palma, Jefe, Depto. Tráfico; (technical) Carlos Paguada, Director del Dpto. Técnico; (heads of administration) Venancio Mejía, Gerente; Nelson Perdomo, Director. Free calendars. Three IRCs or $1 required. Replies to correspondence in English, Spanish, Portuguese and German.

Regional Office, San Pedro Sula: Apartado 2336, San Pedro Sula, Honduras. Phone: +504 57-5030. Contact: Hernán Miranda, Director.

Regional Office, La Ceiba: Apartado 164, La Ceiba, Honduras. Phone: +504 43-2390. Contact: José Banegas, Director.

U.S. Office: Conservative Baptist Home Mission Society, Box 828, Wheaton IL 60187 USA. Phone: +1 (708) 260-3800, ext. 1217. Fax: +1 (708) 653 4936. Contact: Jill W. Smith.

Radio Copán International—HRJA

Station: Apartado 955, Tegucigalpa, M.D.C., Honduras.

Miami Office: P.O. Box 526852, Miami FL 33152 USA. Phone: +1 (305) 267-1728. Fax: +1 (305) 267 9253. E-mail: 71163.1735@compuserve.com. Contact: Jeff White. Sells airtime for $1 per minute to anybody in any language to say pretty much whatever they want.

"Radio Waves" Program: P.O. Box 1176, Pinson AL 35126 USA. Contact: David Williams.

Radio HRET, Misión la Mosquitia, Puerto Lempira, Gracias a Dios 33101, Honduras. Contact: (general) Roberto Gostas Kramer, Grabaciones Nuevas; Delmar Brown, Locutor, Operador y Productor; or Tito Sami Martínez, Locutor y Operador; (head of administration) Mateo McCollum, Gerente General. Return postage necessary. Replies to correspondence in Spanish.

Radio Internacional, Apartado 1473, San Pedro Sula, Honduras. Phone: +504 528-181. Fax: +504 581 070. Contact: Víctor Antonio ("Tito") Handal, Gerente y Propietario; or Hugo Hernández y Claudia Susana Prieto, Locutores del "Desfile de Estrellas", aired Sunday at 0200-0500 World Time. Free stickers, stamps, postcards and one-lempira banknote. $1 helpful. Appears to reply regularly to correspondence in Spanish.

Radio Litoral, La Ceiba, Atlántida Province, Honduras. Contact: José A. Mejía, Gerente y Propietario. Free postcards. $1 or return postage necessary. Replies to correspondence in Spanish.

Radio Luz y Vida—HRPC, Apartado 303, San Pedro Sula, Honduras. Fax: +504 57 0394. Contact: C. Paul Easley, Director; or, to have your letter read over the air, "English Friendship Program." Return postage or $1 appreciated.

Sani Radio, Apartado 113, La Ceiba, Honduras. Contact: Jacinto Molina G., Director; or Mario S. Corzo. Return postage or $1 required.

HONG KONG World Time +8

BBC World Service—Hong Kong Relay, East Asia Relay Company Ltd, Tsang Tsui Broadcasting Station Nim Wan, Tuen Mun, New Territories, Hong Kong. Contact: Miles Ashton; (technical) Phillip Sandell, Resident Engineer. Nontechnical correspondence should be sent to the BBC World Service in London (see). The BBC hopes to keep this facility in operation after Hong Kong reverts to Chinese rule in 1997 (also, see Thailand).

Radio Television Hong Kong, C.P.O. Box 70200, Kowloon Central Office, Hong Kong. Fax: +852 (3) 238 0279. Contact: (general) Jagjit Dillon; (technical) W.K. Li, Telecommunications Engineer. May broadcast brief weather reports every even two years, usually around late March or early April, on 3940 kHz or 7290 khz (e.g., sometime between 1000 and 1200 World Time) for the South China Sea Yacht Race.

HUNGARY World Time +1 (+2 midyear)

Radio Budapest

Station Offices: Bródy Sándor utca 5-7, H-1800 Budapest, Hungary. Phone: (general) +36 (1) 138-7357, +36 (1) 138-8588 or +36 (1) 138-7723; (voice mail) +36 (1) 138-8320; (Editorial Office) +36 (1) 138-8415 or +36 (1) 138-7339; (technical) +36 (1) 138-8923. Fax: (general) +36 (1) 138 8517 or +36 (1) 138 8838; (Editorial Office) +36 (1) 138 8838; (technical) +36 (1) 138 7105. World Wide Web: (shortwave program) http://www.glue.umd.edu/-gotthard/hir/entertainment/radio/. Contact: (English Language Dept.) Louis Horvath, DX Editor; Sándor Laczkó, Journalist; Charles Taylor Coutts, Head of English Section; Ilona Kiss; or Anton Réger, Editor; (Editorial Office) Dr. Zsuzsa Mészáros, Assistant Editor-in-Chief; (technical) Laszlo Fuszfas, Deputy Technical Director, Magyar Radio. Free *Budapest International* program periodical.

Transmission Authority: Ministry of Transport, Communications & Water Management, P.O. Box 87, H-1400 Budapest, Hungary. Phone/fax: +36 (1) 156 3493. Contact: Ferenc Horvath, Radio Communications Engineering Services.

ICELAND World Time exactly

Ríkisútvarpid, International Relations Department, Efstaleiti 1, 150 Reykjavik, Iceland. Fax: +354 (5) 693 010. Contact: Dóra Ingvadóttir, Head of International Relations.

INDIA World Time +5:30

Ministry of Information & Broadcasting, Main Secretariat, A-Wing, Shastri Bhawan, New Delhi-110 001, India. Phone: (general) +91 (11) 384-340, +91 (11) 384-782 or +91 (11) 379-338; (Information & Broadcasting Secretary) +91 (11) 382-639. Fax: +91 (11) 383 513. Contact: (general) B. Ghose, Information & Broadcasting Secretary; (adminsitrative) K.P. Singh Deo, Minister for Information & Broadcasting.

Akashvani—Governing Body for All India Radio

Administration: Directorate General of All India Radio, Akashvani Bhawan, 1 Sansad Marg, New Delhi-110 001, India. Phone: (general) +91 (11) 371-0006; (Engineer-in-Chief) +91 (11) 371-0058; (Frequency Management) +91 (11) 371-0145; (Director General) +91 (11) 371-0300 or +91 (11) 371-4061. Fax: +91 (11) 371-1956. Contact: (general) S.K. Kapoor, Director General; (technical) H.M. Joshi, Engineer-in-Chief; or S.A.S. Abidi, Assistant Director and Frequency Manager.

Audience Research: Audience Research Unit, All India Radio, Press Trust of India Building, 2nd floor, Sansad Marg, New Delhi-110 001, India. Phone: +91 (11) 371-0033. Contact: S.K. Khatri, Director.

International Monitoring Station—Main Office: International Monitoring Station, All India Radio, Dr. K.S. Krishnan Road, Todapur, New Delhi 110 097, India. Phone: (general) +91 (11) 581-461; (Control Room) +91 (11) 680-2362; (administration) +91 (11) 680-2306. Contact: S. Haider, Director.

International Monitoring Station—Frequency Planning: Central Monitoring Station, All India Radio, Ayanagar, New Delhi-100 047, India. Phone: +91 (11) 666-306. Contact: (technical) D.P. Chhabra, Assistant Resident Engineer (Frequency Planning).

All India Radio—Aizawl, Radio Tila, Tuikhuahtlang, Aizawl-796 001, Mizoram, India. Phone: +91 (3652) 2415. Contact: (technical) D.K. Sharma, Station Engineer.

All India Radio—Bangalore
Headquarters: see All India Radio—External Services Division.
AIR Office near Transmitter: P.O. Box 5096, Bangalore-560 001, Karnataka, India. Phone: +96 (80) 261-243. Contact: (technical) C. Iyengar, Supervising Engineer.

All India Radio—Bhopal, Akashvani Bhawan, Shamla Hills, Bhopal-462 002, Madhya Pradesh, India. Phone: +91 (755) 540-041. Contact: (technical) C. Lal, Station Engineer.

All India Radio—Bombay
External Services: see All India Radio—External Services Division.
Domestic Service: P.O. Box 13034, Bombay-400 020, India. Phone: +91 (22) 202-9853. Contact: (general) Sarla Mirchandani, Programme Executive, for Station Director; (technical) S. Sundaram, Supervising Engineer. Return postage helpful.

All India Radio—Calcutta, G.P.O. Box 696, Calcutta—700 001, West Bengal, India. Phone: +91 (33) 281-705. Contact: (technical) R.N. Dam, Supervising Engineer.

All India Radio—Delhi—*see* All India Radio—New Delhi.

All India Radio—External Services Division, Parliament Street, P.O. Box 500, New Delhi-110 001, India. Contact: (general) P. M. Iyer, Director of External Services; A. S. Guin, Director of Frequency Assignments; or S.C. Panda, Audience Relations Officer; (technical) S.A.S. Abidi, Assistant Director Engineering (F.A.). Free monthly *India Calling* magazine and stickers. Replies erratic. Except for stations listed below, correspondence to domestic stations is more likely to be responded to if it is sent via the External Services Division; request that your letter be forwarded to the appropriate domestic station.

All India Radio—Gangtok, Old MLA Hostel, Gangtok—737 101, Sikkim, India. Phone: +91 (3592) 226-36. Contact: N.P. Yolmo, Station Director. This station is currently testing a new 10 kW world band transmitter on 3390 kHz.

All India Radio—Gorakhpur
Nepalese External Service: see All India Radio—External Services Division.
Domestic Service: Post Bag 26, Gorakhpur-273 001, Uttar Pradesh, India. Phone: +91 (551) 337-401. Contact: (technical) S.M. Pradhan, Supervising Engineer.

All India Radio—Guwahati, P.O. Box 28, Chandmari, Guwahati-781 003, Assam, India. Phone: +91 (361) 540-135. Contact: (technical) P.C. Sanghi, Superindent Engineer.

All India Radio—Hyderabad, Rocklands, Saifabad, Hyderabad-500 004, Andhra Pradesh, India. Phone: +91 (842) 234-904. Contact: (technical) N. Srinivasan, Supervising Engineer.

All India Radio—Imphal, Palau Road, Imphal-795 001, Manipur, India. Phone: +91 (385) 220-534. Contact: (technical) M. Jayaraman, Supervising Engineer.

All India Radio—Itanagar, Naharlagun, Itanagar-791 110, Arunachal Pradesh, India. Phone: +91 (3781) 4485. Contact: J.T. Jirdoh, Station Director. Although currently not scheduled to be on shortwave, this station recently has been testing a 50 kW world band transmitter on 9650 kHz.

All India Radio—Jaipur, 5 Park House, Mirza Ismail Road, Jaipur-302 001, Rajasthan, India. Phone: +91 (141) 366-263. Contact: (technical) S.C. Sharma, Station Engineer.

All India Radio—Jammu—*see* Radio Kashmir—Jammu.

All India Radio—Kohima, Kohima-797 001, Nagaland, India. Phone: +91 (3866) 2121. Contact: (technical) K.G. Talwar, Superintending Engineer. Return postage, $1 or IRC helpful.

All India Radio—Kurseong, Mehta Club Building, Kurseong-734 203, Darjeeling District, West Bengal, India. Phone: +91 (3554) 350. Contact: (general) George Kuruvilla, Assistant Director; (technical) R.K. Shina, Station Engineer.

All India Radio—Leh—*see* Radio Kashmir—Leh.

All India Radio—Lucknow, 18 Vidhan Sabha Marg, Lucknow-226 001, Uttar Pradesh, India. Phone: +91 (522) 244-130. Contact: R.K. Singh, Supervising Engineer.

All India Radio—Madras
External Services: see All India Radio—External Services Division.
Domestic Service: Kamrajar Salai, Mylapore, Madras-600 004, Tamil Nadu, India. Phone: +91 (44) 845-975. Contact: (technical) S. Bhatia, Supervising Engineer.

All India Radio—New Delhi, P.O. Box 70, New Delhi-110 011, India. Phone: (voice mail for information in English and Hindi about domestic programs) +91 (11) 376-1166; (general) +91 (11) 371-0113. Contact: (technical) G.C. Tyagi, Supervising Engineer. $1 helpful.

All India Radio—Panaji
Headquarters: see All India Radio—External Services Division, above.
AIR Office near Transmitter: P.O. Box 220, Altinho, Panaji-403 001, Goa, India. Phone: +91 (832) 45-563. Contact: (technical) V.K. Singhla, Station Engineer.
A second 250 kW transmitter is now coming into operation on 15290 kHz but, according to expert Indian radio researcher Manosij Guha, the station continues to be hampered by a lack of staff and an unstable electric supply.

All India Radio—Port Blair, Dilanipur, Port Blair-744 102, South Andaman, Andaman & Nicobar Islands, Union Territory, India. Phone: +91 (3192) 20-682. Contact: (general) P.L. Thakur; (technical) Yuvraj Bajaj, Station Engineer. Registering letter appears to be useful.

All India Radio—Ranchi, 6 Ratu Road, Ranchi-834 001, Bihar, India. Phone: +91 (651) 302-358. Contact: (technical) H.N. Agarwal, Supervising Engineer.

All India Radio—Shillong, P.O. Box 14, Shillong-793 001, Meghalaya, India. Phone: +91 (364) 224-443 or +91 (364) 222-781. Contact: (general) C. Lalsaronga, Director NEIS; (technical) H.K. Agarwal, Supervising Engineer. Free booklet on station's history.

All India Radio—Shimla, Choura Maidan, Shimla-171 004, Himachal Pradesh, India. Phone: +91 (177) 4809. Contact: (technical) B.K. Upadhyay, Supervising Engineer.

All India Radio—Srinagar—*see* Radio Kashmir—Srinagar.

All India Radio—Thiruvananthapuram, P.O. Box 403, Bhakti Vilas, Vazuthacaud, Thiruvananthapuram-695 014, Kerala, India. Phone: +91 (471) 65-009. Contact: (technical) K.M. Georgekutty, Station Engineer.

Radio Kashmir—Jammu, Begum Haveli, Old Palace Road, Jammu-180 001, Jammu & Kashmir, India. Phone: +91 (191) 544-411. Contact: (technical) S.K. Sharma, Station Engineer.

Radio Kashmir—Leh, Leh-194 101, Ladakh District, Jammu & Kashmir, India. Phone: +91 (1982) 2263. Contact: (technical) L.K. Gandotar, Station Engineer.

Radio Kashmir—Srinagar, Sherwani Road, Srinagar—190 001, Jammu & Kashmir, India. Phone: +91 (194) 71-460. Contact: L. Rehman, Station Director.

Radio Tila—*see* All India Radio—Aizawl.

Trans World Radio
Studio: P.O. Box 4407, L-15, Green Park, New Delhi-110 016, India. Phone: +91 (11) 662-058. Fax: +91 (11) 686 8049. Contact: N. Emil Jebasingh, Director.
On-Air Address: P.O. Box 5, Andhra Pradesh, India.

INDONESIA World Time +7 Western: Waktu Indonesia Bagian Barat (Jawa, Sumatera); +8 Central: Waktu

Indonesia Bagian Tengal (Bali, Kalimantan, Sulawesi, Nusa Tenggara); +9 Eastern: Waktu Indonesia Bagian Timur (Irian Jaya, Maluku)

Note: Except where otherwise indicated, Indonesian stations, especially those of the Radio Republik Indonesia (RRI) network, will reply to at least some correspondence in English. However, correspondence in Indonesian is more likely to ensure a reply.

Elkira Radio, Kotak Pos No. 199, JAT, Jakarta 13001, Indonesia. This "amatir" station is unlicensed.

Radio Arista, Jalan Timbangan No. 25., Rt. 005/RW01, Kelurahan Kembangan, Jakarta Barat 10610, Indonesia. This "amatir" station is unlicensed.

Radio Gema Pesona Muda, c/o Wisma Pondok Gede, Jakarta Selatan, Indonesia. This "amatir" station is unlicensed.

Radio Khusus Pemerintah Daerah TK II—RKPD Bima, Jalan A. Yani Atau, Sukarno Hatta No. 2, Nusa Tenggara Barat (NTB), Kode Pos 84116, Indonesia. Fax: +62 (374) 2812. Contact: (general) Baya Asmara Dhana, Publik Relations; or Lalu Suherman; (technical) Mr. Chairil, Technisi RKPD Dati II; or Lara Kawirna, Tehnik Manager. Free stickers. Replies slowly and irregularly to correspondence in Indonesian; return postage required.

Radio Pemerintah Daerah TK II—RPD Bengkalis, Kotak Pos 123, Bengkalis 21751, Riau, Indonesia. Contact: Meiriqal, SMHK; or Ahmad Effendi, Pengelola Siaran Radio Pemda. Return postage required. Replies occasionally to correspondence in Indonesian. Return postage required.

Radio Pemerintah Daerah TK II—RPD Poso, Jalan Jenderal Sudirman 7, Poso, Sulawesi Tengah, Indonesia. Contact: Joseph Tinagari, Kepala Stasiun. Return postage necessary. Replies occasionally to correspondence in Indonesian.

Radio Pemerintah Daerah Kabupaten TK II—RPDK Berau, Jalan SA Maulana, Tanjungredeb, Kalimantan Timur, Indonesia. Contact: Kus Syariman. Return postage necessary.

Radio Pemerintah Daerah Kabupaten TK II—RPDK Bima, Jalan Achmad Yani No. 1, Bima (Raba), Sumbawa, Nusa Tenggara Barat, Indonesia. Free stickers. Return postage required. Replies irregularly to correspondence in Indonesian.

Radio Pemerintah Daerah Kabupaten—RPDK Bolaang Mongondow, Jalan S. Parman 192, Kotamobagu, Sulawesi Utara, Indonesia. Replies occasionally to correspondence in Indonesian.

Radio Pemerintah Daerah Kabupaten TK II—RPDK Buol-Tolitoli, Jalan Mohamed Ismail Bantilan No. 4, Tolitoli 94511, Sulawesi Tengah, Indonesia. Contact: Said Rasjid, Kepala Studio; Wiraswasta, Operator/Penyiar; or Muh. Yasin, SM. Return postage required. Replies extremely irregularly to correspondence in Indonesian.

Radio Pemerintah Daerah Kabupaten TK II—RPDK Ende, Jalan Panglima Sudirman, Ende, Flores, Nusa Tenggara Timor, Indonesia. Contact: (technical) Thomas Keropong, YC9LHD. Return postage required.

Radio Pemerintah Daerah Kabupaten TK II—RPDK Luwu, Kantor Deppen Kabupaten Luwu, Jalan Diponegoro 5, Palopo, Sulawesi Selatan, Indonesia. Contact: Arman Mailangkay.

Radio Pemerintah Daerah Kabupaten TK II—RPDK Manggarai, Ruteng, Flores, Nusa Tenggara Timur, Indonesia. Contact: Simon Saleh, B.A. Return postage required.

Radio Pemerintah Daerah Kabupaten TK II—RPDK Sambas, Jalan M. Sushawary, Sambas, Kalimantan Barat, Indonesia.

Radio Pemerintah Daerah Kabupaten TK II—RPDK Tapanuli Selatan, Kotak Pos No. 9, Padang-Sidempuan, Sumatera Utara, Indonesia. Return postage required.

Radio Pemerintah Kabupaten Daerah TK II—RPKD Belitung, Jalan A. Yani, Tanjungpandan 33412, Belitung, Indonesia. Contact: Drs. H. Fadjri Nashir B., Kepala Stasiun. Free tourist brochure. 1 IRC helpful.

Radio Primadona, Jalan Bintaro Permai Raya No. 5, Jakarta Selatan, Indonesia. This "amatir" station is unlicensed.

Radio Republik Indonesia—RRI Ambon, Jalan Jenderal Akhmad Yani 1, Ambon, Maluku, Indonesia. Contact: Drs. H. Ali Amran or Pirla C. Noija, Kepala Seksi Siaran. A very poor replier to correspondence in recent years. Correspondence in Indonesian and return postage essential.

Radio Republik Indonesia—RRI Banda Aceh, Kotak Pos No. 112, Banda Aceh, Aceh, Indonesia. Contact: S.H. Rosa Kim. Return postage helpful.

Radio Republik Indonesia—RRI Bandung, Stasiun Regional 1, Kotak Pos No. 1055, Bandung 40010, Jawa Barat, Indonesia. Contact: Drs. Idrus Alkaf, Kepala Stasiun; or Eem Suhaemi, Kepala Seksi Siaran. Return postage or IRC helpful.

Radio Republik Indonesia—RRI Banjarmasin, Stasiun Nusantara 111, Kotak Pos No. 117, Banjarmasin 70234, Kalimantan Selatan, Indonesia. Contact: Jul Chaidir, Stasiun Kepala; or Harmyn Husein. Return postage or IRCs helpful.

Radio Republik Indonesia—RRI Bengkulu, Stasiun Regional 1, Kotak Pos No. 13 Kawat, Kotamadya Bengkulu, Indonesia. Contact: Drs. H. Harmyn Husein, Kepala Stasiun. Free picture postcards, decals and tourist literature. Return postage or 2 IRCs helpful.

Radio Republik Indonesia—RRI Biak, Kotak Pos No. 505, Biak, Irian Jaya, Indonesia.

Radio Republik Indonesia—RRI Bukittinggi, Stasiun Regional 1 Bukittinggi, Jalan Prof. Muhammad Yamin No. 199, Aurkuning, Bukittinggi 26131, Propinsi Sumatera Barat, Indonesia. Fax: +62 (752) 367 132. Contact: Mr. Effendi, Sekretaris; Zul Arifin Mukhtar, SH; or Samirwan Sarjana Hukum, Producer, "Phone in Program." Replies to correspondence in Indonesian or English. Return postage helpful.

Radio Republik Indonesia—RRI Cirebon, Jalan Brigjen. Dharsono/By Pass, Cirebon 45132, Jawa Barat, Indonesia. Phone: +62 (231) 204 074. Fax: +62 (231) 207 154. Contact: Ahmad Sugiarto, Kepala Seksi Siaran; Darmadi, Produsennya, "Kantong Surat"; Nasuko, Sub Seksi Periklanan dan Jasa; Gunoto, Kepala Sub Bag. Tata Usaha; or Bagus Giarto, B.Sc. Return postage helpful.

Radio Republik Indonesia—RRI Denpasar, P.O. Box 31, Denpasar, Bali, Indonesia. Replies slowly to correspondence in Indonesian. Return postage or IRCs helpful.

Radio Republik Indonesia—RRI Dili, Stasiun Regional 1 Dili, Jalan Kaikoli, Kotak Pos 103, Dili 88000, Timor-Timur, Indonesia. Contact: Harry A. Silalahi, Kepala Stasiun; Arnoldus Klau; or Paul J. Amalo, BA. Return postage or $1 helpful. Replies occasionally to correspondence in Indonesian.

Radio Republik Indonesia—RRI Fak Fak, Jalan Kapten P. Tendean, Kotak Pos No. 54, Fak-Fak 98601, Irian Jaya, Indonesia. Contact: A. Rachman Syukur, Kepala Stasiun; Bahrum Siregar; Aloys Ngotra, Kepala Seksi Siaran; or Richart Tan, Kepala Sub Seksi Siaran Kata. Return postage required. Replies occasionally.

Radio Republik Indonesia—RRI Gorontalo, Jalan Jenderal Sudirman, Gorontalo, Sulawesi Utara, Indonesia. Contact: Emod. Iskander, Kepala; or Saleh S. Thalib, Technical Manager. Return postage helpful. Replies occasionally, preferably to correspondence in Indonesian.

Radio Republik Indonesia—RRI Jakarta, Stasiun Nasional Jakarta, Kotak Pos No. 356, Jakarta, Jawa Barat, Indonesia. Contact: Drs R. Baskara, Stasiun Kepala. Return postage helpful. Replies irregularly.

Radio Republik Indonesia—RRI Jambi, Jalan Jenderal A. Yani No. 5, Telanaipura, Jambi 36122, Propinsi Jambi, Indonesia. Contact: Marlis Ramali, Manager; M. Yazid, Kepala Siaran; or Adjuzar Tjang Abbas, Kepala Stasiun. Return postage helpful.

Radio Republik Indonesia—RRI Jayapura, Jalan Tasangkapura No. 23, Jayapura 99222, Irian Jaya, Indonesia. Contact: Harry Liborang, Direktorat Radio; or Dr. David Alex Siahainenia, Kepala. Return postage helpful.

Radio Republik Indonesia—RRI Kendari, Kotak Pos No. 7, Kendari, Sulawesi Tenggara, Indonesia. Contact: H. Sjahbuddin, BA; or Drs. Supandi. Return postage required. Replies slowly to correspondence in Indonesian.

Radio Republik Indonesia—RRI Kupang (Regional I), Jalan Tompello No. 8, Kupang, Timor, Indonesia. Contact: Alfonsus Soetarno, BBA, Kepala Stasiun; Qustigap Bagang, Kepala Seksi Siaran; or Said Rasyid, Kepala Studio. Return postage helpful. Correspondence in Indonesian preferred. Replies occasionally.

Radio Republik Indonesia—RRI Madiun, Jalan Mayor Jenderal Panjaitan No. 10, Madiun, Jawa Timur, Indonesia. Fax: +62 (351) 4964. Contact: Imam Soeprapto, Kepala Seksi Siaran. Replies to correspondence in English or Indonesian. Return postage helpful.

Radio Republik Indonesia—RRI Malang, Kotak Pos No. 78, Malang 65112, Jawa Timur, Indonesia. Contact: Ml. Mawahib, Kepala Seksi Siaran; or Dra Hartati Soekemi, Mengetahui. Return postage necessary. Replies to correspondence in Indonesian.

Radio Republik Indonesia—RRI Manado, Kotak Pos No. 1110, Manado 95124 Propinsi Sulawesi Utara, Indonesia. Fax: +62 (431) 63492. Contact: Costher H. Gulton, Kepala Stasiun. Free stickers and postcards. Return postage or $1 required. Replies occasionally to correspondence in Indonesian.

Radio Republik Indonesia—RRI Manokwari, Regional II, Jalan Merdeka No. 68, Manokwari, Irian Jaya, Indonesia. Contact: P.M. Tisera, Kepala Stasiun; or Nurdin Mokogintu. Return postage helpful.

Radio Republik Indonesia—RRI Mataram, Stasiun Regional I Mataram, Jalan Langko No. 83, Mataram 83114, Nusa Tenggara Barat, Indonesia. Contact: Drs. Hamid Djasman, Kepala; or Ketua Dewan, Pimpinan Harian. Free stickers. Return postage required. With sufficient return postage or small token gift, sometimes sends tourist information and Batik print. Replies to correspondence in Indonesian.

Radio Republik Indonesia—RRI Medan, Jalan Letkol Martinus Lubis No. 5, Medan 20232, Sumatera, Indonesia. Phone: +62 (61) 324-222/441. Fax: +62 (61) 512 161. Contact: Kepala Stasiun, Ujamalul Abidin Ass; Drs. Syamsui Muin Harahap; Drs. S. Parlin Tobing, SH, Produsennya, "Kontak Pendengar"; Drs. H. Suryanta Saleh; or Suprato. Free stickers. Return postage required. Replies to correspondence in Indonesian.

Radio Republik Indonesia—RRI Merauke, Stasiun Regional I, Kotak Pos No. 11, Merauke, Irian Jaya, Indonesia. Contact: (general) Achmad Ruskaya B.A., Kepala Stasiun, Tuanakotta Semuel, Kepala Seksi Siaran; or John Manuputty, Kepala Subseksi Pemancar; (technical) Daf'an Kubangun, Kepala Seksi Tehnik. Return postage helpful.

Radio Republik Indonesia—RRI Nabire, Kotak Pos No. 110, Jalan Merdeka 74 Nabire 98801, Irian Jaya, Indonesia. Contact: Muchtar Yushaputra, Kepala Stasiun. Free stickers and occasional free picture postcards. Return postage or IRCs helpful.

Radio Republik Indonesia—RRI Padang, Kotak Pos No. 77, Padang 25121, Sumatera Barat, Indonesia. Phone: +61 (751) 28363. Contact: Marlis Ramali; Syair Siak,

Kepala Stasiun; or Amir Hasan, Kepala Seksi Siaran. Return postage helpful.

Radio Republik Indonesia—RRI Palangkaraya, Jalan M. Husni Thamrin No. 1, Palangkaraya 73111, Kalimantan Tengah, Indonesia. Phone: +62 (514) 21779. Fax: +62 (514) 21778. Contact: Drs Amiruddin; S. Polin; A.F. Herry Purwanto; Meyiwati SH; Supardal Djojosubrojo, Sarjana Hukum; Gumer Kamis; or Ricky D. Wader, Kepala Stasiun. Return postage helpful. Will respond to correspondence in Indonesian or English.

Radio Republik Indonesia—RRI Palembang, Jalan Radio No. 2, Km. 4, Palembang, Sumatera Selatan, Indonesia. Contact: Drs. H. Mursjid Noor; H.A. Syukri Ahkab, Kepala Seksi Siaran; or H.Iskandar Suradilaga. Return postage helpful. Replies slowly and occasionally.

Radio Republik Indonesia—RRI Palu, Jalan R.A. Kartini No. 39, 94112 Palu, Sulawesi Tengah, Indonesia. Phone: +62 (451) 21621. Contact: Akson Boole; Elrick Johannes, Kepala Seksi Siaran; Untung Santoso; Nyonyah Netty Soriton; or M. Hasjim, Head of Programming. Return postage required. Replies slowly to correspondence in Indonesian.

Radio Republik Indonesia—RRI Pekanbaru, Jalan Jenderal Sudirman No. 440, Kotak Pos 51, Pekanbaru, Riau, Indonesia. Phone: +62 (761) 22081. Fax: +62 (761) 23605. Contact: (general) Drs. Mukidi, Kepala Stasiun; Arisun Agus, Kepala Seksi Siaran; or Zainal Abbas; (technical) A. Hutasuhut, Kepala Seksi Teknik. Return postage helpful.

Radio Republik Indonesia—RRI Pontianak, Kotak Pos No. 6, Pontianak 78111, Kalimantan Barat, Indonesia. Contact: Daud Hamzah, Kepala Seksi Siaran; Achmad Ruskaya, BA; Drs. Effendi Afati, Producer, "Dalam Acara Kantong Surat"; Subagio, Kepala Sub Bagian Tata Usaha; Suryadharma, Kepala Sub Seksi Programa; or Muchlis Marzuki B.A. Return postage or $1 helpful. Replies some of the time to correspondence in Indonesian (preferred) or English.

Radio Republik Indonesia—RRI Purwokerto, Stasiun Regional II, Kotak Pos No. 5, Purwokerto 53116, Propinsi Jawa Tengah, Indonesia. Phone: +62 (281) 32336. Fax: +62 (281) 35222. Contact: Yon Maryono, Stasiun Kepala; Moeljono, Kepala Seksi Stasiun; Nur Said, Ka Subsi Siaran Kata; or A.R. Imam Soepardi, Produsennya, "Kontak Pendengar." Return postage helpful. Replies to correspondence in Indonesian or English.

Radio Republik Indonesia—RRI Samarinda, Kotak Pos No. 45, Samarinda, Kalimantan Timur 75001, Indonesia. Phone: +62 (541) 43495. Fax: +62 (541) 41693. Contact: Siti Thomah, Kepala Seksi Siaran; Tyranus Lenjau, English Announcer; S. Yati; or Sunendra, Kepala Stasiun. May send tourist brochures and maps. Return postage helpful. Replies to correspondence in Indonesian.

Radio Republik Indonesia—RRI Semarang, Kotak Pos No. 1073, Semarang Jateng, Jawa Tengah, Indonesia. Phone: +62 (24) 316 501. Contact: Djarwanto, SH; Drs. Sabeni, Doktorandus; Drs. Purwadi, Program Director; Dra. Endang Widiastuti, Kepala Sub Seksi Periklanan Jasa dan Hak Cipta; Bagus Giarto, Kepala Stasiun; or Mardanon, Kepala Teknik. Return postage helpful.

Radio Republik Indonesia—RRI Serui, Jalan Pattimura Kotak Pos 19, Serui 98211, Irian Jaya, Indonesia. Contact: Agus Raunsai, Kepala Stasiun; Ketua Tim Pimpinan Harian, Kepala Seksi Siaran; or Drs. Jasran Abubakar. Replies occasionally to correspondence in Indonesian. IRC or return postage helpful.

Radio Republik Indonesia—RRI Sibolga, Jalan Ade Irma Suryani, Nasution No. 5, Sibolga, Sumatera Utara, Indonesia. Contact: Mrs. Laiya, Mrs. S. Sitoupul or B.A. Tanjung. Return postage required. Replies occasionally to correspondence in Indonesian.

Radio Republik Indonesia—RRI Sorong, Jalan Jenderal Achmad Yani No. 44, Klademak II, Kotak Pos 146, Sorong 98414, Irian Jaya, Indonesia. Phone: +62 (951) 21-003,

+62 (951) 22-111, or +62 (951) 22-611. Contact: Drs. Sallomo Hamid; Tetty Rumbay S., Kasubsi Siaran Kata; Mrs. Tien Widarsanto, Resa Kasi Siaran; Ressa Molle; or Linda Rumbay. Return postage helpful.

Radio Republik Indonesia—RRI Sumenep, Jalan Urip Sumoharjo No. 26, Sumenep, Madura, Jawa Timur, Indonesia. Return postage helpful.

Radio Republik Indonesia—RRI Surabaya, Stasiun Regional 1, Kotak Pos No. 239, Surabaya 60271, Jawa Timur, Indonesia. Phone: +62 (31) 41327. Fax: +62 (31) 42351. Contact: Zainal Abbas, Kepala Stasiun; Drs Agus Widjaja, Kepala Subseksi Programa Siaran; Usmany Johozua, Kepala Seksi Siaran; or Ny Koen Tarjadi. Return postage or IRCs helpful.

Radio Republik Indonesia—RRI Surakarta, Kotak Pos No. 40, Surakarta 57133, Jawa Tengah, Indonesia. Contact: Ton Martono, Head of Broadcasting. Return postage helpful.

Radio Republik Indonesia—RRI Tanjungkarang, Kotak Pos No. 24, Bandar Lampung 35213, Indonesia. Phone: +62 (721) 52280. Fax: +62 (721) 62767. Contact: Hi Hanafie Umar; Djarot Nursinggih, Tech. Transmission; Drs. Zulhaqqi Hafiz, Kepala Sub Seksi Periklanan; Asmara Haidar Manaf; or Sutakno, S.E., Kepala Stasiun. Return postage helpful. Replies in Indonesian to correspondence in English or Indonesian.

Radio Republik Indonesia—RRI Tanjung Pinang, Stasiun RRI Regional II Tanjung Pinang, Kotak Pos No. 8, Tanjung Pinang 29123, Riau, Indonesia. Contact: M. Yazid, Kepala Stasiun; or Wan Suhardi, Produsennya, "Siaran Bahasa Melayu"; or Rosakim, S.H., Sarjana Hukum. Return postage helpful. Replies occasionally to correspondence in Indonesian or English.

Radio Republik Indonesia—RRI Ternate, Jalan Kedaton, Ternate (Ternate), Maluku, Indonesia. Contact: (technical) Rusdy Bachmid, Head of Engineering; or Abubakar Alhadar. Return postage helpful.

Radio Republik Indonesia Tual, Tual, Maluku, Indonesia.

Radio Republik Indonesia—RRI Ujung Pandang, RRI Nusantara IV, Kotak Pos No. 103, Ujung Pandang, Sulawesi Selatan, Indonesia. Contact: H. Kamaruddin Alkaf Yasin, Head of Broadcasting Department; L.A. Rachim Ganie; or Drs. Bambang Pudjono. Return postage, $1 or IRCs helpful. Replies irregularly and sometimes slowly.

Radio Republik Indonesia—RRI Wamena, RRI Regional II, Kotak Pos No. 10, Wamena, Irian Jaya 99501, Indonesia. Contact: Yoswa Kumurawak, Penjab Subseksi Pemancar. Return postage helpful.

Radio Republik Indonesia—RRI Yogyakarta, Jalan Amat Jazuli 4, Kotak Pos 18, Yogyakarta 55224, Jawa Tengah, Indonesia. Fax: +62 (274) 2784. Contact: Phoenix Sudomo Sudaryo; Tris Mulyanti, Seksi Programa Siaran; Drs. H. Hamdan Sjahheni; or Martono, Kepal Stasiun. IRC, return postage or $1 helpful. Replies occasionally to correspondence in Indonesian or English.

Radio Ribubung Subang, Komplex AURI, Subang, Jawa Barat, Indonesia.

Radio Siaran Pemerintah Daerah Kabupaten TK II—RSPDK Halmahera Tengah, Soasio, Pengeloa, RSPD Soasio, Kabupaten Halmaherta Tengah, Propinsi Maluku 97812, Indonesia. Contact: Drs. S. Chalid A., Pengelola.

Radio Siaran Pemerintah Daerah Kabupaten TK II—RSPDK Maluku Tengah, Jalan Pattimura, Masohi, Maluku, Indonesia. Contact: Toto Pramurahardja, BA, Kepala Stasiun. Replies slowly to correspondence in Indonesian.

Radio Suara Kasih Agung, Jalan Trikora No. 30, Dok V, Jayapura, Irian Jaya 99114, Indonesia. Contact: Ny. Setiyono Hadi, Pimpinan Studio. Return postage or $1 helpful. This "amatir" station is unlicensed.

Radio Suara Kencana Broadcasting System, Jalan Yos Sudarso Timur, Gombong, Jawa Tengah, Indonesia. This "amatir" station is unlicensed.

Radio Suara Mitra, Jalan Haji Lut, Gang Kresem No. 15, Cigudak, Tangerang, Jawa Barat, Indonesia. This "amatir" station is unlicensed.

Voice of Indonesia, Kotak Pos No. 1157, Jakarta 10001, Indonesia. Contact: Anastasia Yasmine, Head of Foreign Affairs Section.

IRAN World Time +3:30

Voice of the Islamic Republic of Iran

Main Office: IRIB External Services, P.O. Box 19395-3333, Tehran, Iran. Fax: (External Services) + 98 (21) 291 095; (IRIB central administration) +98 (21) 204 1051. Contact: (general) Hamid Yasamin, Public Affairs; Ali Larijani, Head; or Hameed Barimani, Producer, "Listeners Special; (head of administration) J. Ghanbari, Director General." Free seven-volume set of books on Islam, magazines, calendars, book markers, tourist literature and postcards. Verifications require a minimum of two days' reception data, plus return postage.

Engineering Activities, Tehran: IRIB, P.O. Box 15875-4344, Tehran, Iran. Phone: +98 (21) 2196-6127. Fax: +98 (21) 2196 6268 or +98 (26) 172 924. Contact: Mrs. Niloufar Parviz.

Engineering Activities, Hessarak/Karaj: IRIB, P.O. Box 155, Hessarak/Karaj, Iran. Phone: +98 (21) 204-0008. Fax: +98 (21) 2196 6268. Contact: Mohsen Amiri.

Bonn Bureau, Nontechnical: Puetzsir 34, 53129 Bonn, Postfach 150 140, D-53040 Bonn, Germany. Phone: +49 (228) 231-001. Fax: +49 (228) 231 002.

London Bureau, Nontechnical: c/o WTN, IRIB, The Interchange Oval Road, Camden Lock, London NWI, United Kingdom. Phone: +44 (171) 284-3668. Fax: + 44 (171) 284 3669.

Paris Bureau, Nontechnical: 27 rue de Liège, escalier B, 1e étage, porte D, F-75008 Paris, France. Phone: + 33 (1) 42-93-12-73. Fax: +33 (1) 42 93 05 13.

Mashhad Regional Radio, P.O. Box 555, Mashhad Center, Jomhoriye Eslame, Iran. Contact: J. Ghanbari, General Director.

IRAQ World Time +3 (+4 midyear)

Holy Medina Radio—see Radio Iraq International, below, for contact information.

Radio Iraq International (Idha'at al-Iraq al-Duwaliyah)

Main Office: P.O. Box 8145, Baghdad, Iraq. Contact: Muzaffar 'Abd-al'-Al, Director; or Jamal Al-Samaraie, Head of Department. All broadcasting facilities in Iraq are currently suffering from severe operational difficulties.

India Address: P.O. Box 3044, New Delhi 110003, India.

Radio of Iraq, Call of the Kinfolk (Idha'at al-Iraq, Nida' al-Ahl)—same details as "Radio Iraq International," above.

Voice of Arab Syria—see Radio Iraq International, above, for contact information.

IRELAND World Time exactly (+1 midyear)

Radio Dublin International, P.O. Box 2077, 4 St. Vincent Street West, Dublin 8, Ireland. Contact: (general) Jane Cooke; (technical) Eamon Cooke, Director; or Joe Doyle, Producer, "DX Show." 12-page station history $2 postpaid. Free stickers and calendar. $1 required. Replies irregularly. This station is as yet unlicensed, but those wishing to support it and other potential world band shortwave broadcasts from Ireland may write the Minister for Communications, Dublin 2, Ireland.

ISRAEL World Time +2 (+3 midyear)

Galei Zahal, Zahal, Military Mail No. 01005, Israel. Phone: +972 (3) 512-6666. Fax: +972 (3) 512 6760. Contact: Yitshak Pasternak, Director. Israeli law allows the Galei Zahal, as well as the Israel Broadcasting Authority, to air broadcasts beamed to outside Israel.

Kol Israel (Israel Radio, the Voice of Israel)
Main Office, IBA: Israel Broadcasting Authority, P.O. Box
1082, 91 010 Jerusalem, Israel. Phone: (general) +972 (2) 302-
222; (Engineering Dept.) +972 (2) 535-051; (administration)
+972 (2) 248-715. Fax: (English Service) +972 (2) 253 282;
(other) +972 (2) 248 392. Gopher: gopher://israel-
info.gov.il:70/00/cul/media/950300.med. Contact: (general)
Sara Manobla, Head of English Service; Yishai Eldar,
Senior Editor, English Service; (head of administration)
Shmuel Ben-Zvi, Director; (technical) Ben Dalfen. Various
political, religious, tourist, immigration and language
publications. IRC required for reply. The Jewish Agency
has drastically cut back funding for Kol Israel, which has
resulted in elimination of entire services, including to the
Americas. To cope with this, according to a *Monitoring
Times* report from Israel (6/95), Kol Israel is considering
transmitting via foreign facilities in such places as
Lithuania, Poland and Argentina, rather than via Israeli-
based transmitters, to save money—even though this
means that "commentary will be kept to a minimum" so as
not to upset the sensibilities of host nations.
Transmission Office, Bezeq: Engineering & Planning
Division, Radio & T.V. Broadcasting Section, Bezeq, The
Israel Telecommunication Corp Ltd., P.O. Box 29555, 61 294
Tel-Aviv, Israel. Phone: +972 (3) 519-4479. Fax: +972 (3) 510
0696; +972 (3) 519 4614; or +972 (3) 515 1232. Contact: Johanan
Rotem, Radio Frequency Manager; or Marian Kaminski,
Head of AM Radio Broadcasting. This address only for
pointing out transmitter-related problems (interference,
modulation quality, network mixups, etc.), especially by
fax, of transmitters based in Israel. Verifications not given
out at this office; requests for verification should be sent to
English Department of Kol Israel at the main office, above.
San Francisco Office, Schedules: 2654 17th Avenue, San
Francisco CA 94116 USA. Phone: +1 (415) 564-9968. Contact:
George Poppin. Self-addressed stamped envelope or IRC
required for reply. This address, a volunteer office, only
provides Kol Israel schedules. All other correspondence
should be sent directly to the main office in Jerusalem.

ITALY World Time +1 (+2 midyear)
Adventist World Radio, the Voice of Hope, C.P. 383,
I-47100 Forlì, Italy. Phone: +39 (543) 766-655. Fax: +39 (543)
768 198. E-mail: awritaly@queen.shiny.it. Contact: Lina
Lega, Listener Mail Services; or Stefano Losio, Producer
"DX News" in Italian. Free home study Bible guides and
other religious material, quarterly *AWR Current* newslet-
ter, stickers, pennants, pocket calendars and other small
souvenirs. However Two IRCs, $1 or return postage
requested. Also, *see* USA.
European Christian Radio, Postfach 500, A-2345
Brunn, Austria. Fax: +39 (2) 29 51 74 63. Contact: John
Adams, Director; or C.R. Coleman, Station Manager. $1 or
2 IRCs required.
Italian Radio Relay Service, IRRS-Shortwave, Nexus
IBA, P.O. Box 10980, I-20110 Milan MI, Italy. Fax: +39 (2) 70 63
81 51. E-mail: (general) info@nexus.org; ("Hello There" program) ht@nexus.org; (reception reports of test transmissions) test@nexus.org; (other reception reports)
reports@nexus.org. World Wide Web:
http://www.nexus.org. Contact: (general) Alfredo E.
Cotroneo, President & Producer of "Hello There"; (technical) Ms. Anna S. Boschetti, Verification Manager. Free station literature. Two IRCs or $1 helpful.
Radio Europa International, via Gerardi 6, I-25124
Brescia, Italy. Contact: Mariarosa Zahella. Return postage
helpful.
Radio Europe, via Davanzati 8, I-20158 Milan MI, Italy.
Fax: +39 (2) 670 4900. Contact: Dario Monferini, Director; or
Alex Bertini, General Manager. $30 for a lifetime member-
ship to Radio Europe's Listeners' Club. Membership
includes T-shirt, poster, stickers, flags, gadgets, and so
forth, with a monthly drawing for prizes. Application forms

Lina Lega answers listener mail at Adventist World
Radio in Forlì, Italy.

available from station.
Radio Italia Internazionale, Vicolo Volusio 1, I-06049
Spoleto, Italy. Phone: +39 (743) 223-148. Fax: +39 (743) 223
310. Contact: Nicola Mastoro, Owner. Free stickers. Return
postage helpful.
Radio Roma-RAI (external services)
Main Office: External/Foreign Service, Centro RAI, Saxa
Rubra, I-00188 Rome, Italy; or P.O. Box 320, Correspondence
Sector, 00100 Rome, Italy. Fax: +39 (6) 33 17 18 95 or +39 (6)
322 6070. World Wide Web: http://www.milano.ccr.it/radio/
radioit.html. Contact: (general) Rosaria Vassallo,
Correspondence Sector; or Augusto Milana, Editor-in-
Chief, Shortwave Programs in Foreign Languages; (heads
of administration) Giorgio Brovelli, Director; Gabriella
Tambroni, Assistant Director. Free stickers, banners, calendars and *RAI Calling from Rome* magazine. Can provide supplementary materials for Italian-language course
aired over RAI's Italian-language [sic] external service.
Hopes to obtain eventual approval for a new world band
transmitter complex in Tuscany; if this comes to pass, they
plan to expand news, cultural items and music in various
language services—including Spanish, Portuguese,
Italian, plus new services in Chinese and Japanese.
Responses can be very slow.
Shortwave Frequency Monitoring Office: RAI Monitoring
Station, Centro di Controllo, Via Mirabellino 1, I-20052
Monza (MI), Italy. Phone: +39 (39) 388-389. Phone/fax (ask for
fax): +39 (39) 386-222. Contact: Mrs. Giusy Moretti.
Engineering Office, Rome: Via Teulada 66, I-00195 Rome,
Italy. Phone: +39 (6) 33-17-07-21. Fax: +39 (6) 372 3376.
Contact: Mrs. Clara Isola.
Engineering Office, Turin: Via Cernaia 33, I-10121 Turin,
Italy. Phone: +39 (11) 810-2293. Fax: +39 (11) 575 9610.
Contact: Guiseppe Allamano.
New York Office, Nontechnical: 1350 Avenue of the
Americas —21st floor, New York NY 10019 USA. Phone: +1
(212) 468-2500. Fax: +1 (212) 765 1956. Contact: Umberto
Bonetti, Deputy Director of Radio Division. RAI caps,
aprons and tote bags for sale at Boutique RAI, c/o the
aforementioned New York address.
Radio Speranza (if reactivated), Largo San Giorgio 91,
I-41100 Modena, Italy. Contact: Padre Luigi Cordioli.
RTV Italiana-RAI (domestic services)
Caltanissetta: Radio Uno, Via Cerda 19, I-90139 Palermo,
Sicily, Italy. Contact: Gestione Risorse, Transmission
Quality Control. $1 required.
Rome: Notturno Italiano, Centro RAI, Saxa Rubra, I-00188

Rome, Italy. Fax: +39 (6) 322 6070.
Voice of Europe, P.O. Box 26, I-33170 Pordenone, Italy. IRC or $1 helpful. Fax: +39 (6) 488 0196.

JAPAN   World Time +9
NHK Fukuoka, 1-1-10 Ropponmatsu, Chuo-ku, Fukuoka-shi, Fukuoka, 810-77, Japan.
NHK Osaka, 3-43 Bamba-cho, Chuo-ku, Osaka 540-01 Japan. Fax: +81 (6) 941 0612. Contact: (technical) Technical Bureau. IRC or $1 helpful.
NHK Sapporo, 1-1-1 Ohdori Nishai, Chuo-ku, Sapporo 060, Japan. Fax: +81 (11) 232 5951.
NHK Tokyo/Shobu-Kuki, JOAK, 3047-1 Oaza-Sanga, Shoubu-cho, Minami Saitamagun, Saitama 346-01, Japan. Fax: +81 (3) 3481 4985 or +81 (480) 85 1508. IRC or $1 helpful. Replies occasionally. Letters should be sent via registered mail.
Radio Japan/NHK (external service)
Main Office: 2-2-1 Jinnan, Shibuya-ku, Tokyo 150-01, Japan. Phone: +81 (3) 3465-1111. Fax: (general) +81 (3) 3481 1350; ("Hello from Tokyo" and Production Center) +81 (3) 3465 0966; ("Media Roundup") +81 (3) 3481 1633; (News Department) +81 (3) 3481 1462. Gopher: gopher.ntt.jp. World Wide Web: http://www.ntt.jp:80/japan/nhk. Contact: (general) Akio Horikawa, Producer, "Hello from Tokyo"; Reiko Ijuin, Chief Producer, "Hello from Tokyo"; Mitsunori Matsumura, Director of Public Relations; Tsutomu Aoki, Director of Programming; Matsuo Sekino, Director of News Department; Kenji Sato, Director of Production Center; Mr. H. Misawa, Producer, "Media Roundup"; Ms. Mari Kishi, Presenter, "Media Roundup"; (head of administration) Masaomi Sato, Director General. Free *Radio Japan News* publication, sundry other small souvenirs and "Let's Learn/Practice Japanese" language-course materials. Quizzes with prizes, including beautiful wall calendars, over "Media Roundup."
Washington News Bureau: NHK, 2030 M Street NW, Suite 706, Washington DC 20036 USA. Fax: +1 (202) 828 4571.
London News Bureau: NHK General Bureau for Europe, 4 Millbank Westminster, London SW1P 3JA, United Kingdom. Fax: +44 (171) 393 0193.
Sydney News Bureau: c/o SBS 14, Herbert Street, Artarmon NSW 2064, Australia. Fax: +61 (2) 437 6105.
Singapore News Bureau: NHK, 1 Scotts Road #15-06, Shaw Centre, Singapore 0922. Fax: +65 737 5251.
Bangkok News Bureau: 6F MOT Building (Thai TV CH9), 222 Rama 9 Road, Bangkok 10310, Thailand. Fax: +66 (2) 253 2442.

Radio Tampa/NSB
Main Office: Nihon Shortwave Broadcasting, 9-15 Akasaka 1-chome, Minato-ku, Tokyo 107, Japan. Fax: +81 (3) 3583 9062. Contact: H. Nagao, Public Relations; M. Teshima; Ms. Terumi Onoda; or H. Ono. Free stickers and Japanese stamps. $1 or IRC helpful. Once scheduled to terminate shortwave broadcasting around 1997, Radio Tampa now plans to stay on shortwave until the year 2000 and possibly indefinitely.
New York News Bureau: 1325 Avenue of the Americas #2403, New York NY 10019 USA. Fax: +1 (212) 261 6449. Contact: Noboru Fukui, reporter.

JORDAN   World Time +2 (+3 midyear)
Radio Jordan, P.O. Box 909, Amman, Jordan. Phone: +962 (6) 774-111. Fax: +962 (6) 788 115. Contact: (general) Jawad Zada, Director of English Service & Producer of "Mailbag"; or Qasral Mushatta; (administrative) Radi Alkhas, General Director; or Muwaffaq al-Rahayifah, Director of Shortwave Services; (technical) Fawzi Saleh, Director of Engineering. Free stickers. Replies irregularly and slowly.

KAZAKHSTAN   World Time +6 (+7 midyear)
Kazakh Radio, Kazakh Broadcasting Company, Zheltoksan Str. 175A, 480013 Almaty, Kazakhstan. Contact: B. Shalakhmentov, Chairman; or S.D. Primbetov, Deputy Chairman.
Radio Almaty ("Radio Alma-Ata" in English Service, "Radio Kazakhstan" in Russian Service and some other services), Zheltoksan Str. 175A, 480013 Almaty, Kazakhstan. Fax: +7 (3272) 631 207. Contact: Mr. Gulnar.

KENYA   World Time +3
Kenya Broadcasting Corporation, P.O. Box 30456, Nairobi, Kenya. Fax: +254 (2) 220 675. Contact: (general) Henry Makokha, Liaison Office; (head of administration) Phillip Okundi, Managing Director; (technical) Augustine Kenyanjier Gochui; Lawrence Holnati, Engineering Division; or Manager Technical Services. IRC required. Replies irregularly.

KIRIBATI   World Time +12
Radio Kiribati, P.O. Box 78, Bairiki, Tarawa, Republic of Kiribati. Fax: +686 21096. Contact: Atiota Bauro, Program Organiser; Mrs. Otiri Laboia; or Moia Tetoa, Producer, "Kaoti Ami Iango," a program devoted to listeners views; (head of administration) Teraku Tekanene, Managing Director; (technical) Trakaogo, Engineer-in-Charge; Tooto

Junko Omoto, host of music program "Ongaku o Douzo" over Radio Japan.

Kim Hyo-son

"Media Information" host Kim Hae-Young, left, of the Japanese Service of Radio Korea International, interviews Atsushi Konno of the Japanese BCL Federation.

Kabwebwenibeia, Broadcast Engineer; or T. Fakaofo, Technical Staff. Cassettes of local songs available for purchase. $1 or return postage required for a reply (IRCs not accepted).

KOREA (DPR) World Time +9

Radio Pyongyang, External Service, Korean Central Broadcasting Station, Pyongyang, Democratic People's Republic of Korea (*not* "North Korea"). Phone: +850 (2) 812-301 or +850 (2) 36-344. Fax: +850 (2) 814 418. Phone and fax numbers valid only in those countries with direct telephone service to North Korea. Free book for German speakers to learn Korean, sundry other publications, pennants, calendars, artistic prints and pins. Do not include dutiable items in your envelope. Replies are irregular, as mail from countries not having diplomatic relations with North Korea is sent via circuitous routes and apparently does not always arrive. Indeed, *Passport* readers continue to report that mail to Radio Pyongyang in North Korea results in their receiving anti-communist literature from *South Korea*, which indicates that mail interdiction has not ceased. To get around this, one gambit is to send your correspondence to an associate in a country—such as China, Ukraine or India—having reasonable relations with North Korea, and ask that it be forwarded. Nevertheless, replies from this station appear to be increasingly common, occasionally including to the United States and other countries with which North Korea has no diplomatic relations.

Regional Korean Central Broadcasting Stations—Not known to reply, but a long-shot possibility is to try corresponding in Korean to: Korean Central Broadcasting Station, Ministry of Posts and Telecommunications, Chongsung-dong (Moranbong), Pyongyang, Democratic People's Republic of Korea. Fax: +850 (2) 812 301 (valid only in those countries with direct telephone service to North Korea). Contact: Chong Ha-chol, Chairman, Radio and Television Broadcasting Committee.

KOREA (REPUBLIC) World Time +9

Radio Korea International

Main Office: Overseas Service, Korean Broadcasting System, 18 Yoido-dong, Youngdungpo-gu, Seoul 150-790, Republic of Korea. Phone: (general) +82 (2) 781-3710 or +82 (2) 781-3721; (English Service) +82 (2) 781-3728/29/35;

(Russian Service) +82 (2) 781-3714. Fax: +82 (2) 781 3799. Contact: (general) Chae Hong-Pyo, Director of English Service; Robert Gutnikov, English Service; Ms. Han Hee-joo, Producer/Host, "Shortwave Feedback"; Jong Kyong-Tae, Producer, Russian Service; H.A. Staiger, Deputy Head of German Service; Ms. Lee Hae-Ok, Japanese Service; or Ms. Kim Hae-Young, Producer, Japanese Service; (heads of administration) Kim Joo-Chul, Executive Director; Choi Jang-Hoon, Director. Free stickers, calendars, *Let's Learn Korean* book and a wide variety of other small souvenirs. *Washington News Bureau:* National Press Building, Suite 1076, 529 14th Street NW, Washington DC 20045 USA. Phone: +1 (202) 662-7345. Fax: +1 (202) 662 7347.

KUWAIT World Time +3

Radio Kuwait, P.O. Box 397, 13004 Safat, Kuwait. Phone: +965 241-1422. Fax: +965 241 5498 or +965 245 6660. Contact: (general) Manager, External Service; (technical) Nasser M. Al-Saffar, Controller, Frequency Management. Free stickers and, sometimes, calendars.

Voice of America—Kuwait Relay Station. Phone/fax: +965 487-8822. Fax: +965 252 7562. Contact: Terry Donovan, Relay Station Manager. These numbers for timely and significant technical matters only. All other communications should be directed to the usual VOA address in Washington (*see* USA).

KYRGYZSTAN World Time +5 (+6 midyear)

Kyrgyz Radio, Kyrgyz TV and Radio Center, Prospekt Moloday Gvardil 63, 720 300 Bishkek, Kyrgyzstan. Fax: +7 (3312) 257 930. Contact: A.I. Vitshkov or E.M. Abdukarimov.

LAOS World Time +7

Lao National Radio, Luang Prabang ("Sathani Withayu Kachaisiang Khueng Luang Prabang"), Luang Prabang, Laos; or B.P. 310, Vientiane, Laos. Return postage required (IRCs not accepted). Replies slowly and very rarely. Best bet is to write in Laotian or French directly to Luang Prabang, where the transmitter is located.

Lao National Radio, Vientiane, Laotian National Radio and Television, B.P. 310, Vientiane, Laos. Contact: Bounthan Inthasai, Deputy Managing Director.

LATVIA World Time +2 (+3 midyear)

Latvijas Radio, 8 Doma Laukums, LV-1505 Riga, Latvia. Phone: +371 (2) 206-722. Fax: +371 (2) 206 709. Contact: (general) Aivars Ginters, International Relations; or Ms. Darija Juskevica, Program Director; (head of administration) Arnolds Klotins, Director General; (technical) Aigars Semevics, Technical Director. Replies to nontechnical correspondence in Latvian. Does not issue verification replies.

Radio Latvia, P.O. Box 266, LV-1098 Riga, Latvia. Phone: (Director General) +371 (2) 206-747; (Program Director) +371 (2) 206-750; (Secretary) +371 (2) 206-722. Fax: (International Relations) +371 (8) 820 216; (Secretary) +371 (2) 206 709. Contact: (general) Ms. Fogita Cimcus, Chief Editor (English, German, Swedish); (head of administration) Laimonas Tapinas, Director General; (technical, but not for verifications) Aigars Semevics, Technical Director. Free stickers and pennants. Unlike Latvijas Radio, preceding, Radio Latvia verifies regularly via the Chief Editor.

LEBANON   World Time +2 (+3 midyear)
Voice of Hope, P.O. Box 77, 10292 Metulla, Israel; or P.O. Box 3379, Limassol, Cyprus. Phone: (Israel) +972 (6) 959-174 or +972 (6) 959-889. Fax: (Israel) +972 (6) 997 827. Contact: Gary Hull, General Manager; or Isaac Gronberg, Director. Free stickers. Also, see KVOH—High Adventure Radio, USA.

Voice of Lebanon, La Voix du Liban, B.P. 165271, Al-Ashrafiyah, Beirut, Lebanon. Phone/fax: +961 (1) 323-458. $1 required. Replies extremely irregularly to correspondence in French or Arabic, but usually willing to discuss significant matters by telephone. Operated by the Phalangist organization.

Voice of Orthodoxy—see Belarus.

LESOTHO   World Time +2
Radio Lesotho, P.O. Box 552, Maseru 100, Lesotho. Fax: +266 310 003. Contact: (general) Mrs. Florence Lesenya, Controller of Programs; Sekhonyana Motlohi, Producer, "What Do Listeners Say?"; (head of administration) Ms. Mpine Tente, Director; (technical) B. Moeti, Chief Engineer. Return postage necessary.

LIBERIA   World Time exactly
ELBC, Liberian Broadcasting System, P.O. Box 594, 1000 Monrovia 10, Liberia. Contact: Noah A. Bordolo, Sr., Deputy Director General, Broadcasting; or J. Rufus Kaine, Deputy Project Director. Station has requested that listeners outside Liberia should send their reception reports to LBS, Box 242, Danane, La Cote d'Ivoire, West Africa.

ELWA
Main Office: SIM Radio Coordinator, P.O. Box 10-0192, 1000 Monrovia 10, Liberia. Contact: (technical) Dwight, EL2W; or Cordell Loken, Chief Engineer. Free stickers. An ancient (ca. 1937) General Electric shortwave transmitter, once used by KGEI's now-inactive California site, along with new antennas, is to be fired up shortly; it should be on the air by the time you read this.
U.S. Office: SIM, P.O. Box 7900, Charlotte NC 28241 USA. Contact: Stan Bruning, Radio Coordinator.

LIBYA   World Time +1
Radio Jamahiriya
Main Office: P.O. Box 4677 (or P.O. Box 4396), Tripoli, Libya. Contact: R. Cachia. Arabic preferred.
Malta Office: European Branch Office, P.O. Box 17, Hamrun, Malta. This office replies more consistently than does the main office.

LITHUANIA   World Time +2 (+3 midyear)
Lithuanian Radio, Lietuvos Radijas, Konarskio 49, LT-2674 Vilnius, Lithuania. Fax: +370 (2) 66 05 26. Contact: Nerijus Maliukevicius, Director.
Radio Vilnius, Lietuvos Radijas, Konarskio 49, LT-2674 Vilnius, Lithuania. Fax: +370 (2) 66 05 26. Contact: Ms. Rasa Lukaite, "Letterbox"; Audrius Braukyla, Editor-in-Chief; or Ilonia Rukiene, Head of English Department. Free stickers, pennants, Lithuanian stamps and other souvenirs. Radio

Vilnius Listeners' Club, if still active, may be reached by writing Mary Sabatini, 24 Sherman Terrace #4, Madison WI 53704 USA.

MADAGASCAR   World Time +3
Radio Madagasikara, B.P. 1202, Antananarivo, Madagascar. Contact: Mlle. Rakotoniaina Soa Herimanitia, Secrétaire de Direction, a young lady who collects stamps. $1 required, and enclosing used stamps from various countries may help. Replies very rarely and slowly, preferably to friendly philatelist gentlemen who correspond in French.

Radio Nederland Wereldomroep—Madagascar Relay, B.P. 404, Antananarivo, Madagascar. Contact: (technical) J.A. Ratobimiarana, Chief Engineer. Nontechnical correspondence should be sent to Radio Nederland Wereldomroep in Holland (see).

MALAWI   World Time +2
Malawi Broadcasting Corporation, P.O. Box 30133, Chichiri, Blantyre 3, Malawi. Fax: +265 671 353 or +265 671 257. Contact: Henry R. Chirwa, Head of Production; Ben M. Tembo, Head of Presentations; P. Chinseu; or T.J. Sineta. Return postage or $1 helpful.

MALAYSIA   World Time +8
Radio Malaysia, Kajang, RTM, Angkasapuri, Bukit Putra, 50614 Kuala Lumpur, Peninsular Malaysia, Malaysia. Phone: +60 (3) 282-5333. Fax: +60 (3) 282 4735. Contact: (general) Ahmad Raphay, Director of Radio; (technical) Deputy Director Engineering; Abdullah Bin Shahadan, Engineer, Transmission & Monitoring; or Ong Poh, Chief Engineer. May sell T-shirts and key chains. Return postage required.

Radio Malaysia, Kota Kinabalu, RTM, 88614 Kota Kinabalu, Sabah, Malaysia. Contact: Benedict Janil, Director of Broadcasting; or Hasbullah Latiff. Return postage required.

Radio Malaysia, Sarawak (Kuching), RTM, Broadcasting House, Jalan P. Ramlee, 93614 Kuching, Sarawak, Malaysia. Phone: +60 (82) 248-422. Fax: +60 (82) 241 914. Contact: (general) Tuan Haji Ahmad Shafiee Haji Yaman, Director of Broadcasting; (technical, but also nontechnical) Colin A. Minoi, Technical Correspondence; (technical) Kho Kwang Khoon, Deputy Director of Engineering. Return postage helpful.

Radio Malaysia, Sarawak (Miri), RTM, Miri, Sarawak, Malaysia. Contact: Mohammed Nasir B. Mohammed. $1 or return postage helpful.

Radio Malaysia, Sarawak (Sibu), RTM, Jabatan Penyiaran, Bangunan Penyiaran, 96009 Sibu, Sarawak, Malaysia. Contact: Clement Stia, Divisional Controller, Broadcasting Department. $1 or return postage required. Replies irregularly and slowly.

Voice of Malaysia, Suara Malaysia, Wisma Radio, P.O. Box 11272-KL, 50740 Angkasapuri, Kuala Lumpur, Malaysia. Phone: +60 (3) 282-5333. Fax: +60 (3) 282 4735. Contact: (general) Mrs. Mahani bte Ujang, Supervisor, English Service; Hajjah Wan Chik Othman, English Service; (administration) Santokh Singh Gill, Director; or Mrs. Adilan bte Omar, Assistant Director; (technical) Lin Chew, Director of Engineering. Free calendars and stickers. Two IRCs or return postage helpful. Replies slowly and irregularly.

MALI   World Time exactly
Radiodiffusion Télévision Malienne, B.P. 171, Bamako, Mali. Phone: +223 22-47-27. Fax: +223 22 42 05. Contact: Karamoko Issiaka Daman, Directeur des Programmes; (head of administration) Abdoulaye Sidibe, Directeur General. $1 or IRC helpful. Replies slowly and irregularly to correspondence in French. English is accepted.

MALTA   World Time +1 (+2 midyear)

Deutsche Welle—Relay Station Cyclops—This site may be closed down later in the 1990s.

Voice of the Mediterranean, P.O. Box 143, Valletta, CMR 01, Malta. Fax: +356 241 501. Contact: (general) Ali Abdul Aziz El-Kish, Director of News and Programs; or Charles A. Micallef, Deputy Director of News and Programs; (head of administration) Richard Vella Laurenti, Managing Director. Free monthly English newsletter upon request. Station is a joint venture of the Libyan and Maltese governments.

MAURITANIA World Time exactly

Office de Radiodiffusion-Télévision de Mauritanie, B.P. 200, Nouakchott, Mauritania. Fax: +222 (2) 51264. Contact: Madame Amir Feu; Lemrabott Boukhary; Madame Fatimetou Fall Dite Ami, Secretaire de Direction; or Mr. Hane Abou. Return postage or $1 required. Rarely replies.

MEXICO World Time -6 Central, including México; -7 Mountain; -8 (-7 midyear) Pacific

La Hora Exacta—XEQK, IMER, Margaritas 18, Col. Florida, México, D.F. 01030, Mexico. Contact: Gerardo Romero.

La Voz de Veracruz—XEFT, Apartado Postal 21, 91700-4H. Veracruz, Ver., México. Contact: C.P. Miguel Rodríguez Sáez, Sub-Director; or Lic. Juan de Dios Rodríguez Díaz, Director-Gerente. Free tourist guide to Veracruz. Return postage, IRC or $1 probably helpful. Likely to reply to correspondence in Spanish.

Radio Educación—XEPPM, SPE-333/92, Apartado Postal 21-940, 04021 México, D.F., México. Phone: (general) +52 (5) 559-8075 or +52 (5) 559-3102; (studio) +52 (5) 575-0919. Fax: +52 (5) 559-2301. Contact: (general) Lic. Susana E. Mejía Vázquez, Jefe del Dept. de Audiencia y Evaluación; Ma. Teresa Moya Malfavón, Directora de Producción y Planeación; (head of administration) Luis Ernesto Pi Orozco, Director General; (technical) Ing. Gustavo Carreño López, Subdirector, Dpto. Técnico. Free stickers, station photo and a copy of a local publication, *Audio Tinta*. Return postage or $1 required. Replies slowly to correspondence in English, Spanish, Italian or French.

Radio Huayacocotla—XEJN

Station Address: "Radio Huaya," Dom. Gutierrez Najera s/n, Apartado Postal 13, 92600 Huayacocotla, Veracruz, México. Phone: +52 (775) 8-0067. Fax: +52 (775) 8 0178. E-mail: framos@uibero.uia.mx. Contact: Juan Antonio Vázquez; Alfredo Zepeda; Martha Silvia Ortiz López, Program Director; or Felipe de Jesús Martínez Sosa. Return postage or $1 helpful. Replies irregularly to correspondence in Spanish.

Sponsoring Organization: Fomento Cultural y Educativo, A.C. Miguel Laurent 340, Col. Del Valle, 03100 México, D.F., México. Phone: +2 (5) 559-6000. Fax: +52 (5) 575 8357.

Radio México Internacional (when operating), Apartado Postal No. 19-737, México, D.F. 03900, México.

Radio Mil—XEOI, NRM, Insurgentes Sur 1870, Col. Florida, México, D.F. 01030, México. Phone: (station) +52 (5) 662-1000 or +52 (5) 662-1100; (Núcleo Radio Mil network) +52 (5) 662-6060, +52 (5) 663-0739 or +52 (5) 663 0590. Fax: (station) +52 (5) 662 0974; (Núcleo Radio Mil network) +52 (5) 662 0979. Contact: Guillermo Salas Vargas, Presidente; Srta. Cristina Stivalet, Gerente; or Zoila Quintanar Flores. Free stickers. $1 or return postage required.

Radio Universidad/UNAM—XEUDS, Apartado Postal No. 1817, Hermosillo, Sonora 83000, México. Contact: A. Merino M., Director; or Ing. Miguel Angel González, Director. Free tourist literature. $1 or return postage required. Replies irregularly to correspondence in Spanish.

Radio XEQQ, La Voz de la América Latina (on the rare occasions when operating), Sistema Radiópolis, Ayuntamiento 52, México D.F. 06070, Mexico; or Ejército Nacional No. 579 (6to piso), 11520 México, D.F., Mexico.

Contact: (general) Sra. Martha Sandoval; (technical) Ing. Miguel Angel Barrientos, Director Técnico de Plantas Transmisoras. Free pennants. $1, IRC or return postage required. When operating, replies fairly regularly to correspondence in Spanish.

Radio XEUJ, Apartado Postal 62, 67700 Linares, Nuevo León, México. Contact: (general) Marcelo Becerra González, Director General; or Joel Becerra Pecina; (technical) Ing. Gustavo Martínez de la Cruz. Free stickers, pennants and Mexican tourist cards. Replies irregularly to correspondence in Spanish, English or French. Considering replacing their transmitting equipment and extending hours of transmission.

Radio XEUW, Ocampo 119, 91700 Veracruz, México. Contact: Ing. Baltazar Pazos de la Torre, Director General. Free pennants. Return postage required. Replies occasionally to correspondence in Spanish.

Tus Panteras—XEQM, Apartado Postal No. 217, 97000 Mérida, Yucatán, México. Fax: +52 (99) 28 06 80. Contact: Arturo Iglesias Villalobos; L.C.C Roberto Domínguez Avila, Director General; or Ylmar Pacheco Gómez, Locutor. Replies irregularly to correspondence in Spanish.

"MOLDAVIAN REPUBLIC OF PRIDNESTROVYE" World Time +2 (+3 midyear)

The following stations are radio services of the Russian-speaking separatists in the Pridnestrovye region ("Moldavian Republic of Pridnestrovye") of Moldova. Formal talks are currently underway for the possible separation of "Pridnestrovye" from Moldova. Should these talks result in such separation, Moldova could possibly merge with Romania.

Radio Dniester International (external service), 45 - 25th October Street, 278000 Tiraspol, Pridnestrovye, C.I.S. Contact: A. Komar, Chief Editor.

Radio Pridnestrovye, 10 Rosa Luxemburg Street, 278000 Tiraspol, Pridnestrovye, C.I.S.

MOLDOVA World Time +2 (+3 midyear)

Radio Moldova International

General Correspondence: Str. Miorita 1, 277028 Chisinau, Moldova. Phone: +373 (2) 72-17-92, +373 (2) 72-33-79 or +373 (2) 72-33-85. Fax: +373 (2) 72 33 29 or +373 (2) 72 33 07. Contact: Constantin Marin, International Editor-in-Chief; Alexandru Dorogan, General Director of Radio Broadcasting; or Raisa Gonciar. Transmits via facilities of Radio Romãnia International.

Reception Reports: RMI-Monitoring Action, P.O. Box 9972, 277070 Chisinau-70, Moldova.

MONACO World Time +1 (+2 midyear)

Radio Monte-Carlo

Main Office: 16 Boulevard Princesse Charlotte, MC-98080 Monaco Cedex, Monaco. Phone: +33 (93) 15-16-17. Fax: +33 (93) 15 16 30 or +33 (93) 15 94 48. Contact: Jacques Louret; Bernard Poizat, Service Diffusion; or Caroline Wilson, Director of Communication. Free stickers. This station is on world band only with its Arabic Service.

Main Paris Office, Nontechnical: 12 rue Magellan, F-75008 Paris, France. Phone: +33 (1) 40-69-88-00. Fax: +33 (1) 40 69 88 55 or +33 (1) 45 00 92 45.

Paris Office (Arabic Service): 78 Avenue Raymond Poincairé, F-75008 Paris, France. Phone: +33 (1) 45-01-53-30.

Cyprus Office (Arabic Service)—see Cyprus.

Trans World Radio

Station: B.P. 349, MC-98007 Monte-Carlo, Monaco. Phone: +33 (92) 16-56-00. Fax: +33 (92) 16 56 01. Contact: (general) Mrs. Jeanne Olson; (head of administration) Richard Olson, Station Manager; (technical) Bernhard Schravt, Frequency Coordinator. Free paper pennant. IRC or $1 helpful. Also, see USA.

Holland Office, Nontechnical: Postbus 176, NL-3780 BD Voorthuizen, Holland. Phone: +31 (0) 34-29-27-27. Fax: +31 (0) 34 29 67 27. Contact: Beate Kiebel, Manager Broadcast

Department; or Felix Widmer.

Vienna Office, Technical: Postfach 141, A-1235 Vienna, Austria. Phone: +43 (1) 865-2055. Fax: +43 (1) 865 2093. Contact: Helmut Menzel, Frequency Management Services.

MONGOLIA World Time +8

Radio Ulaanbaatar, External Services, C.P.O. Box 365, Ulaanbaatar, Mongolia. Phone: +976 (1) 27-900. Fax: +976 (1) 323 096. Contact: (general) Mr. Bayasa, Mail Editor, English Department; N. Tuya, Head of English Department; Ms. Tsegmid Burmaa, Japanese Department; (head of administration) Ch. Surenjav, Director; (technical) Ganhuu, Chief of Technical Department. Free pennants, postcards, newspapers and Mongolian stamps.

MOROCCO World Time exactly

Radio Medi Un

Main Office: B.P. 2055, Tangier, Morocco. Two IRCs helpful. Contact: J. Dryk, Responsable Haute Fréquence. Free stickers. Correspondence in French preferred.

Paris Bureau, Nontechnical: 78 Avenue Raymond Poincaré, F-75016 Paris, France. Phone: +33 (1) 45-01-53-30. Correspondence in French preferred.

RTV Marocaine, RTM, 1 rue al-Brihi, Rabat, Morocco. Phone: +212 (7) 70-17-40. Fax +212 (7) 70 32 08. Contact: (non-technical and technical) Mrs. Naaman Khadija, Ingénieur d'Etat en Télécommunication; (technical) Tanone Mohammed Jamaledine, Technical Director; Hammouda Mohamed, Engineer; or N. Read. Correspondence welcomed in English, French, Arabic or Berber—especially suggestions for times, languages and other relevant information concerning possible limited expansion of short-wave transmissions to new targets so Moroccan and North African affairs can be more widely disseminated and understood.

Voice of America—Morocco Relay Station, Briech. Phone: (office) +212 (9) 93-24-81; (transmitter) +212 (9) 93-22-00. Fax: +212 (9) 93 55 71. Contact: Wilfred Cooper. These numbers for urgent technical matters only. Otherwise, does not welcome direct correspondence; see USA for acceptable VOA Washington address and related information.

MOZAMBIQUE World Time +2

Rádio Moçambique, C.P. 2000, Maputo, Mozambique. Phone: +258 (1) 42-18- 14. Fax: +258 (1) 42 18 16. Contact: (general) João de Sousa, Administrador e Diretor Comercial; Machado da Graça, Administrador para o Pelouro da Produção; Orlanda Mendes, Produtor, "Linha Direta"; or Marcos Cuembelo, Administrador e Diretor Financeiro; (head of administration) Manuel Veterano, Presidente do Conselho de Administração; (technical) Rufino de Matos, Administrador e Diretor Técnico. Free medallions and pens. Cassettes featuring local music $15. Return postage, $1 or 2 IRCs required. Replies to correspondence in Portuguese or English.

MYANMAR (BURMA) World Time +6:30

Radio Myanmar

Station: GPO Box 1432, Yangon-11181, Myanmar. Phone: +95 (1) 31-355. Fax: +95 (1) 30 211. Currently does not reply directly to correspondence, but this could change as political events evolve. In the meantime, try the following, which may or may not still work:

Washington Embassy: Embassy of the Union of Myanmar, 2300 S Street NW, Washington DC 20008 USA. Phone: +1 (202) 332-9044. Fax: +1 (202) 332 9046. Contact: Daw Kyi Kyi Sein, Third Secretary. This contact currently replies on behalf of Radio Myanmar, but not to persons of obvious Myanmar origin.

NAMIBIA World Time +3 (+2 midyear)

Radio Namibia/NBC, P.O. Box 321, Windhoek 9000, Namibia. Phone: +264 (61) 291-2209 or 264 (61) 291-3291. Fax:

+264 (61) 291 2156 or +264 (61) 291 2291. Contact: P. Schachtschneider, Manager, Transmitter Maintenance. Free stickers.

NEPAL World Time +5:45

Radio Nepal, P.O. Box 634, Singha Durbar, Kathmandu, Nepal. Fax: +977 (1) 221 952. Contact: (general) B.P. Shivakoti; R.J. Karlei; or S.K. Pant, Producer, "Question, Answer"; (technical) Ram S. Karki, Executive Engineer. Return postage necessary.

NEW ZEALAND World Time +13 (+12 midyear)

Kiwi Radio (unlicensed, but left alone by the government), P.O. Box 3103, Onekawa, Napier, New Zealand. Phone: +64 (6) 844-7640. Contact: Graham J. Barclay. Free stickers, etc. Return postage appreciated.

Radio New Zealand International (Te Reo Irirangi O Aotearoa, O Te Moana-nui-a-kiwa), P.O. Box 123, Wellington, New Zealand. Phone: +64 (4) 474-1437. Fax: +64 (4) 474 1433 or +64 (4) 474 1886. E-mail: (general) rnzi@actrix.gen.nz; (Frequency Manager) adrian@actrix. gen.nz. World Wide Web: http://www.actrix.gen.nz/users/ rnzi. Contact: Florence de Ruiter, Listener Mail; Myra Oh, Producer, "Mailbox"; or Walter Zweifel, News Editor; (head of administration) Ms. Linden Clark, Manager; (technical) Adrian Sainsbury, Frequency Manager. Free stickers. Free schedule/flyer about station, map of New Zealand and tourist literature. English/Maori T-shirts for US$20; interesting variety of CDs, as well as music cassettes and spoken programs, in Domestic "Replay Radio" catalog (VISA/MC). Three IRCs for verification, one IRC for schedule/catalog.

Radio Reading Service—ZLXA, P.O. Box 360, Levin 5500, New Zealand. Phone: +64 (6) 368-2229. Fax: +64 (6) 368 0151. Contact: (general) Ron Harper; Ash Bell; Brian Stokoe, Program Supervisor; or Jim Meecham ZLZ BHF, Producer, "CQ Pacific, Radio about Radio"; (head of administration) Allen J. Little, Station Director. Free brochure, postcards and stickers. $1, return postage or 3 IRCs appreciated.

NICARAGUA World Time -6

Radio Miskut, Correo Central (Bragman's Bluff), Puerto Cabezas, R.A.A.N., Nicaragua. Fax: +505 (267) 3032. Contact: Evaristo Mercado Pérez, Director de Operación y de Programas. $1 helpful. Audio cassettes of Nicaraguan folk music $8 each, T-shirts $10, and *Resumen Mensual del Gobierno y Consejo Regional* and *Revista Informativa Detallada de las Gestiones y Logros* $10 per copy. Replies slowly and irregularly to correspondence in English and Spanish.

NIGER World Time +1

La Voix du Sahel, O.R.T.N., B.P. 361, Niamey, Niger. Fax: +227 72 35 48. Contact: (general) Adamou Oumarou; Zakari Saley; or Mounkaïla Inazadan, Producer, "Inter-Jeunes Variétés"; (head of administration) Oumar Tiello, Directeur; (technical) Afo Sourou Victor. $1 helpful. Correspondence in French preferred. Correspondence by males with this station may result in requests for certain unusual types of magazines and photographs.

NIGERIA World Time +1

Woes of Broadcasters, Part I: According to a report in mid-1995 by Radio France Internationale, "A studio belonging to the state radio in central Nigeria has been entirely destroyed by termites. The little creatures ate the lot and, according to witnesses, it was an amazing sight."

Woes of Listeners, Part I—Mail Theft: For the time being, correspondence from abroad to Nigerian addresses has a relatively high probability of being stolen.

Woes of Listeners, Part II—Confidence Artists: For years, now, correspondence with Nigerian stations has sometimes resulted in letters from highly skilled "pen pal" confidence artists. These typically offer to send you large sums of money, if you will provide details of your bank account or similar information (after which they clean out your account). Other scams are disguised as tempting business proposals; or requests for money, free electronic or other products, publications or immigration sponsorship. Persons thus approached should contact their country's diplomatic offices. For example, Americans should contact the Diplomatic Security Section of the Department of State [phone +1 (202) 647-4000), or an American embassy or consulate.

Radio Nigeria—Enugu, P.M.B. 1051, Enugu (Anambra), Nigeria. Contact: Louis Nnamuchi, Assistant Director Technical Services. Two IRCs, return postage or $1 required. Replies slowly.

Radio Nigeria—Ibadan, P.M.B. 5003, Ibadan, Oyo State, Nigeria. Contact: V.A. Kalejaiye, Technical Services Department. $1 or return postage required. Replies slowly.

Radio Nigeria—Kaduna, P.O. Box 250, Kaduna (Kaduna), Nigeria. Contact: Yusuf Garba or Johnson D. Allen. $1 or return postage required. Replies slowly.

Radio Nigeria—Lagos, P.M.B. 12504, Ikoyi, Lagos, Nigeria. Contact: Babatunde Olalekan Raji, Monitoring Unit. Two IRCs or return postage helpful. Replies slowly and irregularly.

Voice of Nigeria, P.M.B. 40003 Falomo, Ikoyi, Lagos, Nigeria. Phone: +234 (1) 269-3245. Fax: +234 (1) 269 1944. Contact: (general) Alhaji Lawal Yusuf Saulawa, Director of Programmes; Mrs. Stella Bassey, Deputy Director Programmes; or Alhaji Mohammed Okorejior, Acting Director News; (head of administration) Alhaji Mallam Yaya Abubakar, Director General; (technical) J.O. Kurunmi, Deputy Director Engineering Services; or G.C. Ugwa, Director Engineering. Replies from station tend to be erratic, but continue to generate unsolicited correspondence from supposed "pen pals" (see the warning on confidence artists, above); faxes, which are much less likely to be intercepted, may be more fruitful. Two IRCs or return postage helpful.

NORTHERN MARIANA ISLANDS World Time +10
Far Eastern Broadcasting Company—KFBS Saipan
Main Office: FEBC, P.O. Box 209, Saipan, Mariana Islands CM 96950 USA. Phone: +670 322-9088. Fax: +670 322 3060. Contact: Chris Slabaugh, Field Director; Mike Adams; or Robert Springer. Replies sometimes take months.

Monitor Radio International—KHBI, P.O. Box 1387, Saipan, Mariana Islands CM 96950 USA; or write to Boston address (see USA). Fax: +670 234 6515. E-mail: (Station Manager) doming@khbi.csms.com. Contact: Doming Villar, Station Manager. Free stickers. Return postage appreciated if writing to Saipan; no return postage necessary when writing to Boston.

NORWAY World Time +1 (+2 midyear)
Radio Norway International
Main Office, Nontechnical: Utgitt av Utenlandssendingen/ NRK, N-0340 Oslo, Norway. Phone: (general) +47 (22) 45-84-41; (Norwegian-language 24-hour recording of schedule information +47 (22) 45-80-08 (Americas, Europe, Africa), +47 (22) 45-80-09 (elsewhere); (Radio Projects Dept.) +47 (22) 45-95-87. Fax: (general) +47 (22) 45 71 34 or +47 (22) 60 57 19; ("Listener's Corner" and Radio Projects Dept.) +47 (22) 45 72 29. Contact: (general) Kirsten Ruud Salomonsen, Head of External Broadcasting; (technical) Gundel Krauss Dahl, Head of Radio Projects. Free stickers and flags.
Technical Office: Statens Teleforvaltning, P.O. Box 2592 Solli, N-0203 Oslo, Norway. Phone: +47 (22) 92-67-12. Fax: +47 (22) 92 66 94. E-mail: olav.grimdalen@ntra.telemax.no or olavmo@oslonett.no. Contact: Olav M. Grimdalen, Frequency Manager.
Washington News Bureau: Norwegian Broadcasting, 2030 M Street NW, Suite 700, Washington DC 20036 USA. Phone: +1 (202) 785-1481 or +1 (202) 785-1460. Contact: Bjorn Hansen

or Gunnar Myklebust.
Singapore News Bureau: NRK, 325 River Valley Road #01-04, Singapore.

OMAN World Time +4
BBC World Service—Eastern Relay Station, P.O. Box 6898 (or 3716), Ruwi Post Office, Muscat, Oman. Contact: (technical) David P. Bones, Senior Transmitter Engineer; Tim Mullins, Senior Transmitter Engineer; or Dave Plater, G4MZY, Senior Transmitter Engineer. Nontechnical correspondence should be sent to the BBC World Service in London (see).

Radio Oman, P.O. Box 600, Muscat, Oman. Fax: +968 602 055 or +968 602 831. Contact: (general) Director General, Radio; (technical) Rashid Haroon Aljabry or A. Al-Sawafi. Replies irregularly, and responses can take anywhere from two weeks to two years. $1, return postage or 3 IRCs helpful.

PAKISTAN World Time +5
Azad Kashmir Radio, Muzaffarabad, Azad Kashmir, Pakistan. Contact: (technical) M. Sajjad Ali Siddiqui, Director of Engineering; or Liaquatullah Khan, Engineering Manager. Registered mail helpful. Rarely replies to correspondence.

Pakistan Broadcasting Corporation—same address, fax and contact as "Radio Pakistan," below.

Radio Pakistan, P.O. Box 1393, Islamabad 44000, Pakistan. Fax: +92 (51) 811 861. Contact: (technical) Anwer Inayet Khan, Senior Broadcast Engineer, Room No. 324, Frequency Management Cell; Syed Abrar Hussain, Controller Frequency Management; or Nasirahmad Bajwa, Frequency Management. Free stickers, pennants and *Pakistan Calling* magazine. May also send pocket calendar. Plans to replace two 50 kW transmitters with 500 kW units if and when funding is forthcoming.

PALAU World Time +9
KHBN—Voice of Hope, High Adventure Radio—Asia, P.O. Box 66, Koror, Palau 96940, Pacific Islands. Phone: +680 488-2162. Fax: +680 488 2163. Contact: Joseph Tan, On-Air Minister; or Eileen Jay; (technical) Richard Horner, Chief Engineer. Free stickers and publications. IRC requested. Also, see USA.

PAPUA NEW GUINEA World Time +10
National Broadcasting Commission of Papua New Guinea, P.O. Box 1359, Boroko, Papua New Guinea. Phone: +675 253-022. Fax: +675 255 403 or +675 230 404. Contact: (general) Francesca Maredei, Planning Officer; (technical) Bob Kabewa, Sr. Technical Officer. Two IRCs or return postage helpful. Replies irregularly.

Radio Central, P.O. Box 1359, Boroko, NCD, Papua New Guinea. Contact: Steven Gamini, Station Manager; or Amos Langit, Technician. $1, 2 IRCs or return postage helpful. Replies irregularly.

Radio Eastern Highlands (Karai Bilong Kumul), P.O. Box 311, Goroka, EHP, Papua New Guinea. Fax: +675 722 841. Contact: Ignas Yanam, Technical Officer; or Kiri Nige, Engineering Division. $1 or return postage required. Replies irregularly.

Radio East New Britain, P.O. Box 393, Rabaul, ENBP, Papua New Guinea. Fax: +675 923 254. Contact: Esekia Mael, Station Manager; or Otto Malatane, Provincial Program Manager. Return postage required. Replies slowly.

Radio East Sepik, P.O. Box 65, Wewak, E.S.P., Papua New Guinea. Fax: +675 862 405. Contact: Elias Albert, Assistant Provincial Program Manager; or Luke Umbo, Station Manager.

Radio Enga, P.O. Box 196, Wabag, Enga, Papua New Guinea. Fax: +675 571 069. Contact: (general) John Lyein Kur, Station Manager; (technical) Felix Tumun K., Station Technician.

Radio Gulf, P.O. Box 36, Kerema, Gulf, Papua New

Guinea. Contact: Robin Wainetta, Station Manager; or Timothy Akia, Provincial Program Manager.

Radio Madang, P.O. Box 2138, Yomba, Madang, Papua New Guinea. Fax: +675 822 360. Contact: (general) Simon Tiori, Station Manager; D. Boaging, Assistant Manager; or James S. Valakvi, Assistant Provincial Program Manager; (technical) Lloyd Guvil, Technician.

Radio Manus, P.O. Box 505, Lorengau, Manus, Papua New Guinea. Fax: +675 409 079. Contact: John P. Mandrakamu, Acting Provincial Program Director.

Radio Milne Bay, P.O. Box 111, Alotau, Milne Bay, Papua New Guinea. Contact: (general) Trevor Webumo, Assistant Manager; Simon Muraga, Station Manager; or Raka Petuely, Program Officer; (technical) Philip Maik, Technician.

Radio Morobe, P.O. Box 1262, Lae, Morobe, Papua New Guinea. Fax: +675 426 423. Contact: Ken L. Tropu, Assistant Program Manager; Peter W. Manua, Program Manager; or Aloysius R. Nase, Station Manager.

Radio New Ireland, P.O. Box 140, Kavieng, New Ireland, Papua New Guinea. Fax: +675 941 489. Contact: Otto A. Malatana, Station Manager; or Ruben Bale, Provincial Program Manager. Return postage or $1 helpful.

Radio Northern, Voice of Oro, P.O. Box 137, Popondetta, Oro, Papua New Guinea. Contact: Roma Tererembo, Assistant Provincial Programme Manager; or Misael Pendaia, Station Manager. Return postage required.

Radio North Solomons (when operating), P.O. Box 35, Buka, North Solomons Province (NSP), Papua New Guinea. Fax: +675 939 912. Contact: Demas Kumaina, Station Manager; Ms. Christine Talei, Assistant Provincial Manager; or Aloysius Laukai, Senior Programme Officer. Replies irregularly.

Radio Sandaun, P.O. Box 37, Vanimo, West Sepik, Papua New Guinea. Fax: +675 871 305. Contact: Gabriel Deckwalen, Station Manager; Elias Rathley, Provincial Programme Manager; or Miss Norryne Pate, Secretary. $1 helpful.

Radio Simbu, P.O. Box 228, Kundiawa, Chimbu, Papua New Guinea. Phone: +675 751-038 or +675 751-082. Fax: +675 751 012. Contact: (general) Tony Mill Waine, Provincial Programme Manager; or Thomas Ghiyandiule, Producer, "Pasikam Long ol Pipel"; (technical) Gabriel Paiao, Station Technician. Cassette recordings $5. Free two-Kina banknotes.

Radio Southern Highlands, P.O. Box 104, Mendi, SHP, Papua New Guinea. Phone: +675 591-020 or +675 591-137. Fax: +675 591 017. Contact: (general) Andrew Meles, Programme Manager; Miriam Piapo, Programme Officer; Benard Kagaro, Programme Officer; Lucy Aluy, Programme Officer; or Nicholas Sambu, Producer, "Questions & Answers"; (technical) Ronald Helori, Station Technician. $1 or return postage helpful; or donate a wall poster of a rock band, singer or American landscape.

Radio Western, P.O. Box 23, Daru, Western Province, Papua New Guinea. Contact: (general) Geo Gedabing, Provincial Programme Manager; (technical) Samson Tobel, Technician. $1 or return postage required. Replies irregularly.

Radio Western Highlands, P.O. Box 311, Mount Hagen, WHP, Papua New Guinea. Fax: +675 521 279. Contact: (technical) Esau Okole, Technician. $1 or return postage helpful. Replies occasionally.

Radio West New Britain, P.O. Box 412, Kimbe, WNBP, Papua New Guinea. Fax: +675 935 600. Contact: Valuka Lowa, Provincial Station Manager; Lemeck Kuam, Producer, "Questions and Answers"; Esekial Mael; or Ruben Bale, Provincial Program Manager. Return postage required.

PARAGUAY World Time -3 (-4 midyear)

Adventist World Radio—A new facility, AWR-Paraguay, with two shortwave transmitters is planned to commence construction in the near future, assuming the last stage in obtaining official licenses is successfully completed.

La Voz del Chaco Paraguayo, Filadelfia, Dpto. de Boquerón, Chaco, Paraguay. This station, currently only on mediumwave AM, hopes to add a world band transmitter within the 60-meter (5 MHz) band. However, to date nothing concrete has come of this.

Radio Encarnación, Gral. Artigas casi Gral. B. Caballero, Encarnación, Paraguay. Phone: (general) +595 (71) 4376 or +595 (71) 3345; (press) +595 (71) 4120. Fax: +595 (71) 4099. Contact: Ramón Giménez B., Director.

Radio Nacional, Calle Montevideo, esq. Estrella, Asunción, Paraguay. No fax machine because of recent severe budget cutbacks. Contact: Julio César Cardozo, Jefe de Personal; (technical) Carlos Montaner, Director Técnico. $1 or return postage required. Replies, sometimes slowly, to correspondence in Spanish.

PERU World Time -5 year-round in Loreto, Cusco and Puno. Other departments sometimes move to World Time -4 for a few weeks of the year.
Note: Obtaining replies from Peruvian stations calls for creativity, tact, patience—and the proper use of Spanish, not form letters and the like. There are nearly 150 world band stations operating from Perú on any given day. While virtually all of these may be reached simply by using as the address the station's city, as given in the Blue Pages, the following are the only stations known to be replying—even if only occasionally—to correspondence from abroad.

Estación C, Casilla de Correo 210, Moyobamba, San Martín, Perú. Contact: J.R. González, Locutor.

Estación NC, Avenida Nueva Cajamarca 311, Nueva Cajamarca, San Martín, Perú. Contact: David Bustamente Chávez, Locutor.

Estación Tarapoto, Jirón Federico Sánchez 720, Tarapoto, Perú. Phone: +51 (94) 522-709. Contact: Luis Humberto Hidalgo Sánchez, Gerente General; or José Luna Paima, Announcer. Replies occasionally to correspondence in Spanish.

Estación Yurimaguas, Calle Comercio 102, Yurimaguas, Loreto, Perú. Contact: Adolfo Onjanama Tanchiva, Director de Producción. Also, Prof. Ronald Ramírez Vela, Director del programa "Enseñanza, Aprendizaje," is interested in feedback on that program, aired Monday to Friday from 1100 to 1130 World Time. Return postage appreciated.

Frecuencia Líder (Radio Bambamarca), Jirón Jorge Chávez 416, Bambamarca, Hualgayoc, Cajamarca, Perú. Contact: (general) Valentín Peralta Díaz, Gerente; Irma Peralta Rojas; or Carlos Antonio Peralta Rojas; (technical) Oscar Lino Peralta Rojas. Free station photos. *La Historia de Bambamarca* book for 5 Soles; cassettes of Peruvian and Latin American folk music for 4 Soles each; T-shirts for 10 Soles each (sending US$1 per Sol should suffice and cover foreign postage costs, as well). Replies occasionally to correspondence in Spanish. Considering replacing their transmitter to improve reception.

Frecuencia San Ignacio, Jirón Villanueva Pinillos 330, San Ignacio, Cajamarca, Perú. Contact: Franklin R. Hoyos Cóndor, Director Gerente; Oscar Vásquez Chacon, Locutor; Ignacio Gómez Torres, Técnico de Sonido. Replies to correspondence in Spanish. $1 or return postage necessary.

La Voz de Alto Mayo—see Radio La Voz de Alto Mayo.
La Vox de la Amistad, Apartado Postal 1934, Trujillo, Perú.
La Voz de la Selva—see Radio La Voz de la Selva.
La Voz de Celendín—see Radio Frecuencia VH, below.
La Vox de Naranjos—see Radiodifusora Comercial La Voz de Naranjos, below.
Onda Azul—see Radio Onda Azul, below.
Ondas del Suroriente—see Radio Ondas del

Suroriente, below.

Radio Adventista Mundial—La Voz de la Esperanza, Jirón Dos de Mayo No. 218, Celendín, Cajamarca, Perú. Contact: Francísco Goicochea Ortiz, Director; or Lucas Solano Oyarce, Director de Ventas.

Radio Altura (Cerro de Pasco), Casilla de Correo 140, Cerro de Pasco, Pasco, Perú. Contact: Oswaldo de la Cruz Vásquez, Gerente General. Replies to correspondence in Spanish.

Radio Altura (Huarmaca), Distrito de Huarmaca, Provincia de Huancabamba, Piura, Perú.

Radio América, Montero Rosas 1099 Santa Beatriz, Lima, Perú. Phone: +51 (14) 728-985. Fax: +51 (14) 719-909. Contact: Liliana Sugobono F., Directora.

Radio Ancash, Casilla de Correo 210, Huaraz, Perú. Phone: +51 (44) 721-381. Contact: Armando Moreno Romero, Gerente General. Replies to correspondence in Spanish.

Radio Andahuaylas, Jr. Ayacucho No. 248, Andahuaylas, Apurímac, Perú. Contact: Sr. Daniel Andréu C., Gerente. $1 required. Replies irregularly to correspondence in Spanish.

Radio Apurímac, Jirón Cusco 206 (or Ovalo El Olivo No. 23), Abancay, Apurímac, Perú. Contact: Antero Quispe Allca, Director General.

Radio Atlántida, Casilla de Correo 786, Iquitos, Loreto, Perú. Phone: +51 (94) 234-962. Contact: Pablo Rojas Bardales. $1 or return postage required. Replies irregularly to correspondence in Spanish.

Radio Ayaviri (La Voz de Melgar), Apartado 8, Ayaviri, Puno, Perú. Contact: José Aristo Solórzano Mendoza.

Radio Bahía, Jirón Alfonso Ugarte 309, Chimbote, Ancash, Perú. Contact: Margarita Rossel Soria, Administradora; or Miruna Cruz Rossel, Administradora.

Radio Cajamarca, Jirón La Mar 675, Cajamarca, Perú. Phone: +51 (44) 921-014. Contact: Porfirio Cruz Potosí.

Radio Chanchamayo, Jirón Tarma 551, La Merced, Junín, Perú.

Radio Chota, Apartado 3, Chota, Cajamarca, Perú. Contact: Aladino Gavadía Huamán, Administrador. $1 or return postage required. Replies slowly to correspondence in Spanish.

Radio Condorcanqui, Emisora Municipal, Alcaldía de Santa María de Nieva, Provincia de Condorcanqui, Amazonas, Perú. Contact: Eduardo Weepiu Daekat, Director; or Octavia Shacaime Huahua, Mayor.

Radio Cora, Compañía Radiofónica Lima, S.A., Paseo de la República 144, Centro Cívico, Oficina 5, Lima 1, Perú. Fax: +51 (14) 336 134. Contact: (general) Dra. Lylian Ramírez M., Directora de Prensa y Programación; or Ms. Angelina Ma Abie; (technical) Srta. Sylvia Ramírez M., Directora Técnica. Free station sticky-label pads. Audio casettes with extracts from their programs $20 plus $2 postage; T-shirts $10 plus $2.50 postage; sweatshirts $20 plus $5 postage; women's hair bands $2 plus $1 postage. Two IRCs or $1 required. Replies slowly to correspondence in English, Spanish, French, Italian and Portuguese.

Radio Cultura Amauta, Apartado 24, Huanta, Perú. Phone: +51 (64) 932-153. Contact: Vicente Saico Tinco.

Radio Cusco, Apartado 251, Cusco, Perú. Fax: +51 (84) 223 308. Contact: Sra. Juana Huamán Yépez, Administradora; or Raúl Siú Almonte, Gerente General; (technical) Benjamín Yábar Alvarez. Free postcards and key rings; also, limited number of T-shirts. Audio cassettes of Peruvian music $10 plus postage. $1 or return postage required. Replies irregularly to correspondence in English or Spanish. Station is looking for folk music recordings from around the world to use in their programs.

Radio Cutervo (when reactivated), Parque José Gálvez Egusquiza, Cutervo, Cajamarca, Perú. Contact: Redecindo Julca Ramírez, Director General y Propietario. Former transmitter, stolen in 1992, has been replaced, and may start operation before long on 6690 kHz, even though the assigned frequency is 3390 kHz.

Radio Del Pacífico, Casilla de Correo 4236, Lima 1, Perú. Contact: J. Petronio Allauca, Secretario, Depto. de Relaciones Públicas. $1 or return postage required. Replies occasionally to correspondence in Spanish.

Radio Diez (when active), Jirón Elías Aguirre 857, Iquitos, Perú. Phone: +51 (94) 231-230. Contact: Betty Santillán, Locutora; or Luis Ugaz Espinoza, director de los noticieros "El Informativo 10" y "Yo soy la voz del pueblo."

Radiodifusora Comercial La Voz de Naranjos, Av. Cajamarca 464, Pardo Miguel Naranjos, Rioja, San Martín, Perú. Contact: Mario Cuzma Paz, Director Propietario.

Radiodifusoras Huancabamba, Calle Unión 409, Huancabamba, Piura, Perú.

Radio El Sol de los Andes, Jirón 2 de Mayo 257, Juliaca, Perú. Phone/fax: +51 (54) 322-981. Contact: Armando Alarcón Velarde.

Radio Frecuencia VH (La Voz de Celendín), Jirón José Gálvez 730, Celendín, Cajamarca, Perú. Contact: Fernando Vásquez Castro, Propietario.

Radio Frecuencia San Ignacio—see Frecuencia San Ignacio.

Radio Horizonte (Chachapoyas), Apartado 69 (or Jirón Santo Domingo 639), Chachapoyas, Amazonas, Perú. Contact: Dolores Gutiérrez Atienza, Gerente; Lourdes Arce Arguedas, Directora de Programas; or Monseñor Angel Francisco Simón Piorno, Director General. Replies to correspondence in Spanish. $1 required.

Radio Horizonte (Chiclayo), Calle Incanto 387, Distrito José Leonardo Ortiz, Chiclayo, Perú. Phone: +51 (74) 222-486.

Radio Huancabamba, Calle Unión 610, Huancabamba, Piura, Perú. Contact: César Colunche Bustamante, Gerente Director Proprietario. Replies occasionally to correspondence in Spanish.

Radio Huanta 2000, Jirón Gervacio Santillana 455, Huanta, Perú. Phone: +51 (64) 932-105. Contact: Humberto Sapaico Salazar, Director Gerente.

Radio Ilucán, Jirón Lima 290, Cutervo, Región Nororiental del Marañón, Perú. Phone: +51 (74) 220-205 anexo 10. Contact: José Gálvez Salazar, Gerente Administrativo. $1 required. Replies occasionally to correspondence in Spanish, and seems to be friendly with Mr. Takayuki Inoue Nozaki.

Radio Imagen, Casilla de Correo 42, Tarapoto, San Martín, Perú; or Apartado 254, Tarapoto, San Martín, Perú. Contact: Adith Chumbe Vásquez, Secretaria; or Jaime Ríos Tapullima, Gerente General. Replies irregularly to correspondence in Spanish. $1 or return postage helpful.

Radio Imperial, Calle Ayabaca 339-341, Huancabamba, Piura, Perú.

Radio Integración, Av. Seoane 200, Abancay, Apurímac, Perú. Contact: Zenón Hernán Farfán Cruzado, Propietario.

Radio Internacional del Perú, Jirón Bolognesi 532, San Pablo, Cajamarca, Perú.

Radio Jaén (La Voz de la Frontera), Calle Mariscal Castilla 439, Jaén, Cajamarca, Perú.

Radio La Hora, Av. Garcilazo 180, Cusco, Perú. Contact: Edmundo Montesinos Gallo, Gerente General. Free stickers, pins, pennants and postcards of Cusco. Return postage required. Replies occasionally to correspondence in Spanish. Hopes to increase transmitter power if and when the economic situation improves.

Radio La Inmaculada, Parroquia La Inmaculada Concepción, Frente de la Plaza de Armas, Santa Cruz, Provincia de Santa Cruz, Departamento de Cajamarca, Perú.

Radio La Merced, Distrito de Tongod, Provincia de Santa Cruz, Cajamarca, Perú. Contact: Roberto Ramos Chanas, Director Gerente. $1 or return postage required. Replies irregularly to correspondence in Spanish.

Radio La Oroya, Apartado Postal No. 88, La Oroya, Provincia de Yauli, Departamento de Junín, Perú. Contact: Jacinto Manuel Figueroa Yauri, Gerente-Propietario. Free pennants. $1 or return postage necessary. Replies to correspondence in Spanish.

Radio Latina (when active), Av. Sáenz Peña 1558, Chiclayo, Lambayeque, Perú. Phone: +51 (74) 233-140. Contact: Carlos Tipara González, Director General.

Radio La Voz del Alto Mayo (when operating), Av. Cajamarca, Carretera Marginal km 459, Nuevo Cajamarca, Provincia de Rioja, San Martín, Perú. Contact: Víctor Bustamante Sánchez, Gerente Propietario; Pedro Bustamante Carrera, Administrador; or José L. Vásquez Paisig, Locutor y Publicista. Return postage necessary. Replies slowly to correspondence in Spanish.

Radio La Voz de Andamachay, Caserio Andamachay, Celendín, Perú; but because of the lack of suitable local transportation, all correspondence should be sent to the owner at his other station, Radio Frecuencia VH (*see*).

Radio La Voz de Cuervo, Jirón María Elena Medina 644-650, Cuervo, Cajamarca. Perú.

Radio La Voz de Huamanga, Calle El Nazareno, 2do Pasaje No. 161, Ayacucho, Perú. Phone: +51 (64) 912-366. Contact: Sra. Aguida A. Valverde Gonzales. Free pennants and postcards.

Radio La Voz de La Selva, Casilla de Correo 207, Iquitos, Loreto, Perú. Phone: +51 (94) 241-515. Fax: +51 (94) 239 360. Contact: Julia Jauregui Rengifo, Directora; Marcelino Esteban Benito, Director; Pedro Sandoval Guzmán, Announcer; or Mery Blas Rojas. Replies to correspondence in Spanish.

Radio La Voz de Oxapampa, Av. Mullenbruck 469, Oxapampa, Pasco, Perú. Contact: Pascual Villafranca Guzmán, Director Propietario.

Radio La Voz de San Antonio, Jirón Alfonso Ugarte 732, Bambamarca, Cajamarca, Perú. Contact: Valentín Mejía Vásquez, Director General; Mauricio Rodríguez R.; or Wilmer Vásquez Campos, Encargado Administración. $1

or return postage required. Replies to correspondence in Spanish.

Radio La Voz de Santa Cruz, Av. Zarumilla 190, Santa Cruz, Cajamarca, Perú.

Radio Libertad de Junín, Apartado 2, Junín, Perú. Contact: Mauro Chaccha G., Director Gerente. Replies slowly to correspondence in Spanish. Return postage necessary.

Radio Líder, Portal Belén 115, 2do piso, Cuzco, Perú. Contact: Mauro Calvo Acurio, Propietario.

Radio Luz Universal, Baptist Mid-Missions, Apartado 368, Cusco, Perú.

Radio Luz y Sonido, Seminario Mayor San Teodoro, Jirón 2 de Mayo 1260 (or Jirón Dámaso Beraún 749, Plaza de Armas), Huánuco, Perú. Phone: +51 (64) 512-394. Contact: Cirilo Damián, or Willy Campos Soto, Seminaristas; or Prof. Jesús Abad Pereira, Director.

Radio Madre de Dios, Apartado 37, Puerto Maldonado, Madre de Dios, Perú. Phone: +51 (84) 571-050. Contact: Alcides Arguedas Márquez, Director del programa "Un Festival de Música Internacional," heard Mondays 0100 to 0200 World Time. Sr. Arguedas is interested in feedback for this letterbox program. Replies to correspondence in Spanish. $1 or return postage appreciated.

Radio Marañón, Apartado 50, Jaén (via Chiclayo), Perú. Phone/fax: +51 (74) 731-147. Contact: Padre Luis Távara Martín, S.J., Director. Return postage necessary. Replies slowly to correspondence in Spanish.

Radio Melodía, San Camilo 501A, Arequipa, Perú. Contact: J. Elva Alvarez de Delgado, Jefa Administración Personal y Financiera; or Deyssy Torres O. Free stickers, pennants and calendars. $1 or return postage necessary. Replies slowly to correspondence in Spanish.

Radio Mundo, Calle Tecte 245, Cusco, Perú. Phone: + 51 (84) 232-076. Fax: +51 (84) 233 076. Contact: Valentín Olivera Puelles, Gerente. Free postcards and stickers. Return postage necessary. Replies slowly to correspondence in Spanish.

Radio Municipal de Cangallo (when active), Concejo Provincial de Cangallo, Plaza Principal No. 02, Cangallo, Ayacucho, Perú. Contact: Nivardo Barbarán Agüero, Encargado Relaciones Públicas.

Radio Nacional del Perú
Administrative Office: Avenida José Gálvez 1040 Santa Beatriz, Lima, Perú. Fax: +51 (14) 726 799. Contact: Rafael Mego Carrascal, Jefatura de la Administración. Replies occasionally to correspondence in Spanish. Return postage required.
Studio Address: Av. Petit Thouars 447, Lima, Perú.

Radio Naylamp, Avenida Huamachuco 1080, 2do piso, Lambayeque, Perú. Phone +51 (74) 283-353. Phone +51 (74) 282-438. Contact: Dr. Juan José Grández Vargas, Director Gerente; or Delicia Coronel Muñoz, who is interested in receiving postcards and the like. Feedback for Dr. J.J.'s weeknightly program "Buenas Tardes, Ecuador," from 0000 to 0100 World Time, appreciated. Free stickers, pennants and calendars. Return postage necessary.

Radio Nor Agricultura (when active), Av. Manco Kápac 852, Baños del Inca, Cajamarca, Perú.

Radio Nor Andina, Jirón José Gálvez 602, Celendín, Cajamarca, Perú. Contact: Misael Alcántara Guevara, Gerente; or Victor B. Vargas C., Departamento de Prensa. Free calendar. $1 required. Donations (registered mail best) sought for the Committee for Good Health for Children, headed by Sr. Alcántara, which is active in saving the lives of hungry youngsters in poverty-stricken Cajamarca Province. Replies irregularly to casual or technical correspondence in Spanish, but regularly to Children's Committee donors and helpful correspondence in Spanish.

Radio Nor Peruana, Emisora Municipal, Jirón Ortiz Arrieta 588, 2do piso, Chachapoyas, Amazonas, Perú. Phone: +51 (44) 981-027. Contact: Fernando Serván Rocha,

Director. Replies very slowly to correspondence in Spanish. Return postage necessary.

Radio Onda Azul, Apartado 210, Puno, Perú. Phone: +51 (54) 351-562. Fax: +51 (54) 352 233. Contact: (general) Mauricio Rodríguez R., Jefe de Producción y Programación; (technical) Marino Rojas Olazabal, Administrador. Free key rings, calendars and diaries. Return postage required. Replies to correspondence in Spanish.

Radio Onda Imperial, Calle Sacsayhuanan K-10, Urbanización Manuel Prado, Cusco, Perú.

Radio Ondas del Huallaga, Apartado 343, Jirón Leoncio Prado 723, Huánuco, Perú. Phone: +51 (64) 512-428. Contact: Flaviano Llanos M., Representante Legal. $1 or return postage required. Replies to correspondence in Spanish.

Radio Ondas del Río Mayo, Jirón Huallaga 348, Nueva Cajamarca, San Martín, Perú. Contact: Edilberto Lucío Peralta Lozada, Gerente; or Víctor Huaras Rojas, Locutor. Free pennants. Return postage helpful. Replies slowly to correspondence in Spanish.

Radio Ondas del Suroriente, Jirón Ricardo Palma 510, Quillabamba, La Convención, Cusco, Perú.

Radio Oriente, Vicariato Apostólico, Calle Progreso 114, Yurimaguas, Loreto, Perú. Phone: +51 (94) 352-156. Phone/fax (ask to switch over to fax): +51 (94) 352 566. Contact: (general) Juan Antonio López-Manzanares M., Director; (technical) Pedro Capo Moragues, Gerente Técnico. $1 or return postage required. Replies occasionally to correspondence in Spanish.

Radio Origen, Avenida Augusto B. Leguía 126, Huancavelica, Perú. Contact: Oscar Andrez Alvarado Yalico, Director General y Propietario; or Jesús Acuña Quispe, Jefe de Programación. $1 or return postage required. Replies occasionally to correspondence in Spanish.

Radio Paucartambo, Jirón Conde de las Lagunas, 2do piso, Frente al Hostal San José, Paucartambo, Pasco, Perú. Contact: Irwin Junio Berrios Pariona, Gerente General. Replies occasionally to correspondence in Spanish.

Radio Paucartambo, Emisora Municipal
Station Address: Paucartambo, Cusco, Perú.
Staffer Address: Manuel H. Loaiza Canal, Correo Central, Paucartambo, Cusco, Perú. Sr. Loaiza, who hosts the week-nightly music show, "El Bus Musical," heard from 2300-2400 World Time, seeks feedback on the program. Return postage or $1 required.

Radio Quillabamba, Centro de los Medios de la Comunicación Social, Quillabamba, La Convención, Cusco, Perú. Contact: Padre Francisco Panera, Director. Replies very irregularly to correspondence in Spanish.

Radio Reina de la Selva, Jirón Ayacucho 944, Plaza de Armas, Chachapoyas, Amazonas, Perú. Contact: José David Reina N., Director. Replies irregularly to correspondence in Spanish. Return postage necessary.

Radio San Ignacio (La Voz de la Frontera), Jirón Mercado 218, San Ignacio, Cajamarca, Perú.

Radio San Martín, Jirón Progreso 225, Tarapoto, San Martín, Perú. Contact: Fernando Tafur Arévalo, Gerente General. May send stickers and magazines. Return postage required. Replies occasionally to correspondence in Spanish.

Radio San Miguel, Av. Huayna Cápac 146, Huánchac, Cusco, Perú. Replies to correspondence in Spanish.

Radio San Miguel Arcángel, Jirón Bolívar 354, San Miguel de Pallaques, Cajamarca, Perú.

Radio Santa Rosa, Casilla 4451, Lima 1, Perú. Phone: +51 (14) 277-488. Fax: +51 (14) 276 791. Contact: Padre Juan Sokolich Alvarado; or Lucy Palma Barreda. Free stickers and pennants. $1 or return postage necessary. 180-page book commemorating stations 35th anniversary $10. Replies to correspondence in Spanish.

Radio Satélite E.U.C., Jirón Cutervo No. 543, Cajamarca, Santa Cruz, Perú. Contact: Sabino Llamo Chávez, Gerente. Free tourist brochure. $1 or return postage required. Replies irregularly to correspondence in Spanish.

Radio Sicuani, Jirón Condemayo 212, Sicuani, Canchis, Cusco, Perú.

Radio Soledad, Distrito de Parcoy, Provincia de Pataz, La Libertad, Perú. Contact: Vicente Valdivieso, Locutor. Return postage necessary.

Radio Sudamérica, Jirón Ramón Castilla 704, 2° piso, Cutervo, Cajamarca, Perú. Contact: Jorge Paredes Guerra, Administrador; or Amadeo Mario Muñoz Guivar, Propietario.

Radio Superior, Av. Marginal 206, Pardo Miguel Naranjos, Rioja, San Martín, Perú.

Radio Tacna, Casilla de Correo 370, Tacna, Perú. Phone: +51 (54) 714-871.Fax: +51 (54) 723 745. Contact: (nontechnical and technical) Ing. Alfonso Cáceres Contreras, Sub-Gerente/Jefe Técnico; (head of administration) Yolanda Vda. de Cáceres C., Directora Gerente. Free stickers and samples of *Correo* local newspaper. $1 or return postage helpful. Audio cassettes of Peruvian and other music $2 plus postage. Replies irregularly to correspondence in English and Spanish.

Radio Tarma, Casilla de Correo 167, Tarma, Perú. Contact: Mario Monteverde Pumareda, Gerente General. Sometimes sends 100 Inti banknote in return when $1 enclosed. Free stickers, possibly free pennants. $1 or return postage required. Replies irregularly to correspondence in Spanish.

Radio Tayacaja, Distrito de Pampas, Tayacaja, Huancavelica, Perú.

Radio Tingo María, Av. Raimondi No. 592, Casilla de Correo 25, Tingo María, Leoncio Prado, Perú. Contact: Gina A. de la Cruz Ricalde, Administradora; or Ricardo Abad Vásquez, Gerente. Free brochures. $1 required. Replies slowly to correspondence in Spanish.

Radio Tropical, S.A., Casilla de Correo 31, Tarapoto, Perú. Fax: +51 (94) 522-155. Contact: Mery A. Rengifo Tenazoa; or Luis F. Mori Roatogui, Gerente. Free stickers, occasionally free pennants, and station history booklet. $1 or return postage required. Replies occasionally to correspondence in Spanish.

Radio Unión, Apartado 833, Lima 27, Perú. Phone: +51 (14) 408-657. Fax: +51 (14) 407 594. Contact: Juan Carlos Sologuren, Dpto. de Administración, who collects stamps. Free satin pennants and stickers. IRC required, and enclosing used or new stamps from various countries is especially appreciated. Replies irregularly to correspondence and tape recordings, especially from young women, with Spanish preferred.

Radio Universo, Av. Lima 307, Saposoa, Cajamarca, Perú. Contact: Víctor C. Lozano Tantaleán, Gerente.

Radio Victoria, Av. Tacna 225 4to piso, Lima 1, Perú. Fax: +51 (14) 427-1195. This station is owned by the Brazilian-run Pentacostal Church "Dios Es Amor." Their program "La Voz de la Liberación" is produced locally and aired over numerous Peruvian shortwave stations.

Radio Villa Rica
General Correspondence: Jirón Virrey Toledo 544, Huancavelica, Perú. Contact: Srta. Maritza Pozo Manrique. Free informative pamphlets. Local storybooks and poems from Huancavelica $15; cassettes of Peruvian and Andean regional music $20; also sells cloth and wooden folk articles. Replies occasionally to correspondence in Spanish.
Technical Correspondence: Apartado 92, Huancavelica, Perú. Contact: Fidel Hilario Huamani, Director. $3 required in return postage for a reply to a reception report from abroad.

Radio Visión 2000, Radiodifusora Comercial Visión 2000, Jirón Prolongación Mariscal Sucre s/n, Bambamarca, Hualgayoc, Cajamacra, Perú. Contact: Víctor Marino Tello Cruzado, Propietario. Return postage required. Replies slowly to correspondence in Spanish.

PHILIPPINES World Time +8

Note: Philippine stations sometimes send publications with lists of Philippine young ladies seeking "pen pal" courtships.

Far East Broadcasting Company—FEBC Radio International

Main Office: P.O. Box 1, Valenzuela, Metro Manila 0560, Philippines; or P.O. Box 2041, Manila 0902, Philippines. Phone: +63 (2) 292-1152, +63 (2) 292-1351 or +63 (2) 292-1490. Fax: +63 (2) 359 490. E-mail: ("DX Dials") dx@febc.jmf.org.ph. Contact: (general) Peter McIntyre, Manager, International Operations Division, and Host of "DX Dials"; Jane Colley, Head, Audience Relations; Roger Foyle, Correspondence and Verification Manager; Ella McIntyre, Producer, "Mailbag, Let's Hear from You"; Fay Olympia, Producer, "Good Morning from Manila"; Christine D. Johnson, Program Supervisor, Overseas English Department; Daniel Wu, Chinese Service; U Zaw Win Tun, Burmese Service; Mrs. Thē Rivera, Vietnamese Service; Miss. Editha Natalio, Indonesian/Malay Service; Miss. Solina Chy, Cambodian Service; or Helen Saldaña, Chief News Editor, FEB-News Bureau; (head of administration) Efren M. Pallorina, Managing Director; (Engineering) Romualdo Lintag, Chief Engineer. Free stickers, calendar cards and DX Club Registration. Three IRCs appreciated for airmail reply.

New Delhi Bureau, Nontechnical: c/o FEBA, Box 6, New Delhi-110 001, India.

Radyo Pilipinas, the Voice of Democracy,
Philippine Broadcasting Service, PIA Building Visayas Avenue, 1103 Quezon City, Metro Manila, Philippines. Fax: +63 (2) 924 2745. Contact: (general) Evelyn Salvador Agato, Broadcast Program Supervisor; Mercy Lumba; Leo Romano, Producer, "Listeners and Friends"; or Ric Lorenzo; (technical) Mike Pangilinan, Engineer. Free postcards & stickers.

Radio Veritas Asia, P.O. Box 2642, Quezon City 1166, Metro Manila, Philippines. Phone: +63 (2) 900-012. Fax: +63 (2) 907 436. Contact: Ms. Cleofe R. Labindao, Audience Relations Supervisor; (technical) Ing. Floremundo L. Kiguchi, Technical Director. Free caps, T-shirts, stickers, pennants, rulers, pens, postcards and calendars.

Voice of America—Poro and Tinang Relay Stations. Phone: +63 (2) 813-0470/1/2. Fax: +63 (2) 813 0469.
Contact: Frank Smith, Manager; or David Strawman, Deputy Manager. These numbers for urgent technical matters only. Otherwise, does not welcome direct correspondence; *see* USA for acceptable VOA Washington address and related information.

PIRATE

Pirate radio stations are usually one-person operations airing home-brew entertainment and/or iconoclastic viewpoints. In order to avoid detection by the authorities, they tend to appear irregularly, with little concern for the niceties of conventional program scheduling.

Most are found in Europe chiefly on Saturdays, and mainly during evenings in North America, often above 6200 kHz and 7375 kHz. These *sub rosa* stations and their addresses are subject to unusually abrupt change or termination, sometimes as a result of forays—increasingly common in such countries as the United States—by radio authorities. Two worthy sources of current addresses and other information on American pirate radio activity are: *The Pirate Radio Directory* [George Zeller, Tiare Publications, P.O. Box 493, Lake Geneva WI 53147 USA; or for specific inquiries, fax author directly at +1 (216) 696 0770], an excellent annual reference available from the publisher or world band specialty stores; and A·C·E, Box 11201, Shawnee Mission KS 66207 USA, a club which publishes a periodical for serious pirate radio enthusiasts.

A show on a specialized form of American pirate activity—low-powered local (usually FM) stations—is "Micro-Radio

in the U.S.," aired over Radio for Peace International, Costa Rica, some Mondays at 2130 and some Thursdays at 2200 World Time on 6200 or 7385 kHz, plus 9400 USB and 15050 kHz.

For Europirate DX news, try:

SRSNEWS, Ostra Porten 29, S-442 54 Ytterby, Sweden. E-mail: srs@ice.warp.slink.se.

Pirate Connection, Kämnärsvägen 13D:220, S-226 46 Lund, Sweden. Six issues annually for about $23

Pirate Chat, 21 Green Park, Bath, Avon, BA1 1HZ, United Kingdom.

FRS Goes DX, P.O. Box 2727, 6049 ZG Herten, Holland

Free-DX, 3 Greenway, Harold Park, Romford, Essex, RM3 OHH, United Kingdom.

FRC-Finland, P.O. Box 82, SF-40101 Jyvaskyla, Finland.

Pirate Express, P.O. Box 220342, Wuppertal, Germany.

For up-to-date listener discussions and other pirate-radio information on the Internet, the Usenet URL is: news:alt.radio.pirate.

POLAND World Time +1 (+2 midyear)

Polish Radio Warsaw

Station: External Service, P.O. Box 46, 00-950 Warsaw, Poland. Phone: (general) +48 (2) 645-9303; (English Department) +48 (2) 645-9262; (German Department) +48 (2) 645-9333. Fax: (general) +48 (22) 445 280, +48 (22) 447 307 or +48 (22) 444 123; (Director +48 (2) 645 5917. Contact: (general) Jacek Detco, Editor, English Department; María Goc, Editor, English Department; (heads of administration) Jerzy Jagodzinski, Director and Editor-in-Chief; Rafal Kiepuszewski; Miroslaw Lubo, Deputy Director. Free stickers. DX Listeners' Club.

Transmission Authority: National Radiocommunication Agency, ul. Kasprzaka 18/20, 01-211 Warsaw, Poland. Phone: +48 (2) 658-5140. Fax: +48 (2) 658 5175. Contact: Mrs. Filomena Grodzicka or Jan Kondej.

PORTUGAL World Time +1 (+2 midyear); Azores World Time -1 (World Time midyear)

RDP International—Rádio Portugal, Box 1011,
Lisbon 1001, Portugal. Phone: +351 (1) 347-5065 or +351 (1) 347-5068. Fax: +351 (1) 347 4475. Contact: (general) "Listeners' Mailbag," English Service; or Arlindo de Carvalho; (head of administration) João Louro, Chairman; (technical) Winnie Almeida, DX Producer/Host, English Section; or Rui de Jesus, Frequency Manager. Free stickers, paper pennants and calendars. May send literature from the Portuguese National Tourist Office.

Rádio Renascença, Rua Ivens 14, 1294 Lisbon Codex, Portugal. Phone: +351 (1) 347-5270. Fax: +351 (1) 342 2658. Contact: C. Pabil, Director-Manager.

Radio Trans Europe (transmission facilities), 6º esq., Rua Braamcamp 84, 1200 Lisbon, Portugal. Transmitter located at Sines.

Voice of Orthodoxy—*see* Belarus.

QATAR World Time +3

Qatar Broadcasting Service, P.O. Box 3939, Doha, Qatar. Phone: +974 86-48-05. Fax: +974 82 28 88. Contact: Jassem Mohamed Al-Qattan, Head of Public Relations. Rarely replies, but return postage helpful.

ROMANIA World Time +2 (+3 midyear)

Radio România International

Station: P.O. Box 111, 70756 Bucharest, România; or Romanian embassies worldwide. Phone: (general) +40 (1) 615-9350; (engineering) +40 (1) 613-4849. Fax: (general) +40 (1) 223 2613 [if no connection, try via office of the Director General of Radio România, but mark fax "Pentru RRI"; that fax is +40 (1) 222 5641]; (Engineering Services) +40 (1) 312 1056 or +40 (1) 615 6992. Contact: (English, Romanian or German) Frederica Dochinoiu, Producer, "Listeners' Letterbox" and "DX Mailbag," English Department; (French or Romanian/head of administration) Doru Vasile Ionescu, Director; (technical) Radu Ianculescu or Marius

Nisipeanu, Engineering Services. Free stickers, pennants, posters, pins and assorted other items. Can provide supplementary materials for "Romanian by Radio" course on audio cassettes. Listeners' Club. Annual contests. Replies slowly but regularly. Concerns about frequency management should be directed to the PTT (see below), with copies to the Romanian Autonomous Company (see farther below) and to a suitable official at RRI.

Transmission and Frequency Management, PTT: General Directorate of Regulations, Ministry of Communications, 14a Al. Libertatii, 70060 Bucharest, Romania. Phone: +40 (1) 400-1060. Fax: +40 (1) 400 1230. Contact: Mrs. Elena Danila.

Transmission and Frequency Management, Autonomous Company: Romanian Autonomous Company for Radio Communications, 14a Al. Libertatii, 70060 Bucharest, Romania. Phone: +40 (1) 400-1228. Contact: Mr. Marian Ionita.

RUSSIA

(Times given for republics, oblasts and krays):
- World Time +2 (+3 midyear) Kaliningradskaya;
- World Time +3 (+4 midyear) Arkhangel'skaya (incl. Nenetskiy), Astrakhanskaya, Belgorodskaya, Bryanskaya, Ivanovskaya, Kaluzhskaya, Karelia, Kirovskaya, Komi, Kostromskaya, Kurskaya, Lipetskaya, Moscovskaya, Murmanskaya, Nizhegorodskaya, Novgorodskaya, Orlovskaya, Penzenskaya, Pskovskaya, Riazanskaya, Samarskaya, Sankt-Peterburgskaya, Smolenskaya, Tambovskaya, Tulskaya, Tverskaya, Vladimirskaya, Vologodskaya, Volgogradskaya, Voronezhskaya, Yaroslavskaya;
- World Time +4 (+5 midyear) Checheno-Ingushia, Chuvashia, Dagestan, Kabardino-Balkaria, Kalmykia, Krasnodarskiy, Mari-Yel, Mordovia, Severnaya Osetia, Stavropolskiy, Tatarstan, Udmurtia;
- World Time +5 (+6 midyear) Bashkortostan, Chelyabinskaya, Kurganskaya, Orenburgskaya, Permskaya, Yekaterinburgskaya, Tyumenskaya;
- World Time +6 (+7 midyear) Omskaya;
- World Time +7 (+8 midyear) Altayskiy, Kemerovskaya, Krasnoyarskiy (incl. Evenkiyskiy), Novosibirskaya, Tomskaya, Tuva;
- World Time +8 (+9 midyear) Buryatia, Irkutskaya;
- World Time +9 (+10 midyear) Amurskaya, Chitinskaya, Sakha (West);
- World Time +10 (+11 midyear) Khabarovskiy, Primorskiy, Sakha (Center), Yevreyskaya;
- World Time +11 (+12 midyear) Magadanskaya (exc. Chukotskiy), Sakha (East), Sakhalinskaya;
- World Time +12 (+13 midyear) Chukotskiy, Kamchatskaya;
- World Time +13 (+14 midyear) all points east of longtitude 172.30 E.

Warning—Mail Theft: Airmail correspondence containing funds or IRCs from North America and Japan may not arrive safely even if sent by registered air mail, as such mail enters via the Moscow Airport. However, funds sent from Europe, North America and Japan via surface mail enter via St. Petersburg, and thus stand a better chance of arriving safely. Airmail service is otherwise now almost on a par with that of other advanced countries.

E-Mail to Moscow Stations: Although few Moscow stations have e-mail addresses, according to Internet's Patrick Stoddard (stoddard@aztec.asu.edu), they can be reached via the World Wide Web at http://www.elvis.msk.su. One menu option is to send a fax to any designated Moscow fax machine, with the relevant fax numbers being given below in this chapter of *Passport.*

Verification of Stations Using Transmitters in St. Petersburg and Kaliningrad: Transmissions of several world band stations—the Voice of Russia, Golos Rossii, Mayak, Radio Odin, Radio Yunost, the BBC World Service, Radio Nederland Wereldomroep and China Radio International—when emanating from transmitters located in St. Petersburg and Kaliningrad, may be verified directly from: World Band Verification QSL Service, The State Enterprise for Broadcasting and Radio Communications No. 2 (GPR-2), ul. Akademika Pavlova 13A, 197376 St. Petersburg, Russia. Fax: +7 (812) 234 2971 during working hours. Contact: Mikhail V. Sergeyev, Chief Engineer; or Mikhail Timofeyev, verifier. Free stickers. Two IRCs required for a reply, which upon request includes a copy of "Broadcast Schedule," which gives transmission details (excluding powers) for all transmissions emanating from three distinct transmitter locations: Kaliningrad- Bolshakovo, St. Petersburg and St. Petersburg-Popovka. This organization—which has 26 shortwave, three longwave, 15 mediumwave AM and nine FM transmitters—relays broadcasts for clients for the equivalent of about $0.70-1.00 per kW/hour.

Government Radio Agencies

C.I.S. Frequency Management Engineering Office: The Main Centre for Control of Broadcasting Networks, ul. Nikolskaya 7, 103012 Moscow, Russia. +7 (095) 921-2501. Fax: +7 (095) 956 7546 or +7 (095) 921 1624. Contact: Anatoliy T. Titov, Chief Director; or Mrs. Antonina Ostakhova. This office plans the frequency usage for transmitters throughout the C.I.S. Correspondence should be concerned only with significant technical observations or engineering suggestions concerning frequency management improvement—not regular requests for verifications. Correspondence in Russian preferred, but English accepted.

State Enterprise for Broadcasting and Radio Communications No. 2 (GPR-2)—see Verification of Stations Using Transmitters in St. Petersburg and Kaliningrad, above.

State Radio Company: AS "Radioagency Co., Pyatnitskaya 25, 113326 Moscow, Russia. Phone: (Khlebnikov and Petrunicheva) +7 (095) 233-6474; (Komissarova) +7 (095) 233-6660; (Staviskaia) +7 (095) 233-7003. Fax: (Khlebnikov, Petrunicheva and Komissarova) +7 (095) 233 1342; (Staviskaia) +7 (095) 230 2828 or +7 (095) 233 7648. Contact: Valentin Khlebnikov, Mrs. Maris Petrunicheva, Mrs. Lyudmila Komissarova or Mrs. Rachel Staviskaia.

State Transmission Authority: Russian Ministry of Telecommunication, ul. Tverskaya 7, 103375 Moscow, Russia. Phone: +7 (095) 201-6568. Fax: +7 (095) 292 7086 or +7 (095) 292 7128. Contact: Anatoly C. Batiouchkine.

State TV and Radio Company: Russian State TV & Radio Company, ul. Yamskogo 5, Polva 19/21, 125124 Moscow, Russia. Phone: +7 (095) 213-1054 or +7 (095) 213-1054 or +7 (095) 250-0511. Fax: +7 (095) 250 0105. Contact: Ivan Sitilenlov.

Adventist World Radio, the Voice of Hope

Main Office: AWR-Russia Media Centre, P.O. Box 170, 300000 Tula-Centre, Russia. Fax: +7 (087) 233 1218. Contact: Peter Kulakov, Manager; or Igor Revtov, Coordinator. Free home study Bible guides and other religious material, pennants, stickers, calendars and other small souvenirs. However, most letters to the Russia Media Centre wind up being answered by the AWR European Office (see Adventist World Radio, Germany), so correspondence is best directed there.

Arkhangel'sk Radio, Dom Radio, ul. Popova 2, 163000 Arkhangel'sk, Arkhangel'skaya Oblast, Russia; or U1PR, Valentin G. Kalasnikov, ul. Suvorov 2, kv. 16, Arkhangel'sk, Arkhangel'skaya Oblast, Russia. Replies irregularly to correspondence in Russian.

Bashkir Radio, ul. Gafuri 9, 450076 Ufa, Bashkortostan, Russia.

Buryat Radio, Dom Radio, ul. Erbanova 7, 670000 Ulan-Ude, Republic of Buryatia, Russia. Contact: Z.A. Telin or L.S. Shikhanova.

Chita Radio, ul. Kostushko-Grigorovicha 27, 672090 Chita, Chitinskaya Oblast, Russia. Contact: (technical)

V.A. Klimov, Chief Engineer; or A.A. Anufriyev.

Christian Radio Station Alpha and Omega, Izdatelstvo "Protestant," Mukomolnyi pr. 1, kor.2, 123290 Moscow, Russia. Contact: E. Gcuob, Executive Manager. Return postage necessary.

Golos Rossii, ul. Pyatnitskaya 25, 113326 Moscow, Russia. Fax: +7 (095) 233 6449 or +7 (095) 973 2000. Contact: Oleg Maksimovich Poptsov, Chairman of All-Russian State Teleradio Broadcasting Company. Correspondence in Russian preferred. For verification of reception from transmitters located in St. Petersburg and Kaliningrad, see the note, above, shortly after the country heading, "RUSSIA."

Islamskaya Volna (Islamic Wave), Islamic Center of Moscow Region, Moscow Jami Mosque, Vypolzov per. 7, 129090 Moscow, Russia. Phone: +7 (095) 281-4904. Contact: Sheikh Ravil Gainutdin. Return postage necessary.

Kabardino-Balkar Radio, ul. Nogmova 38, 360000 Nalchik, Russia.

Kamchatka Radio, RTV Center, Dom Radio, ul. Sovietskaya 62-G, 683000 Petropavlovsk-Kamchatskiy, Kamchatskaya Oblast, Russia. Contact: A. Borodin, Chief OTK; or V.I. Aibabin. $1 required. Replies in Russian to correspondence in Russian or English.

Khabarovsk Radio, RTV Center, ul. Lenina 71, 680013 Khabarovsk, Khabarovskiy Kray, Russia; or Dom Radio, pl. Slavy, 682632 Khabarovsk, Khabarovskiy Kray, Russia. Contact: (technical) V.N. Kononov, Glavnyy Inzhener.

Khanty-Mansiysk Radio, Dom Radio, ul. Mira 7, 626200 Khanty-Mansiysk, Khanty-Mansiyskiy Autonomous Okrug, Tyumenskaya Oblast, Russia. Contact: (technical) Vladimir Sokolov, Engineer.

Krasnoyarsk Radio, RTV Center, Sovietskaya 128, 660017 Krasnoyarsk, Krasnoyarskiy Kray, Russia. Contact: Valeriy Korotchenko; or Anatoliy A. Potehin, RAØAKE. Free local information booklets in English/Russian. Replies in Russian to correspondence in English or Russian. Return postage helpful.

Magadan Radio, RTV Center, ul. Kommuny 8/12, 685013 Magadan, Magadanskaya Oblast, Russia. Contact: Viktor Loktionov or V.G. Kuznetsov. Return postage helpful. May reply to correspondence in Russian.

Mariy Radio, Mari Yel, ul. Osipenko 50, 424014 Yoshkar-Ola, Russia.

Mayak—see Radio Odin and Mayak, below.

Mukto Probaho—see Thailand.

Murmansk Radio, sopka Varnichnaya, 183042 Murmansk, Murmanskaya Oblast, Russia; or RTV Center, Sopka Varnichaya, 183042 Murmansk, Murmanskaya Oblast, Russia.

Primorsk Radio, RTV Center, ul. Uborevieha 20A, 690000 Vladivostok, Primorskiy Kray, Russia. Contact: A.G. Giryuk. Return postage helpful.

Radio Alef (joint project of Voice of Russia and Yiddish Child's Organization.), P.O. Box 72, 123154 Moscow, Russia.

Radio Al-Risalah (The Message) (when operating), c/o Voice of Russia, ul. Pyatnitskaya 25, 113326 Moscow, Russia. Fax: +7 (095) 233 1342. An Islamic program transmitted in Russian via the facilities of the VOR. Currently off the air.

Radio Kudymkar, 617240 Kudymkar, Komi-Permytskiy Autonomous Okrug, Permskaya Oblast, Russia.

Radio Lena, ul. Semena Dezhneva 75-4, Radiocenter, 677002 Yakutsk, Russia.

Radio Maykop, ul. Zhukovskogo 24, 352700 Maykop, Republic of Adygeya, Russia.

Radio Nalchik, ul. Nogmova 38, 360000 Nalchik, Republic Kabardino-Balkariya, Russia.

Radio Novaya Volna (New Wave Radio, when operating; an independent program last traced over Radio Odin and Golos Rossii), ul. Akademika Koroleva 19, 127427 Moscow, Russia. Fax: +7 (095) 215 0847. Contact: Vladimir Razin, Editor-in-Chief.

Radio Novaya Volna-2 (New Wave Radio-2, when

operating), ul. Vorovskogo 6, 454091 Chelyabinsk, Russia.

Radio Odin and Mayak, ul. Akademika Koroleva 12, 127427 Moscow, Russia. Phone: (general) +7 (095) 217-9340; (English Service) +7 (095) 233-6578; (administration) +7 (095) 217-7888. Fax: +7 (095) 215 0847. Correspondence in Russian preferred, but English increasingly accepted. For verification of reception from transmitters located in St. Petersburg and Kaliningrad, see the note, above, shortly after the country heading, "RUSSIA."

Radio Pamyat—see Radiostantsiya Pamyat, below.

Radio Perm, ul. Teknicheskaya 21, 614600 Perm, Permskaya Oblast, Russia.

Radio Radonezh, Studio 158, ul. Pyatnitskaya 25, 113326 Moscow, Russia. Phone: +7 (095) 233-7258. Fax/phone: +7 (095) 233 6356. Contact: Anton Parshin, Announcer. Although this Orthodox Church station's logo shows Radiostansiya Radonezh, it consistently identifies as Radio Radonezh.

Radio Rossii (Russia's Radio), Room 121, 5-R Ulitsa, 19/21 Yamskogo Polya, 125124 Moscow, Russia. Fax: +7 (095) 250 0105. Contact: Sergei Yerofeyev, Director of International Operations [sic]; or Sergei Davidov, Director. Free English-language information sheet. For verification of reception from transmitters located in St. Petersburg and Kaliningrad, see the note, above, shortly after the country heading, "RUSSIA."

Radio Samara/Radio SBC, Samara Broadcasting Center, ul. Sovietskoy Armii 217, 443011 Samara, Samarskaya Oblast, Russia.

Radio Samorodinka, P.O. Box 898, Center, 101000 Moscow, Russia. Contact: L.S. Shiskin, Editor. This station may be licensed as other than a regular broadcaster.

Radio Seven, ul. Gagarina 6a, 443079 Samara, Samarskaya Oblast, Russia. Contact: A.P. Nenashjev; or Mrs. A.S. Shamsutdinova, Editor.

Radio Shark (when operating), Prospekt Oktyabrya 56/1, 450054 Ufa, Bashkortostan, Russia. Contact: Gergey Anatsky; or Anatskiy Sergey, Director.

Radio Titan Kompani (programs aired via Radio Shark, when operating), ul. Sovietskaya 14, k. 9, 450008 Ufa, Bashkortostan, Russia.

Radio Yunost, ul. Pyatnitskaya 25, 113326 Moscow, Russia. Fax: +7 (095) 233 6244. Although this station's logo shows Radiostansiya Yunost, it consistently identifies as Radio Yunost.

Radiostantsiya Atlantika (program of Murmansk Radio, aired via Golos Rossii), per. Rusanova 7-A, 183767 Murmansk, Russia.

Radiostantsiya Pamyat (Memory Radio Station), ul. Valovaya, d.32, kv.4, 113054 Moscow, Russia; or P.O. Box 23, 113535 Moscow, Russia. Phone/fax: +7 (095) 237 3971. Contact: (general) Dimitriy Vasilyev, Director; (technical) Yuri Oleggovich Miroliubov, Radio Operator. Audio cassettes of broadcasts 5 rubles or $2. Correspondence in Russian preferred, with 2 IRCs being requested for a reply; verification cards feature monarchist and Czarist-era themes. Station of the Pamyat National Patriotic Front, whose "memories" are of monarchist and fascist eras.

Radiostansiya Tikhiy Okean (program of Primorsk Radio, also aired via Voice of Russia transmitters), RTV Center, ul. Uborevieha 20A, 690000 Vladivostok, Primorskiy Kray, Russia.

Radiostantsiya Yakutsk, ul. Semena Dezhneva 75/2, Radiocenter, 677000 Yakutsk, Russia.

Radiostantsiya Yunost—see Radio Yunost.

Sakha Radio, Dom Radio, ul. Ordzhonikidze 48, 677007 Yakutsk, Sakha (Yakutia) Republic, Russia. Fax: +7 (095) 230 2919. Contact: (general) Alexandra Borisova; Lia Sharoborina, Advertising Editor; or Albina Danilova, Producer, "Your Letters"; (technical) Sergei Bobnev, Technical Director. Russian books $15; audio cassettes $10. Free station stickers and original Yakutian souvenirs. Replies to correspondence in English.

Sakhalin Radio, Dom Radio, ul. Komsomolskaya 209, 693000 Yuzhno-Sakhalinsk, Sakhalin Is., Sakhalinskaya Oblast, Russia. Contact: V. Belyaev, Chairman of Sakhalinsk RTV Committee.

Tatar Radio, RTV Center, ul. M. Gorkogo 15, 420015 Kazan', Republic of Tatarstan, Russia. May reply to correspondence in Russian. Return postage helpful.

Tyumen' Radio, RTV Center, ul. Permyakova 6, 625013 Tyumen', Tyumenskaya Oblast, Russia. Contact: (technical) V.D. Kizerov, Engineer, Technical Center. Sometimes replies to correspondence in Russian. Return postage helpful.

Voice of Russia, ul. Pyatnitskaya 25, Moscow 113326, Russia. Phone: (World Service) +7 (095) 233-6980 or +7 (095) 233-6586; (International Relations) +7 (095) 233-7801. Fax: (general) +7 (095) 230 2828; (World Service) +7 (095) 233 7693; (International Relations) +7 (095) 233 7648. Contact: (English Service—listeners' questions to be answered over the air) Joe Adamov; (English Service—all other general correspondence) Ms. Olga Troshina, World Service Letters Department; (general correspondence, all languages) Victor Kopytin, Director of International Relations Department; Vladimir Zhamkin, Editor-in-Chief; Yevgeny Nilov, Deputy Editor-in-Chief; Anatoly Morozov, Deputy Editor-in-Chief; (Japanese) Yelena Sopova, Japanese Department; (verifications, all services) Mrs. Eugena Stepanova, c/o English Service; (heads of administration) Yuri Minayev, First Deputy Chairman, Voice of Russia; Armen Oganesyan, Chairman, World Service, Voice of Russia. For verification of reception from transmitters located in St. Petersburg and Kaliningrad, see the note, above, shortly after the country heading, "RUSSIA." For engineering correspondence concerning frequency management problems, see the note on C.I.S. Frequency Management in that same area, above. Free stickers, booklets and sundry other souvenirs occasionally available upon request. Sells audio cassettes of Russian folk and classical music, as well as a Russian language-learning course.

Voice of the Assyrians (when operating)—see Voice of Russia.

RWANDA World Time +2

Deutsche Welle—Relay Station Kigali—Correspondence should be directed to the main offices in Cologne, Germany (see).

Radio Rwanda, B.P. 404, Kigali, Rwanda. Fax: +250 (7) 6185. Contact: Marcel Singirankabo. $1 required. Before the recent civil conflict, rarely replied, with correspondence in French having been preferred.

SAO TOME E PRINCIPE World Time exactly

Voice of America—São Tomé Relay Station, P.O. Box 522, São Tomé, São Tomé e Príncipe. Phone: +23 912 22-800. Fax: +23 912 22 435. Contact: Jack Fisher, Relay Manager. These numbers for timely and significant technical matters only. All other communications should be directed to the usual VOA address in Washington (see USA).

SAUDI ARABIA World Time +3

Broadcasting Service of The Kingdom of Saudi Arabia, P.O. Box 61718, Riyadh 11575, Saudi Arabia. Phone: (general) +966 (1) 404-2795; (administration) +966 (1) 442-5493; (technical) +966 (1) 442-5170. Fax: (general) +966 (1) 402 8177; (Frequency Management) +966 (1) 404 1692. Contact: (general) Mutlaq A. Albegami, European Service Manager; (technical) Sulaiman Samnan, Director of Frequency Management; or A. Shah, Department of Frequency Management. Free travel information and book on Saudi history.

Radio Islam from Holy Mecca (Idha'at Islam min Mecca al-Mukarama)—program with the same contact details as Broadcasting Service of the Kingdom of Saudi

Arabia, above.

SENEGAL World Time exactly

Office de Radiodiffusion-Télévision du Senegal, B.P. 1765, Dakar, Senegal. Phone: +221 23-63-49. Fax: + 221 22 34 90. Contact: (technical) Joseph Nesseim, Directeur des Services Techniques. Free stickers and Senegalese stamps. Return postage, $1 or 2 IRCs required; as Mr. Nesseim collects stamps, unusual stamps may be even more appreciated. Replies to correspondence in French.

SEYCHELLES World Time +4

BBC World Service—Indian Ocean Relay Station, P.O. Box 448, Victoria, Mahé, Seychelles; or Grand Anse, Mahé, Seychelles. Phone: +248 78-269. Fax: +248 78 500. Contact: (head of administration) Peter J. Loveday, Station Manager; (technical) Peter Lee, Resident Engineer; Steve Welch, Assistant Resident Engineer. Nontechnical correspondence should be sent to the BBC World Service in London (see).

Far East Broadcasting Association—FEBA Radio
Main Office: P.O. Box 234, Seychelles, Indian Ocean. Phone: +248 224-449. Fax: +248 225 171. Contact: Dick Whittington, Schedule Controller. Free stickers and station information sheet. $1 or one IRC helpful.
Canadian Office: Box 2233, Vancouver BC, Canada.
India Office: FEBA India, P.O. Box 2526, 7 Commissariat Road, Bangalore-560 025, India. Contact: Peter Muthl Raj.

SIERRA LEONE World Time exactly

Sierra Leone Broadcasting Service, New England, Freetown, Sierra Leone. Contact: (general) Joshua Nicol, Special Assistant to the Director of Broadcasting; (technical) Emmanuel B. Ehirim, Project Engineer.

SINGAPORE World Time +8

BBC World Service—Far Eastern Relay Station, P.O. Box 434, 26 Olive Road, Singapore. Phone: +65 260-1511. Fax: +65 669 0834. Contact: (technical) Far East Resident Engineer. Nontechnical correspondence should be sent to the BBC World Service in London (see).

Radio Corporation of Singapore, Caldecott Hill, Andrew Road, Singapore 1129, Singapore. Phone: +65 251-8622. Fax: +65 256 9338. Contact: (general) Lillian Tan, Public Relations Division; Lim Heng Tow, Manager, International & Community Relations; Tan Eng Lai, Promotion Executive; Lucy Leong; or Karamjit Kaur, Senior Controller; (head of administration) Anthony Chia, Director General; (technical) Lee Wai Meng. Free stickers and lapel pins. Do not include currency in envelope.

Radio Singapore International, Farrer Road, P.O. Box 5300, Singapore 9128, Singapore. Phone: +65 256-0401 or +65 353-5300. Fax: +65 259 1357 or +65 259 1380. Contact: (general) Anushia Kanagabasai, Producer, "You Asked For It"; Belinda Yeo, Producer, "Dateline RSI"; or Mrs. Sakuntala Gupta, Programme Manager, English Service; (head of administration) S. Chandra Mohan, Station Director; (technical) Selena Kaw, Office of the Administrative Executive; or Yong Wui Pin, Engineer. Free souvenir T-shirts and key chains to selected listeners. Do not include currency in envelope.

SLOVAKIA World Time +1 (+2 midyear)

Radio Slovakia International, Slovensky Rozhlas, Mytna 1, 812 90 Bratislava, Slovakia. Phone: +42 (7) 49-62-81. Phone/fax: (technical) +42 (7) 49-76-59. Fax: (French and English Sections) +42 (7) 49 82 67; (English Section) +42 (7) 49 62 82; (other sections) +42 (7) 49 82 47. Contact: Helga Dingová, Director of English Broadcasting; Paul Kaye, Producer "Listeners Tribune"; or Edita Chocholatá; (head of administration) PhDr. Karol Palkovic, Head of External Broadcasting; (technical) Jozef Krátky, Ing. Free stickers and pennants.

SOLOMON ISLANDS World Time +11

Solomon Islands Broadcasting Corporation, P.O.

Box 654, Honiara, Solomon Islands. Phone: +677 20051. Fax: +677 23159. Contact: (general) Julian Maka'a, Producer, "Listeners From Far Away"; Alison Ofotalau, Voice Performer; Cornelius Teasi; or Program Director; (head of administration) James Kilua, General Manager; (technical) George Tora, Chief Engineer. IRC or $1 helpful.

SOMALIA World Time +3

Radio Mogadishu, Ministry of Information, Private Postbag, Mogadishu, Somalia. Contact: (general) Dr. Abdel-Qadir Muhammad Mursal, Director, Media Department; (head of administration) Abdel-Rahman Umar Ma'Alim Dhagah, Acting Director; (technical) Yusuf Dahir Siyad, Chief Engineer. Replies irregularly. Letters should be via registered mail.

"SOMALILAND" World Time +3

Note: "Somaliland," claimed as a independent nation, is diplomatically recognized only as part of Somalia.
Radio Hargeisa (when operating), P.O. Box 14, Hargeisa, Somaliland, Somalia. Contact: Sulayman Abdel-Rahman, announcer. Most likely to respond to correspondence in Somali or Arabic. As of 1994, Radio Hargeisa was supposedly in the process of installing a new 25 kW shortwave transmitter; however, since then, they been continuing to make do with their usual, and highly erratic, mobile transmitter.

SOUTH AFRICA World Time +2

Channel Africa, P.O. Box 91313, Auckland Park 2006, Republic of South Africa. Phone: + 27 (11) 714-2551 or +27 (11) 714-3942; (technical) +27 (11) 714-3409. Fax: (general) + 27 (11) 714 2546, +27 (11) 714 4956 or +27 (11) 714 6377; (technical) +27 (11) 714 5812. Contact: (general) Tony Machilika, Head of English Service; Robert Michel, Head of Research; Lionel Williams, Executive Editor; M.R. Brink, Acting Executive Editor; or Noeleen Vorster, Corporate Communications Manager; (technical) Mrs. H. Meyer, Supervisor Operations; or Lucienne Libotte, Technology Operations. T-shirts $11 and watches $25. Prices do not include shipping and handling. Free stickers and calendars. Reception reports are best directed to Sentech (see below).

South African Broadcasting Corporation
Studios: P.O. Box 91312, Auckland Park 2006, Republic of South Africa. Phone: (technical) +27 (11) 714-3409. Fax: (general) +27 (11) 714 5055; (technical) +27 (11) 714 3106 or +27 (11) 714 5812. World Wide Web: http://www.sabc.co.za. Contact: *Radio Five:* Helena Boshoff, Public Relations Officer; *Radio Oranje:* Hennie Klopper, Announcer; or Christo Olivier; *Radio 2000:* J.H. Odendaal, Transmitter Manager; *All networks:* Karel van der Merwe, Head of Radio. Free stickers.
Transmitters and Verifications: Sentech (Pty) Ltd, Shortwave Services, Private Bag X06, Honeydew 2040, South Africa. Phone: +27 (11) 475-1596. Fax: +27 (11) 475 5112. Contact: Mr. N. Smuts, Managing Director; or Kathy Otto. Sentech is currently issuing its own set of 8 verification cards, and is the best place to direct reception reports for all South African world band stations.

SPAIN World Time +1 (+2 midyear)

Radio Exterior de España ("Spanish National Radio")
Main Office: Apartado 156.202, E-28080 Madrid, Spain. Phone: +34 (1) 346-1149 or +34 (1) 346-1160. Fax: +34 (1) 346 1815 or +34 (1) 346 1813. Contact: Pilar Salvador M., Relaciones con la Audiencia REE; Nuria Alonso Veiga, Head of Information Service; or Penelope Eades, Foreign Language Programmer. Free stickers, calendars, pennants and tourist information.
Russian Office: P.O Box 88, 109044 Moscow, Russia.
Costa Rican Relay Facility—see Costa Rica.
Washington News Bureau: National Press Building, 529 14th Street NW, Suite 1288, Washington DC 20045 USA.

Phone: +1 (202) 783-0768. Contact: Luz María Rodríguez.

SRI LANKA World Time +5:30

Deutsche Welle—Relay Station Sri Lanka, 92/2 Rt. Hon. D.S. Senanayake Mwts, Colombo 8, Sri Lanka. Nontechnical correspondence should be sent to the Deutsche Welle in Germany (*see*).
Radio Japan/NHK, c/o SLBC, P.O. Box 574, Torrington Square, Colombo 7, Sri Lanka. This address for technical correspondence only. General nontechnical listener correspondence should be sent to the usual Radio Japan address in Japan. News-oriented correspondence may also be sent to the NHK Bangkok Bureau (*see* Radio Japan, Japan).
Sri Lanka Broadcasting Corporation, P.O. Box 574, Colombo 7, Sri Lanka. Phone: (domestic service) +94 (1) 697-491; (external service) +94 (1) 695-661. Fax: +94 (1) 695 488. Contact: N. Jayhweera, Director of Audience Research; Lal Herath, Deputy Director General of Broadcasting; or Icumar Ratnayake, Controller, "Mailbag Program"; (technical) H.M.N.R. Jayawardena, Frequency Engineer.
Voice of America—Colombo Relay Station, 228/1 Galle Road, Colombo 4, Sri Lanka. Phone: +94 (1) 585-0119. Fax: +94 (1) 502 675. Contact: David M. Sites, Relay Station Manager. This address, which verifies correct reception reports, is for technical correspondence only. Nontechnical correspondence should be directed to the regular VOA address (*see* "USA").

ST. HELENA World Time exactly

St. Helena Government Broadcasting Service (when operating once each year), The Castle, Jamestown, St. Helena, South Atlantic Ocean. Phone: +290 4669. Fax: +290 4542. Contact: Tony Leo, Station Manager. $1, return postage or 2 IRCs required. Is on the air only once each year, around October (e.g., October 27th, 1995 from 2000-2300 World Time), on 11092.5 kHz in the upper-sideband (USB) mode.

SUDAN World Time +2

National Unity Radio—see Sudan National Broadcasting Corporation, below, for details.
Sudan National Broadcasting Corporation, P.O. Box 572, Omdurman, Sudan. Phone: +249 (11) 52-100. Contact: (general) Mohammed Elmahdi Khalil or Mohammed Elfatih El Sumoal; (technical) Abbas Sidig, Director General, Engineering and Technical Affairs; or Adil Didahammed, Engineering Department. Replies irregularly. Return postage necessary.

SURINAME World Time -3

Radio Apintie, Postbus 595, Paramaribo, Suriname. Phone: +597 40-05-00. Fax: +597 40 06 84. Contact: Ch. E. Vervuurt, Director. Free pennant. Return postage or $1 required.

SWAZILAND World Time +2

Swaziland Commercial Radio
Nontechnical Correspondence: P.O. Box 5569, Rivonia 2128, Transvaal, South Africa. Phone: +27 (11) 884-8400. Fax: +27 (11) 883 1982. Contact: Rob Vickers, Manager—Religion. IRC helpful. Replies irregularly.
Technical Correspondence: P.O. Box 99, Amsterdam 2375, South Africa. Contact: Guy Doult, Chief Engineer.
Trans World Radio
Main Office: P.O. Box 64, Manzini, Swaziland. Phone: +268 52-781. Fax: +268 55 333. Contact: (general) Dawn-Lynn Prediger, Propagation Secretary; Mrs. L. Stavropoulos; Robert W. Lincoln, Programme Administrator; Robert Upper, Follow-up Department; or Mrs. Carol J. Tatlow; (head of administration) Peter A. Prediger, Director; (technical) Rev. Tom Tatlow. Free stickers, postcards and calendars. $1, return postage or IRC required. Also, see USA.
Kenya Office: P.O. Box 21514 Nairobi, Kenya.
Malawi Office: P. O. Box 52 Lilongwe, Malawi.

South African Office: P.O. Box 36000, Menlo Park 0102, Republic of South Africa.

Zimbabwe Office: P.O. Box H-74, Hatfield, Harare, Zimbabwe.

SWEDEN World Time +1 (+2 midyear)

IBRA Radio (program)

Main Office: International Broadcasting Association, Box 396, S-105 36 Stockholm, Sweden. Fax: +46 (8) 579 029. Free pennants and stickers, plus green-on-white IBRA T-shirt available. IBRA Radio is heard as a program over various world band radio stations, including the Voice of Hope, Lebanon, and Trans World Radio, Monaco.

Canadian Office: P.O. Box 444, Niagara Falls ON, L2E 6T8 Canada.

Radio Sweden

Note: Radio Sweden plans to reduce its shortwave operations to Europe, relying increasingly on program placement via local stations. However, it appears that this is more in the line of experimentation to determine optimum audience-building strategies than a move to promote alternative technologies, such as the proposed Eureka system of satellite broadcasting. Among the two and very different audience strategies under serious consideration for its services to all parts of the world are 1) reaching "ordinary listeners," presumably through programs of a more popular nature, and 2) reaching "opinion makers," apparently with public-service-type programs. Feedback from listeners is very much welcomed.

Main Office: S-105 10 Stockholm, Sweden. Phone: (general) +46 (8) 784-7281 or +46 (8) 784-5000; (listener voice mail) +46 (8) 784-7287; (Technical Department) +46 (8) 784-7286. Fax: (general) +46 (8) 667 6283; (audience contact and Technical Department) +46 (8) 660 2990; (polling to receive schedule) +46 8 667 3701. E-mail: (MediaScan office) wood@stab.sr.se. World Wide Web: http://www.abc.se/~m8914/media.html; (MediaScan page) http://www.abc.se/~m8914/rsprog.html; (English Service page) ftp.funet.fi:pub/sounds/radiosweden/mediascan. Contact: (general) Alan Pryke, Host, "In Touch with Stockholm" [include your telephone number]; Sarah Roxström, Head, English Service; Greta Grandin, Program Assistant, English Service; George Wood, Producer, MediaScan; Olimpia Seldon, Assistant to the Director; Charlotte Adler, Public Relations & Information; (head of administration) Hans Wachholz, Director; (technical) Rolf Beckman, Head, Technical Department. "Moose Gustafsson" T-shirts $17 or £10. Payment for T-shirts may be made by international money order, Swedish postal giro account No. 43 36 56-6 or internationally negotiable bank check.

Transmission Authority: Teracom, Svensk Rundradio AB, P.O. Box 17666, S-118 92 Stockholm, Sweden. Phone: (Nilsson) +46 (8) 671-2066; (Gustavsson) +46 (8) 671-2061. Fax: (Nilsson and Gustavsson) +46 (8) 671 2060 or +46 (8) 671 2080; (Sonesson) +46 (42) 342 268 or +46 (8) 671 2084. E-mail: mni@teracom.se. Contact: (Frequency Planning Dept.—Head Office): Magnus Nilsson, Ms. Clara Gustavsson or Lars Sonesson. Free stickers. Seeks monitoring feedback for new frequency usages.

New York News Bureau: Swedish Broadcasting, 825 Third Avenue, New York NY 10022 USA. Phone: +1 (212) 688-6872 or +1 (212) 643-8855. Fax: +1 (212) 594 6413. Contact: Elizabeth Johansson or Ann Hedengren.

Washington News Bureau: Swedish Broadcasting, 2030 M Street NW, Suite 700, Washington DC 20036 USA. Phone: +1 (202) 785-1727. Contact: Folke Rydén, Lisa Carlsson or Steffan Ekendahl.

SWITZERLAND World Time +1 (+2 midyear)

Die Antwort—see Belarus.

European Broadcasting Union, Case Postal 67, CH-1218 Grand-Saconnex GE, Switzerland. Phone: +41 (22) 717-2111. Fax: +41 (22) 717 2710. Contact: Frank Kozamernik.

Red Cross Broadcasting Service, Département de la Communication, CICR/ICRC, 19 Avenue de la Paix, CH-1202 Geneva, Switzerland. Phone: +41 (22) 734-6001. Fax: +41 (22) 733 2057 or +41 (22) 734 8280. Contact: Patrick Piper, Head; Elisabeth Copson, "Red Crossroads"; or Carlos Bauverd, Chef, Division de la Presse. Free stickers, wall calendar and station information. IRC appreciated. Free program cassettes to interested radio stations. As of September, 1995, the RCBS has been reorganized to have shorter, but more frequent, broadcasts.

Swiss Radio International

Main Office: Giacomettistrasse 1, CH-3000 Berne 15, Switzerland. Phone: +41 (31) 350-9222. Fax: (Public Relations and Marketing) +41 (31) 350 9544; (Programme Department) +41 (31) 350 9569. Contact: (general) Walter Fankhauser, Head, Communication & Marketing Services; M. Blaser, Staff Assistant, Communications & Marketing Services; Gillian Zbinden, Secretary, English Programmes; or Thérèse Schafter, Secrétaire des programmes en langue français; (heads of administration) Ulrich Kündig, General Manager; Nicolas Lombard, Deputy Director and Head of Programme Services; (technical) Bob Zanotti, DX Editor. Free station flyers, posters, stickers and pennants. SRI CDs of Swiss music SF28. Station offers listeners a line of articles for sale that bear the station's SRI logo. These include Swiss watches for SF60, Swiss clocks for SF65, microphone lighters for SF26, letter openers for SF30, books for SF40, T-shirts for SF18, pins for SF7 and Swiss Army knives for SF28. Postal and carrying charges for the above items are: Switzerland SF4; Europe and overseas by surface mail, SF6; and overseas by airmail, SF12. VISA or cash, but no personal checks. To place your order, write with payment to: Swiss Radio International, Merchandising, c/o the above address.

Transmission Authority: Division Radiodiffusion, Swiss Telecom PTT, Speichergaße 6, CH-3030 Berne, Switzerland. Phone: +41 (31) 338-3490. Fax: +41 (31) 338 6554. Contact: (general) Ulrich Wegmüller; (head of administration) Dr. Walter G. Tiedweg, Head Radio Division.

Washington News Bureau: 2030 M Street NW, Washington DC 20554 USA. Phone: (general) +1 (202) 775-0894 or +1 (202) 429-9668; (French-language radio) +1 (202) 296-0277; (German-language radio) +1 (202) 7477. Fax: +1 (202) 833 2777. Contact: Christophe Erbeck, reporter.

United Nations Radio, Room G209, Palais des Nations, CH-1211 Geneva 10, Switzerland. Phone: +41 (22) 917-4222. Fax: +41 (22) 917 0123.

SYRIA World Time +2 (+3 midyear)

Radio Damascus, Syrian Radio & Television, Ommayad Square, Damascus, Syria. Contact: Mr. Afaf, Director General; Lisa Arslanian; or Mrs. Wafa Ghawi. Free stickers, paper pennants and *The Syria Times* newspaper. Replies can be highly erratic, but as of late have been more regular, if sometimes slow.

"Voice of Iraq"—see Radio Damascus, above, for contact information.

TAHITI—see FRENCH POLYNESIA.

TAJIKISTAN World Time +6

Radio Dushanbe, Radio House, 31 Chapayev Street, 735025 Dushanbe, Tajikistan. Contact: Gulom Makhmudovich, Deputy Chairman; or Mrs. Raisa Muhutdinova, Editor-in-Chief, English Department. Correspondence in Russian, Farsi, Dari, Tajik or Uzbek preferred. Used Russian stamps appreciated, for whatever reason, but return postage not really necessary.

Radio Pay-i 'Ajam-see Radio Dushanbe for details.

Tajik Radio, Radio House, 31 Chapayev Street, 735025 Dushanbe, Tajikistan. Contact: Mirbobo Mirrakhimov, Chairman of State Television and Radio Corporation. Correspondence in Russian, Tajik or Uzbek preferred.

TANZANIA World Time +3

Radio Tanzania, Director of Broadcasting, P.O. Box 9191,

Dar es Salaam, Tanzania. Phone: +255 (51) 38-015. Fax: +255 (51) 29 416. Contact: (general) Mrs. Deborah Mwenda; Acting Head of External Service; Abdul Ngarawa, Acting Controller of Programs; B.M. Kapinga, Director of Broadcasting; or Ahmed Jongo, Producer, "Your Answer"; (technical) Head of Research & Planning. Replies to correspondence in English.

Voice of Tanzania Zanzibar, P.O. Box 1178, Zanzibar, Tanzania. Phone: +255 (54) 31-088. Contact: (general) Yusuf Omar Chunda, Director Department of Information and Broadcasting; or Ali Bakari Muombwa; (technical) Nassor M. Suleiman, Maintenance Engineer. Return postage helpful.

THAILAND World Time +7

BBC World Service—Thai Relay Station (in construction). The BBC World Service, which currently possesses no world band transmission facilities in Thailand, is adding a relay facility with four 250 kW transmitters at Nakhon Province in Central Thailand. This is expected to be on the air in 1996, just before Hong Kong (where the BBC World Service currently has a relay facility) is scheduled to revert to Chinese rule.

Mukto Probaho, GPO Box 1605, Bangkok 10501, Thailand. This Moslem religious program is aired via transmission facilities located in Russia.

Radio Thailand World Service, 236 Vibhavadi Rangsit Highway, Din Daeng, Iiuaykhwang, Bangkok 10400, Thailand. Phone: +66 (2) 277-0122, +66 (2) 277-1814 or +66 (2) 277-1840. Fax: +66 (2) 277 7095 or +66 (2) 271 3514. Contact: Mrs. Amporn Samosorn, Chief of External Services; or Patra Lamjiack. Free pennants. Replies irregularly, especially to those who persist.

Voice of America—Udorn Thani Relay Station
Transmitter Site: Phone: +66 (42) 271-490/1. Only matters of urgent importance should be directed to these numbers. Normal technical correspondence should be directed to the Thailand QSL Desk (see following paragraph), or to the regular VOA address in Washington (see USA).
Thailand QSL Desk: Voice of America, Room G-759, Washington DC 20547 USA. Phone: +1 (202) 619-1669. Fax: +1 (202) 619 1680. E-mail: ferguson@beng.voa.gov. Contact: Dan Ferguson.

TOGO World Time exactly
Radio Lomé, Lomé, Togo. Return postage, $1 or 2 IRCs helpful.

TONGA World Time +13
Tonga Broadcasting Commission (if and when antenna, destroyed by a cyclone, is ever repaired or replaced), A3Z, P.O. Box 36, Nuku'alofa, Tonga. Fax: +676 22670 or +676 24417. Contact: (general) Robina Nakao, Producer, "Dedication Program"; Mateaki Heimuli, Controller of Programs; or Tavake Fusimalohi, General Manager; (technical) M. Indiran, Chief Engineer; or Kifitoni Sikulu, Controller, Technical Services.

TUNISIA World Time +1
Radiodiffusion Télévision Tunisienne, Radio Sfax, 71 Avenue de la Liberté, Tunis, Tunisia. Contact: Mongai Caffai, Director General; Mohamed Abdelkafi, Director; or Smaoui Sadok, Le Sous-Directeur Technique. Replies irregularly and slowly to correspondence in French or Arabic.

TURKEY World Time +2 (+3 midyear)
Radio Izmir Cinarli Lisesi Radiosu, Teknik ve Endüstri Meslek Lisesi Deneme Radiosu, Cinarli, 35.110 Izmir, Turkey. Phone: +90 (232) 461-7442. Fax: +90 (232) 435 1032. Contact: Göksel Uysal, Technical Manager. Station is run by the local technical institute. Free studio photos. Correspondence in English accepted.

Turkish Radio-Television Corporation—Voice of Turkey

Main Office, Nontechnical: P.K. 333, 06.443 Yenisehir Ankara, Turkey. Phone: +90 (4) 418-9453. Fax: +90 (4) 431 0322. Contact: (English) Osman Erkan, Host, "Letterbox"; or Ms. Semra Eren, Head of English Department; (other languages) Rafet Esit, Foreign Languages Section Chief; (head of administration) Savas Kiratli, Managing Director; A. Akad Gukuriva, Deputy Director General; (technical) Mete Coskun. Free stickers, pennants, women's embroidery artwork swatches and tourist literature.
Main Office, Technical: Gene Mudurluk Teknik, TRT Sitesi, Kkat : 5/C, Or-An, 06.450 Ankara, Turkey. Phone: +90 (312) 490-1730/2. Fax: +90 (312) 490 1733. Contact: Turgay Cakimci, Frequency Manager; Vural Tekeli, Deputy Director General, Engineering; or Ms. F. Elvan Boratav, International Technical Relations Department.
San Francisco Office, Schedules: 2654 17th Avenue, San Francisco CA 94116 USA. Phone: +1 (415) 564-9968. Contact: George Poppin. Self-addressed stamped envelope or IRC required for reply. This address, a volunteer office, only provides TRT schedules to listeners. All other correspondence should be sent directly to Ankara.

Türkiye Polis Radyosu (Turkish Police Radio), T.C. İçişleri Bakanlığı, Emniyet Genel Müdürlüğü, Ankara, Turkey. Contact: Station Director. Tourist literature for return postage. Replies irregularly.

Meteoroloji Sesi Radyosu (Voice of Meteorology), T.C. Tarim Bakanlığı, Devlet Meteoroloji Işleri, Genel Müdürlüğü, P.K. 401, Ankara, Turkey. Contact: Mehmet Öafgharmeci, Director General. Free tourist literature. Return postage helpful.

TURKMENISTAN World Time +5
Turkmen Radio, Ulitsa Mollanepsa 3, 744000 Ashgabat, Turkmenistan. Contact: K. Karayev; or Yu M. Pashaev, Deputy Chairman of State Television and Radio Company.

UGANDA World Time +3
Radio Uganda
General Office: P.O. Box 7142, Kampala, Uganda. Phone: +256 (41) 254-461, +256 (41) 242-316 or +256 (41) 245-376. Fax: +256 (41) 256 888. Contact: Kikulwe Rashid Harolin or A.K. Mlamizo. $1 or return postage required. Replies infrequently and slowly.
Engineering Office: P.O. Box 2038, Kampala, Uganda. Contact: Yona Hamala, Chief Engineer. Four IRCs or $1 required. Enclosing a self addressed envelope may also help to get a reply.

UKRAINE World Time +2 (+3 midyear)
Warning-Mail Theft: **For the time being, letters to Ukrainian stations, especially containing funds or IRCs, are more likely to arrive safely if sent by registered mail.**
Government Transmission Authority: RRT/Concern of Broadcasting, Radiocommunication & Television, 10 Dorogajtshaya St., 254112 Kiev, Ukraine. Phone: +7 (044) 226-2262 or +7 (044) 440-8688. Fax: +7 (044) 440 8722. Contact: Alexey Karpenko, Nikolai P. Kyryliuk or Mrs. Liudmila Deretskaya.

Radio Ukraine International, ul. Kreshchatik 26, 252001 Kiev, Ukraine. Phone: +7 (044) 229-2870 or +7 (044) 229-1757. Fax: +7 (044) 229 4585. Free stickers, calendars and Ukrainian stamps.

Radio Lugansk, ul. Dem'ochina 25, 348000 Lugansk, Ukraine. Contact: A.N. Mospanova.

Ukrainian Radio, ul. Kreshchatik 26, 252001 Kiev, Ukraine. Contact: Vasyl Yurychek, Vice President of State Television and Radio Company.

UNITED ARAB EMIRATES World Time +4
Capital Radio—see UAE Radio from Abu Dhabi, below, for details.

UAE Radio from Abu Dhabi, Ministry of Information & Culture, P.O. Box 63, Abu Dhabi, United Arab Emirates. Phone: +971 (2) 451-000. Fax: (station) +971 (2) 451 155;

(Ministry of Information & Culture) +971 (2) 452 504. Contact: (general) Aïda Hamza, Director, Foreign Language Services; or Abdul Hadi Mubarak, Producer, "Live Program"; (technical) Ibrahim Rashid, Director General, Technical Department; or Fauzi Saleh, Chief Engineer. Free stickers, postcards and stamps.

UAE Radio in Dubai, P.O. Box 1695, Dubai, United Arab Emirates. Phone: +971 (4) 370-255. Fax: +971 (4) 374 111; +971 (4) 370 283; or +971 (4) 371 079. Contact: Ms. Khulud Halaby; or Sameer Aga, Producer, "Cassette Club Cinarabic"; (technical) K.F. Fenner, Chief Engineer—Radio; or Ahmed Al Muhaideb, Assistant Controller, Engineering. Free pennants.

UNITED KINGDOM World Time exactly (+1 midyear)
Bessemer Broadcasting, 52 Hampton Road, Firvale, Sheffield S5 7AN, United Kingdom. This experimental station has been granted a 12-month test and developement license from the U.K. Radio Communication Agency. Station is a joint venture of the Chapel Green Community College and its radio society, Hatley Antenna Technology of Aberdeen, and Bessemer Broadcasting. Reception reports are welcome.

BBC World Service
Main Office, Nontechnical: P.O. Box 76, Bush House, Strand, London WC2B 4PH, United Kingdom. Phone: (general) +44 (171) 240-3456; (*BBC Worldwide* magazine, Editorial Office) +44 (171) 257-2875 or +44 (171) 257-2803; (*BBC Worldwide* magazine, subscription voice mail outside North America) +44 (171) 257-2211; (*BBC Worldwide* magazine, subscription sales toll-free number within the United States) (800) 875-2997; (*BBC Worldwide* subscription sales within Canada) +1 (201) 627-2997; (World Service Mail Order) +44 (171) 257-2576; (International Broadcasting & Audience Research) +44 (171) 257-8141; (Press Office) +44 (171) 257-2947/1; (administration) +44 (171) 257-2057. Fax: (Audience Correspondence) +44 (171) 257 8258; ("Write On" listeners' letters program) +44 (171) 497 0287; (*BBC Worldwide* magazine) +44 (171) 240 4899; (World Service Mail Order) +44 (171) 497 0498; (World Service Shop) +44 (171) 240 4811; (International Broadcasting & Audience Research) +44 (171) 257-8254; (Press Office) +44 (171) 240 8760; (administration) +44 (171) 379 6841. E-mail: (general listener correspondence) worldservice.letters@bbc.co.uk; (general BBC inquiries concerning domestic and external services) correspondence@bbcnc.org.uk; ("New Ideas") newideas@bbc-sci.demon.co.uk; (other specific programs) format is typically programname@bbc.co.uk, so for example the "Write On" correspondence program is writeon@bbc.co.uk, and so on; (specific individuals) for individuals at Bush House, the format is firstname.lastname@bbc.co.uk, so for example "Wavescan" contributor Simon Spanswick is simon.spanswick@bbc.co.uk, and so on; (BBC World Service Science, Industry and Medicine Unit) editor@bbc-sci.demon.co.uk; (Polish Service) polska.sekcja@bbcnc.org.uk. World Wide Web: (URL) http://www.bbc.org.uk; (World Service frequency information) http://www.bbcnc.org.uk/worldservice/monthly_scheds.html. Contact: ("Write On") Paddy Feeny, Presenter; Ernest Warburton, Editor, World Service in English; Graham L. Mytton, Head of International Broadcasting & Audience Research; or Fritz Groothues, Head, Strategy Development; (head of administration) Sam Younger, Managing Director. Monthly *BBC Worldwide* magazine, which may be subscribed to $49.50 or $30 per year to either the Bush House address, above, or P.O. Box 3000, Denville NJ 07834 USA. Numerous audio/video (video PAL/VHS only) cassettes, publications (including *PASSPORT TO WORLD BAND RADIO*), portable world band radios, T-shirts, sweatshirts and other BBC souvenirs available by mail from BBC World Service Shop; for Mail Order details, contact the above London address (VISA/MC/AX/Access). Cassettes of BBC programs from BBC Topical Tapes, also

at the above London address. *BBC English* magazine, to aid in learning English, from BBC English, P.O. Box 96, Cambridge, United Kingdom. Also, see Antigua, Ascension, Oman, Seychelles and Singapore, which are where technical correspondence concerning these BBC relay transmissions should be sent if you seek a reply with full verification data, as no such data are provided via the London address. The BBC World Service is also constructing a relay facility with four 250 kW transmitters in Nakhon Province in Central Thailand; it is expected to be on the air in 1996, just before Hong Kong (where the BBC World Service currently has another relay facility) is scheduled to revert to Chinese rule.

Main Office, Technical: BBC World Service Coverage Department, Reception Analysis Unit, N.E. Wing, P.O. Box 76, Bush House, Strand, London WC2B 4PH, United Kingdom. Phone: (Reception Analysis) +44 (171) 257-2155; (Control Room) +44 (171) 257-2672. Fax: (Reception Analysis) +44 (171) 240 8926; (Control Room) +44 (171) 379 3205. Contact: (Reception Analysis) Dave Chambers, Engineer; or Dennis Thompson, Chief Assistant to the Chief Engineer; (Control Room) Ashley Jones, Engineer. These offices generally respond only to other broadcasting engineering entities, or to technical reception reports from those interested or involved in regular technical monitoring. Normal listener correspondence should be directed to the Main Office—Nontechnical (*see* above).

Foreign Broadcasts Monitoring: BBC Monitoring, Caversham Park, Reading RG4 8TZ, United Kingdom. Phone: (general) +44 (1734) 472-742; (Marketing) +44 (1734) 469-289; (World Broadcasting Information/monitoring) +44 (1734) 469-261/2. Fax: (general) +44 (1734) 461-954; (World Broadcasting Information/monitoring) +44 (1734) 461 993; (Marketing) +44 (1734) 463 823; (Technical Operations) +44 (1734) 462 414. E-mail: (World Broadcasting Information/ monitoring) 100437.173@compuserve.com; (Marketing) 100431.2524@compuserve.com. World Wide Web: (Sample pages of WBI/BS) http://www.bbc.co.uk/ caversham/home-page.html. Contact: (Marketing) Ann Dubina, Marketing Department; (World Broadcasting Information/ monitoring) Chris Greenway, Manager, World Broadcasting Information; or Dave Kenny, Monitor; (head of administration) Thomas Read, Managing Director. World band schedules ("BS") and weekly *WBI* newsletter via post for an annual cost of £435.75 in the U.K., £473.75 airmail to Europe and £490.75 airmail elsewhere, as well as online for an annual fee; audio and teletype feeds for news agencies and others; and world broadcasting program summaries for researchers. VISA/MC/AX. Works in concert with various other organizations, including the Foreign Broadcast Information Service (*see* USA).

North American BBC Worldwide *Subscription Office:* P.O Box 3000, Denville NJ 07834 USA. Phone: (toll-free within United States) (800) 875-2997; (Canada) +1 (201) 627-2997. VISA/MC/AX. US$49.50 per year.

Paris Office: 155 rue du Faubourg-St. Honoré, F-75008 Paris, France. Phone: +33 (1) 45-61-97-00 or +33 (1) 45-63-15-88. Fax: +33 (1) 45 63 67 12.

Berlin Office: Savingnyplatz 6, Berlin 12, Germany.

Singapore Address: P.O. Box 434, Maxwell Road Post Office, Singapore 9008, Singapore. Fax: +65 253 8131.

Australian Office: Suite 101, 80 William Street, East Sydney, NSW 2011, Australia. Fax: 61 (2) 361 0853. Contact: (general) Michelle Rowland; or Marilyn Eccles, Information Desk.

World Radio Network Ltd, Wyvil Court, 10 Wyvil Road, London SW8 2TY, United Kingdom. Phone: +44 (171) 896-9000. Fax: + 44 (171) 896 9007. E-mail: wrn@cityscape.co.uk. World Wide Web: (sound files) http://town.org/radio/wrn.html. Contact: Karl Miosga, Managing Director; or Jeffrey Cohen, President. Provides program placement via satellite in various countries for a variety of international broadcasters. Sponsors seminars by invitation only.

United Nations Radio, R/S-850, United Nations, New York NY 10017 USA; or write the station over which UN Radio was heard (Radio Myanmar, Radio Cairo, China Radio International, Sierra Leone Broadcasting Service, Radio Zambia, Radio Tanzania, Polish Radio Warsaw, HCJB/Ecuador, IRRS/Italy, All India Radio, RFPI/Costa Rica). Fax: +1 (212) 963 1307. Contact: (general) Sylvester E. Rowe, Chief, Radio and Video Service; Ayman El-Amir, Chief, Radio Section, Department of Public Information; (technical and nontechnical) Sandra Guy, Secretary. Free stamps and *UN Frequency* publication.
Geneva Office: see Switzerland.
Paris Office: UNESCO Radio, 7 Pl.de Fontenoy, 75018 Paris, France. Fax: +33 (1) 45 67 30 72. Contact: Erin Faherty, Executive Radio Producer.

URUGUAY World Time -3
El Espectador (when active), Río Branco 1483, 11100 Montevideo, Uruguay. If no response from this address, try sending your correspondence to the station's correspondent in the USA: Carlos Banales, 5601 Seminary Road, Apartment 806-N, Falls Church, Virginia 22041 USA.
La Voz de Artigas, Av. Lecueder 483, 55000 Artigas, Uruguay. Fax: +598 (642) 4744. Contact: (general) Sra. Solange Murillo Ricciardi, Co-Propietario; (technical) Roberto Murillo Ricciardi. Free stickers and pennants. Replies to correspondence in English, Spanish, French and Portuguese.
Radiodifusion Nacional-*see* SODRE, below.
Radio Monte Carlo, Av. 18 de Julio 1224, 11100 Montevideo, Uruguay. Contact: Ana Ferreira de Errázquin, Secretaria, Departmento de Prensa de la Cooperativa de Radioemisoras; Déborah Ibarra, Secretaria; Emilia Sánchez Vega, Secretaria; or Ulises Graceras. Correspondence in Spanish preferred.
Radio Oriental—Same as Radio Monte Carlo, above.
SODRE
Publicity and Technical: Radiodifusion Nacional, Casilla 1412, 11000 Montevideo, Uruguay. Contact: (Publicity) Daniel Ayala González, Publicidad; (technical) Francisco Escobar, Depto. Técnico.
Other: "Radioactividades," Casilla 801 (or Casilla 6541), 11000 Montevideo, Uruguay. Fax: +598 (2) 48 71 27. Contact: Daniel Muñoz Faccioli.

USA World Time -4 Atlantic, including Puerto Rico and Virgin Islands; -5 (-4 midyear) Eastern, excluding Indiana; -5 Indiana, except northwest and southwest portions; -6 (-5 midyear) Central, including northwest and southwest Indiana; -7 (-6 midyear) Mountain, except Arizona; -7 Arizona; -8 (-7 midyear) Pacific; -9 (-8 midyear) Alaska, except Aleutian Islands; -10 (-9 midyear) Aleutian Islands; -10 Hawaii; -11 Samoa
Note on Disestablishmentarian Programs: Contact and related information for many American politically oriented shows that are of an anti-establishment bent are listed separately earlier in this chapter, under Disestablishmentarian, following the entries for Denmark.
Adventist World Radio, the Voice of Hope
World Headquarters: 12501 Old Columbia Pike, Silver Spring MD 20904 USA. Phone: +1 (301) 680-6304. Fax: +1 (301) 680 6303 or +1 (301) 680 6390. Contact: (general) Gordon Retzer, President. Most correspondence and all reception reports are best sent to the station where the transmission you heard actually emanated (see Costa Rica, Germany, Guam, Guatemala, Italy and Russia), rather than to the World Headquarters. Free religious printed matter, pennants, stickers, program schedules and other small souvenirs. IRC or $1 appreciated. Hopes to establish a new facility in Paraguay *(see)*.
Office of International Relations: 903 Tanninger Drive, Indianapolis IN 46239 USA. Phone/fax: +1 (317) 891-8540. Contact: Dr. Adrian M. Peterson, International Liaison.

Provides publications with regular news releases and technical information. Issues some special verification cards. QSL stamps also available from this address in return for reception reports.
DX Program: "Wavescan," prepared by Adrian Peterson (see preceding).
Listener Newsletter: Current, published quarterly by AWR, is available through AWR stations in the countries listed above; free, but IRCs appreciated. The Adventist church provides educational and food aid to underdeveloped countries and disaster relief via the Adventist Development and Relief Agency.
Public Relations & Development: AWR, c/o Newbold College, Binfield, Bracknell, Berks. RG42 4AN, United Kingdom. Fax: +44 (1344) 304 169. Contact: Andrea Steele, Director PR & Development.
Central Intelligence Agency, Washington DC 20505 USA. Phone: (Press Liason) +1 (703) 482-7668; (general) +1 (703) 482-1100. Contact: Kent Harrington, Press Liason. Although the CIA is not believed to be operating any broadcasting stations at present, it is known to have done so in the past, usually in the form of "black" clandestine stations, and could do so again in the future. Additionally, the Agency is reliably reported to have funded a variety of organizations over the years, and may still be funding a relatively small number of organizations today, which operate, control or influence world band programs and stations. Also, see Foreign Broadcast Information Service, below.
C-SPAN, 400 N Capitol Street NW, Suite 650, Washington DC 20001 USA. Phone: +1 (202) 626-4863 or +1 (202) 737-3220. Fax: +1 (202) 737 3323. Contact: Thomas Patton, Audio Network; or Rayne Pollack, Manager, Press Relations. Relays selected international radio broadcasts over cable systems within the United States.
Disestablishmentarian   Programs—*see* Disestablishmentarian listing earlier in this chapter, following the entries for "Denmark."
Federal Communications Commission
Organization: 2000 M Street NW, Washington DC 20554 USA. Phone: (general) +1 (202) 418-0200; (Public Affairs) +1 (202) 418-0500; (International Bureau, technical) + 1 (202) 739-0509; (International Bureau, administration) +1 (202) 418-0420; (International Bureau, legal) +1 (202) 739-0415. Fax: (Public Affairs) +1 (202) 418 2809; (International Bureau, technical) +1 (202) 887 6124; (International Bureau, administration) +1 (202) 418 2818; (International Bureau, legal) +1 (202) 887 0175. World Wide Web: http://fcc.gov/, but be prepared for huge file size. Contact: (Public Affairs) Patricia Chew or Sharon Hurd; (International Bureau, technical) Thomas E. Polzin, International Broadcasting, Room 892; (International Bureau, legal) Rod Porter, Esq., Deputy International Bureau Chief, Suite 800; (International Bureau, administration) Scott Blake Harris, Esq., International Bureau Chief. The FCC, whose International Bureau has recently been functioning exceptionally well, regulates all private broadcasting within the United States, and is not affiliated with the Voice of America. The FCC is scheduled to move to a new location around the end of 1996.
Potential of Domestic Shortwave Broadcasting: In 1995, the International Bureau discovered, to its surprise, that there may or may not be a valid legal basis for the present FCC rule prohibiting domestic shortwave broadcasting. (Currently, private U.S. world band stations must be configured to broadcast internationally, a relatively costly proposition.) Although the Bureau has no plans to act on its own in this regard, it may do so should forces within the broadcasting industry—such as AM stations wishing to increase audience size via regional shortwave simulcasting—demonstrate a strong interest in having the rule-making procedure opened on that issue.
Foreign Broadcast Information Service, P.O. Box

2604, Washington DC 20013 USA. Phone: +1 (202) 338-6735. Parented by the CIA (see, above) and working in concert with BBC Monitoring (see, United Kingdom) and selected other organizations, the F.B.I.S., with listening posts in various countries outside the United States, monitors broadcasts worldwide for intelligence-gathering purposes. However, it never engages in broadcasting or jamming of any sort, directly or indirectly.

Government Broadcasting Regulatory Authority—see Federal Communications Commission, above; also, see the non-governmental National Association of Shortwave Broadcasters, below.

KAIJ

Administration Office: Two-if-by-Sea Broadcasting Co., 22720 SE 410th St., Enumclaw WA 89022 USA. Phone/fax: (Mike Parker, California) +1 (818) 606-1254; (Washington State office, if and when operating) +1 (206) 825 4517. Contact: Mike Parker (mark envelope, "please forward"). Relays programs of Dr. Gene Scott. Replies occasionally.
Transmitter: RR#3 Box 120, Frisco TX 75034 USA (physical location: Highway 380, 3.6 miles west of State Rt. 289, near Denton TX). Phone: +1 (214) 346-2758. Contact: Walt Green or Fred Bethel. Station encourages mail to be sent to administration office (see above), which seldom replies.

KGEI—Voice of Friendship—The original owners discontinued transmission from Redwood City, California, during last half of 1994 because of the high cost of operation at that location. However, another organization, the Calvary Chapel, reportedly hopes to reactivate operation from near Twin Falls, Idaho, in the United States, although they have not as yet filed an application with the Federal Communications Commission. They plan to use the KGEI—Voice of Friendship call sign and the aging California 250 kW transmitter, donated by the former owners, for religious transmissions to Latin America, especially Mexico.

KJES—King Jesus Eternal Savior

Station: The Lord's Ranch, Star Route Box 300, Mesquite NM 88048 USA. Phone: +1 (505) 233-3725. Fax: +1 (505) 233 3019. Contact: Michael Reuter, Manager. $1 or return postage required.
Sponsoring Organization: Our Lady's Youth Center, P.O. Box 1422, El Paso TX 79948 USA. Phone: +1 (915) 533-9122.

KNLS—New Life Station

Operations Center: World Christian Broadcasting Corporation, P.O. Box 681706, Franklin TN 37068 USA (letters sent to the Alaska transmitter site are usually forwarded to Franklin). Phone: +1 (615) 371-8707. Fax: +1 (615) 371 8791. Contact: (general) Wesley Jones, Manager, Follow-Up Department; or Steven Towell, Senior Producer, English Language Service; (technical) Michael Osborne, Production Manager. Free quarterly newsletter, pennants, stickers, English-language and Russian-language religious tapes and literature, and English-language learning course materials for Russian speakers. Free information about Alaska. DX books available; 2 IRCs appreciated for each book. Special, individually numbered, limited edition, verification cards issued for each new transmission period. Swaps cancelled stamps from different countries to help listeners round out their stamp collections. Accepts faxed reports. Return postage helpful. Also broadcasts via Russia, but is not known to verify reports for those particular transmissions.
Transmitter Site: P.O. Box 473, Anchor Point AK 99556 USA. Phone: +1 (907) 235-8262. Fax: +1 (907) 235 2326. Contact: (technical) Kevin Chambers, Engineer.

KTBN—Trinity Broadcasting Network:

General Correspondence: P.O. Box A, Santa Ana CA 92711 USA. Phone: +1 (714) 832-2950. Fax: +1 (714) 731 4196. E-mail: tbntalk@aol.com. Contact: Cheryl Gilroy, Secretary; Alice Fields; or Jay Jones, Producer, "Music of Praise." Monthly TBN newsletter. Religious merchandise sold. Return postage helpful.

Technical Correspondence: Engineering/QSL Department, 2442 Michelle Drive, Tustin CA 92680 USA. Phone: +1 (714) 665-2145. Fax: +1 (714) 730 0661. Contact: Ben Miller, WB5TLZ, Director of Engineering.

KVOH—High Adventure Radio

Main Office: P.O. Box 93937, Los Angeles CA 90093 USA. Phone: (general) +1 (805) 520-9460; (technical) +1 (805) 527-6529. Fax: +1 (805) 520 7823. E-mail: 73223.1040@compuserve.com. Contact: (general) John Tayloe, International Program Director; or Pat Kowalick, Producer, "Music of Hope"; Ralph McDevit, Airtime Sales; (head of administration) Paul Johnson, General Manager; (technical) Dr. Don Myers, Chief Engineer. Free stickers, Voice of Hope book, "High Adventure Ministries" pamphlet and sample "Voice of Hope" broadcast tape. Also, see Lebanon. Replies as time permits. As of August, 1995, has been accepting inter alia politically oriented disestablishmentarian programs for leased-time broadcast.
California Branch Office, Nontechnical: P.O Box 7466, Van Nuys, CA 91409 USA.
Canadian Branch Office, Nontechnical: Box 425, Station "E", Toronto, M6H 4E3 Canada. Phone: +1 (416) 898-5447. Contact: Don McLaughlin, Director.
London Office, Nontechnical: BM Box 2575, London WC1N 3XX, United Kingdom. Contact: Paul Ogle, Director.
Singapore Office: Orchard Box 796, Singapore 9123, Singapore.

KWHR-World Harvest Radio:

Administration Office: see WHRI, USA, below.
Transmitter: Although located 6 miles southwest of Naalehu, 8 miles north of South Cape, and 2000 feet west of South Point Road on otherwise friendly Big Island, Hawaii, the folks at this rural transmitter site maintain no post office box in or near Naalehu, and their telephone number is unlisted. Best bet is to contact them via their administration office (see WHRI, below), or to drive by unannounced the next time you vacation on lovely Big Island. If you learn more, please let us know!

Monitor Radio International, Shortwave World Service (all locations), P.O. Box 860, Boston MA 02123 USA. Phone: (general, toll-free within U.S.) (800) 288-7090 or (general elsewhere) +1 (617) 450-2929 [with either number, extension 2060 for schedules or 2929 for Shortwave Helpline]; (Listener Line) +1 (617) 450-7777. Fax: +1 (617) 450 2283. E-mail: (general) radio@csps.com; (letters and reception reports) letterbox@csms.com; (technical questions) letterbox-tech@csms.com. Contact: Catherine Aitken-Smith, Director of International Broadcasting, Herald Broadcasting Syndicate; Lisa Dale, Host, "Letterbox"; Tina Hammers, Response Supervisor. Free stickers and information on Christian Science religion. Christian Science Monitor newspaper and full line of Christian Science books available from 1 Norway Street, Boston MA 02115 USA. Science and Health with Key to the Scriptures by Mary Baker Eddy available in English $14.95 paperback ($16.95 in French, German, Portuguese or Spanish paperback; $24.95 in Czech or Russian hardcover) from Science and Health, P.O. Box 1875, Boston MA 02117 USA. Also, see Northern Mariana Islands.

Monitor Radio International, Shortwave World Service—WSHB, Rt. 2, Box 107A, Pineland SC 29934 USA. Phone: +1 (803) 625-5555. Fax: +1 (803) 625 5559. E-mail: (engineering) cee@wshb.csms.com; (QSL Coordinator) judy@wshb.csms.com. Contact: (technical) Tony Kobatake, Chief Transmitter Engineer; C. Ed Evans, Senior Station Manager; or Judy P. Cooke, QSL Coordinator. This address for technical feedback on South Carolina transmissions only; other inquiries should be directed to the usual Boston address.

National Association of Shortwave Broadcasters

Headquarters: 11185 Columbia Pike, Silver Spring MD 20901 USA. Phone: +1 (301) 593-5409. Fax: +1 (301) 681 0099. Contact: Tulio R. Haylock, Secretary-Treasurer.

Association of most private U.S. world band stations, as well as a restricted group of other international broadcasters, equipment manufacturers and organizations related to shortwave broadcasting, but apparently not listener-oriented organizations. Includes committees on various subjects, such as digital shortwave radio. Interfaces with the Federal Communications Commission's International Bureau and other broadcasting-related organizations to advance the interests of its members. Publishes *NASB Newsletter* for members and associate members; free sample upon request on letterhead of an appropriate organization. Annual one-day convention held near Washington DC's National Airport each May; non-members wishing to attend should contact the Secretary-Treasurer in advance; convention fee $50/person. Headquarters plans to move from Silver Spring to Miami in early 1996.

Membership Office: 276 N. Bobwhite, Orange CA 92669 USA. Phone/fax: (membership information) +1 (714) 771-1843. Contact: William E. "Ted" Haney, Membership Chairman, NASB. Membership: (single-transmitter private U.S. broadcasters) $500/year; (multiple-transmitter private U.S. broadcasters) $1,000/year. Associate Membership (international broadcasting and broadcasting- related organizations other than private U.S. stations may be accepted for associate membership, subject to the approval of existing members): $500/year.

Public Radio International, 100 North Sixth Street, Suite 900A, Minneapolis MN 55403 USA. Phone: (general) +1 (612) 338-5000, (New Business Development) +1 (612) 330-9238. Fax: +1 (612) 330 9222. Contact: Beth Talisman, Senior Manager, New Business Development. Makes available selected international broadcasts for those PRI radio stations within the United States which choose to air them in whole or in part, often after having taped them for later replay. Interestingly, PRI's placement of international programs seems to have increased, rather than decreased, the interest in world band listening within the United States.

Radio Martí, 330 Independence Avenue SW, Washington DC 20547 USA. Phone: +1 (202) 401-7013. Fax: +1 (202) 401 3340. Contact: (general) Rolando Bonacher, Director of Radio; Bruce Sherman, Deputy Director of Radio; (technical) Mike Pallone, Technical Director.

RFE-RL
Prague Headquarters: Vinohradská 1, 110 00 Prague 1, Czech Republic. Phone: (switchboard) +42 (2) 24-21-00-00; (President) +42 (2) 24-22-04-88; (Board of Directors) +42 (2) 24-21-14-03; Fax: (Belarussian Service) +42 (2) 24 23 53 00; (Ukrainian Service) +42 (2) 24 23 05 87; (Technical Operations) +42 (2) 24 21 15 01. Contact: Kevin Close, President; Luke Springer, Director; or Robert McMahon, Director of News & Current Affairs.

Washington Office: 1201 Connecticut Avenue NW, Washington DC 20036 USA. Phone: (general) +1 (202) 457-6900. Fax: +1 (202) 457 6992. Contact: Jane Lester, Secretary of the Corporation. This organization has wound down considerably from its Cold War days, with its remaining transmission facilities now being managed by the Voice of America. Programs have increasingly been taking the viewpoint of the target countries, rather than the once largely pro-Western perspective formerly associated with the station.

Trans World Radio, International Headquarters, P.O. Box 8700, Cary NC 27512 USA. Phone: +1 (919) 460-3700. Fax: +1 (919) 460 3702. Contact: (general) John Vaught, Public Relations; Rosemarie Jaszka, Director, Public Relations; or Mark Christensen; (technical) Glenn W. Sink, Assistant Vice President, International Operations. Free "Towers to Eternity" publication for those living in the U.S. Technical correspondence should be sent directly to the country where the transmitter is located—Guam, Monaco, Swaziland.

Voice of America/VOA—All Transmitter Locations
Main Office, Nontechnical: 330 Independence Avenue SW, Washington DC 20547 USA. If contacting the VOA directly is impractical, write c/o the American Embassy or USIS Center in your country. Phone: (to hear VOA-English live) +1 (202) 619-1979; (Office of External Affairs) +1 (202) 619-2358 or +1 (202) 619-2039; (Africa Division) +1 (202) 619-1666 or +1 (202) 619-2879; (Audience Research) +1 (202) 619-3047; (administration) +1 (202) 619-1088. Fax: (general information for listeners outside the United States) +1 (202) 376 1066; (Public Liaison for listeners within the United States) +1 (202) 619 1241; (Office of External Affairs) +1 (202) 205 0634 or +1 (202) 205 2875; (Africa Division) +1 (202) 619 1664; (Audience Research) +1 (202) 619 0211; (administration) +1 (202) 619 0085. E-mail: (general inquires outside the United States) letters@voa.gov; (reception reports) qsl@voa.gov; (general inquires within the United States) letters-usa@voa.gov; (Audience Research) ke@voa.gov. FTP: ftp.voa.gov. Gopher: gopher.voa.gov. Contact: (listeners outside the United States) Mrs. Betty Thompson, Audience Mail Division, Room G-759-C; (listeners anywhere) Audience Mail Division, Room G-759-C; Leo Sarkisian or Rita Rochelle, Africa Division; or Kim Andrew Elliott, Audience Research Officer; (head of administration) Geoffrey Cowan, Director. Free stickers and calendars. Free "Music Time in Africa" calendar, to non-U.S. addresses only, from Mrs. Rita Rochelle, Africa Division, Room 1622. If you're an American and miffed because you can't receive these goodies from the VOA, don't blame the station—they're only following the law. Budget cutbacks at the VOA continue. Further information on these cutbacks may be obtained from the station itself, as well as the VOA employees' union [AFGE Local 1812/USIA, 301 4th Street SW, Room 348, Washington DC 20547 USA; phone +1 (202) 619-4759; Contact: Stacey Rose-Blass]. The VOA occasionally hosts international broadcasting conventions.
Main Office, Technical: 330 Independence Avenue SW, Washington DC 20547 USA. Contact: Mrs. Irene Greene, QSL Desk, Audience Mail Division, Room G-759-C. E-mail: qsl@voa.gov. Also, see Ascension, Botswana, Kuwait, São Tomé e Príncipe and Sri Lanka.
Frequency and Monitoring Office, Technical: SW B/EOF:Frequency Management & Monitoring Division, 4605 Cohen Bldg., 330 Independence Avenue SW, Washington DC 20547 USA. Phone: +1 (202) 619-1669 or +1 (202) 619-1675. Fax: +1 (202) 619 1680 or +1 (202) 619 1781. E-mail: ferguson@beng.voa.gov. Contact: Daniel Ferguson. Enclosing pre-addressed labels will help secure a reply.

Voice of America/VOA—Delano Relay Station, Rt. 1, Box 1350, Delano CA 93215 USA. Phone: +1 (805) 725-0150 or +1 (805) 861-4136. Fax: +1 (805) 725 6511. Contact: (technical) Jim O'Neill, Engineer; or Gene Pitts, Manager. Nontechnical correspondence should be sent to the VOA address in Washington.

Voice of America/VOA—Greenville Relay Station, P.O. Box 1826, Greenville NC 27834 USA. Phone: +1 (919) 758-2171 or +1 (919) 752-7115. Fax: +1 (919) 752 5959. Contact: (technical) Bruce Hunter, Manager. Nontechnical correspondence should be sent to the VOA address in Washington.

WEWN Worldwide Catholic Radio
Station office: Eternal Word Radio Network (ETWN), Catholic Radio Service, P.O. Box 100234, Birmingham AL 35210 USA. Phone: (toll-free within U.S.) (800) 585-9396; (elsewhere) +1 (205) 672-7200. Fax: +1 (205) 951 0340. E-mail: 70413.40@compuserve.com. Contact: (general) William Steltemeier, President; Mrs. Gwen Carr, Office Manager; or W. Glen Tapley, Director of Network Radio Operations; (technical) Frank Phillips, General Manager; Gary Gagnon, Frequency Manager; or Matt Cadak, Chief Engineer. Responds to listener correspondence on-air and by mail. Free *Gabriel's Horn* newsletter. Sells religious publications, such as *Gospel of Life* ($4 or more donation),

as well as T-shirts ($12 or more donation), sweatshirts, WEWN program tapes, Sangean world band radios and related articles. A list of items for sale is available upon request (VISA/MC) by phone, fax or mail. IRC or return postage appreciated for correspondence. Although a Catholic entity, WEWN is not an official station of the Vatican, which operates its own Vatican Radio (see). Rather, WEWN reflects the activities of Mother M. Angelica and the Eternal Word Foundation, Inc. Donations and bequests accepted by the Eternal Word Foundation.

Transmission Facility: P.O. Box 176, Vandiver AL 35176 USA. Phone: +1 (205) 672-7200. Fax: +1 (205) 672 9988. Contact: Norman Williams, Manager, Planning & Installation.

Religious Order: Our Lady of The Angels Monastery, 5817 Old Leeds Road, Birmingham AL 35210 USA. Phone: +1 (205) 956-5987.

WGTG—Glory to God, Box 1131, Copper Hill TN 37517 USA. Phone: +1 (706) 492-5944. Contact: Dave Franz, Manager. Transmitter, 50 kW, is reportedly located just across the state line in McCaysville, Georgia, and should commence regular operation around early 1996.

WHRI—World Harvest Radio, WHRI/KWHR, P.O. Box 12, South Bend IN 46624 USA. Phone: +1 (219) 291-8200. Fax: +1 (219) 291 9043. Contact: (general) Joe Hill, Operations Manager; Pete Sumrall, Vice President; Joe Brashier; or Robert Willinger; (technical) Douglas Garlinger, Chief Engineer. Free stickers. WHRI T-shirts $12 from 61300 S. Ironwood Road, South Bend IN 46614 USA. Return postage appreciated. Carries programs from various political organizations; these may be contacted either directly (see Disestablishmentarian, earlier in this chapter) or via WHRI. As of May 1995, has had guidelines that leased-time programs must meet in order to be aired.

WINB (when replacement transmitters installed), World International Broadcast Network, P.O. Box 88, Red Lion PA 17356 USA. Phone: (general) +1 (717) 244-5360; (administration) +1 (717) 246-1681; (studio) +1 (717) 244-3145. Fax: +1 (717) 244 9316. Contact: (general) Mrs. Sally Spyker, Correspondence Secretary; John Stockdale, Manager; Clyde H. Campbell, C.F.O.; or John H. Norris, Owner; (technical) Fred W. Wise, Technical Director. Return postage helpful outside United States. No giveaways or items for sale. Left the air after having dropped a roster of disestablishmentarian programs and terminating relations with the controversial Pastor Pete Peters, but plans to be back in operation in 1996 with apolitical religious programming, using two energy-efficient 50 kW shortwave transmitters that are currently being installed.

WJCR, P.O. Box 91, Upton KY 42784 USA. Phone: +1 (502) 369-8614. Contact: Pastor Don Powell, President; Gerri Powell; or Trish Powell. Free religious printed matter. Return postage appreciated. Actively solicits listener contributions.

WMLK—Assemblies of Yahweh, P.O. Box C, Bethel PA 19507 USA. Toll free telephone (U.S only) +1 (800) 523 3827; (elsewhere) +1 (717) 933-4518. Contact: (general) Elder Jacob O. Mayer, Manager & Producer of "The Open Door to the Living World"; (technical) Gary McAvin. Free *Yahweh* magazine, stickers and religious material. Bibles, audio tapes and religious paperback books offered for sale. Replies slowly, but enclosing return postage or IRCs helps speed things up.

WRMI—Radio Miami Internacional

Main Office: P.O. Box 526852, Miami FL 33152 USA. Phone: +1 (305) 267-1728. Fax: +1 (305) 819 8756 or +1 (305) 267 9253. E-mail: 71163.175@compuserve.com. Contact: (general) Jeff White, Producer, "Viva Miami!"; (technical) Indalecio "Kiko" Espinosa, Chief Engineer. Free station stickers. T-shirts $15, baseball-style hats $10—both postpaid worldwide. Radio Miami Internacional also acts as a broker for Cuban exile programs aired via U.S. stations WHRI and WRNO. Technical correspondence may be sent to either

WRMI or the station over which the program was heard.

Venezuelan Office: Apartado 2122, Valencia 2001, Venezuela. Phone:/fax: + 58 (45) 810-362. Contact: Yoslen Silva.

WRNO, Box 100, New Orleans LA 70181 USA; or 4539 I-10 Service Road North, Metairie LA 70006 USA. Phone: +1 (504) 889-2424. Fax: +1 (504) 889 0602. Contact: Joseph Mark Costello III, General Manager; David Schneider, Public Relations Manager; Joe Pollett; or Jack Bruce. Single copy of program guide for 2 IRCs or an SASE. Free stickers sometimes available. T-shirts sometimes available for $10. Carries programs from various political organizations; these may be contacted either directly (see Disestablishmentarian, above) or via WRNO. As of May, 1995, following the Oklahoma City bombing, had inaugurated guidelines that leased-time programs must meet in order to be aired; however, within two months some programs that apparently had been dropped as inappropriate were once again being aired. Although this station is not formally up for sale, parties seriously interested in acquiring it should fax +1 (301) 587-8801. Correct reception reports verified for 2 IRCs or an SASE.

WSHB—see Monitor Radio International, above.

WVHA—World Voice of Historic Adventism:

Administration Studio: P.O. Box 1844, Mount Dora FL 32757 USA. Phone: (toll-free phone, USA only) (800) 447-5683; (elsewhere) +1 (904) 735-1844. Fax: +1 (904) 735 4055. Contact: (general) Pastor John Osborne; (technical) Gordon Simkin, Chief Engineer & Producer, "DXTRA." This station is not affiliated with Adventist World Radio or its parent organization. Because of the Federal government's activity against another breakaway Adventist group, the Branch Davidians of Waco, Texas, WVHA reportedly has taken security and stockpiling measures to hold out in the event of a Waco-style attack against them. Audio cassette recordings of sermons available at a starting price of $3. Video recordings available on NTSC and PAL; prices vary; reportedly no longer issues the video, *The Military Takeover of America*, with Mark Koernke. Plans to add a new antenna and possibly a second transmitter for North America.

Transmitter: P.O. Box A, Olamon ME 04467 USA. Phone: +1 (207) 732-9842. Fax: +1 (207) 732 5475. Contact: David L. Evans.

WWCR—World Wide Christian Radio, F.W. Robbert Broadcasting Co., 1300 WWCR Avenue, Nashville TN 37218 USA. Phone: +1 (615) 255-1300. Fax: +1 (615) 255 1311. E-mail: (general) wwcr@aol.com; (Operations Manager) wwcrl@aol.com. Contact: (general) Doug Nathan; Sue O'Neill, Executive Producer, Worldwide Country Radio; Chuck Adair, Sales Representative (heads of administration) George McClintock, K4BTY, General Manager; Adam W. Lock, Sr., WA2JAL, Operations Manager; (technical) Watt Hariston, Chief Engineer. Free program guide, updated monthly. Return postage helpful. Replies as time permits. Carries programs from various political organizations; these may be contacted either directly (see Disestablishmentarian, earlier in this chapter) or via WWCR. As of May, 1995, has had guidelines that leased-time programs must meet in order to be aired.

WWV/WWVB (official time and frequency stations), Frequency-Time Broadcast Services Section, Time and Frequency Division, NIST, Mail Station 847, 325 Broadway, Boulder CO 80303 USA. Phone: (tape recording of latest shortwave technical propagation data and forecast) +1 (303) 497-3235; (live WWV audio) +1 (303) 499-7111; (Broadcast Manager) +1 (303) 497-3281; (Public Affairs) +1 (303) 497-3246; (Institute for Telecommunications Sciences) +1 (303) 497-3484. Phone/fax: (technical, call first before trying to fax) +1 (303) 497 3914. Fax: (Public Affairs) +1 (303) 497-3371. Contact: (general) Fred P. McGehan, Public Affairs Officer; (head of administration) Roger Beehler, Broadcast Manager; (technical) James C. Maxton,

Adam Lock adjusts one of WWCR's 100 kW
Continental transmitters.

Engineer-in-Charge; or Matt Deutsch, Engineer. Along
with branch sister station WWVH in Hawaii (see below),
WWV and WWVB are the official time and frequency stations of the United States, operating over longwave
(WWVB) on 60 kHz, and over shortwave (WWV) on 2500,
5000, 10000, 15000 and 20000 kHz. Free Special Publication
432 "NIST Time & Frequency Services" pamphlet. Plans to
increase power of WWVB, currently 13 kW, before end of
decade.

WWVH (official time and frequency station), NIST—
Hawaii, P.O. Box 417, Kekaha, Kauai HI 96752 USA. Phone:
+1 (808) 335-4361. Fax: +1 (808) 335 4747. Contact: (technical)
Dean T. Okayama, Engineer-in-Charge. E-mail: None
planned. Along with headquarters sister stations WWV
and WWVB (see preceding), WWVH is the official time and
frequency station of the United States, operating on 2500,
5000, 10000 and 15000 kHz. Free Special Publication 432
"NIST Time & Frequency Services" pamphlet.

WYFR—Family Radio

Nontechnical: Family Stations, Inc., 290 Hegenberger
Road, Oakland CA 94621 USA. Phone: (toll-free, U.S. only)
(800) 543-1495; (elsewhere) +1 (510) 568-6200. Fax: +1 (510) 633
7983. Contact: Producer, "Mailbag"; Producer, "Open
Forum"; Steffanie A. Yefimov, Secretary; or Thomas A.
Schaff, Shortwave Program Manager. Free stickers, bookmarks, pocket diaries (sometimes), religious books, booklets, cassettes, and quarterly *Family Radio News* magazine. Return postage or 2 IRCs helpful.

Technical: WYFR/Family Radio, 10400 NW 240th Street,
Okeechobee FL 34972 USA. Phone: +1 (941) 763-0281. Fax: +1
(941) 763 8867. Contact: Dan Elyea, Engineering Manager.

UZBEKISTAN   World Time +5

Warning—Mail Theft: Due to increasing local mail theft,
Radio Tashkent suggests that those wishing to correspond
should try using one of the drop-mailing addresses listed
below.

Radio Tashkent, 49 Khorezm Street, 740047 Tashkent,
Uzbekistan. Contact: V. Danchev, Correspondence Section;
Lenora Hannanowa; Zulfiya Ibragimova; Mrs. G.
Babadjanova, Chief Director of Programs; or Mrs. Florida
Perevertailo, Producer, "At Listeners' Request." Free pen-
nants, badges, wallet calendars and postcards. Books in
English by Uzbek writers are apparently available for pur-
chase. Station offers free membership to two clubs: The
"Salum Aleikum Listeners' Club" is open to anyone who

asks to join, whereas "Radio Tashkent DX Club" is open to
listeners who send in ten reception reports that are verified by the station. Station has tentative plans to expand
its Southeast Asian Service.

London Address: 72 Wigmore Street, London W18 9L,
United Kingdom.

Bangkok Address: 848-850 Ramapur Road, Bangkok 10050,
Thailand.

Uzbek Radio—*see* Radio Tashkent for details.

VANUATU   World Time +12 (+11 midyear)

Radio Vanuatu, Information & Public Relations, P.M.B.
049, Port Vila, Vanuatu. Phone: +678 22-999. Fax: +678 22 026.
Contact: (technical) K.J. Page, Principal Engineer.

VATICAN CITY STATE   World Time +1 (+2 midyear)

Vatican Radio

Main and Promotion Offices: 00120 Città del Vaticano,
Vatican City State. Phone: (general) +39 (6) 698-83551;
(Promotion Office and schedules) +39 (6) 698-83045 or +39 (6)
698-83463; (technical) +39 (6) 698-85258. Fax: (general) +39 (6)
698 83237; (technical) +39 (6) 698 85125 or +39 (6) 698 85062.
Contact: (general) Elizabetta Vitalini Sacconi, Promotion
Office and schedules; Eileen O'Neill, Head of Program
Development, English Service; Fr. Federico Lombardi, S.J.,
Program Manager; P. Moreau, Ufficio Promozione; S. de
Maillardoz, International Relations; or Veronica
Scarisbrick, Producer, "On the Air;" (head of administra-
tion) Fr. Pasquale Borgomeo, S.I., Direttore Generale; (tech-
nical) Umberto Tolaini, Frequency Manager, Direzione
Tecnica; Sergio Salvatori, Assistant Frequency Manager,
Direzione Tecnica; or Giovanni Serra, Frequency
Management Department. Correspondence sought on religious and programming matters, rather than the technical
minutiae of radio. Free station stickers and paper pennants. Music CDs $13 and "Sixty Years...a Single Day" PAL
video on Vatican Radio for 15,000 lire, including postage,
from the Promotion Office.

Tokyo Office: 2-10-10 Shiomi, Koto-ku, Tokyo 135, Japan.
Fax: +81 (3) 5632 4457.

VENEZUELA   World Time -4

Note: According to radio writer/traveler Don Moore,
Venezuelan stations are cutting back on their hours of
operation to save electricity during the current period of
economic recession.

Ecos del Torbes, Apartado 152, San Cristóbal 5001-A,
Táchira, Venezuela. Phone: +58 (76) 438-244. Contact: (gen-
eral) Daphne González Zerpa, Directora; (technical) Ing.
Iván Escobar S., Jefe Técnico.

Radio Frontera (when active), Edificio Radio, San
Antonio del Táchira, Táchira, Venezuela. Phone: +58 (76)
782-92. Fax: +58 (76) 78508. Contact: Modesto Marchena,
Gerente General. May reply to correspondence in Spanish.
$1 or return postage suggested. If no reply, try with $1 via
Sr. Contín at Radio Mara, below.

**Radio Mundial Los Andes (Radio Los Andes
1040)**, Calle 44 No. 3-57, Mérida, Venezuela. Phone: +58
(74) 639-286. Contact: Roger Vivas, Director. May reply to
correspondence in Spanish. $1 or return postage suggest-
ed.

Radio Nacional de Venezuela

Main Office: Apartado 3979, Caracas 1050, Venezuela.
Phone: +58 (2) 745-166. Contact: Martin G. Delfin, English
News Director; Jaime Alsina, Director; or Sra. Haydee
Briceno, Gerente. Free 50th anniversary stickers, while
they last, and other small souvenirs. Lone Star exile Marty
Delfin, a former TV newscaster, hails from San Antonio
and UT/Austin, Texas. If no response, try Apartado 50700,
Caracas 1050, Venezuela.

Miami Postal Address: Jet Cargo International, M-7, P.O.
Box 020010, Miami FL 33102 USA. Contact: Martin G. Delfin,
English News Director.

Radio Occidente (when active), Carrera 4a. No. 6-46,

Tovar 5143, Mérida, Venezuela.

Radio Rumbos
Main Address: Apartado 2618, Caracas 1010A, Venezuela. Phone: +58 (2) 261-0666. Fax: +58 (2) 335 164. Contact: (general) Andrés Felipe Serrano, Vice-Presidente; (technical) Ing. José Corrales. Free pamphlets, keychains and stickers. $1 or IRC required. Replies occasionally to correspondence in Spanish.
Miami Address: P.O. Box 020010, Miami FL 33102 USA.

Radio Táchira, Apartado 152, San Cristóbal 5001-A, Táchira, Venezuela. Phone: +58 (76) 430-009. Contact: Desirée González Zerpa, Directora; or Eleázar Silva Malavé, Gerente.

Radio Valera, Av. 10 No. 9-31, Valera 3102, Trujillo, Venezuela. Phone: +58 (71) 53-744. Replies to correspondence in Spanish. Return postage required. This station has been on the same world band frequency for almost 50 years, which is a record for Latin America.

VIETNAM World Time +7

Bac Thai Broadcasting Service—contact via Voice of Vietnam—Overseas Service, below.

Lai Chau Broadcasting Service—contact via Voice of Vietnam—Overseas Service, below.

Lam Dong Broadcasting Service, Da Lat, Vietnam. Contact: Hoang Van Trung. Replies slowly to correspondence in Vietnamese, but French may also suffice.

Son La Broadcasting Service, Son La, Vietnam. Contact: Nguyen Hang, Director. Replies slowly to correspondence in Vietnamese, but French may also suffice.

Voice of Vietnam—Domestic Service (Dài Tiêng Nói Viêt Nam, TNVN)—Addresses and contact numbers are for all sections of Voice of Vietnam—Overseas Service, below. Contact: Phan Quang, Director General.

Voice of Vietnam—Overseas Service
Transmission Facility (main address for nontechnical correspondence and general verifications): 58 Quán Sú, Hànôi, Vietnam. Phone: +84 (4) 257-870. Fax: +84 (4) 255 765. Contact: Dao Dinh Tuan, Director of External Broadcasting. Free paper pennant and, occasionally upon request, Vietnamese stamps. $1 helpful, but IRCs apparently of no use. Replies slowly.
Studios (nontechnical correspondence and general verifications): 45 Ba Trieu Street, Hànôi, Vietnam. Phone: +84 (4) 255-669. Fax: +84 (4) 261 122. Contact and other data: as in *Transmission Facility*, preceding.
Technical Correspondence: Office of Radio Reception Quality, Central Department of Radio and Television Broadcast Engineering, Vietnam General Corporation of Posts and Telecommunications, Hànôi, Vietnam.

Yen Bai Broadcasting Station— contact via Voice of Vietnam, Overseas Service, above.

YEMEN World Time +3

Republic of Yemen Radio—Program 1, Ministry of Information, San'a, Yemen. Contact: (general) English Service; (technical) Abdullah Farhan, Technical Director.

Republic of Yemen Radio—Program 2 (when operating), P.O. Box 2182, Tawahi, Aden, Yemen. Contact: Ahmed Abdulla Fadaq, Director of Foreign Programs; or Mohammed Aljoridi, General Director of Public Relations. This station's equipment reportedly was completely destroyed during the civil war. However, the present government has promised to make the necessary repairs.

YUGOSLAVIA World Time +1 (+2 midyear)

Radiotelevizija Srbije, Hilendarska 2/IV, 11000 Belgrade, Serbia, Yugoslavia. Fax: +381 (11) 332 014. Contact: (technical) B. Miletic, Operations Manager of HF Broadcasting.

Radio Yugoslavia, Hilendarska 2, P.O. Box 200, 11000 Belgrade, Serbia, Yugoslavia. Phone: +381 (11) 346-884 or +381 (11) 346-801; (listener voice mail) +381 (11) 344-455. Fax: +381 (11) 332 014. Contact: (general) Nikola Ivanovic,

Director; Aleksandar Georgiev; Aleksandar Popovic, Head of Public Relations; Pance Zafirovski, Head of Programs; or Slobodan Topovic, Producer, "Post Office Box 200/Radio Hams' Corner"; (technical) B. Miletic, Operations Manager of HF Broadcasting, Technical Department; or Rodoljub Medan, Chief Engineer. Free pennants, stickers, pins and tourist information. $1 helpful.

ZAIRE World Time +1 Western, including Kinshasa; +2 Eastern

La Voix du Zaire—Bukavu, B.P. 475, Bukavu, Zaïre. Contact: Jacques Nyembo-Kibeya; Kalume Kavue Katumbi; or Baruti Lusongela, Directeur. $1 or return postage required. Replies slowly. Correspondence in French preferred.

La Voix du Zaire—Kinshasa (when operating), B.P. 3171, Kinshasa-Gombe, Zaïre. Contact: Ayimpam Mwan-a-ngo, Directeur des Programmes, Radio; or Faustin Mbula, Ingenieur Technicien. Letters should be sent via registered mail. $1 or 3 IRCs helpful. Correspondence in French preferred.

La Voix du Zaire—Kisangani (when operating), B.P. 1745, Kisangani, Zaïre. Contact: (general) Lumeto lue Lumeto, Le Directeur Regional de l'O.Z.R.T.; (technical) Lukusa Kowumayi Branly, Technician. $1 or 2 IRCs required. Correspondence in French preferred. Replies to North American listeners sometimes are mailed via the Oakland, California, post office.

Radio Lubumbashi, La Voix du Zaire (when operating), B.P. 7296, Lubumbashi, Zaïre. Contact: Senga Lokavu, Le Chef du Service de l'Audiovisuel; Bébé Beshelemu, Le Directeur Regional de l'O.Z.R.T; or Mulenga Kanso, Le Chef du Service Logistique. Letters should be sent via registered mail. $1 or 3 IRCs helpful. Correspondence in French preferred.

ZAMBIA World Time +2

Christian Voice
Station: Private Bag E606, Lusaka, Zambia. Phone/fax: +260 (1) 274-251. Contact: Andrew Flynn, Transmitter Engineer;

or Philip Haggar, Station Manager. Free pens and pins featuring station logo. This station broadcasts Christian teachings and programs on farming, education, health and children's affairs.

United Kingdom Office: Christian Vision, Ryder Street, West Bromwich B70 0EJ, United Kingdom.

Radio Zambia, Broadcasting House, P.O. Box 50015, Lusaka, Zambia. Phone: +260 (1) 220-865. Fax: +260 (1) 254 013. Contact: (general) Willis F. Mulongoti; or Noble C. Makungu; (head of administration) Emmanuel Chayi, Acting Director General; (technical) W. Lukozu, Project Engineer. $1 required, and postal correspondence should be sent via registered mail. Replies slowly and irregularly.

ZIMBABWE World Time +2

Zimbabwe Broadcasting Corporation, P.O. Box HG444, Highlands, Harare, Zimbabwe. Phone: +263 (4) 707-222. Fax: (technical) +263 (4) 498 608. Contact: (technical) I. Magoryo, Engineer.

Credits: Craig Tyson (Australia); also Tony Jones (Paraguay), Henrik Klemetz (Colombia), Marie Lamb (USA), Lawrence Magne (USA), Número Uno (USA) and Radio Nuevo Mundo (Japan); with special thanks to David Crystal (Israel), DX Moscow/Anatoly Klepov (Russia), Jock Elliott (USA), Manosij Guha (India), Takayuki Inoue (Japan/Latin America), Ian McFarland (Canada), Richard McVicar/HCJB (Ecuador), Toshimichi Ohtake (Japan), Sheryl Paszkiewicz (USA), George Poppin (USA) and Dieter K. Riebold (Germany).

Glossary

Terms and Abbreviations Used in World Band Radio

A wide variety of terms and abbreviations are used in world band radio. Some are specialized and may need explanation; several are foreign words that benefit from translation; and yet others are simply adaptations of common usage.

Here, then, is PASSPORT'S guide to what's what in world band buzzwords. For a thorough writeup on the terms used in evaluating how well a world band radio performs, see the RDI White Paper, How to Interpret Receiver Specifications and Lab Tests.

Active Antenna. An antenna that electronically amplifies signals. Active antennas are typically mounted indoors, but some models can also be mounted outdoors. Active antennas take up relatively little space, but their amplification circuits may introduce certain types of problems that can result in unwanted sounds being heard. See Passive Antenna.

Adjacent-Channel Rejection. See Selectivity.

AGC. See Automatic Gain Control.

Alt. Freq. Alternative frequency or channel. Frequency or channel that may be used unexpectedly in place of the regularly scheduled one.

Amateur Radio. See Hams.

AM Band. The local radio band, which currently runs from 520 to 1611 kHz (530–1705 kHz in the Western Hemisphere), within the Medium Frequency (MF) range of the radio spectrum. Outside North America, it is usually called the mediumwave (MW) band. However, in one or two Latin American countries it is sometimes called, by the general public and a few stations, *onda larga*—strictly speaking, a misnomer.

Amplified Antenna. See Active Antenna.

Analog Frequency Readout. Needle-and-dial tuning, greatly inferior to synthesized tuning for scanning the world band airwaves. See Synthesizer.

Audio Quality, Audio Fidelity. For purposes of PASSPORT'S equipment analyses, audio quality means the freedom from distortion—as well as audio bandwidth within the range of audio frequencies appropriate to world band reception of music—of a signal fed through a receiver's entire circuitry (not just the audio stage) from the antenna input through to the speaker terminals. Also, see High Fidelity.

Automatic Gain Control (AGC). Smoothes out fluctuations in signal strength brought about by fading, a regular occurrence with world band signals.

AV. A Voz—Portuguese for "Voice of."

Bandwidth. A key variable that determines selectivity (see), bandwidth is the amount of radio signal at –6 dB a radio's circuitry will let pass through, and thus be heard. With world band channel spacing at 5 kHz, the best single bandwidths are usually in the vicinity of 3 to 6 kHz. Better radios offer two or more selectable bandwidths: one of 5 to 7 kHz or so for when a station is in the clear, and one or more others between 2 to 4 kHz for when a station is hemmed in by other stations next to it. Proper selectivity is a key determinant of the aural quality of what you hear.

Baud. Rate by which radioteletype (see), radiofax (see) and other digital data are transmitted.

BC. Broadcasting, Broadcasting Company, Broadcasting Corporation.

Broadcast. A radio or TV transmission meant for the general public. Compare Utility Stations, Hams.

BS. Broadcasting Station, Broadcasting Service.

Cd. Ciudad—Spanish for "City."

Channel. An everyday term to indicate where a station is supposed to be located on the dial. World band channels are spaced exactly 5 kHz apart. Stations operating outside this norm are "off-channel" (for these, PASSPORT provides resolution to better than 1 kHz to aid in station identification).

Chugging, Chuffing. The sound made by some synthesized tuning systems when the tuning knob is turned. Called "chugging" or "chuffing," as it is suggestive of the rhythmic "chug, chug" sound of a steam engine or "chugalug" gulping.

Cl. Club, Clube.

Cult. Cultura, Cultural.

Default. The setting at which a high-tech radio normally operates, and to which it will eventually return.

Digital Frequency Display, Digital Tuning. See Synthesizer.

Dipole Antenna. See Passive Antenna.

Domestic Service. See DS.

DS. Domestic Service—Broadcasting intended primarily for audiences in the broadcaster's home country. However, some domestic programs are beamed on world band to expatriates and other kinfolk abroad, as well as interested foreigners. Compare ES.

DX, DXers, DXing. From an old telegraph term "to DX"; that is, to communicate over a great distance. Thus, DXers are those who specialize in finding distant or exotic stations. Few world band listeners are considered to be regular DXers, but many others seek out DX stations every now and then—usually by bandscanning, which is greatly facilitated by PASSPORT'S Blue Pages.

Dynamic Range. The ability of a receiver to handle weak signals in the presence of strong competing signals within the same world band segment (see World Band Spectrum). Sets with inferior dynamic range sometimes "overload," causing a mishmash of false signals up and down—and even beyond—the segment being received.

Earliest Heard (or Latest Heard). See key at the bottom of each "Blue Page." If the PASSPORT monitoring team cannot establish the definite sign-on (or sign-off) time of a station, the earliest (or latest) time that the station could be traced is indicated by a triangular "flag." This means that the station almost certainly operates beyond the time shown by that "flag." It also means that, unless you live relatively close to the station, you're unlikely to be able to hear it beyond that "flagged" time.

EBS. Economic Broadcasting Station, a type of station sometimes found in China.

ECSS. Exalted-carrier selectable sideband, a term no longer in general use. See Synchronous Detector.

Ed, Educ. Educational, Educação, Educadora.

Electrical Noise. See Noise.

Em. Emissora, Emisora, Emissor, Emetteur—in effect, "station" in various languages.

Enhanced Fidelity. See High Fidelity.

EP. Emissor Provincial—Portuguese for "Provincial Station."

ER. Emissor Regional—Portuguese for "Regional Station."

Ergonomics. How handy and comfortable a set is to operate, especially hour after hour.

ES. External Service—Broadcasting intended primarily for audiences abroad. Compare DS.

External Service. See ES.

F. Friday.

Fax. See Radiofax.

Feeder. A utility transmission from the broadcaster's home country to a relay site some distance away. Although these specialized transmissions carry world band programming, they are not intended to be received by the general public. Many world band radios can process these quasi-broadcasts anyway. Feeders operate in lower sideband (LSB), upper sideband (USB) or independent sideband (termed ISL if heard on the lower side, ISU if heard on the upper side) modes. See Single Sideband, Utility Stations.

Frequency. The standard term to indicate where a station is located on the dial—regardless of whether it is "on-channel" or "off-channel" (see Channel). Measured in kilohertz (kHz) or Megahertz (MHz). Either measurement is equally valid, but to minimize confusion PASSPORT designates frequencies only in kHz.

GMT. Greenwich Mean Time—See World Time.

Hams. Government-licensed amateur radio hobbyists who *transmit* to each other by radio, often by single sideband (see), for pleasure within special amateur bands. Many of these bands are within the shortwave spectrum (see). This is the same spectrum used by world band radio, but world band and ham radio, which laymen sometimes confuse with each other, are two very separate entities.

Harmonic, Harmonic Radiation, Harmonic Signal. Weak spurious repeat of a signal in multiple(s) of the fundamental, or "real," frequency. Thus, the third harmonic of a mediumwave AM station on 1120 kHz might be heard faintly on 4480 kHz within the world band spectrum. Stations almost always try to avoid harmonic radiation, but in rare cases have been known to amplify a harmonic signal so they can operate inexpensively on a second frequency.

Hash. Electrical noise. See Noise.

High Fidelity, Enhanced Fidelity. Radios with good audio performance and certain high-tech circuits can improve upon the fidelity of world band reception. Among the newer fidelity-enhancing techniques is Synchronous Detection (see).

Image Rejection. A key type of spurious-signal rejection (see).

Independent Sideband. See Single Sideband.

Interference. Sounds from other stations, notably on adjacent channels or the same channel ("co-channel"), that are disturbing the one you are trying to hear. Worthy radios reduce interference by having good selectivity (see).

International Telecommunication Union (ITU). The regulatory body, headquartered in Geneva, for all international telecommunications, including world band radio. Sometimes incorrectly written as "International Telecommunications Union."

Inverted-L Antenna. See Passive Antenna.

Ionosphere. See Propagation.

Irr. Irregular operation or hours of operation; i.e., schedule tends to be unpredictable.

ISB. Independent sideband. See Single Sideband.

ISL. Independent sideband, lower. See Feeder.

ISU. Independent sideband, upper. See Feeder.

ITU. See International Telecommunication Union.

Jamming. Deliberate interference to a transmission with the intent of discouraging listening. Jamming is practiced much less now than it was during the Cold War.

kHz. Kilohertz, the most common unit for measuring where a station is on the world band dial. Formerly known as "kilocycles/second." 1,000 kilohertz equals one Megahertz.

Kilohertz. See kHz.

kW. Kilowatt(s), the most common unit of measurement for transmitter power (see).

LCD. Liquid-crystal display. LCDs, if properly designed, are fairly easily seen in bright light, but require sidelighting (also called "backlighting") under darker conditions. LCDs, being gray on gray, also tend to have mediocre contrast, and sometimes can be read from only a certain angle or angles, but they consume nearly no battery power.

LED. Light-emitting diode. LEDs are very easily read in the dark or in normal room light, but consume battery power and are hard to read in bright light.

Loc. Local.

Location. The physical location of a station's transmitter, which may be different from the studio location. Transmitter location is useful as a guide to reception quality. For example, if you're in Eastern North America and wish to listen to Radio Moscow International, a transmitter located in St. Petersburg will almost certainly provide better reception than one located in Siberia.

Longwave Band. The 148.5–283.5 kHz portion of the low-frequency (LF) radio spectrum used in Europe, the Near East, North Africa, Russia and Mongolia for domestic broadcasting. In general, these longwave signals, which have nothing to do with world band or other shortwave signals, are not audible in other parts of the world.

Longwire Antenna. See Passive Antenna.

LSB. Lower Sideband. See Feeder, Single Sideband.

LV. La Voix, La Voz—French and Spanish for "The Voice."

M. Monday.

Mediumwave Band, Mediumwave AM Band. See AM Band.

Megahertz. See MHz.

Memory, Memories. See Preset.

Meters. An outdated unit of measurement used for individual world band segments of the shortwave spectrum. The frequency range covered by a given meters designation—also known as "wavelength"—can be gleaned from the following formula: frequency (kHz) = 299,792/meters. Thus, 49 meters comes out to a frequency of 6118 kHz—well within the range of frequencies included in that segment (see World Band Spectrum). Inversely, meters can be derived from the following: meters = 299,792/frequency (kHz).

MHz. Megahertz, a common unit to measure where a station is on the dial. Formerly known as "Megacycles/second." One Megahertz equals 1,000 kilohertz.

Mode. Method of transmission of radio signals. World band radio broadcasts are almost always in the AM mode, the same mode used in the mediumwave AM band (see). The AM mode consists of three components: two "sidebands" and one "carrier." Each sideband contains the same programming as the other, and the carrier carries no programming, so a few stations are experimenting with the single-sideband (SSB) mode. SSB contains only one sideband, either the lower sideband (LSB) or upper sideband (USB), and no carrier. It requires special radio circuitry to be demodulated, or made intelligible. There are yet other modes used on shortwave, but not for world band. These include CW (Morse-type code), radiofax, RTTY (radioteletype) and narrow-band FM used by utility and ham stations. Narrow-band FM is not used for music, and is different from usual FM. See Single Sideband, ISB, ISL, ISU, LSB and USB.

N. New, Nueva, Nuevo, Nouvelle, Nacional, National, Nationale.

Nac. Nacional. Spanish and Portuguese for National.

Nat, Natl, Nat'l. National, Nationale.

Noise. Static, buzzes, pops and the like caused by the atmosphere (typically lightning, but also galactic noise), or such man-made sources as electric blankets, fish-tank heaters, heating pads, electrical and gasoline motors, light dimmers, flickering light bulbs, non-incandescent lights, computers, office machines, electrical fences and faulty electrical utility wiring.

Other. Programs are in a language other than one of the world's primary languages.

Overloading. See Dynamic Range.

Passive Antenna. An antenna that is not electronically amplified. Typically, these are mounted outdoors, although the "tape-measure" type that comes as an accessory with some portables is usually strung indoors. For world band reception, virtually all models for consumers are made from wire. The two most common designs are inverted-L (so-called "longwire") and trapped dipole (either horizontal or sloper). These atennas are prefer-able to active antennas (see), and are reviewed in detail in the Radio Database International White Paper, *PASSPORT Evaluation of Popular Outdoor Antennas (Unamplified)*.

PBS. People's Broadcasting Station.

Power. Transmitter power *before* amplification by the antenna, expressed in kilowatts (kW). The present range of world band powers is 0.01 to 1,000 kW.

Power Lock. See Travel Power Lock.

PR. People's Republic.

Preselector. A device—typically outboard, but sometimes inboard—that limits the range of frequencies that can enter a receiver's circuitry or that of an active antenna (see); that is, which improves front-end selectivity (see). For example, a preselector may let in the range 15000-16000 kHz, thus helping ensure that your receiver or active antenna will encounter no problems within that range from, say, 5800-6200 kHz or local mediumwave AM signals (520-1700 kHz). This range usually can be varied, manually or automatically, according to where the receiver is being tuned. A pre-selector may be passive (unamplified) or active (ampli-fied).

Preset. Allows you to select a station pre-stored in a radio's memory. The handiest presets require only one push of a button, as on a car radio.

Propagation. World band signals travel, like a basketball, up and down from the station to your radio. The "floor" below is the earth's surface, whereas the "player's hand" on high is the *ionosphere*, a gaseous layer that envelops the earth. While the earth's surface remains pretty much the same from day to day, the ionosphere—nature's own passive "satellite"—varies in how it propagates radio signals, depending on how much sunlight hits the "bounce points."

Thus, some world band segments do well mainly by day, whereas others are best by night. During winter there's less sunlight, so the "night bands" become unusually active, whereas the "day bands" become correspondingly less useful (see World Band Spectrum). Day-to-day changes in the sun's weather also cause short-term changes in world band radio reception; this explains why some days you can hear rare signals.

Additionally, the 11-year sunspot cycle has a long-term effect on propagation. Currently, the sunspot cycle is in its trough. This means that while the upper world band segments will be less active than usual over the next few years, the lower segments will be even more active and strong. Look for an upturn starting around 1997.

PS. Provincial Station, Pangsong.

Pto. Puerto, Porto.

QSL. See Verification.

R. Radio, Radiodiffusion, Radiodifusora, Radiodifusão, Radiofonikos, Radiostantsiya, Radyo, Radyosu, and so forth.

Radiofax, Radio Facsimile. Like ordinary telefax (facsimile by telephone), but by radio.

Radioteletype, RTTY. Characters, but not illustrations, transmitted by radio. "Radio modem." See Baud.

Receiver. Synonym for a radio, but sometimes—especially when called a "communications receiver"—implying a radio with superior tough-signal performance.

Reduced Carrier. See Single Sideband.

Reg. Regional.

Relay. A retransmission facility, often highlighted in "Worldwide Broadcasts in English" and "Voices from Home" in PASSPORT'S WorldScan section. Relay facilities are generally considered to be located outside the broadcaster's country. Being closer to the target audience, they usually provide superior reception. See Feeder.

Rep. Republic, République, República.

RN. See R and N.

RS. Radio Station, Radiostantsiya, Radiostudiya, Radiofonikos Stathmos.

RT, RTV. Radiodiffusion Télévision, Radio Télévision, and so forth.

RTTY. See Radioteletype.

S. As an icon ⚡ : aired summer only. As an ordinary letter: San, Santa, Santo, São, Saint, Sainte. Also, South.

Sa. Saturday.

Scan, Scanning. Circuitry within a radio that allows it to bandscan or memory-scan automatically.

Segments. See Shortwave Spectrum.

Selectivity. The ability of a radio to reject interference (see) from signals on adjacent channels. Thus, also known as adjacent-channel rejection, a key variable in radio quality. Also, see "Bandwidth" and "Synchronous Detector."

Sensitivity. The ability of a radio to receive weak signals; thus, also known as weak-signal sensitivity. Of special importance if you're listening during the day, or if you're located in such parts of the world as Western North America, Hawaii and Australasia, where signals tend to be relatively weak.

Shortwave Spectrum. The shortwave spectrum—also known as the High Frequency (HF) spectrum—is, strictly speaking, that portion of the radio spectrum from 3-30 MHz (3,000-30,000 kHz). However, common usage places it from 2.3-30 MHz (2,000-30,000 kHz). World band operates on shortwave within 14 discrete segments between 2.3-26.1 MHz, with the rest of the shortwave spectrum being occupied by Hams (see) and Utility Stations (see). Also, see World Band Spectrum and the "Best Times and Frequencies" box at the start of the Blue Pages.

Sideband. See Mode.

Single Sideband, Independent Sideband. Spectrum-and power-conserving modes of transmission commonly used by utility stations and hams. Few broadcasters use, or are expected to use, these modes. Many world band radios are already capable of demodulating single-sideband transmissions, and some can even process independent-sideband signals. Certain single-sideband transmissions operate with reduced carrier, which allows them to be listened to, albeit with some distortion, on ordinary radios not equipped to demodulate single sideband. Properly designed synchronous detectors (see) prevent such distortion. See Feeder, Mode.

Site. See Location.

Slew Controls. Elevator-button-type up and down controls to tune a radio. On many radios with synthesized tuning, slewing is used in lieu of tuning by knob. Better is when slew controls are complemented by a tuning knob, which is more versatile.

Sloper Antenna. See Passive Antenna.

SPR. Spurious (false) extra signal from a transmitter actually operating on another frequency. One such type is harmonic (see).

Spurious-Signal Rejection. The ability of a radio receiver not to produce false, or "ghost," signals that might otherwise interfere with the clarity of the station you're trying to hear. See Image Rejection.

Static. See Noise.

St, Sta, Sto. Abbreviations for words that mean "Saint."

Su. Sunday.

Synchronous Detector. World band radios are increasingly coming equipped with this high-tech circuit that greatly reduces fading distortion. Better synchronous detectors also allow for selectable sideband; that is, the ability to select the clearer of the two sidebands of a world band or other AM-mode signal. See Mode.

Synthesizer. Simple radios often use archaic needle-and-dial tuning that makes it difficult to find a desired channel or to tell which station you are hearing, except by ear. Other models utilize a digital frequency *synthesizer* to tune in signals without your having to hunt and peck. Among other things, synthesizers allow for push-button tuning and presets, and display the exact frequency digitally—pluses that make tuning in the world considerably easier. Virtually a "must" feature.

Target. Where a transmission is beamed.

Th. Thursday.

Travel Power Lock. Control to disable the on/off switch to prevent a radio from switching on accidentally.

Transmitter Power. See Power.

Trapper Dipole Antenna. See Passive Antenna.

Tu. Tuesday.

Universal Day. See World Time.

Universal Time. See World Time.

USB. Upper Sideband. See Feeder, Single Sideband.

UTC. See World Time.

Utility Stations. Most signals within the shortwave spectrum are not world band stations. Rather, they are utility stations—radio telephones, ships at sea, aircraft and the like—that transmit strange sounds (growls, gurgles, dih-dah sounds and the like) point-to-point and are not intended to be heard by the general public. *Compare* Broadcast, Hams and Feeders.

v. Variable frequency; i.e., one that is unstable or drifting because of a transmitter malfunction or to avoid jamming.

Verification. A card or letter from a station verifying that a listener indeed heard that particular station. In order to stand a chance of qualifying for a verification card or letter, you need to provide the station heard with the following information in a three-number "SIO" code, in which "SIO 555" is best and "SIO 111" is worst:

•Signal strength, with 5 being of excellent quality, comparable to that of a local mediumwave AM station, and 1 being inaudible or at least so weak as to be virtually unintelligible. 2 (faint but somewhat intelligible), 3 (moderate strength) and 4 (good strength) represent the signal-strength levels usually encountered with world band stations.

•Interference from other stations, with 5 indicating no interference whatsoever, and 1 indicating such extreme interference that the desired signal is virtually drowned out. 2 (heavy interference), 3 (moderate interference) and 4 (slight interference) represent the differing degrees of interference more typically encountered with world band signals. If possible, indicate the names of the interfering signal(s) and the channel(s) they are on. Otherwise, at least describe what the interference sounds like.

•Overall quality of the signal, with 5 being best, 1 worst.

•In addition to providing SIO findings, you should indicate which programs you've heard, as well as comments on how you liked or disliked those programs. Refer to the "Addresses

PLUS" section of this edition for information on where and to whom your report should be sent, and whether return postage should be included.

Vo. Voice of.

W. As an icon   aired winter only. As a regular letter: Wednesday.

Wavelength. See Meters.

Weak-Signal Sensitivity. See Sensitivity.

World Band Radio. Similar to regular mediumwave AM band and FM band radio, except that world band broadcasters can be heard over enormous distances and thus often carry news, music and entertainment programs created especially for audiences abroad. Some world band stations have audiences of up to 120 million each day. Some 600 million people worldwide are believed to listen to world band radio.

World Band Spectrum. See "Best Times and Fre–quencies" box at the start of the Blue Pages.

World Day. See UTC.

World Time. Also known as Coordinated Universal Time (UTC), Greenwich Mean Time (GMT) and Zulu time (Z). With nearly 170 countries on world band radio, if each announced its own local time you would need a calculator to figure it all out. To get around this, a single international time—World Time—is used. The difference between World Time and local time is detailed in the "Addresses PLUS" section of this edition and in the box below, or determined simply by listening to World Time announcements given on the hour by world band stations—or minute by minute by WWV and WWVH in the United States on such frequencies as 5000, 10000, 15000 and 20000 kHz. A 24-hour clock format is used, so "1800 World Time" means 6:00 PM World Time. If you're in, say, North America, Eastern Time is five hours behind World Time winters and four hours behind World Time summers, so 1800 World Time would be 1:00 PM EST or 2:00 PM EDT. The easiest solution is to use a 24-hour clock set to World Time. Many radios already have these built in, and World Time clocks are also available as accessories.

World Time also applies to the days of the week. So if it's 9:00 PM (21:00) Wednesday in New York during the winter, it's 0200 *Thursday* World Time.

WS. World Service.

Printed in USA

DIRECTORY OF ADVERTISERS

BLUE PAGES—1996

Channel-by-Channel Guide to World Band Schedules

If you scan the world band airwaves, you'll discover lots more than just stations aimed your way. That's because shortwave is a natural phenomenon, capriciously scattering signals from big stations, little stations—even stations intended to be heard only locally.

Blue Pages Help Identify Stations

But just dialing around can be frustrating if you don't have a "map"—*Passport's* Blue Pages. Say, you've stumbled across something Asian-sounding on 11620 kHz at 2035 World Time. The Blue Pages show All India Radio in Hindi beamed to

Western Europe, with a whopping 500 kW of power. These clues suggest this is probably what you're hearing, even if you're not in Europe. It also shows that English will be on in ten minutes.

Schedules for Entire Year

Times and days of the week are in World Time (see Glossary); for local times, see "Addresses PLUS." Some stations are an hour earlier (◀) or later (▶) midyear, and may also extend their hours during holidays or sports events.

To be as helpful as possible throughout the year, *Passport* includes not only observed activity and factual schedules, but also that which we have creatively opined will take place. This latter information is original from us, and is inherently less exact than factual data, even though it is very useful.

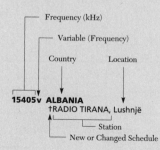

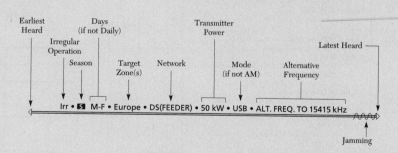

Frequency (kHz) • Variable (Frequency) • Country • Location • Earliest Heard • Irregular Operation • Season • Days (if not Daily) • Target Zone(s) • Network • Transmitter Power • Mode (if not AM) • Alternative Frequency • Latest Heard

15405v †RADIO TIRANA, Lushnjë — ALBANIA — Station — New or Changed Schedule

◀ Irr • **S** • M-F • Europe • DS(FEEDER) • 50 kW • USB • ALT. FREQ. TO 15415 kHz — Jamming

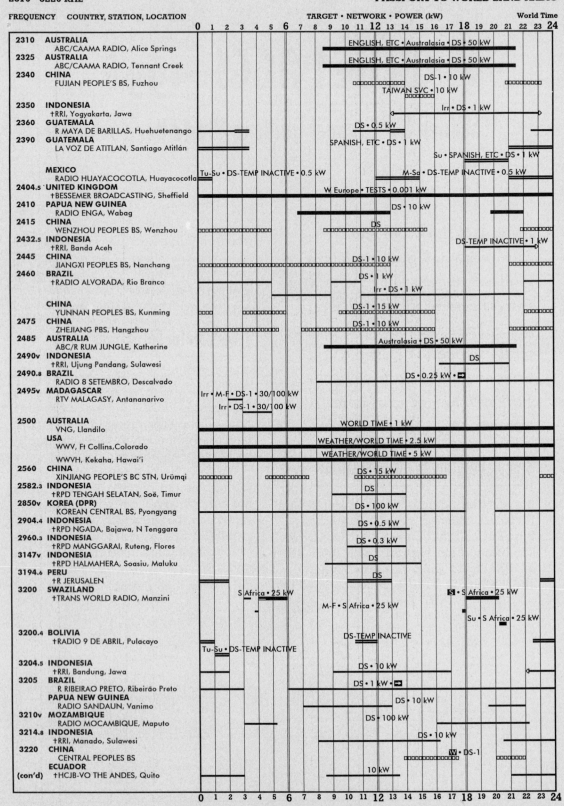

FREQUENCY   COUNTRY, STATION, LOCATION

Frequency	Country / Station / Location	Target · Network · Power (kW)
2310	**AUSTRALIA** ABC/CAAMA RADIO, Alice Springs	ENGLISH, ETC · Australasia · DS · 50 kW
2325	**AUSTRALIA** ABC/CAAMA RADIO, Tennant Creek	ENGLISH, ETC · Australasia · DS · 50 kW
2340	**CHINA** FUJIAN PEOPLE'S BS, Fuzhou	DS-1 · 10 kW / TAIWAN SVC · 10 kW
2350	**INDONESIA** †RRI, Yogyakarta, Jawa	Irr · DS · 1 kW
2360	**GUATEMALA** R MAYA DE BARILLAS, Huehuetenango	DS · 0.5 kW
2390	**GUATEMALA** LA VOZ DE ATITLAN, Santiago Atitlán	SPANISH, ETC · DS · 1 kW / Su · SPANISH, ETC · DS · 1 kW
	MEXICO RADIO HUAYACOCOTLA, Huayacocotla	Tu-Su · DS-TEMP INACTIVE · 0.5 kW / M-Sa · DS-TEMP INACTIVE · 0.5 kW
2404.5	**UNITED KINGDOM** †BESSEMER BROADCASTING, Sheffield	W Europe · TESTS · 0.001 kW
2410	**PAPUA NEW GUINEA** RADIO ENGA, Wabag	DS · 10 kW
2415	**CHINA** WENZHOU PEOPLES BS, Wenzhou	DS
2432.5	**INDONESIA** †RRI, Banda Aceh	DS-TEMP INACTIVE · 1 kW
2445	**CHINA** JIANGXI PEOPLES BS, Nanchang	DS-1 · 10 kW
2460	**BRAZIL** †RADIO ALVORADA, Rio Branco	DS · 1 kW / Irr · DS · 1 kW
	CHINA YUNNAN PEOPLES BS, Kunming	DS-1 · 15 kW
2475	**CHINA** ZHEJIANG PBS, Hangzhou	DS-1 · 10 kW
2485	**AUSTRALIA** ABC/R RUM JUNGLE, Katherine	Australasia · DS · 50 kW
2490v	**INDONESIA** †RRI, Ujung Pandang, Sulawesi	DS
2490.8	**BRAZIL** RADIO 8 SETEMBRO, Descalvado	DS · 0.25 kW · ➡
2495v	**MADAGASCAR** RTV MALAGASY, Antananarivo	Irr · M-F · DS-1 · 30/100 kW / Irr · DS-1 · 30/100 kW
2500	**AUSTRALIA** VNG, Llandilo	WORLD TIME · 1 kW
	USA WWV, Ft Collins, Colorado	WEATHER/WORLD TIME · 2.5 kW
	WWVH, Kekaha, Hawai'i	WEATHER/WORLD TIME · 5 kW
2560	**CHINA** XINJIANG PEOPLE'S BC STN, Urümqi	DS · 15 kW
2582.3	**INDONESIA** †RPD TENGAH SELATAN, Soë, Timur	DS
2850v	**KOREA (DPR)** KOREAN CENTRAL BS, Pyongyang	DS · 100 kW
2904.4	**INDONESIA** †RPD NGADA, Bajawa, N Tenggara	DS · 0.5 kW
2960.3	**INDONESIA** †RPD MANGGARAI, Ruteng, Flores	DS · 0.3 kW
3147v	**INDONESIA** †RPD HALMAHERA, Soasiu, Maluku	DS
3194.6	**PERU** †R JERUSALEN	DS
3200	**SWAZILAND** †TRANS WORLD RADIO, Manzini	S Africa · 25 kW / M-F · S Africa · 25 kW / Ⓢ · S Africa · 25 kW / Su · S Africa · 25 kW
3200.4	**BOLIVIA** †RADIO 9 DE ABRIL, Pulacayo	DS-TEMP INACTIVE / Tu-Su · DS-TEMP INACTIVE
3204.5	**INDONESIA** †RRI, Bandung, Jawa	DS · 10 kW
3205	**BRAZIL** R RIBEIRAO PRETO, Ribeirão Preto	DS · 1 kW · ➡
	PAPUA NEW GUINEA RADIO SANDAUN, Vanimo	DS · 10 kW
3210v	**MOZAMBIQUE** RADIO MOCAMBIQUE, Maputo	DS · 100 kW
3214.8	**INDONESIA** †RRI, Manado, Sulawesi	DS · 10 kW
3220	**CHINA** CENTRAL PEOPLES BS	Ⓦ · DS-1
	ECUADOR	
(con'd)	†HCJB-VO THE ANDES, Quito	10 kW

FREQUENCY   COUNTRY, STATION, LOCATION

TARGET • NETWORK • POWER (kW)

World Time

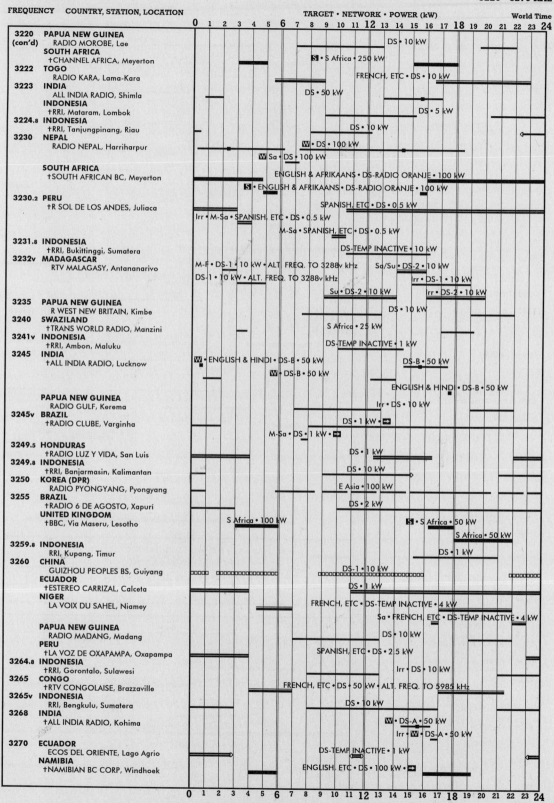

FREQUENCY	COUNTRY, STATION, LOCATION	TARGET • NETWORK • POWER (kW)
3220 (con'd)	PAPUA NEW GUINEA · RADIO MOROBE, Lae	DS • 10 kW
	SOUTH AFRICA · †CHANNEL AFRICA, Meyerton	S • S Africa • 250 kW
3222	TOGO · RADIO KARA, Lama-Kara	FRENCH, ETC • DS • 10 kW
3223	INDIA · ALL INDIA RADIO, Shimla	DS • 50 kW
	INDONESIA · †RRI, Mataram, Lombok	DS • 5 kW
3224.8	INDONESIA · †RRI, Tanjungpinang, Riau	DS • 10 kW
3230	NEPAL · RADIO NEPAL, Harriharpur	W • DS • 100 kW / W • Sa • DS • 100 kW
	SOUTH AFRICA · †SOUTH AFRICAN BC, Meyerton	ENGLISH & AFRIKAANS • DS-RADIO ORANJE • 100 kW / S • ENGLISH & AFRIKAANS • DS-RADIO ORANJE • 100 kW
3230.2	PERU · †R SOL DE LOS ANDES, Juliaca	SPANISH, ETC • DS • 0.5 kW / Irr • M-Sa • SPANISH, ETC • DS • 0.5 kW / M-Sa • SPANISH, ETC • DS • 0.5 kW
3231.8	INDONESIA · †RRI, Bukittinggi, Sumatera	DS-TEMP INACTIVE • 10 kW
3232v	MADAGASCAR · RTV MALAGASY, Antananarivo	M-F • DS-1 • 10 kW • ALT FREQ TO 3288v kHz / Sa/Su • DS-2 • 10 kW / DS-1 • 10 kW • ALT. FREQ. TO 3288v kHz / Irr • DS-1 • 10 kW / Su • DS-2 • 10 kW / Irr • DS-2 • 10 kW
3235	PAPUA NEW GUINEA · R WEST NEW BRITAIN, Kimbe	DS • 10 kW
3240	SWAZILAND · †TRANS WORLD RADIO, Manzini	S Africa • 25 kW
3241v	INDONESIA · †RRI, Ambon, Maluku	DS-TEMP INACTIVE • 1 kW
3245	INDIA · †ALL INDIA RADIO, Lucknow	W • ENGLISH & HINDI • DS-B • 50 kW / DS-B • 50 kW / W • DS-B • 50 kW / ENGLISH & HINDI • DS-B • 50 kW
	PAPUA NEW GUINEA · RADIO GULF, Kerema	Irr • DS • 10 kW
3245v	BRAZIL · †RADIO CLUBE, Varginha	DS • 1 kW • ⇨ / M-Sa • DS • 1 kW • ⇨
3249.5	HONDURAS · †RADIO LUZ Y VIDA, San Luis	DS • 1 kW
3249.8	INDONESIA · †RRI, Banjarmasin, Kalimantan	DS • 10 kW
3250	KOREA (DPR) · RADIO PYONGYANG, Pyongyang	E Asia • 100 kW
3255	BRAZIL · †RADIO 6 DE AGOSTO, Xapuri	DS • 2 kW
	UNITED KINGDOM · †BBC, Via Maseru, Lesotho	S Africa • 100 kW / S • S Africa • 50 kW / S Africa • 50 kW
3259.8	INDONESIA · RRI, Kupang, Timur	DS • 1 kW
3260	CHINA · GUIZHOU PEOPLES BS, Guiyang	DS-1 • 10 kW
	ECUADOR · †ESTEREO CARRIZAL, Calceta	DS • 1 kW
	NIGER · LA VOIX DU SAHEL, Niamey	FRENCH, ETC • DS-TEMP INACTIVE • 4 kW / Sa • FRENCH, ETC • DS-TEMP INACTIVE • 4 kW
	PAPUA NEW GUINEA · RADIO MADANG, Madang	DS • 10 kW
	PERU · †LA VOZ DE OXAPAMPA, Oxapampa	SPANISH, ETC • DS • 2.5 kW
3264.8	INDONESIA · †RRI, Gorontalo, Sulawesi	Irr • DS • 10 kW
3265	CONGO · †RTV CONGOLAISE, Brazzaville	FRENCH, ETC • DS • 50 kW • ALT. FREQ. TO 5985 kHz
3265v	INDONESIA · RRI, Bengkulu, Sumatera	DS • 10 kW
3268	INDIA · †ALL INDIA RADIO, Kohima	W • DS-A • 50 kW / Irr • W • DS-A • 50 kW
3270	ECUADOR · ECOS DEL ORIENTE, Lago Agrio	DS-TEMP INACTIVE • 1 kW
	NAMIBIA · †NAMIBIAN BC CORP, Windhoek	ENGLISH, ETC • DS • 100 kW • ⇨

ENGLISH ▬ ARABIC ⁙ CHINESE □□□ FRENCH ══ GERMAN ▬ RUSSIAN ⹀ SPANISH ══ OTHER ▬

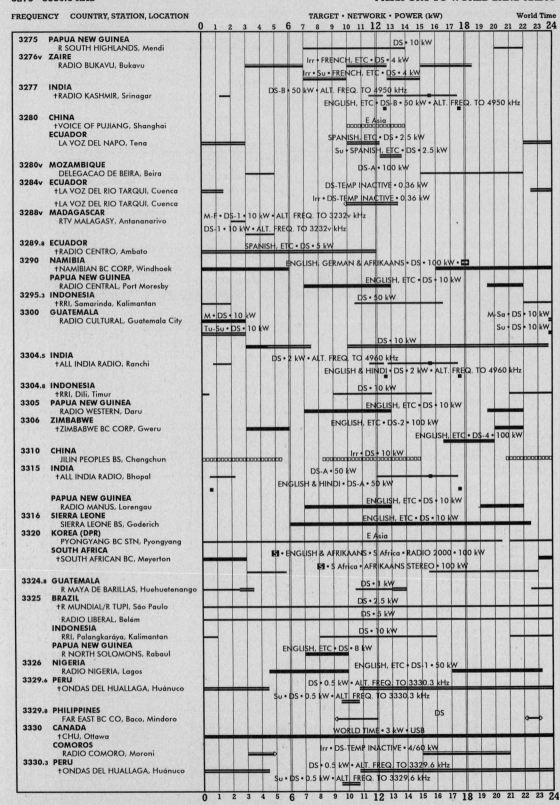

FREQUENCY	COUNTRY, STATION, LOCATION	TARGET • NETWORK • POWER (kW)
3275	**PAPUA NEW GUINEA** R SOUTH HIGHLANDS, Mendi	DS • 10 kW
3276v	**ZAIRE** RADIO BUKAVU, Bukavu	Irr • FRENCH, ETC • DS • 4 kW Irr • Su • FRENCH, ETC • DS • 4 kW
3277	**INDIA** †RADIO KASHMIR, Srinagar	DS-B • 50 kW • ALT. FREQ. TO 4950 kHz ENGLISH, ETC • DS-B • 50 kW • ALT. FREQ. TO 4950 kHz
3280	**CHINA** †VOICE OF PUJIANG, Shanghai	E Asia
	ECUADOR LA VOZ DEL NAPO, Tena	SPANISH, ETC • DS • 2.5 kW Su • SPANISH, ETC • DS • 2.5 kW
3280v	**MOZAMBIQUE** DELEGACAO DE BEIRA, Beira	DS-A • 100 kW
3284v	**ECUADOR** †LA VOZ DEL RIO TARQUI, Cuenca	DS-TEMP INACTIVE • 0.36 kW
	†LA VOZ DEL RIO TARQUI, Cuenca	Irr • DS-TEMP INACTIVE • 0.36 kW
3288v	**MADAGASCAR** RTV MALAGASY, Antananarivo	M-F • DS-1 • 10 kW • ALT. FREQ. TO 3232v kHz DS-1 • 10 kW • ALT. FREQ. TO 3232v kHz
3289.8	**ECUADOR** †RADIO CENTRO, Ambato	SPANISH, ETC • DS • 5 kW
3290	**NAMIBIA** †NAMIBIAN BC CORP, Windhoek	ENGLISH, GERMAN & AFRIKAANS • DS • 100 kW • ➡
	PAPUA NEW GUINEA RADIO CENTRAL, Port Moresby	ENGLISH, ETC • DS • 10 kW
3295.3	**INDONESIA** †RRI, Samarinda, Kalimantan	DS • 50 kW
3300	**GUATEMALA** RADIO CULTURAL, Guatemala City	M • DS • 10 kW M-Sa • DS • 10 kW Tu-Su • DS • 10 kW Su • DS • 10 kW DS • 10 kW
3304.5	**INDIA** †ALL INDIA RADIO, Ranchi	DS • 2 kW • ALT. FREQ. TO 4960 kHz ENGLISH & HINDI • DS • 2 kW • ALT. FREQ. TO 4960 kHz
3304.8	**INDONESIA** †RRI, Dili, Timur	DS • 10 kW
3305	**PAPUA NEW GUINEA** RADIO WESTERN, Daru	ENGLISH, ETC • DS • 10 kW
3306	**ZIMBABWE** †ZIMBABWE BC CORP, Gweru	ENGLISH, ETC • DS-2 • 100 kW ENGLISH, ETC • DS-4 • 100 kW
3310	**CHINA** JILIN PEOPLES BS, Changchun	Irr • DS • 10 kW
3315	**INDIA** †ALL INDIA RADIO, Bhopal	DS-A • 50 kW ENGLISH & HINDI • DS-A • 50 kW
	PAPUA NEW GUINEA RADIO MANUS, Lorengau	ENGLISH, ETC • DS • 10 kW
3316	**SIERRA LEONE** SIERRA LEONE BS, Goderich	ENGLISH, ETC • DS • 10 kW
3320	**KOREA (DPR)** PYONGYANG BC STN, Pyongyang	E Asia
	SOUTH AFRICA †SOUTH AFRICAN BC, Meyerton	[S] • ENGLISH & AFRIKAANS • S Africa • RADIO 2000 • 100 kW [S] • S Africa • AFRIKAANS STEREO • 100 kW
3324.8	**GUATEMALA** R MAYA DE BARILLAS, Huehuetenango	DS • 1 kW
3325	**BRAZIL** †R MUNDIAL/R TUPI, São Paulo	DS • 2.5 kW
	RADIO LIBERAL, Belém	DS • 5 kW
	INDONESIA RRI, Palangkaráya, Kalimantan	DS • 10 kW
	PAPUA NEW GUINEA R NORTH SOLOMONS, Rabaul	ENGLISH, ETC • DS • 8 kW
3326	**NIGERIA** RADIO NIGERIA, Lagos	ENGLISH, ETC • DS-1 • 50 kW
3329.6	**PERU** †ONDAS DEL HUALLAGA, Huánuco	DS • 0.5 kW • ALT. FREQ. TO 3330.3 kHz Su • DS • 0.5 kW • ALT. FREQ. TO 3330.3 kHz
3329.8	**PHILIPPINES** FAR EAST BC CO, Baco, Mindoro	DS
3330	**CANADA** †CHU, Ottawa	WORLD TIME • 3 kW • USB
	COMOROS RADIO COMORO, Moroni	Irr • DS-TEMP INACTIVE • 4/60 kW
3330.3	**PERU** †ONDAS DEL HUALLAGA, Huánuco	DS • 0.5 kW • ALT. FREQ. TO 3329.6 kHz Su • DS • 0.5 kW • ALT. FREQ. TO 3329.6 kHz

World Time 0 1 2 3 4 5 6 7 8 9 10 11 12 13 14 15 16 17 18 19 20 21 22 23 24

FREQUENCY   COUNTRY, STATION, LOCATION

TARGET • NETWORK • POWER (kW)   World Time

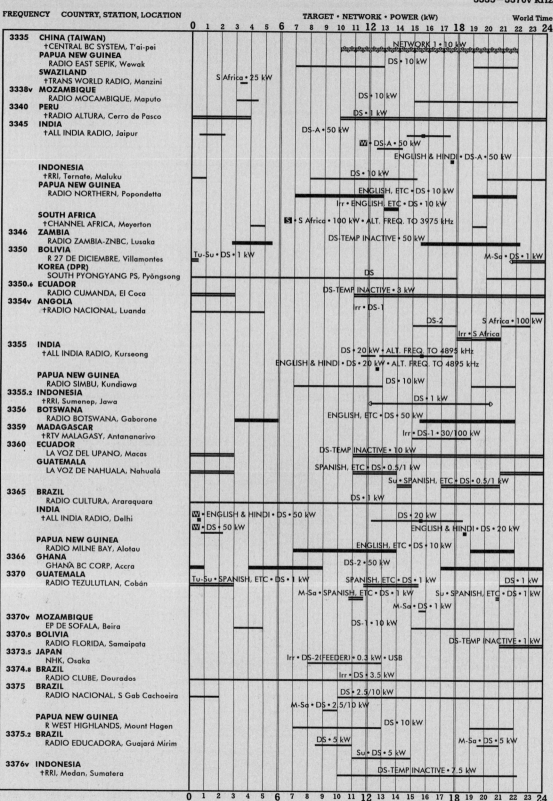

Freq	Country, Station, Location	Schedule Notes
3335	**CHINA (TAIWAN)** †CENTRAL BC SYSTEM, T'ai-pei	NETWORK 1 • 10 kW
	PAPUA NEW GUINEA RADIO EAST SEPIK, Wewak	DS • 10 kW
	SWAZILAND †TRANS WORLD RADIO, Manzini	S Africa • 25 kW
3338v	**MOZAMBIQUE** RADIO MOCAMBIQUE, Maputo	DS • 10 kW
3340	**PERU** †RADIO ALTURA, Cerro de Pasco	DS • 1 kW
3345	**INDIA** †ALL INDIA RADIO, Jaipur	DS-A • 50 kW; W • DS-A • 50 kW; ENGLISH & HINDI • DS-A • 50 kW
	INDONESIA †RRI, Ternate, Maluku	DS • 10 kW
	PAPUA NEW GUINEA RADIO NORTHERN, Popondetta	ENGLISH, ETC • DS 10 kW; Irr • ENGLISH, ETC • DS • 10 kW
	SOUTH AFRICA †CHANNEL AFRICA, Meyerton	S • S Africa • 100 kW • ALT. FREQ. TO 3975 kHz
3346	**ZAMBIA** RADIO ZAMBIA-ZNBC, Lusaka	DS-TEMP INACTIVE • 50 kW
3350	**BOLIVIA** R 27 DE DICIEMBRE, Villamontes	Tu-Su • DS • 1 kW; M-Sa • DS • 1 kW
	KOREA (DPR) SOUTH PYONGYANG PS, Pyŏngsong	DS
3350.6	**ECUADOR** RADIO CUMANDA, El Coca	DS-TEMP INACTIVE • 3 kW
3354v	**ANGOLA** †RADIO NACIONAL, Luanda	Irr • DS-1; DS-2; S Africa • 100 kW; Irr • S Africa
3355	**INDIA** †ALL INDIA RADIO, Kurseong	DS • 20 kW • ALT. FREQ. TO 4895 kHz; ENGLISH & HINDI • DS • 20 kW • ALT. FREQ. TO 4895 kHz
	PAPUA NEW GUINEA RADIO SIMBU, Kundiawa	DS • 10 kW
3355.2	**INDONESIA** †RRI, Sumenep, Jawa	DS • 1 kW
3356	**BOTSWANA** RADIO BOTSWANA, Gaborone	ENGLISH, ETC • DS • 50 kW
3359	**MADAGASCAR** †RTV MALAGASY, Antananarivo	Irr • DS-1 • 30/100 kW
3360	**ECUADOR** LA VOZ DEL UPANO, Macas	DS-TEMP INACTIVE • 10 kW
	GUATEMALA LA VOZ DE NAHUALA, Nahualá	SPANISH, ETC • DS • 0.5/1 kW; Su • SPANISH, ETC • DS • 0.5/1 kW
3365	**BRAZIL** RADIO CULTURA, Araraquara	DS • 1 kW
	INDIA †ALL INDIA RADIO, Delhi	W • ENGLISH & HINDI • DS 50 kW; DS • 20 kW; W • DS 50 kW; ENGLISH & HINDI • DS • 20 kW
	PAPUA NEW GUINEA RADIO MILNE BAY, Alotau	ENGLISH, ETC • DS • 10 kW
3366	**GHANA** GHANA BC CORP, Accra	DS-2 • 50 kW
3370	**GUATEMALA** RADIO TEZULUTLAN, Cobán	Tu-Su • SPANISH, ETC • DS • 1 kW; SPANISH, ETC • DS • 1 kW; DS • 1 kW; M-Sa • SPANISH, ETC • DS • 1 kW; Su • SPANISH, ETC • DS • 1 kW; M-Sa • DS • 1 kW
3370v	**MOZAMBIQUE** EP DE SOFALA, Beira	DS-1 • 10 kW
3370.5	**BOLIVIA** RADIO FLORIDA, Samaipata	DS-TEMP INACTIVE • 1 kW
3373.5	**JAPAN** NHK, Osaka	Irr • DS-2 (FEEDER) • 0.3 kW • USB
3374.8	**BRAZIL** RADIO CLUBE, Dourados	Irr • DS • 3.5 kW
3375	**BRAZIL** RADIO NACIONAL, S Gab Cachoeira	DS • 2.5/10 kW; M-Sa • DS • 2.5/10 kW
	PAPUA NEW GUINEA R WEST HIGHLANDS, Mount Hagen	DS • 10 kW
3375.2	**BRAZIL** RADIO EDUCADORA, Guajará Mirim	DS • 5 kW; Su • DS • 5 kW; M-Sa • DS • 5 kW
3376v	**INDONESIA** †RRI, Medan, Sumatera	DS-TEMP INACTIVE • 7.5 kW

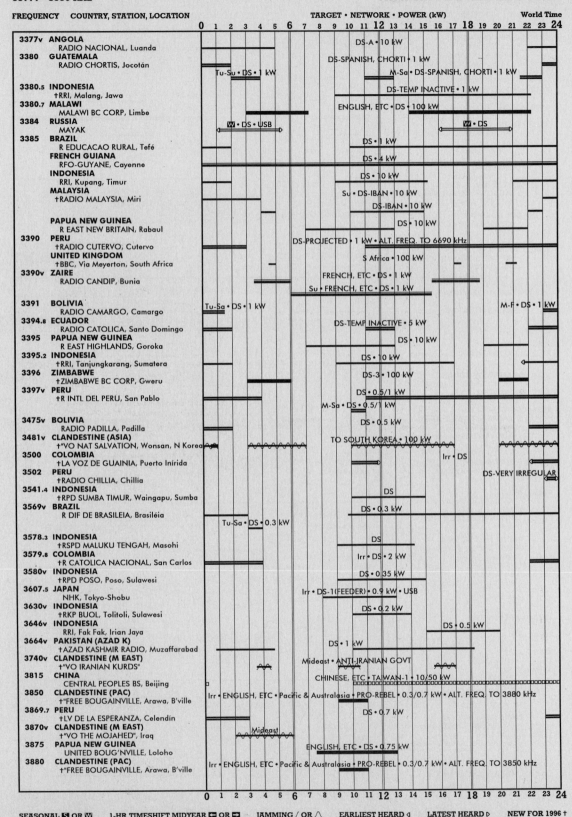

FREQUENCY	COUNTRY, STATION, LOCATION
3377v	**ANGOLA** — RADIO NACIONAL, Luanda
3380	**GUATEMALA** — RADIO CHORTIS, Jocotán
3380.5	**INDONESIA** — †RRI, Malang, Jawa
3380.7	**MALAWI** — MALAWI BC CORP, Limbe
3384	**RUSSIA** — MAYAK
3385	**BRAZIL** — R EDUCACAO RURAL, Tefé
	FRENCH GUIANA — RFO-GUYANE, Cayenne
	INDONESIA — RRI, Kupang, Timur
	MALAYSIA — †RADIO MALAYSIA, Miri
	PAPUA NEW GUINEA — R EAST NEW BRITAIN, Rabaul
3390	**PERU** — †RADIO CUTERVO, Cutervo
	UNITED KINGDOM — †BBC, Via Meyerton, South Africa
3390v	**ZAIRE** — RADIO CANDIP, Bunia
3391	**BOLIVIA** — RADIO CAMARGO, Camargo
3394.8	**ECUADOR** — RADIO CATOLICA, Santo Domingo
3395	**PAPUA NEW GUINEA** — R EAST HIGHLANDS, Goroka
3395.2	**INDONESIA** — †RRI, Tanjungkarang, Sumatera
3396	**ZIMBABWE** — †ZIMBABWE BC CORP, Gweru
3397v	**PERU** — †R INTL DEL PERU, San Pablo
3475v	**BOLIVIA** — RADIO PADILLA, Padilla
3481v	**CLANDESTINE (ASIA)** — †"VO NAT SALVATION, Wonsan, N Korea
3500	**COLOMBIA** — †LA VOZ DE GUAINIA, Puerto Inírida
3502	**PERU** — †RADIO CHILLIA, Chillia
3541.4	**INDONESIA** — †RPD SUMBA TIMUR, Waingapu, Sumba
3569v	**BRAZIL** — R DIF DE BRASILEIA, Brasiléia
3578.3	**INDONESIA** — †RSPD MALUKU TENGAH, Masohi
3579.8	**COLOMBIA** — †R CATOLICA NACIONAL, San Carlos
3580v	**INDONESIA** — †RPD POSO, Poso, Sulawesi
3607.5	**JAPAN** — NHK, Tokyo-Shobu
3630v	**INDONESIA** — †RKP BUOL, Tolitoli, Sulawesi
3646v	**INDONESIA** — RRI, Fak Fak, Irian Jaya
3664v	**PAKISTAN (AZAD K)** — †AZAD KASHMIR RADIO, Muzaffarabad
3740v	**CLANDESTINE (M EAST)** — †"VO IRANIAN KURDS"
3815	**CHINA** — CENTRAL PEOPLES BS, Beijing
3850	**CLANDESTINE (PAC)** — †"FREE BOUGAINVILLE, Arawa, B'ville
3869.7	**PERU** — †LV DE LA ESPERANZA, Celendin
3870v	**CLANDESTINE (M EAST)** — †"VO THE MOJAHED", Iraq
3875	**PAPUA NEW GUINEA** — UNITED BOUG'NVILLE, Loloho
3880	**CLANDESTINE (PAC)** — †"FREE BOUGAINVILLE, Arawa, B'ville

Target · Network · Power (kW) notes:
- DS-A · 10 kW
- DS-SPANISH, CHORTI · 1 kW
- Tu-Su · DS · 1 kW
- M-Sa · DS-SPANISH, CHORTI · 1 kW
- DS-TEMP INACTIVE · 1 kW
- ENGLISH, ETC · DS · 100 kW
- W · DS · USB
- W · DS
- DS · 1 kW
- DS · 4 kW
- DS · 10 kW
- Su · DS-IBAN · 10 kW
- DS-IBAN · 10 kW
- DS · 10 kW
- DS-PROJECTED · 1 kW · ALT. FREQ. TO 6690 kHz
- S Africa · 100 kW
- FRENCH, ETC · DS · 1 kW
- Su · FRENCH, ETC · DS · 1 kW
- Tu-Sa · DS · 1 kW
- M-F · DS · 1 kW
- DS-TEMP INACTIVE · 5 kW
- DS · 10 kW
- DS · 10 kW
- DS-3 · 100 kW
- DS · 0.5/1 kW
- M-Sa · DS · 0.5/1 kW
- DS · 0.5 kW
- TO SOUTH KOREA · 100 kW
- Irr · DS
- DS-VERY IRREGULAR
- DS
- DS · 0.3 kW
- Tu-Sa · DS · 0.3 kW
- DS
- Irr · DS · 2 kW
- DS · 0.35 kW
- Irr · DS-1(FEEDER) · 0.9 kW · USB
- DS · 0.2 kW
- DS · 0.5 kW
- DS · 1 kW
- Mideast · ANTI-IRANIAN GOVT
- CHINESE, ETC · TAIWAN-1 · 10/50 kW
- Irr · ENGLISH, ETC · Pacific & Australasia · PRO-REBEL · 0.3/0.7 kW · ALT. FREQ. TO 3880 kHz
- DS · 0.7 kW
- Mideast
- ENGLISH, ETC · DS · 0.75 kW
- Irr · ENGLISH, ETC · Pacific & Australasia · PRO-REBEL · 0.3/0.7 kW · ALT. FREQ. TO 3850 kHz

FREQUENCY   COUNTRY, STATION, LOCATION

TARGET • NETWORK • POWER (kW)

World Time

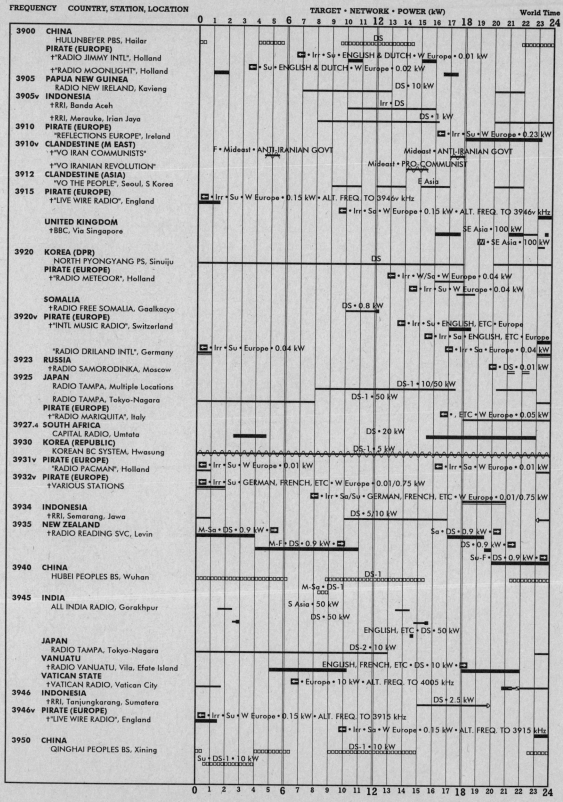

Freq	Country / Station / Location	Details
3900	**CHINA**	
	HULUNBEI'ER PBS, Hailar	DS
	PIRATE (EUROPE)	
	†"RADIO JIMMY INTL", Holland	• Irr • Su • ENGLISH & DUTCH • W Europe • 0.01 kW
	†"RADIO MOONLIGHT", Holland	• Su • ENGLISH & DUTCH • W Europe • 0.02 kW
3905	**PAPUA NEW GUINEA**	
	RADIO NEW IRELAND, Kavieng	DS • 10 kW
3905v	**INDONESIA**	
	†RRI, Banda Aceh	Irr • DS
	†RRI, Merauke, Irian Jaya	DS • 1 kW
3910	**PIRATE (EUROPE)**	
	"REFLECTIONS EUROPE", Ireland	• Irr • Su • W Europe • 0.23 kW
3910v	**CLANDESTINE (M EAST)**	
	†"VO IRAN COMMUNISTS"	F • Mideast • ANTI-IRANIAN GOVT Mideast • ANTI-IRANIAN GOVT
	†"VO IRANIAN REVOLUTION"	Mideast • PRO-COMMUNIST
3912	**CLANDESTINE (ASIA)**	
	"VO THE PEOPLE", Seoul, S Korea	E Asia
3915	**PIRATE (EUROPE)**	
	†"LIVE WIRE RADIO", England	• Irr • Su • W Europe • 0.15 kW • ALT. FREQ. TO 3946v kHz
		• Irr • Sa • W Europe • 0.15 kW • ALT. FREQ. TO 3946v kHz
	UNITED KINGDOM	
	†BBC, Via Singapore	SE Asia • 100 kW
		W • SE Asia • 100 kW
3920	**KOREA (DPR)**	
	NORTH PYONGYANG PS, Sinuiju	DS
	PIRATE (EUROPE)	
	†"RADIO METEOOR", Holland	• Irr • W/Sa • W Europe • 0.04 kW
		• Irr • Su • W Europe • 0.04 kW
	SOMALIA	
	†RADIO FREE SOMALIA, Gaalkacyo	DS • 0.8 kW
3920v	**PIRATE (EUROPE)**	
	†"INTL MUSIC RADIO", Switzerland	• Irr • Su • ENGLISH, ETC • Europe
		• Irr • Sa • ENGLISH, ETC • Europe
	"RADIO DRILAND INTL", Germany	• Irr • Su • Europe • 0.04 kW • Irr • Sa • Europe • 0.04 kW
3923	**RUSSIA**	
	†RADIO SAMORODINKA, Moscow	• DS • 0.01 kW
3925	**JAPAN**	
	RADIO TAMPA, Multiple Locations	DS-1 • 10/50 kW
	RADIO TAMPA, Tokyo-Nagara	DS-1 • 50 kW
	PIRATE (EUROPE)	
	†"RADIO MARIQUITA", Italy	• , ETC • W Europe • 0.05 kW
3927.4	**SOUTH AFRICA**	
	CAPITAL RADIO, Umtata	DS • 20 kW
3930	**KOREA (REPUBLIC)**	
	KOREAN BC SYSTEM, Hwasung	DS-1 • 5 kW
3931v	**PIRATE (EUROPE)**	
	"RADIO PACMAN", Holland	• Irr • Su • W Europe • 0.01 kW • Irr • Sa • W Europe • 0.01 kW
3932v	**PIRATE (EUROPE)**	
	†VARIOUS STATIONS	• Irr • Su • GERMAN, FRENCH, ETC • W Europe • 0.01/0.75 kW
		• Irr • Sa/Su • GERMAN, FRENCH, ETC • W Europe • 0.01/0.75 kW
3934	**INDONESIA**	
	†RRI, Semarang, Jawa	DS • 5/10 kW
3935	**NEW ZEALAND**	
	†RADIO READING SVC, Levin	M-Sa • DS • 0.9 kW • Sa • DS • 0.9 kW •
		M-F • DS • 0.9 kW • DS • 0.9 kW •
		Su-F • DS • 0.9 kW •
3940	**CHINA**	
	HUBEI PEOPLES BS, Wuhan	DS-1
3945	**INDIA**	
	ALL INDIA RADIO, Gorakhpur	M-Sa • DS-1 S Asia • 50 kW DS • 50 kW ENGLISH, ETC • DS • 50 kW
	JAPAN	
	RADIO TAMPA, Tokyo-Nagara	DS-2 • 10 kW
	VANUATU	
	†RADIO VANUATU, Vila, Efate Island	ENGLISH, FRENCH, ETC • DS • 10 kW •
	VATICAN STATE	
	†VATICAN RADIO, Vatican City	• Europe • 10 kW • ALT. FREQ. TO 4005 kHz
3946	**INDONESIA**	
	†RRI, Tanjungkarang, Sumatera	DS • 2.5 kW
3946v	**PIRATE (EUROPE)**	
	†"LIVE WIRE RADIO", England	• Irr • Su • W Europe • 0.15 kW • ALT. FREQ. TO 3915 kHz
		• Irr • Sa • W Europe • 0.15 kW • ALT. FREQ. TO 3915 kHz
3950	**CHINA**	
	QINGHAI PEOPLES BS, Xining	DS-1 • 10 kW Su • DS-1 • 10 kW

ENGLISH ▬   ARABIC ⋙   CHINESE ▭▭▭   FRENCH ══   GERMAN ▭   RUSSIAN ═══   SPANISH ═══   OTHER ▬

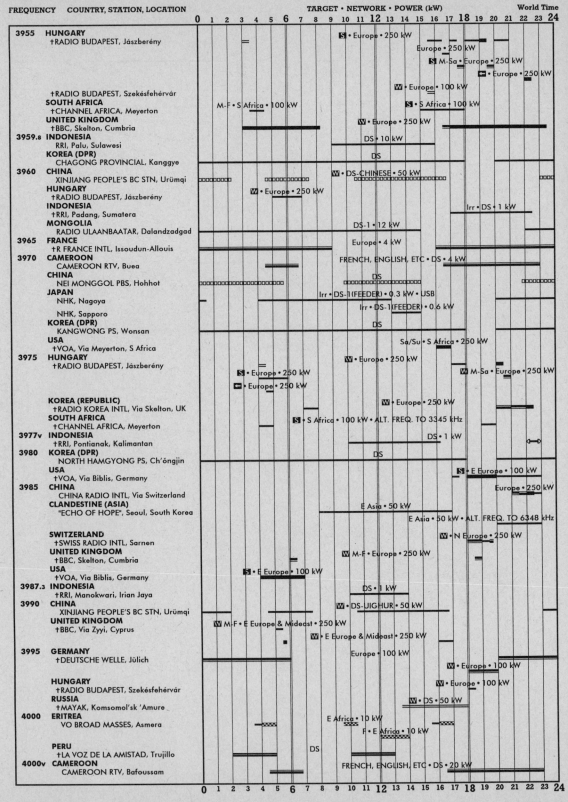

FREQUENCY   COUNTRY, STATION, LOCATION

TARGET • NETWORK • POWER (kW)   World Time

3955	**HUNGARY** †RADIO BUDAPEST, Jászberény
	†RADIO BUDAPEST, Székésfehérvár
	SOUTH AFRICA †CHANNEL AFRICA, Meyerton
	UNITED KINGDOM †BBC, Skelton, Cumbria
3959.8	**INDONESIA** RRI, Palu, Sulawesi
	KOREA (DPR) CHAGONG PROVINCIAL, Kanggye
3960	**CHINA** XINJIANG PEOPLE'S BC STN, Urümqi
	HUNGARY †RADIO BUDAPEST, Jászberény
	INDONESIA †RRI, Padang, Sumatera
	MONGOLIA RADIO ULAANBAATAR, Dalandzadgad
3965	**FRANCE** †R FRANCE INTL, Issoudun-Allouis
3970	**CAMEROON** CAMEROON RTV, Buea
	CHINA NEI MONGGOL PBS, Hohhot
	JAPAN NHK, Nagoya
	NHK, Sapporo
	KOREA (DPR) KANGWONG PS, Wonsan
	USA †VOA, Via Meyerton, S Africa
3975	**HUNGARY** †RADIO BUDAPEST, Jászberény
	KOREA (REPUBLIC) †RADIO KOREA INTL, Via Skelton, UK
	SOUTH AFRICA †CHANNEL AFRICA, Meyerton
3977v	**INDONESIA** †RRI, Pontianak, Kalimantan
3980	**KOREA (DPR)** NORTH HAMGYONG PS, Ch'öngjin
	USA †VOA, Via Biblis, Germany
3985	**CHINA** CHINA RADIO INTL, Via Switzerland
	CLANDESTINE (ASIA) "ECHO OF HOPE", Seoul, South Korea
	SWITZERLAND †SWISS RADIO INTL, Sarnen
	UNITED KINGDOM †BBC, Skelton, Cumbria
	USA †VOA, Via Biblis, Germany
3987.3	**INDONESIA** †RRI, Manokwari, Irian Jaya
3990	**CHINA** XINJIANG PEOPLE'S BC STN, Urümqi
	UNITED KINGDOM †BBC, Via Zyyi, Cyprus
3995	**GERMANY** †DEUTSCHE WELLE, Jülich
	HUNGARY †RADIO BUDAPEST, Székésfehérvár
	RUSSIA †MAYAK, Komsomol'sk 'Amure
4000	**ERITREA** VO BROAD MASSES, Asmera
	PERU †LA VOZ DE LA AMISTAD, Trujillo
4000v	**CAMEROON** CAMEROON RTV, Bafoussam

FREQUENCY   COUNTRY, STATION, LOCATION   TARGET • NETWORK • POWER (kW)   World Time

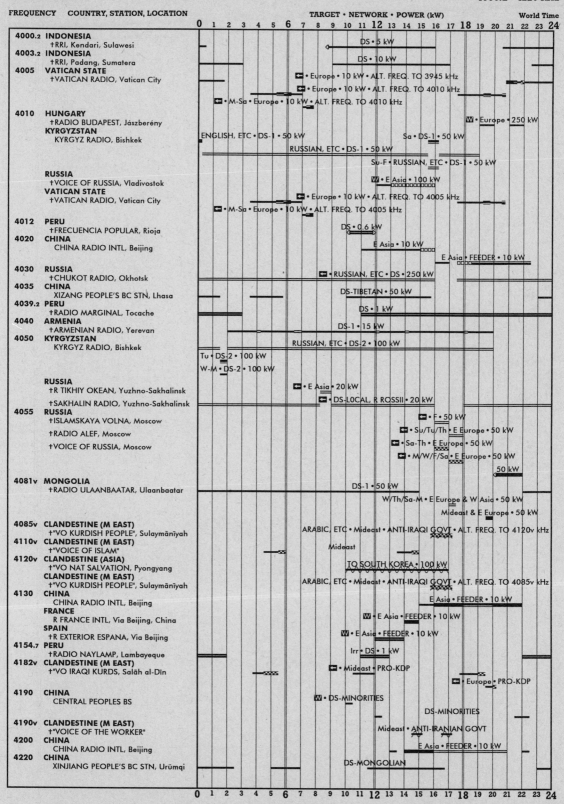

4000.2	INDONESIA
	†RRI, Kendari, Sulawesi
4003.2	INDONESIA
	†RRI, Padang, Sumatera
4005	VATICAN STATE
	†VATICAN RADIO, Vatican City
4010	HUNGARY
	†RADIO BUDAPEST, Jászberény
	KYRGYZSTAN
	KYRGYZ RADIO, Bishkek
	RUSSIA
	†VOICE OF RUSSIA, Vladivostok
	VATICAN STATE
	†VATICAN RADIO, Vatican City
4012	PERU
	†FRECUENCIA POPULAR, Rioja
4020	CHINA
	CHINA RADIO INTL, Beijing
4030	RUSSIA
	†CHUKOT RADIO, Okhotsk
4035	CHINA
	XIZANG PEOPLE'S BC STN, Lhasa
4039.2	PERU
	†RADIO MARGINAL, Tocache
4040	ARMENIA
	†ARMENIAN RADIO, Yerevan
4050	KYRGYZSTAN
	KYRGYZ RADIO, Bishkek
	RUSSIA
	†R TIKHIY OKEAN, Yuzhno-Sakhalinsk
	†SAKHALIN RADIO, Yuzhno-Sakhalinsk
4055	RUSSIA
	†ISLAMSKAYA VOLNA, Moscow
	†RADIO ALEF, Moscow
	†VOICE OF RUSSIA, Moscow
4081v	MONGOLIA
	†RADIO ULAANBAATAR, Ulaanbaatar
4085v	CLANDESTINE (M EAST)
	†"VO KURDISH PEOPLE", Sulaymānīyah
4110v	CLANDESTINE (M EAST)
	†"VOICE OF ISLAM"
4120v	CLANDESTINE (ASIA)
	†VO NAT SALVATION, Pyongyang
	CLANDESTINE (M EAST)
	†"VO KURDISH PEOPLE", Sulaymānīyah
4130	CHINA
	CHINA RADIO INTL, Beijing
	FRANCE
	R FRANCE INTL, Via Beijing, China
	SPAIN
	†R EXTERIOR ESPANA, Via Beijing
4154.7	PERU
	†RADIO NAYLAMP, Lambayeque
4182v	CLANDESTINE (M EAST)
	†"VO IRAQI KURDS, Salāh al-Dīn
4190	CHINA
	CENTRAL PEOPLES BS
4190v	CLANDESTINE (M EAST)
	†"VOICE OF THE WORKER"
4200	CHINA
	CHINA RADIO INTL, Beijing
4220	CHINA
	XINJIANG PEOPLE'S BC STN, Urümqi

DS • 5 kW
DS • 10 kW
• Europe • 10 kW • ALT. FREQ. TO 3945 kHz
• Europe • 10 kW • ALT. FREQ. TO 4010 kHz
• M-Sa • Europe • 10 kW • ALT. FREQ. TO 4010 kHz
W • Europe • 250 kW
ENGLISH, ETC • DS-1 • 50 kW   Sa • DS-1 • 50 kW
RUSSIAN, ETC • DS-1 • 50 kW
Su-F • RUSSIAN, ETC • DS-1 • 50 kW
W • E Asia • 100 kW
• Europe • 10 kW • ALT. FREQ. TO 4005 kHz
• M-Sa • Europe • 10 kW • ALT. FREQ. TO 4005 kHz
DS • 0.6 kW
E Asia • 10 kW
E Asia • FEEDER • 10 kW
• RUSSIAN, ETC • DS • 250 kW
DS-TIBETAN • 50 kW
DS • 1 kW
DS-1 • 15 kW
RUSSIAN, ETC • DS-2 • 100 kW
Tu • DS-2 • 100 kW
W-M • DS-2 • 100 kW
• E Asia • 20 kW
• DS-LOCAL, R ROSSII • 20 kW
• F • 50 kW
• Su/Tu/Th • E Europe • 50 kW
• Sa-Th • E Europe • 50 kW
• M/W/F/Sa • E Europe • 50 kW
50 kW
DS-1 • 50 kW
W/Th/Sa-M • E Europe & W Asia • 50 kW
Mideast & E Europe • 50 kW
ARABIC, ETC • Mideast • ANTI-IRAQI GOVT • ALT. FREQ. TO 4120v kHz
Mideast
TO SOUTH KOREA • 100 kW
ARABIC, ETC • Mideast • ANTI-IRAQI GOVT • ALT. FREQ. TO 4085v kHz
E Asia • FEEDER • 10 kW
W • E Asia • FEEDER • 10 kW
W • E Asia • FEEDER • 10 kW
Irr • DS • 1 kW
• Mideast • PRO-KDP
• Europe • PRO-KDP
W • DS-MINORITIES
DS-MINORITIES
Mideast • ANTI-IRANIAN GOVT
E Asia • FEEDER • 10 kW
DS-MONGOLIAN

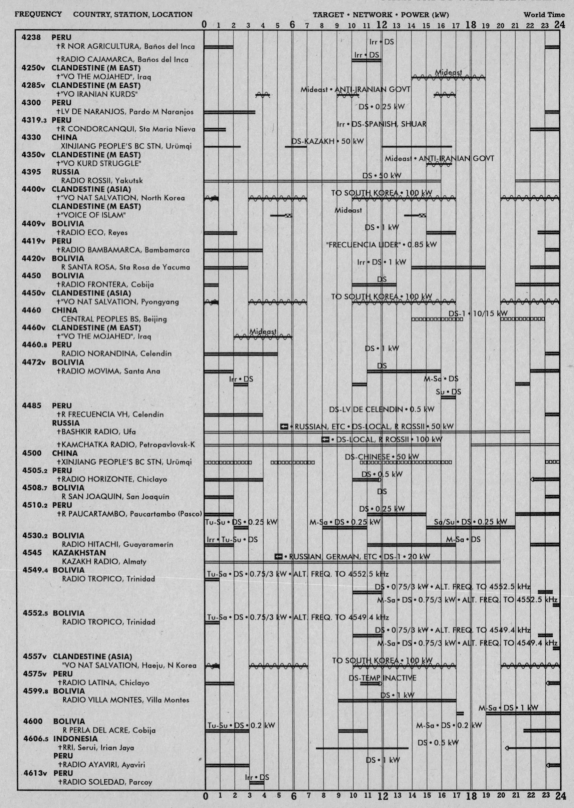

FREQUENCY   COUNTRY, STATION, LOCATION   TARGET • NETWORK • POWER (kW)   World Time

4238	**PERU**
	†R NOR AGRICULTURA, Baños del Inca — Irr • DS
	†RADIO CAJAMARCA, Baños del Inca — Irr • DS
4250v	**CLANDESTINE (M EAST)**
	†"VO THE MOJAHED", Iraq — Mideast
4285v	**CLANDESTINE (M EAST)**
	†"VO IRANIAN KURDS" — Mideast • ANTI-IRANIAN GOVT
4300	**PERU**
	†LV DE NARANJOS, Pardo M Naranjos — DS • 0.25 kW
4319.3	**PERU**
	†R CONDORCANQUI, Sta Maria Nieva — Irr • DS-SPANISH, SHUAR
4330	**CHINA**
	XINJIANG PEOPLE'S BC STN, Urümqi — DS-KAZAKH • 50 kW
4350v	**CLANDESTINE (M EAST)**
	†"VO KURD STRUGGLE" — Mideast • ANTI-IRANIAN GOVT
4395	**RUSSIA**
	RADIO ROSSII, Yakutsk — DS • 50 kW
4400v	**CLANDESTINE (ASIA)**
	†"VO NAT SALVATION, North Korea — TO SOUTH KOREA • 100 kW
	CLANDESTINE (M EAST)
	†"VOICE OF ISLAM" — Mideast
4409v	**BOLIVIA**
	†RADIO ECO, Reyes — DS • 1 kW
4419v	**PERU**
	†RADIO BAMBAMARCA, Bambamarca — "FRECUENCIA LIDER" • 0.85 kW
4420v	**BOLIVIA**
	R SANTA ROSA, Sta Rosa de Yacuma — Irr • DS • 1 kW
4450	**BOLIVIA**
	†RADIO FRONTERA, Cobija — DS
4450v	**CLANDESTINE (ASIA)**
	†"VO NAT SALVATION, Pyongyang — TO SOUTH KOREA • 100 kW
4460	**CHINA**
	CENTRAL PEOPLES BS, Beijing — DS-1 • 10/15 kW
4460v	**CLANDESTINE (M EAST)**
	†"VO THE MOJAHED", Iraq — Mideast
4460.8	**PERU**
	RADIO NORANDINA, Celendín — DS • 1 kW
4472v	**BOLIVIA**
	†RADIO MOVIMA, Santa Ana — DS / Irr • DS / M-Sa • DS / Su • DS
4485	**PERU**
	†R FRECUENCIA VH, Celendín — DS-LV DE CELENDIN • 0.5 kW
	RUSSIA
	†BASHKIR RADIO, Ufa — RUSSIAN, ETC • DS-LOCAL, R ROSSII • 50 kW
	†KAMCHATKA RADIO, Petropavlovsk-K — DS-LOCAL, R ROSSII • 100 kW
4500	**CHINA**
	†XINJIANG PEOPLE'S BC STN, Urümqi — DS-CHINESE • 50 kW
4505.2	**PERU**
	†RADIO HORIZONTE, Chiclayo — DS • 0.5 kW
4508.7	**BOLIVIA**
	R SAN JOAQUIN, San Joaquín — DS
4510.2	**PERU**
	†R PAUCARTAMBO, Paucartambo (Pasco) — DS • 0.25 kW / Tu-Su • DS • 0.25 kW / M-Sa • DS • 0.25 kW / Sa/Su • DS • 0.25 kW
4530.2	**BOLIVIA**
	RADIO HITACHI, Guayaramerín — Irr • Tu-Su • DS / M-Sa • DS
4545	**KAZAKHSTAN**
	KAZAKH RADIO, Almaty — RUSSIAN, GERMAN, ETC • DS-1 • 20 kW
4549.4	**BOLIVIA**
	RADIO TROPICO, Trinidad — Tu-Sa • DS • 0.75/3 kW • ALT. FREQ. TO 4552.5 kHz / DS • 0.75/3 kW • ALT. FREQ. TO 4552.5 kHz / M-Sa • DS • 0.75/3 kW • ALT. FREQ. TO 4552.5 kHz
4552.5	**BOLIVIA**
	RADIO TROPICO, Trinidad — Tu-Sa • DS • 0.75/3 kW • ALT. FREQ. TO 4549.4 kHz / DS • 0.75/3 kW • ALT. FREQ. TO 4549.4 kHz / M-Sa • DS • 0.75/3 kW • ALT. FREQ. TO 4549.4 kHz
4557v	**CLANDESTINE (ASIA)**
	"VO NAT SALVATION, Haeju, N Korea — TO SOUTH KOREA • 100 kW
4575v	**PERU**
	†RADIO LATINA, Chiclayo — DS-TEMP INACTIVE
4599.8	**BOLIVIA**
	RADIO VILLA MONTES, Villa Montes — DS • 1 kW / M-Sa • DS • 1 kW
4600	**BOLIVIA**
	R PERLA DEL ACRE, Cobija — Tu-Su • DS • 0.2 kW / M-Sa • DS • 0.2 kW
4606.5	**INDONESIA**
	†RRI, Serui, Irian Jaya — DS • 0.5 kW
	PERU
	†RADIO AYAVIRI, Ayaviri — DS • 1 kW
4613v	**PERU**
	†RADIO SOLEDAD, Parcoy — Irr • DS

FREQUENCY   COUNTRY, STATION, LOCATION

TARGET • NETWORK • POWER (kW)

World Time

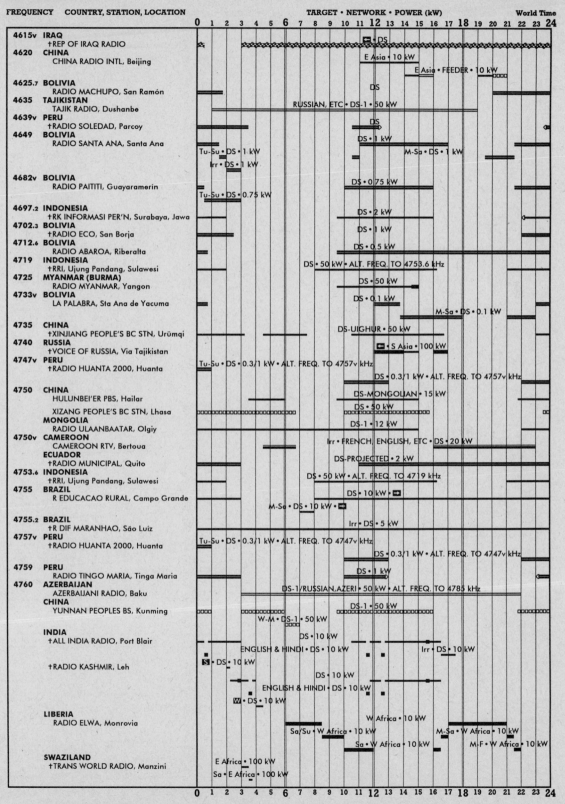

Frequency	Country, Station, Location	Notes
4615v	IRAQ †REP OF IRAQ RADIO	DS
4620	CHINA CHINA RADIO INTL, Beijing	E Asia • 10 kW E Asia • FEEDER • 10 kW
4625.7	BOLIVIA RADIO MACHUPO, San Ramón	DS
4635	TAJIKISTAN TAJIK RADIO, Dushanbe	RUSSIAN, ETC • DS-1 • 50 kW
4639v	PERU †RADIO SOLEDAD, Parcoy	DS
4649	BOLIVIA RADIO SANTA ANA, Santa Ana	DS • 1 kW Tu-Su • DS • 1 kW M-Sa • DS • 1 kW Irr • DS • 1 kW
4682v	BOLIVIA RADIO PAITITI, Guayaramerín	DS • 0.75 kW Tu-Su • DS • 0.75 kW
4697.2	INDONESIA †RK INFORMASI PER'N, Surabaya, Jawa	DS • 2 kW
4702.3	BOLIVIA †RADIO ECO, San Borja	DS • 1 kW
4712.6	BOLIVIA RADIO ABAROA, Riberalta	DS • 0.5 kW
4719	INDONESIA †RRI, Ujung Pandang, Sulawesi	DS • 50 kW • ALT. FREQ. TO 4753.6 kHz
4725	MYANMAR (BURMA) RADIO MYANMAR, Yangon	DS • 50 kW
4733v	BOLIVIA LA PALABRA, Sta Ana de Yacuma	DS • 0.1 kW M-Sa • DS • 0.1 kW
4735	CHINA †XINJIANG PEOPLE'S BC STN, Urümqi	DS-UIGHUR • 50 kW
4740	RUSSIA †VOICE OF RUSSIA, Via Tajikistan	S Asia • 100 kW
4747v	PERU †RADIO HUANTA 2000, Huanta	Tu-Su • DS • 0.3/1 kW • ALT. FREQ. TO 4757v kHz DS • 0.3/1 kW • ALT. FREQ. TO 4757v kHz
4750	CHINA HULUNBEI'ER PBS, Hailar	DS-MONGOLIAN • 15 kW
	XIZANG PEOPLE'S BC STN, Lhasa	DS • 50 kW
	MONGOLIA RADIO ULAANBAATAR, Olgiy	DS-1 • 12 kW
4750v	CAMEROON CAMEROON RTV, Bertoua	Irr • FRENCH, ENGLISH, ETC • DS • 20 kW
	ECUADOR †RADIO MUNICIPAL, Quito	DS-PROJECTED • 2 kW
4753.6	INDONESIA †RRI, Ujung Pandang, Sulawesi	DS • 50 kW • ALT. FREQ. TO 4719 kHz
4755	BRAZIL R EDUCACAO RURAL, Campo Grande	DS • 10 kW M-Sa • DS • 10 kW
4755.2	BRAZIL †R DIF MARANHAO, São Luiz	Irr • DS • 5 kW
4757v	PERU †RADIO HUANTA 2000, Huanta	Tu-Su • DS • 0.3/1 kW • ALT. FREQ. TO 4747v kHz DS • 0.3/1 kW • ALT. FREQ. TO 4747v kHz
4759	PERU RADIO TINGO MARIA, Tinga Maria	DS • 1 kW
4760	AZERBAIJAN AZERBAIJANI RADIO, Baku	DS-1/RUSSIAN, AZERI • 50 kW • ALT. FREQ. TO 4785 kHz
	CHINA YUNNAN PEOPLES BS, Kunming	DS-1 • 50 kW W-M • DS-1 • 50 kW
	INDIA †ALL INDIA RADIO, Port Blair	DS • 10 kW ENGLISH & HINDI • DS • 10 kW Irr • DS • 10 kW
	†RADIO KASHMIR, Leh	S • DS • 10 kW DS • 10 kW ENGLISH & HINDI • DS • 10 kW W • DS • 10 kW
	LIBERIA RADIO ELWA, Monrovia	W Africa • 10 kW Sa/Su • W Africa • 10 kW M-Sa • W Africa • 10 kW Sa • W Africa • 10 kW M-F • W Africa • 10 kW
	SWAZILAND †TRANS WORLD RADIO, Manzini	E Africa • 100 kW Sa • E Africa • 100 kW

ENGLISH ▬   ARABIC ⌇⌇⌇   CHINESE ▯▯▯   FRENCH ▬▬   GERMAN ▬▬   RUSSIAN ══   SPANISH ▬▬   OTHER ▬

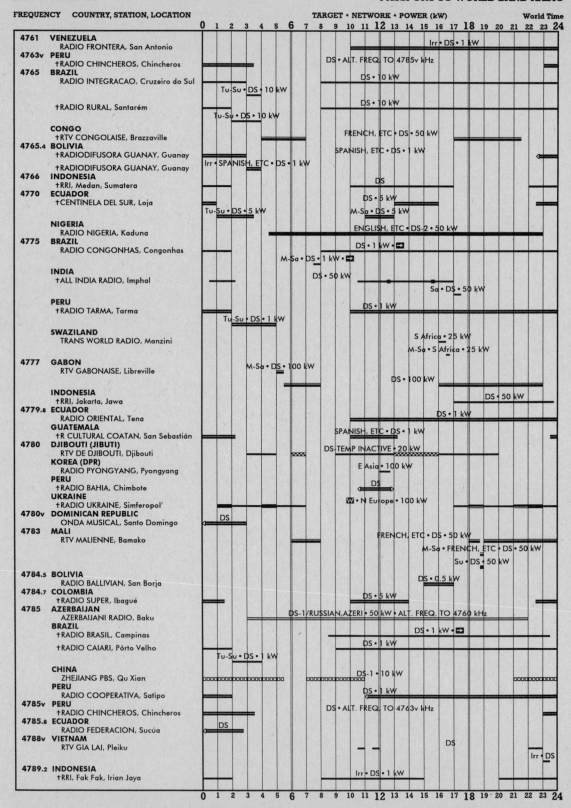

FREQUENCY   COUNTRY, STATION, LOCATION   TARGET • NETWORK • POWER (kW)   World Time

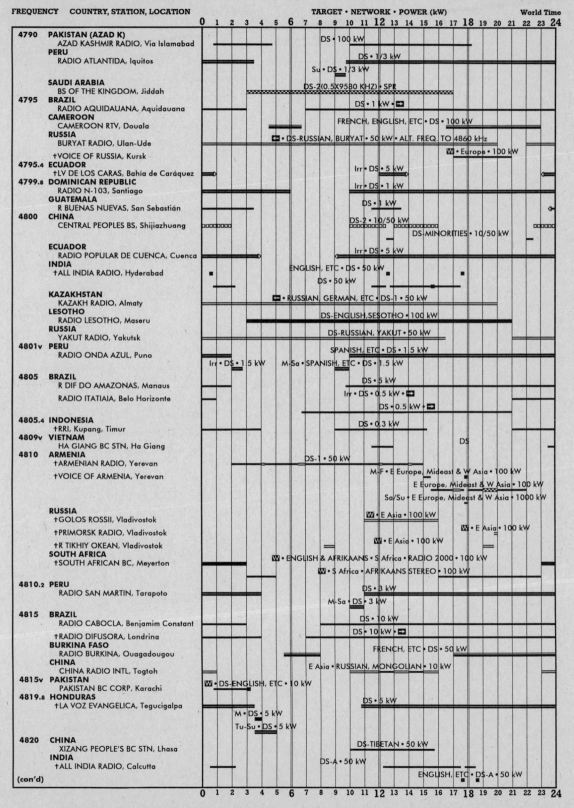

Freq	Country / Station / Location	Notes
4790	**PAKISTAN (AZAD K)** AZAD KASHMIR RADIO, Via Islamabad	DS • 100 kW
	PERU RADIO ATLANTIDA, Iquitos	DS • 1/3 kW / Su • DS • 1/3 kW
	SAUDI ARABIA BS OF THE KINGDOM, Jiddah	DS-2(0.5X9580 KHZ) • SPR
4795	**BRAZIL** RADIO AQUIDAUANA, Aquidauana	DS • 1 kW • ➡
	CAMEROON CAMEROON RTV, Douala	FRENCH, ENGLISH, ETC • DS • 100 kW
	RUSSIA BURYAT RADIO, Ulan-Ude	⬅ • DS-RUSSIAN, BURYAT • 50 kW • ALT. FREQ. TO 4860 kHz
	†VOICE OF RUSSIA, Kursk	W • Europe • 100 kW
4795.4	**ECUADOR** †LV DE LOS CARAS, Bahía de Caráquez	Irr • DS • 5 kW
4799.8	**DOMINICAN REPUBLIC** RADIO N-103, Santiago	Irr • DS • 1 kW
	GUATEMALA R BUENAS NUEVAS, San Sebastián	DS • 1 kW
4800	**CHINA** CENTRAL PEOPLES BS, Shijiazhuang	DS-2 • 10/50 kW / DS-MINORITIES • 10/50 kW
	ECUADOR RADIO POPULAR DE CUENCA, Cuenca	Irr • DS • 5 kW
	INDIA †ALL INDIA RADIO, Hyderabad	ENGLISH, ETC • DS • 50 kW / DS • 50 kW
	KAZAKHSTAN KAZAKH RADIO, Almaty	⬅ • RUSSIAN, GERMAN, ETC • DS-1 • 50 kW
	LESOTHO RADIO LESOTHO, Maseru	DS-ENGLISH, SESOTHO • 100 kW
	RUSSIA YAKUT RADIO, Yakutsk	DS-RUSSIAN, YAKUT • 50 kW
4801v	**PERU** RADIO ONDA AZUL, Puno	SPANISH, ETC • DS • 1.5 kW / Irr • DS • 1.5 kW / M-Sa • SPANISH, ETC • DS • 1.5 kW
4805	**BRAZIL** R DIF DO AMAZONAS, Manaus	DS • 5 kW
	RADIO ITATIAIA, Belo Horizonte	Irr • DS • 0.5 kW • ➡ / DS • 0.5 kW • ➡
4805.4	**INDONESIA** †RRI, Kupang, Timur	DS • 0.3 kW
4809v	**VIETNAM** HA GIANG BC STN, Ha Giang	DS
4810	**ARMENIA** †ARMENIAN RADIO, Yerevan	DS-1 • 50 kW
	†VOICE OF ARMENIA, Yerevan	M-F • E Europe, Mideast & W Asia • 100 kW / E Europe, Mideast & W Asia • 100 kW / Sa/Su • E Europe, Mideast & W Asia • 1000 kW
	RUSSIA †GOLOS ROSSII, Vladivostok	W • E Asia • 100 kW
	†PRIMORSK RADIO, Vladivostok	W • E Asia • 100 kW
	†R TIKHIY OKEAN, Vladivostok	W • E Asia • 100 kW
	SOUTH AFRICA †SOUTH AFRICAN BC, Meyerton	W • ENGLISH & AFRIKAANS • S Africa • RADIO 2000 • 100 kW / W • S Africa • AFRIKAANS STEREO • 100 kW
4810.2	**PERU** RADIO SAN MARTIN, Tarapoto	DS • 3 kW / M-Sa • DS • 3 kW
4815	**BRAZIL** RADIO CABOCLA, Benjamim Constant	DS • 10 kW
	†RADIO DIFUSORA, Londrina	DS • 10 kW • ➡
	BURKINA FASO RADIO BURKINA, Ouagadougou	FRENCH, ETC • DS • 50 kW
	CHINA CHINA RADIO INTL, Togtoh	E Asia • RUSSIAN, MONGOLIAN • 10 kW
4815v	**PAKISTAN** PAKISTAN BC CORP, Karachi	W • DS-ENGLISH, ETC • 10 kW
4819.8	**HONDURAS** †LA VOZ EVANGELICA, Tegucigalpa	DS • 5 kW / M • DS • 5 kW / Tu-Su • DS • 5 kW
4820	**CHINA** XIZANG PEOPLE'S BC STN, Lhasa	DS-TIBETAN • 50 kW
	INDIA †ALL INDIA RADIO, Calcutta	DS-A • 50 kW / ENGLISH, ETC • DS-A • 50 kW

(con'd)

ENGLISH ▬   ARABIC ∾∾   CHINESE □□□   FRENCH ▭▭   GERMAN ▬▬   RUSSIAN ══   SPANISH ▭▭   OTHER ▬

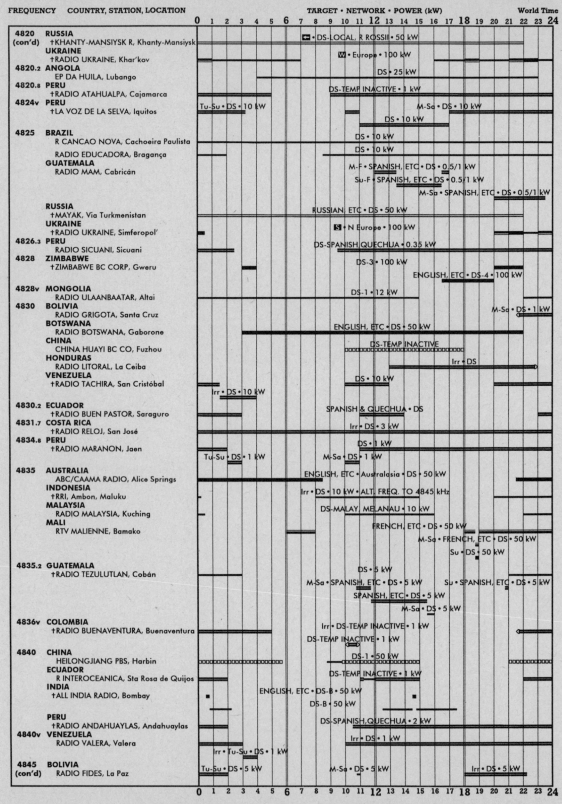

FREQUENCY   COUNTRY, STATION, LOCATION

TARGET • NETWORK • POWER (kW)   World Time

4820	RUSSIA	
(con'd)	†KHANTY-MANSIYSK R, Khanty-Mansiysk	DS-LOCAL, R ROSSII • 50 kW
	UKRAINE	
	†RADIO UKRAINE, Khar'kov	W • Europe • 100 kW
4820.2	ANGOLA	
	EP DA HUILA, Lubango	DS • 25 kW
4820.8	PERU	
	†RADIO ATAHUALPA, Cajamarca	DS-TEMP INACTIVE • 1 kW
4824v	PERU	
	†LA VOZ DE LA SELVA, Iquitos	Tu-Su • DS • 10 kW M-Sa • DS • 10 kW DS • 10 kW
4825	BRAZIL	
	R CANCAO NOVA, Cachoeira Paulista	DS • 10 kW
	RADIO EDUCADORA, Bragança	DS • 10 kW
	GUATEMALA	
	RADIO MAM, Cabricán	M-F • SPANISH, ETC • DS • 0.5/1 kW Su-F • SPANISH, ETC • DS • 0.5/1 kW M-Sa • SPANISH, ETC • DS • 0.5/1 kW
	RUSSIA	
	†MAYAK, Via Turkmenistan	RUSSIAN, ETC • DS • 50 kW
	UKRAINE	
	†RADIO UKRAINE, Simferopol'	S • N Europe • 100 kW
4826.3	PERU	
	RADIO SICUANI, Sicuani	DS-SPANISH QUECHUA • 0.35 kW
4828	ZIMBABWE	
	†ZIMBABWE BC CORP, Gweru	DS-3 • 100 kW ENGLISH, ETC • DS-4 • 100 kW
4828v	MONGOLIA	
	RADIO ULAANBAATAR, Altai	DS-1 • 12 kW
4830	BOLIVIA	
	RADIO GRIGOTA, Santa Cruz	M-Sa • DS • 1 kW
	BOTSWANA	
	RADIO BOTSWANA, Gaborone	ENGLISH, ETC • DS • 50 kW
	CHINA	
	CHINA HUAYI BC CO, Fuzhou	DS-TEMP INACTIVE
	HONDURAS	
	RADIO LITORAL, La Ceiba	Irr • DS
	VENEZUELA	
	†RADIO TACHIRA, San Cristóbal	DS • 10 kW Irr • DS • 10 kW
4830.2	ECUADOR	
	†RADIO BUEN PASTOR, Saraguro	SPANISH & QUECHUA • DS
4831.7	COSTA RICA	
	†RADIO RELOJ, San José	Irr • DS • 3 kW
4834.8	PERU	
	†RADIO MARANON, Jaen	DS • 1 kW Tu-Su • DS • 1 kW M-Sa • DS • 1 kW
4835	AUSTRALIA	
	ABC/CAAMA RADIO, Alice Springs	ENGLISH, ETC • Australasia • DS • 50 kW
	INDONESIA	
	†RRI, Ambon, Maluku	Irr • DS • 10 kW • ALT. FREQ. TO 4845 kHz
	MALAYSIA	
	RADIO MALAYSIA, Kuching	DS-MALAY MELANAU • 10 kW
	MALI	
	RTV MALIENNE, Bamako	FRENCH, ETC • DS • 50 kW M-Sa • FRENCH, ETC • DS • 50 kW Su • DS • 50 kW
4835.2	GUATEMALA	
	†RADIO TEZULUTLAN, Cobán	DS • 5 kW M-Sa • SPANISH, ETC • DS • 5 kW Su • SPANISH, ETC • DS • 5 kW SPANISH, ETC • DS • 5 kW M-Sa • DS • 5 kW
4836v	COLOMBIA	
	†RADIO BUENAVENTURA, Buenaventura	Irr • DS-TEMP INACTIVE • 1 kW DS-TEMP INACTIVE • 1 kW
4840	CHINA	
	HEILONGJIANG PBS, Harbin	DS-1 • 50 kW
	ECUADOR	
	R INTEROCEANICA, Sta Rosa de Quijos	DS-TEMP INACTIVE • 1 kW
	INDIA	
	†ALL INDIA RADIO, Bombay	ENGLISH, ETC • DS-B • 50 kW DS-B • 50 kW
	PERU	
	†RADIO ANDAHUAYLAS, Andahuaylas	DS-SPANISH, QUECHUA • 2 kW
4840v	VENEZUELA	
	RADIO VALERA, Valera	Irr • DS • 1 kW Irr • Tu-Su • DS • 1 kW
4845	BOLIVIA	
(con'd)	RADIO FIDES, La Paz	Tu-Su • DS • 5 kW M-Sa • DS • 5 kW Irr • DS • 5 kW

FREQUENCY	COUNTRY, STATION, LOCATION	TARGET • NETWORK • POWER (kW)	World Time

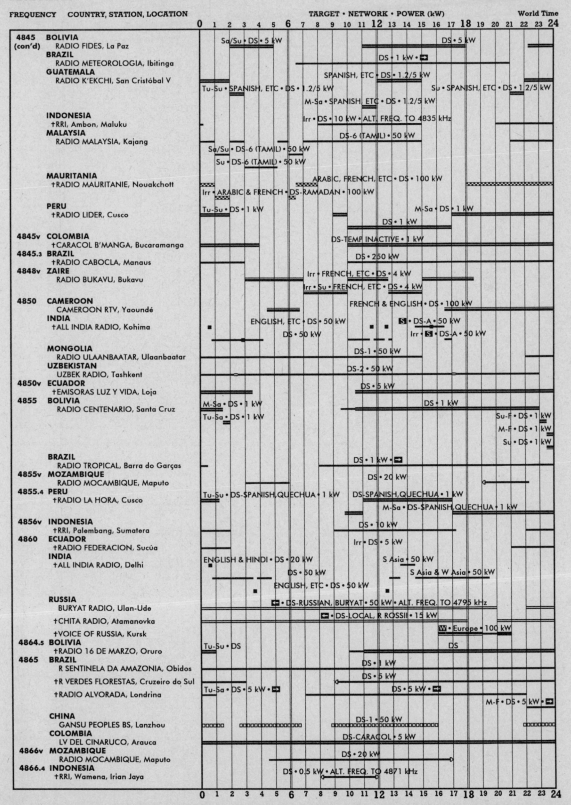

4845 (con'd)	BOLIVIA	
	RADIO FIDES, La Paz	Sa/Su • DS • 5 kW ... DS • 5 kW
	BRAZIL	
	RADIO METEOROLOGIA, Ibitinga	DS • 1 kW • ▣
	GUATEMALA	
	RADIO K'EKCHI, San Cristóbal V	SPANISH, ETC • DS • 1.2/5 kW
		Tu-Su • SPANISH, ETC • DS • 1.2/5 kW ... Su • SPANISH, ETC • DS • 1.2/5 kW
		M-Sa • SPANISH, ETC • DS • 1.2/5 kW
	INDONESIA	
	†RRI, Ambon, Maluku	Irr • DS • 10 kW • ALT. FREQ. TO 4835 kHz
	MALAYSIA	
	RADIO MALAYSIA, Kajang	DS-6 (TAMIL) • 50 kW
		Sa/Su • DS-6 (TAMIL) • 50 kW
		Su • DS-6 (TAMIL) • 50 kW
	MAURITANIA	
	†RADIO MAURITANIE, Nouakchott	ARABIC, FRENCH, ETC • DS • 100 kW
		Irr • ARABIC & FRENCH • DS-RAMADAN • 100 kW
	PERU	
	†RADIO LIDER, Cusco	Tu-Su • DS • 1 kW ... M-Sa • DS • 1 kW
		DS • 1 kW
4845v	COLOMBIA	
	†CARACOL B'MANGA, Bucaramanga	DS-TEMP INACTIVE • 1 kW
4845.3	BRAZIL	
	†RADIO CABOCLA, Manaus	DS • 250 kW
4848v	ZAIRE	
	RADIO BUKAVU, Bukavu	Irr • FRENCH, ETC • DS • 4 kW
		Irr • Su • FRENCH, ETC • DS • 4 kW
4850	CAMEROON	
	CAMEROON RTV, Yaoundé	FRENCH & ENGLISH • DS • 100 kW
	INDIA	
	†ALL INDIA RADIO, Kohima	ENGLISH, ETC • DS • 50 kW ... ▣ • DS-A • 50 kW
		DS • 50 kW ... Irr • ▣ • DS-A • 50 kW
	MONGOLIA	
	RADIO ULAANBAATAR, Ulaanbaatar	DS-1 • 50 kW
	UZBEKISTAN	
	UZBEK RADIO, Tashkent	DS-2 • 50 kW
4850v	ECUADOR	
	†EMISORAS LUZ Y VIDA, Loja	DS • 5 kW
4855	BOLIVIA	
	RADIO CENTENARIO, Santa Cruz	M-Sa • DS • 1 kW ... DS • 1 kW
		Tu-Sa • DS • 1 kW
		Su-F • DS • 1 kW
		M-F • DS • 1 kW
		Su • DS • 1 kW
	BRAZIL	
	RADIO TROPICAL, Barra do Garças	DS • 1 kW • ▣
4855v	MOZAMBIQUE	
	RADIO MOCAMBIQUE, Maputo	DS • 20 kW
4855.4	PERU	
	†RADIO LA HORA, Cusco	Tu-Su • DS-SPANISH, QUECHUA • 1 kW ... DS-SPANISH, QUECHUA • 1 kW
		M-Sa • DS-SPANISH, QUECHUA • 1 kW
4856v	INDONESIA	
	†RRI, Palembang, Sumatera	DS • 10 kW
4860	ECUADOR	
	†RADIO FEDERACION, Sucúa	Irr • DS • 5 kW
	INDIA	
	†ALL INDIA RADIO, Delhi	ENGLISH & HINDI • DS • 20 kW ... S Asia • 50 kW
		DS • 50 kW ... S Asia & W Asia • 50 kW
		ENGLISH, ETC • DS • 50 kW
	RUSSIA	
	BURYAT RADIO, Ulan-Ude	▣ • DS-RUSSIAN, BURYAT • 50 kW • ALT. FREQ. TO 4795 kHz
	†CHITA RADIO, Atamanovka	▣ • DS-LOCAL, R ROSSII • 15 kW
	†VOICE OF RUSSIA, Kursk	▣ • Europe • 100 kW
4864.5	BOLIVIA	
	†RADIO 16 DE MARZO, Oruro	Tu-Su • DS ... DS
4865	BRAZIL	
	R SENTINELA DA AMAZONIA, Obidos	DS • 1 kW
	†R VERDES FLORESTAS, Cruzeiro do Sul	DS • 5 kW
	†RADIO ALVORADA, Londrina	Tu-Sa • DS • 5 kW ... DS • 5 kW • ▣
		M-F • DS • 5 kW • ▣
	CHINA	
	GANSU PEOPLES BS, Lanzhou	DS-1 • 50 kW
	COLOMBIA	
	LV DEL CINARUCO, Arauca	DS-CARACOL • 5 kW
4866v	MOZAMBIQUE	
	RADIO MOCAMBIQUE, Maputo	DS • 20 kW
4866.4	INDONESIA	
	†RRI, Wamena, Irian Jaya	DS • 0.5 kW • ALT. FREQ. TO 4871 kHz

ENGLISH ▬ ARABIC ▨ CHINESE ▦ FRENCH ▬ GERMAN ▬ RUSSIAN ═ SPANISH ▬ OTHER ─

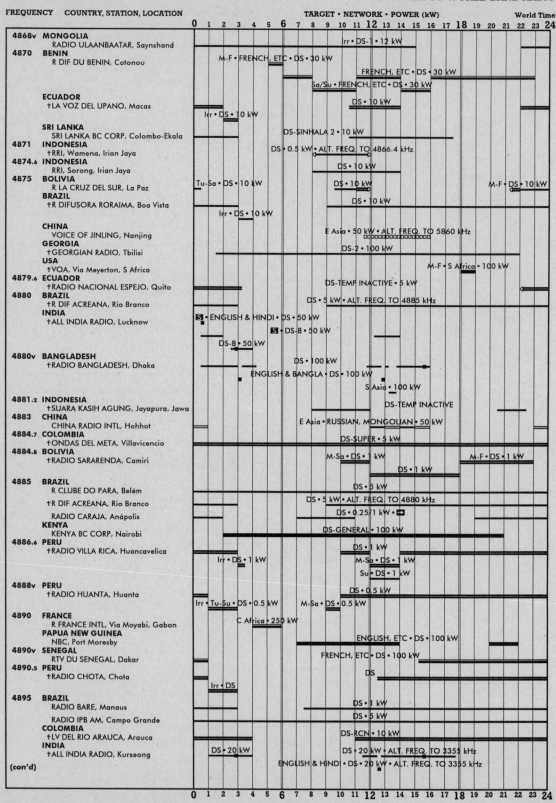

FREQUENCY   COUNTRY, STATION, LOCATION

TARGET • NETWORK • POWER (kW)   World Time

FREQUENCY	COUNTRY, STATION, LOCATION	Notes
4868v	**MONGOLIA** RADIO ULAANBAATAR, Saynshand	Irr • DS-1 • 12 kW
4870	**BENIN** R DIF DU BENIN, Cotonou	M-F • FRENCH, ETC • DS • 30 kW / FRENCH, ETC • DS • 30 kW / Sa/Su • FRENCH, ETC • DS • 30 kW
	ECUADOR †LA VOZ DEL UPANO, Macas	DS • 10 kW / Irr • DS • 10 kW
	SRI LANKA SRI LANKA BC CORP, Colombo-Ekala	DS-SINHALA 2 • 10 kW
4871	**INDONESIA** †RRI, Wamena, Irian Jaya	DS • 0.5 kW • ALT. FREQ. TO 4866.4 kHz
4874.6	**INDONESIA** RRI, Sorong, Irian Jaya	DS • 10 kW
4875	**BOLIVIA** R LA CRUZ DEL SUR, La Paz	Tu-Sa • DS • 10 kW / DS • 10 kW / M-F • DS • 10 kW
	BRAZIL †R DIFUSORA RORAIMA, Boa Vista	DS • 10 kW / Irr • DS • 10 kW
	CHINA VOICE OF JINLING, Nanjing	E Asia • 50 kW • ALT. FREQ. TO 5860 kHz
	GEORGIA †GEORGIAN RADIO, Tbilisi	DS-2 • 100 kW
	USA †VOA, Via Meyerton, S Africa	M-F • S Africa • 100 kW
4879.6	**ECUADOR** †RADIO NACIONAL ESPEJO, Quito	DS-TEMP INACTIVE • 5 kW
4880	**BRAZIL** †R DIF ACREANA, Rio Branco	DS • 5 kW • ALT. FREQ. TO 4885 kHz
	INDIA †ALL INDIA RADIO, Lucknow	S • ENGLISH & HINDI • DS • 50 kW / S • DS-B • 50 kW / DS-B • 50 kW
4880v	**BANGLADESH** †RADIO BANGLADESH, Dhaka	DS • 100 kW / ENGLISH & BANGLA • DS • 100 kW / S Asia • 100 kW
4881.2	**INDONESIA** †SUARA KASIH AGUNG, Jayapura, Jawa	DS-TEMP INACTIVE
4883	**CHINA** CHINA RADIO INTL, Hohhot	E Asia • RUSSIAN, MONGOLIAN • 50 kW
4884.7	**COLOMBIA** †ONDAS DEL META, Villavicencio	DS-SUPER • 5 kW
4884.8	**BOLIVIA** †RADIO SARARENDA, Camiri	M-Sa • DS • 1 kW / DS • 1 kW / M-F • DS • 1 kW
4885	**BRAZIL** R CLUBE DO PARA, Belém	DS • 5 kW
	†R DIF ACREANA, Rio Branco	DS • 5 kW • ALT. FREQ. TO 4880 kHz
	RADIO CARAJA, Anápolis	DS • 0.25/1 kW • □
	KENYA KENYA BC CORP, Nairobi	DS-GENERAL • 100 kW
4886.6	**PERU** †RADIO VILLA RICA, Huancavelica	DS • 1 kW / Irr • DS • 1 kW / M-Sa • DS • 1 kW / Su • DS • 1 kW
4888v	**PERU** †RADIO HUANTA, Huanta	DS • 0.5 kW / Irr • Tu-Su • DS • 0.5 kW / M-Sa • DS • 0.5 kW
4890	**FRANCE** R FRANCE INTL, Via Moyabi, Gabon	C Africa • 250 kW
	PAPUA NEW GUINEA NBC, Port Moresby	ENGLISH, ETC • DS • 100 kW
4890v	**SENEGAL** RTV DU SENEGAL, Dakar	FRENCH, ETC • DS • 100 kW
4890.5	**PERU** †RADIO CHOTA, Chota	DS / Irr • DS
4895	**BRAZIL** RADIO BARE, Manaus	DS • 1 kW
	RADIO IPB AM, Campo Grande	DS • 5 kW
	COLOMBIA †LV DEL RIO ARAUCA, Arauca	DS-RCN • 10 kW
	INDIA †ALL INDIA RADIO, Kurseong	DS • 20 kW / DS • 20 kW • ALT. FREQ. TO 3355 kHz / ENGLISH & HINDI • DS • 20 kW • ALT. FREQ. TO 3355 kHz
(con'd)		

FREQUENCY   COUNTRY, STATION, LOCATION   TARGET • NETWORK • POWER (kW)   World Time

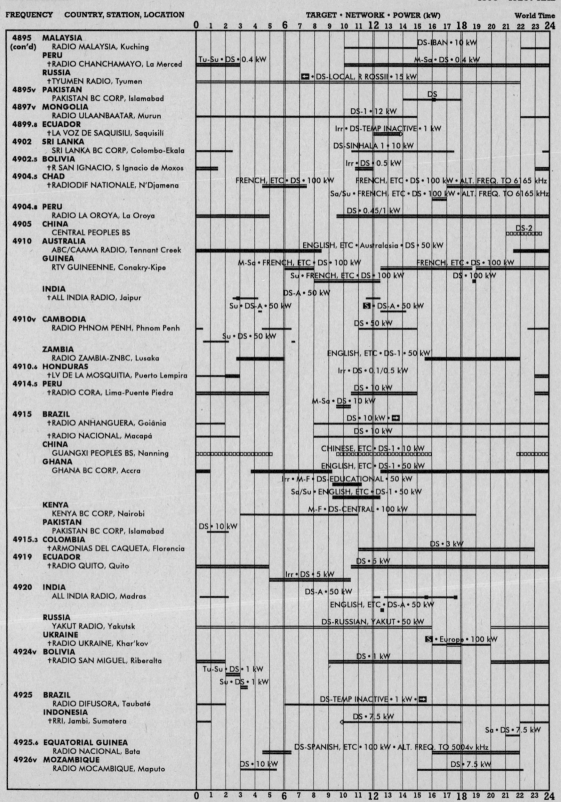

Frequency	Country / Station / Location	Schedule notes
4895 (con'd)	**MALAYSIA** RADIO MALAYSIA, Kuching	DS-IBAN • 10 kW
	PERU †RADIO CHANCHAMAYO, La Merced	Tu-Su • DS • 0.4 kW / M-Sa • DS • 0.4 kW
	RUSSIA †TYUMEN RADIO, Tyumen	• DS-LOCAL, R ROSSII • 15 kW
4895v	**PAKISTAN** PAKISTAN BC CORP, Islamabad	DS
4897v	**MONGOLIA** RADIO ULAANBAATAR, Murun	DS-1 • 12 kW
4899.8	**ECUADOR** †LA VOZ DE SAQUISILI, Saquisilí	Irr • DS-TEMP INACTIVE • 1 kW
4902	**SRI LANKA** SRI LANKA BC CORP, Colombo-Ekala	DS-SINHALA 1 • 10 kW
4902.5	**BOLIVIA** †R SAN IGNACIO, S Ignacio de Moxos	Irr • DS • 0.5 kW
4904.5	**CHAD** †RADIODIF NATIONALE, N'Djamena	FRENCH, ETC • DS • 100 kW / FRENCH, ETC • DS • 100 kW • ALT. FREQ. TO 6165 kHz / Sa/Su • FRENCH, ETC • DS • 100 kW • ALT. FREQ. TO 6165 kHz
4904.8	**PERU** RADIO LA OROYA, La Oroya	DS • 0.45/1 kW
4905	**CHINA** CENTRAL PEOPLES BS	DS-2
4910	**AUSTRALIA** ABC/CAAMA RADIO, Tennant Creek	ENGLISH, ETC • Australasia • DS • 50 kW
	GUINEA RTV GUINEENNE, Conakry-Kipe	M-Sa • FRENCH, ETC • DS • 100 kW / FRENCH, ETC • DS • 100 kW / Su • FRENCH, ETC • DS • 100 kW / DS • 100 kW
	INDIA †ALL INDIA RADIO, Jaipur	DS-A • 50 kW / Su • DS-A • 50 kW / S • DS-A • 50 kW
4910v	**CAMBODIA** RADIO PHNOM PENH, Phnom Penh	DS • 50 kW / Su • DS • 50 kW
	ZAMBIA RADIO ZAMBIA-ZNBC, Lusaka	ENGLISH, ETC • DS-1 • 50 kW
4910.6	**HONDURAS** †LV DE LA MOSQUITIA, Puerto Lempira	Irr • DS • 0.1/0.5 kW
4914.5	**PERU** †RADIO CORA, Lima-Puente Piedra	DS • 10 kW / M-Sa • DS • 10 kW
4915	**BRAZIL** †RADIO ANHANGUERA, Goiânia	DS • 10 kW •
	†RADIO NACIONAL, Macapá	DS • 10 kW
	CHINA GUANGXI PEOPLES BS, Nanning	CHINESE, ETC • DS-1 • 10 kW
	GHANA GHANA BC CORP, Accra	ENGLISH, ETC • DS-1 • 50 kW / Irr • M-F • DS-EDUCATIONAL • 50 kW / Sa/Su • ENGLISH, ETC • DS-1 • 50 kW
	KENYA KENYA BC CORP, Nairobi	M-F • DS-CENTRAL • 100 kW
	PAKISTAN PAKISTAN BC CORP, Islamabad	DS • 10 kW
4915.3	**COLOMBIA** †ARMONIAS DEL CAQUETA, Florencia	DS • 3 kW
4919	**ECUADOR** †RADIO QUITO, Quito	DS • 5 kW / Irr • DS • 5 kW
4920	**INDIA** ALL INDIA RADIO, Madras	DS-A • 50 kW / ENGLISH, ETC • DS-A • 50 kW
	RUSSIA YAKUT RADIO, Yakutsk	DS-RUSSIAN, YAKUT • 50 kW
	UKRAINE †RADIO UKRAINE, Khar'kov	S • Europe • 100 kW
4924v	**BOLIVIA** †RADIO SAN MIGUEL, Riberalta	DS • 1 kW / Tu-Su • DS • 1 kW / Su • DS • 1 kW
4925	**BRAZIL** RADIO DIFUSORA, Taubaté	DS-TEMP INACTIVE • 1 kW •
	INDONESIA †RRI, Jambi, Sumatera	DS • 7.5 kW / Sa • DS • 7.5 kW
4925.6	**EQUATORIAL GUINEA** RADIO NACIONAL, Bata	DS-SPANISH, ETC • 100 kW • ALT. FREQ. TO 5004v kHz
4926v	**MOZAMBIQUE** RADIO MOCAMBIQUE, Maputo	DS • 10 kW / DS • 7.5 kW

ENGLISH ▬▬ ARABIC ≋≋≋ CHINESE □□□ FRENCH ▬▬ GERMAN ▬▬ RUSSIAN ══ SPANISH ▬▬ OTHER ▬

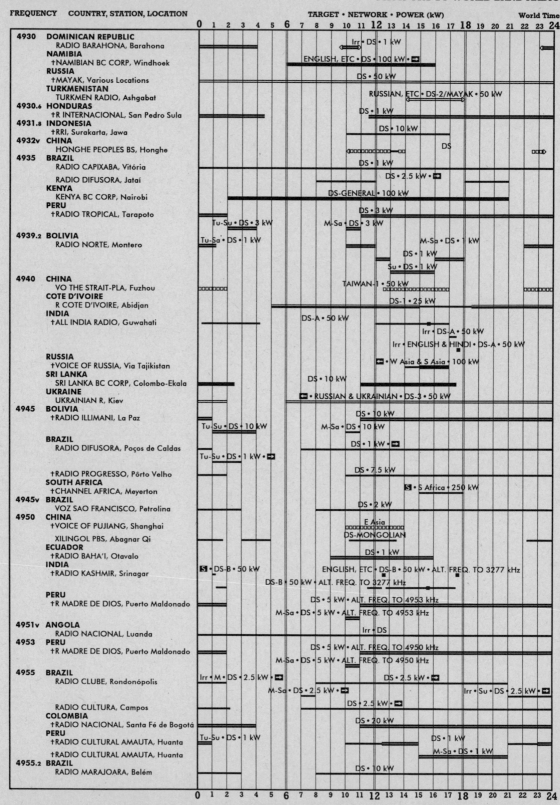

FREQUENCY   COUNTRY, STATION, LOCATION   TARGET • NETWORK • POWER (kW)   World Time

FREQUENCY	COUNTRY, STATION, LOCATION	TARGET • NETWORK • POWER (kW)
4930	**DOMINICAN REPUBLIC**	
	RADIO BARAHONA, Barahona	Irr • DS • 1 kW
	NAMIBIA	
	†NAMIBIAN BC CORP, Windhoek	ENGLISH, ETC • DS • 100 kW • ➡
	RUSSIA	
	†MAYAK, Various Locations	DS • 50 kW
	TURKMENISTAN	
	TURKMEN RADIO, Ashgabat	RUSSIAN, ETC • DS-2/MAYAK • 50 kW
4930.6	**HONDURAS**	
	†R INTERNACIONAL, San Pedro Sula	DS • 1 kW
4931.8	**INDONESIA**	
	†RRI, Surakarta, Jawa	DS • 10 kW
4932v	**CHINA**	
	HONGHE PEOPLES BS, Honghe	DS
4935	**BRAZIL**	
	RADIO CAPIXABA, Vitória	DS • 1 kW
	RADIO DIFUSORA, Jataí	DS • 2.5 kW • ➡
	KENYA	
	KENYA BC CORP, Nairobi	DS-GENERAL • 100 kW
	PERU	
	†RADIO TROPICAL, Tarapoto	DS • 3 kW
		Tu-Su • DS • 3 kW M-Sa • DS • 3 kW
4939.2	**BOLIVIA**	
	RADIO NORTE, Montero	Tu-Sa • DS • 1 kW M-Sa • DS • 1 kW
		DS • 1 kW
		Su • DS • 1 kW
4940	**CHINA**	
	VO THE STRAIT-PLA, Fuzhou	TAIWAN-1 • 50 kW
	COTE D'IVOIRE	
	R COTE D'IVOIRE, Abidjan	DS-1 • 25 kW
	INDIA	
	†ALL INDIA RADIO, Guwahati	DS-A • 50 kW
		Irr • DS-A • 50 kW
		Irr • ENGLISH & HINDI • DS-A • 50 kW
	RUSSIA	
	†VOICE OF RUSSIA, Via Tajikistan	➡ • W Asia & S Asia • 100 kW
	SRI LANKA	
	SRI LANKA BC CORP, Colombo-Ekala	DS • 10 kW
	UKRAINE	
	UKRAINIAN R, Kiev	➡ • RUSSIAN & UKRAINIAN • DS-3 • 50 kW
4945	**BOLIVIA**	
	†RADIO ILLIMANI, La Paz	DS • 10 kW
		Tu-Su • DS • 10 kW M-Sa • DS • 10 kW
	BRAZIL	
	RADIO DIFUSORA, Poços de Caldas	DS • 1 kW • ➡
		Tu-Su • DS • 1 kW • ➡
	†RADIO PROGRESSO, Pôrto Velho	DS • 7.5 kW
	SOUTH AFRICA	
	†CHANNEL AFRICA, Meyerton	🅂 • S Africa • 250 kW
4945v	**BRAZIL**	
	VOZ SAO FRANCISCO, Petrolina	DS • 2 kW
4950	**CHINA**	
	†VOICE OF PUJIANG, Shanghai	E Asia
	XILINGOL PBS, Abagnar Qi	DS-MONGOLIAN
	ECUADOR	
	†RADIO BAHA'I, Otavalo	DS • 1 kW
	INDIA	
	†RADIO KASHMIR, Srinagar	🅂 • DS-B • 50 kW ENGLISH, ETC • DS-B • 50 kW • ALT. FREQ. TO 3277 kHz
		DS-B • 50 kW • ALT. FREQ. TO 3277 kHz
	PERU	
	†R MADRE DE DIOS, Puerto Maldonado	DS • 5 kW • ALT. FREQ. TO 4953 kHz
		M-Sa • DS • 5 kW • ALT. FREQ. TO 4953 kHz
4951v	**ANGOLA**	
	RADIO NACIONAL, Luanda	Irr • DS
4953	**PERU**	
	†R MADRE DE DIOS, Puerto Maldonado	DS • 5 kW • ALT. FREQ. TO 4950 kHz
		M-Sa • DS • 5 kW • ALT. FREQ. TO 4950 kHz
4955	**BRAZIL**	
	RADIO CLUBE, Rondonópolis	Irr • M • DS • 2.5 kW • ➡ DS • 2.5 kW • ➡ Irr • Su • DS • 2.5 kW • ➡
		M-Sa • DS • 2.5 kW • ➡
	RADIO CULTURA, Campos	DS • 2.5 kW • ➡
	COLOMBIA	
	†RADIO NACIONAL, Santa Fé de Bogotá	DS • 20 kW
	PERU	
	†RADIO CULTURAL AMAUTA, Huanta	Tu-Su • DS • 1 kW DS • 1 kW
		M-Sa • DS • 1 kW
	†RADIO CULTURAL AMAUTA, Huanta	
4955.2	**BRAZIL**	
	RADIO MARAJOARA, Belém	DS • 10 kW

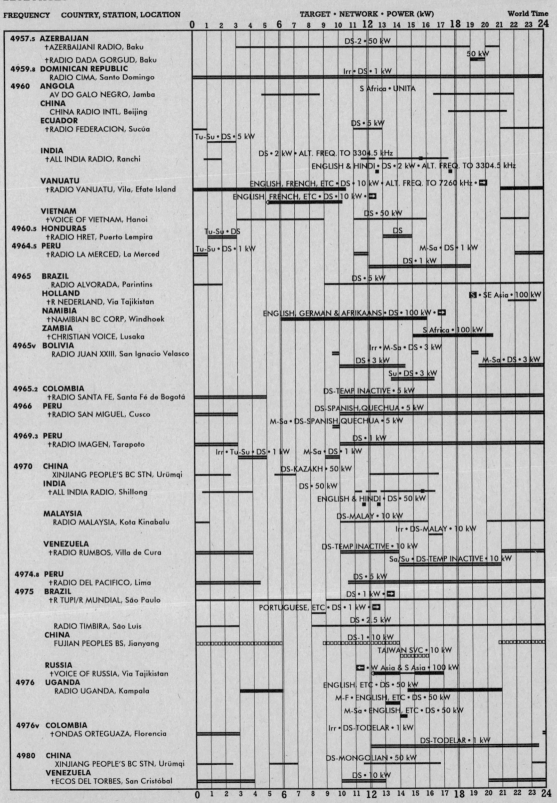

FREQUENCY | COUNTRY, STATION, LOCATION | TARGET • NETWORK • POWER (kW) | World Time

0 1 2 3 4 5 6 7 8 9 10 11 12 13 14 15 16 17 18 19 20 21 22 23 24

4957.5 AZERBAIJAN
†AZERBAIJANI RADIO, Baku — DS-2 • 50 kW
†RADIO DADA GORGUD, Baku — 50 kW

4959.8 DOMINICAN REPUBLIC
RADIO CIMA, Santo Domingo — Irr • DS • 1 kW

4960 ANGOLA
AV DO GALO NEGRO, Jamba — S Africa • UNITA

CHINA
CHINA RADIO INTL, Beijing

ECUADOR
†RADIO FEDERACION, Sucúa — DS • 5 kW; Tu-Su • DS • 5 kW

INDIA
†ALL INDIA RADIO, Ranchi — DS • 2 kW • ALT. FREQ. TO 3304.5 kHz; ENGLISH & HINDI • DS • 2 kW • ALT. FREQ. TO 3304.5 kHz

VANUATU
†RADIO VANUATU, Vila, Efate Island — ENGLISH, FRENCH, ETC • DS • 10 kW • ALT. FREQ. TO 7260 kHz • ➡; ENGLISH, FRENCH, ETC • DS • 10 kW • ➡

VIETNAM
†VOICE OF VIETNAM, Hanoi — DS • 50 kW

4960.5 HONDURAS
†RADIO HRET, Puerto Lempira — Tu-Su • DS; DS

4964.5 PERU
†RADIO LA MERCED, La Merced — Tu-Su • DS • 1 kW; M-Sa • DS • 1 kW; DS • 1 kW

4965 BRAZIL
RADIO ALVORADA, Parintins — DS • 5 kW

HOLLAND
†R NEDERLAND, Via Tajikistan — [S] • SE Asia • 100 kW

NAMIBIA
†NAMIBIAN BC CORP, Windhoek — ENGLISH, GERMAN & AFRIKAANS • DS • 100 kW • ➡

ZAMBIA
†CHRISTIAN VOICE, Lusaka — S Africa • 100 kW

4965v BOLIVIA
RADIO JUAN XXIII, San Ignacio Velasco — Irr • M-Sa • DS • 3 kW; DS • 3 kW; M-Sa • DS • 3 kW; Su • DS • 3 kW

4965.2 COLOMBIA
†RADIO SANTA FE, Santa Fé de Bogotá — DS-TEMP INACTIVE • 5 kW

4966 PERU
†RADIO SAN MIGUEL, Cusco — DS-SPANISH,QUECHUA • 5 kW; M-Sa • DS-SPANISH,QUECHUA • 5 kW

4969.3 PERU
†RADIO IMAGEN, Tarapoto — DS • 1 kW; Irr • Tu-Su • DS • 1 kW; M-Sa • DS • 1 kW

4970 CHINA
XINJIANG PEOPLE'S BC STN, Urümqi — DS-KAZAKH • 50 kW

INDIA
†ALL INDIA RADIO, Shillong — DS • 50 kW; ENGLISH & HINDI • DS • 50 kW

MALAYSIA
RADIO MALAYSIA, Kota Kinabalu — DS-MALAY • 10 kW; Irr • DS-MALAY • 10 kW

VENEZUELA
†RADIO RUMBOS, Villa de Cura — DS-TEMP INACTIVE • 10 kW; Sa/Su • DS-TEMP INACTIVE • 10 kW

4974.8 PERU
†RADIO DEL PACIFICO, Lima — DS • 5 kW

4975 BRAZIL
†R TUPI/R MUNDIAL, São Paulo — DS • 1 kW • ➡; PORTUGUESE, ETC • DS • 1 kW • ➡
RADIO TIMBIRA, São Luís — DS • 2.5 kW

CHINA
FUJIAN PEOPLES BS, Jianyang — DS-1 • 10 kW; TAIWAN SVC • 10 kW

RUSSIA
†VOICE OF RUSSIA, Via Tajikistan — ⬅ • W Asia & S Asia • 100 kW

4976 UGANDA
RADIO UGANDA, Kampala — ENGLISH, ETC • DS • 50 kW; M-F • ENGLISH, ETC • DS • 50 kW; M-Sa • ENGLISH, ETC • DS • 50 kW

4976v COLOMBIA
†ONDAS ORTEGUAZA, Florencia — Irr • DS-TODELAR • 1 kW; DS-TODELAR • 1 kW

4980 CHINA
XINJIANG PEOPLE'S BC STN, Urümqi — DS-MONGOLIAN • 50 kW

VENEZUELA
†ECOS DEL TORBES, San Cristóbal — DS • 10 kW

0 1 2 3 4 5 6 7 8 9 10 11 12 13 14 15 16 17 18 19 20 21 22 23 24

ENGLISH ▬ ARABIC ▭▭▭ CHINESE ▫▫▫ FRENCH ═ GERMAN ═ RUSSIAN ═ SPANISH ═ OTHER —

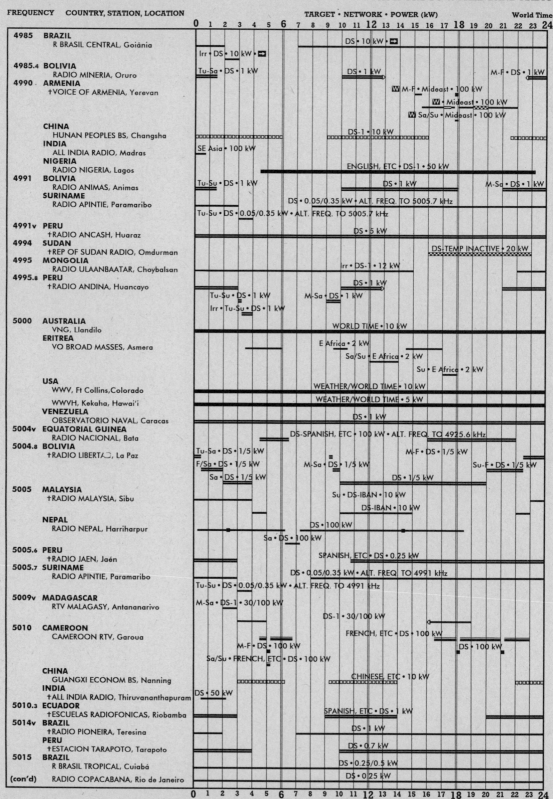

FREQUENCY   COUNTRY, STATION, LOCATION

TARGET • NETWORK • POWER (kW)   World Time

4985   BRAZIL
         R BRASIL CENTRAL, Goiânia

4985.4 BOLIVIA
         RADIO MINERIA, Oruro
4990   ARMENIA
         †VOICE OF ARMENIA, Yerevan

         CHINA
         HUNAN PEOPLES BS, Changsha
         INDIA
         ALL INDIA RADIO, Madras
         NIGERIA
         RADIO NIGERIA, Lagos
4991   BOLIVIA
         RADIO ANIMAS, Animas
         SURINAME
         RADIO APINTIE, Paramaribo

4991v   PERU
         †RADIO ANCASH, Huaraz
4994   SUDAN
         †REP OF SUDAN RADIO, Omdurman
4995   MONGOLIA
         RADIO ULAANBAATAR, Choybalsan
4995.8 PERU
         †RADIO ANDINA, Huancayo

5000   AUSTRALIA
         VNG, Llandilo
         ERITREA
         VO BROAD MASSES, Asmera

         USA
         WWV, Ft Collins, Colorado
         WWVH, Kekaha, Hawai'i
         VENEZUELA
         OBSERVATORIO NAVAL, Caracas
5004v   EQUATORIAL GUINEA
         RADIO NACIONAL, Bata
5004.8 BOLIVIA
         †RADIO LIBERTAD, La Paz

5005   MALAYSIA
         †RADIO MALAYSIA, Sibu

         NEPAL
         RADIO NEPAL, Harriharpur

5005.6 PERU
         †RADIO JAEN, Jaén
5005.7 SURINAME
         RADIO APINTIE, Paramaribo

5009v   MADAGASCAR
         RTV MALAGASY, Antananarivo

5010   CAMEROON
         CAMEROON RTV, Garoua

         CHINA
         GUANGXI ECONOM BS, Nanning
         INDIA
         †ALL INDIA RADIO, Thiruvananthapuram
5010.3 ECUADOR
         †ESCUELAS RADIOFONICAS, Riobamba
5014v   BRAZIL
         †RADIO PIONEIRA, Teresina
         PERU
         †ESTACION TARAPOTO, Tarapoto
5015   BRAZIL
         R BRASIL TROPICAL, Cuiabá
(con'd) RADIO COPACABANA, Rio de Janeiro

FREQUENCY   COUNTRY, STATION, LOCATION

TARGET • NETWORK • POWER (kW)

World Time

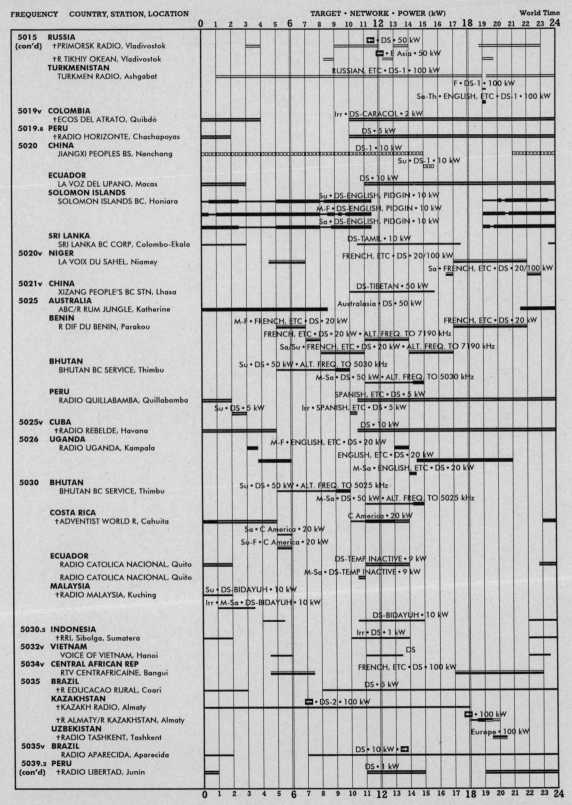

FREQUENCY	COUNTRY, STATION, LOCATION	Notes
5015 (con'd)	RUSSIA †PRIMORSK RADIO, Vladivostok	DS • 50 kW
	†R TIKHIY OKEAN, Vladivostok	E Asia • 50 kW
	TURKMENISTAN TURKMEN RADIO, Ashgabat	RUSSIAN, ETC • DS-1 • 100 kW / F • DS-1 • 100 kW / Sa-Th • ENGLISH, ETC • DS-1 • 100 kW
5019v	COLOMBIA †ECOS DEL ATRATO, Quibdó	Irr • DS-CARACOL • 2 kW
5019.8	PERU †RADIO HORIZONTE, Chachapoyas	DS • 5 kW
5020	CHINA JIANGXI PEOPLES BS, Nanchang	DS-1 • 10 kW / Su • DS-1 • 10 kW
	ECUADOR LA VOZ DEL UPANO, Macas	DS • 10 kW
	SOLOMON ISLANDS SOLOMON ISLANDS BC, Honiara	Su • DS-ENGLISH, PIDGIN • 10 kW / M-F • DS-ENGLISH, PIDGIN • 10 kW / Sa • DS-ENGLISH, PIDGIN • 10 kW
	SRI LANKA SRI LANKA BC CORP, Colombo-Ekala	DS-TAMIL • 10 kW
5020v	NIGER LA VOIX DU SAHEL, Niamey	FRENCH, ETC • DS • 20/100 kW / Sa • FRENCH, ETC • DS • 20/100 kW
5021v	CHINA XIZANG PEOPLE'S BC STN, Lhasa	DS-TIBETAN • 50 kW
5025	AUSTRALIA ABC/R RUM JUNGLE, Katherine	Australasia • DS • 50 kW
	BENIN R DIF DU BENIN, Parakou	M-F • FRENCH, ETC • DS • 20 kW / FRENCH, ETC • DS • 20 kW / FRENCH, ETC • DS • 20 kW • ALT. FREQ. TO 7190 kHz / Sa/Su • FRENCH, ETC • DS • 20 kW • ALT. FREQ. TO 7190 kHz
	BHUTAN BHUTAN BC SERVICE, Thimbu	Su • DS • 50 kW • ALT. FREQ. TO 5030 kHz / M-Sa • DS • 50 kW • ALT. FREQ. TO 5030 kHz
	PERU RADIO QUILLABAMBA, Quillabamba	SPANISH, ETC • DS • 5 kW / Su • DS • 5 kW / Irr • SPANISH, ETC • DS • 5 kW
5025v	CUBA †RADIO REBELDE, Havana	DS • 10 kW
5026	UGANDA RADIO UGANDA, Kampala	M-F • ENGLISH, ETC • DS • 20 kW / ENGLISH, ETC • DS • 20 kW / M-Sa • ENGLISH, ETC • DS • 20 kW
5030	BHUTAN BHUTAN BC SERVICE, Thimbu	Su • DS • 50 kW • ALT. FREQ. TO 5025 kHz / M-Sa • DS • 50 kW • ALT. FREQ. TO 5025 kHz
	COSTA RICA †ADVENTIST WORLD R, Cahuita	C America • 20 kW / Sa • C America • 20 kW / Su-F • C America • 20 kW
	ECUADOR RADIO CATOLICA NACIONAL, Quito	DS-TEMP INACTIVE • 9 kW
	RADIO CATOLICA NACIONAL, Quito	M-Sa • DS-TEMP INACTIVE • 9 kW
	MALAYSIA †RADIO MALAYSIA, Kuching	Su • DS-BIDAYUH • 10 kW / Irr • M-Sa • DS-BIDAYUH • 10 kW / DS-BIDAYUH • 10 kW
5030.5	INDONESIA †RRI, Sibolga, Sumatera	Irr • DS • 1 kW
5032v	VIETNAM VOICE OF VIETNAM, Hanoi	DS
5034v	CENTRAL AFRICAN REP RTV CENTRAFRICAINE, Bangui	FRENCH, ETC • DS • 100 kW
5035	BRAZIL †R EDUCACAO RURAL, Coari	DS • 5 kW
	KAZAKHSTAN †KAZAKH RADIO, Almaty	DS-2 • 100 kW
	†R ALMATY/R KAZAKHSTAN, Almaty	• 100 kW
	UZBEKISTAN †RADIO TASHKENT, Tashkent	Europe • 100 kW
5035v	BRAZIL RADIO APARECIDA, Aparecida	DS • 10 kW •
5039.2 (con'd)	PERU †RADIO LIBERTAD, Junín	DS • 1 kW

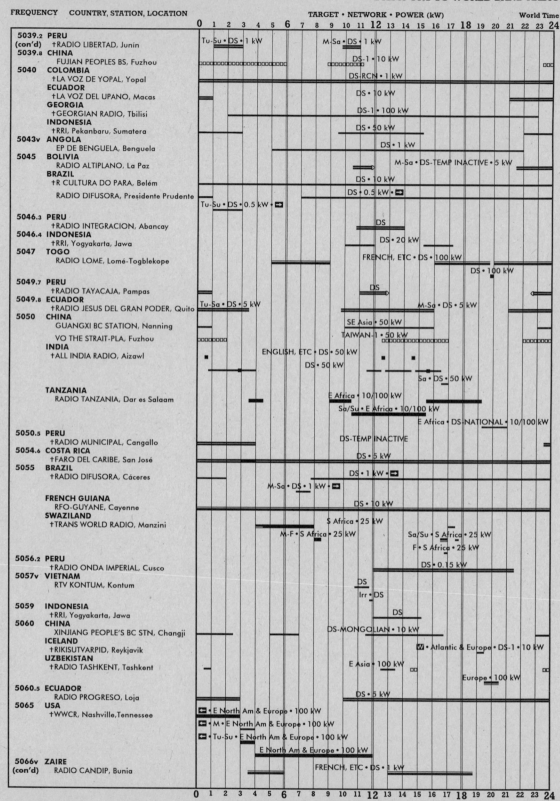

FREQUENCY   COUNTRY, STATION, LOCATION

TARGET • NETWORK • POWER (kW)

World Time

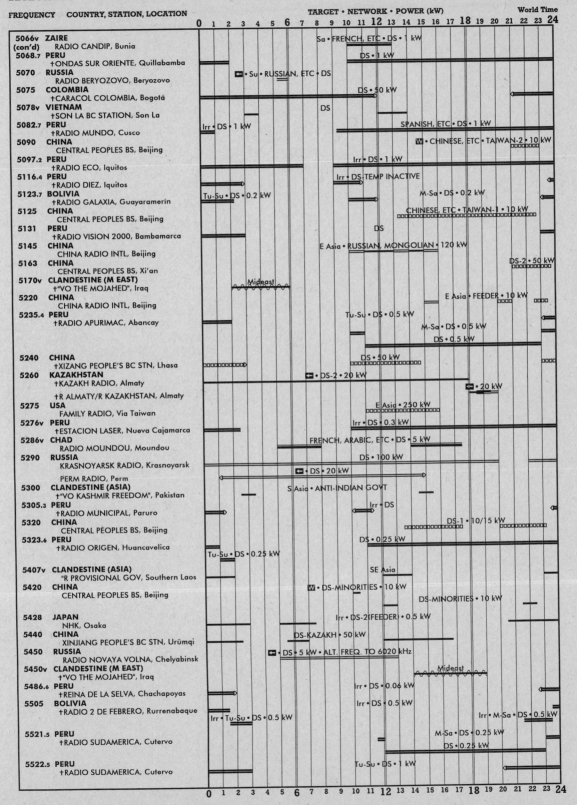

Frequency	Country, Station, Location
5066v **ZAIRE**	
(con'd) RADIO CANDIP, Bunia	Sa • FRENCH, ETC • DS • 1 kW
5068.7 **PERU**	DS • 1 kW
†ONDAS SUR ORIENTE, Quillabamba	
5070 **RUSSIA**	• Su • RUSSIAN, ETC • DS
RADIO BERYOZOVO, Beryozovo	
5075 **COLOMBIA**	DS • 50 kW
†CARACOL COLOMBIA, Bogotá	
5078v **VIETNAM**	DS
†SON LA BC STATION, Son La	
5082.7 **PERU**	Irr • DS • 1 kW SPANISH, ETC • DS • 1 kW
†RADIO MUNDO, Cusco	
5090 **CHINA**	W • CHINESE, ETC • TAIWAN-2 • 10 kW
CENTRAL PEOPLES BS, Beijing	
5097.2 **PERU**	Irr • DS • 1 kW
†RADIO ECO, Iquitos	
5116.4 **PERU**	Irr • DS • TEMP INACTIVE
†RADIO DIEZ, Iquitos	
5123.7 **BOLIVIA**	Tu-Su • DS • 0.2 kW M-Sa • DS • 0.2 kW
†RADIO GALAXIA, Guayaramerín	
5125 **CHINA**	CHINESE, ETC • TAIWAN-1 • 10 kW
CENTRAL PEOPLES BS, Beijing	
5131 **PERU**	DS
†RADIO VISION 2000, Bambamarca	
5145 **CHINA**	E Asia • RUSSIAN, MONGOLIAN • 120 kW
CHINA RADIO INTL, Beijing	
5163 **CHINA**	DS-2 • 50 kW
CENTRAL PEOPLES BS, Xi'an	
5170v **CLANDESTINE (M EAST)**	Mideast
†"VO THE MOJAHED", Iraq	
5220 **CHINA**	E Asia • FEEDER • 10 kW
CHINA RADIO INTL, Beijing	
5235.4 **PERU**	Tu-Su • DS • 0.5 kW
†RADIO APURIMAC, Abancay	M-Sa • DS • 0.5 kW
	DS • 0.5 kW
5240 **CHINA**	DS • 50 kW
†XIZANG PEOPLE'S BC STN, Lhasa	
5260 **KAZAKHSTAN**	• DS-2 • 20 kW
†KAZAKH RADIO, Almaty	
†R ALMATY/R KAZAKHSTAN, Almaty	• 20 kW
5275 **USA**	E Asia • 250 kW
FAMILY RADIO, Via Taiwan	
5276v **PERU**	Irr • DS • 0.3 kW
†ESTACION LASER, Nueva Cajamarca	
5286v **CHAD**	FRENCH, ARABIC, ETC • DS • 5 kW
RADIO MOUNDOU, Moundou	
5290 **RUSSIA**	DS • 100 kW
KRASNOYARSK RADIO, Krasnoyarsk	• DS • 20 kW
PERM RADIO, Perm	
5300 **CLANDESTINE (ASIA)**	S Asia • ANTI-INDIAN GOVT
†"VO KASHMIR FREEDOM", Pakistan	
5305.3 **PERU**	Irr • DS
†RADIO MUNICIPAL, Paruro	
5320 **CHINA**	DS-1 • 10/15 kW
CENTRAL PEOPLES BS, Beijing	
5323.6 **PERU**	DS • 0.25 kW
†RADIO ORIGEN, Huancavelica	Tu-Su • DS • 0.25 kW
5407v **CLANDESTINE (ASIA)**	SE Asia
"R PROVISIONAL GOV, Southern Laos	
5420 **CHINA**	W • DS-MINORITIES • 10 kW
CENTRAL PEOPLES BS, Beijing	DS-MINORITIES • 10 kW
5428 **JAPAN**	Irr • DS-2 (FEEDER) • 0.5 kW
NHK, Osaka	
5440 **CHINA**	DS-KAZAKH • 50 kW
XINJIANG PEOPLE'S BC STN, Urümqi	
5450 **RUSSIA**	• DS • 5 kW • ALT. FREQ. TO 6020 kHz
RADIO NOVAYA VOLNA, Chelyabinsk	
5450v **CLANDESTINE (M EAST)**	Mideast
†"VO THE MOJAHED", Iraq	
5486.6 **PERU**	Irr • DS • 0.06 kW
†REINA DE LA SELVA, Chachapoyas	
5505 **BOLIVIA**	Irr • DS • 0.5 kW
†RADIO 2 DE FEBRERO, Rurrenabaque	Irr • Tu-Su • DS • 0.5 kW Irr • M-Sa • DS • 0.5 kW
5521.5 **PERU**	M-Sa • DS • 0.25 kW
†RADIO SUDAMERICA, Cutervo	DS • 0.25 kW
5522.5 **PERU**	Tu-Su • DS • 1 kW
†RADIO SUDAMERICA, Cutervo	

ENGLISH ▬   ARABIC ⚬⚬⚬   CHINESE ▭▭▭   FRENCH ▬▬   GERMAN ▬   RUSSIAN ══   SPANISH ▬   OTHER ▬

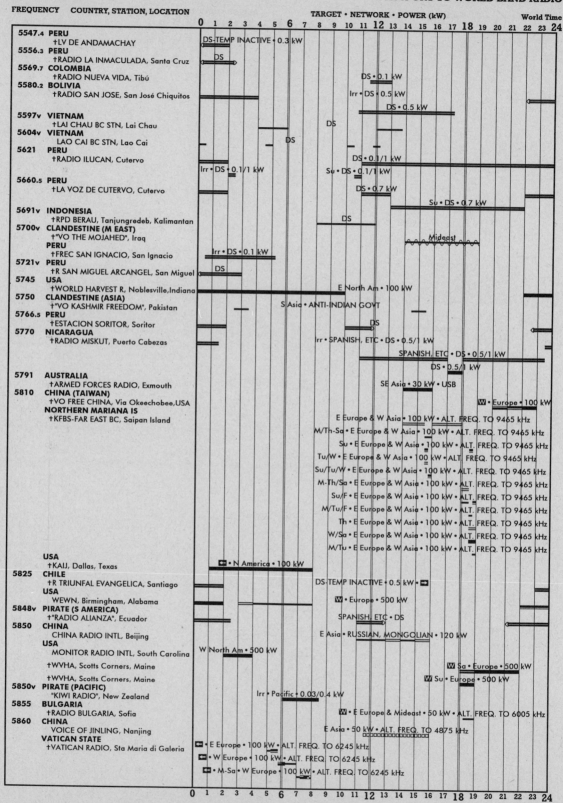

FREQUENCY   COUNTRY, STATION, LOCATION

TARGET • NETWORK • POWER (kW)

World Time

Frequency	Country, Station, Location	Notes
5547.4	**PERU** †LV DE ANDAMACHAY	DS-TEMP INACTIVE • 0.3 kW
5556.3	**PERU** †RADIO LA INMACULADA, Santa Cruz	DS
5569.7	**COLOMBIA** †RADIO NUEVA VIDA, Tibú	DS • 0.1 kW
5580.2	**BOLIVIA** †RADIO SAN JOSE, San José Chiquitos	Irr • DS • 0.5 kW / DS • 0.5 kW
5597v	**VIETNAM** †LAI CHAU BC STN, Lai Chau	DS
5604v	**VIETNAM** LAO CAI BC STN, Lao Cai	DS
5621	**PERU** †RADIO ILUCAN, Cutervo	DS • 0.1/1 kW / Irr • DS • 0.1/1 kW / Su • DS • 0.1/1 kW
5660.5	**PERU** †LA VOZ DE CUTERVO, Cutervo	DS • 0.7 kW / Su • DS • 0.7 kW
5691v	**INDONESIA** †RPD BERAU, Tanjungredeb, Kalimantan	DS
5700v	**CLANDESTINE (M EAST)** †"VO THE MOJAHED", Iraq	Mideast
	PERU †FREC SAN IGNACIO, San Ignacio	Irr • DS • 0.1 kW
5721v	**PERU** †R SAN MIGUEL ARCANGEL, San Miguel	DS
5745	**USA** †WORLD HARVEST R, Noblesville, Indiana	E North Am • 100 kW
5750	**CLANDESTINE (ASIA)** †"VO KASHMIR FREEDOM", Pakistan	S Asia • ANTI-INDIAN GOVT
5766.5	**PERU** †ESTACION SORITOR, Soritor	DS
5770	**NICARAGUA** †RADIO MISKUT, Puerto Cabezas	Irr • SPANISH, ETC • DS • 0.5/1 kW / SPANISH, ETC • DS • 0.5/1 kW / DS • 0.5/1 kW
5791	**AUSTRALIA** †ARMED FORCES RADIO, Exmouth	SE Asia • 30 kW • USB
5810	**CHINA (TAIWAN)** †VO FREE CHINA, Via Okeechobee, USA	W • Europe • 100 kW
	NORTHERN MARIANA IS †KFBS-FAR EAST BC, Saipan Island	E Europe & W Asia • 100 kW • ALT. FREQ. TO 9465 kHz / M/Th-Sa • E Europe & W Asia • 100 kW • ALT. FREQ. TO 9465 kHz / Su • E Europe & W Asia • 100 kW • ALT. FREQ. TO 9465 kHz / Tu/W • E Europe & W Asia • 100 kW • ALT. FREQ. TO 9465 kHz / Su/Tu/W • E Europe & W Asia • 100 kW • ALT. FREQ. TO 9465 kHz / M-Th/Sa • E Europe & W Asia • 100 kW • ALT. FREQ. TO 9465 kHz / Su/F • E Europe & W Asia • 100 kW • ALT. FREQ. TO 9465 kHz / M/Tu/F • E Europe & W Asia • 100 kW • ALT. FREQ. TO 9465 kHz / Th • E Europe & W Asia • 100 kW • ALT. FREQ. TO 9465 kHz / W/Sa • E Europe & W Asia • 100 kW • ALT. FREQ. TO 9465 kHz / M/Tu • E Europe & W Asia • 100 kW • ALT. FREQ. TO 9465 kHz
	USA †KAIJ, Dallas, Texas	• N America • 100 kW
5825	**CHILE** †R TRIUNFAL EVANGELICA, Santiago	DS-TEMP INACTIVE • 0.5 kW •
	USA WEWN, Birmingham, Alabama	W • Europe • 500 kW
5848v	**PIRATE (S AMERICA)** †"RADIO ALIANZA", Ecuador	SPANISH, ETC • DS
5850	**CHINA** CHINA RADIO INTL, Beijing	E Asia • RUSSIAN, MONGOLIAN • 120 kW
	USA MONITOR RADIO INTL, South Carolina	W North Am • 500 kW
	†WVHA, Scotts Corners, Maine	W Sa • Europe • 500 kW
	†WVHA, Scotts Corners, Maine	W Su • Europe • 500 kW
5850v	**PIRATE (PACIFIC)** "KIWI RADIO", New Zealand	Irr • Pacific • 0.03/0.4 kW
5855	**BULGARIA** †RADIO BULGARIA, Sofia	W • E Europe & Mideast • 50 kW • ALT. FREQ. TO 6005 kHz
5860	**CHINA** VOICE OF JINLING, Nanjing	E Asia • 50 kW • ALT. FREQ. TO 4875 kHz
	VATICAN STATE †VATICAN RADIO, Sta Maria di Galeria	• E Europe • 100 kW • ALT. FREQ. TO 6245 kHz / • W Europe • 100 kW • ALT. FREQ. TO 6245 kHz / • M-Sa • W Europe • 100 kW • ALT. FREQ. TO 6245 kHz

FREQUENCY   COUNTRY, STATION, LOCATION

TARGET • NETWORK • POWER (kW)

World Time

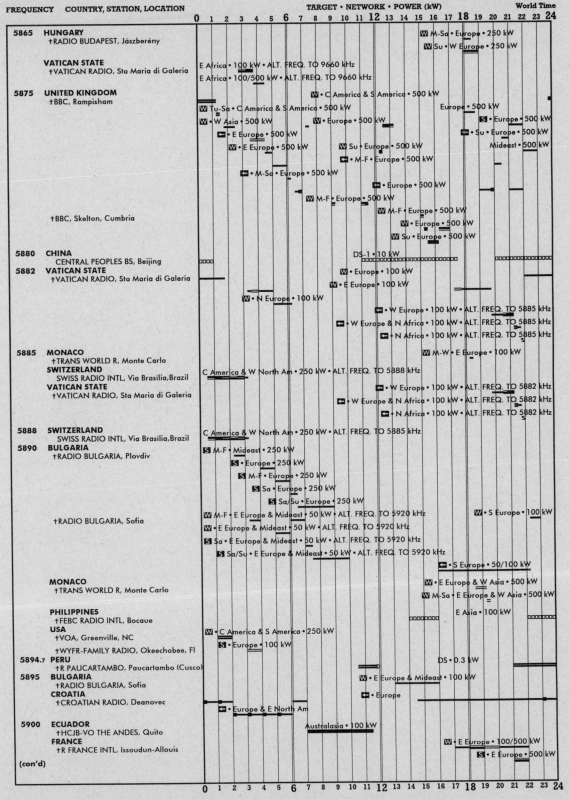

Frequency	Country, Station, Location	Target • Network • Power
5865	HUNGARY †RADIO BUDAPEST, Jászberény	W M-Sa • Europe • 250 kW; W Su • W Europe • 250 kW
	VATICAN STATE †VATICAN RADIO, Sta Maria di Galeria	E Africa • 100 kW • ALT. FREQ. TO 9660 kHz; E Africa • 100/500 kW • ALT. FREQ. TO 9660 kHz
5875	UNITED KINGDOM †BBC, Rampisham	W • C America & S America • 500 kW; W Tu-Sa • C America & S America • 500 kW; Europe • 500 kW; W • W Asia • 500 kW; • Europe • 500 kW; S • Europe • 500 kW; • E Europe • 500 kW; • Su • Europe • 500 kW; W • E Europe • 500 kW; W Su • Europe • 500 kW; Mideast • 500 kW; • M-F • Europe • 500 kW; • M-Sa • Europe • 500 kW; • Europe • 500 kW; W M-F • Europe • 500 kW
	†BBC, Skelton, Cumbria	W M-F • Europe • 500 kW; W • Europe • 500 kW; W Su • Europe • 500 kW
5880	CHINA CENTRAL PEOPLES BS, Beijing	DS-1 • 10 kW
5882	VATICAN STATE †VATICAN RADIO, Sta Maria di Galeria	W • Europe • 100 kW; W • E Europe • 100 kW; W • N Europe • 100 kW; • W Europe • 100 kW • ALT. FREQ. TO 5885 kHz; • W Europe & N Africa • 100 kW • ALT. FREQ. TO 5885 kHz; • N Africa • 100 kW • ALT. FREQ. TO 5885 kHz
5885	MONACO †TRANS WORLD R, Monte Carlo	W M-W • E Europe • 100 kW
	SWITZERLAND SWISS RADIO INTL, Via Brasilia, Brazil	C America & W North Am • 250 kW • ALT. FREQ. TO 5888 kHz
	VATICAN STATE †VATICAN RADIO, Sta Maria di Galeria	• W Europe • 100 kW • ALT. FREQ. TO 5882 kHz; • W Europe & N Africa • 100 kW • ALT. FREQ. TO 5882 kHz; • N Africa • 100 kW • ALT. FREQ. TO 5882 kHz
5888	SWITZERLAND SWISS RADIO INTL, Via Brasilia, Brazil	C America & W North Am • 250 kW • ALT. FREQ. TO 5885 kHz
5890	BULGARIA †RADIO BULGARIA, Plovdiv	S M-F • Mideast • 250 kW; S • Europe • 250 kW; S M-F • Europe • 250 kW; S Sa • Europe • 250 kW; S Sa/Su • Europe • 250 kW
	†RADIO BULGARIA, Sofia	W M-F • E Europe & Mideast • 50 kW • ALT. FREQ. TO 5920 kHz; W • E Europe & Mideast • 50 kW • ALT. FREQ. TO 5920 kHz; S Sa • E Europe & Mideast • 50 kW • ALT. FREQ. TO 5920 kHz; S Sa/Su • E Europe & Mideast • 50 kW • ALT. FREQ. TO 5920 kHz; W • S Europe • 100 kW; • S Europe • 50/100 kW
	MONACO †TRANS WORLD R, Monte Carlo	W • E Europe & W Asia • 500 kW; W M-Sa • E Europe & W Asia • 500 kW
	PHILIPPINES †FEBC RADIO INTL, Bocaue	E Asia • 100 kW
	USA †VOA, Greenville, NC	W • C America & S America • 250 kW
	†WYFR-FAMILY RADIO, Okeechobee, Fl	S • Europe • 100 kW
5894.7	PERU †R PAUCARTAMBO, Paucartambo (Cusco)	DS • 0.3 kW
5895	BULGARIA †RADIO BULGARIA, Sofia	W • E Europe & Mideast • 100 kW
	CROATIA †CROATIAN RADIO, Deanovec	• Europe; • Europe & E North Am
5900	ECUADOR †HCJB-VO THE ANDES, Quito	Australasia • 100 kW
	FRANCE †R FRANCE INTL, Issoudun-Allouis	W • E Europe • 100/500 kW; S • E Europe • 500 kW

(con'd)

ENGLISH ▬   ARABIC ⸗   CHINESE ▭▭▭   FRENCH ▬▬   GERMAN ▬   RUSSIAN =   SPANISH ▭▭   OTHER ▬

FREQUENCY	COUNTRY, STATION, LOCATION	TARGET • NETWORK • POWER (kW)

World Time

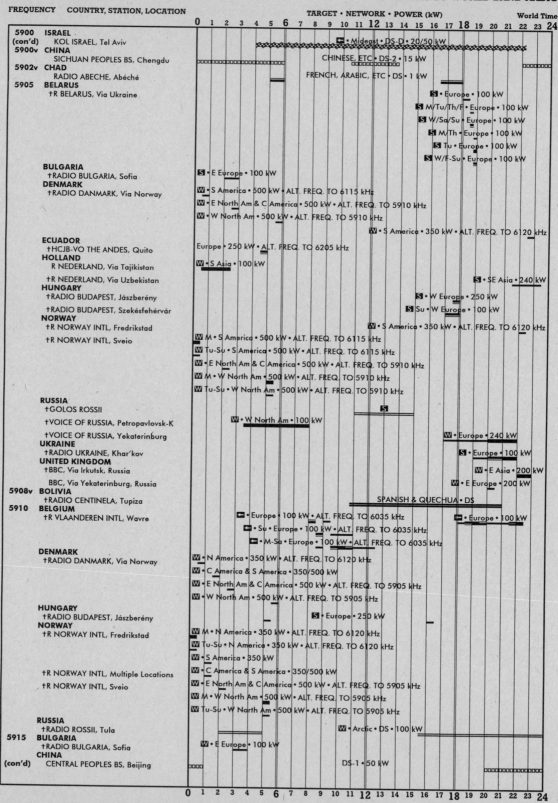

5900 ISRAEL
(con'd)   KOL ISRAEL, Tel Aviv — Mideast • DS-D • 20/50 kW
5900v CHINA
  SICHUAN PEOPLES BS, Chengdu — CHINESE, ETC • DS-2 • 15 kW
5902v CHAD
  RADIO ABECHE, Abéché — FRENCH, ARABIC, ETC • DS • 1 kW
5905 BELARUS
  †R BELARUS, Via Ukraine — S • Europe • 100 kW
  — S M/Tu/Th/F • Europe • 100 kW
  — S W/Sa/Su • Europe • 100 kW
  — S M/Th • Europe • 100 kW
  — S Tu • Europe • 100 kW
  — S W/F-Su • Europe • 100 kW

BULGARIA
  †RADIO BULGARIA, Sofia — S • E Europe • 100 kW
DENMARK
  †RADIO DANMARK, Via Norway — W • S America • 500 kW • ALT. FREQ. TO 6115 kHz
  — W • E North Am & C America • 500 kW • ALT. FREQ. TO 5910 kHz
  — W • W North Am • 500 kW • ALT. FREQ. TO 5910 kHz
  — W • S America • 350 kW • ALT. FREQ. TO 6120 kHz

ECUADOR
  †HCJB-VO THE ANDES, Quito — Europe • 250 kW • ALT. FREQ. TO 6205 kHz
HOLLAND
  R NEDERLAND, Via Tajikistan — W • S Asia • 100 kW
  †R NEDERLAND, Via Uzbekistan — S • SE Asia • 240 kW
HUNGARY
  †RADIO BUDAPEST, Jászberény — S • W Europe • 250 kW
  †RADIO BUDAPEST, Székesfehérvár — S Su • W Europe • 100 kW
NORWAY
  †R NORWAY INTL, Fredrikstad — W • S America • 350 kW • ALT. FREQ. TO 6120 kHz
  †R NORWAY INTL, Sveio — W M • S America • 500 kW • ALT. FREQ. TO 6115 kHz
  — W Tu-Su • S America • 500 kW • ALT. FREQ. TO 6115 kHz
  — W • E North Am & C America • 500 kW • ALT. FREQ. TO 5910 kHz
  — W M • W North Am • 500 kW • ALT. FREQ. TO 5910 kHz
  — W Tu-Su • W North Am • 500 kW • ALT. FREQ. TO 5910 kHz

RUSSIA
  †GOLOS ROSSII — S
  †VOICE OF RUSSIA, Petropavlovsk-K — W • W North Am • 100 kW
  †VOICE OF RUSSIA, Yekaterinburg — W • Europe • 240 kW
UKRAINE
  †RADIO UKRAINE, Khar'kov — S • Europe • 100 kW
UNITED KINGDOM
  †BBC, Via Irkutsk, Russia — W • E Asia • 200 kW
  BBC, Via Yekaterinburg, Russia — W • E Europe • 200 kW
5908v BOLIVIA
  †RADIO CENTINELA, Tupiza — SPANISH & QUECHUA • DS
5910 BELGIUM
  †R VLAANDEREN INTL, Wavre — Europe • 100 kW • ALT. FREQ. TO 6035 kHz
  — Su • Europe • 100 kW • ALT. FREQ. TO 6035 kHz
  — Europe • 100 kW
  — M-Sa • Europe • 100 kW • ALT. FREQ. TO 6035 kHz

DENMARK
  †RADIO DANMARK, Via Norway — W • N America • 350 kW • ALT. FREQ. TO 6120 kHz
  — W • C America & S America • 350/500 kW
  — W • E North Am & C America • 500 kW • ALT. FREQ. TO 5905 kHz
  — W • W North Am • 500 kW • ALT. FREQ. TO 5905 kHz

HUNGARY
  †RADIO BUDAPEST, Jászberény — S • Europe • 250 kW
NORWAY
  †R NORWAY INTL, Fredrikstad — W M • N America • 350 kW • ALT. FREQ. TO 6120 kHz
  — W Tu-Su • N America • 350 kW • ALT. FREQ. TO 6120 kHz
  — W • S America • 350 kW
  †R NORWAY INTL, Multiple Locations — W • C America & S America • 350/500 kW
  — W • E North Am & C America • 500 kW • ALT. FREQ. TO 5905 kHz
  †R NORWAY INTL, Sveio — W M • W North Am • 500 kW • ALT. FREQ. TO 5905 kHz
  — W Tu-Su • W North Am • 500 kW • ALT. FREQ. TO 5905 kHz

RUSSIA
  †RADIO ROSSII, Tula — W • Arctic • DS • 100 kW
5915 BULGARIA
  †RADIO BULGARIA, Sofia — W • E Europe • 100 kW
CHINA
(con'd)   CENTRAL PEOPLES BS, Beijing — DS-1 • 50 kW

FREQUENCY   COUNTRY, STATION, LOCATION   TARGET • NETWORK • POWER (kW)   World Time

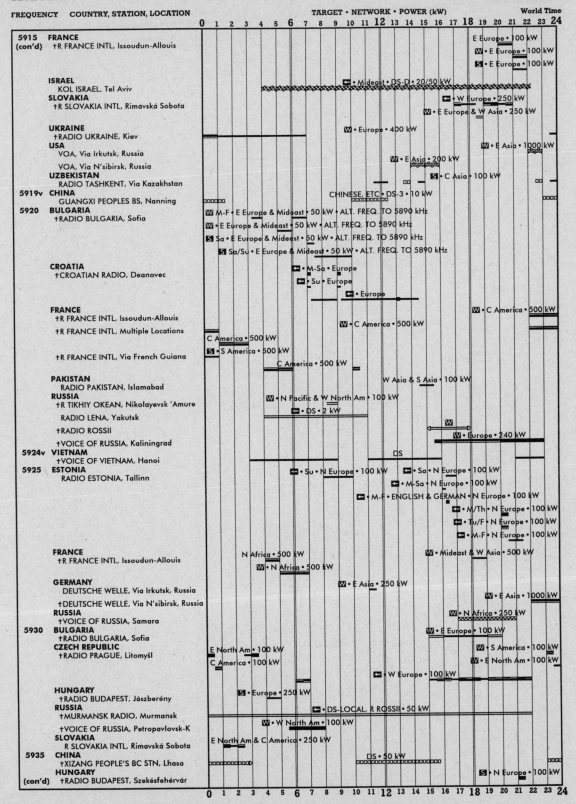

Frequency	Country, Station, Location	Target • Network • Power
5915 (con'd)	FRANCE †R FRANCE INTL, Issoudun-Allouis	E Europe • 100 kW / W • E Europe • 100 kW / S • E Europe • 100 kW
	ISRAEL KOL ISRAEL, Tel Aviv	Mideast • DS-D • 20/50 kW
	SLOVAKIA †R SLOVAKIA INTL, Rimavská Sobota	W Europe • 250 kW / W • E Europe & W Asia • 250 kW
	UKRAINE †RADIO UKRAINE, Kiev	W • Europe • 400 kW
	USA VOA, Via Irkutsk, Russia	W • E Asia • 1000 kW
	VOA, Via N'sibirsk, Russia	W • E Asia • 200 kW
	UZBEKISTAN RADIO TASHKENT, Via Kazakhstan	S • C Asia • 100 kW
5919v	CHINA GUANGXI PEOPLES BS, Nanning	CHINESE, ETC • DS-3 • 10 kW
5920	BULGARIA †RADIO BULGARIA, Sofia	W M-F • E Europe & Mideast • 50 kW • ALT. FREQ. TO 5890 kHz / W • E Europe & Mideast • 50 kW • ALT. FREQ. TO 5890 kHz / S Sa • E Europe & Mideast • 50 kW • ALT. FREQ. TO 5890 kHz / S Sa/Su • E Europe & Mideast • 50 kW • ALT. FREQ. TO 5890 kHz
	CROATIA †CROATIAN RADIO, Deanovec	M-Sa • Europe / Su • Europe / Europe
	FRANCE †R FRANCE INTL, Issoudun-Allouis	W • C America • 500 kW / W • C America • 500 kW
	†R FRANCE INTL, Multiple Locations	C America • 500 kW / S • S America • 500 kW
	†R FRANCE INTL, Via French Guiana	C America • 500 kW
	PAKISTAN RADIO PAKISTAN, Islamabad	W Asia & S Asia • 100 kW
	RUSSIA †R TIKHIY OKEAN, Nikolayevsk 'Amure	W • N Pacific & W North Am • 100 kW
	RADIO LENA, Yakutsk	DS • 2 kW
	†RADIO ROSSII	W
	†VOICE OF RUSSIA, Kaliningrad	W • Europe • 240 kW
5924v	VIETNAM †VOICE OF VIETNAM, Hanoi	DS
5925	ESTONIA RADIO ESTONIA, Tallinn	Su • N Europe • 100 kW / Sa • N Europe • 100 kW / M-Sa • N Europe • 100 kW / M-F • ENGLISH & GERMAN • N Europe • 100 kW / M/Th • N Europe • 100 kW / Tu/F • N Europe • 100 kW / M-F • N Europe • 100 kW
	FRANCE †R FRANCE INTL, Issoudun-Allouis	N Africa • 500 kW / W • N Africa • 500 kW / W • Mideast & W Asia • 500 kW
	GERMANY DEUTSCHE WELLE, Via Irkutsk, Russia	W • E Asia • 250 kW
	†DEUTSCHE WELLE, Via N'sibirsk, Russia	W • E Asia • 1000 kW
	RUSSIA †VOICE OF RUSSIA, Samara	W • N Africa • 250 kW
5930	BULGARIA †RADIO BULGARIA, Sofia	W • E Europe • 100 kW
	CZECH REPUBLIC †RADIO PRAGUE, Litomyšl	E North Am • 100 kW / C America • 100 kW / W • S America • 100 kW / W • E North Am • 100 kW / W Europe • 100 kW
	HUNGARY †RADIO BUDAPEST, Jászberény	S • Europe • 250 kW
	RUSSIA †MURMANSK RADIO, Murmansk	DS-LOCAL, R ROSSII • 50 kW
	†VOICE OF RUSSIA, Petropavlovsk-K	W • W North Am • 100 kW
	SLOVAKIA R SLOVAKIA INTL, Rimavská Sobota	E North Am & C America • 250 kW
5935	CHINA †XIZANG PEOPLE'S BC STN, Lhasa	DS • 50 kW
(con'd)	HUNGARY †RADIO BUDAPEST, Székesfehérvár	S • N Europe • 100 kW

ENGLISH ▬ ARABIC ▨ CHINESE □□□ FRENCH ═ GERMAN ▬ RUSSIAN ═ SPANISH ▬ OTHER ─

FREQUENCY   COUNTRY, STATION, LOCATION

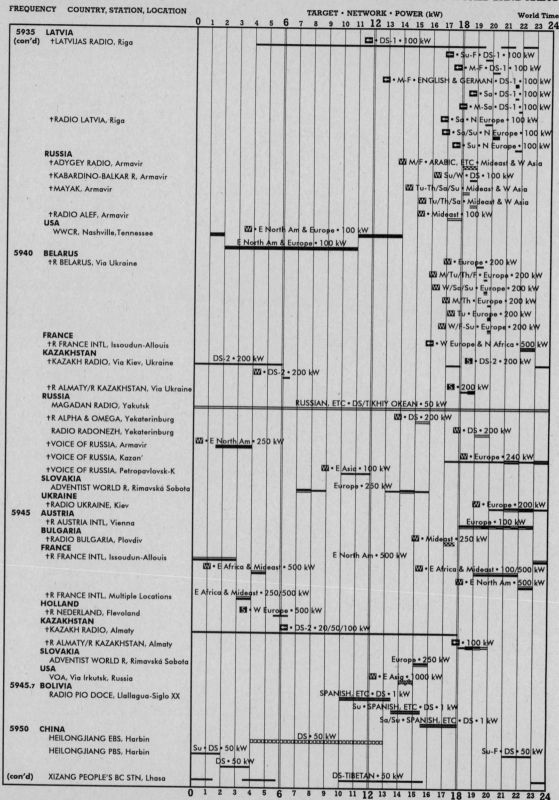

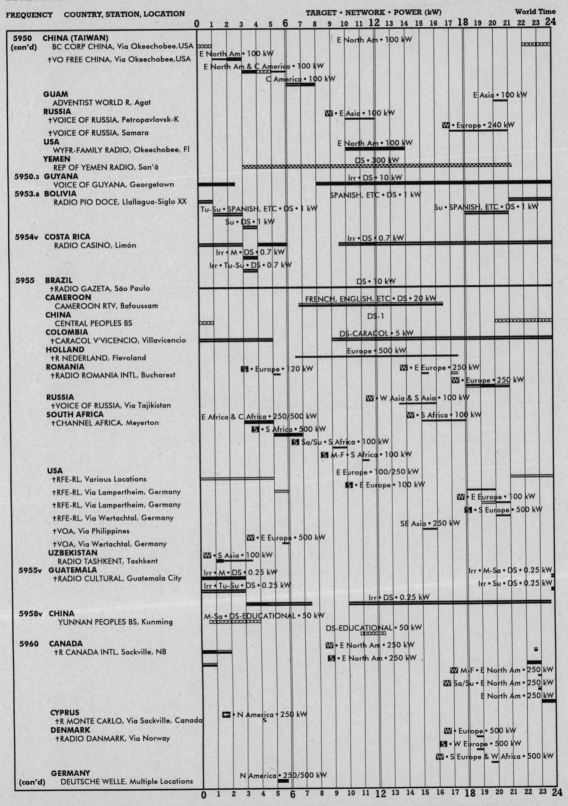

FREQUENCY	COUNTRY, STATION, LOCATION	TARGET • NETWORK • POWER (kW)	World Time

0 1 2 3 4 5 6 7 8 9 10 11 12 13 14 15 16 17 18 19 20 21 22 23 24

5950 **CHINA (TAIWAN)**
(con'd) BC CORP CHINA, Via Okeechobee, USA — E North Am • 100 kW / E North Am • 100 kW

†VO FREE CHINA, Via Okeechobee, USA — E North Am & C America • 100 kW / C America • 100 kW

GUAM
ADVENTIST WORLD R, Agat — E Asia • 100 kW
RUSSIA
†VOICE OF RUSSIA, Petropavlovsk-K — W • E Asia • 100 kW
†VOICE OF RUSSIA, Samara — W • Europe • 240 kW
USA
WYFR-FAMILY RADIO, Okeechobee, Fl — E North Am • 100 kW
YEMEN
REP OF YEMEN RADIO, San'ā — DS • 300 kW
5950.3 GUYANA
VOICE OF GUYANA, Georgetown — Irr • DS • 10 kW
5953.8 BOLIVIA
RADIO PIO DOCE, Llallagua-Siglo XX — SPANISH, ETC • DS • 1 kW / Tu-Su • SPANISH, ETC • DS • 1 kW / Su • SPANISH, ETC • DS • 1 kW / Su • DS • 1 kW

5954v COSTA RICA
RADIO CASINO, Limón — Irr • DS • 0.7 kW / Irr • M • DS • 0.7 kW / Irr • Tu-Su • DS • 0.7 kW

5955 **BRAZIL**
†RADIO GAZETA, São Paulo — DS • 10 kW
CAMEROON
CAMEROON RTV, Bafoussam — FRENCH, ENGLISH, ETC • DS • 20 kW
CHINA
CENTRAL PEOPLES BS — DS-1
COLOMBIA
†CARACOL V'VICENCIO, Villavicencio — DS-CARACOL • 5 kW
HOLLAND
†R NEDERLAND, Flevoland — Europe • 500 kW
ROMANIA
†RADIO ROMANIA INTL, Bucharest — S • Europe • 120 kW / W • E Europe • 250 kW / W • Europe • 250 kW

RUSSIA
†VOICE OF RUSSIA, Via Tajikistan — W • W Asia & S Asia • 100 kW
SOUTH AFRICA
†CHANNEL AFRICA, Meyerton — E Africa & C Africa • 250/500 kW / W • S Africa • 100 kW / S • S Africa • 500 kW / S • Sa/Su • S Africa • 100 kW / S M-F • S Africa • 100 kW

USA
†RFE-RL, Various Locations — E Europe • 100/250 kW
†RFE-RL, Via Lampertheim, Germany — S • E Europe • 100 kW
†RFE-RL, Via Lampertheim, Germany — W • E Europe • 100 kW
†RFE-RL, Via Wertachtal, Germany — S • S Europe • 500 kW
†VOA, Via Philippines — SE Asia • 250 kW
†VOA, Via Wertachtal, Germany — W • E Europe • 500 kW
UZBEKISTAN
RADIO TASHKENT, Tashkent — W • S Asia • 100 kW
5955v GUATEMALA
†RADIO CULTURAL, Guatemala City — Irr • M • DS • 0.25 kW / Irr • M-Sa • DS • 0.25 kW / Irr • Tu-Su • DS • 0.25 kW / Irr • Su • DS • 0.25 kW / Irr • DS • 0.25 kW

5958v CHINA
YUNNAN PEOPLES BS, Kunming — M-Sa • DS-EDUCATIONAL • 50 kW / DS-EDUCATIONAL • 50 kW

5960 **CANADA**
†R CANADA INTL, Sackville, NB — W • E North Am • 250 kW / S • E North Am • 250 kW / W M-F • E North Am • 250 kW / W Sa/Su • E North Am • 250 kW / E North Am • 250 kW

CYPRUS
†R MONTE CARLO, Via Sackville, Canada — N America • 250 kW
DENMARK
†RADIO DANMARK, Via Norway — W • Europe • 500 kW / S • W Europe • 500 kW / W • S Europe & W Africa • 500 kW

GERMANY
(con'd) DEUTSCHE WELLE, Multiple Locations — N America • 250/500 kW

0 1 2 3 4 5 6 7 8 9 10 11 12 13 14 15 16 17 18 19 20 21 22 23 24

ENGLISH ▬ ARABIC ⧖ CHINESE ☐☐☐ FRENCH ▬ GERMAN ▬ RUSSIAN ═ SPANISH ▬ OTHER ▬

FREQUENCY   COUNTRY, STATION, LOCATION

TARGET • NETWORK • POWER (kW)   World Time

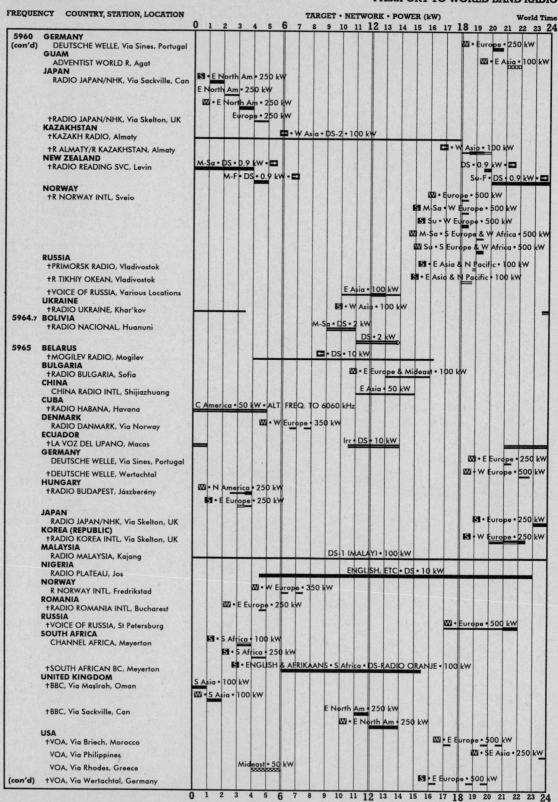

FREQUENCY	COUNTRY, STATION, LOCATION	Schedule details
5960 (con'd)	**GERMANY** DEUTSCHE WELLE, Via Sines, Portugal	W • Europe • 250 kW
	GUAM ADVENTIST WORLD R, Agat	W • E Asia • 100 kW
	JAPAN RADIO JAPAN/NHK, Via Sackville, Can	S • E North Am • 250 kW / E North Am • 250 kW / W • E North Am • 250 kW / Europe • 250 kW
	†RADIO JAPAN/NHK, Via Skelton, UK	
	KAZAKHSTAN †KAZAKH RADIO, Almaty	• W Asia • DS-2 • 100 kW
	†R ALMATY/R KAZAKHSTAN, Almaty	• W Asia • 100 kW
	NEW ZEALAND †RADIO READING SVC, Levin	M-Sa • DS • 0.9 kW • / M-F • DS • 0.9 kW • / DS • 0.9 kW • / Su-F • DS • 0.9 kW •
	NORWAY †R NORWAY INTL, Sveio	W • Europe • 500 kW / S M-Sa • W Europe • 500 kW / S Su • W Europe • 500 kW / W M-Sa • S Europe & W Africa • 500 kW / W Su • S Europe & W Africa • 500 kW
	RUSSIA †PRIMORSK RADIO, Vladivostok	S • E Asia & N Pacific • 100 kW
	†R TIKHIY OKEAN, Vladivostok	S • E Asia & N Pacific • 100 kW
	†VOICE OF RUSSIA, Various Locations	E Asia • 100 kW
	UKRAINE †RADIO UKRAINE, Khar'kov	S • W Asia • 100 kW
5964.7	**BOLIVIA** †RADIO NACIONAL, Huanuni	M-Sa • DS • 2 kW / DS • 2 kW
5965	**BELARUS** †MOGILEV RADIO, Mogilev	• DS • 10 kW
	BULGARIA †RADIO BULGARIA, Sofia	W • E Europe & Mideast • 100 kW
	CHINA CHINA RADIO INTL, Shijiazhuang	E Asia • 50 kW
	CUBA †RADIO HABANA, Havana	C America • 50 kW • ALT FREQ. TO 6060 kHz
	DENMARK RADIO DANMARK, Via Norway	W • W Europe • 350 kW
	ECUADOR †LA VOZ DEL UPANO, Macas	Irr • DS • 10 kW
	GERMANY DEUTSCHE WELLE, Via Sines, Portugal	W • E Europe • 250 kW
	†DEUTSCHE WELLE, Wertachtal	W • W Europe • 500 kW
	HUNGARY †RADIO BUDAPEST, Jászberény	W • N America • 250 kW / S • E Europe • 250 kW
	JAPAN RADIO JAPAN/NHK, Via Skelton, UK	S • Europe • 250 kW
	KOREA (REPUBLIC) †RADIO KOREA INTL, Via Skelton, UK	S • W Europe • 250 kW
	MALAYSIA RADIO MALAYSIA, Kajang	DS-1 (MALAY) • 100 kW
	NIGERIA RADIO PLATEAU, Jos	ENGLISH, ETC • DS • 10 kW
	NORWAY R NORWAY INTL, Fredrikstad	W • W Europe • 350 kW
	ROMANIA †RADIO ROMANIA INTL, Bucharest	W • E Europe • 250 kW
	RUSSIA †VOICE OF RUSSIA, St Petersburg	W • Europe • 500 kW
	SOUTH AFRICA CHANNEL AFRICA, Meyerton	S • S Africa • 100 kW / S • S Africa • 250 kW
	†SOUTH AFRICAN BC, Meyerton	S • ENGLISH & AFRIKAANS • S Africa • DS-RADIO ORANJE • 100 kW
	UNITED KINGDOM †BBC, Via Maşīrah, Oman	S Asia • 100 kW / W • S Asia • 100 kW
	†BBC, Via Sackville, Can	E North Am • 250 kW / W • E North Am • 250 kW
	USA †VOA, Via Briech, Morocco	W • E Europe • 500 kW
	VOA, Via Philippines	W • SE Asia • 250 kW
	VOA, Via Rhodes, Greece	Mideast • 50 kW
(con'd)	†VOA, Via Wertachtal, Germany	S • E Europe • 500 kW

FREQUENCY   COUNTRY, STATION, LOCATION

TARGET • NETWORK • POWER (kW)   World Time

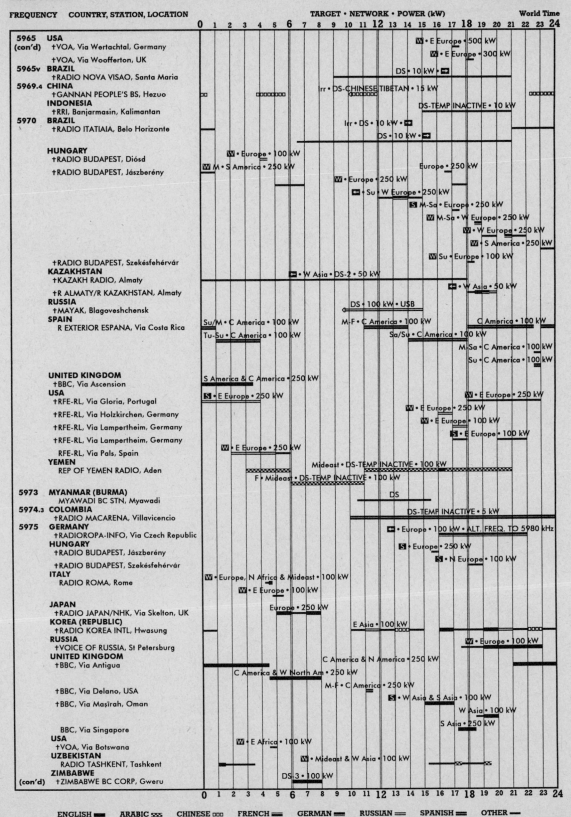

Freq	Country / Station / Location
5965	**USA**
(con'd)	†VOA, Via Wertachtal, Germany
	†VOA, Via Woofferton, UK
5965v	**BRAZIL**
	†RADIO NOVA VISAO, Santa Maria
5969.4	**CHINA**
	†GANNAN PEOPLE'S BS, Hezuo
	INDONESIA
	†RRI, Banjarmasin, Kalimantan
5970	**BRAZIL**
	†RADIO ITATIAIA, Belo Horizonte
	HUNGARY
	†RADIO BUDAPEST, Diósd
	†RADIO BUDAPEST, Jászberény
	†RADIO BUDAPEST, Szekésfehérvár
	KAZAKHSTAN
	†KAZAKH RADIO, Almaty
	†R ALMATY/R KAZAKHSTAN, Almaty
	RUSSIA
	†MAYAK, Blagoveshchensk
	SPAIN
	R EXTERIOR ESPANA, Via Costa Rica
	UNITED KINGDOM
	†BBC, Via Ascension
	USA
	†RFE-RL, Via Gloria, Portugal
	†RFE-RL, Via Holzkirchen, Germany
	†RFE-RL, Via Lampertheim, Germany
	†RFE-RL, Via Lampertheim, Germany
	RFE-RL, Via Pals, Spain
	YEMEN
	REP OF YEMEN RADIO, Aden
5973	**MYANMAR (BURMA)**
	MYAWADI BC STN, Myawadi
5974.3	**COLOMBIA**
	†RADIO MACARENA, Villavicencio
5975	**GERMANY**
	†RADIOROPA-INFO, Via Czech Republic
	HUNGARY
	†RADIO BUDAPEST, Jászberény
	†RADIO BUDAPEST, Szekésfehérvár
	ITALY
	RADIO ROMA, Rome
	JAPAN
	†RADIO JAPAN/NHK, Via Skelton, UK
	KOREA (REPUBLIC)
	†RADIO KOREA INTL, Hwasung
	RUSSIA
	†VOICE OF RUSSIA, St Petersburg
	UNITED KINGDOM
	†BBC, Via Antigua
	†BBC, Via Delano, USA
	†BBC, Via Maşīrah, Oman
	BBC, Via Singapore
	USA
	†VOA, Via Botswana
	UZBEKISTAN
	RADIO TASHKENT, Tashkent
	ZIMBABWE
(con'd)	†ZIMBABWE BC CORP, Gweru

Time markers across top/bottom: 0 1 2 3 4 5 6 7 8 9 10 11 12 13 14 15 16 17 18 19 20 21 22 23 24

Schedule entries (target • network • power):
- USA †VOA Via Wertachtal: W • E Europe • 500 kW
- USA †VOA Via Woofferton: W • E Europe • 300 kW
- BRAZIL RADIO NOVA VISAO: DS • 10 kW
- CHINA GANNAN PEOPLE'S BS: Irr • DS-CHINESE TIBETAN • 15 kW
- INDONESIA RRI: DS-TEMP INACTIVE • 10 kW
- BRAZIL RADIO ITATIAIA: Irr • DS • 10 kW / DS • 10 kW
- HUNGARY RADIO BUDAPEST Diósd: W • Europe • 100 kW
- HUNGARY RADIO BUDAPEST Jászberény: W M • S America • 250 kW; Europe • 250 kW; W • Europe • 250 kW; + Su • W Europe • 250 kW; S M-Sa • Europe • 250 kW; W M-Sa • W Europe • 250 kW; W • W Europe • 250 kW; W • S America • 250 kW; W Su • Europe • 100 kW
- KAZAKHSTAN KAZAKH RADIO: • W Asia • DS-2 • 50 kW
- R ALMATY/R KAZAKHSTAN: • W Asia • 50 kW
- RUSSIA MAYAK: DS • 100 kW • USB
- SPAIN R EXTERIOR ESPANA: Su/M • C America • 100 kW; M-F • C America • 100 kW; C America • 100 kW; Tu-Su • C America • 100 kW; Sa/Su • C America • 100 kW; M Sa • C America • 100 kW; Su • C America • 100 kW
- UK BBC Via Ascension: S America & C America • 250 kW
- USA RFE-RL Via Gloria: S • E Europe • 250 kW; W • E Europe • 250 kW
- RFE-RL Via Holzkirchen: W • E Europe • 250 kW
- RFE-RL Via Lampertheim: W • E Europe • 100 kW
- RFE-RL Via Lampertheim: S • E Europe • 100 kW
- RFE-RL Via Pals: W • E Europe • 250 kW
- YEMEN REP OF YEMEN RADIO: Mideast • DS-TEMP INACTIVE • 100 kW; F • Mideast • DS-TEMP INACTIVE • 100 kW
- MYANMAR MYAWADI BC STN: DS
- COLOMBIA RADIO MACARENA: DS-TEMP INACTIVE • 5 kW
- GERMANY RADIOROPA-INFO: • Europe • 100 kW • ALT. FREQ. TO 5980 kHz
- HUNGARY RADIO BUDAPEST Jászberény: S • Europe • 250 kW
- HUNGARY RADIO BUDAPEST Szekésfehérvár: S • N Europe • 100 kW
- ITALY RADIO ROMA: W • Europe, N Africa & Mideast • 100 kW; W • E Europe • 100 kW
- JAPAN RADIO JAPAN/NHK: Europe • 250 kW
- KOREA RADIO KOREA INTL: E Asia • 100 kW
- RUSSIA VOICE OF RUSSIA: W • Europe • 100 kW
- UK BBC Via Antigua: C America & N America • 250 kW
- BBC Via Delano: C America & W North Am • 250 kW; M-F • C America • 250 kW
- BBC Via Maşīrah: S • W Asia & S Asia • 100 kW; W Asia • 100 kW
- BBC Via Singapore: S Asia • 250 kW
- USA VOA Via Botswana: W • E Africa • 100 kW
- UZBEKISTAN RADIO TASHKENT: W • Mideast & W Asia • 100 kW
- ZIMBABWE ZIMBABWE BC CORP: DS-3 • 100 kW

ENGLISH ▬   ARABIC ⧓   CHINESE □□□   FRENCH ═══   GERMAN ▬▬   RUSSIAN ═   SPANISH ▬   OTHER ─

FREQUENCY   COUNTRY, STATION, LOCATION   TARGET • NETWORK • POWER (kW)   World Time

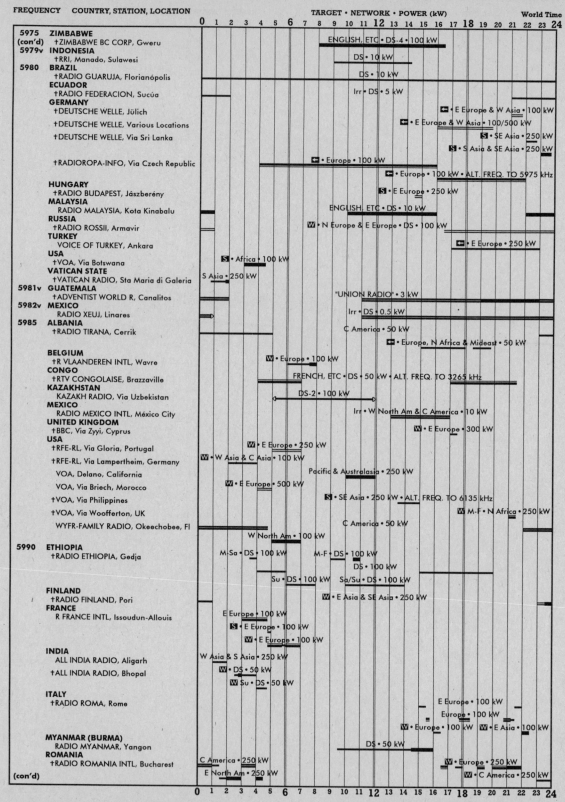

Frequency	Country / Station / Location	Schedule
5975 (con'd)	ZIMBABWE †ZIMBABWE BC CORP, Gweru	ENGLISH, ETC • DS-4 • 100 kW
5979v	INDONESIA †RRI, Manado, Sulawesi	DS • 10 kW
5980	BRAZIL †RADIO GUARUJA, Florianópolis	DS • 10 kW
	ECUADOR †RADIO FEDERACION, Sucúa	Irr • DS • 5 kW
	GERMANY †DEUTSCHE WELLE, Jülich	• E Europe & W Asia • 100 kW
	†DEUTSCHE WELLE, Various Locations	• E Europe & W Asia • 100/500 kW
	†DEUTSCHE WELLE, Via Sri Lanka	S • SE Asia • 250 kW / S • S Asia & SE Asia • 250 kW
	†RADIOROPA-INFO, Via Czech Republic	• Europe • 100 kW / • Europe • 100 kW • ALT. FREQ. TO 5975 kHz
	HUNGARY †RADIO BUDAPEST, Jászberény	S • E Europe • 250 kW
	MALAYSIA RADIO MALAYSIA, Kota Kinabalu	ENGLISH, ETC • DS • 10 kW
	RUSSIA †RADIO ROSSII, Armavir	W • N Europe & E Europe • DS • 100 kW
	TURKEY VOICE OF TURKEY, Ankara	• E Europe • 250 kW
	USA †VOA, Via Botswana	S • Africa • 100 kW
	VATICAN STATE †VATICAN RADIO, Sta Maria di Galeria	S Asia • 250 kW
5981v	GUATEMALA †ADVENTIST WORLD R, Canalitos	"UNION RADIO" • 3 kW
5982v	MEXICO RADIO XEUJ, Linares	Irr • DS • 0.5 kW
5985	ALBANIA †RADIO TIRANA, Cerrik	C America • 50 kW / • Europe, N Africa & Mideast • 50 kW
	BELGIUM †R VLAANDEREN INTL, Wavre	W • Europe • 100 kW
	CONGO †RTV CONGOLAISE, Brazzaville	FRENCH, ETC • DS • 50 kW • ALT. FREQ. TO 3265 kHz
	KAZAKHSTAN KAZAKH RADIO, Via Uzbekistan	DS-2 • 100 kW
	MEXICO RADIO MEXICO INTL, México City	Irr • W North Am & C America • 10 kW
	UNITED KINGDOM †BBC, Via Zyyi, Cyprus	W • E Europe • 300 kW
	USA †RFE-RL, Via Gloria, Portugal	W • E Europe • 250 kW
	†RFE-RL, Via Lampertheim, Germany	W • W Asia & C Asia • 100 kW
	VOA, Delano, California	Pacific & Australasia • 250 kW
	VOA, Via Briech, Morocco	W • E Europe • 500 kW
	†VOA, Via Philippines	S • SE Asia • 250 kW • ALT. FREQ. TO 6135 kHz
	†VOA, Via Woofferton, UK	W • M-F • N Africa • 250 kW
	WYFR-FAMILY RADIO, Okeechobee, Fl	C America • 50 kW / W North Am • 100 kW
5990	ETHIOPIA †RADIO ETHIOPIA, Gedja	M-Sa • DS • 100 kW / M-F • DS • 100 kW / DS • 100 kW / Su • DS • 100 kW / Sa/Su • DS • 100 kW
	FINLAND †RADIO FINLAND, Pori	W • E Asia & SE Asia • 250 kW
	FRANCE R FRANCE INTL, Issoudun-Allouis	E Europe • 100 kW / S • E Europe • 100 kW / W • E Europe • 100 kW
	INDIA ALL INDIA RADIO, Aligarh	W Asia & S Asia • 250 kW
	†ALL INDIA RADIO, Bhopal	W • DS • 50 kW / W • Su • DS • 50 kW
	ITALY †RADIO ROMA, Rome	E Europe • 100 kW / Europe • 100 kW / W • Europe • 100 kW / W • E Asia • 100 kW
	MYANMAR (BURMA) RADIO MYANMAR, Yangon	DS • 50 kW
	ROMANIA †RADIO ROMANIA INTL, Bucharest	C America • 250 kW / E North Am • 250 kW / W • Europe • 250 kW / W • C America • 250 kW
(con'd)		

FREQUENCY   COUNTRY, STATION, LOCATION

TARGET • NETWORK • POWER (kW)

World Time

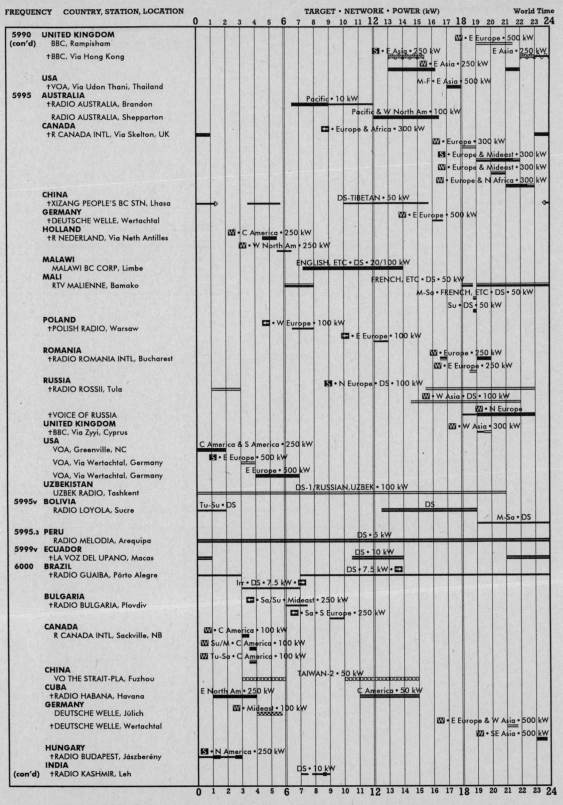

5990	UNITED KINGDOM	
(con'd)	BBC, Rampisham	W • E Europe • 500 kW
		S • E Asia • 250 kW / E Asia • 250 kW
	†BBC, Via Hong Kong	W • E Asia • 250 kW
	USA	
	†VOA, Via Udon Thani, Thailand	M-F • E Asia • 500 kW
5995	AUSTRALIA	
	†RADIO AUSTRALIA, Brandon	Pacific • 10 kW
	RADIO AUSTRALIA, Shepparton	Pacific & W North Am • 100 kW
	CANADA	
	†R CANADA INTL, Via Skelton, UK	• Europe & Africa • 300 kW
		W • Europe • 300 kW
		S • Europe & Mideast • 300 kW
		W • Europe & Mideast • 300 kW
		W • Europe & N Africa • 300 kW
	CHINA	
	†XIZANG PEOPLE'S BC STN, Lhasa	DS-TIBETAN • 50 kW
	GERMANY	
	†DEUTSCHE WELLE, Wertachtal	W • E Europe • 500 kW
	HOLLAND	
	†R NEDERLAND, Via Neth Antilles	W • C America • 250 kW
		W • W North Am • 250 kW
	MALAWI	
	MALAWI BC CORP, Limbe	ENGLISH, ETC • DS • 20/100 kW
	MALI	
	RTV MALIENNE, Bamako	FRENCH, ETC • DS • 50 kW
		M-Sa • FRENCH, ETC • DS • 50 kW
		Su • DS • 50 kW
	POLAND	
	†POLISH RADIO, Warsaw	• W Europe • 100 kW
		• E Europe • 100 kW
	ROMANIA	
	†RADIO ROMANIA INTL, Bucharest	W • Europe • 250 kW
		W • E Europe • 250 kW
	RUSSIA	
	†RADIO ROSSII, Tula	S • N Europe • DS • 100 kW
		W • W Asia • DS • 100 kW
		W • N Europe
	†VOICE OF RUSSIA	
	UNITED KINGDOM	W • W Asia • 300 kW
	†BBC, Via Zyyi, Cyprus	
	USA	
	VOA, Greenville, NC	C America & S America • 250 kW
	VOA, Via Wertachtal, Germany	S • E Europe • 500 kW
	VOA, Via Wertachtal, Germany	E Europe • 500 kW
	UZBEKISTAN	
	UZBEK RADIO, Tashkent	DS-1/RUSSIAN, UZBEK • 100 kW
5995v	BOLIVIA	
	RADIO LOYOLA, Sucre	Tu-Su • DS / DS / M-Sa • DS
5995.3	PERU	
	RADIO MELODIA, Arequipa	DS • 5 kW
5999v	ECUADOR	
	†LA VOZ DEL UPANO, Macas	DS • 10 kW
6000	BRAZIL	
	†RADIO GUAIBA, Pôrto Alegre	DS • 7.5 kW •
		Irr • DS • 7.5 kW •
	BULGARIA	
	†RADIO BULGARIA, Plovdiv	• Sa/Su • Mideast • 250 kW
		• Sa • S Europe • 250 kW
	CANADA	
	R CANADA INTL, Sackville, NB	W • C America • 100 kW
		W Su/M • C America • 100 kW
		W Tu-Sa • C America • 100 kW
	CHINA	
	VO THE STRAIT-PLA, Fuzhou	TAIWAN-2 • 50 kW
	CUBA	
	†RADIO HABANA, Havana	E North Am • 250 kW / C America • 50 kW
	GERMANY	
	DEUTSCHE WELLE, Jülich	W • Mideast • 100 kW
	†DEUTSCHE WELLE, Wertachtal	W • E Europe & W Asia • 500 kW
		W • SE Asia • 500 kW
	HUNGARY	
	†RADIO BUDAPEST, Jászberény	S • N America • 250 kW
	INDIA	
(con'd)	†RADIO KASHMIR, Leh	DS • 10 kW

ENGLISH ▬   ARABIC ⬚⬚⬚   CHINESE ▫▫▫   FRENCH ▭   GERMAN ▬▬   RUSSIAN ══   SPANISH ▬   OTHER ──

| FREQUENCY | COUNTRY, STATION, LOCATION | TARGET • NETWORK • POWER (kW) | World Time |

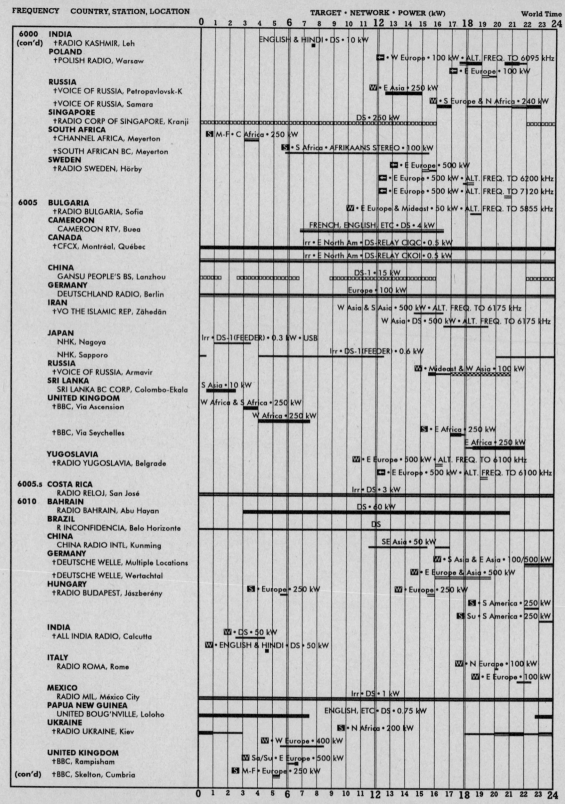

6000
(con'd)
INDIA
†RADIO KASHMIR, Leh — ENGLISH & HINDI • DS • 10 kW
POLAND
†POLISH RADIO, Warsaw — ⬄ • W Europe • 100 kW • ALT. FREQ. TO 6095 kHz
— ⬄ • E Europe • 100 kW
RUSSIA
†VOICE OF RUSSIA, Petropavlovsk-K — Ⓦ • E Asia • 250 kW
†VOICE OF RUSSIA, Samara — Ⓦ • S Europe & N Africa • 240 kW
SINGAPORE
†RADIO CORP OF SINGAPORE, Kranji — DS • 250 kW
SOUTH AFRICA
†CHANNEL AFRICA, Meyerton — Ⓢ M-F • C Africa • 250 kW
†SOUTH AFRICAN BC, Meyerton — Ⓢ • S Africa • AFRIKAANS STEREO • 100 kW
SWEDEN
†RADIO SWEDEN, Hörby — ⬄ • E Europe • 500 kW
— ⬄ • E Europe • 500 kW • ALT. FREQ. TO 6200 kHz
— ⬄ • E Europe • 500 kW • ALT. FREQ. TO 7120 kHz

6005
BULGARIA
†RADIO BULGARIA, Sofia — Ⓦ • E Europe & Mideast • 50 kW • ALT. FREQ. TO 5855 kHz
CAMEROON
CAMEROON RTV, Buea — FRENCH, ENGLISH, ETC • DS • 4 kW
CANADA
†CFCX, Montréal, Québec — Irr • E North Am • DS-RELAY CJQC • 0.5 kW
— Irr • E North Am • DS-RELAY CKOI • 0.5 kW
CHINA
GANSU PEOPLE'S BS, Lanzhou — DS-1 • 15 kW
GERMANY
DEUTSCHLAND RADIO, Berlin — Europe • 100 kW
IRAN
†VO THE ISLAMIC REP, Zāhedān — W Asia & S Asia • 500 kW • ALT. FREQ. TO 6175 kHz
— W Asia • DS • 500 kW • ALT. FREQ. TO 6175 kHz
JAPAN
NHK, Nagoya — Irr • DS-1(FEEDER) • 0.3 kW • USB
NHK, Sapporo — Irr • DS-1(FEEDER) • 0.6 kW
RUSSIA
†VOICE OF RUSSIA, Armavir — Ⓦ • Mideast & W Asia • 100 kW
SRI LANKA
SRI LANKA BC CORP, Colombo-Ekala — S Asia • 10 kW
UNITED KINGDOM
†BBC, Via Ascension — W Africa & S Africa • 250 kW
— W Africa • 250 kW
†BBC, Via Seychelles — Ⓢ • E Africa • 250 kW
— E Africa • 250 kW
YUGOSLAVIA
†RADIO YUGOSLAVIA, Belgrade — Ⓦ • E Europe • 500 kW • ALT. FREQ. TO 6100 kHz
— ⬄ • E Europe • 500 kW • ALT. FREQ. TO 6100 kHz

6005.5
COSTA RICA
RADIO RELOJ, San José — Irr • DS • 3 kW
6010
BAHRAIN
RADIO BAHRAIN, Abu Hayan — DS • 60 kW
BRAZIL
R INCONFIDENCIA, Belo Horizonte — DS
CHINA
CHINA RADIO INTL, Kunming — SE Asia • 50 kW
GERMANY
†DEUTSCHE WELLE, Multiple Locations — Ⓦ • S Asia & E Asia • 100/500 kW
†DEUTSCHE WELLE, Wertachtal — Ⓦ • E Europe & Asia • 500 kW
HUNGARY
†RADIO BUDAPEST, Jászberény — Ⓢ • Europe • 250 kW
— Ⓦ • Europe • 250 kW
— Ⓢ • S America • 250 kW
— Ⓢ Su • S America • 250 kW
INDIA
†ALL INDIA RADIO, Calcutta — Ⓦ • DS • 50 kW
— Ⓦ • ENGLISH & HINDI • DS • 50 kW
ITALY
RADIO ROMA, Rome — Ⓦ • N Europe • 100 kW
— Ⓦ • E Europe • 100 kW
MEXICO
RADIO MIL, México City — Irr • DS • 1 kW
PAPUA NEW GUINEA
UNITED BOUG'NVILLE, Loloho — ENGLISH, ETC • DS • 0.75 kW
UKRAINE
†RADIO UKRAINE, Kiev — Ⓢ • N Africa • 200 kW
— Ⓦ • W Europe • 400 kW
UNITED KINGDOM
†BBC, Rampisham — Ⓦ Sa/Su • E Europe • 500 kW
(con'd)
†BBC, Skelton, Cumbria — Ⓢ M-F • Europe • 250 kW

SEASONAL Ⓢ OR Ⓦ   1-HR TIMESHIFT MIDYEAR ⬄ OR ⬄   JAMMING / OR ∧   EARLIEST HEARD ◁   LATEST HEARD ▷   NEW FOR 1996 †

FREQUENCY   COUNTRY, STATION, LOCATION   TARGET • NETWORK • POWER (kW)   World Time

0 1 2 3 4 5 6 7 8 9 10 11 12 13 14 15 16 17 18 19 20 21 22 23 24

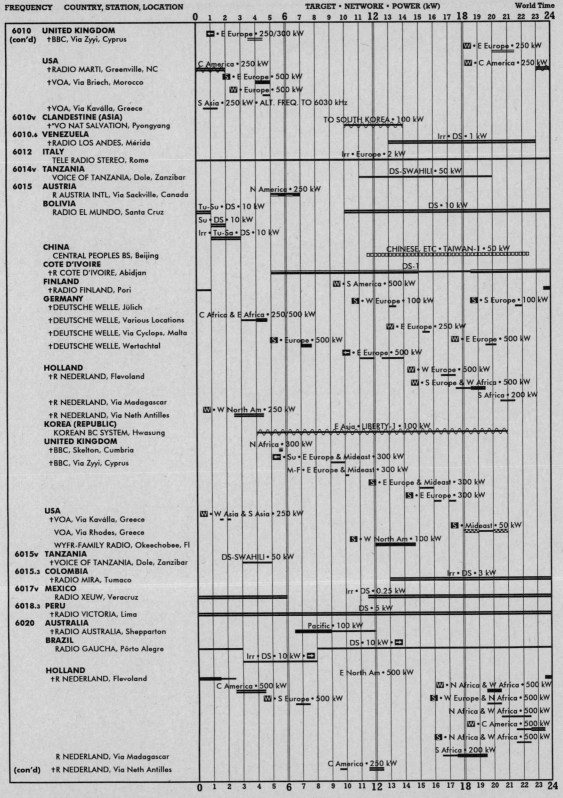

Frequency	Country, Station, Location	Target • Network • Power
6010 (con'd)	**UNITED KINGDOM** †BBC, Via Zyyi, Cyprus	E Europe • 250/300 kW; W • E Europe • 250 kW
	USA †RADIO MARTI, Greenville, NC	C America • 250 kW; W • C America • 250 kW
	†VOA, Via Briech, Morocco	S • E Europe • 500 kW; W • Europe • 500 kW
	†VOA, Via Kaválla, Greece	S Asia • 250 kW • ALT. FREQ. TO 6030 kHz
6010v	**CLANDESTINE (ASIA)** †"VO NAT SALVATION, Pyongyang	TO SOUTH KOREA • 100 kW
6010.6	**VENEZUELA** †RADIO LOS ANDES, Mérida	Irr • DS • 1 kW
6012	**ITALY** TELE RADIO STEREO, Rome	Irr • Europe • 2 kW
6014v	**TANZANIA** VOICE OF TANZANIA, Dole, Zanzibar	DS-SWAHILI • 50 kW
6015	**AUSTRIA** R AUSTRIA INTL, Via Sackville, Canada	N America • 250 kW
	BOLIVIA RADIO EL MUNDO, Santa Cruz	Tu-Su • DS • 10 kW; DS • 10 kW; Su • DS • 10 kW; Irr • Tu-Sa • DS • 10 kW
	CHINA CENTRAL PEOPLES BS, Beijing	CHINESE, ETC • TAIWAN-1 • 50 kW
	COTE D'IVOIRE †R COTE D'IVOIRE, Abidjan	DS-1
	FINLAND †RADIO FINLAND, Pori	W • S America • 500 kW
	GERMANY †DEUTSCHE WELLE, Jülich	S • W Europe • 100 kW; S • S Europe • 100 kW
	†DEUTSCHE WELLE, Various Locations	C Africa & E Africa • 250/500 kW
	†DEUTSCHE WELLE, Via Cyclops, Malta	W • E Europe • 250 kW; W • E Europe • 500 kW
	†DEUTSCHE WELLE, Wertachtal	S • Europe • 500 kW; E Europe • 500 kW
	HOLLAND †R NEDERLAND, Flevoland	W • W Europe • 500 kW; W • S Europe & W Africa • 500 kW; S Africa • 200 kW
	†R NEDERLAND, Via Madagascar	
	†R NEDERLAND, Via Neth Antilles	W • W North Am • 250 kW
	KOREA (REPUBLIC) KOREAN BC SYSTEM, Hwasung	E Asia • LIBERTY-1 • 100 kW
	UNITED KINGDOM †BBC, Skelton, Cumbria	N Africa • 300 kW; Su • E Europe & Mideast • 300 kW
	†BBC, Via Zyyi, Cyprus	M-F • E Europe & Mideast • 300 kW; S • E Europe & Mideast • 300 kW; S • E Europe • 300 kW
	USA †VOA, Via Kaválla, Greece	W • W Asia & S Asia • 250 kW
	VOA, Via Rhodes, Greece	S • Mideast • 50 kW
	WYFR-FAMILY RADIO, Okeechobee, Fl	S • W North Am • 100 kW
6015v	**TANZANIA** †VOICE OF TANZANIA, Dole, Zanzibar	DS-SWAHILI • 50 kW
6015.3	**COLOMBIA** †RADIO MIRA, Tumaco	Irr • DS • 3 kW
6017v	**MEXICO** RADIO XEUW, Veracruz	Irr • DS • 0.25 kW
6018.3	**PERU** †RADIO VICTORIA, Lima	DS • 5 kW
6020	**AUSTRALIA** †RADIO AUSTRALIA, Shepparton	Pacific • 100 kW
	BRAZIL RADIO GAUCHA, Pôrto Alegre	DS • 10 kW; Irr • DS • 10 kW
	HOLLAND †R NEDERLAND, Flevoland	E North Am • 500 kW; C America • 500 kW; W • S Europe • 500 kW; W • N Africa & W Africa • 500 kW; S • W Europe & N Africa • 500 kW; N Africa & W Africa • 500 kW; W • C America • 500 kW; S • N Africa & W Africa • 500 kW; S Africa • 200 kW
	R NEDERLAND, Via Madagascar	
(con'd)	†R NEDERLAND, Via Neth Antilles	C America • 250 kW

0 1 2 3 4 5 6 7 8 9 10 11 12 13 14 15 16 17 18 19 20 21 22 23 24

ENGLISH ▬▬   ARABIC ≈≈≈   CHINESE □□□   FRENCH ═══   GERMAN ▬▬   RUSSIAN ══   SPANISH ══   OTHER ──

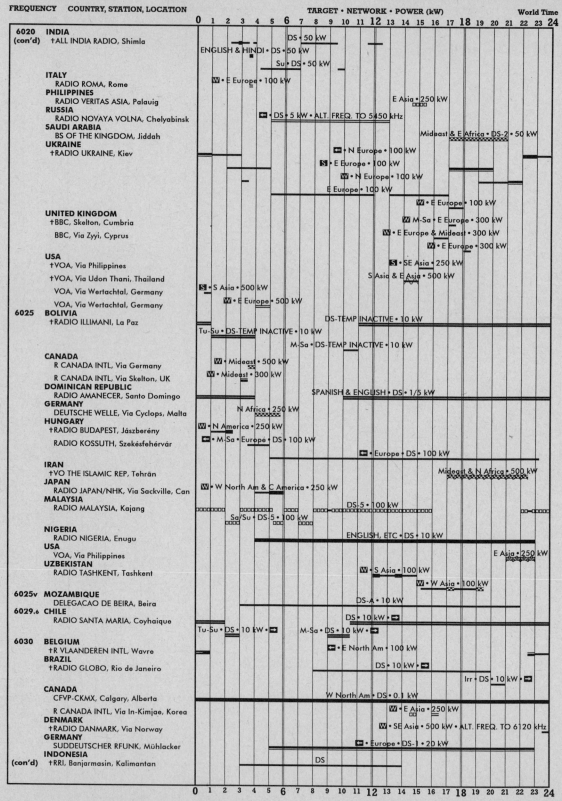

FREQUENCY	COUNTRY, STATION, LOCATION	TARGET • NETWORK • POWER (kW)
6020 (con'd)	**INDIA** †ALL INDIA RADIO, Shimla	DS • 50 kW
		ENGLISH & HINDI • DS • 50 kW
		Su • DS • 50 kW
	ITALY RADIO ROMA, Rome	[W] • E Europe • 100 kW
	PHILIPPINES RADIO VERITAS ASIA, Palauig	E Asia • 250 kW
	RUSSIA RADIO NOVAYA VOLNA, Chelyabinsk	⇐ • DS • 5 kW • ALT. FREQ. TO 5450 kHz
	SAUDI ARABIA BS OF THE KINGDOM, Jiddah	Mideast & E Africa • DS-2 • 50 kW
	UKRAINE †RADIO UKRAINE, Kiev	⇐ • N Europe • 100 kW
		[S] • E Europe • 100 kW
		[W] • N Europe • 100 kW
		E Europe • 100 kW
		[W] • E Europe • 100 kW
	UNITED KINGDOM †BBC, Skelton, Cumbria	[W] M-Sa • E Europe • 300 kW
	BBC, Via Zyyi, Cyprus	[W] • E Europe & Mideast • 300 kW
		[W] • E Europe • 300 kW
	USA †VOA, Via Philippines	[S] • SE Asia • 250 kW
	†VOA, Via Udon Thani, Thailand	S Asia & E Asia • 500 kW
	VOA, Via Wertachtal, Germany	[S] • S Asia • 500 kW
	VOA, Via Wertachtal, Germany	[W] • E Europe • 500 kW
6025	**BOLIVIA** †RADIO ILLIMANI, La Paz	DS-TEMP INACTIVE • 10 kW
		Tu-Su • DS-TEMP INACTIVE • 10 kW
		M-Sa • DS-TEMP INACTIVE • 10 kW
	CANADA R CANADA INTL, Via Germany	[W] • Mideast • 500 kW
	R CANADA INTL, Via Skelton, UK	[W] • Mideast • 300 kW
	DOMINICAN REPUBLIC RADIO AMANECER, Santo Domingo	SPANISH & ENGLISH • DS • 1/5 kW
	GERMANY DEUTSCHE WELLE, Via Cyclops, Malta	N Africa • 250 kW
	HUNGARY †RADIO BUDAPEST, Jászberény	[W] • N America • 250 kW
	RADIO KOSSUTH, Székésfehérvár	⇐ • M-Sa • Europe • DS • 100 kW
		⇐ • Europe • DS • 100 kW
	IRAN †VO THE ISLAMIC REP, Tehrān	Mideast & N Africa • 500 kW
	JAPAN RADIO JAPAN/NHK, Via Sackville, Can	[W] • W North Am & C America • 250 kW
	MALAYSIA RADIO MALAYSIA, Kajang	DS-5 • 100 kW
		Sa/Su • DS-5 • 100 kW
	NIGERIA RADIO NIGERIA, Enugu	ENGLISH, ETC • DS • 10 kW
	USA VOA, Via Philippines	E Asia • 250 kW
	UZBEKISTAN RADIO TASHKENT, Tashkent	[W] • S Asia • 100 kW
		[W] • W Asia • 100 kW
6025v	**MOZAMBIQUE** DELEGACAO DE BEIRA, Beira	DS-A • 10 kW
6029.6	**CHILE** RADIO SANTA MARIA, Coyhaique	DS • 10 kW • ⇒
		Tu-Su • DS • 10 kW • ⇒
		M-Sa • DS • 10 kW • ⇒
6030	**BELGIUM** †R VLAANDEREN INTL, Wavre	⇐ • E North Am • 100 kW
	BRAZIL †RADIO GLOBO, Rio de Janeiro	DS • 10 kW • ⇒
		Irr • DS • 10 kW • ⇒
	CANADA CFVP-CKMX, Calgary, Alberta	W North Am • DS • 0.1 kW
	R CANADA INTL, Via In-Kimjae, Korea	[W] • E Asia • 250 kW
	DENMARK †RADIO DANMARK, Via Norway	[W] • SE Asia • 500 kW • ALT. FREQ. TO 6120 kHz
	GERMANY SUDDEUTSCHER RFUNK, Mühlacker	⇐ • Europe • DS-1 • 20 kW
(con'd)	**INDONESIA** †RRI, Banjarmasin, Kalimantan	DS

World Time 0–24

SEASONAL [S] OR [W] 1-HR TIMESHIFT MIDYEAR ⇐ OR ⇒ JAMMING / OR /\ EARLIEST HEARD ◁ LATEST HEARD ▷ NEW FOR 1996 †

FREQUENCY   COUNTRY, STATION, LOCATION

TARGET • NETWORK • POWER (kW)

World Time

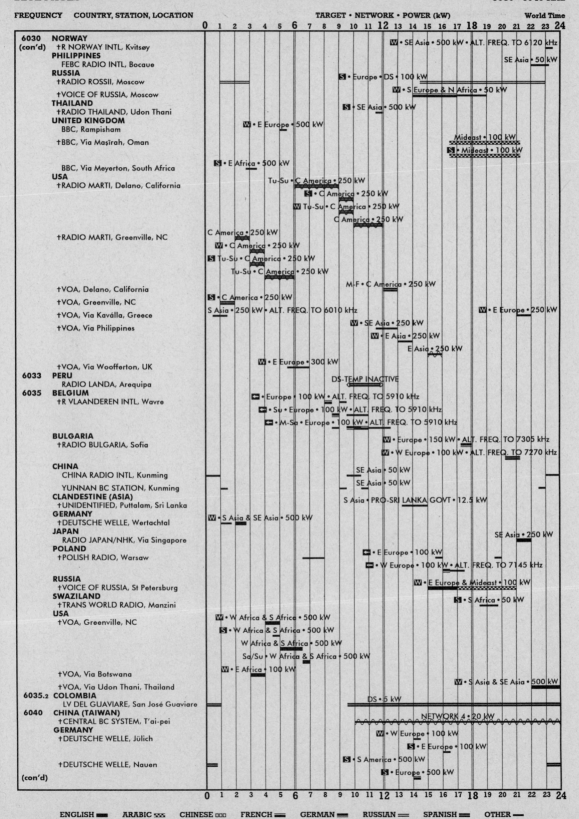

Frequency	Country / Station / Location	Broadcast details
6030 (con'd)	**NORWAY** †R NORWAY INTL, Kvitsøy	W • SE Asia • 500 kW • ALT. FREQ. TO 6120 kHz
	PHILIPPINES FEBC RADIO INTL, Bocaue	SE Asia • 50 kW
	RUSSIA †RADIO ROSSII, Moscow	S • Europe • DS • 100 kW
	†VOICE OF RUSSIA, Moscow	W • S Europe & N Africa • 50 kW
	THAILAND †RADIO THAILAND, Udon Thani	S • SE Asia • 500 kW
	UNITED KINGDOM BBC, Rampisham	W • E Europe • 500 kW
	†BBC, Via Maṣīrah, Oman	Mideast • 100 kW / S • Mideast • 100 kW
	BBC, Via Meyerton, South Africa	S • E Africa • 500 kW
	USA †RADIO MARTI, Delano, California	Tu-Su • C America • 250 kW / S • C America • 250 kW / W Tu-Su • C America • 250 kW / C America • 250 kW
	†RADIO MARTI, Greenville, NC	C America • 250 kW / W • C America • 250 kW / S Tu-Su • C America • 250 kW / Tu-Su • C America • 250 kW
	†VOA, Delano, California	M-F • C America • 250 kW / S • C America • 250 kW
	†VOA, Greenville, NC	S Asia • 250 kW • ALT. FREQ. TO 6010 kHz / W • E Europe • 250 kW
	†VOA, Via Kaválla, Greece	W • SE Asia • 250 kW
	†VOA, Via Philippines	W • E Asia • 250 kW / E Asia • 250 kW
	†VOA, Via Woofferton, UK	W • E Europe • 300 kW
6033	**PERU** RADIO LANDA, Arequipa	DS-TEMP INACTIVE
6035	**BELGIUM** †R VLAANDEREN INTL, Wavre	Europe • 100 kW • ALT. FREQ. TO 5910 kHz / Su • Europe • 100 kW • ALT. FREQ. TO 5910 kHz / M-Sa • Europe • 100 kW • ALT. FREQ. TO 5910 kHz
	BULGARIA †RADIO BULGARIA, Sofia	W • Europe • 150 kW • ALT. FREQ. TO 7305 kHz / W • W Europe • 100 kW • ALT. FREQ. TO 7270 kHz
	CHINA CHINA RADIO INTL, Kunming	SE Asia • 50 kW
	YUNNAN BC STATION, Kunming	SE Asia • 50 kW
	CLANDESTINE (ASIA) †UNIDENTIFIED, Puttalam, Sri Lanka	S Asia • PRO-SRI LANKA GOVT • 12.5 kW
	GERMANY †DEUTSCHE WELLE, Wertachtal	W • S Asia & SE Asia • 500 kW
	JAPAN RADIO JAPAN/NHK, Via Singapore	SE Asia • 250 kW
	POLAND †POLISH RADIO, Warsaw	E Europe • 100 kW / W Europe • 100 kW • ALT. FREQ. TO 7145 kHz
	RUSSIA †VOICE OF RUSSIA, St Petersburg	W • E Europe & Mideast • 100 kW
	SWAZILAND †TRANS WORLD RADIO, Manzini	S • S Africa • 50 kW
	USA †VOA, Greenville, NC	W • W Africa & S Africa • 500 kW / S • W Africa & S Africa • 500 kW / W Africa & S Africa • 500 kW / Sa/Su • W Africa & S Africa • 500 kW
	†VOA, Via Botswana	W • E Africa • 100 kW
	†VOA, Via Udon Thani, Thailand	W • S Asia & SE Asia • 500 kW
6035.2	**COLOMBIA** LV DEL GUAVIARE, San José Guaviare	DS • 5 kW
6040	**CHINA (TAIWAN)** †CENTRAL BC SYSTEM, T'ai-pei	NETWORK 4 • 20 kW
	GERMANY †DEUTSCHE WELLE, Jülich	W • W Europe • 100 kW / S • E Europe • 100 kW
	†DEUTSCHE WELLE, Nauen	S • S America • 500 kW / S • Europe • 500 kW
(con'd)		

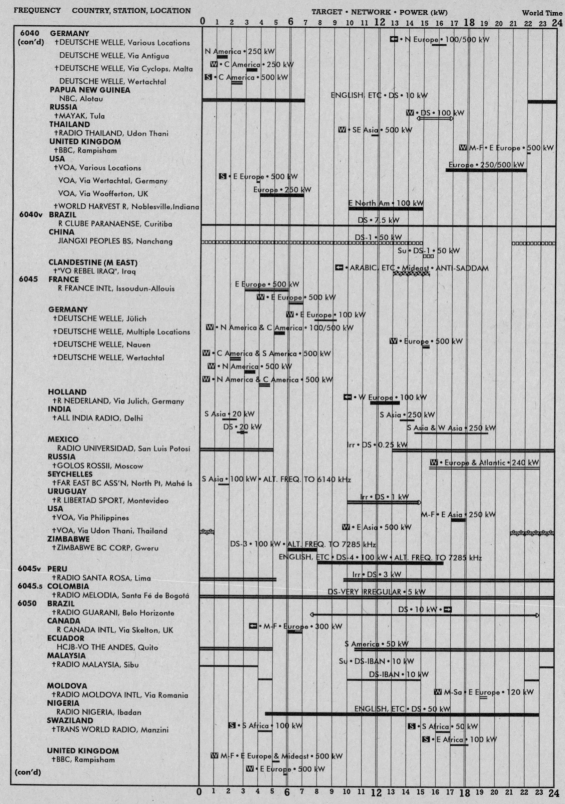

FREQUENCY	COUNTRY, STATION, LOCATION	TARGET • NETWORK • POWER (kW)	World Time

6040
(con'd) **GERMANY**
†DEUTSCHE WELLE, Various Locations — ⇦ • N Europe • 100/500 kW
DEUTSCHE WELLE, Via Antigua — N America • 250 kW
†DEUTSCHE WELLE, Via Cyclops, Malta — Ⓦ • C America • 250 kW
DEUTSCHE WELLE, Wertachtal — Ⓢ • C America • 500 kW
PAPUA NEW GUINEA
NBC, Alotau — ENGLISH, ETC • DS • 10 kW
RUSSIA
†MAYAK, Tula — Ⓦ • DS • 100 kW
THAILAND
†RADIO THAILAND, Udon Thani — Ⓦ • SE Asia • 500 kW
UNITED KINGDOM
†BBC, Rampisham — Ⓦ M-F • E Europe • 500 kW
USA
†VOA, Various Locations — Europe • 250/500 kW
VOA, Via Wertachtal, Germany — Ⓢ • E Europe • 500 kW
VOA, Via Woofferton, UK — Europe • 250 kW
†WORLD HARVEST R, Noblesville, Indiana — E North Am • 100 kW
6040v BRAZIL
R CLUBE PARANAENSE, Curitiba — DS • 7.5 kW
CHINA
JIANGXI PEOPLES BS, Nanchang — DS-1 • 50 kW / Su • DS-1 • 50 kW
CLANDESTINE (M EAST)
†"VO REBEL IRAQ", Iraq — ⇦ • ARABIC, ETC • Mideast • ANTI-SADDAM
6045 FRANCE
R FRANCE INTL, Issoudun-Allouis — E Europe • 500 kW
GERMANY
†DEUTSCHE WELLE, Jülich — Ⓦ • E Europe • 500 kW / Ⓦ • E Europe • 100 kW
†DEUTSCHE WELLE, Multiple Locations — Ⓦ • N America & C America • 100/500 kW
†DEUTSCHE WELLE, Nauen — Ⓦ • Europe • 500 kW
†DEUTSCHE WELLE, Wertachtal — Ⓦ • C America & S America • 500 kW / Ⓦ • N America • 500 kW / Ⓦ • N America & C America • 500 kW
HOLLAND
†R NEDERLAND, Via Julich, Germany — ⇦ • W Europe • 100 kW
INDIA
†ALL INDIA RADIO, Delhi — S Asia • 20 kW / S Asia • 250 kW / DS • 20 kW / S Asia & W Asia • 250 kW
MEXICO
RADIO UNIVERSIDAD, San Luis Potosí — Irr • DS • 0.25 kW
RUSSIA
†GOLOS ROSSII, Moscow — Ⓦ • Europe & Atlantic • 240 kW
SEYCHELLES
†FAR EAST BC ASS'N, North Pt, Mahé Is — S Asia • 100 kW • ALT. FREQ. TO 6140 kHz
URUGUAY
†R LIBERTAD SPORT, Montevideo — Irr • DS • 1 kW
USA
†VOA, Via Philippines — M-F • E Asia • 250 kW
†VOA, Via Udon Thani, Thailand — Ⓦ • E Asia • 500 kW
ZIMBABWE
†ZIMBABWE BC CORP, Gweru — DS-3 • 100 kW • ALT. FREQ. TO 7285 kHz / ENGLISH, ETC • DS-4 • 100 kW • ALT. FREQ. TO 7285 kHz
6045v PERU
†RADIO SANTA ROSA, Lima — Irr • DS • 3 kW
6045.5 COLOMBIA
†RADIO MELODIA, Santa Fé de Bogotá — DS-VERY IRREGULAR • 5 kW
6050 BRAZIL
†RADIO GUARANI, Belo Horizonte — DS • 10 kW • ⇦
CANADA
R CANADA INTL, Via Skelton, UK — ⇦ • M-F • Europe • 300 kW
ECUADOR
HCJB-VO THE ANDES, Quito — S America • 50 kW
MALAYSIA
†RADIO MALAYSIA, Sibu — Su • DS-IBAN • 10 kW / DS-IBAN • 10 kW
MOLDOVA
†RADIO MOLDOVA INTL, Via Romania — Ⓦ M-Sa • E Europe • 120 kW
NIGERIA
RADIO NIGERIA, Ibadan — ENGLISH, ETC • DS • 50 kW
SWAZILAND
†TRANS WORLD RADIO, Manzini — Ⓢ • S Africa • 100 kW / Ⓢ • S Africa • 50 kW / Ⓢ • E Africa • 100 kW
UNITED KINGDOM
†BBC, Rampisham — Ⓦ M-F • E Europe & Mideast • 500 kW / Ⓦ • E Europe • 500 kW
(con'd)

FREQUENCY   COUNTRY, STATION, LOCATION   TARGET • NETWORK • POWER (kW)   World Time

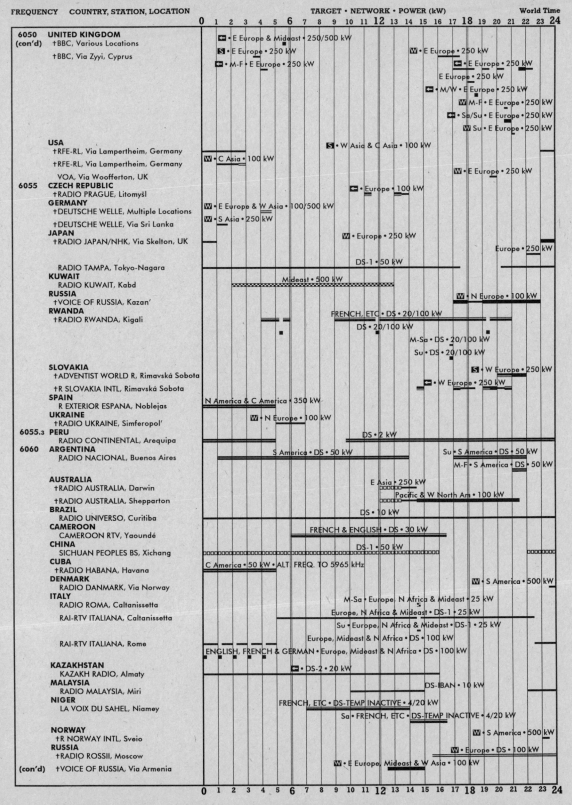

FREQUENCY	COUNTRY, STATION, LOCATION	TARGET • NETWORK • POWER (kW)
6050 (con'd)	**UNITED KINGDOM**	
	†BBC, Various Locations	E Europe & Mideast • 250/500 kW
		E Europe • 250 kW
		W • E Europe • 250 kW
	†BBC, Via Zyyi, Cyprus	M-F • E Europe • 250 kW
		E Europe • 250 kW
		E Europe • 250 kW
		M/W • E Europe • 250 kW
		W • M-F • E Europe • 250 kW
		Sa/Su • E Europe • 250 kW
		W • Su • E Europe • 250 kW
	USA	
	†RFE-RL, Via Lampertheim, Germany	W Asia & C Asia • 100 kW
	†RFE-RL, Via Lampertheim, Germany	W • C Asia • 100 kW
	VOA, Via Woofferton, UK	W • E Europe • 250 kW
6055	**CZECH REPUBLIC**	
	RADIO PRAGUE, Litomyšl	Europe • 100 kW
	GERMANY	
	†DEUTSCHE WELLE, Multiple Locations	W • E Europe & W Asia • 100/500 kW
	†DEUTSCHE WELLE, Via Sri Lanka	W • S Asia • 250 kW
	JAPAN	
	†RADIO JAPAN/NHK, Via Skelton, UK	W • Europe • 250 kW
		Europe • 250 kW
	RADIO TAMPA, Tokyo-Nagara	DS-1 • 50 kW
	KUWAIT	
	RADIO KUWAIT, Kabd	Mideast • 500 kW
	RUSSIA	
	†VOICE OF RUSSIA, Kazan'	W • N Europe • 100 kW
	RWANDA	
	†RADIO RWANDA, Kigali	FRENCH, ETC • DS • 20/100 kW
		DS • 20/100 kW
		M-Sa • DS • 20/100 kW
		Su • DS • 20/100 kW
	SLOVAKIA	
	†ADVENTIST WORLD R, Rimavská Sobota	W Europe • 250 kW
	†R SLOVAKIA INTL, Rimavská Sobota	W Europe • 250 kW
	SPAIN	
	R EXTERIOR ESPANA, Noblejas	N America & C America • 350 kW
	UKRAINE	
	†RADIO UKRAINE, Simferopol'	W • N Europe • 100 kW
6055.3	**PERU**	
	RADIO CONTINENTAL, Arequipa	DS • 2 kW
6060	**ARGENTINA**	
	RADIO NACIONAL, Buenos Aires	S America • DS • 50 kW
		Su • S America • DS • 50 kW
		M-F • S America • DS • 50 kW
	AUSTRALIA	
	†RADIO AUSTRALIA, Darwin	E Asia • 250 kW
	†RADIO AUSTRALIA, Shepparton	Pacific & W North Am • 100 kW
	BRAZIL	
	RADIO UNIVERSO, Curitiba	DS • 10 kW
	CAMEROON	
	CAMEROON RTV, Yaoundé	FRENCH & ENGLISH • DS • 30 kW
	CHINA	
	SICHUAN PEOPLES BS, Xichang	DS-1 • 50 kW
	CUBA	
	†RADIO HABANA, Havana	C America • 50 kW • ALT FREQ. TO 5965 kHz
	DENMARK	
	RADIO DANMARK, Via Norway	W • S America • 500 kW
	ITALY	
	RADIO ROMA, Caltanissetta	M-Sa • Europe, N Africa & Mideast • 25 kW
	RAI-RTV ITALIANA, Caltanissetta	Europe, N Africa & Mideast • DS-1 • 25 kW
		Su • Europe, N Africa & Mideast • DS-1 • 25 kW
	RAI-RTV ITALIANA, Rome	Europe, Mideast & N Africa • DS • 100 kW
		ENGLISH, FRENCH & GERMAN • Europe, Mideast & N Africa • DS • 100 kW
	KAZAKHSTAN	
	KAZAKH RADIO, Almaty	DS-2 • 20 kW
	MALAYSIA	
	RADIO MALAYSIA, Miri	DS-IBAN • 10 kW
	NIGER	
	LA VOIX DU SAHEL, Niamey	FRENCH, ETC • DS-TEMP INACTIVE • 4/20 kW
		Sa • FRENCH, ETC • DS-TEMP INACTIVE • 4/20 kW
	NORWAY	
	†R NORWAY INTL, Sveio	W • S America • 500 kW
	RUSSIA	
	†RADIO ROSSII, Moscow	W • Europe • DS • 100 kW
(con'd)	†VOICE OF RUSSIA, Via Armenia	W • E Europe, Mideast & W Asia • 100 kW

ENGLISH ▬   ARABIC ⨯⨯⨯   CHINESE ▯▯▯   FRENCH ▭▭   GERMAN ━━   RUSSIAN ══   SPANISH ▬▬   OTHER ──

FREQUENCY   COUNTRY, STATION, LOCATION   TARGET • NETWORK • POWER (kW)   **World Time**

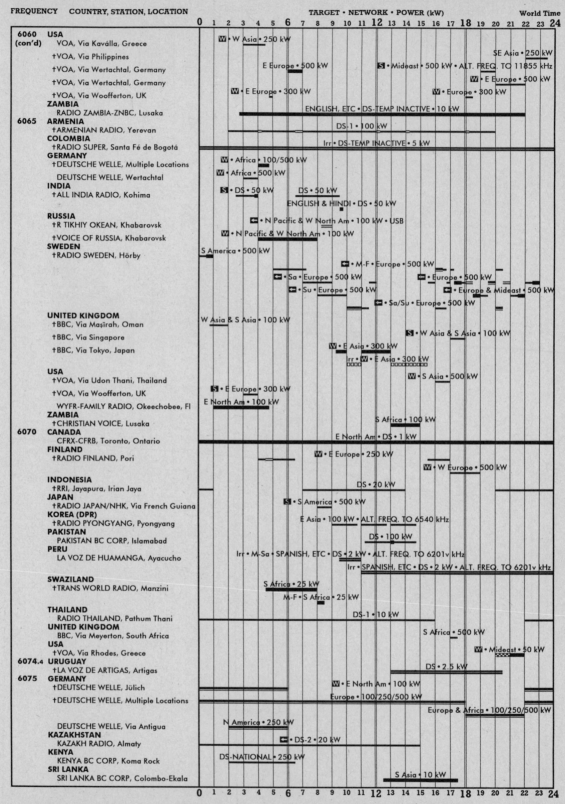

6060	USA	
(con'd)	VOA, Via Kaválla, Greece	W • W Asia • 250 kW
	†VOA, Via Philippines	SE Asia • 250 kW
	†VOA, Via Wertachtal, Germany	E Europe • 500 kW S • Mideast • 500 kW • ALT. FREQ. TO 11855 kHz
	†VOA, Via Wertachtal, Germany	W • E Europe • 500 kW
	†VOA, Via Woofferton, UK	W • E Europe • 300 kW W • Europe • 300 kW
	ZAMBIA	
	RADIO ZAMBIA-ZNBC, Lusaka	ENGLISH, ETC • DS-TEMP INACTIVE • 10 kW
6065	ARMENIA	
	†ARMENIAN RADIO, Yerevan	DS-1 • 100 kW
	COLOMBIA	
	†RADIO SUPER, Santa Fé de Bogotá	Irr • DS-TEMP INACTIVE • 5 kW
	GERMANY	
	†DEUTSCHE WELLE, Multiple Locations	W • Africa • 100/500 kW
	DEUTSCHE WELLE, Wertachtal	W • Africa • 500 kW
	INDIA	
	†ALL INDIA RADIO, Kohima	S • DS • 50 kW DS • 50 kW
		ENGLISH & HINDI • DS • 50 kW
	RUSSIA	
	†R TIKHIY OKEAN, Khabarovsk	• N Pacific & W North Am • 100 kW • USB
	†VOICE OF RUSSIA, Khabarovsk	W • N Pacific & W North Am • 100 kW
	SWEDEN	
	†RADIO SWEDEN, Hörby	S America • 500 kW
		• M-F • Europe • 500 kW
		• Sa • Europe • 500 kW • Europe • 500 kW
		• Su • Europe • 500 kW • Europe & Mideast • 500 kW
		• Sa/Su • Europe • 500 kW
	UNITED KINGDOM	
	†BBC, Via Maṣīrah, Oman	W Asia & S Asia • 100 kW
	†BBC, Via Singapore	S • W Asia & S Asia • 100 kW
	†BBC, Via Tokyo, Japan	W • E Asia • 300 kW
		Irr • W • E Asia • 300 kW
	USA	W • S Asia • 500 kW
	†VOA, Via Udon Thani, Thailand	S • E Europe • 300 kW
	†VOA, Via Woofferton, UK	E North Am • 100 kW
	WYFR-FAMILY RADIO, Okeechobee, Fl	
	ZAMBIA	S Africa • 100 kW
	†CHRISTIAN VOICE, Lusaka	
6070	CANADA	E North Am • DS • 1 kW
	CFRX-CFRB, Toronto, Ontario	
	FINLAND	
	†RADIO FINLAND, Pori	W • E Europe • 250 kW
		W • W Europe • 500 kW
	INDONESIA	
	†RRI, Jayapura, Irian Jaya	DS • 20 kW
	JAPAN	
	†RADIO JAPAN/NHK, Via French Guiana	S • S America • 500 kW
	KOREA (DPR)	E Asia • 100 kW • ALT. FREQ. TO 6540 kHz
	†RADIO PYONGYANG, Pyongyang	
	PAKISTAN	
	PAKISTAN BC CORP, Islamabad	DS • 100 kW
	PERU	
	LA VOZ DE HUAMANGA, Ayacucho	Irr • M-Sa • SPANISH, ETC • DS • 2 kW • ALT. FREQ. TO 6201v kHz
		Irr • SPANISH, ETC • DS • 2 kW • ALT. FREQ. TO 6201v kHz
	SWAZILAND	
	†TRANS WORLD RADIO, Manzini	S Africa • 25 kW
		M-F • S Africa • 25 kW
	THAILAND	
	RADIO THAILAND, Pathum Thani	DS-1 • 10 kW
	UNITED KINGDOM	
	BBC, Via Meyerton, South Africa	S Africa • 500 kW
	USA	
	†VOA, Via Rhodes, Greece	W • Mideast • 50 kW
6074.4	URUGUAY	
	†LA VOZ DE ARTIGAS, Artigas	DS • 2.5 kW
6075	GERMANY	
	†DEUTSCHE WELLE, Jülich	W • E North Am • 100 kW
		Europe • 100/250/500 kW
	†DEUTSCHE WELLE, Multiple Locations	Europe & Africa • 100/250/500 kW
	DEUTSCHE WELLE, Via Antigua	N America • 250 kW
	KAZAKHSTAN	
	KAZAKH RADIO, Almaty	• DS-2 • 20 kW
	KENYA	
	KENYA BC CORP, Koma Rock	DS-NATIONAL • 250 kW
	SRI LANKA	
	SRI LANKA BC CORP, Colombo-Ekala	S Asia • 10 kW

FREQUENCY   COUNTRY, STATION, LOCATION   TARGET • NETWORK • POWER (kW)   World Time

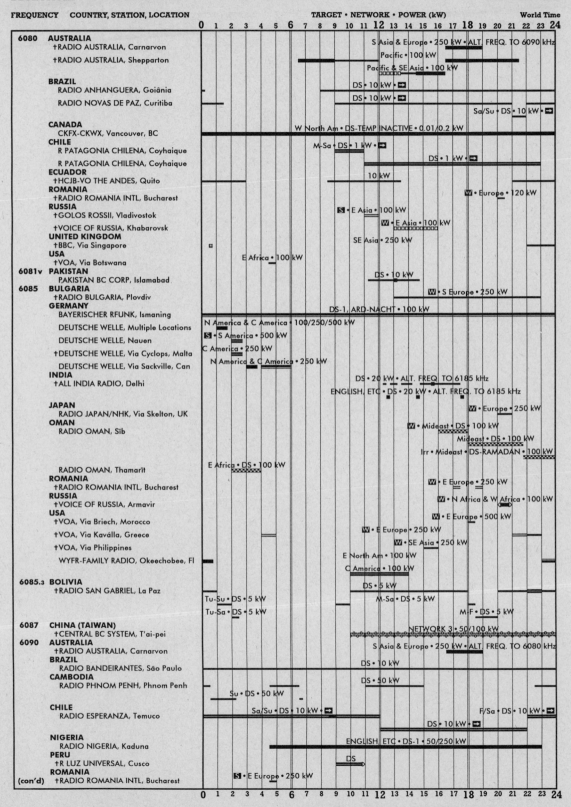

6080	**AUSTRALIA**	
	†RADIO AUSTRALIA, Carnarvon	S Asia & Europe • 250 kW • ALT. FREQ. TO 6090 kHz
	†RADIO AUSTRALIA, Shepparton	Pacific • 100 kW / Pacific & SE Asia • 100 kW
	BRAZIL	
	RADIO ANHANGUERA, Goiânia	DS • 10 kW •
	RADIO NOVAS DE PAZ, Curitiba	DS • 10 kW • / Sa/Su • DS • 10 kW •
	CANADA	
	CKFX-CKWX, Vancouver, BC	W North Am • DS–TEMP INACTIVE • 0.01/0.2 kW
	CHILE	
	R PATAGONIA CHILENA, Coyhaique	M-Sa • DS • 1 kW •
	R PATAGONIA CHILENA, Coyhaique	DS • 1 kW •
	ECUADOR	
	†HCJB-VO THE ANDES, Quito	10 kW
	ROMANIA	
	†RADIO ROMANIA INTL, Bucharest	W • Europe • 120 kW
	RUSSIA	
	†GOLOS ROSSII, Vladivostok	S • E Asia • 100 kW
	†VOICE OF RUSSIA, Khabarovsk	W • E Asia • 100 kW
	UNITED KINGDOM	
	†BBC, Via Singapore	SE Asia • 250 kW
	USA	
	†VOA, Via Botswana	E Africa • 100 kW
6081v	**PAKISTAN**	
	PAKISTAN BC CORP, Islamabad	DS • 10 kW
6085	**BULGARIA**	
	†RADIO BULGARIA, Plovdiv	W • S Europe • 250 kW
	GERMANY	
	BAYERISCHER RFUNK, Ismaning	DS-1, ARD-NACHT • 100 kW
	DEUTSCHE WELLE, Multiple Locations	N America & C America • 100/250/500 kW
	DEUTSCHE WELLE, Nauen	S • S America • 500 kW / C America • 250 kW
	†DEUTSCHE WELLE, Via Cyclops, Malta	
	DEUTSCHE WELLE, Via Sackville, Can	N America & C America • 250 kW
	INDIA	
	†ALL INDIA RADIO, Delhi	DS • 20 kW • ALT. FREQ. TO 6185 kHz / ENGLISH, ETC • DS • 20 kW • ALT. FREQ. TO 6185 kHz
	JAPAN	
	RADIO JAPAN/NHK, Via Skelton, UK	W • Europe • 250 kW
	OMAN	
	RADIO OMAN, Sib	W • Mideast • DS • 100 kW / Mideast • DS • 100 kW / Irr • Mideast • DS–RAMADAN • 100 kW
	RADIO OMAN, Thamarīt	E Africa • DS • 100 kW
	ROMANIA	
	†RADIO ROMANIA INTL, Bucharest	W • E Europe • 250 kW
	RUSSIA	
	†VOICE OF RUSSIA, Armavir	W • N Africa & W Africa • 100 kW
	USA	
	†VOA, Via Briech, Morocco	W • E Europe • 500 kW
	†VOA, Via Kaválla, Greece	W • E Europe • 250 kW
	†VOA, Via Philippines	W • SE Asia • 250 kW
	WYFR-FAMILY RADIO, Okeechobee, Fl	E North Am • 100 kW / C America • 100 kW
6085.3	**BOLIVIA**	
	†RADIO SAN GABRIEL, La Paz	DS • 5 kW / Tu-Su • DS • 5 kW / M-Sa • DS • 5 kW / Tu-Sa • DS • 5 kW / M-F • DS • 5 kW
6087	**CHINA (TAIWAN)**	
	†CENTRAL BC SYSTEM, T'ai-pei	NETWORK 3 • 50/100 kW
6090	**AUSTRALIA**	
	†RADIO AUSTRALIA, Carnarvon	S Asia & Europe • 250 kW • ALT. FREQ. TO 6080 kHz
	BRAZIL	
	RADIO BANDEIRANTES, São Paulo	DS • 10 kW
	CAMBODIA	
	RADIO PHNOM PENH, Phnom Penh	DS • 50 kW / Su • DS • 50 kW
	CHILE	
	RADIO ESPERANZA, Temuco	Sa/Su • DS • 10 kW • / F/Sa • DS • 10 kW • / DS • 10 kW •
	NIGERIA	
	RADIO NIGERIA, Kaduna	ENGLISH, ETC • DS-1 • 50/250 kW
	PERU	
	†R LUZ UNIVERSAL, Cusco	DS
(con'd)	**ROMANIA**	
	†RADIO ROMANIA INTL, Bucharest	S • E Europe • 250 kW

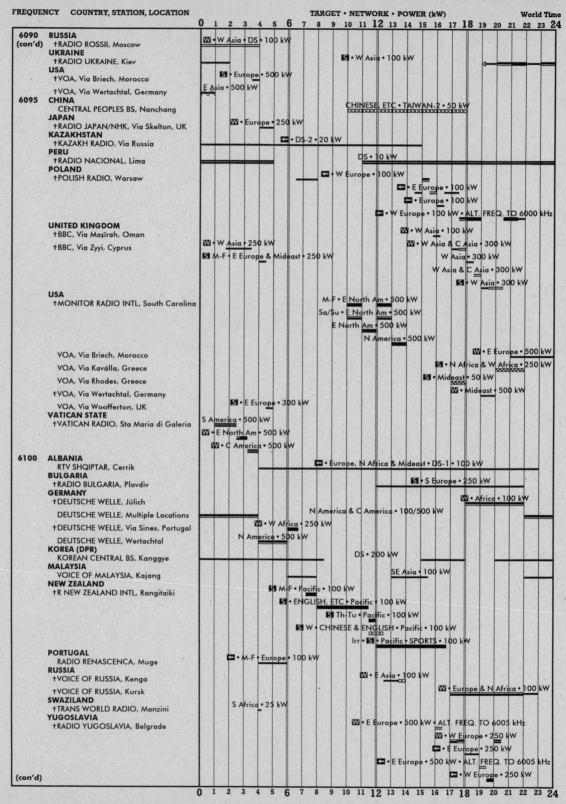

FREQUENCY   COUNTRY, STATION, LOCATION

		TARGET • NETWORK • POWER (kW)		World Time

6090 **RUSSIA**
(con'd) †RADIO ROSSII, Moscow — W • W Asia • DS • 100 kW
         UKRAINE
         †RADIO UKRAINE, Kiev — S • W Asia • 100 kW
         USA
         †VOA, Via Briech, Morocco — S • Europe • 500 kW
         †VOA, Via Wertachtal, Germany — E Asia • 500 kW

6095 **CHINA**
         CENTRAL PEOPLES BS, Nanchang — CHINESE, ETC • TAIWAN-2 • 50 kW
         JAPAN
         †RADIO JAPAN/NHK, Via Skelton, UK — W • Europe • 250 kW
         KAZAKHSTAN
         †KAZAKH RADIO, Via Russia — DS-2 • 20 kW
         PERU
         †RADIO NACIONAL, Lima — DS • 10 kW
         POLAND
         †POLISH RADIO, Warsaw — W Europe • 100 kW
                                    E Europe • 100 kW
                                    Europe • 100 kW
                                    W Europe • 100 kW • ALT. FREQ. TO 6000 kHz

         UNITED KINGDOM
         †BBC, Via Maṣīrah, Oman — W • W Asia • 100 kW
         †BBC, Via Zyyi, Cyprus — W • W Asia • 250 kW
                                  W • W Asia & C Asia • 300 kW
                                  S • M-F • E Europe & Mideast • 250 kW
                                  W Asia • 300 kW
                                  W Asia & C Asia • 300 kW
                                  S • W Asia • 300 kW

         USA
         †MONITOR RADIO INTL, South Carolina — M-F • E North Am • 500 kW
                                               Sa/Su • E North Am • 500 kW
                                               E North Am • 500 kW
                                               N America • 500 kW

         VOA, Via Briech, Morocco — W • E Europe • 500 kW
         VOA, Via Kaválla, Greece — S • N Africa & W Africa • 250 kW
         VOA, Via Rhodes, Greece — S • Mideast • 50 kW
         †VOA, Via Wertachtal, Germany — W • Mideast • 500 kW
         VOA, Via Woofferton, UK — S • E Europe • 300 kW
         VATICAN STATE
         †VATICAN RADIO, Sta Maria di Galeria — S America • 500 kW
                                                W • E North Am • 500 kW
                                                W • C America • 500 kW

6100 **ALBANIA**
         RTV SHQIPTAR, Cerrik — Europe, N Africa & Mideast • DS-1 • 100 kW
         BULGARIA
         †RADIO BULGARIA, Plovdiv — S • S Europe • 250 kW
         GERMANY
         †DEUTSCHE WELLE, Jülich — W • Africa • 100 kW
         DEUTSCHE WELLE, Multiple Locations — N America & C America • 100/500 kW
         †DEUTSCHE WELLE, Via Sines, Portugal — W • W Africa • 250 kW
         DEUTSCHE WELLE, Wertachtal — N America • 500 kW
         KOREA (DPR)
         KOREAN CENTRAL BS, Kanggye — DS • 200 kW
         MALAYSIA
         VOICE OF MALAYSIA, Kajang — SE Asia • 100 kW
         NEW ZEALAND
         †R NEW ZEALAND INTL, Rangitaiki — S • M-F • Pacific • 100 kW
                                           S • ENGLISH, ETC • Pacific • 100 kW
                                           S • Th-Tu • Pacific • 100 kW
                                           S • W • CHINESE & ENGLISH • Pacific • 100 kW
                                           Irr • S • Pacific • SPORTS • 100 kW

         PORTUGAL
         RADIO RENASCENCA, Muge — M-F • Europe • 100 kW
         RUSSIA
         †VOICE OF RUSSIA, Kenga — W • E Asia • 100 kW
         †VOICE OF RUSSIA, Kursk — W • Europe & N Africa • 100 kW
         SWAZILAND
         †TRANS WORLD RADIO, Manzini — S Africa • 25 kW
         YUGOSLAVIA
         †RADIO YUGOSLAVIA, Belgrade — W • E Europe • 500 kW • ALT. FREQ. TO 6005 kHz
                                       W • W Europe • 250 kW
                                       E Europe • 250 kW
                                       E Europe • 500 kW • ALT. FREQ. TO 6005 kHz
                                       W Europe • 250 kW

(con'd)

0 1 2 3 4 5 6 7 8 9 10 11 12 13 14 15 16 17 18 19 20 21 22 23 24

SEASONAL **S** OR **W**   1-HR TIMESHIFT MIDYEAR ⊟ OR ⊞   JAMMING / OR /\   EARLIEST HEARD ◁   LATEST HEARD ▷   NEW FOR 1996 †

FREQUENCY   COUNTRY, STATION, LOCATION

TARGET • NETWORK • POWER (kW)

World Time

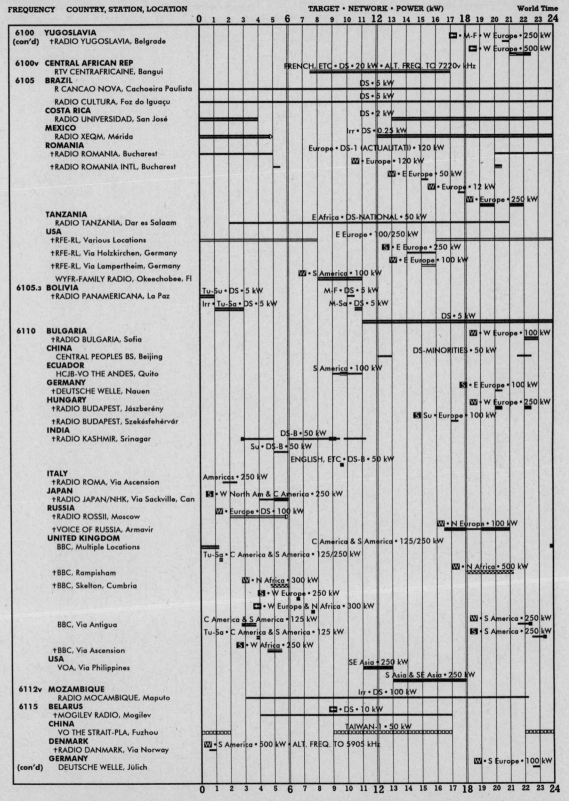

Frequency	Country, Station, Location	Target • Network • Power
6100	YUGOSLAVIA	
(con'd)	†RADIO YUGOSLAVIA, Belgrade	M-F • W Europe • 250 kW
		W Europe • 500 kW
6100v	CENTRAL AFRICAN REP	
	RTV CENTRAFRICAINE, Bangui	FRENCH, ETC • DS • 20 kW • ALT. FREQ. TO 7220v kHz
6105	BRAZIL	
	R CANCAO NOVA, Cachoeira Paulista	DS • 5 kW
	RADIO CULTURA, Foz do Iguaçu	DS • 5 kW
	COSTA RICA	
	RADIO UNIVERSIDAD, San José	DS • 2 kW
	MEXICO	
	RADIO XEQM, Mérida	Irr • DS • 0.25 kW
	ROMANIA	
	†RADIO ROMANIA, Bucharest	Europe • DS-1 (ACTUALITATI) • 120 kW
	†RADIO ROMANIA INTL, Bucharest	W • Europe • 120 kW
		W • E Europe • 50 kW
		W • Europe • 12 kW
		W • Europe • 250 kW
	TANZANIA	
	RADIO TANZANIA, Dar es Salaam	E Africa • DS-NATIONAL • 50 kW
	USA	
	†RFE-RL, Various Locations	E Europe • 100/250 kW
	†RFE-RL, Via Holzkirchen, Germany	S • E Europe • 250 kW
	†RFE-RL, Via Lampertheim, Germany	W • E Europe • 100 kW
	WYFR-FAMILY RADIO, Okeechobee, Fl	W • S America • 100 kW
6105.3	BOLIVIA	Tu-Su • DS • 5 kW M-F • DS • 5 kW
	†RADIO PANAMERICANA, La Paz	Irr • Tu-Sa • DS • 5 kW M-Sa • DS • 5 kW
		DS • 5 kW
6110	BULGARIA	
	†RADIO BULGARIA, Sofia	W • W Europe • 100 kW
	CHINA	
	CENTRAL PEOPLES BS, Beijing	DS-MINORITIES • 50 kW
	ECUADOR	
	HCJB-VO THE ANDES, Quito	S America • 100 kW
	GERMANY	
	†DEUTSCHE WELLE, Nauen	S • E Europe • 100 kW
	HUNGARY	
	†RADIO BUDAPEST, Jászberény	W • W Europe • 250 kW
	†RADIO BUDAPEST, Szekésfehérvár	S Su • Europe • 100 kW
	INDIA	
	†RADIO KASHMIR, Srinagar	DS-B • 50 kW
		Su • DS-B • 50 kW
		ENGLISH, ETC • DS-B • 50 kW
	ITALY	
	†RADIO ROMA, Via Ascension	Americas • 250 kW
	JAPAN	
	†RADIO JAPAN/NHK, Via Sackville, Can	S • W North Am & C America • 250 kW
	RUSSIA	
	†RADIO ROSSII, Moscow	W • Europe • DS • 100 kW
	†VOICE OF RUSSIA, Armavir	W • N Europe • 100 kW
	UNITED KINGDOM	
	BBC, Multiple Locations	C America & S America • 125/250 kW
		Tu-Sa • C America & S America • 125/250 kW
	†BBC, Rampisham	W • N Africa • 500 kW
	†BBC, Skelton, Cumbria	W • N Africa • 300 kW
		S • W Europe • 250 kW
		W Europe & N Africa • 300 kW
	BBC, Via Antigua	C America & S America • 125 kW W • S America • 250 kW
		Tu-Sa • C America & S America • 125 kW S • S America • 250 kW
	†BBC, Via Ascension	S • W Africa • 250 kW
	USA	
	VOA, Via Philippines	SE Asia • 250 kW
		S Asia & SE Asia • 250 kW
6112v	MOZAMBIQUE	
	RADIO MOCAMBIQUE, Maputo	Irr • DS • 100 kW
6115	BELARUS	DS • 10 kW
	†MOGILEV RADIO, Mogilev	
	CHINA	TAIWAN-1 • 50 kW
	VO THE STRAIT-PLA, Fuzhou	
	DENMARK	W • S America • 500 kW • ALT. FREQ. TO 5905 kHz
	†RADIO DANMARK, Via Norway	
	GERMANY	W • S Europe • 100 kW
(con'd)	DEUTSCHE WELLE, Jülich	

ENGLISH ▬▬   ARABIC ⧓⧓⧓   CHINESE □□□   FRENCH ▭▭▭   GERMAN ▬▬▬   RUSSIAN ══   SPANISH ▬▬▬   OTHER ▬

FREQUENCY   COUNTRY, STATION, LOCATION

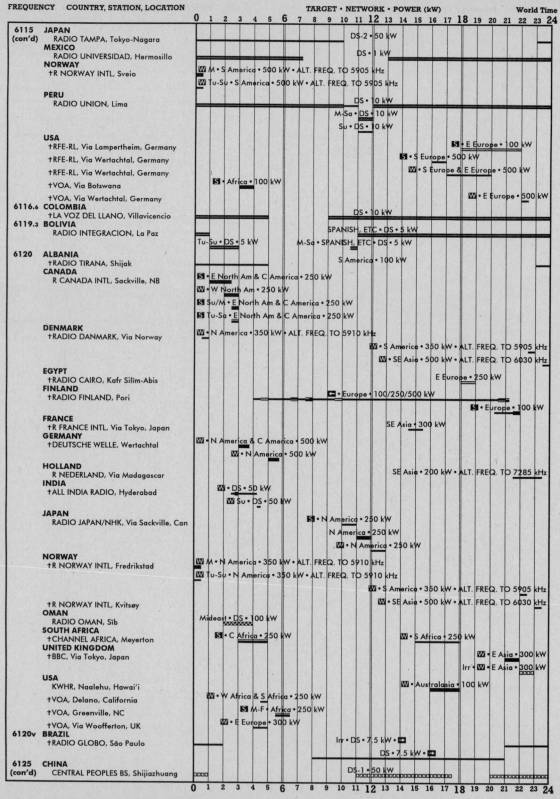

FREQUENCY	COUNTRY, STATION, LOCATION	TARGET • NETWORK • POWER (kW)
6115 (con'd)	**JAPAN** RADIO TAMPA, Tokyo-Nagara	DS-2 • 50 kW
	MEXICO RADIO UNIVERSIDAD, Hermosillo	DS • 1 kW
	NORWAY †R NORWAY INTL, Sveio	W • M • S America • 500 kW • ALT. FREQ. TO 5905 kHz / W • Tu-Su • S America • 500 kW • ALT. FREQ. TO 5905 kHz
	PERU RADIO UNION, Lima	DS • 10 kW / M-Sa • DS • 10 kW / Su • DS • 10 kW
	USA †RFE-RL, Via Lampertheim, Germany	S • E Europe • 100 kW
	†RFE-RL, Via Wertachtal, Germany	S • S Europe • 500 kW
	†RFE-RL, Via Wertachtal, Germany	W • S Europe & E Europe • 500 kW
	†VOA, Via Botswana	S • Africa • 100 kW
	†VOA, Via Wertachtal, Germany	W • E Europe • 500 kW
6116.6	**COLOMBIA** †LA VOZ DEL LLANO, Villavicencio	DS • 10 kW
6119.3	**BOLIVIA** RADIO INTEGRACION, La Paz	SPANISH, ETC • DS • 5 kW / Tu-Su • DS • 5 kW / M-Sa • SPANISH, ETC • DS • 5 kW
6120	**ALBANIA** †RADIO TIRANA, Shijak	S America • 100 kW
	CANADA R CANADA INTL, Sackville, NB	S • E North Am & C America • 250 kW / W • W North Am • 250 kW / S • Su/M • E North Am & C America • 250 kW / S • Tu-Sa • E North Am & C America • 250 kW
	DENMARK †RADIO DANMARK, Via Norway	W • N America • 350 kW • ALT. FREQ. TO 5910 kHz / W • S America • 350 kW • ALT. FREQ. TO 5905 kHz / W • SE Asia • 500 kW • ALT. FREQ. TO 6030 kHz
	EGYPT †RADIO CAIRO, Kafr Silim-Abis	E Europe • 250 kW
	FINLAND †RADIO FINLAND, Pori	⇆ • Europe • 100/250/500 kW / S • Europe • 100 kW
	FRANCE †R FRANCE INTL, Via Tokyo, Japan	SE Asia • 300 kW
	GERMANY †DEUTSCHE WELLE, Wertachtal	W • N America & C America • 500 kW / W • N America • 500 kW
	HOLLAND R NEDERLAND, Via Madagascar	SE Asia • 200 kW • ALT. FREQ. TO 7285 kHz
	INDIA †ALL INDIA RADIO, Hyderabad	W • DS • 50 kW / W • Su • DS • 50 kW
	JAPAN RADIO JAPAN/NHK, Via Sackville, Can	S • N America • 250 kW / N America • 250 kW / W • N America • 250 kW
	NORWAY †R NORWAY INTL, Fredrikstad	W • M • N America • 350 kW • ALT. FREQ. TO 5910 kHz / W • Tu-Su • N America • 350 kW • ALT. FREQ. TO 5910 kHz / W • S America • 350 kW • ALT. FREQ. TO 5905 kHz / W • SE Asia • 500 kW • ALT. FREQ. TO 6030 kHz
	†R NORWAY INTL, Kvitsøy	
	OMAN RADIO OMAN, Sib	Mideast • DS • 100 kW
	SOUTH AFRICA †CHANNEL AFRICA, Meyerton	S • C Africa • 250 kW / W • S Africa • 250 kW
	UNITED KINGDOM †BBC, Via Tokyo, Japan	W • E Asia • 300 kW / Irr • W • E Asia • 300 kW
	USA KWHR, Naalehu, Hawai'i	W • Australasia • 100 kW
	†VOA, Delano, California	W • W Africa & S Africa • 250 kW
	†VOA, Greenville, NC	S • M-F • Africa • 250 kW
	†VOA, Via Woofferton, UK	W • E Europe • 300 kW
6120v	**BRAZIL** †RADIO GLOBO, São Paulo	Irr • DS • 7.5 kW • ⇆ / DS • 7.5 kW • ⇆
6125 (con'd)	**CHINA** CENTRAL PEOPLES BS, Shijiazhuang	DS-1 • 50 kW

SEASONAL **S** OR **W**   1-HR TIMESHIFT MIDYEAR ⇆ OR ⇄   JAMMING / OR ∧   EARLIEST HEARD ◁   LATEST HEARD ▷   NEW FOR 1996 †

FREQUENCY   COUNTRY, STATION, LOCATION   TARGET • NETWORK • POWER (kW)   World Time

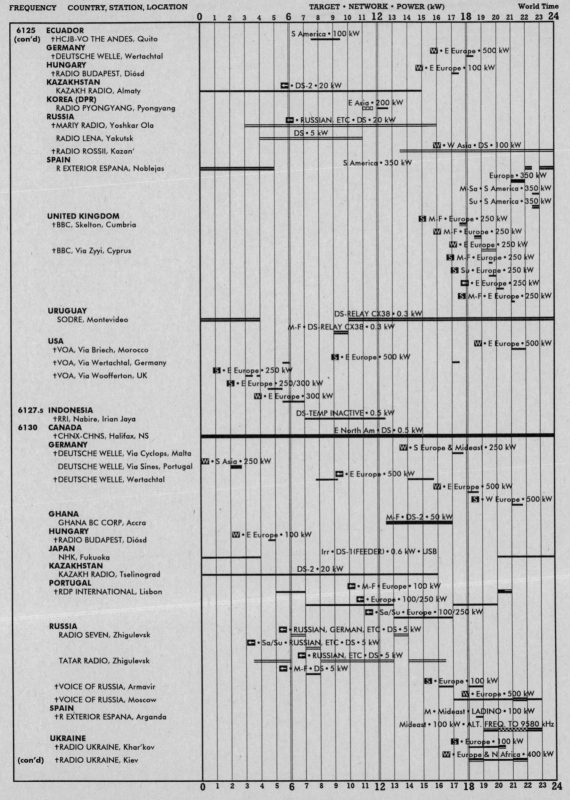

FREQUENCY	COUNTRY, STATION, LOCATION	Details
6125 (con'd)	**ECUADOR** †HCJB-VO THE ANDES, Quito	S America • 100 kW
	GERMANY †DEUTSCHE WELLE, Wertachtal	W • E Europe • 500 kW
	HUNGARY †RADIO BUDAPEST, Diósd	W • E Europe • 100 kW
	KAZAKHSTAN KAZAKH RADIO, Almaty	• DS-2 • 20 kW
	KOREA (DPR) RADIO PYONGYANG, Pyongyang	E Asia • 200 kW
	RUSSIA †MARIY RADIO, Yoshkar Ola	• RUSSIAN, ETC • DS • 20 kW
	RADIO LENA, Yakutsk	DS • 5 kW
	†RADIO ROSSII, Kazan'	W • W Asia • DS • 100 kW
	SPAIN R EXTERIOR ESPANA, Noblejas	S America • 350 kW / Europe • 350 kW / M-Sa • S America • 350 kW / Su • S America • 350 kW
	UNITED KINGDOM †BBC, Skelton, Cumbria	M-F • Europe • 250 kW / W M-F • Europe • 250 kW / W • E Europe • 250 kW
	†BBC, Via Zyyi, Cyprus	M-F • Europe • 250 kW / Su • Europe • 250 kW / • E Europe • 250 kW / M-F • E Europe • 250 kW
	URUGUAY SODRE, Montevideo	DS-RELAY CX38 • 0.3 kW / M-F • DS-RELAY CX38 • 0.3 kW
	USA †VOA, Via Briech, Morocco	W • E Europe • 500 kW
	†VOA, Via Wertachtal, Germany	S • E Europe • 500 kW
	†VOA, Via Woofferton, UK	S • E Europe • 250 kW / S • E Europe • 250/300 kW / W • E Europe • 300 kW
6127.5	**INDONESIA** †RRI, Nabire, Irian Jaya	DS-TEMP INACTIVE • 0.5 kW
6130	**CANADA** †CHNX-CHNS, Halifax, NS	E North Am • DS • 0.5 kW
	GERMANY †DEUTSCHE WELLE, Via Cyclops, Malta	W • S Europe & Mideast • 250 kW
	DEUTSCHE WELLE, Via Sines, Portugal	W • S Asia • 250 kW
	†DEUTSCHE WELLE, Wertachtal	• E Europe • 500 kW / W • E Europe • 500 kW / S • W Europe • 500 kW
	GHANA GHANA BC CORP, Accra	M-F • DS-2 • 50 kW
	HUNGARY †RADIO BUDAPEST, Diósd	W • E Europe • 100 kW
	JAPAN NHK, Fukuoka	Irr • DS-1 (FEEDER) • 0.6 kW • USB
	KAZAKHSTAN KAZAKH RADIO, Tselinograd	DS-2 • 20 kW
	PORTUGAL †RDP INTERNATIONAL, Lisbon	• M-F • Europe • 100 kW / • Europe • 100/250 kW / • Sa/Su • Europe • 100/250 kW
	RUSSIA RADIO SEVEN, Zhigulevsk	• RUSSIAN, GERMAN, ETC • DS • 5 kW / • Sa/Su • RUSSIAN, ETC • DS • 5 kW
	TATAR RADIO, Zhigulevsk	• RUSSIAN, ETC • DS • 5 kW / • M-F • DS • 5 kW
	†VOICE OF RUSSIA, Armavir	S • Europe • 100 kW
	†VOICE OF RUSSIA, Moscow	W • Europe • 500 kW
	SPAIN †R EXTERIOR ESPANA, Arganda	M • Mideast • LADINO • 100 kW / Mideast • 100 kW • ALT. FREQ. TO 9580 kHz
	UKRAINE †RADIO UKRAINE, Khar'kov	S • Europe • 100 kW
(con'd)	†RADIO UKRAINE, Kiev	W • Europe & N Africa • 400 kW

ENGLISH ▬   ARABIC ▨   CHINESE ▭▭▭   FRENCH ═   GERMAN ▬   RUSSIAN ══   SPANISH ▬   OTHER ▬

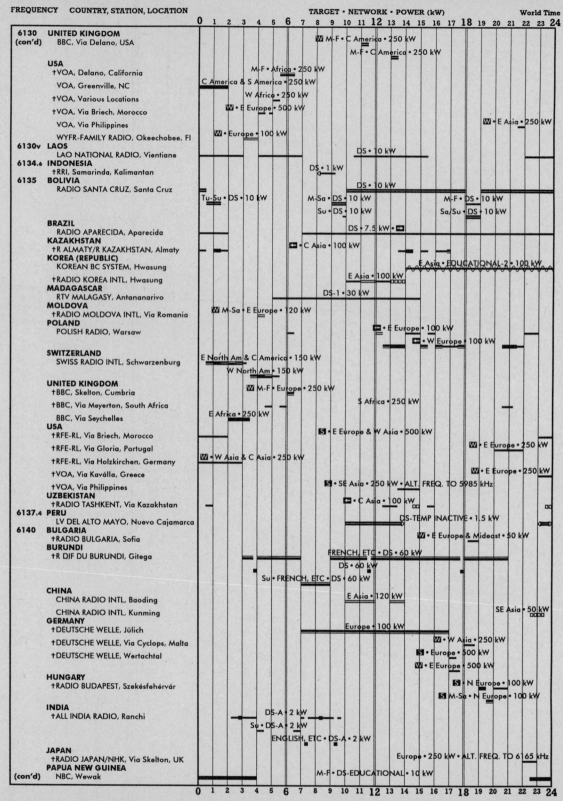

FREQUENCY   COUNTRY, STATION, LOCATION

TARGET • NETWORK • POWER (kW)   World Time

6130 **UNITED KINGDOM**
(con'd)   BBC, Via Delano, USA
    W M-F • C America • 250 kW
    M-F • C America • 250 kW

USA
†VOA, Delano, California — M-F • Africa • 250 kW
VOA, Greenville, NC — C America & S America • 250 kW
†VOA, Various Locations — W Africa • 250 kW
†VOA, Via Briech, Morocco — W • E Europe • 500 kW
VOA, Via Philippines — W • E Asia • 250 kW
WYFR-FAMILY RADIO, Okeechobee, Fl — W • Europe • 100 kW

6130v LAOS
LAO NATIONAL RADIO, Vientiane — DS • 10 kW
6134.6 INDONESIA
†RRI, Samarinda, Kalimantan — DS • 1 kW
6135 BOLIVIA
RADIO SANTA CRUZ, Santa Cruz — DS • 10 kW
    Tu-Su • DS • 10 kW   M-Sa • DS • 10 kW   M-F • DS • 10 kW
    Su • DS • 10 kW   Sa/Su • DS • 10 kW

BRAZIL
RADIO APARECIDA, Aparecida — DS • 7.5 kW • ◻▶
KAZAKHSTAN
†R ALMATY/R KAZAKHSTAN, Almaty — ◻▶ • C Asia • 100 kW
KOREA (REPUBLIC)
KOREAN BC SYSTEM, Hwasung — E Asia • EDUCATIONAL-2 • 100 kW
†RADIO KOREA INTL, Hwasung — E Asia • 100 kW
MADAGASCAR
RTV MALAGASY, Antananarivo — DS-1 • 30 kW
MOLDOVA
†RADIO MOLDOVA INTL, Via Romania — W M-Sa • E Europe • 120 kW
POLAND
POLISH RADIO, Warsaw — ◻▶ • E Europe • 100 kW
    ◻▶ • W Europe • 100 kW

SWITZERLAND
SWISS RADIO INTL, Schwarzenburg — E North Am & C America • 150 kW
    W North Am • 150 kW

UNITED KINGDOM
†BBC, Skelton, Cumbria — W M-F • Europe • 250 kW
†BBC, Via Meyerton, South Africa — S Africa • 250 kW
BBC, Via Seychelles — E Africa • 250 kW
USA
†RFE-RL, Via Briech, Morocco — S • E Europe & W Asia • 500 kW
†RFE-RL, Via Gloria, Portugal — W • E Europe • 250 kW
†RFE-RL, Via Holzkirchen, Germany — W • W Asia & C Asia • 250 kW
    W • E Europe • 250 kW
†VOA, Via Kaválla, Greece — S • SE Asia • 250 kW • ALT. FREQ. TO 5985 kHz
†VOA, Via Philippines
UZBEKISTAN
†RADIO TASHKENT, Via Kazakhstan — ◻▶ • C Asia • 100 kW
6137.4 PERU
LV DEL ALTO MAYO, Nuevo Cajamarca — DS-TEMP INACTIVE • 1.5 kW
6140 BULGARIA
†RADIO BULGARIA, Sofia — W • E Europe & Mideast • 50 kW
BURUNDI
†R DIF DU BURUNDI, Gitega — FRENCH, ETC • DS • 60 kW
    DS • 60 kW
    Su • FRENCH, ETC • DS • 60 kW

CHINA
CHINA RADIO INTL, Baoding — E Asia • 120 kW
CHINA RADIO INTL, Kunming — SE Asia • 50 kW
GERMANY
†DEUTSCHE WELLE, Jülich — Europe • 100 kW
†DEUTSCHE WELLE, Via Cyclops, Malta — W • W Asia • 250 kW
†DEUTSCHE WELLE, Wertachtal — S • Europe • 500 kW
    W • E Europe • 500 kW
HUNGARY
†RADIO BUDAPEST, Székésfehérvár — S • N Europe • 100 kW
    S M-Sa • N Europe • 100 kW
INDIA
†ALL INDIA RADIO, Ranchi — DS-A • 2 kW
    Su • DS-A • 2 kW
    ENGLISH, ETC • DS-A • 2 kW
JAPAN
†RADIO JAPAN/NHK, Via Skelton, UK — Europe • 250 kW • ALT. FREQ. TO 6165 kHz
PAPUA NEW GUINEA
(con'd)   NBC, Wewak — M-F • DS-EDUCATIONAL • 10 kW

FREQUENCY   COUNTRY, STATION, LOCATION   TARGET • NETWORK • POWER (kW)   World Time

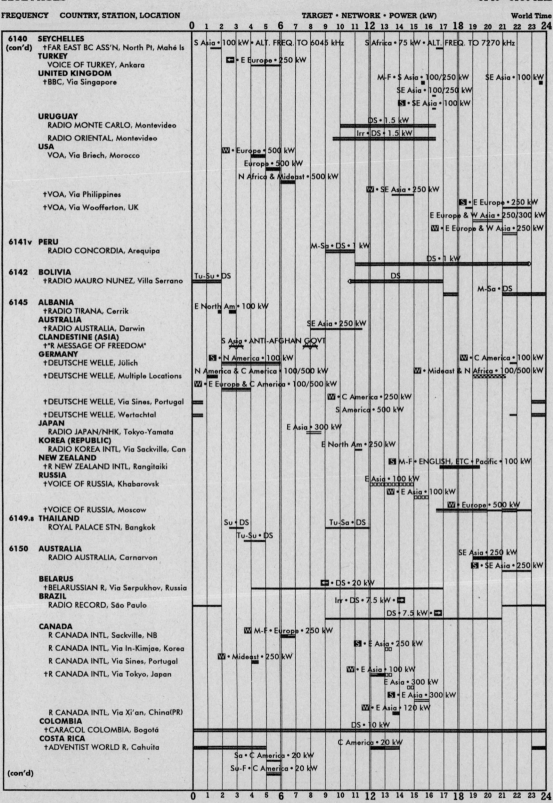

FREQUENCY	COUNTRY, STATION, LOCATION	TARGET • NETWORK • POWER (kW)
6140 (con'd)	SEYCHELLES	
	†FAR EAST BC ASS'N, North Pt, Mahé Is	S Asia • 100 kW • ALT. FREQ. TO 6045 kHz / S Africa • 75 kW • ALT. FREQ. TO 7270 kHz
	TURKEY	
	VOICE OF TURKEY, Ankara	• E Europe • 250 kW
	UNITED KINGDOM	
	†BBC, Via Singapore	M-F • S Asia • 100/250 kW / SE Asia • 100 kW / SE Asia • 100/250 kW / S • SE Asia • 100 kW
	URUGUAY	
	RADIO MONTE CARLO, Montevideo	DS • 1.5 kW
	RADIO ORIENTAL, Montevideo	Irr • DS • 1.5 kW
	USA	
	VOA, Via Briech, Morocco	W • Europe • 500 kW / Europe • 500 kW / N Africa & Mideast • 500 kW
	†VOA, Via Philippines	W • SE Asia • 250 kW
	†VOA, Via Woofferton, UK	S • E Europe • 250 kW / E Europe & W Asia • 250/300 kW / W • E Europe & W Asia • 250 kW
6141v	PERU	
	RADIO CONCORDIA, Arequipa	M-Sa • DS • 1 kW / DS • 1 kW
6142	BOLIVIA	
	†RADIO MAURO NUNEZ, Villa Serrano	Tu-Su • DS / DS / M-Sa • DS
6145	ALBANIA	
	†RADIO TIRANA, Cerrik	E North Am • 100 kW
	AUSTRALIA	
	†RADIO AUSTRALIA, Darwin	SE Asia • 250 kW
	CLANDESTINE (ASIA)	
	†"R MESSAGE OF FREEDOM"	S Asia • ANTI-AFGHAN GOVT
	GERMANY	
	†DEUTSCHE WELLE, Jülich	S • N America • 100 kW / W • C America • 100 kW
	†DEUTSCHE WELLE, Multiple Locations	N America & C America • 100/500 kW / W • Mideast & N Africa • 100/500 kW / W • E Europe & C America • 100/500 kW
	†DEUTSCHE WELLE, Via Sines, Portugal	W • C America • 250 kW
	†DEUTSCHE WELLE, Wertachtal	S America • 500 kW
	JAPAN	
	RADIO JAPAN/NHK, Tokyo-Yamata	E Asia • 300 kW
	KOREA (REPUBLIC)	
	RADIO KOREA INTL, Via Sackville, Can	E North Am • 250 kW
	NEW ZEALAND	
	†R NEW ZEALAND INTL, Rangitaiki	S • M-F • ENGLISH, ETC • Pacific • 100 kW
	RUSSIA	
	†VOICE OF RUSSIA, Khabarovsk	E Asia • 100 kW / W • E Asia • 100 kW
	†VOICE OF RUSSIA, Moscow	W • Europe • 500 kW
6149.8	THAILAND	
	ROYAL PALACE STN, Bangkok	Su • DS / Tu-Sa • DS / Tu-Su • DS
6150	AUSTRALIA	
	RADIO AUSTRALIA, Carnarvon	SE Asia • 250 kW / S • SE Asia • 250 kW
	BELARUS	
	†BELARUSSIAN R, Via Serpukhov, Russia	• DS • 20 kW
	BRAZIL	
	RADIO RECORD, São Paulo	Irr • DS • 7.5 kW • / DS • 7.5 kW •
	CANADA	
	R CANADA INTL, Sackville, NB	W • M-F • Europe • 250 kW
	R CANADA INTL, Via In-Kimjae, Korea	S • E Asia • 250 kW
	R CANADA INTL, Via Sines, Portugal	W • Mideast • 250 kW
	†R CANADA INTL, Via Tokyo, Japan	W • E Asia • 100 kW / E Asia • 300 kW / S • E Asia • 300 kW
	R CANADA INTL, Via Xi'an, China(PR)	W • E Asia • 120 kW
	COLOMBIA	
	†CARACOL COLOMBIA, Bogotá	DS • 10 kW
	COSTA RICA	
	†ADVENTIST WORLD R, Cahuita	C America • 20 kW / Sa • C America • 20 kW / Su-F • C America • 20 kW
(con'd)		

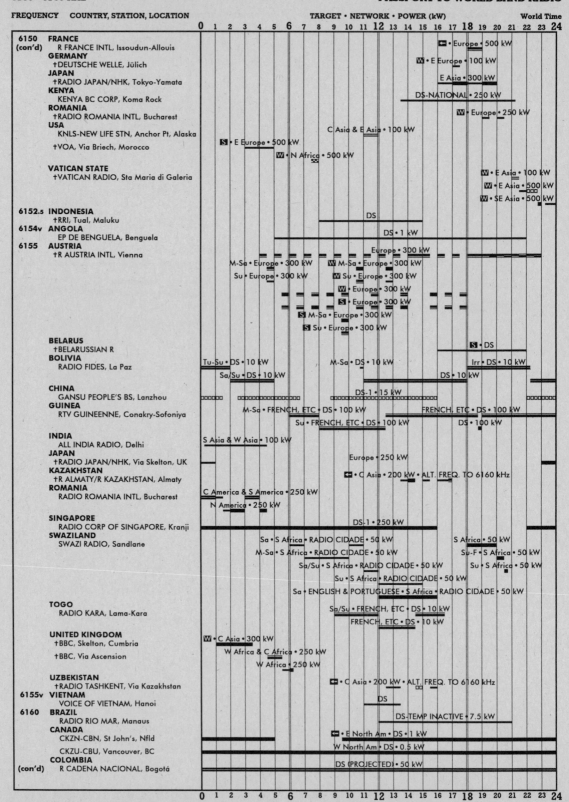

FREQUENCY   COUNTRY, STATION, LOCATION   TARGET • NETWORK • POWER (kW)   World Time

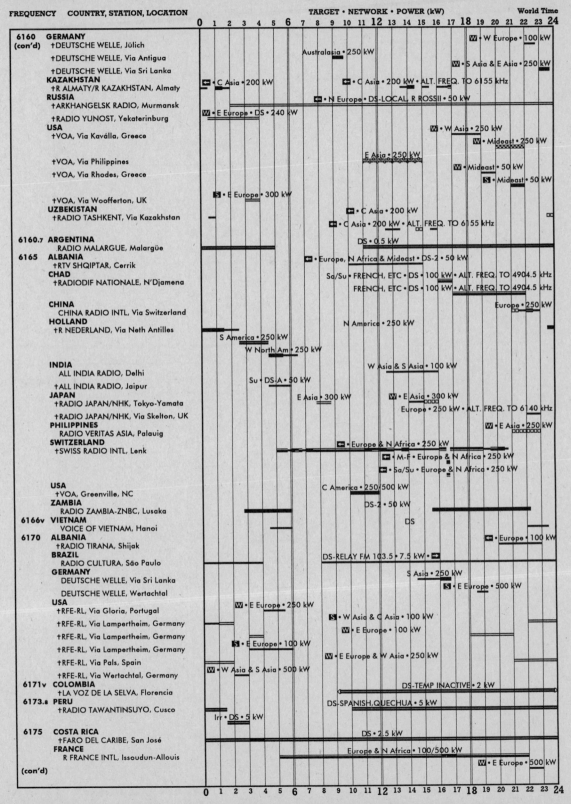

Frequency / Station	Listing
6160 (con'd) **GERMANY**	
†DEUTSCHE WELLE, Jülich	W • W Europe • 100 kW
†DEUTSCHE WELLE, Via Antigua	Australasia • 250 kW
†DEUTSCHE WELLE, Via Sri Lanka	W • S Asia & E Asia • 250 kW
KAZAKHSTAN †R ALMATY/R KAZAKHSTAN, Almaty	• C Asia • 200 kW / • C Asia • 200 kW • ALT. FREQ. TO 6155 kHz
RUSSIA †ARKHANGELSK RADIO, Murmansk	• N Europe • DS-LOCAL R ROSSII • 50 kW
†RADIO YUNOST, Yekaterinburg	W • E Europe • DS • 240 kW
USA †VOA, Via Kaválla, Greece	W • W Asia • 250 kW / W • Mideast • 250 kW
†VOA, Via Philippines	E Asia • 250 kW
†VOA, Via Rhodes, Greece	W • Mideast • 50 kW / S • Mideast • 50 kW
†VOA, Via Woofferton, UK	S • E Europe • 300 kW
UZBEKISTAN †RADIO TASHKENT, Via Kazakhstan	• C Asia • 200 kW / • C Asia • 200 kW • ALT. FREQ. TO 6155 kHz
6160.7 ARGENTINA RADIO MALARGUE, Malargüe	DS • 0.5 kW
6165 ALBANIA †RTV SHQIPTAR, Cerrik	• Europe, N Africa & Mideast • DS-2 • 50 kW
CHAD †RADIODIF NATIONALE, N'Djamena	Sa/Su • FRENCH, ETC • DS • 100 kW • ALT. FREQ. TO 4904.5 kHz / FRENCH, ETC • DS • 100 kW • ALT. FREQ. TO 4904.5 kHz
CHINA CHINA RADIO INTL, Via Switzerland	Europe • 250 kW
HOLLAND †R NEDERLAND, Via Neth Antilles	N America • 250 kW / S America • 250 kW / W North Am • 250 kW
INDIA ALL INDIA RADIO, Delhi	W Asia & S Asia • 100 kW
†ALL INDIA RADIO, Jaipur	Su • DS-A • 50 kW
JAPAN †RADIO JAPAN/NHK, Tokyo-Yamata	E Asia • 300 kW / W • E Asia • 300 kW
†RADIO JAPAN/NHK, Via Skelton, UK	Europe • 250 kW • ALT. FREQ. TO 6140 kHz
PHILIPPINES RADIO VERITAS ASIA, Palauig	W • E Asia • 250 kW
SWITZERLAND †SWISS RADIO INTL, Lenk	• Europe & N Africa • 250 kW / • M-F • Europe & N Africa • 250 kW / • Sa/Su • Europe & N Africa • 250 kW
USA †VOA, Greenville, NC	C America • 250/500 kW
ZAMBIA RADIO ZAMBIA-ZNBC, Lusaka	DS-2 • 50 kW
6166v VIETNAM VOICE OF VIETNAM, Hanoi	DS
6170 ALBANIA †RADIO TIRANA, Shijak	• Europe • 100 kW
BRAZIL RADIO CULTURA, São Paulo	DS-RELAY FM 103.5 • 7.5 kW •
GERMANY DEUTSCHE WELLE, Via Sri Lanka	S Asia • 250 kW
DEUTSCHE WELLE, Wertachtal	S • E Europe • 500 kW
USA †RFE-RL, Via Gloria, Portugal	W • E Europe • 250 kW
†RFE-RL, Via Lampertheim, Germany	S • W Asia & C Asia • 100 kW
†RFE-RL, Via Lampertheim, Germany	W • E Europe • 100 kW
†RFE-RL, Via Lampertheim, Germany	S • E Europe • 100 kW
†RFE-RL, Via Pals, Spain	W • E Europe & W Asia • 250 kW
†RFE-RL, Via Wertachtal, Germany	W • W Asia & S Asia • 500 kW
6171v COLOMBIA †LA VOZ DE LA SELVA, Florencia	DS-TEMP INACTIVE • 2 kW
6173.8 PERU †RADIO TAWANTINSUYO, Cusco	DS-SPANISH, QUECHUA • 5 kW / Irr • DS • 5 kW
6175 COSTA RICA †FARO DEL CARIBE, San José	DS • 2.5 kW
FRANCE R FRANCE INTL, Issoudun-Allouis	Europe & N Africa • 100/500 kW / W • E Europe • 500 kW

(con'd)

ENGLISH ▬   ARABIC ⌇⌇⌇   CHINESE □□□   FRENCH ═══   GERMAN ▬▬   RUSSIAN ══   SPANISH ▬▬   OTHER ──

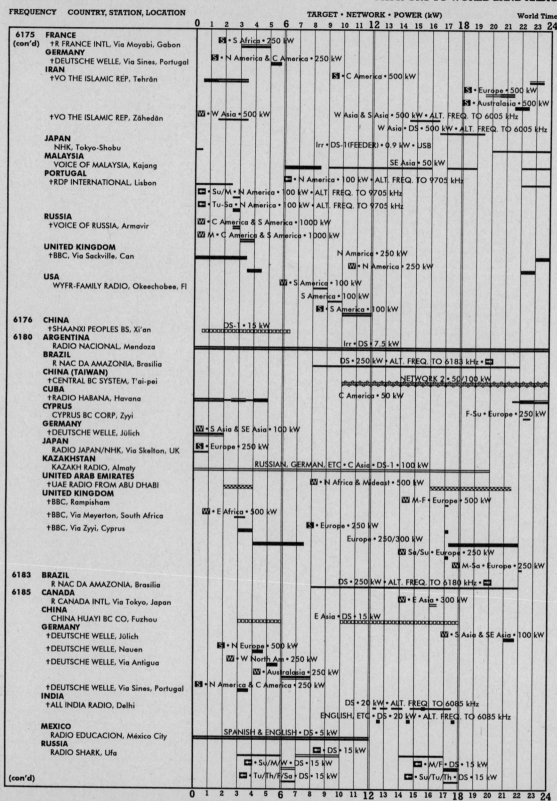

FREQUENCY   COUNTRY, STATION, LOCATION

TARGET • NETWORK • POWER (kW)   World Time

6175
(con'd) **FRANCE**
             †R FRANCE INTL, Via Moyabi, Gabon
             GERMANY
             †DEUTSCHE WELLE, Via Sines, Portugal
             IRAN
             †VO THE ISLAMIC REP, Tehrān

             †VO THE ISLAMIC REP, Zāhedān

             JAPAN
             NHK, Tokyo-Shobu
             MALAYSIA
             VOICE OF MALAYSIA, Kajang
             PORTUGAL
             †RDP INTERNATIONAL, Lisbon

             RUSSIA
             †VOICE OF RUSSIA, Armavir

             UNITED KINGDOM
             †BBC, Via Sackville, Can

             USA
             WYFR-FAMILY RADIO, Okeechobee, Fl

6176   **CHINA**
             †SHAANXI PEOPLES BS, Xi'an
6180   **ARGENTINA**
             RADIO NACIONAL, Mendoza
             BRAZIL
             R NAC DA AMAZONIA, Brasilia
             CHINA (TAIWAN)
             †CENTRAL BC SYSTEM, T'ai-pei
             CUBA
             †RADIO HABANA, Havana
             CYPRUS
             CYPRUS BC CORP, Zyyi
             GERMANY
             †DEUTSCHE WELLE, Jülich
             JAPAN
             RADIO JAPAN/NHK, Via Skelton, UK
             KAZAKHSTAN
             KAZAKH RADIO, Almaty
             UNITED ARAB EMIRATES
             †UAE RADIO FROM ABU DHABI
             UNITED KINGDOM
             †BBC, Rampisham

             †BBC, Via Meyerton, South Africa

             †BBC, Via Zyyi, Cyprus

6183   **BRAZIL**
             R NAC DA AMAZONIA, Brasilia
6185   **CANADA**
             R CANADA INTL, Via Tokyo, Japan
             CHINA
             CHINA HUAYI BC CO, Fuzhou
             GERMANY
             †DEUTSCHE WELLE, Jülich

             †DEUTSCHE WELLE, Nauen

             †DEUTSCHE WELLE, Via Antigua

             †DEUTSCHE WELLE, Via Sines, Portugal
             INDIA
             †ALL INDIA RADIO, Delhi

             MEXICO
             RADIO EDUCACION, México City
             RUSSIA
             RADIO SHARK, Ufa

(con'd)

FREQUENCY   COUNTRY, STATION, LOCATION

TARGET • NETWORK • POWER (kW)

World Time

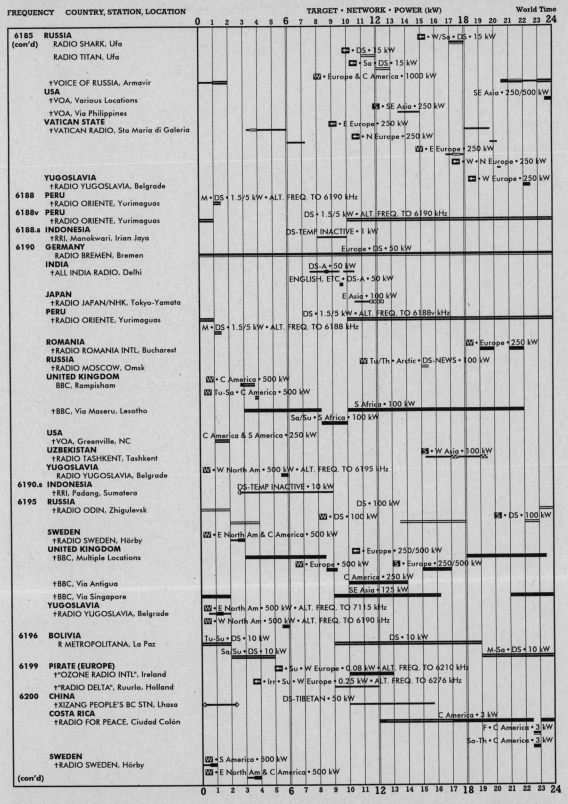

FREQUENCY	COUNTRY, STATION, LOCATION	Notes
6185 (con'd)	RUSSIA	
	RADIO SHARK, Ufa	W/Sa • DS • 15 kW
	RADIO TITAN, Ufa	DS • 15 kW / Sa • DS • 15 kW
	†VOICE OF RUSSIA, Armavir	W • Europe & C America • 1000 kW
	USA	
	†VOA, Various Locations	SE Asia • 250/500 kW
	†VOA, Via Philippines	SE Asia • 250 kW
	VATICAN STATE	
	†VATICAN RADIO, Sta Maria di Galeria	E Europe • 250 kW / N Europe • 250 kW / W • E Europe • 250 kW / W • N Europe • 250 kW / W • Europe • 250 kW
	YUGOSLAVIA	
	†RADIO YUGOSLAVIA, Belgrade	
6188	PERU	
	†RADIO ORIENTE, Yurimaguas	M • DS • 1.5/5 kW • ALT. FREQ. TO 6190 kHz
6188v	PERU	
	†RADIO ORIENTE, Yurimaguas	DS • 1.5/5 kW • ALT. FREQ. TO 6190 kHz
6188.8	INDONESIA	
	†RRI, Manokwari, Irian Jaya	DS-TEMP INACTIVE • 1 kW
6190	GERMANY	
	RADIO BREMEN, Bremen	Europe • DS • 50 kW
	INDIA	
	†ALL INDIA RADIO, Delhi	DS-A • 50 kW / ENGLISH, ETC • DS-A • 50 kW
	JAPAN	
	†RADIO JAPAN/NHK, Tokyo-Yamata	E Asia • 100 kW
	PERU	
	†RADIO ORIENTE, Yurimaguas	DS • 1.5/5 kW • ALT. FREQ. TO 6188v kHz / M • DS • 1.5/5 kW • ALT. FREQ. TO 6188 kHz
	ROMANIA	
	†RADIO ROMANIA INTL, Bucharest	W • Europe • 250 kW
	RUSSIA	
	†RADIO MOSCOW, Omsk	W • Tu/Th • Arctic • DS-NEWS • 100 kW
	UNITED KINGDOM	
	BBC, Rampisham	W • C America • 500 kW / W • Tu-Sa • C America • 500 kW
	†BBC, Via Maseru, Lesotho	S Africa • 100 kW / Sa/Su • S Africa • 100 kW
	USA	
	†VOA, Greenville, NC	C America & S America • 250 kW
	UZBEKISTAN	
	†RADIO TASHKENT, Tashkent	S • W Asia • 100 kW
	YUGOSLAVIA	
	RADIO YUGOSLAVIA, Belgrade	W • W North Am • 500 kW • ALT. FREQ. TO 6195 kHz
6190.8	INDONESIA	
	†RRI, Padang, Sumatera	DS-TEMP INACTIVE • 10 kW
6195	RUSSIA	
	†RADIO ODIN, Zhigulevsk	DS • 100 kW / W • DS • 100 kW / S • DS • 100 kW
	SWEDEN	
	†RADIO SWEDEN, Hörby	W • E North Am & C America • 500 kW
	UNITED KINGDOM	
	†BBC, Multiple Locations	Europe • 250/500 kW / W • Europe • 500 kW / S • Europe • 250/500 kW
	†BBC, Via Antigua	C America • 250 kW
	†BBC, Via Singapore	SE Asia • 125 kW
	YUGOSLAVIA	
	†RADIO YUGOSLAVIA, Belgrade	W • E North Am • 500 kW • ALT. FREQ. TO 7115 kHz / W • W North Am • 500 kW • ALT. FREQ. TO 6190 kHz
6196	BOLIVIA	
	R METROPOLITANA, La Paz	Tu-Su • DS • 10 kW / Sa/Su • DS • 10 kW / DS • 10 kW / M-Sa • DS • 10 kW
6199	PIRATE (EUROPE)	
	†"OZONE RADIO INTL", Ireland	• Su • W Europe • 0.08 kW • ALT. FREQ. TO 6210 kHz
	†"RADIO DELTA", Ruurlo, Holland	• Irr • Su • W Europe • 0.25 kW • ALT. FREQ. TO 6276 kHz
6200	CHINA	
	†XIZANG PEOPLE'S BC STN, Lhasa	DS-TIBETAN • 50 kW
	COSTA RICA	
	†RADIO FOR PEACE, Ciudad Colón	C America • 3 kW / F • C America • 3 kW / Sa-Th • C America • 3 kW
	SWEDEN	
	†RADIO SWEDEN, Hörby	W • S America • 500 kW / W • E North Am & C America • 500 kW
(con'd)		

ENGLISH ▬▬   ARABIC ⁓⁓   CHINESE ▫▫▫   FRENCH ══   GERMAN ▬▬   RUSSIAN ══   SPANISH ▬▬   OTHER ▬▬

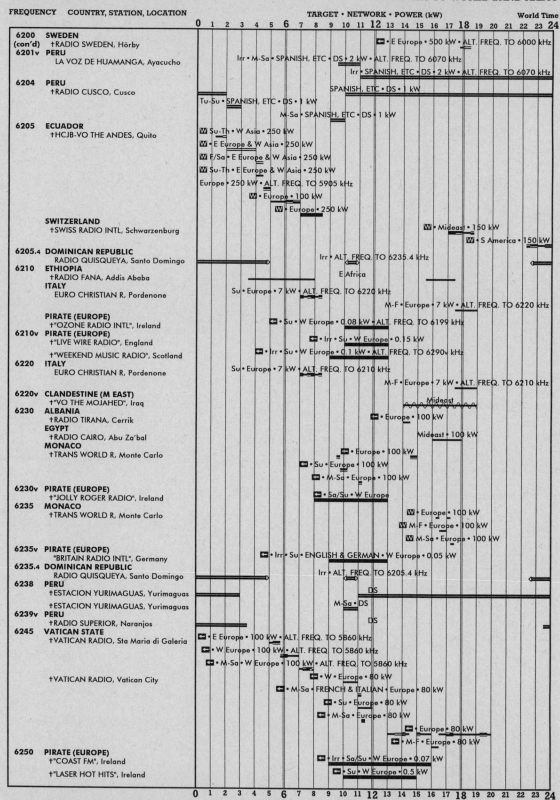

FREQUENCY	COUNTRY, STATION, LOCATION	Details
6200 (con'd)	SWEDEN †RADIO SWEDEN, Hörby	E Europe • 500 kW • ALT. FREQ. TO 6000 kHz
6201v	PERU LA VOZ DE HUAMANGA, Ayacucho	Irr • M-Sa • SPANISH, ETC • DS • 2 kW • ALT. FREQ. TO 6070 kHz; Irr • SPANISH, ETC • DS • 2 kW • ALT. FREQ. TO 6070 kHz
6204	PERU †RADIO CUSCO, Cusco	SPANISH, ETC • DS • 1 kW; Tu-Su • SPANISH, ETC • DS • 1 kW; M-Sa • SPANISH, ETC • DS • 1 kW
6205	ECUADOR †HCJB-VO THE ANDES, Quito	Su-Th • W Asia • 250 kW; E Europe & W Asia • 250 kW; F/Sa • E Europe & W Asia • 250 kW; Su-Th • E Europe & W Asia • 250 kW; Europe • 250 kW • ALT. FREQ. TO 5905 kHz; Europe • 100 kW; Europe • 250 kW
	SWITZERLAND †SWISS RADIO INTL, Schwarzenburg	Mideast • 150 kW; S America • 150 kW
6205.4	DOMINICAN REPUBLIC RADIO QUISQUEYA, Santo Domingo	Irr • ALT. FREQ. TO 6235.4 kHz
6210	ETHIOPIA †RADIO FANA, Addis Ababa	E Africa
	ITALY EURO CHRISTIAN R, Pordenone	Su • Europe • 7 kW • ALT. FREQ. TO 6220 kHz; M-F • Europe • 7 kW • ALT. FREQ. TO 6220 kHz
	PIRATE (EUROPE) †"OZONE RADIO INTL", Ireland	Su • W Europe • 0.08 kW • ALT. FREQ. TO 6199 kHz
6210v	PIRATE (EUROPE) †"LIVE WIRE RADIO", England	Irr • Su • W Europe • 0.15 kW
	†"WEEKEND MUSIC RADIO", Scotland	Irr • Su • W Europe • 0.1 kW • ALT. FREQ. TO 6290v kHz
6220	ITALY EURO CHRISTIAN R, Pordenone	Su • Europe • 7 kW • ALT. FREQ. TO 6210 kHz; M-F • Europe • 7 kW • ALT. FREQ. TO 6210 kHz
6220v	CLANDESTINE (M EAST) †"VO THE MOJAHED", Iraq	Mideast
6230	ALBANIA †RADIO TIRANA, Cerrik	Europe • 100 kW
	EGYPT †RADIO CAIRO, Abu Za'bal	Mideast • 100 kW
	MONACO †TRANS WORLD R, Monte Carlo	Europe • 100 kW; Su • Europe • 100 kW; M-Sa • Europe • 100 kW
6230v	PIRATE (EUROPE) †"JOLLY ROGER RADIO", Ireland	Sa/Su • W Europe
6235	MONACO †TRANS WORLD R, Monte Carlo	Europe • 100 kW; M-F • Europe • 100 kW; M-Sa • Europe • 100 kW
6235v	PIRATE (EUROPE) "BRITAIN RADIO INTL", Germany	Irr • Su • ENGLISH & GERMAN • W Europe • 0.05 kW
6235.4	DOMINICAN REPUBLIC RADIO QUISQUEYA, Santo Domingo	Irr • ALT. FREQ. TO 6205.4 kHz
6238	PERU †ESTACION YURIMAGUAS, Yurimaguas	DS; M-Sa • DS
6239v	PERU †RADIO SUPERIOR, Naranjos	DS
6245	VATICAN STATE †VATICAN RADIO, Sta Maria di Galeria	E Europe • 100 kW • ALT. FREQ. TO 5860 kHz; W Europe • 100 kW • ALT. FREQ. TO 5860 kHz; M-Sa • W Europe • 100 kW • ALT. FREQ. TO 5860 kHz
	†VATICAN RADIO, Vatican City	W • Europe • 80 kW; M-Sa • FRENCH & ITALIAN • Europe • 80 kW; Su • Europe • 80 kW; M-Sa • Europe • 80 kW; Europe • 80 kW; M-F • Europe • 80 kW
6250	PIRATE (EUROPE) †"COAST FM", Ireland	Irr • Sa/Su • W Europe • 0.07 kW
	†"LASER HOT HITS", Ireland	Su • W Europe • 0.5 kW

FREQUENCY   COUNTRY, STATION, LOCATION

TARGET • NETWORK • POWER (kW)

World Time

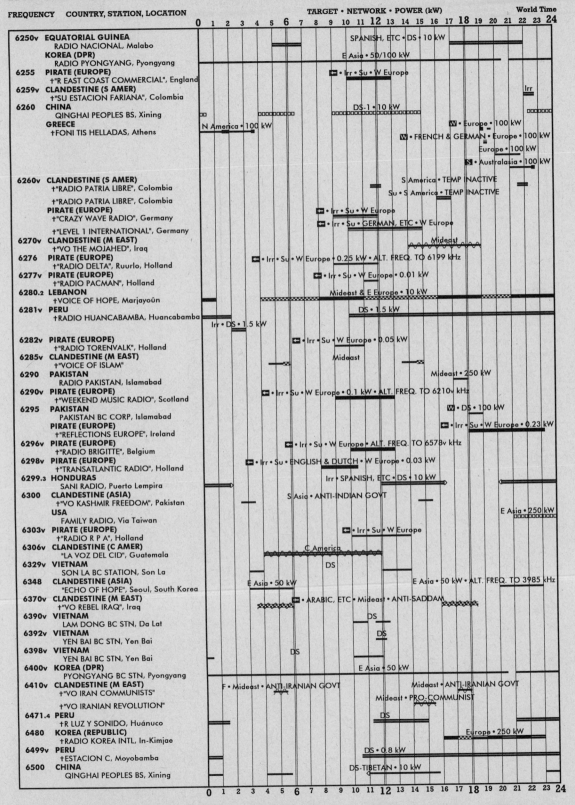

Frequency	Country, Station, Location	Annotation
6250v	**EQUATORIAL GUINEA** — RADIO NACIONAL, Malabo	SPANISH, ETC • DS • 10 kW
	KOREA (DPR) — RADIO PYONGYANG, Pyongyang	E Asia • 50/100 kW
6255	**PIRATE (EUROPE)** — †"R EAST COAST COMMERCIAL", England	Irr • Su • W Europe
6259v	**CLANDESTINE (S AMER)** — †"SU ESTACION FARIANA", Colombia	Irr
6260	**CHINA** — QINGHAI PEOPLES BS, Xining	DS-1 • 10 kW
	GREECE — †FONI TIS HELLADAS, Athens	N America • 100 kW / W • Europe • 100 kW / W • FRENCH & GERMAN • Europe • 100 kW / Europe • 100 kW / S • Australasia • 100 kW
6260v	**CLANDESTINE (S AMER)** — †"RADIO PATRIA LIBRE", Colombia	S America • TEMP INACTIVE / Su • S America • TEMP INACTIVE
	†"RADIO PATRIA LIBRE", Colombia	
	PIRATE (EUROPE) — †"CRAZY WAVE RADIO", Germany	Irr • Su • W Europe
	†"LEVEL 1 INTERNATIONAL", Germany	Irr • Su • GERMAN, ETC • W Europe
6270v	**CLANDESTINE (M EAST)** — †"VO THE MOJAHED", Iraq	Mideast
6276	**PIRATE (EUROPE)** — †"RADIO DELTA", Ruurlo, Holland	Irr • Su • W Europe • 0.25 kW • ALT. FREQ. TO 6199 kHz
6277v	**PIRATE (EUROPE)** — †"RADIO PACMAN", Holland	Irr • Su • W Europe • 0.01 kW
6280.2	**LEBANON** — †VOICE OF HOPE, Marjayoûn	Mideast & E Europe • 10 kW
6281v	**PERU** — †RADIO HUANCABAMBA, Huancabamba	DS • 1.5 kW / Irr • DS • 1.5 kW
6282v	**PIRATE (EUROPE)** — †"RADIO TORENVALK", Holland	Irr • Su • W Europe • 0.05 kW
6285v	**CLANDESTINE (M EAST)** — †"VOICE OF ISLAM"	Mideast
6290	**PAKISTAN** — RADIO PAKISTAN, Islamabad	Mideast • 250 kW
6290v	**PIRATE (EUROPE)** — †"WEEKEND MUSIC RADIO", Scotland	Irr • Su • W Europe • 0.1 kW • ALT. FREQ. TO 6210v kHz
6295	**PAKISTAN** — PAKISTAN BC CORP, Islamabad	W • DS • 100 kW
	PIRATE (EUROPE) — †"REFLECTIONS EUROPE", Ireland	Irr • Su • W Europe • 0.23 kW
6296v	**PIRATE (EUROPE)** — †"RADIO BRIGITTE", Belgium	Irr • Su • W Europe • ALT. FREQ. TO 6578v kHz
6298v	**PIRATE (EUROPE)** — †"TRANSATLANTIC RADIO", Holland	Irr • Su • ENGLISH & DUTCH • W Europe • 0.03 kW
6299.3	**HONDURAS** — SANI RADIO, Puerto Lempira	Irr • SPANISH, ETC • DS • 10 kW
6300	**CLANDESTINE (ASIA)** — †"VO KASHMIR FREEDOM", Pakistan	S Asia • ANTI-INDIAN GOVT
	USA — FAMILY RADIO, Via Taiwan	E Asia • 250 kW
6303v	**PIRATE (EUROPE)** — †"RADIO R P A", Holland	Irr • Su • W Europe
6306v	**CLANDESTINE (C AMER)** — "LA VOZ DEL CID", Guatemala	C America
6329v	**VIETNAM** — SON LA BC STATION, Son La	DS
6348	**CLANDESTINE (ASIA)** — "ECHO OF HOPE", Seoul, South Korea	E Asia • 50 kW / E Asia • 50 kW • ALT. FREQ. TO 3985 kHz
6370v	**CLANDESTINE (M EAST)** — †"VO REBEL IRAQ", Iraq	ARABIC, ETC • Mideast • ANTI-SADDAM
6390v	**VIETNAM** — LAM DONG BC STN, Da Lat	DS
6392v	**VIETNAM** — YEN BAI BC STN, Yen Bai	DS
6398v	**VIETNAM** — YEN BAI BC STN, Yen Bai	DS
6400v	**KOREA (DPR)** — PYONGYANG BC STN, Pyongyang	E Asia • 50 kW
6410v	**CLANDESTINE (M EAST)** — †"VO IRAN COMMUNISTS"	F • Mideast • ANTI-IRANIAN GOVT / Mideast • ANTI-IRANIAN GOVT
	†"VO IRANIAN REVOLUTION"	Mideast • PRO-COMMUNIST
6471.4	**PERU** — †R LUZ Y SONIDO, Huánuco	DS
6480	**KOREA (REPUBLIC)** — †RADIO KOREA INTL, In-Kimjae	Europe • 250 kW
6499v	**PERU** — †ESTACION C, Moyobamba	DS • 0.8 kW
6500	**CHINA** — QINGHAI PEOPLES BS, Xining	DS-TIBETAN • 10 kW

ENGLISH ▬   ARABIC ξξξ   CHINESE □□□   FRENCH ▬   GERMAN ▬   RUSSIAN ═   SPANISH ▬   OTHER ▬

FREQUENCY	COUNTRY, STATION, LOCATION	TARGET • NETWORK • POWER (kW)
6520	**KOREA (DPR)** †RADIO PYONGYANG, Pyongyang	E Asia • 100 kW; Mideast & N Africa • 200 kW • ALT. FREQ. TO 6540 kHz
6535.8	**PERU** †R DIF HUANCABAMBA, Huancabamba	DS • 0.8 kW
6540	**KOREA (DPR)** †RADIO PYONGYANG, Pyongyang	E Asia • 100 kW • ALT. FREQ. TO 6070 kHz; Mideast & N Africa • 200 kW • ALT. FREQ. TO 6520 kHz
6544.7	**PERU** †RADIO IMPERIAL, Huancabamba	DS
6545v	**VIETNAM** †CAO BANG BC STN, Cao Bang	DS
6549.5	**LEBANON** †VOICE OF LEBANON, Beirūt-Ashrafiyah	DS-PHALANGE • 8 kW
6550	**CANADA** †R CANADA INTL, Via Beijing, China	E Asia • FEEDER • 10/50 kW
6552v	**ZAIRE** RADIO BUKAVU, Bukavu	Irr • FRENCH, ETC • DS-2X3276V KHZ • SPR; Irr • Su • FRENCH, ETC • DS-2X3276V KHZ • SPR
6560	**KOREA (DPR)** †RADIO PYONGYANG, Pyongyang	E Asia • 100 kW • ALT. FREQ. TO 9650 kHz
6560v	**IRAQ** †REP OF IRAQ RADIO	DS
6570	**MYANMAR (BURMA)** DEFENSE FORCES BC, Taunggyi	DS • 10 kW
6576	**KOREA (DPR)** RADIO PYONGYANG, Kujang-dong	Americas • 400 kW
	RADIO PYONGYANG, Pyongyang	Europe • 200 kW
6578v	**PIRATE (EUROPE)** †"RADIO BRIGITTE", Belgium	Irr • Su • W Europe • ALT. FREQ. TO 6296v kHz
6600v	**CLANDESTINE (ASIA)** "VO THE PEOPLE", Seoul, S Korea	E Asia
6627.6	**PERU** †LV DE SAN ANTONIO, Bambamarca	DS • 0.25/0.5 kW; Irr • DS • 0.25/0.5 kW
6652v	**VIETNAM** BAC THAI BC STN, Bac Thai	DS
6670.2	**PERU** †R SANTA MONICA, Santiago de Chuco	Irr • DS
6690	**PERU** †RADIO CUTERVO, Cutervo	DS-PROJECTED • 1 kW • ALT. FREQ. TO 3390 kHz
6705v	**VIETNAM** †LAI CHAU BC STN, Lai Chau	DS
6726v	**PERU** †RADIO SATELITE, Santa Cruz	DS • 0.15/1 kW
6750	**CHINA** CENTRAL PEOPLES BS	DS-1
6751.2	**PERU** †RADIO SAN IGNACIO, San Ignacio	DS
6754.7	**PERU** †RADIO LA MERCED, Tongod	Irr • DS
6770	**ETHIOPIA** VO TIGRAY REVOL'N, Mek'ele	E Africa
6790	**CHINA** CENTRAL PEOPLES BS, Beijing	[W] • CHINESE, ETC • TAIWAN-2 • 10 kW
6803v	**PERU** †ONDAS DEL MAYO, Nueva Cajamarca	DS • 1 kW
6805	**RUSSIA** †RADIO ROSSII	[W] • DS(FEEDER) • USB
6815.3	**PERU** †RADIO UNIVERSO, Saposoa	M • DS-TEMP INACTIVE • 0.04 kW; Su • DS-TEMP INACTIVE • 0.04 kW; Irr • M • DS-TEMP INACTIVE • 0.04 kW
6822.5	**RUSSIA** †VOICE OF RUSSIA, Moscow	[W] • 100 kW • USB
6825	**CHINA** CHINA RADIO INTL, Beijing	E Asia • FEEDER • 10 kW
6840	**CHINA** CENTRAL PEOPLES BS, Hohhot	DS-1 • 50 kW; W-M • DS-1 • 50 kW
6870	**SOMALIA** RADIO MOGADISHU, Mogadishu	E Africa • USB
6873	**USA** †VOA, Greenville, NC	[W] • N Africa • (FEEDER) • 50 kW • ISU; [S] • N Africa • (FEEDER) • 50 kW • ISL; [W] • N Africa • (FEEDER) • 50 kW • ISL; N Africa • (FEEDER) • 50 kW • ISU
6890	**CHINA** CENTRAL PEOPLES BS, Beijing	DS-2 • 10 kW
6895.3	**PERU** †RADIO SENSACION, Huancabamba	Irr • DS • 0.5 kW; DS • 0.5 kW
(con'd)		

World Time 0 1 2 3 4 5 6 7 8 9 10 11 12 13 14 15 16 17 18 19 20 21 22 23 24

SEASONAL [S] OR [W]   1-HR TIMESHIFT MIDYEAR ⇐ OR ⇒   JAMMING / OR ⋀   EARLIEST HEARD ◁   LATEST HEARD ▷   NEW FOR 1996 †

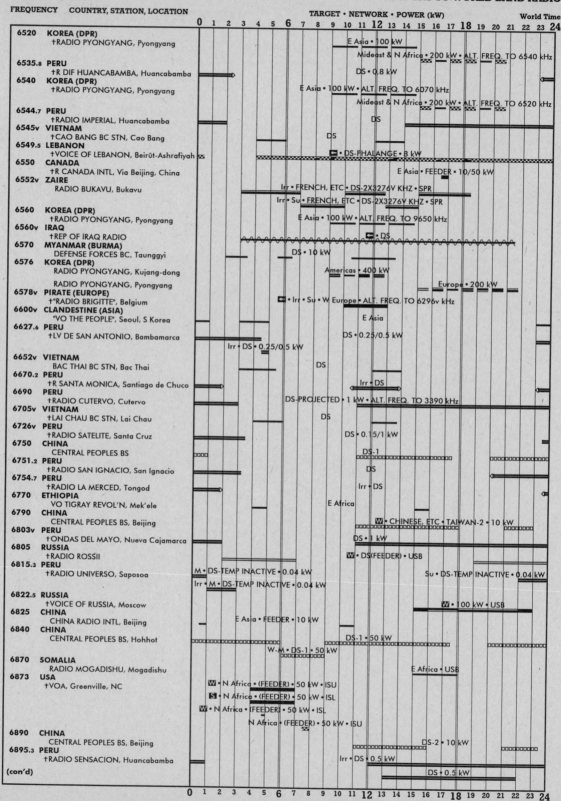

FREQUENCY   COUNTRY, STATION, LOCATION

TARGET • NETWORK • POWER (kW)   World Time

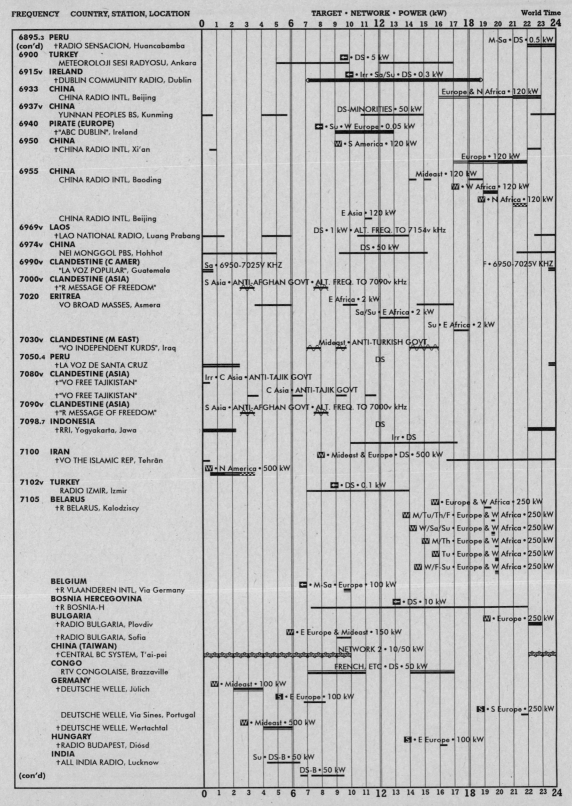

Frequency	Country, Station, Location	Target • Network • Power
6895.3 (con'd)	PERU †RADIO SENSACION, Huancabamba	M-Sa • DS • 0.5 kW
6900	TURKEY METEOROLOJI SESI RADYOSU, Ankara	• DS • 5 kW
6915v	IRELAND †DUBLIN COMMUNITY RADIO, Dublin	• Irr • Sa/Su • DS • 0.3 kW
6933	CHINA CHINA RADIO INTL, Beijing	Europe & N Africa • 120 kW
6937v	CHINA YUNNAN PEOPLES BS, Kunming	DS-MINORITIES • 50 kW
6940	PIRATE (EUROPE) †"ABC DUBLIN", Ireland	• Su • W Europe • 0.05 kW
6950	CHINA †CHINA RADIO INTL, Xi'an	W • S America • 120 kW
6955	CHINA CHINA RADIO INTL, Baoding	Europe • 120 kW / Mideast • 120 kW / W • W Africa • 120 kW / W • N Africa • 120 kW
	CHINA RADIO INTL, Beijing	E Asia • 120 kW
6969v	LAOS †LAO NATIONAL RADIO, Luang Prabang	DS • 1 kW • ALT. FREQ. TO 7154v kHz
6974v	CHINA NEI MONGGOL PBS, Hohhot	DS • 50 kW
6990v	CLANDESTINE (C AMER) "LA VOZ POPULAR", Guatemala	Sa • 6950-7025V KHZ F • 6950-7025V KHZ
7000v	CLANDESTINE (ASIA) †"R MESSAGE OF FREEDOM"	S Asia • ANTI-AFGHAN GOVT • ALT. FREQ. TO 7090v kHz
7020	ERITREA VO BROAD MASSES, Asmera	E Africa • 2 kW / Sa/Su • E Africa • 2 kW / Su • E Africa • 2 kW
7030v	CLANDESTINE (M EAST) "VO INDEPENDENT KURDS", Iraq	Mideast • ANTI-TURKISH GOVT
7050.4	PERU †LA VOZ DE SANTA CRUZ	DS
7080v	CLANDESTINE (ASIA) †"VO FREE TAJIKISTAN"	Irr • C Asia • ANTI-TAJIK GOVT
	†"VO FREE TAJIKISTAN"	C Asia • ANTI-TAJIK GOVT
7090v	CLANDESTINE (ASIA) †"R MESSAGE OF FREEDOM"	S Asia • ANTI-AFGHAN GOVT • ALT. FREQ. TO 7000v kHz
7098.7	INDONESIA †RRI, Yogyakarta, Jawa	DS / Irr • DS
7100	IRAN †VO THE ISLAMIC REP, Tehrān	W • Mideast & Europe • DS • 500 kW / W • N America • 500 kW
7102v	TURKEY RADIO IZMIR, Izmir	• DS • 0.1 kW
7105	BELARUS †R BELARUS, Kalodziscy	W • Europe & W Africa • 250 kW / W M/Tu/Th/F • Europe & W Africa • 250 kW / W/Sa/Su • Europe & W Africa • 250 kW / W M/Th • Europe & W Africa • 250 kW / W Tu • Europe & W Africa • 250 kW / W/F-Su • Europe & W Africa • 250 kW
	BELGIUM †R VLAANDEREN INTL, Via Germany	• M-Sa • Europe • 100 kW
	BOSNIA HERCEGOVINA †R BOSNIA-H	• DS • 10 kW
	BULGARIA †RADIO BULGARIA, Plovdiv	W • Europe • 250 kW
	†RADIO BULGARIA, Sofia	W • E Europe & Mideast • 150 kW
	CHINA (TAIWAN) †CENTRAL BC SYSTEM, T'ai-pei	NETWORK 2 • 10/50 kW
	CONGO RTV CONGOLAISE, Brazzaville	FRENCH, ETC • DS • 50 kW
	GERMANY †DEUTSCHE WELLE, Jülich	W • Mideast • 100 kW / S • E Europe • 100 kW
	DEUTSCHE WELLE, Via Sines, Portugal	S • S Europe • 250 kW
	†DEUTSCHE WELLE, Wertachtal	W • Mideast • 500 kW
	HUNGARY †RADIO BUDAPEST, Diósd	S • E Europe • 100 kW
	INDIA †ALL INDIA RADIO, Lucknow	Su • DS-B • 50 kW / DS-B • 50 kW
(con'd)		

ENGLISH ▬ ARABIC ≈≈≈ CHINESE □□□ FRENCH ▬▬ GERMAN ▬▬ RUSSIAN ══ SPANISH ▬▬▬ OTHER ──

FREQUENCY   COUNTRY, STATION, LOCATION

TARGET • NETWORK • POWER (kW)   World Time

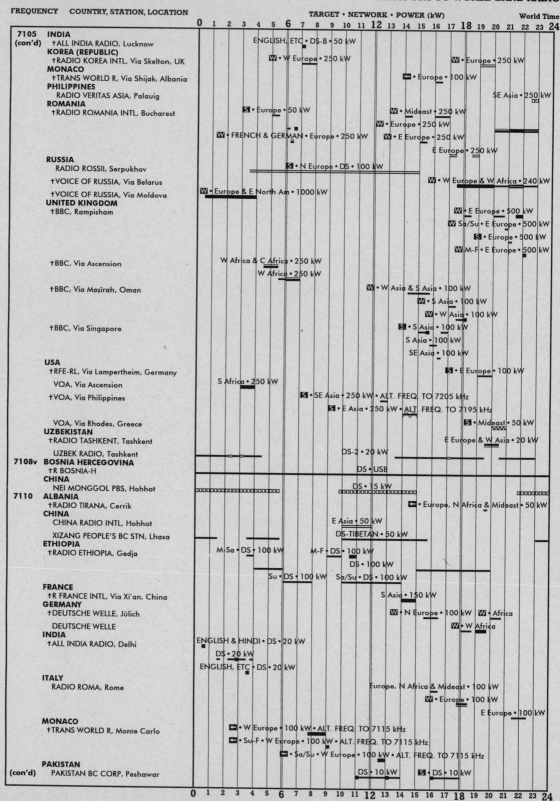

FREQUENCY	COUNTRY, STATION, LOCATION	TARGET • NETWORK • POWER (kW)
7105 (con'd)	INDIA †ALL INDIA RADIO, Lucknow	ENGLISH, ETC • DS-B • 50 kW
	KOREA (REPUBLIC) †RADIO KOREA INTL, Via Skelton, UK	W • W Europe • 250 kW · W • Europe • 250 kW
	MONACO †TRANS WORLD R, Via Shijak, Albania	• Europe • 100 kW
	PHILIPPINES RADIO VERITAS ASIA, Palauig	SE Asia • 250 kW
	ROMANIA †RADIO ROMANIA INTL, Bucharest	S • Europe • 50 kW · W • Mideast • 250 kW · W • Europe • 250 kW · W • FRENCH & GERMAN • Europe • 250 kW · W • E Europe • 250 kW · E Europe • 250 kW
	RUSSIA RADIO ROSSII, Serpukhov	S • N Europe • DS • 100 kW
	†VOICE OF RUSSIA, Via Belarus	W • W Europe & W Africa • 240 kW
	†VOICE OF RUSSIA, Via Moldova	W • Europe & E North Am • 1000 kW
	UNITED KINGDOM †BBC, Rampisham	W • E Europe • 500 kW · W Sa/Su • E Europe • 500 kW · S • Europe • 500 kW · W M-F • E Europe • 500 kW
	†BBC, Via Ascension	W Africa & C Africa • 250 kW · W Africa • 250 kW
	†BBC, Via Maşīrah, Oman	W • W Asia & S Asia • 100 kW · W • S Asia • 100 kW · W • W Asia • 100 kW
	†BBC, Via Singapore	S • S Asia • 100 kW · S Asia • 100 kW · SE Asia • 100 kW
	USA †RFE-RL, Via Lampertheim, Germany	S • E Europe • 100 kW
	VOA, Via Ascension	S Africa • 250 kW
	†VOA, Via Philippines	S • SE Asia • 250 kW • ALT. FREQ. TO 7205 kHz · S • E Asia • 250 kW • ALT. FREQ. TO 7195 kHz
	VOA, Via Rhodes, Greece	S • Mideast • 50 kW
	UZBEKISTAN †RADIO TASHKENT, Tashkent	E Europe & W Asia • 20 kW
	UZBEK RADIO, Tashkent	DS-2 • 20 kW
7108v	BOSNIA HERCEGOVINA †R BOSNIA-H	DS • USB
	CHINA NEI MONGGOL PBS, Hohhot	DS • 15 kW
7110	ALBANIA †RADIO TIRANA, Cerrik	• Europe, N Africa & Mideast • 50 kW
	CHINA CHINA RADIO INTL, Hohhot	E Asia • 50 kW
	XIZANG PEOPLE'S BC STN, Lhasa	DS-TIBETAN • 50 kW
	ETHIOPIA †RADIO ETHIOPIA, Gedja	M-Sa • DS • 100 kW · M-F • DS • 100 kW · DS • 100 kW · Su • DS • 100 kW · Sa/Su • DS • 100 kW
	FRANCE †R FRANCE INTL, Via Xi'an, China	S Asia • 150 kW
	GERMANY †DEUTSCHE WELLE, Jülich	W • N Europe • 100 kW · W • Africa
	DEUTSCHE WELLE	W • W Africa
	INDIA †ALL INDIA RADIO, Delhi	ENGLISH & HINDI • DS • 20 kW · DS • 20 kW · ENGLISH, ETC • DS • 20 kW
	ITALY RADIO ROMA, Rome	Europe, N Africa & Mideast • 100 kW · W • Europe • 100 kW · E Europe • 100 kW
	MONACO †TRANS WORLD R, Monte Carlo	• W Europe • 100 kW • ALT. FREQ. TO 7115 kHz · • Su-F • W Europe • 100 kW • ALT. FREQ. TO 7115 kHz · • Sa/Su • W Europe • 100 kW • ALT. FREQ. TO 7115 kHz
	PAKISTAN	DS • 10 kW · S • DS • 10 kW
(con'd)	PAKISTAN BC CORP, Peshawar	

FREQUENCY   COUNTRY, STATION, LOCATION   TARGET • NETWORK • POWER (kW)   World Time

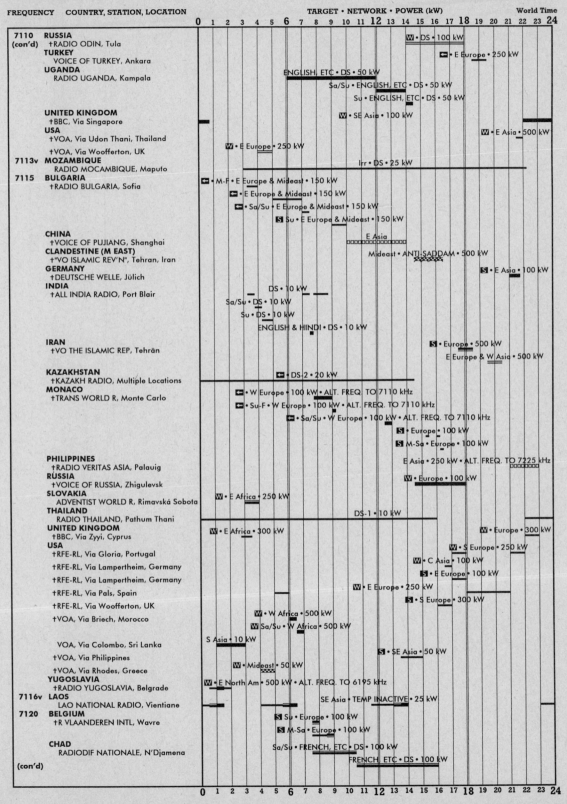

FREQUENCY	COUNTRY, STATION, LOCATION	TARGET • NETWORK • POWER (kW)
7110 (con'd)	RUSSIA †RADIO ODIN, Tula	W • DS • 100 kW
	TURKEY VOICE OF TURKEY, Ankara	☐ • E Europe • 250 kW
	UGANDA RADIO UGANDA, Kampala	ENGLISH, ETC • DS • 50 kW; Sa/Su • ENGLISH, ETC • DS • 50 kW; Su • ENGLISH, ETC • DS • 50 kW
	UNITED KINGDOM †BBC, Via Singapore	W • SE Asia • 100 kW; W • E Asia • 500 kW
	USA †VOA, Via Udon Thani, Thailand	
	†VOA, Via Woofferton, UK	W • E Europe • 250 kW
7113v	MOZAMBIQUE RADIO MOCAMBIQUE, Maputo	Irr • DS • 25 kW
7115	BULGARIA †RADIO BULGARIA, Sofia	☐ • M-F • E Europe & Mideast • 150 kW; ☐ • E Europe & Mideast • 150 kW; ☐ • Sa/Su • E Europe & Mideast • 150 kW; S • Su • E Europe & Mideast • 150 kW
	CHINA †VOICE OF PUJIANG, Shanghai	E Asia
	CLANDESTINE (M EAST) †"VO ISLAMIC REV'N", Tehran, Iran	Mideast • ANTI-SADDAM • 500 kW
	GERMANY †DEUTSCHE WELLE, Jülich	S • E Asia • 100 kW
	INDIA †ALL INDIA RADIO, Port Blair	DS • 10 kW; Sa/Su • DS • 10 kW; Su • DS • 10 kW; ENGLISH & HINDI • DS • 10 kW
	IRAN †VO THE ISLAMIC REP, Tehrān	S • Europe • 500 kW; E Europe & W Asia • 500 kW
	KAZAKHSTAN †KAZAKH RADIO, Multiple Locations	☐ • DS-2 • 20 kW
	MONACO †TRANS WORLD R, Monte Carlo	☐ • W Europe • 100 kW • ALT. FREQ. TO 7110 kHz; ☐ • Su-F • W Europe • 100 kW • ALT. FREQ. TO 7110 kHz; ☐ • Sa/Su • W Europe • 100 kW • ALT. FREQ. TO 7110 kHz; S • Europe • 100 kW; S • M-Sa • Europe • 100 kW
	PHILIPPINES †RADIO VERITAS ASIA, Palauig	E Asia • 250 kW • ALT. FREQ. TO 7225 kHz
	RUSSIA †VOICE OF RUSSIA, Zhigulevsk	W • Europe • 100 kW
	SLOVAKIA ADVENTIST WORLD R, Rimavská Sobota	W • E Africa • 250 kW
	THAILAND RADIO THAILAND, Pathum Thani	DS-1 • 10 kW
	UNITED KINGDOM †BBC, Via Zyyi, Cyprus	W • E Africa • 300 kW; W • Europe • 300 kW
	USA †RFE-RL, Via Gloria, Portugal	W • S Europe • 250 kW
	†RFE-RL, Via Lampertheim, Germany	W • C Asia • 100 kW
	†RFE-RL, Via Lampertheim, Germany	S • E Europe • 100 kW
	†RFE-RL, Via Pals, Spain	W • E Europe • 250 kW
	†RFE-RL, Via Woofferton, UK	S • S Europe • 300 kW
	†VOA, Via Briech, Morocco	W • W Africa • 500 kW; W • Sa/Su • W Africa • 500 kW
	VOA, Via Colombo, Sri Lanka	S Asia • 10 kW
	†VOA, Via Philippines	S • SE Asia • 50 kW
	†VOA, Via Rhodes, Greece	W • Mideast • 50 kW
	YUGOSLAVIA †RADIO YUGOSLAVIA, Belgrade	W • E North Am • 500 kW • ALT. FREQ. TO 6195 kHz
7116v	LAOS LAO NATIONAL RADIO, Vientiane	SE Asia • TEMP INACTIVE • 25 kW
7120	BELGIUM †R VLAANDEREN INTL, Wavre	S • Su • Europe • 100 kW; S • M-Sa • Europe • 100 kW
	CHAD RADIODIF NATIONALE, N'Djamena	Sa/Su • FRENCH, ETC • DS • 100 kW; FRENCH, ETC • DS • 100 kW
(con'd)		

ENGLISH ▄▄   ARABIC ⌇⌇⌇   CHINESE ▫▫▫   FRENCH ▬▬   GERMAN ▬▬   RUSSIAN ══   SPANISH ▬▬   OTHER ──

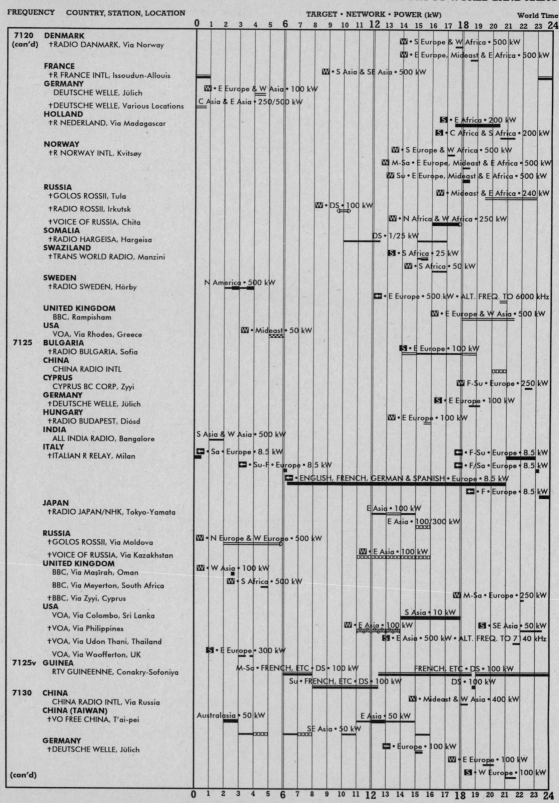

FREQUENCY   COUNTRY, STATION, LOCATION

TARGET • NETWORK • POWER (kW)   World Time

Frequency	Country, Station, Location	Details
7120 (con'd)	DENMARK	
	†RADIO DANMARK, Via Norway	W • S Europe & W Africa • 500 kW / W • E Europe, Mideast & E Africa • 500 kW
	FRANCE	
	†R FRANCE INTL, Issoudun-Allouis	W • S Asia & SE Asia • 500 kW
	GERMANY	
	DEUTSCHE WELLE, Jülich	W • E Europe & W Asia • 100 kW
	†DEUTSCHE WELLE, Various Locations	C Asia & E Asia • 250/500 kW
	HOLLAND	
	†R NEDERLAND, Via Madagascar	S • E Africa • 200 kW / S • C Africa & S Africa • 200 kW
	NORWAY	
	†R NORWAY INTL, Kvitsøy	W • S Europe & W Africa • 500 kW / W M-Sa • E Europe, Mideast & E Africa • 500 kW / W Su • E Europe, Mideast & E Africa • 500 kW
	RUSSIA	
	†GOLOS ROSSII, Tula	W • Mideast & E Africa • 240 kW
	†RADIO ROSSII, Irkutsk	W • DS • 100 kW
	†VOICE OF RUSSIA, Chita	W • N Africa & W Africa • 250 kW
	SOMALIA	
	†RADIO HARGEISA, Hargeisa	DS • 1/25 kW
	SWAZILAND	
	†TRANS WORLD RADIO, Manzini	S • S Africa • 25 kW / W • S Africa • 50 kW
	SWEDEN	
	†RADIO SWEDEN, Hörby	N America • 500 kW / ▭ • E Europe • 500 kW • ALT. FREQ. TO 6000 kHz
	UNITED KINGDOM	
	BBC, Rampisham	W • E Europe & W Asia • 500 kW
	USA	
	VOA, Via Rhodes, Greece	W • Mideast • 50 kW
7125	BULGARIA	
	†RADIO BULGARIA, Sofia	S • E Europe • 100 kW
	CHINA	
	CHINA RADIO INTL	
	CYPRUS	
	CYPRUS BC CORP, Zyyi	W F-Su • Europe • 250 kW
	GERMANY	
	†DEUTSCHE WELLE, Jülich	S • E Europe • 100 kW
	HUNGARY	
	†RADIO BUDAPEST, Diósd	W • E Europe • 100 kW
	INDIA	
	ALL INDIA RADIO, Bangalore	S Asia & W Asia • 500 kW
	ITALY	
	†ITALIAN R RELAY, Milan	▭ • Sa • Europe • 8.5 kW / ▭ • Su-F • Europe • 8.5 kW / ▭ • ENGLISH, FRENCH, GERMAN & SPANISH • Europe • 8.5 kW / ▭ • F-Su • Europe • 8.5 kW / ▭ • F/Sa • Europe • 8.5 kW / ▭ • F • Europe • 8.5 kW
	JAPAN	
	†RADIO JAPAN/NHK, Tokyo-Yamata	E Asia • 100 kW / E Asia • 100/300 kW
	RUSSIA	
	†GOLOS ROSSII, Via Moldova	W • N Europe & W Europe • 500 kW
	†VOICE OF RUSSIA, Via Kazakhstan	W • E Asia • 100 kW
	UNITED KINGDOM	
	BBC, Via Maşīrah, Oman	W • W Asia • 100 kW
	BBC, Via Meyerton, South Africa	W • S Africa • 500 kW
	†BBC, Via Zyyi, Cyprus	W M-Sa • Europe • 250 kW
	USA	
	VOA, Via Colombo, Sri Lanka	S Asia • 10 kW
	†VOA, Via Philippines	W • E Asia • 100 kW / S • SE Asia • 50 kW
	†VOA, Via Udon Thani, Thailand	S • E Asia • 500 kW • ALT. FREQ. TO 7140 kHz
	VOA, Via Woofferton, UK	S • E Europe • 300 kW
7125v	GUINEA	
	RTV GUINEENNE, Conakry-Sofoniya	M-Sa • FRENCH, ETC • DS • 100 kW / FRENCH, ETC • DS • 100 kW / Su • FRENCH, ETC • DS • 100 kW / DS • 100 kW
7130	CHINA	
	CHINA RADIO INTL, Via Russia	W • Mideast & W Asia • 400 kW
	CHINA (TAIWAN)	
	†VO FREE CHINA, T'ai-pei	Australasia • 50 kW / E Asia • 50 kW / SE Asia • 50 kW
	GERMANY	
	†DEUTSCHE WELLE, Jülich	▭ • Europe • 100 kW / W • E Europe • 100 kW / S • W Europe • 100 kW
(con'd)		

FREQUENCY   COUNTRY, STATION, LOCATION   TARGET • NETWORK • POWER (kW)   World Time

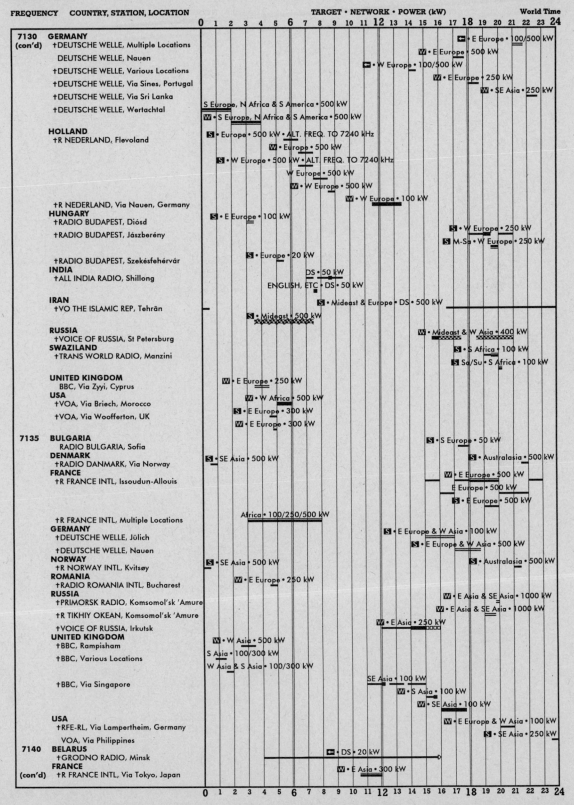

Frequency	Country, Station, Location	
7130 (con'd)	**GERMANY**	
	†DEUTSCHE WELLE, Multiple Locations	▣ • E Europe • 100/500 kW
	DEUTSCHE WELLE, Nauen	W • E Europe • 500 kW
	†DEUTSCHE WELLE, Various Locations	▣ • W Europe • 100/500 kW
	†DEUTSCHE WELLE, Via Sines, Portugal	W • E Europe • 250 kW
	†DEUTSCHE WELLE, Via Sri Lanka	W • SE Asia • 250 kW
	†DEUTSCHE WELLE, Wertachtal	S Europe, N Africa & S America • 500 kW / W • S Europe, N Africa & S America • 500 kW
	HOLLAND	
	†R NEDERLAND, Flevoland	S • Europe • 500 kW • ALT. FREQ. TO 7240 kHz / W • Europe • 500 kW / S • W Europe • 500 kW • ALT. FREQ. TO 7240 kHz / W • Europe • 500 kW / W • W Europe • 500 kW
	†R NEDERLAND, Via Nauen, Germany	W • W Europe • 100 kW
	HUNGARY	
	†RADIO BUDAPEST, Diósd	S • E Europe • 100 kW
	†RADIO BUDAPEST, Jászberény	S • W Europe • 250 kW / S M-Sa • W Europe • 250 kW
	†RADIO BUDAPEST, Szekésfehérvár	S • Europe • 20 kW
	INDIA	
	†ALL INDIA RADIO, Shillong	DS • 50 kW / ENGLISH, ETC • DS • 50 kW
	IRAN	
	†VO THE ISLAMIC REP, Tehrän	S • Mideast & Europe • DS • 500 kW / S • Mideast • 500 kW
	RUSSIA	
	†VOICE OF RUSSIA, St Petersburg	W • Mideast & W Asia • 400 kW
	SWAZILAND	
	†TRANS WORLD RADIO, Manzini	S • S Africa • 100 kW / S Sa/Su • S Africa • 100 kW
	UNITED KINGDOM	
	BBC, Via Zyyi, Cyprus	W • E Europe • 250 kW
	USA	
	†VOA, Via Briech, Morocco	W • W Africa • 500 kW
	†VOA, Via Woofferton, UK	S • E Europe • 300 kW / W • E Europe • 300 kW
7135	**BULGARIA**	
	RADIO BULGARIA, Sofia	S • S Europe • 50 kW
	DENMARK	
	†RADIO DANMARK, Via Norway	S • SE Asia • 500 kW / S • Australasia • 500 kW
	FRANCE	
	†R FRANCE INTL, Issoudun-Allouis	W • E Europe • 500 kW / E Europe • 500 kW / S • E Europe • 500 kW
	†R FRANCE INTL, Multiple Locations	Africa • 100/250/500 kW
	GERMANY	
	†DEUTSCHE WELLE, Jülich	S • E Europe & W Asia • 100 kW
	†DEUTSCHE WELLE, Nauen	S • E Europe & W Asia • 500 kW
	NORWAY	
	†R NORWAY INTL, Kvitsøy	S • SE Asia • 500 kW / S • Australasia • 500 kW
	ROMANIA	
	†RADIO ROMANIA INTL, Bucharest	W • E Europe • 250 kW
	RUSSIA	
	†PRIMORSK RADIO, Komsomol'sk 'Amure	W • E Asia & SE Asia • 1000 kW
	†R TIKHIY OKEAN, Komsomol'sk 'Amure	W • E Asia & SE Asia • 1000 kW
	†VOICE OF RUSSIA, Irkutsk	W • E Asia • 250 kW
	UNITED KINGDOM	
	†BBC, Rampisham	W • W Asia • 500 kW
	†BBC, Various Locations	S Asia • 100/300 kW / W Asia & S Asia • 100/300 kW
	†BBC, Via Singapore	SE Asia • 100 kW / W • S Asia • 100 kW / W • SE Asia • 100 kW
	USA	
	†RFE-RL, Via Lampertheim, Germany	W • E Europe & W Asia • 100 kW
	VOA, Via Philippines	S • SE Asia • 250 kW
7140	**BELARUS**	
	†GRODNO RADIO, Minsk	▣ • DS • 20 kW
	FRANCE	
(con'd)	†R FRANCE INTL, Via Tokyo, Japan	W • E Asia • 300 kW

ENGLISH ▬ ARABIC ⁓⁓⁓ CHINESE ▫▫▫ FRENCH ═ GERMAN ▬ RUSSIAN ═ SPANISH ▬ OTHER ▬

FREQUENCY	COUNTRY, STATION, LOCATION	TARGET • NETWORK • POWER (kW)	World Time

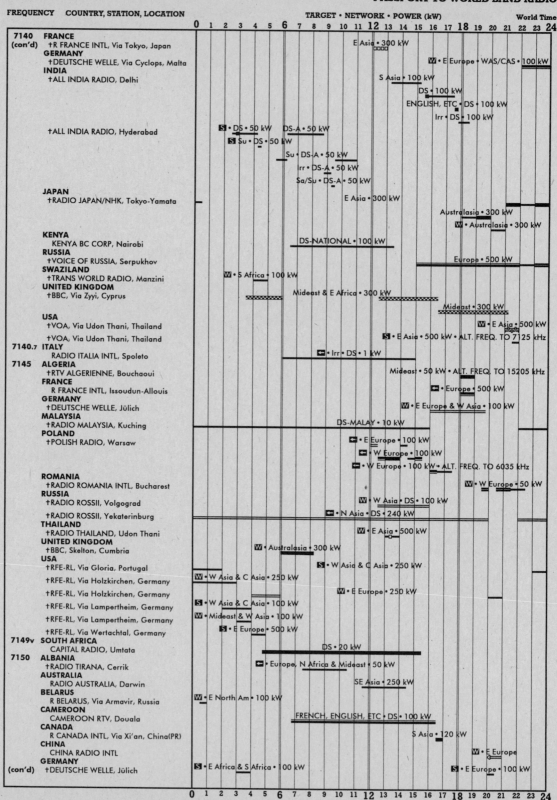

7140
(con'd) †R FRANCE INTL, Via Tokyo, Japan — E Asia • 300 kW
GERMANY
†DEUTSCHE WELLE, Via Cyclops, Malta — W • E Europe • WAS/CAS • 100 kW
INDIA
†ALL INDIA RADIO, Delhi — S Asia • 100 kW / DS • 100 kW / ENGLISH, ETC • DS • 100 kW / Irr • DS • 100 kW

†ALL INDIA RADIO, Hyderabad — S • DS • 50 kW / DS-A • 50 kW / S • Su • DS • 50 kW / Su • DS-A • 50 kW / Irr • DS-A • 50 kW / Sa/Su • DS-A • 50 kW

JAPAN
†RADIO JAPAN/NHK, Tokyo-Yamata — E Asia • 300 kW / Australasia • 300 kW / W • Australasia • 300 kW

KENYA
KENYA BC CORP, Nairobi — DS-NATIONAL • 100 kW
RUSSIA
†VOICE OF RUSSIA, Serpukhov — Europe • 500 kW
SWAZILAND
†TRANS WORLD RADIO, Manzini — W • S Africa • 100 kW
UNITED KINGDOM
†BBC, Via Zyyi, Cyprus — Mideast & E Africa • 300 kW / Mideast • 300 kW

USA
†VOA, Via Udon Thani, Thailand — W • E Asia • 500 kW
†VOA, Via Udon Thani, Thailand — S • E Asia • 500 kW • ALT. FREQ. TO 7125 kHz

7140.7 ITALY
RADIO ITALIA INTL, Spoleto — • Irr • DS • 1 kW

7145 ALGERIA
†RTV ALGERIENNE, Bouchaoui — Mideast • 50 kW • ALT. FREQ. TO 15205 kHz
FRANCE
R FRANCE INTL, Issoudun-Allouis — • Europe • 500 kW
GERMANY
†DEUTSCHE WELLE, Jülich — W • E Europe & W Asia • 100 kW
MALAYSIA
†RADIO MALAYSIA, Kuching — DS-MALAY • 10 kW
POLAND
†POLISH RADIO, Warsaw — • E Europe • 100 kW / • W Europe • 100 kW / • W Europe • 100 kW • ALT. FREQ. TO 6035 kHz

ROMANIA
†RADIO ROMANIA INTL, Bucharest — W • W Europe • 50 kW
RUSSIA
†RADIO ROSSII, Volgograd — W • W Asia • DS • 100 kW

†RADIO ROSSII, Yekaterinburg — • N Asia • DS • 240 kW
THAILAND
†RADIO THAILAND, Udon Thani — W • E Asia • 500 kW
UNITED KINGDOM
†BBC, Skelton, Cumbria — W • Australasia • 300 kW
USA
†RFE-RL, Via Gloria, Portugal — S • W Asia & C Asia • 250 kW
†RFE-RL, Via Holzkirchen, Germany — W • W Asia & C Asia • 250 kW
†RFE-RL, Via Holzkirchen, Germany — W • E Europe • 250 kW
†RFE-RL, Via Lampertheim, Germany — S • W Asia & C Asia • 100 kW
†RFE-RL, Via Lampertheim, Germany — W • Mideast & W Asia • 100 kW
†RFE-RL, Via Wertachtal, Germany — S • E Europe • 500 kW

7149v SOUTH AFRICA
CAPITAL RADIO, Umtata — DS • 20 kW
7150 ALBANIA
†RADIO TIRANA, Cerrik — • Europe, N Africa & Mideast • 50 kW
AUSTRALIA
RADIO AUSTRALIA, Darwin — SE Asia • 250 kW
BELARUS
R BELARUS, Via Armavir, Russia — W • E North Am • 100 kW
CAMEROON
CAMEROON RTV, Douala — FRENCH, ENGLISH, ETC • DS • 100 kW
CANADA
R CANADA INTL, Via Xi'an, China(PR) — S Asia • 120 kW
CHINA
CHINA RADIO INTL — W • E Europe
GERMANY
(con'd) †DEUTSCHE WELLE, Jülich — S • E Africa & S Africa • 100 kW / S • E Europe • 100 kW

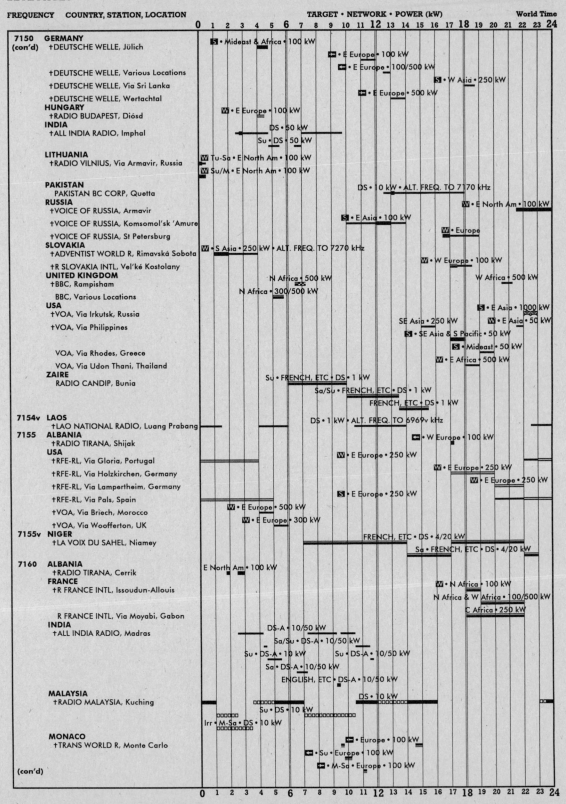

FREQUENCY   COUNTRY, STATION, LOCATION   TARGET • NETWORK • POWER (kW)   World Time

7150 GERMANY
(con'd) †DEUTSCHE WELLE, Jülich — S • Mideast & Africa • 100 kW

†DEUTSCHE WELLE, Various Locations — E Europe • 100 kW

†DEUTSCHE WELLE, Via Sri Lanka — E Europe • 100/500 kW

S • W Asia • 250 kW

†DEUTSCHE WELLE, Wertachtal — E Europe • 500 kW
HUNGARY
†RADIO BUDAPEST, Diósd — W • E Europe • 100 kW
INDIA
†ALL INDIA RADIO, Imphal — DS • 50 kW
Su • DS • 50 kW

LITHUANIA
†RADIO VILNIUS, Via Armavir, Russia — W Tu-Sa • E North Am • 100 kW
W Su/M • E North Am • 100 kW

PAKISTAN
PAKISTAN BC CORP, Quetta — DS • 10 kW • ALT. FREQ. TO 7170 kHz
RUSSIA
†VOICE OF RUSSIA, Armavir — W • E North Am • 100 kW

†VOICE OF RUSSIA, Komsomol'sk 'Amure — S • E Asia • 100 kW

†VOICE OF RUSSIA, St Petersburg — W • Europe
SLOVAKIA
†ADVENTIST WORLD R, Rimavská Sobota — W • S Asia • 250 kW • ALT. FREQ. TO 7270 kHz

†R SLOVAKIA INTL, Vel'ké Kostolany — W • W Europe • 100 kW
UNITED KINGDOM
†BBC, Rampisham — N Africa • 500 kW
W Africa • 500 kW

BBC, Various Locations — N Africa • 300/500 kW
USA
†VOA, Via Irkutsk, Russia — S • E Asia • 1000 kW

†VOA, Via Philippines — SE Asia • 250 kW
W • E Asia • 50 kW
S • SE Asia & S Pacific • 50 kW

VOA, Via Rhodes, Greece — S • Mideast • 50 kW

VOA, Via Udon Thani, Thailand — W • E Africa • 500 kW
ZAIRE
RADIO CANDIP, Bunia — Su • FRENCH, ETC • DS • 1 kW
Sa/Su • FRENCH, ETC • DS • 1 kW
FRENCH, ETC • DS • 1 kW

7154v LAOS
†LAO NATIONAL RADIO, Luang Prabang — DS • 1 kW • ALT. FREQ. TO 6969v kHz
7155 ALBANIA
†RADIO TIRANA, Shijak — W Europe • 100 kW
USA
†RFE-RL, Via Gloria, Portugal — W • E Europe • 250 kW

†RFE-RL, Via Holzkirchen, Germany — W • E Europe • 250 kW

†RFE-RL, Via Lampertheim, Germany — W • E Europe • 250 kW

†RFE-RL, Via Pals, Spain — S • E Europe • 250 kW

†VOA, Via Briech, Morocco — W • E Europe • 500 kW

†VOA, Via Woofferton, UK — W • E Europe • 300 kW
7155v NIGER
†LA VOIX DU SAHEL, Niamey — FRENCH, ETC • DS • 4/20 kW
Sa • FRENCH, ETC • DS • 4/20 kW

7160 ALBANIA
†RADIO TIRANA, Cerrik — E North Am • 100 kW
FRANCE
†R FRANCE INTL, Issoudun-Allouis — W • N Africa • 100 kW
N Africa & W Africa • 100/500 kW
C Africa • 250 kW

R FRANCE INTL, Via Moyabi, Gabon
INDIA
†ALL INDIA RADIO, Madras — DS-A • 10/50 kW
Sa/Su • DS-A • 10/50 kW
Su • DS-A • 10 kW   Su • DS-A • 10/50 kW
Sa • DS-A • 10/50 kW
ENGLISH, ETC • DS-A • 10/50 kW

MALAYSIA
†RADIO MALAYSIA, Kuching — DS • 10 kW
Su • DS • 10 kW
Irr • M-Sa • DS • 10 kW

MONACO
†TRANS WORLD R, Monte Carlo — Europe • 100 kW
Su • Europe • 100 kW
M-Sa • Europe • 100 kW

(con'd)

ENGLISH ▬▬   ARABIC ≋≋≋   CHINESE □□□   FRENCH ══   GERMAN ▬▬   RUSSIAN ═══   SPANISH ▭▭▭   OTHER ──

FREQUENCY   COUNTRY, STATION, LOCATION   TARGET • NETWORK • POWER (kW)   World Time

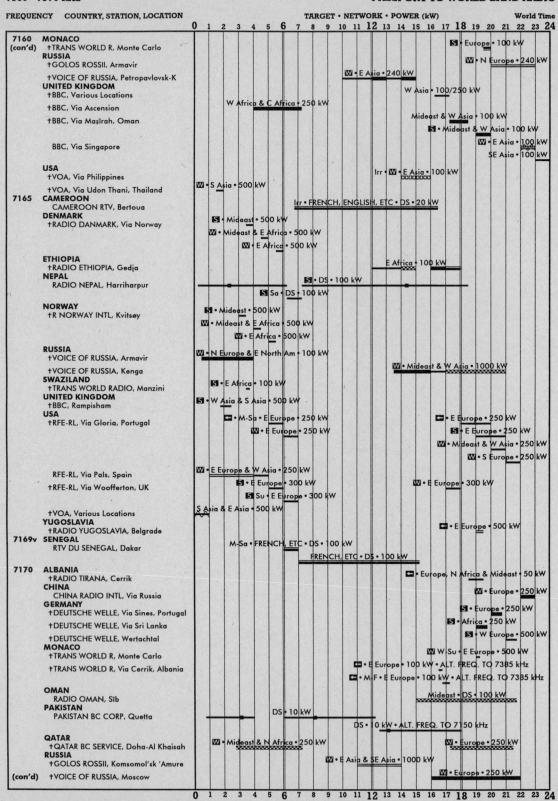

7160 **MONACO**
(con'd)   †TRANS WORLD R, Monte Carlo — S • Europe • 100 kW
          RUSSIA
          †GOLOS ROSSII, Armavir — W • N Europe • 240 kW
          †VOICE OF RUSSIA, Petropavlovsk-K — W • E Asia • 240 kW
          UNITED KINGDOM
          †BBC, Various Locations — W Asia • 100/250 kW
          †BBC, Via Ascension — W Africa & C Africa • 250 kW
          †BBC, Via Maṣīrah, Oman — Mideast & W Asia • 100 kW
                                    S • Mideast & W Asia • 100 kW
          BBC, Via Singapore — W • E Asia • 100 kW
                               SE Asia • 100 kW
          USA
          †VOA, Via Philippines — Irr • W • E Asia • 100 kW
          †VOA, Via Udon Thani, Thailand — W • S Asia • 500 kW
7165 **CAMEROON**
          CAMEROON RTV, Bertoua — Irr • FRENCH, ENGLISH, ETC • DS • 20 kW
          DENMARK
          †RADIO DANMARK, Via Norway — S • Mideast • 500 kW
                                        W • Mideast & E Africa • 500 kW
                                        W • E Africa • 500 kW
          ETHIOPIA
          †RADIO ETHIOPIA, Gedja — E Africa • 100 kW
          NEPAL
          RADIO NEPAL, Harriharpur — S • DS • 100 kW
                                     S Sa • DS • 100 kW
          NORWAY
          †R NORWAY INTL, Kvitsøy — S • Mideast • 500 kW
                                    W • Mideast & E Africa • 500 kW
                                    W • E Africa • 500 kW
          RUSSIA
          †VOICE OF RUSSIA, Armavir — W • N Europe & E North Am • 100 kW
          †VOICE OF RUSSIA, Kenga — W • Mideast & W Asia • 1000 kW
          SWAZILAND
          †TRANS WORLD RADIO, Manzini — S • E Africa • 100 kW
          UNITED KINGDOM
          †BBC, Rampisham — S • W Asia & S Asia • 500 kW
          USA
          †RFE-RL, Via Gloria, Portugal — ⬌ • M-Sa • E Europe • 250 kW
                                          ⬌ • E Europe • 250 kW
                                          W • E Europe • 250 kW
                                          S • E Europe • 250 kW
                                          W • Mideast & W Asia • 250 kW
                                          W • S Europe • 250 kW
          RFE-RL, Via Pals, Spain — W • E Europe & W Asia • 250 kW
          †RFE-RL, Via Woofferton, UK — S • E Europe • 300 kW
                                        W • E Europe • 300 kW
                                        S Su • E Europe • 300 kW
          †VOA, Various Locations — S Asia & E Asia • 500 kW
          YUGOSLAVIA
          †RADIO YUGOSLAVIA, Belgrade — S • E Europe • 500 kW
7169v **SENEGAL**
          RTV DU SENEGAL, Dakar — M-Sa • FRENCH, ETC • DS • 100 kW
                                  FRENCH, ETC • DS • 100 kW
7170 **ALBANIA**
          †RADIO TIRANA, Cerrik — ⬌ • Europe, N Africa & Mideast • 50 kW
          CHINA
          CHINA RADIO INTL, Via Russia — W • Europe • 250 kW
          GERMANY
          †DEUTSCHE WELLE, Via Sines, Portugal — S • Europe • 250 kW
          †DEUTSCHE WELLE, Via Sri Lanka — S • Africa • 250 kW
          †DEUTSCHE WELLE, Wertachtal — S • W Europe • 500 kW
          MONACO
          †TRANS WORLD R, Monte Carlo — W • Su • E Europe • 500 kW
          †TRANS WORLD R, Via Cerrik, Albania — ⬌ • E Europe • 100 kW • ALT. FREQ. TO 7385 kHz
                                                ⬌ • M-F • E Europe • 100 kW • ALT. FREQ. TO 7385 kHz
          OMAN
          RADIO OMAN, Sīb — Mideast • DS • 100 kW
          PAKISTAN
          PAKISTAN BC CORP, Quetta — DS • 10 kW
                                     DS • 10 kW • ALT. FREQ. TO 7150 kHz
          QATAR
          †QATAR BC SERVICE, Doha-Al Khaisah — W • Mideast & N Africa • 250 kW
                                               W • Europe • 250 kW
          RUSSIA
          †GOLOS ROSSII, Komsomol'sk 'Amure — W • E Asia & SE Asia • 1000 kW
(con'd)   †VOICE OF RUSSIA, Moscow — W • Europe • 250 kW

SEASONAL S OR W   1-HR TIMESHIFT MIDYEAR ⬅ OR ➡   JAMMING / OR /\   EARLIEST HEARD ◁   LATEST HEARD ▷   NEW FOR 1996 †

FREQUENCY   COUNTRY, STATION, LOCATION   TARGET • NETWORK • POWER (kW)   World Time

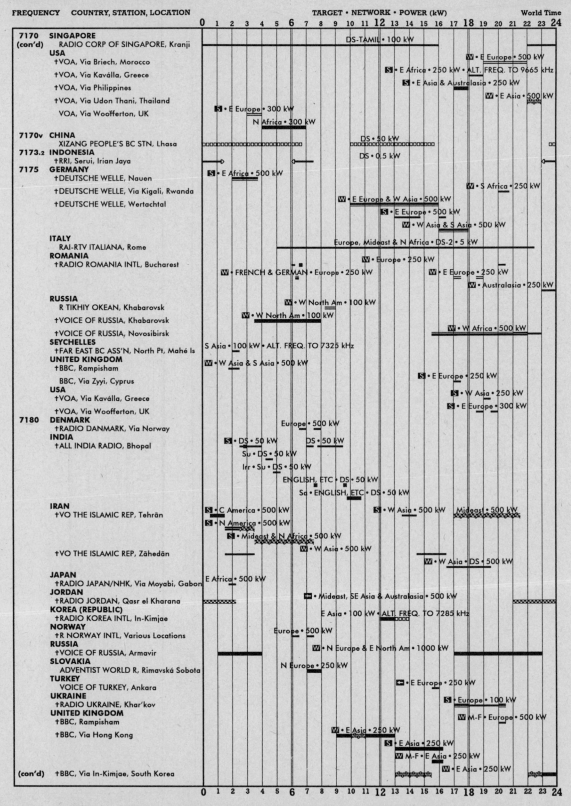

Frequency	Country, Station, Location	Target • Network • Power
7170 (con'd)	**SINGAPORE** RADIO CORP OF SINGAPORE, Kranji	DS-TAMIL • 100 kW
	USA †VOA, Via Briech, Morocco	W • E Europe • 500 kW
	†VOA, Via Kaválla, Greece	S • E Africa • 250 kW • ALT. FREQ. TO 9665 kHz
	†VOA, Via Philippines	S • E Asia & Australasia • 250 kW
	†VOA, Via Udon Thani, Thailand	W • E Asia • 500 kW
	VOA, Via Woofferton, UK	S • E Europe • 300 kW / N Africa • 300 kW
7170v	**CHINA** XIZANG PEOPLE'S BC STN, Lhasa	DS • 50 kW
7173.2	**INDONESIA** †RRI, Serui, Irian Jaya	DS • 0.5 kW
7175	**GERMANY** †DEUTSCHE WELLE, Nauen	S • E Africa • 500 kW
	†DEUTSCHE WELLE, Via Kigali, Rwanda	W • S Africa • 250 kW
	†DEUTSCHE WELLE, Wertachtal	W • E Europe & W Asia • 500 kW / S • E Europe • 500 kW / W • W Asia & S Asia • 500 kW
	ITALY RAI-RTV ITALIANA, Rome	Europe, Mideast & N Africa • DS-2 • 5 kW
	ROMANIA †RADIO ROMANIA INTL, Bucharest	W • Europe • 250 kW / W • FRENCH & GERMAN • Europe • 250 kW / W • E Europe • 250 kW / W • Australasia • 250 kW
	RUSSIA R TIKHIY OKEAN, Khabarovsk	W • W North Am • 100 kW
	†VOICE OF RUSSIA, Khabarovsk	W • W North Am • 100 kW
	†VOICE OF RUSSIA, Novosibirsk	W • W Africa • 500 kW
	SEYCHELLES †FAR EAST BC ASS'N, North Pt, Mahé Is	S Asia • 100 kW • ALT. FREQ. TO 7325 kHz
	UNITED KINGDOM †BBC, Rampisham	W • W Asia & S Asia • 500 kW
	BBC, Via Zyyi, Cyprus	S • E Europe • 250 kW
	USA †VOA, Via Kaválla, Greece	S • W Asia • 250 kW
	†VOA, Via Woofferton, UK	S • E Europe • 300 kW
7180	**DENMARK** †RADIO DANMARK, Via Norway	Europe • 500 kW
	INDIA †ALL INDIA RADIO, Bhopal	S • DS • 50 kW / DS • 50 kW / Su • DS • 50 kW / Irr • Su • DS • 50 kW / ENGLISH, ETC • DS • 50 kW / Sa • ENGLISH, ETC • DS • 50 kW
	IRAN †VO THE ISLAMIC REP, Tehrān	S • C America • 500 kW / W • W Asia • 500 kW / Mideast • 500 kW / S • N America • 500 kW / S • Mideast & N Africa • 500 kW
	†VO THE ISLAMIC REP, Zāhedān	W • W Asia • DS • 500 kW
	JAPAN †RADIO JAPAN/NHK, Via Moyabi, Gabon	E Africa • 500 kW
	JORDAN †RADIO JORDAN, Qasr el Kharana	Mideast, SE Asia & Australasia • 500 kW
	KOREA (REPUBLIC) †RADIO KOREA INTL, In-Kimjae	E Asia • 100 kW • ALT. FREQ. TO 7285 kHz
	NORWAY †R NORWAY INTL, Various Locations	Europe • 500 kW
	RUSSIA †VOICE OF RUSSIA, Armavir	W • N Europe & E North Am • 1000 kW
	SLOVAKIA ADVENTIST WORLD R, Rimavská Sobota	N Europe • 250 kW
	TURKEY VOICE OF TURKEY, Ankara	E Europe • 250 kW
	UKRAINE †RADIO UKRAINE, Khar'kov	S • Europe • 100 kW
	UNITED KINGDOM †BBC, Rampisham	W • M-F • Europe • 500 kW
	†BBC, Via Hong Kong	W • E Asia • 250 kW / S • E Asia • 250 kW / W • M-F • E Asia • 250 kW / W • E Asia • 250 kW
(con'd)	†BBC, Via In-Kimjae, South Korea	

ENGLISH ▬   ARABIC ⧓   CHINESE ▫▫▫   FRENCH ▭   GERMAN ▬   RUSSIAN ═   SPANISH ▬   OTHER ▬

FREQUENCY   COUNTRY, STATION, LOCATION

TARGET • NETWORK • POWER (kW)   World Time

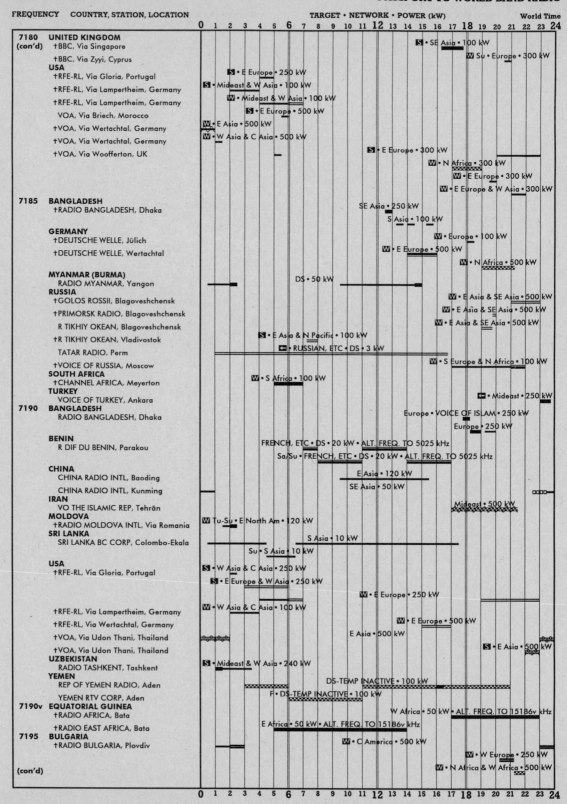

Frequency	Country / Station / Location	Target • Network • Power
7180 (con'd)	**UNITED KINGDOM**	
	†BBC, Via Singapore	S • SE Asia • 100 kW
	†BBC, Via Zyyi, Cyprus	W • Su • Europe • 300 kW
	USA	
	†RFE-RL, Via Gloria, Portugal	S • E Europe • 250 kW
	†RFE-RL, Via Lampertheim, Germany	S • Mideast & W Asia • 100 kW
	†RFE-RL, Via Lampertheim, Germany	W • Mideast & W Asia • 100 kW
	VOA, Via Briech, Morocco	S • E Europe • 500 kW
	†VOA, Via Wertachtal, Germany	W • E Asia • 500 kW
	†VOA, Via Wertachtal, Germany	W • W Asia & C Asia • 500 kW
	†VOA, Via Woofferton, UK	S • E Europe • 300 kW / W • N Africa • 300 kW / W • E Europe • 300 kW / W • E Europe & W Asia • 300 kW
7185	**BANGLADESH**	
	†RADIO BANGLADESH, Dhaka	SE Asia • 250 kW / S Asia • 100 kW
	GERMANY	
	†DEUTSCHE WELLE, Jülich	W • Europe • 100 kW
	†DEUTSCHE WELLE, Wertachtal	W • E Europe • 500 kW / W • N Africa • 500 kW
	MYANMAR (BURMA)	
	RADIO MYANMAR, Yangon	DS • 50 kW
	RUSSIA	
	†GOLOS ROSSII, Blagoveshchensk	W • E Asia & SE Asia • 500 kW
	†PRIMORSK RADIO, Blagoveshchensk	W • E Asia & SE Asia • 500 kW
	R TIKHIY OKEAN, Blagoveshchensk	W • E Asia & SE Asia • 500 kW
	†R TIKHIY OKEAN, Vladivostok	S • E Asia & N Pacific • 100 kW
	TATAR RADIO, Perm	RUSSIAN, ETC • DS • 3 kW
	†VOICE OF RUSSIA, Moscow	W • S Europe & N Africa • 100 kW
	SOUTH AFRICA	
	†CHANNEL AFRICA, Meyerton	W • S Africa • 100 kW
	TURKEY	
	VOICE OF TURKEY, Ankara	• Mideast • 250 kW
7190	**BANGLADESH**	
	RADIO BANGLADESH, Dhaka	Europe • VOICE OF ISLAM • 250 kW / Europe • 250 kW
	BENIN	
	R DIF DU BENIN, Parakou	FRENCH, ETC • DS • 20 kW • ALT. FREQ. TO 5025 kHz / Sa/Su • FRENCH, ETC • DS • 20 kW • ALT. FREQ. TO 5025 kHz
	CHINA	
	CHINA RADIO INTL, Baoding	E Asia • 120 kW
	CHINA RADIO INTL, Kunming	SE Asia • 50 kW
	IRAN	
	VO THE ISLAMIC REP, Tehrān	Mideast • 500 kW
	MOLDOVA	
	†RADIO MOLDOVA INTL, Via Romania	W • Tu-Su • E North Am • 120 kW
	SRI LANKA	
	SRI LANKA BC CORP, Colombo-Ekala	S Asia • 10 kW / Su • S Asia • 10 kW
	USA	
	†RFE-RL, Via Gloria, Portugal	S • W Asia & C Asia • 250 kW / S • E Europe & W Asia • 250 kW / W • E Europe • 250 kW
	†RFE-RL, Via Lampertheim, Germany	W • W Asia & C Asia • 100 kW
	†RFE-RL, Via Wertachtal, Germany	W • E Europe • 500 kW
	†VOA, Via Udon Thani, Thailand	E Asia • 500 kW
	†VOA, Via Udon Thani, Thailand	S • E Asia • 500 kW
	UZBEKISTAN	
	RADIO TASHKENT, Tashkent	S • Mideast & W Asia • 240 kW
	YEMEN	
	REP OF YEMEN RADIO, Aden	DS-TEMP INACTIVE • 100 kW
	YEMEN RTV CORP, Aden	F • DS-TEMP INACTIVE • 100 kW
7190v	**EQUATORIAL GUINEA**	
	†RADIO AFRICA, Bata	W Africa • 50 kW • ALT. FREQ. TO 15186v kHz
	†RADIO EAST AFRICA, Bata	E Africa • 50 kW • ALT. FREQ. TO 15186v kHz
7195	**BULGARIA**	
	†RADIO BULGARIA, Plovdiv	W • C America • 500 kW / W • W Europe • 250 kW / W • N Africa & W Africa • 500 kW
(con'd)		

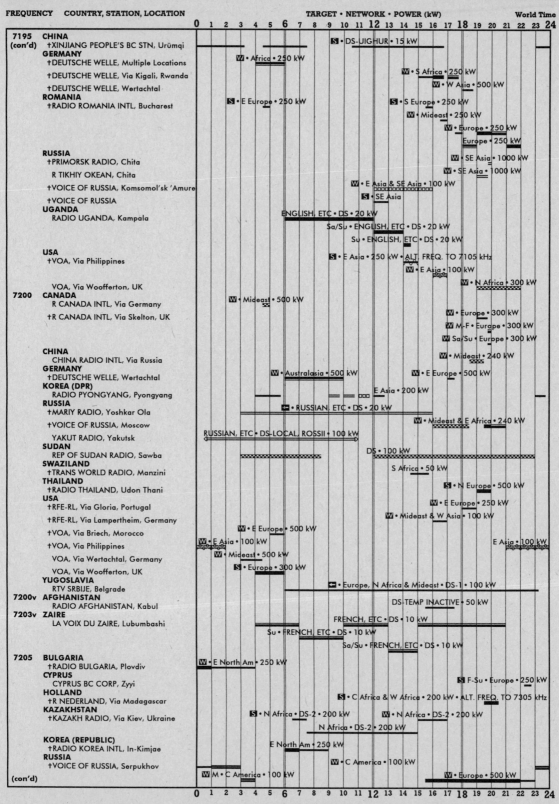

FREQUENCY   COUNTRY, STATION, LOCATION   TARGET • NETWORK • POWER (kW)   World Time

7195 CHINA
(con'd)   †XINJIANG PEOPLE'S BC STN, Urümqi — S • DS-UIGHUR • 15 kW
GERMANY
   †DEUTSCHE WELLE, Multiple Locations — W • Africa • 250 kW
   †DEUTSCHE WELLE, Via Kigali, Rwanda — W • S Africa • 250 kW / W • W Asia • 500 kW
   †DEUTSCHE WELLE, Wertachtal
ROMANIA
   †RADIO ROMANIA INTL, Bucharest — S • E Europe • 250 kW / S • S Europe • 250 kW / W • Mideast • 250 kW / W • Europe • 250 kW / Europe • 250 kW
RUSSIA
   †PRIMORSK RADIO, Chita — W • SE Asia • 1000 kW
   R TIKHIY OKEAN, Chita — W • SE Asia • 1000 kW
   †VOICE OF RUSSIA, Komsomol'sk 'Amure — W • E Asia & SE Asia • 100 kW
   †VOICE OF RUSSIA — S • SE Asia
UGANDA
   RADIO UGANDA, Kampala — ENGLISH, ETC • DS • 20 kW / Sa/Su • ENGLISH, ETC • DS • 20 kW / Su • ENGLISH, ETC • DS • 20 kW
USA
   †VOA, Via Philippines — S • E Asia • 250 kW • ALT. FREQ. TO 7105 kHz / W • E Asia • 100 kW
   VOA, Via Woofferton, UK — W • N Africa • 300 kW
7200 CANADA
   R CANADA INTL, Via Germany — W • Mideast • 500 kW
   †R CANADA INTL, Via Skelton, UK — W • Europe • 300 kW / W • M-F • Europe • 300 kW / W • Sa/Su • Europe • 300 kW
CHINA
   CHINA RADIO INTL, Via Russia — W • Mideast • 240 kW
GERMANY
   †DEUTSCHE WELLE, Wertachtal — W • Australasia • 500 kW / W • E Europe • 500 kW
KOREA (DPR)
   RADIO PYONGYANG, Pyongyang — E Asia • 200 kW
RUSSIA
   †MARIY RADIO, Yoshkar Ola — • RUSSIAN, ETC • DS • 20 kW
   †VOICE OF RUSSIA, Moscow — W • Mideast & E Africa • 240 kW
   YAKUT RADIO, Yakutsk — RUSSIAN, ETC • DS-LOCAL, ROSSII • 100 kW
SUDAN
   REP OF SUDAN RADIO, Sawba — DS • 100 kW
SWAZILAND
   †TRANS WORLD RADIO, Manzini — S Africa • 50 kW
THAILAND
   †RADIO THAILAND, Udon Thani — S • N Europe • 500 kW
USA
   †RFE-RL, Via Gloria, Portugal — W • E Europe • 250 kW
   †RFE-RL, Via Lampertheim, Germany — W • Mideast & W Asia • 100 kW
   †VOA, Via Briech, Morocco — W • E Europe • 500 kW
   †VOA, Via Philippines — W • E Asia • 100 kW / E Asia • 100 kW
   VOA, Via Wertachtal, Germany — W • Mideast • 500 kW
   VOA, Via Woofferton, UK — S • Europe • 300 kW
YUGOSLAVIA
   RTV SRBIJE, Belgrade — • Europe, N Africa & Mideast • DS-1 • 100 kW
7200v AFGHANISTAN
   RADIO AFGHANISTAN, Kabul — DS-TEMP INACTIVE • 50 kW
7203v ZAIRE
   LA VOIX DU ZAIRE, Lubumbashi — FRENCH, ETC • DS • 10 kW / Su • FRENCH, ETC • DS • 10 kW / Sa/Su • FRENCH, ETC • DS • 10 kW
7205 BULGARIA
   †RADIO BULGARIA, Plovdiv — W • E North Am • 250 kW
CYPRUS
   CYPRUS BC CORP, Zyyi — S • F-Su • Europe • 250 kW
HOLLAND
   †R NEDERLAND, Via Madagascar — S • C Africa & W Africa • 200 kW • ALT. FREQ. TO 7305 kHz
KAZAKHSTAN
   †KAZAKH RADIO, Via Kiev, Ukraine — S • N Africa • DS-2 • 200 kW / W • N Africa • DS-2 • 200 kW / N Africa • DS-2 • 200 kW
KOREA (REPUBLIC)
   †RADIO KOREA INTL, In-Kimjae — E North Am • 250 kW
RUSSIA
   †VOICE OF RUSSIA, Serpukhov — W • C America • 100 kW / W • M • C America • 100 kW / W • Europe • 500 kW
(con'd)

ENGLISH ▬   ARABIC ≋   CHINESE □□□   FRENCH ▬   GERMAN ▬   RUSSIAN ═   SPANISH ▬   OTHER ▬

FREQUENCY   COUNTRY, STATION, LOCATION

TARGET • NETWORK • POWER (kW)   World Time

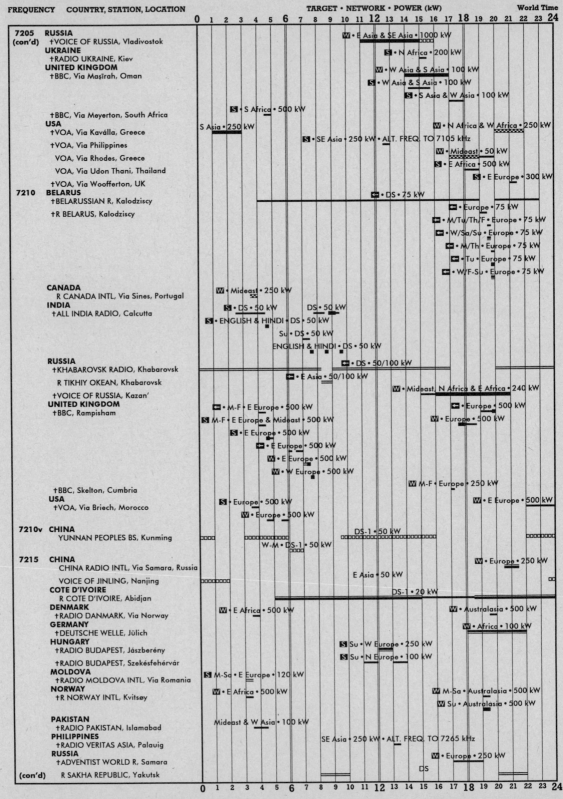

7205	**RUSSIA**
(con'd)	†VOICE OF RUSSIA, Vladivostok
	UKRAINE
	†RADIO UKRAINE, Kiev
	UNITED KINGDOM
	†BBC, Via Maṣīrah, Oman
	†BBC, Via Meyerton, South Africa
	USA
	†VOA, Via Kaválla, Greece
	†VOA, Via Philippines
	VOA, Via Rhodes, Greece
	VOA, Via Udon Thani, Thailand
	†VOA, Via Woofferton, UK
7210	**BELARUS**
	†BELARUSSIAN R, Kalodziscy
	†R BELARUS, Kalodziscy
	CANADA
	R CANADA INTL, Via Sines, Portugal
	INDIA
	†ALL INDIA RADIO, Calcutta
	RUSSIA
	†KHABAROVSK RADIO, Khabarovsk
	R TIKHIY OKEAN, Khabarovsk
	†VOICE OF RUSSIA, Kazan'
	UNITED KINGDOM
	†BBC, Rampisham
	†BBC, Skelton, Cumbria
	USA
	†VOA, Via Briech, Morocco
7210v	**CHINA**
	YUNNAN PEOPLES BS, Kunming
7215	**CHINA**
	CHINA RADIO INTL, Via Samara, Russia
	VOICE OF JINLING, Nanjing
	COTE D'IVOIRE
	R COTE D'IVOIRE, Abidjan
	DENMARK
	†RADIO DANMARK, Via Norway
	GERMANY
	†DEUTSCHE WELLE, Jülich
	HUNGARY
	†RADIO BUDAPEST, Jászberény
	†RADIO BUDAPEST, Székésfehérvár
	MOLDOVA
	†RADIO MOLDOVA INTL, Via Romania
	NORWAY
	†R NORWAY INTL, Kvitsøy
	PAKISTAN
	†RADIO PAKISTAN, Islamabad
	PHILIPPINES
	†RADIO VERITAS ASIA, Palauig
	RUSSIA
	†ADVENTIST WORLD R, Samara
(con'd)	R SAKHA REPUBLIC, Yakutsk

Bars / annotations (left to right by World Time):

- W • E Asia & SE Asia • 1000 kW
- S • N Africa • 200 kW
- W • W Asia & S Asia • 100 kW
- S • W Asia & S Asia • 100 kW
- S Asia & W Asia • 100 kW
- S • S Africa • 500 kW
- S Asia • 250 kW
- W • N Africa & W Africa • 250 kW
- S • SE Asia • 250 kW • ALT. FREQ. TO 7105 kHz
- W • Mideast • 50 kW
- S • E Africa • 500 kW
- S • E Europe • 300 kW
- • DS • 75 kW
- • Europe • 75 kW
- M/Tu/Th/F • Europe • 75 kW
- W/Sa/Su • Europe • 75 kW
- M/Th • Europe • 75 kW
- Tu • Europe • 75 kW
- W/F-Su • Europe • 75 kW
- W • Mideast • 250 kW
- S • DS • 50 kW   DS • 50 kW
- S • ENGLISH & HINDI DS • 50 kW
- Su • DS • 50 kW
- ENGLISH & HINDI • DS • 50 kW
- • DS • 50/100 kW
- • E Asia • 50/100 kW
- W • Mideast, N Africa & E Africa • 240 kW
- • M-F • E Europe • 500 kW   • Europe • 500 kW
- S M-F • E Europe & Mideast • 500 kW   W • Europe • 500 kW
- S • E Europe • 500 kW
- • E Europe • 500 kW
- W • E Europe • 500 kW
- W • W Europe • 500 kW
- W M-F • Europe • 250 kW
- S • Europe • 500 kW   W • E Europe • 500 kW
- W • Europe • 500 kW
- DS-1 • 50 kW
- W-M • DS-1 • 50 kW
- W • Europe • 250 kW
- E Asia • 50 kW
- DS-1 • 20 kW
- W • E Africa • 500 kW   W • Australasia • 500 kW
- W • Africa • 100 kW
- S Su • W Europe • 250 kW
- S Su • N Europe • 100 kW
- S M-Sa • E Europe • 120 kW
- W • E Africa • 500 kW   W M-Sa • Australasia • 500 kW
- W Su • Australasia • 500 kW
- Mideast & W Asia • 100 kW
- SE Asia • 250 kW • ALT. FREQ. TO 7265 kHz
- W • Europe • 250 kW
- DS

FREQUENCY   COUNTRY, STATION, LOCATION   TARGET • NETWORK • POWER (kW)   World Time

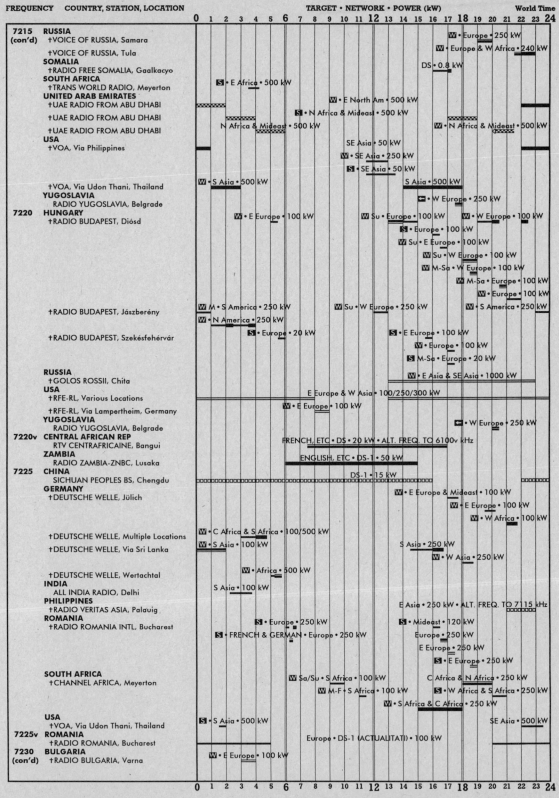

Frequency	Country / Station / Location	Notes
7215 (con'd)	**RUSSIA**	
	†VOICE OF RUSSIA, Samara	W • Europe • 250 kW
	†VOICE OF RUSSIA, Tula	W • Europe & W Africa • 240 kW
	SOMALIA	
	†RADIO FREE SOMALIA, Gaalkacyo	DS • 0.8 kW
	SOUTH AFRICA	
	†TRANS WORLD RADIO, Meyerton	S • E Africa • 500 kW
	UNITED ARAB EMIRATES	
	†UAE RADIO FROM ABU DHABI	W • E North Am • 500 kW
	†UAE RADIO FROM ABU DHABI	S • N Africa & Mideast • 500 kW
	†UAE RADIO FROM ABU DHABI	N Africa & Mideast • 500 kW / W • N Africa & Mideast • 500 kW
	USA	
	†VOA, Via Philippines	SE Asia • 50 kW / W • SE Asia • 250 kW / S • SE Asia • 50 kW
	†VOA, Via Udon Thani, Thailand	W • S Asia • 500 kW / S Asia • 500 kW
	YUGOSLAVIA	
	RADIO YUGOSLAVIA, Belgrade	• W Europe • 250 kW
7220	**HUNGARY**	
	†RADIO BUDAPEST, Diósd	W • E Europe • 100 kW / W Su • Europe • 100 kW / W • W Europe • 100 kW
		S • Europe • 100 kW
		W Su • E Europe • 100 kW
		W Su • W Europe • 100 kW
		W M-Sa • W Europe • 100 kW
		W M-Sa • Europe • 100 kW
		W • Europe • 100 kW
	†RADIO BUDAPEST, Jászberény	W M • S America • 250 kW / W Su • W Europe • 250 kW / W • S America • 250 kW
		W • N America • 250 kW
	†RADIO BUDAPEST, Szekésfehérvár	S • Europe • 20 kW / S • E Europe • 100 kW
		W • Europe • 100 kW
		S M-Sa • Europe • 20 kW
	RUSSIA	
	†GOLOS ROSSII, Chita	W • E Asia & SE Asia • 1000 kW
	USA	
	†RFE-RL, Various Locations	E Europe & W Asia • 100/250/300 kW
	†RFE-RL, Via Lampertheim, Germany	W • E Europe • 100 kW
	YUGOSLAVIA	
	RADIO YUGOSLAVIA, Belgrade	• W Europe • 250 kW
7220v	**CENTRAL AFRICAN REP**	
	RTV CENTRAFRICAINE, Bangui	FRENCH, ETC • DS • 20 kW • ALT. FREQ. TO 6100v kHz
	ZAMBIA	
	RADIO ZAMBIA-ZNBC, Lusaka	ENGLISH, ETC • DS-1 • 50 kW
7225	**CHINA**	
	SICHUAN PEOPLES BS, Chengdu	DS-1 • 15 kW
	GERMANY	
	†DEUTSCHE WELLE, Jülich	W • E Europe & Mideast • 100 kW
		W • E Europe • 100 kW
		W • W Africa • 100 kW
	†DEUTSCHE WELLE, Multiple Locations	W • C Africa & S Africa • 100/500 kW
	†DEUTSCHE WELLE, Via Sri Lanka	W • S Asia • 100 kW / S Asia • 250 kW
		W • W Asia • 250 kW
	†DEUTSCHE WELLE, Wertachtal	W • Africa • 500 kW
	INDIA	
	ALL INDIA RADIO, Delhi	S Asia • 100 kW
	PHILIPPINES	
	†RADIO VERITAS ASIA, Palauig	E Asia • 250 kW • ALT. FREQ. TO 7115 kHz
	ROMANIA	
	†RADIO ROMANIA INTL, Bucharest	S • Europe • 250 kW / S • Mideast • 120 kW
		S • FRENCH & GERMAN • Europe • 250 kW / Europe • 250 kW
		E Europe • 250 kW
		S • E Europe • 250 kW
	SOUTH AFRICA	
	†CHANNEL AFRICA, Meyerton	W Sa/Su • S Africa • 100 kW / C Africa & N Africa • 250 kW
		W M-F • S Africa • 100 kW / S • W Africa & S Africa • 250 kW
		W • S Africa & C Africa • 250 kW
	USA	
	†VOA, Via Udon Thani, Thailand	S • S Asia • 500 kW / SE Asia • 500 kW
7225v	**ROMANIA**	
	†RADIO ROMANIA, Bucharest	Europe • DS-1 (ACTUALITATI) • 100 kW
7230 (con'd)	**BULGARIA**	
	†RADIO BULGARIA, Varna	W • E Europe • 100 kW

ENGLISH ▬▬   ARABIC ▧▧▧   CHINESE ▫▫▫   FRENCH ▭▭   GERMAN ▬▬   RUSSIAN ═══   SPANISH ▬▬   OTHER ▬▬

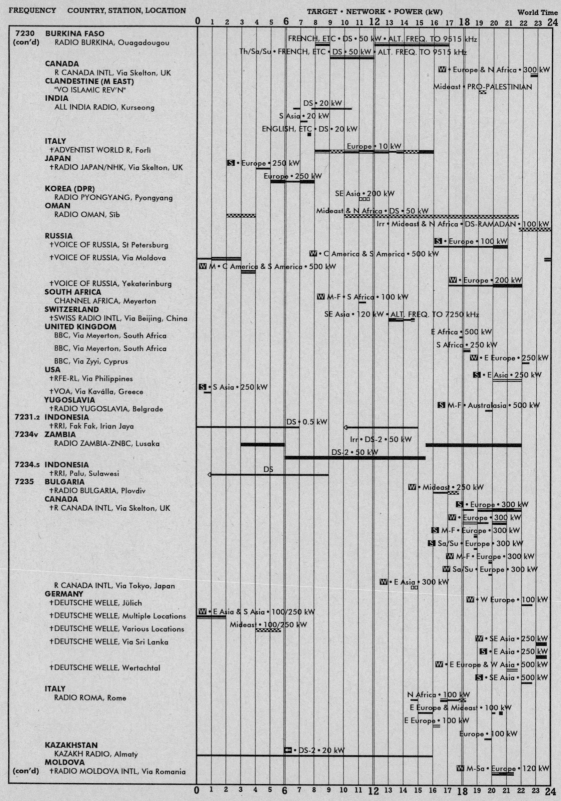

FREQUENCY   COUNTRY, STATION, LOCATION

TARGET • NETWORK • POWER (kW)   World Time

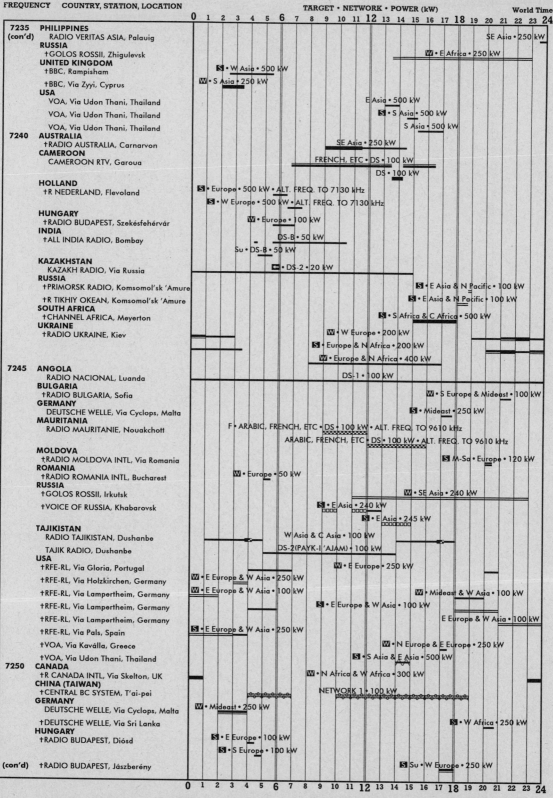

7235	**PHILIPPINES**
(con'd)	RADIO VERITAS ASIA, Palauig
	RUSSIA
	†GOLOS ROSSII, Zhigulevsk
	UNITED KINGDOM
	†BBC, Rampisham
	†BBC, Via Zyyi, Cyprus
	USA
	VOA, Via Udon Thani, Thailand
	VOA, Via Udon Thani, Thailand
	VOA, Via Udon Thani, Thailand
7240	**AUSTRALIA**
	†RADIO AUSTRALIA, Carnarvon
	CAMEROON
	CAMEROON RTV, Garoua
	HOLLAND
	†R NEDERLAND, Flevoland
	HUNGARY
	†RADIO BUDAPEST, Szekésfehérvár
	INDIA
	†ALL INDIA RADIO, Bombay
	KAZAKHSTAN
	KAZAKH RADIO, Via Russia
	RUSSIA
	†PRIMORSK RADIO, Komsomol'sk 'Amure
	†R TIKHIY OKEAN, Komsomol'sk 'Amure
	SOUTH AFRICA
	†CHANNEL AFRICA, Meyerton
	UKRAINE
	†RADIO UKRAINE, Kiev
7245	**ANGOLA**
	RADIO NACIONAL, Luanda
	BULGARIA
	†RADIO BULGARIA, Sofia
	GERMANY
	DEUTSCHE WELLE, Via Cyclops, Malta
	MAURITANIA
	RADIO MAURITANIE, Nouakchott
	MOLDOVA
	†RADIO MOLDOVA INTL, Via Romania
	ROMANIA
	†RADIO ROMANIA INTL, Bucharest
	RUSSIA
	†GOLOS ROSSII, Irkutsk
	†VOICE OF RUSSIA, Khabarovsk
	TAJIKISTAN
	RADIO TAJIKISTAN, Dushanbe
	TAJIK RADIO, Dushanbe
	USA
	†RFE-RL, Via Gloria, Portugal
	†RFE-RL, Via Holzkirchen, Germany
	†RFE-RL, Via Lampertheim, Germany
	†RFE-RL, Via Lampertheim, Germany
	†RFE-RL, Via Lampertheim, Germany
	†RFE-RL, Via Pals, Spain
	†VOA, Via Kaválla, Greece
	†VOA, Via Udon Thani, Thailand
7250	**CANADA**
	†R CANADA INTL, Via Skelton, UK
	CHINA (TAIWAN)
	†CENTRAL BC SYSTEM, T'ai-pei
	GERMANY
	DEUTSCHE WELLE, Via Cyclops, Malta
	†DEUTSCHE WELLE, Via Sri Lanka
	HUNGARY
	†RADIO BUDAPEST, Diósd
(con'd)	†RADIO BUDAPEST, Jászberény

Station schedule annotations:

- SE Asia • 250 kW
- W • E Africa • 250 kW
- S • W Asia • 500 kW
- W • S Asia • 250 kW
- E Asia • 500 kW
- S • S Asia • 500 kW
- S Asia • 500 kW
- SE Asia • 250 kW
- FRENCH, ETC • DS • 100 kW
- DS • 100 kW
- S • Europe • 500 kW • ALT. FREQ. TO 7130 kHz
- S • W Europe • 500 kW • ALT. FREQ. TO 7130 kHz
- W • Europe • 100 kW
- DS-B • 50 kW
- Su • DS-B • 50 kW
- • DS-2 • 20 kW
- S • E Asia & N Pacific • 100 kW
- S • E Asia & N Pacific • 100 kW
- S • S Africa & C Africa • 500 kW
- W • W Europe • 200 kW
- S • Europe & N Africa • 200 kW
- W • Europe & N Africa • 400 kW
- DS-1 • 100 kW
- W • S Europe & Mideast • 100 kW
- S • Mideast • 250 kW
- F • ARABIC, FRENCH, ETC • DS • 100 kW • ALT. FREQ. TO 9610 kHz
- ARABIC, FRENCH, ETC • DS • 100 kW • ALT. FREQ. TO 9610 kHz
- S • M-Sa • Europe • 120 kW
- W • Europe • 50 kW
- W • SE Asia • 240 kW
- S • E Asia • 240 kW
- S • E Asia • 245 kW
- W Asia & C Asia • 100 kW
- DS-2 (PAYK-I 'AJAM) • 100 kW
- W • E Europe • 250 kW
- W • E Europe & W Asia • 250 kW
- W • E Europe & W Asia • 100 kW
- W • Mideast & W Asia • 100 kW
- S • E Europe & W Asia • 100 kW
- E Europe & W Asia • 100 kW
- S • E Europe & W Asia • 250 kW
- W • N Europe & E Europe • 250 kW
- S • S Asia & E Asia • 500 kW
- W • N Africa & W Africa • 300 kW
- NETWORK 1 • 100 kW
- W • Mideast • 250 kW
- S • W Africa • 250 kW
- S • E Europe • 100 kW
- S • S Europe • 100 kW
- S • Su • W Europe • 250 kW

ENGLISH ▬   ARABIC ⧉   CHINESE ⋯   FRENCH ▭   GERMAN ▬   RUSSIAN ═   SPANISH ▬   OTHER ▬

FREQUENCY   COUNTRY, STATION, LOCATION

TARGET • NETWORK • POWER (kW)   World Time

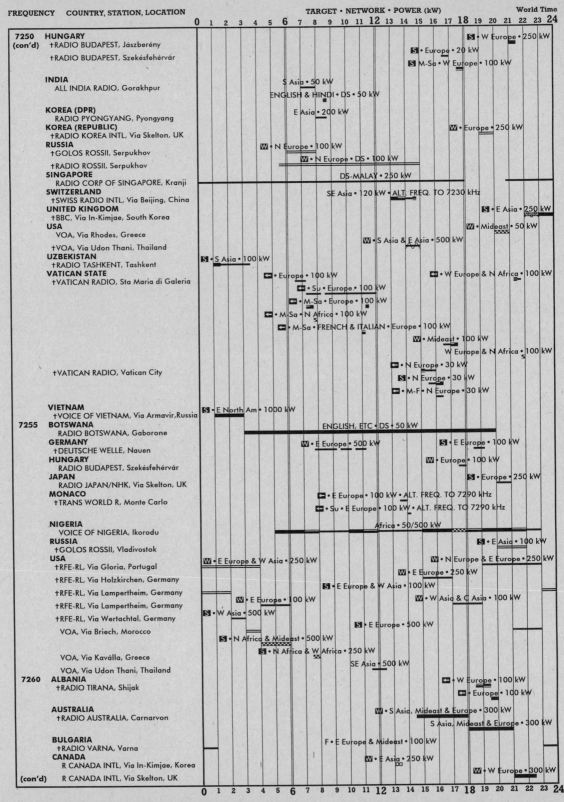

FREQUENCY	COUNTRY, STATION, LOCATION	TARGET • NETWORK • POWER (kW)
7250 (con'd)	HUNGARY	
	†RADIO BUDAPEST, Jászberény	S • W Europe • 250 kW
	†RADIO BUDAPEST, Szekésfehérvár	S • Europe • 20 kW
		S • M-Sa • W Europe • 100 kW
	INDIA	
	ALL INDIA RADIO, Gorakhpur	S Asia • 50 kW
		ENGLISH & HINDI • DS • 50 kW
	KOREA (DPR)	
	RADIO PYONGYANG, Pyongyang	E Asia • 200 kW
	KOREA (REPUBLIC)	
	†RADIO KOREA INTL, Via Skelton, UK	W • Europe • 250 kW
	RUSSIA	
	†GOLOS ROSSII, Serpukhov	W • N Europe • 100 kW
	†RADIO ROSSII, Serpukhov	W • N Europe • DS • 100 kW
	SINGAPORE	
	RADIO CORP OF SINGAPORE, Kranji	DS-MALAY • 250 kW
	SWITZERLAND	
	†SWISS RADIO INTL, Via Beijing, China	SE Asia • 120 kW • ALT. FREQ. TO 7230 kHz
	UNITED KINGDOM	
	†BBC, Via In-Kimjae, South Korea	S • E Asia • 250 kW
	USA	
	VOA, Via Rhodes, Greece	W • Mideast • 50 kW
	†VOA, Via Udon Thani, Thailand	W • S Asia & E Asia • 500 kW
	UZBEKISTAN	
	†RADIO TASHKENT, Tashkent	S • S Asia • 100 kW
	VATICAN STATE	
	†VATICAN RADIO, Sta Maria di Galeria	⊏ • Europe • 100 kW
		⊏ • W Europe & N Africa • 100 kW
		⊏ • Su • Europe • 100 kW
		⊏ • M-Sa • Europe • 100 kW
		⊏ • M-Sa • N Africa • 100 kW
		⊏ • M-Sa • FRENCH & ITALIAN • Europe • 100 kW
		W • Mideast • 100 kW
		W Europe & N Africa • 100 kW
	†VATICAN RADIO, Vatican City	⊏ • N Europe • 30 kW
		S • N Europe • 30 kW
		⊏ • M-F • N Europe • 30 kW
	VIETNAM	
	†VOICE OF VIETNAM, Via Armavir, Russia	S • E North Am • 1000 kW
7255	BOTSWANA	
	RADIO BOTSWANA, Gaborone	ENGLISH, ETC • DS • 50 kW
	GERMANY	
	†DEUTSCHE WELLE, Nauen	W • E Europe • 500 kW
		S • E Europe • 100 kW
	HUNGARY	
	RADIO BUDAPEST, Szekésfehérvár	W • Europe • 100 kW
	JAPAN	
	RADIO JAPAN/NHK, Via Skelton, UK	S • Europe • 250 kW
	MONACO	
	†TRANS WORLD R, Monte Carlo	⊏ • E Europe • 100 kW • ALT. FREQ. TO 7290 kHz
		⊏ • Su • E Europe • 100 kW • ALT. FREQ. TO 7290 kHz
	NIGERIA	
	VOICE OF NIGERIA, Ikorodu	Africa • 50/500 kW
	RUSSIA	
	†GOLOS ROSSII, Vladivostok	S • E Asia • 100 kW
	USA	
	†RFE-RL, Via Gloria, Portugal	W • E Europe & W Asia • 250 kW
		S • N Europe & E Europe • 250 kW
	†RFE-RL, Via Holzkirchen, Germany	W • E Europe • 250 kW
	†RFE-RL, Via Lampertheim, Germany	S • E Europe & W Asia • 100 kW
	†RFE-RL, Via Lampertheim, Germany	W • E Europe • 100 kW
		W • W Asia & C Asia • 100 kW
	†RFE-RL, Via Wertachtal, Germany	S • W Asia • 500 kW
	VOA, Via Briech, Morocco	S • E Europe • 500 kW
		S • N Africa & Mideast • 500 kW
	VOA, Via Kaválla, Greece	S • N Africa & W Africa • 250 kW
	VOA, Via Udon Thani, Thailand	SE Asia • 500 kW
7260	ALBANIA	
	†RADIO TIRANA, Shijak	⊏ • W Europe • 100 kW
		⊏ • Europe • 100 kW
	AUSTRALIA	
	†RADIO AUSTRALIA, Carnarvon	W • S Asia, Mideast & Europe • 300 kW
		S Asia, Mideast & Europe • 300 kW
	BULGARIA	
	†RADIO VARNA, Varna	F • E Europe & Mideast • 100 kW
	CANADA	
	R CANADA INTL, Via In-Kimjae, Korea	W • E Asia • 250 kW
(con'd)	R CANADA INTL, Via Skelton, UK	W • W Europe • 300 kW

SEASONAL S OR W   1-HR TIMESHIFT MIDYEAR ⊏ OR ⊐   JAMMING / OR ∧   EARLIEST HEARD ◁   LATEST HEARD ▷   NEW FOR 1996 †

FREQUENCY   COUNTRY, STATION, LOCATION

TARGET • NETWORK • POWER (kW)

World Time

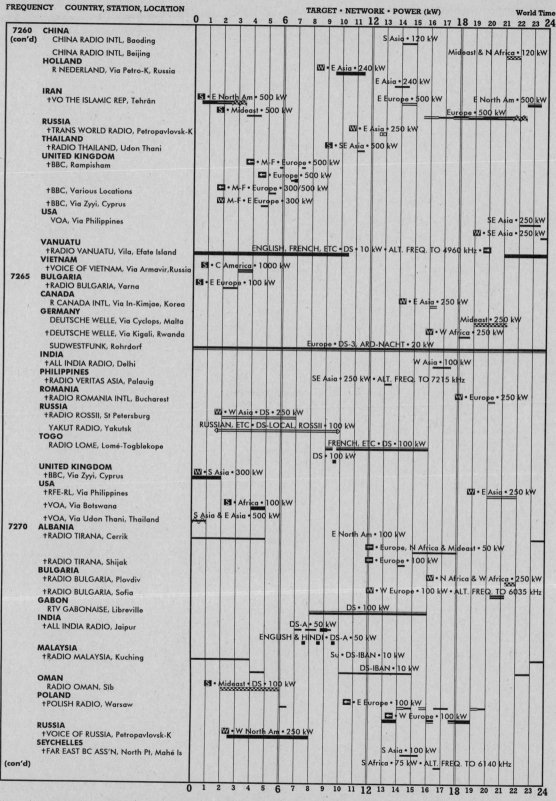

	0 1 2 3 4 5 6 7 8 9 10 11 12 13 14 15 16 17 18 19 20 21 22 23 24
7260 **CHINA**	
(con'd) CHINA RADIO INTL, Baoding	S Asia • 120 kW
CHINA RADIO INTL, Beijing	Mideast & N Africa • 120 kW
HOLLAND	
R NEDERLAND, Via Petro-K, Russia	W • E Asia • 240 kW
	E Asia • 240 kW
IRAN	
†VO THE ISLAMIC REP, Tehrān	S • E North Am • 500 kW E Europe • 500 kW E North Am • 500 kW
	S • Mideast • 500 kW Europe • 500 kW
RUSSIA	
†TRANS WORLD RADIO, Petropavlovsk-K	W • E Asia • 250 kW
THAILAND	
†RADIO THAILAND, Udon Thani	S • SE Asia • 500 kW
UNITED KINGDOM	
†BBC, Rampisham	⇦ • M-F • Europe • 500 kW
	⇦ • Europe • 500 kW
†BBC, Various Locations	⇦ • M-F • Europe • 300/500 kW
†BBC, Via Zyyi, Cyprus	W • M-F • E Europe • 300 kW
USA	
VOA, Via Philippines	SE Asia • 250 kW
	W • SE Asia • 250 kW
VANUATU	
†RADIO VANUATU, Vila, Efate Island	ENGLISH, FRENCH, ETC • DS • 10 kW • ALT. FREQ. TO 4960 kHz • ⇦
VIETNAM	
†VOICE OF VIETNAM, Via Armavir,Russia	S • C America • 1000 kW
7265 **BULGARIA**	
†RADIO BULGARIA, Varna	S • E Europe • 100 kW
CANADA	
R CANADA INTL, Via In-Kimjae, Korea	W • E Asia • 250 kW
GERMANY	
DEUTSCHE WELLE, Via Cyclops, Malta	Mideast • 250 kW
†DEUTSCHE WELLE, Via Kigali, Rwanda	W • W Africa • 250 kW
SUDWESTFUNK, Rohrdorf	Europe • DS-3, ARD-NACHT • 20 kW
INDIA	
†ALL INDIA RADIO, Delhi	W Asia • 100 kW
PHILIPPINES	
†RADIO VERITAS ASIA, Palauig	SE Asia • 250 kW • ALT. FREQ. TO 7215 kHz
ROMANIA	
†RADIO ROMANIA INTL, Bucharest	W • Europe • 250 kW
RUSSIA	
†RADIO ROSSII, St Petersburg	W • W Asia • DS • 250 kW
YAKUT RADIO, Yakutsk	RUSSIAN, ETC • DS-LOCAL, ROSSII • 100 kW
TOGO	
RADIO LOME, Lomé-Togblekope	FRENCH, ETC • DS • 100 kW
	DS • 100 kW
UNITED KINGDOM	
†BBC, Via Zyyi, Cyprus	W • S Asia • 300 kW
USA	
†RFE-RL, Via Philippines	W • E Asia • 250 kW
†VOA, Via Botswana	S • Africa • 100 kW
†VOA, Via Udon Thani, Thailand	S Asia & E Asia • 500 kW
7270 **ALBANIA**	
†RADIO TIRANA, Cerrik	E North Am • 100 kW
†RADIO TIRANA, Shijak	• Europe, N Africa & Mideast • 50 kW
	• Europe • 100 kW
BULGARIA	
†RADIO BULGARIA, Plovdiv	W • N Africa & W Africa • 250 kW
†RADIO BULGARIA, Sofia	W • W Europe • 100 kW • ALT. FREQ. TO 6035 kHz
GABON	
RTV GABONAISE, Libreville	DS • 100 kW
INDIA	
†ALL INDIA RADIO, Jaipur	DS-A • 50 kW
	ENGLISH & HINDI • DS-A • 50 kW
MALAYSIA	
†RADIO MALAYSIA, Kuching	Su • DS-IBAN • 10 kW
	DS-IBAN • 10 kW
OMAN	
RADIO OMAN, Sīb	S • Mideast • DS • 100 kW
POLAND	
†POLISH RADIO, Warsaw	⇦ • E Europe • 100 kW
	⇦ • W Europe • 100 kW
RUSSIA	
†VOICE OF RUSSIA, Petropavlovsk-K	W • W North Am • 250 kW
SEYCHELLES	
†FAR EAST BC ASS'N, North Pt, Mahé Is	S Asia • 100 kW
(con'd)	S Africa • 75 kW • ALT. FREQ. TO 6140 kHz

	0 1 2 3 4 5 6 7 8 9 10 11 12 13 14 15 16 17 18 19 20 21 22 23 24

ENGLISH ▬▬   ARABIC ⦚⦚⦚   CHINESE □□□   FRENCH ▭   GERMAN ▭▭   RUSSIAN ═══   SPANISH ▭▭   OTHER ▬

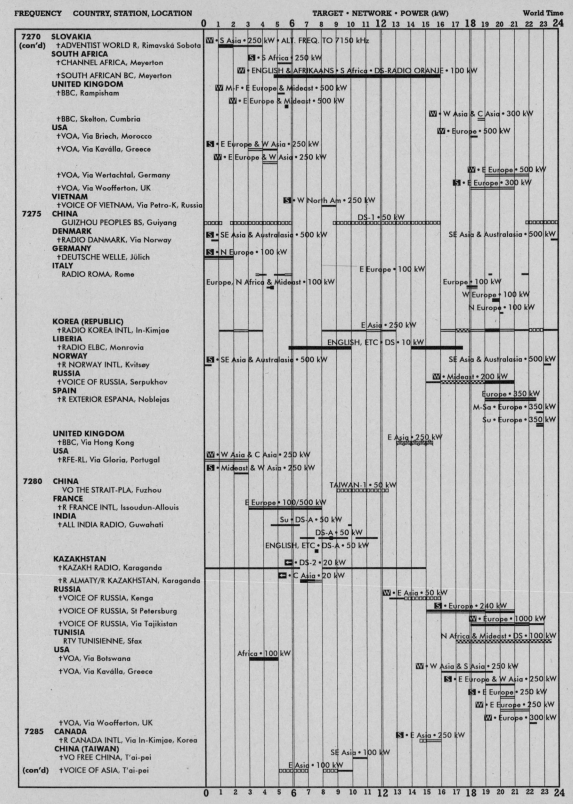

FREQUENCY   COUNTRY, STATION, LOCATION   TARGET • NETWORK • POWER (kW)   World Time

7270 SLOVAKIA
(con'd) †ADVENTIST WORLD R, Rimavská Sobota
SOUTH AFRICA
  †CHANNEL AFRICA, Meyerton
  †SOUTH AFRICAN BC, Meyerton
UNITED KINGDOM
  †BBC, Rampisham

  †BBC, Skelton, Cumbria
USA
  †VOA, Via Briech, Morocco
  †VOA, Via Kaválla, Greece

  †VOA, Via Wertachtal, Germany
  †VOA, Via Woofferton, UK
VIETNAM
  †VOICE OF VIETNAM, Via Petro-K, Russia
7275 CHINA
  GUIZHOU PEOPLES BS, Guiyang
DENMARK
  †RADIO DANMARK, Via Norway
GERMANY
  †DEUTSCHE WELLE, Jülich
ITALY
  RADIO ROMA, Rome

KOREA (REPUBLIC)
  †RADIO KOREA INTL, In-Kimjae
LIBERIA
  †RADIO ELBC, Monrovia
NORWAY
  †R NORWAY INTL, Kvitsøy
RUSSIA
  †VOICE OF RUSSIA, Serpukhov
SPAIN
  †R EXTERIOR ESPANA, Noblejas

UNITED KINGDOM
  †BBC, Via Hong Kong
USA
  †RFE-RL, Via Gloria, Portugal

7280 CHINA
  VO THE STRAIT-PLA, Fuzhou
FRANCE
  †R FRANCE INTL, Issoudun-Allouis
INDIA
  †ALL INDIA RADIO, Guwahati

KAZAKHSTAN
  †KAZAKH RADIO, Karaganda
  †R ALMATY/R KAZAKHSTAN, Karaganda
RUSSIA
  †VOICE OF RUSSIA, Kenga
  †VOICE OF RUSSIA, St Petersburg
  †VOICE OF RUSSIA, Via Tajikistan
TUNISIA
  RTV TUNISIENNE, Sfax
USA
  †VOA, Via Botswana
  †VOA, Via Kaválla, Greece

  †VOA, Via Woofferton, UK
7285 CANADA
  †R CANADA INTL, Via In-Kimjae, Korea
CHINA (TAIWAN)
  †VO FREE CHINA, T'ai-pei
(con'd) †VOICE OF ASIA, T'ai-pei

FREQUENCY　　COUNTRY, STATION, LOCATION　　　　　　TARGET • NETWORK • POWER (kW)　　　World Time

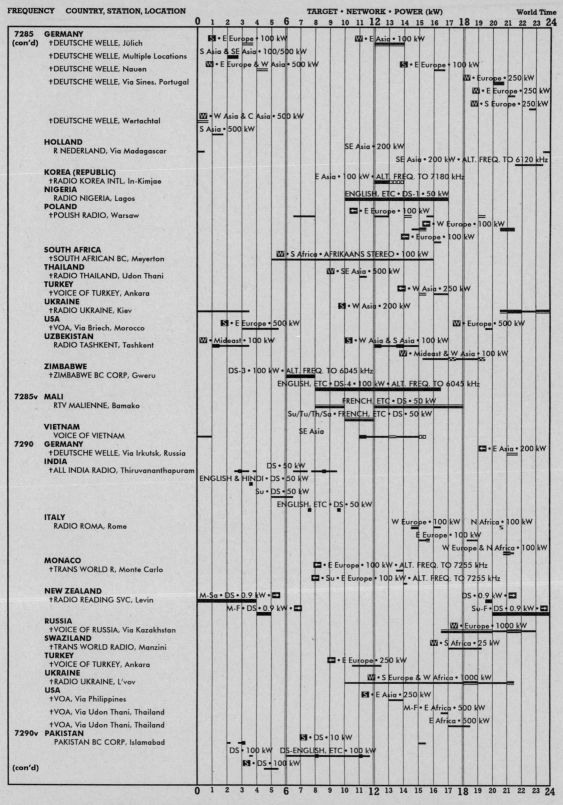

7285	GERMANY	
(con'd)	†DEUTSCHE WELLE, Jülich	S • E Europe • 100 kW　　W • E Asia • 100 kW
	†DEUTSCHE WELLE, Multiple Locations	S Asia & SE Asia • 100/500 kW
	†DEUTSCHE WELLE, Nauen	W • E Europe & W Asia • 500 kW　　S • E Europe • 100 kW
	†DEUTSCHE WELLE, Via Sines, Portugal	W • Europe • 250 kW / W • E Europe • 250 kW / W • S Europe • 250 kW
	†DEUTSCHE WELLE, Wertachtal	W • W Asia & C Asia • 500 kW / S Asia • 500 kW
	HOLLAND	
	R NEDERLAND, Via Madagascar	SE Asia • 200 kW / SE Asia • 200 kW • ALT. FREQ. TO 6120 kHz
	KOREA (REPUBLIC)	
	†RADIO KOREA INTL, In-Kimjae	E Asia • 100 kW • ALT. FREQ. TO 7180 kHz
	NIGERIA	
	RADIO NIGERIA, Lagos	ENGLISH, ETC • DS-1 • 50 kW
	POLAND	
	†POLISH RADIO, Warsaw	• E Europe • 100 kW / • W Europe • 100 kW / • Europe • 100 kW
	SOUTH AFRICA	
	†SOUTH AFRICAN BC, Meyerton	W • S Africa • AFRIKAANS STEREO • 100 kW
	THAILAND	
	†RADIO THAILAND, Udon Thani	W • SE Asia • 500 kW
	TURKEY	
	†VOICE OF TURKEY, Ankara	• W Asia • 250 kW
	UKRAINE	
	†RADIO UKRAINE, Kiev	S • W Asia • 200 kW
	USA	
	†VOA, Via Briech, Morocco	S • E Europe • 500 kW　　W • Europe • 500 kW
	UZBEKISTAN	
	RADIO TASHKENT, Tashkent	W • Mideast • 100 kW　　S • W Asia & S Asia • 100 kW / W • Mideast & W Asia • 100 kW
	ZIMBABWE	
	†ZIMBABWE BC CORP, Gweru	DS-3 • 100 kW • ALT. FREQ. TO 6045 kHz / ENGLISH, ETC • DS-4 • 100 kW • ALT. FREQ. TO 6045 kHz
7285v	MALI	
	RTV MALIENNE, Bamako	FRENCH, ETC • DS • 50 kW / Su/Tu/Th/Sa • FRENCH, ETC • DS • 50 kW
	VIETNAM	
	VOICE OF VIETNAM	SE Asia
7290	GERMANY	
	†DEUTSCHE WELLE, Via Irkutsk, Russia	• E Asia • 200 kW
	INDIA	
	†ALL INDIA RADIO, Thiruvananthapuram	DS • 50 kW / ENGLISH & HINDI • DS • 50 kW / Su • DS • 50 kW / ENGLISH, ETC • DS • 50 kW
	ITALY	
	RADIO ROMA, Rome	W Europe • 100 kW　N Africa • 100 kW / E Europe • 100 kW / W Europe & N Africa • 100 kW
	MONACO	
	†TRANS WORLD R, Monte Carlo	• E Europe • 100 kW • ALT. FREQ. TO 7255 kHz / • Su • E Europe • 100 kW • ALT. FREQ. TO 7255 kHz
	NEW ZEALAND	
	†RADIO READING SVC, Levin	M-Sa • DS • 0.9 kW • / DS • 0.9 kW • / M-F • DS • 0.9 kW • / Su-F • DS • 0.9 kW •
	RUSSIA	
	†VOICE OF RUSSIA, Via Kazakhstan	W • Europe • 1000 kW
	SWAZILAND	
	†TRANS WORLD RADIO, Manzini	W • S Africa • 25 kW
	TURKEY	
	†VOICE OF TURKEY, Ankara	• E Europe • 250 kW
	UKRAINE	
	†RADIO UKRAINE, L'vov	W • S Europe & W Africa • 1000 kW
	USA	
	†VOA, Via Philippines	S • E Asia • 250 kW
	†VOA, Via Udon Thani, Thailand	M-F • E Africa • 500 kW
	†VOA, Via Udon Thani, Thailand	E Africa • 500 kW
7290v	PAKISTAN	
	PAKISTAN BC CORP, Islamabad	S • DS • 10 kW / DS • 100 kW　DS-ENGLISH, ETC • 100 kW / S • DS • 100 kW
(con'd)		

ENGLISH ▬　ARABIC ⊠⊠⊠　CHINESE □□□　FRENCH ▬▬　GERMAN ▬▬　RUSSIAN ══　SPANISH ▬▬　OTHER ──

FREQUENCY   COUNTRY, STATION, LOCATION

TARGET • NETWORK • POWER (kW)

World Time

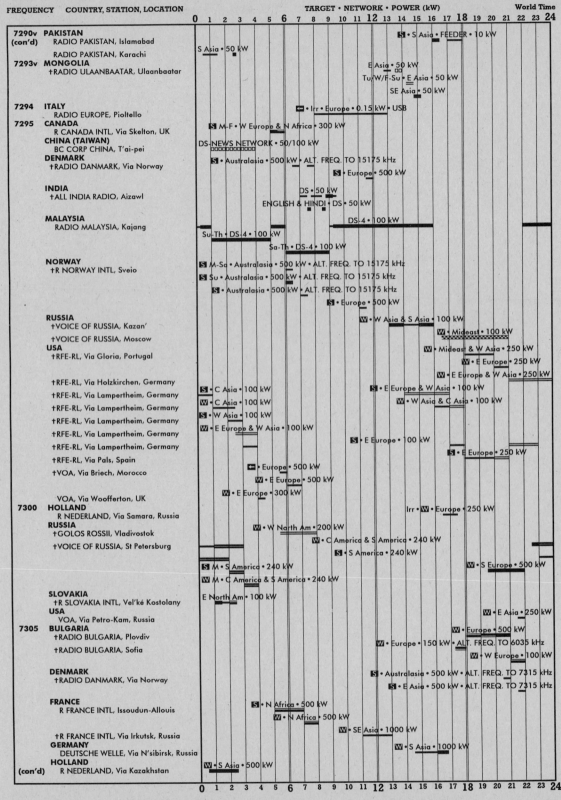

7290v	**PAKISTAN**
(con'd)	RADIO PAKISTAN, Islamabad
	RADIO PAKISTAN, Karachi
7293v	**MONGOLIA**
	†RADIO ULAANBAATAR, Ulaanbaatar
7294	**ITALY**
	RADIO EUROPE, Pioltello
7295	**CANADA**
	R CANADA INTL, Via Skelton, UK
	CHINA (TAIWAN)
	BC CORP CHINA, T'ai-pei
	DENMARK
	†RADIO DANMARK, Via Norway
	INDIA
	†ALL INDIA RADIO, Aizawl
	MALAYSIA
	RADIO MALAYSIA, Kajang
	NORWAY
	†R NORWAY INTL, Sveio
	RUSSIA
	†VOICE OF RUSSIA, Kazan'
	†VOICE OF RUSSIA, Moscow
	USA
	†RFE-RL, Via Gloria, Portugal
	†RFE-RL, Via Holzkirchen, Germany
	†RFE-RL, Via Lampertheim, Germany
	†RFE-RL, Via Lampertheim, Germany
	†RFE-RL, Via Lampertheim, Germany
	†RFE-RL, Via Lampertheim, Germany
	†RFE-RL, Via Lampertheim, Germany
	†RFE-RL, Via Pals, Spain
	†VOA, Via Briech, Morocco
	VOA, Via Woofferton, UK
7300	**HOLLAND**
	R NEDERLAND, Via Samara, Russia
	RUSSIA
	†GOLOS ROSSII, Vladivostok
	†VOICE OF RUSSIA, St Petersburg
	SLOVAKIA
	†R SLOVAKIA INTL, Vel'ké Kostolany
	USA
	VOA, Via Petro-Kam, Russia
7305	**BULGARIA**
	†RADIO BULGARIA, Plovdiv
	†RADIO BULGARIA, Sofia
	DENMARK
	†RADIO DANMARK, Via Norway
	FRANCE
	R FRANCE INTL, Issoudun-Allouis
	†R FRANCE INTL, Via Irkutsk, Russia
	GERMANY
	DEUTSCHE WELLE, Via N'sibirsk, Russia
	HOLLAND
(con'd)	R NEDERLAND, Via Kazakhstan

Schedule annotations (left to right along the time scale):

- RADIO PAKISTAN, Islamabad: S · S Asia · FEEDER · 10 kW
- RADIO PAKISTAN, Karachi: S Asia · 50 kW
- RADIO ULAANBAATAR: E Asia · 50 kW; Tu/W/F-Su · E Asia · 50 kW; SE Asia · 50 kW
- RADIO EUROPE: Irr · Europe · 0.15 kW · USB
- R CANADA INTL: S · M-F · W Europe & N Africa · 300 kW
- BC CORP CHINA: DS-NEWS NETWORK · 50/100 kW
- RADIO DANMARK: S · Australasia · 500 kW · ALT. FREQ. TO 15175 kHz; S · Europe · 500 kW
- ALL INDIA RADIO: DS · 50 kW; ENGLISH & HINDI · DS · 50 kW
- RADIO MALAYSIA: DS-4 · 100 kW; Su-Th · DS-4 · 100 kW; Sa-Th · DS-4 · 100 kW
- R NORWAY INTL: S · M-Sa · Australasia · 500 kW · ALT. FREQ. TO 15175 kHz; S · Su · Australasia · 500 kW · ALT. FREQ. TO 15175 kHz; S · Australasia · 500 kW · ALT. FREQ. TO 15175 kHz; S · Europe · 500 kW
- VOICE OF RUSSIA, Kazan': W · W Asia & S Asia · 100 kW
- VOICE OF RUSSIA, Moscow: W · Mideast · 100 kW
- RFE-RL, Via Gloria, Portugal: W · Mideast & W Asia · 250 kW; W · E Europe · 250 kW; W · E Europe & W Asia · 250 kW
- RFE-RL, Via Holzkirchen: S · C Asia · 100 kW; S · E Europe & W Asia · 100 kW
- RFE-RL, Via Lampertheim: W · C Asia · 100 kW; W · W Asia & C Asia · 100 kW
- RFE-RL, Via Lampertheim: S · W Asia · 100 kW
- RFE-RL, Via Lampertheim: W · E Europe & W Asia · 100 kW
- RFE-RL, Via Lampertheim: S · E Europe · 100 kW
- RFE-RL, Via Lampertheim: S · E Europe · 250 kW
- RFE-RL, Via Pals, Spain: Europe · 500 kW
- VOA, Via Briech, Morocco: W · E Europe · 500 kW
- VOA, Via Woofferton, UK: W · E Europe · 300 kW
- R NEDERLAND, Via Samara: Irr · W · Europe · 250 kW
- GOLOS ROSSII, Vladivostok: W · W North Am · 200 kW; W · C America & S America · 240 kW
- VOICE OF RUSSIA, St Petersburg: W · S America · 240 kW; S · M · S America · 240 kW; W · M · C America & S America · 240 kW; W · S Europe · 500 kW
- R SLOVAKIA INTL: E North Am · 100 kW
- VOA, Via Petro-Kam: W · E Asia · 250 kW
- RADIO BULGARIA, Plovdiv: W · Europe · 500 kW; W · Europe · 150 kW · ALT. FREQ. TO 6035 kHz
- RADIO BULGARIA, Sofia: W · W Europe · 100 kW
- RADIO DANMARK, Via Norway: S · Australasia · 500 kW · ALT. FREQ. TO 7315 kHz; S · E Asia · 500 kW · ALT. FREQ. TO 7315 kHz
- R FRANCE INTL, Issoudun-Allouis: S · N Africa · 500 kW; W · N Africa · 500 kW
- R FRANCE INTL, Via Irkutsk: W · SE Asia · 1000 kW
- DEUTSCHE WELLE, Via N'sibirsk: W · S Asia · 1000 kW
- R NEDERLAND, Via Kazakhstan: W · S Asia · 500 kW

FREQUENCY	COUNTRY, STATION, LOCATION	TARGET • NETWORK • POWER (kW)
7305 (con'd)	**HOLLAND**	
	†R NEDERLAND, Via Madagascar	[S] • C Africa & W Africa • 200 kW • ALT. FREQ. TO 7205 kHz
	NORWAY	
	†R NORWAY INTL, Kvitsøy	[S] • Australasia • 500 kW • ALT. FREQ. TO 7315 kHz
		[S] • E Asia • 500 kW • ALT. FREQ. TO 7315 kHz
	RUSSIA	
	†ADYGEY RADIO, Armavir	[S] M/F • Mideast • 100 kW
	†KABARDINO-BALKAR R, Armavir	[S] W/Su • Mideast • 100 kW
	†MAYAK, Armavir	[S] Tu-Th/Sa/Su • Mideast & W Asia
		[S] Tu/Th/Sa • Mideast & W Asia
	†RADIO ALEF, Armavir	[S] • Mideast • 100 kW
	†RADIO ROSSII, Armavir	[S] • W Asia • DS • 100 kW
	VATICAN STATE	
	†VATICAN RADIO, Sta Maria di Galeria	S America • 250 kW
		[W] • E Africa • 250 kW
		C America & S America • 250 kW
		[W] • Mideast • 100 kW
		E North Am • 250/500 kW
		[W] • E Asia • 500 kW
		E Asia • 500 kW
		SE Asia • 500 kW
7310	**BULGARIA**	
	†RADIO BULGARIA, Varna	[W] • E Europe • 100 kW
	HOLLAND	
	†R NEDERLAND, Via Kaliningrad, Russia	[S] • W Europe • 160 kW
	†R NEDERLAND, Via Madagascar	[S] • E Africa • 200 kW
	RUSSIA	
	†GOLOS ROSSII, Armavir	[W] • Europe • 1000 kW
	†VOICE OF RUSSIA, Kaliningrad	[S] • Europe • 240 kW
	†VOICE OF RUSSIA, Moscow	[W] • S America • 1000 kW
7315	**CHINA**	
	CHINA RADIO INTL, Xi'an	[W] • Europe • 120 kW
	DENMARK	
	†RADIO DANMARK, Via Norway	[S] • Australasia • 500 kW • ALT. FREQ. TO 7305 kHz
		[S] • E Asia • 500 kW • ALT. FREQ. TO 7305 kHz
	FRANCE	
	†R FRANCE INTL, Issoudun-Allouis	Mideast • 500 kW
		[W] • E Africa • 500 kW
		[W] • Mideast • 500 kW
		Africa • 500 kW
	GERMANY	
	†DEUTSCHE WELLE, Via N'sibirsk, Russia	[W] • SE Asia • 1000 kW
	†DEUTSCHE WELLE, Via Samara, Russia	[S] • W Asia & C Asia • 200 kW
		[W] • S Asia • 250 kW
	NORWAY	
	†R NORWAY INTL, Kvitsøy	[S] • Australasia • 500 kW • ALT. FREQ. TO 7305 kHz
		[S] • E Asia • 500 kW • ALT. FREQ. TO 7305 kHz
	SLOVAKIA	
	†ADVENTIST WORLD R, Rimavská Sobota	[W] • N Africa & Mideast • 250 kW • ALT. FREQ. TO 7320 kHz
	USA	
	†VOA, Greenville, NC	W Africa & S Africa • 250 kW
		M-F • W Africa & S Africa • 500 kW
	†WORLD HARVEST R, Noblesville,Indiana	E North Am • 100 kW
		E North Am • 100 kW • ALT. FREQ. TO 9465 kHz
7320	**KAZAKHSTAN**	
	KAZAKH RADIO, Via Russia	⇦ • E Europe • DS-2 • 20 kW
	RUSSIA	
	MAGADAN RADIO, Yakutsk	RUSSIAN, ETC • DS/TIKHIY OKEAN • 100 kW
	MAYAK, Volgograd	[S] • DS • 20 kW
	†VOICE OF RUSSIA, Moscow	[W] • Europe • 500 kW
	SEYCHELLES	
	†FAR EAST BC ASS'N, North Pt, Mahé Is	W Asia & S Asia • 100 kW • ALT. FREQ. TO 7325 kHz
	SLOVAKIA	
	†ADVENTIST WORLD R, Rimavská Sobota	[W] • N Africa & Mideast • 250 kW • ALT. FREQ. TO 7315 kHz
	UNITED KINGDOM	
	†BBC, Rampisham	⇦ • E Europe • 500 kW
7325	**FRANCE**	
	†R FRANCE INTL, Issoudun-Allouis	[W] • N Africa • 100 kW
	MONACO	
	†TRANS WORLD R, Monte Carlo	⇦ • Tu-Sa • Europe • 100 kW • ALT. FREQ. TO 7385 kHz
		[W] M-Sa • Europe • 100 kW • ALT. FREQ. TO 7385 kHz
		⇦ • Su • Europe • 100 kW • ALT. FREQ. TO 7385 kHz
		[W] Sa/Su • Europe • 100 kW • ALT. FREQ. TO 7385 kHz
		[W] Sa • Europe • 100 kW • ALT. FREQ. TO 7385 kHz
	RUSSIA	
	†RADIO ODIN, Kazan'	[S] • DS • 240 kW
	†RADIO ODIN, Moscow	[W] • DS • 100 kW
(con'd)	†RADIO ROSSII, Armavir	[W] • W Asia • DS • 100 kW

World Time: 0 1 2 3 4 5 6 7 8 9 10 11 12 13 14 15 16 17 18 19 20 21 22 23 24

ENGLISH ▬ ARABIC ▭ CHINESE ▫▫▫ FRENCH ═ GERMAN ═ RUSSIAN ═ SPANISH ═ OTHER ─

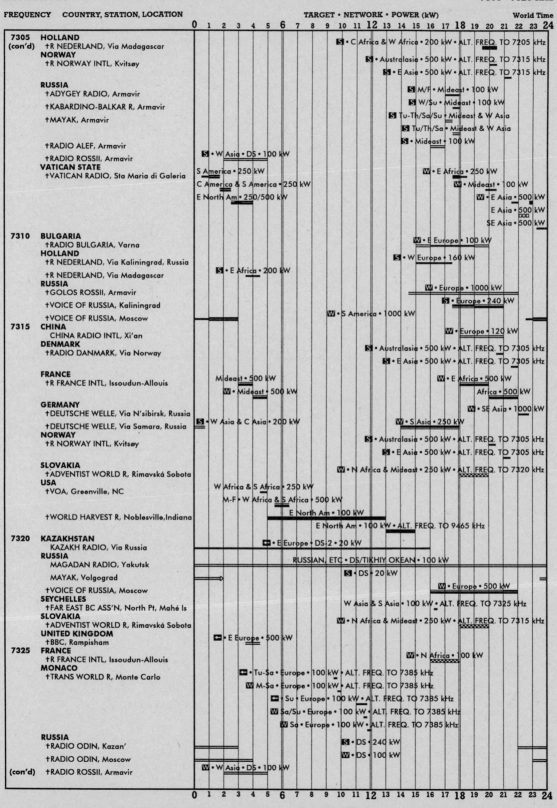

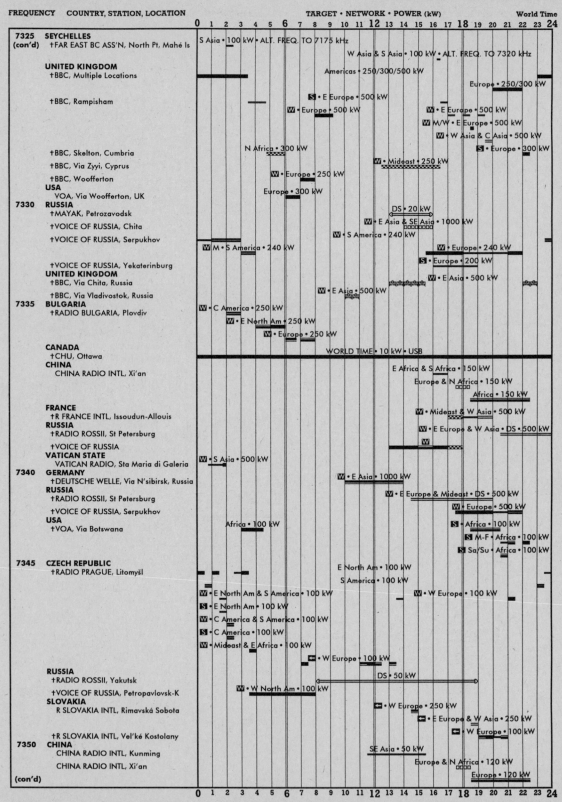

FREQUENCY	COUNTRY, STATION, LOCATION	TARGET • NETWORK • POWER (kW)
7325 (con'd)	**SEYCHELLES**	
	†FAR EAST BC ASS'N, North Pt, Mahé Is	S Asia • 100 kW • ALT. FREQ. TO 7175 kHz
		W Asia & S Asia • 100 kW • ALT. FREQ. TO 7320 kHz
	UNITED KINGDOM	
	†BBC, Multiple Locations	Americas • 250/300/500 kW
		Europe • 250/300 kW
	†BBC, Rampisham	[S] • E Europe • 500 kW
		[W] • Europe • 500 kW
		[W] • E Europe • 500 kW
		[W] M/W • E Europe • 500 kW
		[W] • W Asia & C Asia • 500 kW
	†BBC, Skelton, Cumbria	N Africa • 300 kW
		[S] • Europe • 300 kW
	†BBC, Via Zyyi, Cyprus	[W] • Mideast • 250 kW
	†BBC, Woofferton	[W] • Europe • 250 kW
	USA	
	VOA, Via Woofferton, UK	Europe • 300 kW
7330	**RUSSIA**	
	†MAYAK, Petrozavodsk	DS • 20 kW
	†VOICE OF RUSSIA, Chita	[W] • E Asia & SE Asia • 1000 kW
	†VOICE OF RUSSIA, Serpukhov	[W] • S America • 240 kW
		[W] M • S America • 240 kW
		[W] • Europe • 240 kW
	†VOICE OF RUSSIA, Yekaterinburg	[S] • Europe • 200 kW
	UNITED KINGDOM	
	†BBC, Via Chita, Russia	[W] • E Asia • 500 kW
	†BBC, Via Vladivostok, Russia	[W] • E Asia • 500 kW
7335	**BULGARIA**	
	†RADIO BULGARIA, Plovdiv	[W] • C America • 250 kW
		[W] • E North Am • 250 kW
		[W] • Europe • 250 kW
	CANADA	
	†CHU, Ottawa	WORLD TIME • 10 kW • USB
	CHINA	
	CHINA RADIO INTL, Xi'an	E Africa & S Africa • 150 kW
		Europe & N Africa • 150 kW
		Africa • 150 kW
	FRANCE	
	†R FRANCE INTL, Issoudun-Allouis	[W] • Mideast & W Asia • 500 kW
	RUSSIA	
	†RADIO ROSSII, St Petersburg	[W] • E Europe & W Asia • DS • 500 kW
	†VOICE OF RUSSIA	[W]
	VATICAN STATE	
	VATICAN RADIO, Sta Maria di Galeria	[W] • S Asia • 500 kW
7340	**GERMANY**	
	†DEUTSCHE WELLE, Via N'sibirsk, Russia	[W] • E Asia • 1000 kW
	RUSSIA	
	†RADIO ROSSII, St Petersburg	[W] • E Europe & Mideast • DS • 500 kW
	†VOICE OF RUSSIA, Serpukhov	[W] • Europe • 500 kW
	USA	
	†VOA, Via Botswana	Africa • 100 kW
		[S] • Africa • 100 kW
		[S] M-F • Africa • 100 kW
		[S] Sa/Su • Africa • 100 kW
7345	**CZECH REPUBLIC**	
	†RADIO PRAGUE, Litomyšl	E North Am • 100 kW
		S America • 100 kW
		[W] • E North Am & S America • 100 kW
		[W] • W Europe • 100 kW
		[S] • E North Am • 100 kW
		[W] • C America & S America • 100 kW
		[S] • C America • 100 kW
		[W] • Mideast & E Africa • 100 kW
		⬅ • W Europe • 100 kW
	RUSSIA	
	†RADIO ROSSII, Yakutsk	DS • 50 kW
	†VOICE OF RUSSIA, Petropavlovsk-K	[W] • W North Am • 100 kW
	SLOVAKIA	
	R SLOVAKIA INTL, Rimavská Sobota	⬅ • W Europe • 250 kW
		⬅ • E Europe & W Asia • 250 kW
	†R SLOVAKIA INTL, Vel'ké Kostolany	⬅ • W Europe • 100 kW
7350	**CHINA**	
	CHINA RADIO INTL, Kunming	SE Asia • 50 kW
	CHINA RADIO INTL, Xi'an	Europe & N Africa • 120 kW
		Europe • 120 kW
(con'd)		

World Time: 0 1 2 3 4 5 6 7 8 9 10 11 12 13 14 15 16 17 18 19 20 21 22 23 24

FREQUENCY   COUNTRY, STATION, LOCATION

TARGET • NETWORK • POWER (kW)

World Time

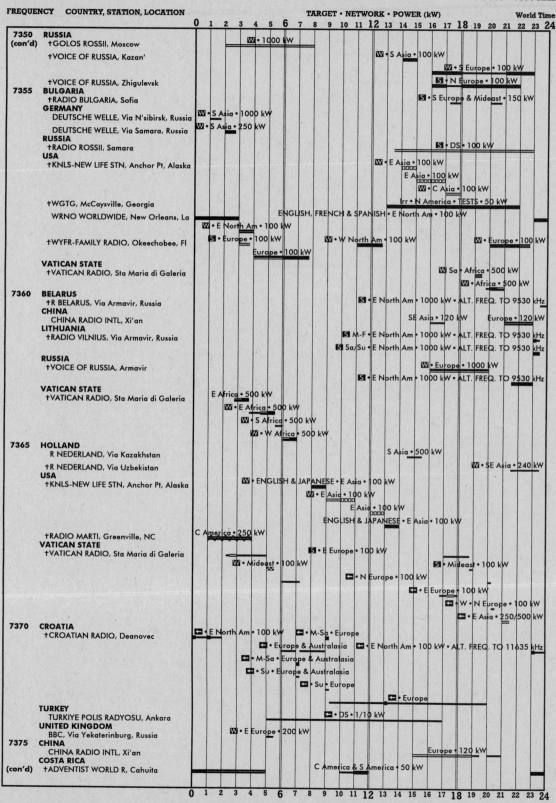

7350	RUSSIA	
(con'd)	†GOLOS ROSSII, Moscow	W • 1000 kW
	†VOICE OF RUSSIA, Kazan'	W • S Asia • 100 kW
		W • S Europe • 100 kW
	†VOICE OF RUSSIA, Zhigulevsk	S • N Europe • 100 kW
7355	BULGARIA	
	†RADIO BULGARIA, Sofia	S • S Europe & Mideast • 150 kW
	GERMANY	
	DEUTSCHE WELLE, Via N'sibirsk, Russia	W • S Asia • 1000 kW
	DEUTSCHE WELLE, Via Samara, Russia	W • S Asia • 250 kW
	RUSSIA	
	†RADIO ROSSII, Samara	S • DS • 100 kW
	USA	
	†KNLS-NEW LIFE STN, Anchor Pt, Alaska	W • E Asia • 100 kW
		E Asia • 100 kW
		W • C Asia • 100 kW
	†WGTG, McCaysville, Georgia	Irr • N America • TESTS • 50 kW
	WRNO WORLDWIDE, New Orleans, La	ENGLISH, FRENCH & SPANISH • E North Am • 100 kW
		W • E North Am • 100 kW
	†WYFR-FAMILY RADIO, Okeechobee, Fl	S • Europe • 100 kW W • W North Am • 100 kW W • Europe • 100 kW
		Europe • 100 kW
	VATICAN STATE	
	†VATICAN RADIO, Sta Maria di Galeria	W • Sa • Africa • 500 kW
		W • Africa • 500 kW
7360	BELARUS	
	†R Belarus, Via Armavir, Russia	S • E North Am • 1000 kW • ALT. FREQ. TO 9530 kHz
	CHINA	
	CHINA RADIO INTL, Xi'an	SE Asia • 120 kW Europe • 120 kW
	LITHUANIA	
	†RADIO VILNIUS, Via Armavir, Russia	S • M-F • E North Am • 1000 kW • ALT. FREQ. TO 9530 kHz
		S • Sa/Su • E North Am • 1000 kW • ALT. FREQ. TO 9530 kHz
	RUSSIA	
	†VOICE OF RUSSIA, Armavir	W • Europe • 1000 kW
	VATICAN STATE	
	†VATICAN RADIO, Sta Maria di Galeria	S • E North Am • 1000 kW • ALT. FREQ. TO 9530 kHz
		E Africa • 500 kW
		W • E Africa • 500 kW
		W • S Africa • 500 kW
		W • W Africa • 500 kW
7365	HOLLAND	
	R NEDERLAND, Via Kazakhstan	S Asia • 500 kW
	†R NEDERLAND, Via Uzbekistan	W • SE Asia • 240 kW
	USA	
	†KNLS-NEW LIFE STN, Anchor Pt, Alaska	W • ENGLISH & JAPANESE • E Asia • 100 kW
		W • E Asia • 100 kW
		E Asia • 100 kW
		ENGLISH & JAPANESE • E Asia • 100 kW
	†RADIO MARTI, Greenville, NC	C America • 250 kW
	VATICAN STATE	
	†VATICAN RADIO, Sta Maria di Galeria	S • E Europe • 100 kW
		W • Mideast • 100 kW
		S • Mideast • 100 kW
		• N Europe • 100 kW
		• E Europe • 100 kW
		• W • N Europe • 100 kW
7370	CROATIA	
	†CROATIAN RADIO, Deanovec	• E Asia • 250/500 kW
		• E North Am • 100 kW • M-Sa • Europe
		• Europe & Australasia • E North Am • 100 kW • ALT. FREQ. TO 11635 kHz
		• M-Sa • Europe & Australasia
		• Su • Europe & Australasia
		• Su • Europe
		• Europe
	TURKEY	
	TURKIYE POLIS RADYOSU, Ankara	• DS • 1/10 kW
	UNITED KINGDOM	
	BBC, Via Yekaterinburg, Russia	W • E Europe • 200 kW
7375	CHINA	
	CHINA RADIO INTL, Xi'an	Europe • 120 kW
	COSTA RICA	
(con'd)	†ADVENTIST WORLD R, Cahuita	C America & S America • 50 kW

ENGLISH ▬▬   ARABIC ⧖⧖⧖   CHINESE □□□   FRENCH ▬ ▬   GERMAN ▬▬   RUSSIAN ══   SPANISH ══   OTHER ──

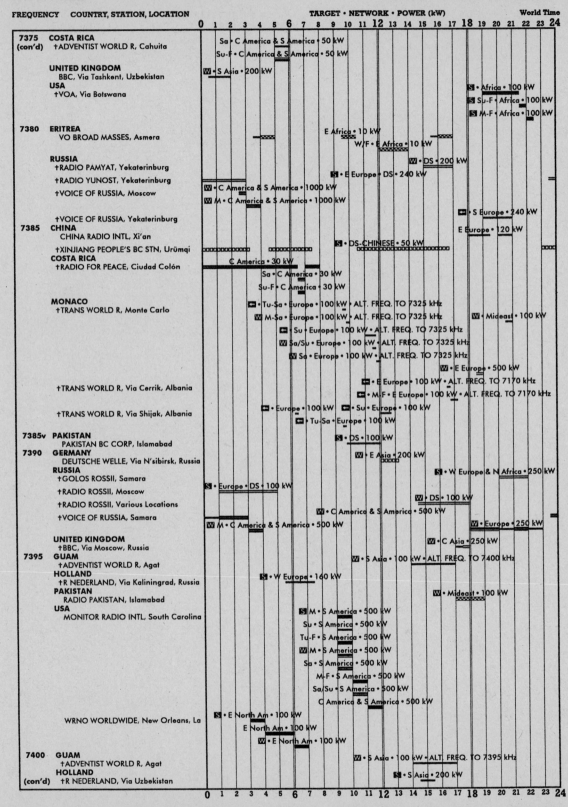

FREQUENCY   COUNTRY, STATION, LOCATION   TARGET • NETWORK • POWER (kW)   World Time

7375	COSTA RICA	Sa • C America & S America • 50 kW
(con'd)	†ADVENTIST WORLD R, Cahuita	Su-F • C America & S America • 50 kW
	UNITED KINGDOM	W • S Asia • 200 kW
	BBC, Via Tashkent, Uzbekistan	
	USA	S • Africa • 100 kW
	†VOA, Via Botswana	S Su-F • Africa • 100 kW
		S M-F • Africa • 100 kW
7380	ERITREA	E Africa • 10 kW
	VO BROAD MASSES, Asmera	W/F • E Africa • 10 kW
	RUSSIA	W • DS • 200 kW
	†RADIO PAMYAT, Yekaterinburg	S • E Europe • DS • 240 kW
	†RADIO YUNOST, Yekaterinburg	W • C America & S America • 1000 kW
	†VOICE OF RUSSIA, Moscow	W M • C America & S America • 1000 kW
	†VOICE OF RUSSIA, Yekaterinburg	S • S Europe • 240 kW
7385	CHINA	E Europe • 120 kW
	CHINA RADIO INTL, Xi'an	S • DS-CHINESE • 50 kW
	†XINJIANG PEOPLE'S BC STN, Urümqi	
	COSTA RICA	C America • 30 kW
	†RADIO FOR PEACE, Ciudad Colón	Sa • C America • 30 kW
		Su-F • C America • 30 kW
	MONACO	S • Tu-Sa • Europe • 100 kW • ALT. FREQ. TO 7325 kHz
	†TRANS WORLD R, Monte Carlo	W M-Sa • Europe • 100 kW • ALT. FREQ. TO 7325 kHz W • Mideast • 100 kW
		S • Su • Europe • 100 kW • ALT. FREQ. TO 7325 kHz
		W • Sa/Su • Europe • 100 kW • ALT. FREQ. TO 7325 kHz
		W • Sa • Europe • 100 kW • ALT. FREQ. TO 7325 kHz
		W • E Europe • 500 kW
	†TRANS WORLD R, Via Cerrik, Albania	S • E Europe • 100 kW • ALT. FREQ. TO 7170 kHz
		S • M-F • E Europe • 100 kW • ALT. FREQ. TO 7170 kHz
	†TRANS WORLD R, Via Shijak, Albania	S • Europe • 100 kW S • Su • Europe • 100 kW
		S • Tu-Sa • Europe • 100 kW
7385v	PAKISTAN	S • DS • 100 kW
	PAKISTAN BC CORP, Islamabad	
7390	GERMANY	W • E Asia • 200 kW
	DEUTSCHE WELLE, Via N'sibirsk, Russia	
	RUSSIA	S • W Europe & N Africa • 250 kW
	†GOLOS ROSSII, Samara	S • Europe • DS • 100 kW
	†RADIO ROSSII, Moscow	W • DS • 100 kW
	†RADIO ROSSII, Various Locations	W • C America & S America • 500 kW
	†VOICE OF RUSSIA, Samara	W M • C America & S America • 500 kW W • Europe • 250 kW
	UNITED KINGDOM	W • C Asia • 250 kW
	†BBC, Via Moscow, Russia	
7395	GUAM	W • S Asia • 100 kW • ALT. FREQ. TO 7400 kHz
	†ADVENTIST WORLD R, Agat	
	HOLLAND	S • W Europe • 160 kW
	†R NEDERLAND, Via Kaliningrad, Russia	
	PAKISTAN	W • Mideast • 100 kW
	RADIO PAKISTAN, Islamabad	
	USA	S M • S America • 500 kW
	MONITOR RADIO INTL, South Carolina	Su • S America • 500 kW
		Tu-F • S America • 500 kW
		W M • S America • 500 kW
		Sa • S America • 500 kW
		M-F • S America • 500 kW
		Sa/Su • S America • 500 kW
		C America & S America • 500 kW
	WRNO WORLDWIDE, New Orleans, La	S • E North Am • 100 kW
		E North Am • 100 kW
		W • E North Am • 100 kW
7400	GUAM	W • S Asia • 100 kW • ALT. FREQ. TO 7395 kHz
	†ADVENTIST WORLD R, Agat	
	HOLLAND	S • S Asia • 200 kW
(con'd)	†R NEDERLAND, Via Uzbekistan	

FREQUENCY   COUNTRY, STATION, LOCATION   TARGET • NETWORK • POWER (kW)   World Time

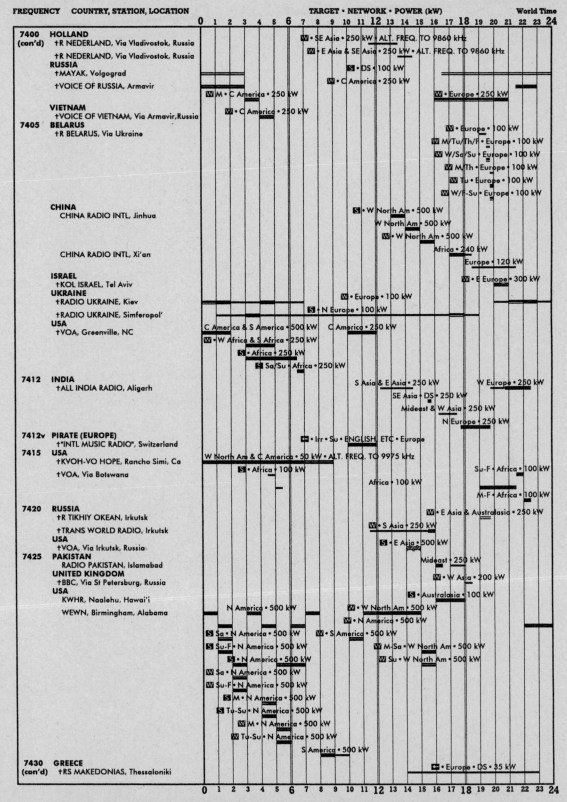

FREQUENCY	COUNTRY, STATION, LOCATION
7400 (con'd)	**HOLLAND**
	†R NEDERLAND, Via Vladivostok, Russia
	†R NEDERLAND, Via Vladivostok, Russia
	RUSSIA
	†MAYAK, Volgograd
	†VOICE OF RUSSIA, Armavir
	VIETNAM
	†VOICE OF VIETNAM, Via Armavir, Russia
7405	**BELARUS**
	†R BELARUS, Via Ukraine
	CHINA
	CHINA RADIO INTL, Jinhua
	CHINA RADIO INTL, Xi'an
	ISRAEL
	†KOL ISRAEL, Tel Aviv
	UKRAINE
	†RADIO UKRAINE, Kiev
	†RADIO UKRAINE, Simferopol'
	USA
	†VOA, Greenville, NC
7412	**INDIA**
	†ALL INDIA RADIO, Aligarh
7412v	**PIRATE (EUROPE)**
	†"INTL MUSIC RADIO", Switzerland
7415	**USA**
	†KVOH-VO HOPE, Rancho Simi, Ca
	†VOA, Via Botswana
7420	**RUSSIA**
	†R TIKHIY OKEAN, Irkutsk
	†TRANS WORLD RADIO, Irkutsk
	USA
	†VOA, Via Irkutsk, Russia
7425	**PAKISTAN**
	RADIO PAKISTAN, Islamabad
	UNITED KINGDOM
	†BBC, Via St Petersburg, Russia
	USA
	KWHR, Naalehu, Hawai'i
	WEWN, Birmingham, Alabama
7430 (con'd)	**GREECE**
	†RS MAKEDONIAS, Thessaloniki

ENGLISH ▬ ARABIC ∽ CHINESE □□□ FRENCH ▬ GERMAN ▬ RUSSIAN ═ SPANISH ▬ OTHER —

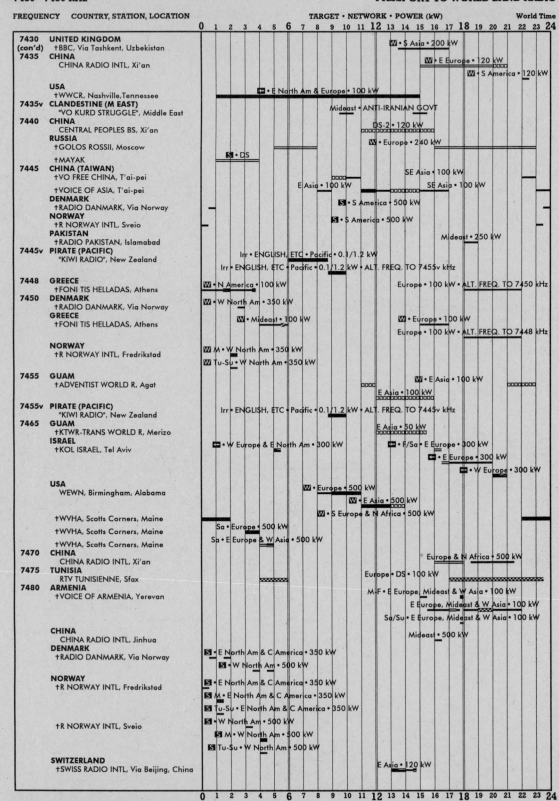

FREQUENCY COUNTRY, STATION, LOCATION

TARGET • NETWORK • POWER (kW)

World Time

7430	UNITED KINGDOM
(con'd)	†BBC, Via Tashkent, Uzbekistan
7435	CHINA
	CHINA RADIO INTL, Xi'an
	USA
	†WWCR, Nashville, Tennessee
7435v	CLANDESTINE (M EAST)
	"VO KURD STRUGGLE", Middle East
7440	CHINA
	CENTRAL PEOPLES BS, Xi'an
	RUSSIA
	†GOLOS ROSSII, Moscow
	†MAYAK
7445	CHINA (TAIWAN)
	†VO FREE CHINA, T'ai-pei
	†VOICE OF ASIA, T'ai-pei
	DENMARK
	†RADIO DANMARK, Via Norway
	NORWAY
	†R NORWAY INTL, Sveio
	PAKISTAN
	†RADIO PAKISTAN, Islamabad
7445v	PIRATE (PACIFIC)
	"KIWI RADIO", New Zealand
7448	GREECE
	†FONI TIS HELLADAS, Athens
7450	DENMARK
	†RADIO DANMARK, Via Norway
	GREECE
	†FONI TIS HELLADAS, Athens
	NORWAY
	†R NORWAY INTL, Fredrikstad
7455	GUAM
	†ADVENTIST WORLD R, Agat
7455v	PIRATE (PACIFIC)
	"KIWI RADIO", New Zealand
7465	GUAM
	†KTWR-TRANS WORLD R, Merizo
	ISRAEL
	†KOL ISRAEL, Tel Aviv
	USA
	WEWN, Birmingham, Alabama
	†WVHA, Scotts Corners, Maine
	†WVHA, Scotts Corners, Maine
	†WVHA, Scotts Corners, Maine
7470	CHINA
	CHINA RADIO INTL, Xi'an
7475	TUNISIA
	RTV TUNISIENNE, Sfax
7480	ARMENIA
	†VOICE OF ARMENIA, Yerevan
	CHINA
	CHINA RADIO INTL, Jinhua
	DENMARK
	†RADIO DANMARK, Via Norway
	NORWAY
	†R NORWAY INTL, Fredrikstad
	†R NORWAY INTL, Sveio
	SWITZERLAND
	†SWISS RADIO INTL, Via Beijing, China

W • S Asia • 200 kW
W • E Europe • 120 kW
W • S America • 120 kW
E North Am & Europe • 100 kW
Mideast • ANTI-IRANIAN GOVT
DS-2 • 120 kW
W • Europe • 240 kW
S • DS
SE Asia • 100 kW
E Asia • 100 kW   SE Asia • 100 kW
S • S America • 500 kW
S • S America • 500 kW
Mideast • 250 kW
Irr • ENGLISH, ETC • Pacific • 0.1/1.2 kW
Irr • ENGLISH, ETC • Pacific • 0.1/1.2 kW • ALT. FREQ. TO 7455v kHz
W • N America • 100 kW   Europe • 100 kW • ALT. FREQ. TO 7450 kHz
W • W North Am • 350 kW
W • Mideast • 100 kW   W • Europe • 100 kW
Europe • 100 kW • ALT. FREQ. TO 7448 kHz
W M • W North Am • 350 kW
W Tu-Su • W North Am • 350 kW
W • E Asia • 100 kW
E Asia • 100 kW
Irr • ENGLISH, ETC • Pacific • 0.1/1.2 kW • ALT. FREQ. TO 7445v kHz
E Asia • 50 kW
W Europe & E North Am • 300 kW   F/Sa • E Europe • 300 kW
E Europe • 300 kW
W Europe • 300 kW
W • Europe • 500 kW
W • E Asia • 500 kW
W • S Europe & N Africa • 500 kW
Sa • Europe • 500 kW
Sa • E Europe & W Asia • 500 kW
Europe & N Africa • 500 kW
Europe • DS • 100 kW
M-F • E Europe, Mideast & W Asia • 100 kW
E Europe, Mideast & W Asia • 100 kW
Sa/Su • E Europe, Mideast & W Asia • 100 kW
Mideast • 500 kW
S • E North Am & C America • 350 kW
S • W North Am • 500 kW
S • E North Am & C America • 350 kW
S M • E North Am & C America • 350 kW
S Tu-Su • E North Am & C America • 350 kW
S • W North Am • 500 kW
S M • W North Am • 500 kW
S Tu-Su • W North Am • 500 kW
E Asia • 120 kW

FREQUENCY   COUNTRY, STATION, LOCATION

TARGET • NETWORK • POWER (kW)

World Time

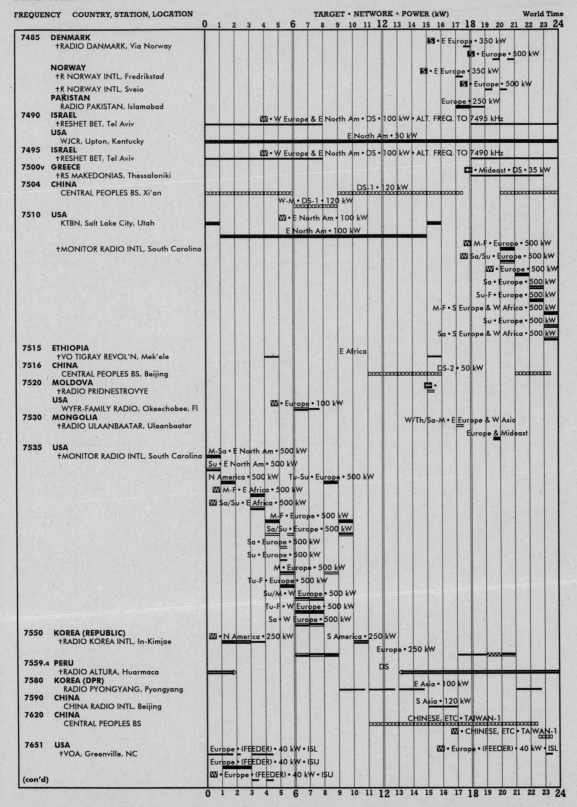

Freq	Country, Station, Location	Details
7485	**DENMARK** †RADIO DANMARK, Via Norway	S • E Europe • 350 kW; S • Europe • 500 kW
	NORWAY †R NORWAY INTL, Fredrikstad	S • E Europe • 350 kW
	†R NORWAY INTL, Sveio	S • Europe • 500 kW
	PAKISTAN RADIO PAKISTAN, Islamabad	Europe • 250 kW
7490	**ISRAEL** †RESHET BET, Tel Aviv	W • W Europe & E North Am • DS • 100 kW • ALT. FREQ. TO 7495 kHz
	USA WJCR, Upton, Kentucky	E North Am • 50 kW
7495	**ISRAEL** †RESHET BET, Tel Aviv	W • W Europe & E North Am • DS • 100 kW • ALT. FREQ. TO 7490 kHz
7500v	**GREECE** †RS MAKEDONIAS, Thessaloniki	• Mideast • DS • 35 kW
7504	**CHINA** CENTRAL PEOPLES BS, Xi'an	DS-1 • 120 kW; W-M • DS-1 • 120 kW
7510	**USA** KTBN, Salt Lake City, Utah	W • E North Am • 100 kW; E North Am • 100 kW
	†MONITOR RADIO INTL, South Carolina	W • M-F • Europe • 500 kW; W • Sa/Su • Europe • 500 kW; W • Europe • 500 kW; Sa • Europe • 500 kW; Su-F • Europe • 500 kW; M-F • S Europe & W Africa • 500 kW; Su • Europe • 500 kW; Sa • S Europe & W Africa • 500 kW
7515	**ETHIOPIA** †VO TIGRAY REVOL'N, Mek'ele	E Africa
7516	**CHINA** CENTRAL PEOPLES BS, Beijing	DS-2 • 50 kW
7520	**MOLDOVA** †RADIO PRIDNESTROVYE	
	USA WYFR-FAMILY RADIO, Okeechobee, Fl	W • Europe • 100 kW
7530	**MONGOLIA** †RADIO ULAANBAATAR, Ulaanbaatar	W/Th/Sa-M • E Europe & W Asia; Europe & Mideast
7535	**USA** †MONITOR RADIO INTL, South Carolina	M-Sa • E North Am • 500 kW; Su • E North Am • 500 kW; N America • 500 kW; Tu-Su • Europe • 500 kW; W • M-F • E Africa • 500 kW; W • Sa/Su • E Africa • 500 kW; M-F • Europe • 500 kW; Sa/Su • Europe • 500 kW; Sa • Europe • 500 kW; Su • Europe • 500 kW; M • Europe • 500 kW; Tu-F • Europe • 500 kW; Su/M • W Europe • 500 kW; Tu-F • W Europe • 500 kW; Sa • W Europe • 500 kW
7550	**KOREA (REPUBLIC)** †RADIO KOREA INTL, In-Kimjae	W • N America • 250 kW; S America • 250 kW; Europe • 250 kW
7559.4	**PERU** †RADIO ALTURA, Huarmaca	DS
7580	**KOREA (DPR)** RADIO PYONGYANG, Pyongyang	E Asia • 100 kW
7590	**CHINA** CHINA RADIO INTL, Beijing	S Asia • 120 kW
7620	**CHINA** CENTRAL PEOPLES BS	CHINESE, ETC • TAIWAN-1; W • CHINESE, ETC • TAIWAN-1
7651	**USA** †VOA, Greenville, NC	Europe • (FEEDER) • 40 kW • ISL; W • Europe • (FEEDER) • 40 kW • ISL; Europe • (FEEDER) • 40 kW • ISU; W • Europe • (FEEDER) • 40 kW • ISU

(con'd)

ENGLISH ▬   ARABIC ▧   CHINESE ▢▢▢   FRENCH ▬   GERMAN ▬   RUSSIAN ═   SPANISH ▬   OTHER ▬

FREQUENCY   COUNTRY, STATION, LOCATION

TARGET • NETWORK • POWER (kW)   World Time

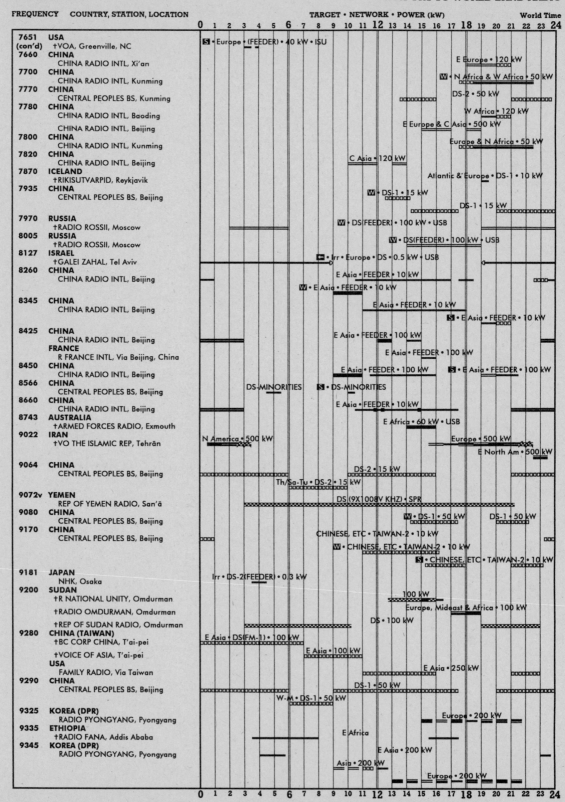

Frequency	Country, Station, Location	Details
7651 (con'd)	USA †VOA, Greenville, NC	S • Europe • (FEEDER) • 40 kW • ISU
7660	CHINA CHINA RADIO INTL, Xi'an	E Europe • 120 kW
7700	CHINA CHINA RADIO INTL, Kunming	W • N Africa & W Africa • 50 kW
7770	CHINA CENTRAL PEOPLES BS, Kunming	DS-2 • 50 kW
7780	CHINA CHINA RADIO INTL, Baoding	W Africa • 120 kW
	CHINA RADIO INTL, Beijing	E Europe & C Asia • 500 kW
7800	CHINA CHINA RADIO INTL, Kunming	Europe & N Africa • 50 kW
7820	CHINA CHINA RADIO INTL, Beijing	C Asia • 120 kW
7870	ICELAND †RIKISUTVARPID, Reykjavik	Atlantic & Europe • DS-1 • 10 kW
7935	CHINA CENTRAL PEOPLES BS, Beijing	W • DS-1 • 15 kW / DS-1 • 15 kW
7970	RUSSIA †RADIO ROSSII, Moscow	W • DS(FEEDER) • 100 kW • USB
8005	RUSSIA †RADIO ROSSII, Moscow	W • DS(FEEDER) • 100 kW • USB
8127	ISRAEL †GALEI ZAHAL, Tel Aviv	Irr • Europe • DS • 0.5 kW • USB
8260	CHINA CHINA RADIO INTL, Beijing	E Asia • FEEDER • 10 kW / W • E Asia • FEEDER • 10 kW
8345	CHINA CHINA RADIO INTL, Beijing	E Asia • FEEDER • 10 kW / S • E Asia • FEEDER • 10 kW
8425	CHINA CHINA RADIO INTL, Beijing	E Asia • FEEDER • 100 kW
	FRANCE R FRANCE INTL, Via Beijing, China	E Asia • FEEDER • 100 kW
8450	CHINA CHINA RADIO INTL, Beijing	E Asia • FEEDER • 100 kW / S • E Asia • FEEDER • 100 kW
8566	CHINA CENTRAL PEOPLES BS, Beijing	DS-MINORITIES / S • DS-MINORITIES
8660	CHINA CHINA RADIO INTL, Beijing	E Asia • FEEDER • 10 kW
8743	AUSTRALIA †ARMED FORCES RADIO, Exmouth	E Africa • 60 kW • USB
9022	IRAN †VO THE ISLAMIC REP, Tehrān	N America • 500 kW / Europe • 500 kW / E North Am • 500 kW
9064	CHINA CENTRAL PEOPLES BS, Beijing	DS-2 • 15 kW / Th/Sa-Tu • DS-2 • 15 kW
9072v	YEMEN REP OF YEMEN RADIO, San'ā	DS (9X1008V KHZ) • SPR
9080	CHINA CENTRAL PEOPLES BS, Beijing	W • DS-1 • 50 kW / DS-1 • 50 kW
9170	CHINA CENTRAL PEOPLES BS, Beijing	CHINESE, ETC • TAIWAN-2 • 10 kW / W • CHINESE, ETC • TAIWAN-2 • 10 kW / S • CHINESE, ETC • TAIWAN-2 • 10 kW
9181	JAPAN NHK, Osaka	Irr • DS-2(FEEDER) • 0.3 kW
9200	SUDAN †R NATIONAL UNITY, Omdurman	100 kW
	†RADIO OMDURMAN, Omdurman	Europe, Mideast & Africa • 100 kW
	†REP OF SUDAN RADIO, Omdurman	DS • 100 kW
9280	CHINA (TAIWAN) †BC CORP CHINA, T'ai-pei	E Asia • DS(FM-1) • 100 kW
	†VOICE OF ASIA, T'ai-pei	E Asia • 100 kW
	USA FAMILY RADIO, Via Taiwan	E Asia • 250 kW
9290	CHINA CENTRAL PEOPLES BS, Beijing	DS-1 • 50 kW / W-M • DS-1 • 50 kW
9325	KOREA (DPR) RADIO PYONGYANG, Pyongyang	Europe • 200 kW
9335	ETHIOPIA †RADIO FANA, Addis Ababa	E Africa
9345	KOREA (DPR) RADIO PYONGYANG, Pyongyang	E Asia • 200 kW / Asia • 200 kW / Europe • 200 kW

FREQUENCY   COUNTRY, STATION, LOCATION   TARGET • NETWORK • POWER (kW)   World Time

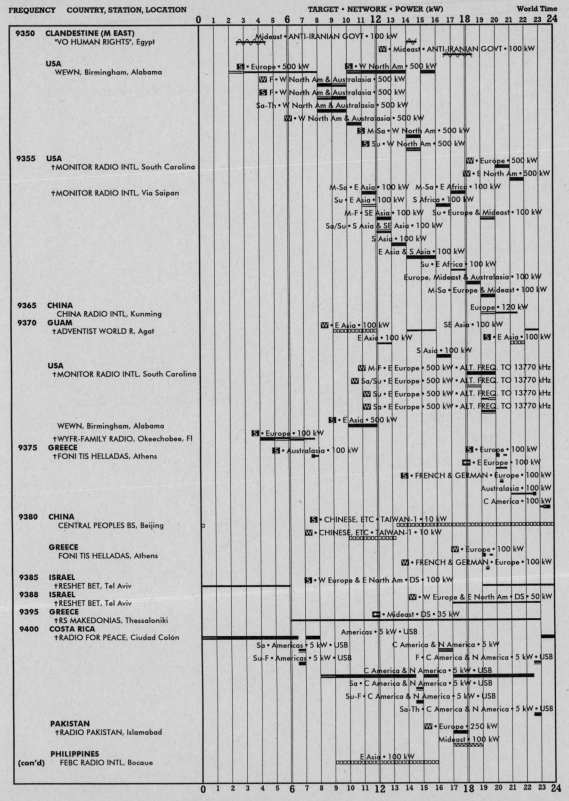

9350	CLANDESTINE (M EAST)	"VO HUMAN RIGHTS", Egypt
	USA	WEWN, Birmingham, Alabama
9355	USA	†MONITOR RADIO INTL, South Carolina
		†MONITOR RADIO INTL, Via Saipan
9365	CHINA	CHINA RADIO INTL, Kunming
9370	GUAM	†ADVENTIST WORLD R, Agat
	USA	†MONITOR RADIO INTL, South Carolina
		WEWN, Birmingham, Alabama
		†WYFR-FAMILY RADIO, Okeechobee, Fl
9375	GREECE	†FONI TIS HELLADAS, Athens
9380	CHINA	CENTRAL PEOPLES BS, Beijing
	GREECE	FONI TIS HELLADAS, Athens
9385	ISRAEL	†RESHET BET, Tel Aviv
9388	ISRAEL	†RESHET BET, Tel Aviv
9395	GREECE	†RS MAKEDONIAS, Thessaloniki
9400	COSTA RICA	†RADIO FOR PEACE, Ciudad Colón
	PAKISTAN	†RADIO PAKISTAN, Islamabad
(con'd)	PHILIPPINES	FEBC RADIO INTL, Bocaue

Mideast • ANTI-IRANIAN GOVT • 100 kW
W • Mideast • ANTI-IRANIAN GOVT • 100 kW

S • Europe • 500 kW
S • W North Am • 500 kW
W F • W North Am & Australasia • 500 kW
S F • W North Am & Australasia • 500 kW
Sa-Th • W North Am & Australasia • 500 kW
W • W North Am & Australasia • 500 kW
S M-Sa • W North Am • 500 kW
S Su • W North Am • 500 kW

W • Europe • 500 kW
W • E North Am • 500 kW
M-Sa • E Asia • 100 kW   M-Sa • E Africa • 100 kW
Su • E Asia • 100 kW   S Africa • 100 kW
M-F • SE Asia • 100 kW   Su • Europe & Mideast • 100 kW
Sa/Su • S Asia & SE Asia • 100 kW
S Asia • 100 kW
E Asia & S Asia • 100 kW
Su • E Africa • 100 kW
Europe, Mideast & Australasia • 100 kW
M-Sa • Europe & Mideast • 100 kW

Europe • 120 kW
W • E Asia • 100 kW   SE Asia • 100 kW
E Asia • 100 kW   S • E Asia • 100 kW
S Asia • 100 kW
W M-F • E Europe • 500 kW • ALT. FREQ. TO 13770 kHz
W Sa/Su • E Europe • 500 kW • ALT. FREQ. TO 13770 kHz
W Su • E Europe • 500 kW • ALT. FREQ. TO 13770 kHz
W Sa • E Europe • 500 kW • ALT. FREQ. TO 13770 kHz
S • E Asia • 500 kW
S • Europe • 100 kW
S • Australasia • 100 kW
S • Europe • 100 kW
E Europe • 100 kW
S • FRENCH & GERMAN • Europe • 100 kW
Australasia • 100 kW
C America • 100 kW

S • CHINESE, ETC • TAIWAN-1 • 10 kW
W • CHINESE, ETC • TAIWAN-1 • 10 kW
W • Europe • 100 kW
W • FRENCH & GERMAN • Europe • 100 kW
S • W Europe & E North Am • DS • 100 kW
W • W Europe & E North Am • DS • 50 kW
• Mideast • DS • 35 kW
Americas • 5 kW • USB
Sa • Americas • 5 kW • USB   C America & N America • 5 kW
Su-F • Americas • 5 kW • USB   F • C America & N America • 5 kW • USB
C America & N America • 5 kW • USB
Sa • C America & N America • 5 kW • USB
Su-F • C America & N America • 5 kW • USB
Sa-Th • C America & N America • 5 kW • USB
W • Europe • 250 kW
Mideast • 100 kW
E Asia • 100 kW

ENGLISH ▬   ARABIC ⌇⌇⌇   CHINESE ▫▫▫   FRENCH ▭▭   GERMAN ▬▬   RUSSIAN ═   SPANISH ▬   OTHER ▬

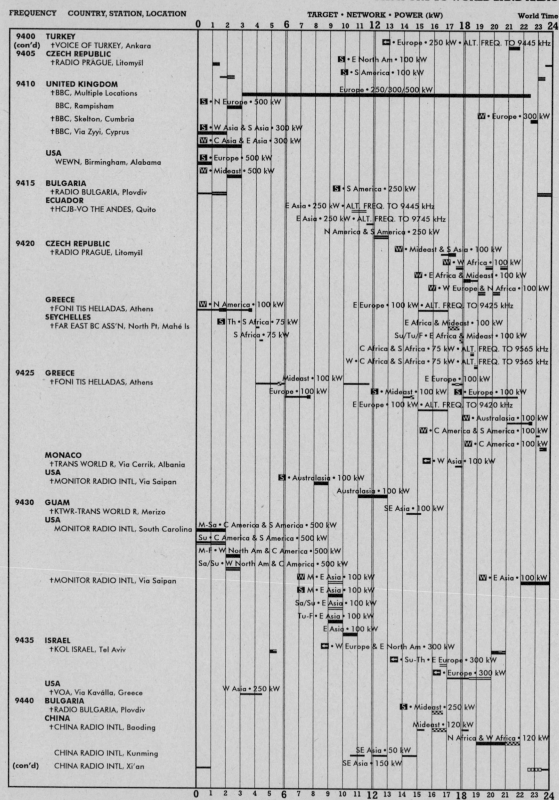

FREQUENCY	COUNTRY, STATION, LOCATION	TARGET • NETWORK • POWER (kW)
9400 (con'd)	TURKEY †VOICE OF TURKEY, Ankara	• Europe • 250 kW • ALT. FREQ. TO 9445 kHz
9405	CZECH REPUBLIC †RADIO PRAGUE, Litomyšl	S • E North Am • 100 kW / S • S America • 100 kW
9410	UNITED KINGDOM †BBC, Multiple Locations	Europe • 250/300/500 kW
	BBC, Rampisham	S • N Europe • 500 kW
	†BBC, Skelton, Cumbria	W • Europe • 300 kW
	†BBC, Via Zyyi, Cyprus	S • W Asia & S Asia • 300 kW / W • C Asia & E Asia • 300 kW
	USA WEWN, Birmingham, Alabama	S • Europe • 500 kW / W • Mideast • 500 kW
9415	BULGARIA †RADIO BULGARIA, Plovdiv	S • S America • 250 kW
	ECUADOR †HCJB-VO THE ANDES, Quito	E Asia • 250 kW • ALT. FREQ. TO 9445 kHz / E Asia • 250 kW • ALT. FREQ. TO 9745 kHz / N America & S America • 250 kW
9420	CZECH REPUBLIC †RADIO PRAGUE, Litomyšl	W • Mideast & S Asia • 100 kW / W • W Africa • 100 kW / W • E Africa & Mideast • 100 kW / W • W Europe & N Africa • 100 kW
	GREECE †FONI TIS HELLADAS, Athens	W • N America • 100 kW / E Europe • 100 kW • ALT. FREQ. TO 9425 kHz
	SEYCHELLES †FAR EAST BC ASS'N, North Pt, Mahé Is	S • Th • S Africa • 75 kW / S Africa • 75 kW / E Africa & Mideast • 100 kW / Su/Tu/F • E Africa & Mideast • 100 kW / C Africa & S Africa • 75 kW • ALT. FREQ. TO 9565 kHz / W • C Africa & S Africa • 75 kW • ALT. FREQ. TO 9565 kHz
9425	GREECE †FONI TIS HELLADAS, Athens	Mideast • 100 kW / E Europe • 100 kW / Europe • 100 kW / S • Mideast • 100 kW S • Europe • 100 kW / E Europe • 100 kW • ALT. FREQ. TO 9420 kHz / W • Australasia • 100 kW / W • C America & S America • 100 kW / W • C America • 100 kW
	MONACO †TRANS WORLD R, Via Cerrik, Albania	• W Asia • 100 kW
	USA †MONITOR RADIO INTL, Via Saipan	S • Australasia • 100 kW / Australasia • 100 kW
9430	GUAM †KTWR-TRANS WORLD R, Merizo	SE Asia • 100 kW
	USA MONITOR RADIO INTL, South Carolina	M-Sa • C America & S America • 500 kW / Su • C America & S America • 500 kW / M-F • W North Am & C America • 500 kW / Sa/Su • W North Am & C America • 500 kW
	†MONITOR RADIO INTL, Via Saipan	W • M • E Asia • 100 kW / W • E Asia • 100 kW / S • M • E Asia • 100 kW / Sa/Su • E Asia • 100 kW / Tu-F • E Asia • 100 kW / E Asia • 100 kW
9435	ISRAEL †KOL ISRAEL, Tel Aviv	• W Europe & E North Am • 300 kW / • Su-Th • E Europe • 300 kW / • Europe • 300 kW
	USA †VOA, Via Kaválla, Greece	W Asia • 250 kW
9440	BULGARIA †RADIO BULGARIA, Plovdiv	S • Mideast • 250 kW
	CHINA †CHINA RADIO INTL, Baoding	Mideast • 120 kW / N Africa & W Africa • 120 kW
	CHINA RADIO INTL, Kunming	SE Asia • 50 kW
(con'd)	CHINA RADIO INTL, Xi'an	SE Asia • 150 kW

FREQUENCY   COUNTRY, STATION, LOCATION

TARGET • NETWORK • POWER (kW)

World Time

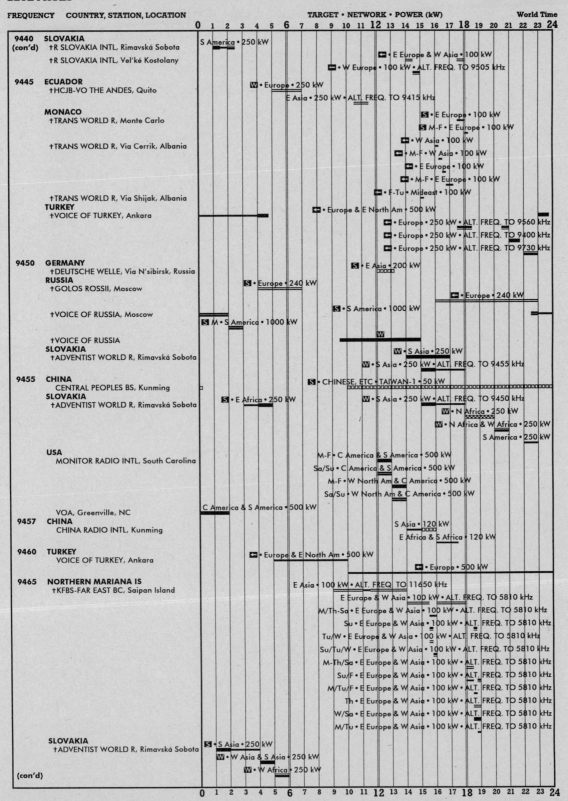

9440 (con'd)	SLOVAKIA
	†R SLOVAKIA INTL, Rimavská Sobota — S America • 250 kW
	†R SLOVAKIA INTL, Vel'ké Kostolany — ⏹ • E Europe & W Asia • 100 kW
	⏹ • W Europe • 100 kW • ALT. FREQ. TO 9505 kHz
9445	ECUADOR
	†HCJB-VO THE ANDES, Quito — W • Europe • 250 kW
	E Asia • 250 kW • ALT. FREQ. TO 9415 kHz
	MONACO
	†TRANS WORLD R, Monte Carlo — S • E Europe • 100 kW
	S M-F • E Europe • 100 kW
	†TRANS WORLD R, Via Cerrik, Albania — ⏹ • W Asia • 100 kW
	⏹ • M-F • W Asia • 100 kW
	⏹ • E Europe • 100 kW
	⏹ • M-F • E Europe • 100 kW
	†TRANS WORLD R, Via Shijak, Albania — ⏹ • F-Tu • Mideast • 100 kW
	TURKEY
	†VOICE OF TURKEY, Ankara — ⏹ • Europe & E North Am • 500 kW
	⏹ • Europe • 250 kW • ALT. FREQ. TO 9560 kHz
	⏹ • Europe • 250 kW • ALT. FREQ. TO 9400 kHz
	⏹ • Europe • 250 kW • ALT. FREQ. TO 9730 kHz
9450	GERMANY
	†DEUTSCHE WELLE, Via N'sibirsk, Russia — S • E Asia • 200 kW
	RUSSIA
	†GOLOS ROSSII, Moscow — S • Europe • 240 kW
	⏹ • Europe • 240 kW
	†VOICE OF RUSSIA, Moscow — S • S America • 1000 kW
	S M • S America • 1000 kW
	†VOICE OF RUSSIA — W
	SLOVAKIA
	†ADVENTIST WORLD R, Rimavská Sobota — W • S Asia • 250 kW
	W • S Asia • 250 kW • ALT. FREQ. TO 9455 kHz
9455	CHINA
	CENTRAL PEOPLES BS, Kunming — S • CHINESE, ETC • TAIWAN-1 • 50 kW
	SLOVAKIA
	†ADVENTIST WORLD R, Rimavská Sobota — S • E Africa • 250 kW
	W • S Asia • 250 kW • ALT. FREQ. TO 9450 kHz
	W • N Africa • 250 kW
	W • N Africa & W Africa • 250 kW
	S America • 250 kW
	USA
	MONITOR RADIO INTL, South Carolina — M-F • C America & S America • 500 kW
	Sa/Su • C America & S America • 500 kW
	M-F • W North Am & C America • 500 kW
	Sa/Su • W North Am & C America • 500 kW
	VOA, Greenville, NC — C America & S America • 500 kW
9457	CHINA
	CHINA RADIO INTL, Kunming — S Asia • 120 kW
	E Africa & S Africa • 120 kW
9460	TURKEY
	VOICE OF TURKEY, Ankara — ⏹ • Europe & E North Am • 500 kW
	⏹ • Europe • 500 kW
9465	NORTHERN MARIANA IS
	†KFBS-FAR EAST BC, Saipan Island — E Asia • 100 kW • ALT. FREQ. TO 11650 kHz
	E Europe & W Asia • 100 kW • ALT. FREQ. TO 5810 kHz
	M/Th-Sa • E Europe & W Asia • 100 kW • ALT. FREQ. TO 5810 kHz
	Su • E Europe & W Asia • 100 kW • ALT. FREQ. TO 5810 kHz
	Tu/W • E Europe & W Asia • 100 kW • ALT. FREQ. TO 5810 kHz
	Su/Tu/W • E Europe & W Asia • 100 kW • ALT. FREQ. TO 5810 kHz
	M-Th/Sa • E Europe & W Asia • 100 kW • ALT. FREQ. TO 5810 kHz
	Su/F • E Europe & W Asia • 100 kW • ALT. FREQ. TO 5810 kHz
	M/Tu/F • E Europe & W Asia • 100 kW • ALT. FREQ. TO 5810 kHz
	Th • E Europe & W Asia • 100 kW • ALT. FREQ. TO 5810 kHz
	W/Sa • E Europe & W Asia • 100 kW • ALT. FREQ. TO 5810 kHz
	M/Tu • E Europe & W Asia • 100 kW • ALT. FREQ. TO 5810 kHz
	SLOVAKIA
	†ADVENTIST WORLD R, Rimavská Sobota — S • S Asia • 250 kW
	W • W Asia & S Asia • 250 kW
	W • W Africa • 250 kW

(con'd)

ENGLISH ▬ ARABIC ⋙ CHINESE ▭▭▭ FRENCH ▭▭ GERMAN ▬▬ RUSSIAN ══ SPANISH ▬▬ OTHER ──

FREQUENCY   COUNTRY, STATION, LOCATION

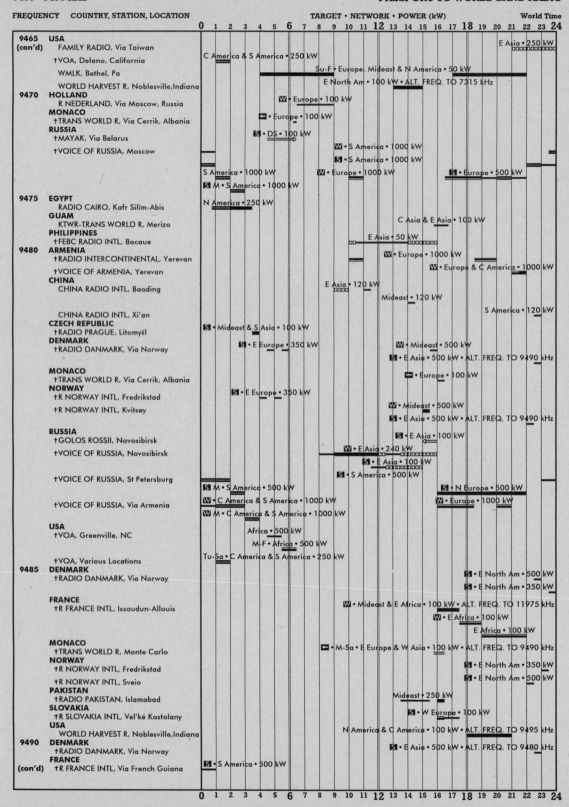

FREQUENCY   COUNTRY, STATION, LOCATION

TARGET • NETWORK • POWER (kW)

World Time

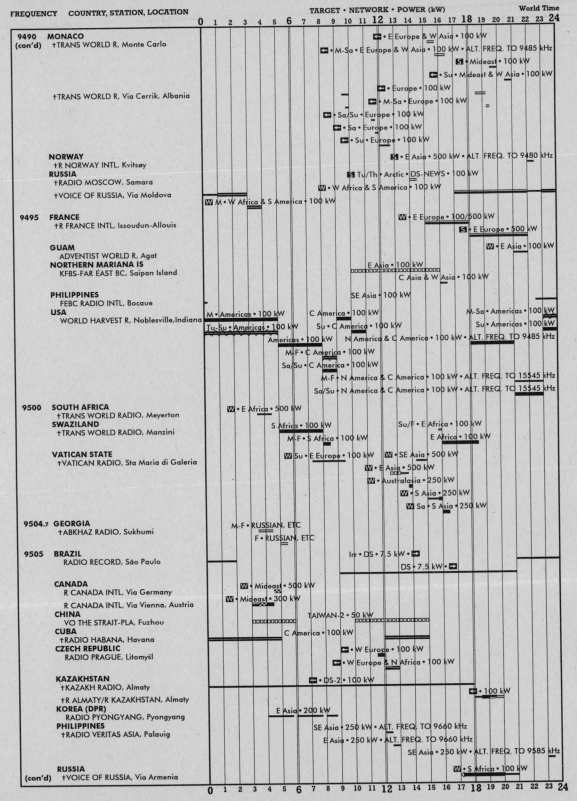

Frequency	Country, Station, Location	Schedule
9490 (con'd)	**MONACO** †TRANS WORLD R, Monte Carlo	• E Europe & W Asia • 100 kW / M-Sa • E Europe & W Asia • 100 kW • ALT. FREQ. TO 9485 kHz / S • Mideast • 100 kW / Su • Mideast & W Asia • 100 kW
	†TRANS WORLD R, Via Cerrik, Albania	• Europe • 100 kW / M-Sa • Europe • 100 kW / Sa/Su • Europe • 100 kW / Sa • Europe • 100 kW / Su • Europe • 100 kW
	NORWAY †R NORWAY INTL, Kvitsøy	S • E Asia • 500 kW • ALT. FREQ. TO 9480 kHz
	RUSSIA †RADIO MOSCOW, Samara	S Tu/Th • Arctic • DS-NEWS • 100 kW
	†VOICE OF RUSSIA, Via Moldova	W • W Africa & S America • 100 kW / W M • W Africa & S America • 100 kW
9495	**FRANCE** †R FRANCE INTL, Issoudun-Allouis	W • E Europe • 100/500 kW / S • E Europe • 500 kW
	GUAM ADVENTIST WORLD R, Agat	W • E Asia • 100 kW
	NORTHERN MARIANA IS KFBS-FAR EAST BC, Saipan Island	E Asia • 100 kW / C Asia & W Asia • 100 kW
	PHILIPPINES FEBC RADIO INTL, Bocaue	SE Asia • 100 kW
	USA WORLD HARVEST R, Noblesville, Indiana	M • Americas • 100 kW / C America • 100 kW / M-Sa • Americas • 100 kW / Tu-Su • Americas • 100 kW / Su • C America • 100 kW / Su • Americas • 100 kW / Americas • 100 kW / N America & C America • 100 kW • ALT. FREQ. TO 9485 kHz / M-F • C America • 100 kW / Sa/Su • C America • 100 kW / M-F • N America & C America • 100 kW • ALT. FREQ. TO 15545 kHz / Sa/Su • N America & C America • 100 kW • ALT. FREQ. TO 15545 kHz
9500	**SOUTH AFRICA** †TRANS WORLD RADIO, Meyerton	W • E Africa • 500 kW
	SWAZILAND †TRANS WORLD RADIO, Manzini	S Africa • 100 kW / Su/F • E Africa • 100 kW / M-F • S Africa • 100 kW / E Africa • 100 kW
	VATICAN STATE †VATICAN RADIO, Sta Maria di Galeria	W Su • E Europe • 100 kW / W • SE Asia • 500 kW / W • E Asia • 500 kW / W • Australasia • 250 kW / W • S Asia • 250 kW / W Sa • S Asia • 250 kW
9504.7	**GEORGIA** †ABKHAZ RADIO, Sukhumi	M-F • RUSSIAN, ETC / F • RUSSIAN, ETC
9505	**BRAZIL** RADIO RECORD, São Paulo	Irr • DS • 7.5 kW • / DS • 7.5 kW •
	CANADA R CANADA INTL, Via Germany	W • Mideast • 500 kW
	R CANADA INTL, Via Vienna, Austria	W • Mideast • 300 kW
	CHINA VO THE STRAIT-PLA, Fuzhou	TAIWAN-2 • 50 kW
	CUBA †RADIO HABANA, Havana	C America • 100 kW
	CZECH REPUBLIC RADIO PRAGUE, Litomyšl	• W Europe • 100 kW / • W Europe & N Africa • 100 kW
	KAZAKHSTAN †KAZAKH RADIO, Almaty	• DS-2 • 100 kW
	†R ALMATY/R KAZAKHSTAN, Almaty	• 100 kW
	KOREA (DPR) RADIO PYONGYANG, Pyongyang	E Asia • 200 kW
	PHILIPPINES †RADIO VERITAS ASIA, Palauig	SE Asia • 250 kW • ALT. FREQ. TO 9660 kHz / E Asia • 250 kW • ALT. FREQ. TO 9660 kHz / SE Asia • 250 kW • ALT. FREQ. TO 9585 kHz
(con'd)	**RUSSIA** †VOICE OF RUSSIA, Via Armenia	W • S Africa • 100 kW

ENGLISH ▬   ARABIC ⧈   CHINESE ▫▫▫   FRENCH ▬   GERMAN ▬   RUSSIAN ═   SPANISH ▬   OTHER ▬

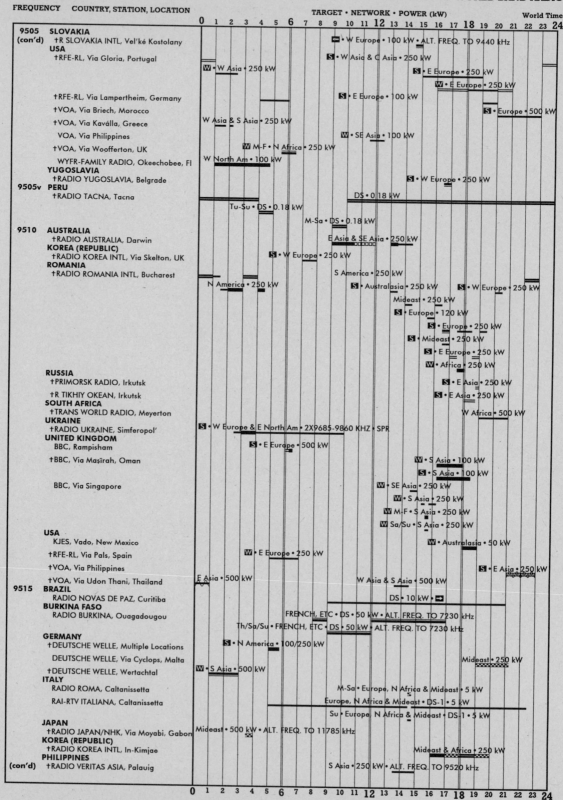

FREQUENCY	COUNTRY, STATION, LOCATION	TARGET • NETWORK • POWER (kW)
9505 (con'd)	**SLOVAKIA**	
	†R SLOVAKIA INTL, Vel'ké Kostolany	⇦ • W Europe • 100 kW • ALT. FREQ. TO 9440 kHz
	USA	
	†RFE-RL, Via Gloria, Portugal	[S] • W Asia & C Asia • 250 kW
		[W] • W Asia • 250 kW
		[S] • E Europe • 250 kW
		[W] • E Europe • 250 kW
	†RFE-RL, Via Lampertheim, Germany	[S] • E Europe • 100 kW
	†VOA, Via Briech, Morocco	[S] • Europe • 500 kW
	†VOA, Via Kaválla, Greece	W Asia & S Asia • 250 kW
	VOA, Via Philippines	[W] • SE Asia • 100 kW
	†VOA, Via Woofferton, UK	[W] M-F • N Africa • 250 kW
	WYFR-FAMILY RADIO, Okeechobee, Fl	W North Am • 100 kW
	YUGOSLAVIA	
	†RADIO YUGOSLAVIA, Belgrade	[S] • W Europe • 250 kW
9505v	**PERU**	
	†RADIO TACNA, Tacna	DS • 0.18 kW
		Tu-Su • DS • 0.18 kW
		M-Sa • DS • 0.18 kW
9510	**AUSTRALIA**	
	†RADIO AUSTRALIA, Darwin	E Asia & SE Asia • 250 kW
	KOREA (REPUBLIC)	
	†RADIO KOREA INTL, Via Skelton, UK	[S] • W Europe • 250 kW
	ROMANIA	
	†RADIO ROMANIA INTL, Bucharest	S America • 250 kW
		N America • 250 kW
		[S] • Australasia • 250 kW
		[S] • W Europe • 250 kW
		Mideast • 250 kW
		[S] • Europe • 120 kW
		[S] • Europe • 250 kW
		[S] • Mideast • 250 kW
		[S] • E Europe • 250 kW
		[W] • Africa • 250 kW
	RUSSIA	
	†PRIMORSK RADIO, Irkutsk	[S] • E Asia • 250 kW
	†R TIKHIY OKEAN, Irkutsk	[S] • E Asia • 250 kW
	SOUTH AFRICA	
	†TRANS WORLD RADIO, Meyerton	W Africa • 500 kW
	UKRAINE	
	†RADIO UKRAINE, Simferopol'	[S] • W Europe & E North Am • 2X9685-9860 KHZ • SPR
	UNITED KINGDOM	
	BBC, Rampisham	[S] • E Europe • 500 kW
	†BBC, Via Maṣīrah, Oman	[W] • S Asia • 100 kW
		[S] • S Asia • 100 kW
	BBC, Via Singapore	[W] • SE Asia • 250 kW
		[W] • S Asia • 250 kW
		[W] M-F • S Asia • 250 kW
		[W] Sa/Su • S Asia • 250 kW
	USA	
	KJES, Vado, New Mexico	[W] • Australasia • 50 kW
	†RFE-RL, Via Pals, Spain	[W] • E Europe • 250 kW
	†VOA, Via Philippines	[S] • E Asia • 250 kW
	†VOA, Via Udon Thani, Thailand	E Asia • 500 kW
		W Asia & S Asia • 500 kW
9515	**BRAZIL**	
	RADIO NOVAS DE PAZ, Curitiba	DS • 10 kW • ⇨
	BURKINA FASO	
	RADIO BURKINA, Ouagadougou	FRENCH, ETC • DS • 50 kW • ALT. FREQ. TO 7230 kHz
		Th/Sa/Su • FRENCH, ETC • DS • 50 kW • ALT. FREQ. TO 7230 kHz
	GERMANY	
	†DEUTSCHE WELLE, Multiple Locations	[S] • N America • 100/250 kW
	DEUTSCHE WELLE, Via Cyclops, Malta	Mideast • 250 kW
	†DEUTSCHE WELLE, Wertachtal	[W] • S Asia • 500 kW
	ITALY	
	RADIO ROMA, Caltanissetta	M-Sa • Europe, N Africa & Mideast • 5 kW
	RAI-RTV ITALIANA, Caltanissetta	Europe, N Africa & Mideast • DS-1 • 5 kW
		Su • Europe, N Africa & Mideast • DS-1 • 5 kW
	JAPAN	
	†RADIO JAPAN/NHK, Via Moyabi, Gabon	Mideast • 500 kW • ALT. FREQ. TO 11785 kHz
	KOREA (REPUBLIC)	
	†RADIO KOREA INTL, In-Kimjae	Mideast & Africa • 250 kW
	PHILIPPINES	
(con'd)	†RADIO VERITAS ASIA, Palauig	S Asia • 250 kW • ALT. FREQ. TO 9520 kHz

World Time 0 1 2 3 4 5 6 7 8 9 10 11 12 13 14 15 16 17 18 19 20 21 22 23 24

SEASONAL [S] OR [W]   1-HR TIMESHIFT MIDYEAR ⇦ OR ⇨   JAMMING / OR ∧   EARLIEST HEARD ◁   LATEST HEARD ▷   NEW FOR 1996 †

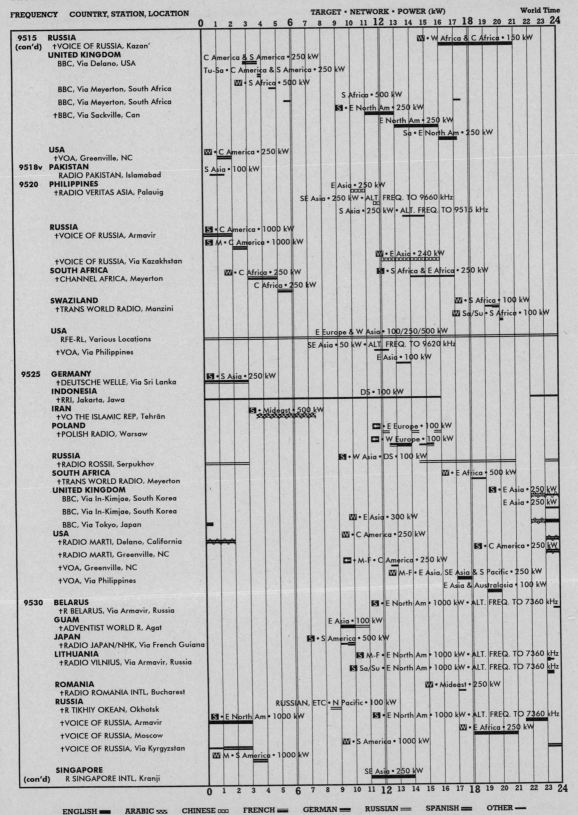

9515 RUSSIA
(con'd) †VOICE OF RUSSIA, Kazan'
UNITED KINGDOM
BBC, Via Delano, USA
C America & S America • 250 kW
Tu-Sa • C America & S America • 250 kW
W • S Africa • 500 kW

BBC, Via Meyerton, South Africa
S Africa • 500 kW
BBC, Via Meyerton, South Africa
S • E North Am • 250 kW
†BBC, Via Sackville, Can
E North Am • 250 kW
Sa • E North Am • 250 kW

USA
†VOA, Greenville, NC   W • C America • 250 kW
9518v PAKISTAN
RADIO PAKISTAN, Islamabad   S Asia • 100 kW
9520 PHILIPPINES
†RADIO VERITAS ASIA, Palauig
E Asia • 250 kW
SE Asia • 250 kW • ALT. FREQ. TO 9660 kHz
S Asia • 250 kW • ALT. FREQ. TO 9515 kHz

RUSSIA
†VOICE OF RUSSIA, Armavir   S • C America • 1000 kW
S • M • C America • 1000 kW

†VOICE OF RUSSIA, Via Kazakhstan   W • E Asia • 240 kW
SOUTH AFRICA
†CHANNEL AFRICA, Meyerton   W • C Africa • 250 kW   S • S Africa & E Africa • 250 kW
C Africa • 250 kW

SWAZILAND
†TRANS WORLD RADIO, Manzini   W • S Africa • 100 kW
W Sa/Su • S Africa • 100 kW

USA
RFE-RL, Various Locations   E Europe & W Asia • 100/250/500 kW
†VOA, Via Philippines   SE Asia • 50 kW • ALT. FREQ. TO 9620 kHz
E Asia • 100 kW

9525 GERMANY
†DEUTSCHE WELLE, Via Sri Lanka   S • S Asia • 250 kW
INDONESIA
†RRI, Jakarta, Jawa   DS • 100 kW
IRAN
†VO THE ISLAMIC REP, Tehrān   S • Mideast • 500 kW
POLAND
†POLISH RADIO, Warsaw   E Europe • 100 kW
W Europe • 100 kW

RUSSIA
†RADIO ROSSII, Serpukhov   S • W Asia • DS • 100 kW
SOUTH AFRICA
†TRANS WORLD RADIO, Meyerton   W • E Africa • 500 kW
UNITED KINGDOM
BBC, Via In-Kimjae, South Korea   S • E Asia • 250 kW
BBC, Via In-Kimjae, South Korea   E Asia • 250 kW
BBC, Via Tokyo, Japan   W • E Asia • 300 kW
USA
†RADIO MARTI, Delano, California   W • C America • 250 kW
†RADIO MARTI, Greenville, NC   S • C America • 250 kW
†VOA, Greenville, NC   M-F • C America • 250 kW
†VOA, Via Philippines   W M-F • E Asia, SE Asia & S Pacific • 250 kW
E Asia & Australasia • 100 kW

9530 BELARUS
†R BELARUS, Via Armavir, Russia   S • E North Am • 1000 kW • ALT. FREQ. TO 7360 kHz
GUAM
†ADVENTIST WORLD R, Agat   E Asia • 100 kW
JAPAN
†RADIO JAPAN/NHK, Via French Guiana   S • S America • 500 kW
LITHUANIA
†RADIO VILNIUS, Via Armavir, Russia   S M-F • E North Am • 1000 kW • ALT. FREQ. TO 7360 kHz
S Sa/Su • E North Am • 1000 kW • ALT. FREQ. TO 7360 kHz

ROMANIA
†RADIO ROMANIA INTL, Bucharest   W • Mideast • 250 kW
RUSSIA
†R TIKHIY OKEAN, Okhotsk   RUSSIAN, ETC • N Pacific • 100 kW
†VOICE OF RUSSIA, Armavir   S • E North Am • 1000 kW   S • E North Am • 1000 kW • ALT. FREQ. TO 7360 kHz
†VOICE OF RUSSIA, Moscow   W • E Africa • 250 kW
†VOICE OF RUSSIA, Via Kyrgyzstan   W • S America • 1000 kW
W M • S America • 1000 kW

SINGAPORE
(con'd) R SINGAPORE INTL, Kranji   SE Asia • 250 kW

ENGLISH ▬ ARABIC ≋ CHINESE ▫▫▫ FRENCH ▬ GERMAN ▬ RUSSIAN ═ SPANISH ▬ OTHER ▬

FREQUENCY   COUNTRY, STATION, LOCATION

TARGET • NETWORK • POWER (kW)

World Time

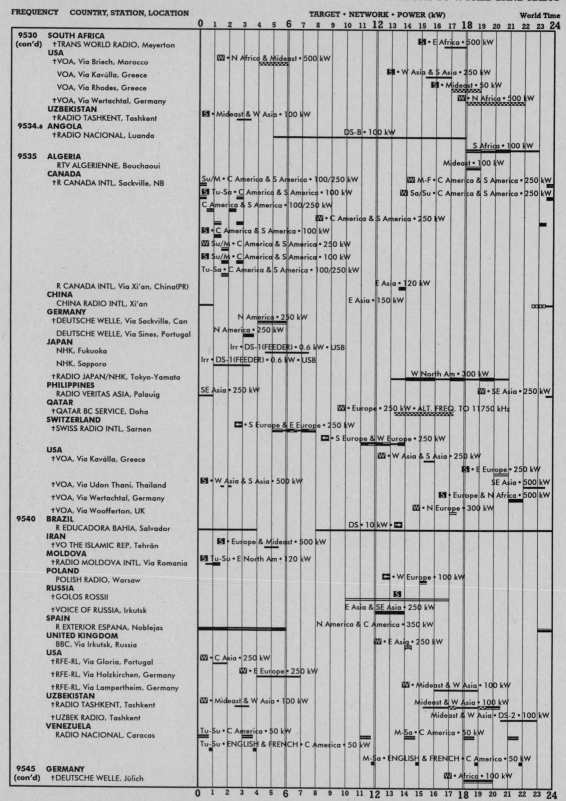

FREQUENCY	COUNTRY, STATION, LOCATION	TARGET • NETWORK • POWER (kW)
9530 (con'd)	SOUTH AFRICA †TRANS WORLD RADIO, Meyerton	S • E Africa • 500 kW
	USA †VOA, Via Briech, Morocco	W • N Africa & Mideast • 500 kW
	VOA, Via Kaválla, Greece	S • W Asia & S Asia • 250 kW
	VOA, Via Rhodes, Greece	S • Mideast • 50 kW
	†VOA, Via Wertachtal, Germany	W • N Africa • 500 kW
	UZBEKISTAN †RADIO TASHKENT, Tashkent	S • Mideast & W Asia • 100 kW
9534.8	ANGOLA †RADIO NACIONAL, Luanda	DS-B • 100 kW S Africa • 100 kW
9535	ALGERIA RTV ALGERIENNE, Bouchaoui	Mideast • 100 kW
	CANADA †R CANADA INTL, Sackville, NB	Su/M • C America & S America • 100/250 kW W M-F • C America & S America • 250 kW
		S Tu-Sa • C America & S America • 100 kW W Sa/Su • C America & S America • 250 kW
		C America & S America • 100/250 kW
		W • C America & S America • 250 kW
		S • C America & S America • 100 kW
		W Su/M • C America & S America • 250 kW
		S Su/M • C America & S America • 100 kW
		Tu-Sa • C America & S America • 100/250 kW
	R CANADA INTL, Via Xi'an, China(PR)	E Asia • 120 kW
	CHINA CHINA RADIO INTL, Xi'an	E Asia • 150 kW
	GERMANY †DEUTSCHE WELLE, Via Sackville, Can	N America • 250 kW
	DEUTSCHE WELLE, Via Sines, Portugal	N America • 250 kW
	JAPAN NHK, Fukuoka	Irr • DS-1(FEEDER) • 0.6 kW • USB
	NHK, Sapporo	Irr • DS-1(FEEDER) • 0.6 kW • USB
	†RADIO JAPAN/NHK, Tokyo-Yamata	W North Am • 300 kW
	PHILIPPINES RADIO VERITAS ASIA, Palauig	SE Asia • 250 kW W • SE Asia • 250 kW
	QATAR †QATAR BC SERVICE, Doha	W • Europe • 250 kW • ALT. FREQ. TO 11750 kHz
	SWITZERLAND †SWISS RADIO INTL, Sarnen	• S Europe & E Europe • 250 kW
		• S Europe & W Europe • 250 kW
	USA †VOA, Via Kaválla, Greece	W • W Asia & S Asia • 250 kW S • E Europe • 250 kW
	†VOA, Via Udon Thani, Thailand	S • W Asia & S Asia • 500 kW SE Asia • 500 kW
	†VOA, Via Wertachtal, Germany	S • Europe & N Africa • 500 kW
	†VOA, Via Woofferton, UK	W • N Europe • 300 kW
9540	BRAZIL R EDUCADORA BAHIA, Salvador	DS • 10 kW •
	IRAN †VO THE ISLAMIC REP, Tehrãn	S • Europe & Mideast • 500 kW
	MOLDOVA †RADIO MOLDOVA INTL, Via Romania	S Tu-Su • E North Am • 120 kW
	POLAND POLISH RADIO, Warsaw	• W Europe • 100 kW
	RUSSIA †GOLOS ROSSII	S
	†VOICE OF RUSSIA, Irkutsk	E Asia & SE Asia • 250 kW
	SPAIN R EXTERIOR ESPANA, Noblejas	N America & C America • 350 kW
	UNITED KINGDOM BBC, Via Irkutsk, Russia	W • E Asia • 250 kW
	USA †RFE-RL, Via Gloria, Portugal	W • C Asia • 250 kW
	†RFE-RL, Via Holzkirchen, Germany	W • E Europe • 250 kW
	†RFE-RL, Via Lampertheim, Germany	W • Mideast & W Asia • 100 kW
	UZBEKISTAN †RADIO TASHKENT, Tashkent	W • Mideast & W Asia • 100 kW Mideast & W Asia • 100 kW
	†UZBEK RADIO, Tashkent	Mideast & W Asia • DS-2 • 100 kW
	VENEZUELA RADIO NACIONAL, Caracas	Tu-Su • C America • 50 kW M-Sa • C America • 50 kW
		Tu-Su • ENGLISH & FRENCH • C America • 50 kW
		M-Sa • ENGLISH & FRENCH • C America • 50 kW
9545 (con'd)	GERMANY †DEUTSCHE WELLE, Jülich	W • Africa • 100 kW

FREQUENCY   COUNTRY, STATION, LOCATION

TARGET • NETWORK • POWER (kW)

World Time

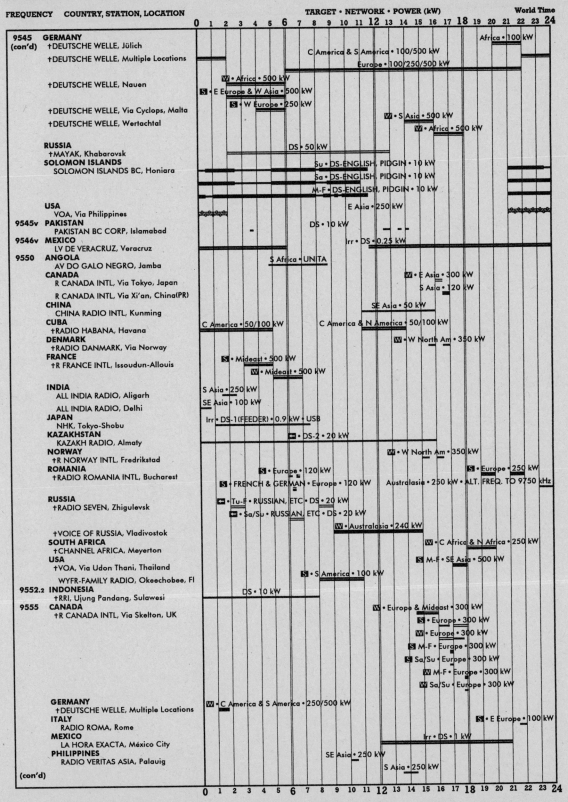

Frequency	Country, Station, Location	Target • Network • Power
9545 (con'd)	**GERMANY**	
	†DEUTSCHE WELLE, Jülich	Africa • 100 kW
	†DEUTSCHE WELLE, Multiple Locations	C America & S America • 100/500 kW; Europe • 100/250/500 kW
	†DEUTSCHE WELLE, Nauen	W • Africa • 500 kW; S • E Europe & W Asia • 500 kW; S • W Europe • 250 kW
	†DEUTSCHE WELLE, Via Cyclops, Malta	W • S Asia • 500 kW
	†DEUTSCHE WELLE, Wertachtal	W • Africa • 500 kW
	RUSSIA	
	†MAYAK, Khabarovsk	DS • 50 kW
	SOLOMON ISLANDS	
	SOLOMON ISLANDS BC, Honiara	Su • DS-ENGLISH, PIDGIN • 10 kW; Sa • DS-ENGLISH, PIDGIN • 10 kW; M-F • DS-ENGLISH, PIDGIN • 10 kW
	USA	
	VOA, Via Philippines	E Asia • 250 kW
9545v	**PAKISTAN**	
	PAKISTAN BC CORP, Islamabad	DS • 10 kW
9546v	**MEXICO**	
	LV DE VERACRUZ, Veracruz	Irr • DS • 0.25 kW
9550	**ANGOLA**	
	AV DO GALO NEGRO, Jamba	S Africa • UNITA
	CANADA	
	R CANADA INTL, Via Tokyo, Japan	W • E Asia • 300 kW; S Asia • 120 kW
	R CANADA INTL, Via Xi'an, China(PR)	
	CHINA	
	CHINA RADIO INTL, Kunming	SE Asia • 50 kW
	CUBA	
	†RADIO HABANA, Havana	C America • 50/100 kW; C America & N America • 50/100 kW
	DENMARK	
	†RADIO DANMARK, Via Norway	W • W North Am • 350 kW
	FRANCE	
	†R FRANCE INTL, Issoudun-Allouis	S • Mideast • 500 kW; W • Mideast • 500 kW
	INDIA	
	ALL INDIA RADIO, Aligarh	S Asia • 250 kW
	ALL INDIA RADIO, Delhi	SE Asia • 100 kW
	JAPAN	
	NHK, Tokyo-Shobu	Irr • DS-1(FEEDER) • 0.9 kW • USB
	KAZAKHSTAN	
	KAZAKH RADIO, Almaty	DS-2 • 20 kW
	NORWAY	
	†R NORWAY INTL, Fredrikstad	W • W North Am • 350 kW
	ROMANIA	
	†RADIO ROMANIA INTL, Bucharest	S • Europe • 120 kW; S • Europe • 250 kW; S • FRENCH & GERMAN • Europe • 120 kW; Australasia • 250 kW • ALT. FREQ. TO 9750 kHz
	RUSSIA	
	†RADIO SEVEN, Zhigulevsk	Tu-F • RUSSIAN, ETC • DS • 20 kW; Sa/Su • RUSSIAN, ETC • DS • 20 kW
	†VOICE OF RUSSIA, Vladivostok	W • Australasia • 240 kW
	SOUTH AFRICA	
	†CHANNEL AFRICA, Meyerton	W • C Africa & N Africa • 250 kW
	USA	
	†VOA, Via Udon Thani, Thailand	S • M-F • SE Asia • 500 kW
	WYFR-FAMILY RADIO, Okeechobee, Fl	S • S America • 100 kW
9552.2	**INDONESIA**	
	†RRI, Ujung Pandang, Sulawesi	DS • 10 kW
9555	**CANADA**	
	†R CANADA INTL, Via Skelton, UK	W • Europe & Mideast • 300 kW; S • Europe • 300 kW; W • Europe • 300 kW; S M-F • Europe • 300 kW; S Sa/Su • Europe • 300 kW; W M-F • Europe • 300 kW; W Sa/Su • Europe • 300 kW
	GERMANY	
	†DEUTSCHE WELLE, Multiple Locations	W • C America & S America • 250/500 kW
	ITALY	
	RADIO ROMA, Rome	S • E Europe • 100 kW
	MEXICO	
	LA HORA EXACTA, México City	Irr • DS • 1 kW
	PHILIPPINES	
	RADIO VERITAS ASIA, Palauig	SE Asia • 250 kW; S Asia • 250 kW
(con'd)		

ENGLISH ▬   ARABIC ⌇⌇⌇   CHINESE ▫▫▫   FRENCH ▬▬   GERMAN ▬▬   RUSSIAN ══   SPANISH ▬▬   OTHER ▬

FREQUENCY   COUNTRY, STATION, LOCATION   TARGET • NETWORK • POWER (kW)   World Time

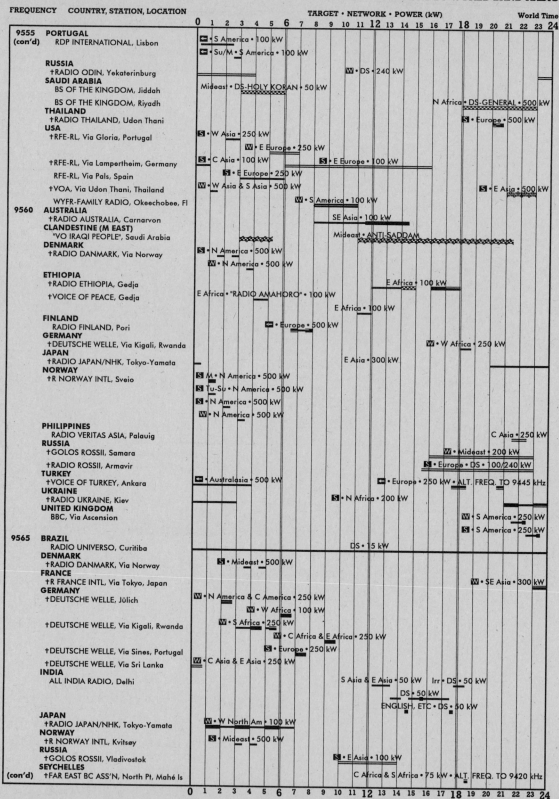

9555 **PORTUGAL**	
(con'd) RDP INTERNATIONAL, Lisbon	⊡ • S America • 100 kW
	⊡ • Su/M • S America • 100 kW
RUSSIA	
†RADIO ODIN, Yekaterinburg	W • DS • 240 kW
SAUDI ARABIA	
BS OF THE KINGDOM, Jiddah	Mideast • DS-HOLY KORAN • 50 kW
BS OF THE KINGDOM, Riyadh	N Africa • DS-GENERAL • 500 kW
THAILAND	
†RADIO THAILAND, Udon Thani	S • Europe • 500 kW
USA	
†RFE-RL, Via Gloria, Portugal	S • W Asia • 250 kW
	W • E Europe • 250 kW
†RFE-RL, Via Lampertheim, Germany	S • C Asia • 100 kW S • E Europe • 100 kW
RFE-RL, Via Pals, Spain	S • E Europe • 250 kW
†VOA, Via Udon Thani, Thailand	W • W Asia & S Asia • 500 kW S • E Asia • 500 kW
WYFR-FAMILY RADIO, Okeechobee, Fl	W • S America • 100 kW
9560 **AUSTRALIA**	
†RADIO AUSTRALIA, Carnarvon	SE Asia • 100 kW
CLANDESTINE (M EAST)	
"VO IRAQI PEOPLE", Saudi Arabia	Mideast • ANTI-SADDAM
DENMARK	
†RADIO DANMARK, Via Norway	S • N America • 500 kW
	W • N America • 500 kW
ETHIOPIA	
†RADIO ETHIOPIA, Gedja	E Africa • 100 kW
†VOICE OF PEACE, Gedja	E Africa • "RADIO AMAHORO" • 100 kW
	E Africa • 100 kW
FINLAND	
RADIO FINLAND, Pori	⊡ • Europe • 500 kW
GERMANY	
†DEUTSCHE WELLE, Via Kigali, Rwanda	W • W Africa • 250 kW
JAPAN	
†RADIO JAPAN/NHK, Tokyo-Yamata	E Asia • 300 kW
NORWAY	
†R NORWAY INTL, Sveio	S • M • N America • 500 kW
	S • Tu-Su • N America • 500 kW
	S • N America • 500 kW
	W • N America • 500 kW
PHILIPPINES	
RADIO VERITAS ASIA, Palauig	C Asia • 250 kW
RUSSIA	
†GOLOS ROSSII, Samara	W • Mideast • 200 kW
†RADIO ROSSII, Armavir	S • Europe • DS • 100/240 kW
TURKEY	
†VOICE OF TURKEY, Ankara	⊡ • Australasia • 500 kW ⊡ • Europe • 250 kW • ALT. FREQ. TO 9445 kHz
UKRAINE	
†RADIO UKRAINE, Kiev	S • N Africa • 200 kW
UNITED KINGDOM	
BBC, Via Ascension	W • S America • 250 kW
	S • S America • 250 kW
9565 **BRAZIL**	
RADIO UNIVERSO, Curitiba	DS • 15 kW
DENMARK	
†RADIO DANMARK, Via Norway	S • Mideast • 500 kW
FRANCE	
†R FRANCE INTL, Via Tokyo, Japan	W • SE Asia • 300 kW
GERMANY	
†DEUTSCHE WELLE, Jülich	W • N America & C America • 250 kW
	W • W Africa • 100 kW
†DEUTSCHE WELLE, Via Kigali, Rwanda	W • S Africa • 250 kW
	W • C Africa & E Africa • 250 kW
†DEUTSCHE WELLE, Via Sines, Portugal	S • Europe • 250 kW
†DEUTSCHE WELLE, Via Sri Lanka	W • C Asia & E Asia • 250 kW
INDIA	
ALL INDIA RADIO, Delhi	S Asia & E Asia • 50 kW Irr • DS • 50 kW
	DS • 50 kW
	ENGLISH, ETC • DS • 50 kW
JAPAN	
†RADIO JAPAN/NHK, Tokyo-Yamata	W • W North Am • 100 kW
NORWAY	
†R NORWAY INTL, Kvitsøy	S • Mideast • 500 kW
RUSSIA	
†GOLOS ROSSII, Vladivostok	S • E Asia • 100 kW
SEYCHELLES	
(con'd) †FAR EAST BC ASS'N, North Pt, Mahé Is	C Africa & S Africa • 75 kW • ALT. FREQ. TO 9420 kHz

0 1 2 3 4 5 6 7 8 9 10 11 12 13 14 15 16 17 18 19 20 21 22 23 24

FREQUENCY   COUNTRY, STATION, LOCATION   TARGET • NETWORK • POWER (kW)   World Time

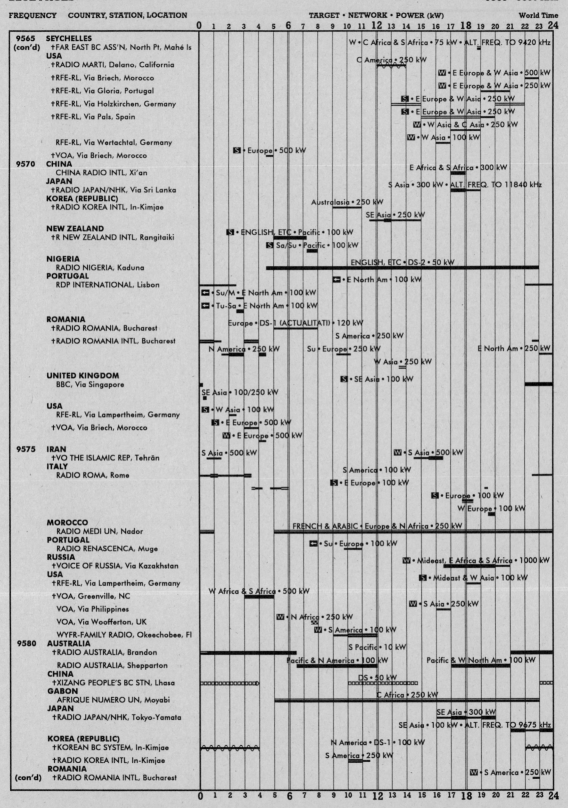

Frequency	Country, Station, Location	Target • Network • Power
9565	**SEYCHELLES**	
(con'd)	†FAR EAST BC ASS'N, North Pt, Mahé Is	W • C Africa & S Africa • 75 kW • ALT. FREQ. TO 9420 kHz
	USA	
	†RADIO MARTI, Delano, California	C America • 250 kW
	†RFE-RL, Via Briech, Morocco	W • E Europe & W Asia • 500 kW
	†RFE-RL, Via Gloria, Portugal	W • E Europe & W Asia • 250 kW
	†RFE-RL, Via Holzkirchen, Germany	S • E Europe & W Asia • 250 kW
	†RFE-RL, Via Pals, Spain	S • E Europe & W Asia • 250 kW
		W • W Asia & C Asia • 250 kW
	RFE-RL, Via Wertachtal, Germany	W • W Asia • 100 kW
	†VOA, Via Briech, Morocco	S • Europe • 500 kW
9570	**CHINA**	
	CHINA RADIO INTL, Xi'an	E Africa & S Africa • 300 kW
	JAPAN	
	†RADIO JAPAN/NHK, Via Sri Lanka	S Asia • 300 kW • ALT. FREQ. TO 11840 kHz
	KOREA (REPUBLIC)	
	†RADIO KOREA INTL, In-Kimjae	Australasia • 250 kW
		SE Asia • 250 kW
	NEW ZEALAND	
	†R NEW ZEALAND INTL, Rangitaiki	S • ENGLISH, ETC • Pacific • 100 kW
		S • Sa/Su • Pacific • 100 kW
	NIGERIA	
	RADIO NIGERIA, Kaduna	ENGLISH, ETC • DS-2 • 50 kW
	PORTUGAL	
	RDP INTERNATIONAL, Lisbon	E North Am • 100 kW
		Su/M • E North Am • 100 kW
		Tu-Sa • E North Am • 100 kW
	ROMANIA	
	†RADIO ROMANIA, Bucharest	Europe • DS-1 (ACTUALITATI) • 120 kW
	†RADIO ROMANIA INTL, Bucharest	S America • 250 kW
		N America • 250 kW
		Su • Europe • 250 kW
		W Asia • 250 kW
		E North Am • 250 kW
	UNITED KINGDOM	
	BBC, Via Singapore	S • SE Asia • 100 kW
		SE Asia • 100/250 kW
	USA	
	RFE-RL, Via Lampertheim, Germany	S • W Asia • 100 kW
	†VOA, Via Briech, Morocco	S • E Europe • 500 kW
		W • E Europe • 500 kW
9575	**IRAN**	
	†VO THE ISLAMIC REP, Tehrān	S Asia • 500 kW
		W • S Asia • 500 kW
	ITALY	
	RADIO ROMA, Rome	S America • 100 kW
		S • E Europe • 100 kW
		S • Europe • 100 kW
		W Europe • 100 kW
	MOROCCO	
	RADIO MEDI UN, Nador	FRENCH & ARABIC • Europe & N Africa • 250 kW
	PORTUGAL	
	RADIO RENASCENCA, Muge	Su • Europe • 100 kW
	RUSSIA	
	†VOICE OF RUSSIA, Via Kazakhstan	W • Mideast, E Africa & S Africa • 1000 kW
	USA	
	†RFE-RL, Via Lampertheim, Germany	S • Mideast & W Asia • 100 kW
	†VOA, Greenville, NC	W Africa & S Africa • 500 kW
	VOA, Via Philippines	W • S Asia • 250 kW
	VOA, Via Woofferton, UK	W • N Africa • 250 kW
	WYFR-FAMILY RADIO, Okeechobee, Fl	W • S America • 100 kW
9580	**AUSTRALIA**	
	†RADIO AUSTRALIA, Brandon	S Pacific • 10 kW
	RADIO AUSTRALIA, Shepparton	Pacific & N America • 100 kW
		Pacific & W North Am • 100 kW
	CHINA	
	†XIZANG PEOPLE'S BC STN, Lhasa	DS • 50 kW
	GABON	
	AFRIQUE NUMERO UN, Moyabi	C Africa • 250 kW
	JAPAN	
	†RADIO JAPAN/NHK, Tokyo-Yamata	SE Asia • 300 kW
		SE Asia • 100 kW • ALT. FREQ. TO 9675 kHz
	KOREA (REPUBLIC)	
	†KOREAN BC SYSTEM, In-Kimjae	N America • DS-1 • 100 kW
	†RADIO KOREA INTL, In-Kimjae	S America • 250 kW
	ROMANIA	
(con'd)	†RADIO ROMANIA INTL, Bucharest	W • S America • 250 kW

ENGLISH ▬▬   ARABIC ⌇⌇⌇   CHINESE □□□   FRENCH ══   GERMAN ▬▬   RUSSIAN ══   SPANISH ▬▬   OTHER ▬

FREQUENCY	COUNTRY, STATION, LOCATION

TARGET • NETWORK • POWER (kW) — World Time

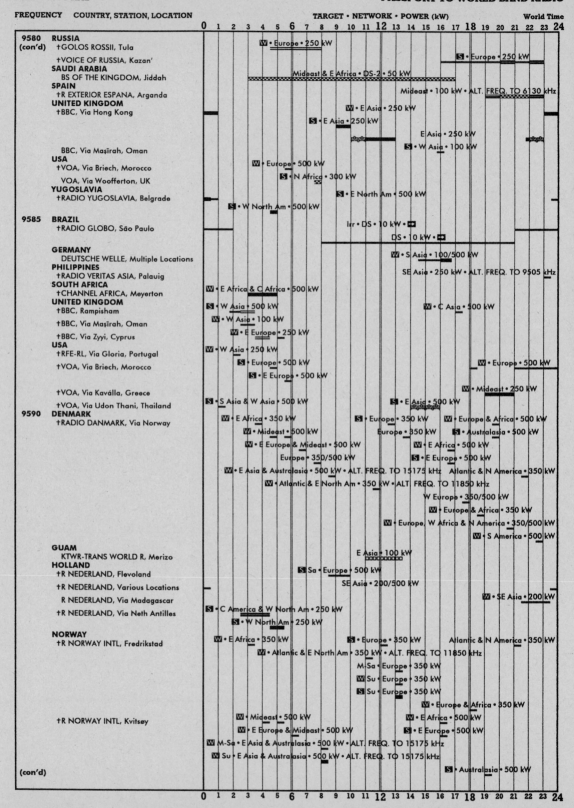

FREQUENCY	COUNTRY, STATION, LOCATION
9580 (con'd)	RUSSIA
	†GOLOS ROSSII, Tula — W • Europe • 250 kW
	†VOICE OF RUSSIA, Kazan' — S • Europe • 250 kW
	SAUDI ARABIA
	BS OF THE KINGDOM, Jiddah — Mideast & E Africa • DS-2 • 50 kW
	SPAIN
	†R EXTERIOR ESPANA, Arganda — Mideast • 100 kW • ALT. FREQ. TO 6130 kHz
	UNITED KINGDOM
	†BBC, Via Hong Kong — W • E Asia • 250 kW / S • E Asia • 250 kW
	BBC, Via Maşīrah, Oman — E Asia • 250 kW / S • W Asia • 100 kW
	USA
	†VOA, Via Briech, Morocco — W • Europe • 500 kW
	VOA, Via Woofferton, UK — S • N Africa • 300 kW
	YUGOSLAVIA
	†RADIO YUGOSLAVIA, Belgrade — S • E North Am • 500 kW / S • W North Am • 500 kW
9585	BRAZIL
	†RADIO GLOBO, São Paulo — Irr • DS • 10 kW / DS • 10 kW
	GERMANY
	DEUTSCHE WELLE, Multiple Locations — W • S Asia • 100/500 kW
	PHILIPPINES
	†RADIO VERITAS ASIA, Palauig — SE Asia • 250 kW • ALT. FREQ. TO 9505 kHz
	SOUTH AFRICA
	†CHANNEL AFRICA, Meyerton — W • E Africa & C Africa • 500 kW
	UNITED KINGDOM
	†BBC, Rampisham — S • W Asia • 500 kW / W • C Asia • 500 kW
	†BBC, Via Maşīrah, Oman — W • W Asia • 100 kW
	†BBC, Via Zyyi, Cyprus — W • E Europe • 250 kW
	USA
	†RFE-RL, Via Gloria, Portugal — W • W Asia • 250 kW
	†VOA, Via Briech, Morocco — S • Europe • 500 kW / W • Europe • 500 kW / S • E Europe • 500 kW
	†VOA, Via Kaválla, Greece — W • Mideast • 250 kW
	†VOA, Via Udon Thani, Thailand — S • S Asia & W Asia • 500 kW / S • E Asia • 500 kW
9590	DENMARK
	†RADIO DANMARK, Via Norway — W • E Africa • 350 kW / S • Europe • 350 kW / W • Europe & Africa • 500 kW
		W • Mideast • 500 kW / Europe • 350 kW / S • Australasia • 500 kW
		W • E Europe & Mideast • 500 kW / W • E Africa • 500 kW
		Europe • 350/500 kW / S • E Europe • 500 kW
		W • E Asia & Australasia • 500 kW • ALT. FREQ. TO 15175 kHz Atlantic & N America • 350 kW
		W • Atlantic & E North Am • 350 kW • ALT. FREQ. TO 11850 kHz
		W Europe • 350/500 kW
		W • Europe & Africa • 350 kW
		W • Europe, W Africa & N America • 350/500 kW
		W • S America • 500 kW
	GUAM
	KTWR-TRANS WORLD R, Merizo — E Asia • 100 kW
	HOLLAND
	†R NEDERLAND, Flevoland — Sa • Europe • 500 kW
	†R NEDERLAND, Various Locations — SE Asia • 200/500 kW
	R NEDERLAND, Via Madagascar — W • SE Asia • 200 kW
	†R NEDERLAND, Via Neth Antilles — S • C America & W North Am • 250 kW / S • W North Am • 250 kW
	NORWAY
	†R NORWAY INTL, Fredrikstad — W • E Africa • 350 kW / S • Europe • 350 kW / Atlantic & N America • 350 kW
		W • Atlantic & E North Am • 350 kW • ALT. FREQ. TO 11850 kHz
		M-Sa • Europe • 350 kW
		W Su • Europe • 350 kW
		S Su • Europe • 350 kW
		W • Europe & Africa • 350 kW
	†R NORWAY INTL, Kvitsøy — W • Mideast • 500 kW / W • E Africa • 500 kW
		W • E Europe & Mideast • 500 kW / S • E Europe • 500 kW
		W M-Sa • E Asia & Australasia • 500 kW • ALT. FREQ. TO 15175 kHz
		W Su • E Asia & Australasia • 500 kW • ALT. FREQ. TO 15175 kHz
		S • Australasia • 500 kW
(con'd)	

FREQUENCY   COUNTRY, STATION, LOCATION   TARGET • NETWORK • POWER (kW)   World Time

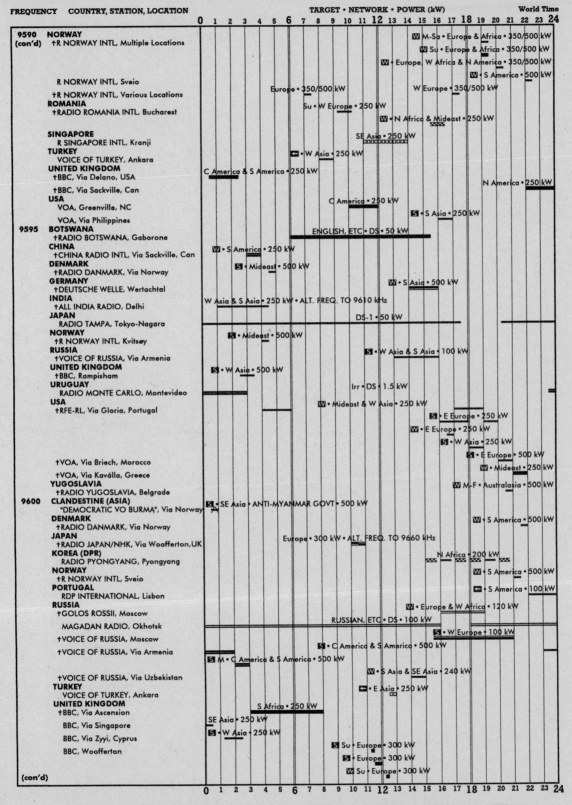

Frequency	Country / Station / Location	Details
9590 (con'd)	**NORWAY** †R NORWAY INTL, Multiple Locations	W • M-Sa • Europe & Africa • 350/500 kW
		W • Su • Europe & Africa • 350/500 kW
		W • Europe, W Africa & N America • 350/500 kW
		W • S America • 500 kW
	R NORWAY INTL, Sveio	W Europe • 350/500 kW
	†R NORWAY INTL, Various Locations	Europe • 350/500 kW
	ROMANIA †RADIO ROMANIA INTL, Bucharest	Su • W Europe • 250 kW
		W • N Africa & Mideast • 250 kW
	SINGAPORE R SINGAPORE INTL, Kranji	SE Asia • 250 kW
	TURKEY VOICE OF TURKEY, Ankara	• W Asia • 250 kW
	UNITED KINGDOM †BBC, Via Delano, USA	C America & S America • 250 kW
	†BBC, Via Sackville, Can	N America • 250 kW
	USA VOA, Greenville, NC	C America • 250 kW
	VOA, Via Philippines	S • S Asia • 250 kW
9595	**BOTSWANA** †RADIO BOTSWANA, Gaborone	ENGLISH, ETC • DS • 50 kW
	CHINA †CHINA RADIO INTL, Via Sackville, Can	W • S America • 250 kW
	DENMARK †RADIO DANMARK, Via Norway	S • Mideast • 500 kW
	GERMANY †DEUTSCHE WELLE, Wertachtal	W • S Asia • 500 kW
	INDIA †ALL INDIA RADIO, Delhi	W Asia & S Asia • 250 kW • ALT. FREQ. TO 9610 kHz
	JAPAN RADIO TAMPA, Tokyo-Nagara	DS-1 • 50 kW
	NORWAY †R NORWAY INTL, Kvitsøy	S • Mideast • 500 kW
	RUSSIA †VOICE OF RUSSIA, Via Armenia	S • W Asia & S Asia • 100 kW
	UNITED KINGDOM †BBC, Rampisham	S • W Asia • 500 kW
	URUGUAY RADIO MONTE CARLO, Montevideo	Irr • DS • 1.5 kW
	USA †RFE-RL, Via Gloria, Portugal	W • Mideast & W Asia • 250 kW
		S • E Europe • 250 kW
		W • E Europe • 250 kW
		S • W Asia • 250 kW
		S • E Europe • 500 kW
	†VOA, Via Briech, Morocco	W • Mideast • 250 kW
	†VOA, Via Kaválla, Greece	W • M-F • Australasia • 500 kW
	YUGOSLAVIA †RADIO YUGOSLAVIA, Belgrade	
9600	**CLANDESTINE (ASIA)** "DEMOCRATIC VO BURMA", Via Norway	S • SE Asia • ANTI-MYANMAR GOVT • 500 kW
	DENMARK †RADIO DANMARK, Via Norway	W • S America • 500 kW
	JAPAN †RADIO JAPAN/NHK, Via Woofferton, UK	Europe • 300 kW • ALT. FREQ. TO 9660 kHz
	KOREA (DPR) RADIO PYONGYANG, Pyongyang	N Africa • 200 kW
	NORWAY †R NORWAY INTL, Sveio	W • S America • 500 kW
	PORTUGAL RDP INTERNATIONAL, Lisbon	• S America • 100 kW
	RUSSIA †GOLOS ROSSII, Moscow	W • Europe & W Africa • 120 kW
	MAGADAN RADIO, Okhotsk	RUSSIAN, ETC • DS • 100 kW
	†VOICE OF RUSSIA, Moscow	S • W Europe • 100 kW
	†VOICE OF RUSSIA, Via Armenia	S • C America & S America • 500 kW
		S • M • C America & S America • 500 kW
	†VOICE OF RUSSIA, Via Uzbekistan	W • S Asia & SE Asia • 240 kW
	TURKEY VOICE OF TURKEY, Ankara	• E Asia • 250 kW
	UNITED KINGDOM †BBC, Via Ascension	S Africa • 250 kW
	BBC, Via Singapore	SE Asia • 250 kW
	BBC, Via Zyyi, Cyprus	S • W Asia • 250 kW
	BBC, Woofferton	S • Su • Europe • 300 kW
		S • Europe • 300 kW
		W • Su • Europe • 300 kW
(con'd)		

0 1 2 3 4 5 6 7 8 9 10 11 12 13 14 15 16 17 18 19 20 21 22 23 24

ENGLISH ▬   ARABIC ∽∽∽   CHINESE □□□   FRENCH ▭▭   GERMAN ▬▬   RUSSIAN ══   SPANISH ▬▬   OTHER ──

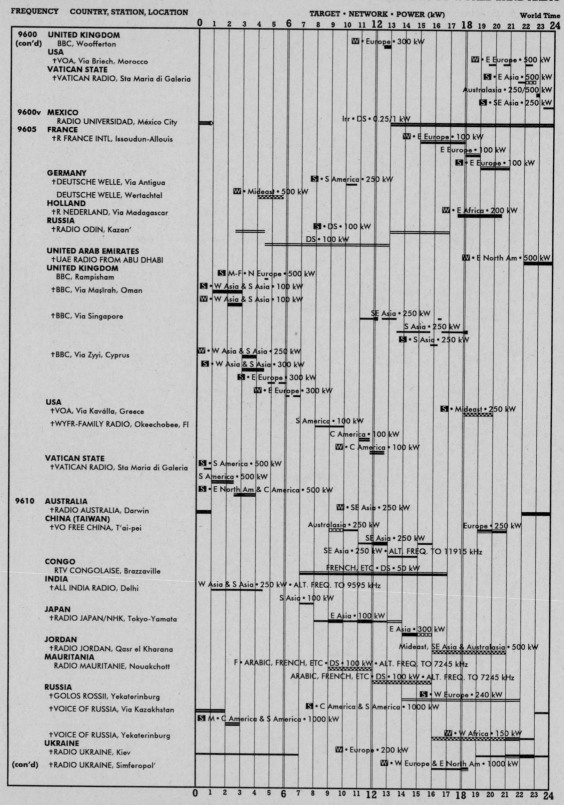

FREQUENCY   COUNTRY, STATION, LOCATION

TARGET • NETWORK • POWER (kW)   World Time

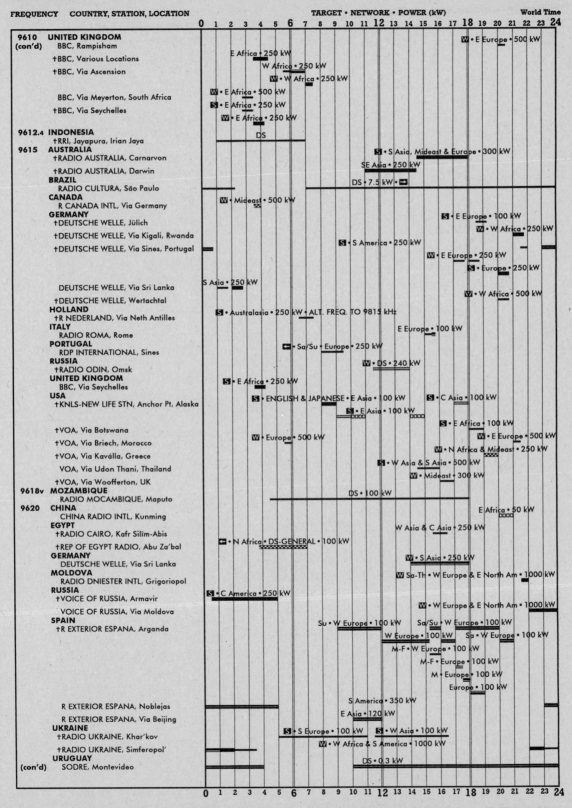

9610 UNITED KINGDOM	
(con'd) BBC, Rampisham	W • E Europe • 500 kW
†BBC, Various Locations	E Africa • 250 kW
†BBC, Via Ascension	W Africa • 250 kW
	W • W Africa • 250 kW
BBC, Via Meyerton, South Africa	W • E Africa • 500 kW
†BBC, Via Seychelles	S • E Africa • 250 kW
	W • E Africa • 250 kW
9612.4 INDONESIA	
†RRI, Jayapura, Irian Jaya	DS
9615 AUSTRALIA	
†RADIO AUSTRALIA, Carnarvon	S • S Asia, Mideast & Europe • 300 kW
†RADIO AUSTRALIA, Darwin	SE Asia • 250 kW
BRAZIL	
RADIO CULTURA, São Paulo	DS • 7.5 kW • ▭
CANADA	
R CANADA INTL, Via Germany	W • Mideast • 500 kW
GERMANY	
†DEUTSCHE WELLE, Jülich	S • E Europe • 100 kW
†DEUTSCHE WELLE, Via Kigali, Rwanda	W • W Africa • 250 kW
†DEUTSCHE WELLE, Via Sines, Portugal	S • S America • 250 kW
	W • E Europe • 250 kW
	S • Europe • 250 kW
DEUTSCHE WELLE, Via Sri Lanka	S Asia • 250 kW
†DEUTSCHE WELLE, Wertachtal	W • W Africa • 500 kW
HOLLAND	
†R NEDERLAND, Via Neth Antilles	S • Australasia • 250 kW • ALT. FREQ. TO 9815 kHz
ITALY	
RADIO ROMA, Rome	E Europe • 100 kW
PORTUGAL	
RDP INTERNATIONAL, Sines	▭ • Sa/Su • Europe • 250 kW
RUSSIA	
†RADIO ODIN, Omsk	W • DS • 240 kW
UNITED KINGDOM	
BBC, Via Seychelles	S • E Africa • 250 kW
USA	
†KNLS-NEW LIFE STN, Anchor Pt, Alaska	S • ENGLISH & JAPANESE • E Asia • 100 kW S • C Asia • 100 kW
	S • E Asia • 100 kW
†VOA, Via Botswana	S • E Africa • 100 kW
†VOA, Via Briech, Morocco	W • Europe • 500 kW W • E Europe • 500 kW
†VOA, Via Kaválla, Greece	W • N Africa & Mideast • 250 kW
VOA, Via Udon Thani, Thailand	S • W Asia & S Asia • 500 kW
†VOA, Via Woofferton, UK	W • Mideast • 300 kW
9618v MOZAMBIQUE	
RADIO MOCAMBIQUE, Maputo	DS • 100 kW
9620 CHINA	
CHINA RADIO INTL, Kunming	E Africa • 50 kW
EGYPT	
†RADIO CAIRO, Kafr Silim-Abis	W Asia & C Asia • 250 kW
†REP OF EGYPT RADIO, Abu Za'bal	▭ • N Africa • DS-GENERAL • 100 kW
GERMANY	
DEUTSCHE WELLE, Via Sri Lanka	W • S Asia • 250 kW
MOLDOVA	
RADIO DNIESTER INTL, Grigoriopol	W Sa-TH • W Europe & E North Am • 1000 kW
RUSSIA	
†VOICE OF RUSSIA, Armavir	S • C America • 250 kW
VOICE OF RUSSIA, Via Moldova	W • W Europe & E North Am • 1000 kW
SPAIN	
†R EXTERIOR ESPANA, Arganda	Su • W Europe • 100 kW Sa/Su • W Europe • 100 kW
	W Europe • 100 kW Sa • W Europe • 100 kW
	M-F • W Europe • 100 kW
	M-F • Europe • 100 kW
	M • Europe • 100 kW
	Europe • 100 kW
R EXTERIOR ESPANA, Noblejas	S America • 350 kW
R EXTERIOR ESPANA, Via Beijing	E Asia • 120 kW
UKRAINE	
†RADIO UKRAINE, Khar'kov	S • S Europe • 100 kW S • W Asia • 100 kW
†RADIO UKRAINE, Simferopol'	W • W Africa & S America • 1000 kW
URUGUAY	
(con'd) SODRE, Montevideo	DS • 0.3 kW

FREQUENCY   COUNTRY, STATION, LOCATION

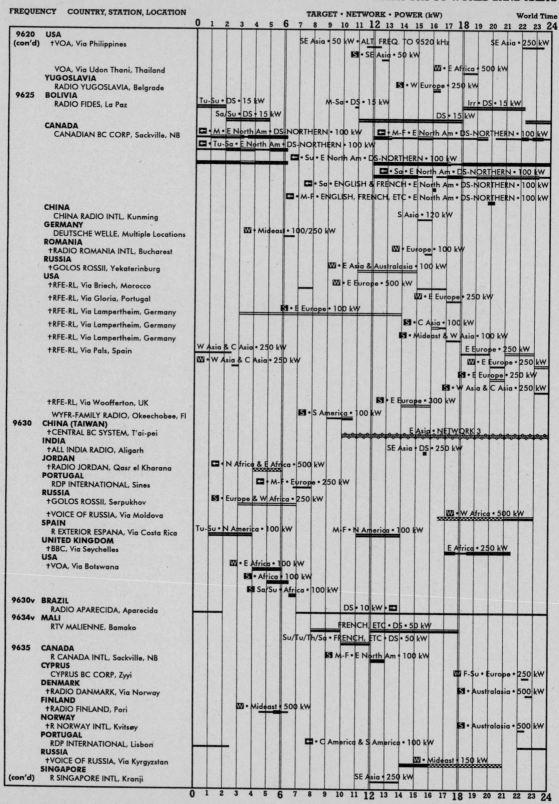

TARGET • NETWORK • POWER (kW)   World Time

9620	USA	
(con'd)	†VOA, Via Philippines	
	VOA, Via Udon Thani, Thailand	
	YUGOSLAVIA	
	RADIO YUGOSLAVIA, Belgrade	
9625	BOLIVIA	
	RADIO FIDES, La Paz	
	CANADA	
	CANADIAN BC CORP, Sackville, NB	
	CHINA	
	CHINA RADIO INTL, Kunming	
	GERMANY	
	DEUTSCHE WELLE, Multiple Locations	
	ROMANIA	
	†RADIO ROMANIA INTL, Bucharest	
	RUSSIA	
	†GOLOS ROSSII, Yekaterinburg	
	USA	
	†RFE-RL, Via Briech, Morocco	
	†RFE-RL, Via Gloria, Portugal	
	†RFE-RL, Via Lampertheim, Germany	
	†RFE-RL, Via Lampertheim, Germany	
	†RFE-RL, Via Lampertheim, Germany	
	†RFE-RL, Via Pals, Spain	
	†RFE-RL, Via Woofferton, UK	
	WYFR-FAMILY RADIO, Okeechobee, Fl	
9630	CHINA (TAIWAN)	
	†CENTRAL BC SYSTEM, T'ai-pei	
	INDIA	
	†ALL INDIA RADIO, Aligarh	
	JORDAN	
	†RADIO JORDAN, Qasr el Kharana	
	PORTUGAL	
	RDP INTERNATIONAL, Sines	
	RUSSIA	
	†GOLOS ROSSII, Serpukhov	
	†VOICE OF RUSSIA, Via Moldova	
	SPAIN	
	R EXTERIOR ESPANA, Via Costa Rica	
	UNITED KINGDOM	
	†BBC, Via Seychelles	
	USA	
	†VOA, Via Botswana	
9630v	BRAZIL	
	RADIO APARECIDA, Aparecida	
9634v	MALI	
	RTV MALIENNE, Bamako	
9635	CANADA	
	R CANADA INTL, Sackville, NB	
	CYPRUS	
	CYPRUS BC CORP, Zyyi	
	DENMARK	
	†RADIO DANMARK, Via Norway	
	FINLAND	
	†RADIO FINLAND, Pori	
	NORWAY	
	†R NORWAY INTL, Kvitsøy	
	PORTUGAL	
	RDP INTERNATIONAL, Lisbon	
	RUSSIA	
	†VOICE OF RUSSIA, Via Kyrgyzstan	
	SINGAPORE	
(con'd)	R SINGAPORE INTL, Kranji	

Chart annotations:

- †VOA, Via Philippines: SE Asia • 50 kW • ALT FREQ TO 9520 kHz / SE Asia • 250 kW
- S • SE Asia • 50 kW
- W • E Africa • 500 kW
- RADIO YUGOSLAVIA: S • W Europe • 250 kW
- RADIO FIDES: Tu-Su • DS • 15 kW / M-Sa • DS • 15 kW / Irr • DS • 15 kW / Sa/Su • DS • 15 kW / DS • 15 kW
- CANADIAN BC CORP: M • E North Am • DS-NORTHERN • 100 kW / M-F • E North Am • DS-NORTHERN • 100 kW / Tu-Sa • E North Am • DS-NORTHERN • 100 kW / Su • E North Am • DS-NORTHERN • 100 kW / Sa • E North Am • DS-NORTHERN • 100 kW / Sa • ENGLISH & FRENCH • E North Am • DS-NORTHERN • 100 kW / M-F • ENGLISH, FRENCH, ETC • E North Am • DS-NORTHERN • 100 kW
- CHINA RADIO INTL: S Asia • 120 kW
- DEUTSCHE WELLE: W • Mideast • 100/250 kW
- RADIO ROMANIA INTL: W • Europe • 100 kW
- GOLOS ROSSII, Yekaterinburg: W • E Asia & Australasia • 100 kW
- RFE-RL, Via Briech: W • E Europe • 500 kW
- RFE-RL, Via Gloria: W • E Europe • 250 kW
- RFE-RL, Via Lampertheim: S • E Europe • 100 kW
- RFE-RL, Via Lampertheim: S • C Asia • 100 kW
- RFE-RL, Via Lampertheim: S • Mideast & W Asia • 100 kW
- RFE-RL, Via Pals: W Asia & C Asia • 250 kW / E Europe • 250 kW / W • W Asia & C Asia • 250 kW / W • E Europe • 250 kW / S • E Europe • 250 kW / S • W Asia & C Asia • 250 kW
- RFE-RL, Via Woofferton: S • E Europe • 300 kW
- WYFR-FAMILY RADIO: S • S America • 100 kW
- CENTRAL BC SYSTEM: E Asia • NETWORK 3
- ALL INDIA RADIO: SE Asia • DS • 250 kW
- RADIO JORDAN: N Africa & E Africa • 500 kW
- RDP INTERNATIONAL, Sines: M-F • Europe • 250 kW
- GOLOS ROSSII, Serpukhov: S • Europe & W Africa • 250 kW
- VOICE OF RUSSIA, Via Moldova: W • W Africa • 500 kW
- R EXTERIOR ESPANA: Tu-Su • N America • 100 kW / M-F • N America • 100 kW
- BBC, Via Seychelles: E Africa • 250 kW
- VOA, Via Botswana: W • E Africa • 100 kW / S • Africa • 100 kW / S Sa/Su • Africa • 100 kW
- RADIO APARECIDA: DS • 10 kW
- RTV MALIENNE: FRENCH, ETC • DS • 50 kW / Su/Tu/Th/Sa • FRENCH, ETC • DS • 50 kW
- R CANADA INTL: S • M-F • E North Am • 100 kW
- CYPRUS BC CORP: W • F-Su • Europe • 250 kW
- RADIO DANMARK: S • Australasia • 500 kW
- RADIO FINLAND: W • Mideast • 500 kW
- R NORWAY INTL: S • Australasia • 500 kW
- RDP INTERNATIONAL, Lisbon: C America & S America • 100 kW
- VOICE OF RUSSIA, Via Kyrgyzstan: W • Mideast • 150 kW
- R SINGAPORE INTL: SE Asia • 250 kW

FREQUENCY   COUNTRY, STATION, LOCATION

TARGET • NETWORK • POWER (kW)

World Time

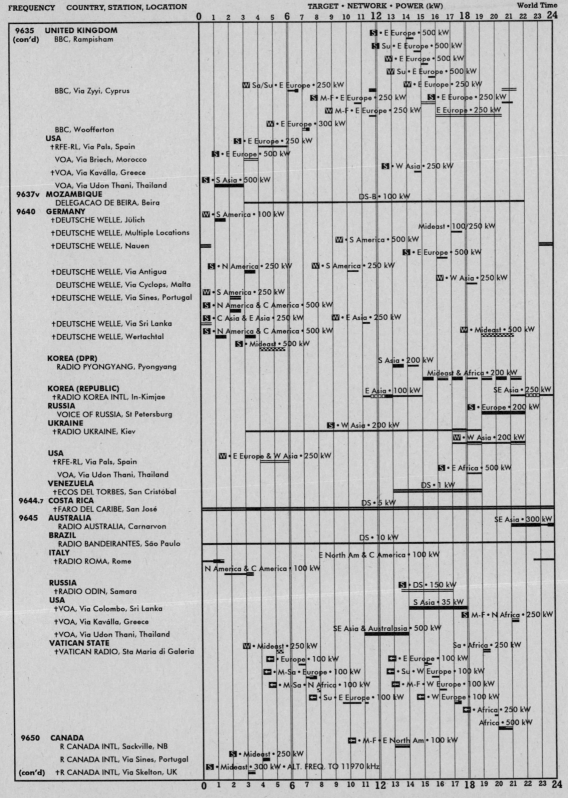

Frequency	Country, Station, Location	Target • Network • Power
9635 (con'd)	**UNITED KINGDOM** BBC, Rampisham	**S** • E Europe • 500 kW; **Su** • E Europe • 500 kW; **W** • E Europe • 500 kW; **W** Su • E Europe • 500 kW
	BBC, Via Zyyi, Cyprus	**W** Sa/Su • E Europe • 250 kW; **W** • E Europe • 250 kW; **S** M-F • E Europe • 250 kW; **S** • E Europe • 250 kW; **W** M-F • E Europe • 250 kW; E Europe • 250 kW
	BBC, Woofferton	**W** • E Europe • 300 kW
	USA †RFE-RL, Via Pals, Spain	**S** • E Europe • 250 kW
	VOA, Via Briech, Morocco	**S** • E Europe • 500 kW
	†VOA, Via Kaválla, Greece	**S** • W Asia • 250 kW
	VOA, Via Udon Thani, Thailand	**S** • S Asia • 500 kW
9637v	**MOZAMBIQUE** DELEGACAO DE BEIRA, Beira	DS-B • 100 kW
9640	**GERMANY** †DEUTSCHE WELLE, Jülich	**W** • S America • 100 kW
	†DEUTSCHE WELLE, Multiple Locations	Mideast • 100/250 kW
	†DEUTSCHE WELLE, Nauen	**W** • S America • 500 kW; **S** • E Europe • 500 kW
	†DEUTSCHE WELLE, Via Antigua	**S** • N America • 250 kW; • S America • 250 kW
	DEUTSCHE WELLE, Via Cyclops, Malta	**W** • W Asia • 250 kW
	†DEUTSCHE WELLE, Via Sines, Portugal	**W** • S America • 250 kW
		S • N America & C America • 500 kW
	†DEUTSCHE WELLE, Via Sri Lanka	**S** • C Asia & E Asia • 250 kW; **W** • E Asia • 250 kW
	†DEUTSCHE WELLE, Wertachtal	**S** • N America & C America • 500 kW; **W** • Mideast • 500 kW
		S • Mideast • 500 kW
	KOREA (DPR) RADIO PYONGYANG, Pyongyang	S Asia • 200 kW; Mideast & Africa • 200 kW
	KOREA (REPUBLIC) †RADIO KOREA INTL, In-Kimjae	E Asia • 100 kW; SE Asia • 250 kW
	RUSSIA VOICE OF RUSSIA, St Petersburg	**S** • Europe • 200 kW
	UKRAINE †RADIO UKRAINE, Kiev	**S** • W Asia • 200 kW; **W** • W Asia • 200 kW
	USA †RFE-RL, Via Pals, Spain	**W** • E Europe & W Asia • 250 kW
	VOA, Via Udon Thani, Thailand	**S** • E Africa • 500 kW
	VENEZUELA †ECOS DEL TORBES, San Cristóbal	DS • 1 kW
9644.7	**COSTA RICA** †FARO DEL CARIBE, San José	DS • 5 kW
9645	**AUSTRALIA** RADIO AUSTRALIA, Carnarvon	SE Asia • 300 kW
	BRAZIL RADIO BANDEIRANTES, São Paulo	DS • 10 kW
	ITALY †RADIO ROMA, Rome	E North Am & C America • 100 kW; N America & C America • 100 kW
	RUSSIA †RADIO ODIN, Samara	**S** • DS • 150 kW
	USA †VOA, Via Colombo, Sri Lanka	S Asia • 35 kW
	†VOA, Via Kaválla, Greece	**S** M-F • N Africa • 250 kW
	†VOA, Via Udon Thani, Thailand	SE Asia & Australasia • 500 kW
	VATICAN STATE †VATICAN RADIO, Sta Maria di Galeria	**W** • Mideast • 250 kW; Sa • Africa • 250 kW
		▭ • Europe • 100 kW; ▭ • E Europe • 100 kW
		▭ • M-Sa • Europe • 100 kW; ▭ • Su • W Europe • 100 kW
		▭ • M Sa • N Africa • 100 kW; ▭ • M-F • W Europe • 100 kW
		▭ • Su • E Europe • 100 kW; ▭ • W Europe • 100 kW
		▭ • Africa • 250 kW; Africa • 500 kW
9650	**CANADA** R CANADA INTL, Sackville, NB	▭ • M-F • E North Am • 100 kW
	R CANADA INTL, Via Sines, Portugal	**S** • Mideast • 250 kW
(con'd)	†R CANADA INTL, Via Skelton, UK	**S** • Mideast • 300 kW • ALT. FREQ. TO 11970 kHz

ENGLISH ▬   ARABIC ⌇⌇   CHINESE ▫▫▫   FRENCH ═   GERMAN ▬   RUSSIAN ═   SPANISH ═   OTHER ▬

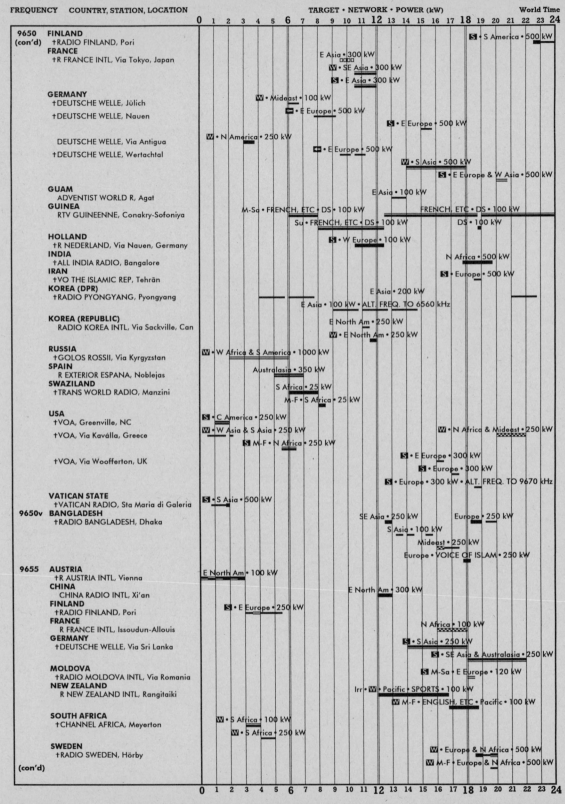

FREQUENCY	COUNTRY, STATION, LOCATION	TARGET • NETWORK • POWER (kW)	World Time

9650 (con'd) FINLAND †RADIO FINLAND, Pori — S • S America • 500 kW

FRANCE †R FRANCE INTL, Via Tokyo, Japan — E Asia • 300 kW; W • SE Asia • 300 kW; S • E Asia • 300 kW

GERMANY †DEUTSCHE WELLE, Jülich — W • Mideast • 100 kW
†DEUTSCHE WELLE, Nauen — E Europe • 500 kW; S • E Europe • 500 kW
DEUTSCHE WELLE, Via Antigua — W • N America • 250 kW
†DEUTSCHE WELLE, Wertachtal — E Europe • 500 kW; W • S Asia • 500 kW; S • E Europe & W Asia • 500 kW

GUAM ADVENTIST WORLD R, Agat — E Asia • 100 kW
GUINEA RTV GUINEENNE, Conakry-Sofoniya — M-Sa • FRENCH, ETC • DS • 100 kW; FRENCH, ETC • DS • 100 kW; Su • FRENCH, ETC • DS • 100 kW; DS • 100 kW

HOLLAND †R NEDERLAND, Via Nauen, Germany — S • W Europe • 100 kW
INDIA †ALL INDIA RADIO, Bangalore — N Africa • 500 kW
IRAN †VO THE ISLAMIC REP, Tehrän — S • Europe • 500 kW
KOREA (DPR) †RADIO PYONGYANG, Pyongyang — E Asia • 200 kW; E Asia • 100 kW • ALT. FREQ. TO 6560 kHz

KOREA (REPUBLIC) RADIO KOREA INTL, Via Sackville, Can — E North Am • 250 kW; W • E North Am • 250 kW

RUSSIA †GOLOS ROSSII, Via Kyrgyzstan — W • W Africa & S America • 1000 kW
SPAIN R EXTERIOR ESPANA, Noblejas — Australasia • 350 kW
SWAZILAND †TRANS WORLD RADIO, Manzini — S Africa • 25 kW; M-F • S Africa • 25 kW

USA †VOA, Greenville, NC — S • C America • 250 kW; W • W Asia & S Asia • 250 kW
†VOA, Via Kavälla, Greece — S • M-F • N Africa • 250 kW; W • N Africa & Mideast • 250 kW
†VOA, Via Woofferton, UK — S • E Europe • 300 kW; S • Europe • 300 kW; S • Europe • 300 kW • ALT. FREQ. TO 9670 kHz

VATICAN STATE †VATICAN RADIO, Sta Maria di Galeria — S • S Asia • 500 kW
9650v BANGLADESH †RADIO BANGLADESH, Dhaka — SE Asia • 250 kW; Europe • 250 kW; S Asia • 100 kW; Mideast • 250 kW; Europe • VOICE OF ISLAM • 250 kW

9655 AUSTRIA †R AUSTRIA INTL, Vienna — E North Am • 100 kW
CHINA CHINA RADIO INTL, Xi'an — E North Am • 300 kW
FINLAND †RADIO FINLAND, Pori — S • E Europe • 250 kW
FRANCE R FRANCE INTL, Issoudun-Allouis — N Africa • 100 kW
GERMANY †DEUTSCHE WELLE, Via Sri Lanka — S • S Asia • 250 kW; S • SE Asia & Australasia • 250 kW
MOLDOVA †RADIO MOLDOVA INTL, Via Romania — S M-Sa • E Europe • 120 kW
NEW ZEALAND R NEW ZEALAND INTL, Rangitaiki — Irr • W • Pacific • SPORTS • 100 kW; W M-F • ENGLISH, ETC • Pacific • 100 kW
SOUTH AFRICA †CHANNEL AFRICA, Meyerton — W • S Africa • 100 kW; W • S Africa • 250 kW
SWEDEN †RADIO SWEDEN, Hörby — W • Europe & N Africa • 500 kW; W M-F • Europe & N Africa • 500 kW

(con'd)

SEASONAL ⓈOR Ⓦ　　1-HR TIMESHIFT MIDYEAR ⊟ OR ⊡　　JAMMING / OR ∧　　EARLIEST HEARD ◁　　LATEST HEARD ▷　　NEW FOR 1996 †

FREQUENCY	COUNTRY, STATION, LOCATION	TARGET • NETWORK • POWER (kW)	World Time

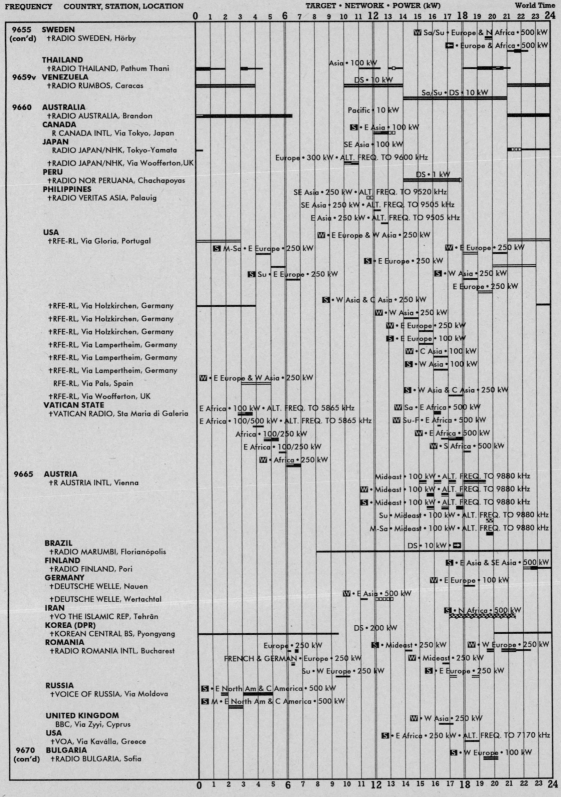

Content listing (frequency / country / station):

9655 **SWEDEN**
(con'd) †RADIO SWEDEN, Hörby
- W Sa/Su • Europe & N Africa • 500 kW
- Europe & Africa • 500 kW

THAILAND
†RADIO THAILAND, Pathum Thani
- Asia • 100 kW

9659v **VENEZUELA**
†RADIO RUMBOS, Caracas
- DS • 10 kW
- Sa/Su • DS • 10 kW

9660 **AUSTRALIA**
†RADIO AUSTRALIA, Brandon
- Pacific • 10 kW

CANADA
R CANADA INTL, Via Tokyo, Japan
- S • E Asia • 100 kW

JAPAN
RADIO JAPAN/NHK, Tokyo-Yamata
- SE Asia • 100 kW

†RADIO JAPAN/NHK, Via Woofferton, UK
- Europe • 300 kW • ALT. FREQ. TO 9600 kHz

PERU
†RADIO NOR PERUANA, Chachapoyas
- DS • 1 kW

PHILIPPINES
†RADIO VERITAS ASIA, Palauig
- SE Asia • 250 kW • ALT. FREQ. TO 9520 kHz
- SE Asia • 250 kW • ALT. FREQ. TO 9505 kHz
- E Asia • 250 kW • ALT. FREQ. TO 9505 kHz

USA
†RFE-RL, Via Gloria, Portugal
- W • E Europe & W Asia • 250 kW
- S M-Sa • E Europe • 250 kW
- W • E Europe • 250 kW
- S • E Europe • 250 kW
- S Su • E Europe • 250 kW
- S • W Asia • 250 kW
- E Europe • 250 kW

†RFE-RL, Via Holzkirchen, Germany
- S • W Asia & C Asia • 250 kW

†RFE-RL, Via Holzkirchen, Germany
- W • W Asia • 250 kW

†RFE-RL, Via Holzkirchen, Germany
- W • E Europe • 250 kW

†RFE-RL, Via Lampertheim, Germany
- S • E Europe • 100 kW

†RFE-RL, Via Lampertheim, Germany
- W • C Asia • 100 kW

†RFE-RL, Via Lampertheim, Germany
- S • W Asia • 100 kW

RFE-RL, Via Pals, Spain
- W • E Europe & W Asia • 250 kW

†RFE-RL, Via Woofferton, UK
- S • W Asia & C Asia • 250 kW

VATICAN STATE
†VATICAN RADIO, Sta Maria di Galeria
- E Africa • 100 kW • ALT. FREQ. TO 5865 kHz
- W Sa • E Africa • 500 kW
- E Africa • 100/500 kW • ALT. FREQ. TO 5865 kHz
- W Su-F • E Africa • 500 kW
- Africa • 100/250 kW
- W • E Africa • 500 kW
- E Africa • 100/250 kW
- W • S Africa • 500 kW
- W • Africa • 250 kW

9665 **AUSTRIA**
†R AUSTRIA INTL, Vienna
- Mideast • 100 kW • ALT. FREQ. TO 9880 kHz
- W • Mideast • 100 kW • ALT. FREQ. TO 9880 kHz
- S • Mideast • 100 kW • ALT. FREQ. TO 9880 kHz
- Su • Mideast • 100 kW • ALT. FREQ. TO 9880 kHz
- M-Sa • Mideast • 100 kW • ALT. FREQ. TO 9880 kHz

BRAZIL
†RADIO MARUMBI, Florianópolis
- DS • 10 kW

FINLAND
†RADIO FINLAND, Pori
- S • E Asia & SE Asia • 500 kW

GERMANY
†DEUTSCHE WELLE, Nauen
- W • E Europe • 100 kW

†DEUTSCHE WELLE, Wertachtal
- W • E Asia • 500 kW

IRAN
†VO THE ISLAMIC REP, Tehrān
- S • N Africa • 500 kW

KOREA (DPR)
†KOREAN CENTRAL BS, Pyongyang
- DS • 200 kW

ROMANIA
†RADIO ROMANIA INTL, Bucharest
- Europe • 250 kW
- S • Mideast • 250 kW
- W • W Europe • 250 kW
- FRENCH & GERMAN • Europe • 250 kW
- W • Mideast • 250 kW
- Su • W Europe • 250 kW
- S • E Europe • 250 kW

RUSSIA
†VOICE OF RUSSIA, Via Moldova
- S • E North Am & C America • 500 kW
- S M • E North Am & C America • 500 kW

UNITED KINGDOM
BBC, Via Zyyi, Cyprus
- W • W Asia • 250 kW

USA
†VOA, Via Kaválla, Greece
- S • E Africa • 250 kW • ALT. FREQ. TO 7170 kHz

9670 **BULGARIA**
(con'd) †RADIO BULGARIA, Sofia
- S • W Europe • 100 kW

ENGLISH ▬ ARABIC ∽∽∽ CHINESE □□□ FRENCH ═ GERMAN ▬▬ RUSSIAN ══ SPANISH ▬▬ OTHER ▬

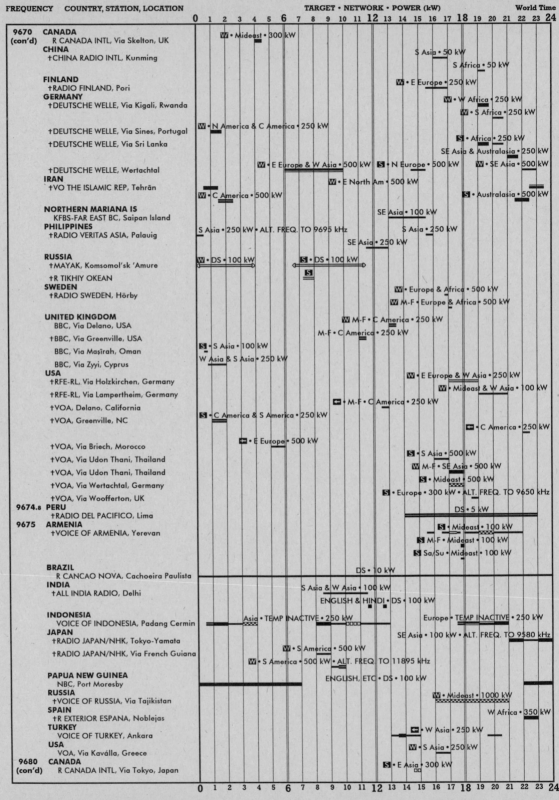

FREQUENCY	COUNTRY, STATION, LOCATION	TARGET • NETWORK • POWER (kW)	World Time

9670 **CANADA**
(con'd)   R CANADA INTL, Via Skelton, UK — W • Mideast • 300 kW

CHINA
†CHINA RADIO INTL, Kunming — S Asia • 50 kW; S Africa • 50 kW

FINLAND
†RADIO FINLAND, Pori — W • E Europe • 250 kW

GERMANY
†DEUTSCHE WELLE, Via Kigali, Rwanda — W • W Africa • 250 kW; W • S Africa • 250 kW

†DEUTSCHE WELLE, Via Sines, Portugal — W • N America & C America • 250 kW

†DEUTSCHE WELLE, Via Sri Lanka — S • Africa • 250 kW; SE Asia & Australasia • 250 kW

†DEUTSCHE WELLE, Wertachtal — W • E Europe & W Asia • 500 kW; S • N Europe • 500 kW; W • SE Asia • 500 kW

IRAN
†VO THE ISLAMIC REP, Tehrān — W • E North Am • 500 kW; W • C America • 500 kW; S • Australasia • 500 kW

NORTHERN MARIANA IS
KFBS-FAR EAST BC, Saipan Island — SE Asia • 100 kW

PHILIPPINES
†RADIO VERITAS ASIA, Palauig — S Asia • 250 kW • ALT. FREQ. TO 9695 kHz; S Asia • 250 kW; SE Asia • 250 kW

RUSSIA
†MAYAK, Komsomol'sk 'Amure — W • DS • 100 kW; S • DS • 100 kW

†R TIKHIY OKEAN — S

SWEDEN
†RADIO SWEDEN, Hörby — W • Europe & Africa • 500 kW; W • M-F • Europe & Africa • 500 kW

UNITED KINGDOM
BBC, Via Delano, USA — W M-F • C America • 250 kW; M-F • C America • 250 kW

†BBC, Via Greenville, USA — S • S Asia • 100 kW

BBC, Via Maṣīrah, Oman — W Asia & S Asia • 250 kW

BBC, Via Zyyi, Cyprus

USA
†RFE-RL, Via Holzkirchen, Germany — W • E Europe & W Asia • 250 kW; W • Mideast & W Asia • 100 kW

†RFE-RL, Via Lampertheim, Germany — ⇆ • M-F • C America • 250 kW

†VOA, Delano, California — S • C America & S America • 250 kW

†VOA, Greenville, NC — ⇆ • C America • 250 kW

†VOA, Via Briech, Morocco — ⇆ • E Europe • 500 kW

†VOA, Via Udon Thani, Thailand — S • S Asia • 500 kW

†VOA, Via Udon Thani, Thailand — W • M-F • SE Asia • 500 kW

†VOA, Via Wertachtal, Germany — S • Mideast • 500 kW

†VOA, Via Woofferton, UK — S • Europe • 300 kW • ALT. FREQ. TO 9650 kHz

9674.8 PERU
†RADIO DEL PACIFICO, Lima — DS • 5 kW

9675 ARMENIA
†VOICE OF ARMENIA, Yerevan — S • Mideast • 100 kW; S M-F • Mideast • 100 kW; S Sa/Su • Mideast • 100 kW

BRAZIL
R CANCAO NOVA, Cachoeira Paulista — DS • 10 kW

INDIA
†ALL INDIA RADIO, Delhi — S Asia & W Asia • 100 kW; ENGLISH & HINDI • DS • 100 kW

INDONESIA
VOICE OF INDONESIA, Padang Cermin — Asia • TEMP INACTIVE • 250 kW; Europe • TEMP INACTIVE • 250 kW

JAPAN
†RADIO JAPAN/NHK, Tokyo-Yamata — SE Asia • 100 kW • ALT. FREQ. TO 9580 kHz; W • S America • 500 kW

†RADIO JAPAN/NHK, Via French Guiana — W • S America • 500 kW • ALT. FREQ. TO 11895 kHz

PAPUA NEW GUINEA
NBC, Port Moresby — ENGLISH, ETC • DS • 100 kW

RUSSIA
†VOICE OF RUSSIA, Via Tajikistan — W • Mideast • 1000 kW

SPAIN
†R EXTERIOR ESPANA, Noblejas — W Africa • 350 kW

TURKEY
VOICE OF TURKEY, Ankara — ⇆ • W Asia • 250 kW

USA
VOA, Via Kaválla, Greece — W • S Asia • 250 kW

9680 CANADA
(con'd)   R CANADA INTL, Via Tokyo, Japan — S • E Asia • 300 kW

SEASONAL S OR W   1-HR TIMESHIFT MIDYEAR ⇆ OR ⇉   JAMMING / OR ∧   EARLIEST HEARD ◁   LATEST HEARD ▷   NEW FOR 1996 †

FREQUENCY	COUNTRY, STATION, LOCATION	TARGET • NETWORK • POWER (kW)	World Time

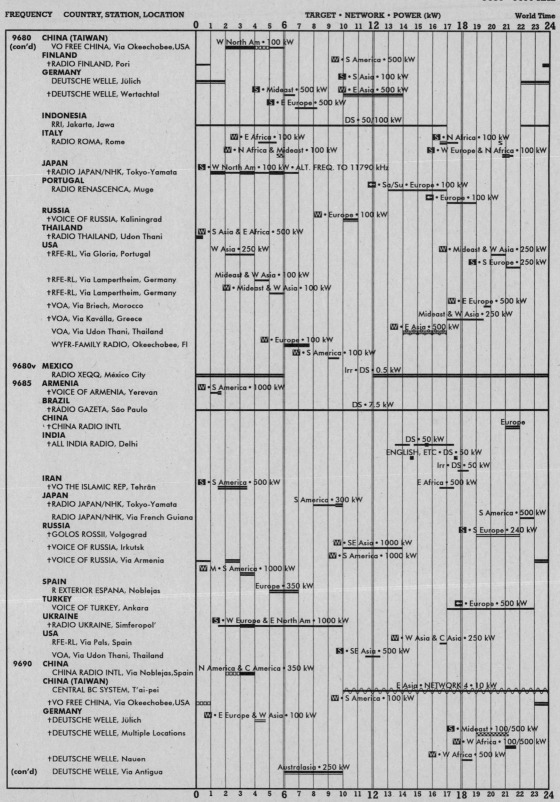

FREQUENCY	COUNTRY, STATION, LOCATION	TARGET • NETWORK • POWER (kW)
9680 (con'd)	**CHINA (TAIWAN)** VO FREE CHINA, Via Okeechobee, USA	W • North Am • 100 kW
	FINLAND †RADIO FINLAND, Pori	W • S America • 500 kW
	GERMANY DEUTSCHE WELLE, Jülich	S • S Asia • 100 kW
	†DEUTSCHE WELLE, Wertachtal	S • Mideast • 500 kW W • E Asia • 500 kW
		S • E Europe • 500 kW
	INDONESIA RRI, Jakarta, Jawa	DS • 50/100 kW
	ITALY RADIO ROMA, Rome	W • E Africa • 100 kW S • N Africa • 100 kW
		W • N Africa & Mideast • 100 kW S • W Europe & N Africa • 100 kW
	JAPAN †RADIO JAPAN/NHK, Tokyo-Yamata	S • W North Am • 100 kW • ALT. FREQ. TO 11790 kHz
	PORTUGAL RADIO RENASCENCA, Muge	Sa/Su • Europe • 100 kW
		Europe • 100 kW
	RUSSIA †VOICE OF RUSSIA, Kaliningrad	W • Europe • 100 kW
	THAILAND †RADIO THAILAND, Udon Thani	W • S Asia & E Africa • 500 kW
	USA †RFE-RL, Via Gloria, Portugal	W Asia • 250 kW W • Mideast & W Asia • 250 kW
		S • S Europe • 250 kW
	†RFE-RL, Via Lampertheim, Germany	Mideast & W Asia • 100 kW
	†RFE-RL, Via Lampertheim, Germany	W • Mideast & W Asia • 100 kW
	†VOA, Via Briech, Morocco	W • E Europe • 500 kW
	†VOA, Via Kaválla, Greece	Mideast & W Asia • 250 kW
	VOA, Via Udon Thani, Thailand	W • E Asia • 500 kW
	WYFR-FAMILY RADIO, Okeechobee, Fl	W • Europe • 100 kW
		W • S America • 100 kW
9680v	**MEXICO** RADIO XEQQ, México City	Irr • DS • 0.5 kW
9685	**ARMENIA** †VOICE OF ARMENIA, Yerevan	W • S America • 1000 kW
	BRAZIL †RADIO GAZETA, São Paulo	DS • 7.5 kW
	CHINA †CHINA RADIO INTL	Europe
	INDIA †ALL INDIA RADIO, Delhi	DS • 50 kW
		ENGLISH, ETC • DS • 50 kW
		Irr • DS • 50 kW
	IRAN †VO THE ISLAMIC REP, Tehrān	S • S America • 500 kW E Africa • 500 kW
	JAPAN †RADIO JAPAN/NHK, Tokyo-Yamata	S America • 300 kW
	RADIO JAPAN/NHK, Via French Guiana	S America • 500 kW
	RUSSIA †GOLOS ROSSII, Volgograd	S • S Europe • 240 kW
	†VOICE OF RUSSIA, Irkutsk	W • SE Asia • 1000 kW
	†VOICE OF RUSSIA, Via Armenia	W • S America • 1000 kW
		W • M • S America • 1000 kW
	SPAIN R EXTERIOR ESPANA, Noblejas	Europe • 350 kW
	TURKEY VOICE OF TURKEY, Ankara	Europe • 500 kW
	UKRAINE †RADIO UKRAINE, Simferopol'	S • W Europe & E North Am • 1000 kW
	USA RFE-RL, Via Pals, Spain	W • W Asia & C Asia • 250 kW
	VOA, Via Udon Thani, Thailand	S • SE Asia • 500 kW
9690	**CHINA** CHINA RADIO INTL, Via Noblejas, Spain	N America & C America • 350 kW
	CHINA (TAIWAN) CENTRAL BC SYSTEM, T'ai-pei	E Asia • NETWORK 4 • 10 kW
	†VO FREE CHINA, Via Okeechobee, USA	W • S America • 100 kW
	GERMANY †DEUTSCHE WELLE, Jülich	W • E Europe & W Asia • 100 kW
	†DEUTSCHE WELLE, Multiple Locations	S • Mideast • 100/500 kW
		W • W Africa • 100/500 kW
	†DEUTSCHE WELLE, Nauen	W • W Africa • 500 kW
(con'd)	DEUTSCHE WELLE, Via Antigua	Australasia • 250 kW

World Time scale: 0 1 2 3 4 5 6 7 8 9 10 11 12 13 14 15 16 17 18 19 20 21 22 23 24

ENGLISH ▬▬　ARABIC ⬚⬚⬚　CHINESE □□□　FRENCH ══　GERMAN ▬▬　RUSSIAN ＝＝　SPANISH ▬▬　OTHER ──

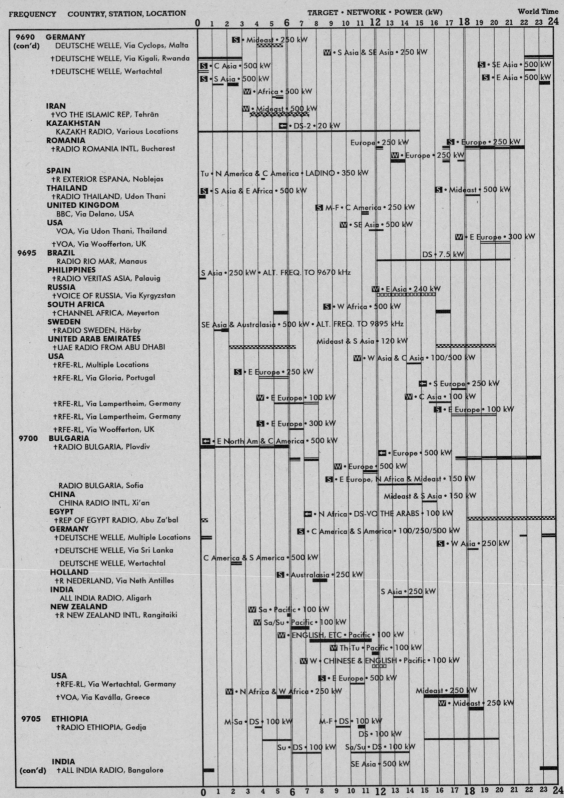

FREQUENCY   COUNTRY, STATION, LOCATION

TARGET • NETWORK • POWER (kW)   World Time

9690 (con'd)	GERMANY	
	DEUTSCHE WELLE, Via Cyclops, Malta	S • Mideast • 250 kW
	†DEUTSCHE WELLE, Via Kigali, Rwanda	W • S Asia & SE Asia • 250 kW
	†DEUTSCHE WELLE, Wertachtal	S • C Asia • 500 kW / S • SE Asia • 500 kW / S • S Asia • 500 kW / S • E Asia • 500 kW / W • Africa • 500 kW
	IRAN	
	†VO THE ISLAMIC REP, Tehrān	W • Mideast • 500 kW
	KAZAKHSTAN	
	KAZAKH RADIO, Various Locations	□ • DS-2 • 20 kW
	ROMANIA	
	†RADIO ROMANIA INTL, Bucharest	Europe • 250 kW / S • Europe • 250 kW / W • Europe • 250 kW
	SPAIN	
	†R EXTERIOR ESPANA, Noblejas	Tu • N America & C America • LADINO • 350 kW
	THAILAND	
	†RADIO THAILAND, Udon Thani	S • S Asia & E Africa • 500 kW / S • Mideast • 500 kW
	UNITED KINGDOM	
	BBC, Via Delano, USA	S • M-F • C America • 250 kW
	USA	
	VOA, Via Udon Thani, Thailand	W • SE Asia • 500 kW
	†VOA, Via Woofferton, UK	W • E Europe • 300 kW
9695	BRAZIL	
	RADIO RIO MAR, Manaus	DS • 7.5 kW
	PHILIPPINES	
	†RADIO VERITAS ASIA, Palauig	S Asia • 250 kW • ALT. FREQ. TO 9670 kHz
	RUSSIA	
	†VOICE OF RUSSIA, Via Kyrgyzstan	W • E Asia • 240 kW
	SOUTH AFRICA	
	†CHANNEL AFRICA, Meyerton	S • W Africa • 500 kW
	SWEDEN	
	†RADIO SWEDEN, Hörby	SE Asia & Australasia • 500 kW • ALT. FREQ. TO 9895 kHz
	UNITED ARAB EMIRATES	
	†UAE RADIO FROM ABU DHABI	Mideast & S Asia • 120 kW
	USA	
	†RFE-RL, Multiple Locations	W • W Asia & C Asia • 100/500 kW
	†RFE-RL, Via Gloria, Portugal	S • E Europe • 250 kW / □ • S Europe • 250 kW
	†RFE-RL, Via Lampertheim, Germany	W • E Europe • 100 kW / W • C Asia • 100 kW
	†RFE-RL, Via Lampertheim, Germany	S • E Europe • 100 kW
	†RFE-RL, Via Woofferton, UK	S • E Europe • 300 kW
9700	BULGARIA	
	†RADIO BULGARIA, Plovdiv	□ • E North Am & C America • 500 kW / □ • Europe • 500 kW / W • Europe • 500 kW
	RADIO BULGARIA, Sofia	S • E Europe, N Africa & Mideast • 150 kW
	CHINA	
	CHINA RADIO INTL, Xi'an	Mideast & S Asia • 150 kW
	EGYPT	
	†REP OF EGYPT RADIO, Abu Za'bal	□ • N Africa • DS-VO THE ARABS • 100 kW
	GERMANY	
	†DEUTSCHE WELLE, Multiple Locations	S • C America & S America • 100/250/500 kW
	†DEUTSCHE WELLE, Via Sri Lanka	S • W Asia • 250 kW
	DEUTSCHE WELLE, Wertachtal	C America & S America • 500 kW
	HOLLAND	
	†R NEDERLAND, Via Neth Antilles	S • Australasia • 250 kW
	INDIA	
	ALL INDIA RADIO, Aligarh	S Asia • 250 kW
	NEW ZEALAND	
	†R NEW ZEALAND INTL, Rangitaiki	W • Sa • Pacific • 100 kW / W • Sa/Su • Pacific • 100 kW / W • ENGLISH, ETC • Pacific • 100 kW / W • Th-Tu • Pacific • 100 kW / W • CHINESE & ENGLISH • Pacific • 100 kW
	USA	
	†RFE-RL, Via Wertachtal, Germany	S • E Europe • 500 kW
	†VOA, Via Kaválla, Greece	W • N Africa & W Africa • 250 kW / Mideast • 250 kW / W • Mideast • 250 kW
9705	ETHIOPIA	
	†RADIO ETHIOPIA, Gedja	M-Sa • DS • 100 kW / M-F • DS • 100 kW / DS • 100 kW / Su • DS • 100 kW / Sa/Su • DS • 100 kW
(con'd)	INDIA	
	†ALL INDIA RADIO, Bangalore	SE Asia • 500 kW

FREQUENCY   COUNTRY, STATION, LOCATION   TARGET • NETWORK • POWER (kW)   World Time

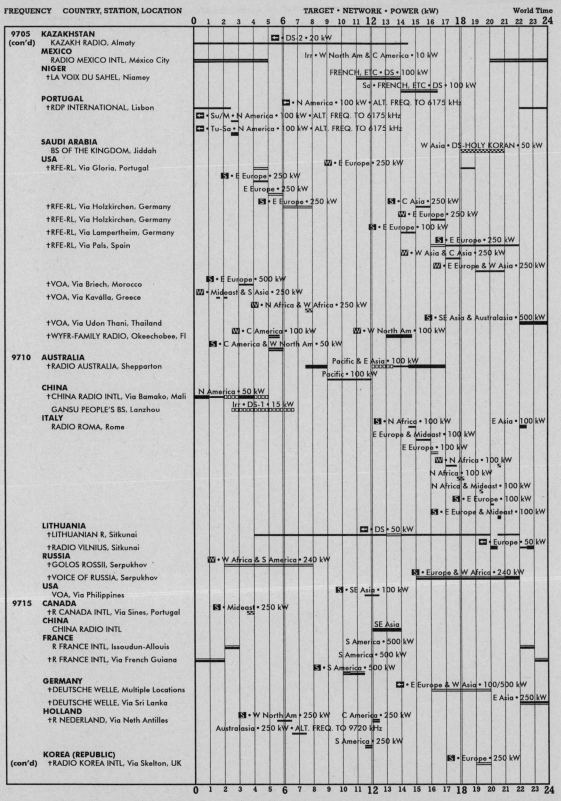

Frequency	Country, Station, Location
9705 (con'd)	**KAZAKHSTAN**
	KAZAKH RADIO, Almaty
	MEXICO
	RADIO MEXICO INTL, México City
	NIGER
	†LA VOIX DU SAHEL, Niamey
	PORTUGAL
	†RDP INTERNATIONAL, Lisbon
	SAUDI ARABIA
	BS OF THE KINGDOM, Jiddah
	USA
	†RFE-RL, Via Gloria, Portugal
	†RFE-RL, Via Holzkirchen, Germany
	†RFE-RL, Via Holzkirchen, Germany
	†RFE-RL, Via Lampertheim, Germany
	†RFE-RL, Via Pals, Spain
	†VOA, Via Briech, Morocco
	†VOA, Via Kaválla, Greece
	†VOA, Via Udon Thani, Thailand
	†WYFR-FAMILY RADIO, Okeechobee, Fl
9710	**AUSTRALIA**
	†RADIO AUSTRALIA, Shepparton
	CHINA
	†CHINA RADIO INTL, Via Bamako, Mali
	GANSU PEOPLE'S BS, Lanzhou
	ITALY
	RADIO ROMA, Rome
	LITHUANIA
	†LITHUANIAN R, Sitkunai
	†RADIO VILNIUS, Sitkunai
	RUSSIA
	†GOLOS ROSSII, Serpukhov
	†VOICE OF RUSSIA, Serpukhov
	USA
	VOA, Via Philippines
9715	**CANADA**
	†R CANADA INTL, Via Sines, Portugal
	CHINA
	CHINA RADIO INTL
	FRANCE
	R FRANCE INTL, Issoudun-Allouis
	†R FRANCE INTL, Via French Guiana
	GERMANY
	†DEUTSCHE WELLE, Multiple Locations
	†DEUTSCHE WELLE, Via Sri Lanka
	HOLLAND
	†R NEDERLAND, Via Neth Antilles
	KOREA (REPUBLIC)
(con'd)	†RADIO KOREA INTL, Via Skelton, UK

Chart annotations:
- DS-2 • 20 kW
- Irr • W North Am & C America • 10 kW
- FRENCH, ETC • DS • 100 kW
- Sa • FRENCH, ETC • DS • 100 kW
- N America • 100 kW • ALT. FREQ. TO 6175 kHz
- Su/M • N America • 100 kW • ALT. FREQ. TO 6175 kHz
- Tu-Sa • N America • 100 kW • ALT. FREQ. TO 6175 kHz
- W Asia • DS-HOLY KORAN • 50 kW
- W • E Europe • 250 kW
- S • E Europe • 250 kW
- E Europe • 250 kW
- S • E Europe • 250 kW
- S • C Asia • 250 kW
- W • E Europe • 250 kW
- S • E Europe • 100 kW
- S • E Europe • 250 kW
- W • W Asia & C Asia • 250 kW
- W • E Europe & W Asia • 250 kW
- S • E Europe • 500 kW
- W • Mideast & S Asia • 250 kW
- W • N Africa & W Africa • 250 kW
- S • SE Asia & Australasia • 500 kW
- W • C America • 100 kW
- W • W North Am • 100 kW
- S • C America & W North Am • 50 kW
- Pacific & E Asia • 100 kW
- Pacific • 100 kW
- N America • 50 kW
- Irr • DS-1 • 15 kW
- S • N Africa • 100 kW
- E Asia • 100 kW
- E Europe & Mideast • 100 kW
- E Europe • 100 kW
- W • N Africa • 100 kW
- N Africa • 100 kW
- N Africa & Mideast • 100 kW
- S • E Europe • 100 kW
- S • E Europe & Mideast • 100 kW
- DS • 50 kW
- Europe • 50 kW
- W • W Africa & S America • 240 kW
- S • Europe & W Africa • 240 kW
- S • SE Asia • 100 kW
- S • Mideast • 250 kW
- SE Asia
- S America • 500 kW
- S America • 500 kW
- S • S America • 500 kW
- E Europe & W Asia • 100/500 kW
- E Asia • 250 kW
- S • W North Am • 250 kW
- C America • 250 kW
- Australasia • 250 kW • ALT. FREQ. TO 9720 kHz
- S America • 250 kW
- S • Europe • 250 kW

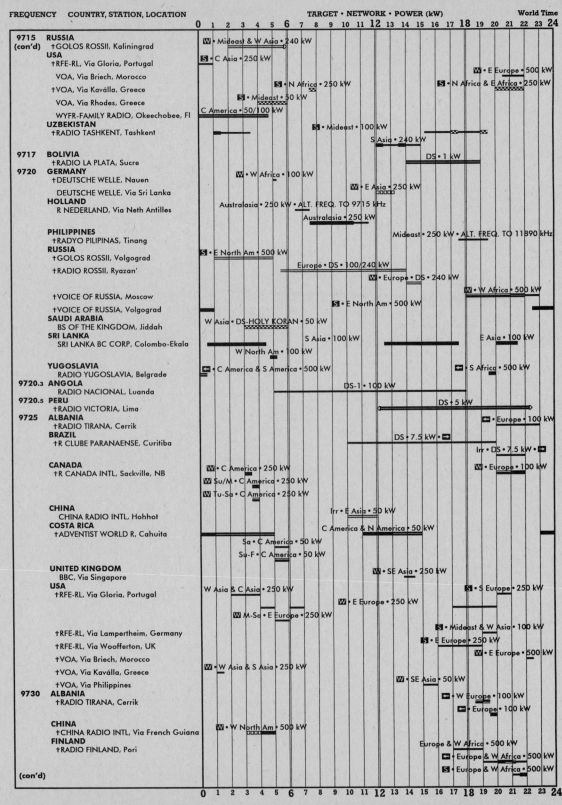

FREQUENCY   COUNTRY, STATION, LOCATION   TARGET • NETWORK • POWER (kW)   World Time

9715	RUSSIA
(con'd)	†GOLOS ROSSII, Kaliningrad
	USA
	†RFE-RL, Via Gloria, Portugal
	VOA, Via Briech, Morocco
	†VOA, Via Kaválla, Greece
	VOA, Via Rhodes, Greece
	WYFR-FAMILY RADIO, Okeechobee, Fl
	UZBEKISTAN
	†RADIO TASHKENT, Tashkent
9717	BOLIVIA
	†RADIO LA PLATA, Sucre
9720	GERMANY
	†DEUTSCHE WELLE, Nauen
	DEUTSCHE WELLE, Via Sri Lanka
	HOLLAND
	R NEDERLAND, Via Neth Antilles
	PHILIPPINES
	†RADYO PILIPINAS, Tinang
	RUSSIA
	†GOLOS ROSSII, Volgograd
	†RADIO ROSSII, Ryazan'
	†VOICE OF RUSSIA, Moscow
	†VOICE OF RUSSIA, Volgograd
	SAUDI ARABIA
	BS OF THE KINGDOM, Jiddah
	SRI LANKA
	SRI LANKA BC CORP, Colombo-Ekala
	YUGOSLAVIA
	RADIO YUGOSLAVIA, Belgrade
9720.3	ANGOLA
	RADIO NACIONAL, Luanda
9720.5	PERU
	†RADIO VICTORIA, Lima
9725	ALBANIA
	†RADIO TIRANA, Cerrik
	BRAZIL
	†R CLUBE PARANAENSE, Curitiba
	CANADA
	†R CANADA INTL, Sackville, NB
	CHINA
	CHINA RADIO INTL, Hohhot
	COSTA RICA
	†ADVENTIST WORLD R, Cahuita
	UNITED KINGDOM
	BBC, Via Singapore
	USA
	†RFE-RL, Via Gloria, Portugal
	†RFE-RL, Via Lampertheim, Germany
	†RFE-RL, Via Woofferton, UK
	†VOA, Via Briech, Morocco
	†VOA, Via Kaválla, Greece
	†VOA, Via Philippines
9730	ALBANIA
	†RADIO TIRANA, Cerrik
	CHINA
	†CHINA RADIO INTL, Via French Guiana
	FINLAND
	†RADIO FINLAND, Pori
(con'd)	

Target/Network/Power notes as charted:

- †GOLOS ROSSII, Kaliningrad — W • Mideast & W Asia • 240 kW
- †RFE-RL, Via Gloria, Portugal — S • C Asia • 250 kW
- VOA, Via Briech, Morocco — W • E Europe • 500 kW
- †VOA, Via Kaválla, Greece — S • N Africa • 250 kW ; S • N Africa & E Africa • 250 kW
- VOA, Via Rhodes, Greece — S • Mideast • 50 kW
- WYFR-FAMILY RADIO — C America • 50/100 kW
- †RADIO TASHKENT — S • Mideast • 100 kW ; S Asia • 240 kW
- †RADIO LA PLATA — DS • 1 kW
- †DEUTSCHE WELLE, Nauen — W • W Africa • 100 kW
- DEUTSCHE WELLE, Via Sri Lanka — W • E Asia • 250 kW
- R NEDERLAND — Australasia • 250 kW • ALT. FREQ. TO 9715 kHz ; Australasia • 250 kW
- †RADYO PILIPINAS — Mideast • 250 kW • ALT. FREQ. TO 11890 kHz
- †GOLOS ROSSII, Volgograd — S • E North Am • 500 kW
- †RADIO ROSSII, Ryazan' — Europe • DS • 100/240 kW ; W • Europe • DS • 240 kW
- †VOICE OF RUSSIA, Moscow — W • W Africa • 500 kW
- †VOICE OF RUSSIA, Volgograd — S • E North Am • 500 kW
- BS OF THE KINGDOM — W Asia • DS-HOLY KORAN • 50 kW
- SRI LANKA BC CORP — S Asia • 100 kW ; E Asia • 100 kW ; W North Am • 100 kW
- RADIO YUGOSLAVIA — C America & S America • 500 kW ; S • S Africa • 500 kW
- RADIO NACIONAL, Luanda — DS-1 • 100 kW
- †RADIO VICTORIA, Lima — DS • 5 kW
- †RADIO TIRANA, Cerrik — Europe • 100 kW
- †R CLUBE PARANAENSE — DS • 7.5 kW ; Irr • DS • 7.5 kW
- †R CANADA INTL — W • C America • 250 kW ; Su/M • C America • 250 kW ; Tu-Sa • C America • 250 kW ; W • Europe • 100 kW
- CHINA RADIO INTL, Hohhot — Irr • E Asia • 50 kW
- †ADVENTIST WORLD R — C America & N America • 50 kW ; Sa • C America • 50 kW ; Su-F • C America • 50 kW
- BBC, Via Singapore — W • SE Asia • 250 kW
- †RFE-RL, Via Gloria, Portugal — W Asia & C Asia • 250 kW ; S • S Europe • 250 kW
- †RFE-RL, Via Lampertheim, Germany — W • E Europe • 250 kW ; M-Sa • E Europe • 250 kW ; S • Mideast & W Asia • 100 kW
- †RFE-RL, Via Woofferton, UK — S • E Europe • 250 kW
- †VOA, Via Briech, Morocco — W • E Europe • 500 kW
- †VOA, Via Kaválla, Greece — W • W Asia & S Asia • 250 kW
- †VOA, Via Philippines — W • SE Asia • 50 kW
- †RADIO TIRANA, Cerrik — W Europe • 100 kW ; Europe • 100 kW
- †CHINA RADIO INTL, Via French Guiana — W • W North Am • 500 kW
- †RADIO FINLAND, Pori — Europe & W Africa • 500 kW ; Europe & W Africa • 500 kW ; S • Europe & W Africa • 500 kW

FREQUENCY   COUNTRY, STATION, LOCATION

TARGET • NETWORK • POWER (kW)

World Time

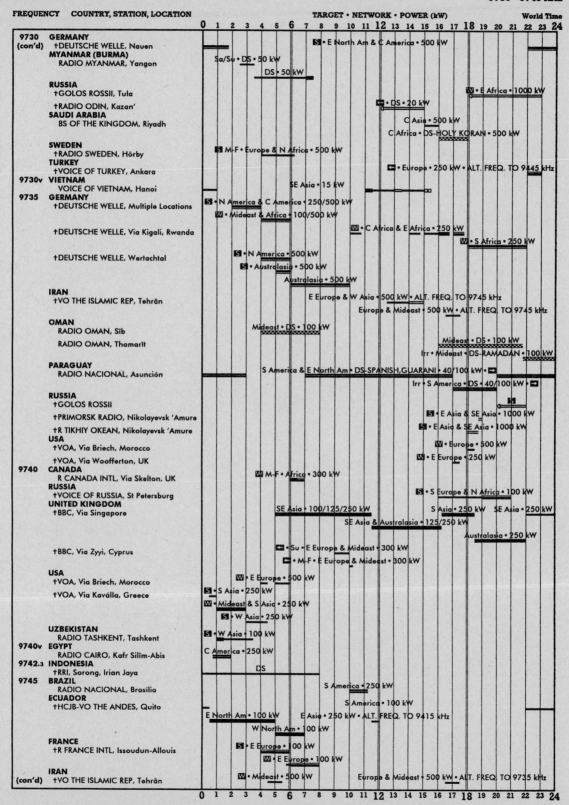

FREQUENCY	COUNTRY, STATION, LOCATION	Details
9730 (con'd)	GERMANY †DEUTSCHE WELLE, Nauen	S • E North Am & C America • 500 kW
	MYANMAR (BURMA) RADIO MYANMAR, Yangon	Sa/Su • DS • 50 kW; DS • 50 kW
	RUSSIA †GOLOS ROSSII, Tula	W • E Africa • 1000 kW
	†RADIO ODIN, Kazan'	DS • 20 kW
	SAUDI ARABIA BS OF THE KINGDOM, Riyadh	C Asia • 500 kW; C Africa • DS-HOLY KORAN • 500 kW
	SWEDEN †RADIO SWEDEN, Hörby	M-F • Europe & N Africa • 500 kW
	TURKEY †VOICE OF TURKEY, Ankara	Europe • 250 kW • ALT. FREQ. TO 9445 kHz
9730v	VIETNAM VOICE OF VIETNAM, Hanoi	SE Asia • 15 kW
9735	GERMANY †DEUTSCHE WELLE, Multiple Locations	S • N America & C America • 250/500 kW; W • Mideast & Africa • 100/500 kW
	†DEUTSCHE WELLE, Via Kigali, Rwanda	W • C Africa & E Africa • 250 kW; W • S Africa • 250 kW
	†DEUTSCHE WELLE, Wertachtal	S • N America • 500 kW; S • Australasia • 500 kW; Australasia • 500 kW
	IRAN †VO THE ISLAMIC REP, Tehrān	E Europe & W Asia • 500 kW • ALT. FREQ. TO 9745 kHz; Europe & Mideast • 500 kW • ALT. FREQ. TO 9745 kHz
	OMAN RADIO OMAN, Sīb	Mideast • DS • 100 kW
	RADIO OMAN, Thamarīt	Mideast • DS • 100 kW; Irr • Mideast • DS-RAMADAN • 100 kW
	PARAGUAY RADIO NACIONAL, Asunción	S America & E North Am • DS-SPANISH, GUARANI • 40/100 kW; Irr • S America • DS • 40/100 kW
	RUSSIA †GOLOS ROSSII	
	†PRIMORSK RADIO, Nikolayevsk 'Amure	S • E Asia & SE Asia • 1000 kW
	†R TIKHIY OKEAN, Nikolayevsk 'Amure	S • E Asia & SE Asia • 1000 kW
	USA †VOA, Via Briech, Morocco	W • Europe • 500 kW
	†VOA, Via Woofferton, UK	W • E Europe • 250 kW
9740	CANADA R CANADA INTL, Via Skelton, UK	W • M-F • Africa • 300 kW
	RUSSIA †VOICE OF RUSSIA, St Petersburg	S • S Europe & N Africa • 100 kW
	UNITED KINGDOM †BBC, Via Singapore	SE Asia • 100/125/250 kW; S Asia • 250 kW; SE Asia • 250 kW; SE Asia & Australasia • 125/250 kW; Australasia • 250 kW
	†BBC, Via Zyyi, Cyprus	Su • E Europe & Mideast • 300 kW; M-F • E Europe & Mideast • 300 kW
	USA †VOA, Via Briech, Morocco	W • E Europe • 500 kW
	†VOA, Via Kaválla, Greece	S • S Asia • 250 kW; W • Mideast & S Asia • 250 kW; S • W Asia • 250 kW
	UZBEKISTAN RADIO TASHKENT, Tashkent	S • W Asia • 100 kW
9740v	EGYPT RADIO CAIRO, Kafr Silīm-Abis	C America • 250 kW
9742.3	INDONESIA †RRI, Sorong, Irian Jaya	DS
9745	BRAZIL RADIO NACIONAL, Brasilia	S America • 250 kW
	ECUADOR †HCJB-VO THE ANDES, Quito	S America • 100 kW; E North Am • 100 kW; E Asia • 250 kW • ALT. FREQ. TO 9415 kHz; W North Am • 100 kW
	FRANCE †R FRANCE INTL, Issoudun-Allouis	S • E Europe • 100 kW; W • E Europe • 100 kW
(con'd)	IRAN †VO THE ISLAMIC REP, Tehrān	W • Mideast • 500 kW; Europe & Mideast • 500 kW • ALT. FREQ. TO 9735 kHz

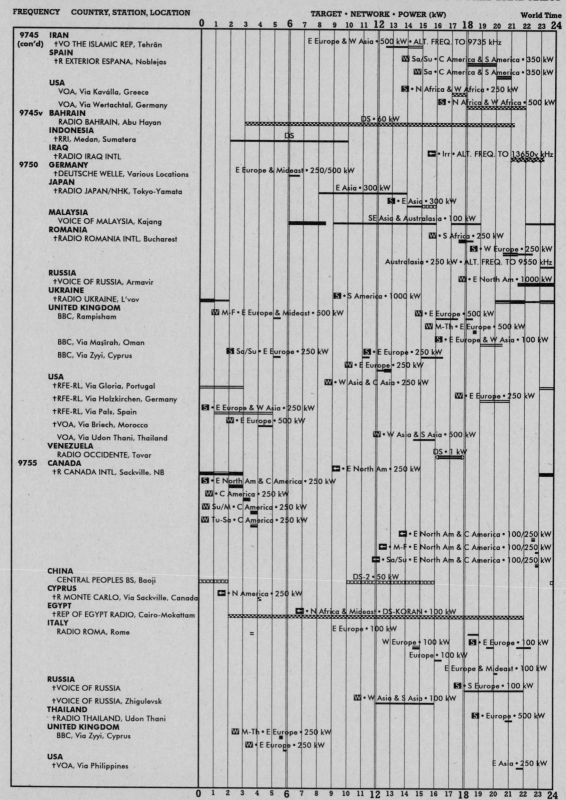

FREQUENCY   COUNTRY, STATION, LOCATION

TARGET • NETWORK • POWER (kW)   World Time

FREQUENCY	COUNTRY, STATION, LOCATION	Details
9745 (con'd)	IRAN †VO THE ISLAMIC REP, Tehrān	E Europe & W Asia • 500 kW • ALT. FREQ. TO 9735 kHz
	SPAIN †R EXTERIOR ESPANA, Noblejas	W Sa/Su • C America & S America • 350 kW ; W Sa • C America & S America • 350 kW
	USA VOA, Via Kaválla, Greece	S • N Africa & W Africa • 250 kW
	VOA, Via Wertachtal, Germany	S • N Africa & W Africa • 500 kW
9745v	BAHRAIN RADIO BAHRAIN, Abu Hayan	DS • 60 kW
	INDONESIA †RRI, Medan, Sumatera	DS
	IRAQ †RADIO IRAQ INTL	• Irr • ALT. FREQ. TO 13650v kHz
9750	GERMANY †DEUTSCHE WELLE, Various Locations	E Europe & Mideast • 250/500 kW
	JAPAN †RADIO JAPAN/NHK, Tokyo-Yamata	E Asia • 300 kW ; S • E Asia • 300 kW
	MALAYSIA VOICE OF MALAYSIA, Kajang	SE Asia & Australasia • 100 kW
	ROMANIA †RADIO ROMANIA INTL, Bucharest	W • S Africa • 250 kW ; S • W Europe • 250 kW ; Australasia • 250 kW • ALT. FREQ. TO 9550 kHz
	RUSSIA †VOICE OF RUSSIA, Armavir	W • E North Am • 1000 kW
	UKRAINE †RADIO UKRAINE, L'vov	S • S America • 1000 kW
	UNITED KINGDOM BBC, Rampisham	W • M-F • E Europe & Mideast • 500 kW ; W • E Europe • 500 kW ; W • M-Th • E Europe • 500 kW
	BBC, Via Maṣīrah, Oman	S • E Europe & W Asia • 100 kW
	BBC, Via Zyyi, Cyprus	S • Sa/Su • E Europe • 250 kW ; S • E Europe • 250 kW ; W • E Europe • 250 kW
	USA †RFE-RL, Via Gloria, Portugal	• W Asia & C Asia • 250 kW
	†RFE-RL, Via Holzkirchen, Germany	W • E Europe • 250 kW
	†RFE-RL, Via Pals, Spain	S • E Europe & W Asia • 250 kW
	†VOA, Via Briech, Morocco	W • E Europe • 500 kW
	VOA, Via Udon Thani, Thailand	W • W Asia & S Asia • 500 kW
	VENEZUELA RADIO OCCIDENTE, Tovar	DS • 1 kW
9755	CANADA †R CANADA INTL, Sackville, NB	• E North Am • 250 kW ; S • E North Am & C America • 250 kW ; W • C America • 250 kW ; W • Su/M • C America • 250 kW ; W • Tu-Sa • C America • 250 kW ; • E North Am & C America • 100/250 kW ; • M-F • E North Am & C America • 100/250 kW ; • Sa/Su • E North Am & C America • 100/250 kW
	CHINA CENTRAL PEOPLES BS, Baoji	DS-2 • 50 kW
	CYPRUS †R MONTE CARLO, Via Sackville, Canada	• N America • 250 kW
	EGYPT †REP OF EGYPT RADIO, Cairo-Mokattam	• N Africa & Mideast • DS-KORAN • 100 kW
	ITALY RADIO ROMA, Rome	E Europe • 100 kW ; W Europe • 100 kW ; S • E Europe • 100 kW ; Europe • 100 kW ; E Europe & Mideast • 100 kW
	RUSSIA †VOICE OF RUSSIA	S • S Europe • 100 kW
	†VOICE OF RUSSIA, Zhigulevsk	W • W Asia & S Asia • 100 kW
	THAILAND †RADIO THAILAND, Udon Thani	S • Europe • 500 kW
	UNITED KINGDOM BBC, Via Zyyi, Cyprus	W • M-Th • E Europe • 250 kW ; W • E Europe • 250 kW
	USA †VOA, Via Philippines	E Asia • 250 kW

FREQUENCY   COUNTRY, STATION, LOCATION   TARGET • NETWORK • POWER (kW)   World Time

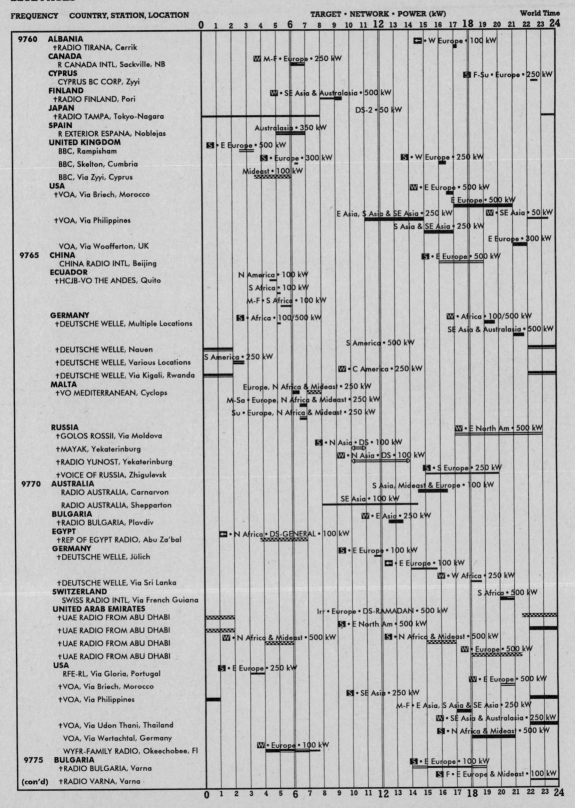

Freq	Country / Station / Location	Schedule
9760	**ALBANIA**	
	†RADIO TIRANA, Cerrik	W Europe • 100 kW
	CANADA	
	R CANADA INTL, Sackville, NB	M-F • Europe • 250 kW
	CYPRUS	
	CYPRUS BC CORP, Zyyi	F-Su • Europe • 250 kW
	FINLAND	
	†RADIO FINLAND, Pori	W • SE Asia & Australasia • 500 kW
	JAPAN	
	†RADIO TAMPA, Tokyo-Nagara	DS-2 • 50 kW
	SPAIN	
	R EXTERIOR ESPANA, Noblejas	Australasia • 350 kW
	UNITED KINGDOM	
	BBC, Rampisham	S • E Europe • 500 kW
	BBC, Skelton, Cumbria	S • Europe • 300 kW
		S • W Europe • 250 kW
	BBC, Via Zyyi, Cyprus	Mideast • 100 kW
	USA	
	†VOA, Via Briech, Morocco	W • E Europe • 500 kW
		E Europe • 500 kW
	†VOA, Via Philippines	E Asia, S Asia & SE Asia • 250 kW
		W • SE Asia • 50 kW
		S Asia & SE Asia • 250 kW
	VOA, Via Woofferton, UK	E Europe • 300 kW
9765	**CHINA**	
	CHINA RADIO INTL, Beijing	S • E Europe • 500 kW
	ECUADOR	
	†HCJB-VO THE ANDES, Quito	N America • 100 kW
		S Africa • 100 kW
		M-F • S Africa • 100 kW
	GERMANY	
	†DEUTSCHE WELLE, Multiple Locations	S • Africa • 100/500 kW
		W • Africa • 100/500 kW
		SE Asia & Australasia • 500 kW
		S America • 500 kW
	†DEUTSCHE WELLE, Nauen	S America • 250 kW
	†DEUTSCHE WELLE, Various Locations	W • C America • 250 kW
	†DEUTSCHE WELLE, Via Kigali, Rwanda	Europe, N Africa & Mideast • 250 kW
	MALTA	
	†VO MEDITERRANEAN, Cyclops	M-Sa • Europe, N Africa & Mideast • 250 kW
		Su • Europe, N Africa & Mideast • 250 kW
	RUSSIA	
	†GOLOS ROSSII, Via Moldova	W • E North Am • 500 kW
	†MAYAK, Yekaterinburg	S • N Asia • DS • 100 kW
	†RADIO YUNOST, Yekaterinburg	W • N Asia • DS • 100 kW
	†VOICE OF RUSSIA, Zhigulevsk	S • S Europe • 250 kW
9770	**AUSTRALIA**	
	RADIO AUSTRALIA, Carnarvon	S Asia, Mideast & Europe • 100 kW
	RADIO AUSTRALIA, Shepparton	SE Asia • 100 kW
	BULGARIA	
	†RADIO BULGARIA, Plovdiv	W • E Asia • 250 kW
	EGYPT	
	†REP OF EGYPT RADIO, Abu Za'bal	N Africa • DS-GENERAL • 100 kW
	GERMANY	
	†DEUTSCHE WELLE, Jülich	S • E Europe • 100 kW
		E Europe • 100 kW
	†DEUTSCHE WELLE, Via Sri Lanka	W • W Africa • 250 kW
	SWITZERLAND	
	SWISS RADIO INTL, Via French Guiana	S Africa • 500 kW
	UNITED ARAB EMIRATES	
	†UAE RADIO FROM ABU DHABI	Irr • Europe • DS-RAMADAN • 500 kW
	†UAE RADIO FROM ABU DHABI	S • E North Am • 500 kW
	†UAE RADIO FROM ABU DHABI	W • N Africa & Mideast • 500 kW
		S • N Africa & Mideast • 500 kW
	†UAE RADIO FROM ABU DHABI	W • Europe • 500 kW
	USA	
	RFE-RL, Via Gloria, Portugal	S • E Europe • 250 kW
	†VOA, Via Briech, Morocco	W • E Europe • 500 kW
	†VOA, Via Philippines	S • SE Asia • 250 kW
		M-F • E Asia, S Asia & SE Asia • 250 kW
	†VOA, Via Udon Thani, Thailand	W • SE Asia & Australasia • 250 kW
	VOA, Via Wertachtal, Germany	S • N Africa & Mideast • 500 kW
	WYFR-FAMILY RADIO, Okeechobee, Fl	W • Europe • 100 kW
9775	**BULGARIA**	
	†RADIO BULGARIA, Varna	S • E Europe • 100 kW
(con'd)	†RADIO VARNA, Varna	S F • E Europe & Mideast • 100 kW

ENGLISH ▬   ARABIC ▧   CHINESE ▫▫▫   FRENCH ═   GERMAN ▬   RUSSIAN ═   SPANISH ▬   OTHER ▬

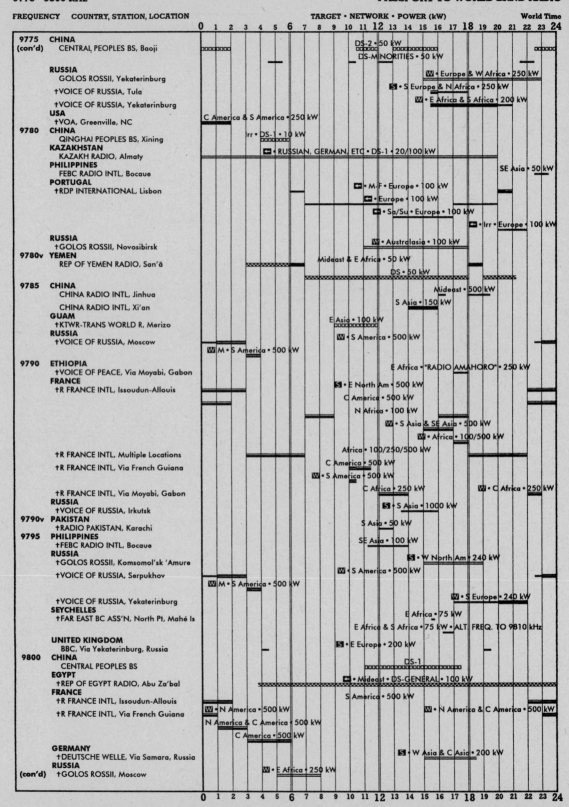

FREQUENCY   COUNTRY, STATION, LOCATION   TARGET • NETWORK • POWER (kW)   World Time

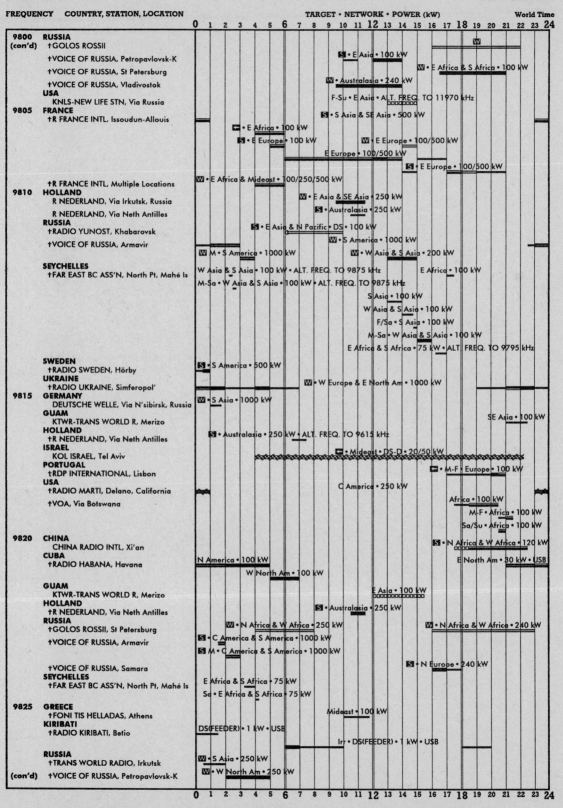

Frequency	Country / Station / Location
9800 (con'd)	**RUSSIA** †GOLOS ROSSII
	†VOICE OF RUSSIA, Petropavlovsk-K
	†VOICE OF RUSSIA, St Petersburg
	†VOICE OF RUSSIA, Vladivostok
	USA KNLS-NEW LIFE STN, Via Russia
9805	**FRANCE** †R FRANCE INTL, Issoudun-Allouis
	†R FRANCE INTL, Multiple Locations
9810	**HOLLAND** R NEDERLAND, Via Irkutsk, Russia
	R NEDERLAND, Via Neth Antilles
	RUSSIA †RADIO YUNOST, Khabarovsk
	†VOICE OF RUSSIA, Armavir
	SEYCHELLES †FAR EAST BC ASS'N, North Pt, Mahé Is
	SWEDEN †RADIO SWEDEN, Hörby
	UKRAINE †RADIO UKRAINE, Simferopol'
9815	**GERMANY** DEUTSCHE WELLE, Via N'sibirsk, Russia
	GUAM KTWR-TRANS WORLD R, Merizo
	HOLLAND †R NEDERLAND, Via Neth Antilles
	ISRAEL KOL ISRAEL, Tel Aviv
	PORTUGAL †RDP INTERNATIONAL, Lisbon
	USA †RADIO MARTI, Delano, California
	†VOA, Via Botswana
9820	**CHINA** CHINA RADIO INTL, Xi'an
	CUBA †RADIO HABANA, Havana
	GUAM KTWR-TRANS WORLD R, Merizo
	HOLLAND †R NEDERLAND, Via Neth Antilles
	RUSSIA †GOLOS ROSSII, St Petersburg
	†VOICE OF RUSSIA, Armavir
	†VOICE OF RUSSIA, Samara
	SEYCHELLES †FAR EAST BC ASS'N, North Pt, Mahé Is
9825	**GREECE** †FONI TIS HELLADAS, Athens
	KIRIBATI †RADIO KIRIBATI, Betio
	RUSSIA †TRANS WORLD RADIO, Irkutsk
(con'd)	†VOICE OF RUSSIA, Petropavlovsk-K

Target • Network • Power notes (as shown on chart):
- VOICE OF RUSSIA, Petropavlovsk-K: S • E Asia • 100 kW
- VOICE OF RUSSIA, St Petersburg: W • E Africa & S Africa • 100 kW
- VOICE OF RUSSIA, Vladivostok: W • Australasia • 240 kW
- KNLS-NEW LIFE STN: F-Su • E Asia • ALT. FREQ. TO 11970 kHz
- R FRANCE INTL, Issoudun-Allouis: S • S Asia & SE Asia • 500 kW; ◨ • E Africa • 100 kW; S • E Europe • 100 kW; W • E Europe • 100/500 kW; E Europe • 100/500 kW; S • E Europe • 100/500 kW
- R FRANCE INTL, Multiple Locations: W • E Africa & Mideast • 100/250/500 kW
- R NEDERLAND, Via Irkutsk: W • E Asia & SE Asia • 250 kW
- R NEDERLAND, Via Neth Antilles: S • Australasia • 250 kW
- RADIO YUNOST, Khabarovsk: S • E Asia & N Pacific • DS • 100 kW
- VOICE OF RUSSIA, Armavir: W • S America • 1000 kW
- FAR EAST BC ASS'N: W • M • S America • 1000 kW; W • W Asia & S Asia • 200 kW; W Asia & S Asia • 100 kW • ALT. FREQ. TO 9875 kHz; E Africa • 100 kW; M-Sa • W Asia & S Asia • 100 kW • ALT. FREQ. TO 9875 kHz; S Asia • 100 kW; W Asia & S Asia • 100 kW; F/Sa • S Asia • 100 kW; M-Sa • W Asia & S Asia • 100 kW; E Africa & S Africa • 75 kW • ALT. FREQ. TO 9795 kHz
- RADIO SWEDEN: S • S America • 500 kW
- RADIO UKRAINE: W • W Europe & E North Am • 1000 kW
- DEUTSCHE WELLE: W • S Asia • 1000 kW
- KTWR-TRANS WORLD R (9815): SE Asia • 100 kW
- R NEDERLAND (9815): S • Australasia • 250 kW • ALT. FREQ. TO 9615 kHz
- KOL ISRAEL: ◨ • Mideast • DS-D • 20/50 kW
- RDP INTERNATIONAL: ◨ • M-F • Europe • 100 kW
- RADIO MARTI: C America • 250 kW
- VOA, Via Botswana: Africa • 100 kW; M-F • Africa • 100 kW; Sa/Su • Africa • 100 kW
- CHINA RADIO INTL: S • N Africa & W Africa • 120 kW
- RADIO HABANA: N America • 100 kW; E North Am • 30 kW • USB; W North Am • 100 kW
- KTWR-TRANS WORLD R (9820): E Asia • 100 kW
- R NEDERLAND (9820): S • Australasia • 250 kW
- GOLOS ROSSII, St Petersburg: W • N Africa & W Africa • 250 kW; W • N Africa & W Africa • 240 kW
- VOICE OF RUSSIA, Armavir (9820): S • C America & S America • 1000 kW; S • M • C America & S America • 1000 kW
- VOICE OF RUSSIA, Samara: S • N Europe • 240 kW
- FAR EAST BC ASS'N (9820): E Africa & S Africa • 75 kW; Sa • E Africa & S Africa • 75 kW
- FONI TIS HELLADAS: Mideast • 100 kW
- RADIO KIRIBATI: DS(FEEDER) • 1 kW • USB; Irr • DS(FEEDER) • 1 kW • USB
- TRANS WORLD RADIO, Irkutsk: W • S Asia • 250 kW
- VOICE OF RUSSIA, Petropavlovsk-K: W • W North Am • 250 kW

ENGLISH ▬▬ **ARABIC** ≋ **CHINESE** ▯▯▯ **FRENCH** ▬▬ **GERMAN** ▬▬ **RUSSIAN** ═ **SPANISH** ▬▬ **OTHER** ▬

FREQUENCY   COUNTRY, STATION, LOCATION

TARGET • NETWORK • POWER (kW)

World Time

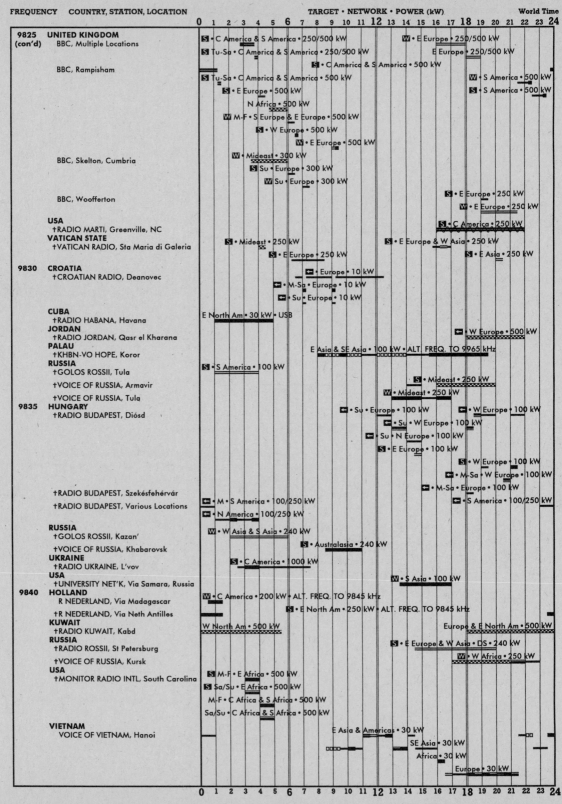

FREQUENCY	COUNTRY, STATION, LOCATION	Schedule details
9825 (con'd)	UNITED KINGDOM BBC, Multiple Locations	S • C America & S America • 250/500 kW W • E Europe • 250/500 kW
		S Tu-Sa • C America & S America • 250/500 kW E Europe • 250/500 kW
		S • C America & S America • 500 kW
	BBC, Rampisham	S Tu-Sa • C America & S America • 500 kW W • S America • 500 kW
		S • E Europe • 500 kW S • S America • 500 kW
		N Africa • 500 kW
		W M-F • S Europe & E Europe • 500 kW
		S • W Europe • 500 kW
		W • E Europe • 500 kW
	BBC, Skelton, Cumbria	W • Mideast • 300 kW
		S Su • Europe • 300 kW
		W Su • Europe • 300 kW
	BBC, Woofferton	S • E Europe • 250 kW
		W • E Europe • 250 kW
	USA †RADIO MARTI, Greenville, NC	S • C America • 250 kW
	VATICAN STATE †VATICAN RADIO, Sta Maria di Galeria	S • Mideast • 250 kW S • E Europe & W Asia • 250 kW
		S • E Europe • 250 kW S • E Asia • 250 kW
9830	CROATIA †CROATIAN RADIO, Deanovec	• Europe • 10 kW
		• M-Sa • Europe • 10 kW
		• Su • Europe • 10 kW
	CUBA †RADIO HABANA, Havana	E North Am • 30 kW • USB
	JORDAN †RADIO JORDAN, Qasr el Kharana	• W Europe • 500 kW
	PALAU †KHBN-VO HOPE, Koror	E Asia & SE Asia • 100 kW • ALT. FREQ. TO 9965 kHz
	RUSSIA †GOLOS ROSSII, Tula	S • S America • 100 kW
	†VOICE OF RUSSIA, Armavir	S • Mideast • 250 kW
	†VOICE OF RUSSIA, Tula	W • Mideast • 250 kW
9835	HUNGARY †RADIO BUDAPEST, Diósd	• Su • Europe • 100 kW • W Europe • 100 kW
		• Su • W Europe • 100 kW
		• Su • N Europe • 100 kW
		S • E Europe • 100 kW
		S • W Europe • 100 kW
		• M-Sa • W Europe • 100 kW
		• M-Sa • Europe • 100 kW
	†RADIO BUDAPEST, Székesfehérvár	• M • S America • 100/250 kW • S America • 100/250 kW
	†RADIO BUDAPEST, Various Locations	• N America • 100/250 kW
	RUSSIA †GOLOS ROSSII, Kazan'	W • W Asia & S Asia • 240 kW
	†VOICE OF RUSSIA, Khabarovsk	S • Australasia • 240 kW
	UKRAINE †RADIO UKRAINE, L'vov	S • C America • 1000 kW
	USA †UNIVERSITY NET'K, Via Samara, Russia	W • S Asia • 100 kW
9840	HOLLAND R NEDERLAND, Via Madagascar	W • C America • 200 kW • ALT. FREQ. TO 9845 kHz
	†R NEDERLAND, Via Neth Antilles	S • E North Am • 250 kW • ALT. FREQ. TO 9845 kHz
	KUWAIT †RADIO KUWAIT, Kabd	W North Am • 500 kW Europe & E North Am • 500 kW
	RUSSIA †RADIO ROSSII, St Petersburg	S • E Europe & W Asia • DS • 240 kW
	†VOICE OF RUSSIA, Kursk	W • W Africa • 250 kW
	USA †MONITOR RADIO INTL, South Carolina	S M-F • E Africa • 500 kW
		S Sa/Su • E Africa • 500 kW
		M-F • C Africa & S Africa • 500 kW
		Sa/Su • C Africa & S Africa • 500 kW
	VIETNAM VOICE OF VIETNAM, Hanoi	E Asia & Americas • 30 kW
		SE Asia • 30 kW
		Africa • 30 kW
		Europe • 30 kW

FREQUENCY   COUNTRY, STATION, LOCATION   TARGET • NETWORK • POWER (kW)   World Time

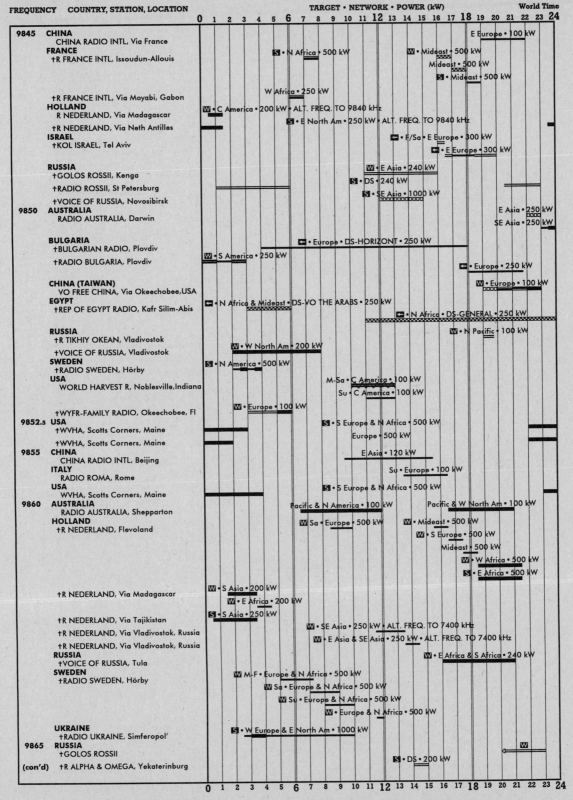

9845	CHINA
	CHINA RADIO INTL, Via France — E Europe • 100 kW
	FRANCE
	†R FRANCE INTL, Issoudun-Allouis — S • N Africa • 500 kW / W • Mideast • 500 kW / Mideast • 500 kW / S • Mideast • 500 kW
	†R FRANCE INTL, Via Moyabi, Gabon — W Africa • 250 kW
	HOLLAND
	R NEDERLAND, Via Madagascar — W • C America • 200 kW • ALT. FREQ. TO 9840 kHz
	†R NEDERLAND, Via Neth Antilles — S • E North Am • 250 kW • ALT. FREQ. TO 9840 kHz
	ISRAEL
	†KOL ISRAEL, Tel Aviv — F/Sa • E Europe • 300 kW / E Europe • 300 kW
	RUSSIA
	†GOLOS ROSSII, Kenga — W • E Asia • 240 kW
	†RADIO ROSSII, St Petersburg — S • DS • 240 kW
	†VOICE OF RUSSIA, Novosibirsk — S • SE Asia • 1000 kW
9850	AUSTRALIA
	RADIO AUSTRALIA, Darwin — E Asia • 250 kW / SE Asia • 250 kW
	BULGARIA
	†BULGARIAN RADIO, Plovdiv — Europe • DS-HORIZONT • 250 kW
	†RADIO BULGARIA, Plovdiv — W • S America • 250 kW / Europe • 250 kW
	CHINA (TAIWAN)
	VO FREE CHINA, Via Okeechobee, USA — W • Europe • 100 kW
	EGYPT
	†REP OF EGYPT RADIO, Kafr Silīm-Abis — N Africa & Mideast • DS-VO THE ARABS • 250 kW / N Africa • DS-GENERAL • 250 kW
	RUSSIA
	†R TIKHIY OKEAN, Vladivostok — W • N Pacific • 100 kW
	†VOICE OF RUSSIA, Vladivostok — W • W North Am • 200 kW
	SWEDEN
	†RADIO SWEDEN, Hörby — S • N America • 500 kW
	USA
	WORLD HARVEST R, Noblesville, Indiana — M-Sa • C America • 100 kW / Su • C America • 100 kW
	†WYFR-FAMILY RADIO, Okeechobee, Fl — W • Europe • 100 kW
9852.5	USA
	†WVHA, Scotts Corners, Maine — S • S Europe & N Africa • 500 kW
	†WVHA, Scotts Corners, Maine — Europe • 500 kW
9855	CHINA
	CHINA RADIO INTL, Beijing — E Asia • 120 kW
	ITALY
	RADIO ROMA, Rome — Su • Europe • 100 kW
	USA
	WVHA, Scotts Corners, Maine — S • S Europe & N Africa • 500 kW
9860	AUSTRALIA
	RADIO AUSTRALIA, Shepparton — Pacific & N America • 100 kW / Pacific & W North Am • 100 kW
	HOLLAND
	†R NEDERLAND, Flevoland — W • Sa • Europe • 500 kW / W • Mideast • 500 kW / W • S Europe • 500 kW / Mideast • 500 kW / W • W Africa • 500 kW / S • E Africa • 500 kW
	†R NEDERLAND, Via Madagascar — W • S Asia • 200 kW
	— W • E Africa • 200 kW
	†R NEDERLAND, Via Tajikistan — S • S Asia • 250 kW
	†R NEDERLAND, Via Vladivostok, Russia — W • SE Asia • 250 kW • ALT. FREQ. TO 7400 kHz
	†R NEDERLAND, Via Vladivostok, Russia — W • E Asia & SE Asia • 250 kW • ALT. FREQ. TO 7400 kHz
	RUSSIA
	†VOICE OF RUSSIA, Tula — W • E Africa & S Africa • 240 kW
	SWEDEN
	†RADIO SWEDEN, Hörby — W • M-F • Europe & N Africa • 500 kW / W • Sa • Europe & N Africa • 500 kW / W • Su • Europe & N Africa • 500 kW / W • Europe & N Africa • 500 kW
	UKRAINE
	†RADIO UKRAINE, Simferopol' — S • W Europe & E North Am • 1000 kW
9865	RUSSIA
	†GOLOS ROSSII — W
(con'd)	†R ALPHA & OMEGA, Yekaterinburg — S • DS • 200 kW

ENGLISH ▬   ARABIC ▧▧▧   CHINESE ▫▫▫   FRENCH ▬▬   GERMAN ▬▬   RUSSIAN ═══   SPANISH ▬▬   OTHER ▬

FREQUENCY   COUNTRY, STATION, LOCATION   TARGET • NETWORK • POWER (kW)   World Time

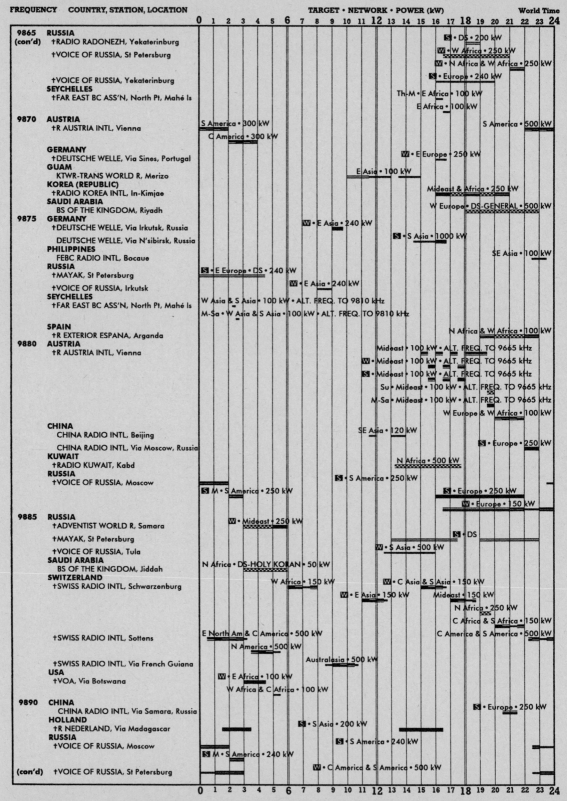

FREQUENCY	COUNTRY, STATION, LOCATION	Target • Network • Power
9865 (con'd)	**RUSSIA** †RADIO RADONEZH, Yekaterinburg	S • DS • 200 kW
	†VOICE OF RUSSIA, St Petersburg	W • W Africa • 250 kW
		W • N Africa & W Africa • 250 kW
	†VOICE OF RUSSIA, Yekaterinburg	S • Europe • 240 kW
	SEYCHELLES †FAR EAST BC ASS'N, North Pt, Mahé Is	Th-M • E Africa • 100 kW
		E Africa • 100 kW
9870	**AUSTRIA** †R AUSTRIA INTL, Vienna	S America • 300 kW
		C America • 300 kW
		S America • 500 kW
	GERMANY †DEUTSCHE WELLE, Via Sines, Portugal	W • E Europe • 250 kW
	GUAM KTWR-TRANS WORLD R, Merizo	E Asia • 100 kW
	KOREA (REPUBLIC) †RADIO KOREA INTL, In-Kimjae	Mideast & Africa • 250 kW
	SAUDI ARABIA BS OF THE KINGDOM, Riyadh	W Europe • DS-GENERAL • 500 kW
9875	**GERMANY** †DEUTSCHE WELLE, Via Irkutsk, Russia	W • E Asia • 240 kW
	DEUTSCHE WELLE, Via N'sibirsk, Russia	S • S Asia • 1000 kW
	PHILIPPINES FEBC RADIO INTL, Bocaue	SE Asia • 100 kW
	RUSSIA †MAYAK, St Petersburg	S • E Europe • DS • 240 kW
	†VOICE OF RUSSIA, Irkutsk	W • E Asia • 240 kW
	SEYCHELLES †FAR EAST BC ASS'N, North Pt, Mahé Is	W Asia & S Asia • 100 kW • ALT. FREQ. TO 9810 kHz
		M-Sa • W Asia & S Asia • 100 kW • ALT. FREQ. TO 9810 kHz
	SPAIN †R EXTERIOR ESPANA, Arganda	N Africa & W Africa • 100 kW
9880	**AUSTRIA** †R AUSTRIA INTL, Vienna	Mideast • 100 kW • ALT. FREQ. TO 9665 kHz
		W • Mideast • 100 kW • ALT. FREQ. TO 9665 kHz
		S • Mideast • 100 kW • ALT. FREQ. TO 9665 kHz
		Su • Mideast • 100 kW • ALT. FREQ. TO 9665 kHz
		M-Sa • Mideast • 100 kW • ALT. FREQ. TO 9665 kHz
		W Europe & W Africa • 100 kW
	CHINA CHINA RADIO INTL, Beijing	SE Asia • 120 kW
	CHINA RADIO INTL, Via Moscow, Russia	S • Europe • 250 kW
	KUWAIT †RADIO KUWAIT, Kabd	N Africa • 500 kW
	RUSSIA †VOICE OF RUSSIA, Moscow	S • S America • 250 kW
		S • M • S America • 250 kW
		S • Europe • 250 kW
		W • Europe • 150 kW
9885	**RUSSIA** †ADVENTIST WORLD R, Samara	W • Mideast • 250 kW
	†MAYAK, St Petersburg	S • DS
	†VOICE OF RUSSIA, Tula	W • S Asia • 500 kW
	SAUDI ARABIA BS OF THE KINGDOM, Jiddah	N Africa • DS-HOLY KORAN • 50 kW
	SWITZERLAND †SWISS RADIO INTL, Schwarzenburg	W Africa • 150 kW
		W • C Asia & S Asia • 150 kW
		W • E Asia • 150 kW
		Mideast • 150 kW
		N Africa • 250 kW
		C Africa & S Africa • 150 kW
	†SWISS RADIO INTL, Sottens	E North Am & C America • 500 kW
		C America & S America • 500 kW
		N America • 500 kW
	†SWISS RADIO INTL, Via French Guiana	Australasia • 500 kW
	USA †VOA, Via Botswana	W • E Africa • 100 kW
		W Africa & C Africa • 100 kW
9890	**CHINA** CHINA RADIO INTL, Via Samara, Russia	S • Europe • 250 kW
	HOLLAND †R NEDERLAND, Via Madagascar	S • S Asia • 200 kW
	RUSSIA †VOICE OF RUSSIA, Moscow	S • S America • 240 kW
		S • M • S America • 240 kW
(con'd)	†VOICE OF RUSSIA, St Petersburg	W • C America & S America • 500 kW

FREQUENCY   COUNTRY, STATION, LOCATION

TARGET • NETWORK • POWER (kW)   World Time

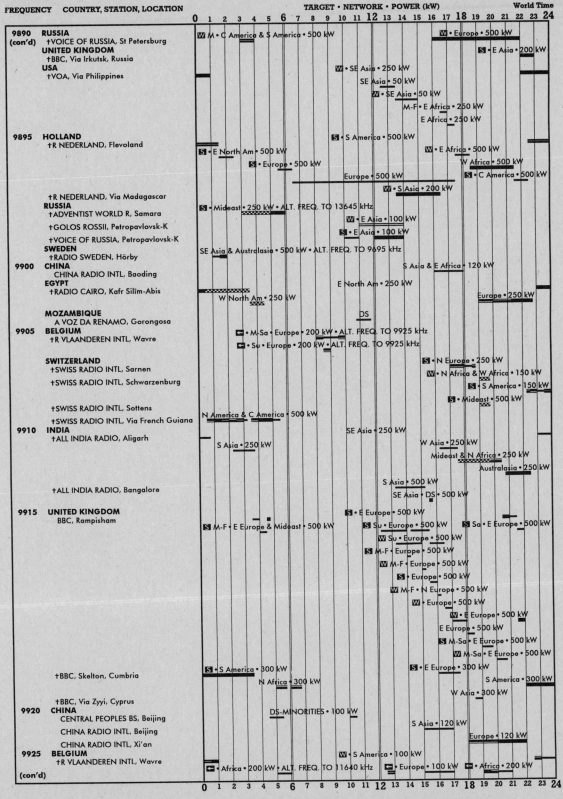

Frequency	Country / Station / Location	Details
9890 (con'd)	**RUSSIA** †VOICE OF RUSSIA, St Petersburg	W • M • C America & S America • 500 kW; W • Europe • 500 kW
	UNITED KINGDOM †BBC, Via Irkutsk, Russia	S • E Asia • 200 kW
	USA †VOA, Via Philippines	W • SE Asia • 250 kW; SE Asia • 50 kW; W • SE Asia • 50 kW; M-F • E Africa • 250 kW; E Africa • 250 kW
9895	**HOLLAND** †R NEDERLAND, Flevoland	S • S America • 500 kW; S • E North Am • 500 kW; S • Europe • 500 kW; Europe • 500 kW; W • E Africa • 500 kW; W Africa • 500 kW; S • C America • 500 kW; W • S Asia • 200 kW
	†R NEDERLAND, Via Madagascar	S • Mideast • 250 kW • ALT. FREQ. TO 13645 kHz
	RUSSIA †ADVENTIST WORLD R, Samara	W • E Asia • 100 kW
	†GOLOS ROSSII, Petropavlovsk-K	S • E Asia • 100 kW
	†VOICE OF RUSSIA, Petropavlovsk-K	
	SWEDEN †RADIO SWEDEN, Hörby	SE Asia & Australasia • 500 kW • ALT. FREQ. TO 9695 kHz
9900	**CHINA** CHINA RADIO INTL, Baoding	S Asia & E Africa • 120 kW
	EGYPT †RADIO CAIRO, Kafr Silim-Abis	E North Am • 250 kW; W North Am • 250 kW; Europe • 250 kW
	MOZAMBIQUE A VOZ DA RENAMO, Gorongosa	DS
9905	**BELGIUM** †R VLAANDEREN INTL, Wavre	• M-Sa • Europe • 200 kW • ALT. FREQ. TO 9925 kHz; • Su • Europe • 200 kW • ALT. FREQ. TO 9925 kHz
	SWITZERLAND †SWISS RADIO INTL, Sarnen	S • N Europe • 250 kW; W • N Africa & W Africa • 150 kW; S • S America • 150 kW; S • Mideast • 500 kW
	†SWISS RADIO INTL, Schwarzenburg	
	†SWISS RADIO INTL, Sottens	
	†SWISS RADIO INTL, Via French Guiana	N America & C America • 500 kW
9910	**INDIA** †ALL INDIA RADIO, Aligarh	SE Asia • 250 kW; S Asia • 250 kW; W Asia • 250 kW; Mideast & N Africa • 250 kW; Australasia • 250 kW
	†ALL INDIA RADIO, Bangalore	S Asia • 500 kW; SE Asia • DS • 500 kW
9915	**UNITED KINGDOM** BBC, Rampisham	S • E Europe • 500 kW; S • M-F • E Europe & Mideast • 500 kW; S • Su • Europe • 500 kW; Sa • E Europe • 500 kW; W • Su • Europe • 500 kW; S • M-F • Europe • 500 kW; W • M-F • Europe • 500 kW; S • Europe • 500 kW; W • M-F • N Europe • 500 kW; W • Europe • 500 kW; W • E Europe • 500 kW; E Europe • 500 kW; S • M-Sa • E Europe • 500 kW; W • M-Sa • E Europe • 500 kW
	†BBC, Skelton, Cumbria	S • S America • 300 kW; N Africa • 300 kW; S • E Europe • 300 kW; W Asia • 300 kW; S America • 300 kW
	†BBC, Via Zyyi, Cyprus	
9920	**CHINA** CENTRAL PEOPLES BS, Beijing	DS-MINORITIES • 100 kW; S Asia • 120 kW; Europe • 120 kW
	CHINA RADIO INTL, Beijing	
	CHINA RADIO INTL, Xi'an	
9925	**BELGIUM** †R VLAANDEREN INTL, Wavre	W • S America • 100 kW; • Africa • 200 kW • ALT. FREQ. TO 11640 kHz; • Europe • 100 kW; • Africa • 200 kW
(con'd)		

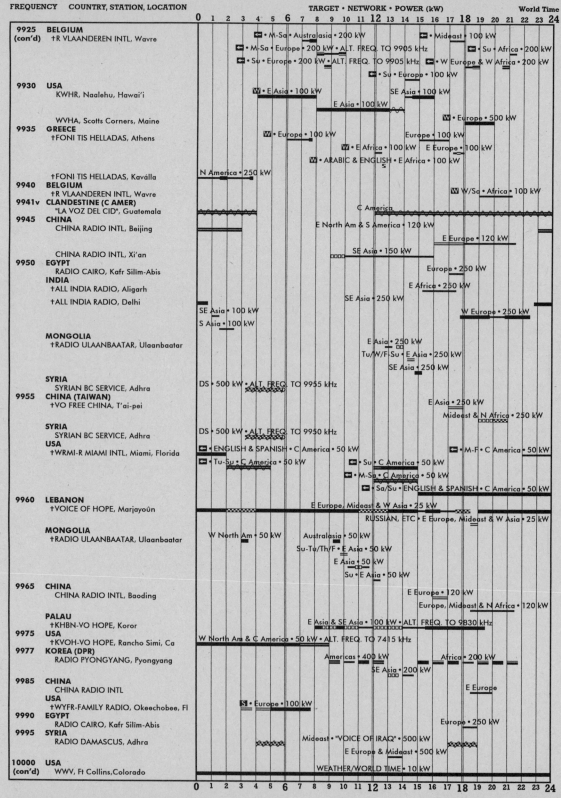

FREQUENCY   COUNTRY, STATION, LOCATION   TARGET • NETWORK • POWER (kW)   World Time

9925   **BELGIUM**
(con'd)   †R VLAANDEREN INTL, Wavre
- ☐• M-Sa • Australasia • 200 kW   ☐• Mideast • 100 kW
- ☐• M-Sa • Europe • 200 kW • ALT. FREQ. TO 9905 kHz   ☐• Su • Africa • 200 kW
- ☐• Su • Europe • 200 kW • ALT. FREQ. TO 9905 kHz   ☐• W Europe & W Africa • 200 kW
- ☐• Su • Europe • 100 kW

9930   **USA**
     KWHR, Naalehu, Hawai'i
- Ⓦ• E Asia • 100 kW   SE Asia • 100 kW
- E Asia • 100 kW

     WVHA, Scotts Corners, Maine
- Ⓦ• Europe • 500 kW

9935   **GREECE**
     †FONI TIS HELLADAS, Athens
- Ⓦ• Europe • 100 kW   Europe • 100 kW
- Ⓦ• E Africa • 100 kW   E Europe • 100 kW
- Ⓦ• ARABIC & ENGLISH • E Africa • 100 kW

     †FONI TIS HELLADAS, Kaválla
- N America • 250 kW

9940   **BELGIUM**
     †R VLAANDEREN INTL, Wavre
- Ⓦ• W/Sa • Africa • 100 kW

9941v   **CLANDESTINE (C AMER)**
     "LA VOZ DEL CID", Guatemala
- C America

9945   **CHINA**
     CHINA RADIO INTL, Beijing
- E North Am & S America • 120 kW
- E Europe • 120 kW

     CHINA RADIO INTL, Xi'an
- SE Asia • 150 kW

9950   **EGYPT**
     RADIO CAIRO, Kafr Silīm-Abis
- Europe • 250 kW

     INDIA
     †ALL INDIA RADIO, Aligarh
- E Africa • 250 kW

     †ALL INDIA RADIO, Delhi
- SE Asia • 250 kW
- SE Asia • 100 kW   W Europe • 250 kW
- S Asia • 100 kW

     MONGOLIA
     †RADIO ULAANBAATAR, Ulaanbaatar
- E Asia • 250 kW
- Tu/W/F-Su • E Asia • 250 kW
- SE Asia • 250 kW

     SYRIA
     SYRIAN BC SERVICE, Adhra
- DS • 500 kW • ALT. FREQ. TO 9955 kHz

9955   **CHINA (TAIWAN)**
     †VO FREE CHINA, T'ai-pei
- E Asia • 250 kW
- Mideast & N Africa • 250 kW

     SYRIA
     SYRIAN BC SERVICE, Adhra
- DS • 500 kW • ALT. FREQ. TO 9950 kHz

     USA
     †WRMI-R MIAMI INTL, Miami, Florida
- ☐• ENGLISH & SPANISH • C America • 50 kW   ☐• M-F • C America • 50 kW
- ☐• Tu-Su • C America • 50 kW   ☐• Su • C America • 50 kW
- ☐• M-Sa • C America • 50 kW
- ☐• Sa/Su • ENGLISH & SPANISH • C America • 50 kW

9960   **LEBANON**
     †VOICE OF HOPE, Marjayoûn
- E Europe, Mideast & W Asia • 25 kW
- RUSSIAN, ETC • E Europe, Mideast & W Asia • 25 kW

     MONGOLIA
     †RADIO ULAANBAATAR, Ulaanbaatar
- W North Am • 50 kW   Australasia • 50 kW
- Su-Tu/Th/F • E Asia • 50 kW
- E Asia • 50 kW
- Su • E Asia • 50 kW

9965   **CHINA**
     CHINA RADIO INTL, Baoding
- E Europe • 120 kW
- Europe, Mideast & N Africa • 120 kW

     PALAU
     †KHBN-VO HOPE, Koror
- E Asia & SE Asia • 100 kW • ALT. FREQ. TO 9830 kHz

9975   **USA**
     †KVOH-VO HOPE, Rancho Simi, Ca
- W North Am & C America • 50 kW • ALT. FREQ. TO 7415 kHz

9977   **KOREA (DPR)**
     RADIO PYONGYANG, Pyongyang
- Americas • 400 kW   Africa • 200 kW
- SE Asia • 200 kW

9985   **CHINA**
     CHINA RADIO INTL
- E Europe

     USA
     †WYFR-FAMILY RADIO, Okeechobee, Fl
- Ⓢ• Europe • 100 kW

9990   **EGYPT**
     RADIO CAIRO, Kafr Silīm-Abis
- Europe • 250 kW

9995   **SYRIA**
     RADIO DAMASCUS, Adhra
- Mideast • "VOICE OF IRAQ" • 500 kW
- E Europe & Mideast • 500 kW

10000   **USA**
(con'd)   WWV, Ft Collins, Colorado
- WEATHER/WORLD TIME • 10 kW

SEASONAL Ⓢ OR Ⓦ   1-HR TIMESHIFT MIDYEAR ☐ OR ☐   JAMMING / OR ∧   EARLIEST HEARD ◁   LATEST HEARD ▷   NEW FOR 1996 †

FREQUENCY   COUNTRY, STATION, LOCATION

TARGET • NETWORK • POWER (kW)

World Time

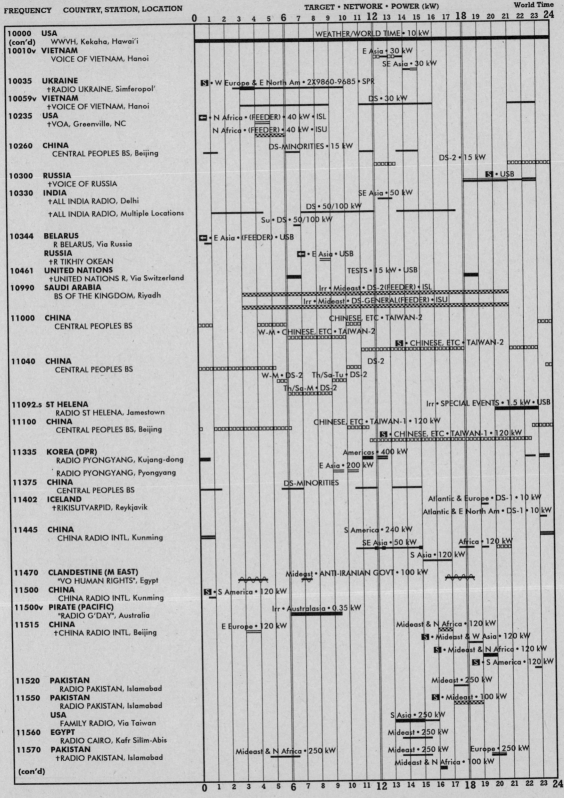

Frequency	Country, Station, Location	Details
10000 (con'd)	USA WWVH, Kekaha, Hawai'i	WEATHER/WORLD TIME • 10 kW
10010v	VIETNAM VOICE OF VIETNAM, Hanoi	E Asia • 30 kW; SE Asia • 30 kW
10035	UKRAINE †RADIO UKRAINE, Simferopol'	S • W Europe & E North Am • 2X9860-9685 • SPR
10059v	VIETNAM †VOICE OF VIETNAM, Hanoi	DS • 30 kW
10235	USA †VOA, Greenville, NC	N Africa • (FEEDER) • 40 kW • ISL; N Africa • (FEEDER) • 40 kW • ISU
10260	CHINA CENTRAL PEOPLES BS, Beijing	DS-MINORITIES • 15 kW; DS-2 • 15 kW
10300	RUSSIA †VOICE OF RUSSIA	S • USB
10330	INDIA †ALL INDIA RADIO, Delhi	SE Asia • 50 kW; DS • 50/100 kW
	†ALL INDIA RADIO, Multiple Locations	Su • DS • 50/100 kW
10344	BELARUS R BELARUS, Via Russia	E Asia • (FEEDER) • USB
	RUSSIA †R TIKHIY OKEAN	E Asia • USB
10461	UNITED NATIONS †UNITED NATIONS R, Via Switzerland	TESTS • 15 kW • USB
10990	SAUDI ARABIA BS OF THE KINGDOM, Riyadh	Irr • Mideast • DS-2(FEEDER) • ISL; Irr • Mideast • DS-GENERAL(FEEDER) • ISU
11000	CHINA CENTRAL PEOPLES BS	CHINESE, ETC • TAIWAN-2; W-M • CHINESE, ETC • TAIWAN-2; S • CHINESE, ETC • TAIWAN-2
11040	CHINA CENTRAL PEOPLES BS	DS-2; W-M • DS-2 Th/Sa-Tu • DS-2; Th/Sa-M • DS-2
11092.5	ST HELENA RADIO ST HELENA, Jamestown	Irr • SPECIAL EVENTS • 1.5 kW • USB
11100	CHINA CENTRAL PEOPLES BS, Beijing	CHINESE, ETC • TAIWAN-1 • 120 kW; S • CHINESE, ETC • TAIWAN-1 • 120 kW
11335	KOREA (DPR) RADIO PYONGYANG, Kujang-dong	Americas • 400 kW; E Asia • 200 kW
	RADIO PYONGYANG, Pyongyang	
11375	CHINA CENTRAL PEOPLES BS	DS-MINORITIES
11402	ICELAND †RIKISUTVARPID, Reykjavik	Atlantic & Europe • DS-1 • 10 kW; Atlantic & E North Am • DS-1 • 10 kW
11445	CHINA CHINA RADIO INTL, Kunming	S America • 240 kW; SE Asia • 50 kW; Africa • 120 kW; S Asia • 120 kW
11470	CLANDESTINE (M EAST) "VO HUMAN RIGHTS", Egypt	Mideast • ANTI-IRANIAN GOVT • 100 kW
11500	CHINA CHINA RADIO INTL, Kunming	S • S America • 120 kW
11500v	PIRATE (PACIFIC) "RADIO G'DAY", Australia	Irr • Australasia • 0.35 kW
11515	CHINA †CHINA RADIO INTL, Beijing	E Europe • 120 kW; Mideast & N Africa • 120 kW; S • Mideast & W Asia • 120 kW; S • Mideast & N Africa • 120 kW; S • S America • 120 kW
11520	PAKISTAN RADIO PAKISTAN, Islamabad	Mideast • 250 kW
11550	PAKISTAN RADIO PAKISTAN, Islamabad	S • Mideast • 100 kW
	USA FAMILY RADIO, Via Taiwan	S Asia • 250 kW
11560	EGYPT RADIO CAIRO, Kafr Silim-Abis	Mideast • 250 kW
11570	PAKISTAN †RADIO PAKISTAN, Islamabad	Mideast & N Africa • 250 kW; Mideast • 250 kW Europe • 250 kW; Mideast & N Africa • 100 kW
(con'd)		

FREQUENCY   COUNTRY, STATION, LOCATION

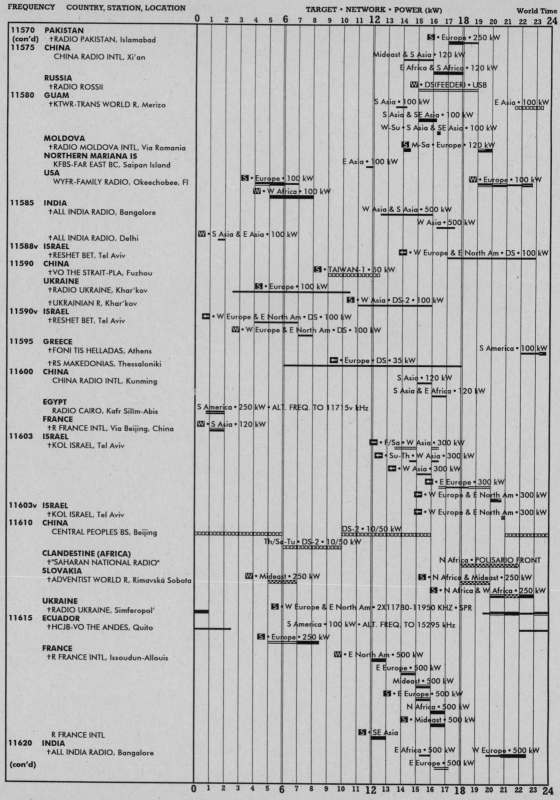

FREQUENCY	COUNTRY, STATION, LOCATION	TARGET • NETWORK • POWER (kW)
11570 (con'd)	PAKISTAN †RADIO PAKISTAN, Islamabad	S • Europe • 250 kW
11575	CHINA CHINA RADIO INTL, Xi'an	Mideast & S Asia • 120 kW; E Africa & S Africa • 120 kW
	RUSSIA †RADIO ROSSII	W • DS(FEEDER) • USB
11580	GUAM †KTWR-TRANS WORLD R, Merizo	S Asia • 100 kW; E Asia • 100 kW; S Asia & SE Asia • 100 kW; W-Su • S Asia & SE Asia • 100 kW
	MOLDOVA †RADIO MOLDOVA INTL, Via Romania	S M-Sa • Europe • 120 kW
	NORTHERN MARIANA IS KFBS-FAR EAST BC, Saipan Island	E Asia • 100 kW
	USA WYFR-FAMILY RADIO, Okeechobee, Fl	S • Europe • 100 kW; W • Europe • 100 kW; W • W Africa • 100 kW
11585	INDIA †ALL INDIA RADIO, Bangalore	W Asia & S Asia • 500 kW; W Asia • 500 kW
	†ALL INDIA RADIO, Delhi	W • S Asia & E Asia • 100 kW
11588v	ISRAEL †RESHET BET, Tel Aviv	⇆ • W Europe & E North Am • DS • 100 kW
11590	CHINA †VO THE STRAIT-PLA, Fuzhou	S • TAIWAN-1 • 50 kW
	UKRAINE †RADIO UKRAINE, Khar'kov	S • Europe • 100 kW
	†UKRAINIAN R, Khar'kov	S • W Asia • DS-2 • 100 kW
11590v	ISRAEL †RESHET BET, Tel Aviv	⇆ • W Europe & E North Am • DS • 100 kW; W • W Europe & E North Am • DS • 100 kW
11595	GREECE †FONI TIS HELLADAS, Athens	S America • 100 kW
	†RS MAKEDONIAS, Thessaloniki	⇆ • Europe • DS • 35 kW
11600	CHINA CHINA RADIO INTL, Kunming	S Asia • 120 kW; S Asia & E Africa • 120 kW
	EGYPT RADIO CAIRO, Kafr Silîm-Abis	S America • 250 kW • ALT. FREQ. TO 11715v kHz
	FRANCE †R FRANCE INTL, Via Beijing, China	W • S Asia • 120 kW
11603	ISRAEL †KOL ISRAEL, Tel Aviv	⇆ • F/Sa • W Asia • 300 kW; ⇆ • Su-Th • W Asia • 300 kW; ⇆ • W Asia • 300 kW; ⇆ • E Europe • 300 kW; ⇆ • W Europe & E North Am • 300 kW
11603v	ISRAEL †KOL ISRAEL, Tel Aviv	⇆ • W Europe & E North Am • 300 kW
11610	CHINA CENTRAL PEOPLES BS, Beijing	DS-2 • 10/50 kW; Th/Sa-Tu • DS-2 • 10/50 kW
	CLANDESTINE (AFRICA) †"SAHARAN NATIONAL RADIO"	N Africa • POLISARIO FRONT
	SLOVAKIA †ADVENTIST WORLD R, Rimavská Sobota	W • Mideast • 250 kW; S • N Africa & Mideast • 250 kW; S • N Africa & W Africa • 250 kW
	UKRAINE †RADIO UKRAINE, Simferopol'	S • W Europe & E North Am • 2X11780-11950 KHZ • SPR
11615	ECUADOR †HCJB-VO THE ANDES, Quito	S America • 100 kW • ALT. FREQ. TO 15295 kHz; S • Europe • 250 kW
	FRANCE †R FRANCE INTL, Issoudun-Allouis	W • E North Am • 500 kW; E Europe • 500 kW; Mideast • 500 kW; S • E Europe • 500 kW; N Africa • 500 kW; S • Mideast • 500 kW
	R FRANCE INTL	S • SE Asia
11620 (con'd)	INDIA †ALL INDIA RADIO, Bangalore	E Africa • 500 kW; W Europe • 500 kW; E Europe • 500 kW

SEASONAL ⓢ OR ⓦ   1-HR TIMESHIFT MIDYEAR ⇆ OR ⇄   JAMMING / OR ∧   EARLIEST HEARD ◁   LATEST HEARD ▷   NEW FOR 1996 †

FREQUENCY   COUNTRY, STATION, LOCATION   TARGET • NETWORK • POWER (kW)   World Time

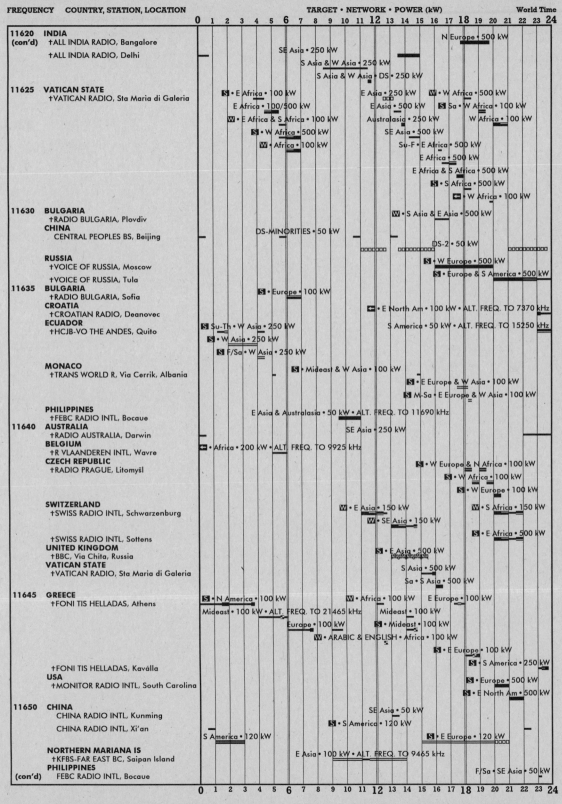

Frequency	Country / Station / Location	Target • Network • Power
11620 (con'd)	**INDIA** †ALL INDIA RADIO, Bangalore	N Europe • 500 kW
	†ALL INDIA RADIO, Delhi	SE Asia • 250 kW
		S Asia & W Asia • 250 kW
		S Asia & W Asia • DS • 250 kW
11625	**VATICAN STATE** †VATICAN RADIO, Sta Maria di Galeria	S • E Africa • 100 kW
		E Africa • 100/500 kW
		W • E Africa & S Africa • 100 kW
		S • W Africa • 500 kW
		W • Africa • 100 kW
		E Asia • 250 kW
		E Asia • 500 kW
		Australasia • 250 kW
		SE Asia • 500 kW
		W • W Africa • 500 kW
		Sa • W Africa • 100 kW
		W Africa • 100 kW
		Su-F • E Africa • 500 kW
		E Africa • 500 kW
		E Africa & S Africa • 500 kW
		S • S Africa • 500 kW
		W Africa • 100 kW
11630	**BULGARIA** †RADIO BULGARIA, Plovdiv	W • S Asia & E Asia • 500 kW
	CHINA CENTRAL PEOPLES BS, Beijing	DS-MINORITIES • 50 kW
		DS-2 • 50 kW
	RUSSIA †VOICE OF RUSSIA, Moscow	S • W Europe • 500 kW
	†VOICE OF RUSSIA, Tula	Europe & S America • 500 kW
11635	**BULGARIA** †RADIO BULGARIA, Sofia	S • Europe • 100 kW
	CROATIA †CROATIAN RADIO, Deanovec	E North Am • 100 kW • ALT. FREQ. TO 7370 kHz
	ECUADOR †HCJB-VO THE ANDES, Quito	S • Su-Th • W Asia • 250 kW
		S America • 50 kW • ALT. FREQ. TO 15250 kHz
		S • W Asia • 250 kW
		S • F/Sa • W Asia • 250 kW
	MONACO †TRANS WORLD R, Via Cerrik, Albania	S • Mideast & W Asia • 100 kW
		S • E Europe & W Asia • 100 kW
		S • M-Sa • E Europe & W Asia • 100 kW
	PHILIPPINES †FEBC RADIO INTL, Bocaue	E Asia & Australasia • 50 kW • ALT. FREQ. TO 11690 kHz
11640	**AUSTRALIA** †RADIO AUSTRALIA, Darwin	SE Asia • 250 kW
	BELGIUM †R VLAANDEREN INTL, Wavre	Africa • 200 kW • ALT. FREQ. TO 9925 kHz
	CZECH REPUBLIC †RADIO PRAGUE, Litomyšl	S • W Europe & N Africa • 100 kW
		S • W Africa • 100 kW
		S • W Europe • 100 kW
	SWITZERLAND †SWISS RADIO INTL, Schwarzenburg	W • E Asia • 150 kW
		W • S Africa • 150 kW
		W • SE Asia • 150 kW
	†SWISS RADIO INTL, Sottens	S • E Africa • 500 kW
	UNITED KINGDOM †BBC, Via Chita, Russia	S • E Asia • 500 kW
	VATICAN STATE †VATICAN RADIO, Sta Maria di Galeria	S Asia • 500 kW
		Sa • S Asia • 500 kW
11645	**GREECE** †FONI TIS HELLADAS, Athens	S • N America • 100 kW
		W • Africa • 100 kW
		E Europe • 100 kW
		Mideast • 100 kW • ALT. FREQ. TO 21465 kHz
		Mideast • 100 kW
		Europe • 100 kW
		S • Mideast • 100 kW
		W • ARABIC & ENGLISH • Africa • 100 kW
		S • E Europe • 100 kW
	†FONI TIS HELLADAS, Kaválla	S • S America • 250 kW
	USA †MONITOR RADIO INTL, South Carolina	S • Europe • 500 kW
		S • E North Am • 500 kW
11650	**CHINA** CHINA RADIO INTL, Kunming	SE Asia • 50 kW
	CHINA RADIO INTL, Xi'an	S • S America • 120 kW
		S America • 120 kW
		S • E Europe • 120 kW
	NORTHERN MARIANA IS †KFBS-FAR EAST BC, Saipan Island	E Asia • 100 kW • ALT. FREQ. TO 9465 kHz
(con'd)	**PHILIPPINES** FEBC RADIO INTL, Bocaue	F/Sa • SE Asia • 50 kW

0 1 2 3 4 5 6 7 8 9 10 11 12 13 14 15 16 17 18 19 20 21 22 23 24

ENGLISH ▬   ARABIC ⋙   CHINESE ▯▯▯   FRENCH ▭   GERMAN ▭   RUSSIAN ═   SPANISH ▬   OTHER ▬

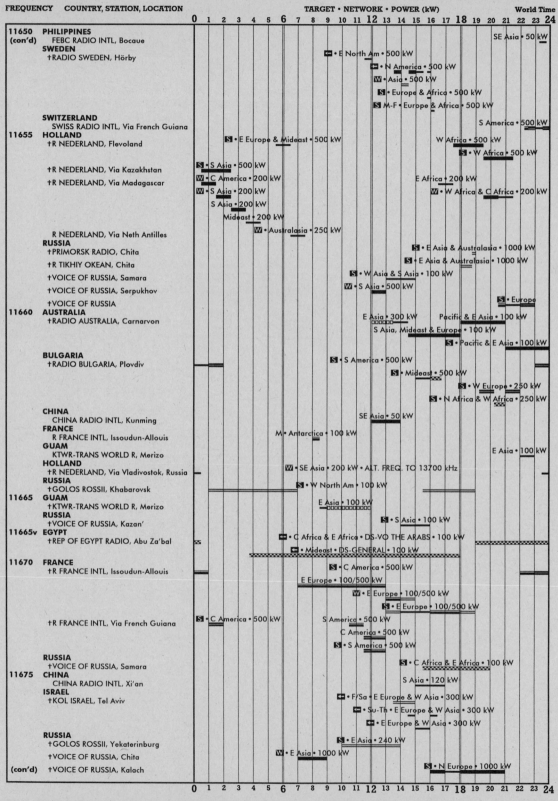

FREQUENCY   COUNTRY, STATION, LOCATION   TARGET • NETWORK • POWER (kW)   World Time

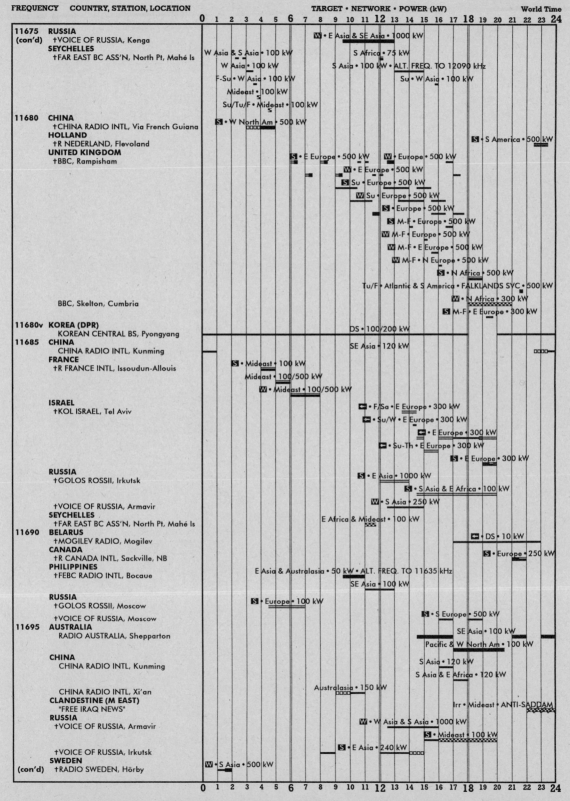

11675	**RUSSIA**
(con'd)	†VOICE OF RUSSIA, Kenga
	SEYCHELLES
	†FAR EAST BC ASS'N, North Pt, Mahé Is
11680	**CHINA**
	†CHINA RADIO INTL, Via French Guiana
	HOLLAND
	†R NEDERLAND, Flevoland
	UNITED KINGDOM
	†BBC, Rampisham
	BBC, Skelton, Cumbria
11680v	**KOREA (DPR)**
	KOREAN CENTRAL BS, Pyongyang
11685	**CHINA**
	CHINA RADIO INTL, Kunming
	FRANCE
	†R FRANCE INTL, Issoudun-Allouis
	ISRAEL
	†KOL ISRAEL, Tel Aviv
	RUSSIA
	†GOLOS ROSSII, Irkutsk
	†VOICE OF RUSSIA, Armavir
	SEYCHELLES
	†FAR EAST BC ASS'N, North Pt, Mahé Is
11690	**BELARUS**
	†MOGILEV RADIO, Mogilev
	CANADA
	†R CANADA INTL, Sackville, NB
	PHILIPPINES
	†FEBC RADIO INTL, Bocaue
	RUSSIA
	†GOLOS ROSSII, Moscow
	†VOICE OF RUSSIA, Moscow
11695	**AUSTRALIA**
	RADIO AUSTRALIA, Shepparton
	CHINA
	CHINA RADIO INTL, Kunming
	CHINA RADIO INTL, Xi'an
	CLANDESTINE (M EAST)
	"FREE IRAQ NEWS"
	RUSSIA
	†VOICE OF RUSSIA, Armavir
	†VOICE OF RUSSIA, Irkutsk
	SWEDEN
(con'd)	†RADIO SWEDEN, Hörby

Target/network/power entries:

- W • E Asia & SE Asia • 1000 kW
- W Asia & S Asia • 100 kW
- S Africa • 75 kW
- W Asia • 100 kW
- S Asia • 100 kW • ALT. FREQ. TO 12090 kHz
- F-Su • W Asia • 100 kW
- Su • W Asia • 100 kW
- Mideast • 100 kW
- Su/Tu/F • Mideast • 100 kW
- S • W North Am • 500 kW
- S • S America • 500 kW
- S • E Europe • 500 kW
- W • Europe • 500 kW
- W • E Europe • 500 kW
- S • Su • Europe • 500 kW
- W • Su • Europe • 500 kW
- S • Europe • 500 kW
- S • M-F • Europe • 500 kW
- W • M-F • Europe • 500 kW
- W • M-F • E Europe • 500 kW
- W • M-F • N Europe • 500 kW
- S • N Africa • 500 kW
- Tu/F • Atlantic & S America • FALKLANDS SVC • 500 kW
- W • N Africa • 300 kW
- S • M-F • E Europe • 300 kW
- DS • 100/200 kW
- SE Asia • 120 kW
- S • Mideast • 100 kW
- Mideast • 100/500 kW
- W • Mideast • 100/500 kW
- F/Sa • E Europe • 300 kW
- Su/W • E Europe • 300 kW
- E Europe • 300 kW
- Su-Th • E Europe • 300 kW
- S • E Europe • 300 kW
- S • E Asia • 1000 kW
- S • S Asia & E Africa • 100 kW
- W • S Asia • 250 kW
- E Africa & Mideast • 100 kW
- DS • 10 kW
- S • Europe • 250 kW
- E Asia & Australasia • 50 kW • ALT. FREQ. TO 11635 kHz
- SE Asia • 100 kW
- S • Europe • 100 kW
- S • S Europe • 500 kW
- SE Asia • 100 kW
- Pacific & W North Am • 100 kW
- S Asia • 120 kW
- S Asia & E Africa • 120 kW
- Australasia • 150 kW
- Irr • Mideast • ANTI-SADDAM
- W • W Asia & S Asia • 1000 kW
- S • Mideast • 100 kW
- S • E Asia • 240 kW
- W • S Asia • 500 kW

ENGLISH ▬▬   ARABIC ※※※   CHINESE □□□   FRENCH ══   GERMAN ▬▬   RUSSIAN ══   SPANISH ▬▬   OTHER ──

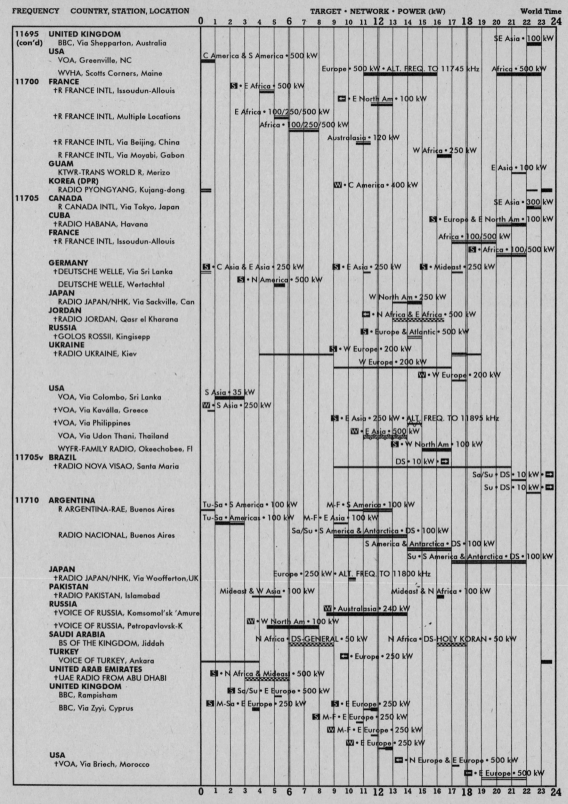

FREQUENCY   COUNTRY, STATION, LOCATION

TARGET • NETWORK • POWER (kW)

World Time

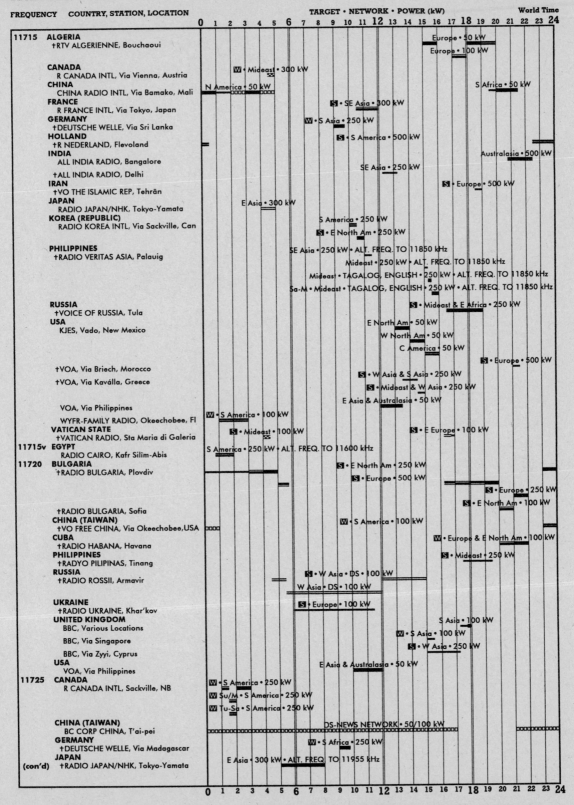

```
0  1  2  3  4  5  6  7  8  9  10 11 12 13 14 15 16 17 18 19 20 21 22 23 24
```

11715 ALGERIA
  †RTV ALGERIENNE, Bouchaoui — Europe • 50 kW / Europe • 100 kW

CANADA
  R CANADA INTL, Via Vienna, Austria — W • Mideast • 300 kW

CHINA
  CHINA RADIO INTL, Via Bamako, Mali — N America • 50 kW / S Africa • 50 kW

FRANCE
  R FRANCE INTL, Via Tokyo, Japan — S • SE Asia • 300 kW

GERMANY
  †DEUTSCHE WELLE, Via Sri Lanka — W • S Asia • 250 kW

HOLLAND
  †R NEDERLAND, Flevoland — S • S America • 500 kW

INDIA
  ALL INDIA RADIO, Bangalore — Australasia • 500 kW

  †ALL INDIA RADIO, Delhi — SE Asia • 250 kW

IRAN
  †VO THE ISLAMIC REP, Tehrān — S • Europe • 500 kW

JAPAN
  RADIO JAPAN/NHK, Tokyo-Yamata — E Asia • 300 kW

KOREA (REPUBLIC)
  RADIO KOREA INTL, Via Sackville, Can — S America • 250 kW / S • E North Am • 250 kW

PHILIPPINES
  †RADIO VERITAS ASIA, Palauig — SE Asia • 250 kW • ALT. FREQ. TO 11850 kHz
    Mideast • 250 kW • ALT. FREQ. TO 11850 kHz
    Mideast • TAGALOG, ENGLISH • 250 kW • ALT. FREQ. TO 11850 kHz
    Sa-M • Mideast • TAGALOG, ENGLISH • 250 kW • ALT. FREQ. TO 11850 kHz

RUSSIA
  †VOICE OF RUSSIA, Tula — S • Mideast & E Africa • 250 kW

USA
  KJES, Vado, New Mexico — E North Am • 50 kW / W North Am • 50 kW / C America • 50 kW / S • Europe • 500 kW

  †VOA, Via Briech, Morocco — S • W Asia & S Asia • 250 kW

  †VOA, Via Kaválla, Greece — S • Mideast & W Asia • 250 kW

  VOA, Via Philippines — E Asia & Australasia • 50 kW

  WYFR-FAMILY RADIO, Okeechobee, Fl — W • S America • 100 kW

VATICAN STATE
  †VATICAN RADIO, Sta Maria di Galeria — S • Mideast • 100 kW / S • E Europe • 100 kW

11715v EGYPT
  RADIO CAIRO, Kafr Silim-Abis — S America • 250 kW • ALT. FREQ. TO 11600 kHz

11720 BULGARIA
  †RADIO BULGARIA, Plovdiv — S • E North Am • 250 kW / S • Europe • 500 kW / S • Europe • 250 kW / S • E North Am • 100 kW

  †RADIO BULGARIA, Sofia

CHINA (TAIWAN)
  †VO FREE CHINA, Via Okeechobee, USA — W • S America • 100 kW

CUBA
  †RADIO HABANA, Havana — W • Europe & E North Am • 100 kW

PHILIPPINES
  †RADYO PILIPINAS, Tinang — S • Mideast • 250 kW

RUSSIA
  †RADIO ROSSII, Armavir — S • W Asia • DS • 100 kW / W Asia • DS • 100 kW

UKRAINE
  †RADIO UKRAINE, Khar'kov — S • Europe • 100 kW

UNITED KINGDOM
  BBC, Various Locations — S Asia • 100 kW

  BBC, Via Singapore — W • S Asia • 100 kW

  BBC, Via Zyyi, Cyprus — S • W Asia • 250 kW

USA
  VOA, Via Philippines — E Asia & Australasia • 50 kW

11725 CANADA
  R CANADA INTL, Sackville, NB — W • S America • 250 kW / W Su/M • S America • 250 kW / W Tu-Sa • S America • 250 kW

CHINA (TAIWAN)
  BC CORP CHINA, T'ai-pei — DS-NEWS NETWORK • 50/100 kW

GERMANY
  †DEUTSCHE WELLE, Via Madagascar — W • S Africa • 250 kW

JAPAN
(con'd) †RADIO JAPAN/NHK, Tokyo-Yamata — E Asia • 300 kW • ALT. FREQ. TO 11955 kHz

```
0  1  2  3  4  5  6  7  8  9  10 11 12 13 14 15 16 17 18 19 20 21 22 23 24
```

ENGLISH ▬   ARABIC ≋   CHINESE ▭▭▭   FRENCH ▬▬   GERMAN ▬   RUSSIAN ══   SPANISH ▬▬   OTHER —

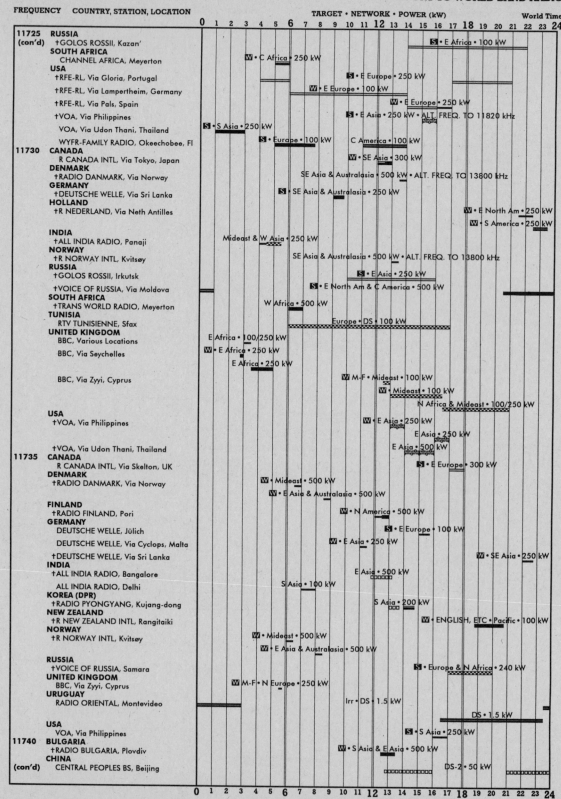

FREQUENCY	COUNTRY, STATION, LOCATION	TARGET • NETWORK • POWER (kW) / World Time
11725 (con'd)	RUSSIA †GOLOS ROSSII, Kazan'	S • E Africa • 100 kW
	SOUTH AFRICA CHANNEL AFRICA, Meyerton	W • C Africa • 250 kW
	USA †RFE-RL, Via Gloria, Portugal	S • E Europe • 250 kW
	†RFE-RL, Via Lampertheim, Germany	W • E Europe • 100 kW
	†RFE-RL, Via Pals, Spain	W • E Europe • 250 kW
	†VOA, Via Philippines	S • E Asia • 250 kW • ALT. FREQ. TO 11820 kHz
	VOA, Via Udon Thani, Thailand	S • S Asia • 250 kW
	WYFR-FAMILY RADIO, Okeechobee, Fl	S • Europe • 100 kW C America • 100 kW
11730	CANADA R CANADA INTL, Via Tokyo, Japan	W • SE Asia • 300 kW
	DENMARK †RADIO DANMARK, Via Norway	SE Asia & Australasia • 500 kW • ALT. FREQ. TO 13800 kHz
	GERMANY †DEUTSCHE WELLE, Via Sri Lanka	S • SE Asia & Australasia • 250 kW
	HOLLAND †R NEDERLAND, Via Neth Antilles	W • E North Am • 250 kW W • S America • 250 kW
	INDIA †ALL INDIA RADIO, Panaji	Mideast & W Asia • 250 kW
	NORWAY †R NORWAY INTL, Kvitsøy	SE Asia & Australasia • 500 kW • ALT. FREQ. TO 13800 kHz
	RUSSIA †GOLOS ROSSII, Irkutsk	S • E Asia • 250 kW
	†VOICE OF RUSSIA, Via Moldova	S • E North Am & C America • 500 kW
	SOUTH AFRICA †TRANS WORLD RADIO, Meyerton	W Africa • 500 kW
	TUNISIA RTV TUNISIENNE, Sfax	Europe • DS • 100 kW
	UNITED KINGDOM BBC, Various Locations	E Africa • 100/250 kW
	BBC, Via Seychelles	W • E Africa • 250 kW E Africa • 250 kW
	BBC, Via Zyyi, Cyprus	W M-F • Mideast • 100 kW W • Mideast • 100 kW N Africa & Mideast • 100/250 kW
	USA †VOA, Via Philippines	W • E Asia • 250 kW E Asia • 250 kW
	†VOA, Via Udon Thani, Thailand	E Asia • 500 kW
11735	CANADA R CANADA INTL, Via Skelton, UK	S • E Europe • 300 kW
	DENMARK †RADIO DANMARK, Via Norway	W • Mideast • 500 kW W • E Asia & Australasia • 500 kW
	FINLAND †RADIO FINLAND, Pori	W • N America • 500 kW
	GERMANY DEUTSCHE WELLE, Jülich	S • E Europe • 100 kW
	DEUTSCHE WELLE, Via Cyclops, Malta	W • E Asia • 250 kW
	†DEUTSCHE WELLE, Via Sri Lanka	W • SE Asia • 250 kW
	INDIA †ALL INDIA RADIO, Bangalore	E Asia • 500 kW
	ALL INDIA RADIO, Delhi	S Asia • 100 kW
	KOREA (DPR) †RADIO PYONGYANG, Kujang-dong	S Asia • 200 kW
	NEW ZEALAND †R NEW ZEALAND INTL, Rangitaiki	W • ENGLISH, ETC • Pacific • 100 kW
	NORWAY †R NORWAY INTL, Kvitsøy	W • Mideast • 500 kW W • E Asia & Australasia • 500 kW
	RUSSIA †VOICE OF RUSSIA, Samara	S • Europe & N Africa • 240 kW
	UNITED KINGDOM BBC, Via Zyyi, Cyprus	W M-F • N Europe • 250 kW
	URUGUAY RADIO ORIENTAL, Montevideo	Irr • DS • 1.5 kW DS • 1.5 kW
	USA VOA, Via Philippines	S • S Asia • 250 kW
11740	BULGARIA †RADIO BULGARIA, Plovdiv	W • S Asia & E Asia • 500 kW
(con'd)	CHINA CENTRAL PEOPLES BS, Beijing	DS-2 • 50 kW

FREQUENCY   COUNTRY, STATION, LOCATION

TARGET • NETWORK • POWER (kW)

World Time

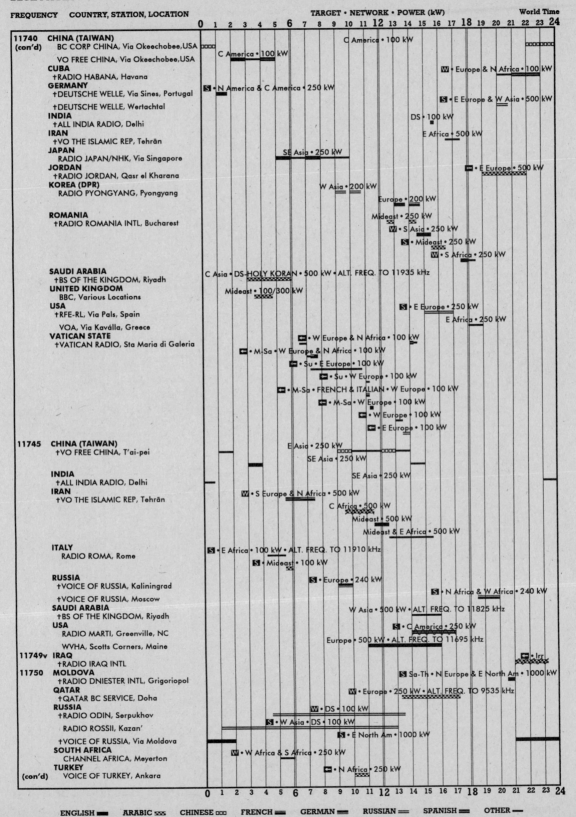

Freq	Country, Station, Location	Target • Network • Power
11740 (con'd)	**CHINA (TAIWAN)** BC CORP CHINA, Via Okeechobee, USA	C America • 100 kW
	VO FREE CHINA, Via Okeechobee, USA	C America • 100 kW
	CUBA †RADIO HABANA, Havana	W • Europe & N Africa • 100 kW
	GERMANY †DEUTSCHE WELLE, Via Sines, Portugal	S • N America & C America • 250 kW
	†DEUTSCHE WELLE, Wertachtal	S • E Europe & W Asia • 500 kW
	INDIA †ALL INDIA RADIO, Delhi	DS • 100 kW
	IRAN †VO THE ISLAMIC REP, Tehrān	E Africa • 500 kW
	JAPAN RADIO JAPAN/NHK, Via Singapore	SE Asia • 250 kW
	JORDAN †RADIO JORDAN, Qasr el Kharana	• E Europe • 500 kW
	KOREA (DPR) RADIO PYONGYANG, Pyongyang	W Asia • 200 kW
		Europe • 200 kW
	ROMANIA †RADIO ROMANIA INTL, Bucharest	Mideast • 250 kW
		W • S Asia • 250 kW
		S • Mideast • 250 kW
		W • S Africa • 250 kW
	SAUDI ARABIA †BS OF THE KINGDOM, Riyadh	C Asia • DS-HOLY KORAN • 500 kW • ALT. FREQ. TO 11935 kHz
	UNITED KINGDOM BBC, Various Locations	Mideast • 100/300 kW
	USA †RFE-RL, Via Pals, Spain	S • E Europe • 250 kW
	VOA, Via Kaválla, Greece	E Africa • 250 kW
	VATICAN STATE †VATICAN RADIO, Sta Maria di Galeria	• W Europe & N Africa • 100 kW
		• M-Sa • W Europe & N Africa • 100 kW
		• Su • E Europe • 100 kW
		• Su • W Europe • 100 kW
		• M-Sa • FRENCH & ITALIAN • W Europe • 100 kW
		• M-Sa • W Europe • 100 kW
		• W Europe • 100 kW
		• E Europe • 100 kW
11745	**CHINA (TAIWAN)** †VO FREE CHINA, T'ai-pei	E Asia • 250 kW
		SE Asia • 250 kW
	INDIA †ALL INDIA RADIO, Delhi	SE Asia • 250 kW
	IRAN †VO THE ISLAMIC REP, Tehrān	W • S Europe & N Africa • 500 kW
		C Africa • 500 kW
		Mideast • 500 kW
		Mideast & E Africa • 500 kW
	ITALY RADIO ROMA, Rome	S • E Africa • 100 kW • ALT. FREQ. TO 11910 kHz
		S • Mideast • 100 kW
	RUSSIA †VOICE OF RUSSIA, Kaliningrad	S • Europe • 240 kW
	†VOICE OF RUSSIA, Moscow	S • N Africa & W Africa • 240 kW
	SAUDI ARABIA †BS OF THE KINGDOM, Riyadh	W Asia • 500 kW • ALT. FREQ. TO 11825 kHz
	USA RADIO MARTI, Greenville, NC	S • C America • 250 kW
	WVHA, Scotts Corners, Maine	Europe • 500 kW • ALT. FREQ. TO 11695 kHz
11749v	**IRAQ** †RADIO IRAQ INTL	• Irr
11750	**MOLDOVA** †RADIO DNIESTER INTL, Grigoriopol	S • Sa-Th • N Europe & E North Am • 1000 kW
	QATAR †QATAR BC SERVICE, Doha	W • Europe • 250 kW • ALT. FREQ. TO 9535 kHz
	RUSSIA †RADIO ODIN, Serpukhov	W • DS • 100 kW
	RADIO ROSSII, Kazan'	S • W Asia • DS • 100 kW
	†VOICE OF RUSSIA, Via Moldova	S • E North Am • 1000 kW
	SOUTH AFRICA CHANNEL AFRICA, Meyerton	W • W Africa & S Africa • 250 kW
(con'd)	**TURKEY** VOICE OF TURKEY, Ankara	• N Africa • 250 kW

FREQUENCY   COUNTRY, STATION, LOCATION

TARGET • NETWORK • POWER (kW)   World Time

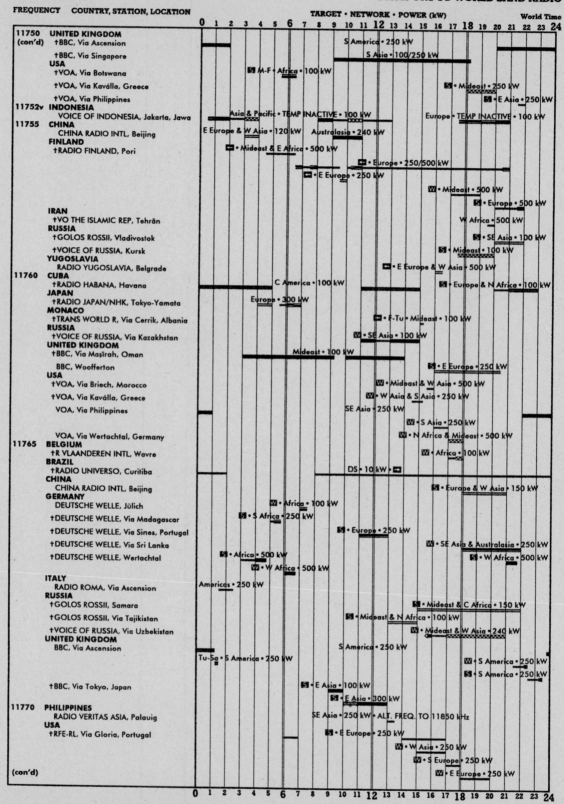

FREQUENCY	COUNTRY, STATION, LOCATION	TARGET • NETWORK • POWER (kW)
11750 (con'd)	UNITED KINGDOM †BBC, Via Ascension	S America • 250 kW
	†BBC, Via Singapore	S Asia • 100/250 kW
	USA †VOA, Via Botswana	M-F • Africa • 100 kW
	†VOA, Via Kaválla, Greece	Mideast • 250 kW
	†VOA, Via Philippines	E Asia • 250 kW
11752v	INDONESIA VOICE OF INDONESIA, Jakarta, Jawa	Asia & Pacific • TEMP INACTIVE • 100 kW Europe • TEMP INACTIVE • 100 kW
11755	CHINA CHINA RADIO INTL, Beijing	E Europe & W Asia • 120 kW Australasia • 240 kW
	FINLAND †RADIO FINLAND, Pori	Mideast & E Africa • 500 kW
		Europe • 250/500 kW
		E Europe • 250 kW
		Mideast • 500 kW
		Europe • 500 kW
	IRAN †VO THE ISLAMIC REP, Tehrān	W Africa • 500 kW
	RUSSIA †GOLOS ROSSII, Vladivostok	SE Asia • 100 kW
	†VOICE OF RUSSIA, Kursk	Mideast • 100 kW
	YUGOSLAVIA RADIO YUGOSLAVIA, Belgrade	E Europe & W Asia • 500 kW
11760	CUBA †RADIO HABANA, Havana	C America • 100 kW Europe & N Africa • 100 kW
	JAPAN †RADIO JAPAN/NHK, Tokyo-Yamata	Europe • 300 kW
	MONACO †TRANS WORLD R, Via Cerrik, Albania	F-Tu • Mideast • 100 kW
	RUSSIA †VOICE OF RUSSIA, Via Kazakhstan	SE Asia • 100 kW
	UNITED KINGDOM †BBC, Via Maşirah, Oman	Mideast • 100 kW
	BBC, Woofferton	E Europe • 250 kW
	USA †VOA, Via Briech, Morocco	Mideast & W Asia • 500 kW
	†VOA, Via Kaválla, Greece	W Asia & S Asia • 250 kW
	VOA, Via Philippines	SE Asia • 250 kW
	VOA, Via Wertachtal, Germany	S Asia • 250 kW N Africa & Mideast • 500 kW
11765	BELGIUM †R VLAANDEREN INTL, Wavre	Africa • 100 kW
	BRAZIL †RADIO UNIVERSO, Curitiba	DS • 10 kW
	CHINA CHINA RADIO INTL, Beijing	Europe & W Asia • 150 kW
	GERMANY DEUTSCHE WELLE, Jülich	Africa • 100 kW
	†DEUTSCHE WELLE, Via Madagascar	S Africa • 250 kW
	†DEUTSCHE WELLE, Via Sines, Portugal	Europe • 250 kW
	†DEUTSCHE WELLE, Via Sri Lanka	SE Asia & Australasia • 250 kW
	†DEUTSCHE WELLE, Wertachtal	Africa • 500 kW W Africa • 500 kW
		W Africa • 500 kW
	ITALY RADIO ROMA, Via Ascension	Americas • 250 kW
	RUSSIA †GOLOS ROSSII, Samara	Mideast & C Africa • 150 kW
	†GOLOS ROSSII, Via Tajikistan	Mideast & N Africa • 100 kW
	†VOICE OF RUSSIA, Via Uzbekistan	Mideast & W Asia • 240 kW
	UNITED KINGDOM BBC, Via Ascension	S America • 250 kW
		Tu-Sa • S America • 250 kW S America • 250 kW
		S America • 250 kW
	†BBC, Via Tokyo, Japan	E Asia • 100 kW
		E Asia • 300 kW
11770	PHILIPPINES RADIO VERITAS ASIA, Palauig	SE Asia • 250 kW • ALT. FREQ. TO 11850 kHz
	USA †RFE-RL, Via Gloria, Portugal	E Europe • 250 kW
		W Asia • 250 kW
(con'd)		S Europe • 250 kW
		E Europe • 250 kW

FREQUENCY   COUNTRY, STATION, LOCATION   TARGET • NETWORK • POWER (kW)   World Time

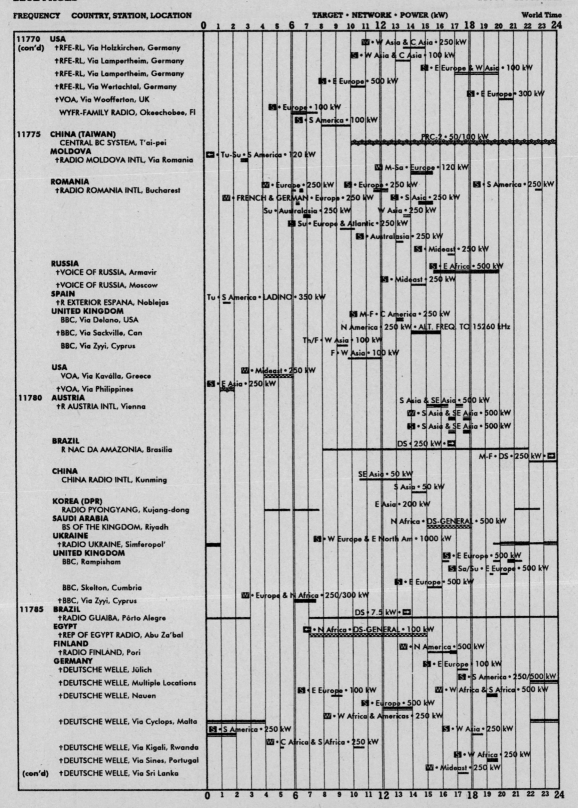

Frequency	Country, Station, Location	Target • Network • Power
11770 (con'd)	**USA**	
	†RFE-RL, Via Holzkirchen, Germany	W • W Asia & C Asia • 250 kW
	†RFE-RL, Via Lampertheim, Germany	S • W Asia & C Asia • 100 kW
	†RFE-RL, Via Lampertheim, Germany	S • E Europe & W Asia • 100 kW
	†RFE-RL, Via Wertachtal, Germany	S • E Europe • 500 kW
	†VOA, Via Woofferton, UK	S • E Europe • 300 kW
		S • Europe • 100 kW
	WYFR-FAMILY RADIO, Okeechobee, Fl	S • S America • 100 kW
11775	**CHINA (TAIWAN)**	
	CENTRAL BC SYSTEM, T'ai-pei	PRC-2 • 50/100 kW
	MOLDOVA	
	†RADIO MOLDOVA INTL, Via Romania	Tu-Su • S America • 120 kW
		W • M-Sa • Europe • 120 kW
	ROMANIA	
	†RADIO ROMANIA INTL, Bucharest	W • Europe • 250 kW S • Europe • 250 kW S • S America • 250 kW
		W • FRENCH & GERMAN • Europe • 250 kW S • S Asia • 250 kW
		Su • Australasia • 250 kW W Asia • 250 kW
		S • Su • Europe & Atlantic • 250 kW
		S • Australasia • 250 kW
		S • Mideast • 250 kW
	RUSSIA	
	†VOICE OF RUSSIA, Armavir	S • E Africa • 500 kW
	†VOICE OF RUSSIA, Moscow	S • Mideast • 250 kW
	SPAIN	
	†R EXTERIOR ESPANA, Noblejas	Tu • S America • LADINO • 350 kW
	UNITED KINGDOM	
	BBC, Via Delano, USA	S • M-F • C America • 250 kW
		N America • 250 kW • ALT. FREQ. TO 15260 kHz
	†BBC, Via Sackville, Can	Th/F • W Asia • 100 kW
	BBC, Via Zyyi, Cyprus	F • W Asia • 100 kW
	USA	
	VOA, Via Kaválla, Greece	W • Mideast • 250 kW
	†VOA, Via Philippines	S • E Asia • 250 kW
11780	**AUSTRIA**	
	†R AUSTRIA INTL, Vienna	S Asia & SE Asia • 500 kW
		W • S Asia & SE Asia • 500 kW
		S • S Asia & SE Asia • 500 kW
	BRAZIL	
	R NAC DA AMAZONIA, Brasilia	DS • 250 kW • →
		M-F • DS • 250 kW • →
	CHINA	
	CHINA RADIO INTL, Kunming	SE Asia • 50 kW
		S Asia • 50 kW
	KOREA (DPR)	
	RADIO PYONGYANG, Kujang-dong	E Asia • 200 kW
	SAUDI ARABIA	
	BS OF THE KINGDOM, Riyadh	N Africa • DS-GENERAL • 500 kW
	UKRAINE	
	†RADIO UKRAINE, Simferopol'	S • W Europe & E North Am • 1000 kW
	UNITED KINGDOM	
	BBC, Rampisham	S • E Europe • 500 kW
		S • Sa/Su • E Europe • 500 kW
	BBC, Skelton, Cumbria	S • E Europe • 500 kW
	†BBC, Via Zyyi, Cyprus	W • Europe & N Africa • 250/300 kW
11785	**BRAZIL**	
	†RADIO GUAIBA, Pôrto Alegre	DS • 7.5 kW • →
	EGYPT	
	†REP OF EGYPT RADIO, Abu Za'bal	N Africa • DS-GENERAL • 100 kW
	FINLAND	
	†RADIO FINLAND, Pori	W • N America • 500 kW
	GERMANY	
	†DEUTSCHE WELLE, Jülich	S • E Europe • 100 kW
		S • S America • 250/500 kW
	†DEUTSCHE WELLE, Multiple Locations	S • E Europe • 100 kW W • W Africa & S Africa • 500 kW
	†DEUTSCHE WELLE, Nauen	S • Europe • 500 kW
		W • W Africa & Americas • 250 kW
	†DEUTSCHE WELLE, Via Cyclops, Malta	S • S America • 250 kW S • W Asia • 250 kW
	†DEUTSCHE WELLE, Via Kigali, Rwanda	W • C Africa & S Africa • 250 kW
	†DEUTSCHE WELLE, Via Sines, Portugal	S • W Africa • 250 kW
(con'd)	†DEUTSCHE WELLE, Via Sri Lanka	W • Mideast • 250 kW

ENGLISH ▬▬   ARABIC ≋≋≋   CHINESE □□□   FRENCH ══   GERMAN ▬▬   RUSSIAN ═══   SPANISH ▬▬   OTHER ▬

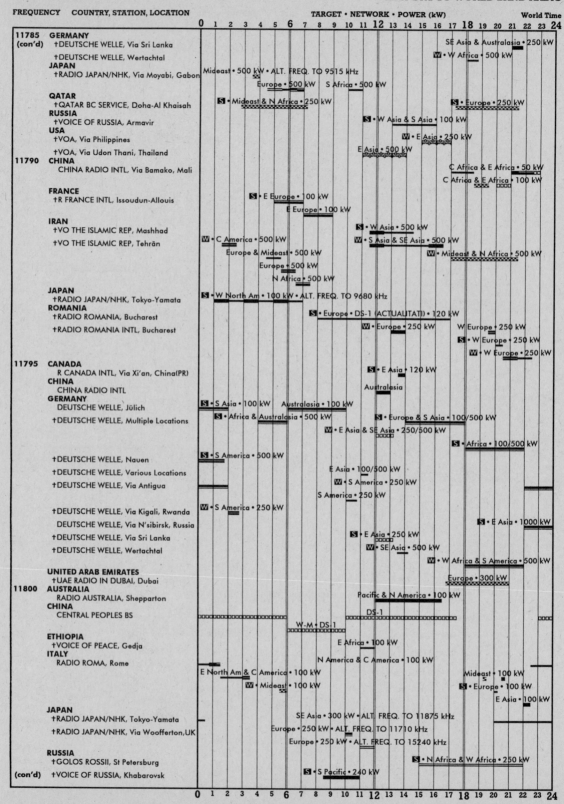

FREQUENCY   COUNTRY, STATION, LOCATION   TARGET • NETWORK • POWER (kW)   World Time

11785	GERMANY
(con'd)	†DEUTSCHE WELLE, Via Sri Lanka — SE Asia & Australasia • 250 kW
	†DEUTSCHE WELLE, Wertachtal — W • W Africa • 500 kW
	JAPAN
	†RADIO JAPAN/NHK, Via Moyabi, Gabon — Mideast • 500 kW • ALT. FREQ. TO 9515 kHz
	Europe • 500 kW S Africa • 500 kW
	QATAR
	†QATAR BC SERVICE, Doha-Al Khaisah — S • Mideast & N Africa • 250 kW S • Europe • 250 kW
	RUSSIA
	†VOICE OF RUSSIA, Armavir — S • W Asia & S Asia • 100 kW
	USA
	†VOA, Via Philippines — W • E Asia • 250 kW
	†VOA, Via Udon Thani, Thailand — E Asia • 500 kW
11790	CHINA
	CHINA RADIO INTL, Via Bamako, Mali — C Africa & E Africa • 50 kW
	C Africa & E Africa • 100 kW
	FRANCE
	†R FRANCE INTL, Issoudun-Allouis — S • E Europe • 100 kW
	E Europe • 100 kW
	IRAN
	†VO THE ISLAMIC REP, Mashhad — S • W Asia • 500 kW
	†VO THE ISLAMIC REP, Tehrān — W • C America • 500 kW W • S Asia & SE Asia • 500 kW
	Europe & Mideast • 500 kW W • Mideast & N Africa • 500 kW
	Europe • 500 kW
	N Africa • 500 kW
	JAPAN
	†RADIO JAPAN/NHK, Tokyo-Yamata — S • W North Am • 100 kW • ALT. FREQ. TO 9680 kHz
	ROMANIA
	†RADIO ROMANIA, Bucharest — S • Europe • DS-1 (ACTUALITATI) • 120 kW
	†RADIO ROMANIA INTL, Bucharest — W • Europe • 250 kW W Europe • 250 kW
	S • W Europe • 250 kW
	W • W Europe • 250 kW
11795	CANADA
	R CANADA INTL, Via Xi'an, China(PR) — S • E Asia • 120 kW
	CHINA
	CHINA RADIO INTL — Australasia
	GERMANY
	DEUTSCHE WELLE, Jülich — S • S Asia • 100 kW Australasia • 100 kW
	†DEUTSCHE WELLE, Multiple Locations — S • Africa & Australasia • 500 kW S • Europe & S Asia • 100/500 kW
	W • E Asia & SE Asia • 250/500 kW
	S • Africa • 100/500 kW
	†DEUTSCHE WELLE, Nauen — S • S America • 500 kW
	†DEUTSCHE WELLE, Various Locations — E Asia • 100/500 kW
	†DEUTSCHE WELLE, Via Antigua — W • S America • 250 kW
	S America • 250 kW
	†DEUTSCHE WELLE, Via Kigali, Rwanda — W • S America • 250 kW
	DEUTSCHE WELLE, Via N'sibirsk, Russia — S • E Asia • 1000 kW
	†DEUTSCHE WELLE, Via Sri Lanka — S • E Asia • 250 kW
	†DEUTSCHE WELLE, Wertachtal — W • SE Asia • 500 kW
	W • W Africa & S America • 500 kW
	UNITED ARAB EMIRATES
	†UAE RADIO IN DUBAI, Dubai — Europe • 300 kW
11800	AUSTRALIA
	RADIO AUSTRALIA, Shepparton — Pacific & N America • 100 kW
	CHINA
	CENTRAL PEOPLES BS — DS-1
	ETHIOPIA
	†VOICE OF PEACE, Gedja — W-M • DS-1 E Africa • 100 kW
	ITALY
	RADIO ROMA, Rome — N America & C America • 100 kW
	E North Am & C America • 100 kW Mideast • 100 kW
	W • Mideast • 100 kW S • Europe • 100 kW
	E Asia • 100 kW
	JAPAN
	†RADIO JAPAN/NHK, Tokyo-Yamata — SE Asia • 300 kW • ALT. FREQ. TO 11875 kHz
	†RADIO JAPAN/NHK, Via Woofferton, UK — Europe • 250 kW • ALT. FREQ. TO 11710 kHz
	Europe • 250 kW • ALT. FREQ. TO 15240 kHz
	RUSSIA
	†GOLOS ROSSII, St Petersburg — S • N Africa & W Africa • 250 kW
(con'd)	†VOICE OF RUSSIA, Khabarovsk — S • S Pacific • 240 kW

FREQUENCY   COUNTRY, STATION, LOCATION

TARGET • NETWORK • POWER (kW)

World Time

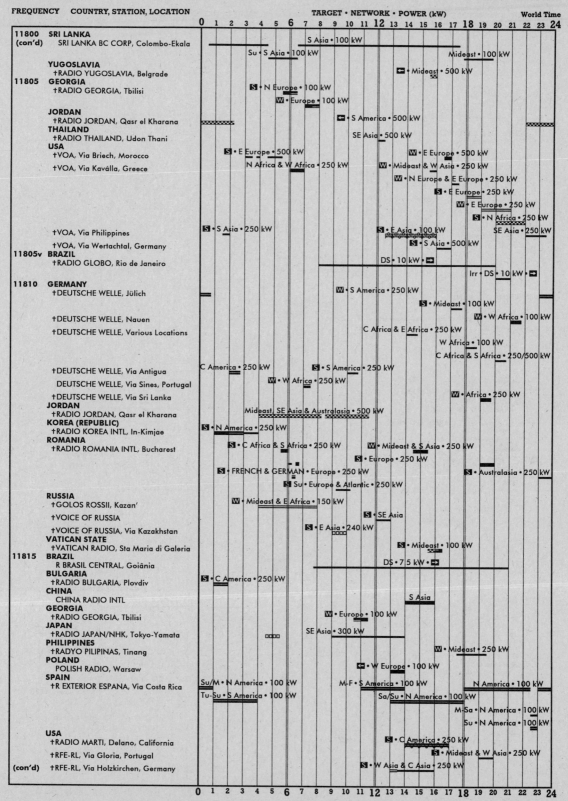

Frequency	Country, Station, Location	Details
11800 (con'd)	**SRI LANKA** — SRI LANKA BC CORP, Colombo-Ekala	S Asia • 100 kW; Su • S Asia • 100 kW; Mideast • 100 kW
	YUGOSLAVIA — †RADIO YUGOSLAVIA, Belgrade	• Mideast • 500 kW
11805	**GEORGIA** — †RADIO GEORGIA, Tbilisi	S • N Europe • 100 kW; W • Europe • 100 kW
	JORDAN — †RADIO JORDAN, Qasr el Kharana	• S America • 500 kW
	THAILAND — †RADIO THAILAND, Udon Thani	SE Asia • 500 kW
	USA — †VOA, Via Briech, Morocco	S • E Europe • 500 kW; W • E Europe • 500 kW
	†VOA, Via Kaválla, Greece	N Africa & W Africa • 250 kW; W • Mideast & W Asia • 250 kW; W • N Europe & E Europe • 250 kW; S • E Europe • 250 kW; W • E Europe • 250 kW; S • N Africa • 250 kW
	†VOA, Via Philippines	S • S Asia • 250 kW; S • E Asia • 100 kW; SE Asia • 250 kW
	†VOA, Via Wertachtal, Germany	S • S Asia • 500 kW
11805v	**BRAZIL** — †RADIO GLOBO, Rio de Janeiro	DS • 10 kW • ; Irr • DS • 10 kW •
11810	**GERMANY** — †DEUTSCHE WELLE, Jülich	W • S America • 250 kW; S • Mideast • 100 kW; W • W Africa • 100 kW
	†DEUTSCHE WELLE, Nauen	C Africa & E Africa • 250 kW
	†DEUTSCHE WELLE, Various Locations	W Africa • 100 kW; C Africa & S Africa • 250/500 kW
	†DEUTSCHE WELLE, Via Antigua	C America • 250 kW; S • S America • 250 kW
	DEUTSCHE WELLE, Via Sines, Portugal	W • W Africa • 250 kW
	†DEUTSCHE WELLE, Via Sri Lanka	W • Africa • 250 kW
	JORDAN — †RADIO JORDAN, Qasr el Kharana	Mideast, SE Asia & Australasia • 500 kW
	KOREA (REPUBLIC) — †RADIO KOREA INTL, In-Kimjae	S • N America • 250 kW
	ROMANIA — †RADIO ROMANIA INTL, Bucharest	S • C Africa & S Africa • 250 kW; W • Mideast & S Asia • 250 kW; W • Europe • 250 kW; S • FRENCH & GERMAN • Europe • 250 kW; S • Australasia • 250 kW; S • Su • Europe & Atlantic • 250 kW
	RUSSIA — †GOLOS ROSSII, Kazan'	W • Mideast & E Africa • 150 kW
	†VOICE OF RUSSIA	S • SE Asia
	†VOICE OF RUSSIA, Via Kazakhstan	S • E Asia • 240 kW
	VATICAN STATE — †VATICAN RADIO, Sta Maria di Galeria	S • Mideast • 100 kW
11815	**BRAZIL** — R BRASIL CENTRAL, Goiânia	DS • 7.5 kW •
	BULGARIA — †RADIO BULGARIA, Plovdiv	S • C America • 250 kW
	CHINA — CHINA RADIO INTL	S Asia
	GEORGIA — †RADIO GEORGIA, Tbilisi	W • Europe • 100 kW
	JAPAN — †RADIO JAPAN/NHK, Tokyo-Yamata	SE Asia • 300 kW
	PHILIPPINES — †RADYO PILIPINAS, Tinang	W • Mideast • 250 kW
	POLAND — POLISH RADIO, Warsaw	• W Europe • 100 kW
	SPAIN — †R EXTERIOR ESPANA, Via Costa Rica	Su/M • N America • 100 kW; M-F • S America • 100 kW; N America • 100 kW; Tu-Su • S America • 100 kW; Sa/Su • N America • 100 kW; M-Sa • N America • 100 kW; Su • N America • 100 kW
	USA — †RADIO MARTI, Delano, California	S • C America • 250 kW
	†RFE-RL, Via Gloria, Portugal	S • Mideast & W Asia • 250 kW
(con'd)	†RFE-RL, Via Holzkirchen, Germany	S • W Asia & C Asia • 250 kW

ENGLISH ▬   ARABIC ⌇⌇⌇   CHINESE ▫▫▫   FRENCH ▬   GERMAN ▬   RUSSIAN ═══   SPANISH ▬   OTHER ▬

FREQUENCY   COUNTRY, STATION, LOCATION

TARGET • NETWORK • POWER (kW)   World Time

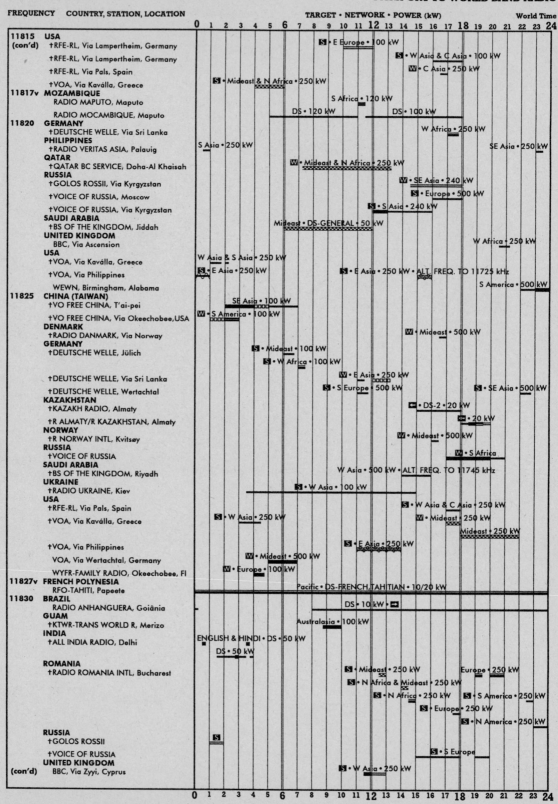

FREQUENCY	COUNTRY, STATION, LOCATION	Schedule
11815 (con'd)	**USA**	
	†RFE-RL, Via Lampertheim, Germany	S • E Europe • 100 kW
	†RFE-RL, Via Lampertheim, Germany	S • W Asia & C Asia • 100 kW
	†RFE-RL, Via Pals, Spain	W • C Asia • 250 kW
	†VOA, Via Kaválla, Greece	S • Mideast & N Africa • 250 kW
11817v	**MOZAMBIQUE**	
	RADIO MAPUTO, Maputo	S Africa • 120 kW
	RADIO MOCAMBIQUE, Maputo	DS • 120 kW DS • 100 kW
11820	**GERMANY**	
	†DEUTSCHE WELLE, Via Sri Lanka	W Africa • 250 kW
	PHILIPPINES	
	†RADIO VERITAS ASIA, Palauig	S Asia • 250 kW SE Asia • 250 kW
	QATAR	
	†QATAR BC SERVICE, Doha-Al Khaisah	W • Mideast & N Africa • 250 kW
	RUSSIA	
	†GOLOS ROSSII, Via Kyrgyzstan	W • SE Asia • 240 kW
	†VOICE OF RUSSIA, Moscow	S • Europe • 500 kW
	†VOICE OF RUSSIA, Via Kyrgyzstan	S • S Asia • 240 kW
	SAUDI ARABIA	
	†BS OF THE KINGDOM, Jiddah	Mideast • DS-GENERAL • 50 kW
	UNITED KINGDOM	
	BBC, Via Ascension	W Africa • 250 kW
	USA	
	†VOA, Via Kaválla, Greece	W Asia & S Asia • 250 kW
	†VOA, Via Philippines	S • E Asia • 250 kW S • E Asia • 250 kW • ALT. FREQ. TO 11725 kHz
	WEWN, Birmingham, Alabama	S America • 500 kW
11825	**CHINA (TAIWAN)**	
	†VO FREE CHINA, T'ai-pei	SE Asia • 100 kW
	†VO FREE CHINA, Via Okeechobee, USA	W • S America • 100 kW
	DENMARK	
	†RADIO DANMARK, Via Norway	W • Mideast • 500 kW
	GERMANY	
	†DEUTSCHE WELLE, Jülich	S • Mideast • 100 kW
		S • W Africa • 100 kW
	†DEUTSCHE WELLE, Via Sri Lanka	W • E Asia • 250 kW
	†DEUTSCHE WELLE, Wertachtal	S • S Europe • 500 kW S • SE Asia • 500 kW
	KAZAKHSTAN	
	†KAZAKH RADIO, Almaty	DS-2 • 20 kW
	†R ALMATY/R KAZAKHSTAN, Almaty	20 kW
	NORWAY	
	†R NORWAY INTL, Kvitsøy	W • Mideast • 500 kW
	RUSSIA	
	†VOICE OF RUSSIA	W • S Africa
	SAUDI ARABIA	
	†BS OF THE KINGDOM, Riyadh	W Asia • 500 kW • ALT. FREQ. TO 11745 kHz
	UKRAINE	
	†RADIO UKRAINE, Kiev	S • W Asia • 100 kW
	USA	
	†RFE-RL, Via Pals, Spain	S • W Asia & C Asia • 250 kW
	†VOA, Via Kaválla, Greece	S • W Asia • 250 kW W • Mideast • 250 kW
		Mideast • 250 kW
	†VOA, Via Philippines	S • E Asia • 250 kW
	VOA, Via Wertachtal, Germany	W • Mideast • 500 kW
	WYFR-FAMILY RADIO, Okeechobee, Fl	W • Europe • 100 kW
11827v	**FRENCH POLYNESIA**	
	RFO-TAHITI, Papeete	Pacific • DS-FRENCH, TAHITIAN • 10/20 kW
11830	**BRAZIL**	
	RADIO ANHANGUERA, Goiânia	DS • 10 kW
	GUAM	
	†KTWR-TRANS WORLD R, Merizo	Australasia • 100 kW
	INDIA	
	†ALL INDIA RADIO, Delhi	ENGLISH & HINDI • DS • 50 kW
		DS • 50 kW
	ROMANIA	
	†RADIO ROMANIA INTL, Bucharest	S • Mideast • 250 kW Europe • 250 kW
		S • N Africa & Mideast • 250 kW
		S • N Africa • 250 kW S • S America • 250 kW
		S • Europe • 250 kW
		S • N America • 250 kW
	RUSSIA	
	†GOLOS ROSSII	S
	†VOICE OF RUSSIA	S • S Europe
	UNITED KINGDOM	
(con'd)	BBC, Via Zyyi, Cyprus	S • W Asia • 250 kW

SEASONAL S OR W   1-HR TIMESHIFT MIDYEAR ⊟ OR ⊟   JAMMING / OR ∧   EARLIEST HEARD ◁   LATEST HEARD ▷   NEW FOR 1996 †

FREQUENCY	COUNTRY, STATION, LOCATION	TARGET • NETWORK • POWER (kW)	World Time

0 1 2 3 4 5 6 7 8 9 10 11 12 13 14 15 16 17 18 19 20 21 22 23 24

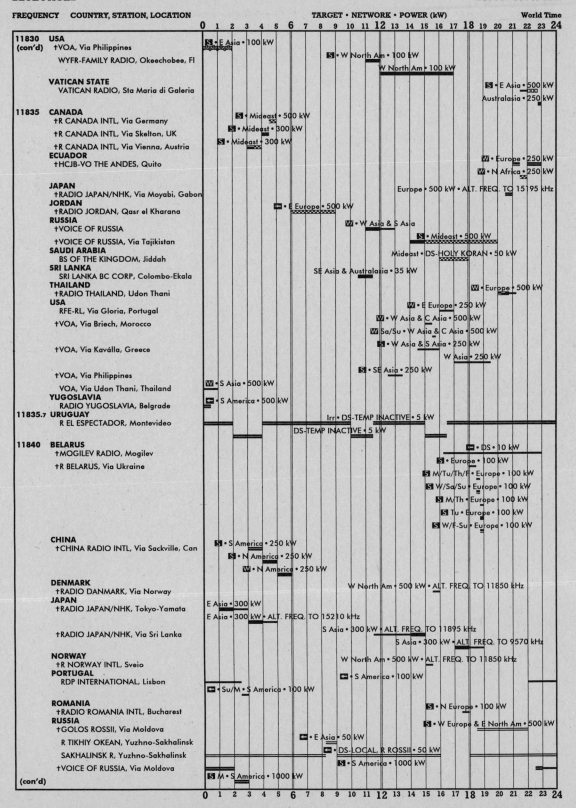

11830 (con'd)	**USA**	
	†VOA, Via Philippines	S • E Asia • 100 kW
	WYFR-FAMILY RADIO, Okeechobee, Fl	S • W North Am • 100 kW / W North Am • 100 kW
	VATICAN STATE	
	VATICAN RADIO, Sta Maria di Galeria	S • E Asia • 500 kW / Australasia • 250 kW
11835	**CANADA**	
	†R CANADA INTL, Via Germany	S • Mideast • 500 kW
	†R CANADA INTL, Via Skelton, UK	S • Mideast • 300 kW
	†R CANADA INTL, Via Vienna, Austria	S • Mideast • 300 kW
	ECUADOR	
	†HCJB-VO THE ANDES, Quito	W • Europe • 250 kW / W • N Africa • 250 kW
	JAPAN	
	†RADIO JAPAN/NHK, Via Moyabi, Gabon	Europe • 500 kW • ALT. FREQ. TO 15195 kHz
	JORDAN	
	†RADIO JORDAN, Qasr el Kharana	• E Europe • 500 kW
	RUSSIA	
	†VOICE OF RUSSIA	W • W Asia & S Asia
	†VOICE OF RUSSIA, Via Tajikistan	S • Mideast • 500 kW
	SAUDI ARABIA	
	BS OF THE KINGDOM, Jiddah	Mideast • DS-HOLY KORAN • 50 kW
	SRI LANKA	
	SRI LANKA BC CORP, Colombo-Ekala	SE Asia & Australasia • 35 kW
	THAILAND	
	†RADIO THAILAND, Udon Thani	W • Europe • 500 kW
	USA	
	RFE-RL, Via Gloria, Portugal	W • E Europe • 250 kW
	†VOA, Via Briech, Morocco	W • W Asia & C Asia • 500 kW
		W Sa/Su • W Asia & C Asia • 500 kW
	†VOA, Via Kaválla, Greece	S • W Asia & S Asia • 250 kW / W Asia • 250 kW
	†VOA, Via Philippines	S • SE Asia • 250 kW
	VOA, Via Udon Thani, Thailand	W • S Asia • 500 kW
	YUGOSLAVIA	
	RADIO YUGOSLAVIA, Belgrade	• S America • 500 kW
11835.7	**URUGUAY**	
	R EL ESPECTADOR, Montevideo	Irr • DS-TEMP INACTIVE • 5 kW / DS-TEMP INACTIVE • 5 kW
11840	**BELARUS**	
	†MOGILEV RADIO, Mogilev	• DS • 10 kW
	†R BELARUS, Via Ukraine	S • Europe • 100 kW
		S M/Tu/Th/F • Europe • 100 kW
		S W/Sa/Su • Europe • 100 kW
		S M/Th • Europe • 100 kW
		S Tu • Europe • 100 kW
		S W/F-Su • Europe • 100 kW
	CHINA	
	†CHINA RADIO INTL, Via Sackville, Can	S • S America • 250 kW
		S • N America • 250 kW
		W • N America • 250 kW
	DENMARK	
	†RADIO DANMARK, Via Norway	W North Am • 500 kW • ALT. FREQ. TO 11850 kHz
	JAPAN	
	†RADIO JAPAN/NHK, Tokyo-Yamata	E Asia • 300 kW
		E Asia • 300 kW • ALT. FREQ. TO 15210 kHz
	†RADIO JAPAN/NHK, Via Sri Lanka	S Asia • 300 kW • ALT. FREQ. TO 11895 kHz
		S Asia • 300 kW • ALT. FREQ. TO 9570 kHz
	NORWAY	
	†R NORWAY INTL, Sveio	W North Am • 500 kW • ALT. FREQ. TO 11850 kHz
	PORTUGAL	
	RDP INTERNATIONAL, Lisbon	• S America • 100 kW
		Su/M • S America • 100 kW
	ROMANIA	
	†RADIO ROMANIA INTL, Bucharest	S • N Europe • 100 kW
	RUSSIA	
	†GOLOS ROSSII, Via Moldova	S • W Europe & E North Am • 500 kW
	R TIKHIY OKEAN, Yuzhno-Sakhalinsk	• E Asia • 50 kW
	SAKHALINSK R, Yuzhno-Sakhalinsk	• DS-LOCAL, R ROSSII • 50 kW
	†VOICE OF RUSSIA, Via Moldova	S • S America • 1000 kW
(con'd)		S M • S America • 1000 kW

0 1 2 3 4 5 6 7 8 9 10 11 12 13 14 15 16 17 18 19 20 21 22 23 24

ENGLISH ▬   ARABIC ▨   CHINESE ☐☐☐   FRENCH ▭   GERMAN ▭   RUSSIAN ═   SPANISH ▭   OTHER ──

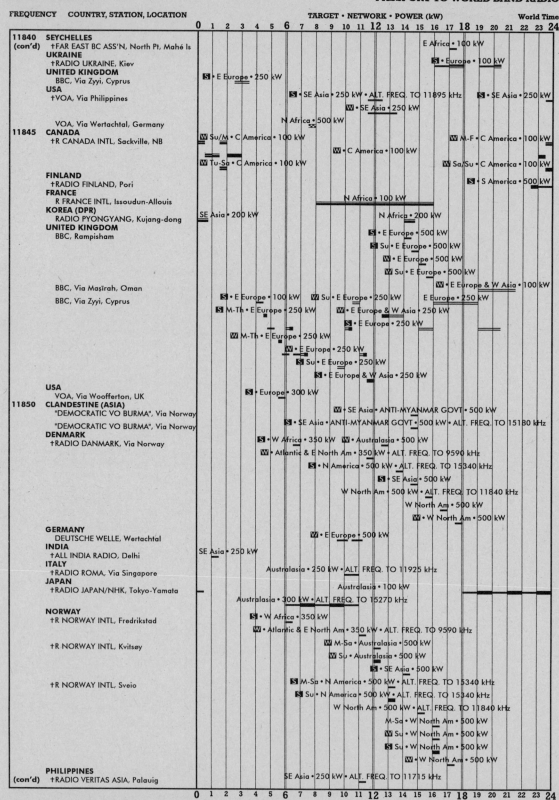

11840 SEYCHELLES
(con'd)   †FAR EAST BC ASS'N, North Pt, Mahé Is   E Africa • 100 kW
    UKRAINE
        †RADIO UKRAINE, Kiev   S • Europe • 100 kW
    UNITED KINGDOM
        BBC, Via Zyyi, Cyprus   S • E Europe • 250 kW
    USA
        †VOA, Via Philippines   S • SE Asia • 250 kW • ALT. FREQ. TO 11895 kHz   S • SE Asia • 250 kW
                                       S • SE Asia • 250 kW

        VOA, Via Wertachtal, Germany   N Africa • 500 kW
11845 CANADA
        †R CANADA INTL, Sackville, NB   W Su/M • C America • 100 kW   W M-F • C America • 100 kW

                                W Tu-Sa • C America • 100 kW   W Sa/Su • C America • 100 kW

    FINLAND
        †RADIO FINLAND, Pori   S • S America • 500 kW
    FRANCE
        R FRANCE INTL, Issoudun-Allouis   N Africa • 100 kW
    KOREA (DPR)
        RADIO PYONGYANG, Kujang-dong   SE Asia • 200 kW   N Africa • 200 kW
    UNITED KINGDOM
        BBC, Rampisham   S • E Europe • 500 kW
                                              S Su • E Europe • 500 kW
                                              W • E Europe • 500 kW
                                              W Su • E Europe • 500 kW

                                                   W • E Europe & W Asia • 100 kW
        BBC, Via Maṣīrah, Oman   S • E Europe • 100 kW   W Su • E Europe • 250 kW   E Europe • 250 kW
        BBC, Via Zyyi, Cyprus   S M-Th • E Europe • 250 kW   W • E Europe & W Asia • 250 kW
                                                   S • E Europe • 250 kW

                                       W M-Th • E Europe • 250 kW
                                              W • E Europe • 250 kW
                                              S Su • E Europe • 250 kW
                                                   S • E Europe & W Asia • 250 kW
    USA
        VOA, Via Woofferton, UK   S • Europe • 300 kW
11850 CLANDESTINE (ASIA)
        "DEMOCRATIC VO BURMA", Via Norway   W • SE Asia • ANTI-MYANMAR GOVT • 500 kW
        "DEMOCRATIC VO BURMA", Via Norway   S • SE Asia • ANTI-MYANMAR GOVT • 500 kW • ALT. FREQ. TO 15180 kHz
    DENMARK
        †RADIO DANMARK, Via Norway   S • W Africa • 350 kW   W • Australasia • 500 kW
                                       W • Atlantic & E North Am • 350 kW • ALT. FREQ. TO 9590 kHz
                                              S • N America • 500 kW • ALT. FREQ. TO 15340 kHz
                                                   S • SE Asia • 500 kW
                                              W North Am • 500 kW • ALT. FREQ. TO 11840 kHz
                                                   W North Am • 500 kW
                                                   W • W North Am • 500 kW

    GERMANY
        DEUTSCHE WELLE, Wertachtal   W • E Europe • 500 kW
    INDIA
        †ALL INDIA RADIO, Delhi   SE Asia • 250 kW
    ITALY
        †RADIO ROMA, Via Singapore   Australasia • 250 kW • ALT. FREQ. TO 11925 kHz
    JAPAN
        †RADIO JAPAN/NHK, Tokyo-Yamata   ▬   Australasia • 100 kW
                                Australasia • 300 kW • ALT. FREQ. TO 15270 kHz
    NORWAY
        †R NORWAY INTL, Fredrikstad   S • W Africa • 350 kW
                                       W • Atlantic & E North Am • 350 kW • ALT. FREQ. TO 9590 kHz

        †R NORWAY INTL, Kvitsøy   W M-Sa • Australasia • 500 kW
                                       W Su • Australasia • 500 kW
                                              S • SE Asia • 500 kW
        †R NORWAY INTL, Sveio   S M-Sa • N America • 500 kW • ALT. FREQ. TO 15340 kHz
                                       S Su • N America • 500 kW • ALT. FREQ. TO 15340 kHz
                                              W North Am • 500 kW • ALT. FREQ. TO 11840 kHz
                                                   M-Sa • W North Am • 500 kW
                                                   W Su • W North Am • 500 kW
                                                   S Su • W North Am • 500 kW
                                                   W • W North Am • 500 kW

    PHILIPPINES
(con'd)   †RADIO VERITAS ASIA, Palauig   SE Asia • 250 kW • ALT. FREQ. TO 11715 kHz

SEASONAL ⑤ OR Ⓦ   1-HR TIMESHIFT MIDYEAR ⊏ OR ⊐   JAMMING / OR ∧   EARLIEST HEARD ◁   LATEST HEARD ▷   NEW FOR 1996 †

FREQUENCY	COUNTRY, STATION, LOCATION	TARGET • NETWORK • POWER (kW)	World Time

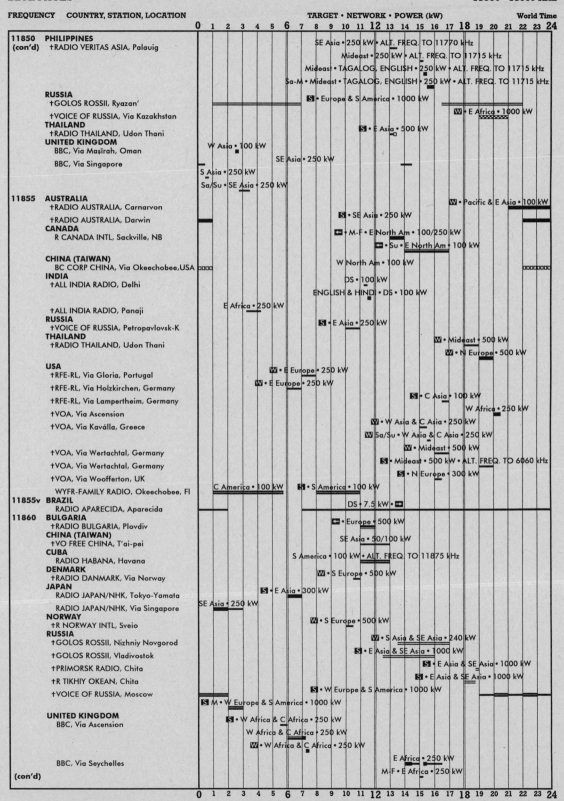

11850 **PHILIPPINES**
(con'd) †RADIO VERITAS ASIA, Palauig
- SE Asia • 250 kW • ALT. FREQ. TO 11770 kHz
- Mideast • 250 kW • ALT. FREQ. TO 11715 kHz
- Mideast • TAGALOG, ENGLISH • 250 kW • ALT. FREQ. TO 11715 kHz
- Sa-M • Mideast • TAGALOG, ENGLISH • 250 kW • ALT. FREQ. TO 11715 kHz

RUSSIA
†GOLOS ROSSII, Ryazan' — S • Europe & S America • 1000 kW
†VOICE OF RUSSIA, Via Kazakhstan — W • E Africa • 1000 kW
THAILAND
†RADIO THAILAND, Udon Thani — S • E Asia • 500 kW
UNITED KINGDOM
BBC, Via Maşīrah, Oman — W Asia • 100 kW
BBC, Via Singapore — SE Asia • 250 kW
— S Asia • 250 kW
— Sa/Su • SE Asia • 250 kW

11855 **AUSTRALIA**
†RADIO AUSTRALIA, Carnarvon — W • Pacific & E Asia • 100 kW
†RADIO AUSTRALIA, Darwin — S • SE Asia • 250 kW
CANADA
R CANADA INTL, Sackville, NB — M-F • E North Am • 100/250 kW
— Su • E North Am • 100 kW
CHINA (TAIWAN)
BC CORP CHINA, Via Okeechobee,USA — W North Am • 100 kW
INDIA
†ALL INDIA RADIO, Delhi — DS • 100 kW
— ENGLISH & HINDI • DS • 100 kW
†ALL INDIA RADIO, Panaji — E Africa • 250 kW
RUSSIA
†VOICE OF RUSSIA, Petropavlovsk-K — S • E Asia • 250 kW
THAILAND
†RADIO THAILAND, Udon Thani — W • Mideast • 500 kW
— W • N Europe • 500 kW
USA
†RFE-RL, Via Gloria, Portugal — W • E Europe • 250 kW
†RFE-RL, Via Holzkirchen, Germany — W • E Europe • 250 kW
†RFE-RL, Via Lampertheim, Germany — S • C Asia • 100 kW
†VOA, Via Ascension — W Africa • 250 kW
†VOA, Via Kaválla, Greece — W • W Asia & C Asia • 250 kW
— W Sa/Su • W Asia & C Asia • 250 kW
†VOA, Via Wertachtal, Germany — W • Mideast • 500 kW
†VOA, Via Wertachtal, Germany — S • Mideast • 500 kW • ALT. FREQ. TO 6060 kHz
†VOA, Via Woofferton, UK — S • N Europe • 300 kW
WYFR-FAMILY RADIO, Okeechobee, Fl — C America • 100 kW
— S • S America • 100 kW
11855v **BRAZIL**
RADIO APARECIDA, Aparecida — DS • 7.5 kW •
11860 **BULGARIA**
†RADIO BULGARIA, Plovdiv — Europe • 500 kW
CHINA (TAIWAN)
†VO FREE CHINA, T'ai-pei — SE Asia • 50/100 kW
CUBA
RADIO HABANA, Havana — S America • 100 kW • ALT. FREQ. TO 11875 kHz
DENMARK
†RADIO DANMARK, Via Norway — W • S Europe • 500 kW
JAPAN
RADIO JAPAN/NHK, Tokyo-Yamata — S • E Asia • 300 kW
RADIO JAPAN/NHK, Via Singapore — SE Asia • 250 kW
NORWAY
†R NORWAY INTL, Sveio — W • S Europe • 500 kW
RUSSIA
†GOLOS ROSSII, Nizhniy Novgorod — W • S Asia & SE Asia • 240 kW
†GOLOS ROSSII, Vladivostok — S • E Asia & SE Asia • 1000 kW
†PRIMORSK RADIO, Chita — S • E Asia & SE Asia • 1000 kW
†R TIKHIY OKEAN, Chita — S • E Asia & SE Asia • 1000 kW
†VOICE OF RUSSIA, Moscow — S • W Europe & S America • 1000 kW
— S M • W Europe & S America • 1000 kW
UNITED KINGDOM
BBC, Via Ascension — S • W Africa & C Africa • 250 kW
— W Africa & C Africa • 250 kW
— W • W Africa & C Africa • 250 kW
BBC, Via Seychelles — E Africa • 250 kW
— M-F • E Africa • 250 kW

(con'd)

0 1 2 3 4 5 6 7 8 9 10 11 12 13 14 15 16 17 18 19 20 21 22 23 24

ENGLISH ▬ ARABIC ⊠⊠ CHINESE ▢▢▢ FRENCH ▬▬ GERMAN ▬▬ RUSSIAN ══ SPANISH ▬▬ OTHER ▬▬

FREQUENCY　　COUNTRY, STATION, LOCATION　　　　　　TARGET • NETWORK • POWER (kW)　　　World Time

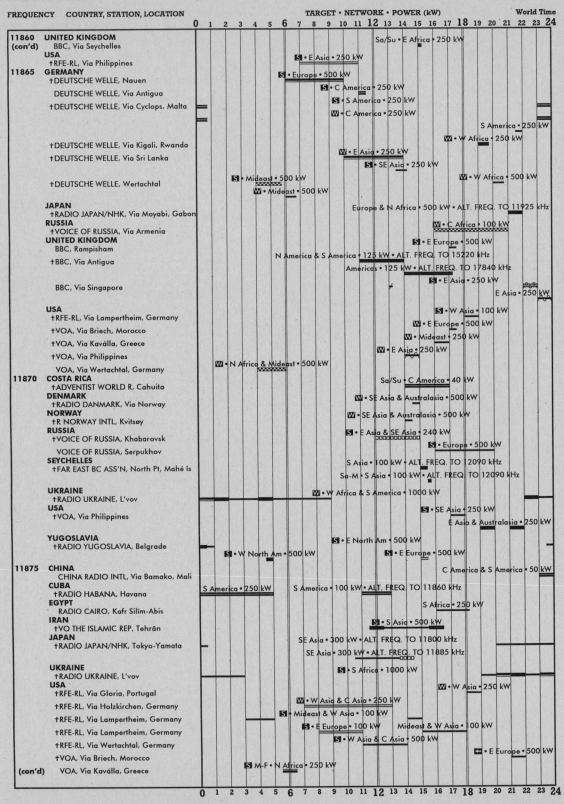

FREQUENCY	COUNTRY, STATION, LOCATION	TARGET • NETWORK • POWER (kW)
11860 (con'd)	UNITED KINGDOM BBC, Via Seychelles	Sa/Su • E Africa • 250 kW
	USA †RFE-RL, Via Philippines	S • E Asia • 250 kW
11865	GERMANY †DEUTSCHE WELLE, Nauen	S • Europe • 500 kW
	DEUTSCHE WELLE, Via Antigua	S • C America • 250 kW
	†DEUTSCHE WELLE, Via Cyclops, Malta	S • S America • 250 kW W • C America • 250 kW S America • 250 kW
	†DEUTSCHE WELLE, Via Kigali, Rwanda	W • W Africa • 250 kW
	†DEUTSCHE WELLE, Via Sri Lanka	W • E Asia • 250 kW S • SE Asia • 250 kW
	†DEUTSCHE WELLE, Wertachtal	S • Mideast • 500 kW W • Mideast • 500 kW W • W Africa • 500 kW
	JAPAN †RADIO JAPAN/NHK, Via Moyabi, Gabon	Europe & N Africa • 500 kW • ALT. FREQ. TO 11925 kHz
	RUSSIA †VOICE OF RUSSIA, Via Armenia	W • C Africa • 100 kW
	UNITED KINGDOM BBC, Rampisham	S • E Europe • 500 kW
	†BBC, Via Antigua	N America & S America • 125 kW • ALT. FREQ. TO 15220 kHz Americas • 125 kW • ALT. FREQ. TO 17840 kHz
	BBC, Via Singapore	S • E Asia • 250 kW E Asia • 250 kW
	USA †RFE-RL, Via Lampertheim, Germany	S • W Asia • 100 kW
	†VOA, Via Briech, Morocco	W • E Europe • 500 kW
	†VOA, Via Kaválla, Greece	W • Mideast • 250 kW
	†VOA, Via Philippines	W • E Asia • 250 kW
	VOA, Via Wertachtal, Germany	W • N Africa & Mideast • 500 kW
11870	COSTA RICA †ADVENTIST WORLD R, Cahuita	Sa/Su • C America • 40 kW
	DENMARK †RADIO DANMARK, Via Norway	W • SE Asia & Australasia • 500 kW
	NORWAY †R NORWAY INTL, Kvitsøy	W • SE Asia & Australasia • 500 kW
	RUSSIA †VOICE OF RUSSIA, Khabarovsk	S • E Asia & SE Asia • 240 kW
	VOICE OF RUSSIA, Serpukhov	S • Europe • 500 kW
	SEYCHELLES †FAR EAST BC ASS'N, North Pt, Mahé Is	S Asia • 100 kW • ALT. FREQ. TO 12090 kHz Sa-M • S Asia • 100 kW • ALT. FREQ. TO 12090 kHz
	UKRAINE †RADIO UKRAINE, L'vov	W • W Africa & S America • 1000 kW
	USA †VOA, Via Philippines	S • SE Asia • 250 kW E Asia & Australasia • 250 kW
	YUGOSLAVIA †RADIO YUGOSLAVIA, Belgrade	S • E North Am • 500 kW S • W North Am • 500 kW S • E Europe • 500 kW
11875	CHINA CHINA RADIO INTL, Via Bamako, Mali	C America & S America • 50 kW
	CUBA †RADIO HABANA, Havana	S America • 250 kW S America • 100 kW • ALT. FREQ. TO 11860 kHz
	EGYPT RADIO CAIRO, Kafr Silim-Abis	S Africa • 250 kW
	IRAN †VO THE ISLAMIC REP, Tehrãn	S • S Asia • 500 kW
	JAPAN †RADIO JAPAN/NHK, Tokyo-Yamata	SE Asia • 300 kW • ALT. FREQ. TO 11800 kHz SE Asia • 300 kW • ALT. FREQ. TO 11885 kHz
	UKRAINE †RADIO UKRAINE, L'vov	S • S Africa • 1000 kW
	USA †RFE-RL, Via Gloria, Portugal	W • W Asia • 250 kW
	†RFE-RL, Via Holzkirchen, Germany	W • W Asia & C Asia • 250 kW
	†RFE-RL, Via Lampertheim, Germany	S • Mideast & W Asia • 100 kW
	†RFE-RL, Via Lampertheim, Germany	S • E Europe • 100 kW Mideast & W Asia • 100 kW
	†RFE-RL, Via Wertachtal, Germany	S • W Asia & C Asia • 500 kW
	†VOA, Via Briech, Morocco	E Europe • 500 kW
(con'd)	VOA, Via Kaválla, Greece	S • M-F • N Africa • 250 kW

0 1 2 3 4 5 6 7 8 9 10 11 12 13 14 15 16 17 18 19 20 21 22 23 24

FREQUENCY   COUNTRY, STATION, LOCATION

TARGET • NETWORK • POWER (kW)

World Time

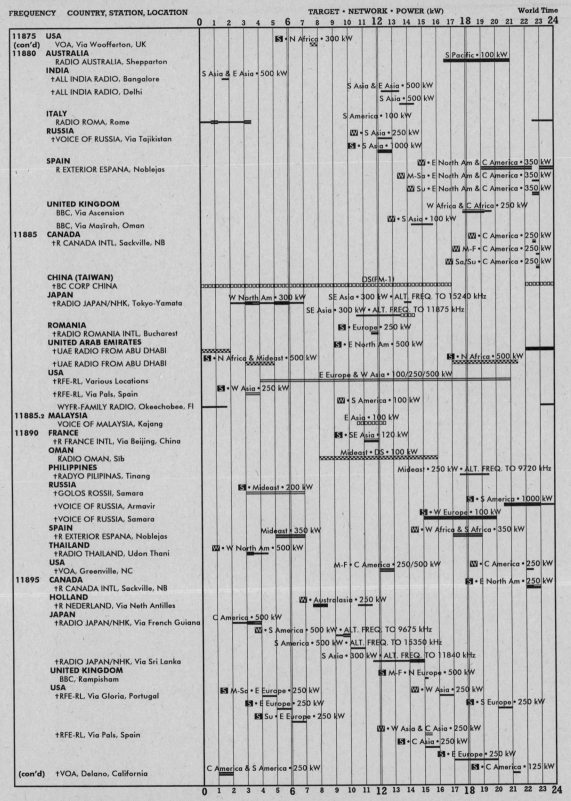

Frequency	Country, Station, Location	Target • Network • Power
11875 (con'd)	USA — VOA, Via Woofferton, UK	N Africa • 300 kW
11880	AUSTRALIA — RADIO AUSTRALIA, Shepparton	S Pacific • 100 kW
	INDIA — †ALL INDIA RADIO, Bangalore	S Asia & E Asia • 500 kW
	†ALL INDIA RADIO, Delhi	S Asia & E Asia • 500 kW
		S Asia • 500 kW
	ITALY — RADIO ROMA, Rome	S America • 100 kW
	RUSSIA — †VOICE OF RUSSIA, Via Tajikistan	W • S Asia • 250 kW
		S • S Asia • 1000 kW
	SPAIN — R EXTERIOR ESPANA, Noblejas	W • E North Am & C America • 350 kW
		W-Sa • E North Am & C America • 350 kW
		W-Su • E North Am & C America • 350 kW
	UNITED KINGDOM — BBC, Via Ascension	W Africa & C Africa • 250 kW
	BBC, Via Maṣīrah, Oman	W • S Asia • 100 kW
11885	CANADA — †R CANADA INTL, Sackville, NB	W • C America • 250 kW
		W M-F • C America • 250 kW
		W Sa/Su • C America • 250 kW
	CHINA (TAIWAN) — †BC CORP CHINA	DS(FM-1)
	JAPAN — †RADIO JAPAN/NHK, Tokyo-Yamata	W North Am • 300 kW SE Asia • 300 kW • ALT. FREQ. TO 15240 kHz
		SE Asia • 300 kW • ALT. FREQ. TO 11875 kHz
	ROMANIA — †RADIO ROMANIA INTL, Bucharest	S • Europe • 250 kW
	UNITED ARAB EMIRATES — †UAE RADIO FROM ABU DHABI	S • E North Am • 500 kW
		S • N Africa & Mideast • 500 kW
	†UAE RADIO FROM ABU DHABI	S • N Africa • 500 kW
	USA — †RFE-RL, Various Locations	E Europe & W Asia • 100/250/500 kW
	†RFE-RL, Via Pals, Spain	S • W Asia • 250 kW
	WYFR-FAMILY RADIO, Okeechobee, Fl	W • S America • 100 kW
11885.2	MALAYSIA — VOICE OF MALAYSIA, Kajang	E Asia • 100 kW
11890	FRANCE — †R FRANCE INTL, Via Beijing, China	S • SE Asia • 120 kW
	OMAN — RADIO OMAN, Sīb	Mideast • DS • 100 kW
	PHILIPPINES — †RADYO PILIPINAS, Tinang	Mideast • 250 kW • ALT. FREQ. TO 9720 kHz
	RUSSIA — †GOLOS ROSSII, Samara	S • Mideast • 200 kW
	†VOICE OF RUSSIA, Armavir	S • S America • 1000 kW
	†VOICE OF RUSSIA, Samara	S • W Europe • 100 kW
	SPAIN — †R EXTERIOR ESPANA, Noblejas	Mideast • 350 kW W • W Africa & S Africa • 350 kW
	THAILAND — †RADIO THAILAND, Udon Thani	W • W North Am • 500 kW
	USA — †VOA, Greenville, NC	M-F • C America • 250/500 kW W • C America • 250 kW
11895	CANADA — †R CANADA INTL, Sackville, NB	S • E North Am • 250 kW
	HOLLAND — †R NEDERLAND, Via Neth Antilles	W • Australasia • 250 kW
	JAPAN — †RADIO JAPAN/NHK, Via French Guiana	C America • 500 kW
		W • S America • 500 kW • ALT. FREQ. TO 9675 kHz
		S America • 500 kW • ALT. FREQ. TO 15350 kHz
	†RADIO JAPAN/NHK, Via Sri Lanka	S Asia • 300 kW • ALT. FREQ. TO 11840 kHz
	UNITED KINGDOM — BBC, Rampisham	S M-F • N Europe • 500 kW
	USA — †RFE-RL, Via Gloria, Portugal	S M-Sa • E Europe • 250 kW W • W Asia • 250 kW
		S • E Europe • 250 kW S • S Europe • 250 kW
		S Su • E Europe • 250 kW
	†RFE-RL, Via Pals, Spain	W • W Asia & C Asia • 250 kW
		S • C Asia • 250 kW
		S • E Europe • 250 kW
(con'd)	†VOA, Delano, California	C America & S America • 250 kW S • C America • 125 kW

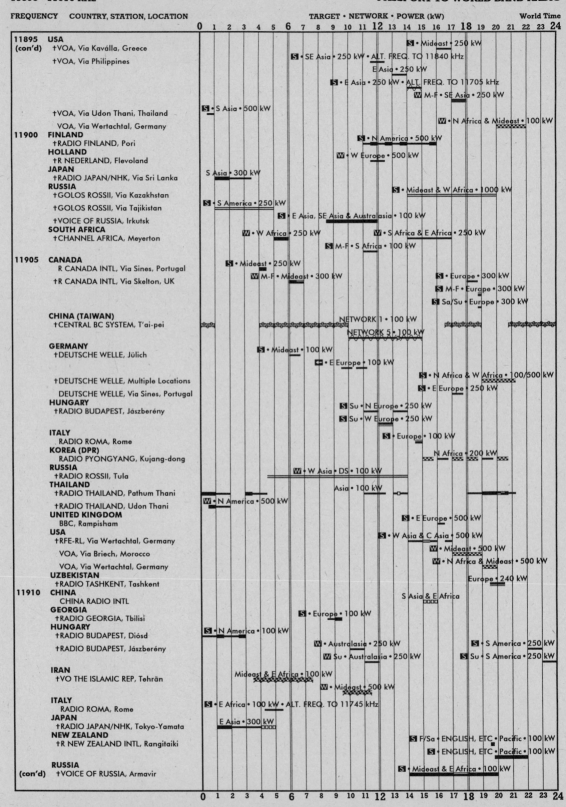

| FREQUENCY | COUNTRY, STATION, LOCATION | TARGET • NETWORK • POWER (kW) | World Time |

11895 **USA**
(con'd) †VOA, Via Kaválla, Greece — S • Mideast • 250 kW
†VOA, Via Philippines — S • SE Asia • 250 kW • ALT. FREQ. TO 11840 kHz
E Asia • 250 kW
S • E Asia • 250 kW • ALT. FREQ. TO 11705 kHz
W • M-F • SE Asia • 250 kW
†VOA, Via Udon Thani, Thailand — S • S Asia • 500 kW
VOA, Via Wertachtal, Germany — W • N Africa & Mideast • 100 kW

11900 **FINLAND**
†RADIO FINLAND, Pori — S • N America • 500 kW
HOLLAND
†R NEDERLAND, Flevoland — W • W Europe • 500 kW
JAPAN
†RADIO JAPAN/NHK, Via Sri Lanka — S Asia • 300 kW
RUSSIA
†GOLOS ROSSII, Via Kazakhstan — S • Mideast & W Africa • 1000 kW
†GOLOS ROSSII, Via Tajikistan — S • S America • 250 kW
†VOICE OF RUSSIA, Irkutsk — S • E Asia, SE Asia & Australasia • 100 kW
SOUTH AFRICA
†CHANNEL AFRICA, Meyerton — W • W Africa • 250 kW   W • S Africa & E Africa • 250 kW
S • M-F • S Africa • 100 kW

11905 **CANADA**
R CANADA INTL, Via Sines, Portugal — S • Mideast • 250 kW
†R CANADA INTL, Via Skelton, UK — W M-F • Mideast • 300 kW   S • Europe • 300 kW
S • M-F • Europe • 300 kW
S • Sa/Su • Europe • 300 kW

CHINA (TAIWAN)
†CENTRAL BC SYSTEM, T'ai-pei — NETWORK 1 • 100 kW
NETWORK 5 • 100 kW

GERMANY
†DEUTSCHE WELLE, Jülich — S • Mideast • 100 kW
• E Europe • 100 kW
†DEUTSCHE WELLE, Multiple Locations — S • N Africa & W Africa • 100/500 kW
DEUTSCHE WELLE, Via Sines, Portugal — S • E Europe • 250 kW
HUNGARY
†RADIO BUDAPEST, Jászberény — S Su • N Europe • 250 kW
S Su • W Europe • 250 kW

ITALY
RADIO ROMA, Rome — S • Europe • 100 kW
KOREA (DPR)
RADIO PYONGYANG, Kujang-dong — N Africa • 200 kW
RUSSIA
†RADIO ROSSII, Tula — W • W Asia • DS • 100 kW
THAILAND
†RADIO THAILAND, Pathum Thani — Asia • 100 kW
†RADIO THAILAND, Udon Thani — W • N America • 500 kW
UNITED KINGDOM
BBC, Rampisham — S • E Europe • 500 kW
USA
†RFE-RL, Via Wertachtal, Germany — S • W Asia & C Asia • 500 kW
VOA, Via Briech, Morocco — W • Mideast • 500 kW
VOA, Via Wertachtal, Germany — W • N Africa & Mideast • 500 kW
UZBEKISTAN
†RADIO TASHKENT, Tashkent — Europe • 240 kW

11910 **CHINA**
CHINA RADIO INTL — S Asia & E Africa
GEORGIA
†RADIO GEORGIA, Tbilisi — S • Europe • 100 kW
HUNGARY
†RADIO BUDAPEST, Diósd — S • N America • 100 kW
†RADIO BUDAPEST, Jászberény — W • Australasia • 250 kW   S • S America • 250 kW
W Su • Australasia • 250 kW   S Su • S America • 250 kW
IRAN
†VO THE ISLAMIC REP, Tehrān — Mideast & E Africa • 100 kW
W • Mideast • 500 kW
ITALY
RADIO ROMA, Rome — S • E Africa • 100 kW • ALT. FREQ. TO 11745 kHz
JAPAN
†RADIO JAPAN/NHK, Tokyo-Yamata — E Asia • 300 kW
NEW ZEALAND
†R NEW ZEALAND INTL, Rangitaiki — S F/Sa • ENGLISH, ETC • Pacific • 100 kW
S • ENGLISH, ETC • Pacific • 100 kW
RUSSIA
(con'd) †VOICE OF RUSSIA, Armavir — S • Mideast & E Africa • 100 kW

FREQUENCY   COUNTRY, STATION, LOCATION   TARGET • NETWORK • POWER (kW)   World Time

Frequency	Country / Station / Location	Target • Network • Power
11910 (con'd)	**SAUDI ARABIA** †BS OF THE KINGDOM, Riyadh	W Europe • DS-GENERAL • 500 kW • ALT. FREQ. TO 11965 kHz
	SPAIN R EXTERIOR ESPANA, Via Xi'an, China	SE Asia • 120 kW
	UNITED KINGDOM BBC, Via Delano, USA	C America & S America • 250 kW; Tu-Sa • C America & S America • 250 kW
11915	**BRAZIL** RADIO GAUCHA, Pôrto Alegre	DS • 7.5 kW • →
	CANADA R CANADA INTL, Via Sines, Portugal	W • Europe • 250 kW; W • E Europe • 250 kW
	CHINA (TAIWAN) †VO FREE CHINA, T'ai-pei	SE Asia • 250 kW; SE Asia • 250 kW • ALT. FREQ. TO 9610 kHz
	GERMANY †DEUTSCHE WELLE, Jülich	S • W Africa • 100 kW; S • E Europe • 100 kW
	†DEUTSCHE WELLE, Wertachtal	S • E Europe & W Asia • 500 kW
	HUNGARY †RADIO BUDAPEST, Jászberény	S • N Europe • 250 kW
	JAPAN †RADIO JAPAN/NHK, Tokyo-Yamata	SE Asia • 100 kW; SE Asia • 300 kW
	RUSSIA †GOLOS ROSSII, Petropavlovsk-K	S • E Asia • 100 kW
	USA †RFE-RL, Via Briech, Morocco	W • E Europe • 500 kW
	†RFE-RL, Via Gloria, Portugal	S • W Asia & C Asia • 250 kW; W • W Asia & C Asia • 250 kW; S • E Europe • 250 kW; W • E Europe • 250 kW
	VOA, Via Briech, Morocco	S • W Africa • 500 kW; S • M-F • W Africa • 500 kW; S • Sa/Su • W Africa • 500 kW
	VOA, Via Kaválla, Greece	W • M-F • N Africa & W Africa • 250 kW
	†WINB-WORLD INTL BC, Red Lion, Pa	W • Europe & N Africa • 14/50 kW; W • F • Europe & N Africa • 14/50 kW; W • Th/Sa-Tu • Europe & N Africa • 14/50 kW; W • W • Europe & N Africa • 14/50 kW
	WYFR-FAMILY RADIO, Okeechobee, Fl	W • Europe • 100 kW
11920	**ARMENIA** †VOICE OF ARMENIA, Yerevan	S • S America • 1000 kW; S • W Europe & C America • 1000 kW
	BELARUS †BELARUSSIAN R	W • DS
	COTE D'IVOIRE R COTE D'IVOIRE, Abidjan	DS-2 • 25 kW
	INDIA †ALL INDIA RADIO, Delhi	ENGLISH, ETC • DS • 50 kW
	MOROCCO RTV MAROCAINE, Briech	N Africa & Mideast • 500 kW
	RUSSIA †VOICE OF RUSSIA, Samara	S • S Europe • 100 kW
	SPAIN R EXTERIOR ESPANA, Noblejas	Europe • 350 kW
	UNITED KINGDOM BBC, Via Singapore	SE Asia • 100 kW; S Asia • 100 kW; S • S Asia • 100 kW; S • M-F • S Asia • 100 kW; S • Sa/Su • S Asia • 100 kW
	BBC, Via Zyyi, Cyprus	W • S Asia & W Asia • 100 kW
	USA VOA, Via Udon Thani, Thailand	Sa/Su • E Africa • 500 kW
	VOA, Via Udon Thani, Thailand	E Africa • 500 kW
11925	**BRAZIL** R JURATEL/R BANDEIRANTES, São Paulo	DS • 10 kW
	GERMANY †DEUTSCHE WELLE, Via Sines, Portugal	W • Europe • 250 kW
	ITALY †RADIO ROMA, Via Singapore	Australasia • 250 kW • ALT. FREQ. TO 11850 kHz
	JAPAN †RADIO JAPAN/NHK, Via Moyabi, Gabon	Europe & N Africa • 500 kW • ALT. FREQ. TO 11865 kHz
	MALTA †VO MEDITERRANEAN, Cyclops	Europe, N Africa & Mideast • 250 kW; M-Sa • Europe, N Africa & Mideast • 250 kW; Su • Europe, N Africa & Mideast • 250 kW
(con'd)	**TURKEY** VOICE OF TURKEY, Ankara	→ • W Asia • 250 kW

ENGLISH ▬   ARABIC ≋   CHINESE ▭▭▭   FRENCH ▬▬   GERMAN ▬▬   RUSSIAN ═══   SPANISH ▬▬   OTHER ▬

FREQUENCY   COUNTRY, STATION, LOCATION   TARGET • NETWORK • POWER (kW)   World Time

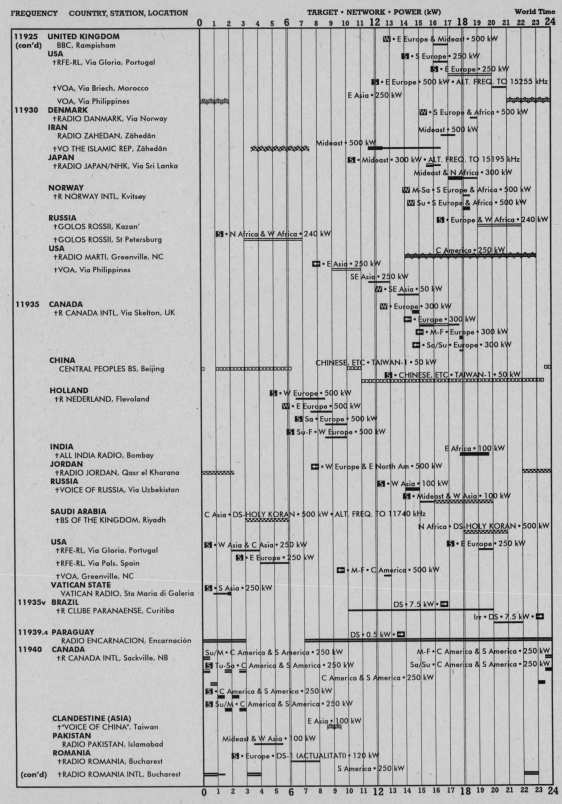

FREQUENCY	COUNTRY, STATION, LOCATION	TARGET • NETWORK • POWER (kW)
11925 (con'd)	UNITED KINGDOM / BBC, Rampisham	W • E Europe & Mideast • 500 kW
	USA / †RFE-RL, Via Gloria, Portugal	S • S Europe • 250 kW / S • E Europe • 250 kW
	†VOA, Via Briech, Morocco	S • E Europe • 500 kW • ALT. FREQ. TO 15255 kHz
	VOA, Via Philippines	E Asia • 250 kW
11930	DENMARK / †RADIO DANMARK, Via Norway	W • S Europe & Africa • 500 kW
	IRAN / RADIO ZAHEDAN, Zāhedān	Mideast • 500 kW
	†VO THE ISLAMIC REP, Zāhedān	Mideast • 500 kW
	JAPAN / †RADIO JAPAN/NHK, Via Sri Lanka	S • Mideast • 300 kW • ALT. FREQ. TO 15195 kHz / Mideast & N Africa • 300 kW
	NORWAY / †R NORWAY INTL, Kvitsøy	W M-Sa • S Europe & Africa • 500 kW / W Su • S Europe & Africa • 500 kW
	RUSSIA / †GOLOS ROSSII, Kazan'	S • Europe & W Africa • 240 kW
	†GOLOS ROSSII, St Petersburg	S • N Africa & W Africa • 240 kW
	USA / †RADIO MARTI, Greenville, NC	C America • 250 kW
	†VOA, Via Philippines	E Asia • 250 kW / SE Asia • 250 kW
11935	CANADA / †R CANADA INTL, Via Skelton, UK	W • SE Asia • 50 kW / W • Europe • 300 kW / Europe • 300 kW / M-F • Europe • 300 kW / Sa/Su • Europe • 300 kW
	CHINA / CENTRAL PEOPLES BS, Beijing	CHINESE, ETC • TAIWAN-1 • 50 kW / S • CHINESE, ETC • TAIWAN-1 • 50 kW
	HOLLAND / †R NEDERLAND, Flevoland	S • W Europe • 500 kW / W • E Europe • 500 kW / S Sa • Europe • 500 kW / Su-F • W Europe • 500 kW
	INDIA / †ALL INDIA RADIO, Bombay	E Africa • 100 kW
	JORDAN / †RADIO JORDAN, Qasr el Kharana	W Europe & E North Am • 500 kW
	RUSSIA / †VOICE OF RUSSIA, Via Uzbekistan	S • W Asia • 100 kW / S • Mideast & W Asia • 100 kW
	SAUDI ARABIA / †BS OF THE KINGDOM, Riyadh	C Asia • DS-HOLY KORAN • 500 kW • ALT. FREQ. TO 11740 kHz / N Africa • DS-HOLY KORAN • 500 kW
	USA / †RFE-RL, Via Gloria, Portugal	S • W Asia & C Asia • 250 kW / S • E Europe • 250 kW
	†RFE-RL, Via Pals, Spain	S • E Europe • 250 kW
	†VOA, Greenville, NC	M-F • C America • 500 kW
	VATICAN STATE / VATICAN RADIO, Sta Maria di Galeria	S • S Asia • 250 kW
11935v	BRAZIL / †R CLUBE PARANAENSE, Curitiba	DS • 7.5 kW • / Irr • DS • 7.5 kW •
11939.4	PARAGUAY / RADIO ENCARNACION, Encarnación	DS • 0.5 kW •
11940	CANADA / †R CANADA INTL, Sackville, NB	Su/M • C America & S America • 250 kW / M-F • C America & S America • 250 kW / S Tu-Sa • C America & S America • 250 kW / Sa/Su • C America & S America • 250 kW / C America & S America • 250 kW / S • C America & S America • 250 kW / S Su/M • C America & S America • 250 kW
	CLANDESTINE (ASIA) / †"VOICE OF CHINA", Taiwan	E Asia • 100 kW
	PAKISTAN / RADIO PAKISTAN, Islamabad	Mideast & W Asia • 100 kW
	ROMANIA / †RADIO ROMANIA, Bucharest	S • Europe • DS-1 (ACTUALITATI) • 120 kW
(con'd)	†RADIO ROMANIA INTL, Bucharest	S America • 250 kW

FREQUENCY   COUNTRY, STATION, LOCATION

TARGET • NETWORK • POWER (kW)

World Time

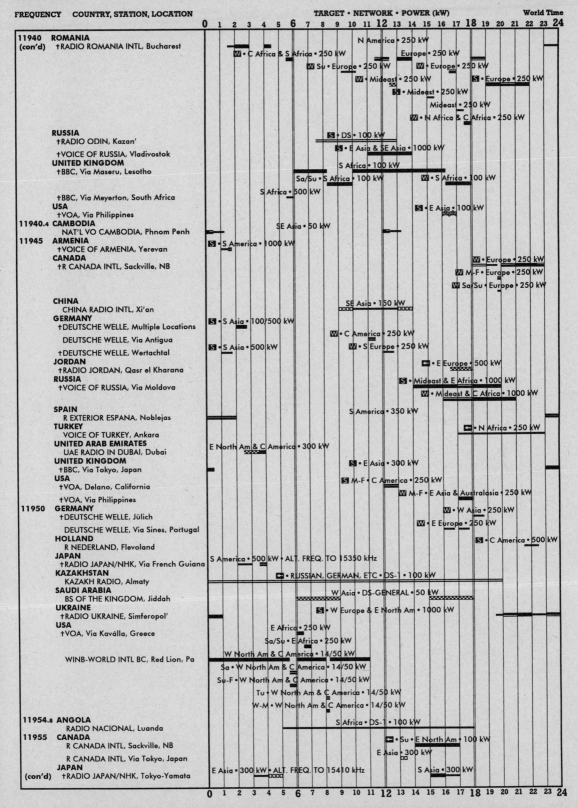

FREQUENCY	COUNTRY, STATION, LOCATION	TARGET • NETWORK • POWER (kW)
11940 (con'd)	**ROMANIA** †RADIO ROMANIA INTL, Bucharest	N America • 250 kW
		W • C Africa & S Africa • 250 kW / Europe • 250 kW
		W Su • Europe • 250 kW / W • Europe • 250 kW
		W • Mideast • 250 kW / S • Europe • 250 kW
		S • Mideast • 250 kW
		Mideast • 250 kW
		W • N Africa & C Africa • 250 kW
	RUSSIA †RADIO ODIN, Kazan'	S • DS • 100 kW
	†VOICE OF RUSSIA, Vladivostok	S • E Asia & SE Asia • 1000 kW
	UNITED KINGDOM †BBC, Via Maseru, Lesotho	S Africa • 100 kW
		Sa/Su • S Africa • 100 kW / W • S Africa • 100 kW
	†BBC, Via Meyerton, South Africa	S Africa • 500 kW
	USA †VOA, Via Philippines	S • E Asia • 100 kW
11940.4	**CAMBODIA** NAT'L VO CAMBODIA, Phnom Penh	SE Asia • 50 kW
11945	**ARMENIA** †VOICE OF ARMENIA, Yerevan	S • S America • 1000 kW
	CANADA †R CANADA INTL, Sackville, NB	W • Europe • 250 kW
		W • M-F • Europe • 250 kW
		W Sa/Su • Europe • 250 kW
	CHINA CHINA RADIO INTL, Xi'an	SE Asia • 150 kW
	GERMANY †DEUTSCHE WELLE, Multiple Locations	S • S Asia • 100/500 kW
	DEUTSCHE WELLE, Via Antigua	W • C America • 250 kW
	†DEUTSCHE WELLE, Wertachtal	S • S Asia • 500 kW / W • S Europe • 250 kW
	JORDAN †RADIO JORDAN, Qasr el Kharana	• E Europe • 500 kW
	RUSSIA †VOICE OF RUSSIA, Via Moldova	S • Mideast & E Africa • 1000 kW
		W • Mideast & C Africa • 1000 kW
	SPAIN R EXTERIOR ESPANA, Noblejas	S America • 350 kW
	TURKEY VOICE OF TURKEY, Ankara	• N Africa • 250 kW
	UNITED ARAB EMIRATES UAE RADIO IN DUBAI, Dubai	E North Am & C America • 300 kW
	UNITED KINGDOM †BBC, Via Tokyo, Japan	S • E Asia • 300 kW
	USA †VOA, Delano, California	S M-F • C America • 250 kW
	†VOA, Via Philippines	W M-F • E Asia & Australasia • 250 kW
11950	**GERMANY** †DEUTSCHE WELLE, Jülich	W • W Asia • 250 kW
	DEUTSCHE WELLE, Via Sines, Portugal	W • E Europe • 250 kW
	HOLLAND R NEDERLAND, Flevoland	S • C America • 500 kW
	JAPAN †RADIO JAPAN/NHK, Via French Guiana	S America • 500 kW • ALT. FREQ. TO 15350 kHz
	KAZAKHSTAN KAZAKH RADIO, Almaty	• RUSSIAN, GERMAN, ETC • DS-1 • 100 kW
	SAUDI ARABIA BS OF THE KINGDOM, Jiddah	W Asia • DS-GENERAL • 50 kW
	UKRAINE †RADIO UKRAINE, Simferopol'	S • W Europe & E North Am • 1000 kW
	USA †VOA, Via Kaválla, Greece	E Africa • 250 kW
		Sa/Su • E Africa • 250 kW
	WINB-WORLD INTL BC, Red Lion, Pa	W North Am & C America • 14/50 kW
		Sa • W North Am & C America • 14/50 kW
		Su-F • W North Am & C America • 14/50 kW
		Tu • W North Am & C America • 14/50 kW
		W-M • W North Am & C America • 14/50 kW
11954.8	**ANGOLA** RADIO NACIONAL, Luanda	S Africa • DS-1 • 100 kW
11955	**CANADA** R CANADA INTL, Sackville, NB	• Su • E North Am • 100 kW
	R CANADA INTL, Via Tokyo, Japan	E Asia • 300 kW
	JAPAN (con'd) †RADIO JAPAN/NHK, Tokyo-Yamata	E Asia • 300 kW • ALT. FREQ. TO 15410 kHz / S Asia • 300 kW

ENGLISH ▬▬   ARABIC ∼∼∼   CHINESE □□□   FRENCH ═══   GERMAN ▬▬   RUSSIAN ══   SPANISH ▬▬   OTHER ──

FREQUENCY   COUNTRY, STATION, LOCATION

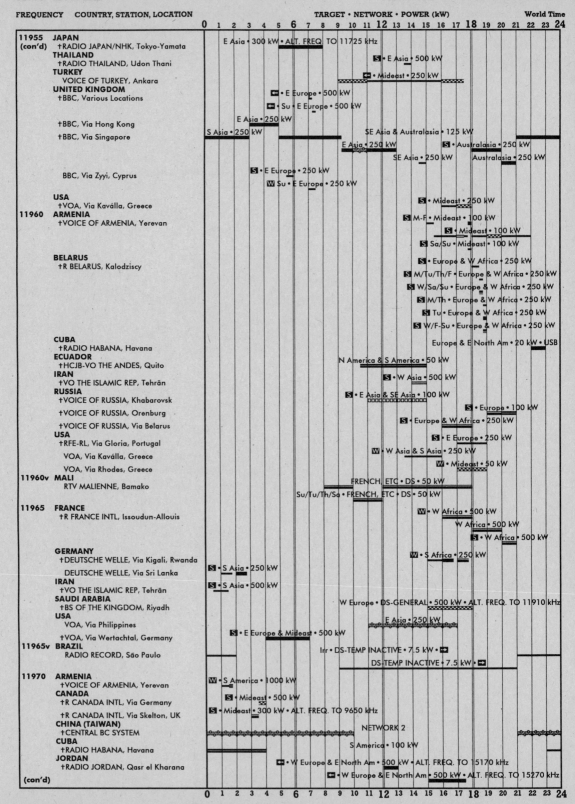

FREQUENCY	COUNTRY, STATION, LOCATION	TARGET • NETWORK • POWER (kW)
11955 (con'd)	**JAPAN** †RADIO JAPAN/NHK, Tokyo-Yamata	E Asia • 300 kW • ALT. FREQ. TO 11725 kHz
	THAILAND †RADIO THAILAND, Udon Thani	S • E Asia • 500 kW
	TURKEY VOICE OF TURKEY, Ankara	• Mideast • 250 kW
	UNITED KINGDOM †BBC, Various Locations	• E Europe • 500 kW / Su • E Europe • 500 kW
	†BBC, Via Hong Kong	E Asia • 250 kW
	†BBC, Via Singapore	S Asia • 250 kW / SE Asia & Australasia • 125 kW / E Asia • 250 kW / S • Australasia • 250 kW / SE Asia • 250 kW / Australasia • 250 kW
	BBC, Via Zyyi, Cyprus	S • E Europe • 250 kW / W Su • E Europe • 250 kW
	USA †VOA, Via Kaválla, Greece	S • Mideast • 250 kW
11960	**ARMENIA** †VOICE OF ARMENIA, Yerevan	S M-F • Mideast • 100 kW / S • Mideast • 100 kW / S Sa/Su • Mideast • 100 kW
	BELARUS †R BELARUS, Kalodziscy	S • Europe & W Africa • 250 kW / S M/Tu/Th/F • Europe & W Africa • 250 kW / S W/Sa/Su • Europe & W Africa • 250 kW / S M/Th • Europe & W Africa • 250 kW / S Tu • Europe & W Africa • 250 kW / S W/F-Su • Europe & W Africa • 250 kW
	CUBA †RADIO HABANA, Havana	Europe & E North Am • 20 kW • USB
	ECUADOR †HCJB-VO THE ANDES, Quito	N America & S America • 50 kW
	IRAN †VO THE ISLAMIC REP, Tehrān	S • W Asia • 500 kW
	RUSSIA †VOICE OF RUSSIA, Khabarovsk	S • E Asia & SE Asia • 100 kW
	†VOICE OF RUSSIA, Orenburg	S • Europe • 100 kW
	†VOICE OF RUSSIA, Via Belarus	S • Europe & W Africa • 250 kW
	USA †RFE-RL, Via Gloria, Portugal	S • E Europe • 250 kW
	VOA, Via Kaválla, Greece	W • W Asia & S Asia • 250 kW
	VOA, Via Rhodes, Greece	W • Mideast • 50 kW
11960v	**MALI** RTV MALIENNE, Bamako	FRENCH, ETC • DS • 50 kW / Su/Tu/Th/Sa • FRENCH, ETC • DS • 50 kW
11965	**FRANCE** †R FRANCE INTL, Issoudun-Allouis	W • W Africa • 500 kW / W Africa • 500 kW / S • W Africa • 500 kW
	GERMANY †DEUTSCHE WELLE, Via Kigali, Rwanda	W • S Africa • 250 kW
	DEUTSCHE WELLE, Via Sri Lanka	S • S Asia • 250 kW
	IRAN †VO THE ISLAMIC REP, Tehrān	S • S Asia • 500 kW
	SAUDI ARABIA †BS OF THE KINGDOM, Riyadh	W Europe • DS-GENERAL • 500 kW • ALT. FREQ. TO 11910 kHz
	USA VOA, Via Philippines	E Asia • 250 kW
	†VOA, Via Wertachtal, Germany	S • E Europe & Mideast • 500 kW
11965v	**BRAZIL** RADIO RECORD, São Paulo	Irr • DS-TEMP INACTIVE • 7.5 kW • / DS-TEMP INACTIVE • 7.5 kW •
11970	**ARMENIA** †VOICE OF ARMENIA, Yerevan	W • S America • 1000 kW
	CANADA †R CANADA INTL, Via Germany	S • Mideast • 500 kW
	†R CANADA INTL, Via Skelton, UK	S • Mideast • 300 kW • ALT. FREQ. TO 9650 kHz
	CHINA (TAIWAN) †CENTRAL BC SYSTEM	NETWORK 2
	CUBA †RADIO HABANA, Havana	S America • 100 kW
	JORDAN †RADIO JORDAN, Qasr el Kharana	• W Europe & E North Am • 500 kW • ALT. FREQ. TO 15170 kHz / • W Europe & E North Am • 500 kW • ALT. FREQ. TO 15270 kHz
(con'd)		

FREQUENCY   COUNTRY, STATION, LOCATION   TARGET • NETWORK • POWER (kW)   World Time

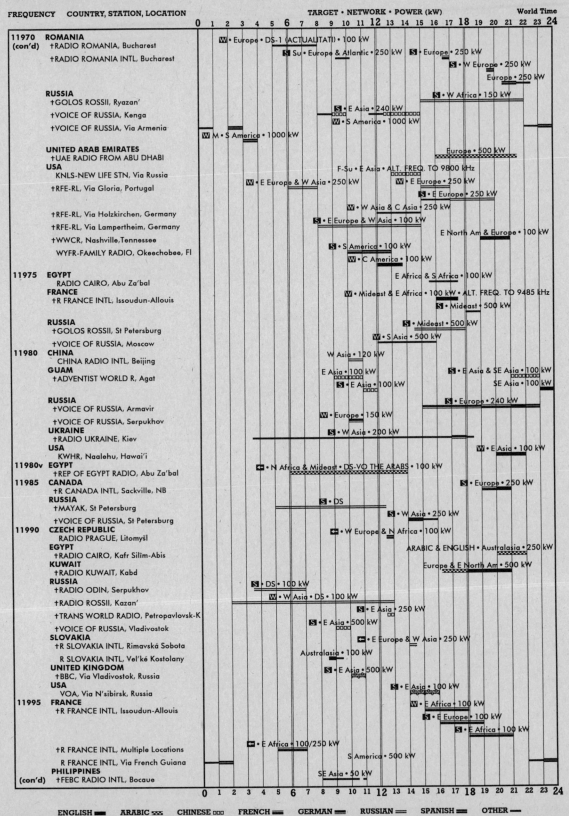

11970	**ROMANIA**	
(con'd)	†RADIO ROMANIA, Bucharest	W • Europe • DS-1 (ACTUALITATI) • 100 kW
	†RADIO ROMANIA INTL, Bucharest	Su • Europe & Atlantic • 250 kW S • Europe • 250 kW
		S • W Europe • 250 kW
		Europe • 250 kW
	RUSSIA	
	†GOLOS ROSSII, Ryazan'	S • W Africa • 150 kW
	†VOICE OF RUSSIA, Kenga	S • E Asia • 240 kW
	†VOICE OF RUSSIA, Via Armenia	W • S America • 1000 kW
		W • M • S America • 1000 kW
	UNITED ARAB EMIRATES	
	†UAE RADIO FROM ABU DHABI	Europe • 500 kW
	USA	
	KNLS-NEW LIFE STN, Via Russia	F-Su • E Asia • ALT. FREQ. TO 9800 kHz
	†RFE-RL, Via Gloria, Portugal	W • E Europe & W Asia • 250 kW W • E Europe • 250 kW
		S • E Europe • 250 kW
	†RFE-RL, Via Holzkirchen, Germany	W • W Asia & C Asia • 250 kW
	†RFE-RL, Via Lampertheim, Germany	S • E Europe & W Asia • 100 kW
	†WWCR, Nashville, Tennessee	E North Am & Europe • 100 kW
	WYFR-FAMILY RADIO, Okeechobee, Fl	S • S America • 100 kW
		W • C America • 100 kW
11975	**EGYPT**	
	RADIO CAIRO, Abu Za'bal	E Africa & S Africa • 100 kW
	FRANCE	
	†R FRANCE INTL, Issoudun-Allouis	W • Mideast & E Africa • 100 kW • ALT. FREQ. TO 9485 kHz
		S • Mideast • 500 kW
	RUSSIA	
	†GOLOS ROSSII, St Petersburg	S • Mideast • 500 kW
	†VOICE OF RUSSIA, Moscow	W • S Asia • 500 kW
11980	**CHINA**	
	CHINA RADIO INTL, Beijing	W Asia • 120 kW
	GUAM	
	†ADVENTIST WORLD R, Agat	E Asia • 100 kW S • E Asia & SE Asia • 100 kW
		S • E Asia • 100 kW SE Asia • 100 kW
	RUSSIA	
	†VOICE OF RUSSIA, Armavir	S • Europe • 240 kW
	†VOICE OF RUSSIA, Serpukhov	W • Europe • 150 kW
	UKRAINE	
	†RADIO UKRAINE, Kiev	S • W Asia • 200 kW
	USA	
	KWHR, Naalehu, Hawai'i	W • E Asia • 100 kW
11980v	**EGYPT**	
	†REP OF EGYPT RADIO, Abu Za'bal	• N Africa & Mideast • DS-VO THE ARABS • 100 kW
11985	**CANADA**	
	†R CANADA INTL, Sackville, NB	S • Europe • 250 kW
	RUSSIA	
	†MAYAK, St Petersburg	S • DS
	†VOICE OF RUSSIA, St Petersburg	S • W Asia • 250 kW
11990	**CZECH REPUBLIC**	
	RADIO PRAGUE, Litomyšl	• W Europe & N Africa • 100 kW
	EGYPT	
	†RADIO CAIRO, Kafr Silim-Abis	ARABIC & ENGLISH • Australasia • 250 kW
	KUWAIT	
	†RADIO KUWAIT, Kabd	Europe & E North Am • 500 kW
	RUSSIA	
	†RADIO ODIN, Serpukhov	S • DS • 100 kW
	†RADIO ROSSII, Kazan'	W • W Asia • DS • 100 kW
	†TRANS WORLD RADIO, Petropavlovsk-K	S • E Asia • 250 kW
	†VOICE OF RUSSIA, Vladivostok	S • E Asia • 500 kW
	SLOVAKIA	
	†R SLOVAKIA INTL, Rimavská Sobota	• E Europe & W Asia • 250 kW
	R SLOVAKIA INTL, Vel'ké Kostolany	Australasia • 100 kW
	UNITED KINGDOM	
	†BBC, Via Vladivostok, Russia	S • E Asia • 500 kW
	USA	
	VOA, Via N'sibirsk, Russia	S • E Asia • 100 kW
11995	**FRANCE**	
	†R FRANCE INTL, Issoudun-Allouis	W • E Africa • 100 kW
		S • E Europe • 100 kW
		S • E Africa • 100 kW
	†R FRANCE INTL, Multiple Locations	• E Africa • 100/250 kW
	R FRANCE INTL, Via French Guiana	S America • 500 kW
	PHILIPPINES	
(con'd)	†FEBC RADIO INTL, Bocaue	SE Asia • 50 kW

ENGLISH ▬▬ **ARABIC** ⌇⌇⌇ **CHINESE** ▫▫▫ **FRENCH** ▬▬ **GERMAN** ▬▬ **RUSSIAN** ═══ **SPANISH** ▬▬ **OTHER** ▬▬

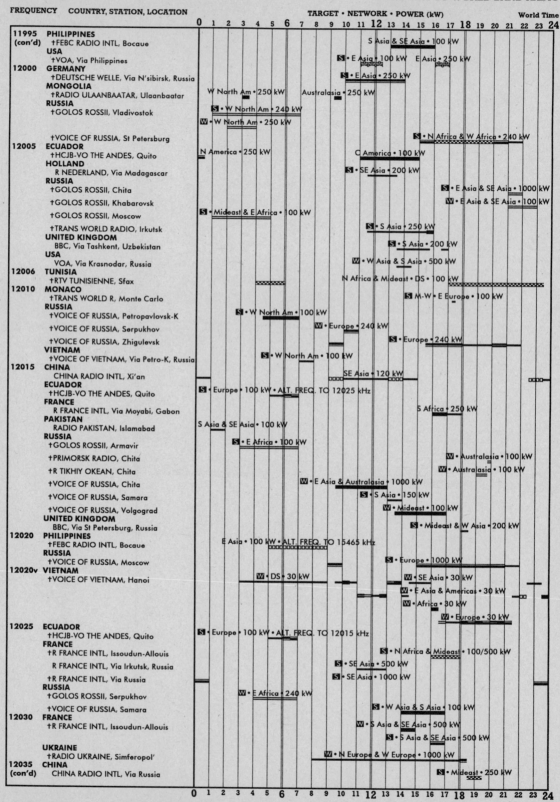

FREQUENCY   COUNTRY, STATION, LOCATION   TARGET • NETWORK • POWER (kW)   World Time

		0 ... 12 ... 18 ... 24

11995 **PHILIPPINES**
(con'd)   †FEBC RADIO INTL, Bocaue — S Asia & SE Asia • 100 kW
USA
  †VOA, Via Philippines — Ⓢ E Asia • 100 kW   E Asia • 250 kW
12000 **GERMANY**
  †DEUTSCHE WELLE, Via N'sibirsk, Russia — Ⓢ • E Asia • 250 kW
MONGOLIA
  †RADIO ULAANBAATAR, Ulaanbaatar — W North Am • 250 kW   Australasia • 250 kW
RUSSIA
  †GOLOS ROSSII, Vladivostok — Ⓢ • W North Am • 240 kW
                                   Ⓦ • W North Am • 250 kW

  †VOICE OF RUSSIA, St Petersburg — Ⓢ • N Africa & W Africa • 240 kW
12005 **ECUADOR**
  †HCJB-VO THE ANDES, Quito — N America • 250 kW   C America • 100 kW
HOLLAND
  R NEDERLAND, Via Madagascar — Ⓢ • SE Asia • 200 kW
RUSSIA
  †GOLOS ROSSII, Chita — Ⓢ • E Asia & SE Asia • 1000 kW
  †GOLOS ROSSII, Khabarovsk — Ⓦ • E Asia & SE Asia • 100 kW
  †GOLOS ROSSII, Moscow — Ⓢ • Mideast & E Africa • 100 kW
  †TRANS WORLD RADIO, Irkutsk — Ⓢ • S Asia • 250 kW
UNITED KINGDOM
  BBC, Via Tashkent, Uzbekistan — Ⓢ • S Asia • 200 kW
USA
  VOA, Via Krasnodar, Russia — Ⓦ • W Asia & S Asia • 500 kW
12006 **TUNISIA**
  †RTV TUNISIENNE, Sfax — N Africa & Mideast • DS • 100 kW
12010 **MONACO**
  †TRANS WORLD R, Monte Carlo — Ⓢ M-W • E Europe • 100 kW
RUSSIA
  †VOICE OF RUSSIA, Petropavlovsk-K — Ⓢ • W North Am • 100 kW
  †VOICE OF RUSSIA, Serpukhov — Ⓦ • Europe • 240 kW
  †VOICE OF RUSSIA, Zhigulevsk — Ⓢ • Europe • 240 kW
VIETNAM
  †VOICE OF VIETNAM, Via Petro-K, Russia — Ⓢ • W North Am • 100 kW
12015 **CHINA**
  CHINA RADIO INTL, Xi'an — SE Asia • 120 kW
ECUADOR
  †HCJB-VO THE ANDES, Quito — Ⓢ • Europe • 100 kW • ALT. FREQ. TO 12025 kHz
FRANCE
  R FRANCE INTL, Via Moyabi, Gabon — S Africa • 250 kW
PAKISTAN
  RADIO PAKISTAN, Islamabad — S Asia & SE Asia • 100 kW
RUSSIA
  †GOLOS ROSSII, Armavir — Ⓢ • E Africa • 100 kW
  †PRIMORSK RADIO, Chita — Ⓦ • Australasia • 100 kW
  †R TIKHIY OKEAN, Chita — Ⓦ • Australasia • 100 kW
  †VOICE OF RUSSIA, Chita — Ⓦ • E Asia & Australasia • 1000 kW
  †VOICE OF RUSSIA, Samara — Ⓢ • S Asia • 150 kW
  †VOICE OF RUSSIA, Volgograd — Ⓦ • Mideast • 100 kW
UNITED KINGDOM
  BBC, Via St Petersburg, Russia — Ⓢ • Mideast & W Asia • 200 kW
12020 **PHILIPPINES**
  †FEBC RADIO INTL, Bocaue — E Asia • 100 kW • ALT. FREQ. TO 15465 kHz
RUSSIA
  †VOICE OF RUSSIA, Moscow — Ⓢ • Europe • 1000 kW
12020v **VIETNAM**
  †VOICE OF VIETNAM, Hanoi — Ⓦ • DS • 30 kW
                              Ⓦ • SE Asia • 30 kW
                              Ⓦ • E Asia & Americas • 30 kW
                              Ⓦ • Africa • 30 kW
                              Ⓦ • Europe • 30 kW
12025 **ECUADOR**
  †HCJB-VO THE ANDES, Quito — Ⓢ • Europe • 100 kW • ALT. FREQ. TO 12015 kHz
FRANCE
  †R FRANCE INTL, Issoudun-Allouis — Ⓢ • N Africa & Mideast • 100/500 kW
  R FRANCE INTL, Via Irkutsk, Russia — Ⓢ • SE Asia • 500 kW
  †R FRANCE INTL, Via Russia — Ⓢ • SE Asia • 1000 kW
RUSSIA
  †GOLOS ROSSII, Serpukhov — Ⓦ • E Africa • 240 kW
  †VOICE OF RUSSIA, Samara — Ⓢ • W Asia & S Asia • 100 kW
12030 **FRANCE**
  †R FRANCE INTL, Issoudun-Allouis — Ⓦ • S Asia & SE Asia • 500 kW
                                      Ⓢ • S Asia & SE Asia • 500 kW
UKRAINE
  †RADIO UKRAINE, Simferopol' — Ⓦ • N Europe & W Europe • 1000 kW
12035 **CHINA**
(con'd)   CHINA RADIO INTL, Via Russia — Ⓢ • Mideast • 250 kW

		0 ... 12 ... 18 ... 24

SEASONAL Ⓢ OR Ⓦ   1-HR TIMESHIFT MIDYEAR ⮜ OR ⮞   JAMMING / OR ∧   EARLIEST HEARD ◁   LATEST HEARD ▷   NEW FOR 1996 †

FREQUENCY   COUNTRY, STATION, LOCATION

TARGET • NETWORK • POWER (kW)

World Time

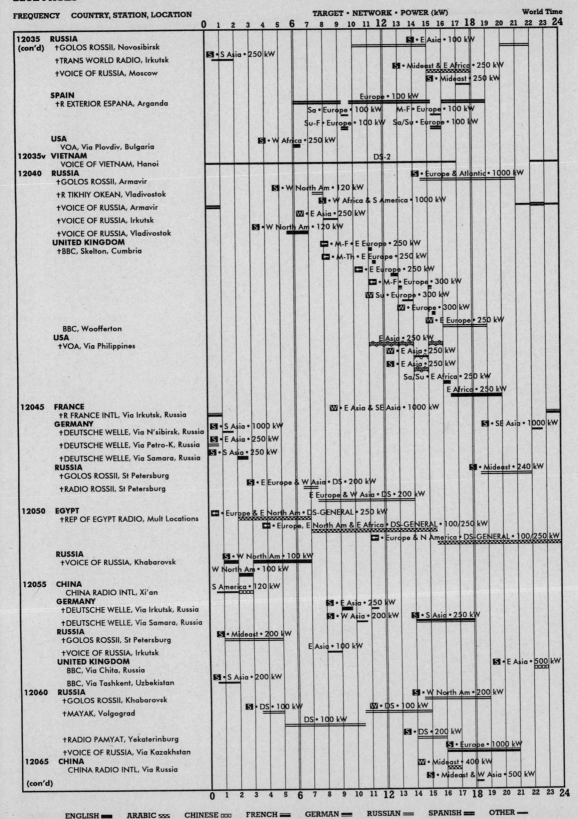

Frequency	Country, Station, Location	Broadcast Details
12035 (con'd)	**RUSSIA**	
	†GOLOS ROSSII, Novosibirsk	S • E Asia • 100 kW
	†TRANS WORLD RADIO, Irkutsk	S • S Asia • 250 kW
	†VOICE OF RUSSIA, Moscow	S • Mideast & E Africa • 250 kW
		S • Mideast • 250 kW
	SPAIN	
	†R EXTERIOR ESPANA, Arganda	Europe • 100 kW
		Sa • Europe • 100 kW M-F • Europe • 100 kW
		Su-F • Europe • 100 kW Sa/Su • Europe • 100 kW
	USA	
	VOA, Via Plovdiv, Bulgaria	S • W Africa • 250 kW
12035v	**VIETNAM**	DS-2
	VOICE OF VIETNAM, Hanoi	
12040	**RUSSIA**	
	†GOLOS ROSSII, Armavir	S • Europe & Atlantic • 1000 kW
	†R TIKHIY OKEAN, Vladivostok	S • W North Am • 120 kW
	†VOICE OF RUSSIA, Armavir	S • W Africa & S America • 1000 kW
	†VOICE OF RUSSIA, Irkutsk	W • E Asia • 250 kW
	†VOICE OF RUSSIA, Vladivostok	S • W North Am • 120 kW
	UNITED KINGDOM	
	†BBC, Skelton, Cumbria	M-F • E Europe • 250 kW
		M-Th • E Europe • 250 kW
		E Europe • 250 kW
		M-F • Europe • 300 kW
		W Su • Europe • 300 kW
		W • Europe • 300 kW
		W • E Europe • 250 kW
	BBC, Woofferton	E Asia • 250 kW
	USA	W • E Asia • 250 kW
	†VOA, Via Philippines	S • E Asia • 250 kW
		Sa/Su • E Africa • 250 kW
		E Africa • 250 kW
12045	**FRANCE**	
	†R FRANCE INTL, Via Irkutsk, Russia	W • E Asia & SE Asia • 1000 kW
	GERMANY	
	†DEUTSCHE WELLE, Via N'sibirsk, Russia	S • S Asia • 1000 kW S • SE Asia • 1000 kW
	†DEUTSCHE WELLE, Via Petro-K, Russia	S • E Asia • 250 kW
	†DEUTSCHE WELLE, Via Samara, Russia	S • S Asia • 250 kW
	RUSSIA	S • Mideast • 240 kW
	†GOLOS ROSSII, St Petersburg	S • E Europe & W Asia • DS • 200 kW
	†RADIO ROSSII, St Petersburg	E Europe & W Asia • DS • 200 kW
12050	**EGYPT**	
	†REP OF EGYPT RADIO, Mult Locations	E • Europe & E North Am • DS-GENERAL • 250 kW
		E • Europe, E North Am & E Africa • DS-GENERAL • 100/250 kW
		E • Europe & N America • DS-GENERAL • 100/250 kW
	RUSSIA	
	†VOICE OF RUSSIA, Khabarovsk	S • W North Am • 100 kW
		W North Am • 100 kW
12055	**CHINA**	
	CHINA RADIO INTL, Xi'an	S America • 120 kW
	GERMANY	
	†DEUTSCHE WELLE, Via Irkutsk, Russia	S • E Asia • 250 kW
	†DEUTSCHE WELLE, Via Samara, Russia	S • W Asia • 200 kW S • S Asia • 250 kW
	RUSSIA	
	†GOLOS ROSSII, St Petersburg	S • Mideast • 200 kW
	†VOICE OF RUSSIA, Irkutsk	E Asia • 100 kW
	UNITED KINGDOM	
	BBC, Via Chita, Russia	S • E Asia • 500 kW
	BBC, Via Tashkent, Uzbekistan	S • S Asia • 200 kW
12060	**RUSSIA**	
	†GOLOS ROSSII, Khabarovsk	S • W North Am • 200 kW
	†MAYAK, Volgograd	S • DS • 100 kW W • DS • 100 kW
		DS • 100 kW
	†RADIO PAMYAT, Yekaterinburg	S • DS • 200 kW
	†VOICE OF RUSSIA, Via Kazakhstan	S • Europe • 1000 kW
12065	**CHINA**	
	CHINA RADIO INTL, Via Russia	W • Mideast • 400 kW
		S • Mideast & W Asia • 500 kW
(con'd)		

ENGLISH ▬ ARABIC ≋ CHINESE ▭▭▭ FRENCH ▬ GERMAN ▬ RUSSIAN ═ SPANISH ▬ OTHER ▬

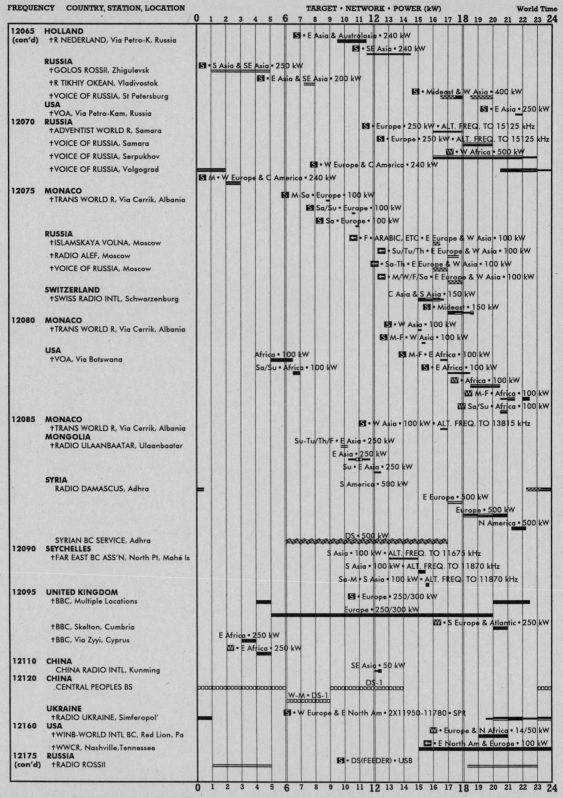

FREQUENCY	COUNTRY, STATION, LOCATION	TARGET • NETWORK • POWER (kW)
12065 (con'd)	**HOLLAND**	
	†R NEDERLAND, Via Petro-K, Russia	[S] • E Asia & Australasia • 240 kW
		[S] • SE Asia • 240 kW
	RUSSIA	
	†GOLOS ROSSII, Zhigulevsk	[S] • S Asia & SE Asia • 250 kW
	†R TIKHIY OKEAN, Vladivostok	[S] • E Asia & SE Asia • 200 kW
	†VOICE OF RUSSIA, St Petersburg	[S] • Mideast & W Asia • 400 kW
	USA	
	†VOA, Via Petro-Kam, Russia	[S] • E Asia • 250 kW
12070	**RUSSIA**	
	†ADVENTIST WORLD R, Samara	[S] • Europe • 250 kW • ALT. FREQ. TO 15125 kHz
	†VOICE OF RUSSIA, Samara	[S] • Europe • 250 kW • ALT. FREQ. TO 15125 kHz
	†VOICE OF RUSSIA, Serpukhov	[W] • W Africa • 500 kW
	†VOICE OF RUSSIA, Volgograd	[S] • W Europe & C America • 240 kW
		[S] M • W Europe & C America • 240 kW
12075	**MONACO**	
	†TRANS WORLD R, Via Cerrik, Albania	[S] M-Sa • Europe • 100 kW
		[S] Sa/Su • Europe • 100 kW
		[S] Sa • Europe • 100 kW
	RUSSIA	
	†ISLAMSKAYA VOLNA, Moscow	⇦ • F • ARABIC, ETC • E Europe & W Asia • 100 kW
	†RADIO ALEF, Moscow	⇦ • Su/Tu/Th • E Europe & W Asia • 100 kW
	†VOICE OF RUSSIA, Moscow	⇦ • Sa-Th • E Europe & W Asia • 100 kW
		⇦ • M/W/F/Sa • E Europe & W Asia • 100 kW
	SWITZERLAND	
	†SWISS RADIO INTL, Schwarzenburg	C Asia & S Asia • 150 kW
		[S] • Mideast • 150 kW
12080	**MONACO**	
	†TRANS WORLD R, Via Cerrik, Albania	[S] • W Asia • 100 kW
		[S] M-F • W Asia • 100 kW
	USA	
	†VOA, Via Botswana	Africa • 100 kW
		Sa/Su • Africa • 100 kW
		[S] M-F • E Africa • 100 kW
		[S] • E Africa • 100 kW
		[W] • Africa • 100 kW
		[W] M-F • Africa • 100 kW
		[W] Sa/Su • Africa • 100 kW
12085	**MONACO**	
	†TRANS WORLD R, Via Cerrik, Albania	[S] • W Asia • 100 kW • ALT. FREQ. TO 13815 kHz
	MONGOLIA	
	†RADIO ULAANBAATAR, Ulaanbaatar	Su-Tu/Th/F • E Asia • 250 kW
		E Asia • 250 kW
		Su • E Asia • 250 kW
	SYRIA	
	RADIO DAMASCUS, Adhra	S America • 500 kW
		E Europe • 500 kW
		Europe • 500 kW
		N America • 500 kW
	SYRIAN BC SERVICE, Adhra	DS • 500 kW
12090	**SEYCHELLES**	
	†FAR EAST BC ASS'N, North Pt, Mahé Is	S Asia • 100 kW • ALT. FREQ. TO 11675 kHz
		S Asia • 100 kW • ALT. FREQ. TO 11870 kHz
		Sa-M • S Asia • 100 kW • ALT. FREQ. TO 11870 kHz
12095	**UNITED KINGDOM**	
	†BBC, Multiple Locations	[S] • Europe • 250/300 kW
		Europe • 250/300 kW
	†BBC, Skelton, Cumbria	[W] • S Europe & Atlantic • 250 kW
	†BBC, Via Zyyi, Cyprus	E Africa • 250 kW
		[W] • E Africa • 250 kW
12110	**CHINA**	
	CHINA RADIO INTL, Kunming	SE Asia • 50 kW
12120	**CHINA**	
	CENTRAL PEOPLES BS	DS-1
		W-M • DS-1
	UKRAINE	
	†RADIO UKRAINE, Simferopol'	[S] • W Europe & E North Am • 2X11950-11780 • SPR
12160	**USA**	
	†WINB-WORLD INTL BC, Red Lion, Pa	[W] • Europe & N Africa • 14/50 kW
	†WWCR, Nashville, Tennessee	⇦ • E North Am & Europe • 100 kW
12175 (con'd)	**RUSSIA**	
	†RADIO ROSSII	[S] • DS(FEEDER) • USB

World Time: 0 1 2 3 4 5 6 7 8 9 10 11 12 13 14 15 16 17 18 19 20 21 22 23 24

FREQUENCY　　COUNTRY, STATION, LOCATION　　　　　　　TARGET • NETWORK • POWER (kW)　　　　World Time

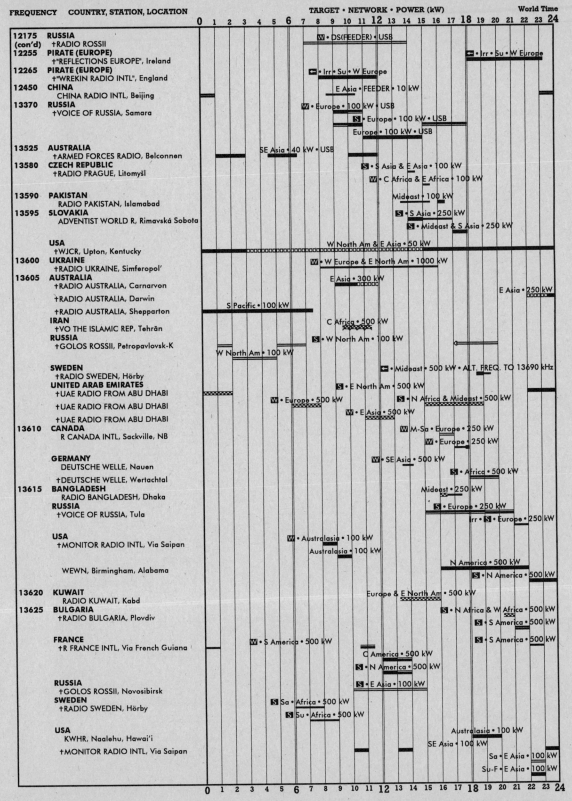

Frequency	Country, Station, Location	Details
12175 (con'd)	**RUSSIA** †RADIO ROSSII	W • DS(FEEDER) • USB
12255	**PIRATE (EUROPE)** †"REFLECTIONS EUROPE", Ireland	Irr • Su • W Europe
12265	**PIRATE (EUROPE)** †"WREKIN RADIO INTL", England	Irr • Su • W Europe
12450	**CHINA** CHINA RADIO INTL, Beijing	E Asia • FEEDER • 10 kW
13370	**RUSSIA** †VOICE OF RUSSIA, Samara	W • Europe • 100 kW • USB; S • Europe • 100 kW • USB; Europe • 100 kW • USB
13525	**AUSTRALIA** †ARMED FORCES RADIO, Belconnen	SE Asia • 40 kW • USB
13580	**CZECH REPUBLIC** †RADIO PRAGUE, Litomyšl	S • S Asia & E Asia • 100 kW; W • C Africa & E Africa • 100 kW
13590	**PAKISTAN** RADIO PAKISTAN, Islamabad	Mideast • 100 kW
13595	**SLOVAKIA** ADVENTIST WORLD R, Rimavská Sobota	S • S Asia • 250 kW; S • Mideast & S Asia • 250 kW
	USA †WJCR, Upton, Kentucky	W North Am & E Asia • 50 kW
13600	**UKRAINE** †RADIO UKRAINE, Simferopol'	W • W Europe & E North Am • 1000 kW
13605	**AUSTRALIA** †RADIO AUSTRALIA, Carnarvon	E Asia • 300 kW; E Asia • 250 kW
	†RADIO AUSTRALIA, Darwin	
	†RADIO AUSTRALIA, Shepparton	S Pacific • 100 kW
	IRAN †VO THE ISLAMIC REP, Tehrān	C Africa • 500 kW
	RUSSIA †GOLOS ROSSII, Petropavlovsk-K	S • W North Am • 100 kW; W North Am • 100 kW
	SWEDEN †RADIO SWEDEN, Hörby	Mideast • 500 kW • ALT. FREQ. TO 13690 kHz
	UNITED ARAB EMIRATES †UAE RADIO FROM ABU DHABI	S • E North Am • 500 kW
	†UAE RADIO FROM ABU DHABI	W • Europe • 500 kW; S • N Africa & Mideast • 500 kW
	†UAE RADIO FROM ABU DHABI	W • E Asia • 500 kW
13610	**CANADA** R CANADA INTL, Sackville, NB	W M-Sa • Europe • 250 kW; W • Europe • 250 kW
	GERMANY DEUTSCHE WELLE, Nauen	W • SE Asia • 500 kW; S • Africa • 500 kW
	†DEUTSCHE WELLE, Wertachtal	
13615	**BANGLADESH** RADIO BANGLADESH, Dhaka	Mideast • 250 kW
	RUSSIA †VOICE OF RUSSIA, Tula	S • Europe • 250 kW; Irr • S • Europe • 250 kW
	USA †MONITOR RADIO INTL, Via Saipan	W • Australasia • 100 kW; Australasia • 100 kW
	WEWN, Birmingham, Alabama	N America • 500 kW; S • N America • 500 kW
13620	**KUWAIT** RADIO KUWAIT, Kabd	Europe & E North Am • 500 kW
13625	**BULGARIA** †RADIO BULGARIA, Plovdiv	S • N Africa & W Africa • 500 kW; S • S America • 500 kW; S • S America • 500 kW
	FRANCE †R FRANCE INTL, Via French Guiana	W • S America • 500 kW; C America • 500 kW; S • N America • 500 kW
	RUSSIA †GOLOS ROSSII, Novosibirsk	S • E Asia • 100 kW
	SWEDEN †RADIO SWEDEN, Hörby	Sa • Africa • 500 kW; Su • Africa • 500 kW
	USA KWHR, Naalehu, Hawai'i	Australasia • 100 kW; SE Asia • 100 kW
	†MONITOR RADIO INTL, Via Saipan	Sa • E Asia • 100 kW; Su-F • E Asia • 100 kW

ENGLISH ▬　ARABIC ≋　CHINESE ▯▯▯　FRENCH ▭▭　GERMAN ▬▬　RUSSIAN ═　SPANISH ▬▬　OTHER ▬

FREQUENCY   COUNTRY, STATION, LOCATION

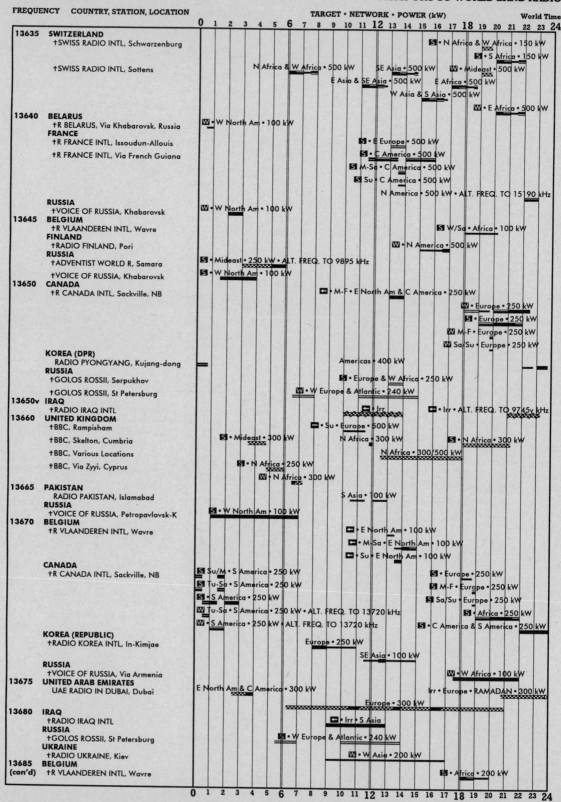

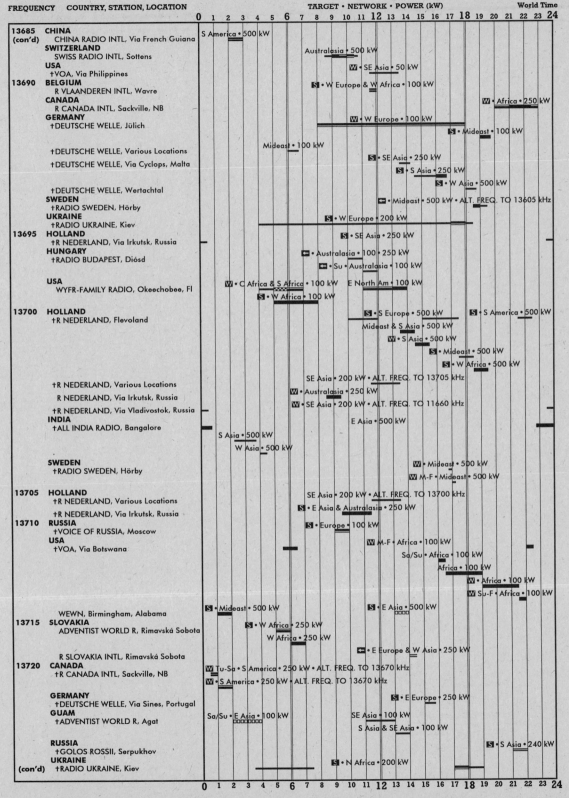

FREQUENCY　　COUNTRY, STATION, LOCATION　　　　　　TARGET • NETWORK • POWER (kW)　　　　World Time

Frequency	Country, Station, Location	Target • Network • Power
13685 (con'd)	**CHINA** CHINA RADIO INTL, Via French Guiana	S America • 500 kW
	SWITZERLAND SWISS RADIO INTL, Sottens	Australasia • 500 kW
	USA †VOA, Via Philippines	W • SE Asia • 50 kW
13690	**BELGIUM** R VLAANDEREN INTL, Wavre	S • W Europe & W Africa • 100 kW
	CANADA R CANADA INTL, Sackville, NB	W • Africa • 250 kW
	GERMANY †DEUTSCHE WELLE, Jülich	W • W Europe • 100 kW
		S • Mideast • 100 kW
	†DEUTSCHE WELLE, Various Locations	Mideast • 100 kW
	†DEUTSCHE WELLE, Via Cyclops, Malta	S • SE Asia • 250 kW
		S • S Asia • 250 kW
	†DEUTSCHE WELLE, Wertachtal	W • W Asia • 500 kW
	SWEDEN †RADIO SWEDEN, Hörby	Mideast • 500 kW • ALT. FREQ. TO 13605 kHz
	UKRAINE †RADIO UKRAINE, Kiev	S • W Europe • 200 kW
13695	**HOLLAND** †R NEDERLAND, Via Irkutsk, Russia	S • SE Asia • 250 kW
	HUNGARY †RADIO BUDAPEST, Diósd	Australasia • 100 • 250 kW
		Su • Australasia • 100 kW
	USA WYFR–FAMILY RADIO, Okeechobee, Fl	W • C Africa & S Africa • 100 kW E North Am • 100 kW
		S • W Africa • 100 kW
13700	**HOLLAND** †R NEDERLAND, Flevoland	S • S Europe • 500 kW S • S America • 500 kW
		Mideast & S Asia • 500 kW
		W • S Asia • 500 kW
		S • Mideast • 500 kW
		S • W Africa • 500 kW
	†R NEDERLAND, Various Locations	SE Asia • 200 kW • ALT. FREQ. TO 13705 kHz
	R NEDERLAND, Via Irkutsk, Russia	W • Australasia • 250 kW
	†R NEDERLAND, Via Vladivostok, Russia	W • SE Asia • 200 kW • ALT. FREQ. TO 11660 kHz
	INDIA †ALL INDIA RADIO, Bangalore	E Asia • 500 kW
		S Asia • 500 kW
		W Asia • 500 kW
	SWEDEN †RADIO SWEDEN, Hörby	W • Mideast • 500 kW
		M-F • Mideast • 500 kW
13705	**HOLLAND** †R NEDERLAND, Various Locations	SE Asia • 200 kW • ALT. FREQ. TO 13700 kHz
	†R NEDERLAND, Via Irkutsk, Russia	S • E Asia & Australasia • 250 kW
13710	**RUSSIA** †VOICE OF RUSSIA, Moscow	S • Europe • 100 kW
	USA †VOA, Via Botswana	W • M-F • Africa • 100 kW
		Sa/Su • Africa • 100 kW
		Africa • 100 kW
		W • Africa • 100 kW
		W • Su-F • Africa • 100 kW
	WEWN, Birmingham, Alabama	S • Mideast • 500 kW S • E Asia • 500 kW
13715	**SLOVAKIA** ADVENTIST WORLD R, Rimavská Sobota	S • W Africa • 250 kW
		W Africa • 250 kW
	R SLOVAKIA INTL, Rimavská Sobota	E Europe & W Asia • 250 kW
13720	**CANADA** †R CANADA INTL, Sackville, NB	W • Tu-Sa • S America • 250 kW • ALT. FREQ. TO 13670 kHz
		W • S America • 250 kW • ALT. FREQ. TO 13670 kHz
	GERMANY †DEUTSCHE WELLE, Via Sines, Portugal	S • E Europe • 250 kW
	GUAM †ADVENTIST WORLD R, Agat	Sa/Su • E Asia • 100 kW SE Asia • 100 kW
		S Asia & SE Asia • 100 kW
	RUSSIA †GOLOS ROSSII, Serpukhov	S • S Asia • 240 kW
	UKRAINE	S • N Africa • 200 kW
(con'd)	†RADIO UKRAINE, Kiev	

ENGLISH ▬　ARABIC ▨　CHINESE ▢▢▢　FRENCH ▭▭　GERMAN ▬▬　RUSSIAN ══　SPANISH ▭▭　OTHER ▬

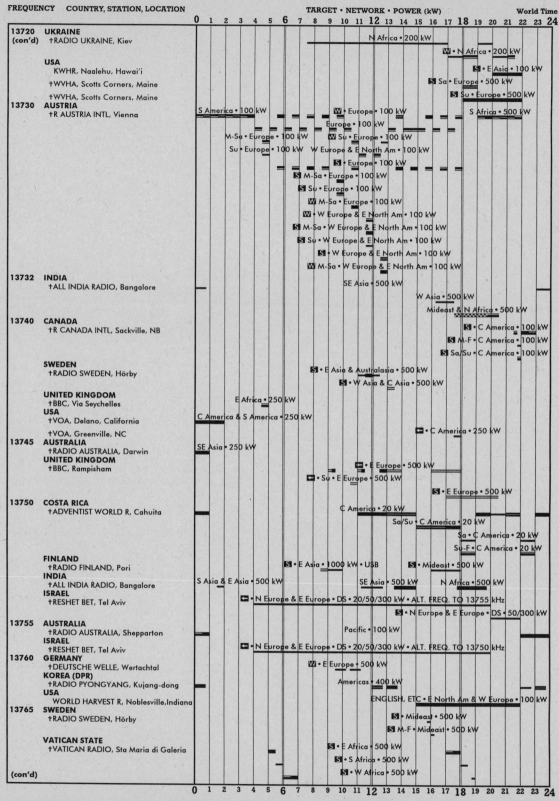

FREQUENCY   COUNTRY, STATION, LOCATION

TARGET • NETWORK • POWER (kW)   World Time

13720 UKRAINE
(con'd) †RADIO UKRAINE, Kiev

       USA
         KWHR, Naalehu, Hawai'i
         †WVHA, Scotts Corners, Maine
         †WVHA, Scotts Corners, Maine
13730 AUSTRIA
         †R AUSTRIA INTL, Vienna

13732 INDIA
         †ALL INDIA RADIO, Bangalore

13740 CANADA
         †R CANADA INTL, Sackville, NB

       SWEDEN
         †RADIO SWEDEN, Hörby

       UNITED KINGDOM
         †BBC, Via Seychelles
       USA
         †VOA, Delano, California
         †VOA, Greenville, NC
13745 AUSTRALIA
         †RADIO AUSTRALIA, Darwin
       UNITED KINGDOM
         †BBC, Rampisham

13750 COSTA RICA
         †ADVENTIST WORLD R, Cahuita

       FINLAND
         †RADIO FINLAND, Pori
       INDIA
         †ALL INDIA RADIO, Bangalore
       ISRAEL
         †RESHET BET, Tel Aviv

13755 AUSTRALIA
         †RADIO AUSTRALIA, Shepparton
       ISRAEL
         †RESHET BET, Tel Aviv
13760 GERMANY
         †DEUTSCHE WELLE, Wertachtal
       KOREA (DPR)
         †RADIO PYONGYANG, Kujang-dong
       USA
         WORLD HARVEST R, Noblesville, Indiana
13765 SWEDEN
         †RADIO SWEDEN, Hörby

       VATICAN STATE
         †VATICAN RADIO, Sta Maria di Galeria

(con'd)

FREQUENCY   COUNTRY, STATION, LOCATION

TARGET • NETWORK • POWER (kW)   World Time

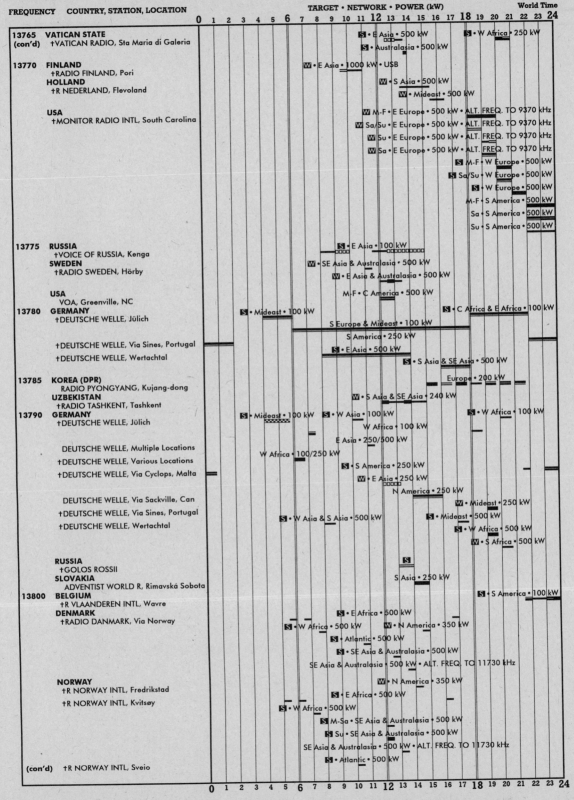

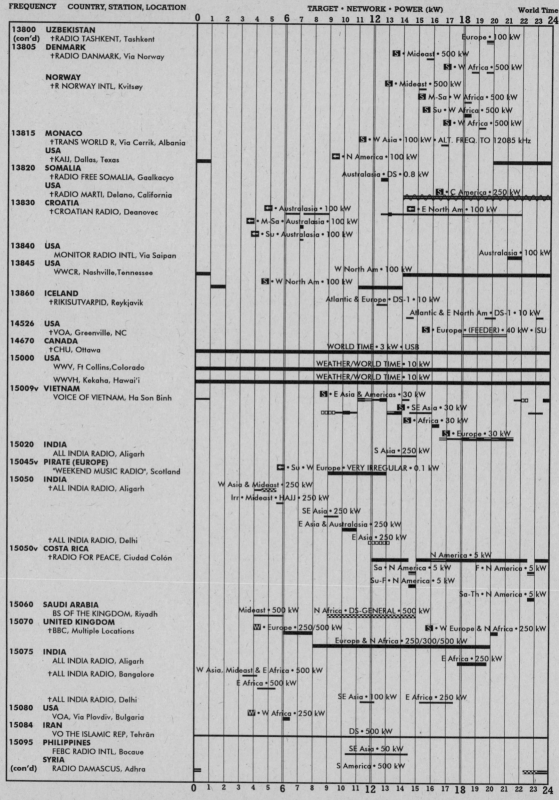

FREQUENCY   COUNTRY, STATION, LOCATION   TARGET • NETWORK • POWER (kW)   World Time

13800 UZBEKISTAN
(con'd) †RADIO TASHKENT, Tashkent   Europe • 100 kW
13805 DENMARK
         †RADIO DANMARK, Via Norway   S • Mideast • 500 kW
                                                              S • W Africa • 500 kW
       NORWAY
         †R NORWAY INTL, Kvitsøy   S • Mideast • 500 kW
                                                        S • M-Sa • W Africa • 500 kW
                                                        S • Su • W Africa • 500 kW
                                                              S • W Africa • 500 kW
13815 MONACO
         †TRANS WORLD R, Via Cerrik, Albania   S • W Asia • 100 kW • ALT. FREQ. TO 12085 kHz
       USA
         †KAIJ, Dallas, Texas   ⇔ • N America • 100 kW
13820 SOMALIA
         †RADIO FREE SOMALIA, Gaalkacyo   Australasia • DS • 0.8 kW
       USA
         †RADIO MARTI, Delano, California   S • C America • 250 kW
13830 CROATIA
         †CROATIAN RADIO, Deanovec   ⇔ • Australasia • 100 kW   ⇔ • E North Am • 100 kW
                                                        ⇔ • M-Sa • Australasia • 100 kW
                                                        ⇔ • Su • Australasia • 100 kW
13840 USA
         MONITOR RADIO INTL, Via Saipan   Australasia • 100 kW
13845 USA
         WWCR, Nashville, Tennessee   W North Am • 100 kW
                                                        S • W North Am • 100 kW
13860 ICELAND
         †RIKISUTVARPID, Reykjavik   Atlantic & Europe • DS-1 • 10 kW
                                                              Atlantic & E North Am • DS-1 • 10 kW
14526 USA
         †VOA, Greenville, NC   S • Europe • (FEEDER) • 40 kW • SU
14670 CANADA
         †CHU, Ottawa   WORLD TIME • 3 kW • USB
15000 USA
         WWV, Ft Collins, Colorado   WEATHER/WORLD TIME • 10 kW
         WWVH, Kekaha, Hawai'i   WEATHER/WORLD TIME • 10 kW
15009v VIETNAM
         VOICE OF VIETNAM, Ha Son Binh   S • E Asia & Americas • 30 kW
                                                        S • SE Asia • 30 kW
                                                        S • Africa • 30 kW
                                                              S • Europe • 30 kW
15020 INDIA
         ALL INDIA RADIO, Aligarh   S Asia • 250 kW
15045v PIRATE (EUROPE)
         "WEEKEND MUSIC RADIO", Scotland   ⇔ • Su • W Europe • VERY IRREGULAR • 0.1 kW
15050 INDIA
         †ALL INDIA RADIO, Aligarh   W Asia & Mideast • 250 kW
                                                        Irr • Mideast • HAJJ • 250 kW
                                                        SE Asia • 250 kW
                                                        E Asia & Australasia • 250 kW
                                                        E Asia • 250 kW
         †ALL INDIA RADIO, Delhi
15050v COSTA RICA
         †RADIO FOR PEACE, Ciudad Colón   N America • 5 kW
                                                        Sa • N America • 5 kW   F • N America • 5 kW
                                                        Su-F • N America • 5 kW
                                                              Sa-Th • N America • 5 kW
15060 SAUDI ARABIA
         BS OF THE KINGDOM, Riyadh   Mideast • 500 kW   N Africa • DS-GENERAL • 500 kW
15070 UNITED KINGDOM
         †BBC, Multiple Locations   W • Europe • 250/500 kW   S • W Europe & N Africa • 250 kW
                                                        Europe & N Africa • 250/300/500 kW
15075 INDIA
         ALL INDIA RADIO, Aligarh   E Africa • 250 kW
         †ALL INDIA RADIO, Bangalore   W Asia, Mideast & E Africa • 500 kW
                                                        E Africa • 500 kW
         †ALL INDIA RADIO, Delhi   SE Asia • 100 kW   E Africa • 250 kW
15080 USA
         VOA, Via Plovdiv, Bulgaria   W • W Africa • 250 kW
15084 IRAN
         VO THE ISLAMIC REP, Tehrãn   DS • 500 kW
15095 PHILIPPINES
         FEBC RADIO INTL, Bocaue   SE Asia • 50 kW
       SYRIA
(con'd) RADIO DAMASCUS, Adhra   S America • 500 kW

SEASONAL S OR W   1-HR TIMESHIFT MIDYEAR ⇔ OR ⇒   JAMMING / OR ∧   EARLIEST HEARD ◁   LATEST HEARD ▷   NEW FOR 1996 †

FREQUENCY   COUNTRY, STATION, LOCATION   TARGET • NETWORK • POWER (kW)   World Time

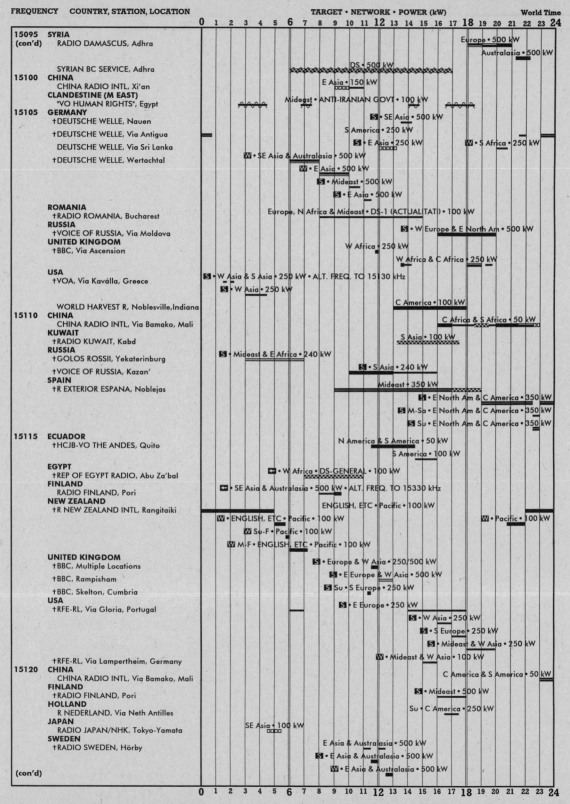

15095 SYRIA
(con'd)   RADIO DAMASCUS, Adhra — Europe • 500 kW; Australasia • 500 kW

           SYRIAN BC SERVICE, Adhra — DS • 500 kW
15100 CHINA
           CHINA RADIO INTL, Xi'an — E Asia • 150 kW
       CLANDESTINE (M EAST)
           "VO HUMAN RIGHTS", Egypt — Mideast • ANTI-IRANIAN GOVT • 100 kW
15105 GERMANY
          †DEUTSCHE WELLE, Nauen — S • SE Asia • 500 kW
          †DEUTSCHE WELLE, Via Antigua — S America • 250 kW
           DEUTSCHE WELLE, Via Sri Lanka — S • E Asia • 250 kW; W • S Africa • 250 kW
          †DEUTSCHE WELLE, Wertachtal — W • SE Asia & Australasia • 500 kW
                                        W • E Asia • 500 kW
                                        S • Mideast • 500 kW
                                        S • E Asia • 500 kW
       ROMANIA
          †RADIO ROMANIA, Bucharest — Europe, N Africa & Mideast • DS-1 (ACTUALITAT) • 100 kW
       RUSSIA
          †VOICE OF RUSSIA, Via Moldova — S • W Europe & E North Am • 500 kW
       UNITED KINGDOM
          †BBC, Via Ascension — W Africa • 250 kW; W Africa & C Africa • 250 kW
       USA
          †VOA, Via Kaválla, Greece — S • W Asia & S Asia • 250 kW • ALT. FREQ. TO 15130 kHz
                                        S • W Asia • 250 kW

           WORLD HARVEST R, Noblesville, Indiana — C America • 100 kW
15110 CHINA
           CHINA RADIO INTL, Via Bamako, Mali — C Africa & S Africa • 50 kW
       KUWAIT
          †RADIO KUWAIT, Kabd — S Asia • 100 kW
       RUSSIA
          †GOLOS ROSSII, Yekaterinburg — S • Mideast & E Africa • 240 kW
          †VOICE OF RUSSIA, Kazan' — S • S Asia • 240 kW
       SPAIN
          †R EXTERIOR ESPANA, Noblejas — Mideast • 350 kW
                                        S • E North Am & C America • 350 kW
                                        S M-Sa • E North Am & C America • 350 kW
                                        S Su • E North Am & C America • 350 kW

15115 ECUADOR
          †HCJB-VO THE ANDES, Quito — N America & S America • 50 kW
                                        S America • 100 kW

       EGYPT
          †REP OF EGYPT RADIO, Abu Za'bal — • W Africa • DS-GENERAL • 100 kW
       FINLAND
           RADIO FINLAND, Pori — • SE Asia & Australasia • 500 kW • ALT. FREQ. TO 15330 kHz
       NEW ZEALAND
          †R NEW ZEALAND INTL, Rangitaiki — ENGLISH, ETC • Pacific • 100 kW
                                        W • ENGLISH, ETC • Pacific • 100 kW; W • Pacific • 100 kW
                                        W Su-F • Pacific • 100 kW
                                        W M-F • ENGLISH, ETC • Pacific • 100 kW

       UNITED KINGDOM
          †BBC, Multiple Locations — S • Europe & W Asia • 250/500 kW
          †BBC, Rampisham — S • E Europe & W Asia • 500 kW
          †BBC, Skelton, Cumbria — S Su • S Europe • 250 kW
       USA
          †RFE-RL, Via Gloria, Portugal — S • E Europe • 250 kW
                                        S • W Asia • 250 kW
                                        S • S Europe • 250 kW
                                        S • Mideast & W Asia • 250 kW
          †RFE-RL, Via Lampertheim, Germany — W • Mideast & W Asia • 100 kW
15120 CHINA
           CHINA RADIO INTL, Via Bamako, Mali — C America & S America • 50 kW
       FINLAND
          †RADIO FINLAND, Pori — S • Mideast • 500 kW
       HOLLAND
           R NEDERLAND, Via Neth Antilles — Su • C America • 250 kW
       JAPAN
           RADIO JAPAN/NHK, Tokyo-Yamata — SE Asia • 100 kW
       SWEDEN
          †RADIO SWEDEN, Hörby — E Asia & Australasia • 500 kW
                                        S • E Asia & Australasia • 500 kW
                                        W • E Asia & Australasia • 500 kW

(con'd)

ENGLISH ▬   ARABIC ⌇⌇⌇   CHINESE ▫▫▫   FRENCH ▭▭   GERMAN ▬▬   RUSSIAN ▬   SPANISH ▬▬   OTHER ▬

FREQUENCY   COUNTRY, STATION, LOCATION

TARGET • NETWORK • POWER (kW)

World Time

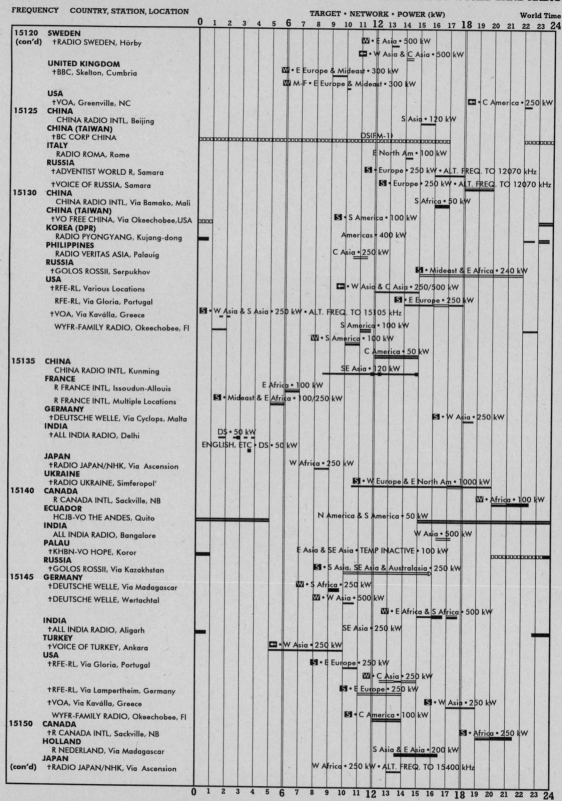

FREQUENCY	COUNTRY, STATION, LOCATION	TARGET • NETWORK • POWER (kW)
15120 (con'd)	SWEDEN †RADIO SWEDEN, Hörby	W • E Asia • 500 kW / W Asia & C Asia • 500 kW
	UNITED KINGDOM †BBC, Skelton, Cumbria	W • E Europe & Mideast • 300 kW / W M-F • E Europe & Mideast • 300 kW
	USA †VOA, Greenville, NC	C America • 250 kW
15125	CHINA CHINA RADIO INTL, Beijing	S Asia • 120 kW
	CHINA (TAIWAN) †BC CORP CHINA	DS(FM-1)
	ITALY RADIO ROMA, Rome	E North Am • 100 kW
	RUSSIA †ADVENTIST WORLD R, Samara	S • Europe • 250 kW • ALT. FREQ. TO 12070 kHz
	†VOICE OF RUSSIA, Samara	S • Europe • 250 kW • ALT. FREQ. TO 12070 kHz
15130	CHINA CHINA RADIO INTL, Via Bamako, Mali	S Africa • 50 kW
	CHINA (TAIWAN) †VO FREE CHINA, Via Okeechobee, USA	S • S America • 100 kW
	KOREA (DPR) RADIO PYONGYANG, Kujang-dong	Americas • 400 kW
	PHILIPPINES RADIO VERITAS ASIA, Palauig	C Asia • 250 kW
	RUSSIA †GOLOS ROSSII, Serpukhov	S • Mideast & E Africa • 240 kW
	USA †RFE-RL, Various Locations	W Asia & C Asia • 250/500 kW
	RFE-RL, Via Gloria, Portugal	S • E Europe • 250 kW
	†VOA, Via Kaválla, Greece	S • W Asia & S Asia • 250 kW • ALT. FREQ. TO 15105 kHz
	WYFR-FAMILY RADIO, Okeechobee, Fl	S America • 100 kW / W • S America • 100 kW
15135	CHINA	C America • 50 kW
	CHINA RADIO INTL, Kunming	SE Asia • 120 kW
	FRANCE R FRANCE INTL, Issoudun-Allouis	E Africa • 100 kW
	R FRANCE INTL, Multiple Locations	S • Mideast & E Africa • 100/250 kW
	GERMANY †DEUTSCHE WELLE, Via Cyclops, Malta	S • W Asia • 250 kW
	INDIA †ALL INDIA RADIO, Delhi	DS • 50 kW / ENGLISH, ETC • DS • 50 kW
	JAPAN †RADIO JAPAN/NHK, Via Ascension	W Africa • 250 kW
	UKRAINE †RADIO UKRAINE, Simferopol'	S • W Europe & E North Am • 1000 kW
15140	CANADA R CANADA INTL, Sackville, NB	W • Africa • 100 kW
	ECUADOR HCJB-VO THE ANDES, Quito	N America & S America • 50 kW
	INDIA ALL INDIA RADIO, Bangalore	W Asia • 500 kW
	PALAU †KHBN-VO HOPE, Koror	E Asia & SE Asia • TEMP INACTIVE • 100 kW
	RUSSIA †GOLOS ROSSII, Via Kazakhstan	S • S Asia, SE Asia & Australasia • 250 kW
15145	GERMANY †DEUTSCHE WELLE, Via Madagascar	W • S Africa • 250 kW
	†DEUTSCHE WELLE, Wertachtal	W • W Asia • 500 kW / W • E Africa & S Africa • 500 kW
	INDIA †ALL INDIA RADIO, Aligarh	SE Asia • 250 kW
	TURKEY †VOICE OF TURKEY, Ankara	W Asia • 250 kW
	USA †RFE-RL, Via Gloria, Portugal	S • E Europe • 250 kW / W • C Asia • 250 kW
	†RFE-RL, Via Lampertheim, Germany	S • E Europe • 250 kW
	†VOA, Via Kaválla, Greece	S • W Asia • 250 kW
	WYFR-FAMILY RADIO, Okeechobee, Fl	S • C America • 100 kW
15150	CANADA †R CANADA INTL, Sackville, NB	S • Africa • 250 kW
	HOLLAND R NEDERLAND, Via Madagascar	S Asia & E Asia • 200 kW
	JAPAN (con'd) †RADIO JAPAN/NHK, Via Ascension	W Africa • 250 kW • ALT. FREQ. TO 15400 kHz

FREQUENCY   COUNTRY, STATION, LOCATION

TARGET • NETWORK • POWER (kW)

World Time

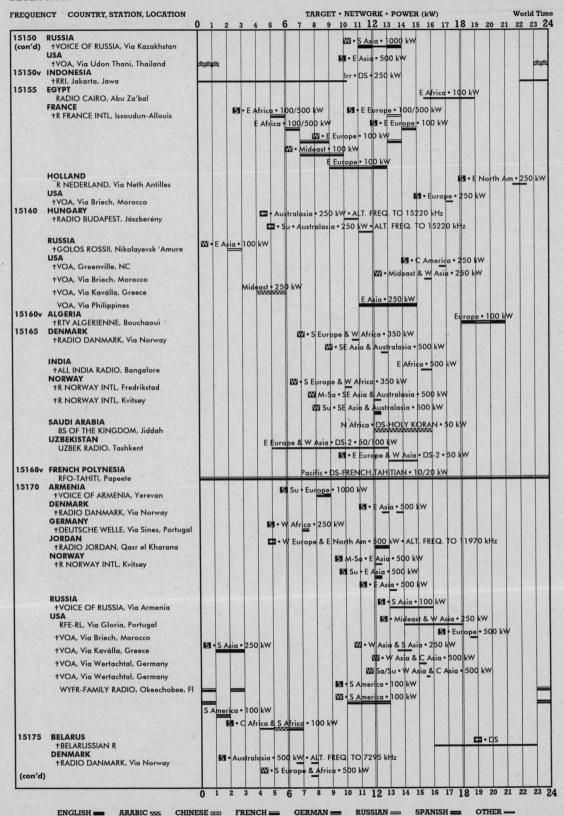

	15150	**RUSSIA**
	(con'd)	†VOICE OF RUSSIA, Via Kazakhstan
		USA
		†VOA, Via Udon Thani, Thailand
	15150v	**INDONESIA**
		†RRI, Jakarta, Jawa
	15155	**EGYPT**
		RADIO CAIRO, Abu Za'bal
		FRANCE
		†R FRANCE INTL, Issoudun-Allouis
		HOLLAND
		†R NEDERLAND, Via Neth Antilles
		USA
		†VOA, Via Briech, Morocco
	15160	**HUNGARY**
		†RADIO BUDAPEST, Jászberény
		RUSSIA
		†GOLOS ROSSII, Nikolayevsk 'Amure
		USA
		†VOA, Greenville, NC
		†VOA, Via Briech, Morocco
		†VOA, Via Kaválla, Greece
		VOA, Via Philippines
	15160v	**ALGERIA**
		†RTV ALGERIENNE, Bouchaoui
	15165	**DENMARK**
		†RADIO DANMARK, Via Norway
		INDIA
		†ALL INDIA RADIO, Bangalore
		NORWAY
		†R NORWAY INTL, Fredrikstad
		†R NORWAY INTL, Kvitsøy
		SAUDI ARABIA
		BS OF THE KINGDOM, Jiddah
		UZBEKISTAN
		UZBEK RADIO, Tashkent
	15168v	**FRENCH POLYNESIA**
		RFO-TAHITI, Papeete
	15170	**ARMENIA**
		†VOICE OF ARMENIA, Yerevan
		DENMARK
		†RADIO DANMARK, Via Norway
		GERMANY
		†DEUTSCHE WELLE, Via Sines, Portugal
		JORDAN
		†RADIO JORDAN, Qasr el Kharana
		NORWAY
		†R NORWAY INTL, Kvitsøy
		RUSSIA
		†VOICE OF RUSSIA, Via Armenia
		USA
		RFE-RL, Via Gloria, Portugal
		†VOA, Via Briech, Morocco
		†VOA, Via Kaválla, Greece
		†VOA, Via Wertachtal, Germany
		†VOA, Via Wertachtal, Germany
		WYFR-FAMILY RADIO, Okeechobee, Fl
	15175	**BELARUS**
		†BELARUSSIAN R
		DENMARK
		†RADIO DANMARK, Via Norway
	(con'd)	

Data points from chart:

- VOICE OF RUSSIA, Via Kazakhstan: W • S Asia • 1000 kW
- VOA, Via Udon Thani: S • E Asia • 500 kW
- RRI, Jakarta: Irr • DS • 250 kW
- RADIO CAIRO: E Africa • 100 kW
- R FRANCE INTL: S • E Africa • 100/500 kW; S • E Europe • 100/500 kW; E Africa • 100/500 kW; S • E Europe • 100 kW; W • E Europe • 100 kW; W • Mideast • 100 kW; E Europe • 100 kW
- R NEDERLAND: S • E North Am • 250 kW
- VOA, Via Briech, Morocco: S • Europe • 250 kW
- RADIO BUDAPEST: ⎘ • Australasia • 250 kW • ALT. FREQ. TO 15220 kHz; ⎘ • Su • Australasia • 250 kW • ALT. FREQ. TO 15220 kHz
- GOLOS ROSSII: W • E Asia • 100 kW
- VOA, Greenville, NC: S • C America • 250 kW
- VOA, Via Briech, Morocco: W • Mideast & W Asia • 250 kW
- VOA, Via Kaválla, Greece: Mideast • 250 kW
- VOA, Via Philippines: E Asia • 250 kW
- RTV ALGERIENNE: Europe • 100 kW
- RADIO DANMARK, Via Norway: W • S Europe & W Africa • 350 kW; W • SE Asia & Australasia • 500 kW
- ALL INDIA RADIO: E Africa • 500 kW
- R NORWAY INTL, Fredrikstad: W • S Europe & W Africa • 350 kW
- R NORWAY INTL, Kvitsøy: W • M-Sa • SE Asia & Australasia • 500 kW; W • Su • SE Asia & Australasia • 500 kW
- BS OF THE KINGDOM: N Africa • DS-HOLY KORAN • 50 kW
- UZBEK RADIO: E Europe & W Asia • DS-2 • 50/100 kW; S • E Europe & W Asia • DS-2 • 50 kW
- RFO-TAHITI: Pacific • DS-FRENCH, TAHITIAN • 10/20 kW
- VOICE OF ARMENIA: S • Su • Europe • 1000 kW
- RADIO DANMARK, Via Norway: S • E Asia • 500 kW
- DEUTSCHE WELLE: S • W Africa • 250 kW
- RADIO JORDAN: ⎘ • W Europe & E North Am • 500 kW • ALT. FREQ. TO 11970 kHz
- R NORWAY INTL, Kvitsøy: S • M-Sa • E Asia • 500 kW; S • Su • E Asia • 500 kW; S • E Asia • 500 kW
- VOICE OF RUSSIA, Via Armenia: S • S Asia • 100 kW
- RFE-RL, Via Gloria, Portugal: S • Mideast & W Asia • 250 kW
- VOA, Via Briech, Morocco: S • Europe • 500 kW
- VOA, Via Kaválla, Greece: S • S Asia • 250 kW; W • W Asia & S Asia • 250 kW
- VOA, Via Wertachtal, Germany: W • W Asia & C Asia • 500 kW
- VOA, Via Wertachtal, Germany: W • Sa/Su • W Asia & C Asia • 500 kW
- WYFR-FAMILY RADIO: S • S America • 100 kW; W • S America • 100 kW; S America • 100 kW; S • C Africa & S Africa • 100 kW
- BELARUSSIAN R: ⎘ • DS
- RADIO DANMARK, Via Norway: S • Australasia • 500 kW • ALT. FREQ. TO 7295 kHz; W • S Europe & Africa • 500 kW

ENGLISH ■■■   ARABIC ⋙   CHINESE □□□   FRENCH ▬   GERMAN ═   RUSSIAN ══   SPANISH ▬   OTHER ▬

FREQUENCY	COUNTRY, STATION, LOCATION	TARGET • NETWORK • POWER (kW)	World Time

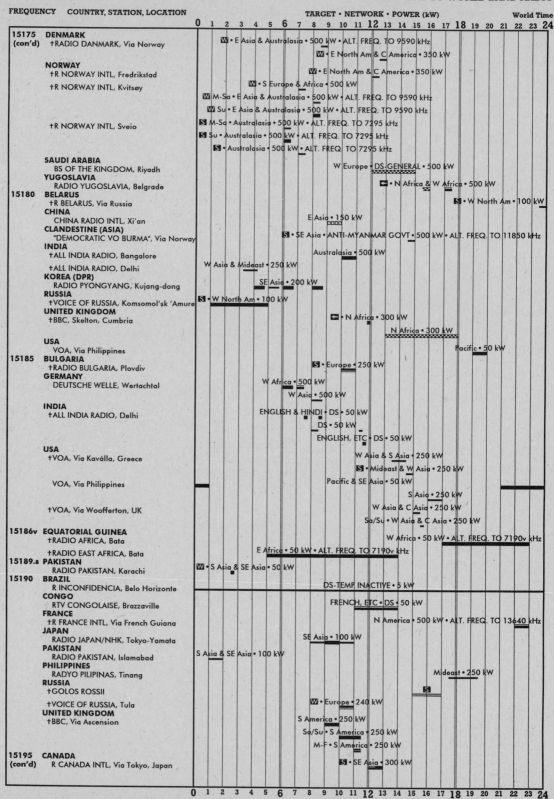

Chart entries (World Time scale 0–24):

15175 DENMARK
(con'd) †RADIO DANMARK, Via Norway — W • E Asia & Australasia • 500 kW • ALT. FREQ. TO 9590 kHz
— W • E North Am & C America • 350 kW

NORWAY
†R NORWAY INTL, Fredrikstad — W • E North Am & C America • 350 kW
— W • S Europe & Africa • 500 kW
†R NORWAY INTL, Kvitsøy — W M-Sa • E Asia & Australasia • 500 kW • ALT. FREQ. TO 9590 kHz
— W Su • E Asia & Australasia • 500 kW • ALT. FREQ. TO 9590 kHz
†R NORWAY INTL, Sveio — S M-Sa • Australasia • 500 kW • ALT. FREQ. TO 7295 kHz
— S Su • Australasia • 500 kW • ALT. FREQ. TO 7295 kHz
— S • Australasia • 500 kW • ALT. FREQ. TO 7295 kHz

SAUDI ARABIA
BS OF THE KINGDOM, Riyadh — W Europe • DS-GENERAL • 500 kW
YUGOSLAVIA
RADIO YUGOSLAVIA, Belgrade — • N Africa & W Africa • 500 kW

15180 BELARUS
†R BELARUS, Via Russia — S • W North Am • 100 kW
CHINA
CHINA RADIO INTL, Xi'an — E Asia • 150 kW
CLANDESTINE (ASIA)
"DEMOCRATIC VO BURMA", Via Norway — S • SE Asia • ANTI-MYANMAR GOVT • 500 kW • ALT. FREQ. TO 11850 kHz
INDIA
†ALL INDIA RADIO, Bangalore — Australasia • 500 kW
†ALL INDIA RADIO, Delhi — W Asia & Mideast • 250 kW
KOREA (DPR)
RADIO PYONGYANG, Kujang-dong — SE Asia • 200 kW
RUSSIA
†VOICE OF RUSSIA, Komsomol'sk 'Amure — S • W North Am • 100 kW
UNITED KINGDOM
†BBC, Skelton, Cumbria — • N Africa • 300 kW
— N Africa • 300 kW

USA
VOA, Via Philippines — Pacific • 50 kW
15185 BULGARIA
†RADIO BULGARIA, Plovdiv — S • Europe • 250 kW
GERMANY
DEUTSCHE WELLE, Wertachtal — W Africa • 500 kW
— W Asia • 500 kW

INDIA
†ALL INDIA RADIO, Delhi — ENGLISH & HINDI • DS • 50 kW
— DS • 50 kW
— ENGLISH, ETC • DS • 50 kW

USA
†VOA, Via Kavála, Greece — W Asia & S Asia • 250 kW
— S • Mideast & W Asia • 250 kW
VOA, Via Philippines — Pacific & SE Asia • 50 kW
— S Asia • 250 kW
†VOA, Via Woofferton, UK — W Asia & C Asia • 250 kW
— Sa/Su • W Asia & C Asia • 250 kW

15186v EQUATORIAL GUINEA
†RADIO AFRICA, Bata — W Africa • 50 kW • ALT. FREQ. TO 7190v kHz
†RADIO EAST AFRICA, Bata — E Africa • 50 kW • ALT. FREQ. TO 7190v kHz
15189.8 PAKISTAN
RADIO PAKISTAN, Karachi — W • S Asia & SE Asia • 50 kW
15190 BRAZIL
R INCONFIDENCIA, Belo Horizonte — DS-TEMP INACTIVE • 5 kW
CONGO
RTV CONGOLAISE, Brazzaville — FRENCH, ETC • DS • 50 kW
FRANCE
†R FRANCE INTL, Via French Guiana — N America • 500 kW • ALT. FREQ. TO 13640 kHz
JAPAN
RADIO JAPAN/NHK, Tokyo-Yamata — SE Asia • 100 kW
PAKISTAN
RADIO PAKISTAN, Islamabad — S Asia & SE Asia • 100 kW
PHILIPPINES
RADYO PILIPINAS, Tinang — Mideast • 250 kW
RUSSIA
†GOLOS ROSSII — S
†VOICE OF RUSSIA, Tula — W • Europe • 240 kW
UNITED KINGDOM
†BBC, Via Ascension — S America • 250 kW
— Sa/Su • S America • 250 kW
— M-F • S America • 250 kW

15195 CANADA
(con'd) R CANADA INTL, Via Tokyo, Japan — S • SE Asia • 300 kW

SEASONAL **S** OR **W**   1-HR TIMESHIFT MIDYEAR ◱ OR ◲   JAMMING / OR ∧   EARLIEST HEARD ◁   LATEST HEARD ▷   NEW FOR 1996 †

| FREQUENCY | COUNTRY, STATION, LOCATION | TARGET • NETWORK • POWER (kW) | World Time |

0 1 2 3 4 5 6 7 8 9 10 11 12 13 14 15 16 17 18 19 20 21 22 23 24

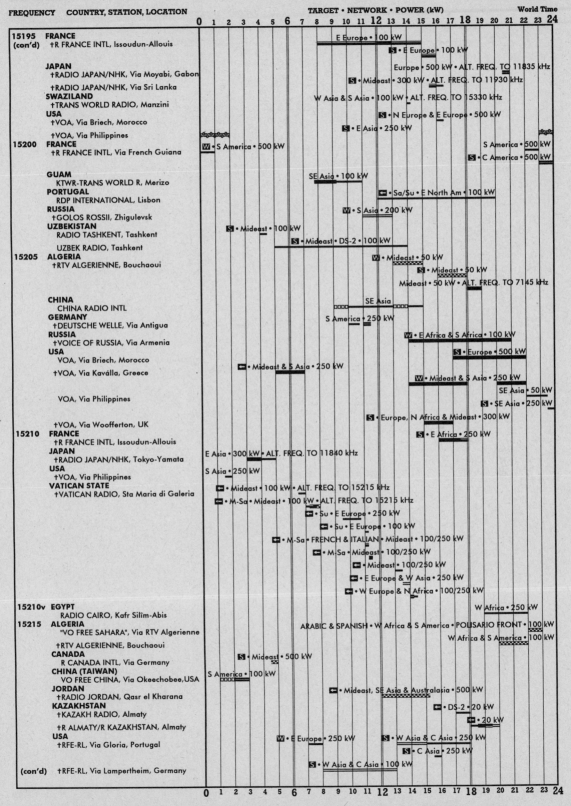

15195 FRANCE
(con'd) †R FRANCE INTL, Issoudun-Allouis — E Europe • 100 kW ; S • E Europe • 100 kW

JAPAN
†RADIO JAPAN/NHK, Via Moyabi, Gabon — Europe • 500 kW • ALT. FREQ. TO 11835 kHz
†RADIO JAPAN/NHK, Via Sri Lanka — S • Mideast • 300 kW • ALT. FREQ. TO 11930 kHz

SWAZILAND
†TRANS WORLD RADIO, Manzini — W Asia & S Asia • 100 kW • ALT. FREQ. TO 15330 kHz

USA
†VOA, Via Briech, Morocco — S • N Europe & E Europe • 500 kW
†VOA, Via Philippines — S • E Asia • 250 kW

15200 FRANCE
†R FRANCE INTL, Via French Guiana — W • S America • 500 kW ; S America • 500 kW ; S • C America • 500 kW

GUAM
KTWR-TRANS WORLD R, Merizo — SE Asia • 100 kW

PORTUGAL
RDP INTERNATIONAL, Lisbon — S • Sa/Su • E North Am • 100 kW

RUSSIA
†GOLOS ROSSII, Zhigulevsk — W • S Asia • 200 kW

UZBEKISTAN
RADIO TASHKENT, Tashkent — S • Mideast • 100 kW
UZBEK RADIO, Tashkent — S • Mideast • DS-2 • 100 kW

15205 ALGERIA
†RTV ALGERIENNE, Bouchaoui — W • Mideast • 50 kW ; S • Mideast • 50 kW ; Mideast • 50 kW • ALT. FREQ. TO 7145 kHz

CHINA
CHINA RADIO INTL — SE Asia

GERMANY
†DEUTSCHE WELLE, Via Antigua — S America • 250 kW

RUSSIA
†VOICE OF RUSSIA, Via Armenia — W • E Africa & S Africa • 100 kW

USA
VOA, Via Briech, Morocco — S • Europe • 500 kW
†VOA, Via Kaválla, Greece — Mideast & S Asia • 250 kW ; W • Mideast & S Asia • 250 kW
VOA, Via Philippines — SE Asia • 50 kW ; S • SE Asia • 250 kW
†VOA, Via Woofferton, UK — S • Europe, N Africa & Mideast • 300 kW

15210 FRANCE
†R FRANCE INTL, Issoudun-Allouis — S • E Africa • 250 kW

JAPAN
†RADIO JAPAN/NHK, Tokyo-Yamata — E Asia • 300 kW • ALT. FREQ. TO 11840 kHz

USA
†VOA, Via Philippines — S Asia • 250 kW

VATICAN STATE
†VATICAN RADIO, Sta Maria di Galeria — Mideast • 100 kW • ALT. FREQ. TO 15215 kHz ; M-Sa • Mideast • 100 kW • ALT. FREQ. TO 15215 kHz ; Su • E Europe • 250 kW ; Su • E Europe • 100 kW ; M-Sa • FRENCH & ITALIAN • Mideast • 100/250 kW ; M-Sa • Mideast • 100/250 kW ; Mideast • 100/250 kW ; E Europe & W Asia • 250 kW ; W Europe & N Africa • 100/250 kW

15210v EGYPT
RADIO CAIRO, Kafr Silim-Abis — W Africa • 250 kW

15215 ALGERIA
"VO FREE SAHARA", Via RTV Algerienne — ARABIC & SPANISH • W Africa & S America • POLISARIO FRONT • 100 kW ; W Africa & S America • 100 kW
†RTV ALGERIENNE, Bouchaoui

CANADA
R CANADA INTL, Via Germany — S • Mideast • 500 kW

CHINA (TAIWAN)
VO FREE CHINA, Via Okeechobee, USA — S America • 100 kW

JORDAN
†RADIO JORDAN, Qasr el Kharana — Mideast, SE Asia & Australasia • 500 kW

KAZAKHSTAN
†KAZAKH RADIO, Almaty — DS-2 • 20 kW
†R ALMATY/R KAZAKHSTAN, Almaty — 20 kW

USA
†RFE-RL, Via Gloria, Portugal — W • E Europe • 250 kW ; S • W Asia & C Asia • 250 kW ; S • C Asia • 250 kW

(con'd) †RFE-RL, Via Lampertheim, Germany — S • W Asia & C Asia • 100 kW

0 1 2 3 4 5 6 7 8 9 10 11 12 13 14 15 16 17 18 19 20 21 22 23 24

ENGLISH ▬ ARABIC ⧠ CHINESE ⧠⧠⧠ FRENCH ▬ GERMAN ▬ RUSSIAN ═ SPANISH ▬ OTHER ▬

FREQUENCY   COUNTRY, STATION, LOCATION   TARGET • NETWORK • POWER (kW)   World Time

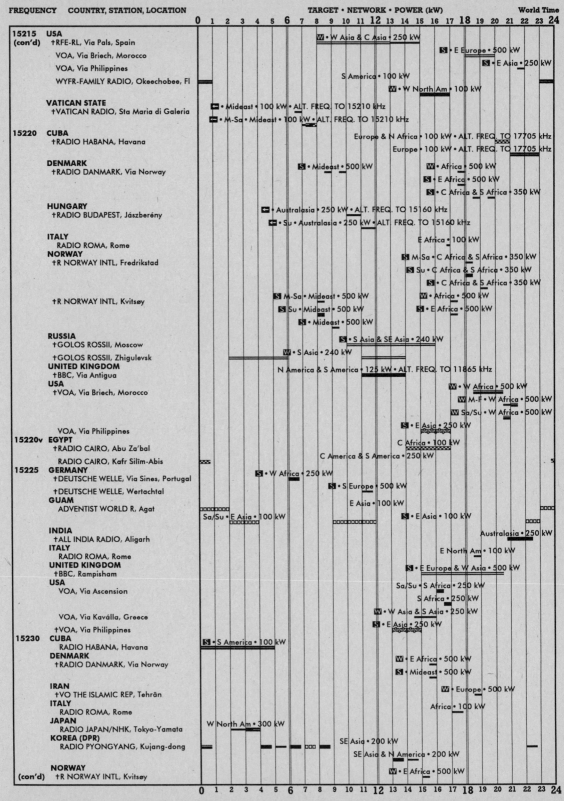

Frequency	Country, Station, Location	Target • Network • Power
15215 (con'd)	USA	
	†RFE-RL, Via Pals, Spain	W • W Asia & C Asia • 250 kW
		S • E Europe • 500 kW
	VOA, Via Briech, Morocco	S • E Asia • 250 kW
	VOA, Via Philippines	S America • 100 kW
	WYFR-FAMILY RADIO, Okeechobee, Fl	W • W North Am • 100 kW
	VATICAN STATE	
	†VATICAN RADIO, Sta Maria di Galeria	• Mideast • 100 kW • ALT. FREQ. TO 15210 kHz
		• M-Sa • Mideast • 100 kW • ALT. FREQ. TO 15210 kHz
15220	CUBA	
	†RADIO HABANA, Havana	Europe & N Africa • 100 kW • ALT. FREQ. TO 17705 kHz
		Europe • 100 kW • ALT. FREQ. TO 17705 kHz
	DENMARK	
	†RADIO DANMARK, Via Norway	S • Mideast • 500 kW
		W • Africa • 500 kW
		S • E Africa • 500 kW
		S • C Africa & S Africa • 350 kW
	HUNGARY	
	†RADIO BUDAPEST, Jászberény	• Australasia • 250 kW • ALT. FREQ. TO 15160 kHz
		• Su • Australasia • 250 kW • ALT. FREQ. TO 15160 kHz
	ITALY	
	RADIO ROMA, Rome	E Africa • 100 kW
	NORWAY	
	†R NORWAY INTL, Fredrikstad	S M-Sa • C Africa & S Africa • 350 kW
		S Su • C Africa & S Africa • 350 kW
		S • C Africa & S Africa • 350 kW
	†R NORWAY INTL, Kvitsøy	S M-Sa • Mideast • 500 kW
		W • Africa • 500 kW
		S Su • Mideast • 500 kW
		S • E Africa • 500 kW
		S • Mideast • 500 kW
	RUSSIA	
	†GOLOS ROSSII, Moscow	S • S Asia & SE Asia • 240 kW
	†GOLOS ROSSII, Zhigulevsk	W • S Asia • 240 kW
	UNITED KINGDOM	
	†BBC, Via Antigua	N America & S America • 125 kW • ALT. FREQ. TO 11865 kHz
	USA	
	†VOA, Via Briech, Morocco	W • W Africa • 500 kW
		W M-F • W Africa • 500 kW
		W Sa/Su • W Africa • 500 kW
	VOA, Via Philippines	S • E Asia • 250 kW
15220v	EGYPT	
	†RADIO CAIRO, Abu Za'bal	C Africa • 100 kW
	RADIO CAIRO, Kafr Silīm-Abis	C America & S America • 250 kW
15225	GERMANY	
	†DEUTSCHE WELLE, Via Sines, Portugal	S • W Africa • 250 kW
	†DEUTSCHE WELLE, Wertachtal	S • S Europe • 500 kW
	GUAM	
	ADVENTIST WORLD R, Agat	E Asia • 100 kW
		Sa/Su • E Asia • 100 kW
		S • E Asia • 100 kW
	INDIA	
	†ALL INDIA RADIO, Aligarh	Australasia • 250 kW
	ITALY	
	RADIO ROMA, Rome	E North Am • 100 kW
	UNITED KINGDOM	
	†BBC, Rampisham	S • E Europe & W Asia • 500 kW
	USA	
	VOA, Via Ascension	Sa/Su • S Africa • 250 kW
		S Africa • 250 kW
	VOA, Via Kaválla, Greece	W • W Asia & S Asia • 250 kW
	†VOA, Via Philippines	S • E Asia • 250 kW
15230	CUBA	
	RADIO HABANA, Havana	S • S America • 100 kW
	DENMARK	
	†RADIO DANMARK, Via Norway	W • E Africa • 500 kW
		S • Mideast • 500 kW
	IRAN	
	†VO THE ISLAMIC REP, Tehrān	W • Europe • 500 kW
	ITALY	
	RADIO ROMA, Rome	Africa • 100 kW
	JAPAN	
	RADIO JAPAN/NHK, Tokyo-Yamata	W North Am • 300 kW
	KOREA (DPR)	
	RADIO PYONGYANG, Kujang-dong	SE Asia • 200 kW
		SE Asia & N America • 200 kW
	NORWAY	
(con'd)	†R NORWAY INTL, Kvitsøy	W • E Africa • 500 kW

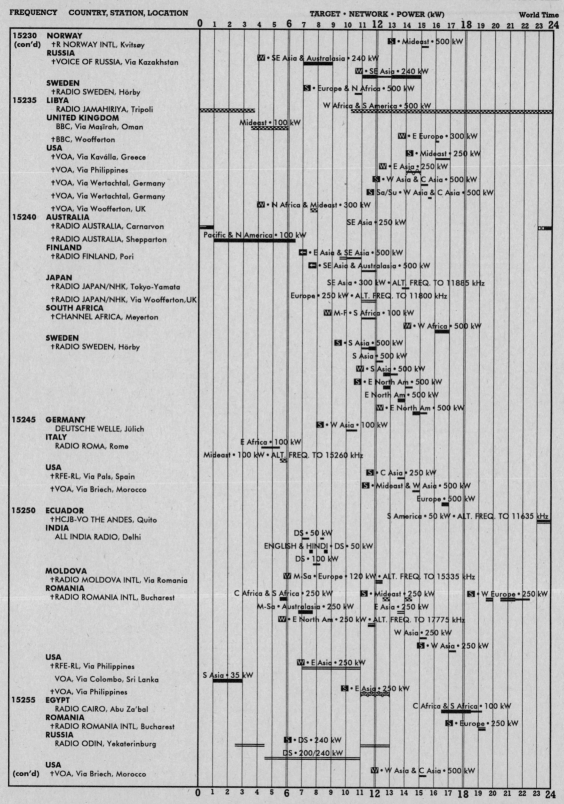

FREQUENCY	COUNTRY, STATION, LOCATION	TARGET • NETWORK • POWER (kW)
15230 (con'd)	**NORWAY**	
	†R NORWAY INTL, Kvitsøy	[S] • Mideast • 500 kW
	RUSSIA	
	†VOICE OF RUSSIA, Via Kazakhstan	[W] • SE Asia & Australasia • 240 kW
		[W] • SE Asia • 240 kW
	SWEDEN	
	†RADIO SWEDEN, Hörby	[S] • Europe & N Africa • 500 kW
15235	**LIBYA**	
	RADIO JAMAHIRIYA, Tripoli	W Africa & S America • 500 kW
	UNITED KINGDOM	
	BBC, Via Maṣīrah, Oman	Mideast • 100 kW
	†BBC, Woofferton	[W] • E Europe • 300 kW
	USA	
	†VOA, Via Kaválla, Greece	[S] • Mideast • 250 kW
	†VOA, Via Philippines	[W] • E Asia • 250 kW
	†VOA, Via Wertachtal, Germany	[S] • W Asia & C Asia • 500 kW
	†VOA, Via Wertachtal, Germany	[S] Sa/Su • W Asia & C Asia • 500 kW
	†VOA, Via Woofferton, UK	[W] • N Africa & Mideast • 300 kW
15240	**AUSTRALIA**	
	†RADIO AUSTRALIA, Carnarvon	SE Asia • 250 kW
	†RADIO AUSTRALIA, Shepparton	Pacific & N America • 100 kW
	FINLAND	
	†RADIO FINLAND, Pori	← • E Asia & SE Asia • 500 kW
		← • SE Asia & Australasia • 500 kW
	JAPAN	
	†RADIO JAPAN/NHK, Tokyo-Yamata	SE Asia • 300 kW • ALT. FREQ. TO 11885 kHz
	†RADIO JAPAN/NHK, Via Woofferton, UK	Europe • 250 kW • ALT. FREQ. TO 11800 kHz
	SOUTH AFRICA	
	†CHANNEL AFRICA, Meyerton	[W] M-F • S Africa • 100 kW
		[W] • W Africa • 500 kW
	SWEDEN	
	†RADIO SWEDEN, Hörby	[S] • S Asia • 500 kW
		S Asia • 500 kW
		[W] • S Asia • 500 kW
		[S] • E North Am • 500 kW
		E North Am • 500 kW
		[W] • E North Am • 500 kW
15245	**GERMANY**	
	DEUTSCHE WELLE, Jülich	[S] • W Asia • 100 kW
	ITALY	
	RADIO ROMA, Rome	E Africa • 100 kW
		Mideast • 100 kW • ALT. FREQ. TO 15260 kHz
	USA	
	†RFE-RL, Via Pals, Spain	[S] • C Asia • 250 kW
	†VOA, Via Briech, Morocco	[S] • Mideast & W Asia • 500 kW
		Europe • 500 kW
15250	**ECUADOR**	
	†HCJB-VO THE ANDES, Quito	S America • 50 kW • ALT. FREQ. TO 11635 kHz
	INDIA	
	ALL INDIA RADIO, Delhi	DS • 50 kW
		ENGLISH & HINDI • DS • 50 kW
		DS • 100 kW
	MOLDOVA	
	†RADIO MOLDOVA INTL, Via Romania	[W] M-Sa • Europe • 120 kW • ALT. FREQ. TO 15335 kHz
	ROMANIA	
	†RADIO ROMANIA INTL, Bucharest	C Africa & S Africa • 250 kW
		[S] • Mideast • 250 kW
		[S] • W Europe • 250 kW
		M-Sa • Australasia • 250 kW
		E Asia • 250 kW
		[W] • E North Am • 250 kW • ALT. FREQ. TO 17775 kHz
		W Asia • 250 kW
		[S] • W Asia • 250 kW
	USA	
	†RFE-RL, Via Philippines	[W] • E Asia • 250 kW
	VOA, Via Colombo, Sri Lanka	S Asia • 35 kW
	†VOA, Via Philippines	[S] • E Asia • 250 kW
15255	**EGYPT**	
	RADIO CAIRO, Abu Za'bal	C Africa & S Africa • 100 kW
	ROMANIA	
	†RADIO ROMANIA INTL, Bucharest	[S] • Europe • 250 kW
	RUSSIA	
	RADIO ODIN, Yekaterinburg	[S] • DS • 240 kW
		DS • 200/240 kW
	USA	
(con'd)	†VOA, Via Briech, Morocco	[W] • W Asia & C Asia • 500 kW

World Time 0 1 2 3 4 5 6 7 8 9 10 11 12 13 14 15 16 17 18 19 20 21 22 23 24

ENGLISH ARABIC CHINESE FRENCH GERMAN RUSSIAN SPANISH OTHER

FREQUENCY   COUNTRY, STATION, LOCATION   TARGET • NETWORK • POWER (kW)   **World Time**

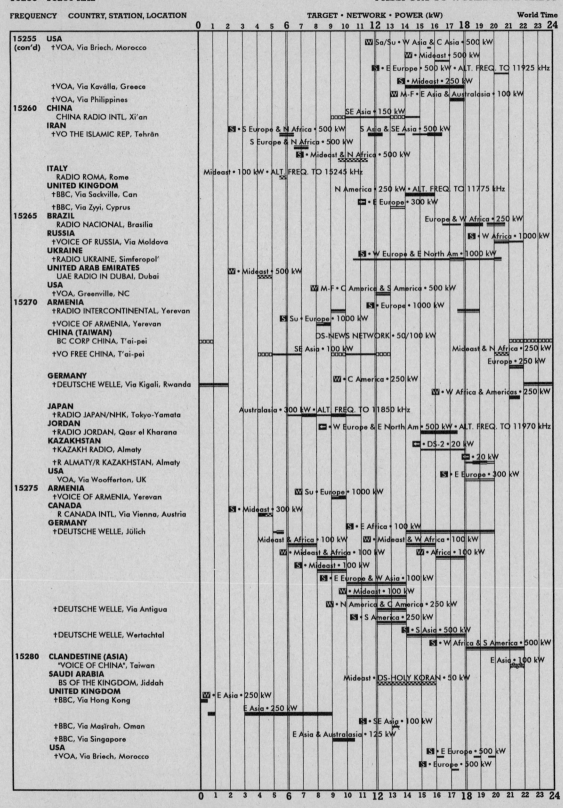

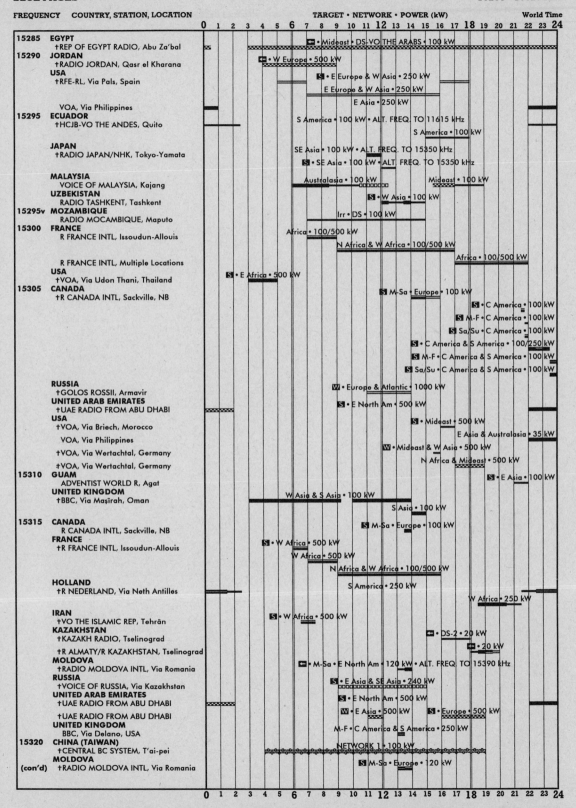

FREQUENCY   COUNTRY, STATION, LOCATION   TARGET • NETWORK • POWER (kW)   World Time

Frequency	Country, Station, Location	Target • Network • Power
15285	**EGYPT** †REP OF EGYPT RADIO, Abu Za'bal	◫ • Mideast • DS-VO THE ARABS • 100 kW
15290	**JORDAN** †RADIO JORDAN, Qasr el Kharana	◫ • W Europe • 500 kW
	USA †RFE-RL, Via Pals, Spain	⑤ • E Europe & W Asia • 250 kW; E Europe & W Asia • 250 kW
	VOA, Via Philippines	E Asia • 250 kW
15295	**ECUADOR** †HCJB-VO THE ANDES, Quito	S America • 100 kW • ALT. FREQ. TO 11615 kHz; S America • 100 kW
	JAPAN †RADIO JAPAN/NHK, Tokyo-Yamata	SE Asia • 100 kW • ALT. FREQ. TO 15350 kHz; ⑤ • SE Asia • 100 kW • ALT. FREQ. TO 15350 kHz
	MALAYSIA VOICE OF MALAYSIA, Kajang	Australasia • 100 kW; Mideast • 100 kW
	UZBEKISTAN RADIO TASHKENT, Tashkent	⑤ • W Asia • 100 kW
15295v	**MOZAMBIQUE** RADIO MOCAMBIQUE, Maputo	Irr • DS • 100 kW
15300	**FRANCE** R FRANCE INTL, Issoudun-Allouis	Africa • 100/500 kW; N Africa & W Africa • 100/500 kW
	R FRANCE INTL, Multiple Locations	Africa • 100/500 kW
	USA †VOA, Via Udon Thani, Thailand	⑤ • E Africa • 500 kW
15305	**CANADA** †R CANADA INTL, Sackville, NB	⑤ • M-Sa • Europe • 100 kW; ⑤ • C America • 100 kW; ⑤ • M-F • C America • 100 kW; ⑤ • Sa/Su • C America • 100 kW; ⑤ • C America & S America • 100/250 kW; ⑤ • M-F • C America & S America • 100 kW; ⑤ • Sa/Su • C America & S America • 100 kW
	RUSSIA †GOLOS ROSSII, Armavir	◫ • Europe & Atlantic • 1000 kW
	UNITED ARAB EMIRATES †UAE RADIO FROM ABU DHABI	⑤ • E North Am • 500 kW
	USA †VOA, Via Briech, Morocco	⑤ • Mideast • 500 kW
	VOA, Via Philippines	E Asia & Australasia • 35 kW
	†VOA, Via Wertachtal, Germany	◫ • Mideast & W Asia • 500 kW
	‡VOA, Via Wertachtal, Germany	N Africa & Mideast • 500 kW
15310	**GUAM** ADVENTIST WORLD R, Agat	⑤ • E Asia • 100 kW
	UNITED KINGDOM †BBC, Via Maşirah, Oman	W Asia & S Asia • 100 kW; S Asia • 100 kW
15315	**CANADA** R CANADA INTL, Sackville, NB	⑤ • M-Sa • Europe • 100 kW
	FRANCE †R FRANCE INTL, Issoudun-Allouis	⑤ • W Africa • 500 kW; W Africa • 500 kW; N Africa & W Africa • 100/500 kW
	HOLLAND †R NEDERLAND, Via Neth Antilles	S America • 250 kW; W Africa • 250 kW
	IRAN †VO THE ISLAMIC REP, Tehrān	⑤ • W Africa • 500 kW
	KAZAKHSTAN †KAZAKH RADIO, Tselinograd	◫ • DS-2 • 20 kW
	†R ALMATY/R KAZAKHSTAN, Tselinograd	◫ • 20 kW
	MOLDOVA †RADIO MOLDOVA INTL, Via Romania	◫ • M-Sa • E North Am • 120 kW • ALT. FREQ. TO 15390 kHz
	RUSSIA †VOICE OF RUSSIA, Via Kazakhstan	⑤ • E Asia & SE Asia • 240 kW
	UNITED ARAB EMIRATES †UAE RADIO FROM ABU DHABI	⑤ • E North Am • 500 kW
	†UAE RADIO FROM ABU DHABI	◫ • E Asia • 500 kW; ◫ • Europe • 500 kW
	UNITED KINGDOM BBC, Via Delano, USA	M-F • C America & S America • 250 kW
15320	**CHINA (TAIWAN)** †CENTRAL BC SYSTEM, T'ai-pei	NETWORK 1 • 100 kW
(con'd)	**MOLDOVA** †RADIO MOLDOVA INTL, Via Romania	⑤ • M-Sa • Europe • 120 kW

ENGLISH ▬   ARABIC ▨   CHINESE ▢▢▢   FRENCH ▬   GERMAN ▬   RUSSIAN ═   SPANISH ▬   OTHER ▬

FREQUENCY   COUNTRY, STATION, LOCATION   TARGET • NETWORK • POWER (kW)   World Time

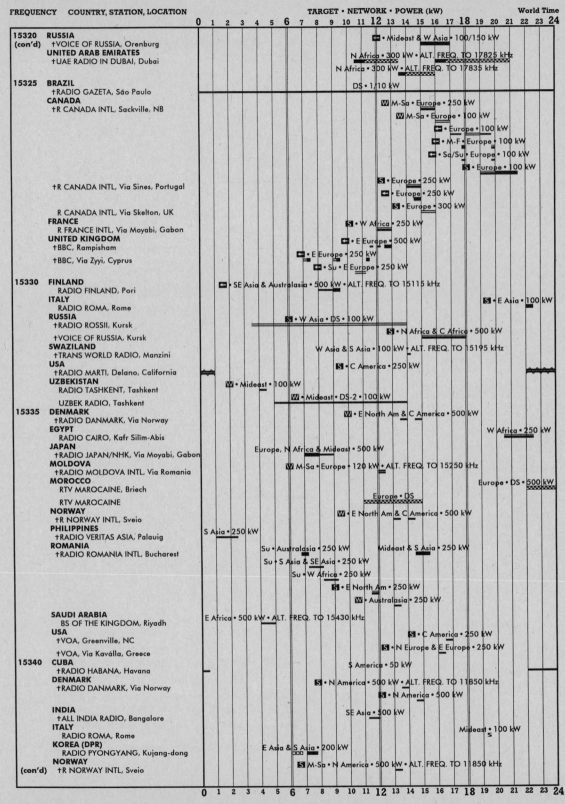

15320 RUSSIA	
(con'd) †VOICE OF RUSSIA, Orenburg	• Mideast & W Asia • 100/150 kW
UNITED ARAB EMIRATES	N Africa • 300 kW • ALT. FREQ. TO 17825 kHz
†UAE RADIO IN DUBAI, Dubai	N Africa • 300 kW • ALT. FREQ. TO 17835 kHz
15325 BRAZIL	
†RADIO GAZETA, São Paulo	DS • 1/10 kW
CANADA	
†R CANADA INTL, Sackville, NB	M-Sa • Europe • 250 kW
	M-Sa • Europe • 100 kW
	• Europe • 100 kW
	• M-F • Europe • 100 kW
	• Sa/Su • Europe • 100 kW
	• Europe • 100 kW
†R CANADA INTL, Via Sines, Portugal	• Europe • 250 kW
	• Europe • 250 kW
	• Europe • 300 kW
R CANADA INTL, Via Skelton, UK	
FRANCE	
R FRANCE INTL, Via Moyabi, Gabon	• W Africa • 250 kW
UNITED KINGDOM	
†BBC, Rampisham	• E Europe • 500 kW
†BBC, Via Zyyi, Cyprus	• E Europe • 250 kW
	• Su • E Europe • 250 kW
15330 FINLAND	
RADIO FINLAND, Pori	• SE Asia & Australasia • 500 kW • ALT. FREQ. TO 15115 kHz
ITALY	
RADIO ROMA, Rome	• E Asia • 100 kW
RUSSIA	
†RADIO ROSSII, Kursk	• W Asia • DS • 100 kW
†VOICE OF RUSSIA, Kursk	• N Africa & C Africa • 500 kW
SWAZILAND	
†TRANS WORLD RADIO, Manzini	W Asia & S Asia • 100 kW • ALT. FREQ. TO 15195 kHz
USA	
†RADIO MARTI, Delano, California	• C America • 250 kW
UZBEKISTAN	
RADIO TASHKENT, Tashkent	• Mideast • 100 kW
UZBEK RADIO, Tashkent	• Mideast • DS-2 • 100 kW
15335 DENMARK	
†RADIO DANMARK, Via Norway	• E North Am & C America • 500 kW
EGYPT	
RADIO CAIRO, Kafr Silim-Abis	W Africa • 250 kW
JAPAN	
†RADIO JAPAN/NHK, Via Moyabi, Gabon	Europe, N Africa & Mideast • 500 kW
MOLDOVA	
†RADIO MOLDOVA INTL, Via Romania	M-Sa • Europe • 120 kW • ALT. FREQ. TO 15250 kHz
MOROCCO	
RTV MAROCAINE, Briech	Europe • DS • 500 kW
RTV MAROCAINE	Europe • DS
NORWAY	
†R NORWAY INTL, Sveio	• E North Am & C America • 500 kW
PHILIPPINES	
†RADIO VERITAS ASIA, Palauig	S Asia • 250 kW
ROMANIA	
†RADIO ROMANIA INTL, Bucharest	Su • Australasia • 250 kW
	Mideast & S Asia • 250 kW
	Su • S Asia & SE Asia • 250 kW
	Su • W Africa • 250 kW
	• E North Am • 250 kW
	• Australasia • 250 kW
SAUDI ARABIA	
BS OF THE KINGDOM, Riyadh	E Africa • 500 kW • ALT. FREQ. TO 15430 kHz
USA	
†VOA, Greenville, NC	• C America • 250 kW
†VOA, Via Kaválla, Greece	• N Europe & E Europe • 250 kW
15340 CUBA	
†RADIO HABANA, Havana	S America • 50 kW
DENMARK	
†RADIO DANMARK, Via Norway	• N America • 500 kW • ALT. FREQ. TO 11850 kHz
	• N America • 500 kW
INDIA	
†ALL INDIA RADIO, Bangalore	SE Asia • 500 kW
ITALY	
RADIO ROMA, Rome	Mideast • 100 kW
KOREA (DPR)	
RADIO PYONGYANG, Kujang-dong	E Asia & S Asia • 200 kW
NORWAY	
(con'd) †R NORWAY INTL, Sveio	M-Sa • N America • 500 kW • ALT. FREQ. TO 11850 kHz

SEASONAL ⬛S OR ⬛W   1-HR TIMESHIFT MIDYEAR ⬛ OR ⬛   JAMMING / OR /\   EARLIEST HEARD ◁   LATEST HEARD ▷   NEW FOR 1996 †

FREQUENCY	COUNTRY, STATION, LOCATION	TARGET • NETWORK • POWER (kW) World Time

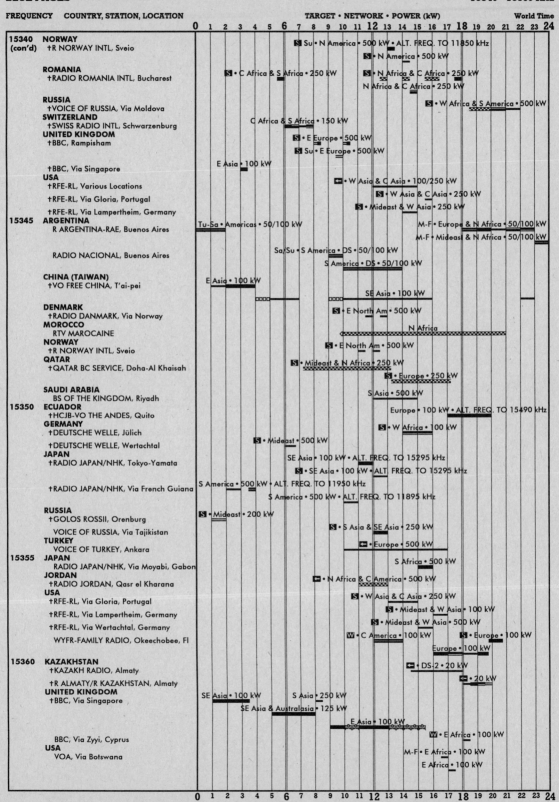

15340 **NORWAY**
(con'd) †R NORWAY INTL, Sveio — Su • N America • 500 kW • ALT. FREQ. TO 11850 kHz
 N America • 500 kW

ROMANIA
†RADIO ROMANIA INTL, Bucharest — C Africa & S Africa • 250 kW — N Africa & C Africa • 250 kW
 N Africa & C Africa • 250 kW

RUSSIA
†VOICE OF RUSSIA, Via Moldova — W Africa & S America • 500 kW
SWITZERLAND
†SWISS RADIO INTL, Schwarzenburg — C Africa & S Africa • 150 kW
UNITED KINGDOM
†BBC, Rampisham — E Europe • 500 kW
 Su • E Europe • 500 kW

†BBC, Via Singapore — E Asia • 100 kW
USA
†RFE-RL, Various Locations — W Asia & C Asia • 100/250 kW
†RFE-RL, Via Gloria, Portugal — W Asia & C Asia • 250 kW
†RFE-RL, Via Lampertheim, Germany — Mideast & W Asia • 250 kW

15345 **ARGENTINA**
 R ARGENTINA-RAE, Buenos Aires — Tu-Sa • Americas • 50/100 kW — M-F • Europe & N Africa • 50/100 kW
 M-F • Mideast & N Africa • 50/100 kW

 RADIO NACIONAL, Buenos Aires — Sa/Su • S America • DS • 50/100 kW
 S America • DS • 50/100 kW

CHINA (TAIWAN)
†VO FREE CHINA, T'ai-pei — E Asia • 100 kW
 SE Asia • 100 kW

DENMARK
†RADIO DANMARK, Via Norway — E North Am • 500 kW
MOROCCO
 RTV MAROCAINE — N Africa
NORWAY
†R NORWAY INTL, Sveio — E North Am • 500 kW
QATAR
†QATAR BC SERVICE, Doha-Al Khaisah — Mideast & N Africa • 250 kW
 Europe • 250 kW

SAUDI ARABIA
 BS OF THE KINGDOM, Riyadh — S Asia • 500 kW
15350 **ECUADOR**
†HCJB-VO THE ANDES, Quito — Europe • 100 kW • ALT. FREQ. TO 15490 kHz
GERMANY
 †DEUTSCHE WELLE, Jülich — W Africa • 100 kW
†DEUTSCHE WELLE, Wertachtal — Mideast • 500 kW
JAPAN
†RADIO JAPAN/NHK, Tokyo-Yamata — SE Asia • 100 kW • ALT. FREQ. TO 15295 kHz
 SE Asia • 100 kW • ALT. FREQ. TO 15295 kHz
†RADIO JAPAN/NHK, Via French Guiana — S America • 500 kW • ALT. FREQ. TO 11950 kHz
 S America • 500 kW • ALT. FREQ. TO 11895 kHz

RUSSIA
†GOLOS ROSSII, Orenburg — Mideast • 200 kW
 VOICE OF RUSSIA, Via Tajikistan — S Asia & SE Asia • 250 kW
TURKEY
 VOICE OF TURKEY, Ankara — Europe • 500 kW
15355 **JAPAN**
 RADIO JAPAN/NHK, Via Moyabi, Gabon — S Africa • 500 kW
JORDAN
†RADIO JORDAN, Qasr el Kharana — N Africa & C America • 500 kW
USA
†RFE-RL, Via Gloria, Portugal — W Asia & C Asia • 250 kW
†RFE-RL, Via Lampertheim, Germany — Mideast & W Asia • 100 kW
†RFE-RL, Via Wertachtal, Germany — Mideast & W Asia • 500 kW
 WYFR-FAMILY RADIO, Okeechobee, Fl — C America • 100 kW — Europe • 100 kW
 Europe • 100 kW

15360 **KAZAKHSTAN**
†KAZAKH RADIO, Almaty — DS-2 • 20 kW
†R ALMATY/R KAZAKHSTAN, Almaty — 20 kW
UNITED KINGDOM
†BBC, Via Singapore — SE Asia • 100 kW — S Asia • 250 kW
 SE Asia & Australasia • 125 kW
 E Asia • 100 kW

 BBC, Via Zyyi, Cyprus — E Africa • 100 kW
USA
 VOA, Via Botswana — M-F • E Africa • 100 kW
 E Africa • 100 kW

ENGLISH ▬ ARABIC ⋙ CHINESE ▫▫▫ FRENCH ▬ GERMAN ▬ RUSSIAN ═ SPANISH ▬ OTHER ▬

FREQUENCY   COUNTRY, STATION, LOCATION

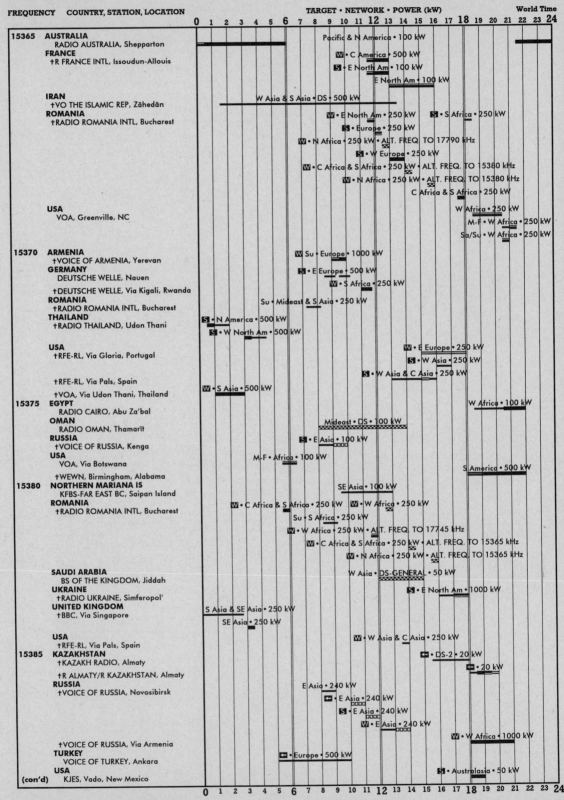

		TARGET • NETWORK • POWER (kW)
15365	**AUSTRALIA**	
	RADIO AUSTRALIA, Shepparton	Pacific & N America • 100 kW
	FRANCE	
	†R FRANCE INTL, Issoudun-Allouis	W • C America • 500 kW
		S • E North Am • 100 kW
		E North Am • 100 kW
	IRAN	
	†VO THE ISLAMIC REP, Zāhedān	W Asia & S Asia • DS • 500 kW
	ROMANIA	
	†RADIO ROMANIA INTL, Bucharest	W • E North Am • 250 kW S • S Africa • 250 kW
		S • Europe • 250 kW
		W • N Africa • 250 kW • ALT. FREQ. TO 17790 kHz
		S • W Europe • 250 kW
		W • C Africa & S Africa • 250 kW • ALT. FREQ. TO 15380 kHz
		W • N Africa • 250 kW • ALT. FREQ. TO 15380 kHz
		C Africa & S Africa • 250 kW
	USA	
	VOA, Greenville, NC	W Africa • 250 kW
		M-F • W Africa • 250 kW
		Sa/Su • W Africa • 250 kW
15370	**ARMENIA**	
	†VOICE OF ARMENIA, Yerevan	W • Su • Europe • 1000 kW
	GERMANY	
	DEUTSCHE WELLE, Nauen	S • E Europe • 500 kW
	†DEUTSCHE WELLE, Via Kigali, Rwanda	W • S Africa • 250 kW
	ROMANIA	
	†RADIO ROMANIA INTL, Bucharest	Su • Mideast & S Asia • 250 kW
	THAILAND	
	†RADIO THAILAND, Udon Thani	S • N America • 500 kW
		S • W North Am • 500 kW
	USA	
	†RFE-RL, Via Gloria, Portugal	W • E Europe • 250 kW
		S • W Asia • 250 kW
	†RFE-RL, Via Pals, Spain	S • W Asia & C Asia • 250 kW
	†VOA, Via Udon Thani, Thailand	W • S Asia • 500 kW
15375	**EGYPT**	W Africa • 100 kW
	RADIO CAIRO, Abu Za'bal	
	OMAN	
	RADIO OMAN, Thamarīt	Mideast • DS • 100 kW
	RUSSIA	
	†VOICE OF RUSSIA, Kenga	S • E Asia • 100 kW
	USA	
	VOA, Via Botswana	M-F • Africa • 100 kW
		S America • 500 kW
	†WEWN, Birmingham, Alabama	
15380	**NORTHERN MARIANA IS**	SE Asia • 100 kW
	KFBS-FAR EAST BC, Saipan Island	
	ROMANIA	
	†RADIO ROMANIA INTL, Bucharest	W • C Africa & S Africa • 250 kW W • W Africa • 250 kW
		Su • S Africa • 250 kW
		W • W Africa • 250 kW • ALT. FREQ. TO 17745 kHz
		W • C Africa & S Africa • 250 kW • ALT. FREQ. TO 15365 kHz
		W • N Africa • 250 kW • ALT. FREQ. TO 15365 kHz
	SAUDI ARABIA	
	BS OF THE KINGDOM, Jiddah	W Asia • DS-GENERAL • 50 kW
	UKRAINE	
	†RADIO UKRAINE, Simferopol'	S • E North Am • 1000 kW
	UNITED KINGDOM	
	†BBC, Via Singapore	S Asia & SE Asia • 250 kW
		SE Asia • 250 kW
	USA	
	†RFE-RL, Via Pals, Spain	W • W Asia & C Asia • 250 kW
15385	**KAZAKHSTAN**	
	†KAZAKH RADIO, Almaty	DS-2 • 20 kW
	†R ALMATY/R KAZAKHSTAN, Almaty	20 kW
	RUSSIA	
	†VOICE OF RUSSIA, Novosibirsk	E Asia • 240 kW
		E Asia • 240 kW
		S • E Asia • 240 kW
		W • E Asia • 240 kW
		W • W Africa • 1000 kW
	†VOICE OF RUSSIA, Via Armenia	
	TURKEY	
	VOICE OF TURKEY, Ankara	Europe • 500 kW
	USA	
(con'd)	KJES, Vado, New Mexico	S • Australasia • 50 kW

World Time: 0 1 2 3 4 5 6 7 8 9 10 11 12 13 14 15 16 17 18 19 20 21 22 23 24

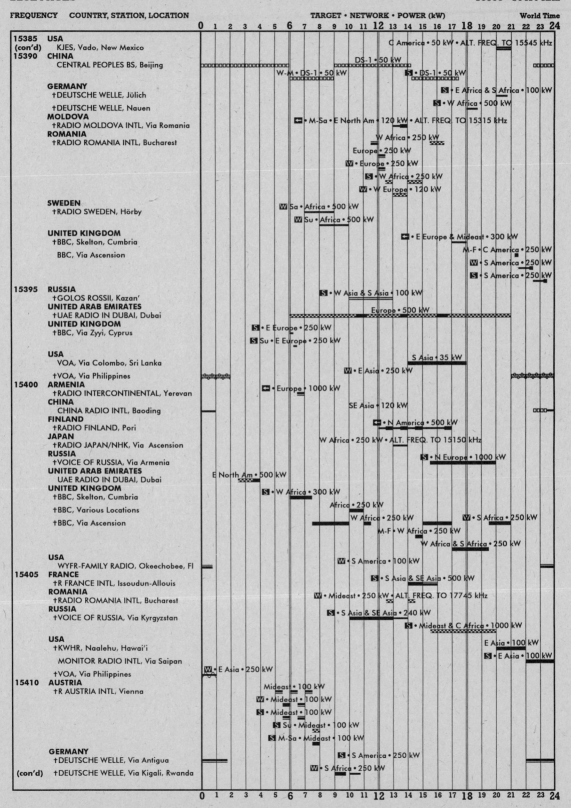

FREQUENCY   COUNTRY, STATION, LOCATION

Frequency	Country, Station, Location	Target • Network • Power (kW)
15385 (con'd)	USA KJES, Vado, New Mexico	C America • 50 kW • ALT. FREQ. TO 15545 kHz
15390	CHINA CENTRAL PEOPLES BS, Beijing	DS-1 • 50 kW / W-M • DS-1 • 50 kW / S • DS-1 • 50 kW
	GERMANY †DEUTSCHE WELLE, Jülich	S • E Africa & S Africa • 100 kW
	†DEUTSCHE WELLE, Nauen	S • W Africa • 500 kW
	MOLDOVA †RADIO MOLDOVA INTL, Via Romania	• M-Sa • E North Am • 120 kW • ALT. FREQ. TO 15315 kHz
	ROMANIA †RADIO ROMANIA INTL, Bucharest	W Africa • 250 kW
		Europe • 250 kW
		W • Europe • 250 kW
		S • W Africa • 250 kW
		W • W Europe • 120 kW
	SWEDEN †RADIO SWEDEN, Hörby	W Sa • Africa • 500 kW
		W Su • Africa • 500 kW
	UNITED KINGDOM †BBC, Skelton, Cumbria	• E Europe & Mideast • 300 kW
	BBC, Via Ascension	M-F • C America • 250 kW
		S • S America • 250 kW
		S • S America • 250 kW
15395	RUSSIA †GOLOS ROSSII, Kazan'	S • W Asia & S Asia • 100 kW
	UNITED ARAB EMIRATES †UAE RADIO IN DUBAI, Dubai	Europe • 500 kW
	UNITED KINGDOM †BBC, Via Zyyi, Cyprus	S • E Europe • 250 kW
		S Su • E Europe • 250 kW
	USA VOA, Via Colombo, Sri Lanka	S Asia • 35 kW
	†VOA, Via Philippines	W • E Asia • 250 kW
15400	ARMENIA †RADIO INTERCONTINENTAL, Yerevan	• Europe • 1000 kW
	CHINA CHINA RADIO INTL, Baoding	SE Asia • 120 kW
	FINLAND †RADIO FINLAND, Pori	• N America • 500 kW
	JAPAN †RADIO JAPAN/NHK, Via Ascension	W Africa • 250 kW • ALT. FREQ. TO 15150 kHz
	RUSSIA †VOICE OF RUSSIA, Via Armenia	S • N Europe • 1000 kW
	UNITED ARAB EMIRATES UAE RADIO IN DUBAI, Dubai	E North Am • 500 kW
	UNITED KINGDOM †BBC, Skelton, Cumbria	S • W Africa • 300 kW
	†BBC, Various Locations	Africa • 250 kW
	†BBC, Via Ascension	W Africa • 250 kW
		W • S Africa • 250 kW
		M-F • W Africa • 250 kW
		W Africa & S Africa • 250 kW
	USA WYFR-FAMILY RADIO, Okeechobee, Fl	W • S America • 100 kW
15405	FRANCE †R FRANCE INTL, Issoudun-Allouis	S • S Asia & SE Asia • 500 kW
	ROMANIA †RADIO ROMANIA INTL, Bucharest	W • Mideast • 250 kW • ALT. FREQ. TO 17745 kHz
	RUSSIA †VOICE OF RUSSIA, Via Kyrgyzstan	S • S Asia & SE Asia • 240 kW
		S • Mideast & C Africa • 1000 kW
	USA †KWHR, Naalehu, Hawai'i	E Asia • 100 kW
	MONITOR RADIO INTL, Via Saipan	S • E Asia • 100 kW
	†VOA, Via Philippines	W • E Asia • 250 kW
15410	AUSTRIA †R AUSTRIA INTL, Vienna	Mideast • 100 kW
		W • Mideast • 100 kW
		S • Mideast • 100 kW
		S Su • Mideast • 100 kW
		S M-Sa • Mideast • 100 kW
	GERMANY †DEUTSCHE WELLE, Via Antigua	S • S America • 250 kW
(con'd)	†DEUTSCHE WELLE, Via Kigali, Rwanda	W • S Africa • 250 kW

ENGLISH ▬   ARABIC ⧓   CHINESE ▯▯▯   FRENCH ▭▭   GERMAN ▬▬   RUSSIAN ══   SPANISH ▬▬   OTHER ▬

FREQUENCY	COUNTRY, STATION, LOCATION

TARGET • NETWORK • POWER (kW)   World Time

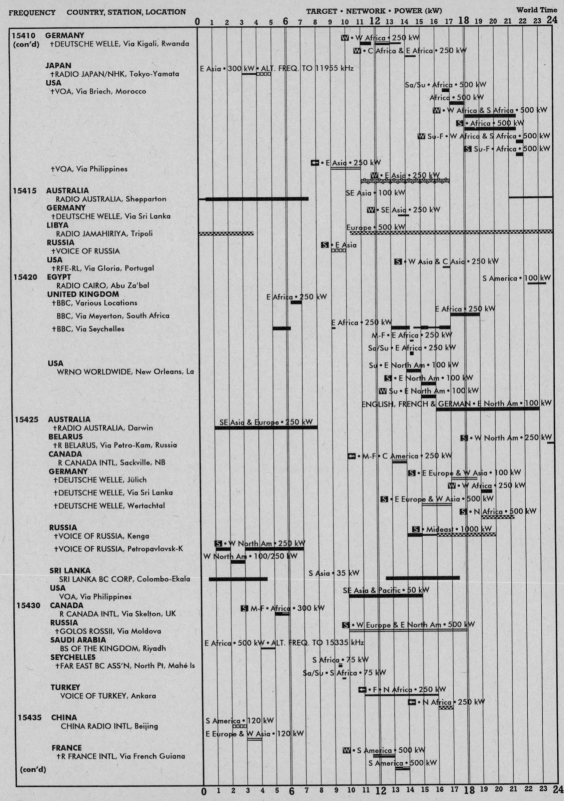

15410 (con'd)	**GERMANY** †DEUTSCHE WELLE, Via Kigali, Rwanda
	JAPAN †RADIO JAPAN/NHK, Tokyo-Yamata
	USA †VOA, Via Briech, Morocco
	†VOA, Via Philippines
15415	**AUSTRALIA** RADIO AUSTRALIA, Shepparton
	GERMANY †DEUTSCHE WELLE, Via Sri Lanka
	LIBYA RADIO JAMAHIRIYA, Tripoli
	RUSSIA †VOICE OF RUSSIA
	USA †RFE-RL, Via Gloria, Portugal
15420	**EGYPT** RADIO CAIRO, Abu Za'bal
	UNITED KINGDOM †BBC, Various Locations
	BBC, Via Meyerton, South Africa
	†BBC, Via Seychelles
	USA WRNO WORLDWIDE, New Orleans, La
15425	**AUSTRALIA** †RADIO AUSTRALIA, Darwin
	BELARUS †R BELARUS, Via Petro-Kam, Russia
	CANADA R CANADA INTL, Sackville, NB
	GERMANY †DEUTSCHE WELLE, Jülich
	†DEUTSCHE WELLE, Via Sri Lanka
	†DEUTSCHE WELLE, Wertachtal
	RUSSIA †VOICE OF RUSSIA, Kenga
	†VOICE OF RUSSIA, Petropavlovsk-K
	SRI LANKA SRI LANKA BC CORP, Colombo-Ekala
	USA VOA, Via Philippines
15430	**CANADA** R CANADA INTL, Via Skelton, UK
	RUSSIA †GOLOS ROSSII, Via Moldova
	SAUDI ARABIA BS OF THE KINGDOM, Riyadh
	SEYCHELLES †FAR EAST BC ASS'N, North Pt, Mahé Is
	TURKEY VOICE OF TURKEY, Ankara
15435	**CHINA** CHINA RADIO INTL, Beijing
	FRANCE †R FRANCE INTL, Via French Guiana
(con'd)	

FREQUENCY	COUNTRY, STATION, LOCATION	TARGET • NETWORK • POWER (kW)
15435 (con'd)	**GERMANY** †DEUTSCHE WELLE, Jülich	S • W Asia & S Asia • 100 kW
	LIBYA RADIO JAMAHIRIYA, Tripoli	N Africa & Mideast • 500 kW
	RUSSIA †GOLOS ROSSII	S
	†R TIKHIY OKEAN, Irkutsk	S • Australasia • 1000 kW
	†VOICE OF RUSSIA	S • S Asia
	UNITED ARAB EMIRATES UAE RADIO IN DUBAI, Dubai	Australasia • 500 kW
	USA †VOA, Via Briech, Morocco	S • E Europe • 500 kW
	VOA, Via Kavália, Greece	S • Mideast • 250 kW
15440	**CHINA** CHINA RADIO INTL, Kunming	Australasia • 120 kW
	CHINA (TAIWAN) BC CORP CHINA, Via Okeechobee,USA	C America • 100 kW
	FINLAND †RADIO FINLAND, Pori	S • Mideast • 500 kW
		W • Mideast • 500 kW
		S • Europe • 500 kW
	FRANCE †R FRANCE INTL, Via Beijing, China	S • S Asia • 120 kW
	†R FRANCE INTL, Via Tokyo, Japan	S • SE Asia • 300 kW
	USA WYFR-FAMILY RADIO, Okeechobee, Fl	C America • 100 kW
15445	**BRAZIL** RADIO NACIONAL, Brasília	N America & C America • 250 kW
	CHINA CHINA RADIO INTL, Via Brasília, Brazil	C America & S America • 250 kW
	PAKISTAN RADIO PAKISTAN, Islamabad	Mideast • 100 kW
	SEYCHELLES †FAR EAST BC ASS'N, North Pt, Mahé Is	W Asia & S Asia • 100 kW
		Sa • S Asia • 100 kW
		F • W Asia & S Asia • 100 kW
		S Asia • 100 kW
	USA †RFE-RL, Via Gloria, Portugal	S • W Asia & C Asia • 250 kW
	VOA, Via Ascension	W • C Africa • 250 kW
		W Su-F • C Africa • 250 kW
	VOA, Via Botswana	Sa/Su • C Africa & E Africa • 100 kW
		C Africa & E Africa • 100 kW
		W • C Africa & E Africa • 100 kW
	†VOA, Via Briech, Morocco	S • Africa • 500 kW
		S Su-F • Africa • 500 kW
	†VOA, Via Udon Thani, Thailand	◄ • E Asia • 500 kW
	†VOA, Via Woofferton, UK	S • W Asia & C Asia • 300 kW
		S Sa/Su • W Asia & C Asia • 300 kW
15450	**AUSTRIA** †R AUSTRIA INTL, Vienna	E Asia • 500 kW
		W • E Asia • 500 kW
		S • E Asia • 500 kW
	PHILIPPINES FEBC RADIO INTL, Bocaue	S Asia & SE Asia • 100 kW
	RUSSIA †GOLOS ROSSII, Serpukhov	S • S Asia & SE Asia • 1000 kW
	TUNISIA RTV TUNISIENNE, Sfax	N Africa & Mideast • DS • 100 kW
15455	**CHINA** CHINA RADIO INTL, Beijing	S • S Asia • 120 kW
	RUSSIA †GOLOS ROSSII, Komsomol'sk 'Amure	S • W North Am • 200 kW
	†VOICE OF RUSSIA, Tula	S • Europe • 240 kW
		S • Europe & W Africa • 240 kW
15460	**COSTA RICA** †ADVENTIST WORLD R, Cahuita	Sa/Su • C America & S America • 50 kW
		Sa • C America & S America • 50 kW
		Su-F • C America & S America • 50 kW
		C America & S America • 50 kW
	FRANCE †R FRANCE INTL, Issoudun-Allouis	W • E Africa • 100 kW
		S • E Africa • 100 kW
	RUSSIA †VOICE OF RUSSIA, Moscow	S • SE Asia • 240 kW
		W • SE Asia • 250 kW
	SWITZERLAND †SWISS RADIO INTL, Schwarzenburg	S • SE Asia • 150 kW • ALT. FREQ. TO 15545 kHz

World Time: 0 1 2 3 4 5 6 7 8 9 10 11 12 13 14 15 16 17 18 19 20 21 22 23 24

ENGLISH ▬ ARABIC ▦ CHINESE ▫▫▫ FRENCH ▬ GERMAN ▬ RUSSIAN ═ SPANISH ▬ OTHER —

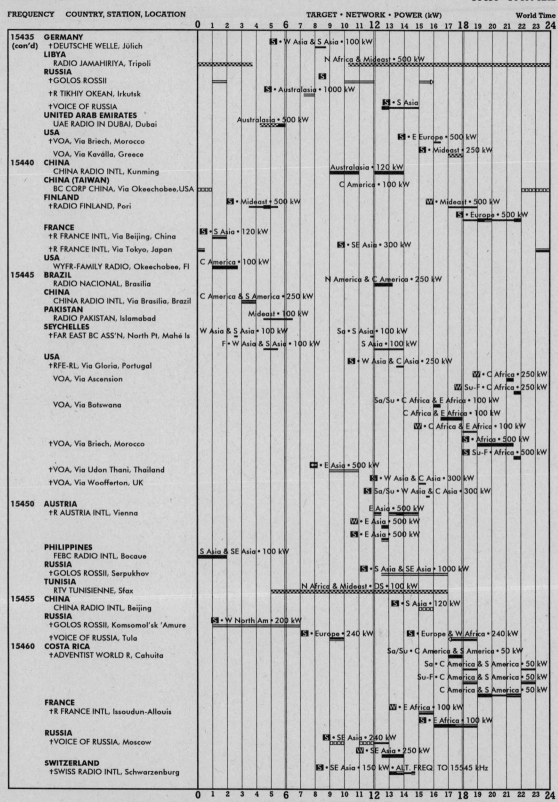

FREQUENCY   COUNTRY, STATION, LOCATION

TARGET • NETWORK • POWER (kW)   World Time

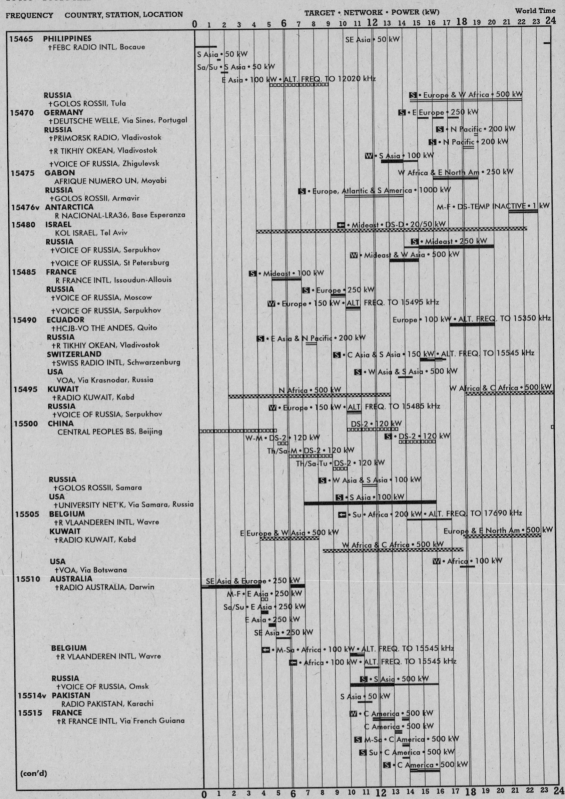

Freq	Country, Station, Location	Schedule details
15465	**PHILIPPINES** †FEBC RADIO INTL, Bocaue	SE Asia • 50 kW / S Asia • 50 kW / Sa/Su • S Asia • 50 kW / E Asia • 100 kW • ALT. FREQ. TO 12020 kHz
	RUSSIA †GOLOS ROSSII, Tula	S • Europe & W Africa • 500 kW
15470	**GERMANY** †DEUTSCHE WELLE, Via Sines, Portugal	S • E Europe • 250 kW
	RUSSIA †PRIMORSK RADIO, Vladivostok	S • N Pacific • 200 kW
	†R TIKHIY OKEAN, Vladivostok	S • N Pacific • 200 kW
	†VOICE OF RUSSIA, Zhigulevsk	W • S Asia • 100 kW
15475	**GABON** AFRIQUE NUMERO UN, Moyabi	W Africa & E North Am • 250 kW
	RUSSIA †GOLOS ROSSII, Armavir	S • Europe, Atlantic & S America • 1000 kW
15476v	**ANTARCTICA** R NACIONAL-LRA36, Base Esperanza	M-F • DS-TEMP INACTIVE • 1 kW
15480	**ISRAEL** KOL ISRAEL, Tel Aviv	• Mideast • DS-D • 20/50 kW
	RUSSIA †VOICE OF RUSSIA, Serpukhov	S • Mideast • 250 kW
	†VOICE OF RUSSIA, St Petersburg	W • Mideast & W Asia • 500 kW
15485	**FRANCE** R FRANCE INTL, Issoudun-Allouis	S • Mideast • 100 kW
	RUSSIA †VOICE OF RUSSIA, Moscow	S • Europe • 250 kW
	†VOICE OF RUSSIA, Serpukhov	W • Europe • 150 kW • ALT. FREQ. TO 15495 kHz
15490	**ECUADOR** †HCJB-VO THE ANDES, Quito	Europe • 100 kW • ALT. FREQ. TO 15350 kHz
	RUSSIA †R TIKHIY OKEAN, Vladivostok	S • E Asia & N Pacific • 200 kW
	SWITZERLAND †SWISS RADIO INTL, Schwarzenburg	S • C Asia & S Asia • 150 kW • ALT. FREQ. TO 15545 kHz
	USA VOA, Via Krasnodar, Russia	S • W Asia & S Asia • 500 kW
15495	**KUWAIT** †RADIO KUWAIT, Kabd	N Africa • 500 kW / W Africa & C Africa • 500 kW
	RUSSIA †VOICE OF RUSSIA, Serpukhov	W • Europe • 150 kW • ALT. FREQ. TO 15485 kHz
15500	**CHINA** CENTRAL PEOPLES BS, Beijing	DS-2 • 120 kW / W-M • DS-2 • 120 kW / S • DS-2 • 120 kW / Th/Sa•M • DS-2 • 120 kW / Th/Sa-Tu • DS-2 • 120 kW
	RUSSIA †GOLOS ROSSII, Samara	S • W Asia & S Asia • 100 kW
	USA †UNIVERSITY NET'K, Via Samara, Russia	S • S Asia • 100 kW
15505	**BELGIUM** †R VLAANDEREN INTL, Wavre	• Su • Africa • 200 kW • ALT. FREQ. TO 17690 kHz
	KUWAIT †RADIO KUWAIT, Kabd	E Europe & W Asia • 500 kW / Europe & E North Am • 500 kW / W Africa & C Africa • 500 kW
	USA †VOA, Via Botswana	W • Africa • 100 kW
15510	**AUSTRALIA** †RADIO AUSTRALIA, Darwin	SE Asia & Europe • 250 kW / M-F • E Asia • 250 kW / Sa/Su • E Asia • 250 kW / E Asia • 250 kW / SE Asia • 250 kW
	BELGIUM †R VLAANDEREN INTL, Wavre	• M-Sa • Africa • 100 kW • ALT. FREQ. TO 15545 kHz / • Africa • 100 kW • ALT. FREQ. TO 15545 kHz
	RUSSIA †VOICE OF RUSSIA, Omsk	S • S Asia • 500 kW
15514v	**PAKISTAN** RADIO PAKISTAN, Karachi	S Asia • 50 kW
15515	**FRANCE** †R FRANCE INTL, Via French Guiana	W • C America • 500 kW / C America • 500 kW / S • M-Sa • C America • 500 kW / S • Su • C America • 500 kW / S • C America • 500 kW

(con'd)

FREQUENCY   COUNTRY, STATION, LOCATION   TARGET • NETWORK • POWER (kW)

World Time
0 1 2 3 4 5 6 7 8 9 10 11 12 13 14 15 16 17 18 19 20 21 22 23 24

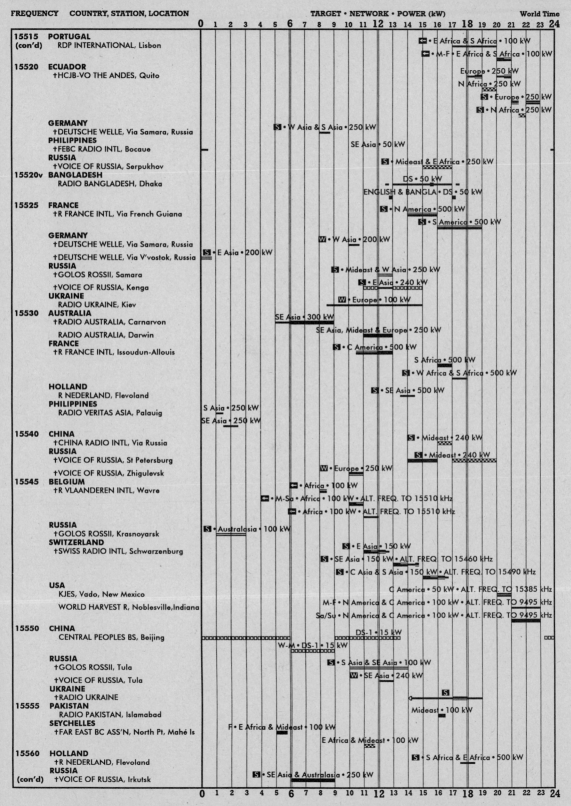

Frequency	Country, Station, Location	Details
15515 (con'd)	**PORTUGAL** †RDP INTERNATIONAL, Lisbon	E Africa & S Africa • 100 kW; M-F • E Africa & S Africa • 100 kW
15520	**ECUADOR** †HCJB-VO THE ANDES, Quito	Europe • 250 kW; N Africa • 250 kW; S • Europe • 250 kW; S • N Africa • 250 kW
	GERMANY †DEUTSCHE WELLE, Via Samara, Russia	S • W Asia & S Asia • 250 kW
	PHILIPPINES †FEBC RADIO INTL, Bocaue	SE Asia • 50 kW
	RUSSIA †VOICE OF RUSSIA, Serpukhov	S • Mideast & E Africa • 250 kW
15520v	**BANGLADESH** RADIO BANGLADESH, Dhaka	DS • 50 kW; ENGLISH & BANGLA • DS • 50 kW
15525	**FRANCE** †R FRANCE INTL, Via French Guiana	S • N America • 500 kW; S • S America • 500 kW
	GERMANY †DEUTSCHE WELLE, Via Samara, Russia	W • W Asia • 200 kW
	†DEUTSCHE WELLE, Via V'vostok, Russia	S • E Asia • 200 kW
	RUSSIA †GOLOS ROSSII, Samara	S • Mideast & W Asia • 250 kW
	†VOICE OF RUSSIA, Kenga	S • E Asia • 240 kW
	UKRAINE RADIO UKRAINE, Kiev	W • Europe • 100 kW
15530	**AUSTRALIA** †RADIO AUSTRALIA, Carnarvon	SE Asia • 300 kW
	RADIO AUSTRALIA, Darwin	SE Asia, Mideast & Europe • 250 kW
	FRANCE †R FRANCE INTL, Issoudun-Allouis	S • C America • 500 kW; S Africa • 500 kW; S • W Africa & S Africa • 500 kW
	HOLLAND R NEDERLAND, Flevoland	S • SE Asia • 500 kW
	PHILIPPINES RADIO VERITAS ASIA, Palauig	S Asia • 250 kW; SE Asia • 250 kW
15540	**CHINA** †CHINA RADIO INTL, Via Russia	S • Mideast • 240 kW
	RUSSIA †VOICE OF RUSSIA, St Petersburg	S • Mideast • 240 kW
	†VOICE OF RUSSIA, Zhigulevsk	W • Europe • 250 kW
15545	**BELGIUM** †R VLAANDEREN INTL, Wavre	Africa • 100 kW; M-Sa • Africa • 100 kW • ALT. FREQ. TO 15510 kHz; Africa • 100 kW • ALT. FREQ. TO 15510 kHz
	RUSSIA †GOLOS ROSSII, Krasnoyarsk	S • Australasia • 100 kW
	SWITZERLAND †SWISS RADIO INTL, Schwarzenburg	S • E Asia • 150 kW; S • SE Asia • 150 kW • ALT. FREQ. TO 15460 kHz; S • C Asia & S Asia • 150 kW • ALT. FREQ. TO 15490 kHz
	USA KJES, Vado, New Mexico	C America • 50 kW • ALT. FREQ. TO 15385 kHz
	WORLD HARVEST R, Noblesville, Indiana	M-F • N America & C America • 100 kW • ALT. FREQ. TO 9495 kHz; Sa/Su • N America & C America • 100 kW • ALT. FREQ. TO 9495 kHz
15550	**CHINA** CENTRAL PEOPLES BS, Beijing	DS-1 • 15 kW; W-M • DS-1 • 15 kW
	RUSSIA †GOLOS ROSSII, Tula	S • S Asia & SE Asia • 100 kW
	†VOICE OF RUSSIA, Tula	W • SE Asia • 240 kW
	UKRAINE †RADIO UKRAINE	S
15555	**PAKISTAN** RADIO PAKISTAN, Islamabad	Mideast • 100 kW
	SEYCHELLES †FAR EAST BC ASS'N, North Pt, Mahé Is	F • E Africa & Mideast • 100 kW; E Africa & Mideast • 100 kW
15560	**HOLLAND** †R NEDERLAND, Flevoland	S • S Africa & E Africa • 500 kW
(con'd)	**RUSSIA** †VOICE OF RUSSIA, Irkutsk	S • SE Asia & Australasia • 250 kW

0 1 2 3 4 5 6 7 8 9 10 11 12 13 14 15 16 17 18 19 20 21 22 23 24

ENGLISH ▬   ARABIC ▧   CHINESE ▫▫▫   FRENCH ▬   GERMAN ▬   RUSSIAN ═   SPANISH ═   OTHER ▬

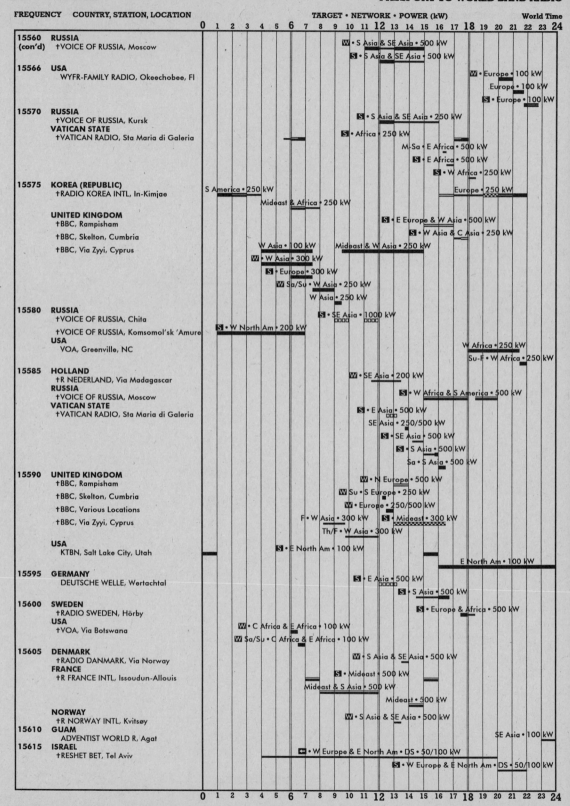

FREQUENCY   COUNTRY, STATION, LOCATION

TARGET • NETWORK • POWER (kW)   World Time

15560	RUSSIA
(con'd)	†VOICE OF RUSSIA, Moscow
15566	USA
	WYFR-FAMILY RADIO, Okeechobee, Fl
15570	RUSSIA
	†VOICE OF RUSSIA, Kursk
	VATICAN STATE
	†VATICAN RADIO, Sta Maria di Galeria
15575	KOREA (REPUBLIC)
	†RADIO KOREA INTL, In-Kimjae
	UNITED KINGDOM
	†BBC, Rampisham
	†BBC, Skelton, Cumbria
	†BBC, Via Zyyi, Cyprus
15580	RUSSIA
	†VOICE OF RUSSIA, Chita
	†VOICE OF RUSSIA, Komsomol'sk 'Amure
	USA
	VOA, Greenville, NC
15585	HOLLAND
	†R NEDERLAND, Via Madagascar
	RUSSIA
	†VOICE OF RUSSIA, Moscow
	VATICAN STATE
	†VATICAN RADIO, Sta Maria di Galeria
15590	UNITED KINGDOM
	†BBC, Rampisham
	†BBC, Skelton, Cumbria
	†BBC, Various Locations
	†BBC, Via Zyyi, Cyprus
	USA
	KTBN, Salt Lake City, Utah
15595	GERMANY
	DEUTSCHE WELLE, Wertachtal
15600	SWEDEN
	†RADIO SWEDEN, Hörby
	USA
	†VOA, Via Botswana
15605	DENMARK
	†RADIO DANMARK, Via Norway
	FRANCE
	†R FRANCE INTL, Issoudun-Allouis
	NORWAY
	†R NORWAY INTL, Kvitsøy
15610	GUAM
	ADVENTIST WORLD R, Agat
15615	ISRAEL
	†RESHET BET, Tel Aviv

FREQUENCY   COUNTRY, STATION, LOCATION   TARGET • NETWORK • POWER (kW)   World Time

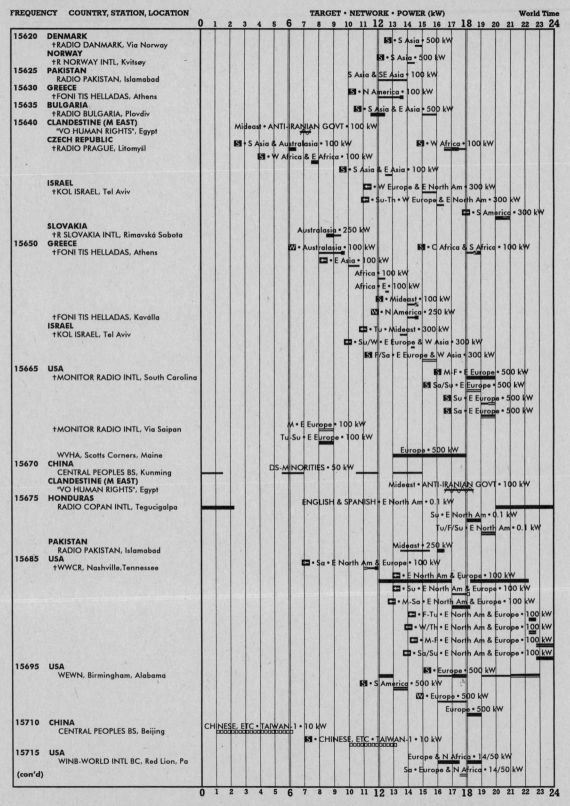

Freq	Country, Station, Location	Target • Network • Power
15620	**DENMARK** †RADIO DANMARK, Via Norway	S • S Asia • 500 kW
	NORWAY †R NORWAY INTL, Kvitsøy	S • S Asia • 500 kW
15625	**PAKISTAN** RADIO PAKISTAN, Islamabad	S Asia & SE Asia • 100 kW
15630	**GREECE** †FONI TIS HELLADAS, Athens	S • N America • 100 kW
15635	**BULGARIA** †RADIO BULGARIA, Plovdiv	S • S Asia & E Asia • 500 kW
15640	**CLANDESTINE (M EAST)** "VO HUMAN RIGHTS", Egypt	Mideast • ANTI-IRANIAN GOVT • 100 kW
	CZECH REPUBLIC †RADIO PRAGUE, Litomyšl	S • S Asia & Australasia • 100 kW S • W Africa • 100 kW
		S • W Africa & E Africa • 100 kW
		S • S Asia & E Asia • 100 kW
	ISRAEL †KOL ISRAEL, Tel Aviv	• W Europe & E North Am • 300 kW
		• Su-Th • W Europe & E North Am • 300 kW
		• S America • 300 kW
	SLOVAKIA †R SLOVAKIA INTL, Rimavská Sobota	Australasia • 250 kW
15650	**GREECE** †FONI TIS HELLADAS, Athens	W • Australasia • 100 kW S • C Africa & S Africa • 100 kW
		• E Asia • 100 kW
		Africa • 100 kW
		Africa • E • 100 kW
		S • Mideast • 100 kW
		W • N America • 250 kW
	†FONI TIS HELLADAS, Kaválla	• Tu • Mideast • 300 kW
	ISRAEL †KOL ISRAEL, Tel Aviv	• Su/W • E Europe & W Asia • 300 kW
		S • F/Sa • E Europe & W Asia • 300 kW
15665	**USA** †MONITOR RADIO INTL, South Carolina	S • M-F • E Europe • 500 kW
		S • Sa/Su • E Europe • 500 kW
		S • Su • E Europe • 500 kW
		S • Sa • E Europe • 500 kW
	†MONITOR RADIO INTL, Via Saipan	M • E Europe • 100 kW
		Tu-Su • E Europe • 100 kW
	WVHA, Scotts Corners, Maine	Europe • 500 kW
15670	**CHINA** CENTRAL PEOPLES BS, Kunming	DS-MINORITIES • 50 kW
	CLANDESTINE (M EAST) "VO HUMAN RIGHTS", Egypt	Mideast • ANTI-IRANIAN GOVT • 100 kW
15675	**HONDURAS** RADIO COPAN INTL, Tegucigalpa	ENGLISH & SPANISH • E North Am • 0.1 kW
		Su • E North Am • 0.1 kW
		Tu/F/Su • E North Am • 0.1 kW
	PAKISTAN RADIO PAKISTAN, Islamabad	Mideast • 250 kW
15685	**USA** †WWCR, Nashville, Tennessee	• Sa • E North Am & Europe • 100 kW
		• E North Am & Europe • 100 kW
		• Su • E North Am & Europe • 100 kW
		• M-Sa • E North Am & Europe • 100 kW
		• F-Tu • E North Am & Europe • 100 kW
		• W/Th • E North Am & Europe • 100 kW
		• M-F • E North Am & Europe • 100 kW
		• Sa/Su • E North Am & Europe • 100 kW
15695	**USA** WEWN, Birmingham, Alabama	S • Europe • 500 kW
		S • S America • 500 kW
		W • Europe • 500 kW
		Europe • 500 kW
15710	**CHINA** CENTRAL PEOPLES BS, Beijing	CHINESE, ETC • TAIWAN-1 • 10 kW
		S • CHINESE, ETC • TAIWAN-1 • 10 kW
15715	**USA** WINB-WORLD INTL BC, Red Lion, Pa	Europe & N Africa • 14/50 kW
(con'd)		Sa • Europe & N Africa • 14/50 kW

ENGLISH ▬   ARABIC ⧓⧓⧓   CHINESE ▢▢▢   FRENCH ▬   GERMAN ▬   RUSSIAN ═   SPANISH ▬   OTHER ▬

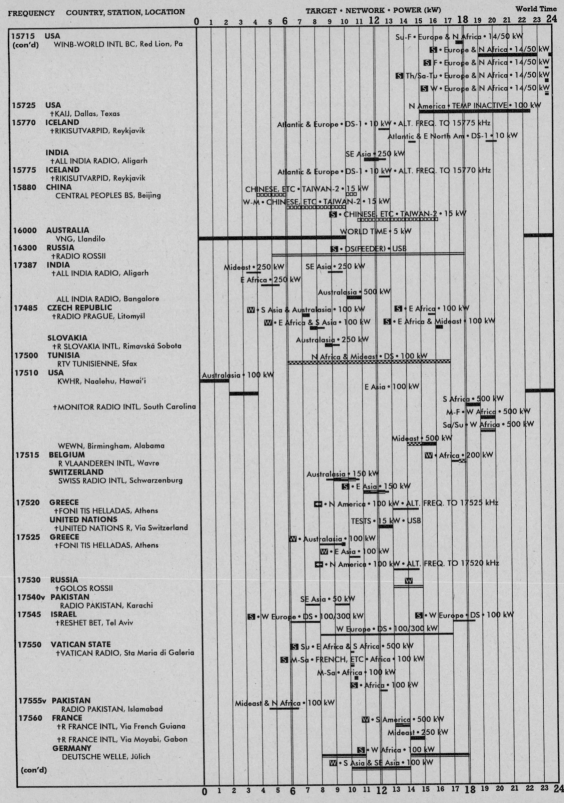

FREQUENCY	COUNTRY, STATION, LOCATION
15715 (con'd)	USA WINB-WORLD INTL BC, Red Lion, Pa
15725	USA †KAIJ, Dallas, Texas
15770	ICELAND †RIKISUTVARPID, Reykjavik
	INDIA †ALL INDIA RADIO, Aligarh
15775	ICELAND †RIKISUTVARPID, Reykjavik
15880	CHINA CENTRAL PEOPLES BS, Beijing
16000	AUSTRALIA VNG, Llandilo
16300	RUSSIA †RADIO ROSSII
17387	INDIA †ALL INDIA RADIO, Aligarh
	ALL INDIA RADIO, Bangalore
17485	CZECH REPUBLIC †RADIO PRAGUE, Litomyšl
	SLOVAKIA †R SLOVAKIA INTL, Rimavská Sobota
17500	TUNISIA RTV TUNISIENNE, Sfax
17510	USA KWHR, Naalehu, Hawai'i
	†MONITOR RADIO INTL, South Carolina
	WEWN, Birmingham, Alabama
17515	BELGIUM R VLAANDEREN INTL, Wavre
	SWITZERLAND SWISS RADIO INTL, Schwarzenburg
17520	GREECE †FONI TIS HELLADAS, Athens
	UNITED NATIONS †UNITED NATIONS R, Via Switzerland
17525	GREECE †FONI TIS HELLADAS, Athens
17530	RUSSIA †GOLOS ROSSII
17540v	PAKISTAN RADIO PAKISTAN, Karachi
17545	ISRAEL †RESHET BET, Tel Aviv
17550	VATICAN STATE †VATICAN RADIO, Sta Maria di Galeria
17555v	PAKISTAN RADIO PAKISTAN, Islamabad
17560	FRANCE †R FRANCE INTL, Via French Guiana
	†R FRANCE INTL, Via Moyabi, Gabon
	GERMANY DEUTSCHE WELLE, Jülich
(con'd)	

FREQUENCY   COUNTRY, STATION, LOCATION | TARGET • NETWORK • POWER (kW) | World Time

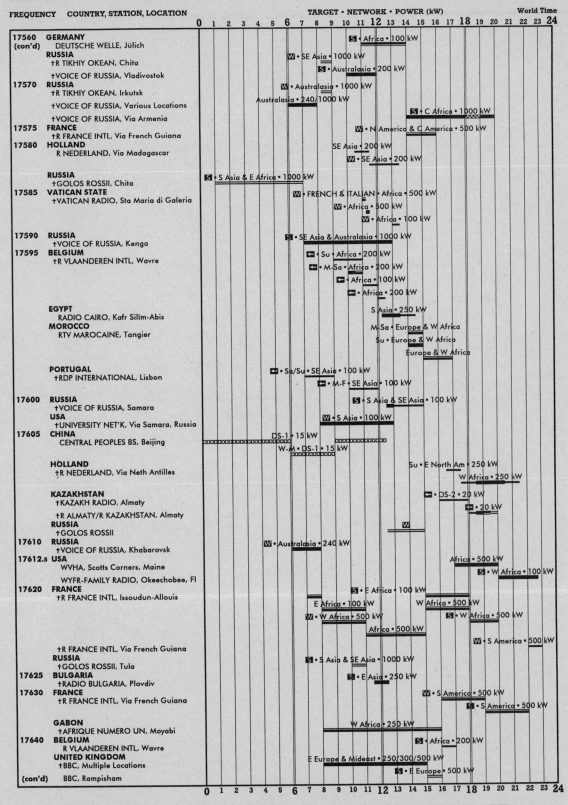

Freq	Country / Station / Location	Schedule
17560 (con'd)	**GERMANY** DEUTSCHE WELLE, Jülich	S • Africa • 100 kW
	RUSSIA †R TIKHIY OKEAN, Chita	W • SE Asia • 1000 kW
	†VOICE OF RUSSIA, Vladivostok	S • Australasia • 200 kW
17570	**RUSSIA** †R TIKHIY OKEAN, Irkutsk	W • Australasia • 1000 kW
	†VOICE OF RUSSIA, Various Locations	Australasia • 240/1000 kW
	†VOICE OF RUSSIA, Via Armenia	S • C Africa • 1000 kW
17575	**FRANCE** †R FRANCE INTL, Via French Guiana	W • N America & C America • 500 kW
17580	**HOLLAND** R NEDERLAND, Via Madagascar	SE Asia • 200 kW / W • SE Asia • 200 kW
	RUSSIA †GOLOS ROSSII, Chita	S • S Asia & E Africa • 1000 kW
17585	**VATICAN STATE** †VATICAN RADIO, Sta Maria di Galeria	W • FRENCH & ITALIAN • Africa • 500 kW / W • Africa • 500 kW / W • Africa • 100 kW
17590	**RUSSIA** †VOICE OF RUSSIA, Kenga	S • SE Asia & Australasia • 1000 kW
17595	**BELGIUM** †R VLAANDEREN INTL, Wavre	• Su • Africa • 200 kW / • M-Sa • Africa • 200 kW / • Africa • 100 kW / • Africa • 200 kW
	EGYPT RADIO CAIRO, Kafr Silim-Abis	S Asia • 250 kW
	MOROCCO RTV MAROCAINE, Tangier	M-Sa • Europe & W Africa / Su • Europe & W Africa / Europe & W Africa
	PORTUGAL †RDP INTERNATIONAL, Lisbon	• Sa/Su • SE Asia • 100 kW / • M-F • SE Asia • 100 kW
17600	**RUSSIA** †VOICE OF RUSSIA, Samara	S • S Asia & SE Asia • 100 kW
	USA †UNIVERSITY NET'K, Via Samara, Russia	W • S Asia • 100 kW
17605	**CHINA** CENTRAL PEOPLES BS, Beijing	DS-1 • 15 kW / W-M • DS-1 • 15 kW
	HOLLAND †R NEDERLAND, Via Neth Antilles	Su • E North Am • 250 kW / W Africa • 250 kW
	KAZAKHSTAN †KAZAKH RADIO, Almaty	• DS-2 • 20 kW
	†R ALMATY/R KAZAKHSTAN, Almaty	• 20 kW
	RUSSIA †GOLOS ROSSII	W
17610	**RUSSIA** †VOICE OF RUSSIA, Khabarovsk	W • Australasia • 240 kW
17612.5	**USA** WVHA, Scotts Corners, Maine	Africa • 500 kW
	WYFR-FAMILY RADIO, Okeechobee, Fl	S • W Africa • 100 kW
17620	**FRANCE** †R FRANCE INTL, Issoudun-Allouis	S • E Africa • 100 kW / E Africa • 100 kW / W • W Africa • 500 kW / W Africa • 500 kW / Africa • 500 kW
	†R FRANCE INTL, Via French Guiana	W • S America • 500 kW
	RUSSIA †GOLOS ROSSII, Tula	S • S Asia & SE Asia • 1000 kW
17625	**BULGARIA** †RADIO BULGARIA, Plovdiv	S • E Asia • 250 kW
17630	**FRANCE** †R FRANCE INTL, Via French Guiana	W • S America • 500 kW / S • S America • 500 kW
	GABON †AFRIQUE NUMERO UN, Moyabi	W Africa • 250 kW
17640	**BELGIUM** R VLAANDEREN INTL, Wavre	S • Africa • 200 kW
	UNITED KINGDOM †BBC, Multiple Locations	E Europe & Mideast • 250/300/500 kW
(con'd)	BBC, Rampisham	S • E Europe • 500 kW

ENGLISH ▬   ARABIC ▨   CHINESE ▫▫▫   FRENCH ═   GERMAN ▬   RUSSIAN ═   SPANISH ▬   OTHER ▬

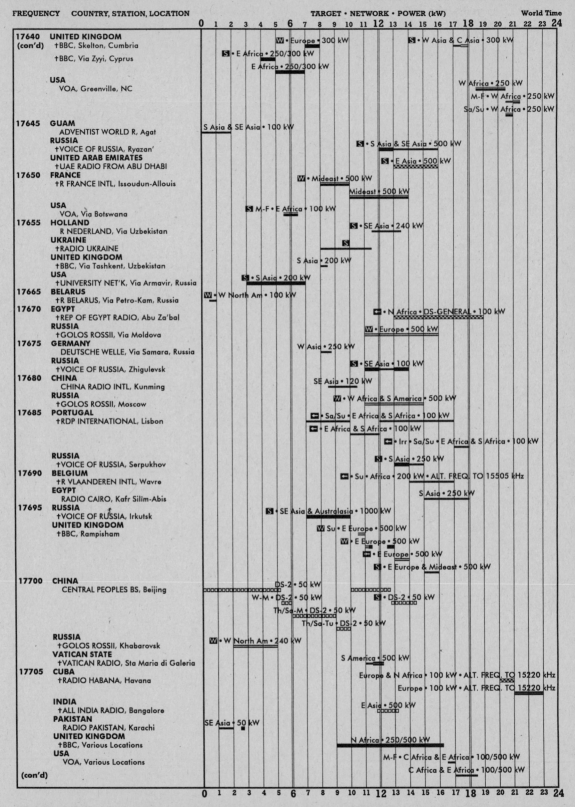

FREQUENCY   COUNTRY, STATION, LOCATION   TARGET • NETWORK • POWER (kW)   World Time

Frequency	Country, Station, Location	Target • Network • Power
17640 (con'd)	**UNITED KINGDOM** †BBC, Skelton, Cumbria	W • Europe • 300 kW; S • W Asia & C Asia • 300 kW; S • E Africa • 250/300 kW
	†BBC, Via Zyyi, Cyprus	E Africa • 250/300 kW
	USA VOA, Greenville, NC	W Africa • 250 kW; M-F • W Africa • 250 kW; Sa/Su • W Africa • 250 kW
17645	**GUAM** ADVENTIST WORLD R, Agat	S Asia & SE Asia • 100 kW
	RUSSIA †VOICE OF RUSSIA, Ryazan'	S • S Asia & SE Asia • 500 kW
	UNITED ARAB EMIRATES †UAE RADIO FROM ABU DHABI	S • E Asia • 500 kW
17650	**FRANCE** †R FRANCE INTL, Issoudun-Allouis	W • Mideast • 500 kW; Mideast • 500 kW
	USA VOA, Via Botswana	S • M-F • E Africa • 100 kW
17655	**HOLLAND** R NEDERLAND, Via Uzbekistan	S • SE Asia • 240 kW
	UKRAINE †RADIO UKRAINE	S
	UNITED KINGDOM †BBC, Via Tashkent, Uzbekistan	S Asia • 200 kW
	USA †UNIVERSITY NET'K, Via Armavir, Russia	S • S Asia • 200 kW
17665	**BELARUS** †R BELARUS, Via Petro-Kam, Russia	W • W North Am • 100 kW
17670	**EGYPT** †REP OF EGYPT RADIO, Abu Za'bal	• N Africa • DS-GENERAL • 100 kW
	RUSSIA †GOLOS ROSSII, Via Moldova	W • Europe • 500 kW
17675	**GERMANY** DEUTSCHE WELLE, Via Samara, Russia	W Asia • 250 kW
	RUSSIA †VOICE OF RUSSIA, Zhigulevsk	S • SE Asia • 100 kW
17680	**CHINA** CHINA RADIO INTL, Kunming	SE Asia • 120 kW
	RUSSIA †GOLOS ROSSII, Moscow	W • W Africa & S America • 500 kW
17685	**PORTUGAL** †RDP INTERNATIONAL, Lisbon	• Sa/Su • E Africa & S Africa • 100 kW; • E Africa & S Africa • 100 kW; • Irr • Sa/Su • E Africa & S Africa • 100 kW
	RUSSIA †VOICE OF RUSSIA, Serpukhov	S • S Asia • 250 kW
17690	**BELGIUM** †R VLAANDEREN INTL, Wavre	• Su • Africa • 200 kW • ALT. FREQ. TO 15505 kHz
	EGYPT RADIO CAIRO, Kafr Silim-Abis	S Asia • 250 kW
17695	**RUSSIA** †VOICE OF RUSSIA, Irkutsk	S • SE Asia & Australasia • 1000 kW
	UNITED KINGDOM †BBC, Rampisham	W • Su • E Europe • 500 kW; W • E Europe • 500 kW; • E Europe • 500 kW; S • E Europe & Mideast • 500 kW
17700	**CHINA** CENTRAL PEOPLES BS, Beijing	DS-2 • 50 kW; W-M • DS-2 • 50 kW; S • DS-2 • 50 kW; Th/Sa-M • DS-2 • 50 kW; Th/Sa-Tu • DS-2 • 50 kW
	RUSSIA †GOLOS ROSSII, Khabarovsk	W • W North Am • 240 kW
	VATICAN STATE †VATICAN RADIO, Sta Maria di Galeria	S America • 500 kW
17705	**CUBA** †RADIO HABANA, Havana	Europe & N Africa • 100 kW • ALT. FREQ. TO 15220 kHz; Europe • 100 kW • ALT. FREQ. TO 15220 kHz
	INDIA †ALL INDIA RADIO, Bangalore	E Asia • 500 kW
	PAKISTAN RADIO PAKISTAN, Karachi	SE Asia • 50 kW
	UNITED KINGDOM †BBC, Various Locations	N Africa • 250/500 kW
	USA VOA, Various Locations	M-F • C Africa & E Africa • 100/500 kW; C Africa & E Africa • 100/500 kW
(con'd)		

FREQUENCY   COUNTRY, STATION, LOCATION

TARGET • NETWORK • POWER (kW)

World Time

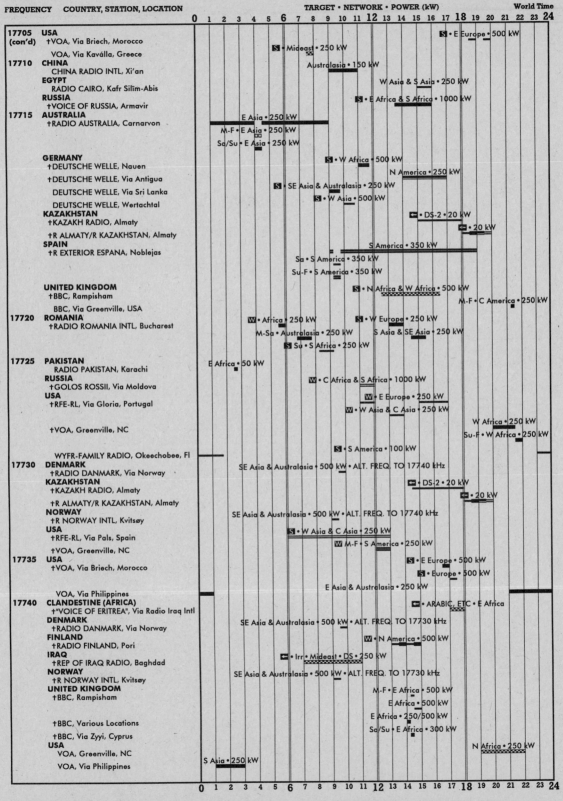

Frequency	Country / Station / Location	Target • Network • Power
17705 (con'd)	**USA**	
	†VOA, Via Briech, Morocco	🅂 • E Europe • 500 kW
	VOA, Via Kaválla, Greece	🅂 • Mideast • 250 kW
17710	**CHINA**	
	CHINA RADIO INTL, Xi'an	Australasia • 150 kW
	EGYPT	
	RADIO CAIRO, Kafr Silim-Abis	W Asia & S Asia • 250 kW
	RUSSIA	
	†VOICE OF RUSSIA, Armavir	🅂 • E Africa & S Africa • 1000 kW
17715	**AUSTRALIA**	
	†RADIO AUSTRALIA, Carnarvon	E Asia • 250 kW
		M-F • E Asia • 250 kW
		Sa/Su • E Asia • 250 kW
	GERMANY	
	†DEUTSCHE WELLE, Nauen	🅂 • W Africa • 500 kW
	†DEUTSCHE WELLE, Via Antigua	N America • 250 kW
	DEUTSCHE WELLE, Via Sri Lanka	🅂 • SE Asia & Australasia • 250 kW
	DEUTSCHE WELLE, Wertachtal	🅂 • W Asia • 500 kW
	KAZAKHSTAN	
	†KAZAKH RADIO, Almaty	⊡ • DS-2 • 20 kW
	†R ALMATY/R KAZAKHSTAN, Almaty	⊡ • 20 kW
	SPAIN	
	†R EXTERIOR ESPANA, Noblejas	S America • 350 kW
		Sa • S America • 350 kW
		Su-F • S America • 350 kW
	UNITED KINGDOM	
	†BBC, Rampisham	🅂 • N Africa & W Africa • 500 kW
	BBC, Via Greenville, USA	M-F • C America • 250 kW
17720	**ROMANIA**	
	†RADIO ROMANIA INTL, Bucharest	🅆 • Africa • 250 kW 🅂 • W Europe • 250 kW
		M-Sa • Australasia • 250 kW S Asia & SE Asia • 250 kW
		Su • S Africa • 250 kW
17725	**PAKISTAN**	
	RADIO PAKISTAN, Karachi	E Africa • 50 kW
	RUSSIA	
	†GOLOS ROSSII, Via Moldova	🅆 • C Africa & S Africa • 1000 kW
	USA	
	†RFE-RL, Via Gloria, Portugal	🅆 • E Europe • 250 kW
		🅆 • W Asia & C Asia • 250 kW
	†VOA, Greenville, NC	W Africa • 250 kW
		Su-F • W Africa • 250 kW
	WYFR-FAMILY RADIO, Okeechobee, Fl	🅂 • S America • 100 kW
17730	**DENMARK**	
	†RADIO DANMARK, Via Norway	SE Asia & Australasia • 500 kW • ALT. FREQ. TO 17740 kHz
	KAZAKHSTAN	
	†KAZAKH RADIO, Almaty	⊡ • DS-2 • 20 kW
	†R ALMATY/R KAZAKHSTAN, Almaty	⊡ • 20 kW
	NORWAY	
	†R NORWAY INTL, Kvitsøy	SE Asia & Australasia • 500 kW • ALT. FREQ. TO 17740 kHz
	USA	
	†RFE-RL, Via Pals, Spain	🅂 • W Asia & C Asia • 250 kW
	†VOA, Greenville, NC	🅆 M-F • S America • 250 kW
17735	**USA**	
	†VOA, Via Briech, Morocco	🅂 • E Europe • 500 kW
		🅂 • Europe • 500 kW
	VOA, Via Philippines	E Asia & Australasia • 250 kW
17740	**CLANDESTINE (AFRICA)**	
	†"VOICE OF ERITREA", Via Radio Iraq Intl	⊡ • ARABIC, ETC • E Africa
	DENMARK	
	†RADIO DANMARK, Via Norway	SE Asia & Australasia • 500 kW • ALT. FREQ. TO 17730 kHz
	FINLAND	
	†RADIO FINLAND, Pori	🅆 • N America • 500 kW
	IRAQ	
	†REP OF IRAQ RADIO, Baghdad	⊡ • Irr • Mideast • DS • 250 kW
	NORWAY	
	†R NORWAY INTL, Kvitsøy	SE Asia & Australasia • 500 kW • ALT. FREQ. TO 17730 kHz
	UNITED KINGDOM	
	†BBC, Rampisham	M-F • E Africa • 500 kW
		E Africa • 500 kW
	†BBC, Various Locations	E Africa • 250/500 kW
	†BBC, Via Zyyi, Cyprus	Sa/Su • E Africa • 300 kW
	USA	
	VOA, Greenville, NC	N Africa • 250 kW
	VOA, Via Philippines	S Asia • 250 kW

FREQUENCY   COUNTRY, STATION, LOCATION

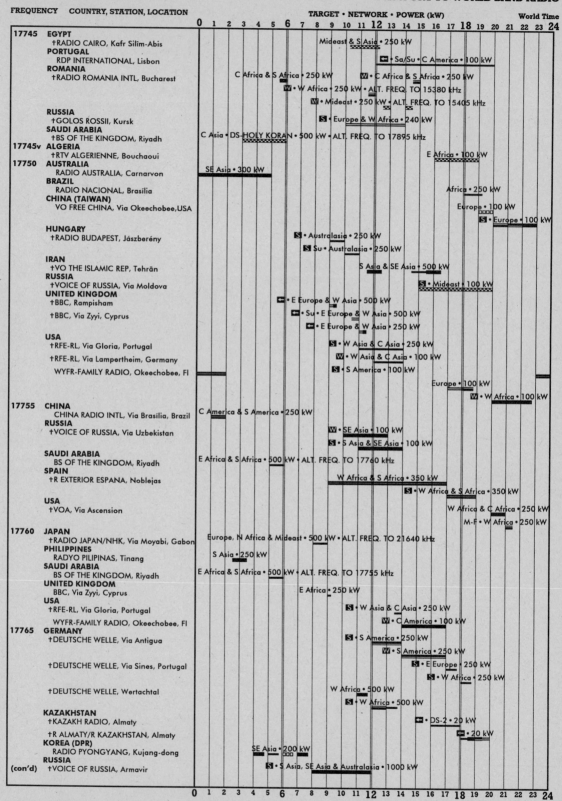

TARGET • NETWORK • POWER (kW)   World Time

FREQUENCY	COUNTRY, STATION, LOCATION
17745	**EGYPT**
	†RADIO CAIRO, Kafr Silîm-Abis
	PORTUGAL
	RDP INTERNATIONAL, Lisbon
	ROMANIA
	†RADIO ROMANIA INTL, Bucharest
	RUSSIA
	†GOLOS ROSSII, Kursk
	SAUDI ARABIA
	†BS OF THE KINGDOM, Riyadh
17745v	**ALGERIA**
	†RTV ALGERIENNE, Bouchaoui
17750	**AUSTRALIA**
	RADIO AUSTRALIA, Carnarvon
	BRAZIL
	RADIO NACIONAL, Brasilia
	CHINA (TAIWAN)
	VO FREE CHINA, Via Okeechobee, USA
	HUNGARY
	†RADIO BUDAPEST, Jászberény
	IRAN
	†VO THE ISLAMIC REP, Tehrān
	RUSSIA
	†VOICE OF RUSSIA, Via Moldova
	UNITED KINGDOM
	†BBC, Rampisham
	†BBC, Via Zyyi, Cyprus
	USA
	†RFE-RL, Via Gloria, Portugal
	†RFE-RL, Via Lampertheim, Germany
	WYFR-FAMILY RADIO, Okeechobee, Fl
17755	**CHINA**
	CHINA RADIO INTL, Via Brasilia, Brazil
	RUSSIA
	†VOICE OF RUSSIA, Via Uzbekistan
	SAUDI ARABIA
	BS OF THE KINGDOM, Riyadh
	SPAIN
	†R EXTERIOR ESPANA, Noblejas
	USA
	†VOA, Via Ascension
17760	**JAPAN**
	†RADIO JAPAN/NHK, Via Moyabi, Gabon
	PHILIPPINES
	RADYO PILIPINAS, Tinang
	SAUDI ARABIA
	BS OF THE KINGDOM, Riyadh
	UNITED KINGDOM
	BBC, Via Zyyi, Cyprus
	USA
	†RFE-RL, Via Gloria, Portugal
	WYFR-FAMILY RADIO, Okeechobee, Fl
17765	**GERMANY**
	†DEUTSCHE WELLE, Via Antigua
	†DEUTSCHE WELLE, Via Sines, Portugal
	†DEUTSCHE WELLE, Wertachtal
	KAZAKHSTAN
	†KAZAKH RADIO, Almaty
	†R ALMATY/R KAZAKHSTAN, Almaty
	KOREA (DPR)
	RADIO PYONGYANG, Kujang-dong
	RUSSIA
(con'd)	†VOICE OF RUSSIA, Armavir

FREQUENCY	COUNTRY, STATION, LOCATION	TARGET • NETWORK • POWER (kW)	World Time

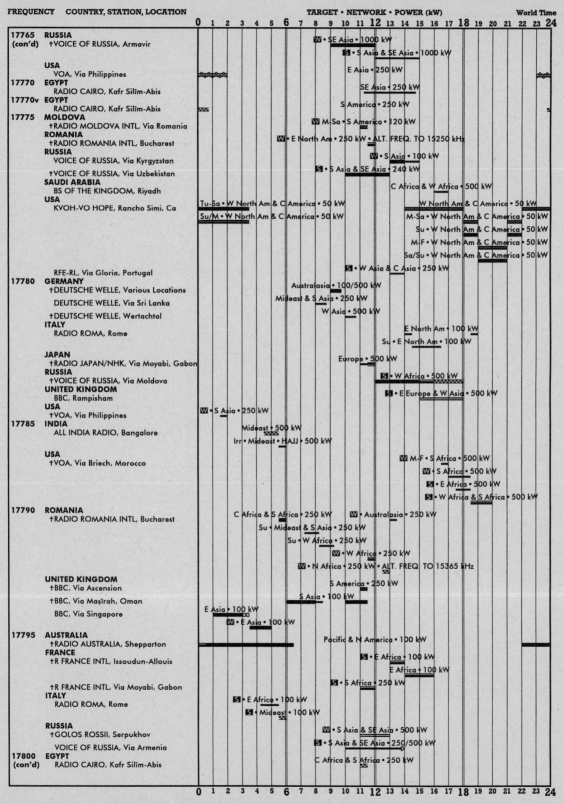

17765 **RUSSIA**
(con'd) †VOICE OF RUSSIA, Armavir
　　W • SE Asia • 1000 kW
　　S • S Asia & SE Asia • 1000 kW

　　USA
　　VOA, Via Philippines
　　E Asia • 250 kW

17770 **EGYPT**
　　RADIO CAIRO, Kafr Silim-Abis
　　SE Asia • 250 kW

17770v **EGYPT**
　　RADIO CAIRO, Kafr Silim-Abis
　　S America • 250 kW

17775 **MOLDOVA**
　　†RADIO MOLDOVA INTL, Via Romania
　　W • M-Sa • S America • 120 kW
　　ROMANIA
　　†RADIO ROMANIA INTL, Bucharest
　　W • E North Am • 250 kW • ALT. FREQ. TO 15250 kHz
　　RUSSIA
　　VOICE OF RUSSIA, Via Kyrgyzstan
　　W • S Asia • 100 kW

　　†VOICE OF RUSSIA, Via Uzbekistan
　　S • S Asia & SE Asia • 240 kW
　　SAUDI ARABIA
　　BS OF THE KINGDOM, Riyadh
　　C Africa & W Africa • 500 kW
　　USA
　　KVOH-VO HOPE, Rancho Simi, Ca
　　Tu-Sa • W North Am & C America • 50 kW　　W North Am & C America • 50 kW
　　Su/M • W North Am & C America • 50 kW
　　　　M-Sa • W North Am & C America • 50 kW
　　　　Su • W North Am & C America • 50 kW
　　　　M-F • W North Am & C America • 50 kW
　　　　Sa/Su • W North Am & C America • 50 kW

　　RFE-RL, Via Gloria, Portugal
　　S • W Asia & C Asia • 250 kW

17780 **GERMANY**
　　†DEUTSCHE WELLE, Various Locations
　　Australasia • 100/500 kW
　　DEUTSCHE WELLE, Via Sri Lanka
　　Mideast & S Asia • 250 kW

　　†DEUTSCHE WELLE, Wertachtal
　　W Asia • 500 kW
　　ITALY
　　RADIO ROMA, Rome
　　E North Am • 100 kW
　　　　Su • E North Am • 100 kW

　　JAPAN
　　†RADIO JAPAN/NHK, Via Moyabi, Gabon
　　Europe • 500 kW
　　RUSSIA
　　†VOICE OF RUSSIA, Via Moldova
　　S • W Africa • 500 kW
　　UNITED KINGDOM
　　BBC, Rampisham
　　S • E Europe & W Asia • 500 kW
　　USA
　　†VOA, Via Philippines
　　W • S Asia • 250 kW

17785 **INDIA**
　　ALL INDIA RADIO, Bangalore
　　Mideast • 500 kW
　　Irr • Mideast • HAJJ • 500 kW

　　USA
　　†VOA, Via Briech, Morocco
　　W • M-F • S Africa • 500 kW
　　　　W • S Africa • 500 kW
　　　　S • E Africa • 500 kW
　　　　S • W Africa & S Africa • 500 kW

17790 **ROMANIA**
　　†RADIO ROMANIA INTL, Bucharest
　　C Africa & S Africa • 250 kW　　W • Australasia • 250 kW
　　Su • Mideast & S Asia • 250 kW
　　Su • W Africa • 250 kW
　　W • W Africa • 250 kW
　　W • N Africa • 250 kW • ALT. FREQ. TO 15365 kHz

　　UNITED KINGDOM
　　†BBC, Via Ascension
　　S America • 250 kW

　　†BBC, Via Masirah, Oman
　　S Asia • 100 kW

　　BBC, Via Singapore
　　E Asia • 100 kW
　　W • E Asia • 100 kW

17795 **AUSTRALIA**
　　†RADIO AUSTRALIA, Shepparton
　　Pacific & N America • 100 kW
　　FRANCE
　　†R FRANCE INTL, Issoudun-Allouis
　　S • E Africa • 100 kW
　　E Africa • 100 kW

　　†R FRANCE INTL, Via Moyabi, Gabon
　　S • S Africa • 250 kW
　　ITALY
　　RADIO ROMA, Rome
　　S • E Africa • 100 kW
　　S • Mideast • 100 kW

　　RUSSIA
　　†GOLOS ROSSII, Serpukhov
　　W • S Asia & SE Asia • 500 kW
　　VOICE OF RUSSIA, Via Armenia
　　S • S Asia & SE Asia • 250/500 kW

17800 **EGYPT**
(con'd) RADIO CAIRO, Kafr Silim-Abis
　　C Africa & S Africa • 250 kW

FREQUENCY   COUNTRY, STATION, LOCATION

TARGET • NETWORK • POWER (kW)   World Time

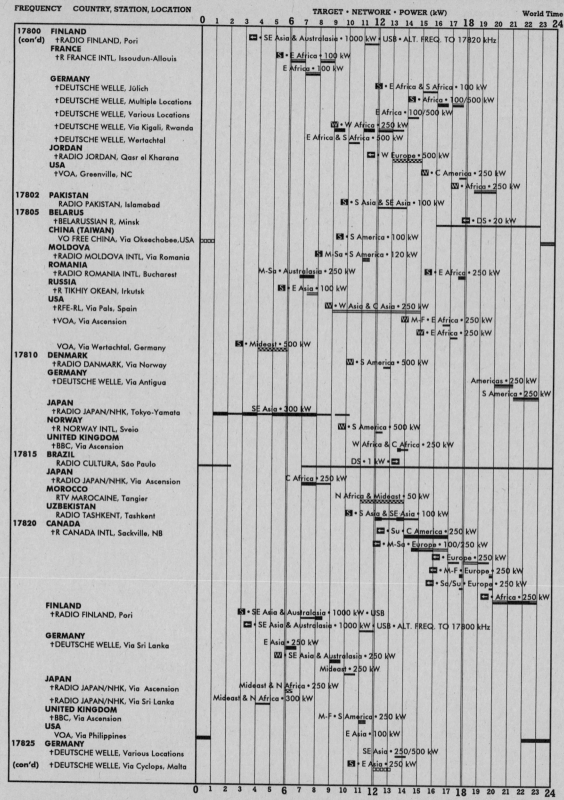

FREQUENCY	COUNTRY, STATION, LOCATION	TARGET • NETWORK • POWER (kW)
17800 (con'd)	FINLAND †RADIO FINLAND, Pori	SE Asia & Australasia • 1000 kW • USB • ALT. FREQ. TO 17820 kHz
	FRANCE †R FRANCE INTL, Issoudun-Allouis	E Africa • 100 kW / E Africa • 100 kW
	GERMANY †DEUTSCHE WELLE, Jülich	E Africa & S Africa • 100 kW
	†DEUTSCHE WELLE, Multiple Locations	Africa • 100/500 kW
	†DEUTSCHE WELLE, Various Locations	E Africa • 100/500 kW
	†DEUTSCHE WELLE, Via Kigali, Rwanda	W Africa • 250 kW
	†DEUTSCHE WELLE, Wertachtal	E Africa & S Africa • 500 kW
	JORDAN †RADIO JORDAN, Qasr el Kharana	W Europe • 500 kW
	USA †VOA, Greenville, NC	C America • 250 kW
		Africa • 250 kW
17802	PAKISTAN RADIO PAKISTAN, Islamabad	S Asia & SE Asia • 100 kW
17805	BELARUS †BELARUSSIAN R, Minsk	DS • 20 kW
	CHINA (TAIWAN) VO FREE CHINA, Via Okeechobee, USA	S America • 100 kW
	MOLDOVA †RADIO MOLDOVA INTL, Via Romania	M-Sa • S America • 120 kW
	ROMANIA †RADIO ROMANIA INTL, Bucharest	M-Sa • Australasia • 250 kW / E Africa • 250 kW
	RUSSIA †R TIKHIY OKEAN, Irkutsk	E Asia • 100 kW
	USA †RFE-RL, Via Pals, Spain	W • W Asia & C Asia • 250 kW
	†VOA, Via Ascension	M-F • E Africa • 250 kW / E Africa • 250 kW
	VOA, Via Wertachtal, Germany	Mideast • 500 kW
17810	DENMARK †RADIO DANMARK, Via Norway	S America • 500 kW
	GERMANY †DEUTSCHE WELLE, Via Antigua	Americas • 250 kW / S America • 250 kW
	JAPAN †RADIO JAPAN/NHK, Tokyo-Yamata	SE Asia • 300 kW
	NORWAY †R NORWAY INTL, Sveio	S America • 500 kW
	UNITED KINGDOM †BBC, Via Ascension	W Africa & C Africa • 250 kW
17815	BRAZIL RADIO CULTURA, São Paulo	DS • 1 kW
	JAPAN †RADIO JAPAN/NHK, Via Ascension	C Africa • 250 kW
	MOROCCO RTV MAROCAINE, Tangier	N Africa & Mideast • 50 kW
	UZBEKISTAN RADIO TASHKENT, Tashkent	S Asia & SE Asia • 100 kW
17820	CANADA †R CANADA INTL, Sackville, NB	Su • C America • 250 kW
		M-Sa • Europe • 100/250 kW
		Europe • 250 kW
		M-F • Europe • 250 kW
		Sa/Su • Europe • 250 kW
		Africa • 250 kW
	FINLAND †RADIO FINLAND, Pori	SE Asia & Australasia • 1000 kW • USB
		SE Asia & Australasia • 1000 kW • USB • ALT. FREQ. TO 17800 kHz
	GERMANY †DEUTSCHE WELLE, Via Sri Lanka	E Asia • 250 kW
		SE Asia & Australasia • 250 kW
		Mideast • 250 kW
	JAPAN †RADIO JAPAN/NHK, Via Ascension	Mideast & N Africa • 250 kW
	†RADIO JAPAN/NHK, Via Sri Lanka	Mideast & N Africa • 300 kW
	UNITED KINGDOM †BBC, Via Ascension	M-F • S America • 250 kW
	USA VOA, Via Philippines	E Asia • 100 kW
17825	GERMANY †DEUTSCHE WELLE, Various Locations	SE Asia • 250/500 kW
(con'd)	†DEUTSCHE WELLE, Via Cyclops, Malta	E Asia • 250 kW

FREQUENCY   COUNTRY, STATION, LOCATION   TARGET • NETWORK • POWER (kW)   World Time

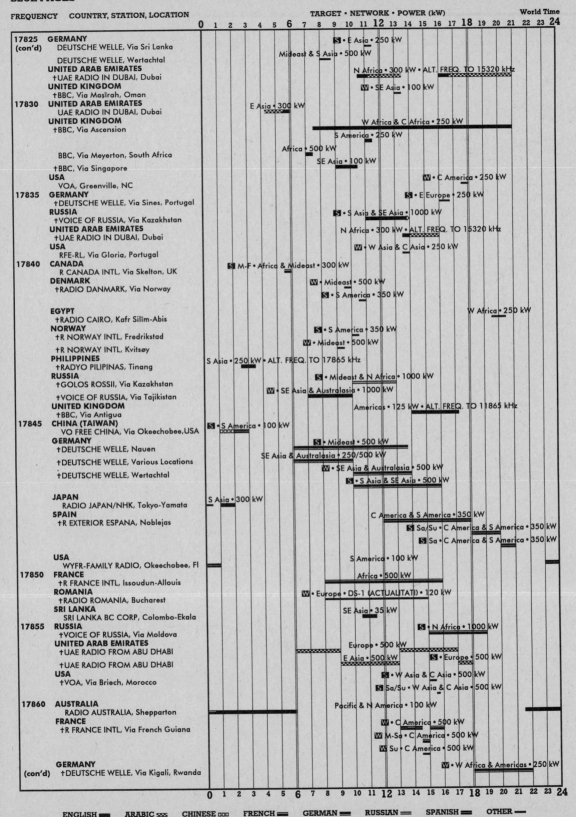

Frequency	Country, Station, Location	Target • Network • Power
17825 (con'd)	**GERMANY** DEUTSCHE WELLE, Via Sri Lanka	S • E Asia • 250 kW
	DEUTSCHE WELLE, Wertachtal	Mideast & S Asia • 500 kW
	UNITED ARAB EMIRATES †UAE RADIO IN DUBAI, Dubai	N Africa • 300 kW • ALT. FREQ. TO 15320 kHz
	UNITED KINGDOM †BBC, Via Maṣīrah, Oman	W • SE Asia • 100 kW
17830	**UNITED ARAB EMIRATES** UAE RADIO IN DUBAI, Dubai	E Asia • 300 kW
	UNITED KINGDOM †BBC, Via Ascension	W Africa & C Africa • 250 kW
		S America • 250 kW
	BBC, Via Meyerton, South Africa	Africa • 500 kW
	†BBC, Via Singapore	SE Asia • 100 kW
	USA VOA, Greenville, NC	W • C America • 250 kW
17835	**GERMANY** †DEUTSCHE WELLE, Via Sines, Portugal	S • E Europe • 250 kW
	RUSSIA †VOICE OF RUSSIA, Via Kazakhstan	S • S Asia & SE Asia • 1000 kW
	UNITED ARAB EMIRATES †UAE RADIO IN DUBAI, Dubai	N Africa • 300 kW • ALT. FREQ. TO 15320 kHz
	USA RFE-RL, Via Gloria, Portugal	W • W Asia & C Asia • 250 kW
17840	**CANADA** R CANADA INTL, Via Skelton, UK	S • M-F • Africa & Mideast • 300 kW
	DENMARK †RADIO DANMARK, Via Norway	W • Mideast • 500 kW
		S • S America • 350 kW
	EGYPT †RADIO CAIRO, Kafr Silīm-Abis	W Africa • 250 kW
	NORWAY †R NORWAY INTL, Fredrikstad	S • S America • 350 kW
	†R NORWAY INTL, Kvitsøy	W • Mideast • 500 kW
	PHILIPPINES †RADYO PILIPINAS, Tinang	S Asia • 250 kW • ALT. FREQ. TO 17865 kHz
	RUSSIA †GOLOS ROSSII, Via Kazakhstan	S • Mideast & N Africa • 1000 kW
	†VOICE OF RUSSIA, Via Tajikistan	W • SE Asia & Australasia • 1000 kW
	UNITED KINGDOM †BBC, Via Antigua	Americas • 125 kW • ALT. FREQ. TO 11865 kHz
17845	**CHINA (TAIWAN)** VO FREE CHINA, Via Okeechobee,USA	S • S America • 100 kW
	GERMANY †DEUTSCHE WELLE, Nauen	S • Mideast • 500 kW
	†DEUTSCHE WELLE, Various Locations	SE Asia & Australasia • 250/500 kW
	†DEUTSCHE WELLE, Wertachtal	W • SE Asia & Australasia • 500 kW
		S • S Asia & SE Asia • 500 kW
	JAPAN RADIO JAPAN/NHK, Tokyo-Yamata	S Asia • 300 kW
	SPAIN †R EXTERIOR ESPANA, Noblejas	C America & S America • 350 kW
		S • Sa/Su • C America & S America • 350 kW
		S • Sa • C America & S America • 350 kW
	USA WYFR-FAMILY RADIO, Okeechobee, Fl	S America • 100 kW
17850	**FRANCE** †R FRANCE INTL, Issoudun-Allouis	Africa • 500 kW
	ROMANIA †RADIO ROMANIA, Bucharest	W • Europe • DS-1 (ACTUALITATI) • 120 kW
	SRI LANKA SRI LANKA BC CORP, Colombo-Ekala	SE Asia • 35 kW
17855	**RUSSIA** †VOICE OF RUSSIA, Via Moldova	S • N Africa • 1000 kW
	UNITED ARAB EMIRATES †UAE RADIO FROM ABU DHABI	Europe • 500 kW
	†UAE RADIO FROM ABU DHABI	E Asia • 500 kW / S • Europe • 500 kW
	USA †VOA, Via Briech, Morocco	S • W Asia & C Asia • 500 kW
		S • Sa/Su • W Asia & C Asia • 500 kW
17860	**AUSTRALIA** RADIO AUSTRALIA, Shepparton	Pacific & N America • 100 kW
	FRANCE †R FRANCE INTL, Via French Guiana	W • C America • 500 kW
		W • M-Sa • C America • 500 kW
		W • Su • C America • 500 kW
(con'd)	**GERMANY** †DEUTSCHE WELLE, Via Kigali, Rwanda	W • W Africa & Americas • 250 kW

ENGLISH ▬   ARABIC ⧆⧆   CHINESE ▫▫▫   FRENCH ▬▬   GERMAN ▬▬   RUSSIAN ═══   SPANISH ▬▬   OTHER ▬

FREQUENCY   COUNTRY, STATION, LOCATION

TARGET • NETWORK • POWER (kW)   World Time

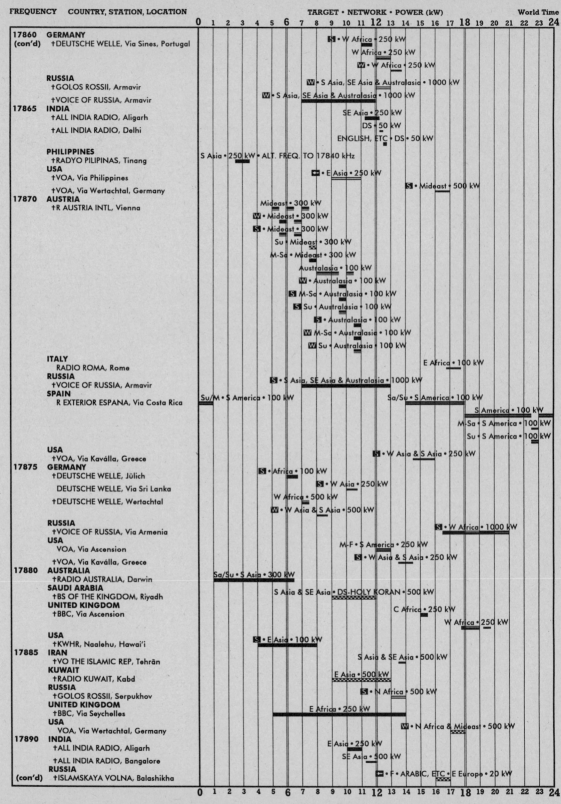

17860	**GERMANY**
(con'd)	†DEUTSCHE WELLE, Via Sines, Portugal
	RUSSIA
	†GOLOS ROSSII, Armavir
	†VOICE OF RUSSIA, Armavir
17865	**INDIA**
	†ALL INDIA RADIO, Aligarh
	†ALL INDIA RADIO, Delhi
	PHILIPPINES
	†RADYO PILIPINAS, Tinang
	USA
	†VOA, Via Philippines
	†VOA, Via Wertachtal, Germany
17870	**AUSTRIA**
	†R AUSTRIA INTL, Vienna
	ITALY
	RADIO ROMA, Rome
	RUSSIA
	†VOICE OF RUSSIA, Armavir
	SPAIN
	R EXTERIOR ESPANA, Via Costa Rica
	USA
	†VOA, Via Kaválla, Greece
17875	**GERMANY**
	†DEUTSCHE WELLE, Jülich
	DEUTSCHE WELLE, Via Sri Lanka
	†DEUTSCHE WELLE, Wertachtal
	RUSSIA
	†VOICE OF RUSSIA, Via Armenia
	USA
	VOA, Via Ascension
	†VOA, Via Kaválla, Greece
17880	**AUSTRALIA**
	†RADIO AUSTRALIA, Darwin
	SAUDI ARABIA
	†BS OF THE KINGDOM, Riyadh
	UNITED KINGDOM
	†BBC, Via Ascension
	USA
	†KWHR, Naalehu, Hawai'i
17885	**IRAN**
	†VO THE ISLAMIC REP, Tehrān
	KUWAIT
	†RADIO KUWAIT, Kabd
	RUSSIA
	†GOLOS ROSSII, Serpukhov
	UNITED KINGDOM
	†BBC, Via Seychelles
	USA
	VOA, Via Wertachtal, Germany
17890	**INDIA**
	†ALL INDIA RADIO, Aligarh
	†ALL INDIA RADIO, Bangalore
	RUSSIA
(con'd)	†ISLAMSKAYA VOLNA, Balashikha

Target/Network/Power notes (by station):

- DEUTSCHE WELLE, Via Sines: S • W Africa • 250 kW; W Africa • 250 kW; W • W Africa • 250 kW
- GOLOS ROSSII, Armavir: W • S Asia, SE Asia & Australasia • 1000 kW
- VOICE OF RUSSIA, Armavir: W • S Asia, SE Asia & Australasia • 1000 kW
- ALL INDIA RADIO, Aligarh: SE Asia • 250 kW; DS • 50 kW
- ALL INDIA RADIO, Delhi: ENGLISH, ETC • DS • 50 kW
- RADYO PILIPINAS, Tinang: S Asia • 250 kW • ALT. FREQ. TO 17840 kHz
- VOA, Via Philippines: E Asia • 250 kW
- VOA, Via Wertachtal: S • Mideast • 500 kW
- R AUSTRIA INTL, Vienna: Mideast • 300 kW; W • Mideast • 300 kW; S • Mideast • 300 kW; Su • Mideast • 300 kW; M-Sa • Mideast • 300 kW; Australasia • 100 kW; W • Australasia • 100 kW; S M-Sa • Australasia • 100 kW; S Su • Australasia • 100 kW; S • Australasia • 100 kW; W M-Sa • Australasia • 100 kW; W Su • Australasia • 100 kW
- RADIO ROMA, Rome: E Africa • 100 kW
- VOICE OF RUSSIA, Armavir: S • S Asia, SE Asia & Australasia • 1000 kW
- R EXTERIOR ESPANA: Su/M • S America • 100 kW; Sa/Su • S America • 100 kW; S America • 100 kW; M-Sa • S America • 100 kW; Su • S America • 100 kW
- VOA, Via Kaválla: S • W Asia & S Asia • 250 kW
- DEUTSCHE WELLE, Jülich: S • Africa • 100 kW
- DEUTSCHE WELLE, Via Sri Lanka: S • W Asia • 250 kW
- DEUTSCHE WELLE, Wertachtal: W Africa • 500 kW; W • W Asia & S Asia • 500 kW
- VOICE OF RUSSIA, Via Armenia: S • W Africa • 1000 kW
- VOA, Via Ascension: M-F • S America • 250 kW
- VOA, Via Kaválla: S • W Asia & S Asia • 250 kW
- RADIO AUSTRALIA, Darwin: Sa/Su • S Asia • 300 kW
- BS OF THE KINGDOM, Riyadh: S Asia & SE Asia • DS-HOLY KORAN • 500 kW
- BBC, Via Ascension: C Africa • 250 kW; W Africa • 250 kW
- KWHR, Naalehu: S • E Asia • 100 kW
- VO THE ISLAMIC REP: S Asia & SE Asia • 500 kW
- RADIO KUWAIT, Kabd: E Asia • 500 kW
- GOLOS ROSSII, Serpukhov: S • N Africa • 500 kW
- BBC, Via Seychelles: E Africa • 250 kW
- VOA, Via Wertachtal: W • N Africa & Mideast • 500 kW
- ALL INDIA RADIO, Aligarh: E Asia • 250 kW
- ALL INDIA RADIO, Bangalore: SE Asia • 500 kW
- ISLAMSKAYA VOLNA, Balashikha: F • ARABIC, ETC • E Europe • 20 kW

FREQUENCY   COUNTRY, STATION, LOCATION   TARGET • NETWORK • POWER (kW)   World Time

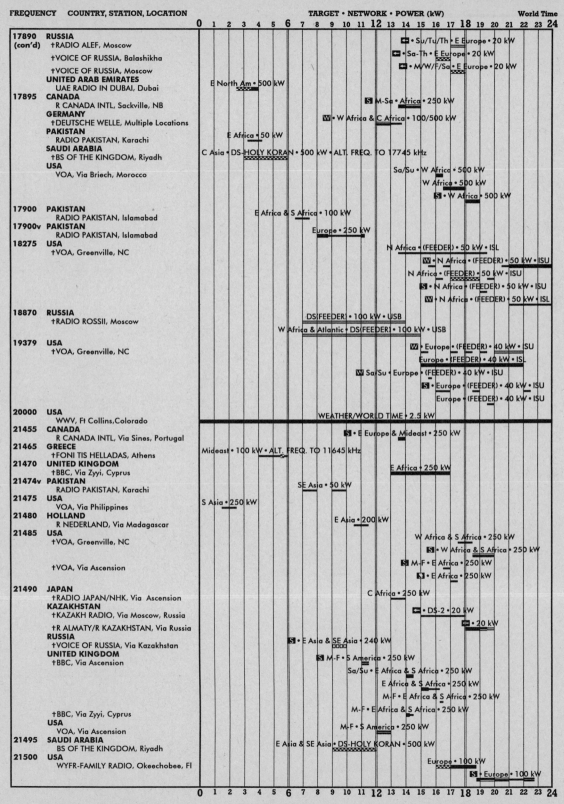

Frequency	Country / Station / Location	Target • Network • Power
17890 (con'd)	**RUSSIA** †RADIO ALEF, Moscow	• Su/Tu/Th • E Europe • 20 kW
	†VOICE OF RUSSIA, Balashikha	• Sa-Th • E Europe • 20 kW
	†VOICE OF RUSSIA, Moscow	• M/W/F/Sa • E Europe • 20 kW
	UNITED ARAB EMIRATES UAE RADIO IN DUBAI, Dubai	E North Am • 500 kW
17895	**CANADA** R CANADA INTL, Sackville, NB	S M-Sa • Africa • 250 kW
	GERMANY †DEUTSCHE WELLE, Multiple Locations	W • W Africa & C Africa • 100/500 kW
	PAKISTAN RADIO PAKISTAN, Karachi	E Africa • 50 kW
	SAUDI ARABIA †BS OF THE KINGDOM, Riyadh	C Asia • DS-HOLY KORAN • 500 kW • ALT. FREQ. TO 17745 kHz
	USA VOA, Via Briech, Morocco	Sa/Su • W Africa • 500 kW / W Africa • 500 kW / S • W Africa • 500 kW
17900	**PAKISTAN** RADIO PAKISTAN, Islamabad	E Africa & S Africa • 100 kW
17900v	**PAKISTAN** RADIO PAKISTAN, Islamabad	Europe • 250 kW
18275	**USA** †VOA, Greenville, NC	N Africa • (FEEDER) • 50 kW • ISL / W • N Africa • (FEEDER) • 50 kW • ISU / N Africa • (FEEDER) • 50 kW • ISU / S • N Africa • (FEEDER) • 50 kW • ISU / W • N Africa • (FEEDER) • 50 kW • ISL
18870	**RUSSIA** †RADIO ROSSII, Moscow	DS(FEEDER) • 100 kW • USB / W Africa & Atlantic • DS(FEEDER) • 100 kW • USB
19379	**USA** †VOA, Greenville, NC	W • Europe • (FEEDER) • 40 kW • SU / Europe • (FEEDER) • 40 kW • ISL / W Sa/Su • Europe • (FEEDER) • 40 kW • ISU / S • Europe • (FEEDER) • 40 kW • ISU / Europe • (FEEDER) • 40 kW • ISU
20000	**USA** WWV, Ft Collins, Colorado	WEATHER/WORLD TIME • 2.5 kW
21455	**CANADA** R CANADA INTL, Via Sines, Portugal	S • E Europe & Mideast • 250 kW
21465	**GREECE** †FONI TIS HELLADAS, Athens	Mideast • 100 kW • ALT. FREQ. TO 11645 kHz
21470	**UNITED KINGDOM** †BBC, Via Zyyi, Cyprus	E Africa • 250 kW
21474v	**PAKISTAN** RADIO PAKISTAN, Karachi	SE Asia • 50 kW
21475	**USA** VOA, Via Philippines	S Asia • 250 kW
21480	**HOLLAND** R NEDERLAND, Via Madagascar	E Asia • 200 kW
21485	**USA** †VOA, Greenville, NC	W Africa & S Africa • 250 kW / S • W Africa & S Africa • 250 kW
	†VOA, Via Ascension	S M-F • E Africa • 250 kW / S • E Africa • 250 kW
21490	**JAPAN** †RADIO JAPAN/NHK, Via Ascension	C Africa • 250 kW
	KAZAKHSTAN †KAZAKH RADIO, Via Moscow, Russia	• DS-2 • 20 kW
	†R ALMATY/R KAZAKHSTAN, Via Russia	• 20 kW
	RUSSIA †VOICE OF RUSSIA, Via Kazakhstan	S • E Asia & SE Asia • 240 kW
	UNITED KINGDOM †BBC, Via Ascension	S M-F • S America • 250 kW / Sa/Su • E Africa & S Africa • 250 kW / E Africa & S Africa • 250 kW / M-F • E Africa & S Africa • 250 kW
	†BBC, Via Zyyi, Cyprus	M-F • E Africa & S Africa • 250 kW
	USA VOA, Via Ascension	M-F • S America • 250 kW
21495	**SAUDI ARABIA** BS OF THE KINGDOM, Riyadh	E Asia & SE Asia • DS-HOLY KORAN • 500 kW
21500	**USA** WYFR-FAMILY RADIO, Okeechobee, Fl	Europe • 100 kW / S • Europe • 100 kW

ENGLISH ▬ ARABIC ⌇⌇⌇ CHINESE ▫▫▫ FRENCH ▬ GERMAN ▬ RUSSIAN ═ SPANISH ▬ OTHER ▬

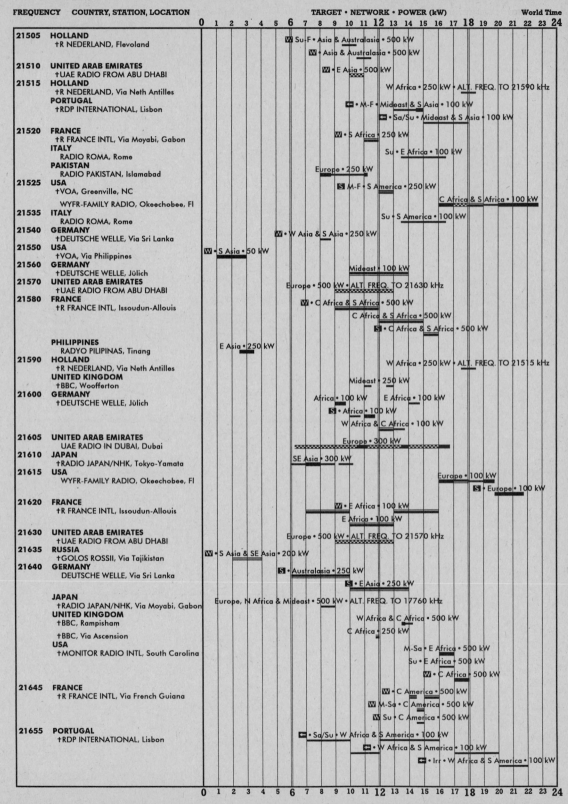

FREQUENCY	COUNTRY, STATION, LOCATION	TARGET • NETWORK • POWER (kW)	World Time

21505 **HOLLAND**
      †R NEDERLAND, Flevoland
      W • Su-F • Asia & Australasia • 500 kW
      W • Asia & Australasia • 500 kW

21510 **UNITED ARAB EMIRATES**
      †UAE RADIO FROM ABU DHABI
      W • E Asia • 500 kW

21515 **HOLLAND**
      †R NEDERLAND, Via Neth Antilles
      W Africa • 250 kW • ALT. FREQ. TO 21590 kHz
      PORTUGAL
      †RDP INTERNATIONAL, Lisbon
      M-F • Mideast & S Asia • 100 kW
      Sa/Su • Mideast & S Asia • 100 kW

21520 **FRANCE**
      †R FRANCE INTL, Via Moyabi, Gabon
      W • S Africa • 250 kW
      ITALY
      RADIO ROMA, Rome
      Su • E Africa • 100 kW
      PAKISTAN
      RADIO PAKISTAN, Islamabad
      Europe • 250 kW

21525 **USA**
      †VOA, Greenville, NC
      S • M-F • S America • 250 kW
      WYFR-FAMILY RADIO, Okeechobee, Fl
      C Africa & S Africa • 100 kW

21535 **ITALY**
      RADIO ROMA, Rome
      Su • S America • 100 kW

21540 **GERMANY**
      †DEUTSCHE WELLE, Via Sri Lanka
      W • W Asia & S Asia • 250 kW

21550 **USA**
      †VOA, Via Philippines
      W • S Asia • 50 kW

21560 **GERMANY**
      †DEUTSCHE WELLE, Jülich
      Mideast • 100 kW

21570 **UNITED ARAB EMIRATES**
      †UAE RADIO FROM ABU DHABI
      Europe • 500 kW • ALT. FREQ. TO 21630 kHz

21580 **FRANCE**
      †R FRANCE INTL, Issoudun-Allouis
      W • C Africa & S Africa • 500 kW
      C Africa & S Africa • 500 kW
      S • C Africa & S Africa • 500 kW

      PHILIPPINES
      RADYO PILIPINAS, Tinang
      E Asia • 250 kW

21590 **HOLLAND**
      †R NEDERLAND, Via Neth Antilles
      W Africa • 250 kW • ALT. FREQ. TO 21515 kHz
      UNITED KINGDOM
      †BBC, Woofferton
      Mideast • 250 kW

21600 **GERMANY**
      †DEUTSCHE WELLE, Jülich
      Africa • 100 kW   E Africa • 100 kW
      S • Africa • 100 kW
      W Africa & C Africa • 100 kW

21605 **UNITED ARAB EMIRATES**
      UAE RADIO IN DUBAI, Dubai
      Europe • 300 kW

21610 **JAPAN**
      †RADIO JAPAN/NHK, Tokyo-Yamata
      SE Asia • 300 kW

21615 **USA**
      WYFR-FAMILY RADIO, Okeechobee, Fl
      Europe • 100 kW
      S • Europe • 100 kW

21620 **FRANCE**
      †R FRANCE INTL, Issoudun-Allouis
      W • E Africa • 100 kW
      E Africa • 100 kW

21630 **UNITED ARAB EMIRATES**
      †UAE RADIO FROM ABU DHABI
      Europe • 500 kW • ALT. FREQ. TO 21570 kHz

21635 **RUSSIA**
      †GOLOS ROSSII, Via Tajikistan
      W • S Asia & SE Asia • 200 kW

21640 **GERMANY**
      DEUTSCHE WELLE, Via Sri Lanka
      S • Australasia • 250 kW
      S • E Asia • 250 kW

      JAPAN
      †RADIO JAPAN/NHK, Via Moyabi, Gabon
      Europe, N Africa & Mideast • 500 kW • ALT. FREQ. TO 17760 kHz
      UNITED KINGDOM
      †BBC, Rampisham
      W Africa & C Africa • 500 kW
      †BBC, Via Ascension
      C Africa • 250 kW
      USA
      †MONITOR RADIO INTL, South Carolina
      M-Sa • E Africa • 500 kW
      Su • E Africa • 500 kW
      W • C Africa • 500 kW

21645 **FRANCE**
      †R FRANCE INTL, Via French Guiana
      W • C America • 500 kW
      W • M-Sa • C America • 500 kW
      W • Su • C America • 500 kW

21655 **PORTUGAL**
      †RDP INTERNATIONAL, Lisbon
      Sa/Su • W Africa & S America • 100 kW
      W Africa & S America • 100 kW
      Irr • W Africa & S America • 100 kW

SEASONAL **S** OR **W**   1-HR TIMESHIFT MIDYEAR ⇦ OR ⇨   JAMMING / OR ∧   EARLIEST HEARD ◁   LATEST HEARD ▷   NEW FOR 1996 †

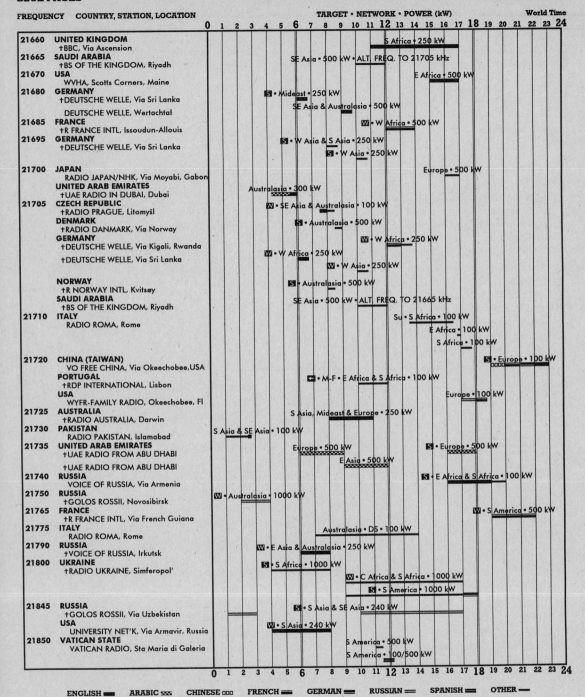

FREQUENCY	COUNTRY, STATION, LOCATION	TARGET • NETWORK • POWER (kW)	World Time

21660 **UNITED KINGDOM** — †BBC, Via Ascension — S Africa • 250 kW

21665 **SAUDI ARABIA** — †BS OF THE KINGDOM, Riyadh — SE Asia • 500 kW • ALT. FREQ. TO 21705 kHz

21670 **USA** — WVHA, Scotts Corners, Maine — E Africa • 500 kW

21680 **GERMANY** — †DEUTSCHE WELLE, Via Sri Lanka — S • Mideast • 250 kW

DEUTSCHE WELLE, Wertachtal — SE Asia & Australasia • 500 kW

21685 **FRANCE** — †R FRANCE INTL, Issoudun-Allouis — W • W Africa • 500 kW

21695 **GERMANY** — †DEUTSCHE WELLE, Via Sri Lanka — S • W Asia & S Asia • 250 kW

S • W Asia • 250 kW

21700 **JAPAN** — RADIO JAPAN/NHK, Via Moyabi, Gabon — Europe • 500 kW

UNITED ARAB EMIRATES — †UAE RADIO IN DUBAI, Dubai — Australasia • 300 kW

21705 **CZECH REPUBLIC** — †RADIO PRAGUE, Litomyšl — W • SE Asia & Australasia • 100 kW

DENMARK — †RADIO DANMARK, Via Norway — S • Australasia • 500 kW

GERMANY — †DEUTSCHE WELLE, Via Kigali, Rwanda — W • W Africa • 250 kW

†DEUTSCHE WELLE, Via Sri Lanka — W • W Africa • 250 kW

W • W Asia • 250 kW

NORWAY — †R NORWAY INTL, Kvitsøy — S • Australasia • 500 kW

SAUDI ARABIA — †BS OF THE KINGDOM, Riyadh — SE Asia • 500 kW • ALT. FREQ. TO 21665 kHz

21710 **ITALY** — RADIO ROMA, Rome — Su • S Africa • 100 kW

E Africa • 100 kW

S Africa • 100 kW

21720 **CHINA (TAIWAN)** — VO FREE CHINA, Via Okeechobee, USA — S • Europe • 100 kW

PORTUGAL — †RDP INTERNATIONAL, Lisbon — • M-F • E Africa & S Africa • 100 kW

USA — WYFR-FAMILY RADIO, Okeechobee, Fl — Europe • 100 kW

21725 **AUSTRALIA** — †RADIO AUSTRALIA, Darwin — S Asia, Mideast & Europe • 250 kW

21730 **PAKISTAN** — RADIO PAKISTAN, Islamabad — S Asia & SE Asia • 100 kW

21735 **UNITED ARAB EMIRATES** — †UAE RADIO FROM ABU DHABI — Europe • 500 kW

S • Europe • 500 kW

†UAE RADIO FROM ABU DHABI — E Asia • 500 kW

21740 **RUSSIA** — VOICE OF RUSSIA, Via Armenia — S • E Africa & S Africa • 100 kW

21750 **RUSSIA** — †GOLOS ROSSII, Novosibirsk — W • Australasia • 1000 kW

21765 **FRANCE** — †R FRANCE INTL, Via French Guiana — W • S America • 500 kW

21775 **ITALY** — RADIO ROMA, Rome — Australasia • DS • 100 kW

21790 **RUSSIA** — †VOICE OF RUSSIA, Irkutsk — W • E Asia & Australasia • 250 kW

21800 **UKRAINE** — †RADIO UKRAINE, Simferopol' — S • S Africa • 1000 kW

W • C Africa & S Africa • 1000 kW

S • S America • 1000 kW

21845 **RUSSIA** — †GOLOS ROSSII, Via Uzbekistan — S • S Asia & SE Asia • 240 kW

USA — UNIVERSITY NET'K, Via Armavir, Russia — W • S Asia • 240 kW

21850 **VATICAN STATE** — VATICAN RADIO, Sta Maria di Galeria — S America • 500 kW

S America • 100/500 kW

ENGLISH ▬ ARABIC ᚶᚶᚶ CHINESE □□□ FRENCH ══ GERMAN ▬▬ RUSSIAN ══ SPANISH ▬▬ OTHER ──

Setting Your World Time Clock

"Addresses PLUS," found elsewhere in this edition, lets you arrive at the local time in another country by adding or subtracting from World Time. Use that section to determine the time within a country you are listening to.

This box, however, gives it from the other direction. That is, it tells you what to add or subtract from your local time *to determine World Time.* Use this box to set your World Time clock.

Where You Are	To Determine World Time
Europe	
United Kingdom and Ireland London, Dublin	Same time as World Time winter, subtract 1 hour summer
Continental Western Europe; also, some other parts of non-western Continental Europe Berlin, Stockholm, Prague	Subtract 1 hour winter, 2 hours summer
Elsewhere in Continental Europe Belarus, Bulgaria, Cyprus, Estonia, Finland, Greece, Latvia, Lithuania, Moldova, Romania, Russia (westernmost only), Turkey and Ukraine	Subtract 2 hours winter, 3 hours summer
North America	
Eastern Montréal	Add 5 hours winter, 4 hours New York, summer
Central	Add 6 hours winter, 5 hours Chicago, Winnipeg summer
Mountain	Add 7 hours winter, 6 hours Denver, Calgary summer
Pacific Vancouver	Add 8 hours winter, 7 hours San Francisco, summer
Alaska Fairbanks	Add 9 hours winter, 8 hours Anchorage, summer
Hawaii Honolulu, Hilo	Add 10 hours year round
East Asia & Australasia	
China, including Hong Kong and Taiwan	Subtract 8 hours year round
Japan	Subtract 9 hours year round
Australia: Victoria, New South Wales, Tasmania	Subtract 11 hours local summer, 10 local winter (midyear)
Australia: South Australia	Subtract 10½ hours local summer, 9½ hours local winter (midyear)
Australia: Queensland	Subtract 10 hours year round
Australia: Northern Territory	Subtract 9 hours year round
Australia: Western Australia	Subtract 8 hours year round
New Zealand	Subtract 13 hours local summer, 12 hours local winter (midyear)